TRADITIONS & ENCOUNTERS

To access the *Traditions & Encounters* online resource package please visit
www.mhhe.com/bentleybrief and use the following code: **G8JR-Y9P7-TTEH-9487-THW4**

TRADITIONS & ENCOUNTERS

A Brief Global History

Jerry H. Bentley
University of Hawai'i

Herbert F. Ziegler
University of Hawai'i

Heather E. Streets
Washington State University

Boston   Burr Ridge, IL   Dubuque, IA   Madison, WI   New York
San Francisco   St. Louis   Bangkok   Bogotá   Caracas   Kuala Lumpur
Lisbon   London   Madrid   Mexico City   Milan   Montreal   New Delhi
Santiago   Seoul   Singapore   Sydney   Taipei   Toronto

ISBN: 978-0-07-353453-4
MHID: 0-07-353453-6

Editor in Chief: *Emily Barrosse*
Publisher: *Lisa Moore*
Sponsoring Editor: *Jon-David Hague*
Marketing Manager: *Jennifer Reed*
Director of Development: *Lisa Pinto*
Developmental Editor: *Angela Kao*
Editorial Coordinator: *Nicole Caddigan*
Project Manager: *Christina Gimlin*
Manuscript Editor: *Carole Crouse*
Art Director: *Jeanne Schreiber*
Design Manager: *Kim Menning*
Text Designer: *Linda Robertson*
Art Editor: *Katherine McNab*
Manager, Photo Research: *Brian J. Pecko*
Supplements Producer: *Louis Swaim*
Production Supervisor: *Richard DeVitto*
Composition: *10/12 Galliard by Thompson Type*
Printing: *45 # Publisher's Matte, R. R. Donnelley & Sons*

Cover credits: Royal Standard of Ur, © Erich Lessing/Art Resource, NY; Han emperor with Confucian scholars, © Bibliotheque Nationale, Paris, France/The Bridgeman Art Library; faithful before the Kaaba in Mecca, © Topkapi Palace Museum, Istanbul, Turkey, Bildarchiv Steffens/The Bridgeman Art Library; merchants and customers in a town market, © Scala/Art Resource, NY; Doña Marina, Hernán Cortés, and Tlaxcala, © The Granger Collection, New York; young woman at work in a mechanized mill, © Bettmann/Corbis; Himid, Lubaina (b. 1954), *Between the two my heart is balanced*, 1991, © Tate Gallery, London/Art Resource, NY. Used by permission of Lubaina Himid.

Credits: The credits section for this book begins on page C-1 and is considered an extension of the copyright page.

Library of Congress Cataloging-in-Publication Data

Bentley, Jerry H., 1949–
    Traditions and encounters : a brief global history / by Jerry H. Bentley, Herbert F. Ziegler, and Heather E. Streets.
        p. cm.
    Brief ed. of: Traditions and encounters / Jerry H. Bentley, Herbert F. Ziegler. 3rd ed.
    Includes index.
    ISBN-13: 978-0-07-353453-4 (alk. paper)
    ISBN-10: 0-07-353453-6 (alk. paper)
    1. World history. 2. Intercultural communication--History. I. Ziegler, Herbert F., 1949– II. Streets, Heather E. III. Title.
    IV. Title: Traditions and encounters.

D20.B42 2006
909—dc22   2006046708

The Internet addresses listed in the text were accurate at the time of publication. The inclusion of a Web site does not indicate an endorsement by the authors or McGraw-Hill, and McGraw-Hill does not guarantee the accuracy of the information presented at these sites.

www.mhhe.com

Brief Table of Contents

Table of Contents

PART I

THE EARLY COMPLEX SOCIETIES, 3500 TO 500 B.C.E. 2

PART II

THE FORMATION OF CLASSICAL SOCIETIES, 500 B.C.E. to 500 C.E. 81

PART III

THE POSTCLASSICAL ERA, 500 TO 1000 C.E. 175

PART IV

AN AGE OF CROSS CULTURAL INTERACTION, 1000 TO 1500 c.e. 265

PART V

THE ORIGINS OF GLOBAL INTERDEPENDENCE, 1500–1800 354

Primary Sources from the Past

Preface

How is it possible to make sense of the entire human past?

The study of world history is an exhilarating project that offers unparalleled opportunities to understand oneself and one's society in relation to the larger world. Given the range of human diversity, however, world history also presents a daunting challenge. Human communities have adopted widely varying forms of political, social, and economic organization, and they have elaborated even more diverse cultural, religious, and philosophical legacies.

We wrote *Traditions & Encounters* to offer a global perspective on the past—a vision of history that is meaningful and appropriate for the interdependent world we live in today. During an era when peoples from all parts of the earth meet, interact, and do business with one another, a global perspective has become an essential tool for informed and responsible citizenship. Because global interactions profoundly influence the fortunes of peoples in all lands, it is impossible to understand the contemporary world by approaching it exclusively from the viewpoint of western Europe, the United States, Japan, or any other individual society, or the historical experience of any one society.

We wrote *Traditions & Encounters: A Brief Global History* to offer an option to instructors who want to provide a global perspective to their students with a briefer text, allowing more flexibility in the way they present the exciting stories of world history to their students.

Of course, a brief text must offer more than just brevity. It must also provide a sound organizational structure, strong themes that provide a systematic framework for interpreting history, an engaging narrative, strong visual appeal, and solid pedagogy. *Traditions & Encounters: A Brief Global History* offers all of these elements.

ORGANIZATIONAL STRUCTURE

We discuss the world's development through time by organizing it into ***seven eras of global history.*** These eras, treated successively in the seven parts of this book, represent coherent epochs that form the larger architecture of world history as we see it. The eras owe their coherence in large part to the networks of transportation, communication, and exchange that have linked peoples of different societies at different times in the past. This structure allows us to make cross-cultural comparisons that help frame world history for students to put events in a perspective that renders them more understandable.

UNIFYING THEMES

The themes of traditions and encounters that give this book its title bring focus to the human experience. Together they account for much of the historical development of human societies.

The theme of *tradition* draws attention to the dynamics of individual societies. From their earliest days on earth, human groups have generated distinctive political, social, economic, and cultural traditions that have guided affairs in their own societies. Some of these traditions arose and disappeared relatively quickly, while others influenced human affairs over the centuries and millennia, sometimes down to the present day.

The world's peoples have interacted with one another since the earliest days of history. The theme of *encounters* directs attention to the elements that have linked individual societies to their neighbors and others in the larger world. Whether in the form of mass migrations, the spread of infectious diseases, imperial expansion, long-distance trade, or the multitude of other ways in which peoples interact, these encounters have profoundly influenced the experiences of individual societies and the development of the world as a whole.

Like the structure, the strong themes illuminate the events of history for students, enhancing their understanding of and appreciation for world history in a way they can use and apply to their point of view as world events unfold throughout their lives.

ENGAGING NARRATIVE

The structure and themes provide a strong foundation on which the story of global history can be told in an engrossing way. Each chapter-opening narrative tells the story of a man or woman caught in the currents of movement and exchange. Whether it be Xuanzang, a Chinese monk who illegally travels to India to study Buddhism and bring it back to his native land, or Doña Marina, a slave girl of noble descent in Central Mexico who serves as translator and aid to the Spanish conquistador, Hernán Cortés, as he conquers her native land, each story serves as portal to engage students and to foster their enthusiasm for the study of the world's past.

STRONG VISUAL APPEAL

Throughout the book, *images* are seamlessly integrated into the narrative to enhance and support the stories of history that unfold through the themes of traditions and encounters. Students interested in the story of Xuanzang can see a scroll depicting his return to China with caravan of oxen carrying 657 books, relics, and images.

And in Chapter Twenty-two a depiction of the controversial figure, Doña Marina, shows her standing centrally between Hernán Cortés and a Tlax-cala ruler as they enter into an alliance against the Aztecs. All of the images in the book were carefully researched and chosen to support and enlighten the stories of the past.

Each *map* in the book provides a clear pedagogical purpose to enrich student's understanding of the relationship between geography and history. Interactive maps are also available on the book's website, and they are called out throughout the text with this icon.

Interactive Map

The Ottoman empire

SOLID PEDAGOGY

This text contains a carefully selected range of tools to enhance student comprehension and enthusiasm.

    Part openers explain the rationale behind a major era of human history, and all part openers combine to provide a cohesive summary of the seven-era scheme, the larger interpretive framework of the book.

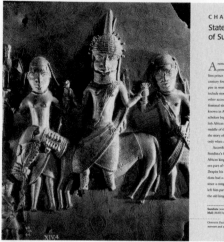

Chapter-opening vignettes draw the reader into the larger story and allow students to remember that world history is really about people.

Sources from the Past, a primary source excerpt, are in every chapter. These excerpts were selected to illustrate fundamental ideas raised in the text and to provide individual voices from the human past.

SOURCES FROM THE PAST

First Impressions of Spanish Forces

As the Spanish army made its way to Tenochtitlan, Motecuzoma dispatched a series of emissaries to communicate with Cortés and learn his intentions. The reports that came back were not reassuring. They brought disturbing news about Spanish weapons, armor, horses, and dogs that were much larger and more aggressive than the small, barkless animals that were native to Mexico.

And when [Motecuzoma] had heard what the messengers reported, he was terrified, he was astounded. . . .

Especially did it cause him to faint away when he heard how the gun, at [the Spaniards'] command, discharged [the shot]; how it resounded as if it thundered when it went off. It indeed bereft one of strength; it shut off one's ears. And when it discharged, something like a round pebble came forth from within. Fire went showering forth; sparks went blazing forth. And its smoke smelled very foul; it had a fetid odor which verily wounded the head. And when [the shot] struck a mountain, it was as if it were destroyed, dissolved. And a tree was pulverized; it was as if it vanished; it was as if someone blew it away.

All iron was their war array. In iron they clothed themselves. With iron they covered their heads. Iron were their swords. Iron were their crossbows. Iron were their shields. Iron were their lances.

And those which bore them upon their backs, their deer [that is, horses], were as tall as roof terraces.

And their bodies were everywhere covered; only their faces appeared. They were very white; they had chalky faces; they had yellow hair, though the hair of some was black. Long were their beards; they also were yellow. They were yellow-headed. [The black men's hair] was kinky, like maize stalks, good-tasting as if of maize stalk flour; a little sweet, a little honeyed. It was honeyed to eat; it was sweet to eat.

And their dogs were very large. They had ears folded over; great dragging jowls. They had fiery eyes—blazing eyes; they had yellow eyes—fiery yellow eyes. They had thin flanks—flanks with ribs showing. They had gaunt stomachs. They were very tall. They were nervous; they went about panting, with tongues hanging out. They were spotted like ocelots; they were varicolored.

And when Motecuzoma heard all this, he was much terrified. It was as if he fainted away. His heart saddened; his heart failed him.

• *In light of the reports that he received, what were Motecuzoma's options for dealing with the Spanish threat?*

SOURCE: Bernardino de Sahagún. *Florentine Codex: General History of the Things of New Spain,* 13 vols. Trans. by Arthur J. O. Anderson and Charles E. Dibble. Salt Lake City: University of Utah Press, 1950–82, 13:19–20. (Translation slightly modified.)

Running Pronunciation Guide at the bottom of each page helps readers with unfamiliar words and names. An audio version is also available online.

formed sacrifices similar to those conducted by the *brahmins* in India. Like the Aryans, the ancient Persians glorified strength and martial virtues, and the cults of both peoples sought principally to bring about a comfortable material existence for their practitioners.

During the classical era Persian religion underwent considerable change, as moral and religious thinkers *Zarathustra* sought to adapt their messages to the circumstances of a complex, cosmopolitan society. One result was Zoroastrianism, which emerged from the teachings of Zarathustra. Though Zarathustra was undoubtedly a historical person, little certain information survives about his life and career. It is not even clear when he lived, though most scholars date his life to the late seventh and early sixth centuries

Avesta. Nevertheless, many of Zarathustra's own compositions survive because of the diligence by which *magi* preserved them through oral transmission. Known as the *Gathas,* Zarathustra's works were hymns that he composed in honor of the various deities that he recognized. Apart from the *Gathas,* ancient Zoroastrian literature included a wide variety of hymns, liturgical works, and treatises on moral and theological themes. Though some of these works survive, the arrival of Islam in the seventh century C.E. and the subsequent decline of Zoroastrianism resulted in the loss of most of the Avesta and later Zoroastrian works.

Zarathustra and his followers were not strict monotheists. They recognized Ahura Mazda as a supreme

Zoroastrianism (zohr-oh-ASS-tree-ahn-iz'm)

Zarathustra (zar-uh-THOO-struh)
Gathas (GATH-uhs)

Liu Bang called the new dynasty the Han, in honor of his native land. The Han dynasty turned out to be one of the longest and most influential in all of Chinese history. It lasted for more than four hundred years, from 206 B.C.E. to 220 C.E., although for a brief period (9–23 C.E.) a usurper temporarily displaced Han rule. Thus historians conventionally divide the dynasty into the Former Han (206 B.C.E.–9 C.E.) and the Later Han (25–220 C.E.).

The Han dynasty consolidated the tradition of centralized imperial rule that the Qin dynasty had pioneered. During the Former Han, emperors ruled from Chang'an, a cosmopolitan city near modern Xi'an that became the cultural capital of China. During the Later Han, the emperors moved their capital east to Luoyang, also a cosmopolitan city and second in importance only to Chang'an throughout much of Chinese history.

During the early days of the Han dynasty, Liu Bang attempted to follow a middle path between the decentralized political alliances of the Zhou dynasty and the tightly centralized state of the *Early Han Policies* Qin to save the advantages and avoid the excesses of both. On the one hand, he allotted large landholdings to members of the imperial family, in the expectation that they would provide a reliable network

Domestically, Han Wudi worked strenuously to increase the authority and prestige of the central government. He built an enormous bureaucracy to administer his empire, *Han Centralization* and he relied on Legalist principles of government. He also continued the Qin policy of building roads and canals to facilitate trade and communication between China's regions. To finance the vast machinery of his government, he levied taxes on agriculture, trade, and craft industries, and he established imperial monopolies on the production of essential goods such as iron and salt. In building such an enormous governmental structure, Han Wudi faced a serious problem of recruitment. He needed thousands of reliable, intelligent, educated individuals to run his bureaucracy, but there was no institutionalized educational system in China that could provide a continuous supply of such people.

Han Wudi addressed that problem in 124 B.C.E. by establishing an imperial university that prepared young men for government service. Personally, *The Confucian Educational System* the Martial Emperor cared little for learning. In that respect he resembled all the other early Han emperors: Liu Bang once emptied his bladder in the distinctive cap worn by Confucian scholars in order to demonstrate his con-

The Marginal Key Terms highlight events and concepts as they appear within the narrative.

A *Chronology* at the end of each chapter lists the key dates and events of the chapter to provide an easy overview.

CHRONOLOGY	
1ST TO 6TH CENTURY	Kingdom of Funan
606–648	Reign of Harsha
670–1025	Kingdom of Srivijaya
711	Conquest of Sind by Umayyad forces
850–1267	Chola kingdom
889–1431	Kingdom of Angkor
1001–1027	Raids on India by Mahmud of Ghazni
11TH TO 12TH CENTURY	Life of Ramanuja
12TH CENTURY	Beginning of the bhakti movement
1206–1526	Sultanate of Delhi
1336–1565	Kingdom of Vijayanagar

SUMMARY

After gaining independence from European colonial powers, the states of the western hemisphere worked to build stable and prosperous societies. The independent American states faced difficult challenges as they sought to construct viable societies on the Enlightenment principles of freedom, equality, and constitutional government. The United States and Canada built large federal societies in North America, whereas a series of smaller states governed affairs in Latin America. Throughout the hemisphere descendants of European settlers subdued indigenous American peoples and built societies dominated by Euro-American peoples. They established agricultural economies, exploited natural resources, and in some lands launched processes of industrialization. They accepted streams of European and Asian migrants, who contributed to American cultural diversity. All American lands experienced tensions arising from social, economic, cultural, and ethnic differences, which led occasionally to violent civil conflict and often to smoldering resentments and grievances. The making of independent American societies was not a smooth process, but it reflected the increasing interdependence of all the world's peoples.

Summaries: Each chapter ends with a clearly written, paragraph-long summary to remind students of the highlights they have just read.

And, finally, *For Further Reading* provides an annotated list of references that students can use for research assignments or their own study.

FOR FURTHER READING

Colin G. Calloway. *First Peoples: A Documentary Survey of American Indian History.* Boston, 1999. A fine text on native American history, written by a knowledgeable scholar in the field.

Fernando Henrique Cardoso and Enzo Faletto. *Dependency and Development in Latin America.* Berkeley, 1979. A sophisticated treatment of economic development in Latin America.

William Cronon. *Nature's Metropolis: Chicago and the Great West.* New York, 1991. A valuable study exploring the role of Chicago in the economic development of the American west.

Tulio Halperín Donghi. *The Contemporary History of Latin America.* Trans. by J. C. Chasteen. Durham, 1993. An influential general history of Latin America from a Latin American point of view.

Ellen C. DuBois. *Feminism and Suffrage: The Emergence of an Independent Women's Movement in America, 1848–1869.* Ithaca, 1984. Traces the rise and character of the U.S. women's movement in the nineteenth century.

Patricia Nelson Limerick. *The Legacy of Conquest: The Unbroken Past of the American West.* New York, 1987. A provocative work exploring the influences of race, class, and gender in the conquest of the American west.

Leon F. Litwack. *Been in the Storm So Long: The Aftermath of Slavery.* New York, 1979. The best study of the promises and perils of life for freed slaves after the U.S. Civil War.

J. R. Miller. *Skyscrapers Hide the Heavens: A History of Indian-White Relations in Canada.* Toronto, 1989. An important study of Canadian policies toward indigenous peoples.

Walter Nugent. *Crossings: The Great Transatlantic Migrations, 1870–1914.* Bloomington, 1992. Provides an overview and analysis of the mass migrations to North America in the nineteenth and twentieth centuries.

Ronald Takaki. *A Different Mirror: A History of Multicultural America.* Boston, 1993. A spirited account of the contributions made by peoples of European, African, Asian, and Native American ancestry to the modern American society.

Throughout the three editions of *Traditions & Encounters: A Global Perspective on the Past,* upon which this text is based, we have benefited from the feedback of instructors and students. Our approach to world history and the manner in which it resonates in the text has been honed by classroom experiences that many others have so generously shared with us. We hope the dialogue continues with the publication of *Traditions & Encounters: A Brief Global History* and that our approach can continue to evolve. World history is a passion for all three of us, and we hope that our texts help to instill in students today a lifelong appreciation for the field as well.

Jerry H. Bentley
Herbert F. Ziegler
Heather E. Streets

Acknowledgments

Many individuals have contributed to this book, and the authors take pleasure in recording deep thanks for all the comments, criticism, advice, and suggestions that helped to improve the work. Special thanks to the editorial and production teams at McGraw-Hill: Lyn Uhl, Jon-David Hague, Angela Kao, Lisa Pinto, Christina Gimlin, Kim Menning, and Brian Pecko who provided crucial support by helping the authors work through difficult issues and solve the innumerable problems of content, style, and organization that arise in any project to produce a history of the world. Finally, we would like to express our appreciation for the advice of the following individuals who read and commented on the original manuscript and previous editions of this text.

Heather J. Abdelnur
Blackburn College

Wayne Ackerson
Salisbury University

William H. Alexander
Norfolk State University

Michael Balyo
Chemeketa Community College

Diane Barefoot
Caldwell Community College, Watauga Campus

Gene Barnett
Calhoun Community College

John Boswell
San Antonio College

W. H. Bragg
Georgia College and State University

Robert Brown
UNC Pembroke

Gayle Brunelle
California State University, Fullerton

Marybeth Carlson
University of Dayton

Kay J. Carr
Southern Illinois University

Jon Davidann
Hawaii Pacific University

Mitch Driebe
Andrew College

Shannon Duffy
Loyola University of New Orleans

Shawn Dry
Oakland Community College

Robert J. Flynn
Portland Community College

Deanna D. Forsman
North Hennepin Community College

Kristine Frederickson
Brigham Young University

James Fuller
University of Indianapolis

Jessie Ruth Gaston
California State University, Sacramento

George W. Gawrych
Baylor University

Deborah Gerish
Emporia State University

Gary G. Gibbs
Roanoke College

Candace Gregory
California State University, Sacramento

Jillian Hartley
Arkansas Northeastern College

Gregory Havrilcsak
The University of Michigan, Flint

John K. Hayden
Southwest Oklahoma State University

Thomas J. Hegarty
University of Tampa

Michael Hickey
Bloomsburg University

Tamara Hunt
University of Southern Indiana

Wallace Hutcheon
Northern Virginia Community College

Karen Irizarry
Southwestern College

Christopher Johnson
Palomar College

Roger L. Jungmeyer
Lincoln University of Missouri

Carole A. Keller
San Antonio College

Charles Keller
Southern Arkansas University

Mee-Ae Kim
Albertson College of Idaho

Mark Konnerty
University of Calgary

Alan D. Lane
Barton College

Marcus Larsen
University of Wisconsin–Eau Claire

Laurence W. Marvin
*Evans School of Humanities,
Berry College*

Ken Millen-Penn
Fairmont State University

April Najjaj
Greensboro College

Kenneth Osgood
Florida Atlantic University

Patrick Peebles
University of Missouri, Kansas City

Phyllis E. Pobst
Arkansas State University

Ronald E. Powaski
Cleveland State University

Dave Pretty
Winthrop University

Tracie Provost
Middle Georgia College

Paul C. Rosier
Villanova University

Margaret Sankey
Minnesota State Moorhead

Daniel Sarefield
Ohio State University

Thomas Saylor
Concordia University, St. Paul

Stuart Schaar
Brooklyn College

Timothy Schroer
University of West Georgia

Francis M. Stackenwalt
East Central University

Gordon C. Thomasson
Broome Community College

John Tucker
East Carolina University

Sara Tucker
Washburn University

Wendy Turner
August State University

David Ulbrich
Ball State University

Rick Whisonant
York Technical College

Pingchao Zhu
University of Idaho

About the Authors

Jerry H. Bentley is professor of history at the University of Hawai'i and editor of the *Journal of World History*. He has written extensively on the cultural history of early modern Europe and on cross-cultural interactions in world history. His research on the religious, moral, and political writings of the Renaissance led to the publication of *Humanists and Holy Writ: New Testament Scholarship in the Renaissance* (1983) and *Politics and Culture in Renaissance Naples* (1987). His more recent research has concentrated on global history and particularly on processes of cross-cultural interaction. His book *Old World Encounters: Cross-Cultural Contacts and Exchanges in Pre-Modern Times* (1993) studies processes of cultural exchange and religious conversion before modern times, and his pamphlet *Shapes of World History in Twentieth-Century Scholarship* (1996) discusses the historiography of world history. His current interests include processes of cross-cultural interaction and cultural exchange in modern times.

Herbert F. Ziegler is an associate professor of history at the University of Hawai'i. He has taught world history since 1980 and currently serves as director of the world history program at the University of Hawai'i. He also serves as book review editor of the *Journal of World History*. His interest in twentieth-century European social and political history led to the publication of *Nazi Germany's New Aristocracy* (1990). He is at present working on a study that explores from a global point of view the demographic trends of the past ten thousand years, along with their concomitant technological, economic, and social developments. His other current research project focuses on the application of complexity theory to a comparative study of societies and their internal dynamics.

Heather Streets is an associate professor of history at Washington State University, where she teaches world history at the graduate and undergraduate levels. She has been teaching at WSU since 1998 and is the director of the WSU history department's world history Ph.D. program. Streets is also co-editor of *World History Connected: the ejournal of Learning and Teaching*. Recent publications include *Martial Races: The Military, Race, and Masculinity in British Imperial Culture, 1857–1914* (2004). She is currently researching 19th and 20th century imperialism as a global phenomenon rather than as a strictly national issue. Her next book will explore the connections between French Indochina, the Dutch East Indies, and British India as a way of demonstrating that the various national empires learned from, imitated, and stayed in contact with one another.

Connections in History, Connections in Class:
Resources for Students and Instructors

Texts these days abound in print and media resources for students and instructors, and we begin to wonder what instructor or student has time to sort through all of the resources available and make use of them in class or for studying. As we developed the text, we worked to discover exactly what tools instructors and students need to be successful in the course, and how to make these resources as easy to use as possible.

As a result of extensive research, we have streamlined the traditional laundry list of ancillary items available with texts these days onto a single rich Web site to support teaching and learning with *Traditions & Encounters: A Brief Global History*.

THE ONLINE LEARNING CENTER FOR STUDENTS

We have created tools for students that reinforce the text's chapters and encourage their interest in world history. The Online Learning Center, or OLC, serves two purposes: 1) Help students prepare for exams, and 2) Help students conduct research for papers and presentations. The OLC is a complete, straightforward media resource that provides a multitude of practice quizzes as well as readings and images for outside research.

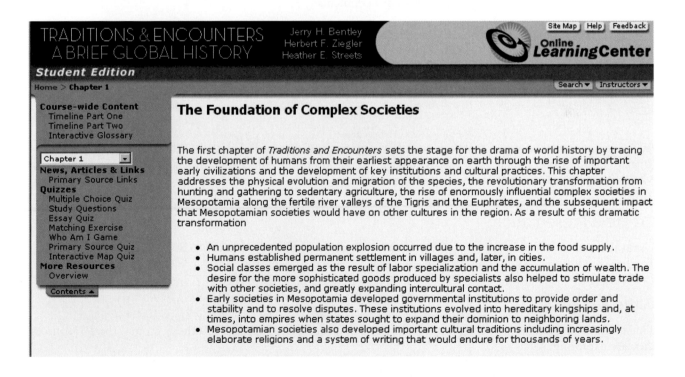

To simplify matters for instructors, we provide a map of every feature on the OLC in a downloadable Faculty Guide, so that instructors can see exactly what kind of study tools the student is using and coordinate those tools with their own class assignments. (See below for more information.)

Primary Source Investigator (PSI) on the Online Learning Center

Beginning historians must learn to use primary and secondary sources to formulate and defend their arguments. Available online for the first time, McGraw-Hill's *Primary Source Investigator (PSI)* is designed to support and enrich the text discussion in *Traditions & Encounters: A Brief Global History*.

Access to Sources:

A selection of the resources available through PSI are integrated into the text itself. Throughout the text, marginal icons show that an additional source is available for free on the OLC.

Primary Source
"Battuta in China"

Image
The Diamond Sutra

Interactive Map
The Silk Roads

- **Primary Source Documents**: Documents include contemporary accounts of events that appeared in books, newspapers, or private letters of an era as well as government documents.

- **Images:** These include photographs of artifacts and buildings as well as contemporary paintings, engravings, and drawings.

- **Interactive Maps:** These maps actively illustrate historical changes over time.

Additional secondary sources materials such as videos are available on PSI but not integrated into the text. Informative and of high quality, the videos engage student interest in topics such as Islamic scientific advances or Mesoamerican civilizations.

Create a Presentation:

Using the sources available through *PSI*, students and teachers can choose sources to build a custom presentation. Teachers can use this tool for presentations during lectures and students for in-class presentation assignments.

Write a Paper:

This useful tool guides students through the process of creating and supporting a thesis around the *PSI* sources they are exploring.

Study Tools on the Online Learning Center

We understand that research is only part of a world history course. This portion of the OLC provides students with study tools to aid in exam preparation.

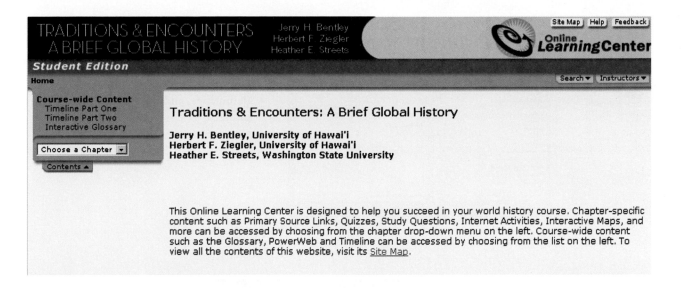

- **Blank Maps:** All of the maps from the book are available for download without any labels, keys, or captions. Students can print these out to quiz themselves on geography.

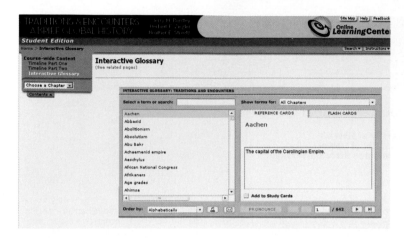

- **Interactive Glossary:** A textbook for world history naturally spans many different countries and languages. This interactive glossary is formatted in a flashcard template with over 600 terms, definitions, and an audio pronunciation guide.

- **Practice Quizzes:** Each chapter contains a variety of quizzes with questions in a variety of formats: multiple choice, true/false, short answer, and essay.

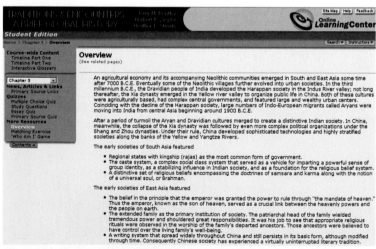

- **Review Summaries:** A chapter outline and overview help to reinforce the big picture of each chapter.

- **Interactive Maps with Quizzes:** Created directly from the maps in the book, the online interactive maps in each chapter are accompanied by critical thinking questions.

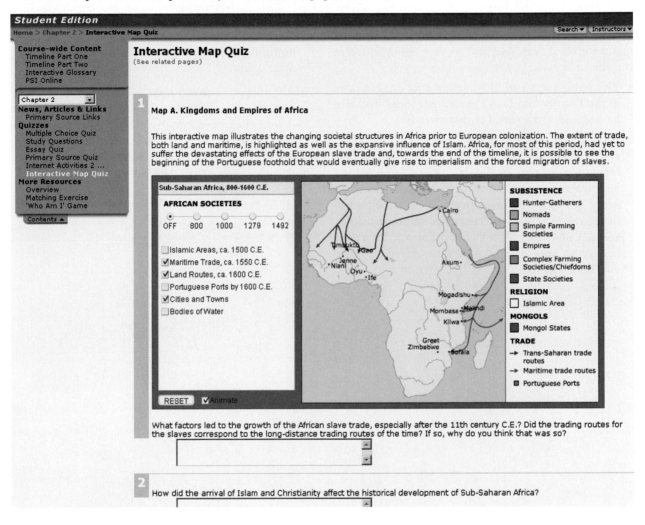

EFFORTLESS TEACHING TOOLS: THE ONLINE *FACULTY GUIDE* WITH INSTRUCTOR'S RESOURCE

This instructor's tool contains the best of the premier resources that are traditionally available for the larger version of this text:

- Image bank
- Premier PowerPoint Slides with over 100 images and maps
- Instructor's Manual

- Test Bank
- EZ TEST (a computerized test bank)
- Classroom Performance System questions (see below)
- New *Faculty Guide* to resources

The *Faculty Guide* provides easy reference to all learning assets available to both teachers and students. McGraw-Hill resources are organized within chapter outlines to streamline lecture and assignment preparation. Faculty will see the options and sources at a glance, and where to find them on the Web site.

ADDITIONAL TOOLS
FOR THE INSTRUCTOR

We identified two other resources that are in high demand for classroom use, and so they are included in the resource package for instructors as well:

- The same maps and illustrations that are available in the Faculty Guide as PowerPoint slides may also be ordered as *overhead transparencies.*

- A *classroom response system* using electronic "clickers" is available. McGraw-Hill's Classroom Performance System (CPS) by eInstruction allows instructors to gauge immediately what students are learning during lectures. Instructors can ask questions, take polls, host classroom demonstrations, and get instant feedback. In addition, CPS makes it easy to take attendance, give and grade pop quizzes, or give formal paper-based class tests with multiple versions of the test using CPS for immediate grading.

Instructors can contact their McGraw-Hill sales representative for all of the above resources. You can find your sales representative at www.mhhe.com/rep.

We hope that these tightly integrated resources make the teaching and learning of world history more manageable than ever before.

J. H. B.
H. F. Z.
H. E. S.

TRADITIONS & ENCOUNTERS

For thousands of years after the emergence of the human species, human beings lived in tiny communities, and they traveled regularly in pursuit of game and edible plants. Yet intelligence set human beings apart from the other members of the animal kingdom and enabled human groups to invent tools and techniques that enhanced their ability to exploit the natural environment.

Although humans altered the earth to suit their needs even in remote prehistoric times, they crossed an important threshold when they began to experiment with agriculture about twelve thousand years ago. Soon it became clear that cultivation provided a larger and more reliable food supply than foraging. Groups that turned to agriculture experienced rapid population growth, and they settled in permanent communities. Some of these developed into cities: the world's first complex societies.

The term *complex society* refers to a form of large-scale social organization in which productive agricultural economies resulted in surplus food. That surplus allowed some people to devote their time to specialized tasks other than food production, and to congregate in urban settlements. During the centuries from 3500 to 500 B.C.E., complex societies arose independently in several regions of the world, including Mesopotamia, Egypt, northern India, China, Mesoamerica, and the central Andean region of South America. All established political authorities, built states with formal governmental institutions, collected surplus agricultural production in the form of taxes or tribute, and redistributed wealth. Complex societies also traded with other peoples, and they often sought to extend their authority to surrounding territories.

1

Complex societies were able to generate and preserve much more wealth than smaller societies. When bequeathed to heirs and held within particular families, this accumulated wealth became the foundation for social distinctions. These societies developed different kinds of social distinctions, but all recognized several classes of people, including ruling elites, common people, and slaves.

All early complex societies also created sophisticated cultural traditions. Most of them either invented or borrowed a system of writing, which quickly came to be used to construct traditions of literature, learning, and reflection. All the complex societies

THE EARLY COMPLEX SOCIETIES, 3500 TO 500 B.C.E.

organized systems of formal education that introduced intellectual elites to skills such as writing and astronomical observation deemed necessary for their societies' survival. In many cases individuals also produced works that explored the nature of humanity, the world, and the gods. Some of these works inspired religious and philosophical traditions for two millennia or more.

Complex society was not the only form of social organization that early human groups constructed, but it was an unusually important and influential type of society. Indeed, complex societies deployed their power, pursued their interests, and promoted their values over much larger regions than did smaller societies. Because of that, most of the world's peoples have led their lives under the influence of complex societies.

CHAPTER 1

The Foundations of Complex Societies

By far, the best-known individual of ancient Mesopotamian society was a man named Gilgamesh. According to historical sources, Gilgamesh was the fifth king of the city of Uruk. He ruled about 2750 B.C.E., and he led his community in its conflicts with Kish, a nearby city that was the principal rival of Uruk.

Gilgamesh was a figure of Mesopotamian mythology and folklore as well as history. He was the subject of numerous poems and legends, and Mesopotamian bards made him the central figure in a cycle of stories known collectively as the *Epic of Gilgamesh*. As a figure of legend, Gilgamesh became the greatest hero figure of ancient Mesopotamia. According to the stories, the gods granted Gilgamesh a perfect body and endowed him with superhuman strength and courage. The legends declare that he constructed the massive city walls of Uruk as well as several of the city's magnificent temples to Mesopotamian deities.

The stories that make up the *Epic of Gilgamesh* recount the adventures of this hero and his cherished friend Enkidu as they sought fame. They killed an evil monster, rescued Uruk from a ravaging bull, and matched wits with the gods. In spite of their heroic deeds, Enkidu offended the gods and fell under a sentence of death. His loss profoundly affected Gilgamesh, who sought for some means to cheat death and gain eternal life. He eventually found a magical plant that had the power to confer immortality, but a serpent stole the plant and carried it away, forcing Gilgamesh to recognize that death is the ultimate fate

---

Uruk (OO-rook)

OPPOSITE PAGE: The Royal Standard of Ur, *a painting dating from about 2700 B.C.E., depicts scenes from daily life in the Sumerian city-state of Ur.*

of all human beings. Thus, while focusing on the activities of Gilgamesh and Enkidu, the stories explored themes of friendship, loyalty, ambition, fear of death, and longing for immortality. In doing so they reflected the interests and concerns of the complex, urban-based society that had recently emerged in Mesopotamia.

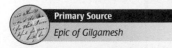

Primary Source
Epic of Gilgamesh

Yet such interests and concerns had their foundation deep in the human past. By the time Mesopotamian society emerged, our own species of human, *Homo sapiens,* had existed for about two hundred thousand years. These humans, who themselves descended from earlier hominids, were already accomplished problem solvers and thinkers long before urban societies developed. In fact, early human communities were responsible for laying the social, economic, and cultural foundations on which their descendants built increasingly complex societies—especially through the domestication of plants and animals and by establishing agricultural economies.

Indeed, productive agricultural economies supported the development of the first known complex societies during the fourth millennium B.C.E. Such societies, in which sizable numbers of people lived in cities and extended their political, social, economic, and cultural influence over large regions, emerged first in southwest Asia, particularly in Mesopotamia. As these complex societies developed and grew, people found that they needed to resolve disputes that inevitably arose as individual and group interests conflicted. In Mesopotamia, settled agricultural peoples in search of order recognized political authorities and built states. The establishment of states in turn encouraged the creation of empires, as some states sought to extend their power by imposing their rule on neighboring lands.

Apart from stimulating the establishment of states, urban society in Mesopotamia also promoted the emergence of social classes, thus giving rise to increasingly complex social and economic structures. Cities fostered specialized labor, and the efficient production of high-quality goods in turn stimulated trade. Furthermore, early Mesopotamia also developed distinctive cultural traditions as Mesopotamians invented a system of writing and supported organized religions.

Mesopotamian and other peoples regularly interacted with one another, which helped further the geographic reach of Mesopotamian society. Some Indo-European peoples also had direct dealings with their Mesopotamian contemporaries, with effects crucial for both Indo-European and Mesopotamian societies. Other Indo-European peoples never heard of Mesopotamia, but they employed Mesopotamian inventions such as wheels and metallurgy when undertaking extensive migrations that profoundly influenced historical development throughout much of Eurasia from western Europe to India and beyond. Even in the earliest days of city life, the world was the site of frequent and intense interaction between peoples of different societies.

THE TRANSITION TO AGRICULTURE

Between twelve and six thousand years ago, humans crossed a critical threshold of immense significance for the species, and the earth more generally, when they began to domesticate plants and animals. That transition to agriculture led to a population explosion, which enabled human communities to establish themselves in far greater numbers around the world than ever before. Agriculture also led to new forms of social organization, which ultimately resulted in the birth of the world's first urban centers.

The Paleolithic Era

Homo sapiens ("consciously thinking human")—the direct ancestor of our own subspecies, *Homo sapiens sapiens*—evolved about two hundred thousand years ago from a hominid ancestry that originated in east Africa about four to five million years ago. *Homo sapiens* possessed larger brains and greater intelligence than earlier hominids—a feature that enabled them to adapt to widely varying environmental conditions and to displace earlier hominid species. More than one hundred thousand years ago, communities of *Homo sapiens* began to spread throughout the temperate lands of the eastern hemisphere. Using their intelligence to make warm clothes and shelters, *Homo sapiens* soon

Homo sapiens

Interactive Map
Spread of the earliest humans

---

hominid (HAW-mih-nihd)

Homo sapiens (HOH-moh SAY-pyans)
Homo sapiens sapiens (HOH-moh SAY-pyans SAY-pyans)

established communities in progressively colder regions. Then, between sixty and fifteen thousand years ago, *Homo sapiens* took advantage of land bridges exposed by lowered sea levels and spread to Indonesia, New Guinea, Australia, and finally, the Americas. Thus by about fifteen thousand years ago, communities of *Homo sapiens* had appeared in almost every habitable region of the world.

For most of human existence—indeed, from the evolution of the first hominids until about twelve thousand years ago—our ancestors foraged for their food. In other words, they hunted wild animals or gathered edible products of naturally growing plants. That reliance on foraging characterized what historians and archaeologists call the *paleolithic era,* or the "old stone age."

The conditions of foraging economies decisively influenced all dimensions of the human experience during the paleolithic era. For instance, because of constant mobility in the search for food, a foraging economy virtually prohibits individuals from accumulating private property and basing social distinctions on wealth. In the absence of accumulated wealth, hunters and gatherers of paleolithic times probably lived a relatively egalitarian existence. Some scholars believe that this relative social equality also extended to relations between the sexes, because all members of a paleolithic group made important contributions to the survival of the community. Although meat from the hunt (provided by men) was the most highly prized item in the paleolithic diet, plant foods (provided by women) were essential to survival and sustained communities when the hunt did not succeed. Because of the thorough interdependence of the sexes from the viewpoint of food production, paleolithic society probably did not encourage the domination of one sex by the other.

The Neolithic Era

Between twelve and six thousand years ago, human communities in a variety of locations underwent profound economic, social, and political changes when they began to experiment with the domestication of plants and animals. Scientists refer to this period as the *neolithic era,* or "new stone age," because of the polished stone tools associated with peoples who relied on cultivation for subsistence.

Neolithic peoples sought to ensure themselves of more regular food supplies by encouraging the growth of edible crops and bringing wild animals

into dependence on human keepers. Many scholars believe that women most likely began the systematic care of plants. As the principal gatherers in foraging communities, women in neolithic societies probably began to nurture plants instead of simply collecting available foods in the wild. Meanwhile, instead of just stalking game with the intention of killing it for meat, neolithic men began to capture animals and domesticate them by providing for their needs and supervising their breeding. Over a period of decades and centuries, these practices gradually led to the formation of agricultural economies.

The transition to agriculture—including both the cultivation of crops and the domestication of animals—emerged independently in several parts of the world. The earliest evidence of agricultural activity discovered so far dates to the era after 9000 B.C.E. in southwest Asia (modern-day Iraq, Syria, and Turkey). Between 9000 and 7000 B.C.E., agriculture also emerged among African peoples inhabiting the southeastern margin of the Sahara desert (modern-day Sudan), and then among the peoples of sub-Saharan west Africa (in the vicinity of modern Nigeria) between 8000 and 6000 B.C.E. In east Asia, residents of the Yangzi River valley began to cultivate crops as early as 6500 B.C.E., and their neighbors to the north in the Yellow River valley did the same after 5500 B.C.E. In southeast Asia the cultivation of crops dates from an indeterminate but very early time, probably 3000 B.C.E. or earlier. In the western hemisphere, inhabitants of Mesoamerica (central Mexico) cultivated plants as early as 4000 B.C.E., and residents of the central Andean region of South America (modern Peru) followed suit after 3000 B.C.E. It is also possible that the Amazon River valley was yet another site of independently invented agriculture.

The Early Spread of Agriculture

Once established, agriculture spread rapidly. As a result, foods originally cultivated in only one region also spread widely, as merchants, migrants, or other travelers carried knowledge of these foods to agricultural lands that previously had relied on different crops. However, agriculture did not spread rapidly because it was easier than foraging. On the contrary, agriculture involved long hours of hard physical labor—clearing land, preparing fields, planting seeds, pulling weeds, and harvesting crops—and thus probably required more work than paleolithic foraging. Yet agriculture had its own appeal in that it made possible the production of abundant food supplies, which in turn allowed human populations to grow to unprecedented levels. For example, historians estimate that before agriculture, about 10,000 B.C.E., the earth's human population was about four million. By 500 B.C.E., after agriculture had spread to most world regions, the human population had risen to about one hundred million.

Such rapidly increasing populations encouraged neolithic peoples to adopt new forms of social organiza-

The Development of Social Distinctions

tion. Because they devoted their time to cultivation rather than to foraging, neolithic peoples did not continue the migratory life of their paleolithic pre-decessors but, rather, settled near their fields in permanent villages. Most people in neolithic villages cultivated crops or kept animals, and many even continued to hunt and forage for wild plants. But a surplus of food enabled some individuals to concentrate their time and talents on enterprises that had nothing to do with the production of food, especially pottery making, metallurgy, and textile production. Moreover, the concentration of people into permanent settlements and the increasing specialization of labor provided the first opportunity for individuals to accumulate considerable wealth. The institutionalization of privately owned landed property—which occurred at an uncertain date after the introduction of agriculture—enhanced the significance of accumulated wealth. Because land was (and remains) the ultimate source of wealth in any agricultural society, ownership of land carried enormous economic power. When especially successful individuals managed to consolidate wealth in their families' hands and kept it there for several generations, clearly defined social classes emerged.

Within four thousand years of its introduction, agriculture had dramatically transformed the face of the

Çatal Hüyük

earth. Human beings multiplied prodigiously, congregated in densely populated quarters, placed the surrounding lands under cultivation, and domesticated several species of animals. Besides altering the physical appearance of the earth, agriculture transformed the lives of human beings. Even a modest neolithic village dwarfed a paleolithic band of a few dozen hunters and gatherers. In larger villages and towns, with their populations of several thousand people, their specialized labor, and their craft industries, social relationships became more complex than would have been conceivable during paleolithic times.

Excavations carried out at Çatal Hüyük, one of the best-known neolithic settlements, have helped confirm that view. Located in south-central Anatolia (modern Turkey), Çatal Hüyük grew from a small village to a bustling town of five thousand inhabitants between its

settlement in 7250 B.C.E. and its abandonment in 5400 B.C.E. Archaeological evidence indicates that because the site was close to large obsidian deposits, Çatal Hüyük became a center for production and trade in obsidian tools. The wealth generated from such trade in turn allowed increasing specialization of labor, so that residents eventually manufactured and traded pots, textiles, leather, beads, and jewelry at the site. Gradually, dense populations, specialized labor, and complex social relations such as those that developed at Çatal Hüyük gave rise to an altogether new form of social organization—the city.

THE QUEST FOR ORDER

The earliest known cities grew out of agricultural villages and towns in the valleys of the Tigris and Euphrates rivers in Mesopotamia (modern-day Iraq). During the fourth millennium B.C.E., human population increased rapidly in the area, which in turn presented inhabitants with the challenge of keeping order in a large-scale society. Over time, by experimentation and adaptation, they created states and governmental machinery that brought political and social order to their territories. Moreover, effective political and military organization enabled them to build regional empires and extend their authority to neighboring peoples.

Mesopotamia: "The Land between the Rivers"

The place-name *Mesopotamia* comes from two Greek words meaning "the land between the rivers." Mesopotamia receives little rainfall, but the Tigris and the Euphrates brought large volumes of fresh water to the region. Early cultivators realized that by tapping these rivers, building reservoirs, and digging canals, they could irrigate fields of barley, wheat, and peas. Small-scale irrigation began in Mesopotamia soon after 6000 B.C.E.

Artificial irrigation led to increased food supplies, which in turn supported a rapidly increasing human population and attracted migrants from other

Sumer

regions. Human numbers grew especially fast in the land of Sumer in the southern half of Mesopotamia. By about 5000 B.C.E. the Sumerians were constructing elaborate irrigation networks that helped them realize abundant agricultural harvests. By 3000 B.C.E. the population of Sumer approached one hun-

Map 1.1 Territories of early Mesopotamia between 3000 and 2000 B.C.E. Note that the borders of this society centered on the Euphrates and Tigris rivers. Why would the rivers have been important to early settlement?

dred thousand—an unprecedented concentration of people in ancient times—and the Sumerians were the dominant people of Mesopotamia.

Semitic Migrants

While supporting a growing population, the wealth of Sumer also attracted migrants from other regions. Most of the new arrivals were Semitic peoples—so called because they spoke tongues in the Semitic family of languages, including Akkadian, Aramaic, Hebrew, and Phoenician. Semitic peoples were nomadic herders who went to Mesopotamia from the Arabian and Syrian deserts to the south and west. They often intermarried with the Sumerians, and they largely adapted to Sumerian ways.

Sumerian City-States

Beginning about 4000 B.C.E., as human numbers increased in southern Mesopotamia, the Sumerians built the world's first cities. These cities differed markedly from the neolithic villages that preceded them. Unlike the earlier settlements, the Sumerian cities were centers of political and military authority, and their jurisdiction extended into the surrounding regions. Moreover, bustling marketplaces that drew buyers and sellers from near and far turned the cities

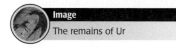

into economic centers as well. Finally, the cities also served as cultural centers where priests maintained organized religions and scribes developed traditions of writing and formal education. For almost a millennium, from 3200 to 2350 B.C.E., a dozen Sumerian cities—Eridu, Ur, Uruk, Lagash, Nippur, Kish, and others—dominated public affairs in Mesopotamia.

These cities all experienced internal and external pressures that prompted them to establish states—formal governmental institutions that wielded authority throughout their territories. Internally, the cities needed recognized authorities to maintain order and ensure that inhabitants cooperated on community projects. With their expanding populations, the cities also needed to prevent conflicts between urban residents from escalating into serious civic disorder. In addition, because agriculture was crucial to the welfare of urban residents, the cities all became city-states: they not only controlled public life within the city walls but also oversaw affairs in surrounding agricultural regions.

While preserving the peace, recognized authorities were also needed to organize work on projects of value to the entire community. Palaces, temples, and defensive walls dominated all the Sumerian cities. Particularly impressive were the ziggurats—distinctive stepped pyramids that housed temples and altars to the principal local deity. More important, however, were the irrigation systems that supported productive agriculture

Sumerians (soo-MEHR-ee-uhns)
Semitic (suh-MIHT-ihk)

The massive temple of the moon god Nanna-Suen (sometimes known as Sin) dominated the Sumerian city of Ur. Constructing temples of this size required a huge investment of resources and thousands of laborers.

and urban society. As their population grew, the Sumerians expanded their networks of reservoirs and canals, whose construction and maintenance required untold thousands of laborers and provided precious water for Sumerian crops.

As the wealth of Sumerian cities grew, they began to face increasing external problems from raiders outside the cities. The cities responded

Sumerian Kings   to that threat by building defensive walls and organizing military forces. Thus the need to recruit, train, equip, maintain, and deploy military forces created another demand for recognized authority. To answer that demand, the earliest Sumerian governments were probably made up of assemblies of prominent men who made decisions on behalf of the whole community. By about 3000 B.C.E., however, most Sumerian cities were ruled by individual kings who claimed absolute authority within their realms. By 2500 B.C.E. city-states ruled by kings dominated public life in Sumer.

---

ziggurats (ZIG-uh-rahts)

The Course of Empire

Conflicts between city-states often led to war between ambitious or aggrieved kings. However, after 2350 B.C.E. a series of conquerors sought to put an end to these constant conflicts by building empires that supervised the affairs of numerous subject cities and peoples.

The first of these conquerors was Sargon of Akkad. A talented administrator and brilliant warrior, Sargon (2370–2315 B.C.E.) began   *Sargon of Akkad* his career as a minister to the king of Kish. About 2334 B.C.E. he organized a coup against the king, recruited an army, and went on the offensive against the Sumerian city-states. He conquered the cities one by one, destroyed their defensive walls, and placed them under his own governors and administrators. Sargon financed his empire by seizing control of trade routes and taxing the goods that traveled along them, which allowed him to transform his capital at Akkad into the wealthiest and most powerful city in the world. At the high point of his reign, his empire embraced all of Mesopotamia, and his armies had ventured as far afield as the Mediterranean and the Black Sea.

By about 2150 B.C.E. Sargon's empire had collapsed in the midst of rebellion from within and invasion from outsiders. Yet the memory of his deeds, recorded in legends and histories as well as in his own works of propaganda, inspired later conquerors to follow his example. Most prominent of these later conquerors was the Babylonian Hammurabi (reigned 1792–1750 B.C.E.), who styled himself "king of the four quarters of the world." Hammurabi improved on Sargon's administrative techniques by relying on centralized bureaucratic rule and regular taxation rather than on suppression and plunder.

By these means Hammurabi developed a more efficient and predictable government than his predecessors and also spread its costs more evenly over the population. Hammurabi also sought to maintain his empire by providing it with a code of law, which became the most extensive and complete Mesopotamian law code up to that point. In the prologue to his laws, Hammurabi proclaimed that the gods had chosen him "to promote the welfare of the people, . . . to cause justice to prevail in the land, to destroy the wicked and evil, [so] that the strong might not oppress the weak, to rise like the sun over the people, and to light up the land." Hammurabi's laws established high standards of behavior and stern punishments for violators. They prescribed death penalties for murder, theft, fraud, false accusations, sheltering of runaway slaves, failure to obey royal orders, adultery, and incest. Civil laws regulated prices, wages, commercial dealings, marital relationships, and the conditions of slavery.

Hammurabi's Laws

The code relied heavily on the principle that offenders should suffer punishments resembling their violations. However, the code did not treat all social classes equally and demanded lesser punishments for those of higher classes who committed crimes against those of lower classes. In addition, local judges did not always follow the prescriptions of Hammurabi's code: indeed, they frequently relied on their own judgment when deciding cases that came before them. Nevertheless, Hammurabi's laws established a set of common standards that lent some degree of cultural unity to the far-flung Babylonian empire.

Eventually, the wealth of the Babylonian empire attracted invaders. Foremost among them were the Hittites, who had built a powerful empire in Anatolia

Hammurabi (hahm-uh-RAH-bee)

This handsome basalt stele shows Hammurabi receiving his royal authority from the sun god, Shamash. Some four thousand lines of Hammurabi's laws are inscribed below.

(modern-day Turkey). By about 1595 B.C.E. the Babylonian empire had crumbled before Hittite assaults. For several centuries after the fall of Babylon, southwest Asia was a land of considerable turmoil, as regional states competed for power and position while migrants and invaders struggled to establish footholds for themselves in Mesopotamia and neighboring regions.

Imperial rule returned to Mesopotamia with the Assyrians, a people from northern Mesopotamia who had built a compact state in the Tigris River valley during the nineteenth century B.C.E. Taking advantage of their location on trade routes running both north-south and east-west, the Assyrians built flourishing cities at Assur and Nineveh. They built a powerful and intimidating army by organizing their forces into standardized units and placing them under the command of professional officers chosen on the basis of merit and skill. They supplemented infantry with cavalry forces and light, swift, horse-drawn chariots, which they borrowed from the Hittites. These chariots were devastating instruments of war that allowed archers to attack their enemies from rapidly moving platforms.

The Assyrian Empire

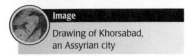
Image
Drawing of Khorsabad, an Assyrian city

Many states jockeyed for power following the collapse of the Babylonian empire, but after about 1300 B.C.E. the Assyrians gradually extended their authority to much of southwest Asia. At its high point, during the eighth and seventh centuries B.C.E., the Assyrian empire embraced not only Mesopotamia but also Syria, Palestine, much of Anatolia, and most of Egypt.

Like most other Mesopotamian peoples, the Assyrians relied on the administrative techniques pioneered by their Babylonian predecessors, and they

---

Assyrians (uh-SEER-ee-uhns)

followed laws much like those enshrined in the code of Hammurabi. They also preserved a great deal of Mesopotamian literature in huge libraries maintained at their large and lavish courts. Yet Assyrian domination was extremely unpopular and proved impossible to maintain. In 612 B.C.E. a combination of internal unrest and external assault brought the empire down.

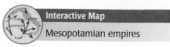
Interactive Map
Mesopotamian empires

For half a century, from 600 to 550 B.C.E., Babylon once again dominated Mesopotamia during the New Babylonian empire, sometimes called the Chaldean empire. King Nebuchadnezzar (reigned 605–562 B.C.E.) lavished wealth and resources on his capital city. Babylon occupied some 850 hectares (more than 2,100 acres), and the city's defensive walls were reportedly so thick that a four-horse chariot could turn around on top of them. Within the walls there were enormous palaces and 1,179 temples, some of them faced with gold and decorated with thousands of statues. When one of the king's wives longed for flowering shrubs from her mountain homeland, Nebuchadnezzar had them planted in terraces above the city walls, and the hanging gardens of Babylon have symbolized the city's luxuriousness ever since.

The New Babylonian Empire

By this time, however, peoples beyond Mesopotamia had acquired advanced weapons and were ex-

---

Map 1.2 Boundaries and major cities of the Mesopotamian empires between 1800 and 1600 B.C.E. Observe the position of these empires in relation to major rivers and seas. How might access to water, either for transport or for agriculture, have played a role in the power of these early empires?

perimenting with techniques of administering large territories. As a result, in the mid–sixth century B.C.E. Mesopotamians largely lost control of their affairs, and foreign conquerors absorbed them into their own empires.

THE FORMATION OF A COMPLEX SOCIETY AND SOPHISTICATED CULTURAL TRADITIONS

With the emergence of cities and the congregation of dense populations in urban spaces, specialized labor proliferated. The Mesopotamian economy became increasingly diverse, and trade linked the region with distant peoples. Clearly defined social classes emerged, as small groups of people concentrated wealth and power in their own hands, and Mesopotamia developed into a patriarchal society that vested authority largely in adult males. Mesopotamians also allocated some of their resources to individuals who worked to develop sophisticated cultural traditions, including the invention of writing, which enabled them to record information for future retrieval. Indeed, writing soon became a foundation for education, science, literature, and religious reflection.

Economic Specialization and Trade

When large numbers of people began to congregate in cities and work at tasks other than agriculture, they vastly expanded the stock of human skills. Craftsmen refined techniques inherited from earlier generations and experimented with new ways of doing things. Pottery making, textile manufacture, woodworking, leather production, brick making, stonecutting, and masonry all became distinct occupations in the world's earliest cities.

Metallurgical innovations ranked among the most important developments that came about because of specialized labor. About 4000 B.C.E. experimentation with copper metallurgy led to the invention of bronze when Mesopotamian metalworkers learned to alloy copper with tin. Unlike pure copper, bronze is both hard and strong, and it quickly became the preferred metal for military weaponry as craftsmen turned out swords, spears, axes, shields, and armor made of the recently invented metal. And although bronze was expensive, over a long period Mesopotamian farmers also began to use

Bronze Metallurgy

bronze knives and bronze-tipped plows instead of tools made of bone, wood, stone, or obsidian.

After about 1000 B.C.E. Mesopotamian craftsmen began to manufacture effective tools and weapons with iron as well as bronze. Whereas early experimentation with iron metallurgy resulted in products that were too brittle for heavy-duty uses, by about 1300 B.C.E. craftsmen from Hittite society in Anatolia (discussed later in this chapter) developed techniques of forging exceptionally strong iron tools and weapons. As knowledge of those techniques spread, Assyrian conquerors made particularly effective use of them by forging iron weapons to build their empire. Iron also had the advantage of being less expensive than bronze, which quickly made it the metal of choice for weapons and tools.

Iron Metallurgy

Other craftsmen focused on devising efficient means of transportation based on wheeled vehicles and sailing ships, both of which facilitated long-distance trade. The first use of wheels probably took place about 3500 B.C.E., and Sumerians were building wheeled carts by 3000 B.C.E. Wheeled carts and wagons enabled people to haul heavy loads of bulk goods over much longer distances than human porters or draft animals could manage. The wheel rapidly diffused from Sumer to neighboring lands, and within a few centuries it had become a standard means of overland transportation.

The Wheel

Sumerians also experimented with technologies of maritime transportation. By 3500 B.C.E. they had built watercraft that allowed them to venture into the Persian Gulf and beyond. By 2300 B.C.E. they were trading regularly with merchants of Harappan society in the Indus River valley of northern India (discussed in chapter 3), which they reached by sailing through the Persian Gulf and the Arabian Sea. During the time of the Babylonian empire, Mesopotamians traded extensively with peoples in all directions: they imported silver from Anatolia, cedar wood from Lebanon, copper from Arabia, gold from Egypt, tin from Persia, lapis lazuli from Afghanistan, and semiprecious stones from northern India.

Shipbuilding

The Emergence of a Stratified Patriarchal Society

With their increasingly specialized labor and long-distance trade, cities provided many more opportunities for the accumulation of wealth than ever before. As a result, social distinctions in Mesopotamia became much more sharply defined than those of neolithic villages.

A silver model of a boat discovered in a royal tomb at Ur throws light on Sumerian transportation of grain and other goods on the rivers, canals, and marshes of southern Mesopotamia about 2700 B.C.E.

In early Mesopotamia the ruling classes originally consisted of kings and nobles who were elected to their positions because of their valor and success as warriors. However, royal status soon became hereditary, as kings arranged for their sons to succeed them. Nobles were mostly members of royal families and other close supporters of the kings and thus controlled significant wealth and power. Members of the ruling class displayed their high status through large-scale construction projects and by lavishly decorating their capital cities.

Social Classes

Closely allied with the ruling elites were priests and priestesses, many of whom were younger relatives of the rulers. The principal role of the priestly elites was to intervene with the gods to ensure good fortune for their communities. In exchange for those services, priests and priestesses lived in temple communities and received offerings of food, drink, and clothing from city inhabitants. Temples also generated their own income from vast tracts of land that they owned and large workshops that they maintained. Because of their wealth, temples provided comfortable livings for their inhabitants, and they also served the needs of the larger community. For instance, temples functioned as banks where individuals could store wealth, and they helped underwrite trading ventures to distant lands. They also helped those in need by taking

Temple Communities

in orphans, supplying grain in times of famine, and providing ransoms for community members captured in battle.

Apart from the ruling and priestly elites, Mesopotamian society included less privileged classes of free commoners, dependent clients, and slaves. Free commoners mostly worked as peasant cultivators in the countryside on land owned by their families, although some also worked in the cities as builders, craftsmen, or professionals. Dependent clients possessed no property and usually worked as agricultural laborers on estates owned by others. Free commoners and dependent clients all paid taxes—usually in the form of surplus agricultural production—that supported the ruling classes, military forces, and temple communities. In addition, free commoners and dependent clients were also subject to conscription by ruling authorities to provide labor services for large-scale construction projects such as roads, city walls, irrigation systems, temples, and public buildings.

Gypsum carving of an elderly couple from the city of Nippur about 2500 B.C.E.

Slaves came from three main sources: prisoners of

war, convicted criminals, and heavily indebted individuals who sold themselves into slavery to satisfy their obligations. Some slaves worked as agricultural laborers on the estates of nobles or temple communities, but most were domestic servants in wealthy households. Many masters granted slaves their freedom, often with a financial bequest, after several years of good service.

Slaves

In addition to recognizing differences of rank, wealth, and social status, Mesopotamians built a patriarchal society that vested authority over public and private affairs in adult men. Men made most of the important decisions within households and dominated public life as well. In effect, men ruled as kings, and decisions about policies and public affairs rested almost entirely in their hands.

Hammurabi's laws throw considerable light on sex and gender relations in ancient Mesopotamia. The laws recognized men as heads of their households and entrusted all major family decisions to their judgment. Men even had the power to sell their wives and children into slavery to satisfy their debts. In the interests of protecting the reputations of husbands and the legitimacy of offspring, the laws prescribed death by drowning as the punishment for adulterous wives, as well as for their partners, while permitting men to engage in consensual sexual relations with concubines, slaves, or prostitutes without penalty.

Gender Roles

In spite of their subordinate legal status, women made their influence felt in Mesopotamian society. At ruling courts women sometimes advised kings and their governments. A few women wielded great power as high priestesses who managed the enormous estates belonging to their temples. Others obtained a formal education and worked as scribes—literate individuals who prepared administrative and legal documents for governments and private parties. Women also pursued careers as midwives, shopkeepers, brewers, bakers, tavern keepers, and textile manufacturers.

During the second millennium B.C.E., however, Mesopotamian men progressively tightened their control over the social and sexual behavior of women. To protect family fortunes and guarantee the legitimacy of heirs, Mesopotamians insisted on the virginity of brides at marriage, and they forbade casual socializing between married women and men outside their family. By 1500 B.C.E. and probably even earlier, married women in Mesopotamian cities had begun to wear veils when they ventured beyond their own house-

holds in order to discourage the attention of men from other families. This concern to control women's social and sexual behavior spread throughout much of southwest Asia and the Mediterranean basin, where it reinforced patriarchal social structures.

The Development of Written Cultural Traditions

The world's earliest known writing came from Mesopotamia. Sumerians invented a system of writing about the middle of the fourth millennium B.C.E. to keep track of commercial transactions and tax collections. They first experimented with pictographs representing animals, agricultural products, and trade items that figured prominently in tax and commercial transactions. By 3100 B.C.E. conventional signs representing specific words had spread throughout Mesopotamia.

A writing system that depends on pictures is useful for purposes such as keeping records, but it is a cumbersome way to communicate abstract ideas. Beginning about 2900 B.C.E. the Sumerians developed a more flexible system of writing that used graphic symbols to represent sounds, syllables, and ideas as well as physical objects. By combining pictographs and other symbols, the Sumerians created a powerful writing system.

When writing, a Sumerian scribe used a stylus fashioned from a reed to impress symbols on wet clay. Because the stylus left lines and wedge-shaped marks, Sumerian writing is known as *cuneiform*, a term that comes from two Latin words meaning "wedge-shaped." When dried in the sun or baked in an oven, the clay hardened and preserved a permanent record of the scribe's message. Babylonians, Assyrians, and other peoples later adapted the Sumerians' script to their own languages, and the tradition of cuneiform writing continued for more than three thousand years.

Cuneiform Writing

Though originally invented for purposes of keeping records, writing clearly had potential that went far beyond the purely practical matter of storing information. Mesopotamians relied on writing to communicate complex ideas about the world, the gods, human beings, and their relationships with one another. Indeed, writing made possible the emergence of a distinctive cultural tradition that shaped Mesopotamian values for almost three millennia.

Literacy led to a rapid expansion of knowledge. Mesopotamian scholars devoted themselves to the study of astronomy and mathematics—both important

SOURCES FROM THE PAST

Hammurabi's Laws on Family Relationships

By the time of Hammurabi, Mesopotamian marriages had come to represent important business and economic relationships between families. Hammurabi's laws reflect a concern to ensure the legitimacy of children and to protect the economic interests of both marital partners and their families. While placing women under the authority of their fathers and husbands, the laws also protected women against unreasonable treatment by their husbands or other men.

■   ■   ■

128: If a seignior acquired a wife, but did not draw up the contracts for her, that woman is no wife.

129: If the wife of a seignior has been caught while lying [i.e., having sexual relations] with another man, they shall bind them and throw them into the water. If the husband of the woman wishes to spare his wife, then the king in turn may spare his subject.

Primary Source
Code of Hammurabi

130: If a seignior bound the (betrothed) wife of a(nother) seignior, who had no intercourse with a male and was still living in her father's house, and he has lain in her bosom and they have caught him, that seignior shall be put to death, while that woman shall go free.

131: If a seignior's wife was accused by her husband, but she was not caught while lying with another man, she shall make affirmation by god and return to her house. . . .

138: If a seignior wishes to divorce his wife who did not bear him children, he shall give her money to the full amount of her marriage-price [money or goods that the husband paid to the bride's family in exchange for the right to marry her] and he shall also make good to her the dowry [money or goods that the bride brought to the marriage] which she brought from her father's house and then he may divorce her.

139: If there was no marriage-price, he shall give her one mina of silver as the divorce-settlement.

140: If he is a peasant, he shall give her one-third mina of silver.

141: If a seignior's wife, who was living in the house of the seignior, has made up her mind to leave in order that she may engage in business, thus neglecting her house (and) humiliating her husband, they shall prove it against her; and if her husband has then decided on her divorce, he may divorce her, with nothing to be given her as her divorce-settlement upon her departure. If her husband has not decided on her divorce, her husband may marry another woman, with the former woman living in the house of her husband like a maidservant.

142: If a woman so hated her husband that she has declared, "You may not have me," her record shall be investigated at her city council, and if she was careful and was not at fault, even though her husband has been going out and disparaging her greatly, that woman, without incurring any blame at all, may take her dowry and go off to her father's house.

143: If she was not careful, but was a gadabout, thus neglecting her house [and] humiliating her husband, they shall throw that woman into the water.

• *Discuss the extent to which Hammurabi's various provisions on family relationships protected the interests of different groups—husbands, wives, and the family itself.*

SOURCE: James B. Pritchard, ed. *Ancient Near Eastern Texts Relating to the Old Testament*. Princeton: Princeton University Press, 1955, pp. 171–72.

sciences for agricultural societies. Knowledge of astronomy helped them prepare accurate calendars,

Astronomy and Mathematics

which in turn enabled them to chart the rhythms of the seasons and determine the appropriate times for planting and harvesting crops. They used their mathematical skills to survey agricultural lands and allocate them to the proper owners or tenants. Some Mesopotamian conventions persist to the present day: Mesopotamian scientists divided the year into twelve months, for example, and they divided the hours of the day into sixty minutes, each composed of sixty seconds.

Mesopotamians also used writing to communicate abstract ideas, investigate intellectual problems,

The Epic of Gilgamesh

and reflect on human beings and their place in the world. Best known of the reflective literature from Mesopotamia is the *Epic of Gilgamesh,* completed after 2000 B.C.E. In recounting the experiences of Gilgamesh and Enkidu, the epic explored themes of friendship, relations between humans and the gods, and especially the meaning of life and death. The stories of Gilgamesh and Enkidu resonated so widely that for some two thousand years—from the time of the Sumerian city-states to the fall of the Assyrian empire—they were the principal vehicles for Mesopotamian reflections on moral issues.

THE BROADER INFLUENCE OF MESOPOTAMIAN SOCIETY

While building cities and regional states, Mesopotamians deeply influenced the development and experiences of peoples living far beyond their own lands. Often their wealth and power attracted the attention of neighboring peoples. Sometimes Mesopotamians projected their power to foreign lands and imposed their ways by force. Occasionally migrants left Mesopotamia and carried their inherited traditions to new lands. Mesopotamian influence did not completely transform other peoples and turn them into carbon copies of Mesopotamians. On the contrary, other peoples adopted Mesopotamian ways selectively and adapted them to their own needs and interests. Yet the broader impact of Mesopotamian society shows that even in early times, complex agricultural societies organized around cities had strong potential to influence the development of distant human communities.

Hebrews, Israelites, and Jews

The best-known cases of early Mesopotamian influence involved Hebrews, Israelites, and Jews, who preserved memories of their historical experiences in an extensive collection of sacred writings. Hebrews were speakers of the ancient Hebrew language. Israelites formed a branch of Hebrews who settled in Palestine (modern-day Israel) after 1300 B.C.E. Jews descended from southern Israelites who inhabited the kingdom of Judah. For more than two thousand years, Hebrews, Israelites, and Jews interacted constantly with Mesopotamians and other peoples as well, with profound consequences for the development of their own societies.

The earliest Hebrews were pastoral nomads who inhabited lands between Mesopotamia and Egypt during the second millennium B.C.E. As Meso-

The Early Hebrews

potamia prospered, some of the Hebrews settled in the region's cities. There, they recognized many of the deities, values, and customs common to Mesopotamian peoples and participated fully in the larger society of Mesopotamia. Hebrew law, for example, borrowed heavily from Hammurabi's code. The Hebrews also told the story of a devastating flood that had destroyed all early human society, which was a variation on similar flood stories related from the earliest days of Sumerian society.

According to their scriptures (the Old Testament of the Christian Bible), some Hebrews migrated from Palestine to Egypt during the eighteenth century B.C.E. About 1300 B.C.E., however, this branch of the Hebrews departed under the leadership of

Migrations and Settlement in Palestine

Moses and returned to Palestine. Organized into a loose federation of twelve tribes, those Hebrews, known as the Israelites, fought bitterly with other inhabitants of Palestine and carved out a territory for themselves. Eventually the Israelites abandoned their inherited tribal structure in favor of a Mesopotamian-style monarchy that brought all their twelve tribes under unified rule. During the reigns of King David (1000–970 B.C.E.) and King Solomon (970–930 B.C.E.), Israelites dominated the territory between Syria and the Sinai peninsula. They built an elaborate and cosmopolitan capital city at Jerusalem and entered into diplomatic and commercial relations with Mesopotamians, Egyptians, and Arabian peoples. Like other peoples of southwest Asia, the Israelites made use of iron technology to strengthen their military forces and produce tough agricultural implements.

After the time of Moses, however, the religious beliefs of the Israelites developed along increasingly distinctive lines. Whereas the early Hebrews had recognized many of the same gods as their Mesopotamian neighbors, Moses embraced monotheism: he taught that there was only one god, known as Yahweh, who was a supremely powerful deity, the creator and sustainer of the world. Yahweh expected his followers to worship him alone, and he demanded that they observe high moral and ethical standards. In the Ten Commandments, a set of religious and ethical principles that Moses announced to the Israelites, Yahweh warned his followers against destructive and antisocial behavior such as lying, theft, adultery, and murder. Between about 1000 and 400 B.C.E., the Israelites' religious leaders compiled their teachings in a set of holy scriptures known as the Torah (Hebrew for "doctrine" or "teaching"), which laid down Yahweh's laws and outlined his role in creating the world and guiding human affairs. The Torah taught that Yahweh would reward those who obeyed his will and punish those who did not.

Moses and Monotheism

After the tenth century B.C.E., the Israelites experienced a series of political and military setbacks. Following King Solomon's reign, tribal tensions led to the division of the community into a large kingdom of Israel in the north and a smaller kingdom of Judah in the land known as Judea to the south. In 722 B.C.E. Assyrian forces conquered the northern kingdom and deported many of its inhabitants to other regions, many of whom lost their identity as Israelites. In 586 B.C.E., the New Babylonian empire toppled the kingdom of Judah and destroyed Jerusalem, forcing many residents into exile. Unlike their cousins to the north, however, most of these Israelites maintained their religious identity, and many of the deportees eventually returned to Judea, where they became known as Jews.

Assyrian and Babylonian Conquests

The exiles who returned to Judea built a distinctive religious community based on their conviction that they had a special relationship with Yahweh, their devotion to Yahweh's teachings as expressed in the Torah, and their concern for justice and righteousness. These elements enabled the Jews to maintain a strong sense of identity as a people distinct from Mesopotamians and others, even as they participated fully in the

The Early Jewish Community

development of a larger complex society in southwest Asia. Over the longer term, Jewish monotheism, scriptures, and moral concerns also profoundly influenced the development of Christianity and Islam.

The Phoenicians

North of the Israelites' kingdom in Palestine, the Phoenicians occupied a narrow coastal plain between the Mediterranean Sea and the Lebanon Mountains. They spoke a Semitic language, referring to themselves as Canaanites and their land as Canaan. (The term *Phoenician* comes from early Greek references.) Sometime after 3000 B.C.E., the Phoenicians established a series of city-states ruled by local kings, the most important of which were Tyre, Sidon, Beirut, and Byblos. Though not a numerous or militarily powerful people, the Phoenicians influenced societies throughout the Mediterranean basin because of their trade and communication networks. Their meager lands did not permit development of a large agricultural society, so after about 2500 B.C.E. the Phoenicians turned increasingly to industry and trade. Although the Phoenicians traded overland, they were also excellent sailors, and they built the best ships of their times. Between 1200 and 800 B.C.E., they dominated Mediterranean trade. They established commercial colonies in Rhodes, Cyprus, Sicily, Sardinia, Spain, and north Africa. They sailed far and wide in search of raw materials, which took them well beyond the Mediterranean: Phoenician merchant ships visited the Canary Islands, coastal ports in Portugal and France, and even the distant British Isles, and adventurous Phoenician mariners made exploratory voyages to the Azores Islands and down the west coast of Africa as far as the Gulf of Guinea.

Phoenician Trade Networks

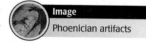

Image

Phoenician artifacts

Like the Hebrews, the Phoenicians largely adapted Mesopotamian cultural traditions to their own needs. Their gods, for example, were mostly adapted from Mesopotamian gods. The Phoenicians also creatively adapted the Mesopotamian practice of writing by experimenting with simpler alternatives to cuneiform. By 1500 B.C.E. Phoenician scribes had devised an early alphabetic script consisting of twenty-two symbols representing consonants (the Phoenician alphabet had no symbols for vowels). Learning twenty-two letters and building words with them was much

Alphabetic Writing

---

monotheism (mah-noh-THEE-iz'm)
Yahweh (YAH-way)

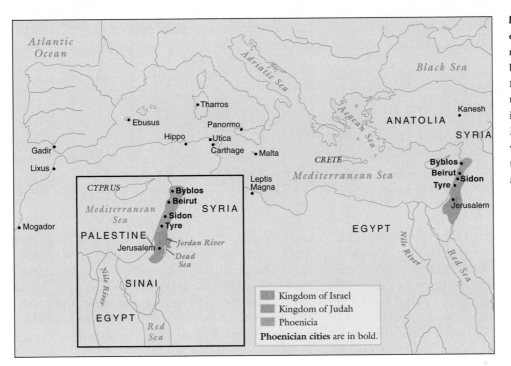

Map 1.3 The kingdoms of Israel and Judah and major Phoenician cities between 1500 and 600 B.C.E. Note the position of these kingdoms and cities in relation to the rest of the Mediterranean Sea. Why would people have wanted to create settlements in that area?

easier than memorizing the hundreds of symbols employed in cuneiform. Because alphabetic writing required much less investment in education than did cuneiform writing, more people were able to become literate than ever before.

Alphabetic writing spread widely as the Phoenicians traveled and traded throughout the Mediterranean basin. About the ninth century B.C.E., for example, Greeks modified the Phoenician alphabet and added symbols representing vowels. Romans later adapted the Greek alphabet to their own language and passed it along to their cultural heirs in Europe. In later centuries alphabetic writing spread to central Asia, south Asia, and southeast Asia, and ultimately throughout most of the world.

THE INDO-EUROPEAN MIGRATIONS

After 3000 B.C.E. Mesopotamia was a prosperous, productive region where peoples from many different communities mixed and mingled. But Mesopotamia was only one region in a much larger world of interaction and exchange. Mesopotamians and their neighbors all dealt frequently with peoples from regions far beyond southwest Asia. Among the most influential of these peoples in the third and second millennia

B.C.E. were those who spoke various Indo-European languages. Their migrations throughout much of Eurasia profoundly influenced historical development in both southwest Asia and the larger world.

Indo-European Origins

During the eighteenth and nineteenth centuries, linguists noticed that many languages of Europe, southwest Asia, and India featured remarkable similarities in vocabulary and grammatical structure. *Indo-European Languages* Ancient languages displaying these similarities included Sanskrit (the sacred language of ancient India), Old Persian, Greek, and Latin. Because of the geographic regions where these tongues are found, scholars refer to them as Indo-European languages. Major subgroups of the Indo-European family of languages include Indo-Iranian, Greek, Balto-Slavic, Germanic, Italic, and Celtic. English belongs to the Germanic subgroup of the Indo-European family of languages.

After noticing linguistic similarities, scholars sought a way to explain the close relationship between the Indo-European languages. The only persuasive explanation for the high degree of linguistic coincidence was that speakers of Indo-European languages were all descendants of ancestors who spoke a common

Phoenician, Greek, Hebrew, and Roman letters.

NORTH SEMITIC			GREEK		ETRUSCAN	LATIN	
EARLY PHOENICIAN	EARLY HEBREW	PHOENICIAN	EARLY	CLASSICAL	EARLY	EARLY	CLASSICAL
K	K	X	ᐱ	A	A	A	A
9	9	9	8	B	B		B
1	1	1	1	Γ	ꙅ		C
△	ᖴ	ᖴ	Δ	Δ	ᐃ	ᗡ	D

tongue and migrated from their original homeland. As migrants established their own separate communities and lost touch with one another, their languages evolved along different lines, adding new words, pronunciations, and spellings but retaining the basic grammatical structure of their original speech.

The Indo-European Homeland

The original homeland of Indo-European speakers was probably the steppe region of modern-day Ukraine and southern Russia, where the earliest of them built a society between about 4500 and 2500 B.C.E. A central feature of Indo-European society was the domestication of wild horses from the Eurasian steppe about 4000 B.C.E. Horses were initially used for food and soon thereafter for riding as well. When Sumerian knowledge of bronze metallurgy spread to the Indo-European homeland about 3000 B.C.E., Indo-European speakers devised ways to hitch horses to carts, wagons, and chariots. The possession of domesticated horses vastly magnified the power of the Indo-Europeans. Horses enabled them to develop transportation technologies that were much faster and more efficient than other alternatives. Furthermore, because of their strength and speed, horses provided Indo-European

speakers with a tremendous military advantage over peoples they encountered. It is perhaps significant that many groups of Indo-European speakers considered themselves superior to other peoples: the terms *Aryan, Iran,* and *Eire* (the official name of the modern Republic of Ireland) all derive from the Indo-European word *aryo,* meaning "nobleman" or "lord."

Indo-European Expansion and Its Effects

Horses also provided Indo-European speakers with a means of expanding far beyond their original homeland. As they flourished in southern Russia, Indo-European speakers experienced a population explosion, which prompted some of them to move into the sparsely inhabited eastern steppe or even beyond the grasslands altogether. The earliest Indo-European migrations began about 3000 B.C.E. and continued until about 1000 B.C.E. Like early movements of other peoples, these were not mass migrations so much as gradual and incremental processes that resulted in the spread of

The Nature of Indo-European Migration

Similarities in Vocabulary Indicating Close Relationships between Select Indo-European Languages

English	German	Spanish	Greek	Latin	Sanskrit
father	vater	padre	pater	pater	pitar
one	ein	uno	hen	unus	ekam
fire	feuer	fuego	pyr	ignis	agnis
field	feld	campo	agros	ager	ajras
sun	sonne	sol	helios	sol	surya
king	könig	rey	basileus	rex	raja
god	gott	dios	theos	deus	devas

Indo-European languages and ethnic communities, as small groups of people established settlements in new lands, which then became foundations for further expansion.

The most influential Indo-European migrants in ancient times were the Hittites. About 1900 B.C.E.

The Hittites the Hittites migrated to the central plain of Anatolia, where they imposed their language and rule on the region's inhabitants. During the seventeenth and sixteenth centuries B.C.E., they built a powerful kingdom and established close relations with Mesopotamian peoples. They traded with Babylonians and Assyrians, adapted cuneiform writing to their Indo-European language, and accepted many Mesopotamian deities into their own pantheon. In 1595 B.C.E. the Hittites toppled the mighty Babylonian empire of Mesopotamia, and for several centuries thereafter they were the dominant power in southwest Asia. Between 1450 and 1200 B.C.E. their authority extended to eastern Anatolia, northern Mesopotamia, and Syria down to Phoenicia. After 1200 B.C.E. the unified Hittite state dissolved, but a Hittite identity survived, along with the Hittite language, throughout the era of the Assyrian empire and beyond.

The Hittites were responsible for two technological innovations—the construction of light, horse-

War Chariots drawn war chariots and the refinement of iron metallurgy—that greatly strengthened their own society and influenced other peoples throughout much of the ancient world. The Hittites' speedy chariots were crucial in their campaign to es-

tablish a state in Anatolia. Following the Hittites' example, Mesopotamians soon added chariot teams to their own armies, and Assyrians made especially effective use of chariots in building their empire. Indeed, chariot warfare was so effective—and its techniques spread so widely—that charioteers became the elite strike forces in armies throughout much of the ancient world from Rome to China.

After about 1300 B.C.E. the Hittites also refined the technology of iron metallurgy, which enabled them to produce effective weapons *Iron Metallurgy* cheaply and in large quantities. Hittite methods of iron production diffused rapidly and eventually spread throughout all of Eurasia. (Peoples of sub-Saharan Africa independently invented iron metallurgy.) Hittites were not the original inventors either of horse-drawn chariots or of iron metallurgy: in both cases they built on Mesopotamian precedents. But in both cases they clearly improved on existing technologies and introduced innovations that other peoples readily adopted.

While the Hittites were building a state in Anatolia, other Indo-European speakers migrated from the steppe to different regions. Some *Indo-European* went east into central Asia, venturing *Migrations to the* as far as the Tarim Basin (now west- *West and East* ern China) by 2000 B.C.E. Meanwhile, other Indo-European migrants moved west. One wave of migration took Indo-European speakers into Greece after 2200 B.C.E., with their descendants moving into central Italy by 1000 B.C.E. Another migratory wave established an Indo-European presence

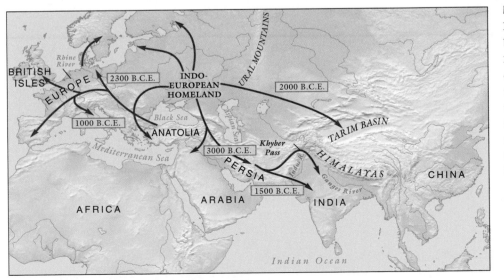

Map 1.4 Routes of the Indo-European migrations between 3000 and 1000 B.C.E. Notice the great distances Indo-Europeans traveled over the course of two millennia. How would the gradual influx of such migrants have affected existing populations across Eurasia?

farther to the west. By 2300 B.C.E. some Indo-European speakers had made their way from southern Russia into central Europe (modern Germany and Austria), by 1200 B.C.E. to western Europe (modern France), and shortly thereafter to the British Isles, the Baltic region, and the Iberian peninsula. Yet another, later wave of migrations established an Indo-European presence in Iran and India. About 1500 B.C.E. the Medes and the Persians migrated into the Iranian plateau, while the Aryans began filtering into northern India. As in earlier migrations, Indo-European migrants borrowed from, influenced, and mixed with the settled peoples they discovered and in so doing shaped future historical developments in each area.

Aryans (AYR-ee-uhns)

SUMMARY

Building on neolithic foundations, Mesopotamian peoples constructed societies much more complex, powerful, and influential than those of their predecessors. Through their city-states, kingdoms, and regional empires, Mesopotamians created formal institutions of government that extended the authority of ruling elites to all corners of their states, and they occasionally mobilized forces that projected their power to distant lands. They generated several distinct social classes. Specialized labor fueled productive economies and encouraged the establishment of long-distance trade networks. They devised systems of writing, which enabled them to develop sophisticated cultural traditions. They deeply influenced other peoples, such as the Hebrews and the Phoenicians, throughout southwest Asia and the eastern Mediterranean basin. They had frequent dealings also with Indo-European peoples. Although Indo-European society emerged far to the north of Mesopotamia, speakers of Indo-European languages migrated widely and established societies throughout much of Eurasia. Sometimes they drew inspiration from Mesopotamian practices, and sometimes they developed their own practices that influenced Mesopotamians and others as well. Thus, already in remote antiquity, the various peoples of the world profoundly influenced one another through cross-cultural interaction and exchange.

CHRONOLOGY

4 MILLION–1 MILLION YEARS AGO	Era of first hominids, *Australopithecus*
2.5 MILLION–200,000 YEARS AGO	Era of *Homo erectus*
200,000 YEARS AGO	Early evolution of *Homo sapiens*
40,000 YEARS AGO	First appearance of *Homo sapiens sapiens*
10,000–8000 B.C.E.	Early experimentation with agriculture
4000–3500 B.C.E.	Appearance of cities in southwest Asia
3200–2350 B.C.E.	Era of Sumerian dominance in Mesopotamia
3000 B.C.E.–1000 C.E.	Era of Indo-European migrations
2350–1600 B.C.E.	Era of Babylonian dominance in Mesopotamia
2334–2315 B.C.E.	Reign of Sargon of Akkad
1792–1750 B.C.E.	Reign of Hammurabi
1450–1200 B.C.E.	Hittite state based in Anatolia
1000–970 B.C.E.	Reign of Hebrew king David
1000–612 B.C.E.	Era of Assyrian dominance in Mesopotamia
970–930 B.C.E.	Reign of Hebrew king Solomon
722 B.C.E.	Assyrian conquest of the kingdom of Israel
605–562 B.C.E.	Reign of Nebuchadnezzar
600–550 B.C.E.	New Babylonian empire
586 B.C.E.	New Babylonian conquest of the kingdom of Judah

FOR FURTHER READING

Elizabeth Wayland Barber. *Women's Work: The First 20,000 Years.* New York, 1994. Fascinating study of ancient textiles, which the author argues was a craft industry dominated by women from the earliest times.

David Christian. *Maps of Time: An Introduction to Big History.* Berkeley, 2004. A brilliant study that considers human history in the context of natural history since the big bang.

Jared Diamond. *The Third Chimpanzee: Evolution and the Future of the Human Animal.* New York, 1992. An insightful guide to human evolution and its significance for human behavior.

Andrew George, trans. *The Epic of Gilgamesh.* London, 1999. A careful study and fresh translation of the best-known Mesopotamian literary work prepared on the basis of recently discovered texts.

J. P. Mallory. *In Search of the Indo-Europeans: Language, Archaeology, and Myth.* London, 1989. Carefully reviews modern theories about early Indo-European speakers in light of both the linguistic and the archaeological evidence.

Hans J. Nissen. *The Early History of the Ancient Near East, 9000–2000 B.C.* Trans. by E. Lutzeier. Chicago, 1988. A brilliant synthesis of scholarship on the development of cities and complex society in Mesopotamia and neighboring regions.

J. N. Postgate. *Early Mesopotamia: Society and Economy at the Dawn of History.* London, 1992. Outstanding synthesis that draws on both archaeological and textual sources.

James B. Pritchard, ed. *Ancient Near Eastern Texts Relating to the Old Testament.* 2 vols. 3rd ed. Princeton, 1975. Important collection of primary sources in translation, emphasizing parallels between the ancient Hebrews and other peoples.

Michael Roaf. *Cultural Atlas of Mesopotamia and the Ancient Near East.* New York, 1990. Richly illustrated volume with well-informed essays on all dimensions of Mesopotamian history.

Bruce D. Smith. *The Emergence of Agriculture.* New York, 1995. Concentrates on the initial domestication of plant and animal species in world regions where agriculture developed.

CHAPTER 2

Early African Societies
and the Bantu Migrations

For almost three thousand years, Egyptian embalmers preserved the bodies of deceased individuals through a process of mummification. Egyptian records rarely mention the techniques of mummification, but the Greek historian Herodotus traveled in Egypt about 450 B.C.E. and briefly explained the craft. The embalmer first used a metal hook to draw the brain of the deceased out through a nostril, then re-moved the internal organs through an incision made alongside the ab-domen, washed them in palm wine, and sealed them with preser-vatives in stone vessels. Next, the embalmer washed the body, filled it with spices and aromatics, and covered it for about two months with natron, a naturally occurring salt substance. When the natron had extracted all moisture from the body, the embalmer cleansed it again and wrapped it with strips of fine linen covered with resin. Adorned with jewelry, the preserved body then went into a coffin bearing a painting or a sculpted likeness of the deceased.

Careful preservation of the body was only a part of the funer-ary ritual for prominent Egyptians. Ruling elites, wealthy individuals, and sometimes common people as well laid their de-ceased to rest in expensive tombs equipped with furniture, tools, weapons, and ornaments that the departed would need in their next lives. Relatives periodically brought food and wine to nourish the deceased in their new dimen-sion of existence.

Egyptian funerary customs were reflections of a prosperous agricultural society. Food offerings

Canopic Coffinette of Tutankhamon

OPPOSITE PAGE: *Excavations surrounding the pyramids, as seen from the air.*

consisted mostly of local agricultural products, and scenes painted on tomb walls often depicted workers preparing fields or cultivating crops. Moreover, bountiful harvests explained the accumulation of wealth that supported elaborate funerary practices, and they also enabled some individuals to devote their efforts to specialized tasks such as embalming. Agriculture even influenced religious beliefs. Many Egyptians believed fervently in a life beyond the grave, and they likened the human experience of life and death to the agricultural cycle in which crops grow, die, and come to life again in another season.

As Mesopotamians built a productive agricultural society in southwest Asia and as Indo-European peoples introduced domesticated horses to much of Eurasia, cultivation and herding also transformed African societies. African agriculture first took root in the Sudan, then moved into the Nile River valley and also to most parts of sub-Saharan Africa. Agriculture flourished particularly in the fertile Nile valley, and abundant harvests soon supported fast-growing populations. That agricultural bounty underwrote the development of Egypt, the most prosperous and powerful of the early agricultural societies in Africa, and also of Nubia, Egypt's neighbor to the south.

Distinctive Egyptian and Nubian societies began to take shape in the valley of the Nile River during the late fourth millennium B.C.E., shortly after the emergence of complex society in Mesopotamia. Like their Mesopotamian counterparts, Egyptians and Nubians drew on agricultural surpluses to organize formal states, support specialized laborers, and develop distinctive cultural traditions. Also like Mesopotamians, Egyptian and Nubian residents of the Nile valley had regular dealings with peoples from other societies. They drew inspiration for political and social organization both from Mesopotamia and from their African neighbors to the south. In addition, they both traded with and competed against Mesopotamians, Phoenicians, Africans, and others, which resulted in increasing connections with other societies as well as intermittent military conflict.

Indeed, like their counterparts in Mesopotamia, Egyptian and Nubian societies developed from their earliest days in a larger world of interaction and exchange. Just as the peoples of southwest Asia influenced one another, so inhabitants of the Nile valley mixed and mingled with peoples from the eastern Mediterranean, southwest Asia, and sub-Saharan Africa. Just as Indo-European peoples migrated to new lands and established communities that transformed much of Eurasia, so Bantu peoples migrated from their original homeland in west Africa and established settlements that brought profound change to much of sub-Saharan Africa. By no means were Egypt and Nubia isolated centers of social development. Instead, they were only a small part of a much larger world of interacting societies.

EARLY AGRICULTURAL SOCIETY IN AFRICA

Egypt was the most prominent of early African societies, but it was by no means the only agricultural society, or even the only complex, city-based society of ancient Africa. On the contrary, Egypt emerged alongside Nubia and other agricultural societies in sub-Saharan Africa. Indeed, agricultural crops and domesticated animals reached Egypt from sub-Saharan Africa by way of Nubia as well as from southwest Asia. Favorable geographic conditions enabled Egyptians to build an especially productive agricultural economy that supported a powerful state, while Nubia became home to a somewhat less prosperous but nonetheless sophisticated society. After taking shape as distinctive societies, Egypt had regular dealings with both eastern Mediterranean and southwest Asian peoples, and Nubia linked Egypt and the eastern Mediterranean basin with the peoples and societies of sub-Saharan Africa.

Climatic Change and the Development of Agriculture in Africa

African agriculture emerged in the context of gradual but momentous changes in climatic conditions. About 10,000 B.C.E., after the end of the last ice age, the area now occupied by the Sahara desert was mostly a grassy steppe land with numerous lakes, rivers, and streams. Indeed, climatic and geographic conditions were similar to those of the Sudan—a region of savanna and grassland that stretches across the African continent

---

Nubia (NOO-bee-uh)

Bantu (BAHN-too)

between the Sahara to the north and the tropical rain forest to the south. Many human inhabitants of the Sahara and the Sudan lived by hunting wild cattle and collecting wild grains, and others subsisted on fish and aquatic resources from the region's waters.

After about 9000 B.C.E., peoples of the eastern Sudan domesticated cattle and became nomadic herders *Early Sudanic* but also continued to collect wild grains. *Agriculture* After 7500 B.C.E. they established permanent settlements and began to cultivate sorghum. Meanwhile, after about 8000 B.C.E., inhabitants of the western Sudan began to cultivate yams in the region between the Niger and Congo rivers. Sudanic agriculture became increasingly diverse over the following centuries: sheep and goats arrived from southwest Asia after 7000 B.C.E., and Sudanic peoples began to cultivate gourds, watermelons, and cotton after 6500 B.C.E.

Agricultural productivity—and the need for order—led Sudanic peoples to organize small-scale states. By about 5000 B.C.E. many Sudanic peoples had formed small monarchies ruled by kings who were viewed as divine or semidivine beings. Sudanic peoples also developed religious beliefs that reflected their agricultural society. They recognized a single divine force as the source of good and evil, and they associated it with rain—a matter of concern for any agricultural society.

After 5000 B.C.E. the northern half of Africa became much hotter and drier than before—a change that profoundly influenced social organization *Climatic Change* and agriculture throughout the region. The Sahara desert in particular became increasingly arid and uninhabitable. This process of desiccation drove both humans and animals to regions that offered reliable sources of water such as lakes and rivers. One of those regions was the valley of the Nile River, the principal source of water flowing through north Africa.

Fed by rain and snow in the mountains of east Africa, the Nile, which is the world's longest river, *The Nile River Valley* courses some 6,695 kilometers (4,160 miles) from its source at Lake Victoria to its outlet through the delta to the Mediterranean Sea. Each spring, rain and melting snow swell the river, which surges north through the Sudan and Egypt. Until the completion of the high dam at Aswan in 1968, every year the Nile flooded the plains downstream. When the waters receded, they left behind a layer of rich, fertile muck, and those alluvial deposits supported a remarkably productive agricultural economy throughout the Nile River valley.

Egypt and Nubia: "Gifts of the Nile"

Agriculture transformed the entire Nile River valley, with effects that were most dramatic in Egypt. In ancient times, Egypt referred not to the territory embraced by the modern state of Egypt but, rather, to the ribbon of land bordering the lower third of the Nile between the Mediterranean and the river's first cataract (an unnavigable stretch of rapids and waterfalls) near Aswan. Egypt enjoyed a much larger floodplain than most of the land to the south known as Nubia, the middle stretches of the Nile valley between the river's first and sixth cataracts. As the Sahara became increasingly arid, cultivators flocked to the Nile valley and established societies that depended on intensive agriculture. Because of their broad floodplains, Egyptians were able to take better advantage of the Nile's annual floods than their neighbors to

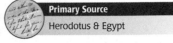
Primary Source
Herodotus & Egypt

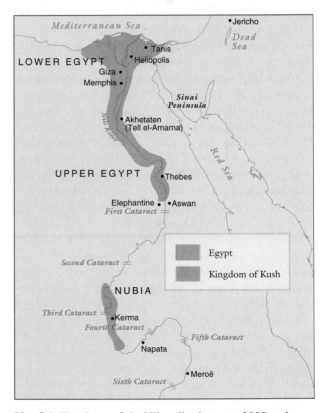

Map 2.1 Kingdoms of the Nile valley between 3000 and 2000 B.C.E. Observe the absence of large kingdoms between the first and second cataracts of the Nile. Why did the boundaries of Egypt end at the first cataract?

the south, and they turned Egypt into an especially productive agricultural region that was capable of supporting a much larger population than were Nubian lands. Because of its prosperity, the Greek historian Herodotus proclaimed Egypt "the gift of the Nile."

Early Agriculture in the Nile Valley Geography ensured that both Egypt and Nubia would come under the influence of both sub-Saharan Africa and the eastern Mediterranean basin, since the Nile River links the two regions. About 10,000 B.C.E. migrants from the Red Sea hills in northern Ethiopia traveled down the Nile valley and introduced to Egypt and Nubia the practice of collecting wild grains as well as their language, which became the language of ancient Egypt. After 5000 B.C.E., as the African climate grew hotter and drier, Sudanic peoples moved down the Nile, introducing Egypt and Nubia to crops such as gourds and watermelons and domesticated animals such as cattle and donkeys. About the same time, wheat and barley reached Egypt and Nubia from Mesopotamia by traveling up the Nile from the Mediterranean.

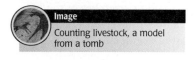
Counting livestock, a model from a tomb

Both Egyptians and Nubians relied heavily on agriculture at least by 5000 B.C.E. Egyptian cultivators went into the floodplains in the late summer, after the recession of the Nile's annual flood, sowed their seeds without extensive preparation of the soil, allowed their crops to mature during the cool months of the year, and harvested them during the winter and early spring. With less extensive floodplains, Nubians relied more on prepared fields and irrigation by waters diverted from the Nile. As in Mesopotamia, high agricultural productivity led to a rapid increase in population throughout the Nile valley. Demographic pressures soon forced Egyptians in particular to develop more intense and sophisticated methods of agriculture as cultivators found it necessary to move beyond the Nile's immediate floodplains to areas that required careful preparation and irrigation. By 4000 B.C.E. agricultural villages dotted the Nile's shores from the Mediterranean in the north to the river's fourth cataract in the south. As in Mesopotamia, dense human population in Egypt and Nubia brought a need for formal organization of public affairs. Although geographical barriers in the form of seas and desert meant that neither area faced external dangers to the extent that Mesopotamia did, the two areas still faced the need to maintain order and organize community projects. As a result, both

A painting from the tomb of a priest who lived about the fifteenth century B.C.E. depicts agricultural workers plowing and sowing crops in southern Egypt.

Egyptians and Nubians created states and recognized official authorities.

The earliest Egyptian and Nubian states were small kingdoms much like those instituted in the Sudan after 5000 B.C.E. Indeed, it is likely that the notion of divine or semidivine rulers reached Egypt and Nubia from the eastern and central Sudan. In any case, small kingdoms appeared first in southern Egypt and Nubia after 4000 B.C.E., and by 3300 B.C.E. small local kingdoms organized public life throughout Egypt as well as Nubia.

The Unification of Egypt

By 3500 B.C.E. political and economic competition fueled numerous skirmishes and small-scale wars between the Nile kingdoms. Some kingdoms overcame their neighbors and gradually expanded until they controlled sizable territories. About 3100 *Menes* B.C.E. Egyptian rulers drew on the considerable agricultural and demographic advantages of Egypt's large population and broad floodplains to forge all the territory between the Nile delta and the river's first cataract into a powerful and unified kingdom. Tradition holds that unified rule came to Egypt in the person of a conqueror named Menes (sometimes identified with an early Egyptian ruler called Narmer). Menes was an ambitious minor official from southern Egypt (known as Upper Egypt, since the Nile flows north) who rose to power and extended his authority north and into the delta (known as Lower Egypt). According to tradition, Menes founded the city of Memphis, near modern Cairo, which stood at the junction of Upper and Lower Egypt. Memphis served as Menes' capital and eventually became the cultural as well as the political center of ancient Egypt.

Menes and his successors built a centralized state ruled by the pharaoh, the Egyptian king. The early pharaohs claimed to be gods living on the earth in human form, the owners and absolute rulers of all the land. In that respect, they continued the tradition of divine kingship inherited from the early agricultural societies of the Sudan. Over time, Egyptians viewed rulers as offspring of Amon, a sun god. They considered the ruling pharaoh a human sun overseeing affairs on the earth, just as Amon was the sun supervising the larger cosmos, and they believed that after his death the pharaoh actually merged with Amon.

The power of the pharaohs was greatest during the first millennium of Egyptian history—the eras known as *The Archaic Period and the Old Kingdom* the Archaic Period (3100–2660 B.C.E.) and the Old Kingdom (2660–2160 B.C.E.). The most enduring symbols of their authority and divine status are the massive pyramids constructed during the Old Kingdom as royal tombs, most of them during the century from 2600 to 2500 B.C.E. These enormous monuments stand

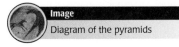
Image — Diagram of the pyramids

today at Giza, near Cairo, as testimony to the pharaohs' ability to marshal Egyptian resources. The largest is the pyramid of Khufu (also known as Cheops), which involved the precise cutting and fitting of 2.3 million limestone blocks weighing up to 15 tons, with an average weight of 2.5 tons. Scholars estimate that construction of Khufu's pyramid required the services of some eighty-four thousand laborers working eighty days per year for twenty years.

Even after the emergence of the strong pharaonic state, the fortunes of Egypt and Nubia remained *Relations between Egypt and Nubia* closely intertwined. Egyptians had strong interests in Nubia for both political and commercial reasons: they were wary of Nubian kingdoms that might threaten Upper Egypt, and they desired products such as gold, ivory, ebony, and precious stones that were available only from southern lands. Meanwhile, Nubians had equally strong interests in Egypt: they wanted to protect their independence from their large and powerful neighbor to the north, and they sought to profit by controlling trade down the Nile.

Tensions led to frequent violence between Egypt and Nubia throughout the Archaic Period and the Old

Kingdom. The early pharaohs organized at least five military campaigns to Nubia between 3100 and 2600 B.C.E. Indeed, Egypt dominated *The Early Kingdom of Kush* Lower Nubia (the land between the first and second cataracts of the Nile) for more than half a millennium, from about 3000 to 2400 B.C.E. This Egyptian presence in the north forced Nubian leaders to concentrate their efforts at political organization farther to the south in Upper Nubia. By about 2500 B.C.E. they had established a powerful kingdom, called Kush, with a capital at Kerma, about 700 kilometers (435 miles) south of Aswan. Though not as powerful as united Egypt, the kingdom of Kush became a formidable and wealthy state in its own right.

In spite of constant tension and frequent hostilities, Egypt and Nubia remained connected in many ways. About 2300 B.C.E., for example, the Egyptian explorer Harkhuf made four expeditions to Nubia. He returned from one of his trips with a caravan of some three hundred donkeys bearing exotic products from tropical Africa, as well as a dancing dwarf, and his cargo stimulated Egyptian desire for trade with southern lands. Meanwhile, by the end of the Old Kingdom, Nubian mercenaries had become quite prominent in Egyptian armies. In fact, they often married Egyptian women and assimilated into Egyptian society.

Turmoil and Empire

Toward the end of the Old Kingdom, high agricultural productivity made several regions of Egypt so prosperous and powerful that they were able to ignore the pharaohs and pursue their own *The Middle Kingdom* interests. As a result, the central state declined and eventually disappeared altogether during a long season of upheaval and unrest (2160–2040 B.C.E.). Pharaonic authority returned with the establishment of the Middle Kingdom (2040–1640 B.C.E.). Pharaohs of the Middle Kingdom were not as powerful as their predecessors of the Old Kingdom, but they effectively stabilized Egypt and supervised relations with neighboring lands.

Gradually, however, Egypt came under the pressure of foreign peoples from southwest Asia, particularly a Semitic people whom Egyptians *The Hyksos* called the Hyksos ("foreign rulers"). Little information survives about the Hyksos, but it is clear that they were horse-riding nomads. Indeed, their horse-drawn chariots, which they learned about from Hittites and Mesopotamians, provided them with a

SOURCES FROM THE PAST

Harkhuf's Expeditions to Nubia

Many Egyptians wrote brief autobiographies that they or their descendants had carved into their tombs. One of the most famous autobiographies from the Old Kingdom is that of Harkhuf, a royal official who became governor of Upper Egypt before 2300 B.C.E. The inscriptions in his tomb mention his four expeditions to Nubia to seek valuable items and report on political conditions there. The inscriptions also include the text of a letter from the boy-pharaoh Neferkare expressing his appreciation for Harkhuf's fourth expedition and his desire to see the dancing dwarf that Harkhuf had brought back from Nubia.

The majesty of [Pharaoh] Mernere, my lord, sent me together with my father . . . to [the Upper Nubian kingdom of] Yam to open the way to that country. I did it in seven months; I brought from it all kinds of beautiful and rare gifts, and was praised for it greatly.

His majesty sent me a second time alone. . . . I came down [the Nile] bringing gifts from that country in great quantity, the likes of which had never before been brought back to this land [Egypt]. . . .

Then his majesty sent me a third time to Yam. . . . I came down with three hundred donkeys laden with incense, ebony, . . . panther skins, elephant's tusks, throw sticks, and all sorts of good products.

[The letter of Pharaoh Neferkare to Harkhuf:] Notice has been taken of this dispatch of yours which you made for the King of the Palace, to let one know that you have come down in safety from Yam with the army that was with you. You have said in this dispatch of yours that you have brought all kinds of great and beautiful gifts. . . . You have said in this dispatch of yours that you have brought a pygmy of the god's dances from the land of the horizon-dwellers [the region of Nubia southeast of Egypt], like the pygmy whom the [royal official] Bawerded brought from Punt [Ethiopia and Somalia] in the time of King Isesi. You have said to my majesty that his like has never been brought by anyone who [visited] Yam previously.

Truly you know how to do what your lord loves and praises. Truly you spend day and night planning to do what your lord loves, praises, and commands. His majesty will provide you many worthy honors for the benefit of your son's son for all time, so that all people will say, when they hear what my majesty did for you: "Does anything equal what was done for the sole companion Harkhuf when he came down from Yam, on account of the vigilance he showed in doing what his lord loved, praised, and commanded?"

Come north to the residence at once! Hurry and bring with you this pygmy whom you brought from the land of the horizon-dwellers live, hale, and healthy, for the dances of the god, to gladden the heart, to delight the heart of King Neferkare who lives forever! When he goes down with you into the ship, get worthy men to be around him on deck, lest he fall into the water! When he lies down at night, get worthy men to lie around him in his tent. Inspect ten times at night! My majesty desires to see this pygmy more than the gifts of the mineland [the Sinai peninsula] and of Punt!

When you arrive at the residence and this pygmy is with you live, hale, and healthy, my majesty will do great things for you, more than was done for the [royal official] Bawerded in the time of King Isesi, in accordance with my majesty's wish to see this pygmy. Orders have been brought to the chief of the new towns and the companion, overseer of priests to command that supplies be furnished from what is under the charge of each from every storage depot and every temple that has not been exempted.

• *How does Harkhuf's autobiography illuminate early Egyptian interest in Nubia and the processes by which Egyptians of the Old Kingdom developed knowledge about Nubia?*

SOURCE: Miriam Lichtheim, ed. *Ancient Egyptian Literature.* 3 vols. Berkeley: University of California Press, 1973, 1:25–27.

significant military advantage over Egyptian forces. They enjoyed an advantage also in their weaponry: the Hyksos used bronze weapons and bronze-tipped arrows, whereas Egyptians relied mostly on wooden weapons and arrows with stone heads. About 1674 B.C.E. the Hyksos captured Memphis and levied tribute throughout Egypt.

Hyksos rule provoked a strong reaction especially in Upper Egypt, where disgruntled nobles organized revolts against the foreigners. They adopted horses and chariots for their own military forces. They also equipped their troops with bronze weapons. Working from Thebes and later from Memphis, Egyptian leaders gradually pushed the Hyksos out of the Nile delta and founded a powerful state known as the New Kingdom (1550–1070 B.C.E.).

Pharaohs of the New Kingdom presided over a prosperous and productive society. Agricultural surpluses supported a population of perhaps four million people as well as an army and an elaborate bureaucracy that divided responsibilities among different offices.

Pharaohs of the New Kingdom also worked to extend Egyptian authority well beyond the Nile valley and the delta. After expelling the Hyksos, they sought to prevent new invasions by seizing control of regions that might pose threats in the future.
Egyptian Imperialism Most vigorous of the New Kingdom pharaohs was Tuthmosis III (reigned 1479–1425 B.C.E.). After seventeen campaigns that he personally led to Palestine and Syria, Tuthmosis dominated the coastal regions of the eastern Mediterranean as well as north Africa. Rulers of the New Kingdom also turned their attention to the south and restored Egyptian dominance in Nubia. Thus for half a millennium Egypt was an imperial power throughout much of the eastern Mediterranean basin and southwest Asia as well as most of the Nile River valley.

After the New Kingdom, Egypt entered a long period of political and military decline. Just as Hyksos rule provoked a reaction in Egypt, so Egyptian rule provoked reactions in the regions subdued by pharaonic armies. Local resistance drove Egyptian forces out of Nubia and southwest Asia; then Kushite and Assyrian armies invaded Egypt itself.

By 1100 B.C.E. Egyptian forces were in full retreat from Nubia, and in the tenth century B.C.E. Nubian leaders organized a new kingdom of Kush with a cap-

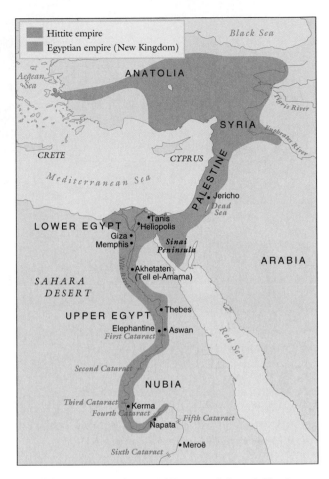

Map 2.2 Territories of imperial Egypt and the neighboring Hittite empire about 1400 B.C.E. Compare this map with Map 2.1. How did the boundaries of Egypt change, and why did they not expand east to the Red Sea or west into the Sahara?

ital at Napata, located just below the Nile's fourth cataract. By the eighth century B.C.E., rulers of this revived kingdom of Kush were powerful enough to invade Egypt. *The Revived Kingdom of Kush* King Kashta conquered Thebes about 760 B.C.E. and founded a Kushite dynasty that ruled Egypt for almost a century. Kashta's successors consolidated Kushite authority in Upper Egypt, claimed the title of pharaoh, and eventually extended their rule to the Nile delta and beyond.

Meanwhile, as Kushites pushed into Egypt from the south, Assyrian armies equipped with iron weapons bore down from the north. During the mid–seventh century B.C.E., while building their vast empire, the Assyrians invaded Egypt, campaigned as far south as Thebes, drove out the Kushites, and subjected Egypt to Assyrian rule. After the mid–sixth century B.C.E.,

---

Hyksos (HICK-sohs)

A wall painting from the tomb of an Egyptian imperial official in Nubia depicts a delegation of Nubians bringing tribute in the forms of exotic beasts, animal skins, and rings of gold.

like Mesopotamia, Egypt fell to a series of foreign conquerors who built vast empires throughout southwest Asia and the eastern Mediterranean region.

THE FORMATION OF COMPLEX SOCIETIES AND SOPHISTICATED CULTURAL TRADITIONS

As in Mesopotamia, cities and the congregation of dense populations encouraged the emergence of specialized labor in the early agricultural societies of Africa. Clearly defined social classes emerged throughout the Nile valley, and both Egypt and Nubian lands built patriarchal societies that placed authority largely in the hands of their adult males. The Egyptian economy was especially productive, and because of both its prosperity and its geographic location, Egypt figured as a center of trade, linking lands in southwest Asia, the eastern Mediterranean, and sub-Saharan Africa. Meanwhile, like southwest Asia, the Nile valley was a site of sophisticated cultural development. Writing systems appeared in both Egypt and Nubia, and writing soon became a principal medium of literary expression and religious reflection as well as a

means for preserving governmental records and commercial information.

The Emergence of Cities and Stratified Societies

Cities were not as prominent in early societies of the Nile River valley as they were in ancient Mesopotamia. Nevertheless, several major cities emerged and guided affairs in both Egypt and Nubia. In Egypt, Memphis, Thebes, Heliopolis, and Tanis all became important political, administrative, or cultural centers. In Nubia, Kerma, Napata, and Meroë all took their turn as political capitals between about 2500 B.C.E. and 100 C.E.   *Cities of the Nile Valley*

In Egypt and Nubia alike, ancient cities were centers of considerable accumulated wealth, which encouraged the development of social distinctions and hierarchies. Like the   *Social Classes* Mesopotamians, ancient Egyptians recognized a series of well-defined social classes. Egyptian peasants and slaves played roles in society similar to those of their Mesopotamian counterparts: they supplied the hard labor that made complex agricul-

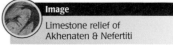

Image
Limestone relief of Akhenaten & Nefertiti

tural society possible. The organization of the ruling classes, however, differed considerably between Mesopotamia and Egypt. Instead of a series of urban kings, as in Mesopotamia, Egyptians recognized the pharaoh as a supreme central ruler. In addition, rather than depending on nobles who owed their positions to their birth, Egypt relied on professional military forces and an elaborate bureaucracy of administrators and tax collectors who served the central government. Thus, in Egypt much more than in Mesopotamia, individuals of common birth could attain high positions in society through government service.

Surviving information illuminates Egyptian society much better than Nubian, but it is clear that Nubia also was the site of a complex, hierarchical society in ancient times. Indeed, cemeteries associated with Nubian cities clearly reveal social and economic distinctions. Tombs of wealthy and powerful individuals were often elaborate structures—comfortable dwelling places tastefully decorated with paintings and filled with expensive goods such as gold jewelry, gems, fine furniture, and abundant supplies of food. In contrast, graves of commoners were much simpler, although they usually contained jewelry, pottery, personal ornaments, and other goods to accompany the departed.

Like their Mesopotamian counterparts, both Egyptian and Nubian peoples built patriarchal societies that vested authority over public and private affairs in their men. With rare exceptions men were the rulers in both Egyptian and Nubian private as well as public life, and decisions about government policies rested mostly in men's hands.

Patriarchal Society

Yet women made their influence felt in ancient Egyptian and Nubian societies much more than in contemporary Mesopotamia. In Egypt, women of the royal family sometimes served as regents for young rulers. In one notable case, a woman took power as pharaoh herself: Queen Hatshepsut (reigned 1473–1458 B.C.E.) served as coruler with her stepson Tuthmosis III. However, the notion of a female ruler may have been unsettling to many Egyptians. In what seems to have been an effort to present her in unthreatening guise, a monumental statue of Queen Hatshepsut depicts her wearing the stylized beard traditionally associated with the pharaohs. In Nubia, in contrast, there is abundant evidence of many women rulers in the kingdom of Kush. Some ruled in their own right, others reigned jointly with male kings, and many governed also in the capacity of regents. Meanwhile, other women wielded considerable power as priestesses in the numerous religious cults observed in Egypt and Nubia. A few women also obtained a formal education and worked as scribes.

Building pyramids and other large structures involved heavy work, especially by the less privileged classes. Here an Egyptian manuscript painting produced about 1000 B.C.E. depicts a supervisor overseeing a group of laborers as they drag a sled loaded with building blocks.

Economic Specialization and Trade

With the formation of complex, city-based societies, peoples of the Nile valley were able to draw on a rapidly expanding stock of human skills. Bronze metallurgy made its way from Mesopotamia to both Egypt and Nubia, and Sudanic peoples independently developed a technology of iron production that eventually spread to most parts of sub-Saharan Africa. Pottery, textile manufacture, woodworking, leather production, stonecutting, and masonry all became distinct occupations in cities throughout the Nile valley. Specialized labor and the invention of efficient transportation technologies encouraged the development of trade networks that linked the Nile valley to a much larger world.

Nile societies were much slower than their Mesopotamian counterparts to adopt metal tools and weapons. Whereas the production *Bronze Metallurgy* of bronze flourished in Mesopotamia by 3000 B.C.E., use of bronze implements became widespread in Egypt only after the seventeenth century B.C.E., when the Hyksos relied on bronze weapons to impose their authority on the Nile delta. Although Egyptians equipped their own forces with bronze weapons after expelling the Hyksos, the high cost of copper and tin kept bronze out of the hands of most people. Indeed, bronze was considered so valuable that officers weighed the bronze tools issued to workers at royal tombs to ensure that craftsmen did not shave slivers off them for personal uses.

Bronze was even less prominent in Nubian societies than in Egypt. During the centuries after 1000 B.C.E., *Iron Metallurgy* however, the southern Nile societies made up for their lack of bronze with the emergence of large-scale iron production. The Hittites had developed techniques for forging iron in Anatolia about 1300 B.C.E., but iron metallurgy in Africa arose independently about 1000 B.C.E. in the Great Lakes region of east Africa (modern-day Burundi and Rwanda) and on the southern side of Lake Chad (in modern-day Cameroon). From there, iron metallurgy quickly spread throughout most of sub-Saharan Africa. Furnaces churned out iron implements both in Nubia and in west Africa at least by 500 B.C.E. Meroë in particular became a site of large-scale iron production. Indeed, archaeologists who excavated Meroë in the early twentieth century C.E. found enormous mounds of slag still remaining from ancient times.

Nile craftsmen also worked from the early days of agricultural society to devise efficient means of trans-portation. Before 3500 B.C.E. Egyptians already traveled up and down the Nile with ease. Because the Nile flows north, boats could ride the currents from Upper to Lower Egypt. *Transportation* Meanwhile, prevailing winds blow almost year-round from the north, so that by raising a sail, boats could easily make their way upriver from Lower to Upper Egypt. Soon after 3000 B.C.E. Egyptians sailed beyond the Nile into the Mediterranean, and by about 2000 B.C.E. they had also thoroughly explored the waters of the Red Sea, the Gulf of Aden, and the western portion of the Arabian Sea. Egyptians also made use of Mesopotamian-style wheeled vehicles for local transport as well as donkey caravans for overland transport.

In Nubia, navigation on the Nile was less convenient than in Egypt because unnavigable cataracts made it necessary to transport goods overland before continuing on the river. Moreover, sailing ships heading upriver could not negotiate a long stretch of the Nile around the fourth cataract because winds blow the same direction that currents flow. As a result, Nubian societies had to rely more than Egyptians on overland transport by wheeled vehicles and donkey caravan.

In both Egypt and Nubia, specialized labor and efficient means of transportation encouraged the development of long-distance trade. By the *Trade Networks* time of the Old Kingdom, trade flowed regularly between Egypt and Nubia. Exotic African goods such as ivory, ebony, leopard skins, ostrich feathers, gemstones, gold, and slaves went down the Nile in exchange for pottery, wine, honey, and finished products from Egypt. Among the most prized Egyptian exports were fine linen textiles woven from the flax that flourished in the Nile valley as well as high-quality decorative and ornamental objects such as boxes, furniture, and jewelry produced by skilled artisans. Commerce linked Egypt and Nubia throughout ancient times, even when tensions or hostilities complicated relations between the two societies.

Egyptian merchants looked north as well as south. They traded with Mesopotamians as early as 3500 B.C.E., and after 3000 B.C.E. they were active throughout the eastern Mediterranean basin. Since Egypt has very few trees, Egyptian ships regularly imported huge loads from Lebanon. Pharaohs especially prized aromatic cedar for their tombs, and one record from about 2600 B.C.E. mentions an expedition of forty ships hauling cedar logs. In exchange for cedar, Egyptians offered gold, silver, linen textiles, leather goods, and dried foods such as lentils.

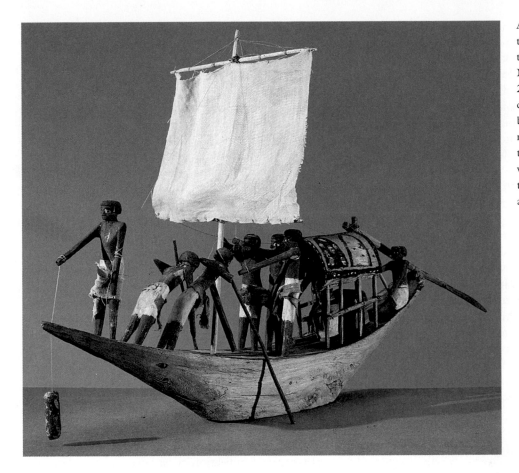

A wooden model found in a tomb shows how Egyptians traveled up and down the Nile River. Produced about 2000 B.C.E., this sculpture depicts a relatively small boat with a mast, sail, rudder, and poles to push the vessel through shallow waters. Many wall and tomb paintings confirm the accuracy of this model.

After the establishment of the New Kingdom, Egyptians also traded through the Red Sea and the Gulf of Aden with an east African land they called Punt—probably modern-day Somalia and Ethiopia. From Punt they imported gold, ebony, ivory, cattle, aromatics, and slaves. Thus, as in southwest Asia, specialization of labor and efficient technologies of transportation not only quickened the economies of complex societies in Egypt and Nubia but also encouraged their interaction with peoples of distant lands.

Early Writing in the Nile Valley

Writing appeared in Egypt at least by 3200 B.C.E., possibly as a result of Mesopotamian influence. As in Mesopotamia, the earliest Egyptian writing was pictographic, but Egyptians soon supplemented their pictographs with symbols representing sounds and ideas. Early Greek visitors to Egypt marveled at the large and handsome pictographs that adorned Egyptian monuments and buildings. Since the symbols were particularly prominent on temples, the visitors called them hieroglyphs, from two Greek words meaning "holy inscriptions." Hieroglyphic writing also survives on sheets of papyrus, a paper-like material fashioned from the insides of papyrus reeds, which flourish along the Nile River. The hot, dry climate of Egypt has preserved large numbers of papyrus texts bearing administrative and commercial records as well as literary and religious texts.

Hieroglyphic Writing

Although striking and dramatic, hieroglyphs were also somewhat cumbersome. Egyptians went to the trouble of using hieroglyphs for formal writing and monumental inscriptions, but for everyday affairs they commonly relied on the hieratic ("priestly") script, a simplified, cursive form of hieroglyphs. Hieratic appeared in the early centuries of the third millennium B.C.E., and Egyptians made extensive use of the script for more than three thousand years, from about 2600

---

hieroglyphics (heye-ruh-GLIPH-iks)

B.C.E. to 600 C.E. Hieratic largely disappeared after the middle of the first millennium C.E., when Egyptians adapted the Greek alphabet to their own language and developed alphabetic scripts known as the demotic ("popular") and Coptic ("Egyptian") scripts.

Nubian peoples spoke their own languages, but all early writing in Nubia was Egyptian hieroglyphic writing. Indeed, over the centuries, Egypt wielded great cultural influence in Nubia, especially during times when Egyptian political and military influence was strong in southern lands. After about the fifth century B.C.E., however, Egyptian cultural influence declined noticeably in Nubia. After the transfer of the Kushite capital from Napata to Meroë, Nubian scribes even devised an alphabetic script for the Meroitic language. They borrowed Egyptian hieroglyphs but used them to represent sounds rather than ideas and so created a flexible writing system. Many Meroitic inscriptions survive, both on monuments and on papyrus. However, although scholars have ascertained the sound values of the alphabet, the Meroitic language itself is so different from other known languages that no one has been able to decipher Meroitic texts.

Meroitic Writing

The Development of Organized Religious Traditions

Like their counterparts in other world regions, Egyptians and Nubians believed that deities played prominent roles in the world and that proper cultivation of the gods was an important community responsibility. The principal gods revered in ancient Egypt were Amon and Re. Amon was originally a local Theban deity associated with the sun, creation, fertility, and reproductive forces, and Re was a sun god worshiped at Heliopolis. During the Old Kingdom and the Middle Kingdom, priests increasingly associated the two gods with each other and honored them in the combined cult of Amon-Re. At Heliopolis a massive temple complex supported priests who tended to the cult of Amon-Re and studied the heavens for astronomical purposes. When Egypt became an imperial power during the New Kingdom, some devotees suggested that Amon-Re might even be a universal god who presided over all the earth.

Amon and Re

For a brief period the cult of Amon-Re faced a monotheistic challenge from the god Aten, another deity associated with the sun. Aten's champion was Pharaoh Amenhotep IV (reigned 1353–1335 B.C.E.), who changed his name to Akhenaten in honor of his preferred deity. Akhenaten considered Aten the world's "sole god, like whom there is no other." This faith represented one of the world's earliest expressions of monotheism—the belief that a single god rules over all creation. As long as Akhenaten lived, the cult of Aten flourished. But when the pharaoh died, traditional priests mounted a fierce counterattack, restored the cult of Amon-Re to privileged status, and nearly annihilated the worship and even the memory of Aten.

Aten and Monotheism

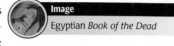

Image
Egyptian *Book of the Dead*

Whereas Mesopotamians believed with Gilgamesh that death brought an end to an individual's existence, many Egyptians believed that death was not an end so much as a transition to a new dimension of existence. The yearning for immortality helps to explain the Egyptian practice of mummifying the dead. During the Old Kingdom, Egyptians believed that only the ruling elites would survive the grave, so they mummified only pharaohs and their close relatives. During the Middle and New Kingdoms, however, Egyptians came to think of eternal life as a condition available to normal mortals as well as members of the ruling classes. Mummification never became general practice in Egypt, but with or without preservation of the body, a variety of religious cults promised to lead individuals of all classes to immortality.

Mummification

The cult of Osiris attracted particularly strong popular interest. According to the myths surrounding the cult, Osiris's evil brother Seth murdered him and scattered his dismembered parts throughout the land, but the victim's loyal wife, Isis, retrieved his parts and gave her husband a proper burial. Impressed by her devotion, the gods restored Osiris to life as god of the underworld, the dwelling place of the departed.

Cult of Osiris

Egyptians also associated Osiris with immortality and honored him through a religious cult that demanded observance of high moral standards. Following their deaths, individual souls faced the judgment of Osiris, who had their hearts weighed against a feather symbolizing justice. Those with heavy hearts carrying a burden of evil and guilt did not merit immortality, whereas those of pure heart and honorable deeds gained the gift of eternal life. Thus Osiris's cult held out hope of eternal reward for those who behaved according to high moral standards.

Amon-Re (AH-mohn RRAY)

Osiris (seated at right) receives a recently deceased individual, while attendants weigh the heart of another individual against a feather. This illustration comes from a papyrus copy of the *Book of the Dead* that was buried with a royal mummy.

Nubian peoples observed their own religious traditions, but very little written information survives to throw light on their religious beliefs. The most prominent of the Nubian deities was the lion-god Apedemak, often depicted with a bow and arrows, who served as war god for the kingdom of Kush. Another deity, Sebiumeker, was a creator god and divine guardian of his human devotees. Alongside native traditions, Egyptian religious cults were quite prominent in Nubia, especially after the aggressive pharaohs of the New Kingdom imposed Egyptian rule on the southern lands. Nubian peoples did not mummify the remains of their deceased, but they built pyramids similar to those of Egypt, although smaller, and they embraced several Egyptian gods. Amon was the preeminent Egyptian deity in Nubia as in Egypt itself. Osiris was also popular in Nubia, where he sometimes appeared in association with the native deity Sebiumeker. However, Egyptian gods did not displace native gods so much as they joined them in the Nubian pantheon. Indeed, Nubians often identified Egyptian gods with their own deities or endowed the foreign gods with traits important in Nubian society.

Nubian Religious Beliefs

BANTU MIGRATIONS AND EARLY AGRICULTURAL SOCIETIES OF SUB-SAHARAN AFRICA

Like their counterparts in southwest Asia, Egyptian and Nubian societies participated in a much larger world of interaction and exchange. Mesopotamian societies developed under the strong influences of long-distance trade, diffusions of technological innovations, the spread of cultural traditions, and the far-flung migrations of Semitic and Indo-European peoples. Similarly, quite apart from their dealings with southwest Asian and Mediterranean peoples, Egyptian and Nubian societies developed in the context of widespread interaction and exchange in sub-Saharan Africa. The most prominent processes unfolding in sub-Saharan Africa during ancient times were the migrations of Bantu-speaking peoples and the establishment of agricultural societies in regions where Bantu speakers settled. Just as Sudanic agriculture spread to the Nile valley and provided an economic foundation for the development of Egyptian and Nubian societies, it also spread to most other regions of Africa south of the Sahara and supported the emergence of distinctive agricultural societies.

The Dynamics of Bantu Expansion

Among the most influential peoples of sub-Saharan Africa in ancient times were those who spoke Bantu languages. The original Bantu language was one of many related tongues in the larger Niger-Congo family of languages widely spoken in west Africa after 4000 B.C.E. The earliest Bantu speakers inhabited a region embracing the eastern part of modern Nigeria and the southern part of modern Cameroon. Members of this community referred to themselves as *bantu* (meaning "persons" or "people"). The earliest Bantu speakers settled mostly along the banks of rivers, which they navigated in canoes, and in open areas of the region's forests. They cultivated yams and oil palms, and in later centuries they added millet and sorghum. They also kept goats

The Bantu

and raised guinea fowl. They lived in clan-based villages headed by chiefs who conducted religious rituals and represented their communities in dealings with neighboring villages. They traded regularly with hunting and gathering peoples who inhabited the tropical forests. Bantu cultivators provided these forest peoples with pottery and stone axes in exchange for meat, honey, and other forest products.

Unlike most of their neighbors, the Bantu displayed an early readiness to migrate to new territories. By 3000

Bantu Migrations   B.C.E. they were slowly spreading south into the west African forest, and after 2000 B.C.E. they expanded rapidly to the south toward the Congo River basin and east toward the Great Lakes, absorbing local populations of hunting, gathering, and fishing peoples into their own agricultural societies. Over the centuries, as some groups of Bantu speakers settled and others moved on to new territories, their languages differentiated into more than five hundred distinct but related tongues. (Today more than ninety million people speak Bantu languages, which collectively constitute the most prominent family of languages in sub-Saharan Africa.) Like the Indo-European migrations discussed in chapter 1, the Bantu migrations were not mass movements of peoples. Instead, they were intermittent and incremental processes that resulted in the gradual spread of Bantu languages and ethnic communities, as small groups moved to new territories and established settlements, which then became foundations for further expansion. By 1000 C.E. Bantu-speaking peoples occupied most of Africa south of the equator.

The precise motives of the early Bantu migrants are unknown, but it seems likely that population pressures drove the migrations. When settlements grew uncomfortably large and placed strains on available resources, small groups left their parent communities and moved to new territories. As they moved, Bantu migrants placed pressures on the forest dwellers, sometimes clashing with them over land resources but often intermarrying and absorbing them into Bantu agricultural society.

After about 1000 B.C.E., the pace of Bantu migrations quickened, as Bantu peoples began to produce

Iron and   iron tools and weapons. Iron tools enabled
Migration   Bantu cultivators to clear land and expand the zone of agriculture more effectively than before, while iron weapons strengthened the hand of Bantu groups against adversaries and competitors for lands or other resources. Thus iron metallurgy sup-

Map 2.3 Bantu migrations in sub-Saharan Africa between 2000 B.C.E. and 1000 B.C.E. Note the direction of Bantu migrations to the south and east of the Bantu homeland. Why didn't the migrations move north and west as well?

ported rapid population growth among the Bantu while also lending increased momentum to their continuing migrations.

Early Agricultural Societies of Sub-Saharan Africa

Several smaller migrations took place alongside the spread of Bantu peoples in sub-Saharan Africa. Between 3500 and 1000 B.C.E., southern Kushite herders pushed into parts of east Africa (modern-day Kenya and Tanzania), while Sudanese cultivators and herders moved into the upper reaches of the Nile River (now southern Sudan and northern Uganda). Meanwhile, Mande-speaking peoples who cultivated African rice established communities along the Atlantic estuaries of west Africa, and other peoples speaking Niger-Congo languages spread the cultivation of okra from forest regions throughout much of west Africa.

Among the most important effects of Bantu and other migrations was the establishment of agricultural societies throughout most of sub-Saharan Africa. Between 1000 and 500 B.C.E., cultivators ex-

Spread of Agriculture

tended the cultivation of yams and grains deep into east and south Africa (modern-day Kenya, Malawi, Mozambique, Zimbabwe, and South Africa), while herders introduced sheep and cattle to the region. About the same time, Bantu and other peoples speaking Niger-Congo languages spread the intensive cultivation of yams, oil palms, millet, and sorghum throughout west and central Africa while also introducing sheep, pigs, and cattle to the region. By the late centuries B.C.E., agriculture had reached almost all of sub-Saharan Africa except for densely forested regions and deserts.

As cultivation and herding spread throughout sub-Saharan Africa, agricultural peoples built distinctive societies and cultural traditions. Most Bantu and other peoples lived in communities of a few hundred individuals led by chiefs. Many peoples recognized groups known as age sets, or age grades, consisting of individuals born within a few years of one another. Members of each age set jointly assumed responsibility for tasks appropriate to their levels of strength, energy, maturity, and experience. During their early years, for example, members of an age set might perform light public chores. At maturity, members jointly underwent elaborate initiation rites that introduced them to adult society. Older men cultivated fields and provided military service, and women tended to domestic chores and sometimes traded at markets. In later years, members of age sets served as community leaders and military officers.

African cultivators and herders also developed distinctive cultural and religious traditions. Both Sudanic and Niger-Congo peoples (including Bantu speakers), for example, held monotheistic religious beliefs by 5000 B.C.E. Sudanic peoples recognized a single, impersonal divine force that they regarded as the source of both good and evil. They believed that this divine force could take the form of individual

African Cultivators

spirits, and they often addressed the divine force through prayers to intermediary spirits. The divine force itself, however, was ultimately responsible for rewards and punishments meted out to human beings. For their part, Niger-Congo peoples recognized a single god originally called Nyamba who created the world and established the principles that would govern its development, then stepped back and allowed the world to proceed on its own. Individuals did not generally address this distant creator god directly but, rather, offered their prayers to ancestor spirits and local territorial spirits believed to inhabit the world and influence the fortunes of living humans. Proper attention to these spirits would ensure them good fortune, they believed, whereas their neglect would bring punishment or adversity from disgruntled spirits.

Individual communities frequently borrowed religious elements from other communities and adapted their beliefs to changing circumstances or fresh understandings of the world. Migrations of Bantu and other peoples in particular resulted in a great deal of cultural mixing and mingling, and religious beliefs often spread to new communities in the wake of population movements. After 1000 B.C.E., for example, as they encountered Sudanic peoples and their reverence of a single divine force that was the source of good and evil, many Bantu peoples associated the god Nyamba with goodness. As a result, this formerly distant creator god took on a new moral dimension that brought him closer to the lives of individuals. Thus changing religious beliefs sometimes reflected widespread interactions among African societies.

SUMMARY

Like other world regions, Africa was a land in which peoples of different societies regularly traded, communicated, and interacted with one another from ancient times. African agriculture and herding first emerged in the Sudan, then spread both to the Nile River valley and to arable lands throughout sub-Saharan Africa. Agricultural crops and domesticated animals from southwest Asia soon made their way into the Nile valley. With its broad floodplains, Egypt became an especially productive land, while Nubia supported a smaller but flourishing society. Throughout the Nile valley, abundant agricultural surpluses supported dense populations and the construction of prosperous societies with sophisticated cultural traditions. Elsewhere in sub-Saharan Africa, populations were less dense, but the migrations of Bantu and other peoples facilitated the spread of agriculture, and later iron metallurgy as well, throughout most of the region. Meanwhile, the Nile River served as a route of trade and communication linking Egypt and the Mediterranean basin to the north with the Sudan and sub-Saharan Africa to the south. Only in the context of migration, trade, communication, and interaction is it possible to understand the early development of African societies.

CHRONOLOGY

9000 B.C.E.	Origins of Sudanic herding
7500 B.C.E.	Origins of Sudanic cultivation
3100 B.C.E.	Unification of Egypt
3100–2660 B.C.E.	Archaic Period of Egyptian history
2660–2160 B.C.E.	Egyptian Old Kingdom
2600–2500 B.C.E.	Era of pyramid building in Egypt
2500–1450 B.C.E.	Early kingdom of Kush with capital at Kerma
2040–1640 B.C.E.	Egyptian Middle Kingdom
2000 B.C.E.	Beginnings of Bantu migrations
1550–1070 B.C.E.	Egyptian New Kingdom
1479–1425 B.C.E.	Reign of Pharaoh Tuthmosis III
1473–1458 B.C.E.	Reign of Queen Hatshepsut (coruler with Tuthmosis III)
1353–1335 B.C.E.	Reign of Pharaoh Amenhotep IV (Akhenaten)
900 B.C.E.	Invention of iron metallurgy in sub-Saharan Africa
760 B.C.E.	Conquest of Egypt by King Kashta of Kush

FOR FURTHER READING

Cyril Aldred. *The Egyptians*. Rev. ed. New York, 1984. A popular, well-illustrated, and reliable survey of ancient Egyptian history.

Christopher Ehret. *An African Classical Age: Eastern and Southern Africa in World History, 1000 B.C. to A.D. 400*. Charlottesville, Va., 1998. A pathbreaking volume focusing on eastern and southern Africa and drawing on both linguistic and archaeological evidence.

———. *The Civilizations of Africa: A History to 1800*. Charlottesville, Va., 2001. An important contribution that views Africa in the context of world history.

Robert W. July. *Precolonial Africa: An Economic and Social History*. New York, 1975. Excellent short analysis of African social and economic history.

Miriam Lichtheim, ed. *Ancient Egyptian Literature*. 3 vols. Berkeley, 1973–80. An important collection of primary sources in translation that reflects the results of recent scholarship.

Roderick James McIntosh. *The Peoples of the Middle Niger: The Island of Gold*. Oxford, 1998. Fascinating volume emphasizing the environmental context of west African history.

Jan Vansina. *Paths in the Rainforests: Toward a History of Political Tradition in Equatorial Africa*. Madison, 1990. A brilliant synthesis concentrating on central Africa by one of the world's foremost historians of Africa.

Derek A. Welsby. *The Kingdom of Kush: The Napatan and Meroitic Empires*. London, 1996. Draws on both written and archaeological sources in tracing the development of ancient Nubia and charting its relationship with Egypt.

CHAPTER 3

Early Societies in South and East Asia

For a god, Indra was a very rambunctious fellow. According to the stories told about him by the Aryans, Indra had few if any peers in fighting, feasting, or drinking. The Aryans were a herding people who spoke an Indo-European language and who migrated to south Asia in large numbers after 1500 B.C.E. In the early days of their migrations they took Indra as their chief deity. The Aryans told dozens of stories about Indra and sang hundreds of hymns in his honor. One favorite story described how Indra brought rain to the earth by killing a dragon who lived in the sky and hoarded water in the clouds. When the dragon fell to earth, its weight caused such turmoil in the atmosphere that it rained enough to fill seven rivers in northern India. Those rivers, in turn, brought life-giving waters to inhabitants of the region.

A warrior such as Indra was a useful god for the Aryans, because as they migrated into south Asia they came into frequent conflict with Dravidian peoples already living there. For a thousand years and more, Aryans looked upon the rowdy, raucous war god as a ready source of inspiration as they sought to build a society in an already occupied land.

In ancient China, heroic figures were quite different. Legends tell stories of heroes who invented agriculture, domesticated animals, taught people to marry and live in families, created music, introduced the calendar, and instructed people in the arts and crafts. Most dashing of those heroes was a sage-king named Yu, who helped lay the foundations of Chinese society by rescuing China from the devastating flood waters of the Yellow River. Rather than dam the

OPPOSITE PAGE: *Sandstone bust of a distinguished man, perhaps a priest-king, from Mohenjo-daro.*

river as his predecessors had done, Yu dredged it and dug canals parallel to the river to allow the flood waters to flow harmlessly out to sea.

The legends say that Yu worked on the river for thirteen years without ever returning home. Once, he passed by the gate to his home and heard his wife and children crying out of loneliness, but he continued on his way rather than interrupt his flood-control work. Because he tamed the Yellow River, Yu became a popular hero, and poets praised the man who protected fields and villages from deadly and destructive floods. By exalting Yu as an exemplar of virtue, Chinese moralists promoted the values of social harmony and selfless, dedicated work that the sage-king represented.

Archaeological excavations show that China was a site of paleolithic communities as early as four hundred thousand years ago. In south Asia, humans appeared at least two hundred thousand years ago, long before the Aryans introduced Indra to south Asia. Yet, as in Mesopotamia and Egypt, population pressures in both east and south Asia induced human groups to begin experimenting with agriculture. By 7000 B.C.E. agriculture had taken root in India's Indus River valley, and by 3000 B.C.E. it had spread throughout much of the Indian subcontinent. In roughly the same period, between 7000 and 5000 B.C.E., people in China's Yangzi River valley domesticated and became dependent on rice, while people farther north in the Yellow River valley learned to cultivate and depend on millet.

In both south and east Asia, agricultural surpluses encouraged the growth of complex societies. Indeed, people in both locations developed bustling cities. By 3000 B.C.E. people in India's Indus River valley built south Asia's first cities in what has come to be known as Harappan society. Harappan society collapsed about 1500 B.C.E., just as Aryans moved into India in large numbers, which created a period of turmoil and conflict. Eventually, however, Aryan peoples interacted and intermarried with the indigenous Dravidians, and that combination led to the development of a distinctive society and a rich cultural tradition. In China, three dynastic states based in the Yellow River valley brought much of China under their authority during the second millennium B.C.E. in the process forged many local communities into a larger Chinese society. At the same time, all three dynasties had frequent dealings with neighboring peoples to the west, who linked China to

other societies and brought knowledge and technologies from afar. As in early Mesopotamia and Egypt, then, complex society in both south and east Asia promoted the development of distinctive social and cultural traditions in the context of cross-cultural interaction and exchange.

HARAPPAN SOCIETY

Like societies in Mesopotamia and Egypt, the earliest urban society in south Asia was built by Dravidian peoples in the valley of a river, the Indus, whose waters were available for irrigation of crops. This society—called Harappan society after one of its two chief cities—thrived between about 3000 B.C.E. and 1900 B.C.E. As it fell into decline over the next four hundred years, Indo-European migrants from the northwest began to settle in south Asia. Although Indo-Europeans initially clashed with the indigenous Dravidians, over time the two groups mixed and became indistinguishable from each other. In the process, they created a unique social and religious order that helped shape south Asian society until modern times.

Although scholars know that cities were evolving in the Indus region by 3000 B.C.E., it is impossible to follow the development of Harappan society in detail. One reason is that many of the earliest Harappan physical remains lie below the existing water table and thus are inaccessible to archaeologists. Another reason is the lack of deciphered written records, because scholars have so far been unable to understand the complex pictographic Harappan script. As a result, our understanding of Harappan society depends entirely on the study of accessible material remains.

If the Greek historian Herodotus had known of Harappan society, he might have called it "the gift of the Indus." Like the Nile, the Indus *The Indus River* draws its waters from rain and melting snow in towering mountains—in this case, the Hindu Kush and the Himalayas. As the waters reach the lowlands, the Indus deposits huge quantities of silt on its banks. Although the Indus periodically caused extensive destruction from flooding, it did make agricultural society possible in northern India. Early cultivators sowed their crops along its banks in September, after the flood receded, and harvested their crops the following spring.

Yu (yoo)

Harappan (huh-RUHP-puhn)

As in Mesopotamia and Egypt, agricultural surpluses in India vastly increased the food supply, stimulated population growth, and supported the establishment of cities and specialized labor. Between 3000 and 2500 B.C.E., the agricultural surplus of the Indus valley fed two large cities, Harappa and Mohenjo-daro, as well as subordinate cities and a vast agricultural hinterland. Harappan society embraced much of modern-day Pakistan and a large part of northern India as well—a territory of about 1.3 million square kilometers (502,000 square miles)—and thus was considerably larger than either Mesopotamian or Egyptian society.

Harappa and Mohenjo-daro

No evidence survives concerning the Harappan political system, although archaeological excavations do not suggest a royal or imperial authority. However, both Harappa and Mohenjo-daro had city walls, a fortified citadel, and a large granary, suggesting that they served as centers of political authority and sites for the collection and redistribution of taxes paid in the form of grain. The two cities represented a considerable investment of

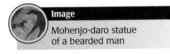
Mohenjo-daro statue of a bearded man

human labor and other resources: both featured marketplaces, temples, public buildings, extensive residential districts, and broad streets laid out on a carefully planned grid.

The two cities clearly established the patterns that shaped the larger society: weights, measures, architectural styles, and even brick sizes were consistent throughout the land. This standardization no doubt reflects the prominence of Harappa and Mohenjo-daro as powerful and wealthy cities whose influence touched all parts of Harappan society, as well as the degree to which the Indus River facilitated trade, travel, and communication among the far-flung regions of Harappan society.

Specialized Labor and Trade

Like other complex societies in ancient times, Harappa engaged in trade, both domestic and foreign. Pottery, tools, and decorative items produced in Harappa and Mohenjo-daro found their way to all corners of the Indus valley, while the cities imported precious metals and stones from neighboring peoples in Persia and the Hindu Kush mountains. During the period about 2300 to 1750 B.C.E., they also traded with Mesopotamians, mostly via ships that followed the coastline of the Arabian Sea between the mouth of the Indus River and the Persian Gulf.

Harappan Society and Culture

Like societies in Mesopotamia and Egypt, Harappan society generated considerable wealth. Excavations at Mohenjo-daro show that at its high point, from about 2500 to 2000 B.C.E., the city was a thriving economic center with a population of about forty thousand. The wealth of Harappan society, like that in Mesopotamia and Egypt, encouraged the formation of social distinctions. It is clear from Harappan dwellings that rich and poor lived in very different styles. In Mohenjo-daro, for example, many people lived in one-room tenements in barracks-like structures, but there were also individual houses of two and three stories with a

Social Distinctions

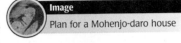
Plan for a Mohenjo-daro house

dozen rooms and an interior courtyard, as well as a few even larger houses. Almost all houses had private bathrooms with showers and toilets that drained into city sewage systems, which themselves were among the most sophisticated of the ancient world.

In the absence of deciphered writing, Harappan beliefs and values are very difficult to interpret. Even without written texts, however, material remains shed some tantalizing light on Harappan society. Like other early agricultural societies, Harappans venerated gods and goddesses they associated with creation and procreation. They recognized a mother goddess and a horned fertility god, and they held trees and animals sacred because of their associations with vital forces. In fact, many scholars believe that some Harappan deities survived the collapse of the larger society and later found places in the Hindu pantheon, because they have noticed striking similarities between Harappan and Hindu deities—especially those associated with fertility and procreation.

Sometime after 1900 B.C.E. Harappan society entered a period of decline. A primary cause was ecological degradation: in clearing the land for cultivation and firewood, Harappans deforested the Indus valley. In the process, they facilitated soil erosion and desertification. Over a period of half a millennium or more, most of the Indus valley became a desert: agriculture is possible there today only with the aid of artificial irrigation. These climatic and ecological changes reduced agricultural yields, and Harappan society faced a subsistence crisis during the centuries after 1900 B.C.E. By about 1700 B.C.E. the populations of Harappa and Mohenjo-daro had abandoned the cities, and by

Harappan Decline

Map 3.1   Harappan society and its neighbors about 2000 B.C.E. Observe the way in which Harappan society maintained trade connections with both Egypt and Mesopotamia. What conditions would have been necessary to allow trading parties to successfully traverse the land and sea routes depicted in this map?

1500 B.C.E. even the smaller Harappan cities had almost entirely collapsed.

THE INDO-EUROPEAN MIGRATIONS AND EARLY ARYAN INDIA

During the second millennium B.C.E., just as Harappan society declined, bands of foreigners filtered into the Indian subcontinent via the Hindu Kush mountains and settled throughout the Indus valley and beyond. Most prominent were nomadic and pastoral peoples speaking Indo-European languages who called themselves Aryans ("noble people"). By about 1500 B.C.E. they had begun to establish small herding and agricultural communities throughout northern India.

Their migrations took place over several centuries and thus did not constitute an invasion or a military campaign. Even so, it is clear that Indo-European migrants clashed with Dravidians and other peoples already settled in India. However, in the centuries after 1500 B.C.E., Dravidian and Indo-European peoples increasingly intermingled, in the process laying the social and cultural foundations that would influence Indian society to the present day.

The Aryans and India

When they entered India, the Aryans depended heavily on a pastoral economy. They especially prized their horses and herds of cattle. Horses were quite valuable because of their expense and rarity: horses do not breed well in India, so it was necessary for Aryans to replenish their stock by importing animals from central Asia. Like their Indo-European cousins to the north, the Aryans harnessed

The Early Aryans

This aerial view of the excavations at Mohenjo-daro illustrates the careful planning and precise layout of the city.

horses to carts, and they also hitched them to chariots for use in warfare. Meanwhile, cattle became the principal measure of wealth in early Aryan society. The Aryans consumed both dairy products and beef, and they often calculated prices in terms of cattle.

The Vedas   The early Aryans did not use writing but instead preserved extensive collections of religious and literary works by transmitting them orally from one generation to another in their sacred language, Sanskrit. The earliest of these orally transmitted works were the Vedas, which were collections of hymns, songs, prayers, and rituals honoring the various gods of the Aryans. There are four Vedas, the earliest and most important of which is the *Rig Veda*, a collection of 1,028 hymns addressed to Aryan gods. Although it was compiled between about 1400 and 900 B.C.E., Aryan priests committed the *Rig Veda* to writing only in about 600 B.C.E.

While the Vedas represent a priestly perspective on affairs because of their function in transmitting religious knowledge, they also shed considerable light on early Aryan society in India. Indeed, in view of their importance as historical sources, scholars refer to Indian history during the millennium between 1500 and 500 B.C.E. as the Vedic age.

The Vedic Age   The Vedas reflect a boisterous society in which the Aryans clashed repeatedly with the Dravidians and other peoples—referred to in the texts as *dasas*, meaning "enemies" or "subject peoples"—already living in India. The Vedas identify Indra, the Aryan war god and military hero, as one who ravaged citadels, smashed dams, and destroyed forts the way age consumes cloth garments. These characterizations suggest that competition over land and resources fueled intermittent conflict between Aryan and Dravidian peoples. The Aryans also fought ferociously among themselves. They did not have a state or common government but, rather, formed hundreds of chiefdoms organized around herding communities and agricultural villages. Because of their close proximity, this practice encouraged competition for resources and created enormous potential for conflict.

Vedas (VAY-duhs)

During the early centuries of the Vedic age, Aryan groups settled in the Punjab, the upper Indus River valley that straddles the modern-day border between northern India and Pakistan. After 1000 B.C.E. they began to settle in the area between the Himalayan foothills and the Ganges River, where they learned to make iron tools and to practice agriculture. Agricultural surpluses encouraged larger populations and more complex social organization, and by about 750 B.C.E., Aryans had established the first small cities in the Ganges River valley. Population growth also encouraged further migration. Thus, by 500 B.C.E. Aryan groups had migrated as far south as the northern Deccan, a plateau region in the southern cone of the Indian subcontinent about 1,500 kilometers (950 miles) south of the Punjab.

Aryan Migrations in India

As they settled into permanent communities and began to rely more on agriculture than on herding, the Aryans gradually lost the tribal political organization they had brought into India and instead evolved more formal political institutions. Indeed, between 1000 and 500 B.C.E., tribal chiefdoms increasingly developed into regional kingdoms, and for centuries these became the most common form of political organization on the subcontinent.

Origins of the Caste System

Although the Aryans did not build large imperial states, they did construct a well-defined social order. In fact, in some ways their social hierarchy served to maintain the order and stability that states and political structures guaranteed in other societies. The Aryan social structure, known today as the caste system, rested on sharp hereditary distinctions between individuals and groups, according to their occupations and roles in society.

Caste identities developed gradually as the Aryans established settlements throughout India. Initially, increased interaction with Dravidian peoples probably prompted Aryans to base social distinctions on either Aryan or Dravidian ancestry. In part, those distinctions may have arisen from differences in complexion between the Aryans, who referred to themselves as "wheat-colored," and the darker-skinned Dravidians. Indeed, the Aryan term *varna,* which refers to the major social classes, comes from the Sanskrit word meaning "color." However, over time Aryans and Dravidians mixed, mingled,

Caste and Varna

This bronze sword manufactured by Aryan craftsmen was a much stronger and more effective weapon than those available to Harappan defenders.

interacted, and intermarried to the point that distinguishing between them was impossible.

After about 1000 B.C.E. the Aryans increasingly recognized four main *varnas:* priests *(brahmins);* warriors and aristocrats *(kshatriyas);* cultivators, artisans,

varna (VUHR-nuh)
brahmins (BRAH-minz)

and merchants *(vaishyas);* and landless peasants and serfs *(shudras).* Some centuries later, probably about the end of the Vedic age, they added the category of the untouchables—people who performed dirty or un-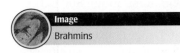pleasant tasks, such as butchering animals or handling dead bodies, and who theoretically became so polluted from their work that their very touch could defile individuals of higher status.

Until about the sixth century B.C.E., the four *varnas* described Vedic society reasonably well. Because

Subcastes and Jati

they did not live in cities and did not yet pursue many specialized occupations, the Aryans had little need for a more complicated social order. Over the longer term, however, a much more elaborate scheme of social classification emerged. As Vedic society became more complex and generated increasingly specialized occupations, the caste system served as the umbrella for a complicated hierarchy of subcastes known as *jati,* which were hereditary categories largely determined by occupation. By the eighteenth and nineteenth centuries C.E., in its most fully articulated form, the system featured several thousand *jati,* which prescribed individuals' roles in society in minute detail.

Castes and subcastes deeply influenced the lives of individual Indians through much of history. Members of a *jati* ate with one another and intermarried, and they cared for those who became ill or fell on hard times. Elaborate rules dictated forms of address and specific behavior appropriate for communication between members of different castes and subcastes. Violation of *jati* rules could result in expulsion from the larger group. That penalty was serious, since an outcast individual could not function well and sometimes could not even survive when shunned by members of the larger society.

The caste system never functioned in an absolutely rigid or inflexible manner but, rather, operated so as to

Caste and Social Mobility

accommodate social change. Individuals sometimes prospered on the basis of their own initiative, or else they could fall on hard times and move down in the social hierarchy. More often, however, social mobility came about as members of *jati* improved their condition collec-

kshatriyas (SHUHT-ree-uhs)
vaishyas (VEYESH-yuhs)
shudras (SHOO-druhs)

tively. Achieving upward mobility was not an easy matter—it often entailed moving to a new area, or at least taking on a new line of work—but the possibility of improving individual or group status helped to dissipate social tensions. In addition, the caste system also enabled foreign peoples to find a place in Indian society by allowing newcomers to organize into well-defined groups that eventually came to adopt caste identities.

By the end of the Vedic age, caste distinctions had become central institutions in Aryan India. Whereas in other lands, states and empires maintained public order, in India the caste system served as a principal foundation of social stability. Individuals have often identified more closely with their *jati* than with their cities or states, and castes have played a large role in maintaining social discipline in India.

While building an elaborate social hierarchy on the foundations of caste and *varna* distinctions, the Aryans also constructed a strongly patriarchal so-

The Lawbook of Manu

cial order on the basis of gender distinctions. At the time of their migrations into India, men already dominated Aryan society. All priests, warriors, and tribal chiefs were men, and the Aryans recognized descent through the male line. Women influenced affairs within their own families but enjoyed no public authority. As the Aryans settled in agricultural communities throughout India, they maintained this thoroughly patriarchal society. Only males could inherit property, unless a family had no male heirs, and only men could preside over family rituals that honored departed ancestors.

A text from about the first century B.C.E., called the *Lawbook of Manu,* illustrates the patriarchal ideologies that helped structure Indian society. Although composed after the Vedic age, the *Lawbook of Manu* reflected the society constructed earlier under Aryan influence. The author advised men to treat women with honor and respect, but he insisted that women remain subject to the guidance of the principal men in their lives. The *Lawbook* also specified that the most important duties of women were to bear children and maintain wholesome homes for their families.

RELIGION IN THE VEDIC AGE

As the caste system emerged and helped to organize Indian society, distinctive cultural and religious traditions also took shape. The Aryans entered India with

This greenish blue schist carving illustrates the devotion of a mother to her child.

traditions and beliefs that met the needs of a mobile and often violent society. As they spread throughout India and mixed with the Dravidians, however, the Aryans encountered new religious ideas they considered intriguing and persuasive. The resulting fusion of Aryan traditions with Dravidian beliefs and values laid the foundation for Hinduism, a faith immensely popular in India and parts of southeast Asia for more than two millennia.

Aryan Religion

As in Mesopotamia, Egypt, and other lands, religious values in India reflected the larger society. For example, during the early centuries following the Aryan migrations, the focus on Indra the war god testified to the instability and turbulence of early Vedic society. Also important to those early beliefs was the proper performance of ritual sacrifices. Through sacrifices, Aryans hoped to win the favor of the gods to ensure military success, large families, long life, and abundant herds of cattle. But those rewards required constant attention to religious ritual: proper honor for the gods called for households to have *brahmins* perform no fewer than five sacrifices per day—a time-consuming and expensive obligation.

As the centuries passed, many Aryans became dissatisfied with the sacrificial cults of the Vedas, which increasingly seemed like sterile rituals rather than a genuine means of communicating with the gods. Beginning about 800 B.C.E. many thoughtful individuals left their villages and retreated to the forests of the Ganges valley, where they lived as hermits and reflected on the relationships between human beings, the world, and the gods. These mystics drew considerable inspiration from the religious beliefs of Dravidian peoples, who often worshiped nature spirits that they associated with fertility and the generation of new life. Dravidians also believed that human souls took on new physical forms after the deaths of their bodily hosts. The notion that souls could experience transmigration and reincarnation— that an individual soul could depart one body at death and become associated with another body through a new birth—intrigued thoughtful people and encouraged them to try to understand the principles that governed the fate of souls. As a result, a remarkable tradition of religious speculation emerged.

Spirituality

The Blending of Aryan and Dravidian Values

This tradition achieved its fullest development in a body of works known as the Upanishads, which began to appear late in the Vedic age, about 800 to 400 B.C.E. The word *upanishad* literally means "a sitting in front of," and it refers to the practice of disciples gathering before a sage for discussion of religious issues. The Upanishads often took the form of dialogues that explored the Vedas and the religious issues that they raised.

The Upanishads taught that each person participates in a larger cosmic order and forms a small part of a universal soul, known as *Brahman.* Whereas the physical world is a theater of change, instability, and illusion, Brahman is an eternal, unchanging, permanent foundation for all things that exist—hence the only genuine reality. The authors of the Upanishads believed that individual souls were born into the physical world, not once, but many times: they believed that souls appeared most often as humans, but sometimes as animals, and possibly even occasionally as plants or other vegetable matter.

Brahman, the Universal Soul

Upanishads (oo-pah-NIH-shuhds)

The Upanishads developed several specific doctrines that helped to explain this line of thought. One was the

Teachings of the Upanishads

doctrine of *samsara*, which held that upon death, individual souls go temporarily to the World of the Fathers and then return to earth in a new incarnation. Another was the doctrine of *karma*, which accounted for the specific incarnations that souls experienced. According to this doctrine, individuals who lived virtuous lives and fulfilled all their duties could expect rebirth into a purer and more honorable existence—for example, into a higher and more distinguished caste. Those who accumulated a heavy burden of karma, however, would suffer in a future incarnation by being reborn into a difficult existence, or perhaps even into the body of an animal or an insect.

The Upanishads also encouraged the cultivation of personal integrity—a self-knowledge that would incline individuals naturally toward both ethical behavior and union with Brahman. In addition, they taught respect for all living things, animal as well as human. Animal bodies, after all, might well hold incarnations of unfortunate souls suffering the effects of a heavy debt of karma. A vegetarian diet thus became a common feature of the ascetic regime.

Yet even under the best of circumstances, the cycle of rebirth involved a certain amount of pain and suffering. The authors of the Upanishads sought to escape the cycle altogether and attain the state of *moksha,* which they characterized as a deep, dreamless sleep that came with permanent liberation from physical incarnation. This goal was difficult to reach, since it entailed severing all ties to the physical world and identifying with the ultimate reality of Brahman, the universal soul. The two principal means to the goal were asceticism and meditation, which could help individuals purge themselves of desire for the comforts of the physical world.

Just as the Aryan focus on Indra reflected early Aryan society, so the religious views of the Upani-

Religion and Vedic Society

shads dovetailed with the social order of the late Vedic age. Indeed, the doctrines of samsara and karma certainly reinforced the Vedic social order: they explained why individuals were born into their castes, and they encouraged individuals to observe their caste duties in hopes of enjoying a more comfortable and honorable

incarnation in the future. However, these doctrines were not simply cynical means of controlling Vedic society. Indeed, the sages who gave voice to these doctrines were conscientiously attempting to deal with meaningful spiritual and intellectual problems. Like Greek philosophers, Christian theologians, and many others, the authors of the Upanishads sought ultimate truth and certain knowledge in an ideal world that transcends our own.

POLITICAL ORGANIZATION IN EARLY CHINA

As in the Indus River valley of India, fertile river valleys in China allowed villages and towns to flourish along their banks. The most important of these valleys were those of the Yellow and Yangzi rivers, which supported settlements of agriculturalists after about 7000 B.C.E. By the late years of the third millennium B.C.E., these small settlements began to give way to much larger regional states. Among the most notable were those of the Xia, Shang, and Zhou dynasties, which progressively brought much of China under their authority and laid a political foundation for the development of a distinctive Chinese society.

Like the Indus, the Yellow River is boisterous and unpredictable. It rises in the mountains bordering the high plateau of Tibet, and it courses

The Yellow River

almost 4,700 kilometers (2,920 miles) before emptying into the Yellow Sea. It takes its name, Huang He, meaning "Yellow River," from the vast quantities of light-colored soil that it picks up along its route. So much soil becomes suspended in the Yellow River that the water turns yellow. The soil gradually builds up, raising the river bed and forcing the water out of its established path, periodically unleashing tremendous floods. The Yellow River has caused so much destruction that it has earned the nickname "China's Sorrow." Despite the periodic damage caused by the Yellow River, however, the soil it deposits is extremely fertile and easy to work, so even before the introduction of metal tools, cultivators using wooden implements could bring in generous harvests. As in India, agricultural surpluses resulted in increased population, which eventually gave rise to complex societies.

---

samsara (suhm-SAH-ruh)
karma (KAHR-mah)

Yangzi (YAHNG-zuh)

Chinese legends speak of three ancient dynasties—the Xia, the Shang, and the Zhou—that arose before the Qin and Han dynasties brought China under unified rule in the third century B.C.E. These dynasties were hereditary states that extended their control over progressively larger regions, although none of them embraced all the territory claimed by later Chinese dynasties.

The Xia and Shang Dynasties

The Xia dynasty emerged about 2200 B.C.E. and was one of the earliest to organize public life in China on a large scale. Ancient legends credit the dynasty's founder,

The Xia Dynasty the sage-king Yu, with the organization of effective flood-control projects on the Yellow River: thus here, as in Mesopotamia and Egypt, the need to organize large-scale public works projects helped to establish recognized authorities and formal political institutions. Although no information survives about the political institutions of the Xia, the dynasty's rulers probably exercised power throughout the middle Yellow River valley by controlling the leaders of individual villages. By extending formal control over this region, the Xia dynasty established a precedent for hereditary monarchical rule in China.

According to the legends, the last Xia king was an oppressive despot who lost his realm to the founder

The Shang Dynasty of the Shang dynasty. In fact, the Xia state probably gave way gradually before the Shang, which arose in a region to the south and east of the Xia realm. Tradition assigns the Shang dynasty to the period 1766 to 1122 B.C.E., and archaeological discoveries have largely confirmed those dates. Because the Shang dynasty left written records as well as material remains, the basic features of early Chinese society come into much clearer focus than they did during the Xia.

Technology helps to explain the rise and success of the Shang dynasty. Bronze metallurgy transformed

Bronze Metallurgy and Chariots Chinese society during Shang times and indeed may well have enabled Shang rulers to displace the Xia dynasty. Bronze metallurgy—together with horses, horse-drawn chariots, and other wheeled vehicles—came to China with Indo-European migrants from southwest Asia. Although the Xia dynasty already made limited use of bronze tools and weapons, Shang ruling elites

Xia (shyah)

Map 3.2 Boundaries and major cities of the Xia, Shang, and Zhou dynasties between 2200 and 256 B.C.E. Note how each dynasty progressively claimed larger territories over time. What would be the advantages and the disadvantages of administering these differently sized territories?

managed to monopolize the production of bronze in the Yellow River valley. Thus, control over bronze production strengthened Shang forces against those of the Xia, and they had little difficulty imposing their rule on agricultural villages and extending their influence throughout much of the Yellow River valley.

Shang kings extended their rule to a large portion of northeastern China centered on the modern-day province of Henan. Like state builders in other parts of the world, the kings claimed a generous portion of the surplus agricultural production from the regions they controlled and then used that surplus to support military forces, political allies, and others who could help them maintain their rule.

The Shang state rested on a vast network of walled towns whose local rulers recognized the authority of the Shang kings. During the course of the dynasty, Shang kings may have controlled one thousand or more towns. *Shang Political Organization* According to tradition, the Shang capital moved six times during the course of the dynasty. Though originally chosen for political and military reasons, in each case the capital also became an important social, economic, and cultural center—the site not only of admin-

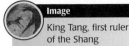
King Tang, first ruler of the Shang

istration and military command but also of bronze foundries, arts, crafts, trade, and religious observances.

Excavations have revealed much about the workings of the Shang dynasty. One remarkable site is Yin, near modern Anyang, which was the Shang capital during the last two or three centuries of the dynasty. Archaeologists working at Yin have identified a complex of royal palaces, archives with written documents, several residential neighborhoods, two large bronze foundries, several workshops used by craftsmen, and scattered burial grounds. Eleven large and lavish tombs constructed

The Shang Capital at Yin

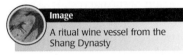
A ritual wine vessel from the Shang Dynasty

for Shang kings have received particular attention. The graves included thousands of objects—chariots, weapons, bronze goods, pottery, carvings, and sacrificial victims, including dogs, horses, and scores of human beings intended to serve the deceased royals in another existence. One tomb alone contained skeletons of more than three hundred sacrificial victims who joined the Shang king in death.

The Xia and Shang dynasties were not the only states that developed in ancient China, although legendary and historical accounts paid special attention to them because of their location in the Yellow River valley, where the first Chinese imperial states rose in later times. Indeed, archaeological excavations are making it clear that similar states dominated other regions at the same time the Xia and the Shang ruled the Yellow River valley. Recent excavations, for example, have unearthed evidence of a very large city at Sanxingdui in modern-day Sichuan province (southwestern China). Occupied about 1700 to 1000 B.C.E., the city was roughly contemporaneous with the Shang dynasty, and it probably served as capital of a regional kingdom.

The Zhou Dynasty

Although little information survives to illustrate the principles of law, justice, and administration by which Shang rulers maintained order, the picture becomes more clear in the practices of the Zhou dynasty, which succeeded the Shang as the preeminent political authority in northern China. Dwelling in the Wei River valley of northwestern China (modern Shaanxi province), the Zhou were a tough people who battled Shang forces and eventually won recognition as kings of the western regions.

The Rise of the Zhou

But the ambitions of the two dynasties collided in the late twelfth century B.C.E. According to Zhou accounts, the last Shang king was a criminal fool who gave himself over to wine, women, tyranny, and greed. As a result, many of the towns and political districts subject to the Shang transferred their loyalties to the Zhou, who toppled his government in 1122 B.C.E. and replaced it with their own state. The new dynasty ruled most of northern and central China, at least nominally, until 256 B.C.E.

In justifying the deposition of the Shang, spokesmen for the Zhou dynasty articulated a set of principles that influenced Chinese thinking about government and political legitimacy until the twentieth century. The Zhou theory of politics rested on the assumption that heavenly powers granted the right to govern—"the mandate of heaven"—to an especially deserving individual known as the son of heaven. The ruler had the duty to govern conscientiously, to observe high standards of honor and justice, and to maintain order and harmony within his realm. As long as he did so, the heavenly powers would approve of his work, the cosmos would enjoy stability, and the ruling dynasty would retain its mandate to govern. If a ruler failed in his duties, however, chaos and suffering would afflict his realm, the cosmos would fall out of balance, and the displeased heavenly powers would withdraw the mandate to rule and transfer it to a more deserving candidate. On the basis of that reasoning, spokesmen for the new dynasty explained the fall of the Shang and the transfer of the mandate of heaven to the Zhou.

The Mandate of Heaven

The Zhou state was much larger than the Shang. In fact, it was so extensive that a single central court could not rule the entire land effectively. As a result, Zhou rulers relied on a decentralized administration: they entrusted power, authority, and responsibility to subordinates who in return owed allegiance, tribute, and military support to the central government. During the early days of the dynasty, that system worked reasonably well. Gradually, however, subordinates established their own bases of power, which allowed them to become more independent of the Zhou dynasty. In addition, iron production spread rapidly across China in the first millennium B.C.E., and Zhou subordinates took advantage of the technology to outfit their own forces with weapons to resist the central government.

Political Organization

Zhou (JOH)

Decline of the Zhou

After the early eighth century B.C.E., Zhou rule deteriorated as nomadic invaders forced the royal court from their capital at Hao. Although the dynasty survived, it never regained its authority, and competing states fought ferociously with one another in hopes of establishing themselves as leaders of a new political order. So violent were the last centuries of the Zhou dynasty that they are known as the Period of the Warring States (403–221 B.C.E.). The Zhou dynasty officially ended in 256 B.C.E. when the last king abdicated his position under pressure from his ambitious subordinate the king of Qin. Only with the establishment of the Qin dynasty in 221 B.C.E. did effective central government return to China.

SOCIETY AND FAMILY IN ANCIENT CHINA

In China, as in India, the introduction of agriculture enabled individuals to accumulate wealth and preserve it within their families. Social distinctions began to appear during neolithic times, and after the establishment of the Xia, Shang, and Zhou dynasties the distinctions became even sharper. Throughout China the patriarchal family emerged as the institution that most directly influenced individuals' lives and their roles in the larger society.

The Social Order

Ruling Elites

Already during the Xia dynasty, but especially under the Shang and the early Zhou, the royal family and allied noble families occupied the most honored positions in Chinese society. They resided in large, palatial compounds made of pounded earth, and they lived on the agricultural surplus and taxes delivered by their subjects. One of the hallmarks of these elites was their conspicuous consumption of bronze, which was far too expensive for most people to afford. Indeed, ruling elites controlled much of the bronze weaponry that existed in northern China and also supplied their households with elaborately decorated cast-bronze utensils and vessels. Ruling elites consumed bronze in such staggering quantities that the tomb of Marquis Yi of Zeng, a provincial governor of the late Zhou dynasty, contained a collection of bronze weapons and decorative objects that weighed almost eleven tons.

A privileged class of hereditary aristocrats rose from the military allies of Shang and Zhou rulers. These aristocrats possessed extensive landholdings, and their standard of living was much more refined than that of the commoners and slaves who worked their fields and served their needs. They were served by a small class of free artisans and craftsmen, including bronzesmiths, jewelers, jade workers, and silk manufacturers, who enjoyed a reasonably comfortable existence because of aristocratic patronage.

Peasants

Far less comfortable was a large class of semiservile peasants who populated the Chinese countryside. They owned no land but provided agricultural, military, and labor services for their lords in exchange for plots to cultivate, security, and a portion of the harvest. They lived like their neolithic predecessors in small subterranean houses excavated to a depth of about one meter (three feet) and protected from the elements by thatched walls and roofs. Women's duties included mostly indoor activities such as wine making,

The delicate design of this bronze wine vessel displays the high level of craftsmanship during the late Shang dynasty.

SOURCES FROM THE PAST

Peasants' Protest

Peasants in ancient China mostly did not own their own land. Instead, they worked as tenants on plots allotted to them by royal or aristocratic owners, who took sizable portions of the harvest for their own uses. In the following poem from the Book of Songs, a collection of verses dating from Zhou times, peasants liken their lords to rodents, protest the bite lords take from the peasants' agricultural production, and threaten to abandon the lords' lands for a neighboring state where conditions are better.

■   ■   ■

Large rats! Large rats!
Do not eat our millet.
Three years have we had to do with you.
And you have not been willing to show any regard
    for us.
We will leave you,
And go to that happy land.
Happy land! Happy land!
There shall we find our place.
Large rats! Large rats!
Do not eat our wheat.
Three years have we had to do with you.
And you have not been willing to show any kindness
    to us.

We will leave you,
And go to that happy state.
Happy state! Happy state!
There shall we find ourselves aright.
Large rats! Large rats!
Do not eat our springing grain!
Three years have we had to do with you,
And you have not been willing to think of our toil.
We will leave you,
And go to those happy borders.
Happy borders! Happy borders!
Who will there make us always to groan?

• *How might you go about judging the extent to which these verses throw reliable light on class relations in ancient China?*

SOURCE: James Legge, trans. *The Chinese Classics,* 5 vols. London: Henry Frowde, 1893, 4:171–72.

weaving, and cultivation of silkworms, whereas men spent most of their time outside working in the fields, hunting, and fishing.

Finally, there was a sizable class of slaves, most of whom were enemy warriors captured during battles be-*Slaves* tween the many competing states of ancient China. Slaves performed hard labor, such as the clearing of new fields or the building of city walls, that required a large workforce.

Family and Patriarchy

Throughout human history the family has served as the principal institution for the socialization of children and the preservation of cultural traditions. In China the extended family emerged as a particularly

influential institution during neolithic times, and it continued to play a prominent role in shaping both private and public affairs after the appearance of the Xia, Shang, and Zhou states. Indeed, the early dynasties ruled their territories largely through family and kinship groups.

One reason for the pronounced influence of the Chinese family was the veneration of ancestors, a practice with roots in neolithic times. This *Veneration* practice was based on the belief that dead *of Ancestors* ancestors had the power to support and protect their surviving families, but only if their descendants displayed proper respect and ministered to the spirits' needs. A family could expect to prosper only if all its members—dead as well as living—worked cooperatively toward common interests. Thus, the family became an institution linking departed generations to the living and helped build a strong ethic of family solidarity.

Patriarchal Society
In the absence of organized religion or official priesthood in ancient China, the patriarchal head of the family presided at ceremonies honoring ancestors' spirits. As mediator between the family's dead and living members, the family patriarch possessed tremendous authority. Indeed, Chinese society vested authority principally in elderly males who headed their households. And, like its counterparts in other regions, Chinese patriarchy intensified with the emergence of large states. During neolithic times Chinese men wielded public authority, but they won their rights to it by virtue of the female line of their descent. Gradually, however, Chinese society lost its matrilineal character. By the later Shang and Zhou dynasties, women lived increasingly in the shadow of men, and even queens and empresses were honored only as a result of being associated with their illustrious husbands.

EARLY CHINESE WRITING AND CULTURAL DEVELOPMENT

Early Chinese myths and legends explained the origins of the world, the human race, agriculture, and the various arts and crafts. But Chinese thinkers saw no need to organize those ideas into systematic religious traditions. Although they often spoke of an impersonal heavenly power, they did not recognize a personal supreme deity who intervened in human affairs or took special interest in human behavior. Nor did ancient China support a large class of priests like those of Mesopotamia, Egypt, and India. As a result, it was family patriarchs who represented the interests of living generations to the spirits of departed ancestors.

In that environment, writing served as the foundation for a distinctive secular cultural tradition in ancient China. Surviving evidence suggests that writing came into extensive use during the Shang dynasty. As in other lands, writing in east Asia quickly became an indispensable tool of government as well as a means of expressing ideas and offering reflections on human beings and their world.

patriarch (PAY-tree-ahrk)

Oracle Bones and Early Chinese Writing

In Mesopotamia and India, merchants pioneered the use of writing. In China, however, the earliest known writing served the interests of rulers rather than traders. Writing in China goes back at least to the early part of the second millennium B.C.E. Surviving records indicate that scribes at the Shang royal court kept written accounts of important events on strips of bamboo or pieces of silk. Unfortunately, almost all those materials have perished, along with their messages. Yet one medium employed by ancient Chinese scribes has survived the ravages of time. Recognized just over a century ago, inscriptions on so-called oracle bones have thrown tremendous light both on the Shang dynasty and on the early stages of Chinese writing.

Oracle Bones
Oracle bones were the principal instruments used by fortune-tellers in ancient China. Diviners inscribed a question on a specially prepared broad bone—such as the shoulder blade of a sheep—and then subjected it to heat. When heated, the bone developed networks of splits and cracks. The fortune-teller then studied the patterns and determined the answer to the question inscribed on the bone. Often the diviner recorded the answer on the bone, and later scribes occasionally added further information about the events that actually came to pass.

Most of the oracle bones have come from royal archives, and the questions posed on them clearly reveal the day-to-day concerns of the Shang royal court. Will the season's harvest be abundant or poor? Will the queen bear a son or a daughter? Taken together, bits of information preserved on the oracle bones have allowed historians to piece together an understanding of the political and social order of Shang times.

Even more important, the oracle bones offer the earliest glimpse into the tradition of Chinese writing. The earliest form of Chinese writing, like Sumerian and Egyptian writing, was the pictograph—a conventional or stylized representation of an object. The characters used in contemporary Chinese writing are direct descendants of those used in Shang times. Scholars have identified more than two thousand characters inscribed on oracle bones, most of which have a modern counterpart. Over the centuries, written Chinese characters have undergone considerable modification: generally speaking, they have become

Oracle bone from Shang times with an inscribed question and cracks caused by exposure of the bone to heat.

more stylized, conventional, and abstract. Yet the affinities between Shang and later Chinese written characters are apparent at a glance.

The political interests of the Shang kings may have accounted for the origin of Chinese writing, but once established, the technology was available for other uses. Because Shang writing survives only on oracle bones and a small number of bronze inscriptions, however, evidence for the expanded uses of writing comes only from the Zhou dynasty and later times.

Indeed, the Zhou dynasty produced books of poetry and history, manuals of divination and ritual, and *Zhou Literature* essays dealing with moral, religious, philosophical, and political themes. Best known of these works are the reflections of Confucius and other late Zhou thinkers (discussed in chapter 6), which served as the intellectual foundation of classical Chinese society. But many works won recognition in Zhou society, including the popular *Book of Changes* (a manual instructing diviners in the art of foretelling the future), the *Book of History* (a collection of documents that justified the Zhou state), the *Book of Etiquette* (a manual in the arts of polite behavior), and—most notable of all—the *Book of Songs* (a collection of verses).

Unfortunately, most other Zhou writings have perished. One important reason for this is that when the imperial house of Qin ended the chaos of the Period of the Warring States and brought all of China under tightly centralized rule in 221 B.C.E., the victorious emperor ordered the destruction of all writings that did not have some immediate utilitarian value. Only a few items escaped, hidden away for a decade or more until scholars and writers could once again work without fear of persecution. These few survivors represent the earliest development of Chinese literature and moral thought.

ANCIENT CHINA AND THE LARGER WORLD

High mountain ranges, forbidding deserts, and turbulent seas stood between China and other early societies of the eastern hemisphere. These geographic features did not entirely prevent communication between China and other lands, but they hindered the establishment of direct long-distance trade relations such as those linking Mesopotamia with Harappan India or those between the Phoenicians and other peoples of the Mediterranean basin. Nevertheless, like other early societies, ancient China developed in the context of a larger world of interaction and exchange.

	Turtle	Horse
Oracle bone script of the Shang dynasty (16th century–11th century B.C.E.)		
Zhou dynasty script (11th century–3rd century B.C.E.)		
Qin dynasty script (221–207 B.C.E.)		
Han dynasty script (207 B.C.E.–220 C.E.)		
Modern script (3rd century C.E.–present)		
Contemporary script, People's Republic of China (1950–the present)		

The evolution of Chinese characters from the Shang dynasty to the present.

Trade, migration, and the expansion of Chinese agricultural society all ensured that peoples of the various east Asian and central Asian societies would have regular dealings with one another. Chinese cultivators had particularly intense relations—sometimes friendly and sometimes hostile—with their neighbors to the north, the west, and the south.

Relations with Nomadic Peoples of Central Asia

From the valley of the Yellow River, Chinese agriculture spread to the north and west. As this expansion occurred, Chinese cultivators encountered nomadic peoples who had built pastoral societies in the grassy steppe lands of central Asia. These lands were too arid to sustain large agricultural societies, but their grasses supported large herds of livestock. By 2200 B.C.E. these nomads were already experienced horseback riders, had learned the technology of bronze metallurgy, and had introduced large numbers of heavy wagons into the steppes. After about 1000 B.C.E. several clusters of nomadic peoples organized powerful herding societies on the Eurasian steppes.

Steppe Nomads

Nomadic peoples did little farming but instead concentrated on herding their animals, driving them to regions where they could find food and water. Because nomadic peoples ranged widely over the grassy steppes of central Asia, they served as links between agricultural societies to the east and west. They were prominent intermediaries in trade networks spanning central Asia. They also brought knowledge of bronze metallurgy and horse-drawn chariots from southwest Asia. Nomadic peoples depended on agricultural societies for grains and finished products, such as textiles and metal goods, which they could not readily produce for themselves. In exchange for those products, they offered horses, which flourished on the steppes, and their services as links to other societies. Yet the Chinese and nomadic peoples always had tense relations. Indeed, they often engaged in bitter wars, and nomadic raids posed a constant threat to the northern and western regions of China.

Nomadic Society

The Southern Expansion of Chinese Society

Chinese influence spread to the south as well as to the north and west. There was no immediate barrier to cultivation in the south: indeed, the valley of the Yangzi River supports even more intensive agriculture than is possible in the Yellow River basin. In fact, the moist, subtropical climate of southern China lent itself readily to the cultivation of rice: ancient cultivators sometimes raised two crops of rice per year.

The Yangzi Valley

But intensive cultivation of rice depended on the construction and maintenance of an elaborate irrigation system that allowed cultivators to flood their paddies and release the waters at the appropriate time. The Shang and Zhou states provided sources of au-

Terraced rice paddies in the river valleys of southern China have long produced abundant harvests.

thority that could supervise a complex irrigation system, and harvests in southern China—along with the population—increased dramatically during the second and first millennia B.C.E.

Agricultural surpluses and growing populations led to the emergence of cities, states, and complex societies in the Yangzi as well as the Yellow River valley. During the late Zhou *The State of Chu* dynasty, the powerful state of Chu, situated in the central region of the Yangzi, governed its affairs autonomously and challenged the Zhou for supremacy. By the end of the Zhou dynasty, Chu and other states in southern China were in regular communication with their counterparts in the Yellow River valley. They adopted Chinese political and social traditions as well as Chinese writing, and they built societies closely resembling those of the Yellow River valley. As a result, although only the northern portions of the Yangzi River valley fell under the authority of the Shang and Zhou states, by the end of the Zhou dynasty all of southern China formed part of an emerging larger Chinese society.

SUMMARY

Agricultural peoples in south and east Asia built complex societies that in broad outline were much like those to the west. Particularly in the valleys of the Yellow River, the Yangzi River, and the Indus River, early Chinese and Indian cultivators organized states, developed social distinctions, and established sophisticated cultural traditions. Their languages, writing, beliefs, and values differed considerably from one another and from those of their contemporaries in other societies, and these cultural elements lent distinctiveness to both Chinese and Indian society. Moreover, inhabitants of both ancient China and India managed to trade and communicate with peoples of other societies. As a result, wheat cultivation, bronze and iron metallurgy, horse-drawn chariots, and wheeled vehicles all made their way from southwest Asia in ancient times. Thus, in south and east Asia, as in other parts of the eastern hemisphere, agriculture demonstrated its potential to provide a foundation for large-scale social organization and to support interaction and exchange between peoples of different societies.

CHRONOLOGY

SOUTH ASIA	
8000–7000 B.C.E.	Beginnings of agriculture in south Asia
2500–2000 B.C.E.	High point of Harappan society
1900 B.C.E.	Beginning of Harappan decline
1500 B.C.E.	Beginning of Aryan migration to India
1500–500 B.C.E.	Vedic age
1400–900 B.C.E.	Composition of the *Rig Veda*
1000 B.C.E.	Aryan migrations into the Ganges River valley
1000 B.C.E.	Emergence of *varna* distinctions
1000–500 B.C.E.	Formation of regional kingdoms in northern India
800–400 B.C.E.	Composition of the principal Upanishads
750 B.C.E.	Establishment of first Aryan cities in the Ganges valley
500 B.C.E.	Aryan migrations to the Deccan Plateau
EAST ASIA	
5000–3000 B.C.E.	Yangshao society
2200–1766 B.C.E.	Xia dynasty
1766–1122 B.C.E.	Shang dynasty
1122–256 B.C.E.	Zhou dynasty
403–221 B.C.E.	Period of the Warring States

FOR FURTHER READING

F. R. Allchin. *The Archaeology of Early Historic South Asia: The Emergence of Cities and States.* Cambridge, 1995. A collection of scholarly essays on the roles of cities and states in ancient India.

Cyril Birch, ed. *Anthology of Chinese Literature.* 2 vols. New York, 1965. Collection of primary sources in translation.

Kwang-chih Chang. *The Archaeology of Ancient China.* 4th ed. New Haven, 1986. Brings the results of archaeological excavations to bear on ancient Chinese history.

Nicola di Cosmo. *Ancient China and Its Enemies: The Rise of Nomadic Power in East Asian History.* Cambridge, 2002. An insightful study analyzing the emergence of pastoral nomadism and relations between Chinese cultivators and nomadic peoples in ancient times.

David N. Keightley, ed. *The Origins of Chinese Civilization.* Berkeley, 1983. An important collection of scholarly articles dealing with all aspects of early Chinese society.

Jonathan Mark Kenoyer. *Ancient Cities of the Indus Valley Civilization.* Oxford, 1998. A well-illustrated volume that synthesizes recent archaeological and linguistic scholarship on Harappan society.

J. P. Mallory. *In Search of the Indo-Europeans: Language, Archaeology, and Myth.* London, 1989. Carefully reviews modern theories about early Indo-European speakers in light of both the linguistic and the archaeological evidence.

Juan Mascaró, trans. *The Upanishads.* London, 1965. A superb English version of selected Upanishads by a gifted translator.

Shereen Ratnagar. *Encounters: The Westerly Trade of the Harappan Civilization.* Delhi, 1981. Relies on archaeological discoveries in examining commercial relations between Harappan society and Mesopotamia.

Jessica Rawson. *Ancient China: Art and Archaeology.* New York, 1980. An outstanding and well-illustrated volume with especially strong treatment of archaeological discoveries.

CHAPTER 4

Early Societies in the Americas and Oceania

In early September of the year 683 C.E., a Maya man named Chan Bahlum grasped a sharp obsidian knife and cut three deep slits into the skin of his penis. He inserted into each slit a strip of paper made from beaten tree bark so as to encourage a continuing flow of blood. His younger brother Kan Xul performed a similar rite, and other members of his family also drew blood from their own bodies.

The bloodletting observances of September 683 C.E. were political and religious rituals, acts of deep piety performed as Chan Bahlum presided over funeral services for his recently deceased father, Pacal, king of the Maya city of Palenque in the Yucatan peninsula. The Maya believed that the shedding of royal blood was essen-tial to the world's survival. Thus, as Chan Bahlum prepared to succeed his father as king of Palenque, he let his blood flow copiously.

Throughout Mesoamerica, Maya and other peoples performed similar rituals for a millennium and more. Maya rulers and their family members regularly spilled their own blood. Men commonly drew blood from the penis, like Chan Bahlum, and women often drew from the tongue. Both sexes occa-sionally drew blood also from the earlobes, lips, or cheeks, and they sometimes increased the flow by pulling long, thick cords through their wounds.

According to Maya priests, the gods had shed their own blood to water the earth and nourish crops of maize, and they expected

---

Maya (MAH-uh)
Yucatan (yoo-kah-TAN)

OPPOSITE PAGE: *Figure of a Mayan warrior with facial tattooing.*

63

human beings to honor them by imitating their sacrifice. By spilling human blood the Maya hoped to please the gods and ensure that life-giving waters would bring bountiful harvests to their fields. By inflicting painful wounds not just on their enemies but on their own bodies as well, the Maya demonstrated their conviction that bloodletting rituals were essential to the coming of rain and the survival of their agricultural society.

This agricultural society was the product of a distinctive tradition. Human groups migrated to the Americas and Oceania long after they had established communities throughout most of the eastern hemisphere, but long before any people began to experiment with agriculture. Their migrations took place during ice ages, when glaciers locked up much of the earth's water, causing sea levels all over the world to decline precipitously—sometimes by as much as 300 meters (984 feet). For thousands of years, temporary land bridges joined regions that both before and after the ice ages were separated by the seas. One land bridge linked Siberia with Alaska. Another joined the continent of Australia to the island of New Guinea. Human groups took advantage of those bridges by migrating to new lands.

When the earth's temperature rose and the glaciers melted, beginning about eighteen thousand years ago, the waters returned and flooded low-lying lands around the world. Eventually, the seas once again divided Asia from America by the body of water known as the Bering Strait, and they also separated Australia and New Guinea. By that time, however, human communities had become well established in each of those areas.

The return of high waters did not put an end to human migrations. Human groups fanned out from Alaska and ventured to all corners of North, Central, and South America. Beginning about 3000 B.C.E. coastal peoples of southeast Asia built large sailing canoes and established human settlements in the previously uninhabited islands of the Pacific Ocean. By about 700 C.E. human beings had established communities in almost every habitable part of the world.

Although they were separated by large bodies of water, by no means did human migrants to the Americas and Oceania lead completely isolated lives. On the contrary, there were frequent and sometimes regular interactions between peoples of different societies within the Americas and within Oceania. It is likely that at least fleeting encounters took place as well between peoples of the eastern and western hemispheres, although very little evidence survives to throw light on the nature of those encounters in early times. Yet even as they dealt with peoples of other societies, the first inhabitants of the Americas and Oceania also established distinctive societies of their own.

Despite their different origins and their distinctive political, social, and cultural traditions, peoples of the Americas and Oceania built societies that in some ways resembled those of the eastern hemisphere. Human communities independently discovered agriculture in several regions of North America and South America, and migrants introduced cultivation to the inhabited Pacific islands as well. With agriculture came increasing populations, settlement in towns, specialized labor, formal political authorities, hierarchical social orders, long-distance trade, and organized religious traditions. The Americas also generated large, densely populated societies featuring cities, monumental public works, imperial states, and sometimes traditions of writing as well. Thus, like their counterparts in the eastern hemisphere, the earliest societies of the Americas and Oceania reflected a common human tendency toward the development of increasingly complex social forms.

EARLY SOCIETIES OF MESOAMERICA

Much is unclear about the early population of the Americas by human communities. Several archaeological excavations suggest that at least a few human groups had made their way to the Americas by 15,000 B.C.E. or earlier, although it is not clear whether they arrived by land or by water. However, it is clear that large-scale migration to the Americas began after 13,000 B.C.E., as humans made their way in large numbers across the Bering land bridge. Once in the Americas, humans quickly populated all habitable regions of the western hemisphere. By 9500 B.C.E. they had reached the southernmost part of South America, more than 17,000 kilometers (10,566 miles) from the Bering land bridge.

The earliest human inhabitants of the Americas lived exclusively by hunting and gathering. Beginning about 8000 B.C.E., however, large game animals became scarce, partly because they did not adapt well to the rapidly warming climate and partly because of overhunting by expanding human communities. By 7500 B.C.E. many species of large animals in the Americas were well on the road to extinction. To survive, some human communities supplemented the foods they gathered with fish and small game. Others turned to agriculture, and they gave rise to the first complex societies in the Americas.

The Olmecs

By 8000 to 7000 B.C.E. the peoples of Mesoamerica—the region from the central portion of modern Mexico to Honduras and El Salvador—had begun to experi-

Early Agriculture in Mesoamerica

ment with the cultivation of beans, chili peppers, avocados, squashes, and gourds. By 4000 B.C.E. they had discovered the agricultural potential of maize, which soon became the staple food of the region. Later they added tomatoes to the crops they cultivated. Agricultural villages appeared soon after 3000 B.C.E., and by 2000 B.C.E. agriculture had spread throughout Mesoamerica.

Early Mesoamerican peoples had a diet rich in cultivated foods, but most large animals of the western hemisphere were not susceptible to domestication. For that reason, Mesoamericans were unable to harness animal energy as did the peoples of the eastern hemisphere. As a result, human laborers prepared fields for cultivation, and human porters carried trade goods on their backs. Mesoamericans had no need for wheeled vehicles, which would have been useful only if draft animals had been available to pull them.

Toward the end of the second millennium B.C.E., the tempo of Mesoamerican life quickened as elaborate ceremonial centers with monumental pyramids, temples, and palaces arose alongside the agricultural villages. These were not cities like those that existed in the eastern hemisphere, because only members of the ruling elite, priests, and those who tended to their needs were permanent residents. Instead, most people lived in surrounding villages and gathered in the ceremonial centers only on special occasions or on market days.

Ceremonial Centers

The earliest known ceremonial centers of the ancient Americas appeared on the coast of the Gulf of Mexico, near the modern Mexican city of Veracruz, and they served as the nerve center of the Olmecs, the

Olmecs: The "Rubber People"

first complex society of the Americas. Historians and archaeologists have systematically studied Olmec society only since the 1940s, and many questions about them remain unanswered. Even their proper name is unknown: the term *Olmec* (meaning "rubber people") did not come from the ancient people themselves but derives instead from the rubber trees that flourish in the region they inhabited. Nevertheless, some of the basic features of Olmec society have become reasonably clear, and it is certain that Olmec cultural traditions influenced all complex societies of Mesoamerica until the arrival of European peoples in the sixteenth century C.E.

The first Olmec ceremonial center arose about 1200 B.C.E. on the site of the modern town of San Lorenzo, and it served as their capital for some four hundred years. When the influence of San Lorenzo waned, leadership passed to new ceremonial centers at

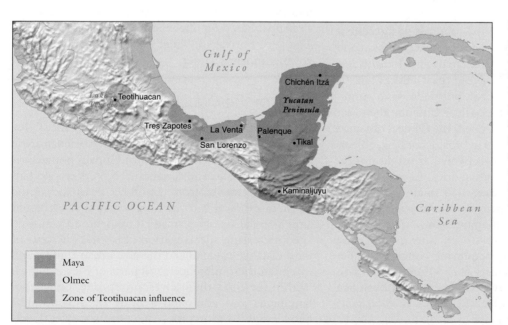

Map 4.1 Boundaries and major cities of the early Mesoamerican societies from 1200 B.C.E. to 1100 C.E. Observe the position of these early societies on the narrow isthmus connecting North and South America. What advantages would such a location have afforded Mesoamericans?

La Venta (800–400 B.C.E.) and Tres Zapotes (400–100 B.C.E.). These sites defined the heartland of Olmec society, where agriculture produced rich harvests. The entire region receives abundant rainfall, so, like the Harappans, the Olmecs constructed elaborate drainage systems to divert waters that otherwise might have flooded their fields or destroyed their settlements.

Olmec society was probably authoritarian in nature. Common subjects delivered a portion of their harvests for the maintenance of the elite classes living in the ceremonial centers and provided labor for large-scale construction projects. Indeed, untold thousands of laborers were required to build the temples, pyramids, altars, sculptures, and tombs that characterized each Olmec ceremonial center.

Olmec Society

Common subjects also provided appropriate artistic adornment for the elites in Olmec capitals. The most distinctive artistic creations of the Olmecs were colossal human heads—possibly likenesses of rulers—sculpted from basalt rock. The largest of these sculptures stands 3 meters (almost 10 feet) tall and weighs some twenty tons. In the absence of draft animals and wheels, human laborers had to move rocks to the ceremonial centers. The largest sculptures required the services of about one thousand laborers. Apart from the colossal heads, the Olmec capitals featured many other large stone sculptures and monumental buildings that required the services of laborers by the hundreds and thousands.

Image
Olmec altar from La Venta

Olmec influence extended to much of the central and southern regions of modern Mexico and beyond to modern Guatemala and El Salvador. The Olmecs spread their influence partly by military force, but trade was a prominent link between the Olmec heartland and the other regions of Mesoamerica. Indeed, the Olmecs obtained both jade and obsidian—used for decorative objects and for cutting tools, respectively—from distant regions in the interior of Mesoamerica. In exchange for such imports, the Olmecs traded small works of art fashioned from jade, basalt, or ceramics and perhaps also local products such as animal skins.

Trade in Jade and Obsidian

Among the many mysteries surrounding the Olmecs, one of the most perplexing concerns the decline and fall of their society. The Olmecs systematically destroyed their ceremonial centers at both San

La Venta (lah BEHN-tah)

Colossal Olmec head carved from basalt rock between 1000 and 600 B.C.E. and discovered at La Venta. Olmecs carved similar heads for their ceremonial centers at San Lorenzo and Tres Zapotes.

Lorenzo and La Venta and then deserted the sites. Archaeologists studying those sites found statues broken and buried, monuments defaced, and the capitals themselves burned. Although intruders may have ravaged the ceremonial centers, many scholars believe that the Olmecs deliberately destroyed their capitals, perhaps because of civil conflicts or doubts about the effectiveness and legitimacy of the ruling classes. In any case, Olmec society collapsed soon after 400 B.C.E.

Yet later Mesoamerican societies adopted several Olmec traditions. They cultivated maize, built ceremonial centers with temple pyramids, and maintained a calendar based on one inherited from Olmec priests. They also borrowed Olmec ball games and rituals involving human sacrifice.

Heirs of the Olmecs: The Maya

During the thousand years following the Olmecs' disappearance about 400 B.C.E., complex societies arose in several Mesoamerican regions. Human population grew dramatically, and ceremonial centers cropped up at sites far removed from the Olmec heartland. Some of them evolved into genuine cities that attracted large populations of permanent residents and encouraged increasing specialization of labor. Networks of long-distance trade linked the new urban centers and extended their influence to all parts of Mesoamerica. Within the cities themselves, priests devised written languages and compiled a body of astronomical knowledge. In short, Mesoamerican societies developed in a manner roughly parallel to that of their counterparts in the eastern hemisphere.

The Maya   The earliest heirs of the Olmecs were the Maya, who created a remarkable society in the region now occupied by southern Mexico, Guatemala, Belize, Honduras, and El Salvador. Although Maya society originally appeared in the fertile Guatemalan highlands beginning in the third century B.C.E., after the fourth century it flourished mostly in the poorly drained Mesoamerican lowlands, where thin, tropical soils quickly lost their fertility. To enhance the agricultural potential of their region, the Maya built terraces designed to trap silt carried by the numerous rivers passing through the lowlands. By artificially retaining rich earth, they dramatically increased the agricultural productivity of their lands. They harvested maize in abundance, and they also cultivated cotton, from which they wove fine textiles highly prized both in their own society and by trading partners in other parts of Mesoamerica. Maya cultivators also raised cacao, the large bean that is the source of chocolate. Cacao was a precious commodity consumed mostly by nobles in Maya society. They whisked powdered cacao into water to create a stimulating beverage, and they sometimes even ate the bitter cacao beans as snacks. The product was so valuable that Maya used cacao beans as money.

Tikal   The Maya organized themselves politically into scores of small city-kingdoms. From about 300 to 900 C.E., the Maya built more than eighty large ceremonial centers in the lowlands—all with pyramids, palaces, and temples—as well as numerous smaller settlements. Some of the larger centers attracted dense populations and evolved into genuine cities. Foremost among them was

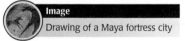
Drawing of a Maya fortress city

Tikal, the most important Maya political center between the fourth and ninth centuries C.E. At its height, roughly 600 to 800 C.E., Tikal was a wealthy and bustling city with a population approaching forty thousand. It boasted enormous paved plazas and scores of temples, pyramids, palaces, and public buildings. The Temple of the Giant Jaguar, a stepped pyramid rising sharply to a height of 47 meters (154 feet), dominated the skyline and represented Tikal's control over the surrounding region, which had a population of about five hundred thousand.

Tikal (tee-KAHL)

Maya Warfare   The Maya kingdoms fought constantly with one another. Victors generally destroyed the peoples they defeated and took over their ceremonial centers, but the purpose of Maya warfare was not so much to kill enemies as to capture them in hand-to-hand combat on the battlefield. Warriors won enormous prestige when they brought back important captives from neighboring kingdoms. Ultimately, most captives ended their lives either as slaves or as sacrificial victims to Maya gods. High-ranking captives in particular often underwent ritual torture and sacrifice in public ceremonies on important occasions.

Chichén Itzá   Bitter conflicts between small kingdoms were a source of constant tension in Maya society. Only about the ninth century C.E. did the state of Chichén Itzá in the northern Yucatan peninsula seek to construct a larger society by integrating captives into their own society instead of killing

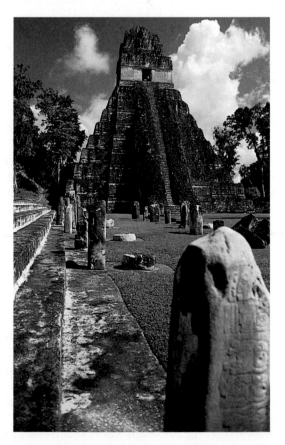

Temple of the Giant Jaguar at Tikal, which served as the funerary pyramid for Lord Cacao, a prominent Maya ruler of the late sixth and early seventh centuries C.E.

them. Some captives refused the opportunity and went to their deaths as proud warriors, but many agreed to recognize the authority of Chichén Itzá. Between the ninth and eleventh centuries C.E., Chichén Itzá organized a loose empire that brought a measure of political stability to the northern Yucatan.

Maya Decline   By about 800 B.C.E., however, most Maya populations had begun to desert their cities. Within a century Maya society was in full decline everywhere except the northern Yucatan, where Chichén Itzá continued to flourish. Historians have suggested many possible causes of the decline, including invasion, internal dissension and civil war, failure of the system of water control, ecological problems caused by destruction of the forests, the spread of epidemic diseases, and natural catastrophes such as earthquakes. Possibly several problems combined to destroy Maya society. It is likely that debilitating civil conflict and excessive siltation of agricultural terraces caused particularly difficult problems for the Maya. In any case, the population declined, the people abandoned their cities, and long-distance trade came to a halt. Meanwhile, the tropical jungles of the lowlands encroached on human settlements and gradually smothered the cities, temples, pyramids, and monuments of a once-vibrant society.

Maya Society and Religion

In addition to kings and ruling families, Maya society included a large class of priests who maintained an elaborate calendar and transmitted knowledge of writing, astronomy, and mathematics. A hereditary nobility owned most land and cooperated with the kings and the priests by organizing military forces and participating in religious rituals. Maya merchants also came from the ruling and noble classes, because they served not only as traders but also as ambassadors to neighboring lands and allied peoples. Apart from the ruling and priestly elites, Maya society generated several other distinct social classes. Professional architects and sculptors oversaw construction of large monuments and public buildings. Artisans specialized in the production of pottery, tools, and cotton textiles. Finally, large classes of peasants and slaves fed the entire society and provided physical labor for the construction of cities and monuments.

Building on the achievements of their Olmec predecessors, Maya priests studied astronomy and mathematics, and they devised both a sophisticated calendar and an elaborate system of writing. They understood the movements of heavenly bodies well enough to plot planetary cycles and to predict eclipses of the sun and the moon. They invented the concept of zero and used a symbol to represent zero mathematically, which facilitated their manipulation of large numbers. By combining their astronomical and mathematical observations, Maya priests calculated the length of the solar year at 365.242 days—about seventeen seconds shorter than the figure reached by modern astronomers.

The Maya Calendar   Maya priests constructed the most elaborate calendar of the ancient Americas, which reflected a powerful urge to identify meaningful cycles of time. The Maya calendar interwove two kinds of year: a solar year of 365 days governed the agricultural cycle, and a ritual year of 260 days governed daily affairs by organizing time into twenty "months" of thirteen days apiece. The Maya believed that each day derived certain specific characteristics from its position in both the solar and the ritual calendar and that the combined attributes of each day would determine the fortune of activities undertaken on that day. It took fifty-two years for the two calendars to work through all possible combinations of days and return simultaneously to their respective starting points. Maya priests carefully studied the various opportunities and dangers that would come together on a given day in hopes that they could determine which activities were safe to initiate. The Maya attributed especially great significance to the fifty-two-year periods in which the two calendars ran. They believed that the end of a cycle would bring monumental changes and that ultimately the world would end after one such cycle.

Maya Writing   The Maya also expanded on the Olmec tradition of written inscriptions. In doing so they created the most flexible and sophisticated of all the early American systems of writing. The Maya script contained both ideographic elements (like Chinese characters) and symbols for syllables. Scholars have begun to decipher this script only since the 1960s, and it has become clear that writing was just as important to the Maya as it was to early complex societies in the eastern hemisphere. Most Maya writing survives today in the form of inscriptions on temples and monuments, because sixteenth-century Spanish conquerors and missionaries destroyed untold numbers of books in hopes of undermining native religious beliefs. Today only four books of the ancient Maya survive, all dealing with astronomical and calendrical matters.

Surviving inscriptions and other writings shed considerable light on Maya religious and cultural traditions.

Maya Religious Thought The *Popol Vuh*, a Maya creation myth, taught that the gods had created human beings out of maize and water, the ingredients that became human flesh and blood. Thus Maya religious thought reflected the fundamental role of agriculture in their society, much like religious thought in early complex societies of the eastern hemisphere. Maya priests also taught that the gods kept the world going and maintained the agricultural cycle in exchange for honors and sacrifices performed for them by human beings.

The most important of those sacrifices involved the shedding of human blood, which the Maya be-

---

Popol Vuh (paw-pawl vuh)

In this stone relief sculpture, a Maya king from Yaxchilán (between Tikal and Palenque in the southern Yucatan peninsula) holds a torch over a woman from the royal family as she draws a thorn-studded rope through a hole in her tongue, so as to shed her blood in honor of the Maya gods.

lieved would prompt the gods to send rain to water their crops of maize. Some bloodletting rituals centered on war captives. Before sacrificing the victims by decapitation, their captors cut off the ends of their fingers or lacerated their bodies so as to cause a copious flow of blood in honor of the gods. Yet the Maya did not look on these rituals simply as opportunities to torture their enemies. Indeed, the ruling classes also frequently and voluntarily shed their own blood as a means of displaying reverence to their gods.

Bloodletting Rituals

Apart from the calendar and sacrificial rituals, the Maya also inherited a distinctive ball game from the Olmecs. The game sometimes pitted two men against each other, but it often involved teams of two to four members apiece. The object of the game was for players to score points by propelling a rubber ball through a ring or onto a marker without using their hands. The Maya used a solid rubber ball about 20 centimeters (8 inches) in diameter, which was

The Maya Ball Game

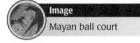
Mayan ball court

both heavy and hard. Players needed great dexterity and skill to maneuver it accurately using only their feet, legs, hips, torso, shoulders, or elbows. The game was extremely popular: almost all Maya ceremonial centers, towns, and cities had stone-paved courts on which players performed publicly.

The Maya played the ball game for several reasons. Sometimes individuals competed for sporting purposes, and sometimes the game was used as a ritual that honored the conclusion of treaties. High-ranking captives often engaged in forced public competition in which the stakes were their very lives: losers became sacrificial victims and faced torture and execution immediately following the match. Alongside some ball courts were skull racks that bore the decapitated heads of losing players. Thus Maya concerns to please the gods by shedding human blood extended even to the realm of sport.

Heirs of the Olmecs: Teotihuacan

While the Maya flourished in the Mesoamerican lowlands, a different society arose to the north in the highlands of Mexico. For most of human history, the valley of central Mexico, situated some two kilometers (more than a mile) above sea level, was the site of several large lakes fed by the waters coming off the surrounding mountains. Although environmental changes have caused most of the lakes to disappear, in earlier times their abundant supplies of freshwater, fish, and waterfowl attracted human settlers.

The earliest settlers in the valley of Mexico channeled some of the waters from the mountain streams into their fields and established a productive agricultural society. Soon the resulting expanding human population led to the emergence of a complex society. The earliest center of this society was the large and bustling city of Teotihuacan, located about 50 kilometers (31 miles) northeast of modern Mexico City.

The City of Teotihuacan

Teotihuacan was probably a large agricultural village by 500 B.C.E., but by the end of the millennium its population approached fifty thousand. By the year 100 C.E., the city's two most prominent monuments, the colossal pyramids of the sun and the moon, dominated the skyline. The Pyramid of the Sun is the largest single structure in Mesoamerica. It occupies nearly as much space as the pyramid of Khufu in Egypt, though it stands only half as tall. At its high point, about 400 to 600 C.E., Teotihuacan was home to almost

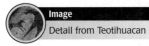

two hundred thousand inhabitants, a thriving metropolis with scores of temples, several palatial residences, neighborhoods with small apartments for the masses, busy markets, and hundreds of workshops for artisans and craftsmen.

Teotihuacan (tay-oh-tee-wa-KAHN)

The organization of a large urban population, along with the hinterland that supported it, required a recognized source of authority. Unfortunately, scholars have little information about the character of that authority, since books and written records from the city did not survive. Yet paintings and murals suggest that Teotihuacan was a theocracy of sorts. Priests figure prominently in the works of art, and scholars interpret many figures as representations of deities.

Apart from rulers and priests, Teotihuacan's population included cultivators, artisans, and merchants. Perhaps as many as two-thirds of the city's inhabitants worked during the day in fields surrounding Teotihuacan and returned to their small apartments in the city at night. Artisans of Teotihuacan were especially famous for their obsidian tools and fine orange pottery. Professional merchants traded the products of Teotihuacan throughout Mesoamerica, from the region of modern Guatemala City in the south to Durango and beyond in the north.

The Society of Teotihuacan

Until about 500 C.E. there was little sign of military organization in Teotihuacan. The city did not have defensive walls, and works of art rarely depicted warriors. Yet the influence of Teotihuacan extended to much of modern Mexico and beyond. Apparently, the city's influence derived less from military might than from its ability to produce fine manufactured goods that appealed to consumers in distant markets.

Like the Maya, the residents of Teotihuacan built on cultural foundations established by the Olmecs. They played the ball game, adapted the Olmec calendar

Aerial view of Teotihuacan, looking toward the Pyramid of the Moon (top center) from the Pyramid of the Sun (bottom left). Shops and residences occupied the spaces surrounding the main street and the pyramids.

The Popol Vuh *on the Creation of Human Beings*

The Popol Vuh *outlines traditional Maya views on the creation of the world and human beings. The version of the work that survives today dates from the mid–sixteenth century, but it reflects beliefs of a much earlier era. According to the* Popol Vuh, *the gods wanted to create intelligent beings that would recognize and praise them. Three times they tried to fashion such beings out of animals, mud, and wood, but without success. Then they decided to use maize and water as their ingredients.*

■   ■   ■

And here is the beginning of the conception of humans, and of the search for the ingredients of the human body. So they spoke, the [gods] Bearer, Begetter, the Makers, Modelers named Sovereign Plumed Serpent:

"The dawn has approached, preparations have been made, and morning has come for the provider, nurturer, born in the light, begotten in the light. Morning has come for humankind, for the people of the face of the earth," they said. It all came together as they went on thinking in the darkness, in the night, as they searched and they sifted, they thought and they wondered.

And here their thoughts came out in clear light. They sought and discovered what was needed for human flesh. . . . Broken Place, Bitter Water Place is the name: the yellow corn, white corn came from there. . . .

And these were the ingredients for the flesh of the human work, the human design, and the water was for the blood. It became human blood, and corn was also used by the Bearer, Begetter. . . .

And then the yellow corn and white corn were ground, and Xmucane did the grinding nine times. Corn was used, along with the water she rinsed her hands with, for the creation of grease; it became human fat when it was worked by the Bearer, Begetter, Sovereign Plumed Serpent, as they are called. . . .

It was staples alone that made up their flesh.

These are the names of the first people who were made and modeled.

This is the first person: Jaguar Quitze.

And now the second: Jaguar Night.

And now the third: Mahucutah.

And the fourth: True Jaguar.

And these are the names of our first mother-fathers. They were simply made and modeled, it is said; they had no mother and no father. We have named the men by themselves. No woman gave birth to them, nor were they begotten by the builder, sculptor, Bearer, Begetter. By sacrifice alone, by genius alone they were made, they were modeled by the Maker, Modeler, Bearer, Begetter, Sovereign Plumed Serpent. And when they came to fruition, they came out human:

They talked and they made words.

They looked and they listened.

They walked, they worked. . . .

And then their wives and women came into being. Again, the same gods thought of it. It was as if they were asleep when they received them, truly beautiful women were there with Jaguar Quitze, Jaguar Night, Mahucutah, and True Jaguar. With their women there they became wider awake. Right away they were happy at heart again, because of their wives.

Celebrated Seahouse is the name of the wife of Jaguar Quitze.

Prawn House is the name of the wife of Jaguar Night.

Hummingbird House is the name of the wife of Mahucutah.

Macaw House is the name of the wife of True Jaguar.

So these are the names of their wives, who became ladies of rank, giving birth to the people of the tribes, small and great.

• *Discuss the extent to which this account of human creation reflects the influences on Maya society of both agriculture and the untamed natural world.*

SOURCE: Dennis Tedlock, trans. *Popol Vuh: The Definitive Edition of the Mayan Book of the Dawn of Life and the Glories of Gods and Kings.* New York: Simon and Schuster, 1985, pp. 163–65, 167.

to their own uses, and expanded the Olmecs' graphic symbols into a complete system of writing. Unfortu-

Cultural Traditions

nately, because their books have all perished, it is impossible to know exactly how they viewed the world and their place in it. Works of art suggest that they recognized an earth god and a rain god, and it is certain that they carried out human sacrifices during their religious rituals.

Teotihuacan began to experience increasing military pressure from other peoples about 500 C.E. After about

Decline of Teotihuacan

650 C.E. Teotihuacan entered a period of decline. About the middle of the eighth century, invaders sacked and burned the city, destroying its books and monuments. After that catastrophe most residents deserted Teotihuacan, and the city slowly fell into ruin.

EARLY SOCIETIES OF SOUTH AMERICA

By about 12,000 B.C.E. hunting and gathering peoples had made their way across the narrow isthmus of Central America and into South America. Those who migrated into the region of the northern and central Andes mountains hunted deer, llama, alpaca, and other large animals. Both the mountainous highlands and the coastal regions below benefited from a cool and moist climate that provided natural harvests of squashes, gourds, and wild potatoes. Beginning about 8000 B.C.E., however, the climate of this whole region became increasingly warm and dry, and the changes placed pressure on natural food supplies. To maintain their numbers, the human communities of the region began to experiment with agriculture. Here, as elsewhere, agriculture encouraged population growth, the establishment of villages and cities, the building of states, and the elaboration of organized cultural traditions. During the centuries after 1000 B.C.E., the central Andean region generated complex societies parallel to those of Mesoamerica.

Early Andean Society and the Chavín Cult

Although they were exact contemporaries, early Mesoamerican and Andean societies developed largely independently. Geography discouraged the establishment of communications between the Andean region and Mesoamerica because neither society possessed abundant pack animals or a technology to facilitate long-

distance transportation. Although some agricultural products and technologies diffused slowly from one area to the other, neither the Andes mountains nor the lowlands of modern Panama and Nicaragua offered an attractive highway linking the two regions.

Geography even made communications within the central Andean region difficult. Deep valleys crease the western flank of the Andes mountains as rivers drain waters from the highlands to the Pacific Ocean, so transportation and communication between the valleys have always been very difficult. Nevertheless, powerful Andean states sometimes overcame the difficulties and influenced human affairs over a broad geographical range.

Most of the early Andean heartland came under cultivation between 2500 and 2000 B.C.E. The coastal regions probably developed complex societies first, since cultivators there experienced abundant harvests as a result of crops such as beans, peanuts, and sweet potatoes, and supplemented them with the rich marine life of the Pacific Ocean. Settle-

Image
A ceramic effigy of a shaman

ments likely appeared somewhat later in the Andean highlands, but it is clear that potatoes were being cultivated in the region after about 2000 B.C.E. By 1800 B.C.E. peoples in all the Andean regions had begun to fashion distinctive styles of pottery and to build temples and pyramids in large ceremonial centers.

Shortly after the year 1000 B.C.E., a new religion appeared suddenly in the central Andes. The Chavín cult, which enjoyed enormous popularity during the period 900 to 800

The Chavín Cult

B.C.E., spread through most of the territory occupied by modern Peru and then vanished about 300 B.C.E. Although scholars do not understand the precise significance of the cult, it is clear that Andean society became increasingly complex during this period. Weavers devised techniques of producing elaborate, intricately patterned cotton textiles. Artisans manufactured large, light, and strong fishnets from cotton string. Craftsmen experimented with minerals and discovered techniques of gold, silver, and copper metallurgy and used them to make jewelry as well as small tools.

There is no evidence to suggest that Chavín cultural and religious beliefs led to the establishment of a state or any organized political order. Indeed,

Early Cities

they probably inspired the building of ceremonial centers rather than the making of true cities. As the population increased and society became more

Map 4.2 Early societies of Andean South America from 1000 B.C.E. to 700 C.E. Note the long, narrow outline of early Andean settlement boundaries. Why didn't early Andean societies expand further to the east in this period?

highlands, the central valleys, and the coastal regions together. Each region contributed its own products to the larger economy of the valley: from the highlands came potatoes, llama meat, and alpaca wool; the central valleys supplied maize, beans, and squashes; and the coasts provided sweet potatoes, fish, and cotton.

Because early Andean societies did not make use of writing, their beliefs, values, and ways of life remain largely hidden. Surviving fortifications as well as art suggest that early Andean states relied heavily on arms to introduce order and maintain stability within their realms. In addition, art from the early Andean state of Mochica—which dominated the coasts and valleys of northern Peru from about 300 to 700 C.E.—offers a detailed

The Mochica State

Mochica (moh-CHEE-kah)

Many Mochica pots portray human figures and often depict distinctive characteristics of individuals or typical scenes from daily life. This pot represents two women helping a man who consumed a little too much maize beer.

complex, however, cities began to appear shortly after the disappearance of the Chavín cult. Beginning about 200 B.C.E. large cities emerged at the modern-day sites of Huari, Pucara, and Tiahuanaco. Each of these early Andean cities had a population exceeding ten thousand, and each also featured large public buildings, ceremonial plazas, and extensive residential districts.

Early Andean States: Mochica

Along with cities there appeared regional states. The earliest Andean states arose in the many valleys on the western side of the mountains. These states emerged when conquerors unified the valleys and organized them into integrated societies. They coordinated the building of irrigation systems so that the lower valleys could support intensive agriculture, and they established trade and exchange networks that tied the and expressive depiction of early Andean society in all its variety. Most Mochica art survives in the form of pottery vessels, many of which depict individuals' heads or represent the major gods and various subordinate deities and demons. Most interesting, perhaps, are those that illustrate scenes in the everyday life of the Mochica people: aristocrats embarking on a hunting party, warriors leading captives bound by ropes, women working in a textile factory under the careful eye of a supervisor, rulers receiving messengers or ambassadors from neighboring states, and beggars looking for handouts on a busy street. Even in the absence of writing, Mochica artists left abundant evidence of a complex society with considerable specialization of labor.

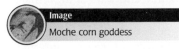

Image
Moche corn goddess

Mochica was only one of several large states that dominated the central Andean region during the first millennium C.E. Although they integrated the regional economies of the various Andean valleys, none of these early states was able to impose order on the entire region or even to dominate a portion of it for very long. The exceedingly difficult geographical barriers posed by the Andes mountains presented challenges that ancient technology and social organization simply could not meet. As a result, at the end of the first millennium C.E., Andean society exhibited regional differences much sharper than those of Mesoamerica and early complex societies in the eastern hemisphere.

EARLY SOCIETIES OF OCEANIA

Human migrants entered Australia and New Guinea at least 60,000 years ago, and possibly earlier than that. They arrived in watercraft—probably canoes fitted with sails—but because of the low sea levels of that era, the migrants did not have to cross large stretches of open ocean. These earliest inhabitants of Oceania also migrated—perhaps over land when sea levels were still low—to the Bismarcks, the Solomons, and other small island groups near New Guinea. Beginning about 5,000 years ago, seafaring peoples from southeast Asia settled the northern coast of New Guinea and then ventured farther and established communities in the island groups of the western Pacific Ocean. By the middle centuries of the first millennium C.E., their descendants had established human communities in all the habitable islands of the Pacific Ocean.

Early Societies in Australia and New Guinea

Human migrants reached Australia and New Guinea long before any people had begun to cultivate crops or keep herds of domesticated animals. As a result, the earliest inhabitants of Australia and New Guinea lived by hunting and gathering. Once rising seas covered the land bridge connecting Australia and New Guinea about ten thousand years ago, however, human societies in each area followed radically different paths. While the aboriginal peoples of Australia continued as hunting and gathering societies, in New Guinea human communities turned to agriculture: beginning about 3000 B.C.E. the cultivation of root crops such as yams and taro and the keeping of pigs and chickens spread rapidly throughout the island.

Like hunting and gathering peoples elsewhere, the aboriginal Australians lived in small, mobile communities that undertook seasonal migrations in search of food. Over the centuries, they learned to exploit the resources of the various ecological regions of Australia. Plant foods, including fruits, berries, roots, nuts, seeds, shoots, and green leaves, constituted the bulk of their diet. To supplement their plant-based diet, they used axes, spears, clubs, nets, lassos, snares, and boomerangs to bring down animals ranging in size from rats to giant kangaroos, which grew to a height of 3 meters (almost 10 feet), and to catch fish, waterfowl, and small birds.

Early Hunting and Gathering Societies in Australia

In New Guinea, seafaring peoples from southeast Asia introduced agriculture to the island about five thousand years ago when they began to establish trading and settlement communities on the northern coast. These sailors spoke Austronesian languages (whose modern relatives include Malayan, Indonesian, and Polynesian) and were highly skilled in seafaring technologies. They sailed the open ocean in large canoes equipped with outriggers, which stabilized their craft and reduced the risks of long voyages. By paying close attention to winds, currents, stars, cloud formations, and other natural indicators, they learned how to find distant lands reliably and return home safely.

Austronesian Peoples

Austronesian seafarers came from societies that depended on the cultivation of root crops and the herding of animals. When they settled in New Guinea, they introduced yams, taro, pigs, and chickens to the island, and the indigenous peoples themselves soon followed

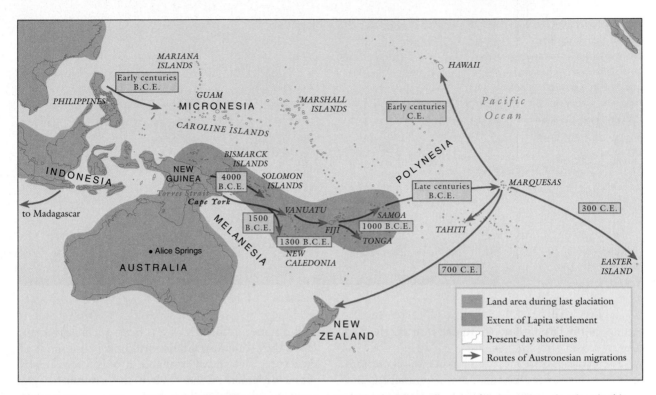

Map 4.3 **Early societies of Oceania from 1500 B.C.E. to 700 C.E.** Note the direction and extent of Austronesian migrations in this period. How was it possible for migrants to travel such long distances over water without the aid of modern technology?

suit. Within a few centuries agriculture and herding had spread to all parts of New Guinea. There, as in other lands, agriculture brought population growth and specialization of labor: after the change to agriculture, permanent settlements, pottery, and carefully crafted tools appeared throughout the island.

Early Agriculture in New Guinea

The Peopling of the Pacific Islands

Austronesian-speaking peoples possessed a sophisticated maritime technology as well as agricultural expertise, and they established human settlements in the islands of the Pacific Ocean. Their outrigger canoes enabled them to sail safely over long distances of open ocean, and their food crops and domesticated animals enabled them to establish agricultural societies in the islands. Once they had established coastal settlements in New Guinea, Austronesian seafarers sailed easily to the Bismarck and Solomon islands east of New Guinea. From there they undertook exploratory voyages that led them to previously unpopulated islands.

Austronesian Migrations to Polynesia

By about 1500 B.C.E. Austronesian mariners had arrived at Vanuatu (formerly called New Hebrides) and New Caledonia, by 1300 B.C.E. at Fiji, and by 1000 B.C.E. at Tonga and Samoa. During the late centuries of the first millennium B.C.E., they established settlements in Tahiti and the Marquesas. From there they launched ventures that took them to the most remote outposts of Polynesia, which required them to sail over thousands of nautical miles of blue water. They reached the islands of Hawai`i in the early centuries C.E., Easter Island by 300 C.E., and the large islands of New Zealand by 700 C.E.

While one branch of the Austronesian-speaking peoples populated the islands of Polynesia, other branches sailed in different directions. From the Philippines some ventured to the region of Micronesia, which includes small islands and atolls such as the Mariana, Caroline, and Marshall islands of the western Pacific. Others looked west from their homelands in Indonesia, sailed throughout the Indian Ocean, and became the first human

Austronesian Migrations to Micronesia and Madagascar

Austronesian mariners sailed double-hulled voyaging canoes much like this one from Ra'iatea in the Society Islands drawn in 1769 by an artist who accompanied Captain James Cook on his first voyage in the Pacific Ocean.

settlers of the large island of Madagascar off the east African coast.

The Lapita Peoples

The earliest Austronesian migrants to sail out into the blue water of the Pacific Ocean and establish human settlements in Pacific islands are known as the Lapita peoples. No one knows what they called themselves: the name *Lapita* comes from a beach in New Caledonia where some of the earliest recognizable Lapita artifacts came to the attention of archaeologists. It is clear, however, that between about 1500 and 500 B.C.E., Lapita peoples maintained communication and exchange networks throughout a large region extending about 4,500 kilometers (2,800 miles) from New Guinea and the Bismarck Archipelago to Samoa and Tonga.

Wherever they settled, Lapita peoples established agricultural villages where they raised pigs and chickens and introduced the suite of crops they inherited from their Austronesian ancestors. They supplemented their crops and domesticated animals with fish and seaweed from nearby waters, and they soon killed off most of the large land animals and birds that were suitable for human consumption. They left abundant evidence of their presence in the form of their distinctive pottery decorated with stamped geometric designs.

For about one thousand years, Lapita peoples maintained extensive networks of trade and communication across vast stretches of open ocean. Their agricultural settlements were largely self-sufficient, but they placed high value on some objects from distant islands. Their pottery was a principal item of

long-distance exchange, as was high-quality obsidian, which they sometimes transported over thousands of kilometers, since it was available at only a few sites of Lapita settlement. Other trade items brought to light by archaeologists include shell jewelry and stone tools. Indeed, it is clear that, like their counterparts in other regions of the world, the earliest inhabitants of the Pacific islands maintained regular contacts with peoples well beyond their own societies.

After about 500 B.C.E. Lapita trade networks fell into disuse, probably because the various Lapita settlements had grown large enough that they could supply their own needs. By the middle part of the first

Chiefly Political Organization

millennium B.C.E., Lapita and other Austronesian peoples had established hierarchical chiefdoms in the Pacific islands. Contests for power and influence between ambitious subordinates frequently caused tension and turmoil, but the possibility of migration offered an alternative to conflict. Indeed, the spread of Austronesian peoples throughout the Pacific islands came about partly because of population pressures and conflicts that encouraged small parties to seek fresh opportunities in more hospitable lands.

Over the longer term, descendants of Lapita peoples built strong, chiefly societies, particularly on large islands with relatively dense populations, such as those of the Tongan, Samoan, and Hawaiian groups. In Hawai`i, for example, militarily skilled chiefs cooperated closely with priests, administrators, soldiers, and servants in ruling their districts. Chiefs and their retinues claimed a portion of the agricultural surplus produced by their subjects, and they sometimes required subjects to deliver additional products, such as fish, birds, or timber. Chiefs and their administrators also vied with the ruling classes of neighboring districts, led public ritual observances, and oversaw irrigation systems that watered the taro plants that were crucial to the survival of Hawaiian society. Eventually, the chiefly and aristocratic classes became so entrenched and powerful that they regarded themselves as divine or semidivine, and the law of the land prohibited common subjects from even gazing directly at them.

Summary

Very little writing survives to illuminate the historical development of early societies in the Americas and Oceania. Thus it is impossible to offer the sort of richly detailed account of their political organization, social structures, and cultural traditions that historians commonly provide for societies of the eastern hemisphere. Nevertheless, it is clear that migrations to the Americas and Oceania represented continuations of population movements that began with *Homo erectus* and early *Homo sapiens,* resulting eventually in the establishment of human communities in almost all habitable parts of the earth. Moreover, it is also clear that the earliest inhabitants of the Americas and Oceania built productive and vibrant societies whose development roughly paralleled that of their counterparts in the eastern hemisphere. Many communities depended on an agricultural economy, and with their surplus production they supported dense populations, engaged in specialized labor, established formal political authorities, constructed hierarchical social orders, carried on long-distance trade, and formed distinctive cultural traditions. The early historical development of the Americas and Oceania demonstrates once again the tendency of agriculture to encourage human communities to construct ever more elaborate and complex forms of social organization.

CHRONOLOGY

AMERICAS	
13,000 B.C.E.	Human migration to North America from Siberia
8000–7000 B.C.E.	Origins of agriculture in Mesoamerica
4000 B.C.E.	Origins of maize cultivation in Mesoamerica
3000 B.C.E.	Origins of agriculture in South America
1200–100 B.C.E.	Olmec society
1000–300 B.C.E.	Chavín cult
300–1100 C.E.	Maya society
300–700 C.E.	Mochica society
500 B.C.E.–750 C.E.	Teotihuacan society
OCEANIA	
60,000 B.C.E.	Human migration to Australia and New Guinea
3000 B.C.E.	Origins of agriculture in New Guinea
3000 B.C.E.	Austronesian migrations to New Guinea
1500–500 B.C.E.	Lapita society
1500 B.C.E.–700 C.E.	Austronesian migrations to Pacific islands

FOR FURTHER READING

Robert McC. Adams. *The Evolution of Urban Society.* Chicago, 1966. Provocative analysis comparing the development of Mesopotamian and Mesoamerican societies by a leading archaeologist.

Ignacio Bernal. *Mexico before Cortez: Art, History, and Legend.* Trans. by W. Barnstone. Garden City, 1963. Judicious survey by a leading student of ancient Mesoamerica.

Geoffrey Blainey. *Triumph of the Nomads: A History of Aboriginal Australia.* Melbourne, 1975. A sympathetic account of Australia before European arrival, well informed by archaeological discoveries.

Michael D. Coe. *The Maya.* 4th ed. London, 1987. Well-illustrated popular account by one of the world's leading scholars of the Maya.

David Freidel, Linda Schele, and Joy Parker. *Maya Cosmos: Three Thousand Years on the Shaman's Path.* New York, 1993. Fascinating investigation of Maya conceptions of the world and their continuing influence in the present day.

K. R. Howe. *The Quest for Origins: Who First Discovered and Settled the Pacific Islands?* Honolulu, 2003. Reviews the numerous theories advanced to explain the arrival of human populations and the establishment of human societies in the remote islands of the Pacific Ocean.

Jesse D. Jennings, ed. *The Prehistory of Polynesia.* Cambridge, Mass., 1979. Brings together essays by prominent scholars on Polynesia before the arrival of Europeans in the Pacific Ocean.

Friedrich Katz. *The Ancient American Civilizations.* Trans. by K. M. L. Simpson. New York, 1972. Detailed survey that compares the experiences of Mesoamerica and Andean South America.

Edward P. Lanning. *Peru before the Incas.* Englewood Cliffs, 1967. Summarizes the results of archaeological research that has transformed scholars' understanding of ancient Andean societies.

Linda Schele and Mary Ellen Miller. *The Blood of Kings: Dynasty and Ritual in Maya Art.* New York, 1986. A richly illustrated volume that explores Maya society through works of art and architecture as well as writing.

Dennis Tedlock, trans. *Popol Vuh: The Definitive Edition of the Mayan Book of the Dawn of Life and the Glories of Gods and Kings.* New York, 1985. The best translation of the *Popol Vuh,* with an excellent introduction.

Muriel Porter Weaver. *The Aztecs, Maya, and Their Predecessors: Archaeology of Mesoamerica.* 3rd ed. San Diego, 1993. An up-to-date survey based on recent historical and archaeological research.

Toward the end of the first millennium B.C.E., several early complex societies achieved particularly high degrees of internal organization, extended their authority over extremely large regions, and elaborated especially influential cultural traditions. The most prominent of these societies developed in Persia, China, India, and the Mediterranean basin. Because their legacies have endured so long and have influenced the ways that literally billions of people have led their lives, historians often refer to them as classical societies.

The classical societies of Persia, China, India, and the Mediterranean basin differed from one another in many ways. However, despite their differences, these societies faced several common problems. They all confronted the challenge, for example, of administering vast territories without advanced technologies of transportation and communication. To meet that challenge, classical rulers built roads and supported networks of trade and communication that linked the sometimes far-flung regions under their authority.

The classical societies all faced military challenges, and they raised powerful armies for both defensive and offensive purposes, and for both internal and external threats. In hopes of securing their borders and enhancing the welfare of their lands, rulers of most classical societies launched campaigns of expansion that ultimately produced massive imperial states.

The bureaucracies and armies that enabled classical societies to address some problems effectively created difficulties as well. Most classical societies forced subjects to pay taxes to finance state bureaucracies and armies and required compulsory labor for large-scale public projects. And, while some members of classical societies grew rich from taxes and imperial expansion, others grew increasingly impoverished. Growing economic distinctions in turn gave rise to tensions that fueled bitter class conflict. In some cases, conflicts escalated into rebellions and civil wars that threatened the very survival of the classical societies.

All the classical societies engaged in long-distance trade. This trade encouraged economic integration within and between societies, and various regions came to depend on one another for agricultural products and manufactured items. Indeed, long-distance trade became common enough that a well-established network of land and sea routes,

THE FORMATION OF CLASSICAL SOCIETIES, 500 B.C.E. to 500 C.E.

known collectively as the silk roads, linked lands as distant as China and Europe.

Finally, all the classical societies generated sophisticated cultural and religious traditions. Different societies held widely varying beliefs and values, but their cultural and religious traditions offered guidance on moral, religious, political, and social issues. Several cultural and religious traditions also attracted large popular followings and created institutional structures that enabled them to survive over the very long term.

Over the centuries, specific political, social, economic, and cultural features of the classical societies have disappeared. Yet their legacies deeply influenced future societies and in many ways continue to influence the lives of the world's peoples. Appreciation of the legacies of classical societies is thus crucial to understanding the world's historical development.

CHAPTER 5

The Empires of Persia

The Greek historian Herodotus relished a good story, and he related many a tale about the Persian empire and its conflicts with other peoples, including Greeks. One story had to do with a struggle between Cyrus, leader of the expanding Persian realm, and Croesus, ruler of the powerful and wealthy kingdom of Lydia in southwestern Anatolia (modern Turkey). Croesus noted the growth of Persian influence with concern and asked the Greek oracle at Delphi whether to go to war against Cyrus. The oracle responded that an attack on Cyrus would destroy a great kingdom.

Overjoyed, Croesus lined up his allies and prepared for war. In 546 B.C.E. he provoked Cyrus to engage the formidable Lydian cavalry. The resulting battle was hard fought but inconclusive. Because winter was approaching, Croesus disbanded his troops and returned to his capital at Sardis, expecting Cyrus to retreat as well. But Cyrus was a vigorous and unpredictable warrior, and he pursued Croesus to Sardis. When he learned of the pursuit, Croesus hastily assembled an army to confront the invaders. Cyrus threw it into disarray, however, by advancing a group of warriors mounted on camels, which spooked the Lydian horses and sent them into headlong flight. Cyrus's army then surrounded Sardis and took the city after a siege of only two weeks. Croesus was taken captive and afterward became an advisor to Cyrus. Herodotus could not resist pointing out that events proved the Delphic oracle right: Croesus's attack on Cyrus did indeed lead to the destruction of a great kingdom—his own.

OPPOSITE PAGE: *Gold plaque depicting a figure who was perhaps a priest in Achaemenid times.*

The victory over Lydia was a major turning point in the development of the Persian empire. Lydia had a reputation as a kingdom of fabulous wealth, partly because it conducted maritime trade with Greece, Egypt, and Phoenicia as well as overland trade with Mesopotamia and Persia. Lydian wealth and resources gave Cyrus tremendous momentum as he extended Persian authority to new lands and built the earliest of the vast imperial states of classical times.

Classical Persian society began to take shape during the sixth century B.C.E. when warriors conquered an enormous region from the Indus River to Egypt and southeastern Europe. Indeed, the very size of the Persian empire created political and administrative problems for its rulers. Once they solved those problems, however, a series of Persian-based empires governed much of the territory between India and the Mediterranean Sea for more than a millennium—from the mid–sixth century B.C.E. until the early seventh century C.E.—and brought centralized political organization to many distinct peoples living over vast geographic spaces.

In organizing their realm, Persian rulers relied heavily on Mesopotamian techniques of administration, but they also created new institutions and administrative procedures of their own. In addition, they invested resources in the construction of roads and highways to improve communications and mobility across the empire. As a result of those efforts, central administrators were able to send instructions throughout the empire, dispatch armies in times of turmoil, and ensure that local officials would carry out imperial policies.

The organization of the vast territories embraced by the classical Persian empires had important social, economic, and cultural implications. Because high agricultural productivity allowed more people to work at tasks other than cultivation, classes of bureaucrats, administrators, priests, craftsmen, and merchants increased in number. Meanwhile, social extremes between the wealthy and the poor became more pronounced. In addition, good roads across the empire allowed Persian society to serve as a commercial and cultural bridge between Indian and Mediterranean societies. As a result, Persia became an important link in long-distance trade networks as well as a conduit for the exchange of philosophical and religious ideas. Indeed, Persian religious traditions inspired religious thinkers subject to Persian rule and deeply influenced Judaism, Christianity, and Islam.

THE RISE AND FALL OF THE PERSIAN EMPIRES

The empires of Persia arose in the arid land of Iran. For centuries Iran had developed under the shadow of the wealthier and more productive Mesopotamia to the west while absorbing migrations and invasions of nomadic peoples coming out of central Asia. During the sixth century B.C.E., rulers of the province of Persia in southwestern Iran embarked on a series of conquests that resulted in the formation of an enormous empire. For more than a millennium, four ruling dynasties—the Achaemenids (558–330 B.C.E.), the Seleucids (323–83 B.C.E.), the Parthians (247 B.C.E.–224 C.E.), and the Sasanids (224–651 C.E.)—maintained a continuous tradition of imperial rule in much of southwest Asia.

The Achaemenid Empire

The origins of classical Persian society trace back to the late stages of Mesopotamian society. During the centuries before 1000 B.C.E., two closely related Indo-European peoples known as the Medes and the Persians migrated from central Asia to Persia, where they lived *The Medes and the Persians* in loose subjection to the Babylonian and Assyrian empires. The Medes and the Persians shared many cultural traits with their distant cousins the Aryans, who had migrated into India.

Interactive Map
Achaemenid and Seleucid empires

Like the Aryans, they were mostly pastoralists, although they also practiced a limited amount of agriculture. They also possessed considerable military power: like other Indo-Europeans, they were skilled equestrians and expert archers. They also organized themselves by clans rather than by states, although they did recognize leaders who collected taxes and delivered tribute to their Mesopotamian overlords.

When the Assyrian and Babylonian empires weakened in the sixth century B.C.E., the Medes and the Persians launched their first bid for empire in the person of Cyrus the *Cyrus's Conquests* Achaemenid (reigned 558–530 B.C.E.). Cyrus proved to be a tough, wily leader and an outstanding military

---

Achaemenid (ah-KEE-muh-nid)
Medes (meeds)

Map 5.1 Boundaries and major cities of the Achaemenid and Seleucid empires between 558 and 83 B.C.E. Note the location of the Royal Road, which extended from Sardis in Anatolia to Susa near the Persian Gulf. What role did the Royal Road play in the maintenance of the empires?

strategist, whose conquests laid the foundation for the first Persian empire. In 558 B.C.E. Cyrus became king of the Persian tribes, which he ruled from his mountain fortress at Pasargadae. In 553 B.C.E. he initiated a rebellion against his Median overlord, whom he crushed within three years. By 548 B.C.E. he had brought all of Iran under his control, and he began to look for opportunities to expand. In 546 B.C.E., as we know, he conquered the powerful kingdom of Lydia in Anatolia. Between 545 B.C.E. and 539 B.C.E. he campaigned in central Asia and Bactria (modern Afghanistan). In a swift campaign of 539 B.C.E., he seized Babylonia, whose vassal states immediately recognized him as their lord. Within twenty years Cyrus went from minor regional king to ruler of an empire that stretched from India to the borders of Egypt. Had he lived long enough, Cyrus no doubt would have mounted a campaign against Egypt, the largest and wealthiest neighboring state outside his control. But in 530 B.C.E. he fell, mortally wounded, while protecting his northeastern frontier from nomadic raiders.

Darius Cyrus's empire survived and expanded during the reigns of his successors. His son Cambyses (reigned 530–522 B.C.E.) conquered Egypt in 525 B.C.E. His younger kinsman Darius (reigned 521–486 B.C.E.) then extended the empire both east and west. Indeed, Darius's armies pushed into northwestern India as far as the Indus River, absorbing the northern Indian kingdom of Gandhara, while also capturing Thrace, Macedonia, and the western coast of the Black Sea in southeastern Europe. By the late sixth century B.C.E., Darius presided over an empire stretching some 3,000 kilometers (1,865 miles) from the Indus River in the east to the Aegean Sea in the west and 1,500 kilometers (933 miles) from Armenia in the north to the first cataract of the Nile River in the south. With a population of some thirty-five million, Darius's realm was by far the largest empire the world had yet seen.

Yet Darius was more important as an administrator than as a conqueror. Governing a far-flung empire of so many ethnic groups, languages, and traditions was a much more difficult challenge than conquering it. To maintain their empire, the Achaemenids needed to establish lines of communication with all parts of their realm and design institutions that would enable them to administer their territories efficiently. Their solutions not only made it possible for the Achaemenid empire to survive but also pioneered administrative techniques that would outlast their own dynasty and influence political life in southwestern Asia for centuries to come.

Soon after his rise to power, Darius began to centralize his administration. About 520 B.C.E. he started to build a new capital of astonishing magnificence at Persepolis. Darius intended Persep- *Persepolis* olis to serve not only as an administrative center but also as a monument to the Achaemenid dynasty. From the time of Darius to the end of the Achaemenid dynasty in 330 B.C.E., Persepolis served as the nerve center of the Persian empire—a resplendent capital bustling with advisors, ministers, diplomats, scribes, accountants, translators, and bureaucratic officers of all descriptions. Even today, massive columns and other ruins bespeak the grandeur of Darius's capital.

The government of the Achaemenid empire depended on a finely tuned balance between central initiative and local administration. Like their Mesopotamian predecessors, the Achaemenids appointed governors to serve as agents of the central administration and oversee affairs in the various regions. Darius divided his realm into twenty-three administrative and taxation districts he called satrapies, with each governed by an official satrap. Yet the Achaemenids did not try to push direct rule on their subjects: although most satraps were Persian, the Achaemenids recruited local officials to fill almost all other administrative posts.

Achaemenid Administration: The Satrapies

The Achaemenid rulers employed two strategies to discourage distant satraps from allying with local groups or trying to become independent of Achaemenid authority. First, each satrapy had a contingent of military officers and tax collectors who served as checks on the satraps' power and independence. Second, the rulers created a new category of officials—essentially imperial spies—known as "the eyes and ears of the king." These agents traveled throughout the empire with their own military forces, conducting surprise audits of accounts and procedures in the provinces and collecting intelligence reports. Taken together, these two strategies helped prevent the vast Achaemenid empire from splitting into a series of independent kingdoms.

Darius also sought to improve administrative efficiency by regularizing tax levies and standardizing laws. Instead of exacting irregular tribute payments from subject lands as his predecessors had done, Darius instituted regular, formal tax levies. Each satrapy was now required to pay a set quantity of silver to the imperial court every year. To simplify the process, Darius issued standardized coins—a move that also fostered trade throughout his empire. Equally important, beginning in 520 B.C.E., Darius also sought to bring the many legal systems of his empire closer to a single standard. The point was not to abolish the existing laws of individual lands or peoples to impose a uniform law code on his entire

Taxation and Law

---

satraps (SAY-traps)

Ruins of Persepolis, showing the imperial reception hall and palaces.

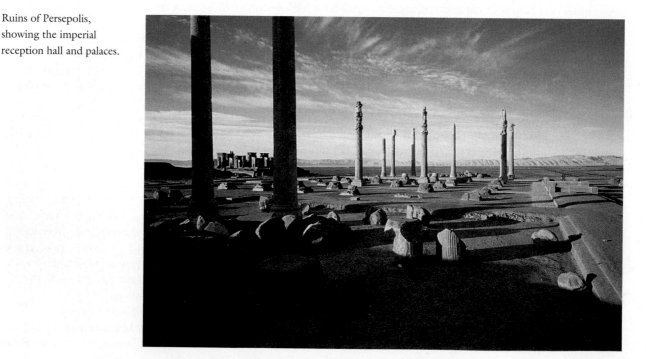

empire. Rather, Darius wished to codify the laws of his subject peoples, modifying them when necessary to harmonize them with the legal principles observed in the empire as a whole.

Alongside administrative and legal policies, the Achaemenid rulers took other measures to knit their far-flung realm into a coherent whole. *Roads and Communications* They built good roads across their realm, notably the so-called Persian Royal Road, which stretched some 2,575 kilometers (1,600 miles) from the Aegean port of Ephesus to Sardis in Anatolia, through Mesopotamia along the Tigris River, to Susa in Iran, with an extension to Pasargadae and Persepolis. Caravans took some ninety days to travel this road, lodging at inns along the well-policed route.

The imperial government also organized a courier service and built 111 postal stations at intervals of 40 to 50 kilometers (25 to 30 miles) along the Royal Road. Each station kept a supply of fresh horses, enabling couriers to speed from one end of the Royal Road to the other in a week's time. The Achaemenids also improved existing routes between Mesopotamia and Egypt, and they built a new road between Persia and the Indus River to link the imperial center with the satrapy of Gandhara in northwestern India. In addition to improving communications, these roads facilitated trade, which helped to integrate the empire's various regions into a larger economy.

Decline and Fall of the Achaemenid Empire

The Achaemenids' roads and administrative machinery enabled them to govern a vast empire and extend Persian influences throughout their territories. Persian concepts of law and justice administered by trained imperial officials linked peoples from the Mediterranean Sea to the Indus River in a larger Persian society. *The Achaemenid Commonwealth* Political stability made it possible to undertake enormous public works projects such as the construction of *qanat* (underground canals), which led to enhanced agricultural production and population growth. Iron metallurgy spread to all parts of the empire, and by the end of the Achaemenid dynasty, iron tools were common in Persian agricultural communities. Peoples in the various regions of the Achaemenid empire maintained their ethnic identities, but all participated in a larger Persian commonwealth.

Eventually, however, difficulties between rulers and subject peoples undermined the integrity of the empire. Cyrus and Darius both consciously pursued a policy of toleration in administering their vast multicultural empire: they took great care to respect the values and cultural traditions of the peoples they ruled. In Mesopotamia, for example, they portrayed

qanat (kah-NAHT)

Carving from Persepolis showing an enthroned Darius (with his son Xerxes standing behind him) receiving a high court official, as incense burners perfume the air.

themselves not as Persian conquerors but, rather, as legitimate Babylonian rulers and representatives of Marduk, the patron deity of Babylon. Darius also won high praise from Jews in the Achaemenid empire, since he allowed them to return to Jerusalem and rebuild the temple that Babylonian conquerors had destroyed in 587 B.C.E.

Darius's successor, Xerxes (reigned 486–465 B.C.E.), retreated from this policy of toleration, however, flaunted his Persian identity, and sought to impose his own values on conquered lands. That policy caused enormous ill will, especially in Mesopotamia and Egypt, where peoples with their own cultural traditions resented Xerxes' pretensions. Although Xerxes successfully repressed rebellions against his rule in Mesopotamia and Egypt, resentment of Persian conquerors continued to fester, and it caused serious problems for the later Achaemenids.

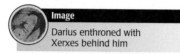
Darius enthroned with Xerxes behind him

In fact, efforts to control their ethnic Greek subjects helped to bring about the collapse of the Achaemenid empire. Ethnic Greeks inhabited many of the cities in Anatolia—particularly in the region of Ionia on the Aegean coast of western Anatolia—and they maintained close economic and commercial ties with their cousins in the peninsula of Greece itself. The Ionian Greeks fell under Persian domination during the reign of Cyrus. They became restive under Darius's Persian governors who oversaw their affairs, and in 500 B.C.E. the Ionian cities rebelled, expelled or executed their governors, and asserted their independence. Their rebellion launched a series of conflicts known as the Persian Wars (500–479 B.C.E.).

The Persian Wars

The conflict between the Ionian Greeks and the Persians expanded considerably when the cities of peninsular Greece sent fleets to aid their kinsmen in Ionia. Darius managed to put down the rebellion and reassert Achaemenid authority, but he and his successors became entangled in a difficult and ultimately destructive effort to extend their authority to the Greek peninsula. Indeed, after some initial successes against the Greeks, the Persians suffered a rout at the battle of Marathon (490 B.C.E.), and they returned home without achieving their goals. Ten years later, in 480 B.C.E., a renewed Persian attempt to conquer the Greek cities ended in costly defeats for the Persians. Thereafter, for almost 150 years the Persian empire continued to spar intermittently with the Greek cities without achieving victory.

A coin issued by Alexander with an image of the conqueror.

The standoff ended with the rise of Alexander of Macedon, often called Alexander the Great (discussed more fully in chapter 8). In 334 B.C.E. Alexander invaded Persia with an army of some forty-eight thousand tough, battle-hardened Macedonians. Though far smaller than the Persian army in numbers, the well-disciplined Macedonians carried heavier arms and employed more sophisticated military tactics than their opponents. As a result, they sliced through the Persian empire and dealt their adversaries a series of devastating defeats. In 331 B.C.E. Alexander shattered Achaemenid forces at the battle of Gaugamela, and within a year the empire founded by Cyrus had dissolved.

Alexander of Macedon

Alexander led his forces into Persepolis and proclaimed himself heir to the Achaemenid rulers. After a brief season of celebration, Alexander and his forces ignited a blaze—perhaps intentionally—that destroyed Persepolis. The conflagration was so great that when archaeologists first began to explore the ruins of Persepolis in the eighteenth century, they found layers of ash and charcoal up to 1 meter (3 feet) deep.

The Achaemenid empire had crumbled, but its legacy was by no means exhausted. Alexander portrayed himself in Persia and Egypt as a legitimate successor of the Achaemenids who observed their precedents and deserved their honors. He retained the Achaemenid administrative structure, and he even confirmed the appointments of many satraps and other officials. As it happened, Alexander had little time to enjoy his conquests, because he died in 323 B.C.E. after a brief effort to extend his empire to India. But the states that succeeded him—the Seleucid, Parthian, and Sasanid empires—continued to employ a basically Achaemenid structure of imperial administration.

The Seleucid, Parthian, and Sasanid Empires

After Alexander died, his chief generals carved his empire into three large realms, which they divided among themselves. The choicest realm, which included most of the former Achaemenid empire, went to Seleucus (reigned 305–281 B.C.E.), who had com-

The Seleucids manded an elite corps of guards in Alexander's army. Like Alexander, Seleucus and his successors retained the Achaemenid systems of administration and taxation as well as the imperial roads and postal service. The Seleucids also founded new cities throughout the realm and attracted Greek colonists to occupy them. These new cities greatly stimulated trade and economic development both within the Seleucid empire and beyond.

As foreigners, the Seleucids faced opposition from native Persians. Satraps often revolted against Seleucid rule and tried to establish their independence. The Seleucids soon lost their holdings in northern India, and the seminomadic Parthians progressively took over Iran during the third century B.C.E. The Seleucids continued to rule a truncated empire until 83 B.C.E., when Roman conquerors put an end to their empire.

Meanwhile, the Parthians established themselves as lords of a powerful empire based in Iran that they

The Parthians extended to Mesopotamia. The Parthians had occupied the region of eastern Iran around Khurasan since Achaemenid times. They retained many of the customs and traditions of nomadic peoples from the steppes of central Asia. They did not have a centralized government, for example, but organized themselves into a federation of clans. They were also skillful warriors, accustomed to defending themselves against constant threats from nomadic peoples farther east.

As they settled and turned increasingly to agriculture, the Parthians discovered that they could resist nomadic invasions better by feeding their horses on alfalfa during the winter. The alfalfa allowed the animals to grow much larger and stronger than the small horses and ponies of nomadic peoples who had to forage on the steppes in winter. The larger Parthian horses could then support heavily armed warriors outfitted with metal armor, which served as an effective shield against the arrows of the steppe nomads. Indeed, few existing forces could stand up to Parthian heavy cavalry.

As early as the third century B.C.E., the Parthians began to wrest their independence from the Seleucids. The Parthian satrap revolted against his Seleucid overlord in 238 B.C.E., and during the following decades his successors gradually enlarged their holdings. Mithradates I, the Parthians' greatest conqueror, came

Seleucids (sih-LOO-sihds)

Gold sculpture of a nomadic horseman discharging an arrow. This figurine dates from the fifth or fourth century B.C.E. and might well represent a Parthian.

to the throne about 171 B.C.E. and transformed his state into a mighty empire. By about 155 B.C.E. he had consolidated his hold on Iran and had also extended Parthian rule to Mesopotamia.

The Parthians portrayed themselves as enemies of the foreign Seleucids, as restorers of rule in the Persian tradition. To some extent that characterization was accurate. The Parthians largely followed the example of the Achaemenids in structuring their empire: they governed through satraps, employed Achaemenid techniques of administration and taxation, and built a lavish capital city. But the Parthians also retained elements of their own steppe traditions. For example, they did not develop nearly as cen-

Parthian Government

Image
A coin with Mithradates I

tralized a regime as the Achaemenids or the Seleucids but, rather, vested a great deal of authority and responsibility in their clan leaders. These men—who frequently served as satraps—could be troublesome, because they frequently rebelled against the imperial government from their regional bases.

For about three centuries the Parthians presided over a powerful empire between India and the Mediterranean. Beginning in the first century C.E., they faced pressure in the west from the expanding Roman empire. On three occasions in the second century C.E., Roman armies captured the Parthian capital at Ctesiphon. Combined with internal difficulties caused by rebellious satraps, Roman pressure contributed to the weakening of the Parthian state. During the early third century C.E., internal rebellion brought it down.

Once again, though, the tradition of imperial rule continued, this time under the Sasanids, who came *The Sasanids* from Persia and claimed direct descent from the Achaemenids. The Sasanids toppled the Parthians in 224 C.E. and ruled until the year 651, re-creating much of the splendor of the Achaemenid empire. From their cosmopolitan capital at Ctesiphon, the Sasanid "king of kings" provided strong rule from Parthia to Mesopotamia. Sasanid merchants traded actively with peoples to both the east and the west, and they introduced into Iran the cultivation of crops such as rice, sugarcane, citrus fruits, eggplant, and cotton that came west over the trade routes from India and China.

During the reign of Shapur I (239–272 C.E.), the Sasanids stabilized their western frontier and created a series of buffer states between themselves and the Roman empire. After Shapur, the Sasanids did not expand militarily but entered into a standoff relationship with the Kushan empire in the east and the Roman and Byzantine empires in the west. None of those

Sasanids (suh-SAH-nids)

large empires was strong enough to overcome the others, but they contested border areas and buffer states, sometimes engaging in lengthy and bitter disputes that sapped the energies of all involved.

These continual conflicts seriously weakened the Sasanid empire in particular. The empire came to an end in 651 C.E. when Arab warriors killed the last Sasanid ruler, overran his realm, and incorporated it into their rapidly expanding Islamic empire. Yet even conquest by external invaders did not end the legacy of classical Persia, since Arab conquerors adopted Persian administrative techniques and cultural traditions for their own use in building a new Islamic society.

IMPERIAL SOCIETY AND ECONOMY

Throughout the eastern hemisphere during the classical era, public life and social structure became much more complicated than they had been during the days of the early complex societies. Centralized imperial governments needed large numbers of administrative officials, which led to the emergence of educated classes of bureaucrats. Stable empires also enabled many individuals to engage in trade or other

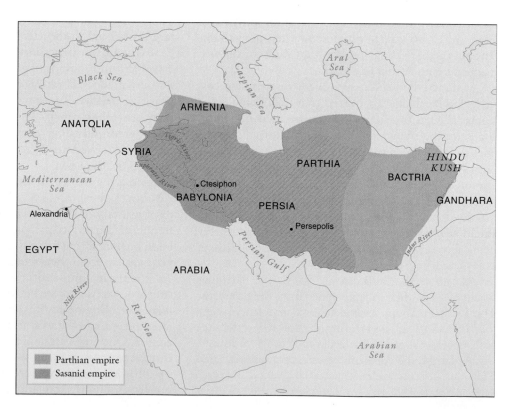

Map 5.2 Boundaries and major cities of the Parthian and Sasanid empires from 247 B.C.E. to 651 C.E. Observe the position of these empires between the Black Sea and Mediterranean in the west to the Indus River in the east. Would the existence of such large empires have helped or hindered trade relations across Eurasia?

specialized labor. Some of these individuals accumulated vast wealth, which led to increased distance and tensions between rich and poor. Meanwhile, slavery became more common than in earlier times. The prominence of slavery had to do partly with the expansion of imperial states, which often enslaved conquered foes, but it also reflected the increasing gulf between rich and poor, which placed such great economic pressure on some individuals that they had to give up their freedom in order to survive. All these developments had implications for the social structures of classical societies in Persia as well as China, India, and the Mediterranean basin.

Social Development in Classical Persia

During the early days of the Achaemenid empire, Persian society reflected its nomadic steppe origins. When the Medes and the Persians migrated to Iran, their social structure was very similar to that of the Aryans in India, consisting primarily of warriors, priests, and peasants. Family and clan relationships were extremely important in the organization of Persian political and social affairs. Male warriors headed the clans, which retained much of their influence long after the establishment of the Achaemenid empire.

Imperial Bureaucrats

The development of a cosmopolitan empire and the requirements of imperial administration, however, called for a new class of educated bureaucrats, who to a large extent undermined the position of the old warrior elite. Although the bureaucrats did not directly challenge the patriarchal warriors, their crucial role in running the day-to-day affairs of the empire guaranteed them a prominent and comfortable place in Persian society. By the time of the later Achaemenids and the Seleucids, Persian cities were home to masses of administrators, tax collectors, and record keepers. The bureaucracy even included a substantial corps of translators, who facilitated communications among the empire's many linguistic groups. Imperial survival depended on these literate professionals, and high-ranking bureaucrats came to share power and influence with warriors and clan leaders.

Free Classes

The bulk of Persian society consisted of free individuals such as artisans, craftsmen, merchants, and low-ranking civil servants. Priests and priestesses were also prominent urban residents, along with servants who maintained the temple communities in which they lived. In Persian society, as in earlier Mesopotamian societies, members of the free classes participated in religious observances conducted at local temples, and they had the right to share in the income that temples generated from their agricultural operations and from craft industries such as textile production that the temples organized. The weaving of textiles was mostly the work of women, who received rations of grain, wine, beer, and sometimes meat from the imperial and temple workshops that employed them.

In the countryside the free classes included peasants who owned their own land as well as landless cultivators who worked on properties owned by the state, temple communities, or other individuals. Free residents of rural areas had the right to marry and move as they wished, and they could seek better opportunities in the cities or in military service. The Persian empires embraced a great deal of parched land that received little rainfall, and free residents of the countryside contributed much of the labor that went into the building and maintenance of irrigation systems. Most remarkable of those systems were underground canals known as *qanat,* which allowed cultivators to distribute water to fields without losing large quantities to evaporation through exposure to the sun and open air. Numerous *qanat* crisscrossed the Iranian plateau in the heartland of the Persian empire, where extreme scarcity of water justified the enormous investment of human labor required to build the canals.

Slaves

A large class of slaves also worked in both the cities and the countryside. Individuals passed into slavery by two main routes. Most were prisoners of war who became slaves as the price of survival. Other slaves came from the ranks of free subjects who accumulated debts that they could not satisfy. In the cities, for example, merchants, artisans, and craftsmen borrowed funds to purchase goods or open shops, while in the countryside small farmers facing competition from large-scale cultivators borrowed against their property and liberty to purchase tools, seed, or food. Failure to repay those debts in a timely fashion often forced the borrowers not only to forfeit their property but also to sell their children, their spouses, or themselves into slavery.

Slave status deprived individuals of their personal freedom. Slaves became the property of an individual, the state, or an institution such as a temple community; they worked at tasks set by their owners, and they could not move or marry at will. Most slaves probably worked as domestic servants or skilled laborers in the households of the wealthy. However, state-owned

In this sculpture from Persepolis, Persian nobles dressed in fine cloaks and hats ascend the staircase leading to the imperial reception hall.

slaves provided much of the manual labor for large-scale construction projects such as roads, irrigation systems, city walls, and palaces, whereas slaves owned by temples worked at agricultural tasks and performed administrative chores for their priestly masters.

Economic Foundations of Classical Persia

Agriculture was the economic foundation of classical Persian society. Like other classical societies, Persia needed large agricultural surpluses to support military forces and administrative specialists as well as residents of cities who were artisans, crafts workers, and merchants rather than cultivators. The Persian empires embraced several regions of exceptional fertility—notably Mesopotamia, Egypt, Anatolia, and northern India—and they prospered by mobilizing the agricultural surpluses of those lands.

Barley and wheat were the grains cultivated most commonly in the Persian empires. Peas, lentils, mustard, garlic, onions, cucumbers, dates, apples, pomegranates, pears, and apricots supplemented the cereals in diets throughout Persian society, and beer and wine were the most common beverages. In most years agricultural production far exceeded the needs of cultivators, making sizable surpluses available for sale in the cities or for distribution to state servants through the imperial bu-

Agricultural Production

reaucracy. Vast quantities of produce flowed into the imperial court from state-owned lands. Even though they are incomplete, surviving records show that, for example, in 500 B.C.E., during the middle period of Darius's reign, the imperial court received almost eight hundred thousand liters of grain, quite apart from vegetables, fruits, meat, poultry, fish, oil, beer, wine, and textiles. Officials distributed some of this produce to the imperial staff as wages in kind, but much of it also found its way into the enormous banquets that Darius organized for as many as ten thousand guests.

Agriculture was the foundation of the Persian economy, but long-distance trade grew rapidly during the course of the Persian empires and linked lands from India to Egypt in a vast commercial zone. Each region of the Persian empire contributed particular products to the imperial economy, from the gold and ivory of India to the semiprecious stones of Iran, and from the metals of Anatolia to the textiles and grain of Egypt. Several conditions promoted the growth of trade: the relative political stability maintained by the Persian empires, the general prosperity of the realm, the use of standardized coins, and the availability of good trade routes, including long-established routes, newly constructed highways such as the Persian Royal Road, and sea routes through the Red Sea, the Persian Gulf, and the Arabian Sea. Markets operated regularly in all the larger cities of the Persian empires, and the largest cities,

Trade

such as Babylon, also were home to banks and companies that invested in commercial ventures.

Long-distance trade of this sort became especially prominent during the reigns of Alexander of Macedon and his Seleucid successors. The cities they established and the colonists they attracted stimulated trade throughout the whole region from the Mediterranean to northern India. Indeed, Greek migrants facilitated cultural as well as commercial exchanges by encouraging the mixing and mingling of religious faiths, art styles, and philosophical speculation throughout the Persian realm.

RELIGIONS OF SALVATION IN CLASSICAL PERSIAN SOCIETY

Cross-cultural influences were especially noticeable in the development of Persian religion. Persians came from the family of peoples who spoke Indo-European languages, and their earliest religion closely resembled that of the Aryans of India. During the classical era, however, the new faith of Zoroastrianism emerged and became widely popular in Iran and to a lesser extent also in the larger Persian empires. Zoroastrianism reflected the cosmopolitan society of the empires, and it profoundly influenced the beliefs and values of Judaism, Christianity, and Islam.

Zarathustra and His Faith

The earliest Persian religion recognized many of the same gods as the ancient Aryans, and their priests performed sacrifices similar to those conducted by the *brahmins* in India. Like the Aryans, the ancient Persians glorified strength and martial virtues, and the cults of both peoples sought principally to bring about a comfortable material existence for their practitioners.

During the classical era Persian religion underwent considerable change, as moral and religious thinkers *Zarathustra* sought to adapt their messages to the circumstances of a complex, cosmopolitan society. One result was Zoroastrianism, which emerged from the teachings of Zarathustra. Though Zarathustra was undoubtedly a historical person, little certain information survives about his life and career. It is not even clear when he lived, though most scholars date his life to the late seventh and early sixth centuries

Zoroastrianism (zohr-oh-ASS-tree-ahn-iz'm)

A gold clasp or button of the fifth century B.C.E. with the symbol of Ahura Mazda as a winged god.

B.C.E. He came from an aristocratic family, and he probably was a priest who became disenchanted with the traditional religion. In any case, when he was about twenty years old, Zarathustra left his family and home in search of wisdom. After about ten years of travel, he experienced a series of visions and became convinced that the supreme god, whom he called Ahura Mazda ("the wise lord"), had chosen him to serve as his prophet and spread his message.

Like his life, Zarathustra's doctrine remains largely unknown, since many of the earliest Zoroastrian teachings were not preserved in writing. Only *The Gathas* during the Seleucid dynasty did Zoroastrian priests, known as *magi*, begin to preserve religious texts in writing, and only under the Sasanids did they compile their scriptures in a holy book known as the Avesta. Nevertheless, many of Zarathustra's own compositions survive because of the diligence by which *magi* preserved them through oral transmission. Known as the *Gathas*, Zarathustra's works were hymns that he composed in honor of the various deities that he recognized. Apart from the *Gathas*, ancient Zoroastrian literature included a wide variety of hymns, liturgical works, and treatises on moral and theological themes. Though some of these works survive, the arrival of Islam in the seventh century C.E. and the subsequent decline of Zoroastrianism resulted in the loss of most of the Avesta and later Zoroastrian works.

Zarathustra and his followers were not strict monotheists. They recognized Ahura Mazda as a supreme

Zarathustra (zar-uh-THOO-struh)
Gathas (GATH-uhs)

deity, and the creator of all good things, but Zarathustra also praised six lesser deities in the *Gathas*. Furthermore, he believed that Ahura Mazda engaged in a cosmic conflict with an independent adversary, an evil and malign spirit known as Angra Mainyu ("the destructive spirit" or "the hostile spirit"). Following a struggle of some twelve thousand years, Zarathustra believed, Ahura Mazda and the forces of good would ultimately prevail, and Angra Mainyu and the principle of evil would disappear forever. At that time individual human souls would undergo judgment and would experience the rewards or punishments they deserved. Honest and moral individuals would enter into a heavenly paradise, whereas demons would fling their evil brethren into a hellish realm of pain and suffering.

Zoroastrian Teachings

Zarathustra did not call for ascetic renunciation of the world in favor of a future heavenly existence. On the contrary, he considered the material world a blessing that reflected the benevolent nature of Ahura Mazda. His moral teachings allowed human beings to enjoy the world and its fruits—including wealth, sexual pleasure, and social prestige—as long as they did so in moderation and behaved honestly toward others. Zoroastrians have often summarized their moral teachings in the simple formula "good words, good thoughts, good deeds."

Zarathustra's teachings began to attract large numbers of followers during the sixth century B.C.E., particularly among Persian aristocrats and ruling elites. Wealthy patrons donated land and established endowments for the support of Zoroastrian temples. The Achaemenid era saw the emergence of a sizable priesthood, whose members conducted religious rituals, maintained a calendar, taught Zoroastrian values, and preserved Zoroastrian doctrine through oral transmission.

Popularity of Zoroastrianism

Beginning with Darius, the Achaemenid emperors closely associated themselves with Ahura Mazda and claimed divine sanction for their rule. Darius ordered stone inscriptions celebrating his achievements, and in those monuments he clearly revealed his devotion to Ahura Mazda and his opposition to the principle of evil. In one of his inscriptions, Darius praised Ahura Mazda as the great god who created the earth, the sky, and humanity and who moreover elevated Darius himself to the imperial honor. With the aid of imperial sponsorship, Zoroastrian temples cropped up throughout the Achaemenid

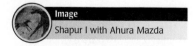
Shapur I with Ahura Mazda

realm. The faith was most popular in Iran, but it attracted sizable followings also in Mesopotamia, Anatolia, Egypt, and other parts of the Achaemenid empire even though there was no organized effort to spread it beyond its original homeland.

Religions of Salvation in a Cosmopolitan Society

The arrival of Alexander of Macedon inaugurated a difficult era for the Zoroastrian community. During his Persian campaign, Alexander's forces burned many temples and killed numerous *magi*. Because at that time the *magi* still transmitted Zoroastrian doctrines orally, an untold number of hymns and holy verses disappeared. The Zoroastrian faith survived, however, and the Parthians cultivated it to rally support against the Seleucids. Once established in power, the Parthians observed Zoroastrian rituals, though they did not support the faith as enthusiastically as their predecessors had done.

During the Sasanid dynasty, however, Zoroastrianism experienced a revival. As self-proclaimed heirs to the Achaemenids, the Sasanids identified closely with Zoroastrianism and supported it zealously. Indeed, the Sasanids often persecuted other faiths if they seemed likely to become popular enough to challenge the supremacy of Zoroastrianism.

Officially Sponsored Zoroastrianism

With generous imperial backing, the Zoroastrian faith and the *magi* flourished as never before. Theologians prepared written versions of the holy texts and collected them in the Avesta. They also explored points of doctrine and addressed difficult questions of morality and theology. Ordinary people flocked to Zoroastrian temples, where they prayed to Ahura Mazda and participated in rituals. The Zoroastrian faith faced severe difficulties in the seventh century C.E. when Islamic conquerors toppled the Sasanid empire. The conquerors did not outlaw the religion altogether, but they placed political and financial pressure on the *magi* and Zoroastrian temples. Some Zoroastrians fled their homeland and found refuge in India, where their descendants, known as Parsis ("Persians"), continue even today to observe Zoroastrian traditions. But most Zoroastrians remained in Iran and eventually converted to Islam. Only a few thousand faithful maintain a Zoroastrian community in modern-day Iran.

Parsis (pahr-SEES)

SOURCES FROM THE PAST

Zarathustra on Good and Evil

Like many other religious faiths of classical times, Zoroastrianism encouraged the faithful to observe high moral and ethical standards. In this hymn from the Gathas, *Zarathustra relates how Ahura Mazda and Angra Mainyu—representatives of good and evil, respectively—made choices about how to behave based on their fundamental natures. Human beings did likewise, according to Zarathustra, and ultimately all would experience the rewards and punishments that their choices merited.*

■ ■ ■

In the beginning, there were two Primal Spirits,
    Twins spontaneously active;
These are the Good and the Evil, in thought, and
    in word, and in deed:
Between these two, let the wise choose aright;
Be good, not base.

And when these Twin Spirits came together at
    first,
They established Life and Non-Life,
And so shall it be as long as the world shall last;
The worst existence shall be the lot of the
    followers of evil,
And the Good Mind shall be the reward of the
    followers of good.

Of these Twin Spirits, the Evil One chose to do
    the worst;
While the bountiful Holy Spirit of Goodness,
Clothing itself with the mossy heavens for a
    garment, chose the Truth;
And so will those who [seek to] please Ahura
    Mazda with righteous deeds, performed
    with faith in Truth. . . .

And when there cometh Divine Retribution for
    the Evil One,
Then at Thy command shall the Good Mind
    establish the Kingdom of Heaven, O
    Mazda,
For those who will deliver Untruth into the
    hands
    of Righteousness and Truth.

Then truly cometh the blow of destruction on
    Untruth,
And all those of good fame are garnered up in
    the Fair Abode,
The Fair Abode of the Good Mind, the Wise
    Lord, and of Truth!

O ye mortals, mark these commandments—
The commandments which the Wise Lord has
    given, for Happiness and for Pain;
Long punishment for the evil-doer, and bliss for
    the follower of Truth,
The joy of salvation for the Righteous ever
    afterwards!

• *What assumptions does Zarathustra make about human nature and the capacity of human beings to make morally good choices out of their own free will?*

SOURCE: D. J. Irani. *The Divine Songs of Zarathustra.* London: George Allen & Unwin, 1924.

Meanwhile, even though Zoroastrianism ultimately declined in its homeland, the cosmopolitan character of the Persian realm offered it opportunities to influence other religious faiths. In particular, Jews living in Persia during Achaemenid times adopted several specific teachings of Zoroastrianism, which later found their way into the faiths of Christianity and Islam as well.

Influence of Zoroastrianism

These teachings included the notion that an omnipotent and beneficent deity was responsible for all creation, the idea that a purely evil being worked against the creator god, the conviction that the forces of good will ultimately prevail over the power of evil after a climactic struggle, the belief that human beings must strive to observe the highest moral standards, and the doctrine that individuals will undergo judgment, after which the morally upright will experience rewards in paradise while evildoers will suffer punishments in hell. These teachings, which have profoundly influenced Judaism, Christianity, and Islam, all derived ultimately from the faith of Zarathustra and his followers.

Summary

The Achaemenid empire inaugurated a new era of world history. The Achaemenids borrowed military and administrative techniques devised earlier by Babylonian and Assyrian rulers, but they applied those techniques on a much larger scale than did any of their Mesopotamian predecessors. In doing so they conquered a vast empire and then governed its diverse lands and peoples with tolerable success for more than two centuries. The Achaemenids demonstrated how it was possible to build and maintain a massive imperial state, and their example inspired later efforts to establish similar large-scale imperial states based in Persia and other Eurasian lands as well. The Achaemenid and later Persian empires integrated much of the territory from the Mediterranean Sea to the Indus River into a commonwealth in which peoples of different regions and ethnic groups participated in a larger economy and society. By sponsoring regular and systematic interactions between peoples of different communities, the Persian empires wielded tremendous cultural as well as political, social, and economic influence. Indeed, Persian religious beliefs helped to shape moral and religious thought throughout much of southwest Asia and the Mediterranean basin. Zoroastrian teachings were particularly influential: although Zoroastrianism declined after the Sasanid dynasty, its doctrines decisively influenced the fundamental teachings of Judaism, Christianity, and Islam.

CHRONOLOGY

7TH–6TH CENTURIES B.C.E. (?)	Life of Zarathustra
558–330 B.C.E.	Achaemenid dynasty
558–530 B.C.E.	Reign of Cyrus the Achaemenid
521–486 B.C.E.	Reign of Darius
334–330 B.C.E.	Invasion and conquest of the Achaemenid empire by Alexander of Macedon
323–83 B.C.E.	Seleucid dynasty
247 B.C.E–224 C.E.	Parthian dynasty
224–651 C.E.	Sasanid dynasty

FOR FURTHER READING

Mary Boyce, ed. *Textual Sources for the Study of Zoroastrianism.* Totowa, N.J., 1984. Sources in translation with numerous explanatory comments by the author.

Maria Brosius. *Women in Ancient Persia, 559–331 B.C.* Oxford, 1996. Carefully examines both Persian and Greek sources for information about women and their role in Achaemenid society.

J. M. Cook. *The Persian Empire.* New York, 1983. A popular account of the Achaemenid empire.

Muhammad A. Dandamaev and Vladimir G. Lukonin. *The Culture and Social Institutions of Ancient Iran.* Ed. by P. L. Kohl. Cambridge, 1989. Scholarly account that brings the results of Russian research to bear on the Achaemenid empire.

Richard C. Foltz. *Spirituality in the Land of the Noble: How Iran Shaped the World's Religions.* Oxford, 2004. Includes an accessible discussion of the Zoroastrian faith.

Richard N. Frye. *The Heritage of Central Asia: From Antiquity to the Turkish Expansion.* Princeton, 1996. Briefly sketches the history of various Iranian-speaking peoples in the steppes of central Asia as well as on the Iranian plateau.

A. T. Olmstead. *History of the Persian Empire (Achaemenid Period).* Chicago, 1948. An older study concentrating on political history; exceptionally well written and still valuable.

Susan Sherwin-White and Amélie Kuhrt. *From Samarkhand to Sardis: A New Approach to the Seleucid Empire.* Berkeley, 1993. Detailed scholarly analysis of the Seleucid empire concentrating on political and economic matters.

Mortimer Wheeler. *Flames over Persepolis.* New York, 1968. Deals with Alexander's conquest of the Achaemenid empire and especially the spread of Greek art styles throughout the Persian empire.

Robert C. Zaehner. *The Dawn and Twilight of Zoroastrianism.* London, 1961. An important interpretation of Zoroastrianism that concentrates on the Achaemenid and Sasanid periods.

CHAPTER 6
The Unification of China

In the year 99 B.C.E., Chinese imperial officials sentenced the historian Sima Qian to punishment by castration. For just over a decade, Sima Qian had worked on a project that he had inherited from his father, a history of China from earliest times to his own day. That project brought Sima Qian high prominence at the imperial court. Thus, when he spoke in defense of a dishonored general, his views attracted widespread attention. The emperor reacted furiously when he learned that Sima Qian had publicly expressed opinions that contradicted the ruler's judgment and ordered the historian to undergo his humiliating punishment.

Human castration was by no means uncommon in premodern times. Thousands of boys and young men of undistinguished birth underwent voluntary castration in China and many other lands as well to pursue careers as eunuchs. Ruling elites often appointed eunuchs, rather than nobles, to sensitive posts because eunuchs did not sire families and so could not build power bases to challenge established authorities. As personal servants of ruling elites, eunuchs sometimes came to wield enormous power.

Castration was not an appealing alternative, however, to educated elites and other prominent individuals: indeed, Chinese men of honor normally avoided the penalty by taking their own lives. Yet Sima Qian chose to endure his punishment. In a letter to a friend he explained that suicide would mean that his work would go forever unwritten. To transmit his understanding of the Chinese past, then, Sima Qian opted to live and work in disgrace until his death about 90 B.C.E.

OPPOSITE PAGE: *The Han emperor discusses classical texts with Confucian scholars.*

During his last years Sima Qian completed a massive work consisting of 130 chapters, most of which survive. He composed historical accounts of the emperors' reigns and biographical sketches of notable figures, including ministers, statesmen, generals, empresses, aristocrats, scholars, officials, merchants, and rebels. He even described the societies of neighboring peoples with whom Chinese sometimes conducted trade and sometimes made war. As a result, Sima Qian's efforts still provide the best information available about the development of early imperial China.

A rich body of political and social thought prepared the way for the unification of China under the Qin and Han dynasties. Confucians, Daoists, Legalists, and others formed schools of thought and worked to bring political and social stability to China during the chaotic years of the late Zhou dynasty and the Period of the Warring States. Legalist ideas contributed directly to unification by outlining means by which rulers could strengthen their states. The works of the Confucians and the Daoists were not directly concerned with unification, but both schools of thought profoundly influenced Chinese political and cultural traditions over the long term.

Rulers of the Qin and Han dynasties adopted Legalist principles and imposed centralized imperial rule on all of China. Like the Achaemenids of Persia, the Qin and Han emperors ruled through an elaborate bureaucracy, and they built roads that linked the various regions of China. They went further than the Persian emperors in their efforts to foster cultural unity in their realm. They imposed a common written language throughout China and established an educational system based on Confucian thought and values. For almost 450 years the Qin and Han dynasties guided the fortunes of China and established a strong precedent for centralized imperial rule.

Especially during the Han dynasty, political stability brought economic prosperity. High agricultural productivity supported the development of iron and silk industries, and Chinese goods found markets in central Asia, India, the Persian Empire, and even the Mediterranean basin. In spite of economic prosperity, however, later Han society experienced deep divisions between rich landowners and poor peasants. Those divisions eventually led to civil disorder and the emergence of political factions, which ultimately brought the Han dynasty to an end.

IN SEARCH OF POLITICAL AND SOCIAL ORDER

The late centuries of the Zhou dynasty led eventually to the chaos associated with the Period of the Warring States (403–221 B.C.E.). Yet the political turmoil of that period also resulted in a remarkable cultural flowering, because it forced thoughtful people to reflect on the proper roles of human beings in society. Some sought to identify principles that would restore political and social order. Others concerned themselves with a search for individual tranquility apart from society. Three schools of thought that emerged during those centuries of confusion and chaos— Confucianism, Daoism, and Legalism—exercised a particularly deep influence on Chinese political and cultural traditions.

Confucius and His School

The first Chinese thinker who addressed the problem of political and social order in a straightforward and self-conscious way was Kong Fuzi (551–479 B.C.E.)— "Master Philosopher Kong," as his disciples called him, or Confucius, as he is known in *Confucius* English. He came from an aristocratic family in the state of Lu in northern China, and for many years he sought an influential post at the Lu court. But Confucius was a strong-willed man who often did not get along well with others. He could be quite cantankerous: he was known to lodge bitter complaints, for example, if someone undercooked or overcooked his rice. Not surprisingly, then, he refused to compromise his beliefs in the interest of political expediency, and he insisted on observing principles that frequently clashed with state policy. As a result, Confucius was unable to obtain a high position at the Lu court. Confucius then sought employment with other courts in northern China but after a decade of travel found none willing to accept his services. In 484 B.C.E., bitterly disappointed, he returned to Lu, where he died five years later.

Although Confucius never realized his ambition, he left an enduring mark on Chinese society through his work as an educator and a political advisor. He attracted numerous disciples who aspired to political careers, and those disciples compiled the master's say-

Confucianism (kuhn-FEW-shuhn-iz'm)

ings and teachings in a book known as the *Analects*—a work that has profoundly influenced Chinese political and cultural traditions.

Confucius's thought was fundamentally moral, ethical, and political in character. It was also thoroughly practical: Confucius did not address philosophical or religious questions but focused instead on the proper ordering of human relationships. In an age when bureaucratic institutions were not yet well developed, Confucius believed that the best way to promote good government was to fill official positions with individuals who were both well educated and extraordinarily conscientious. Thus Confucius concentrated on the formation of what he called *junzi*—"superior individuals"—who did not allow personal interests to influence their judgments.

Confucian Ideas

In the absence of an established educational system and a formal curriculum, Confucius had his disciples study works of poetry and history that provided insight into human nature. He and his students carefully examined works produced during the Zhou dynasty, such as the *Book of Songs*, the *Book of History*, and the *Book of Rites*, concentrating especially on their practical value for prospective administrators. As a result of Confucius's influence, literary works of the Zhou dynasty became the core texts of the traditional Chinese education. For more than two thousand years, until the early twentieth century C.E., talented Chinese seeking government posts followed a program of study deriving from the one developed by Confucius in the fifth century B.C.E.

Confucian Values

For Confucius, though, ideal government officials needed more than an advanced education: they also needed a strong sense of moral integrity and a capacity to deliver wise and fair judgments. Several qualities were particularly important to Confucius. One of them he called *ren*, by which he meant an attitude of kindness and benevolence or a sense of humanity. Confucius explained that individuals possessing *ren* were courteous, respectful, diligent, and loyal—characteristics desperately needed in government officials. Another quality of central importance was *li,* a sense of propriety, which called for individuals to behave appropriately: they should treat all other human beings with courtesy, while showing special respect and deference to elders or superiors. Yet another quality that Confucius emphasized was *xiao,*

li (LEE)
xiao (SHAYOH)

No contemporary portrait of Confucius survives, but artists have used their imaginations and depicted him in many ways over the years. This portrait of 1735 identifies Confucius as "the Sage and Teacher" and represents him in the distinctive dress of an eighteenth-century Confucian scholar-bureaucrat.

filial piety, which obliged children to respect their parents and other family elders, look after their welfare, support them in old age, and remember them along with other ancestors after their deaths.

Confucius emphasized personal qualities such as *ren, li,* and *xiao* because he believed that individuals who possessed those traits would gain influence in the larger society and in the process would lead others by their own example. Only through enlightened leadership by morally strong individuals, Confucius believed, was there any hope for the restoration of political and social order in China. Thus his goal was not simply the cultivation of personal morality for its own sake but also the creation of *junzi* who could bring order and stability to China.

Because Confucius expressed his thought in general terms, later disciples could adapt it to the particular problems of their times. Indeed, the flexibility of

SOURCES FROM THE PAST

Confucius on Good Government

Confucius never composed formal writings, but his disciples collected his often pithy remarks into a work known as the Analects *("sayings"). Referred to as "the Master" in the following excerpts from the* Analects, *Confucius consistently argued that only good men possessing moral authority could rule effectively.*

■   ■   ■

The Master said, "He who exercises government by means of his virtue may be compared to the north polar star, which keeps its place, while all the stars turn toward it. . . ."

The Master said, "If the people be led by laws, and uniformity be imposed on them by punishments, they will try to avoid the punishment, but will have no sense of shame."

"If they be led by virtue, and uniformity be provided for them by the rules of propriety, they will have the sense of shame, and moreover will become good. . . ."

The duke Ai asked, saying, "What should be done in order to secure the submission of the people?" Confucius replied, "Advance the upright and set aside the crooked, and then the people will submit. Advance the crooked and set aside the upright, and then the people will not submit."

Ji Kang asked how to cause the people to reverence their ruler, to be faithful to him, and to go on to seek virtue. The Master said, "Let him preside over them with gravity; then they will reverence him. Let him be filial and kind to all; then they will be faithful to him. Let him advance the good and teach the incompetent; then they will eagerly seek to be virtuous. . . ."

Zigong asked about government. The Master said, "The requisites of government are that there be sufficiency of food, sufficiency of military equipment, and the confidence of the people in their ruler." Zigong said, "If it cannot be helped, and one of these must be dispensed with, which of the three should be foregone first?" "The military equipment," said the Master.

Zigong again asked, "If it cannot be helped, and one of the remaining two must be dispensed with, which of them should be foregone?" The Master answered, "Part with the food. From olden times, death has been the lot of all men; but if the people have no faith in their rulers, there is no standing for the state. . . ."

Ji Kang asked Confucius about government, saying, "What do you say to killing the unprincipled for the good of the principled?" Confucius replied, "Sir, in carrying on your government, why should you use killing at all? Let your evinced desires be for what is good, and the people will be good. The relation between superiors and inferiors is like that between the wind and the grass. The grass must bend when the wind blows across it. . . ."

The Master said, "When a prince's personal conduct is correct, his government is effective without the issuing of orders. If his personal conduct is not correct, he may issue orders, but they will not be followed."

• *Compare Confucius's understanding of moral virtue with Zarathustra's notion of morality discussed in the previous chapter.*

SOURCE: James Legge, trans. *The Chinese Classics,* 7 vols. Oxford: Clarendon Press, 1893, 1:145, 146, 152, 254, 258–59, 266. (Translations slightly modified.)

Confucian thought helps to account for its remarkable longevity and influence in China. Two later disciples of Confucius—Mencius and Xunzi—illustrate especially well the ways in which Confucian thought lent itself to adaptation.

Mencius (372–289 B.C.E.) was the most learned man of his age and the principal spokesman for the Confucian school. During the Period of the Warring States, he traveled widely throughout China as a political advisor. Mencius firmly be-

Mencius

lieved that human nature was basically good; thus he placed special emphasis on the Confucian virtue of *ren* and advocated government by benevolence and humanity. This principle implied that rulers would levy light taxes, avoid wars, support education, and encourage harmony and cooperation. In his own lifetime, Mencius's advice had little practical effect, and critics charged that his views about human nature were naïve. Over the long term, however, his ideas deeply influenced the Confucian tradition. Since about the tenth century C.E., many Chinese scholars have considered Mencius the most authoritative of Confucius's early expositors.

Xunzi Like Confucius and Mencius, Xunzi (298–238 B.C.E.) was a man of immense learning, but unlike his predecessors, he also served for many years as a government administrator. His practical experience encouraged him to develop a less optimistic view of human nature than Mencius's. Xunzi believed that human beings selfishly pursued their own interests and resisted making any voluntary contribution to the larger society. He considered strong social discipline the best means to bring order to society. Thus, whereas Mencius emphasized the Confucian quality of *ren*, Xunzi emphasized *li*. He advocated the establishment of clear, well-publicized standards of conduct that would set limits on the pursuit of individual interests and punish those who neglected their obligations to the larger society.

Like Confucius and Mencius, however, Xunzi also believed that it was possible to improve human beings and restore order to society. That fundamental optimism was a basic characteristic of Confucian thought. It explains the high value that Confucian thinkers placed on education and public behavior, and it accounts also for their activist approach to public affairs. Confucians involved themselves in society: they sought government positions and made conscientious efforts to solve political and social problems and to promote harmony in public life.

Daoism

Some contemporaries, however, regarded Confucian activism as little more than misspent energy. Among the most prominent of these critics were the Daoists. Like Confucianism, Daoist thought developed in response to the turbulence of the late Zhou dynasty and the Period of the Warring States. But unlike the Confucians, the Daoists considered it pointless to waste time on social activism. Instead, the Daoists devoted their energies to reflection and introspec-

tion, in hopes that they could understand how to live in harmony with the natural principles that governed the world. The Daoists believed that over time, this approach would bring harmony to society as a whole, as people ceased to meddle in affairs that they could not understand or control.

Laozi and the Daodejing According to Chinese tradition, the founder of Daoism was a sixth-century B.C.E. sage named Laozi. Although Laozi has been credited with composing the *Daodejing (Classic of the Way and of Virtue)*, the basic exposition of Daoist beliefs, it is almost certain that the book acquired its definitive form over several centuries. After the *Daodejing*, the most important Daoist work was the *Zhuangzi*, named after its author, the philosopher Zhuangzi (369–286 B.C.E.), which provided a well-reasoned compendium of Daoist views.

The Dao Daoism represented an effort to understand the fundamental character of the world and nature. The central concept of Daoism is the elusive concept of *dao*, meaning "the way," or more specifically "the way of nature" or "the way of the cosmos." In the *Daodejing*, *dao* figures as the original force of the cosmos, an eternal principle that governs all the workings of the world. Yet the *Daodejing* envisioned *dao* as a supremely passive force and spoke of it mostly in negative terms: *dao* does nothing, and yet it accomplishes everything. *Dao* resembles water, which is soft and yielding, yet is also so powerful that it eventually erodes even the hardest rock placed in its path. *Dao* also resembles the cavity of a pot: although it is nothing more than an empty space, it makes the pot a useful tool.

Daoists believed that human beings should live in harmony with the passive and yielding nature of *dao*. To the Daoists, that meant retreating from the world of politics and administration. Ambition and activism had only brought the world to a state of chaos. The proper response to that situation was to cease frantic striving and live in as simple a manner as possible.

The Doctrine of Wuwei Thus early Daoists recognized as the chief moral virtue the trait of *wuwei*—disengagement from active involvement in worldly affairs. *Wuwei* required that individuals refrain from advanced education and personal striving, and that they live simply, unpretentiously, and in harmony with nature.

Daoism (DOW-iz'm)
Daodejing (DOW-DAY-JIHNG)
wuwei (woo-WAY)

Wuwei also had implications for state and society: the less government, the better. Instead of expansive kingdoms, the *Daodejing* envisioned a world of tiny, self-sufficient communities where people had no desire to conquer their neighbors or even to trade or visit with them.

Although Daoist thought opposed the activism of Confucianism, in fact the Daoist encouragement of self-knowledge appealed strongly to many Confucians. And, since neither Confucianism nor Daoism was an exclusive faith, it was possible for individuals to study the Confucian curriculum and take administrative posts in the government while devoting their private hours to reflection on human nature and the place of humans in the larger world—to live as Confucians by day, as it were, and Daoists by night.

Legalism

Ultimately, neither Confucian activism nor Daoist retreat was able to solve the problems of the Period of the Warring States. Order returned to China only after the emergence of a third school of thought—that of the Legalists—which promoted a practical and ruthlessly efficient approach to statecraft. Unlike the Confucians, the Legalists did not concern themselves with ethics, morality, or propriety. Unlike the Daoists, the Legalists cared nothing about the place of human beings in nature. Instead, they devoted their attention exclusively to the state, which they sought to strengthen and expand at all costs.

Legalist doctrine emerged from the insights of men who were active in Chinese political affairs during the late fourth century B.C.E. Most notable of them was Shang Yang (ca. 390–338 B.C.E.), who served as *Shang Yang and Han Feizi* chief minister to the duke of the Qin state in western China. His policies survive in a work titled *The Book of Lord Shang*. Though a clever and efficient administrator, Shang Yang was despised because of his power and ruthlessness. Thus, when his patron died, Shang's enemies at court executed him, mutilated his body, and annihilated his family. Another Legalist theorist, Han Feizi (ca. 280–233 B.C.E.) also fell afoul of ambitious men at the Qin court. During his life, Han Feizi synthesized Legalist ideas in a collection of powerful and well-argued essays on statecraft. However, his enemies forced him to commit suicide by taking poison. Thus, the Legalist state itself consumed the two foremost exponents of Legalist doctrine.

Shang Yang, Han Feizi, and other Legalists reasoned that the foundations of a state's strength were agriculture and armed forces. Since both lines of work directly advanced *Legalist Doctrine* the interests of the state, Legalists sought to channel as many individuals as possible into cultivation or military service. Meanwhile, they discouraged others from pursuing what they believed were less useful ca-

A jade statue produced about the tenth century C.E. depicts the sage Laozi on an ox. Legends reported that Laozi rode a blue ox from China to central Asia when spreading his teachings.

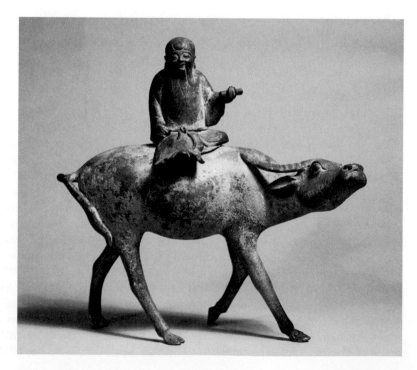

reers as merchants, entrepreneurs, scholars, educators, philosophers, poets, or artists.

The Legalists expected to harness subjects' energy by means of clear and strict laws—hence the name "Legalist." Their faith in laws distinguished the Legalists clearly from the Confucians, who relied on education and example to induce individuals to behave appropriately. The Legalists believed that this was not enough: to persuade individuals to serve the needs of the state, they imposed a strict legal regimen that clearly outlined expectations and provided severe punishment for violators. They believed that if people feared to commit small crimes, they would hesitate all the more before committing great crimes. Thus Legalists imposed harsh penalties even for minor infractions: individuals could suffer amputation of their hands or feet, for example, for disposing of trash in the street. The Legalists also established the principle of collective responsibility before the law, whereby all members of a family or a community were liable to be punished along with the actual violator.

The Legalists' principles of government did not win them much popularity. Yet Legalist doctrine lent itself readily to practical application, and Legalist principles of government quickly produced remarkable results for rulers who adopted them. In fact, Legalist methods put an end to the Period of the Warring States and brought about the unification of China.

THE UNIFICATION OF CHINA

During the Period of the Warring States, rulers of several regional states adopted elements of the Legalist program. Legalist doctrines met the most enthusiastic response in the state of Qin, in western China, where 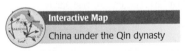 Shang Yang and Han Feizi oversaw the implementation of Legalist policies. The Qin state soon dominated its neighbors and imposed centralized imperial rule throughout China. Qin rule survived only for a few years, but the succeeding Han dynasty followed the Qin example by governing China through a centralized imperial administration.

The Qin Dynasty

During the fourth and third centuries B.C.E., the Qin state underwent a remarkable round of economic, political, and military development. Shang Yang encouraged peasant cultivators to migrate to the sparsely populated state by granting them private plots. That policy dramatically boosted agricultural production while it simultaneously weakened the economic position of the hereditary aristocratic classes. As a result, Qin *The Kingdom of Qin* rulers found fewer obstacles to establishing centralized, bureaucratic rule throughout their state. Meanwhile, they devoted their newfound wealth to the organization of a powerful army equipped with the most effective iron weapons available. During the third century B.C.E., Qin rulers attacked one state after another, absorbing each new conquest into their centralized structure, until finally they had brought China for the first time under the sway of a single state.

In 221 B.C.E., Qin Shihuangdi, the king of Qin (reigned 221–210 B.C.E.), proclaimed himself the First Emperor and decreed that his descendants *The First Emperor* would reign for thousands of generations. In fact, the dynasty lasted only fourteen years, dissolving in 207 B.C.E. because of civil insurrections. Yet the Qin dynasty had a significance out of proportion to its short life, because like the Achaemenid empire in Persia, the Qin dynasty established a tradition of centralized imperial rule that later rulers sought to emulate.

Like his ancestors in the kingdom of Qin, the First Emperor of China ignored the nobility and ruled his empire through a centralized bureaucracy. He governed from his capital at Xianyang, near the modern city of Xi'an. The remainder of China he divided into administrative provinces and districts, and he entrusted the implementation of his policies to officers of the central government who served at his

The Great Wall

pleasure. He disarmed regional military forces, and he built roads to facilitate communications and the movement of armies. He also drafted laborers by the hundreds of thousands to build a massive defensive barrier that was a precursor to the Great Wall of China.

It is likely that many Chinese welcomed the political stability introduced by the Qin dynasty, but it did not win universal acceptance. Confucians, Daoists, and others launched a vigorous campaign of criticism. In an effort *Resistance to Qin Policies* to reassert his authority, Qin Shihuangdi ordered execution for those who criticized his regime. In the year following this decree, for example, he sentenced some 460 scholars residing in the capital to be buried alive

---

Qin (chihn)
Xianyang (SHYAHN-YAHNG)

Map 6.1 The territory of China under the Qin dynasty between 221 and 207 B.C.E. Locate the defensive walls on the northern boundaries of this territory. Who or what were the walls designed to protect against, and why were they positioned on the border of the Gobi desert?

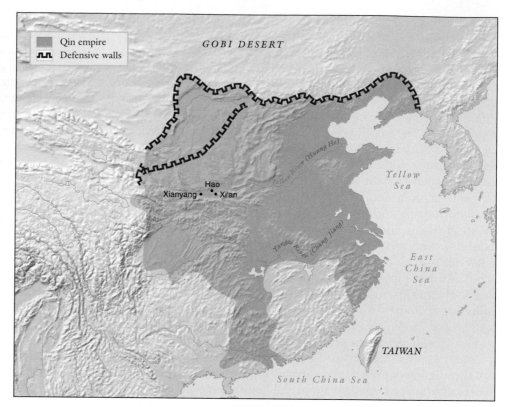

for their criticism of his regime. Qin Shihuangdi also demanded that all books of philosophy, ethics, history, and literature be burned. Although he spared some works on medicine, fortune-telling, and agriculture on the grounds that they had some utilitarian value, many classical literary or philosophical works were lost.

The First Emperor launched several initiatives that enhanced the unity of China. In keeping with his pol-
Qin Centralization icy of centralization, he standardized the laws, currencies, weights, and measures of the various regions of China. Previously, regional states had organized their own legal and economic systems, which often hampered commerce and communications across state boundaries. Uniform coinage and legal standards encouraged the integration of China's various regions into a society more tightly knit than ever before. The roads and bridges that Qin Shihuangdi built throughout his realm, like those built in other classical societies, also encouraged economic integration because they facilitated interregional commerce.

Perhaps even more important than his legal and economic policies was the First Emperor's standardization of Chinese script. Before the Qin dynasty, regional Chinese scripts had developed along different lines and had

become mutually unrecognizable. In hopes of ensuring better understanding and uniform application of his policies, Qin Shihuangdi mandated the use of a common script throughout his *Standardized Script* empire. The regions of China continued to use different spoken languages, as they do today, but they wrote those languages with a common script—just as if Europeans spoke English, French, German, and other languages but wrote them all down in Latin. In China, speakers of different languages use the same written symbols, which enables them to communicate in writing across linguistic boundaries.

In spite of his ruthlessness, Qin Shihuangdi ranks as one of the most important figures in Chinese history. The First Emperor established a precedent for centralized imperial rule, which remained the norm in China until the early twentieth century. He also pointed China in the direction of political and cultural unity, and with some periods of interruption, China has remained politically and culturally unified to the present day.

Qin Shihuangdi died in 210 B.C.E. His final resting place was a lavish tomb constructed by some seven hundred thousand drafted laborers as a permanent monument to the First Emperor. Rare and expensive

One detachment of the formidable, life-size, terra-cotta army buried in the vicinity of Qin Shihuangdi's tomb to protect the emperor after his death.

grave goods accompanied the emperor in burial, along with sacrificed slaves, concubines, and many of the craftsmen who designed and built the tomb. Qin Shihuangdi was laid to rest in an elaborate underground palace lined with bronze and protected by traps and crossbows rigged to fire at intruders. Buried in the vicinity of the tomb itself was an entire army of magnificently detailed life-size pottery figures to guard the emperor in death.

Tomb of the First Emperor

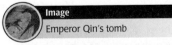

The terra-cotta army of Qin Shihuangdi protected his tomb, but it could not save his successors or his empire. The First Emperor had conscripted millions of laborers from all parts of China to work on massive public works projects. Although these projects increased productivity and promoted the integration of China's various regions, they also generated tremendous ill will among the drafted laborers.

Revolts began in the year after Qin Shihuangdi's death, and in 207 B.C.E. waves of rebels overwhelmed the Qin court, slaughtering government officials and burning state buildings. The Qin dynasty quickly dissolved in chaos.

The Early Han Dynasty

The bloody end of the Qin dynasty might well have ended the experiment with centralized imperial rule in China. However, centralized rule returned almost immediately, largely because of a determined commander named Liu Bang. Judging from the historian Sima Qian's account, Liu Bang was not a colorful or charismatic figure, but he was a persistent man and a methodical planner. He surrounded himself with brilliant advisors and enjoyed the unwavering loyalty of his troops. By 206 B.C.E. he had restored order throughout China and established himself at the head of a new dynasty.

Liu Bang

Liu Bang called the new dynasty the Han, in honor of his native land. The Han dynasty turned out to be one of the longest and most influential in all of Chinese history. It lasted for more than four hundred years, from 206 B.C.E. to 220 C.E., although for a brief period (9–23 C.E.) a usurper temporarily displaced Han rule. Thus historians conventionally divide the dynasty into the Former Han (206 B.C.E.–9 C.E.) and the Later Han (25–220 C.E.).

The Han dynasty consolidated the tradition of centralized imperial rule that the Qin dynasty had pioneered. During the Former Han, emperors ruled from Chang'an, a cosmopolitan city near modern Xi'an that became the cultural capital of China. During the Later Han, the emperors moved their capital east to Luoyang, also a cosmopolitan city and second in importance only to Chang'an throughout much of Chinese history.

During the early days of the Han dynasty, Liu Bang attempted to follow a middle path between the decentralized political alliances of the Zhou dynasty and the tightly centralized state of the Qin to save the advantages and avoid the excesses of both. On the one hand, he allotted large landholdings to members of the imperial family, in the expectation that they would provide a reliable network of support for his rule. On the other hand, he divided the empire into administrative districts governed by officials who served at the emperor's pleasure.

Early Han Policies

Liu Bang learned quickly that reliance on his family did not guarantee support for the emperor. In 200 B.C.E. an army of nomadic Xiongnu warriors besieged Liu Bang and almost captured him. He managed to escape—but without receiving the support he had expected from his family members. From that point forward, Liu Bang and his successors followed a policy of centralization. They reclaimed lands from family members, absorbed those lands into the imperial domain, and entrusted political responsibilities to an administrative bureaucracy. Thus, despite a brief flirtation with a decentralized government, the Han dynasty left as its principal political legacy a tradition of centralized imperial rule.

Much of the reason for the Han dynasty's success was the long reign of the dynasty's greatest and most energetic emperor, Han Wudi, the "Martial Emperor," who occupied the throne for fifty-four years, from 141 to 87 B.C.E. Han Wudi ruled his empire with vision and vigor. He pursued two policies in particular: administrative centralization and imperial expansion.

The Martial Emperor: Han Wudi

Domestically, Han Wudi worked strenuously to increase the authority and prestige of the central government. He built an enormous bureaucracy to administer his empire, and he relied on Legalist principles of government. He also continued the Qin policy of building roads and canals to facilitate trade and communication between China's regions. To finance the vast machinery of his government, he levied taxes on agriculture, trade, and craft industries, and he established imperial monopolies on the production of essential goods such as iron and salt. In building such an enormous governmental structure, Han Wudi faced a serious problem of recruitment. He needed thousands of reliable, intelligent, educated individuals to run his bureaucracy, but there was no institutionalized educational system in China that could provide a continuous supply of such people.

Han Centralization

Han Wudi addressed that problem in 124 B.C.E. by establishing an imperial university that prepared young men for government service. Personally, the Martial Emperor cared little for learning. In that respect he resembled all the other early Han emperors: Liu Bang once emptied his bladder in the distinctive cap worn by Confucian scholars in order to demonstrate his contempt for academic pursuits! Yet Han Wudi recognized that the success of his efforts at bureaucratic centralization would depend on a corps of educated officeholders. The imperial university took Confucianism—the only Chinese cultural tradition developed enough to provide rigorous intellectual discipline—as the basis for its curriculum. Ironically, then, although he relied on Legalist principles of government, Han Wudi ensured the long-term survival of the Confucian tradition by establishing it as the official imperial ideology.

The Confucian Educational System

While he moved aggressively to centralize power and authority at home, Han Wudi pursued an equally vigorous foreign policy of imperial expansion. He invaded northern Vietnam and Korea, subjected them to Han rule, and brought them into the orbit of Chinese society. He ruled both lands through a Chinese-style government, and Confucian values followed the Han armies into the new colonies. Over the course of the centuries, the educational systems of both northern Vietnam and Korea drew their inspiration almost entirely from Confucianism.

Han Imperial Expansion

The greatest foreign challenge that Han Wudi faced came from the Xiongnu, a nomadic people from the steppes of central Asia. Like most of the other

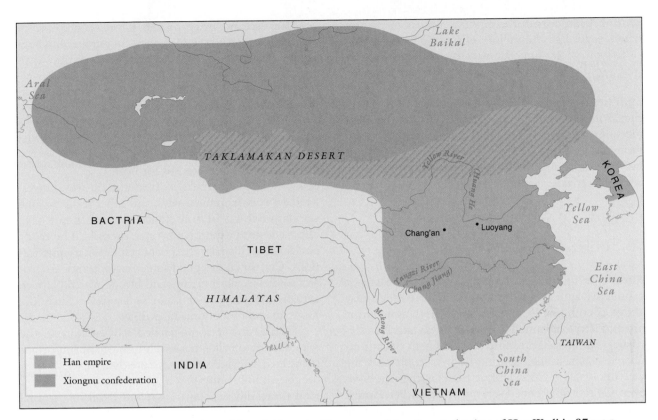

Map 6.2 **Boundaries of the Han empire and its neighbor, the Xiongnu confederation, at the time of Han Wudi in 87** B.C.E. Compare this map with Map 6.1. Notice the extension of Chinese territory to the Taklamakan desert in the west and to Korea in the east. What was the strategic value of such territorial claims?

nomadic peoples of central Asia, the Xiongnu were superb horsemen. Although their weaponry was not *The Xiongnu* as sophisticated as that of the Chinese, their mobility offered the Xiongnu a distinct advantage. When they could not satisfy their needs through peaceful trade, they mounted sudden raids into villages or trading areas, where they commandeered supplies and then rapidly departed. Because they had no cities or settled places to defend, the Xiongnu could quickly disperse when confronted by a superior force.

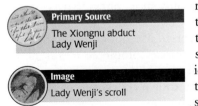

Primary Source

The Xiongnu abduct Lady Wenji

Image

Lady Wenji's scroll

During the reign of Maodun (210–174 B.C.E.), their most successful leader, the Xiongnu ruled a vast federation of nomadic peoples that stretched from the Aral Sea to the Yellow Sea. Maodun brought strict military discipline to the Xiongnu. According to Sima Qian, Maodun once instructed his forces to shoot their arrows at whatever target he himself selected. He aimed in succession at his favorite horse, one of his wives, and his father's best horse, and he summarily executed those who failed to discharge their arrows. When his forces reliably followed his orders, Maodun targeted his father, who immediately fell under a hail of arrows, leaving Maodun as the Xiongnu chief.

With its highly disciplined army, the Xiongnu empire was a source of concern to the Han emperors. During the early days of the dynasty, they attempted to pacify the Xiongnu by paying them tribute—providing them with food and finished goods in hopes that they would refrain from mounting raids in China—or by arranging marriages between the ruling houses of the two peoples in hopes of establishing peaceful diplomatic relations. Neither method succeeded for long.

Ultimately, Han Wudi decided to go on the offensive against the Xiongnu. He invaded central Asia with vast armies and brought much of the Xiongnu empire under Chinese military control. He pacified a long central Asian corridor extending almost to Bactria, which served as the lifeline of a trade network that linked much of the Eurasian landmass. He even planted colonies of Chinese cultivators in the oasis communities of central Asia. As a result of those efforts, the Xiongnu empire soon fell into disarray. For the moment, the Han state enjoyed uncontested hegemony in both east Asia and central Asia. Before long, however, economic and social problems within China brought serious problems for the Han dynasty itself.

Han Expansion into Central Asia

FROM ECONOMIC PROSPERITY TO SOCIAL DISORDER

Already during the Xia, Shang, and Zhou dynasties, a productive agricultural economy supported the emergence of complex society in China. High agricultural productivity continued during the Qin and Han dynasties, and it supported the development of craft industries such as the forging of iron tools and the weaving of silk textiles. During the Han dynasty, however, China experienced serious social and economic problems as land became concentrated in the hands of a small, wealthy elite class. Social tensions generated banditry, rebellion, and even the temporary deposition of the Han state itself. Although Han rulers regained the throne, they presided over a much-weakened realm. By the early third century C.E., social and political problems brought the Han dynasty to an end.

Productivity and Prosperity during the Former Han

The structure of Chinese society during the Qin and Han dynasties was very similar to that of the Zhou era. Patriarchal households averaged five inhabitants, although several generations of aristocratic families sometimes lived together in large compounds. During the Han dynasty, moralists sought to enhance the authority of patriarchal family heads by emphasizing the importance of filial piety and women's subordination to their menfolk. A widely read treatise titled *Admonitions for Women,* for example, emphasized humility, obedience, subservience, and devotion to their husbands as the virtues most appropriate for women. To Confucian moralists and government authorities alike, orderly, patriarchal families were the foundations of a stable society.

Patriarchal Social Order

The vast majority of the Chinese population worked in the countryside cultivating grains and vegetables, which they harvested in larger quantities than ever before. The increased agricultural surplus allowed many Chinese to produce fine manufactured goods and to engage in trade.

During the Han dynasty, the iron industry entered a period of rapid growth. Han artisans experimented with production techniques and learned to craft fine utensils for both domestic and military uses. Iron pots, stoves, knives, needles, axes, hammers, saws, and other tools became standard fixtures in households that could not have afforded more expensive bronze utensils. The ready availability of iron also had important military implications. Craftsmen designed suits of iron armor to protect soldiers against arrows and blows, which helps to explain the success of Chinese armies against the Xiongnu and other nomadic peoples.

Iron Metallurgy

Textile production—particularly sericulture, the manufacture of silk—became an especially important industry. The origins of sericulture date to the fourth millennium B.C.E., but only in Han times did sericulture expand from its original home in the Yellow River valley to most parts of China. Although silkworms inhabited much of Eurasia, Chinese silk was especially fine because of advanced sericulture techniques. Chinese producers bred their silkworms, fed them on finely chopped mulberry leaves, and carefully unraveled their cocoons so as to obtain long fibers of raw silk which they wove into light, strong, lustrous fabrics. (In other lands, producers relied on wild silkworms that ate a variety of leaves and chewed through their cocoons, leaving only short fibers that yielded lower-quality fabrics.) Chinese silk became a prized commodity in India, Persia, Mesopotamia, and even the distant Roman empire. Commerce in silk and other products led to the establishment of an intricate network of trade routes known collectively as the silk roads (discussed in chapter 9).

Silk Textiles

Interactive Map
The silk roads

While expanding the iron and silk industries, Han craftsmen also invented paper. In earlier times Chinese scribes had written mostly on bamboo strips and silk fabrics, but about 100 C.E. Chinese craftsmen began to fashion hemp, bark, and textile fibers into sheets of paper. Although wealthy elites continued to read books written on silk rolls, paper soon became the preferred medium for most writing.

Paper

Clay model of an aristocratic house of the sort inhabited by a powerful clan during the Han dynasty. This model came from a tomb near the city of Guangzhou in southern China.

High agricultural productivity supported rapid demographic growth and general prosperity during the early part of the Han dynasty. Historians

Population Growth

estimate that about 220 B.C.E., just after the founding of the Qin dynasty, the Chinese population was twenty million. By the year 9 C.E., at the end of the Former Han dynasty, it had tripled to sixty million. Meanwhile, taxes claimed only a small portion of production, yet state granaries bulged so much that their contents sometimes spoiled before they could be consumed.

Economic and Social Difficulties

In spite of general prosperity, China began to experience economic and social difficulties in the Former Han period. The military adventures and the central Asian policy of Han Wudi caused severe economic strain. To finance his ventures, Han Wudi raised taxes and confiscated land and personal property from wealthy individuals, sometimes on the pretext that they had violated imperial laws. Those measures discouraged investment in manufacturing and trading enterprises, which in turn had a dampening effect on the larger economy.

Distinctions between rich and poor hardened during the course of the Han dynasty. Wealthy individuals wore fine silk garments and ate rich foods, whereas the poor classes

Social Tensions

made do with rough hemp clothing and a diet of mostly grain. By the first century B.C.E., social and economic differences had generated serious tensions, and peasants in hard-pressed regions began to organize rebellions in hopes of gaining a larger share of Han society's resources.

A particularly difficult problem concerned the distribution of land. Economic problems forced many small landowners to sell their property

Land Distribution

under unfavorable conditions or even to forfeit it in exchange for cancellation of their debts. In extreme cases, individuals had to sell themselves and their families into slavery to satisfy their creditors. Owners of large estates not only increased the size of their holdings by absorbing the property of their less fortunate neighbors but also increased the efficiency of their operations by employing cheap labor.

By the end of the first century B.C.E., land had accumulated in the hands of a relatively small number of individuals who owned vast estates, while ever-increasing numbers of peasant cultivators led difficult lives with few prospects for improvement. Landless peasants became restive, and Chinese society faced growing problems of banditry and sporadic rebellion.

Tensions came to a head during the early first century C.E. when a powerful and respected Han minister named Wang Mang undertook a thoroughgoing program of reform. In 6 C.E. a two-year-old boy inherited the Han impe-

The Reign of Wang Mang

rial throne. Because the boy was unable to govern, Wang Mang served as his regent. Many officials regarded Wang as more capable than members of the Han family and urged him to claim the imperial honor for himself. In 9 C.E. he did just that: announcing that the mandate of heaven had passed from the Han to his own family, he seized the throne. Wang Mang then introduced a series of wide-ranging reforms that have prompted historians to refer to him as the "socialist emperor."

The most important reforms concerned landed property: Wang Mang limited the amount of land that a family could hold and ordered officials to break

In Han times the wealthiest classes enjoyed the privilege of being buried in suits of jade plaques sewn together with gold threads, like the burial dress of Liu Sheng, who died in 113 B.C.E. at Manzheng in Hebei Province. Legend held that jade prevented decomposition of the deceased's body. Scholars have estimated that a jade burial suit like this one required ten years' worth of labor.

up large estates, redistribute them, and provide landless individuals with property to cultivate. Despite his good intentions, the socialist emperor attempted to impose his policy without adequate preparation and communication. The result was confusion: landlords resisted a policy that threatened their holdings, and even peasants found its application inconsistent and unsatisfactory. After several years of chaos, in 23 C.E. a coalition of disgruntled landlords and desperate peasants ended both his dynasty and his life.

The Later Han Dynasty

Within two years a recovered Han dynasty returned to power, but it ruled over a weakened realm. Nevertheless, during the early years of the Later Han, emperors ruled vigorously in the manner of Liu Bang and Han Wudi. They regained control of the centralized administration and reorganized the state bureaucracy. They also maintained the Chinese presence in central Asia, continued to keep the Xiongnu in submission, and exercised firm control over the silk roads.

However, the Later Han emperors did not seriously address the problem of land distribution that had helped to bring down the Former Han dynasty.

The wealthy classes still lived in relative luxury while peasants worked under difficult conditions. The empire continued to suffer the effects of banditry and rebellions organized by desperate peasants with few opportunities to improve their lot.

In addition, the Later Han emperors were unable to prevent the development of factions at court that paralyzed the central government. Factions of imperial family members, Confucian scholar-bureaucrats, and court *Collapse of the Han Dynasty* eunuchs sought to increase their influence, protect their own interests, and destroy their rivals. On several occasions relations between the various factions became so strained that they made war against one another. In 189 C.E., for example, a faction led by an imperial relative descended on the Han palace and slaughtered more than two thousand eunuchs in an effort to destroy them as a political force. In that respect the attack succeeded. From the unmeasured violence of the operation, however, it is clear that the Later Han dynasty had reached a point of internal weakness from which it could not easily recover. Indeed, early in the next century, the central government disintegrated, and for almost four centuries China remained divided into several large regional kingdoms.

SUMMARY

The Qin state lasted for a short fourteen years, but it opened a new era in Chinese history. Qin conquerors imposed unified rule on a series of politically independent kingdoms and launched an ambitious program to forge culturally distinct regions into a larger Chinese society. The Han dynasty endured for more than four centuries and largely completed the project of unifying China. Han rulers built a centralized bureaucracy that administered a unified empire, thus establishing a precedent for centralized imperial rule in China. They also entered into a close alliance with Confucian moralists who organized a system of advanced education that provided recruits for the imperial bureaucracy. Moreover, on the basis of a highly productive economy stimulated by technological innovations, Han rulers projected Chinese influence abroad to Korea, Vietnam, and central Asia. Thus, like classical societies in Persia, India, and the Mediterranean basin, Han China produced a set of distinctive political and cultural traditions that shaped Chinese and neighboring societies over the long term.

CHRONOLOGY

SIXTH CENTURY B.C.E. (?)	Laozi
551–479 B.C.E.	Confucius
403–221 B.C.E.	Period of the Warring States
390–338 B.C.E.	Shang Yang
372–289 B.C.E.	Mencius
298–238 B.C.E.	Xunzi
280–233 B.C.E.	Han Feizi
221–207 B.C.E.	Qin dynasty
206 B.C.E.–9 C.E.	Former Han dynasty
141–87 B.C.E.	Reign of Han Wudi
9–23 C.E.	Reign of Wang Mang
25–220 C.E.	Later Han dynasty

FOR FURTHER READING

Thomas J. Barfield. *The Perilous Frontier: Nomadic Empires and China.* Cambridge, Mass., 1989. A provocative analysis of the relations between Chinese and central Asian peoples.

Sebastian De Grazia, ed. *Masters of Chinese Political Thought from the Beginnings to the Han Dynasty.* New York, 1973. A valuable collection of primary sources in translation, all of them bearing on political themes.

Mark Elvin. *The Pattern of the Chinese Past.* Stanford, 1973. A remarkable analysis of Chinese history by an economic historian who brings a comparative perspective to his work.

Cho-yun Hsu. *Han Agriculture: The Formation of Early Chinese Agrarian Economy (206 B.C.–A.D. 220).* Seattle, 1980. Studies the development of intensive agriculture in Han China and provides English translations of more than two hundred documents illustrating the conditions of rural life.

Michael Loewe. *Everyday Life in Early Imperial China.* London, 1968. Deals with the social, economic, and cultural history of China during the Han dynasty.

Victor H. Mair, trans. *Tao Te Ching: The Classic Book of Integrity and the Way.* New York, 1990. A fresh and lively translation of the Daoist classic *Daodejing,* based on recently discovered manuscripts.

Frederick W. Mote. *Intellectual Foundations of China.* 2nd ed. New York, 1989. A compact and concise introduction to the cultural history of classical China.

Michele Pirazzoli-t'Serstevens. *The Han Dynasty.* Trans. by J. Seligman. New York, 1982. An excellent and well-illustrated survey of Han China that draws on archaeological discoveries.

Benjamin I. Schwartz. *The World of Thought in Ancient China.* Cambridge, Mass., 1985. A synthesis of classical Chinese thought by a leading scholar.

Arthur Waley, trans. *The Analects of Confucius.* New York, 1938. An English version of Confucius's sayings by a gifted translator.

CHAPTER 7

State, Society, and the Quest for Salvation in India

The earliest description of India by a foreigner came from the pen of a Greek ambassador named Megasthenes. As the diplomatic representative of the Seleucid emperor, Megasthenes lived in India for many years during the late fourth and early third centuries B.C.E., and he traveled throughout much of northern India. Although Megasthenes' book, the *Indika*, has long been lost, many quotations from it survive in Greek and Latin literature. These fragments clearly show that Megasthenes had great respect for the Indian land, people, and society.

Like travel writers of all times, Megasthenes included a certain amount of spurious information in his account of India. He wrote, for example, of ants the size of foxes that mined gold from the earth and fiercely defended their hoards from any humans who

tried to steal them. Only by distracting them with slabs of meat, Megasthenes said, could humans safely make away with their treasure. He also reported races of monstrous human beings: some with no mouth who survived by breathing in the odors of fruits, flowers, and roots, others with the heads of dogs who communicated by barking.

Beyond the tall tales, Megasthenes offered a great deal of reliable information. He portrayed India as a fertile land that supported two harvests of grain per year. He described the capital of Pataliputra as a rectangle-shaped city situated along the Ganges River and surrounded by a moat and a massive timber wall with 570 towers and sixty-four gates. He mentioned large armies that used elephants as war animals. He pointed out the strongly

OPPOSITE PAGE: *Manuscript depicting the birth of Mahavira, founder of Jainism.*

hierarchical character of Indian society. He noted that two main schools of "philosophers" (Hindus and Buddhists) enjoyed special prominence as well as exemption from taxes, and he described the ascetic lifestyles and vegetarian diets followed by particularly devout individuals. In short, Megasthenes portrayed India as a wealthy land that supported a distinctive society with well-established cultural traditions.

In India as in Persia and China, the centuries after 500 B.C.E. witnessed the development of a classical society whose influence has persisted over the centuries. Its most prominent features were a well-defined social structure, which left individuals with few doubts about their position and role in society, and several popular religious traditions that helped to shape Indian beliefs and values. Two religions, Buddhism and Hinduism, also appealed strongly to peoples beyond the subcontinent.

For the most part, classical India fell under the sway of regional kingdoms rather than centralized empires. Yet the empires that did arise were crucial for the consolidation of Indian cultural traditions, because they sponsored cultural leaders and promoted their ideals throughout the subcontinent and beyond. The spread of Buddhism is a case in point: imperial support helped the faith secure its position in India and attract converts in other lands. Thus, even in the absence of a continuous imperial tradition like that of Persia or China, the social and cultural traditions of classical India not only shaped the lives and experiences of the subcontinent's inhabitants but also influenced peoples in distant lands.

THE FORTUNES OF EMPIRE IN CLASSICAL INDIA

Following their migrations to India after 1500 B.C.E., the Aryans established a series of small kingdoms throughout the subcontinent. By the sixth century B.C.E., wars of expansion between these small kingdoms had resulted in the consolidation of several large regional kingdoms that dominated much of the subcontinent. Despite strenuous efforts, none of these kingdoms was able to establish hegemony over the others until the classical era, when the Mauryan and the Gupta dynasties founded centralized, imperial states that embraced much of India. However, neither empire survived long enough to establish centralized rule as a lasting feature of Indian political life.

The Mauryan Dynasty and the Temporary Unification of India

The unification of India came about partly as a result of intrusion from beyond the subcontinent. About 520 B.C.E. the Persian emperor Darius crossed the Hindu Kush Mountains, conquered parts of northwestern India, and made the kingdom of Gandhara in the northern Punjab (the northern part of modern-day Pakistan) a province of the Achaemenid empire. Almost two centuries later, in 327 B.C.E., after overrunning the Persian empire, Alexander of Macedon crossed the Indus River and crushed the states he found there. Alexander remained in India for only two years, and he did not make a deep impression on the Punjabi people. Yet his campaign had an important effect on Indian history, since he created a political vacuum in northwestern India by destroying the existing states and then withdrawing his own forces.

Poised to fill the vacuum was the dynamic kingdom of Magadha, located in the central portion of the Ganges plain. By about 500 B.C.E. Magadha had emerged as the most important state in northeastern India. During the next two centuries, the kings of Magadha conquered the neighboring states and gained control of Indian commerce passing through the Ganges valley as well as overseas trade between India and Burma passing across the Bay of Bengal. The withdrawal of Alexander from the Punjab presented Magadha with a rare opportunity to expand.

Kingdom of Magadha

During the late 320s B.C.E., an ambitious adventurer named Chandragupta Maurya exploited that opportunity and laid the foundation for the Mauryan empire, the first state to bring a centralized and unified government to most of the Indian subcontinent. Chandragupta began by seizing control of small, remote regions of Magadha and then worked his way gradually toward the center. By 321

Chandragupta Maurya

Interactive Map
Mauryan & Gupta empires

B.C.E. he had overthrown the ruling dynasty and consolidated his hold on the kingdom. He then moved into the Punjab and brought northwestern India under his control. Next he ventured beyond the Indus River and conquered the Greek state in Bactria. By the end of the fourth century B.C.E., Chandragupta's empire embraced all of northern India from the Indus to the Ganges.

Map 7.1   Mauryan and Gupta empires from 321 B.C.E. **until 550** C.E. Observe the trade routes that connected both empires to the west and east, via both land and sea. How might these trade routes have affected the power of Mauryan and Gupta rulers? How might they have affected common people in south Asia?

Chandragupta's Government

A careful and systematic advisor named Kautalya devised procedures for the governance of Chandragupta's realm. Some of Kautalya's advice survives in the ancient Indian political handbook known as the *Arthashastra*. The *Arthashastra* outlined methods of administering the empire, overseeing trade and agriculture, collecting taxes, maintaining order, conducting foreign relations, and waging war. Kautalya also advised Chandragupta to make abundant use of spies, and he even included prostitutes in his stable of informants. Like the emperors of Persia and China, Chandragupta and Kautalya built a bureaucratic administrative system that enabled them to implement policies throughout the state.

Tradition holds that Chandragupta abdicated his throne to become a monk and led such an ascetic life that he starved himself to death. Whether that report

Arthashastra (UHRR-th-sha-strah)

is true or not, it is certain that his son succeeded him in 297 B.C.E. and added most of southern India to the growing empire. The high point of the Mauryan empire, however, came during the reign of Chandragupta's grandson Ashoka.

Ashoka Maurya

Ashoka began his reign (268–232 B.C.E.) as a conqueror. When he came to power, the only major region that remained independent of the Mauryan empire was the kingdom of Kalinga (modern Orissa) in the east-central part of the subcontinent. Kalinga was desirable territory for Ashoka because it controlled both land and sea trade routes between the Ganges plain and southern India. Thus Ashoka's first major undertaking as emperor was to conquer Kalinga and bring it under Mauryan control, which he did in a bloody campaign in 260 B.C.E. By Ashoka's estimate, 100,000 Kalingans died in the fighting, 150,000 were driven from their homes, and untold numbers of others perished in the ruined land.

In spite of that campaign, Ashoka is much better known as a governor than as a conqueror. With

Kalinga subdued, Ashoka ruled almost the entire subcontinent—only the southernmost region escaped his control—and he turned his attention to the responsible government of his realm. As heir to the administrative structure that Chandragupta and Kautalya had instituted, Ashoka ruled through a tightly organized bureaucracy. He established his capital at the fortified and cosmopolitan city of Pataliputra (near modern Patna), where a central administration developed policies for the whole empire. A central treasury oversaw the efficient collection of taxes—a hallmark of Kautalya's influence—which supported legions of officials, accountants, clerks, soldiers, and other imperial employees. Ashoka communicated his policies throughout his realm by inscribing edicts in natural stone formations or on pillars that he ordered erected. In those promulgations, known as the rock and pillar edicts, Ashoka issued imperial decrees, encouraged his subjects to observe Buddhist values, and expressed his intention to serve as a fair, just, and humane ruler.

As a result of Ashoka's policies, the various regions of India became well integrated, and the subcontinent

benefited from both an expanding economy and a stable government. Ashoka encouraged the expansion of agriculture by building irrigation systems. He encouraged trade by building roads, most notably a highway of more than 1,600 kilometers (1,000 miles) linking Pataliputra with Taxila, the chief political and commercial center of northern India, which offered access to Bactria, Persia, and other points west. Ashoka also provided comforts for administrators, merchants, and other travelers by planting banyan trees to offer shade, digging wells, and establishing inns along the roads.

Ashoka's policies did not long survive his rule, nor did his empire. Ashoka died in 232 B.C.E., and decline set in almost immediately. During its later years the Mauryan empire suffered from acute financial and economic difficulties. The empire depended on a strong army and a large corps of officials to administer imperial policy. Salaries for soldiers and bureaucrats were very expensive, and soon administrative costs outstripped the revenues that flowed into the central treasury. Because of their financial difficulties, the later Mauryan emperors were unable to hold the realm together. By about 185 B.C.E., just fifty years after Ashoka's death, the Mauryan empire had disappeared.

Decline of the Mauryan Empire

As a symbol of his rule, Ashoka had this sculpture of four lions mounted atop a column about 20 meters (66 feet) tall. The lion capital is the official symbol of the modern Republic of India.

The Emergence of Regional Kingdoms and the Revival of Empire

Although the Mauryan empire came to an end, India did not crumble into anarchy. Instead, local rulers formed a series of kingdoms that brought order to large regions. Although regional kingdoms emerged throughout the subcontinent, historical records and archaeological excavations have thrown clearest light on developments in northern India. For almost two centuries after the collapse of the Mauryan empire, northwestern India fell under the rule of Greek-speaking conquerors from Bactria—Alexander of Macedon's imperial heirs who had mingled with local populations since establishing an independent Bactrian kingdom in the third century B.C.E. Bactria was a thriving commercial center linking lands from China in the east to the Mediterranean basin in the west, so Bactrian rule had the effect of promoting cross-cultural interaction and exchange in northern India. Large volumes of trade provided sources of revenue for the Bactrian rulers, and the city of Taxila flourished because of its strategic loca-

Bactrian Rule in Northwestern India

tion on trade routes leading from northern India to Bactria.

Beginning in the late second century B.C.E., several groups of nomadic conquerors from central Asia attacked Bactria and eventually put an end to the Indo-Greek kingdom there. The most successful of those conquerors were the Kushans, who ruled a sizable empire embracing much of northern India and central Asia from about 1 to 300 C.E. Under Kanishka, the most prominent of the Kushan emperors (reigned 78–103 C.E.), the Kushan empire embraced modern-day Pakistan, Afghanistan, and northern India to Gujarat and the central part of the Ganges valley. Like the Indo-Greek Bactrians, the Kushans facilitated commerce between India and lands to the north. Indeed, the Kushan empire played a crucial role in the silk roads network (discussed in chapter 9) by pacifying much of the large region between Persia and China, thus making it possible for merchants to travel safely across long distances.

The Kushan Empire

In about 320 C.E., a new power—the Guptas—arose in the Ganges region and established a dynamic kingdom. Like the Mauryas, the Guptas based their state in Magadha, a crucial region because of its wealth, its dominance of the Ganges valley, and its role as intermediary between the various regions of the subcontinent. The empire was founded by Chandra Gupta (not related to Chandragupta Maurya), who forged alliances with powerful families in the Ganges region. His successors, Samudra Gupta (reigned 335–375 C.E.) and Chandra Gupta II (reigned 375–415 C.E.), took the former Mauryan capital of Pataliputra as their own, conquered many of the regional kingdoms of India, and established tributary alliances with others that elected not to fight. Only the Deccan Plateau and the southernmost part of the subcontinent remained outside the orbit of Gupta influence.

The Gupta Dynasty

The Gupta empire was somewhat smaller in size than the Mauryan, and it also differed considerably in organization. Ashoka had insisted on knowing the details of regional affairs, which he closely monitored from his court at Pataliputra. The Guptas left local government and administration, and even the making of basic policy, in the hands of their allies in the various regions of their empire. Nevertheless, during the late fourth and early fifth centuries C.E., the Gupta dynasty brought stability and prosperity to much of the subcontinent.

The Guptas were eventually overcome, however, by the White Huns, a nomadic people from central Asia. For the first half of the fifth century, the Guptas repelled the Huns as they tried to invade across the Hindu Kush mountains from Bactria, but the defense cost them dearly in resources and eventually weakened their state. By the end of the fifth century, the Huns moved across the Hindu Kush almost at will and had established several kingdoms in northern and western India.

Gupta Decline

The Gupta dynasty continued in name only: regional governors progressively usurped imperial rights and powers, and contemporary documents do not even record the names of all the later Gupta emperors. Once again, imperial government survived only for a short term in India. Not until the establishment of the Mughal dynasty in the sixteenth century C.E. did any state rule as much of India as the Mauryan and Gupta empires ruled. Memories of empire remained, to be sure, but for the most part large regional kingdoms dominated political life in India during the millennium between the Gupta and the Mughal dynasties.

ECONOMIC DEVELOPMENT AND SOCIAL DISTINCTIONS

After spreading through the subcontinent, Aryan migrants turned increasingly from herding to agriculture. Once they learned the techniques of iron metallurgy after about 1000 B.C.E., they used iron axes and tools to advance into previously inaccessible regions, notably the jungle-covered valley of the Ganges River. Agricultural surpluses from these fertile lands supported large-scale states such as the regional kingdoms and the Mauryan and Gupta empires that organized Indian public life. Agricultural surpluses also encouraged the emergence of towns, the growth of trade, and further development of the caste system.

Towns and Trade

After about 600 B.C.E. towns dotted the Indian countryside, especially in the northwestern corner of the subcontinent. These towns served the needs of a productive agricultural society by providing manufactured products for local consumption—pots, textiles, iron tools, and other metal utensils—as well as luxury goods such as jewelry destined for the wealthy and elite classes.

Gupta (GOOP-tah)

Flourishing towns maintained marketplaces and encouraged the development of trade. Within the subcontinent itself trade was most active along the Ganges River, although trade routes also passed through the Ganges delta east to Burma and down the east Indian coast to the Deccan and southern India. Roads built by Ashoka also facilitated overland commerce within the subcontinent.

Meanwhile, the volume of long-distance trade also grew as large imperial states in China, southwest Asia, and the Mediterranean basin provided a political foundation enabling merchants to deal with their counterparts in distant lands. From India, long-distance trade passed overland in two directions: through the Hindu Kush mountains and the Gandharan capital of Taxila to Persia and the Mediterranean basin, and across the silk roads of central Asia to markets in China. Cotton, aromatics, black pepper, pearls, and gems were the principal Indian exports, in exchange for which Indian merchants imported horses and bullion from western lands and silk from China.

Long-Distance Trade

During the Mauryan era merchants continued to use land routes, but they increasingly turned to the sea to transport their goods. Seaborne trade benefited especially from the rhythms of the monsoon winds that govern weather and the seasons in the Indian Ocean basin. During the spring and summer, the winds blow from the southwest, and during the fall and winter, they come from the northeast. Once mariners recognized these rhythms, they could sail easily and safely before the wind to any part of the Indian Ocean basin.

Trade in the Indian Ocean Basin

As early as the fifth century B.C.E., Indian merchants had traveled to the islands of Indonesia and the southeast Asian mainland, where they exchanged pearls, cotton, black pepper, and Indian manufactured goods for spices and exotic local products. Many of those goods then traveled west through the Arabian Sea to the lands bordering the Persian Gulf and the Red Sea. Indian products also found markets in the Mediterranean basin. Indian pepper became so popular there that the Romans established direct commercial relations and built several trading settlements in southern India. Archaeologists in southern India have unearthed hoards of Roman coins that testify to the large volume of trade between classical India and Mediterranean lands.

Jewel-bedecked flying goddesses drop flowers on the earth from their perch in the heavens. Their gems and personal adornments reflect the tastes of upper-class women during the Gupta dynasty. This painting on a rock wall, produced about the sixth century C.E., survives in modern Sri Lanka.

Family Life and the Caste System

In the midst of urban growth and economic development, Indian moralists sought to promote stability by encouraging respect for strong patriarchal families and

Gender Relations to promote the maintenance of a social order in which all members played well-defined roles. Although most people lived with members of their nuclear family, among the higher castes several generations of a family often lived in large compounds ruled by powerful patriarchs. Literary works suggest that women were largely subordinate to men. The two great Indian epics, the *Mahabharata* and the *Ramayana*, commonly portrayed women as weak-willed and emotional creatures and exalted wives who devoted themselves to their husbands.

During the early centuries C.E., patriarchal dominance became more pronounced in India. By the Gupta era child marriage was common: when girls were eight or nine years of age, their parents betrothed them to men in their twenties. Formal marriage took place just after the girls reached puberty. Wives often came to dominate domestic affairs in their households, but the practice of child marriage placed them under the control of older men and encouraged them to devote themselves to family matters rather than to public affairs in the larger society.

After their arrival in India, the Aryans recognized four main castes, or classes of people: priests *(brah-*

Social Order *mins),* warriors and aristocrats *(kshatri-yas),* peasants and merchants *(vaishyas),* and serfs *(shudras). Brahmins* in particular endorsed this social order, which brought them honor, prestige, and sometimes considerable wealth as well.

However, as trade and industrial activity expanded, new groups of artisans, craftsmen, and merchants ap-

Castes and Guilds peared, many of whom did not fit easily into the established structure. Individuals working in the same craft or trade usually joined together to form a guild, a corporate body that supervised prices and wages in a given industry and provided for the welfare of members and their families. Guild members lived in the same quarter of town, socialized with one another, intermarried, and cared for the group's widows, orphans, and needy.

In effect, the guilds functioned as subcastes based on occupation, known as *jati.* These *jati,* in turn, as-

Buddhist art often depicted individuals as models of proper social relationships. Here a sculpture from a Buddhist temple at Karli, produced about the first century C.E., represents an ideal Buddhist married couple.

sumed much of the responsibility for maintaining social order in India. *Jati* regularly organized their own courts, through which they disciplined members, resolved differences, and regulated community affairs. Individuals who did not abide by group rules were liable to expulsion from the community. Thus Indian guilds and *jati* performed services that central governments provided in other lands. The tendency for individuals and their families to associate closely with others of the same occupation remained a prominent feature of Indian society well into modern times.

Beyond encouraging further development of the caste system, economic development in the subcontinent also generated tremendous wealth, which posed a serious challenge to the social order that arose in India follow-

Wealth and the Social Order

ing the Aryan migrations. Traditional social theory accorded special honor to the *brahmins* and the *kshatriyas* because of the worthy lives they had led during previous incarnations and the heavy responsibilities they assumed as priests, warriors, and rulers during their

---

Mahabharata (mah-hah-BAH-'rah-tah)

Ramayana (rah-MAY-yuh-nah)

vaishyas (VEYESH-yuhs)

shudras (SHOO-druhs)

current incarnations. Members of the *vaishya* and *shudra* castes, on the other hand, had the obligation to work as directed by the higher castes. During the centuries after 600 B.C.E., however, trade and industry brought prosperity to many *vaishyas* and even *shudras,* who sometimes became wealthier and more influential in society than their *brahmin* and *kshatriya* contemporaries.

Economic development and social change in classical India had profound implications for the established cultural as well as the social order. The beliefs, values, and rituals that were meaningful in early Aryan society seemed increasingly irrelevant during the centuries after 600 B.C.E. Along with emerging towns, growing trade, increasing wealth, and a developing social structure, classical India saw the appearance of new religions that addressed the needs of the changing times.

RELIGIONS OF SALVATION IN CLASSICAL INDIA

Ancient Indian religion revolved around ritual sacrifices offered by *brahmin* priests. Because the *brahmins* performed services deemed crucial for the survival of society, they enjoyed exemption from taxation and received generous gifts in return for their services. As the Indian economy developed, however, those services seemed less meaningful than they had before, especially to the newly wealthy classes of merchants and artisans from the lower castes.

During the sixth and fifth centuries B.C.E., new religions and philosophies rejected the *brahmins'* cults and appealed to the interests of new social classes. Some of them tended toward atheistic materialism: members of the Charvaka sect, for example, believed that the gods were figments of the imagination, that *brahmins* were charlatans who enriched themselves by hoodwinking others, and that human beings came from dust and returned to dust like any other animal in the natural world. Others, such as the Jains, the Buddhists, and the Hindus, turned to intense spirituality as an alternative to the mechanical rituals of the *brahmins.*

Jainism and the Challenge to the Established Cultural Order

Among the most influential of the new religions was Jainism. Although Jainist doctrines first appeared during the seventh century B.C.E., they became popular only when the great teacher Vardhamana Mahavira turned to Jainism in the late sixth century B.C.E. Mahavira ("the great hero") was born in northern India about 540 B.C.E. to a prominent *kshatriya* family. According to *Vardhamana Mahavira* the semilegendary accounts of his life, he left home at the age of thirty to seek salvation by escaping from the cycle of incarnation. For twelve years he led an ascetic life wandering throughout the Ganges valley, after which he gained enlightenment. He abandoned all his worldly goods, even his clothes, and taught an ascetic doctrine of detachment from the world. For the next thirty years, until his death about 468 B.C.E., he expounded his thought to a group of disciples who formed a monastic order to perpetuate and spread his message. These disciples referred to Mahavira as *Jina* ("the conqueror"), and borrowing from this title his followers referred to themselves as *Jains.*

Much of the inspiration for Jainist doctrine came from the Upanishads. Jains believed that everything in the universe—humans, animals, plants, the air, bodies of water, and even inanimate physical objects—possessed a soul. As long as they remained trapped in terrestrial bodies, these souls experienced both physical and psychological suffering. Only by purification from selfish behavior could souls gain release from their imprisonment and attain a state of bliss.

Individuals underwent purification by observing the principle of *ahimsa,* or nonviolence to other souls. Devout Jainist monks went to extremes to avoid harming the millions of souls *Jainist Ethics* they encountered each day. They swept the ground before them as they walked to avoid causing harm to insects; they strained their drinking water through cloth filters to remove tiny animals they might unwittingly consume; they followed an abstemious and strictly vegetarian diet; they even wore masks and avoided making sudden movements so that they would not bruise or otherwise disturb the tiny souls inhabiting the surrounding air.

Jainist ethics were so demanding that few people other than devout monks could hope to observe them closely. For certain groups, however, Jainism represented an attractive alternative to the traditional cults. Indeed, since Jains believed all creatures had souls that should be protected equally, Jains did not recognize human social hierarchies based on caste or *jati.* It is not surprising, then, that their faith became

---

Jainism (JEYEN-iz'm)

Upanishads (oo-pan-NIH-shuhds)

ahimsa (uh-HIM-suh)

Early Buddhism

Like Mahavira, the founder of Buddhism, Siddhartha Gautama, came from a *kshatriya* family but gave up his position and inheritance to seek salvation. He was born about 563 B.C.E. in a small tribal state governed by his father in the foothills of the Himalayas. According to early accounts, Gautama lived a pampered and sheltered life in palaces and parks, because his father had determined that Gautama would never know misery. He married his cousin and excelled in the program of studies that would prepare him to succeed his father as governor.

Siddhartha Guatama

Eventually, however, Gautama became dissatisfied with his comfortable life. One day, according to an early legend, while riding toward a park in his chariot, Gautama saw a man made miserable by age and infirmity. When he asked for an explanation of this unsettling sight, Gautama learned from his chariot driver that all human beings grow old and weak. On later outings Gautama learned that disease and death were also inevitable features of the human condition. When he then came into contact with a monk traveling by foot, Gautama learned that some individuals withdraw from the active life of the world to lead holy lives. Inspired, Gautama determined to take up a similar life for himself in the hope that it would help him to understand the phenomenon of suffering.

About 534 B.C.E. Gautama left his wife and family and the comforts of home to lead the existence of a holy man. He wandered throughout the Ganges valley searching for spiritual enlightenment and an explanation for suffering. He sought enlightenment first by means of intense meditation and later through the rigors of extreme asceticism. None of those tactics satisfied him. Then, according to Buddhist legends, as he sat one day beneath a large bo tree in Bodh Gaya, southwest of Pataliputra, Gautama decided that he would remain exactly where he was until he understood the problem of suffering. For forty-nine days he sat in meditation as various demons tempted and threatened him to shake his resolution. On the forty-ninth day Gautama prevailed and received enlightenment: he understood both

Gautama's Search for Enlightenment

the problem of suffering and the means by which humans could eliminate it from the world. At that point, Gautama became the Buddha—"the enlightened one."

Mahavira with one of his disciples. Representations of the early Jains often depicted them in the nude because of their ascetic way of life.

popular especially among members of lower castes, including merchants, scholars, and literary figures. These people provided substantial lay support for the Jainist monks and helped to maintain the ideal of *ahimsa* as a prominent concern of Indian ethics. Indeed, the doctrine of *ahimsa* has been an especially influential teaching over the long term, both in India and beyond. Quite apart from some two million Indian individuals who maintain Jainist traditions in the present day, many Buddhists and Hindus recognize *ahimsa* as a fundamental element of their beliefs, and prominent reformers of the twentieth century C.E. such as Mohandas K. Gandhi and Martin Luther King Jr. relied on the doctrine of *ahimsa* when promoting social reform by nonviolent means.

In spite of the moral respect it has commanded and the influence it has wielded through the centuries, however, Jainism has always been the faith of a small minority. It has simply been too difficult for most people to observe. A more popular and practical alternative to the *brahmins'* cults came in the form of Buddhism.

Siddhartha Gautama (sih-DHAR-tuh GAHW-tah-mah)

The Buddha publicly announced his doctrine for the first time about 528 B.C.E. at the Deer Park of Sarnath, near the Buddhist holy city of Banaras (modern Varanasi), in a sermon delivered to friends. Buddhists refer to this sermon as the "Turning of the Wheel of the Law" because it represented the beginning of the Buddha's quest to promulgate the law of righteousness. His teachings quickly attracted attention, and disciples came from all parts of the Ganges valley. He organized them into a community of monks who owned only their yellow robes and their begging bowls. For more than forty years, the Buddha himself led his disciples throughout much of northern India in hopes of bringing spiritual enlightenment to others.

The Buddha and His Followers

The core of the Buddha's doctrine, known as the Four Noble Truths, teaches that all life involves suffering; that desire is the cause of suffering; that elimination of desire brings an end to suffering; and that a disciplined life conducted in accordance with the Noble Eightfold Path brings the elimination of desire. The Noble Eightfold Path calls for individuals to lead balanced and moderate lives, rejecting both devotion to luxury and regimes of extreme asceticism. Specifically, the Noble Eightfold Path demands right belief, right resolve, right speech, right behavior, right occupation, right effort, right contemplation, and right meditation. Taken together, the teachings of the Four Noble Truths and the Noble Eightfold Path constitute the Buddhist *dharma*—the basic doctrine shared by Buddhists of all sects.

Buddhist Doctrine: The Dharma

Ultimately, Buddhists believed that a lifestyle based on the Buddhist *dharma* would lead to personal salvation, which meant an escape from the cycle of incarnation and attainment of *nirvana*, a state of perfect spiritual independence. Like the Jains, the Buddhists sought to escape the cycle of incarnation without depending on the services of the *brahmins*. Like the Jains, too, they did not recognize social distinctions based on caste or *jati*. As a result, their message appealed strongly to members of lower castes. Yet, because it did not demand the rigorous asceticism of Jainism, Buddhism became far more popular, especially with merchants.

A confident and serene Buddha preaches his first sermon after his enlightenment at the Deer Park of Sarnath.

Apart from the social implications of the doctrine, there were several other reasons for the popularity of early Buddhism in India. One has to do with language. Following the example of the Buddha himself, early Buddhist monks and preachers avoided the use of Sanskrit, the literary language of the Vedas that the *brahmins* employed in their rituals, in favor of vernacular tongues that reached a much larger popular audience. Furthermore, early Buddhists recognized holy sites that served as focal points for devotion. Even in the early days of Buddhism, pilgrims flocked to Bodh Gaya, where Gautama received enlightenment, and the Deer Park of Sarnath, where as the Buddha he preached his first sermon. Also popular with the faithful were stupas—shrines housing relics of the Buddha and his first disciples that pilgrims venerated while meditating on Buddhist values.

Appeal of Buddhism

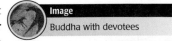

Image
Buddha with devotees

Buddha (BOO-duh)
dharma (DHUHR-muh)
Buddhism (BOO-diz'm)

Yet another reason for the early popularity of Buddhism was the organization of the Buddhist movement. From the days of the Buddha himself, the most enthusiastic and highly motivated converts joined monastic communities where they dedicated their lives 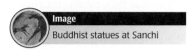 to the search for enlightenment and to preaching the Buddhist *dharma* to lay audiences. During the centuries following the Buddha's death, this monastic organization proved to be extremely efficient at spreading the Buddhist message and winning converts to the faith.

The early Buddhist movement also benefited from the official patronage and support of the Mauryan dynasty. The precise reason for Ashoka's conversion to Buddhism is unclear. Ashoka's own account, as preserved in one of his edicts, explains that the emperor adopted Buddhism about 260 B.C.E. after the war against Kalinga. Saddened by the violence of the war and the suffering of the Kalingans, Ashoka said that he decided to pursue his aims henceforth by means of virtue, benevolence, and humanity rather than arms. Quite apart from his sincere religious convictions, it is also likely that

Ashoka's Support

stupas (STOO-pahs)

Ashoka found Buddhism appealing as a faith that could lend unity to his culturally diverse and far-flung realm. In any case, in honor of *ahimsa,* the doctrine of nonviolence, Ashoka banned animal sacrifices in Pataliputra, gave up his beloved hunting expeditions, and eliminated most meat dishes from the tables of his court. Ashoka rewarded Buddhists with grants of land, and he encouraged them to spread their faith throughout India. He built monasteries and stupas and made pilgrimages to the holy sites of Buddhism. Ashoka also sent missionaries to Bactria and Ceylon (modern Sri Lanka), thus inaugurating a process by which Buddhism attracted large followings in central Asia, east Asia, and southeast Asia.

Mahayana Buddhism

From its earliest days Buddhism attracted merchants, artisans, and others of low rank in the traditional Indian social order. Its appeal was due both to its disregard for social classes and to its concern for ethical behavior instead of complicated ceremonies. Yet, even though it vastly simplified religious observances, early Buddhism made heavy demands on individuals seeking to escape from the cycle of incarnation. A truly righteous existence involved considerable sacrifice: giving up personal property, forsaking the search

The famous Buddhist stupa at Sanchi, originally built by Ashoka and enlarged in later times.

for social standing, and resolutely detaching oneself from the charms of family and the world. Although perhaps more attractive than the religion of the *brahmins,* Buddhism did not promise to make life easy for its adherents.

Between the third century B.C.E. and the first century C.E., however, three new developments in Buddhist thought and practice reduced obligations of believers, opened new avenues to salvation, and brought explosive popularity to the faith. In the first place, whereas the Buddha had not considered himself divine, some of his later followers began to worship him as a god. Thus Buddhism acquired a devotional focus that helped converts channel their spiritual energies. In the second place, theologians articulated the notion of the *boddhisatva* ("an enlightened being"). *Boddhisatvas* were individuals who had reached spiritual perfection and merited the reward of nirvana, but who intentionally delayed their entry into nirvana to help others who were still struggling. Like Christian saints, *boddhisatvas* served as examples of spiritual excellence, and they provided a source of inspiration. Finally, Buddhist monasteries began to accept gifts from wealthy individuals and to regard the bequests as acts of generosity that merited salvation. Thus wealthy individuals could avoid the sacrifices demanded by early Buddhist teachings and still ensure their salvation.

Development of Buddhism

Because these innovations opened the road to salvation for large numbers of people, their proponents called their faith the *Mahayana* ("the greater vehicle," which could carry more people to salvation), as opposed to the *Hinayana* ("the lesser vehicle"), a pejorative term for the earlier and stricter doctrine known also as Theravada Buddhism. During the early centuries C.E., Mahayana Buddhism spread rapidly throughout India and attracted many converts. In later centuries Mahayana Buddhism became established also in central Asia, China, Japan, and Korea. The stricter Theravada faith did not disappear, but since the first century C.E. most of the world's Buddhists have practiced Mahayana Buddhism.

The Spread of Mahayana Buddhism

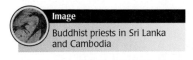

Image
Buddhist priests in Sri Lanka and Cambodia

boddhisatvas (BOH-dih-SAT-vuhs)
Mahayana (mah-huh-YAH-nah)
Hinayana (HEE-nah-yah-nuh)

Carving of a *boddhisatva* from the second or third century C.E. This carving perhaps represents Avalokitesvara, also known as the Lord of Compassion. Almost as perfect as the Buddha, Avalokitesvara had a reputation for protecting merchants and sailors, helping women conceive, and turning enemies into kindhearted friends.

Mahayana Buddhism flourished partly because of educational institutions that promoted the faith. During the Vedic era, Indian education was mostly an informal affair involving a sage and his students. When Jains and Buddhists organized monasteries, however, they began to establish educational institutions. Most monasteries provided basic education, and larger communities offered advanced instruction as well. Best known of all was the Buddhist monastery at Nalanda, founded during the Gupta dynasty in the Ganges River valley near Pataliputra. At Nalanda it was possible to study not only Buddhism but also the Vedas, Hindu philosophy, logic, mathematics, astronomy, and medicine. Nalanda soon became famous, and by the end of the Gupta dynasty, several thousand students may have been in residence there.

Nalanda

The Emergence of Popular Hinduism

As Buddhism generated new ideas and attracted widespread popular interest, Hinduism underwent a similar evolution that transformed it into a popular religion of salvation. Although drawing inspiration from the Vedas and the Upanishads, popular Hinduism increasingly departed from the older traditions of the *brahmins* to meet the needs of ordinary people.

A short poetic work known as the *Bhagavad Gita* ("song of the lord") best illustrates both the expectations that Hinduism made of individuals and the promise of salvation that it held out to them. Scholars have dated the work at various points between 300 B.C.E. and 300 C.E., and it most likely underwent several rounds of revision before taking on its final form about 400

The Bhagavad Gita

Bhagavad Gita (BHUHG-vuhd GEE-tuh)

C.E. Yet it eloquently evokes the cultural climate of India between the Mauryan and the Gupta dynasties.

The work is a self-contained episode of the *Mahabharata,* one of the great epic poems of India. It presents a dialogue between Arjuna, a *kshatriya* warrior about to enter battle, and his charioteer Krishna, who was in fact a human incarnation of the god Vishnu. The immediate problem addressed in the work was Arjuna's reluctance to fight: the enemy included many of his friends and relatives, and even though he recognized the justice of his cause, he shrank from the conflict. In an effort to persuade the warrior to fight, Krishna presented Arjuna with several lines of argument. In the first place, he said, Arjuna must not worry about harming his friends and relatives, because the soul does not die with the human body, and Arjuna's weapons did not have the power to touch the soul.

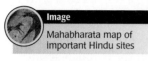
Mahabharata map of important Hindu sites

Krishna also held that Arjuna's caste imposed specific moral duties and social responsibilities on him. The duty of *shudras* was to serve, of *vaishyas* to work, of *brahmins* to learn the scriptures and seek wisdom. Similarly, Krishna argued, the duty of *kshatriyas* was to govern and fight. Indeed, Krishna went further and held that failure to fulfill caste duties was a grievous sin, whereas their observance brought spiritual benefits.

Finally, Krishna taught that Arjuna would attain everlasting peace if he devoted himself to the love, adoration, and service of Krishna himself. Arjuna should abandon his selfish and superficial personal concerns and surrender to the deeper wisdom of the god. As a reward, Arjuna would receive eternal salvation through unity with his god. Alongside understanding of the soul and caste duties, then, unquestioning faith and devotion would put Arjuna in the proper state of mind for the conflict by aligning his actions with divine wisdom and will. Krishna's teaching that faith would bring salvation helped inspire a tradition of ecstatic and unquestioning devotion in popular Hinduism.

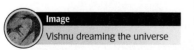
Vishnu dreaming the universe

Hindu ethics thus differed considerably from those of earlier Indian moralists. The Upanishads had taught that only through renunciation and detachment from the world could individuals escape the cycle of incarnation. As represented in the *Bhagavad Gita,* however, Hindu ethical teachings also held out the promise of salvation to those who participated actively in the world and met their caste responsibilities. To be sure, Krishna taught that individuals should meet their responsibilities in detached fashion and that they should not strive for material reward or recognition. Rather, they should perform their duties faithfully, with no thought as to their consequences.

Hindu Ethics

Other works by early Hindu moralists acknowledged even more openly than did the *Bhagavad Gita* that individuals could lead honorable lives in the world. Indeed, Hindu ethics commonly recognized four principal aims of human life: obedience to religious and moral laws *(dharma),* the pursuit of economic well-being and honest prosperity *(artha),* the enjoyment of social, physical, and sexual pleasure *(kama),* and the salvation of the soul *(moksha).* According to Hindu moral precepts, a proper balance of *dharma, artha,* and *kama* would help an individual to attain *moksha.*

As devotional Hinduism evolved and became increasingly distinct from the teachings of the Upanishads and the older traditions of the *brahmins,* it also enhanced its appeal to all segments of Indian society. Hinduism offered salvation to masses of people who, as a matter of practical necessity, had to lead active lives in the world and thus could not even hope to achieve the detachment envisioned in the Upanishads.

Hinduism gradually displaced Buddhism as the most popular religion in India. Later Buddhist monks did not seek to communicate their message to the larger society in the zealous way of their predecessors but increasingly confined themselves to the comforts of monasteries richly endowed by wealthy patrons. Meanwhile, devotional Hinduism attracted political support and patronage, particularly from the Gupta emperors. The Guptas and their successors bestowed grants of land on Hindu *brahmins* and supported an educational system that promoted Hindu values. Just as Ashoka Maurya had advanced the cause of Buddhism, the Guptas and their successors later helped Hinduism become the dominant religious and cultural tradition in India. By about 1000 C.E., Buddhism had entered a noticeable decline in India, while Hinduism was growing in popularity. Within a few centuries devotional Hinduism and the more recently introduced faith of Islam almost completely eclipsed Buddhism in its homeland.

Popularity of Hinduism

SOURCES FROM THE PAST

Caste Duties According to the Bhagavad Gita

In urging Arjuna to enter battle, Krishna pointed out that Arjuna could not harm the immortal souls of his family and friends on the other side. Beyond that, however, Krishna emphasized the duty to fight that Arjuna inherited as a member of the kshatriya *caste. Yet Krishna also counseled Arjuna to perform his duty in a spirit of detachment, not caring for victory or defeat.*

■ ■ ■

As a man, casting off old clothes, puts on others and new ones, so the embodied self, casting off old bodies, goes to others and new ones. Weapons do not divide the self into pieces; fire does not burn it; waters do not moisten it; the wind does not dry it up. It is not divisible; it is not combustible; it is not to be moistened; it is not to be dried up. It is everlasting, all-pervading, stable, firm, and eternal. It is said to be unperceived, to be unthinkable, to be unchangeable. Therefore knowing it to be such, you ought not to grieve. But even if you think that the self is constantly born, and constantly dies, still, O you of mighty arms, you ought not to grieve thus. For to one that is born, death is certain; and to one that dies, birth is certain. Therefore about this unavoidable thing, you ought not to grieve. . . .

Having regard to your own duty, you ought not to falter, for there is nothing better for a *kshatriya* than a righteous battle. Happy those *kshatriyas* who can find such a battle—an open door to heaven! But if you will not fight this righteous battle, then you will have abandoned your own duty and your fame, and you will incur sin. All beings, too, will tell of your everlasting infamy; and to one who has been honored, infamy is a greater evil than death. Warriors who are masters of great chariots will think that you have abstained from the battle through fear, and having been highly thought of by

them, you will fall down to littleness. Your enemies, too, decrying your power, will speak much about you that should not be spoken. And what, indeed, could be more lamentable than that? Killed, you will obtain heaven; victorious, you will enjoy the earth. Therefore arise, resolved to engage in battle. Looking on pleasure and pain, on gain and loss, on victory and defeat as the same, prepare for battle, and thus you will not incur sin. . . .

The state of mind that consists in firm understanding regarding steady contemplation does not belong to those who are strongly attached to worldly pleasures and power, and whose minds are drawn away by that flowery talk that is full of specific acts for the attainment of pleasures and power, and that promises birth as the fruit of actions—that flowery talk uttered by unwise ones who are enamored of Vedic words, who say there is nothing else, who are full of desires, and whose goal is heaven. . . .

Your business is with action alone, not by any means with the fruit of the action. Let not the fruit of action be your motive to action. Let not your attachment be fixed on inaction. Having recourse to devotion, perform actions, casting off all attachment, and being equable in success or ill success.

• *How do these reflections on caste duties and detachment in the* Bhagavad Gita *compare and contrast with the moral and ethical teachings of Zarathustra and Confucius discussed in earlier chapters?*

SOURCE: *The Bhagavad Gita*. Trans. by Kashinath Trimbak Telang. In F. Max Müller, ed., *The Sacred Books of the East*, vol. 8. Oxford: Clarendon Press, 1908, pp. 45–48. (Translation slightly modified.)

SUMMARY

In India, as in classical Persia and China, a robust agricultural economy supported the creation of large-scale states and interregional trade. Although an imperial state did not become a permanent feature of Indian political life, the peoples of the subcontinent maintained an orderly society based on the caste system and regional states. Indian cultural and religious traditions reflected the conditions of the larger society in which they developed. Mahayana Buddhism and devotional Hinduism in particular addressed the needs of the increasingly prominent lay classes, and the two faiths profoundly influenced the religious life of Asian peoples over the long term of history.

CHRONOLOGY

563–483 B.C.E.	Life of Siddhartha Gautama, the Buddha
540–468 B.C.E.	Life of Vardhamana Mahavira
520 B.C.E.	Invasion of India by Darius of Persia
327 B.C.E.	Invasion of India by Alexander of Macedon
321–185 B.C.E.	Mauryan dynasty
321–297 B.C.E.	Reign of Chandragupta Maurya
268–232 B.C.E.	Reign of Ashoka Maurya
182 B.C.E.–1 C.E.	Bactrian rule in northern India
1–300 C.E.	Kushan empire in northern India and central Asia
78–103 C.E.	Reign of Kushan emperor Kanishka
320–550 C.E.	Gupta dynasty

FOR FURTHER READING

Roy C. Amore and Larry D. Shinn. *Lustful Maidens and Ascetic Kings.* New York, 1981. Translations of stories and moral tales from Hindu and Buddhist writings.

Jeannine Auboyer. *Daily Life in Ancient India.* Trans. by S. W. Taylor. New York, 1965. An excellent and well-researched, though somewhat dated, introduction to Indian social history during the classical era.

Edward Conze. *Buddhism: Its Essence and Development.* New York, 1959. Systematic account of Buddhism from a theological point of view.

William Theodore De Bary, ed. *Sources of Indian Tradition.* 2 vols. 2nd ed. New York, 1988. Important collection of sources in translation.

Xinru Liu. *Ancient India and Ancient China: Trade and Religious Exchanges, A.D. 1–600.* Delhi, 1988. Important study exploring the early spread of Buddhism from India to central Asia and China.

Juan Mascaró, trans. *The Bhagavad Gita.* Harmondsworth, 1962. Brilliant and evocative English version by a gifted translator.

Jean W. Sedlar. *India and the Greek World: A Study in the Transmission of Culture.* Totowa, N.J., 1980. Important study of relations between India and Greece, based on solid research.

Romila Thapar. *Ashoka and the Decline of the Mauryas.* London, 1961. The best scholarly study of Ashoka and his reign.

———. *A History of India,* vol. 1. Harmondsworth, 1966. Popular account by one of the leading scholars of early Indian history.

———, ed. *Recent Perspectives of Early Indian History.* New Delhi, 1995. A valuable collection of essays discussing recent scholarship on early Indian history.

CHAPTER 8

Mediterranean Society under the Greeks and the Romans

For a man who perhaps never existed, Homer has been a profoundly influential figure. According to tradition, Homer composed the two great epic poems of ancient Greece, the *Iliad* and the *Odyssey*. In fact, scholars now know that bards recited both poems for generations before Homer, and some believe that Homer was simply a convenient name for the otherwise anonymous scribes who committed the *Iliad* and the *Odyssey* to writing. Whether Homer ever really lived or not, the epics attributed to him deeply influenced the development of classical Greek thought and literature. The *Iliad* offered a Greek perspective on a campaign waged by a band of Greek warriors against the city of Troy in Anatolia during the twelfth century B.C.E. The *Odyssey* recounted the experiences of the Greek hero Odysseus as he sailed home after the Trojan War. The two works described scores of difficulties faced by Greek warriors, including battles, monsters, and conflicts among themselves. Between them, the two epics preserved a rich collection of stories that literary figures mined for more than a millennium.

The *Iliad* and the *Odyssey* also testify to the frequency and normality of travel, communication, and interaction in the Mediterranean basin during the second and first millennia B.C.E. Both works portray Greeks as expert and fearless seamen, almost as comfortable aboard their ships as on land, who did not hesitate to venture into the waters of what Homer called the "wine-dark sea." Homer lovingly described the sleek galleys in which Greek warriors raced across the waters, and

OPPOSITE PAGE: *The theater at Delphi.*

he even had Odysseus construct a sailing ship single-handedly when he found himself shipwrecked on an island inhabited only by a goddess. The *Iliad* and the *Odyssey* make it clear that maritime links touched peoples throughout the Mediterranean basin in Homer's time and, further, that Greeks were among the most prominent seafarers of the age.

The maritime links established by the Greeks lived on long after the decline of classical Greek society. Indeed, the Romans took advantage of those links and used them to build a powerful society that dominated the whole Mediterranean basin by the first century C.E. By that time, Roman citizens found themselves living in a cosmopolitan world in which Roman administrators oversaw affairs from Anatolia and Palestine in the east to Spain and Morocco in the west.

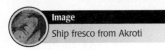
Ship fresco from Akroti

Just as Homer's epics recall the world of the Greeks, the story of Paul of Tarsus reflects the cosmopolitan world of the Romans. Born in the first century C.E., Paul was a devout Jew from Anatolia who accepted the Christian teachings of Jesus of Nazareth. Paul was a principal figure in the development of Christianity to an independent religious faith, largely because of his zealous missionary efforts to attract converts from outside as well as within the Jewish community. While promoting his adopted faith in Jerusalem about 55 C.E., however, Paul was attacked by a crowd of his enemies who believed his views were a threat to Judaism. The disturbance was so severe that Roman authorities intervened to restore order.

Under normal circumstances, Roman authorities would have delivered Paul to the leaders of his own ethnic community, where he would be dealt with according to custom. But knowing that Jewish leaders would probably execute him, Paul asserted his rights as a Roman citizen to appeal his case in Rome. Paul had never been to Rome, but this Anatolian traveling in Palestine called on the laws of the imperial center to determine his fate. Paul traveled across the Mediterranean to Rome, but his appeal did not succeed. Tradition holds that he was executed by imperial authorities out of concern that Christianity was a threat to the peace and stability of the empire.

Under both the Greeks and the Romans, the Mediterranean basin became much more tightly integrated than before as both societies organized commercial exchange and sponsored interaction throughout the region. In fact, under Greek and then Roman

supervision, the Mediterranean served not as a barrier but, rather, as a highway. Moreover, this highway carried more than soldiers, citizens, and goods: it also carried ideas. Indeed, Greek philosophy—which generated a remarkable body of moral thought and philosophical reflection—shaped the cultural foundations of the Roman republic and empire, as educated Roman thinkers drew inspiration from their neighbors to the east. Later, this highway carried the Christian religion to all corners of the Roman empire.

Yet Greek and Roman societies also differed substantially, both in organization and in outlook. Early in the classical era, the Greeks lived in independent, autonomous city-states. Only after the late third century B.C.E. did they play prominent roles in the large, centralized empire established by their neighbors to the north in Macedon. Until then, the Greeks had integrated the societies and economies of distant lands mainly through energetic commercial activity over the Mediterranean sea lanes. In contrast to the Greeks, the Romans built an extensive, centralized land empire. At its high point the Roman empire dominated the entire Mediterranean basin and parts of southwest Asia as well as north Africa and much of continental Europe and Britain. In addition, whereas Greek authorities did not sponsor an evangelical religion, Christianity eventually became the official religion of the Roman empire, which allowed the new religion to spread much more effectively than before.

EARLY DEVELOPMENT OF GREEK SOCIETY

During the third millennium B.C.E., the peoples of the Balkan region and the Greek peninsula increasingly met and mingled with peoples from different societies who traveled and traded in the Mediterranean basin. As a result, early inhabitants of the Greek peninsula built their societies under the influence of Mesopotamians, Egyptians, Phoenicians, and others active in the region. Beginning in the ninth century B.C.E., the Greeks organized a series of city-states, which served as the political context for the development of classical Greek society.

Minoan and Mycenaean Societies

During the late third millennium B.C.E., a sophisticated society arose on the island of Crete. Scholars refer to it as Minoan society, after Minos, a legendary king of ancient Crete. Between 2000 and 1700 B.C.E., the inhabitants of Crete built a series of lavish palaces throughout the island, most notably the enor-

Knossos

mous complex at Knossos decorated with vivid frescoes depicting Minoans at work and play. These palaces were the nerve centers of Minoan society: they were residences of rulers, and they also served as storehouses where officials collected taxes in kind from local cultivators.

Between 2200 and 1450 B.C.E., Crete was a principal center of Mediterranean commerce. By 2200 B.C.E. Cretans were traveling aboard advanced sailing craft of Phoenician design. Minoan ships sailed to Greece, Anatolia, Phoenicia, and Egypt, where they exchanged Cretan wine, olive oil, and wool for grains, textiles, and manufactured goods. After 1600 B.C.E. Cretans established colonies on Cyprus and many islands in the Aegean Sea.

After 1700 B.C.E. Minoan society experienced a series of earthquakes, volcanic eruptions, and tidal waves.

Decline of Minoan Society

Between 1600 and 1450 B.C.E., Cretans embarked on a new round of palace building to replace structures destroyed by those natural catastrophes: they built luxurious complexes with indoor plumbing and drainage systems and even furnished some of them with flush toilets. After 1450 B.C.E., however, the wealth of Minoan society attracted a series of invaders, and by 1100 B.C.E. Crete had fallen under foreign domination. Yet Minoan traditions deeply influenced the inhabitants of nearby Greece.

Beginning about 2200 B.C.E. migratory Indo-European peoples filtered into the Greek peninsula.

Mycenaean Society

By 1600 B.C.E. they had begun to trade with Minoan merchants and visit Crete, where they learned about writing and large-scale construction. After 1450 B.C.E. they also built massive stone fortresses and palaces throughout the southern part of the Greek peninsula, known as the Peloponnesus. Because the fortified sites offered protection, they soon attracted settlers, who built small agricultural communities. Their society is known as Mycenaean, after Mycenae, one of their most important settlements.

From 1500 to 1100 B.C.E., the Mycenaeans expanded their influence beyond peninsular Greece. They largely overpowered Minoan society, and they took over the Cretan palaces. The Mycenaeans also established settlements in Anatolia, Sicily, and southern Italy. About 1200 B.C.E. the Mycenaeans engaged in a conflict with the city of Troy in Anatolia. This Trojan War, which Homer recalled from a Greek perspective in his *Iliad,* coincided with

Chaos in the Eastern Mediterranean

invasions of foreign mariners in the Mycenaean homeland. Indeed, from 1100 to 800 B.C.E., chaos reigned throughout the eastern Mediterranean region. Invasions and civil disturbances made it impossible to maintain stable governments or even productive agricultural societies. Mycenaean palaces fell into ruin, the population sharply declined, and people abandoned most settlements.

The World of the Polis

In the absence of a centralized state or empire, local institutions took the lead in restoring political order in Greece after the decline of Mycenaean society. The most important institution was the city-state, or polis. Over time, many of these poleis (the plural of *polis*) became lively commercial centers. They took on an increasingly urban character and extended their authority over surrounding regions. By about 800 B.C.E. many poleis had become bustling city-states that functioned as the principal centers of Greek society. The most important of the poleis were Sparta and Athens, whose contrasting constitutions help to illustrate the variety of political styles in classical Greece.

Sparta was situated in a fertile region of the Greek peninsula, whose lands the Spartans exploited by forcing neighboring peoples to perform agricultural

Sparta

labor. These *helots*, or servants of the Spartan state, were not slaves, but neither were they free to leave the land. Their role in society was to keep Sparta supplied with food. By the sixth century B.C.E., the helots probably outnumbered the Spartan citizens by more than ten to one, which meant that the Spartans constantly had to guard against rebellion. As a result, the Spartans devoted most of their resources to maintaining a powerful and disciplined military machine.

In theory, Spartan citizens were equal in status. To discourage the development of economic and social distinctions, Spartans observed an extraordinarily austere lifestyle. They

Spartan Society

did not wear jewelry or elaborate clothes, nor did they pamper themselves with luxuries or accumulate private wealth on a large scale. It is for good reason,

---

Minoan (mih-NOH-uhn)
Mycenaean (meye-suh-NEE-uhn)

polis (POH-lihs)

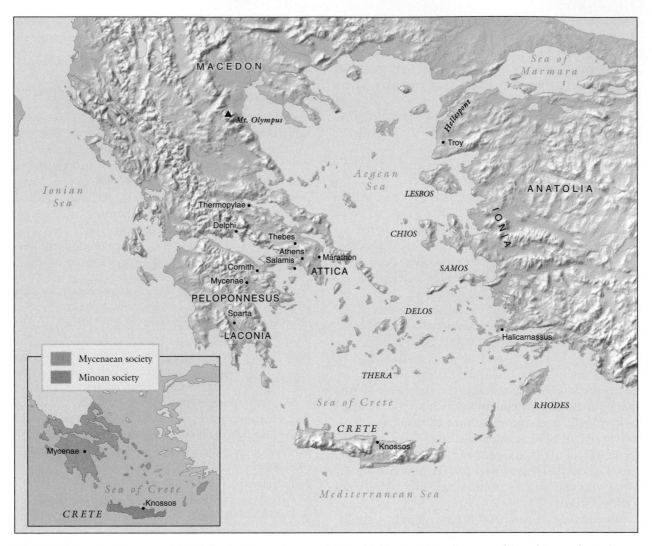

Map 8.1 Major city-states, or poleis, of classical Greece between 800 and 350 B.C.E. Note that some of the poleis were located in coastal areas and others were located inland. How might proximity to or distance from the sea have shaped the economic and social development of individual poleis?

then, that our adjective *spartan* refers to a lifestyle characterized by simplicity, frugality, and austerity.

Distinction among the ancient Spartans came by prowess, discipline, and military talent, which the Spartan educational system cultivated from an early age. All Spartans, men and women, underwent a rigorous regime of physical training. The sons of Spartan citizens left their homes at age seven and went to live in military barracks. At age twenty they began active military service, which they continued until retirement. Spartan women married when they reached eighteen to twenty years of age but did not live with

their husbands. Only at about age thirty did men leave the barracks and set up a household with their wives and children. Although Spartan society had lost much of its ascetic rigor by the fourth century B.C.E., Spartan institutions nevertheless continued to reflect the larger society's commitment to military values.

Whereas Sparta sought to impose order by military means, Athenians relieved social tensions by establishing a government based on democratic principles. Indeed, Athenians opened government offices to all citizens and broadened the base of political participation in classical Greece. Citizenship was by

Athens

A painted cup produced in Sparta about 550 B.C.E. depicts hunters attacking a boar. Spartans regarded hunting as an exercise that helped to sharpen fighting skills and aggressive instincts.

no means open to all residents, however: only free adult males from Athens played a role in public affairs, leaving foreigners, slaves, and women with no direct voice in government.

During the seventh century B.C.E., the gap between rich and poor around Athens widened considerably as increased trade brought prosperity to wealthy landowners. By the early sixth century B.C.E., a large class of underprivileged people were unhappy enough to wage war against their wealthy neighbors. To avert civil war, an Athenian aristocrat named Solon devised a solution to class conflict in Attica, the region around Athens.

Athenian Society

Solon forged a compromise between the classes. He allowed aristocrats to keep their lands, but he cancelled debts, forbade debt slavery, and liberated those already enslaved for debt. Solon also provided representation for the common classes in the Athenian government by opening the councils of the polis to any citizen wealthy enough to devote time to public affairs. During the late sixth and fifth centuries B.C.E., these reforms went even further as Athenian leaders paid salaries to officeholders so financial hardship would not exclude anyone from service.

Solon and Athenian Democracy

These reforms gradually transformed Athens into a democratic state. The high tide of Athenian democracy

came under the leadership of the statesman Pericles, who became the most popular Athenian leader from 461 B.C.E. until his death in 429 B.C.E. Under the leadership of Pericles, Athens became the most sophisticated of the poleis, with a vibrant community of scientists, philosophers, poets, dramatists, artists, and architects.

Pericles

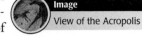
Image
View of the Acropolis

GREECE AND THE LARGER WORLD

As the poleis prospered, Greeks became increasingly prominent in the larger world of the Mediterranean basin. They established colonies along the shores of the Mediterranean Sea and the Black Sea, and they traded throughout the region. Eventually, their political and economic interests brought them into conflict with the expanding Persian empire. After a century of intermittent war, in the fourth century B.C.E. Alexander of Macedon toppled the Achaemenid empire and built an empire stretching from India to Egypt and Greece. His conquests created a vast zone of trade and communication that encouraged commercial and cultural exchange on an unprecedented scale.

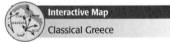
Interactive Map
Classical Greece

Greek Colonization

To relieve population pressures in the rocky Greek peninsula, Greeks began to establish colonies in other parts of the Mediterranean basin. Between the mid–eighth and the late sixth centuries B.C.E., they founded more than four hundred colonies along the shores of the Mediterranean Sea and the Black Sea.

The Greeks established their first colonies in the central Mediterranean during the early eighth century B.C.E. The most popular sites were Sicily and southern Italy, particularly the region around modern Naples, which was itself originally a Greek colony called Neapolis ("new polis"). These colonies provided merchants not only with fertile fields that yielded large agricultural surpluses but also with convenient access to the copper, zinc, tin, and iron ores of central Italy.

Greek Colonies

During the eighth and seventh centuries B.C.E., Greeks ventured into the Black Sea in large numbers and established colonies all along its shores. These

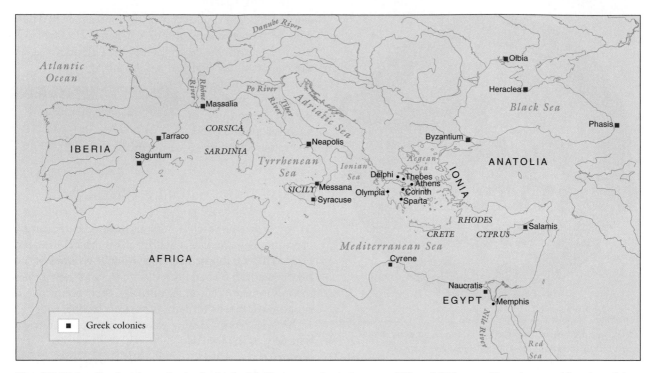

Map 8.2 Major Greek cities and colonies in the Mediterranean basin between 800 and 500 B.C.E. Note the coastal location of the many Greek colonies. What does that suggest about their purpose?

settlements offered merchants access to rich supplies of grain, fish, furs, timber, honey, wax, gold, and amber as well as slaves captured in southern Russia and transported to markets in the Mediterranean.

Unlike their counterparts in classical Persia, China, and India, the Greeks did not build a centralized imperial state. Instead, colonies relied on their own resources and charted their own courses. Nevertheless, Greek colonization sponsored more communication, interaction, and exchange than ever before among Mediterranean lands and peoples. From the early eighth century B.C.E., colonies facilitated trade between their own regions and the Greek poleis. At the same time, colonization spread Greek language as well as cultural and political traditions throughout the Mediterranean basin. Thus Greek colonization had important political and social effects throughout the Mediterranean basin.

Conflict with Persia

During the fifth century B.C.E., their links abroad brought the poleis of the Greek peninsula into direct conflict with the Persian empire in a long struggle known as the Persian Wars (500–479 B.C.E.). As the Persian emperors Cyrus and Darius tightened their grip on Anatolia, the Greek cities on the Ionian coast became increasingly restless. In 500 B.C.E. they revolted against Persian rule and expelled the Achaemenid administrators. In support of their fellow Greeks and commercial partners, the Athenians sent a fleet of ships to aid the Ionian effort.

Despite Athenian assistance, Darius repressed the Ionian rebellion in 493 B.C.E. Three years later, he mounted a campaign against peninsular Greece to punish them for their interference. Although greatly outnumbered, the Athenians routed the Persian army at the battle of Marathon and then marched back to Athens in time to fight off the Persian fleet. In spite of success in individual battles, however, neither side could secure a definitive victory over the other, and for more than a century Greeks and Persians continued to skirmish intermittently without decisive results.

The Persian Wars

Yet the Persian Wars did initiate serious conflict among the Greek poleis themselves. The cause was an alliance between the poleis known as the Delian League, which was formed to discourage further Persian actions in Greece. Because of its superior fleet, Athens became the leader of the alliance, benefiting greatly from the

The Delian League

financial contributions of other poleis. However, once it was clear that the Persian threat no longer existed, the other poleis resented having to make contributions that seemed to benefit only the Athenians.

Ultimately, the tensions resulted in a bitter civil conflict known as the Peloponnesian War (431–404 B.C.E.). Poleis divided into two armed camps under the leadership of Athens and Sparta, the principal contenders for hegemony in the Greek world. By 404 B.C.E. the Spartans and their allies had forced the Athenians to unconditional surrender. However, Sparta's victory soon generated new jealousies, and new conflicts quickly broke out between the poleis. Meanwhile, as internal struggles weakened the poleis, a formidable power took shape in the north.

The Peloponnesian War

The Macedonians and the Coming of Empire

Until the fourth century B.C.E., the kingdom of Macedon was a frontier state north of peninsular Greece. During the reign of King Philip II (359–336 B.C.E.), however, Macedon became a powerful, unified state with an impressive military machine. When Philip had consolidated his hold on Macedon, he turned his attention to two larger prizes: Greece and the Persian empire. Greece proved relatively easy to conquer: the Peloponnesian War had poisoned the poleis against one another, which hampered organized resistance. Thus in 338 B.C.E., after a campaign of twelve years, Philip had all of Greece under his control.

The Kingdom of Macedon

Philip intended to use his conquest of Greece as a launching pad for an invasion of Persia but was prevented from doing so by an assassin who brought him down in 336 B.C.E. The invasion of Persia thus fell to his twenty-year-old son, Alexander of Macedon, often called Alexander the Great. Alexander soon assembled an army to invade the Persian empire. Alexander was a brilliant strategist and an inspired leader, and he inherited a well-equipped and highly spirited veteran force from his father. By 333 B.C.E. Alexander had subjected Ionia and Anatolia to his control; within another year he held Syria, Palestine, and Egypt; by 331 B.C.E. he controlled Mesopotamia and prepared to invade the Persian homeland. He took Pasargadae and burned the Achaemenid palace at Persepolis late in 331 B.C.E., and in 330 B.C.E. Alexander established himself as the new emperor of Persia.

Alexander of Macedon

By 327 B.C.E. Alexander had larger ambitions: he took his army into India but was forced to return home when his troops refused to proceed any farther. By 324 B.C.E. Alexander and his army had returned to Susa in Mesopotamia. In June of 323 B.C.E., however, after an extended round of feasting and drinking, he suddenly fell ill and died at the age of thirty-three. Thus, although Alexander proved to be a brilliant conqueror, he did not live long enough to develop a system of administration for his vast realm.

Alexander's Conquests

The Hellenistic Empires

When Alexander died, his generals divided the empire into three large states. Antigonus took Greece and Macedon, which his Antigonid successors ruled until replaced by the Romans in the second century B.C.E. Ptolemy took Egypt, which the Ptolemaic dynasty ruled until the Roman conquest of Egypt in 31 B.C.E. Seleucus took the largest portion, the former Achaemenid empire stretching from Bactria to Anatolia, which his successors ruled until the Parthians displaced them during the second century B.C.E.

Interactive Map
Achaemenid & Seleucid Empires

Historians refer to the age of Alexander and his successors as the Hellenistic age—an era when Greek cultural traditions expanded their influence *(Hellas)* to a much larger world. Indeed, the Hellenistic empires governed cosmopolitan societies and sponsored interactions between peoples from Greece to India. Like imperial states in classical Persia, China, and India, the Hellenistic empires facilitated trade, and they made it possible for beliefs, values, and religions to spread over greater distances than ever before.

The Hellenistic Era

Primary Source
Arrian's *The Life of Alexander*

All the Hellenistic empires benefited handsomely from the new order through the supervision of extensive trade networks and efficient tax collection. Yet perhaps the wealthiest of the Hellenistic empires was Ptolemaic Egypt. Greek and Macedonian overlords did not interfere in Egyptian society, contenting themselves with the efficient organization of agriculture, industry, and tax

The Ptolemaic Empire

Ptolemaic (TAWL-oh-may-ihk)

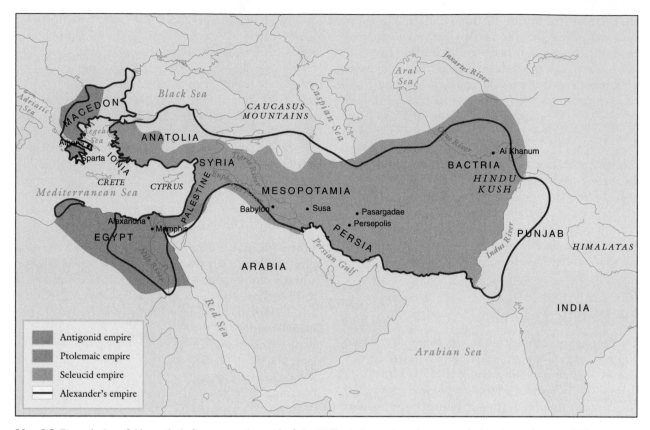

Map 8.3 **Boundaries of Alexander's former empire and of the Hellenistic empires that succeeded it about the year 275 B.C.E.**
Notice the difference in size between the three Hellenistic empires. What would have been the economic and political advantages and disadvantages of each?

collection. They maintained the irrigation networks and monitored the cultivation of crops and the payment of taxes. They also established royal monopolies over the most lucrative industries, such as textiles, salt making, and the brewing of beer.

Much of Egypt's wealth flowed to the Ptolemaic capital of Alexandria. Founded by Alexander at the mouth of the Nile, Alexandria served as the Ptolemies' administrative headquarters, but it became much more than a bureaucratic center. Alexandria's enormous harbor was able to accommodate 1,200 ships simultaneously, and the city soon became the most important port in the Mediterranean. Alongside Greeks, Macedonians, and Egyptians lived sizable communities of Phoenicians, Jews, Arabs, and Babylonians. The city was indeed an early megalopolis, where peoples of different ethnic, religious, and cultural traditions conducted their affairs. Under the Ptolemies, Alexandria also became the cultural capital of the Hellenistic world. It was the site of the famous Alexandrian Museum—a state-financed

Alexandria

institute of higher learning where philosophical, literary, and scientific scholars carried on advanced research—and of the equally famous Alexandrian Library, which supported the scholarship sponsored by the museum and which, by the first century B.C.E., boasted a collection of more than seven hundred thousand works.

It was in the Seleucid realm, however, that Greek influence reached its greatest extent. The principal channels of that influence were the numerous cities that Alexander and his successors founded in the former Persian empire. Greek and Macedonian colonists flocked to these cities, where they created a Mediterranean-style urban society that left its mark on lands as distant as Bactria and India. Many Seleucids became familiar with Greek language, dress, literature, philosophy, art, and architecture. Emperor Ashoka of India himself had his edicts promulgated in Greek and Aramaic, the two most commonly

The Seleucid Empire

Seleucids (sih-LOO-sihds)

used languages of the Hellenistic empires. Indeed, although the societies under Hellenistic domination did not lose their own customs, the Hellenistic empires, like classical states in Persia, China, and India, nevertheless brought distant lands into interaction by way of trade and cultural exchange.

THE FRUITS OF TRADE: GREEK ECONOMY AND SOCIETY

The mountainous and rocky terrain of the Greek peninsula yielded only small harvests of grain, and the southern Balkan mountains hindered travel and communication. Indeed, until the construction of modern roads, much of Greece was more accessible by sea than by land. As a result, early Greek society depended heavily on maritime trade.

Trade and the Integration of the Mediterranean Basin

Although it produced little grain, much of Greece is ideally suited to the cultivation of olives and grapes. After the establishment of the poleis, the Greeks dis-

Trade
covered that they could profitably concentrate their efforts on the production of olive oil and wine. Greek merchants traded these products around the Mediterranean, returning with abundant supplies of grain and other items as well.

By the early eighth century B.C.E., trade had generated considerable prosperity in the Greek world. Merchants and mariners linked Greek communities throughout the Mediterranean world—not only those in the Greek peninsula but also those in Anatolia, the Mediterranean islands, and the Black Sea region. These trade links contributed to a sense of a larger Greek community. Colonists recognized the same gods as their cousins in the Greek peninsula. They spoke Greek dialects, and they maintained commercial relationships with their native communities.

Greeks from all parts gathered periodically to participate in panhellenic festivals that reinforced their common bonds. Many of these festivals

The Olympic Games
featured athletic, literary, or musical contests in which individuals sought to win glory for their polis. Best known of the panhellenic festivals were the Olympic games. According to tradition, in 776 B.C.E. Greek communities from all parts of the Mediterranean sent their best athletes to the polis of Olympia to engage in contests of speed,

Harvesting olives. In this painting on a vase, two men knock fruit off the branches while a third climbs the tree to shake the limbs, and another gathers olives from the ground.

strength, and skill. Events included footracing, long jump, boxing, wrestling, javelin tossing, and discus throwing. Winners of events received olive wreaths, and they became celebrated heroes in their home poleis. The ancient Olympic games took place every four years for more than a millennium before quietly disappearing from Greek life. So, although they were not united politically, by the sixth century B.C.E. Greek communities had nevertheless established a sense of collective identity.

Family and Society

With the establishment of poleis in the eighth century B.C.E., the nature of Greek family and society came into focus. Like urban societies in southwest Asia and Anatolia, the Greek poleis adopted strictly patriarchal family structures. Male family heads ruled their households, and fathers even had the right to decide whether or not to keep infants born to their wives.

Patriarchal Society They could not legally kill infants, but they could abandon newborns in the mountains or the countryside, where they would soon die of exposure.

Greek women fell under the authority of their fathers, husbands, or sons. Upper-class Greek women spent most of their time in the family home and frequently wore veils when they ventured outside. In most of the poleis, women could not own landed property, but they sometimes operated small businesses such as shops and food stalls. The only public position open to Greek women was that of priestess of a religious cult. Sparta was something of a special case when it came to gender relations: there women participated in athletic contests, went about town by themselves, and sometimes even took up arms to defend the polis. Even in Sparta, however, men were family authorities, and men alone determined state policies.

Literacy was common among upper-class Greek women, and a few women earned reputations for literary talent. Most famous of them was the poet *Sappho* Sappho, who was active during the years around 600 B.C.E. Sappho, probably a widow from an aristocratic family, invited young women into her home for instruction in music and literature. Critics charged her with homosexual activity, and her surviving verse speaks of her strong physical attraction to young women. Greek society readily tolerated sexual relationships between men but frowned on female homosexuality. As a result, Sappho fell under a moral cloud, and only fragments of her poetry survive.

Aristocratic families with extensive landholdings could afford to provide girls with a formal education, but in less privileged families all hands contributed to the welfare of the household. In rural families, men performed most of the outside work, while women took care of domestic chores and wove wool textiles. In artisan families living in the poleis, both men and women often participated in businesses and maintained stands or booths in the marketplace.

Throughout the Greek world, as in other classical societies, slavery was a prominent means of mobilizing labor. Slaves came from several different *Slavery* backgrounds. Some entered slavery because they could not pay their debts. Many were soldiers captured in war. A large number came from the peoples with whom the Greeks traded: slave markets at Black Sea ports sold seminomadic Scythians captured in Russia, and Egyptians provided African slaves.

Greek law regarded all slaves as the private chattel property of their owners, and the conditions of slaves' lives depended on the needs and the temperament of their owners. In general, however, slaves who possessed special skills fared better than unskilled slaves. A slave named Pasion, for example, worked first as a porter and then as a clerk at a prominent Athenian bank during the late fifth and early fourth centuries B.C.E. Ultimately, Pasion gained his freedom, took over management of the bank, outfitted five warships from his own pocket, and won a grant of Athenian citizenship.

THE CULTURAL LIFE OF CLASSICAL GREECE

During the eighth and seventh centuries B.C.E., as Greek merchants ventured throughout the Mediterranean basin, they became acquainted with the sophisticated cultural traditions of Mesopotamia and Egypt. They learned astronomy, science, mathematics, medicine, and magic from the Babylonians as well as geometry, medicine, and divination from the Egyptians. They also drew inspiration from the myths, religious beliefs, art motifs, and architectural styles of Mesopotamia and Egypt. About 800 B.C.E. they adapted the Phoenician alphabet to their own language. To the Phoenicians' consonants they added symbols for vowels and thus created an exceptionally flexible system for representing human speech in written form.

During the fifth and fourth centuries B.C.E., the Greeks combined those borrowed cultural elements with their own intellectual interests to elaborate a rich cultural tradition that exercised enormous influence in the Mediterranean basin and western Europe. The most distinctive feature of classical Greek culture was the effort to construct a consistent system of philosophy based purely on human reason.

Rational Thought and Philosophy

The pivotal figure in the development of philosophy was Socrates (470–399 B.C.E.), a thoughtful Athenian driven by a powerful urge to understand human beings in all their complexity. Socrates did not *Socrates* commit his thought to writing, but his disciple Plato later composed dialogues that represented Socrates' views. He suggested that honor was far more important than wealth, fame, or other superficial attributes. He scorned those who preferred public accolades to personal integrity, and he insisted on the need to reflect on the purposes and goals of life. "The unexamined life is not worth living," he held, implying that human beings had an obligation to strive for personal integrity, behave honorably toward others, and work toward the construction of a just society.

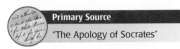
In elaborating those views, Socrates often subjected traditional ethical teachings to critical scrutiny. That outraged some of his fellow citizens, who brought him to trial on charges that he corrupted the Athenian youths who joined him in the marketplace to discuss moral and ethical issues. A jury of Athenian citizens decided that Socrates had indeed passed the bounds of propriety and condemned him to death. In 399 B.C.E. Socrates drank a potion of hemlock sap and died in the company of his friends.

Tradition holds that Socrates was not a physically attractive man, but this statue emphasizes his sincerity and simplicity.

Socrates' influence survived in the work of his most zealous disciple, Plato (430–347 B.C.E.), and in Plato's disciple Aristotle (384–322 B.C.E.). Inspired by his mentor's reflections, Plato elaborated a systematic philosophy of great subtlety. He presented his thought in a series of dialogues in which Socrates figured as the principal speaker. As time passed, Plato gradually formulated his thought into a systematic vision of the world and human society. *Plato*

The cornerstone of Plato's thought was his theory of Forms, or Ideas. It disturbed Plato that he could not gain satisfactory intellectual control over the world. The quality of virtue, for example, meant different things in different situations, as did honesty, courage, truth, and beauty. How was it possible, then, to understand virtue as an abstract quality? In seeking an answer to that question, Plato developed his belief that the world in which we live is not the world of genuine reality, but only a pale and imperfect reflection of the world of Forms or Ideas. The secrets of this world, Plato argued, were available only to philosophers—those who applied their rational faculties to the pursuit of wisdom.

Though abstract, Plato's thought had important political and social implications. In his dialogue *The Republic,* for example, Plato argued that since philosophers were in the best position to understand ultimate reality, they would also be the best rulers. In effect, Plato advocated an intellectual aristocracy: the philosophical elite would rule, and less intelligent classes would work at functions for which their talents best suited them.

During the generation after Plato, Aristotle elaborated a systematic philosophy that equaled Plato's work in its long-term influence. Unlike Plato, Aristotle believed that philosophers could rely on their senses to provide accurate information about the world and then depend on reason to sort out its mysteries. Aristotle explored the nature of reality in subtle metaphysical works, and he devised rigorous rules of logic in an effort to construct powerful and compelling arguments. His work provided such a coherent and comprehensive vision of the world that his later disciples called him "the master of those who know." *Aristotle*

The Greek philosophers deeply influenced the development of European and Islamic cultural traditions. Until the seventeenth century C.E., most European philosophers regarded the Greeks as intellectual authorities. Christian and Islamic theologians alike went

SOURCES FROM THE PAST

Socrates' View of Death

In one of his earliest dialogues, The Apology, *Plato offered an account of Socrates' defense of himself during his trial before a jury of Athenian citizens. After the jury had convicted him and condemned him to death, Socrates reflected on the nature of death and reemphasized his commitment to virtue rather than to wealth or fame.*

And if we reflect in another way we shall see that we may well hope that death is a good thing. For the state of death is one of two things: either the dead man wholly ceases to be and loses all sensation; or, according to the common belief, it is a change and a migration of the soul unto another place. And if death is the absence of all sensation, like the sleep of one whose slumbers are unbroken by any dreams, it will be a wonderful gain. For if a man had to select that night in which he slept so soundly that he did not even see any dreams, and had to compare with it all the other nights and days of his life, and then had to say how many days and nights in his life he had slept better and more pleasantly than this night, I think that a private person, nay, even the great king of Persia himself, would find them easy to count, compared with the others. If that is the nature of death, I for one count it a gain. For then it appears that eternity is nothing more than a single night.

But if death is a journey to another place, and the common belief be true, that all who have died dwell there, what good could be greater than this, my judges? Would a journey not be worth taking if at the end of it, in the other world, we should be released from the self-styled judges of this world, and should find the true judges who are said to sit in judgment below? . . . It would be an infinite happiness to converse with them, and to live with them, and to examine them. Assuredly there they do not put men to death for doing that. For besides the other ways in which they are happier than we are, they are immortal, at least if the common belief be true.

And you too, judges, must face death with a good courage, and believe this as a truth, that no evil can happen to a good man, either in life, or after death. His fortunes are not neglected by the gods, and what has come to me today has not come by chance. I am persuaded that it is better for me to die now, and to be released from trouble. . . . And so I am hardly angry with my accusers, or with those who have condemned me to die. Yet it was not with this mind that they accused me and condemned me, but rather they meant to do me an injury. Only to that extent do I find fault with them.

Yet I have one request to make of them. When my sons grow up, visit them with punishment, my friends, and vex them in the same way that I have vexed you if they seem to you to care for riches or for anything other than virtue: and if they think that they are something when they are nothing at all, reproach them as I have reproached you for not caring for what they should and for thinking that they are great men when in fact they are worthless. And if you will do this, I myself and my sons will have received our deserts at your hands. But now the time has come, and we must go hence: I to die, and you to live. Whether life or death is better is known to God, and to God only.

* *How does Socrates' understanding of personal morality and its rewards compare and contrast with the Zoroastrian, Buddhist, and Hindu views discussed in earlier chapters?*

SOURCE: F. J. Church, trans. *The Trial and Death of Socrates,* 2nd ed. London: Macmillan, 1886, pp. 76–78. (Translation slightly modified.)

to great lengths to harmonize their religious convictions with the philosophical views of Plato and Aristotle. Thus, like philosophical and religious figures in other classical societies, Plato and Aristotle provided a powerful intellectual framework that shaped thought about the world and human affairs for two millennia and more.

Popular Religion and Greek Drama

Because most Greeks of the classical era did not have an advanced education, they turned to traditions of popular culture and popular religion rather than philosophy to seek guidance for human behavior.

Deities The Greeks did not recognize a single, exclusive, all-powerful god. Rather, they believed that in the beginning there was the formless void of chaos out of which emerged the earth, the mother and creator of all things. The earth then generated the sky, and together they produced night, day, sun, moon, and other natural phenomena. Struggles between the deities led to bitter heavenly battles, and ultimately Zeus, grandson of the earth and sky gods, emerged as paramount ruler of the divine realm. Zeus's heavenly court included scores of subordinate deities who had various responsibilities: the god Apollo promoted wisdom and justice, for example; the goddess Fortune brought unexpected opportunities and difficulties; and the Furies wreaked vengeance on those who violated divine law.

Like religious traditions in other lands, Greek myths sought to explain the world and the forces that shape it. They served also as founda-

Religious Cults tions for religious cults based on individual poleis that contributed to a powerful sense of community in classical Greece. These religious cults varied widely: many conducted ritual observances in special places, for example, and some were open to only one sex. Before the fifth century B.C.E., many cults inspired emotional displays and spirited—sometimes frenzied—song and dance.

During the fifth century B.C.E., however, as the poleis strengthened their grip on public and political life, the religious cults became progres-

Tragic Drama sively more tame. Instead of festivals, religious cults marked the year with the presentation of plays that examined relations between humans and the gods or reflected on ethics and morality. That transformation set the stage for the emergence of Greek dramatic literature, which sought to engage audiences in subtle reflection on complicated themes.

The great tragedians—Aeschylus, Sophocles, and Euripides—whose lives spanned the fifth century B.C.E., explored the possibilities and limitations of human action. Comic dramatists such as Aristophanes also dealt with serious issues of human striving and responsible behavior by ridiculing the foibles of prominent public figures and calling attention to the absurd consequences of ill-considered action.

Hellenistic Philosophy and Religion

As the Hellenistic empires seized the political initiative in the Mediterranean basin and eclipsed the poleis, residents ceased to regard their polis as the focus of individual and religious loyalties. Instead, they increasingly looked toward cultural and religious alternatives that ministered to the needs and interests of individuals living in a cosmopolitan society.

The most popular Hellenistic philosophers—the Epicureans, the Skeptics, and the Stoics—addressed individual needs by searching for per-

sonal tranquility and serenity. Epicure- *The Hellenistic Philosophers*
ans, for example, identified pleasure as

the greatest good. By *pleasure* they meant not unbridled hedonism but, rather, a state of quiet satisfaction that would shield them from the pressures of the Hellenistic world. Skeptics refused to take strong positions on political, moral, and social issues because they doubted the possibility of certain knowledge. The most respected and influential of the Hellenistic philosophers, however, were the Stoics. Unlike the Epicureans and the Skeptics, the Stoics did not seek to withdraw from the pressures of the world. Rather, they taught that individuals had the duty to aid others and lead virtuous lives in harmony with reason and nature.

Whereas the philosophers' doctrines appealed to educated elites, religions of salvation spread across the

trade routes of the Hellenistic empires and *Religions of*
enjoyed surging popularity in Hellenistic *Salvation*
society. Mystery religions promised eternal

bliss for initiates who observed their rites and lived in accordance with their doctrines. Some of these faiths spread across the trade routes and found followers far from their homelands. The Egyptian cult of Osiris, for example, became extraordinarily popular because it

---

Aeschylus (ES-kuh-luhs)
Epicureans (ehp-ih-KYOOR-eeuhns)
Stoics (STOH-ihks)

promised salvation for those who led honorable lives. Cults from Persia, Mesopotamia, Anatolia, and Greece also attracted disciples throughout the Hellenistic world.

Many of the mystery religions involved the worship of a savior whose death and resurrection would lead the way to eternal salvation for devoted followers. Some philosophers and religious thinkers speculated that a single, universal god might rule the entire universe, and that this god had a plan for the salvation of all humankind. Like the Hellenistic philosophies, then, religions of salvation addressed the interests of individuals searching for security in a complex world. Indeed, those interests continued to be of concern to peoples in the Mediterranean basin long after political dominance passed from the Greek to the Italian peninsula.

ROME: FROM KINGDOM TO REPUBLIC

Founded in the eighth century B.C.E., the city of Rome was originally a small city-state ruled by a single king. In 509 B.C.E., however, the city's aristocrats deposed the king, ended the monarchy, and instituted a republic—a form of government in which delegates represent the interests of various constituencies. The Roman republic survived for more than five hundred years, and it was under the republican constitution that Rome came to establish itself as the dominant power in the Mediterranean basin.

The Etruscans and Rome

According to legend, the city of Rome was founded by Romulus, who—along with his twin brother, Remus—was abandoned as a baby by an evil uncle near the

Romulus and Remus

flooded Tiber River. Before the infants could drown, a kindly she-wolf found them and nursed them to health. The boys grew strong and courageous, and in 753 B.C.E. Romulus founded the city and established himself as its first king.

Image
Capitoline wolf with Romulus & Remus

Modern scholars do not tell so colorful a tale, but they do agree that bands of Indo-European migrants crossed the Alps and settled throughout the Italian peninsula beginning about 2000 B.C.E. Like their distant cousins in India, Greece, and northern Europe, these migrants blended with the neolithic inhabitants of the region, adopted agriculture, and established tribal federations. Sheepherders and small farmers oc-

cupied much of the Italian peninsula, including the future site of Rome itself. Bronze metallurgy appeared about 1800 B.C.E. and iron about 900 B.C.E.

The Etruscans, a dynamic people, dominated much of Italy between the eighth and fifth centuries B.C.E. The Etruscans probably migrated to Italy from Anatolia. They settled first in Tuscany, the region around modern Florence, but they soon controlled much of Italy. They built thriving cities and established political and economic alliances between their settlements. They manufactured high-quality bronze and iron goods, and they worked gold and silver into jewelry. They built a fleet and traded actively in the western Mediterranean. During the late sixth century B.C.E., however, the Etruscans encountered a series of challenges from other peoples, and their society began to decline.

The Etruscans

The Etruscans deeply influenced the early development of Rome. Like the Etruscan cities, Rome was a monarchy during the early days after its foundation, and several Roman kings were Etruscans. The kings ruled Rome through the seventh and sixth centuries B.C.E., and they provided the city with paved streets, public buildings, defensive walls, and large temples.

The Kingdom of Rome

Etruscan merchants drew a large volume of traffic to Rome, thanks partly to the city's geographical advantages. Rome enjoyed easy access to the Mediterranean by way of the Tiber River, but since it was not on the coast, it did not run the risk of invasion or attack from the sea. Already during the period of Etruscan dominance, trade routes from all parts of Italy converged on Rome. When Etruscan society declined, Rome was in a strong position to play a more prominent role both in Italy and in the larger Mediterranean world.

The Roman Republic and Its Constitution

When the Roman nobility deposed the last Etruscan king and replaced him with a republic, they built the Roman forum at the heart of the city—a political and civic center filled with temples and public buildings where leading citizens tended to government business. They also instituted a republican constitution that entrusted executive responsibilities to two consuls who wielded

Establishment of the Republic

Etruscans (ih-TRUHS-kuhns)

civil and military power. Consuls were elected by an assembly dominated by the wealthy classes, known in Rome as the patricians, and they served one-year terms. The powerful Senate, whose members were mostly aristocrats with extensive political experience, advised the consuls and ratified all major decisions. When faced with crises, however, the Romans appointed an official, known as a dictator, who wielded absolute power for a term of six months. By providing for strong leadership during times of extraordinary difficulty, the republican constitution enabled Rome to maintain a reasonably stable society throughout most of the republic's history.

Conflicts between Patricians and Plebeians

Because the consuls and the Senate both represented the interests of the patricians, there was constant tension between the wealthy classes and the common people, known as the plebeians. Indeed, during the early fifth century B.C.E., relations between the classes became so strained that the plebeians threatened to secede from Rome. To maintain the integrity of the Roman state, the patricians granted plebeians the right to elect officials, known as tribunes, who represented their interests in the Roman government. Originally plebeians chose two tribunes, but the number eventually rose to ten. Tribunes had the power to intervene in all political matters, and they possessed the right to veto measures that they judged unfair.

Although tensions between the classes never disappeared, during the fourth century B.C.E. plebeians

plebeians (plih-BEE-uhns)

became eligible to hold almost all state offices and gained the right to have one of the consuls come from their ranks. By the early third century, plebeian-dominated assemblies won the power to make decisions binding on all of Rome. Thus, like fifth-century Athens, republican Rome gradually broadened the base of political participation.

The Expansion of the Republic

Between the fourth and second centuries B.C.E., the people of Rome transformed their city from a small and vulnerable city-state to the center of an enormous empire. They began by consolidating their power in the Italian peninsula itself. Indeed, by the later fourth century they had emerged as the predominant power in the Italian peninsula. Roman success in the peninsula was partly a matter of military power and partly a matter of generous policies toward the peoples they conquered. Instead of ruling them as vanquished subjects, the Romans allowed conquered people to govern their internal affairs as long as they provided military support and did not enter into hostile alliances. In addition, conquered peoples were allowed to trade in Rome, to take Roman spouses, and even to gain Roman citizenship. These policies both provided Rome with essential support and eased the pain of conquest.

With Italy under its control, Rome began to play a major role in the affairs of the larger Mediterranean basin and to experience conflicts with other Mediterranean powers. The principal power in the western

Ruins of the Roman forum, where political leaders conducted public affairs during the era of the republic, still stand today.

Map 8.4 Territories of the Roman republic to 133 B.C.E. Notice that some of its territories were quite distant from the city of Rome. Why might the acquisition of so much territory have affected the political stability of the republic?

Mediterranean during the fourth and third centuries B.C.E. was the city-state of Carthage, located near modern Tunis. Originally established as a

Expansion in the Mediterranean

Phoenician colony, Carthage enjoyed a strategic location that enabled it to trade actively throughout the Mediterranean. From the wealth generated by this commerce, Carthage became the dominant political power in north Africa (excluding Egypt), the southern part of the Iberian peninsula, and the western region of grain-rich Sicily as well. Meanwhile, the three Hellenistic empires that succeeded Alexander of Macedon continued to dominate the eastern Mediterranean.

Economic and political competition brought the Romans into conflict with Carthage first. Between

The Punic Wars

264 and 146 B.C.E., they fought three devastating conflicts known as the Punic Wars with the Carthaginians. The rivalry ended after Roman forces subjected Carthage to a long siege, conquered and burned the city, and forced some fifty thousand survivors into slavery. The Romans then annexed Carthaginian possessions in north Africa and Iberia—rich in grain, oil, wine, silver, and gold—and used those resources to finance continued imperial expansion.

Shortly after the beginning of the Carthaginian conflict, Rome became embroiled in conflicts with the Antigonids and the Seleucids in the eastern Mediter-

ranean. Between 215 and 148 B.C.E., Rome fought five major wars, mostly in Macedon and Anatolia, against these opponents. As a result of these conflicts, Rome emerged as the preeminent power in the eastern as well as the western Mediterranean by the middle of the second century B.C.E.

FROM REPUBLIC TO EMPIRE

Imperial expansion brought wealth and power to Rome, but these brought problems as well as benefits. Unequal distribution of wealth aggravated class tensions and gave rise to conflict over political and social policies. Meanwhile, the need to administer conquered lands efficiently strained the capacities of the republican constitution. During the first century B.C.E. and the first century C.E., Roman civil and military leaders gradually dismantled the republican constitution and imposed a centralized imperial form of government on the city of Rome and its empire.

Imperial Expansion and Domestic Problems

In Rome, as in classical China and Greece, patterns of land distribution caused serious political and social tensions. Conquered lands fell largely into the hands of wealthy elites, who organized enormous plantations known as *latifundia*. Because they enjoyed economies of scale and often employed slave labor, owners of *latifundia* operated at lower costs than did owners of smaller holdings, who often had to sell out to their wealthier neighbors.

During the second and first centuries B.C.E., relations between the classes became so strained that they led to violent social conflict and civil war. *Civil War* Roman politicians and generals jockeyed for power in support of either social reform or the privileged position of the wealthy elites, with bloody results on both sides. By the middle of the first century B.C.E., it had become increasingly clear that the Roman republic was not suitable for a large and growing empire. In this chaotic context Gaius Julius Caesar inaugurated the process by which Rome replaced its republican constitution with a centralized imperial form of government.

The Foundation of Empire

Julius Caesar recognized the need for social reform and favored liberal policies that would ease the suffering of the poor. During the decade of the 60s B.C.E., he played an active role in Roman politics. He spent enormous sums of money sponsoring public spectacles—such as battles between gladiators and wild animals—which helped him build a reputation and win election to posts in the republican government. This activity kept him in the public eye and helped to publicize his interest in social reform. During the next decade Caesar led a Roman army to Gaul, which he conquered and brought into the still-growing Roman empire.

In 49 B.C.E. Caesar turned his army toward Rome itself after conservative leaders in the city sought to maneuver him out of power. By early 46 B.C.E. he had made himself master of the Roman state and named himself dictator—an office that he claimed for life rather than for the constitutional six-month term. Caesar then centralized military and political functions and brought them under his own control. He confiscated property from conservatives and distributed it to veterans of his armies and other supporters. He launched large-scale building projects in Rome as a way to provide employment for the urban poor. He

A bust of Julius Caesar depicts a trim conqueror and a canny political leader.

also extended Roman citizenship to peoples in the imperial provinces.

Caesar never had the chance to consolidate his government, however, because in 44 B.C.E. members of the Roman elite stabbed him to death in the hopes of reestablishing the republic. Instead, *Augustus* they plunged Rome into thirteen more years of civil conflict. When the struggles ended, power belonged to Octavian, Caesar's nephew and adopted son. In a naval battle at Actium in Greece (31 B.C.E.), Octavian defeated his principal rival, Mark Antony, who had joined forces with Cleopatra, last of the Ptolemaic rulers of Egypt. He then moved quickly to consolidate his rule. In 27 B.C.E. the Senate bestowed on him the title Augustus, a term with strong religious connotations suggesting the divine or semi-divine nature of its holder.

Augustus's government was a monarchy disguised as a republic. He preserved traditional republican offices and forms of government and included members of the Roman elite in *Augustus's Administration* his government while at the same time fundamentally altering the nature of that government.

---

latifundia (lah-tee-FOON-dya)

He accumulated vast powers for himself and ultimately took responsibility for all important governmental functions. He reorganized the military system, creating a new standing army with commanders who owed allegiance directly to himself. He also was careful to place individuals loyal to him in all important positions. During his forty-five years of virtually unopposed rule, Augustus fashioned an imperial government that guided Roman affairs for the next three centuries.

Continuing Expansion and Integration of the Empire

During the two centuries following Augustus's rule, Roman armies conquered distant lands and integrated them into a larger economy and society. At its high point, during the early second century C.E., the Roman empire embraced much of Britain and continental Europe as well as a continuous belt of possessions surrounding the Mediterranean and extending to rich agricultural regions inland, including Mesopotamia.

Interactive Map

Expansion of the Roman republic & empire

Within the boundaries of the Roman empire itself, a long era of peace—known as the *pax romana*, or "Roman peace"—facilitated economic and political integration from the first to the middle of the third century C.E. Like their Persian, Chinese, Indian, and Hellenistic counterparts, the Romans integrated their empire by building networks of transportation and communication. Indeed, roads linked all parts of the Roman empire. One notable highway stretched more than 2,500 kilometers (1,554 miles) along the northeast imperial frontier from the Black Sea to the North Sea, parallel to the Danube and Rhine rivers. The roads permitted urgent travel and messages to proceed with remark-

Roman Roads

Map 8.5 Territories of the Roman empire about 117 C.E. Compare this map with Maps 8.3 and 8.4. Notice that the Roman empire in this period dominated the entire Mediterranean, and—complemented by its system of roads—facilitated connections among peoples and places from Britain to Egypt.

able speed: Tiberius, successor of Augustus as Roman emperor, once traveled 290 kilometers (180 miles) in a single day over Roman roads.

As armies spread Roman influence throughout the Mediterranean, jurists also worked to construct a rational body of law that would apply to all peoples under Roman rule. During the late republic and especially during the empire, the jurists articulated standards of justice and gradually applied them throughout Roman territory. They established the principle that defendants were innocent until proven guilty, and they ensured that defendants had a right to challenge their accusers before a judge in a court of law. Like transportation and communication networks, Roman law helped to integrate the diverse lands that made up the empire, and the principles of Roman law continued to shape Mediterranean and European society long after the empire had disappeared.

Roman Law

ECONOMY AND SOCIETY IN THE ROMAN MEDITERRANEAN

The rapid expansion of Roman influence and the imposition of Roman imperial rule brought economic and social changes to peoples throughout the Mediterranean basin. Good roads and the *pax romana* encouraged trade between regions. Existing cities benefited handsomely from the wealth generated by trade, and in the lands they conquered, the Romans founded new cities to serve as links between local regions and the larger Mediterranean economy. Meanwhile, like most other peoples of classical times, the Romans built a strictly patriarchal society and made extensive use of slave labor.

Trade and Urbanization

As the Roman empire became more integrated, agricultural production grew increasingly commercialized as well as specialized. Because it was possible to import grain at favorable prices from lands that routinely produced large surpluses, other regions could concentrate on the cultivation of fruits and vegetables or on the production of manufactured items. Greece, for example, concentrated on olives and vines, and Italy became a center for the production of pottery, glassware, and bronze goods.

Commercial Agriculture

Specialized production of agricultural commodities and manufactured goods set the stage for vigorous trade. Sea lanes linked ports from Syria and Palestine to

Spain and north Africa. Roman military and naval power kept the seas largely free of pirates so that sizable cargoes could move safely over long distances. Indeed, the Mediterranean became essentially a Roman lake, which the Romans called *mare nostrum* ("our sea").

Mediterranean Trade

Much of the profit from Mediterranean trade flowed to Rome, where it fueled remarkable urban development. In the first century C.E., some ten thousand statues and seven hundred pools decorated the city. The Roman state financed the construction of temples, bath houses, public buildings, stadiums, and, perhaps

The City of Rome

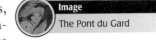
Image
The Pont du Gard

most important of all, aqueducts—built with concrete invented by Roman engineers—that brought fresh water into the city from the neighboring mountains.

In addition to the spectacular growth of Rome, urban growth and development took place in cities all over the empire. And, as wealth concentrated in the cities, urban residents came to expect a variety of comforts not available in rural areas. Roman cities enjoyed abundant supplies of fresh water and elaborate sewage and plumbing systems. All sizable cities and even many smaller towns had public baths and often swimming pools and gymnasia as well. Enormous circuses, stadiums, and amphitheaters provided sites for the entertainment of the urban masses. Entertainment in stadiums often took forms now considered coarse and cruel— battles to the death between gladiators or between humans and wild animals—but urban populations flocked to such events, which they looked on as exciting diversions from daily routine. The Roman Colosseum, a magnificent marble stadium and sports arena opened in 80 C.E., provided seating for about fifty thousand spectators.

Roman Cities and Their Attractions

Family and Society in Roman Times

Roman law vested immense authority in male heads of families, known as the *pater familias*—"father of the family." Roman law gave the *pater familias* the authority to arrange marriages for his children, determine the work or duties they would perform, and punish them for offenses. He had rights also to sell them into slavery and even to execute them.

The Pater Familias

---

pater familias (PAH-tehr fah-MEE-lyas)

Although the *pater familias* was legally endowed with extraordinary powers, women usually supervised domestic affairs in Roman households, and by the time they reached middle age they generally wielded considerable influence within their families. Also, although Roman law placed strict limits on the ability of women to receive inheritances, clever individuals found ways to evade the law. During the third and second centuries B.C.E., women came to possess a great deal of property, and by the first century B.C.E., many women supervised the financial affairs of family businesses and wealthy estates.

Slavery   Roman society made extensive use of slave labor: by the second century C.E., slaves may have represented as much as one-third of the population of the Roman empire. In the countryside they worked mostly on *latifundia* under extremely harsh conditions, often chained together in teams. In fact, discontent among rural slaves led to several large-scale revolts, especially during the second and first centuries B.C.E. During the most serious uprising, in 73 B.C.E., the escaped slave Spartacus assembled an army of seventy thousand rebellious slaves. The Roman army dispatched eight legions, comprising more than forty thousand well-equipped, veteran troops, to quell the revolt.

In the cities, conditions were much less difficult. Female slaves commonly worked as domestic servants while males toiled as servants, laborers, craftsmen, shopkeepers, or business agents for their owners. As in Greece, slaves who had an education or possessed some particular talent had the potential to lead comfortable lives. In urban areas it was also common, though not mandatory, for masters to free slaves about the time they reached thirty years of age. Until freed, however, slaves remained under the strict authority of their masters, who had the right to sell them, arrange their family affairs, punish them, and even execute them for serious offenses.

The Cosmopolitan Mediterranean

The integration of the Mediterranean basin had important effects not only for the trade and economy of the Roman empire but also for its cultural and religious traditions. Roads and communication networks favored the spread of new popular religions. Most important of these over the long run was Christianity, which became the official religion of the Roman empire and the predominant faith of the Mediterranean basin.

Greek Philosophy and Religions of Salvation

During the early days of their history, the Romans recognized many gods and goddesses, who they believed intervened directly in human affairs. Jupiter was the principal god, lord of the heavens, and Mars was the god of war, Ceres the   *Roman Deities* goddess of grain, Janus the god who watched the threshold of individual houses, and Vesta the goddess of the hearth. In addition to those major deities, most Roman households honored tutelary deities, gods who looked after the welfare of individual families.

As the Romans expanded their political influence and built an empire, they encountered the religious and cultural traditions of other peoples. Often they adopted the deities of other peoples and used them for their own purposes. From the Etruscans, for example, they learned of Juno, the moon goddess, and Minerva, the goddess of wisdom, as well as certain religious practices, such as divination of the future through examination of the internal organs of ritually sacrificed animals.

The Romans also drew deep inspiration from the Greek tradition of rational thought and philosophy, especially Stoicism. The Stoics' desire to identify a set of universal moral   *Greek Influence* standards based on nature and reason appealed strongly to Roman intellectuals. Indeed, thinkers such as Marcus Tullius Cicero (106–43 B.C.E.) readily adopted Stoic values. His letters and treatises emphasized the individual's duty to live in accordance with nature and reason. He argued that the pursuit of justice was the individual's highest public duty, and he scorned those who sought to accumulate wealth or to become powerful through immoral, illegal, or unjust means. Through his speeches and especially his writings, Cicero helped to establish Stoicism as the most prominent school of moral philosophy in Rome.

Whereas educated thinkers drew inspiration from the Greeks, the masses found comfort in religions of salvation that established their presence throughout the Mediterranean basin and   *Religions of Salvation* beyond. These religions became prominent features in Rome during the late republic as well as under the empire. Many originated in the far-flung realms of the empire, including the popular Anatolian cult of Mithras, the Anatolian cult of the mother goddess Cybele, and the Egyptian cult of the goddess Isis.

The Mithraic religion provided divine sanction for human life and especially for purposeful moral behavior. It brought together a community that welcomed

Built between 118 and 125 C.E., the Pantheon in Rome was a temple honoring all gods, and it survives as one of the outstanding examples of Roman architecture. With a diameter of 43 meters (141 feet), the building's dome was the largest constructed until the twentieth century.

and nurtured like-minded individuals. Finally, it offered hope for individuals who conscientiously observed the cult's teachings by promising them ecstatic and mysterious union with Mithras—who was strongly associated with military virtues such as strength, courage, and discipline—himself. During the late republic, Mithraic altars and temples appeared in military garrisons throughout the empire. During the early centuries C.E., administrators and merchants also became enchanted with Mithras, and his cult attracted followers among the male populations of all sizable communities and commercial centers in the Roman empire.

Mithraism

The cult of Mithras did not admit women, but cults dedicated to the Anatolian mother goddess Cybele, the Egyptian goddess Isis, and other deities made a place for both men and women. Indeed, the cult of Isis may have been the most popular of all the Mediterranean religions of salvation before the rise of Christianity. Devotees built temples to

Cult of Isis

Isis throughout the Roman empire, and they adored the Egyptian goddess as a benevolent and protective deity who nurtured her worshipers and helped them cope with the stresses of life in cosmopolitan society. Like the Mithraic religion, the cult of Isis and other religions of salvation attracted followers in Rome and other cities throughout the Mediterranean basin. The immense popularity of these religions of salvation provides a context that helps to explain the remarkable success of Christianity in the Roman empire.

Judaism and Early Christianity

After the dissolution of the Jewish kingdom of David and Solomon in the early tenth century B.C.E., the Jewish people maintained their faith and their communities under various imperial regimes. At times, Jewish communities clashed with their imperial overlords, especially because monotheistic Jews refused to revere emperors as gods. As the Romans extended their empire in the eastern Mediterranean and brought the Jews in Palestine under their control, relations between the two became especially tense. Between 66 and 70 C.E., relations deteriorated to such a point that Palestinian Jews rose in rebellion against the Romans in what became known as the Jewish War.

The Jews and the Empire

The Jews were decisively defeated in the war, which prompted some Jews to found new sects that looked for saviors to deliver them from Roman rule so they could practice their faith without interference. The early Christians were one such sect. The Christians formed their community around Jesus of Nazareth, a charismatic Jewish teacher whom they recognized as their savior. Born about the year 4 B.C.E., Jesus grew up at a time of high tension between Roman overlords and their Jewish subjects. He was a peaceful man who taught devotion to God and love for fellow human beings. He attracted large crowds because of a reputation for wisdom and miraculous powers, especially the ability to heal the sick.

Jesus of Nazareth

Yet Jesus alarmed the Romans because he also taught that "the kingdom of God is at hand." To Jesus, the kingdom of God was a spiritual realm in which God would gather those faithful to him. To Roman administrators, however, his message sounded like a threat to Roman rule in Palestine, especially since crowds routinely accompanied Jesus. In an effort to forestall a new round of rebellion, Roman administrators executed Jesus by fixing him to a cross in the early 30s C.E.

Jesus' crucifixion did not put an end to his movement. Even after his execution Jesus' close followers strongly felt his presence and proclaimed that he had triumphed over death by rising from his grave. They called him "Christ," meaning "the anointed one," the savior who would bring individuals into the kingdom of God. They taught that he was the son of God and that his sacrifice served to offset the sins of those who had faith in him. They taught further that, like Jesus, the faithful would survive death and would experience eternal life in the spiritual kingdom of God. Following Jesus' teachings, the early Christians observed a demanding moral code and devoted themselves uncompromisingly to God. They also compiled a body of writings—accounts of Jesus' life, reports of his followers' works, and letters outlining Christian teachings—that gained recognition as the New Testament. Together with the Jews' Hebrew scriptures, which Christians referred to as the Old Testament, the New Testament became the holy book of Christianity.

Jesus' Early Followers

Jesus and his earliest followers were all Jews. Beginning about the middle of the first century C.E., however, some Christians avidly sought converts from non-Jewish communities in the Hellenistic world and the Roman empire. The principal figure in the expansion of Christianity beyond Judaism was Paul of Tarsus, a Jew from Anatolia who zealously preached his faith, especially in the Greek-speaking eastern region of the Roman empire. Paul taught a Christianity that attracted the urban masses in the same way as other religions of salvation that spread widely in the Roman empire. His doctrine called for individuals to observe high moral standards and to place their faith ahead of personal and family interests. His teaching also explained the world and human history as the results of God's purposeful activity so that it provided a framework of meaning for individuals' lives. Furthermore, Paul's doctrine promised a glorious future existence for those who conscientiously observed the faith.

Paul of Tarsus

Yet for two centuries after the crucifixion of Jesus, there was no central authority for the fledgling church. Rather, individual communities selected their own supervisors, known as *bishops,* who oversaw priests and governed their jurisdictions according to their own best understanding of Christian doctrine. As a result, until the emergence of Rome as the principal seat of church authority in the third century C.E., Christians held doctrinal views and followed practices that varied considerably from one community to the next. Some religious leaders taught that Jesus had literally risen from the dead and come back to life, for example, and others held that his resurrection was a spiritual rather than physical matter. Only gradually did believers agree to recognize certain texts as authoritative scripture—the New Testament—and adopt them as fundamental guides for Christian doctrine and practice.

Early Christian Communities

Like the Jews from whose ranks they had sprung, the early Christians refused to honor the Roman state cults or revere the emperor as a god. As a result, Roman imperial authorities launched sporadic campaigns of persecution designed to eliminate Christianity as a threat to the empire. In spite of this repression, Christian numbers grew rapidly. During the first three centuries of the faith's existence, Christianity found its way to almost all parts of the Roman empire, and Christians established thriving communities throughout the Mediterranean basin and farther east in Mesopotamia and Iran. The remarkable growth of Christianity reflected the new faith's appeal particularly to the lower classes, urban populations, and women. Christianity accorded honor and dignity to individuals who did not enjoy high standing in Roman society, and it endowed them with a sense of spiritual freedom more meaningful than wealth, power, or social prominence. It taught the spiritual equality of the sexes and welcomed the contributions of both men and women. And it provided a promise of future glory for those who placed their faith in Jesus. Thus, although Christianity originated as a minor sect of Judaism, urban populations in the Roman empire embraced the new faith with such enthusiasm that by the third century C.E. it had become the most dynamic and influential religious faith in the Mediterranean basin.

The Growth of Early Christianity

SUMMARY

Under Greek and Roman influence, Mediterranean lands became a tightly integrated society. Although the Greeks did not build a centralized empire, they dotted the Mediterranean and Black Sea shorelines with their colonies, and their merchant fleets stimulated both commercial and cultural interactions between peoples of distant lands. Greek merchants, soldiers, and administrators also played prominent roles in the extensive empires of Alexander and the Hellenistic rulers, and they left a remarkably rich and enduring cultural legacy. Building in part on both the cultural and the economic legacies of the Greeks, the Romans proceeded to construct a republic, and then an empire, that eventually administered lands as distant as Mesopotamia and Britain. Highly organized trade networks enabled peoples throughout the empire to concentrate on specialized agricultural or industrial production. Popular religions spread widely and attracted enthusiastic converts. Like Confucianism and Buddhism in classical China and India, rational philosophy and Christianity became prominent sources of intellectual and religious authority in the classical Mediterranean and continued to influence cultural development in the Mediterranean, Europe, and southwest Asia over the long term.

CHRONOLOGY

2200–1100 B.C.E.	Minoan society
1600–1100 B.C.E.	Mycenaean society
800–338 B.C.E.	Era of the classical Greek polis
509 B.C.E.	Establishment of the Roman republic
500–479 B.C.E.	Persian Wars
470–399 B.C.E.	Life of Socrates
443–429 B.C.E.	Pericles' leadership in Athens
431–404 B.C.E.	Peloponnesian War
430–347 B.C.E.	Life of Plato
384–322 B.C.E.	Life of Aristotle
359–336 B.C.E.	Reign of Philip II of Macedon
336–323 B.C.E.	Reign of Alexander of Macedon
264–146 B.C.E.	Roman expansion in the Mediterranean basin
106–43 B.C.E.	Life of Marcus Tullius Cicero
FIRST CENTURY B.C.E.	Civil war in Rome
46–44 B.C.E.	Rule of Gaius Julius Caesar as dictator
31 B.C.E.–14 C.E.	Rule of Augustus
4 B.C.E.–EARLY 30s C.E.	Life of Jesus of Nazareth
FIRST CENTURY C.E.	Life of Paul of Tarsus
66–70 C.E.	Jewish War

FOR FURTHER READING

Martin Bernal. *Black Athena: The Afroasiatic Roots of Classical Civilization.* 2 vols. to date. New Brunswick, 1987–. Provocative and controversial study arguing for Egyptian and Semitic influences on early Greek society.

Henry C. Boren. *Roman Society.* 2nd ed. Lexington, 1992. An authoritative synthesis that places social and economic history in its political context.

Keith R. Bradley. *Discovering the Roman Family: Studies in Roman Social History.* New York, 1991. A provocative analysis of Roman family life with illustrations from individual experiences.

Peter Brown. *The Rise of Western Christendom: Triumph and Diversity, A.D. 200–1000.* 2nd ed. Oxford, 2003. A landmark analysis of early Christian history that incorporates the findings of recent scholarship.

F. M. Cornford. *Before and after Socrates.* Cambridge, 1965. A short but brilliant synthesis of classical Greek philosophy.

M. I. Finley. *Ancient Slavery and Modern Ideology.* Expanded ed. Princeton, 1998. Presents a thoughtful analysis of Greek and Roman slavery in light of modern slavery and contemporary debates.

Frederick C. Grant, ed. *Hellenistic Religions: The Age of Syncretism.* Indianapolis, 1953. Fascinating collection of translated documents and texts that throw light on religious and philosophical beliefs of the Hellenistic era.

Michael Grant. *Cities of Vesuvius: Pompeii and Herculaneum*. London, 1971. Fascinating glimpse of Roman society as reconstructed by archaeologists working at sites destroyed by the eruption of Vesuvius in 79 C.E.

Naphtali Lewis and Meyer Reinhold, eds. *Roman Civilization: Selected Readings*. 2 vols. 3rd ed. New York, 1990. A rich collection of translated texts and documents that illuminate Roman history and society.

Sarah B. Pomeroy. *Goddesses, Whores, Wives, and Slaves: Women in Classical Antiquity*. New York, 1995. Outstanding study analyzing the status and role of women in classical Greece and Rome.

CHAPTER 9

Cross-Cultural Exchanges on the Silk Roads

In the year 139 B.C.E., the Chinese emperor Han Wudi sent an envoy named Zhang Qian on a mission to lands west of China. The emperor's purpose was to find allies who could help combat the nomadic Xiongnu, who menaced the northern and western borders of the Han empire. From captives he had learned that other nomadic peoples in far western lands bore grudges against the Xiongnu, and he reasoned that they might ally with Han forces to pressure their common enemy.

The problem for Zhang Qian was that to communicate with potential allies against the Xiongnu, he had to pass directly through lands they controlled. Soon after Zhang Qian left Han territory, Xiongnu forces captured him. For ten years the Xiongnu held him in comfortable captivity: they allowed him to keep his personal servant,

and they provided him with a Xiongnu wife, with whom he had a son. When suspicions about him subsided, however, Zhang Qian escaped with his family and servant. He even had the presence of mind to keep with him the yak tail that Han Wudi had given him as a sign of his ambassadorial status. He fled to the west and traveled as far as Bactria, but he did not succeed in lining up allies against the Xiongnu. While returning to China, Zhang Qian again fell into Xiongnu hands but managed to escape after one year's detention when the death of the Xiongnu leader led to a period of turmoil. In 126 B.C.E. Zhang Qian and his party returned to China and a warm welcome from Han Wudi.

Although his diplomatic efforts did not succeed, Zhang Qian's mission had far-reaching consequences. Apart from political

OPPOSITE PAGE: *Tomb figure of a camel and a foreign rider. The majority of the Silk Road trade was handled by the nomadic peoples of central and western Asia.*

and military intelligence about western lands and their peoples, Zhang Qian also brought back information of immense commercial value. While in Bactria about 128 B.C.E., he noticed Chinese goods—textiles and bamboo articles—offered for sale in local markets. Upon inquiry he learned that they had come from southwest China by way of Bengal. From that information he deduced the possibility of establishing trade relations between China and Bactria through India.

Han Wudi responded enthusiastically to this idea and dreamed of trading with peoples inhabiting lands west of China. From 102 to 98 B.C.E., he mounted an ambitious campaign that broke the power of the Xiongnu and pacified central Asia. His conquests simplified trade relations, since it became unnecessary to route commerce through India. The intelligence that Zhang Qian gathered during his travels thus contributed to the opening of the silk roads—the network of trade routes that linked lands as distant as China and the Roman empire—and more generally to the establishment of relations between China and lands to the west.

China and other classical societies imposed political and military control over vast territories. They promoted trade and communication within their own empires, bringing regions that had previously been self-sufficient into a larger economy and society. They also fostered the spread of cultural, religious, and political traditions to distant regions, and they encouraged the construction of institutional frameworks that promoted the long-term survival of those traditions.

The classical societies established a broad zone of communication and exchange throughout much of the earth's eastern hemisphere. Trade networks crossed the deserts of central Asia and the depths of the Indian Ocean. Long-distance trade passed through much of Eurasia and north Africa, from China to the Mediterranean basin, and to parts of sub-Saharan Africa as well. That long-distance trade profoundly influenced the experiences of peoples and the development of societies throughout the eastern hemisphere. It brought wealth and access to foreign products, and it facilitated the spread of religious traditions beyond their original homelands. It also facilitated the transmission of disease. Indeed, the transmission of disease over the silk roads helped bring an end to the classical societies, since infectious and contagious diseases sparked devastating epidemics that caused political, social, and economic havoc. Long-distance trade thus had deep political, social, and cultural as well as economic and commercial implications for classical societies.

LONG-DISTANCE TRADE AND THE SILK ROADS NETWORK

Ever since the earliest days of history, human communities have traded with one another, sometimes over long distances. Before classical times, however, long-distance trade was a risky venture. Ancient societies often policed their own realms effectively, but extensive regions lay beyond their control. Trade passing between societies was therefore liable to interception by bandits or pirates. That risk increased the costs of long-distance transactions in ancient times.

During the classical era, two developments reduced the risks associated with travel and stimulated long-distance trade. First, rulers invested heavily in the construction of roads and bridges. They undertook these expensive projects primarily for military and administrative reasons, but roads also had the effect of encouraging trade within individual societies and facilitating exchanges between different societies. Second, classical societies pacified large stretches of Eurasia and north Africa. As a result, merchants did not face such great risk as in previous eras, the costs of long-distance trade dropped, and its volume rose dramatically.

Trade Networks of the Hellenistic Era

The tempo of long-distance trade increased noticeably during the Hellenistic era, partly because of the many colonies established by Alexander of Macedon and the Seleucid rulers in Persia and Bactria. Though originally populated by military forces and administrators, these settlements soon attracted Greek merchants and bankers who linked the recently conquered lands to the Mediterranean basin. The Seleucid rulers controlled land routes linking Bactria, which offered access to Indian markets, to Mediterranean ports in Syria and Palestine.

Like the Seleucids, the Ptolemies maintained land routes—in their case, routes going south from Egypt to the kingdom of Nubia and Meroë in east Africa—but they also paid close attention to sea lanes and maritime trade. They ousted pirates from sea lanes linking the Red Sea to the Arabian Sea and the Indian Ocean. They also built several new ports, the most important being Berenice on the Red Sea, while Alexandria served as their principal window on the Mediterranean.

Even more important, perhaps, mariners from Ptolemaic Egypt learned from Arab and Indian seamen about the monsoon winds that governed sailing and shipping in the Indian Ocean. During the summer the winds blow regularly from the southwest, whereas in the winter they come from the northeast. Knowledge of these winds enabled mariners to sail safely and reliably to all parts of the Indian Ocean basin.

The Monsoon System

Establishment and maintenance of these trade routes was an expensive affair calling for substantial investment in military forces, construction, and bureaucracies to administer the commerce that passed over the routes. But the investment paid handsome dividends. Long-distance trade stimulated economic development within the Hellenistic realms themselves, bringing benefits to local economies throughout the empires. Moreover, Hellenistic rulers closely supervised foreign trade and levied taxes on it, thereby deriving income even from foreign products. Thus with official encouragement, a substantial trade developed throughout the Hellenistic world, from Bactria and India in the east to the Mediterranean basin in the west.

Trade in the Hellenistic World

Indeed, maritime trade networks through the Indian Ocean linked not only the large classical societies of Eurasia and North Africa but also smaller societies in east Africa. During the late centuries B.C.E., the port of Rhapta (located near Dar es Salaam in Tanzania) emerged as the principal commercial center on the east African coast. With increasing trade, groups of professional merchants and entrepreneurs emerged at Rhapta, and coins came into general use on the east African coast. Merchants of Rhapta imported iron goods such as spears, axes, and knives from southern Arabia and the eastern Mediterranean region in exchange for ivory, rhinoceros horn, tortoise shell, and slaves obtained from interior regions.

The Silk Roads

The establishment of classical empires greatly expanded the scope of long-distance trade, as much of Eurasia and north Africa fell under the sway of one classical society or another. The Han empire maintained order in China and pacified much of central Asia, including a sizable corridor offering access to Bactria and western markets. The Parthian empire displaced the Seleucids in Persia and

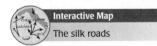

Interactive Map
The silk roads

Ptolemaic (TAWL-oh-may-ihk)

extended its authority to Mesopotamia. The Roman empire brought order to the Mediterranean basin. With the decline of the Mauryan dynasty, India lacked a strong imperial state, but the Kushan empire and other regional states provided stability and security, particularly in northern India, which favored long-distance trade.

As the classical empires expanded, merchants and travelers created an extensive network of trade routes that linked much of Eurasia and north Africa. Historians refer to these routes collectively as the silk roads, since high-quality silk from China was one of the principal commodities exchanged over the roads. The overland silk roads took caravan trade from China to the Roman empire, thus linking the extreme ends of the Eurasian landmass. From the Han capital of Chang'an, the main silk road went west until it arrived at the Taklamakan desert, also known as the Tarim Basin. The silk road then split into two main branches that skirted the desert proper and passed through oasis towns that ringed it to the north and south. The branches came together at Kashgar (now known as Kashi, located in the westernmost corner of modern China). From there the reunited road went west to Bactria, where a branch forked off to offer access to Taxila and northern India, while the principal route continued across northern Iran. There it joined with roads to ports on the Caspian Sea and the Persian Gulf and proceeded to Palmyra (in modern Syria), where it met roads coming from Arabia and ports on the Red Sea. Continuing west, it terminated at the Mediterranean ports of Antioch (in modern Turkey) and Tyre (in modern Lebanon).

Overland Trade Routes

The silk roads also included a network of sea lanes that sustained maritime commerce throughout much of the eastern hemisphere. From Guangzhou in southern China, sea lanes through the South China Sea linked the east Asian seaboard to the mainland and the islands of southeast Asia. Routes linking southeast Asia with Ceylon (modern Sri Lanka) and India were especially busy during classical times. From India, sea lanes passed through the Arabian Sea to Persia and Arabia, and through the Persian Gulf and the Red Sea they offered access to land routes and the Mediterranean basin, which already possessed a well-developed network of trade routes.

Sea Lanes and Maritime Trade

A wide variety of manufactured products and agricultural commodities traveled over the silk roads. Silk and spices traveled west from producers in southeast

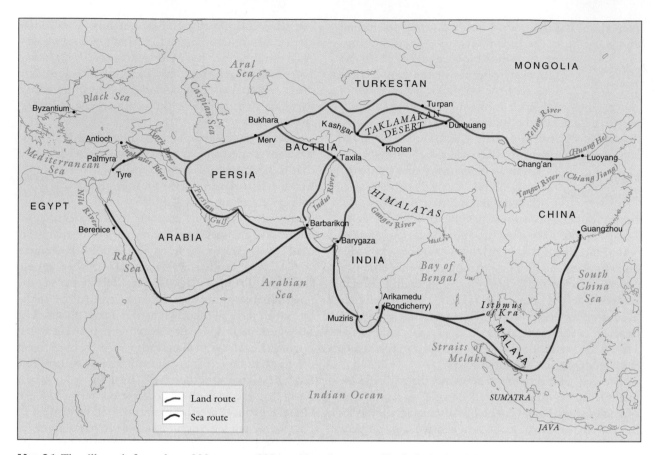

Map 9.1 The silk roads from about 200 B.C.E. to 300 C.E. Note the extent of both the land and the sea routes across Eurasia. What conditions would have made successful travel across these routes possible?

Asia, China, and India to consumers in central Asia, Iran, Arabia, and the Roman empire. Silk came mostly from China, and the fine spices—cloves, nutmeg, mace, and cardamom—all came from southeast Asia. Ginger came from China, cinnamon from China and southeast Asia, pepper from India, and sesame oil from India, Arabia, and southwest Asia. Spices were extremely important commodities in classical times because they had many more uses than they do in the modern world. They served not only as condiments and flavoring agents but also as drugs, anesthetics, aphrodisiacs, perfumes, aromatics, and magical potions. For the silk and spices they imported, western lands exchanged a variety of manufactured goods and other commodities, including horses and jade from central Asia and glassware, jewelry, textiles, and pottery from the Roman empire.

Trade Goods

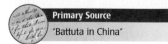

Primary Source

"Battuta in China"

Zhang Qian was only one of many individuals who made very long journeys during classical times. Indeed, records indicate that merchants and diplomats from central Asia, China, India, southeast Asia, and the Roman empire traveled long distances in pursuit of trade and diplomacy. On a few occasions individuals even traveled across much or all of the eastern hemisphere between China and the Roman empire. A Chinese ambassador named Gang Ying embarked on a mission to distant western lands in 97 C.E. and proceeded as far as Mesopotamia before reports of the long and dangerous journey ahead persuaded him to return home. And Chinese sources reported the arrival in 166 C.E. of a delegation claiming to represent the Roman emperor Marcus Aurelius.

Individual merchants did not usually travel from one end of Eurasia to the other, either by land or by sea. Instead, they handled long-distance trade in stages. On the caravan routes between China and Bactria, for example, Chinese and central Asian nomadic peoples dominated trade. Farther west, however, the Parthians took advantage of their power and geographic position to control overland trade within their boundaries. Once merchandise reached Palmyra, it passed mostly into the hands of Roman subjects such as Greeks, Jews, and Armenians, who were especially active in the commercial life of the Mediterranean basin.

The Organization of Long-Distance Trade

On the seas, the situation was similar: Malay and Indian mariners dominated trade in southeast Asian and south Chinese water, Persians and subjects of the Roman empire dominated the Arabian Sea, Parthians controlled the Persian Gulf, and the Roman empire dominated the Red Sea. Indeed, after Roman emperors absorbed Egypt in the first century C.E., their subjects carried on an especially brisk trade between India and the Mediterranean. The Greek geographer Strabo reported in the early first century C.E. that as many as 120 ships departed annually from the Red Sea for India. Meanwhile, since the mid–first century C.E., the Romans also had dominated both the eastern and the western regions of *mare nostrum,* the Mediterranean.

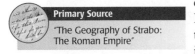

It is impossible to determine the quantity or the value of trade that passed over the silk roads in classical times, but it clearly made a deep impression on contemporaries. By the first century C.E., pepper, cinnamon, and other spices graced the tables of the wealthy classes in the Roman empire, where silk garments had become items of high fashion. Some Romans fretted that see-through silk attire would lead to moral decay, and others worried that hefty expenditures for luxury items would ruin the imperial economy. In both cases their anxieties testified to the powerful attraction of imported silks and spices for Roman consumers.

As it happened, long-distance trade more likely stimulated rather than threatened local economies. Yet long-distance trade did not occur in a vacuum. Commercial exchanges encouraged cultural and biological exchanges, some of which had large implications for classical societies.

CULTURAL AND BIOLOGICAL EXCHANGES ALONG THE SILK ROADS

The silk roads served as magnificent highways for merchants and their commodities, but others also took advantage of the opportunities they offered to travel in relative safety over long distances. Merchants, missionaries, and other travelers carried their beliefs, values, and religious convictions to distant lands: Buddhism, Hinduism, and Christianity all traveled the silk roads

During the first century B.C.E. Romans developed advanced glass-blowing techniques that enabled them to produce wares like this jar that were popular with wealthy consumers.

A Roman coin dated 189 C.E. depicts a merchant ship near the lighthouse at Alexandria. Ships like this one regularly picked up pepper and cinnamon from India along with other cargoes.

and attracted converts far from their original home-lands. Meanwhile, invisible travelers such as disease pathogens also crossed the silk roads and touched off devastating epidemics when they found fresh populations to infect. Toward the end of the classical era, epidemic disease that was spread over the silk roads caused dramatic demographic decline, especially in China and the Mediterranean basin and to a lesser extent in other parts of Eurasia as well.

The Spread of Buddhism and Hinduism

By the third century B.C.E., Buddhism had become well established in northern India, and with the sponsorship of the emperor Ashoka the faith spread to Bactria and Ceylon. Buddhism was particularly successful in attracting merchants as converts. When they traveled, Buddhist merchants observed their faith among themselves and explained it to others. Gradually, Buddhism made its way along the silk roads to Iran, central Asia, China, and southeast Asia.

Buddhism in Central Asia   Buddhism first established a presence in the oasis towns along the silk roads where merchants and their caravans found food, rest, lodging, and markets. The oases depended heavily on trade for their prosperity, and they allowed merchants to build monasteries and invite monks and scribes into their communities. Because they hosted travelers who came from different lands, spoke different languages, and observed different religious practices, the oasis towns became cosmopolitan centers. As early as the second century B.C.E., many residents of the oases themselves adopted Buddhism, which was the most prominent faith of silk roads merchants for almost a millennium, from about 200 B.C.E. to 700 C.E.

Buddhism in China   From the oasis communities Buddhism spread to the steppe lands of central Asia and to China via the nomadic peoples who visited the oases to trade. In the early centuries C.E., they increasingly responded to the appeal of Buddhism, and by the fourth century C.E., they had sponsored the spread of Buddhism throughout much of central Asia. Foreign merchants also brought their faith to China in about the first century B.C.E. Although the religion remained unpopular among native Chinese for several centuries, the presence of

Buddhism (BOO-diz'm)

Early Buddhist sculpture in Bactria reflected the influence of Mediterranean and Greek artistic styles. This seated Buddha from the first or second century C.E. bears Caucasian features and wears Mediterranean-style dress.

Buddhist monasteries and missionaries in China's major cities did attract some converts. Then, in about the fifth century C.E., the Chinese began to respond enthusiastically to Buddhism. Indeed, during the post-classical era Buddhism became the most popular religious faith throughout all of east Asia, including Japan and Korea as well as China.

As Buddhism spread north from India into central Asia and China, both Buddhism and Hinduism also began to attract a following in southeast Asia. Once again, merchants traveling the silk roads—in this case the sea lanes through the Indian Ocean—played prominent roles in spreading these faiths. By the first century C.E., clear signs of Indian cultural influence had appeared in many parts of southeast Asia. Many rulers converted to Buddhism, and others promoted

Buddhism and Hinduism in Southeast Asia

Image
The Diamond Sutra

the Hindu cults of Shiva and Vishnu. They built walled cities around lavish temples constructed in the Indian style, they adopted Sanskrit as a means of written communication, and they appointed Buddhist or Hindu advisors.

The Spread of Christianity

Early Christians faced intermittent persecution from Roman officials. During the early centuries C.E., Roman authorities launched a series of campaigns to stamp out Christianity, because most Christians refused to observe the state cults that honored emperors as divine beings. Imperial officials also considered Christianity a menace to society because zealous missionaries attacked other religions and generated sometimes violent conflict. Nevertheless, Christian missionaries took full advantage of the Romans' magnificent network of roads and sea lanes, which enabled them to carry their message throughout the Roman empire and the Mediterranean basin.

During the second and third centuries C.E., countless missionaries worked zealously to attract converts.

One of the more famous was Gregory the Wonderworker, a tireless missionary with a reputation for performing miracles, who popularized Christianity in central Anatolia during the mid–third century C.E. Contemporaries reported that Gregory not only preached Christian doctrine but also had access to impressive supernatural powers. Gregory and his fellow missionaries helped to make Christianity an enormously popular religion of salvation in the Roman empire. By the late third century C.E., in spite of continuing imperial opposition, devout Christian communities flourished throughout the Mediterranean basin in Anatolia, Syria, Palestine, Egypt, and north Africa as well as in Greece, Italy, Spain, and Gaul.

Christianity in the Mediterranean Basin

The young faith also traveled the trade routes and found followers beyond the Mediterranean basin. By the second century C.E., sizable Christian communities flourished throughout Mesopotamia and Iran, and a few Christian churches had appeared as far away as India. Christians also attracted large numbers of converts in

Christianity in Southwest Asia

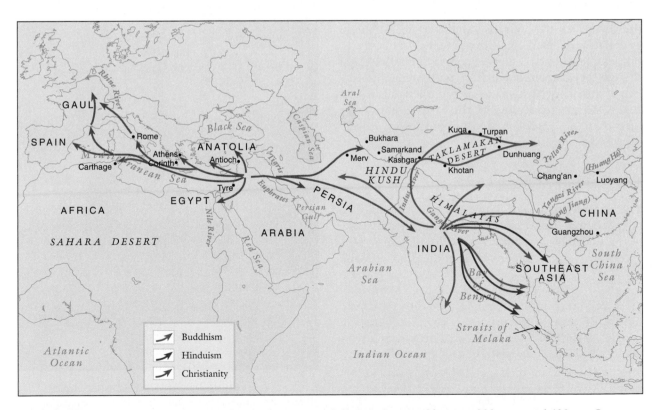

Map 9.2 Major routes through which Buddhism, Hinduism, and Christianity spread between 200 B.C.E. and 400 C.E. Compare this map with Map 9.1. What similarities do you notice between the silk roads and the spread of religion?

southwest Asia and came to constitute—along with Jews and Zoroastrians—one of the major religious communities in the region.

Christian communities in Mesopotamia and Iran deeply influenced Christian practices in the Roman empire. To demonstrate utter loyalty to their faith, Christians in southwest Asia often followed strict ascetic regimes and sometimes even withdrew from family life and society. By the third century C.E., some Mediterranean Christians were so impressed by these practices that they began to live as hermits in isolated locations, or to live exclusively among like-minded individuals who devoted their efforts to prayer and praise of God. Thus ascetic practices of Christians living in lands east of the Roman empire helped to inspire the formation of Christian monastic communities in the Mediterranean basin.

After the fifth century C.E., Christian communities in southwest Asia and the Mediterranean basin increasingly went separate ways. Most of the faithful in southwest Asia became Nestorians—followers of the Greek theologian Nestorius, who lived during the early fifth century 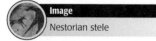 and emphasized the human as opposed to the divine nature of Jesus. Mediterranean church authorities rejected Nestorius's views, and many of his disciples departed for Mesopotamia and Iran. Although they had limited dealings with Mediterranean Christians, the Nestorians spread their faith east across the silk roads, and by the early seventh century they had established communities in central Asia, India, and China.

The Spread of Manichaeism

The explosive spread of Manichaeism dramatically illustrated how missionary religions made effective use of the silk roads trading network. Manichaeism was *Mani and Manichaeism* the faith derived from the prophet Mani (216–272 C.E.), a devout Zoroastrian from Babylon in Mesopotamia who also drew deep inspiration from Christianity and Buddhism. Because of the intense interaction between peoples of different societies, Mani promoted a syncretic blend of Zoroastrian, Christian, and Buddhist

elements as a religious faith that would serve the needs of a cosmopolitan world.

Mani was a dualist: he viewed the world as the site of a cosmic struggle between the forces of light and darkness, good and evil. He urged his followers to reject worldly pleasures and to observe high ethical standards. Devout Manichaeans, known as "the elect," abstained from marriage, sexual relations, and personal comforts, dedicating themselves instead to prayer, fasting, and ritual observances. Less zealous Manichaeans, known as "hearers," led more conventional lives, but they followed a strict moral code and provided food and gifts to sustain the elect. Mani's doctrine had strong appeal because it offered a rational explanation

Manichaean Ethics

A cave painting from about the seventh century C.E. depicts a group of devout Manichaean faithful, whose austere regimen called for them to dress in plain white garments and keep their hair uncut and untrimmed.

Zoroastrian (zohr-oh-ASS-tree-ahn)
Nestorian (neh-STOHR-eeuhn)
Manichaeism (man-ih-KEE-iz'm)

for the presence of good and evil in the world while also providing a means for individuals to achieve personal salvation.

Mani was a fervent missionary and traveled widely to promote his faith. He also created a Manichaean church with its own services, rituals, hymns, and liturgies. His doctrine attracted converts first in Mesopotamia, and before Mani's death it had spread throughout the Sasanid empire and into the eastern Mediterranean region. In spite of its asceticism, Manichaeism appealed especially strongly to merchants, who adopted the faith as hearers and supported the Manichaean church. By the end of the third century C.E., Manichaean communities had appeared in all the large cities and trading centers of the Roman empire.

Decline of Manichaeism

Manichaeism soon came under tremendous pressure in both the Zoroastrian Sasanid state and the Roman empire. Mani himself died in chains as a prisoner of the Sasanid emperor, who saw Manichaeism as a threat to the public order. Authorities in the Roman empire also persecuted Manichaeans and largely exterminated the faith in the Mediterranean basin over the course of the fifth and sixth centuries. Yet Manichaeism survived in central Asia, where it attracted converts among nomadic Turkish peoples who traded with merchants from China, India, and southwest Asia. Like Buddhism, Hinduism, and Christianity, then, Manichaeism relied on the trade routes of classical times to extend its influence to new lands and peoples.

The Spread of Epidemic Disease

Like religious faiths, infectious and contagious diseases also spread along the trade routes of the classical world. Aided by long-distance travelers, pathogens had opportunities to spread beyond their original environments and attack populations with no inherited or acquired immunities to the diseases they caused. The resulting epidemics took a ferocious toll in human lives.

Epidemic Diseases

During the second and third centuries C.E., the Han and Roman empires suffered large-scale outbreaks of epidemic disease. The most destructive of these diseases were probably smallpox and measles, and epidemics of bubonic plague may also have erupted. All three diseases are devastating when they break out in populations without resis-

tance, immunities, or medicines to combat them. As disease ravaged the two empires, Chinese and Roman populations declined sharply.

During the reign of Augustus, the population of the Roman empire stood at about sixty million people. During the second century C.E., epidemics reduced Roman population to forty-five million. Most devastating was an outbreak of smallpox that spread throughout the Mediterranean basin during the years 165 to 180 C.E. In combination with war and invasions, by 400 C.E. continuing outbreaks caused the population to decline even further, to about forty million. Whereas population in the eastern Mediterranean probably stabilized by the sixth century C.E., western Mediterranean lands experienced demographic stagnation until the tenth century.

Epidemics appeared slightly later in China than in the Mediterranean region. From fifty million people at the beginning of the millennium, Chinese population rose to sixty million in 200 C.E. As diseases found their way east, however, Chinese numbers fell back to fifty million by 400 C.E. and to forty-five million by 600 C.E. Thus by 600 C.E. both Mediterranean and Chinese populations had fallen by a quarter to a third from their high points during classical times.

Effects of Epidemic Diseases

Demographic decline in turn brought economic and social change. Trade within the empires declined, and both the Chinese and the Roman economies contracted. Both economies also moved toward regional self-sufficiency: whereas previously the Chinese and Roman states had integrated the various regions of their empires into a larger network of trade and exchange, after about 200 C.E. they increasingly embraced several smaller regional economies that concentrated on their own needs instead of the larger imperial market. Indeed, epidemic disease contributed to serious instability in China after the collapse of the Han dynasty, and in weakening Mediterranean society, it helped bring about the decline and fall of the western Roman empire.

CHINA AFTER THE HAN DYNASTY

By the time epidemic diseases struck China, internal political problems had already begun to weaken the Han dynasty. By the late second century C.E., Han authorities had largely lost their ability to maintain order. Early in the third century C.E., the central

---

Sasanid (suh-SAH-nid)

SOURCES FROM THE PAST

St. Cyprian on Epidemic Disease in the Roman Empire

St. Cyprian, bishop of Carthage, was an outspoken proponent of Christianity during the early and middle decades of the third century C.E. *When epidemic disease struck the Roman empire in 251* C.E., *imperial authorities blamed the outbreak on Christians who refused to honor pagan gods. Cyprian refuted this charge in his treatise* On Mortality, *which described the symptoms of epidemic disease and reflected on its significance for the Christian community.*

It serves as validation of the [Christian] faith when the bowels loosen and drain the body's strength, when fever generated in bone marrow causes sores to break out in the throat, when continuous vomiting roils the intestines, when blood-shot eyes burn, when the feet or other bodily parts are amputated because of infection by putrefying disease, when through weakness caused by injuries to the body either mobility is impeded, or hearing is impaired, or sight is obscured. It requires enormous greatness of heart to struggle with resolute mind against so many onslaughts of destruction and death. It requires great loftiness to stand firm amidst the ruins of the human race, not to concede defeat with those who have no hope in God, but rather to rejoice and embrace the gift of the times. With Christ as our judge, we should receive this gift as the reward of his faith, as we vigorously affirm our faith and, having suffered, advance toward Christ by Christ's narrow path. . . .

Many of us [Christians] are dying in this epidemic—that is, many of us are being liberated from the world. The epidemic is a pestilence for the Jews and the pagans and the enemies of Christ, but for the servants of God it is a welcome event. True, without any discrimination, the just are dying alongside the unjust, but you should not imagine that the evil and the good face a common destruction. The just are called to refreshment, while the unjust are herded off to punishment: the faithful receive protection, while the faithless receive retribution. We are unseeing and ungrateful for divine favors, beloved brethren, and we do not recognize what is granted to us. . . .

How suitable and essential it is that this plague and pestilence, which seems so terrible and ferocious, probes the justice of every individual and examines the minds of the human race to determine whether the healthy care for the ill, whether relatives diligently love their kin, whether masters show mercy to their languishing slaves, whether physicians do not abandon those seeking their aid, whether the ferocious diminish their violence, whether the greedy in the fear of death extinguish the raging flames of their insatiable avarice, whether the proud bend their necks, whether the shameless mitigate their audacity, whether the rich will loosen their purse strings and give something to others as their loved ones perish all around them and as they are about to die without heirs.

• *To what extent do you think St. Cyprian was effective in his efforts to bring inherited Christian teachings to bear on the unprecedented conditions he and his followers faced?*

SOURCE: Wilhelm von Hartel, ed. *S. Thasci Caecili Cypriani opera omnia* in *Corpus scriptorum ecclesiasticorum latinorum.* Vienna, 1868, vol. 3, pp. 305–6. (Translation by Jerry H. Bentley.)

government dissolved, and a series of autonomous regional kingdoms took the place of the Han state. With the disappearance of the Han dynasty, China experienced significant cultural change, most notably an increasing interest in Buddhism.

Internal Decay of the Han State

The Han dynasty collapsed largely because of internal problems that its rulers could not solve. One problem involved the development of factions within

Map 9.3 China after the Han dynasty. Note the division of China into three large kingdoms. What would have been the advantages to such a division? Would there also have been disadvantages?

the ranks of the ruling elites. The desire of some elites to advance their own prospects in the imperial government at the cost of others led to constant infighting and backstabbing among the ruling elites, which reduced the effectiveness of the central government. An even more difficult problem had to do with the perennial issue of land and its equitable distribution. In the last two centuries of the Han dynasty, large landowners gained new influence in the government. They reduced their share of taxes and shifted the burden onto peasants. They even formed private armies to advance the interests of their class.

Peasant Rebellion These developments provoked widespread unrest among peasants, who found themselves under increasing economic pressure with no means to influence the government. Pressures became particularly acute during the late second and third centuries when epidemics began to take their toll. In 184 C.E. peasant discontent fueled a large-scale uprising known as the Yellow Turban rebellion, so called because the rebels wore yellow headbands that represented the color of the Chinese earth and symbolized their peasant origins. Although quickly suppressed, the rebellion proved to be only the first in a series of insurrections that plagued the late Han dynasty.

Meanwhile, Han generals increasingly usurped political authority. By 190 C.E. the Han emperor had become a mere puppet, and the generals effectively ruled the regions controlled by their armies. They allied with wealthy landowners of their regions and established themselves as warlords who maintained a kind of rough order based on force of arms. In 220 C.E. they abolished the Han dynasty altogether and divided the empire into three large kingdoms.

Collapse of the Han Dynasty

Once the dynasty had disappeared, large numbers of nomadic peoples migrated into China, especially the northern regions, and they helped to keep China disunited for more than 350 years. Between the fourth and sixth centuries C.E., nomadic peoples established large kingdoms that dominated much of northern China as well as the steppe lands.

Cultural Change in Post-Han China

In some ways the centuries following the fall of the Han dynasty present a spectacle of chaos and disorder. One kingdom toppled another, only to fall in its turn to a temporary successor. War and nomadic invasions led to population decline in much of northern China. By the mid–fifth century, contemporaries reported, the Former Han capital of Chang'an had no more than one hundred households and the Later Han capital of Luoyang resembled a trash heap more than a city.

Beneath the disorderly surface of political events, however, several important social and cultural changes were taking place. First, nomadic peoples increasingly adapted to the Chinese environment and culture, and as the generations passed, distinctions between peoples of nomadic and Chinese ancestry became less and less obvious. Partly because of that development, a new imperial dynasty was eventually able to reconstitute a centralized imperial state in north China.

Sinicization of Nomadic Peoples

Second, with the disintegration of political order, the Confucian tradition lost much of its credibility. The original goal of Confucius and his early followers was to find some means to move from chaos to stability during the Period of the Warring States. When the Han dynasty collapsed, Confucianism seemed both ineffective and irrelevant.

Individuals who in earlier centuries might have committed themselves to Confucian values turned instead to Daoism and Buddhism. Daoism, from its origins in the Period of the Warring States, had originally appealed mostly to an educated elite. After the fall of the Han, however, Daoist sages widened its appeal by promising salvation to those who observed their doctrines and rituals and by offering the use of elixirs made of spices, herbs, and drugs that supposedly conferred health and immortality. Daoism attracted widespread interest among a population afflicted by war and disease and became much more popular than before, especially because it faced less competition from the Confucian tradition.

Even more important than Daoism for Chinese cultural history was Buddhism. After the fall of the Han empire, Buddhism received strong support from nomadic peoples who migrated into northern China and who in many cases had long been familiar with Buddhism in central Asia. Meanwhile, as a result of missionary efforts, the Indian faith began to attract a following among native Chinese as well. Indeed, between the fourth and sixth centuries C.E., Buddhism became well established in China. When a centralized imperial state took shape in the late sixth century C.E.,

Popularity of Buddhism

Buddhism provided an important cultural foundation for the restoration of a unified political order.

THE FALL OF THE ROMAN EMPIRE

A combination of internal problems and external pressures weakened the Roman empire and brought an end to its authority in the western portion of the empire, whereas in the eastern Mediterranean imperial rule continued until the fifteenth century C.E. In the Mediterranean basin as in China, imperial weakness and collapse coincided with significant cultural change, notably the increasing popularity of Christianity.

Internal Decay in the Roman Empire

As in the case of the Han dynasty, internal political problems go a long way toward explaining the fall of the Roman empire. Like their Han counterparts, the Roman emperors faced internal opposition. During the half century from 235 to 284 C.E., there were no fewer than twenty-six claimants to the imperial throne. Known as the "barracks emperors," most of them were generals who seized power, held it briefly, and then suddenly lost it when they were displaced by rivals or their own mutinous troops. Not surprisingly, most of the barracks emperors died violently. Only one is known for sure to have succumbed to natural causes.

The Barracks Emperors

The Roman empire also faced problems because of its sheer size. Even during the best of times, when the emperors could count on abundant revenues and disciplined armed forces, the sprawling empire posed a challenge for central governors. After the third century, as epidemics spread throughout the empire and its various regions moved toward local, self-sufficient economies, the empire as a whole became increasingly unmanageable.

The emperor Diocletian (reigned 284–305 C.E.) attempted to deal with this problem by dividing the empire into two administrative districts: one in the east and one in the west. A co-emperor ruled each district with the aid of a powerful lieutenant, and the four officials, known as the tetrarchs, were able to administer the vast empire more effectively than an individual emperor could. Diocletian was a skillful administrator. He managed to bring Rome's many armies, including un-

The Emperor Diocletian

Confucianism (kuhn-FEW-shun-iz'm)

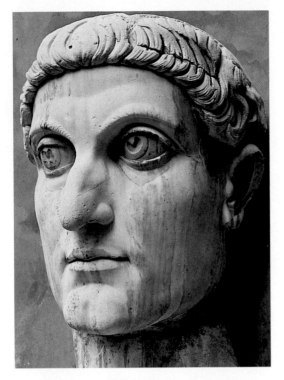

Only the colossal head of Constantine survives from a statue that originally stood about 14 meters (46 feet) tall.

empire, however, he and his successors faced the same sort of administrative difficulties that Diocletian had attempted to solve by dividing the empire. As population declined and the economy contracted, emperors found it increasingly difficult to marshall the resources needed to govern and protect the vast Roman empire.

Constantine

Germanic Invasions and the Fall of the Western Roman Empire

Apart from internal problems, the Roman empire faced a formidable military threat from migratory Germanic peoples. Indeed, during the fifth century C.E., Germanic invasions brought an end to Roman authority in the western half of the empire, although imperial rule survived for an additional millennium in the eastern Mediterranean.

Germanic peoples had migrated from their homelands in northern Europe and lived on the eastern and northern borders of the Roman empire since the second century C.E. Most notable were the Visigoths, who came originally from Scandinavia and Russia. Like the nomadic peoples who moved into northern China after the fall of the Han dynasty, the Visigoths settled, adopted agriculture, and drew deep inspiration from Roman society. In the interests of social order, however, the Romans discouraged settlement of the Visigoths and other Germanic peoples within the empire, preferring that they constitute buffer societies outside imperial borders.

Germanic Migrations

During the late fourth century, the relationship between Visigoths and Romans changed dramatically when the nomadic Huns began an aggressive westward migration from their homeland in central Asia. The Huns were probably cousins of the nomadic Xiongnu who inhabited the central Asian steppe lands west of China. During the mid–fifth century C.E., the warrior-king Attila organized the Huns into a virtually unstoppable military juggernaut. Under Attila, the Huns invaded Hungary, probed Roman frontiers in the Balkan region, menaced Gaul and northern Italy, and attacked Germanic peoples living on the borders of the Roman empire.

The Huns

Attila did not create a set of political institutions or a state structure, and the Huns disappeared as a political and military force soon after his death in 453 C.E. By that time, however, the Huns had placed such pressure on Visigoths and other Germanic peoples

predictable maverick forces, under firm imperial control. He also tried to deal with a crumbling economy by strengthening the imperial currency, forcing the government to adjust its expenditures to its income, and imposing price caps to dampen inflation. His economic measures were less successful than his administrative reforms, but they helped stabilize an economy ravaged by half a century of civil unrest.

Yet Diocletian's reforms encouraged ambition among the tetrarchs and their generals, and his retirement from the imperial office in 305 C.E. set off a round of internal struggles and bitter civil war. Already in 306 C.E. Constantine, son of Diocletian's coruler Constantius, moved to stake his claim as sole emperor. Once he had consolidated his grip on power in 324 C.E., Constantine ordered the construction of a new capital city, Constantinople, at a strategic site overlooking the Bosporus, the strait linking the Black Sea to the Sea of Marmara and beyond to the wealthy eastern Mediterranean. After 340 C.E. Constantinople became the capital of a united Roman empire.

Constantine himself was an able emperor. With the reunion of the eastern and western districts of the

Map 9.4 Germanic invasions and the fall of the western Roman empire between 450 and 476 C.E. Notice the many different groups that moved into western Roman territory in this period. What might have motivated such movement, and why couldn't the western Roman empire prevent it?

that they streamed en masse into the Roman empire in search of refuge. Once inside imperial boundaries, they encountered little effective resistance and moved around almost at will. They established settlements throughout the western half of the empire—Italy, Gaul, Spain, Britain, and north Africa—where populations were less dense than in the eastern Mediterranean. Under the command of Alaric, the Visigoths even stormed and sacked Rome in 410 C.E. By the middle of the fifth century, the western part of the Roman empire was in a shambles. In 476 C.E. imperial authority came to an ignominious end when the Germanic general Odovacer deposed Romulus Augustulus, the last of the Roman emperors in the western half of the empire.

Unlike the Han dynasty, the Roman empire did not entirely disintegrate: imperial authority survived for another millennium in the eastern half of the empire, known after the fifth century C.E. as the Byzantine empire. In the western half, however, Roman

Collapse of the Western Roman Empire

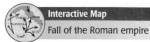

Interactive Map
Fall of the Roman empire

Byzantine (BIHZ-uhn-teen)

authority dissolved, and nomadic peoples built successor states in regions formerly subject to Rome. Vandals and then Visigoths governed Spain, Franks ruled Gaul, Angles and Saxons invaded Britain, and Italy fell under the sway of a variety of peoples, including Visigoths, Vandals, and Lombards.

Cultural Change in the Late Roman Empire

In the Roman empire, as in China, the collapse of the imperial state coincided with important social and cultural changes. The Germanic peoples who toppled the empire looked to their own traditions for purposes of organizing society and government. When they settled in the regions of the former empire, however, they absorbed a good deal of Roman influence. Over time, the mingling of Roman and Germanic traditions led to the emergence of an altogether new society—medieval Europe.

Christianity was perhaps the most prominent survivor of the western Roman empire. During the

Prominence of Christianity

fourth century C.E., several developments enhanced its influence throughout the Mediterranean basin. In the first place, Christianity won recognition as a legitimate religion in the Roman empire. In 312 C.E., while seeking to establish himself as sole Roman emperor, Constantine experienced a vision that impressed upon him the power of the Christian God. He believed that the Christian God helped him to prevail over his rivals, and he promulgated the Edict of Milan, which allowed Christians to practice their faith openly in the Roman empire. At some point during his reign, perhaps after his edict, Constantine himself converted to Christianity, and in 380 C.E. the emperor Theodosius proclaimed Christianity the official religion of the Roman empire. By the mid–fourth century, Christians held important political and military positions, and imperial sponsorship helped their faith to attract more converts than ever before.

Christianity also began to attract thoughtful and talented converts who articulated a Christian message for the intellectual elites of the Roman empire. The earliest Christians had come largely from the ranks of ordinary working people, and for three centuries the new faith grew as a popular religion of salvation favored by the masses, rather than as a reasoned doctrine of intellectual substance. During the fourth century, however, intellectual elites began

Portrait of St. Augustine holding a copy of his most famous work, *The City of God*, which sought to explain the meaning of history and the world from a Christian point of view.

to articulate Christianity in terms that were familiar and persuasive to the educated classes.

The most important and influential of those figures was St. Augustine (354–430 C.E.), bishop of the north African city of Hippo (modern-day Annaba in Algeria). Augustine had

St. Augustine

a fine education, and he was conversant with the leading intellectual currents of the day. During his youth he drew great inspiration from Stoicism and Platonism, and for nine years he belonged to a community of Manichaeans. Eventually he became disillusioned with both the Hellenistic philosophical school and Manichaeism, and in 387 C.E., while studying in Italy, he converted to Christianity. For the remainder of his life, he worked to reconcile Christianity with Greek and Roman philosophical traditions. More than any others, Augustine's writings helped make Christianity an intellectually respectable alternative to Hellenistic philosophy and to popular religions of salvation.

Besides winning the right to practice their faith openly and attracting intellectual talent, Christian leaders constructed an institutional apparatus that transformed a popular religion of salvation into a powerful church. In the absence of recognized leadership, the earliest Christians generated a range of conflicting and sometimes contradictory doctrines. To standardize their faith, Christian leaders instituted a hierarchy of church officials. At the top were five religious authorities—the bishop of Rome and the patriarchs of Jerusalem, Antioch, Alexandria, and Constantinople—who resided in the most important spiritual and political centers of the Roman empire. Subordinate to the five principal authorities were bishops, who presided over religious affairs in their districts, known as dioceses, which included all the prominent cities of the Roman empire. When theological disputes arose, the patriarchs and the bishops assembled in church councils to determine which views would prevail as official doctrine. The councils at Nicaea (325 C.E.) and Chalcedon (451 C.E.), for example, took up the difficult and contentious issue of Jesus' nature. Delegates at

The Institutional Church

these councils proclaimed that Jesus was both fully human and fully divine at the same time, in contrast to Nestorians, Arians, and other Christian groups who held that Jesus was either primarily human or primarily divine.

As Roman imperial authority crumbled, the bishop of Rome, known as the pope (from the Latin *papa,* meaning "father"), emerged as spiritual leader of Christian communities in the western regions of the empire. As the only sources of established and recognized authority, the popes and the bishops of other important cities organized local government and defensive measures for their communities. They also mounted missionary campaigns to convert Germanic peoples to Christianity. Although Roman imperial authority disappeared, Roman Christianity survived and served as a foundation for cultural unity in lands that had formerly made up the western half of the Roman empire.

SUMMARY

By 500 C.E. classical societies in Persia, China, India, and the Mediterranean basin had either collapsed or fallen into decline. Yet all the classical societies left rich legacies that shaped political institutions, social orders, and cultural traditions for centuries to come. Moreover, by sponsoring commercial and cultural relations between different peoples, the classical societies laid a foundation for intensive and systematic cross-cultural interaction in later times. After the third century C.E., the decline of the Han and Roman empires resulted in less activity over the silk roads than in the preceding three hundred years. But the trade routes survived, and when a new series of imperial states reestablished order throughout much of Eurasia and north Africa in the sixth century C.E., the peoples of the eastern hemisphere avidly resumed their crossing of cultural boundary lines in the interests of trade and communication.

CHRONOLOGY

THIRD CENTURY B.C.E.	Spread of Buddhism and Hinduism to southeast Asia
SECOND CENTURY B.C.E.	Introduction of Buddhism to central Asia
139–126 B.C.E.	Travels of Zhang Qian in central Asia
FIRST CENTURY B.C.E.	Introduction of Buddhism to China
SECOND CENTURY C.E.	Spread of Christianity in the Mediterranean basin and southwest Asia
184 C.E.	Yellow Turban rebellion
216–272 C.E.	Life of Mani
220 C.E.	Collapse of the Han dynasty
284–305 C.E.	Reign of Diocletian
313–337 C.E.	Reign of Constantine
313 C.E.	Edict of Milan and the legalization of Christianity in the Roman empire
325 C.E.	Council of Nicaea
451 C.E.	Council of Chalcedon
476 C.E.	Collapse of the western Roman empire

FOR FURTHER READING

Thomas J. Barfield. *The Perilous Frontier: Nomadic Empires and China*. Cambridge, Mass., 1989. Provocative study of the Xiongnu and other central Asian peoples.

Jerry H. Bentley. *Old World Encounters: Cross-Cultural Contacts and Exchanges in Pre-modern Times*. New York, 1993. Studies the spread of cultural and religious traditions before 1500 C.E.

Averil Cameron. *The Later Roman Empire, A.D. 284–430*. Cambridge, Mass., 1993. A lively synthesis.

———. *The Mediterranean World in Late Antiquity, A.D. 395–600*. London, 1993. Like its companion volume just cited, a well-informed synthesis.

Edward Gibbon. *The Decline and Fall of the Roman Empire*. Many editions available. A classic account, still well worth reading, by a masterful historical stylist of the eighteenth century.

C. D. Gordon, ed. *The Age of Attila: Fifth-Century Byzantium and the Barbarians*. Ann Arbor, 1972. Translations of primary sources on the society and history of nomadic and migratory peoples.

Samuel Hugh Moffett. *A History of Christianity in Asia*, vol. 1. San Francisco, 1992. An important volume that surveys the spread of early Christianity east of the Roman empire.

Joseph A. Tainter. *The Collapse of Complex Societies*. Cambridge, 1988. Scholarly review of theories and evidence bearing on the fall of empires and societies.

Susan Whitfield. *Life along the Silk Road*. Berkeley, 1999. Focuses on the experiences of ten individuals who lived or traveled along the silk roads.

Francis Wood. *The Silk Road: Two Thousand Years in the Heart of Asia*. Berkeley, 2002. A brilliantly illustrated volume discussing the history of the silk roads from antiquity to the twentieth century.

The postclassical era was a period of major readjustment for societies throughout the eastern hemisphere. The early centuries C.E. brought turbulence and instability to classical societies in China, India, southwest Asia, and the Mediterranean basin. Most of the classical empires collapsed under the strain. During the postclassical era the settled societies of the eastern hemisphere underwent political, social, economic, and cultural change that would shape their experiences over the long term. Indeed, the influence of the postclassical era continues to the present day.

The first task that settled societies faced in the postclassical era was the need to restore political and social order. They went about this task in very different ways. In the eastern Mediterranean the eastern half of the Roman empire survived as the Byzantine empire but underwent political and social reorganization in order to deal with external pressures. In southwest Asia, Arab conquerors inspired by the recently founded Islamic faith overcame the Sasanid empire of Persia. In China the Sui and Tang dynasties restored centralized imperial authority after almost four centuries of rule by competing regional kingdoms and nomadic conquerors. In India, in contrast, centralized imperial rule did not return: authority devolved instead to a series of regional kingdoms.

The reestablishment of political and social order enabled postclassical societies to revive networks of long-distance trade and participate more actively in processes of cross-cultural communication and exchange. As a result, the postclassical era was a time of rapid economic growth in most of the eastern hemisphere. Meanwhile, increased

3

trade facilitated biological and technological as
well as commercial exchanges: agricultural crops
migrated far beyond the lands of their origin, and improved
techniques of irrigation and cultivation spread through much of Eurasia. As agricultural
production increased, so did human population, which allowed growing numbers of
people to devote their efforts to trade and manufacturing rather than cultivation.

The postclassical era was also crucially important for the formation and
development of cultural and religious traditions. Islam first appeared during the
postclassical era, and it soon became the foundation of an expansive empire stretching

THE POSTCLASSICAL ERA, 500 TO 1000 C.E.

from North Africa to northern India. Buddhism expanded beyond the Indian
subcontinent and central Asia, attracting converts in east and southeast Asia.
Christianity was the official faith of the Byzantine empire, where the Eastern Orthodox
church emerged and gave shape to a distinctive form of Christianity that eventually
spread to much of eastern Europe and Russia.

The empires and regional states of the postclassical era disappeared long ago, but
the social, economic, and cultural legacies of the age are noticeable even today. Most
notable, perhaps, religious and cultural traditions continue to flourish in lands where
they first attracted converts in postclassical times. In some ways, then, the postclassical
age survives even in the modern world.

CHAPTER 10

The Commonwealth of Byzantium

According to the Byzantine historian Procopius, two Christian monks from Persia set out on a momentous journey about the middle of the sixth century C.E. The result of their travels was the introduction of high-quality silk production to the eastern Mediterranean. Although local crafts workers had long produced coarse fabrics from the cocoons of wild silkworms, fine silks had come to the Mediterranean only from China, where manufacturers closely guarded both their carefully bred strains of silkworms and the complex technology that yielded high-quality textiles. Mediterranean consumers obtained silk not directly from Chinese producers but, rather, through intermediaries subject to the Sasanid empire of Persia.

According to Procopius's account, the two Christian monks observed the techniques of silk production during the course of a mission to China. Upon departure they hollowed out their walking staffs and filled them with silkworm eggs, which they smuggled out of China, through their native land of Persia, and into the Byzantine empire.

The monks' motives are unknown. Whatever they may have been, though, it is certain that the monks by themselves could not have introduced a full-blown silk industry to Byzantium. The production of fine, Chinese-style silks required more than a few silkworm eggs. It also required understanding sophisticated technologies and elaborate procedures that must have reached the Byzantine empire by several different routes. Thus it seems that Procopius simplified a much more complex story.

OPPOSITE PAGE: *A sixth-century icon depicting an enthroned Virgin Mary and infant Jesus attended by angels and saints.*

In any case, Byzantine crafts workers did indeed learn how to produce high-quality silk fabrics. By the late sixth century, Byzantine silks matched Chinese silks in quality. Mediterranean consumers no longer relied on Chinese producers and Persian intermediaries, and local production of high-quality silk greatly strengthened the Byzantine economy. Thus Procopius's anonymous monks participated in a momentous transfer of technology between distant lands. Their efforts contributed to the vibrance of Byzantine society, and their story highlights the significance of cross-cultural interactions during the postclassical era.

During the centuries after 200 C.E., most of the classical societies faced a series of problems—epidemic disease, declining population, economic contraction, social and political turmoil, and military threats—that brought about their collapse. Only in the eastern Mediterranean did a classical empire survive. The eastern half of the Roman empire, known as the Byzantine empire, withstood the various problems that brought down other classical societies and survived for almost a millennium after the collapse of the western Roman empire in the fifth century C.E.

The Byzantine empire did not reconstitute the larger Mediterranean society of classical times. The Roman empire had dominated an integrated Mediterranean basin; the Byzantine empire mostly faced a politically and culturally fragmented Mediterranean region. After the seventh century C.E., Islamic states controlled lands to the east and south of the Mediterranean, Slavic peoples dominated lands to the north, and western Europeans organized increasingly powerful states in lands to the west.

Nevertheless, the Byzantine empire was a political and economic powerhouse of the postclassical era. Until the twelfth century, Byzantine authority dominated the wealthy and productive eastern Mediterranean region. Manufactured goods from the Byzantine empire enjoyed a reputation for high quality in markets from the Mediterranean basin to India. The Byzantine empire also deeply influenced the historical development of the Slavic peoples of eastern Europe and Russia by introducing writing, Christianity, codified law, and sophisticated political organization into their lands. Because Byzantine political, economic, and cultural influence stretched so far, historians often refer to it as the "Byzantine commonwealth." Just as Greek and Roman initiative brought Mediterranean lands into a larger integrated society during classical times, Byzantine policies led to the formation of a large, multicultural zone of trade, communication, interaction, and exchange in eastern Europe and the eastern Mediterranean basin during the postclassical era.

THE EARLY BYZANTINE EMPIRE

The Byzantine empire takes its name from Byzantion—latinized as Byzantium—a modest village that occupied a site of enormous strategic significance. Situated on a defensible peninsula and blessed with a magnificent natural harbor known as the Golden Horn, Byzantion had the potential to control the Bosporus, the strait of water leading from the Black Sea to the Sea of Marmara and beyond to the Dardanelles, the Aegean Sea, and the Mediterranean. Apart from its maritime significance, Byzantion also offered convenient access to the rich lands of Anatolia, southwestern Asia, and southeastern Europe.

Because of its strategic value, the Roman emperor Constantine designated Byzantion as the site of a new imperial capital, which he named Constantinople ("city of Constantine"). The imperial government moved to Constantinople in 340 C.E., and the new capital rapidly reached metropolitan dimensions. By the late fourth century, it was the most important political and military center of the eastern Roman empire, and it soon became the dominant economic and commercial center in the eastern Mediterranean basin. The city kept the name Constantinople until 1453 C.E., when it fell to the Ottoman Turks, who renamed it Istanbul. By convention, however, historians refer to the realm governed from Constantinople between the fifth and fifteenth centuries C.E. as the Byzantine empire, or simply as Byzantium, in honor of the original settlement.

The Later Roman Empire and Byzantium

The Byzantine empire originated as the eastern half of the classical Roman empire, which survived the collapse of the western Roman empire in the fifth century C.E. In its early days the Byzantine empire embraced Greece, the Balkan region, Anatolia, Syria, Palestine, Egypt, and northeast Africa. During the seventh and eighth centuries C.E., however, the southern regions

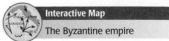

Interactive Map
The Byzantine empire

Byzantine (BIHZ-uhn-teen)

Map 10.1 The boundaries of the Byzantine empire and its neighbors between 527 and 554 C.E. Compare this map with Map 8.4. In what ways do the territories of the Byzantines and the classical Romans differ? How might this have affected trade in the Mediterranean basin?

of the empire fell into the hands of Arab Muslim conquerors. Nevertheless, Byzantium figured as a major power of the eastern Mediterranean basin until the thirteenth century C.E.

The Later Roman Empire As the western Roman empire crumbled, the eastern half of the empire remained intact, complete with roads, communications, lines of authority, and a set of functioning imperial institutions, all inherited from Roman predecessors. Yet the early Byzantine emperors faced challenges different from those of their predecessors, and they built a state significantly different from the classical Roman empire.

The principal challenges that confronted the late Roman and early Byzantine empires were the consolidation of the dynamic Sasanid dynasty (226–641 C.E.) in Persia and the invasions of migratory peoples from the north and east. The Sasanid emperors sought to

rebuild the Achaemenid empire of classical Persia, a goal that brought them into conflict with Roman forces in Mesopotamia and Syria. Germanic invasions also menaced the late Roman empire. Because they did not have adequate resources to respond strongly to the threat on all fronts, Roman authorities concentrated on maintaining the integrity of the wealthy eastern portion of the empire.

The Byzantine emperors built a distinctive tradition of statecraft. Its most important feature was tightly centralized rule that concentrated power in the hands of a highly exalted emperor. This characteristic *The Early Byzantine State* was noticeable already in the time of Constantine, who built his new capital to lavish standards. He filled it with libraries, museums, and artistic treasures, and he constructed magnificent marble structures—all in an effort to create a new Rome fit for the ruler of a mighty empire.

Constantine also set a precedent by hedging his rule with an aura of divinity. Although he did not claim

---

Sasanid (suh-SAH-nid)

divine status as some of his imperial predecessors had, as the first Christian emperor he did claim divine favor and sanction for his rule. He intervened in theological disputes and used his political position to support views that he considered orthodox and condemn those he regarded as heretical. Constantine initiated a policy that historians call "caesaropapism," whereby the emperor not only ruled as secular lord but also played an active and prominent role in ecclesiastical affairs.

Caesaropapism

Particularly after the sixth century, Byzantine emperors became absolute rulers. According to Roman law, emperors stood above the law: theoretically, they wielded absolute authority in political, military, judicial, financial, and religious matters. They also enjoyed the services of a large and complex bureaucracy. In combination, law and bureaucracy produced an exceptionally centralized state.

Even dress and court etiquette drew attention to the lofty status of Byzantine rulers. The emperors wore heavily bejeweled crowns and dressed in magnificent silk robes dyed a dark, rich purple—a color reserved strictly for imperial use. High officials presented themselves to the emperor as slaves and before taking up matters of business prostrated themselves before him three times and kissed his hands and feet. By the tenth century, engineers had contrived a series of mechanical devices that worked dazzling effects and impressed foreign envoys at the Byzantine court: mechanical lions roared and swished their tails as ambassadors approached the emperor, and sometimes the imperial throne itself moved up and down to emphasize the awesome splendor of the emperor.

The Byzantine Court

Justinian and His Legacy

The most important of the early Byzantine emperors was Justinian (527–565 C.E.), an energetic and tireless worker known to his subjects as "the sleepless emperor," who profoundly influenced the development of the Byzantine empire with the aid of his ambitious wife Theodora. Both were intelligent, strong willed, and

Justinian and Theodora

Justinian wears imperial purple robes in this mosaic from the church of San Vitale in Ravenna, which depicts him in the company of ecclesiastical, military, and court officials.

The interior of the church of Hagia Sophia ("Holy Wisdom"), built by Justinian and transformed into a mosque in the fifteenth century. The dome rises almost 60 meters (197 feet) above the floor, and its windows allow abundant light to enter the massive structure.

disciplined and used those qualities to build a strong empire and a grand imperial court.

Like Constantine, Justinian lavished resources on the imperial capital. During the early years of his rule, riots against high taxes had destroyed much of Constantinople. After Theodora persuaded him to deploy the imperial army and quash the disturbances, Justinian embarked on an ambitious construction program that thoroughly remade the city. The most notable building erected during that campaign was 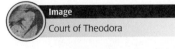 the church of Hagia Sophia, a magnificent domed structure that ranks as one of the world's most important examples of Christian architecture. Visitors marveled at the church's enormous dome, which they likened to the heavens encircling the earth, and they expressed awe at the gold, silver, and gems that decorated and illuminated Hagia Sophia. Over time, the church even acquired a reputation for working miraculous cures: its columns and doors reportedly healed the illnesses of people who stood beside them or touched them.

Justinian's most significant political contribution was his codification of Roman law. Almost immediately on taking the throne, Justinian ordered a thorough and systematic review of Roman law. On the basis of that work, he issued the *Corpus iuris civilis* (*Body of the Civil Law*), which immediately won recognition as a definitive work. Later emperors updated Roman law by adding new provisions, but Justinian's code continued to serve as a source of legal inspiration and went on to influence civil law codes throughout much of western Europe.

Justinian's most ambitious venture was his effort to reconquer the western Roman empire from Germanic

Justinian's Code

Hagia Sophia (HAH-yah soh-FEE-uh)

Corpus iuris civilis (KOR-poos EW-rees sih-BEE-lees)

peoples and reestablish Roman authority throughout the Mediterranean basin. Beginning in 533 he sent his brilliant general Belisarius on military campaigns that returned Italy, Sicily, northwestern Africa, and southern Spain to imperial hands. By the end of his reign in 565, Justinian had reconstituted a good portion of the classical Roman empire.

Belisarius and Byzantine Conquests

Justinian's accomplishment, however, did not long survive his own rule. Byzantium simply did not possess the resources to sustain Belisarius's conquests. Although Byzantium managed to hold on to a few areas in the Italian peninsula, Justinian's dream of restoring Roman authority throughout the Mediterranean basin soon faded. Indeed, Justinian's efforts clearly showed that the classical Roman empire was beyond recovery. While Justinian devoted his attention to the western Mediterranean, the Sasanids threatened Byzantium from the east and Slavic peoples approached from the north. Justinian's successors had no choice but to withdraw their resources from the western Mediterranean and redeploy them in the east. Even though Belisarius's reconquest of the western Roman empire was a spectacular military accomplishment, it was also something of an anachronism, since the lands of the eastern and western Mediterranean had already begun to follow different historical trajectories.

Islamic Conquests and Byzantine Revival

After the seventh century C.E., the emergence of Islam and the development of a powerful and expansive Islamic state (topics discussed in chapter 11) posed a serious challenge to Byzantium. Inspired by their Islamic faith, Arab peoples conquered the Sasanid empire and overran Byzantine Syria, Palestine, Egypt, and north Africa. During the late seventh and early eighth centuries, Islamic forces even subjected Constantinople itself to prolonged siege (in 674–678 and again in 717–718). Byzantium resisted this northern thrust of Islam partly because of military technology. Byzantine forces used a weapon known as "Greek fire"—a devastating incendiary weapon compounded of sulphur, lime, and petroleum—which they launched at both the fleets and the ground forces of the invaders. Greek fire burned even when floating on water and thus created a serious hazard when deployed around wooden ships. On land it caused panic among enemy forces, since it was very difficult to extinguish and often burned troops to death. As a result of this defensive effort, the Byzantine empire retained its hold on Anatolia, Greece, and the Balkan region.

Though much reduced by the Islamic conquests, the Byzantine empire after the eighth century was also more compact and manageable. In addition, Byzantine rulers initiated political and social adjustments that strengthened the empire that remained in their hands. The most important innovation was the reorganization of Byzantine society under the *theme* system. The *theme* system placed an imperial province *(theme)* under the jurisdiction of a general, who assumed responsibility for both its military defense and its civil administration. Generals received their appointments from the imperial government, which closely supervised their activities to prevent decentralization of power and authority. Generals recruited armies from the ranks of free peasants,

Imperial Organization

Illustration in a manuscript depicts Byzantine naval forces turning Greek fire on their Arab enemies.

who received allotments of land in exchange for military service. The armies proved to be effective military forces, and the system as a whole strengthened the class of free peasants, which in turn solidified Byzantium's agricultural economy. The *theme* system enabled Byzantine forces to mobilize quickly and resist further Islamic advances and also undergirded the political order and the social organization of the empire from the eighth through the twelfth century.

Indeed, Byzantium vastly expanded its influence between the late ninth and the late eleventh centuries. During the tenth century Byzantine forces shored up defenses in Anatolia and reconquered Syria from Arab Muslims. During the reign of Basil II (976–1025 C.E.), known as "Basil the Bulgar-Slayer," Byzantine armies turned west and crushed the neighboring Bulgars, who had built a large kingdom in the Balkans. After his victory at the battle of Kleidion in 1014 C.E., Basil reportedly commanded his forces to blind fourteen thousand Bulgarian survivors, though he spared one eye in a few, who then guided the others home. By the mid–eleventh century the Byzantine empire embraced lands from Syria and Armenia in the east to southern Italy in the west, from the Danube River in the north to Cyprus and Crete in the south. Byzantine expansion brought in so much wealth that Basil was able to waive the collection of taxes for two years. Once again, Byzantium dominated the eastern Mediterranean.

Byzantium and Western Europe

While they went to war with their Arab Muslim and pagan Slavic neighbors, Byzantines also experienced tense relations with their Christian counterparts in the western Mediterranean. The Christian church of Constantinople conducted its affairs in Greek and bowed to the will of the caesaropapist emperors, whereas the Christian church of Rome conducted its affairs in Latin and rejected imperial interference in ecclesiastical matters. Church authorities in Byzantium regarded Roman Christians as poorly educated and uncouth. In return, church leaders in Rome considered their Byzantine counterparts insincere and insufficiently wary of heresy.

Tensions between Byzantium and Western European States

Political grievances also strained relations between Byzantium and western European lands. During the fifth and sixth centuries, imperial authorities could do little more than watch as Germanic peoples established successor states to the western Roman empire—lands that Byzantine emperors regarded as their rightful inheritance. Worse yet, some of the upstart powers claimed imperial authority for themselves. In 800, for example, the Frankish ruler Charlemagne received an imperial crown from the pope in Rome, thereby directly challenging Byzantine claims to imperial authority over western lands. Charlemagne's empire soon dissolved, but in 962 Otto of Saxony lodged his own claim to rule as emperor over the western lands of the former Roman empire. Adding injury to insult, Otto then attacked lands in southern Italy that had been in Byzantine possession since the days of Justinian.

BYZANTINE ECONOMY AND SOCIETY

Byzantium dominated the political and military affairs of the eastern Mediterranean largely because of its strong economy. Ever since classical times, the territories embraced by the Byzantine empire had produced abundant agricultural surpluses, supported large numbers of crafts workers, and participated in trade with lands throughout the Mediterranean. Even after the collapse of the Roman empire, those territories continued to provide a solid material foundation for Byzantium, and they helped to make the Byzantine empire an economic powerhouse of the postclassical era.

Rural Economy and Society

Until its conquest by Arab forces, Egypt was the major source of grain for Byzantium. Afterward, Anatolia and the lower Danube region served as the imperial breadbasket. All those lands produced reliable and abundant harvests of wheat, which supported large populations in Byzantium's major cities. Indeed, between the fifth and the early thirteenth centuries, Constantinople's population alone approached or exceeded one million people.

Byzantine economy and society were strongest when the empire supported a large class of free peasants who owned small plots of land. Besides serving as the backbone of the *The Peasantry* Byzantine military system, free peasants cultivated their land intensively in hopes of improving their families' fortunes. As in other societies, however, wealthy families sought to accumulate land and to control the labor of peasants for their own interests. Especially in the early centuries of the Byzantine empire, wealthy cultivators worked to bind peasants to their estates or to force them into sharecropping arrangements from which it was difficult to break free.

However, the invasions of the sixth and seventh centuries broke up many large estates and afforded peasants an opportunity to rebuild small holdings. The *theme* system strengthened the free peasantry by making land available to those who performed military service. The imperial government also made periodic efforts to prevent wealthy landowners from gaining control over peasant lands. Over the long term, however, wealthy landowners built ever larger estates. From the eleventh century onward, they transformed the peasants into an increasingly dependent class, and by the thirteenth century free peasants accounted for only a small portion of the rural population.

Decline of the Free Peasantry   The accumulation of landholdings in the hands of the wealthy had important implications for financial and military affairs. For one thing, large estates often received tax exemptions and so did not contribute their fair share to imperial coffers. Moreover, the decline of the free peasantry diminished the pool of recruits available for service in military forces organized under the *theme* system. Thus, the concentration of land and rural resources worked against the financial interests of the central government, and it caused political, military, and economic difficulties for the Byzantine state during the last three centuries of its existence.

Industry and Trade

In spite of social and economic problems, Byzantium remained a wealthy land. Byzantine prosperity derived both from the empire's productive capacity and from the importance of Constantinople as a center of trade.

Indeed, Constantinople was home to many artisans and crafts workers who enjoyed a reputation especially for their glassware, linen and woolen textiles, gems, jewelry, and fine work in gold and silver. In addition, after the *Manufacturing Enterprises* arrival of silkworms, crafts workers added high-quality silk textiles to the list of products manufactured in the Byzantine empire. Silk was a most important addition to the economy, and Byzantium became the principal supplier of this fashionable fabric to lands in the Mediterranean basin. The silk industry was so important to the Byzantine economy that the government closely supervised every step in its production and sale. Regulations allowed individuals to participate in only one activity—such as weaving, dyeing, or sales—to prevent the creation of a monopoly in the industry by a few wealthy or powerful entrepreneurs.

Situated astride routes going east and west as well as north and south, Constantinople also served as the main clearinghouse for trade in the western part of Eurasia. The merchants of Constantino- *Trade* ple maintained direct commercial links with manufacturers and merchants in central Asia, Russia, Scandinavia, northern Europe, and the lands of the Black Sea and the Mediterranean basin. Byzantium dominated trade to such an extent that trading peoples recognized the Byzantine gold coin, the *bezant,* as the standard currency of the Mediterranean basin for more than half a millennium, from the sixth through the twelfth century.

A manuscript illustration depicts one Byzantine woman weaving cloth (left) while another spins thread (right). Both women veil their hair for modesty. Women workers were prominent in Byzantine textile production.

Byzantium drew enormous wealth simply from the control of trade and the levying of customs duties on merchandise that passed through its lands. More important, Byzantium served as the western anchor of a Eurasian trading network that revived the silk roads of classical times. Silk and porcelain came to Constantinople from China, spices from India and southeast Asia. Carpets arrived from Persia, woolen textiles from western Europe, and timber, furs, honey, amber, and slaves from Russia and Scandinavia.

Banks helped to fuel Byzantine trade by advancing loans to individuals seeking to launch business ventures, and Byzantine merchants often formed partnerships that allowed them to pool their resources and limit their risks. Although neither banking nor partnership was an altogether new technique, Byzantine businessmen made much more extensive use of them than their predecessors had. In doing so, they both supported and stimulated a dynamic commercial economy.

The Organization of Trade

Urban Life

Constantinople had no rival among Byzantine cities. Subjects of the Byzantine empire referred to it simply as "the City." The heart of the City was the imperial palace, which employed twenty thousand workers as palace staff. Peacocks strutted through gardens filled with sculptures and fountains. Most famous was a gold fountain in the shape of a pineapple that spouted wine for imperial guests.

Aristocrats maintained enormous palaces that included courtyards, reception halls, libraries, and chapels. Women lived in separate apartments and did not receive male visitors from outside the household. Indeed, women often did not participate in banquets and parties, especially when wine flowed freely or when the affairs were likely to become so festive that they could compromise a woman's honor.

Housing in Constantinople

The less privileged classes of Constantinople occupied less splendid dwellings. Artisans and crafts workers usually lived in rooms above their shops, and clerks and government officials lived in multistory apartment buildings. Workers and the poor occupied dangerous and rickety tenements, sharing kitchens and sanitary facilities with their neighbors.

Even for the poor, though, the City had its attractions. As the heir to Rome, Constantinople was a city of baths, which were sites of relaxation and exercise as well as hygienic bathing. Taverns and restaurants offered settings for social gatherings—checkers, chess, and dice games were especially popular activities at taverns—and theaters provided entertainment in the form of song, dance, and striptease. Mass entertainment took place in the Hippodrome, a large stadium adjacent to the imperial palace. There Byzantine subjects watched chariot races, athletic matches, contests between wild animals, and circuses featuring clowns, jugglers, acrobats, and dwarfs.

Attractions of Constantinople

CLASSICAL HERITAGE AND ORTHODOX CHRISTIANITY

The first Christian emperor of the Roman empire gave both his name and his faith to Constantinople. Like the Byzantine state, however, Byzantine Christianity developed along distinctive lines, and it became a faith different from the early Christianity of the Roman empire. For one thing, the philosophy and literature of classical Greece had a much deeper influence in Byzantium than in western Europe. Byzantine church leaders also disagreed with their western counterparts on matters of doctrine, ritual, and church authority. By the mid–eleventh century, differences between the eastern and western churches had become so great that their leaders formally divided Mediterranean Christianity into the Eastern Orthodox and Roman Catholic churches.

The Legacy of Classical Greece

Although local inhabitants spoke Greek, the official language of early Constantinople was Latin, the language of Rome. After the sixth century, however, Greek replaced Latin as the language of government in the Byzantine empire. Byzantine scholars often did not learn to read Latin, and they drew intellectual inspiration from the New Testament (originally composed in Greek) and the philosophy and literature of classical Greece rather than classical Rome.

The legacy of classical Greece was especially noticeable in Byzantine education. The Byzantine state considered education vitally important, since its bureaucracy called for large numbers of literate individuals to administer the empire. As a result, the state organized a school system that offered a primary education in reading, writing, and grammar, followed by studies of classical Greek

Byzantine Education

iterature, philosophy, and science. Because of this, basic literacy was widespread in Byzantine society.

Byzantine Scholarship   Like the educational system, Byzantine scholarship reflected the cultural legacy of classical Greece. Byzantine scholars concentrated on the humanities—literature, history, and philosophy—rather than on the natural sciences or medicine. Byzantines with a literary education considered themselves the direct heirs of classical Greece, and they went to great lengths to preserve and transmit the classical legacy. Indeed, almost all literary and philosophical works of classical Greece that survive have come down to the present in copies made between the tenth and twelfth centuries in the Byzantine empire.

The Byzantine Church

The most distinctive feature of Byzantine Christianity was its close relationship with the imperial government. From the time of Constantine on, caesaropapist emperors participated actively in religious and theological matters. In 325 C.E., for example, Constantine organized the Council of Nicaea, which brought together bishops, spokesmen, and leaders from all the important Christian churches to consider the views of the Arians, who believed that Jesus had been a mortal human rather than a divine being coeternal with God. Although Constantine originally favored Arian views, he came to accept the view that Jesus was both human and divine and personally attended sessions of the Council of Nicaea to support it. His presence encouraged the council to endorse his preferred view as orthodox and to condemn Arianism as heresy.

Church and State

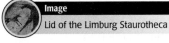
Lid of the Limburg Staurotheca

The Byzantine emperors, in fact, treated the church as a department of state. They appointed individuals to serve as patriarch of Constantinople—the highest ecclesiastical official in the Byzantine church, counterpart of the pope in Rome—and they instructed patriarchs, bishops, and priests to deliver sermons that supported imperial policy. This caesaropapism was a source of constant conflict between imperial and ecclesiastical authorities, and sometimes even between emperors and their subjects. For example, Emperor Leo III (reigned 717–741 C.E.) sparked riots throughout the empire when he embarked on a policy of iconoclasm (literally, "the breaking of icons") in an attempt to prohibit the use of religious images and icons in churches. Although the policy was ultimately unsuccessful, it generated tremendous bitterness among ordinary people who were deeply attached to the religious imagery in their churches.

In its theology, Byzantine Christianity reflected the continuing influence of classical Greek philosophy. Theologians invested a great deal of time and intellectual energy in the examination of religious questions from a philosophical point of view. They looked to classical philosophy, for example, when seeking to understand the nature of Jesus and the extent to which he possessed both human and divine characteristics. Although these debates often became extremely technical, they illustrated an effort to understand Christian doctrine in light of the terms and concepts that classical philosophers had employed in their analysis of the world. A school maintained by the patriarch of Constantinople provided instruction for clergy and church officials in advanced theology of this sort. Thus, although it differed in many ways from Mediterranean society of classical times, Byzantium built its own cultural and religious traditions on a solid classical foundation.

Greek Philosophy and Byzantine Theology

Monasticism and Popular Piety

Caesaropapist emperors, powerful patriarchs, and other high church officials concerned themselves with theological and ritual matters and rarely dealt directly with the lay population of the Byzantine church. Nor did the Byzantine laity have much interest in fine points of theology, and they positively resented policies such as iconoclasm that infringed on cherished patterns of worship. For religious inspiration, then, the laity looked not to the church hierarchy but to the local monasteries.

Byzantine monasticism grew out of the efforts of devout individuals to lead especially holy lives. Drawing inspiration from early Christian ascetics in Egypt, Mesopotamia, and Persia, these individuals observed regimes of extreme asceticism and self-denial. During the fifth century, for example, a few men and at least two women demonstrated their ascetic commitments by perching for years at a time atop tall pillars. Because of the extreme dedication of ascetics, disciples often gathered around them and es-

Asceticism

---

patriarch (PAY-tree-ahrk)

iconoclasts (eye-KAHN-oh-klasts)

tablished communities of men and women determined to follow their example. These communities became the earliest monasteries of the Byzantine church. They had few rules until St. Basil of Caesarea (329–379 C.E.), the patriarch of Constantinople during the mid–fourth century, urged them to give up their personal possessions and live communally, to observe the rule of elected superiors, and to devote themselves to work and prayer. After the fourth century, Basilian monasticism spread rapidly throughout the Byzantine empire.

Byzantine Monasticism
Unlike their counterparts in western Europe and other lands, Byzantine monasteries for the most part did not become centers of education, study, learning, and scholarship. Yet monasteries under the rule of St. Basil had a reputation for piety and devotion that endeared them to the Byzantine laity. Basilian monks went to great lengths in search of mystical union with God through meditation and prayer. Some retired to remote destinations to lead lives of strict asceticism. The devotion of Basilian monks, in turn, inspired piety among the Byzantine laity because they represented a religious faith more immediate and meaningful than that of the theologians and ecclesiastical bureaucrats of Constantinople.

Monks and nuns also provided social services to their communities. They provided spiritual counsel to local laity, and they organized relief efforts by bringing food and medical attention to communities struck by disasters. They won the support of the Byzantine populace, too, when they vigorously opposed the policy of iconoclasm and fought to restore icons to churches and monasteries. Indeed, by setting examples of devotion and by tending to the needs and interests of the laity, monks helped to maintain support for their faith in the Byzantine empire.

Tensions between Eastern and Western Christianity

Byzantine Christianity developed in tension particularly with the Christian faith of western Europe. During the centuries following Constantine's legalization of Christianity, church leaders in Jerusalem, Alexandria, Antioch, Constantinople, and Rome exercised great influence in the larger Christian community. Yet after Arab peoples conquered most of southwest Asia and introduced Islam there in the seventh century, the influence of the patriarchs in Jerusalem, Alexandria, and Antioch declined, leaving only Constantinople and Rome as the principal centers of Christian authority.

The specific issues that divided the two Christian communities in Constantinople and Rome were religious and theological. Some ritual and doctrinal differences were relatively minor concerns over forms of worship *Constantinople and Rome* and the precise wording of theological teachings. Byzantine theologians objected, for example, to the fact that western priests shaved their beards and used unleavened instead of leavened bread when saying Mass. Other differences concerned substantive theological matters, such as the precise relationship between God, Jesus, and the Holy Spirit.

Alongside these ritual and doctrinal differences, the Byzantine patriarchs and Roman popes disputed their respective rights and powers. Patriarchs argued for the autonomy of all major Christian *Schism* jurisdictions, including that of Constantinople, whereas popes asserted the primacy of Rome as the sole seat of authority for all Christendom. Ultimately, relations became so strained that the eastern and western churches went separate ways. In 1054 C.E. the patriarch and the pope excommunicated each other, each refusing to recognize the other's church as properly Christian. Despite efforts at reconciliation, the resulting schism between eastern and western churches persists to the present day. In recognition of the split, historians refer to the eastern Christian church after 1054 as the Eastern Orthodox church and its western counterpart as the Roman Catholic church.

THE INFLUENCE OF BYZANTIUM IN EASTERN EUROPE

By the second millennium C.E., a dynamic society founded on the Islamic faith had seized control of the lands on the Mediterranean's southern and eastern rims, and Byzantines and western Europeans contested the northern rim. Hemmed in and increasingly pressured by Islamic and western European societies, Byzantium entered a period of decline beginning about the late eleventh century.

As its Mediterranean influence waned, however, Byzantium turned its attention to eastern Europe and Russia. Through political, commercial, and cultural relations, Byzantium decisively influenced the history of Slavic peoples. The Byzantine state itself came to an end in the fifteenth century C.E. But because of the Byzantine commonwealth—the larger collection of societies in eastern Europe and the eastern Mediterranean basin that developed under

Anna Comnena on the Suppression of Bogomil Heretics

Anna Comnena (1083–1148), daughter of the Byzantine emperor Alexius I (reigned 1081–1118), wrote the Alexiad, *a laudatory history of her father's reign. In the following selection, she discusses his prosecution in 1110 of Bogomil heretics, who revived the dualist teachings of the Manichaeans. Her account makes it clear that the caesaropapist Byzantine emperors took seriously their commitment to the Orthodox church and their obligation to protect its interests.*

Later . . . there arose an extraordinary "cloud of heretics," a new hostile group, hitherto unknown to the Church. . . . Apparently it was in existence before my father's time, but was unperceived (for the Bogomils' sect is most adept at feigning virtue). No worldly hairstyles are to be seen among Bogomils: their wickedness is hidden beneath cloak and cowl. Your Bogomil wears a somber look; muffled up to the nose, he walks with a stoop, quietly muttering to himself—but inside he's a ravening wolf. This unpleasant race, like a serpent lurking in its hole, was brought to the light and lured out by my father with magical incantations. . . .

The fame of the Bogomils had by now spread to all parts, for the impious sect was controlled with great cunning by a certain monk called Basil. He had twelve followers whom he called "apostles" and also dragged along with him certain female disciples, women of bad character, utterly depraved. In all quarters he made his wicked influence felt and when the evil, like some consuming fire, devoured many souls, the emperor could no longer bear it. He instituted a thorough inquiry into the heresy. . . .

. . . Alexius condemned the heretics out of hand: chorus and chorus-leader alike were to suffer death by burning. When the Bogomils had been hunted down and brought together in one place, some clung to the heresy, but others denied the charges completely, protesting strongly against their accusers and rejecting the Bogomilian heresy with scorn. . . .

The emperor glared at them and said, "Two pyres will have to be lit today. By one a cross will be planted firmly in the ground. Then a choice will be offered to all: those who are prepared to die for their Christian faith will separate themselves from the rest and take up position by the pyre with the cross; the Bogomilian adherents will be thrown on the other. Surely it is better that even Christians should die than live to be hounded down as Bogomils and offend the conscience of the majority. Go away, then, all of you, to whichever pyre you choose". . . .

A huge crowd gathered and stood all about them. Fires were then lit, burning seven times more fiercely than usual. . . . The flames leapt to the heavens. By one pyre stood the cross. Each of the condemned was given his choice, for all were to be burnt. Now that escape was clearly impossible, the orthodox to a man moved over to the pyre with the cross, truly prepared to suffer martyrdom; the godless adherents of the abominable heresy went off to the other. Just as they were about to be thrown on the flames, all the bystanders broke into mourning for the Christians; they were filled with indignation against the emperor (they did not know of his plan). But an order came from him just in time to stop the executioners. Alexius had in this way obtained firm evidence of those who were really Bogomils. The Christians, who were victims of calumny, he released after giving them much advice; the rest [i.e., the Bogomils] were committed once again to prison, but the [Bogomil] "apostles" were kept apart. Later he sent for some of these men every day and personally taught them, with frequent exhortations to abandon their abominable cult. . . . And some did change for the better and were freed from prison, but others died in their heresy, still incarcerated, although they were supplied with plentiful food and clothing.

• *Why did Byzantine rulers go to such lengths to suppress heresy?*

SOURCE: Anna Comnena. *The Alexiad of Anna Comnena.* Trans. by E. R. A. Sewter. Harmondsworth: Penguin, 1969, pp. 496–505. (Translation slightly modified.)

Byzantine influence—the legacy of Byzantium survives and continues to shape the lives of millions of people in Russia and eastern Europe.

Domestic Problems and Foreign Pressures

When Basil II, "the Bulgar-Slayer," died in 1025 C.E., the Byzantine empire was a political, military, and economic dynamo. Within fifty years, however, the empire was suffering from serious internal weaknesses and had endured a series of military reverses. Both domestic and foreign problems help to explain this decline.

Domestic problems arose, ironically, from the success of the *theme* system. Generals who governed the *Social Problems* *themes* were natural allies of local aristocrats who held large tracts of land, and together they began to resist the policies of the imperial government. At times, they even mounted rebellions against central authorities. Moreover, by the mid–eleventh century aristocrats had accumulated vast estates that placed the free peasantry under increasing pressure. Since peasants provided the backbone of Byzantium's military system and agricultural economy, this caused both fiscal and military problems for the imperial government.

As domestic problems mounted, Byzantium also faced fresh foreign challenges. From the west came the Normans—a Scandinavian people who had seized and settled in Normandy (in northern France). During the early eleventh century, they established themselves as an independent power in southern Italy, and by midcentury they had taken control of southern Italy and expelled Byzantine authorities there.

Challenges from the West

During the twelfth and thirteenth centuries, the Normans and other western European peoples mounted a series of crusades—vast military campaigns intended to recapture Jerusalem and other sites holy to Christians from Muslims—and took the opportunity to carve out states in the heart of the Byzantine empire. They even conquered and sacked

Map 10.2 The boundaries of the Byzantine empire and its neighbors about 1100 C.E. Compare this map with Map 10.1. Notice the difference in the extent of Byzantine territory in these maps. How might these differences have affected the economics and politics of the Byzantine empire?

Constantinople in 1204. Although Byzantine forces recaptured the capital in 1261, the destruction of Constantinople dealt the Byzantine empire a blow from which it never completely recovered.

As Europeans expanded into Byzantine territory from the west, nomadic Turkish peoples invaded from the east. Most important among them *Challenges from* were the Muslim Saljuqs, who begin- *the East* ning in the eleventh century sent waves of invaders into Anatolia. Given the military and financial problems of the Byzantine empire, the Saljuqs found Anatolia ripe for plunder. In 1071 they subjected the Byzantine army to a demoralizing defeat at the battle of Manzikert. Byzantine factions then turned on one another in civil war, allowing the Saljuqs almost free rein in Anatolia. By the late twelfth century, the Saljuqs had seized much of Anatolia, and crusaders from western Europe held most of the remainder.

The loss of Anatolia—the principal source of Byzantine grain, wealth, and military forces—sealed the fate of the Byzantine empire. A territorially truncated Byzantium survived until the mid–fifteenth century, but the late Byzantine empire enjoyed little autonomy and continually faced fresh challenges from Italian merchants, western European adventurers, and Turkish nomads. In 1453, after a long era of decline, the Byzantine empire came to an end when Ottoman Turks captured Constantinople and absorbed its territories into their own expanding realm.

Early Relations between Byzantium and Slavic Peoples

By the time Constantinople fell, Byzantine traditions had deeply influenced the political and cultural development of Slavic peoples in eastern Europe and Russia. Close relations between Byzantium and Slavic peoples date from the sixth century. When Justinian deployed Byzantium's military resources in the western Mediterranean, Slavic peoples from the north took advantage of the opportunity to move into Byzantine territory. Serbs and Croats moved into the Balkan peninsula, and Bulgars established a powerful kingdom in the lower Danube region.

Relations between Byzantium and Bulgaria were especially tense. By the eighth century, however, Byzantium had begun to influence Bulgarian politics

Saljuqs (sahl-JYOOKS)

and society. Byzantium and Bulgaria entered into political, commercial, and cultural relations. Members of Bulgarian ruling families often went to Constantinople for a formal education in Greek language and literature and followed Byzantine examples in organizing their court and capital.

Byzantium also sent missionaries to Balkan lands, and Bulgars and other Slavic peoples began to convert to Orthodox Christianity. The most famous of the missionaries to the Slavs were Saints *Cyril and* Cyril and Methodius, two brothers from *Methodius* Thessaloniki in Greece. During the mid–ninth century Cyril and Methodius conducted missions in Bulgaria and Moravia (which included much of the modern Czech, Slovakian, and Hungarian territories). While there, they devised an alphabet, known as the Cyrillic alphabet, for the previously illiterate Slavic peoples.

This illustration from a twelfth-century manuscript depicts ninth-century incursions of Bulgarians into Byzantine territory, culminating in a lecture by the Bulgarian king to the Byzantine emperor, shown here with bound hands.

Though adapted from written Greek, the Cyrillic alphabet represented the sounds of Slavic languages more precisely than did the Greek, and it remained in use in much of eastern Europe until supplanted by the Roman alphabet in the twentieth century. In Russia and most other parts of the former Soviet Union, the Cyrillic alphabet survives to the present day.

Mission to the Slavs

The Cyrillic alphabet stimulated conversion to Orthodox Christianity. Missionaries translated the Christian scriptures and church rituals into Slavonic, and Cyrillic writing helped them explain Christian values and ideas in Slavic terms. Meanwhile, schools organized by missionaries ensured that Slavs would receive religious instruction alongside their introduction to basic literacy. As a result, Orthodox Christianity deeply influenced the cultural traditions of many Slavic peoples.

Byzantium and Russia

North of Bulgaria another Slavic people began to organize large states: the Russians. About the mid–ninth century Russians created several principalities governed from thriving trading centers, notably Kiev. Strategically situated on the Dnieper River along the main trade route linking Scandinavia and Byzantium, Kiev became a wealthy and powerful center, and it dominated much of the territory between the Volga and the Dnieper from the tenth to the thirteenth century. Russian merchants visited Constantinople in large numbers and became well acquainted with Byzantine society. Russian princes sought alliances with Byzantine rulers and began to express an interest in Orthodox Christianity.

About 989 Prince Vladimir of Kiev converted to Orthodox Christianity and ordered his subjects to follow his example. After his conversion, Byzantine influences flowed rapidly into Russia. Cyrillic writing, literacy, and Orthodox missions all spread quickly throughout Russia. Byzantine teachers traveled north to establish schools, and Byzantine priests conducted services for Russian converts. For two centuries Kiev served as a conduit for the spread of Byzantine cultural and religious influence in Russia. Indeed, Byzantine art and architecture dominated Kiev and other Russian cities. The onion domes that are a distinctive feature of early Russian churches were the result of architects' efforts to imitate the domed structures of Constantinople using wood as their principal building material.

The Conversion of Prince Vladimir

Church of the Resurrection

The princes of Kiev established firm, caesaropapist control over the Russian Orthodox church—so called to distinguish it from the Eastern Orthodox church of the Byzantine empire. They also drew inspiration from Byzantine legal tradition and compiled a written law code for their lands. By controlling trade with Byzantium and other lands, they gained financial resources to build a flourishing society.

The Growth of Kiev

Eventually, Russians even claimed to inherit the imperial mantle of Byzantium. According to a popular theory of the sixteenth century, Moscow was the world's third Rome: the first Rome had fallen to Germanic invaders in the fifth century, whereas the second Rome, Constantinople, had fallen to the Turks a thousand years later. Moscow survived as the third Rome, the cultural and religious beacon that would guide the world to Orthodox Christian righteousness. Inspired by that theory, missionaries took their Russian Orthodox faith to distant lands. Thus, long after the collapse of the eastern Roman empire, the Byzantine legacy continued to work its influence through the outward reach of the Russian Orthodox church.

SUMMARY

The Byzantine empire originated as a survivor of the classical era. Byzantium inherited a hardy economy, a set of governing institutions, an imperial bureaucracy, an official religion, an established church, and a rich cultural tradition from classical Mediterranean society and the Roman empire. Byzantine leaders drew heavily on that legacy as they dealt with new challenges. Throughout Byzantine history, classical inspiration was especially noticeable in the imperial office, the bureaucracy, the church, and the educational system. Yet in many ways Byzantium changed profoundly over the course of its thousand-year history. After the seventh century the Byzantine empire shrank dramatically in size, and after the eleventh century it faced relentless foreign pressure from western Europeans and nomadic Turkish peoples. Changing times also brought transformations in Byzantine social and economic organization. Yet from the fifth to the twelfth century and beyond, Byzantium brought political stability and economic prosperity to the eastern Mediterranean basin, and Byzantine society served as a principal anchor supporting commercial and cultural exchanges in the postclassical world. Through its political, economic, and cultural influence, Byzantium also helped shape the development of the larger Byzantine commonwealth in eastern Europe and the eastern Mediterranean basin.

CHRONOLOGY

313–337	Reign of Constantine
325	Council of Nicaea
329–379	Life of St. Basil of Caesarea
340	Transfer of Roman government to Constantinople
527–565	Reign of Justinian
717–741	Reign of Leo III
726–843	Iconoclastic controversy
NINTH CENTURY	Missions of St. Cyril and St. Methodius to the Slavs
976–1025	Reign of Basil II, "the Bulgar-Slayer"
989	Conversion of Prince Vladimir of Kiev to Orthodox Christianity
1054	Beginning of the schism between the eastern and western Christian churches
1071	Battle of Manzikert
1202–1204	Fourth crusade
1453	Fall of Constantinople

FOR FURTHER READING

Averil Cameron. *The Mediterranean World in Late Antiquity, A.D. 395–600.* London, 1993. A thoughtful synthesis that places Byzantium in the context of the late Roman empire.

John V. A. Fine Jr. *The Early Medieval Balkans: A Critical Survey from the Sixth to the Late Twelfth Century.* Ann Arbor, 1983. An excellent introduction to Balkan history in the postclassical era.

Garth Fowden. *Empire to Commonwealth: Consequences of Monotheism in Late Antiquity.* Princeton, 1993. A provocative volume that interprets Byzantine political and cultural development as a monotheist Christian society.

Deno John Geanakoplos. *Byzantium: Church, Society, and Civilization Seen through Contemporary Eyes.* Chicago, 1984. Rich collection of translated documents that throw light on all aspects of Byzantine society.

J. M. Hussey. *The Byzantine World.* London, 1982. A brief and reliable survey.

Dimitri Obolensky. *The Byzantine Commonwealth: Eastern Europe, 500–1453.* New York, 1971. A well-informed overview of early Slavic history and relations between Byzantine and Slavic peoples.

Procopius. *History of the Wars, Secret History, and Buildings.* Trans. by A. Cameron. New York, 1967. Translations of writings by the most important historian in the time of Justinian.

Michael Psellus. *Fourteen Byzantine Rulers.* Trans. by E. R. A. Sewter. Harmondsworth, 1966. Memoirs of eleventh-century Byzantium by a highly placed advisor to several emperors.

Speros Vryonis Jr. *Byzantium and Europe.* London, 1967. Well-illustrated and well-written perusal of Byzantine history and Byzantine relations with western Europe.

Mark Whittow. *The Making of Byzantium, 600–1025.* Berkeley, 1996. Concentrates on Byzantine military and political relations with neighboring societies.

CHAPTER 11
The Expansive Realm of Islam

In 632 C.E. the prophet Muhammad visited his native city of Mecca from his home in exile at Medina, and in doing so he set an example that devout Muslims have sought to emulate ever since. The *hajj*—the holy pilgrimage to Mecca—draws Muslims by the hundreds of thousands from all parts of the world to Saudi Arabia. Each year Muslims travel to Mecca by land, sea, and air to make the pilgrimage and visit the holy sites of Islam.

In centuries past the numbers of pilgrims were smaller, but their observance of the hajj was no less conscientious. By the ninth century, pilgrimage had become so popular that Muslim rulers went to some lengths to meet the needs of travelers passing through their lands. With the approach of the pilgrimage season, crowds gathered at major trading centers such as Baghdad, Damascus, and Cairo. There they lived in tent cities, surviving on food and water provided by government officials, until they could join caravans bound for Mecca. Muslim rulers invested considerable sums in the maintenance of roads, wells, cisterns, and lodgings that accommodated pilgrims—as well as police forces that protected travelers—on their journeys to Mecca and back.

The hajj was not only solemn observance but also an occasion for joy and celebration. Muslim rulers and wealthy pilgrims often made lavish gifts to caravan companions and others they met en route to Mecca. During her famous hajj of 976–977, for example, the Mesopotamian princess Jamila bint Nasir al-Dawla provided food and fresh green vegetables for her fellow

---

hajj (HAHJ)

OPPOSITE PAGE: *A fifteenth-century Persian manuscript depicts pilgrims praying at Mecca in the mosque surrounding the Ka'ba.*

pilgrims and furnished five hundred camels for handicapped travelers. She also purchased freedom for five hundred slaves and distributed fifty thousand fine robes among the common people of Mecca.

Most pilgrims did not have the resources to match Jamila's generosity, but for common travelers, too, the hajj became a special occasion. Merchants and craftsmen arranged business deals with pilgrims from other lands. Students and scholars exchanged ideas during their weeks of traveling together. For all pilgrims, participation in ritual activities lent new meaning and significance to their faith.

The word *Islam* means "submission," signifying obedience to the rule and will of Allah, the only deity recognized in the strictly monotheistic Islamic religion. An individual who accepts the Islamic faith is a *Muslim,* meaning "one who has submitted." Though it began as one man's expression of unqualified faith in Allah, Islam quickly attracted followers. During the first century of the new faith's existence, Islam reached far beyond its Arabian homeland, bringing Sasanid Persia and parts of the Byzantine empire into its orbit. By the eighth century the realm of Islam stood alongside the Byzantine empire as a political and economic anchor of the postclassical world.

Islamic society originally reflected the nomadic and mercantile Arabian society from which Islam arose. Yet over time, Muslims drew deep inspiration from other societies as well. After toppling the Sasanid dynasty, Muslim conquerors adopted Persian techniques of government and finance to administer their lands. Persian literature, science, and religious values also found a place in Islamic society. During later centuries Muslims drew inspiration from Greek and Indian traditions as well.

While drawing influence from other societies, however, the Islamic faith thoroughly transformed the cultural traditions that it absorbed. The expansive realm of Islam eventually provided a political framework for trade and diplomacy over a vast portion of the eastern hemisphere, from west Africa to the islands of Southeast Asia. Many lands of varied cultural background thus became part of a larger society often called the *dar al-Islam*—an Arabic term that means the "house of Islam" and that refers to lands under Islamic rule.

A Prophet and His World

Islam arose in the Arabian peninsula, and the new religion faithfully reflected the social and cultural conditions of its homeland. Desert covers most of the peninsula, and agriculture is possible only in the well-watered area of Yemen in the south and in a few other places, such as the city of Medina, where oases provide water. Yet human communities have occupied Arabia for millennia. Nomadic peoples known as bedouin migrated through the deserts to find grass and water for their herds of sheep, goats, and camels. The bedouin organized themselves in family and clan groups. Individuals and their immediate families depended heavily on those kinship networks for support in times of need. In an environment as harsh and unforgiving as the Arabian desert, cooperation with kin often made the difference between life and death. As a result, bedouin peoples developed a strong sense of loyalty to their clans. Indeed, clan loyalties survived for centuries after the appearance of Islam.

Arabia also figured prominently in the long-distance trade networks of the postclassical era. Commodities arrived at ports on the Persian Gulf (near modern Bahrain), the Arabian Sea (near modern Aden), and the Red Sea (near Mecca), and then traveled overland by camel caravan to Palmyra or Damascus, which offered access to the Mediterranean basin. After the third century C.E., Arabia became an increasingly important link in long-distance trade networks. With the weakening of classical empires, trade routes across central Asia became increasingly insecure. In response, merchants abandoned the overland routes in favor of sea lanes connecting with land routes in the Arabian peninsula. In the process, their trade allowed Arabian cities to thrive.

Muhammad and His Message

The prophet Muhammad came into this world of nomadic bedouin herders and merchants. Born about 570 C.E. into a reputable family of merchants in Mecca, Muhammad ibn Abdullah lost both of his parents as a young child. His grandfather and his uncle raised him and *Muhammad's Early Life* provided him with an education, but Muhammad's early life was difficult. As a young man, he worked for a woman named Khadija, a wealthy widow whom he married about the year 595. Through this marriage he gained a position of some prominence in Meccan society.

By age thirty Muhammad had established himself as a merchant. He made a comfortable life for himself

---

bedouin (BEHD-oh-ihn)
Muhammad (muh-HAHM-mahd)

in Arabian society, where peoples of different religious and cultural traditions regularly dealt with one another. Most Arabs recognized many gods, goddesses, demons, and nature spirits, whose favor they sought through prayers and sacrifices. Large communities of Jewish merchants also worked throughout Arabia, and many Arabs had converted to Christianity by Muhammad's time. Although he was not deeply knowledgeable about Judaism or Christianity, Muhammad had a basic understanding of both faiths.

About 610 C.E., as he approached age forty, Muhammad underwent a profound spiritual experience that transformed his life and left a deep mark on world history. His experience left him with the convictions that in all the world there was only one true deity, Allah ("God"), that he ruled the universe, that idolatry and the recognition of other gods amounted to wickedness, and that Allah would soon bring his judgment on the world. Muhammad experienced visions, which he understood as messages or revelations from Allah, delivered through the archangel Gabriel (also recognized by Jews and Christians as a special messenger of God), instructing him to explain his faith to others. In accordance with instructions transmitted to him by Gabriel, Muhammad began to expound his faith to his family and close friends. Gradually, others showed interest in his message, and by about 620 C.E. a zealous and expanding minority of Mecca's citizenry had joined his circle.

Muhammad's Spiritual Transformation

Muhammad originally presented oral recitations of the revelations he received during his visions. As the Islamic community grew, his followers prepared written texts of his teachings. During the early 650s devout Muslims compiled these written versions of Muhammad's revelations and issued them as the Quran ("recitation"), the holy book of Islam. A work of magnificent poetry, the Quran communicates in powerful and moving terms Muhammad's understanding of Allah and his relation to the world, and it serves as the definitive authority for Islamic religious doctrine and social organization.

The Quran

Apart from the Quran, several other sources have provided moral and religious guidance for the Islamic community. Most important after the Quran itself are traditions known as *hadith,* which include sayings attributed to Muhammad and accounts of his deeds. Regarded as less authoritative than the Quran and the *hadith,* but still important as inspirations for Islamic thought, were early works describing social and legal customs, biographies of Muhammad, and pious commentaries on the Quran.

Muhammad's Migration to Medina

The growing popularity of Muhammad's preaching brought him into conflict with the ruling elites at Mecca. Muhammad's insistence that Allah was the only divine power in the universe struck many polytheistic Arabs as offensive and dangerous, since it disparaged long-recognized deities and spirits thought to wield influence over human affairs. The tensions also had a personal dimension. Mecca's ruling elites, who were also the city's wealthiest merchants, took it as a personal affront when

Conflict at Mecca

Quran (koorr-AHN)

Current Islamic doctrine forbids artistic representations of Muhammad and Allah to prevent the worship of their images as idols. Although artists of previous centuries occasionally produced paintings of Muhammad, Islamic art has emphasized geometric design and calligraphy. This handsome page from a Quran written on vellum dates from the ninth or early tenth century.

Muhammad denounced greed as moral wickedness that Allah would punish.

Muhammad's attack on idolatry also represented an economic threat to those who owned and profited from the many shrines to deities that attracted merchants and pilgrims to Mecca. The best known of these shrines was a large black rock long considered to be the 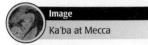 dwelling of a powerful deity. Housed in a cube-shaped building known as the Ka'ba, it drew worshipers from all over Arabia and brought considerable wealth to Mecca. As Muhammad relentlessly condemned the idolatry officially promoted at the Ka'ba and other shrines, the ruling elites of Mecca began to persecute the prophet and his followers.

The pressure became so great that Muhammad and his followers had to flee Mecca in 622 C.E. They *The Hijra* established themselves in Yathrib, a rival trading city north of Mecca, which they renamed Medina ("the city," meaning "the city of the prophet"). Known as the *hijra* ("migration"), Muhammad's move to Medina serves as the starting point of the official Islamic calendar.

Once in Medina, Muhammad found himself at the head of a small but growing society in exile that needed *The Umma* guidance in practical as well as spiritual affairs. He organized his followers into a cohesive community called the *umma* ("community of the faithful") and provided it with a comprehensive legal and social code. He led this community both in daily prayers to Allah and in battle with enemies at Medina, Mecca, and other places. Remembering the difficult days of his own youth, he provided relief for widows, orphans, and the poor, and he made almsgiving a prime moral virtue.

Muhammad's understanding of his religious mission expanded during his years at Medina. He began *The "Seal of the Prophets"* to refer to himself as a prophet, indeed as the "seal of the prophets"—the final prophet through whom Allah would reveal his message to humankind. Muhammad accepted the authority of earlier Jewish and Christian prophets, including Abraham, Moses, and Jesus, and he held the Hebrew scriptures and the Christian New Testament in high esteem. He also believed that Allah was one and the same as the Jews' Yahweh and the Christians' God. Muhammad taught, however, that the message entrusted to him was a more complete revelation of Allah and his will than Jewish and Christian faiths had made available. Thus, while at Medina, Muhammad came to see himself consciously as the messenger who communicated Allah's wishes and his plan for the world to all humankind.

The Establishment of Islam in Arabia

Throughout their sojourn at Medina, Muhammad and his followers planned ultimately to return to their home in Mecca. In 629 C.E. they arranged with the authorities to participate in the annual pilgrimage to the Ka'ba, but *Muhammad's Return to Mecca* they were not content with a short visit. In 630 they attacked Mecca and conquered the city. They forced the elites to adopt Muhammad's faith, and they imposed a government dedicated to Allah. They also destroyed the pagan shrines and replaced them with mosques, buildings that sought to instill a sense of sacredness and community where Muslims gathered for prayers. Only the Ka'ba escaped their efforts to cleanse Mecca of pagan monuments.

Muhammad and his followers denied that the Ka'ba was the home of a deity, but they preserved the black rock and its housing as a symbol of Mecca's greatness. In 632 Muhammad himself led the first Islamic pilgrimage to the Ka'ba, thus establishing the hajj as an example for all devout Muslims. Building on the conquest of Mecca, Muhammad and his followers launched campaigns against other towns and bedouin clans, and by the time of the prophet's death in 632, shortly after his hajj, they had brought most of Arabia under their control.

Muhammad's faith and his personal leadership decisively shaped the values and the development of the Islamic community. The foundation of the Islamic faith as elaborated by *The Five Pillars of Islam* Muhammad consists of obligations known as the Five Pillars of Islam: (1) Muslims must acknowledge Allah as the only god and Muhammad as his prophet. (2) They must pray to Allah daily while facing Mecca. (3) They must observe a fast during the daylight hours of the month of Ramadan. (4) They must contribute alms for the relief of the weak and the poor. (5) Finally, those who are physically and financially able must undertake the hajj and make at least one pilgrimage to Mecca. Although Islam has generated many schools and sects in the centuries since its appearance, the Five Pillars of Islam constitute a powerful framework that has bound the *umma* as a whole into a cohesive community of faith.

Ka'ba (KAH-bah)
umma (UM-mah)

SOURCES FROM THE PAST

The Quran on Allah and His Expectations of Humankind

The foundation of the Islamic faith is the understanding of Allah, his nature, and his plan for the world as outlined in the Quran. Through his visions Muhammad came to understand Allah as the one and only god, the creator and sustainer of the world in the manner of the Jews' Yahweh and the Christians' God. Those who rejected Allah and his message would suffer eternal punishment, whereas those who recognized and obeyed him would receive his mercy and secure his blessings.

■ ■ ■

In the name of Allah, most benevolent, ever-merciful.
All praise be to Allah,
Lord of all the worlds,
Most beneficent, ever-merciful,
King of the Day of Judgement.
You alone we worship, and to You
alone turn for help.
Guide us (O Lord) to the path that is straight,
The path of those You have blessed,
Not of those who have earned Your anger,
nor those who have gone astray. . . .
Verily men and women who have come to submission,
men and women who are believers,
men and women who are devout,
truthful men and women,
men and women with endurance,
men and women who are modest,
men and women who give alms,
men and women who observe fasting,
men and women who guard their private parts,
and those men and women who remember God a great deal,
for them God has forgiveness and a great reward.
No believing men and women have any choice in a matter
after God and His Apostle [i.e., Muhammad] have decided it.
Whoever disobeys God and His Apostle
has clearly lost the way and gone astray. . . .

O you who believe, remember God a great deal,
And sing His praises morning and evening.
It is He who sends His blessings on you,
as (do) His angels, that He may lead you out of darkness into light,
for He is benevolent to the believers. . . .
I call to witness
the early hours of the morning,
And the night when dark and still,
Your Lord has neither left you,
nor despises you.
What is to come is better for you
than what has gone before;
For your Lord will certainly give you,
and you will be content.
Did He not find you an orphan
and take care of you?
Did He not find you poor
and enrich you?
So do not oppress the orphan,
And do not drive
the beggar away,
And keep recounting the favours of your Lord. . . .
Say: "He is God
the one the most unique,
God the immanently indispensable.
He has begotten no one,
and is begotten of none.
There is no one comparable to Him."

- *Compare the Quran's teachings on the relationship between Allah and human beings with the views of Zoroastrians, Jews, and Christians discussed in earlier chapters.*

SOURCE: *Al-Qur'an: A Contemporary Translation.* Trans. by Ahmed Ali. Princeton: Princeton University Press, 1984, pp. 11, 358, 359, 540, 559.

Some Muslims, though by no means all, have taken *jihad* as an additional obligation for the faith-

Jihad

ful. The term *jihad* literally means "struggle," and Muslims have understood its imperatives in various ways. In one sense, *jihad* imposes obligations on Muslims by requiring them to combat vice and evil. In another sense, *jihad* calls on Muslims to struggle against unbelief by spreading the word of Islam and seeking converts to the faith. In some circumstances, *jihad* also obliges Muslims to take up the sword and wage war against unbelievers who threaten Islam.

Islamic Law: The Sharia

Beyond the general obligations prescribed by the Five Pillars, Islamic holy law, known as the *sharia*, emerged during the centuries after Muhammad and offered detailed guidance on proper behavior in almost every aspect of life. Inspired by the Quran and elaborated by jurists and legal scholars, the *sharia* offered precise guidance on matters as diverse as marriage and family life, inheritance, slavery, business relationships, political authority, and crime. Through the *sharia*, Islam became more than a religious doctrine: it developed into a way of life.

---

sharia (shah-REE-ah)

THE EXPANSION OF ISLAM

After Muhammad's death the Islamic community might well have unraveled and disappeared. Muhammad had made no provision for a successor, and there was serious division within the *umma* concerning the selection of a new leader. Many of the towns and bedouin clans that had recently accepted Islam took the opportunity of Muhammad's death to renounce the faith, reassert their independence, and break free from Mecca's control. Within a short time, however, the Islamic community had embarked on a stunningly successful

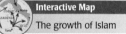

Interactive Map
The growth of Islam

round of military expansion that extended its political and cultural influence far beyond the boundaries of Arabia. Those conquests laid the foundation for the rapid growth of Islamic society.

The Early Caliphs and the Umayyad Dynasty

Because Muhammad was the "seal of the prophets," it was inconceivable that another prophet should succeed him. Shortly after Muhammad's death his advi-

Map 11.1 How Islam expanded in western Asia and the Mediterranean between 632 and 733 C.E. Notice the extensive territories gained by Islamic leaders in this period. Consider the ways in which this expansion might have influenced culture and politics in non-Islamic areas such as the Byzantine empire and the Lombard and Frankish kingdoms.

sors selected Abu Bakr, a genial man who was one of the prophet's closest friends and most devoted disci-

The Caliph   ples, to serve as *caliph* ("deputy"). Thus Abu Bakr and later caliphs led the *umma* not as prophets but as substitutes for Muhammad. Abu Bakr became head of state for the Islamic community as well as chief judge, religious leader, and military commander. Under the new caliph's leadership, the *umma* went on the offensive against people who had renounced Islam after Muhammad's death, and within a year it had compelled them to recognize the faith of Islam and the rule of the caliph.

Indeed, during the century after Muhammad's death, Islamic armies carried their religion and author-

The Expansion of Islam   ity throughout Arabia into Byzantine and Sasanid territories and beyond. Although much less powerful than either the Byzantine empire or the Sasanid empire, early Islamic warriors fought with the zeal of new converts. Moreover, they attacked at a moment when the larger empires were preoccupied with internal difficulties. Between 633 and 637 C.E., Muslim forces seized Byzantine Syria and Palestine and took most of Mesopotamia from the Sasanids. During the 640s they conquered Byzantine Egypt and north Africa. In 651 they toppled the Sasanid dynasty and incorporated Persia into their expanding empire. In 711 they conquered the Hindu kingdom of Sind in northwestern India. Between 711 and 718 they extended their authority to northwest Africa and crossed the Strait of Gibraltar,

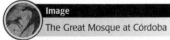
The Great Mosque at Córdoba

conquering most of the Iberian peninsula and threatening the Frankish kingdom in Gaul. By the mid–eighth century an immense Islamic empire ruled lands from India and the central Asian steppe lands in the east to northwest Africa and Iberia in the west.

During this rapid expansion the empire's rulers encountered problems of governance and administration. One problem had to do with the selection of caliphs. During the early decades after Muhammad's death, leaders of the most powerful Arab clans appointed the first four caliphs. Political ambitions, personal differences, and clan loyalties, however, soon led to the rise of factions and parties within the Islamic community.

Disagreements over succession led to the emergence of the Shia sect, the most important and enduring of all the alternatives to the faith observed by

the majority of Muslims, known as Sunni Islam. The Shia sect originated as a party supporting the appointment of Ali—a cousin and son-in-law

The Shia

of Muhammad—and his descendants as caliphs. Ali did serve briefly as the fourth caliph (656–661 C.E.), but his enemies assassinated him, killed many of his relatives, and imposed their own candidate as caliph. Partisans of Ali then organized the Shia ("party") and furiously struggled to return the caliphate to the line of Ali. Although persecuted, the Shia survived and strengthened its identity by adopting doctrines and rituals distinct from those of the Sunnis ("traditionalists"), who accepted the legitimacy of the early caliphs. Shia partisans, for example, observed

Shia pilgrims

holy days in honor of their leaders and martyrs to their cause, and they taught that descendants of Ali were infallible, sinless, and divinely appointed to rule the Islamic community.

After the assassination of Ali, the establishment of the Umayyad dynasty (661–750 C.E.) temporarily solved the problem of succession. The

The Umayyad Dynasty

Umayyads ranked among the most prominent of the Meccan merchant clans, and their reputation and network of alliances helped them bring stability to the Islamic community. Despite their association with Mecca, the Umayyads established their capital at Damascus, a thriving commercial city in Syria, whose central location enabled them to maintain better communication with the vast and still-expanding Islamic empire.

Although the Umayyads' dynasty solved the problem of succession, their tightly centralized rule and the favor they showed to their fellow

Policy toward Conquered Peoples

Arabs generated an administrative problem. The Umayyads ruled the *dar al-Islam* as conquerors, and their policies favored the Arab military aristocracy by distributing both lands and positions of power among this privileged class. Such policies caused severe discontent among the scores of ethnic and religious groups embraced by the Umayyad empire. In addition, although the Arabs mostly allowed conquered peoples to observe their own religions, they levied a special head tax, called the *jizya,* on those who did not convert to Islam.

---

caliph (KHA-leef)

Shia (SHEE-'ah)
Sunni (SOON-nee)
Umayyad (oo-MEYE-ah)
jizya (JIHZ-yah)

The early expansion of Islam was a bloody affair. This illustration from an Arabic manuscript of the thirteenth century depicts a battle between Muhammad's cousin Ali and his adversaries.

Moreover, even those who converted did not enjoy access to wealth and positions of authority, which the Umayyads reserved almost exclusively for members of the Arab military aristocracy.

Beginning in the early eighth century, the Umayyad caliphs became alienated even from other Arabs as they devoted themselves increasingly to luxurious living rather than to moral leadership of the *umma*. By midcentury the Umayyad caliphs faced not only the continued resistance of the Shia faction but also the discontent of conquered peoples throughout their empire and even the disillusionment of Muslim Arab military leaders.

Umayyad Decline

The Abbasid Dynasty

Rebellion in Persia brought the Umayyad dynasty to an end. The chief leader of the rebellion was Abu al-Abbas, a descendant of Muhammad's uncle. Although he was a Sunni Arab, Abu al-Abbas allied readily with Shias and with non-Arab Muslims. During the 740s Abu al-Abbas's party seized control of Persia and Mesopotamia. In 750 his army shattered Umayyad forces in a great battle. Afterward Abu al-Abbas invited the remaining members of the Umayyad clan to a banquet under the pretext of reconciling their differences. Instead, during the festivities his troops slaughtered the Umayyads and annihilated the clan. Abu al-Abbas then founded the Abbasid dynasty, which was the principal source of authority in the *dar al-Islam* until the Mongols toppled it in 1258 C.E.

Abu al-Abbas

The Abbasid dynasty differed considerably from the Umayyad. For one thing, the Abbasid rulers did not show special favor to the Arab military aristocracy. Arabs continued to play a large role in government, but Persians, Egyptians, Mesopotamians, and others also rose to positions of wealth and power.

The Abbasid Dynasty

The Abbasid dynasty differed from the Umayyad also in that it was not a conquering dynasty. The Abbasids did clash intermittently with the Byzantine empire and nomadic peoples from central Asia, and in 751 they defeated a Chinese army at Talas River near Samarkand. The battle of Talas River was exceptionally important: it ended the expansion of China's Tang dynasty into central Asia (discussed in chapter 12), and it opened the door for the spread of Islam among Turkish peoples. Overall, however, the Abbasids did not expand their empire by conquest. The *dar al-Islam* as a whole continued to grow during the Abbasid era, but that was a result of largely autonomous Islamic forces rather than the policies of the caliphs.

Instead of conquering new lands, the Abbasids largely contented themselves with administration—a considerable challenge given the empire's diversity of linguistic, ethnic, and cultural groups. In designing their administration, the Abbasids relied heavily on Persian techniques of statecraft. Central authority came from the court at the magnificent new city of Baghdad (capital of modern Iraq). From Baghdad, instructions flowed to the distant reaches of the Abbasid realm. In the provinces, governors represented

Abbasid Administration

Abbasid (ah-BAH-sih)

the caliph and implemented his political and financial policies.

Learned officials known as *ulama* ("people with religious knowledge") and *qadis* ("judges") set moral standards in local communities and resolved disputes. *Ulama* and *qadis* were not priests—Islam does not recognize priests—but they had a formal education that emphasized study of the Quran and the *sharia*. *Ulama* were pious scholars who sought to develop public policy in accordance with the Quran and the *sharia*. *Qadis* heard cases at law and rendered decisions based on the Quran and the *sharia*. Because of their moral authority, *ulama* and *qadis* became extremely influential officials who helped to ensure widespread observance of Islamic values. The Abbasid caliphs also kept a standing army, maintained the network of roads they inherited from the Sasanids, and established bureaucratic ministries in charge of taxation, finance, coinage, and postal services.

Abbasid Decline In the early ninth century, however, the Abbasid empire entered a period of decline, and disputes over succession seriously damaged its authority. Provincial governors took advantage of disorder in the ruling house by acting independently of the caliphs and building up local bases of power. Meanwhile, popular uprisings and peasant rebellions further weakened the empire.

As a result of these difficulties, the Abbasid caliphs became mere figureheads long before the Mongols extinguished the dynasty in 1258. In 945 members of a Persian noble family seized control of Baghdad and established their clan as the power behind the Abbasid throne. Later, imperial authorities in Baghdad fell under the control of the Saljuq Turks, a nomadic people from central Asia who also invaded the Byzantine empire. By the mid–eleventh century the Saljuqs took possession of Baghdad, and during the following decades they extended their authority to Syria, Palestine, and Anatolia. They retained Abbasid caliphs as nominal sovereigns, but for two centuries, until the arrival of the Mongols, the Saljuq *sultan* ("ruler") was the true source of power in the Abbasid empire.

ECONOMY AND SOCIETY OF THE EARLY ISLAMIC WORLD

In the *dar al-Islam,* as in other agricultural societies, peasants tilled the land while manufacturers and merchants supported a thriving urban economy. Here, as in other lands, the creation of large empires had dramatic economic implications. The Umayyad and Abbasid empires created a zone of trade, exchange, and communication stretching from India to Iberia. Commerce throughout this zone served as a vigorous economic stimulus for both the countryside and the cities of the early Islamic world.

New Crops, Agricultural Experimentation, and Urban Growth

As soldiers, administrators, diplomats, and merchants traveled throughout the *dar al-Islam,* they encountered plants, animals, and agricultural techniques peculiar to the empire's various regions. They often introduced particularly useful crops to new regions. The most important of the transplants traveled west from India and included staple crops such as sugarcane, rice, and new varieties of sorghum and wheat; vegetables such as spinach and artichokes; fruits such as oranges, bananas, coconuts, and mangoes; and industrial crops such as cotton, indigo, and henna.

The Spread of Food and Industrial Crops

The introduction of these crops into the western regions of the Islamic world had wide-ranging effects. New food crops led to a richer and more varied diet. They also increased quantities of food available because they enabled cultivators to extend the growing season: since most of the transplanted crops grew well in high heat, cultivators in southwest Asia and other hot zones could plant an additional crop in the summer months instead of leaving their fields fallow. The result was a dramatic increase in food supplies.

Effects of New Crops

Travel and communication in the *dar al-Islam* also encouraged experimentation with agricultural methods. Cultivators paid close attention to methods of irrigation, fertilization, crop rotation, and the like, and they outlined their findings in hundreds of agricultural manuals. The combined effect of new crops and improved techniques was a far more productive agricultural economy, which in turn supported vigorous economic growth throughout the *dar al-Islam.*

Agricultural Experimentation

Increased agricultural production contributed to the rapid growth of cities in all parts of the Islamic world from India to Spain. All these cities—including, for example, Delhi, Merv, Isfahan, Damascus,

Cairo, Córdoba, and Tangier—had flourishing markets supporting thousands of artisans, craftsmen, and merchants. Most of them were also important centers of industrial production, particularly of textiles, pottery, glassware, leather, iron, and steel.

Urban Growth

A mosque lamp

One new industry appeared in Islamic cities during the Abbasid era: paper manufacture. When Arab forces defeated a Chinese army at the battle of Talas River in 751, they took prisoners skilled in paper production and learned the technique from them. Paper soon became popular throughout the Islamic world. Paper facilitated the keeping of administrative and commercial records, and it made possible the dissemination of books and treatises in larger quantities than ever before. By the tenth century, mills produced paper in Persia, Mesopotamia, Arabia, Egypt, and Spain, and the industry soon spread to western Europe.

In a thirteenth-century manuscript illustration, a fictional Muslim traveler passes a lively agricultural village. On the left a woman spins cotton thread. Sheep, goats, chickens, and date palms figure prominently in the local economy.

The Formation of a Hemispheric Trading Zone

From its earliest days Islamic society drew much of its prosperity from commerce. Muhammad himself was a merchant, and he held merchants in high esteem. By the time of the Abbasid caliphate, elaborate trade networks linked all the regions of the Islamic world and joined it to a larger, hemispheric economy.

When they overran the Sasanid empire, Muslim conquerors brought the prosperous trading cities of central Asia under control of the expanding *dar al-Islam*. Muslim merchants were then able to take advantage of the extensive road networks originally built during the classical era by imperial authorities in India, Persia, and the Mediterranean basin. To be sure, Umayyad and Abbasid rulers maintained the roads for military and administrative purposes, but those same roads also made excellent highways for merchants as well as missionaries and pilgrims.

Overland Trade

Overland trade traveled mostly by camel caravan. Although they are uncooperative beasts, camels endure the rigors of desert travel much better than horses or donkeys. Moreover, camels can carry heavy loads. During the early centuries C.E., camels became the favored beasts of burden in deserts and other dry regions. As camel transport became more common, the major cities of the Islamic world and central Asia built and maintained caravanserais—inns offering lodging for caravan merchants as well as food, water, and care for their animals.

Camels and Caravans

Meanwhile, innovations in nautical technology contributed to a steadily increasing volume of maritime trade in the Red Sea, Persian Gulf, Arabian Sea, and Indian Ocean. Arab and Persian mariners borrowed the compass from its Chinese inventors and used it to guide them on the high seas. From southeast Asian and Indian mariners they borrowed the lateen sail, a triangular sail that increased a ship's maneuverability. From the Hellenistic Mediterranean they borrowed the astrolabe, an instrument that enabled them to calculate latitude. Thus equipped, Arab and Persian mariners ventured throughout the Indian Ocean basin.

Maritime Trade

Banking also stimulated the commercial economy of the Islamic world. Banks had operated since classical antiquity, but Islamic banks of the Abbasid period conducted business on a much larger scale than their predecessors. They not only lent money to entrepreneurs but also served as bro-

Banks

A map produced in the eleventh century by the Arab geographer al-Idrisi shows the lands known and reported by Muslim merchants and travelers. Note that, in accordance with Muslim cartographic convention, this map places south at the top and north at the bottom.

Sahara desert by camel caravan to trade salt, steel, copper, and glass for gold and slaves from the kingdoms of west Africa. They visited the coastal regions of east Africa, where they obtained slaves and exotic local commodities such as animal skins. They engaged in trade with Russia and Scandinavia by way of the Dnieper and Volga rivers and obtained commodities such as animal skins, furs, honey, amber, and slaves as well as bulk goods such as timber and livestock. The vigorous economy of the Abbasid empire thus helped to establish networks of communication and exchange throughout much of the eastern hemisphere.

The prosperity of Islamic Spain, known as al-Andalus, illustrates the far-reaching effects of long-distance trade during the Abbasid era. *Al-Andalus* Most of the Iberian peninsula had fallen into the hands of Muslim Berber conquerors from

al-Andalus (al-ahn-duh-LUHS)

kers for investments and exchanged different currencies. They established multiple branches that honored letters of credit known as *sakk* drawn on the parent bank. Thus merchants could settle accounts with distant business partners without having to deal in cash.

Trade benefited also from refined techniques of business organization. Usually Islamic businessmen pre-*The Organization of Trade* ferred not to embark on solo ventures, since an individual could face financial ruin if an entire cargo of commodities fell prey to pirates or went down with a ship that sank in a storm. Instead, like their counterparts in other postclassical societies, Abbasid entrepreneurs often pooled their resources in a variety of group investments designed to distribute individual risks.

As a result of improved transportation, expanded banking services, and refined techniques of business organization, long-distance trade surged in the early Islamic world. Muslim merchants dealt in silk and ceramics from China, spices and aromatics from India and southeast Asia, and jewelry and fine textiles from the Byzantine empire. Merchants also ventured beyond settled societies in China, India, and the Mediterranean basin to distant lands that previously had not engaged systematically in long-distance trade. They crossed the

In this thirteenth-century manuscript illustration, merchants at a slave market in southern Arabia deal in black slaves captured in sub-Saharan Africa. Slaves traded in Islamic markets also came from Russia and eastern Europe.

north Africa during the early eighth century. As allies of the Umayyads, the governors of al-Andalus refused to recognize the Abbasid dynasty, and beginning in the tenth century they styled themselves caliphs in their own right rather than governors subject to Abbasid authority. Despite political and diplomatic tensions, al-Andalus participated actively in the commercial life of the larger Islamic world, which enabled merchants and manufacturers in al-Andalus to conduct thriving businesses in cities such as Córdoba, Toledo, and Seville.

The Changing Status of Women

A patriarchal society had emerged in Arabia long before Muhammad's time, but Arab women enjoyed rights not accorded to women in many other lands. They could legally inherit property, divorce husbands on their own initiative, and engage in business ventures. Khadija, the first of Muhammad's four wives, managed a successful commercial business.

In some respects the Quran enhanced the security of women in Arabian society. It outlawed female infanticide, and it provided that dowries go directly to brides rather than to their husbands and male guardians. It portrayed women not as the property of their menfolk but as honorable individuals, equal to men before Allah, with their own rights and needs. Muhammad's own kindness and generosity toward his wives also served as an example that may have improved the lives of Muslim women.

The Quran and Women

For the most part, however, the Quran—and later the *sharia* as well—reinforced male dominance. The Quran and Islamic holy law recognized descent through the male line, and to guarantee proper inheritance, they placed a high premium on genealogical purity. To ensure the legitimacy of heirs, they subjected the social and sexual lives of women to the strict control of male guardians. The Quran and the *sharia* also permitted men to take up to four wives, whereas women could have only one husband. The Quran and the *sharia* thus provided a religious and legal foundation for a decisively patriarchal society.

When Islam expanded into the Byzantine and Sasanid empires, it encountered strong patriarchal traditions, and Muslims readily adopted longstanding customs such as the veiling of women. Social and family pressures had induced upper-class urban women to veil themselves in Mesopotamia as early as the thirteenth century B.C.E., and long before Muhammad the practice of veiling had spread to Persia and the eastern Mediterranean.

Veiling of Women

When Muslim Arabs conquered these lands, they adopted the practice. A conspicuous symbol of male authority thus found a prominent place in the early Islamic community.

Although the Quran served as the preeminent source of authority in the Islamic world, over the centuries jurists and legal scholars interpreted the Quran in ways that progressively limited the rights of women. To a large extent the increased emphasis on male authority in Islamic law reflected the influence of the strongly hierarchical and patriarchal societies of Mesopotamia, Persia, and eastern Mediterranean lands as Islam developed from a local faith to a large-scale complex society.

ISLAMIC VALUES AND CULTURAL EXCHANGES

Since the seventh century C.E., the Quran has served as the cornerstone of Islamic society. Arising from a rich tradition of bedouin poetry and song, the Quran established Arabic as a flexible and powerful medium of communication. When carrying their faith to new lands during the era of Islamic expansion, Muslim missionaries spread the message of Allah and provided instruction in the Quran's teachings, although they also permitted continued observance of pre-Islamic traditions. Muslim intellectuals drew freely from the long-established cultural traditions of Persia, India, and Greece, which they became acquainted with during the Umayyad and Abbasid eras.

The Formation of an Islamic Cultural Tradition

Muslim theologians and jurists looked to the Quran and other sources of Islamic doctrine in their efforts to formulate moral guidelines appropriate for their society. The body of civil and criminal law embodied in the *sharia* provided a measure of cultural unity for the vastly different lands of the Islamic world. Islamic law did not by any means erase differences, but it established a common cultural foundation that facilitated dealings between peoples of various Islamic lands and that lent substance to the concept of the *dar al-Islam.*

On a more popular level, *ulama, qadis,* and missionaries helped to spread Islamic values throughout the *dar al-Islam. Ulama* and *qadis* held positions at all Islamic courts. By resolving disputes according to Islamic law and ordering public observance of Islamic *Promotion of* social and moral standards, they helped *Islamic Values* to bring the values of the Quran and the *sharia* into the lives of peoples living far from the birthplace of Islam.

Formal educational institutions also helped promote Islamic values. For example, many mosques maintained schools that provided an elementary education and religious instruction. By the tenth century, institutions of higher education known as *madrasas* had begun to appear, and by the twelfth century they had become established in the major cities of the Islamic world. Muslim rulers often supported the *madrasas* in the interests of recruiting literate and learned students for administrative positions.

Among the most effective Islamic missionaries were mystics known as Sufis. The term *Sufi* probably *Sufis* came from the patched woolen garments favored by the mystics. Sufis did not deny Islamic doctrine, but they also did not find formal religious teachings to be especially meaningful. Thus, instead of concerning themselves with fine points of doctrine, Sufis worked to deepen their spiritual awareness. Most Sufis led pious and ascetic lives. Some devoted themselves to helping the poor. Many sought a mystical, ecstatic union with Allah, relying on rousing sermons, passionate singing, or spirited dancing to bring them to a state of high emotion. Muslim theologians sometimes mistrusted Sufis, fearing that in their lack of concern for doctrine they would adopt erroneous beliefs. Nevertheless, after the ninth century Sufis became increasingly popular in Muslim societies because of their piety, devotion, and eagerness to minister to the needs of their fellow human beings.

Sufis were especially effective as missionaries because they emphasized devotion to Allah above *Sufi Missionaries* mastery of doctrine. They sometimes encouraged individuals to revere Allah in their own ways, even if their methods did not have a basis in the Quran. They tolerated the continued observance of pre-Islamic customs, for example, as well as the association of Allah with deities recognized and revered in other faiths. Because of their kindness, holiness, tolerance, and charismatic appeal, Sufis attracted numerous converts, particularly in lands such as Persia and India, where long-established religious faiths such as Zoroastrianism, Christianity, Bud-

madrasas (MAH-drahs-ahs)
Sufis (SOO-fees)

Through song, dance, and ecstatic experiences, sometimes enhanced by wine, Persian Sufis expressed their devotion to Allah, as in this sixteenth-century painting.

dhism, and Hinduism had enjoyed a mass following for centuries.

The symbol of Islamic cultural unity was the Ka'ba at Mecca, which from an early date attracted pilgrims from all parts of the Islamic world. Indeed, indi- *Hajj* viduals from far-flung regions made their way to Mecca, visited the holy sites, and learned firsthand the traditions of Islam. Over the centuries these pilgrims helped to spread Islamic beliefs and values to all parts of the Islamic world, and alongside the work of *ulama*, *qadis*, and Sufi missionaries, their efforts helped to make the *dar al-Islam* not just a name but also a reality.

Islam and the Cultural Traditions of Persia, India, and Greece

As the Islamic community expanded, Muslims of Arab ancestry interacted regularly with peoples from other cultural traditions, especially those of Persia, India, and Greece. In some cases, particularly in lands ruled by the Umayyad and Abbasid dynasties, large numbers of conquered peoples converted to Islam, and they brought elements of their inherited cultural traditions into Islamic society. In other cases, particularly in lands beyond the authority of Islamic rulers, Muslims became acquainted with the literary, artistic, philosophical, and scientific traditions of peoples who chose not to convert.

Persian Influences on Islam
Persian traditions quickly found a place in Islamic society, since the culturally rich land fell under Islamic rule at an early date. After the establishment of the Abbasid dynasty and the founding of its capital at Baghdad, Persian administrative techniques were crucial for the organization of the imperial structure through which rulers governed their vast empire. Meanwhile, Persian ideas of kingship—in which kings were wise, benevolent, but nonetheless absolute rulers—profoundly influenced Islamic political thought.

Persian influence was also noticeable in literary works from the Abbasid dynasty. Whereas Arabic served as the language of religion, theology, philosophy, and law, Persian was the principal language of literature, poetry, history, and political reflection. The marvelous collection of stories known as *The Arabian Nights* or *The Thousand and One Nights,* for example, presented popular tales of adventure and romance set in the Abbasid empire and the court of Harun al-Rashid.

Indian Influences on Islam
Indian mathematics, science, and medicine also captured the attention of Arab and Persian Muslims who established Islamic states in northern India. Muslims readily adopted what they called "Hindi" numerals, which European peoples later called "Arabic" numerals, since they learned about them through Arab Muslims. Hindi numerals enabled Muslim scholars to develop an impressive tradition of advanced mathematics, concentrating on algebra (an Arabic word) as well as trigonometry and geometry. From a more practical point of view, Indian numerals vastly simplified bookkeeping for Muslim merchants.

Muslims also found much to appreciate in the scientific and medical thought they encountered in India. With the aid of their powerful and flexible mathematics, Indian scholars were able to carry out precise astronomical calculations, which helped inspire the development of Muslim astronomy. Similarly, Indian medicine appealed to Muslims because of its treatments for specific ailments and its use of antidotes for poisons.

Greek Influences on Islam
Muslims also admired the philosophical, scientific, and medical writings of classical Greece. They became especially interested in Plato and Aristotle, whose works they translated and interpreted in commentaries. For example, Ibn Rushd (1126–1198), *qadi* of Seville in the caliphate of Córdoba, followed Aristotle in seeking to articulate a purely rational understanding of the world. Ibn Rushd's work not only helped to shape Islamic philosophy but also found its way to the schools and universities of western Europe, where Christian scholars knew Ibn Rushd as Averroës. During the thirteenth century, his work profoundly influenced the development of scholasticism, the effort of medieval European philosophers to harmonize Christianity with Aristotelian thought. However, after the thirteenth century, Greek philosophy fell out of favor with Muslim philosophers and theologians, who turned instead to teachings from the Quran and Sufi mystics.

Quite apart from philosophy, Greek mathematics, science, and medicine also appealed strongly to Muslims. Greek mathematics did not make use of Indian numerals, but it offered a solid body of powerful reasoning, particularly when dealing with calculations in algebra and geometry. Greek mathematics supported the development of astronomical and geographical scholarship, and studies of anatomy and physiology served as foundations for medical thought. Muslim scholars quickly absorbed these Greek traditions, combined them with influences from India, and used them as points of departure for their own studies. The result was a brilliant flowering of mathematical, scientific, and medical scholarship that provided Muslim societies with powerful tools for understanding the natural world.

SUMMARY

The prophet Muhammad did not intend to found a new religion. Instead, his intention was to express his faith in Allah and perfect the teachings of earlier Jewish and Christian prophets by announcing a revelation more comprehensive than those Allah had entrusted to his predecessors. His message soon attracted a circle of devout and committed disciples, and by the time of his death most of Arabia had accepted Islam. During the two centuries following the prophet's death, Arab conquerors spread Islam throughout southwest Asia and north Africa and introduced their faith to central Asia, India, the Mediterranean islands, and Iberia. This rapid expansion of Islam encouraged the development of an extensive trade and communications network: merchants, diplomats, and other travelers moved easily throughout the Islamic world exchanging goods and introducing agricultural crops to new lands. Rapid expansion also led to encounters between Islam and long-established religious and cultural traditions, Persian literature and political thought, and classical Greek philosophy and science. Muslim rulers built a society that made a place for those of different faiths, and Muslim thinkers readily adapted earlier traditions to their own needs. As a result of its expansion, its extensive trade and communications networks, and its engagement with other religious and cultural traditions, the *dar al-Islam* became one of the most prosperous and cosmopolitan societies of the postclassical world.

CHRONOLOGY

570–632	Life of Muhammad
622	The *hijra*
632	Muhammad's hajj
650s	Compilation of the Quran
661–750	Umayyad dynasty
750–1258	Abbasid dynasty
1050s	Establishment of Saljuq control over the Abbasid dynasty
1058–1111	Life of al-Ghazali
1126–1198	Life of Ibn Rushd

FOR FURTHER READING

Richard C. Foltz. *Spirituality in the Land of the Noble: How Iran Shaped the World's Religions.* Oxford, 2004. Includes an accessible discussion of Persian influences on the Islamic faith.

Abu Hamid Muhammad al-Ghazzali. *The Alchemy of Happiness.* Trans. by Claude Field. Rev. by Elton L. Daniel. New York, 1991. Translation of one of the classic works of early Islamic religious and moral thought.

Mahmood Ibrahim. *Merchant Capital and Islam.* Austin, 1990. Examines the role of trade in Arabia during Muhammad's time and in early Islamic society.

Ira M. Lapidus. *A History of Islamic Societies.* Cambridge, 1988. Authoritative survey of Islamic history, concentrating on social and cultural issues.

M. Lombard. *The Golden Age of Islam.* Princeton, 2004. Concentrates on the social and economic history of the Abbasid period.

William H. McNeill and Marilyn R. Waldman, eds. *The Islamic World.* New York, 1973. An excellent collection of primary sources in translation.

F. E. Peters. *The Hajj: The Muslim Pilgrimage to Mecca and the Holy Places.* Princeton, 1994. Draws on scores of travelers' reports in studying the Muslim practice through the ages of making a pilgrimage to Mecca.

Al Qur'an: A Contemporary Translation. Trans. by Ahmed Ali. Princeton, 1984. A sensitive translation of the holy book of Islam.

Francis Robinson, ed. *The Cambridge Illustrated History of the Islamic World.* Cambridge, 1996. An excellent and lavishly illustrated introduction to Islam and the Muslim world.

Frances Wood. *The Silk Road: Two Thousand Years in the Heart of Asia.* Berkeley, 2002. A brilliantly illustrated volume discussing the history of the silk roads from antiquity to the twentieth century.

CHAPTER 12

The Resurgence of Empire in East Asia

Early in the seventh century C.E., the emperor of China issued an order forbidding his subjects to travel beyond Chinese borders into central Asia. In 629, however, a young Buddhist monk slipped past imperial watchtowers under cover of darkness and made his way west. His name was Xuanzang, and his destination was India, homeland of Buddhism. As a young man, Xuanzang had followed his older brother into a monastery, where he became devoted to Buddhism. While studying the Sanskrit language, Xuanzang noticed that Chinese writings on Buddhism contained many teachings that were confusing or even contradictory to those of Indian Buddhist texts. He decided to travel to India, visit the holy sites of Buddhism, and study with the most knowledgeable Buddhist teachers and sages to learn about his faith from the purest sources.

Xuanzang could not have imagined the difficulties he would face. Immediately after his departure from China, his guide abandoned him in the Gobi desert. After losing his water bag and collapsing in the heat, Xuanzang made his way to the oasis town of Turpan on the silk roads. The Buddhist ruler of Turpan provided the devout pilgrim with travel supplies and rich gifts to support his mission. Among the presents were twenty-four letters of introduction to rulers of lands on the way to India (each one attached to a bolt of silk) thirty horses, twenty-five laborers, and five hundred bolts of silk, along with gold, silver, and

---

Xuanzang (SHWEN-ZAHNG)
Buddhism (BOO-diz'm)

OPPOSITE PAGE: *The features of the emperor Tang Taizong reflect his Turkish and Chinese ancestry.*

silk clothes for Xuanzang to use as travel funds. After departing from Turpan, Xuanzang crossed three of the world's highest mountain ranges—the Tian Shan, Hindu Kush, and Pamir ranges—and lost one-third of his party to exposure and starvation in the Tian Shan.

Yet Xuanzang persisted and arrived in India in 630. He lived there for more than twelve years, devoting himself to the study of languages and Buddhist doctrine, especially at Nalanda, the center of advanced Buddhist education in India. He also amassed a huge collection of relics and images as well as some 657 books, all of which he transported back to China to advance the understanding of Buddhism in his native land.

By the time of his return in 645, Xuanzang had logged more than 16,000 kilometers (10,000 miles) on the road. News of the holy monk's efforts had reached the imperial court, and even though Xuanzang had violated the ban on travel, he received a hero's welcome and an audience with the emperor. Until his death in 664, Xuanzang translated Buddhist treatises into Chinese and promoted his faith. His efforts helped to popularize Buddhism and bring about nearly universal adoption of the faith throughout China.

Xuanzang undertook his journey at a propitious time. For more than 350 years after the fall of the Han dynasty, war, invasion, conquest, and foreign rule disrupted Chinese society. Toward the end of the sixth century, however, centralized imperial rule returned to China. The Sui and Tang dynasties restored order and presided over an era of rapid economic growth in China, especially in the areas of agricultural yields and technological innovations. As a result, China stood alongside the Byzantine and Abbasid empires as a political and economic anchor of the postclassical world.

For China the postclassical era was an age of intense interaction with other peoples. Chinese merchants participated in trade networks that linked most regions of the eastern hemisphere. Buddhism spread beyond its homeland of India and attracted a large popular following in China. A resurgent China also made its influence felt throughout east Asia, especially in Korea, Vietnam, and Japan. Although these lands retained their distinctiveness, each drew deep inspiration from China and participated in a larger east Asian society centered on China.

THE RESTORATION OF CENTRALIZED IMPERIAL RULE IN CHINA

For several centuries following the Han dynasty, none of the remaining regional kingdoms was able to assert lasting authority over all of China. In the late sixth century, however, Yang Jian, an ambitious ruler in northern China, embarked on a series of military campaigns that brought all of China once again under centralized imperial rule. Yang Jian's Sui dynasty survived less than thirty years, but the tradition of centralized rule outlived his house. The Tang dynasty replaced the Sui, and the Song succeeded the Tang. The Tang and Song dynasties organized Chinese society so efficiently that China became a center of exceptional agricultural and industrial production, creating an economy so powerful that it affected much of the eastern hemisphere.

The Sui Dynasty

Like Qin Shihuangdi some eight centuries earlier, Yang Jian imposed tight political discipline on his own state and then extended his rule to the rest of China. Yang Jian began his rise to power when a Turkish ruler appointed him duke of Sui in northern China. In 580 Yang Jian's patron died, and one year later he claimed both the throne and the Mandate of Heaven for himself. During the next decade Yang Jian sent military expeditions into central Asia and southern China. By 589 the house of Sui ruled all of China.

Establishment of the Sui Dynasty

Like the rulers of the Qin dynasty, the emperors of the Sui dynasty (589–618 C.E.) built a strong, centralized government, but only at great human and financial cost. Indeed, the Sui emperors ordered construction projects, repaired defensive walls, and conducted military campaigns, but did so by levying high taxes and demanding compulsory labor services from their subjects.

The most elaborate project undertaken during the Sui dynasty was the construction of the Grand Canal, which was one of the world's largest waterworks projects before modern times. The second emperor, Sui Yangdi (reigned 604–618 C.E.), wanted the canal to facilitate trade between northern and southern China, particularly to make the abundant supplies of rice and other food crops from the Yangzi River valley available to residents of northern regions. Since Chinese rivers generally flow

The Grand Canal

from west to east, only an artificial waterway could support such a large volume of bulky trade goods trade between north and south.

The Grand Canal was a series of artificial waterways that ultimately reached from Hangzhou in the south to the imperial capital of Chang'an in the west to a terminus near modern Beijing in the north. Sui Yangdi used canals dug as early as the Zhou dynasty, but he linked them into a network that served much of China. When completed, the Grand Canal extended almost 2,000 kilometers (1,240 miles) and reportedly was forty paces wide, with roads running parallel to it on either side.

Though expensive to construct, Sui Yangdi's investment in the Grand Canal paid dividends for more than a thousand years. It integrated the economies of northern and southern China, thereby establishing an economic foundation for political and cultural unity. Until the arrival of railroads in the twentieth century, the Grand Canal served as the principal conduit for internal trade. Indeed, the canal continues to function even today.

Sui Yangdi's construction projects served China well for a long time, but their dependence on high taxes and forced labor generated hostility toward his rule. The Grand Canal alone required the services of conscripted laborers by the millions. In the late 610s, discontented subjects began to revolt against Sui rule. In 618 a disgruntled minister assassinated the emperor and brought the dynasty to an end.

The Tang Dynasty

Soon after Sui Yangdi's death, a rebel leader seized Chang'an and proclaimed himself emperor of a new dynasty that he named Tang after his hereditary title. The dynasty survived for almost three hundred years (618–907 C.E.), and Tang rulers organized China into a powerful, productive, and prosperous society.

Much of the Tang success was due to the energy, ability, and policies of the dynasty's second emperor, Tang Taizong (reigned 627–649 C.E.). *Tang Taizong* Taizong was both ambitious and ruthless: in making his way to the imperial throne, he

Map 12.1 Territories of the Sui and Tang dynasties, as well as Korea's Silla kingdom, between 589 and 907 C.E. Notice the extent of the borders of the Tang empire. How did Tang rulers maintain control over such vast territories?

In a painting that dates probably from about the seventeenth century, workers build dikes to hold back a river. Construction of the Grand Canal also involved heavy work by large numbers of conscripted laborers.

murdered two of his brothers and pushed his father aside. Once on the throne, however, he displayed a high sense of duty and strove conscientiously to provide an effective, stable government. He built a splendid capital at Chang'an, and he saw himself as a Confucian ruler who heeded the interests of his subjects. Contemporaries reported that banditry ended during his reign, that the price of rice remained low, and that taxes levied on peasants amounted to only one-fortieth of the annual harvest—a 2.5 percent tax rate. These reports suggest that China enjoyed an era of unusual stability and prosperity during the reign of Tang Taizong.

Three policies in particular help to explain the success of the early Tang dynasty: maintenance of a well-articulated transportation and communications network, distribution of land according to the principles of the equal-field system, and reliance on a bureaucracy based on merit. All three policies originated in the Sui dynasty, but Tang rulers applied them more systematically and effectively than their predecessors.

Apart from the Grand Canal, which served as the principal route for long-distance transportation within China, Tang rulers maintained an extensive network of roads. Along the main routes, Tang officials maintained inns, postal stations, and stables. Using couriers traveling by horse, the Tang court

Transportation and Communications

could communicate with the most distant cities in the empire in about eight days. Even human runners provided speedy services: relay teams of some 9,600 runners supplied the Tang court at Chang'an with fresh seafood from Ningbo, more than 1,000 kilometers (620 miles) away!

The equal-field system governed the allocation of agricultural land. Its purpose was to ensure an equitable distribution of land and to avoid the concentration of landed property that had caused social problems during the Han dynasty. The system allotted land to individuals and their families according to the land's fertility and the recipients' needs. About one-fifth of the land became the hereditary possession of the recipients, and the rest remained available for redistribution when the original recipients' needs and circumstances changed.

The Equal-Field System

For about a century, administrators were able to apply the principles of the equal-field system relatively consistently. By the early eighth century, however, a rapidly rising population brought pressure on the land available for distribution. Meanwhile, influential families found ways to retain land scheduled for redistribution. Furthermore, large parcels of land fell out of the system altogether when Buddhist monasteries acquired them. Nevertheless, during the first half of the

Tang dynasty, the system provided a foundation for stability and prosperity in the Chinese countryside.

The Tang dynasty also relied heavily on a bureaucracy based on merit. Following the example of the *Bureaucracy* Han dynasty, Sui and Tang rulers re-*of Merit* cruited government officials from the ranks of candidates who had progressed through the Confucian educational system based on the classic works of Chinese literature and philosophy. As a result, most officeholders won their posts because of intellectual ability. Members of this talented class were generally loyal to the dynasty, and they worked to preserve and strengthen the state. In fact, the Confucian educational system and the related civil service served Chinese governments so well that with modifications and an occasional interruption, they survived until the collapse of the Qing dynasty in the early twentieth century.

Soon after its foundation, the powerful and dynamic Tang state began to flex its military muscles. *Military* In the north, Tang forces brought Man-*Expansion* churia under imperial authority and forced the Silla kingdom in Korea to acknowledge the Tang emperor as overlord. To the south, Tang armies conquered the northern part of Vietnam. To the west, they extended Tang authority as far as the Aral Sea and brought a portion of the high plateau of Tibet under Tang control. Territorially, the Tang empire ranks among the largest in Chinese history.

In an effort to fashion a stable diplomatic order, the Tang emperors revived the Han dynasty's practice *Tang Foreign* of the tribute system. According to Chi-*Relations* nese political theory, China was the Middle Kingdom and had the responsibility of bringing order to subordinate lands through a system of tributary relationships. Neighboring lands and peoples would recognize Chinese emperors as their overlords, and envoys from those states would regularly deliver gifts to the court of the Middle Kingdom and perform the kowtow—a ritual prostration during which subordinates knelt before the emperor and touched their foreheads to the ground. In return, tributary states received confirmation of their authority as well as lavish gifts. Because Chinese authorities often had little real influence in these supposedly subordinate lands, there was always something of a fictional quality to the system. Nevertheless, it was extremely important because it institutionalized relations between China and neighboring lands, fostering trade and cultural exchanges as well as diplomatic contacts.

Under able rulers such as Taizong, the Tang dynasty flourished. During the mid–eighth century, however, the careless leadership of an *Tang Decline* emperor more interested in music and his favorite concubine brought the dynasty to a crisis. In 755 one of the dynasty's foremost military commanders, An Lushan, mounted a rebellion and captured the capital at Chang'an and the secondary capital at Luoyang. His revolt was short-lived: by 763 Tang forces had suppressed An Lushan's army and recovered their capitals. But the rebellion left the dynasty gravely weakened, because Tang commanders had to ask a nomadic Turkish people, the Uighurs, to help them win back their capitals. In return, the Uighurs demanded the right to sack Chang'an and Luoyang after the expulsion of the rebels.

The Tang imperial house never again regained control of affairs. The equal-field system deteriorated, and tax receipts dwindled. Imperial armies were unable to resist invasions of Turkish peoples in the late eighth century. During the ninth century a series of rebellions devastated the Chinese countryside. In an effort to control the rebellions, the Tang emperors granted progressively greater power and authority to regional military commanders, who gradually became the effective rulers of China. In 907 the last Tang emperor abdicated his throne, and the dynasty came to an end.

The Song Dynasty

Following the Tang collapse, warlords ruled China until the Song dynasty reimposed centralized imperial rule in the late tenth century. Though it survived for more than three centuries, the Song dynasty (960–1279 C.E.) never built a very powerful state. Song rulers mistrusted military leaders, and they placed much more emphasis on civil administration, industry, education, and the arts than on military affairs.

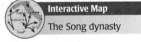

The first Song emperor, Song Taizu (reigned 960–976 C.E.), inaugurated this policy. Song Taizu began his career as a junior military officer for a powerful warlord in northern *Song Taizu* China. He had a reputation for honesty and effectiveness, and in 960 his troops proclaimed him emperor.

Uighurs (WEE-goors)
Song (SOHNG)

During the next several years, he and his army subjected the warlords to their authority and consolidated Song control throughout China. He then set about organizing a centralized administration that placed military forces under tight supervision.

Song rulers vastly expanded the bureaucracy by creating more opportunities for individuals to seek a Confucian education and take civil service examinations. They accepted many more candidates into the bureaucracy than their Sui and Tang predecessors, and they provided generous salaries for those who qualified for government appointments. They even placed civil bureaucrats in charge of military forces.

The Song approach to administration resulted in a more centralized imperial government than earlier Chinese dynasties had enjoyed, but it *Song Weaknesses* caused two big problems that eventually caused the dynasty to fall. The first problem was financial: as the number of bureaucrats and the size of their rewards grew, the imperial treasury came under tremendous pressure. That pressure, in turn, aggravated the peasantry, who were expected to shoulder increased taxes.

The second problem was military. Scholar bureaucrats generally had little talent for military affairs, yet they led Song armies in the field and made military decisions. It was no coincidence that nomadic peoples flourished along China's northern border throughout the Song dynasty. In the early twelfth century, the nomadic Jurchen overran northern China, captured the Song capital at Kaifeng, and proclaimed establishment of the Jin empire. Thereafter the Song dynasty moved its capital to the prosperous port city of Hangzhou and survived only in southern China, so that the latter part of the dynasty is commonly known as the Southern Song. This truncated Southern Song shared a border with the Jin empire about midway between the Yellow River and the Yangzi River until 1279, when Mongol forces ended the dynasty altogether.

Map 12.2 Territories of the Song dynasty between 960 and 1279 C.E. Notice that the Southern Song dynasty moved its capital from Chang'an to Hangzhou after the Jin empire was established. Why would Hangzhou have been a good choice for a new capital?

THE ECONOMIC DEVELOPMENT OF TANG AND SONG CHINA

Although the Song dynasty did not develop a strong military capacity, it benefited from a remarkable series of agricultural, technological, industrial, and commercial developments. This economic development originated in the Tang dynasty, but its results became most clear during the Song, which presided over a land of enormous prosperity. The economic surge of Tang and Song times had implications that went well beyond China, since it stimulated trade and production throughout much of the eastern hemisphere for more than half a millennium, from about 600 to 1300 C.E.

Agricultural Development

The foundation of economic development in Tang and Song China was a surge in agricultural production. When Sui and Tang armies ventured into Vietnam, they encountered new strains of fast-ripening rice that enabled cultivators to harvest two crops per year.

Fast-Ripening Rice

Transferred to the fertile fields of southern China, fast-ripening rice quickly resulted in an expanded supply of food.

Chinese cultivators also increased their productivity by adopting improved agricultural techniques. They made increased use of heavy iron plows, and they harnessed oxen (in the north) and water buffaloes (in the south) to help prepare land for cultivation. They enriched the soil with manure and composted organic matter. They also organized extensive irrigation systems. Artificial irrigation made it possible to extend cultivation to new lands, including terraced mountainsides—a development that vastly expanded China's agricultural potential.

New Agricultural Techniques

Increased agricultural production resulted in rapid population growth. After the fall of the Han dynasty, the population of China reached a low point of about 45 million in 600 C.E. By 1000 C.E. it had increased to 60 million. By 1127, when the Jurchen conquered the northern half of the Song state, the Chinese population had passed the 100 million mark, and by 1200 it stood at about 115 million.

Population Growth

A wall painting in a Buddhist cave depicts a peasant plowing his field in the rain with the aid of an ox and a heavy plow. Other peasants have found shelter from the rain and consume a midday meal brought to them by their wives.

Increased food supplies encouraged the growth of cities. During the Tang dynasty the imperial capital of Chang'an was the world's most
Urbanization   populous city with as many as two million residents. During the Song dynasty, China was the most urbanized land in the world. In the late thirteenth century, Hangzhou, capital of the Southern Song dynasty, had more than one million residents. They supported hundreds of restaurants, taverns, teahouses, brothels, music halls, theaters, clubhouses, gardens, markets, craft shops, and specialty stores dealing in silk, gems, porcelain, lacquerware, and other goods.

Another result of increased food production was the emergence of a commercialized agricultural economy. Because fast-ripening rice yielded bountiful harvests, many cultivators could purchase inexpensive rice and raise vegetables and fruits for sale on the commercial market. Cultivators specialized in crops that grew well in their own regions, and they often exported their harvests to distant regions. By the twelfth century, for example, the wealthy southern province of Fujian imported rice and devoted its land to the production of lychees, oranges, and sugarcane, which fetched high prices in northern markets.

Alongside increasing wealth and agricultural productivity, Tang and especially Song China experienced
Patriarchal Social Structures   a tightening of patriarchal social structures. During the Song dynasty, for example, the veneration of family ancestors became much more elaborate than before. Indeed, descendants diligently sought the graves of their earliest traceable forefathers and then arranged elaborate graveside rituals in their honor. Whole extended families often traveled great distances to attend annual rituals venerating deceased ancestors—a practice that strengthened the sense of family identity and cohesiveness.

Strengthened patriarchal authority also helps to explain the popularity of foot binding, which spread
Foot Binding   among privileged classes during the Song era. Foot binding involved the tight wrapping of young girls' feet with strips of cloth, which prevented natural growth and resulted in tiny, malformed, curved feet. Women with bound feet

Image
Foot binding
could not walk easily or naturally. Usually they needed canes to walk by themselves, and sometimes they depended on servants to carry them around in litters. Foot binding never became universal in China—it was im-

practical for peasants or lower-class working women in the cities—but wealthy families often bound the feet of their daughters to enhance their attractiveness, display their high social standing, and gain increased control over the girls' behavior. Like the practice of veiling women in the Islamic world, foot binding placed women of privileged classes under tight supervision of their male guardians, who then managed the women's affairs in the interests of the larger family.

Technological and Industrial Development

Abundant supplies of food enabled many people to pursue technological and industrial interests. During the Tang and Song dynasties, Chinese crafts workers generated a remarkable range of technological innovations. During Tang times they
Porcelain   discovered techniques for producing high-quality porcelain, which was lighter, thinner, and adaptable to more uses than earlier pottery. Porcelain technology gradually diffused to other societies, yet demand for Chinese porcelain remained high, and the Chinese exported vast quantities of porcelain during the Tang and Song dynasties. Indeed, Chinese porcelain graced the tables of wealthy and refined households in southeast Asia, India, Persia, and the port cities of east Africa. Tang and Song products gained such a reputation that fine porcelain has come to be known generally as *chinaware*.

Tang and Song craftsmen also improved metallurgical technologies, which resulted in a surge of iron and steel production. Chinese craftsmen
Metallurgy   discovered that they could use coke instead of coal in their furnaces and produce stronger and more useful grades of metal. Between the early ninth and the early twelfth centuries, iron production increased almost tenfold, according to official records. Most of the increased supply of iron and steel went into weaponry and agricultural tools: during the early Song dynasty, imperial armaments manufacturers produced 16.5 million iron arrowheads per year. As in the case of porcelain technology, metallurgical techniques soon diffused to lands beyond China. Indeed, Song military difficulties stemmed partly from the fact that nomadic peoples quickly learned Chinese techniques and fashioned their own iron weapons for use in campaigns against them.

Tang and Song craftsmen also invented entirely new products, tools, and techniques, most notably gun-

A printed book from the twelfth century presents a Chinese translation of a Buddhist text along with a block-printed illustration of the Buddha addressing his followers.

powder, printing, and naval technologies. During the Tang dynasty, Daoist alchemists seeking elixirs to prolong life soon learned that it was unwise to mix charcoal, saltpeter, sulphur, and arsenic because of the volatility of the resulting compound. Military officials, however, recognized opportunity in the explosive mixture. By the mid–tenth century they were using gunpowder in bamboo "fire lances," a kind of flamethrower, and by the eleventh century they had fashioned primitive bombs.

Gunpowder

The earliest gunpowder weapons had limited military effectiveness. Over time, however, refinements enhanced their capabilities. Knowledge of gunpowder chemistry quickly diffused through Eurasia, and by the late thirteenth century peoples of southwest Asia and Europe were experimenting with metal-barreled cannons.

The precise origins of printing are obscure. It is clear, however, that it became common during the Tang era. The earliest printers employed block-printing techniques: they carved a reverse image of an entire page into a wooden block, inked the block, and then pressed a sheet of paper on top. By the mid–eleventh century, printers had also begun to experiment with reusable, movable type: instead of carving images into blocks, they fashioned dies in the shape of ideographs, arranged them in a frame, inked them, and pressed the frame over paper sheets. Printing made it possible to produce texts quickly, cheaply, and in huge quantities. By the late ninth century, printed copies of Buddhist texts, Con-

Printing

fucian works, calendars, agricultural treatises, and popular works were abundant, particularly in southwestern China (modern Sichuan province).

Chinese inventiveness extended also to naval technology. Before Tang times, Chinese mariners did not venture very far from land, relying instead on foreign ships for long-distance maritime trade. During the Tang dynasty, however, Chinese consumers developed a taste for the spices and exotic products of southeast Asian islands, and Chinese mariners increasingly visited those lands in their own ships. By the time of the Song dynasty, Chinese seafarers sailed ships fastened with iron nails, waterproofed with oils, furnished with watertight bulkheads, driven by canvas and bamboo sails, steered by rudders, and navigated with the aid of the "south-pointing needle"—the magnetic compass. Chinese ships mostly plied the waters between Japan and the Malay peninsula, but some of them called at ports in India, Ceylon, Persia, and east Africa. These long-distance travels helped to diffuse elements of Chinese naval technology, particularly the compass, which soon became the common property of mariners throughout the Indian Ocean basin.

Naval Technology

The Emergence of a Market Economy

Increased agricultural production, improved transportation systems, population growth, urbanization, and industrial production combined to stimulate the

Chinese economy. China's various regions increasingly specialized in the cultivation of particular food crops or the production of particular manufactured goods. To be sure, the government played an important role in the Chinese economy by regulating the distribution of staple foods and the production of militarily sensitive enterprises such as the iron industry. Nevertheless, millions of cultivators produced fruits and vegetables for sale on the open market, and manufacturers of silk, porcelain, and other goods supplied both domestic and foreign markets. The Chinese economy became more tightly integrated than ever before, and foreign demand for Chinese products fueled rapid economic expansion.

In fact, trade grew so rapidly during Tang and Song times that China experienced a shortage of the copper coins that served as money for most transactions. To alleviate the shortage, letters of credit came into common use during the early Tang dynasty. Later developments included the use of promissory notes, checks, and even paper money. Indeed, wealthy merchants pioneered the use of printed paper money in the late ninth century. In return for cash deposits from their clients, they issued printed notes that the clients could redeem for merchandise. In a society short of cash, these notes greatly facilitated commercial transactions. Yet they also caused disorder, and sometimes even riots, in the event that merchants were not able to honor their notes.

Financial Instruments

In the eleventh century, in an effort to forestall such disorder, the Chinese government stepped in and assumed the sole right to issue paper money. The first government-issued paper money appeared in 1024 in Sichuan province, and by the end of the eleventh century it existed throughout imperial China. In spite of continuing problems with paper currency—including counterfeit notes and lapses of public confidence in the government's ability to honor its own notes—printed paper money provided a powerful stimulus to the Chinese economy under the Song.

Trade and urbanization transformed Tang and Song China into a prosperous, cosmopolitan society. Trade came to China both by land and by sea. Muslim merchants from the Abbasid empire and central Asia—and even subjects of the Byzantine empire—helped to revive the silk roads network and flocked to large Chinese trading centers. Residents of large Chinese cities such as Chang'an and Luoyang became quite ac-

A Cosmopolitan Society

customed to merchants from foreign lands. Indeed, musicians and dancers from Persia became popular entertainers in the cities of the Tang dynasty. Meanwhile, Arab, Persian, Indian, and Malay mariners arriving by way of the Indian Ocean and South China Sea established sizable merchant communities in the bustling southern Chinese port cities of Guangzhou and Quanzhou.

Indeed, high productivity and trade brought the Tang and Song economy a dynamism that China's borders could not restrain. Chinese consumers developed a taste for exotic goods, which stimulated trade throughout much of the eastern hemisphere. Spices from the islands of southeast Asia made their way to China, along with products as diverse as kingfisher feathers and tortoise shell from Vietnam, pearls and incense from India, and horses and melons from central Asia. In exchange for such exotic items, Chi-

China and the Hemispheric Economy

Foreign music and dance were very popular in the large cities of Tang China. This ceramic model depicts a troupe of musicians from southwest Asia performing on a platform mounted on a camel. Many such models survive from Tang times.

SOURCES FROM THE PAST

The Arab Merchant Suleiman on Business Practices in Tang China

The Arab merchant Suleiman made several commercial ventures by ship to India and China during the early ninth century C.E. In 851 an Arab geographer wrote an account of Suleiman's travels, describing India and China for Muslim readers in southwest Asia. His report throws particularly interesting light on the economic conditions and business practices of Tang China.

■ ■ ■

Young and old Chinese all wear silk clothes in both winter and summer, but silk of the best quality is reserved for the kings. . . . During the winter, the men wear two, three, four, five pairs of pants, and even more, according to their means. This practice has the goal of protecting the lower body from the high humidity of the land, which they fear. During the summer, they wear a single shirt of silk or some similar material. They do not wear turbans. . . .

In China, commercial transactions are carried out with the aid of copper coins. The Chinese royal treasury is identical to that of other kings, but only the king of China has a treasury that uses copper coins as a standard. These copper coins serve as the money of the land. The Chinese have gold, silver, fine pearls, fancy silk textiles, raw silk, and all this in large quantities, but they are considered commodities, and only copper coins serve as money.

Imports into China include ivory, incense, copper ingots, shells of sea turtles, and rhinoceros horn, with which the Chinese make ornaments. . . .

The Chinese conduct commercial transactions and business affairs with equity. When someone lends money to another person, he writes up a note documenting the loan. The borrower writes up another note on which he affixes an imprint of his index finger and middle finger together. Then they put the two notes together, roll them up, and write a formula at the point where one touches the other [so that part of the written formula appears on each note]. Next, they separate the notes and entrust to the lender the one on which the borrower recognizes his debt. If the borrower denies his debt later on, they say to him, "Present the note that the lender gave to you." If the borrower maintains that he has no such note from the lender, and denies that he ever agreed to the note with his fingerprints on it, and if the lender's note has disappeared, they say to him, "Declare in writing that you have not contracted this debt, but if later the lender brings forth proof that you have contracted this debt that you deny, you will receive twenty blows of the cane on the back and you will be ordered to pay a penalty of twenty million copper coins." This sum is equal to about 2,000 dinars [gold coins used in the Abbasid empire]. Twenty blows of the cane brings on death. Thus no one in China dares to make such a declaration for fear of losing at the same time both life and fortune. We have seen no one who has agreed when invited to make such a declaration. The Chinese are thus equitable to each other. No one in China is treated unjustly.

• *In what ways might Chinese policies have encouraged business and trade during the Tang dynasty?*

SOURCE: Gabriel Ferrand, trans. *Voyage du marchand arabe Sulayman en Inde et en Chine.* Paris, 1922, pp. 45, 53–54, 60–61. (Translated into English by Jerry H. Bentley.)

nese sent abroad vast quantities of silk, porcelain, and lacquerware. In central Asia, southeast Asia, India, Persia, and the port cities of east Africa, wealthy merchants and rulers wore Chinese silk and set their tables with Chinese porcelain. China's economic surge during the Tang and Song dynasties thus promoted trade and economic growth throughout much of the eastern hemisphere.

CULTURAL CHANGE IN TANG AND SONG CHINA

Interactions with peoples of other societies encouraged cultural change in postclassical China. The Confucian and Daoist traditions did not disappear, but they made way for a foreign religion—Mahayana Buddhism—and they developed along new lines that reflected the conditions of Tang and Song society.

The Establishment of Buddhism

Buddhist merchants traveling the ancient silk roads visited China as early as the second century B.C.E. During the Han dynasty their faith attracted little interest: Confucianism, Daoism, and cults that honored family ancestors were the most popular cultural alternatives. During the unsettled centuries following the fall of the Han, however, several foreign religions—including Nestorian Christianity, Manichaeism, Zoroastrianism, and Islam—established communities in China. Yet these religions of salvation mostly served the needs of foreign merchants trading in China and converts from nomadic societies and did not win a large popular following.

Foreign Religions in China

Mahayana Buddhism was different in that it gradually found a popular following in Tang and Song China. Buddhism came to China over the silk roads via the oasis cities of central Asia, and by the fourth century C.E., a sizable Buddhist community had emerged at Dunhuang in western China (modern Gansu province). Between about 600 and 1000 C.E., Buddhists built hundreds of cave temples in the vicinity of Dunhuang and decorated them with murals depicting events in the lives of the Buddha and the *boddhisattvas*. They also assembled libraries of religious literature and operated scriptoria to produce Buddhist texts. Missions supported by establishments such as those at Dunhuang helped Buddhism to establish a foothold in China.

Dunhuang

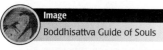
Boddhisattva Guide of Souls

Buddhism attracted Chinese interest partly because of its high standards of morality, its intellectual sophistication, and its promise of salvation. Yet practical concerns also help to account for its appeal. Buddhist monastic communities in China accumulated sizable estates donated by wealthy converts, and they commonly stored a portion of their harvests for distribution among local residents during hard times. As a result, Buddhist monasteries became important elements in the local economies of Chinese communities.

Buddhism in China

In some ways Buddhism posed a challenge to Chinese cultural and social traditions. Buddhist theologians typically placed great emphasis on written texts and used them to explore elaborate investigations into metaphysical themes such as the nature of the soul. Among Chinese intellectuals, however, only the Confucians placed equal emphasis on written texts, and they devoted their energies mostly to practical rather than metaphysical issues. Meanwhile, Daoists had limited interest in written texts of any kind. Buddhist morality also called for individuals to observe an ascetic ideal by following a celibate, monastic lifestyle. In contrast, Chinese morality centered on the family unit and strongly encouraged procreation so that generations of offspring would be available to venerate family ancestors. Some Chinese held that Buddhist monasteries were economically harmful, since they paid no taxes, whereas others scorned Buddhism because of its foreign origins.

Buddhism and Daoism

Because of these differences and concerns, Buddhist missionaries sought to tailor their message to Chinese audiences. They explained Buddhist concepts in vocabulary borrowed from Chinese cultural traditions, particularly Daoism. They translated the Indian term *dharma* (the basic Buddhist doctrine) as *dao* ("the way" in the Daoist sense of the term), and they translated the Indian term *nirvana* (personal salvation that comes after an individual soul escapes from the cycle of incarnation) as *wuwei* (the Daoist ethic of noncompetition). While encouraging the establishment of monasteries and the observance of celibacy, they also recognized the validity of family life and offered Buddhism as a religion that would benefit the extended Chinese family: one son in the monastery, they taught, would bring salvation for ten generations of his kin.

Mount Wudang

Confucianism (kuhn-FYEW-shuhn-iz'm)

nirvana (nuhr-VAH-nuh)
wuwei (woo-WAY)

The result was a syncretic faith, a Buddhism with Chinese characteristics. One of the more popular *Chan Buddhism* schools of Buddhism in China, for example, was the Chan (also known by its Japanese name, Zen). Chan Buddhists had little interest in written texts but, instead, emphasized sudden flashes of insight in their search for spiritual enlightenment. In that respect they resembled Daoists as much as they did Buddhists.

During the Tang and Song dynasties, this syncretic Buddhism became an immensely popular and influential faith in China. Monasteries appeared in all the major cities, and stupas dotted the Chinese landscape. The monk Xuanzang (602–664) was only one of many devout pilgrims who traveled to India to visit holy sites and learn about Buddhism in its homeland. Like Xuanzang, many of those pilgrims returned with copies of treatises that deepened the understanding of Buddhism in China. In the process, they played significant roles in establishing Buddhism as a popular faith in China.

In spite of its popularity, Buddhism met determined resistance from Daoists and Confucians. Daoists *Hostility to Buddhism* resented the popular following of Buddhism, which resulted in diminished resources available for their own tradition. Confucians despised Buddhists' exaltation of celibacy, and they denounced the faith as an alien superstition.

During the late Tang dynasty, Daoist and Confucian critics of Buddhism found allies in the imperial court. Beginning in the 840s the Tang emperors ordered the closure of monasteries and the expulsion of Buddhists as well as Zoroastrians, Nesto-*Persecution* rian Christians, and Manichaeans. Yet Tang rulers did not implement the policy in a thorough way, and foreign faiths were not eradicated. Buddhism in particular enjoyed continued support that enabled it not only to survive but also to influence the development of Confucianism during the Song dynasty.

Neo-Confucianism

The Song emperors did not persecute Buddhists, but they actively supported native Chinese cultural traditions in hopes of limiting the influence of foreign religions. They contributed particularly generously to the Confucian tradition by sponsoring the studies of Confucian scholars and subsidizing the printing and dissemination of Confucian writings.

Yet the Confucian tradition of the Song dynasty differed from that of earlier times. The earliest Confucians had concentrated resolutely on practical issues of politics and morality, since *Confucians and Buddhism* they were mainly concerned with establishing social order. Confucians of the Song dynasty studied the classic works of their tradition, but they also were inspired by many aspects of Buddhist thought. Indeed, Buddhism both offered a tradition of logical thought and argumentation and dealt with issues not systematically explored by Confucian thinkers, such as

---

Chan Buddhism (CHAHN BOO-diz'm)

neo-Confucianism (nee-oh-kuhn-FYEW-shuhn-iz'm)

This scroll painting depicts the return of the monk Xuanzang to China. His baggage included 657 books, mostly Buddhist treatises but also a few works on grammar and logic, as well as hundreds of relics and images.

the nature of the soul. Because Confucian thought during the Song dynasty reflected the influence of Buddhism as well as original Confucian values, it has come to be known as neo-Confucianism.

Neo-Confucianism ranks as an important cultural development for two reasons. First, it illustrates the deep influence of Buddhism in Chinese society. Even though the neo-Confucians rejected Buddhism as a faith, their writings adapted Buddhist themes and reasoning to Confucian interests and values. Second, neo-Confucianism influenced east Asian thought over a very long term. In China, neo-Confucianism enjoyed the status of an officially recognized creed from the Song dynasty until the early twentieth century, and in lands that fell within China's cultural orbit—particularly Korea, Vietnam, and Japan—neo-Confucianism shaped philosophical, political, and moral thought for half a millennium and more.

Neo-Confucian Influence

CHINESE INFLUENCE IN EAST ASIA

Like societies in Byzantium and the *dar al-Islam,* Chinese society influenced the development of neighboring lands during postclassical times. Chinese armies periodically invaded Korea and Vietnam, and Chinese merchants established commercial relations with Japan as well as with Korea and Vietnam. Chinese techniques of government and administration helped shape public life in all three lands, as did Chinese values and cultural traditions. By no means did these lands become absorbed into China: all maintained distinctive identities. Yet they also drew deep inspiration from Chinese examples and built societies that reflected their participation in a larger east Asian society revolving around China.

Korea and Vietnam

During the Tang dynasty, Chinese imperial armies followed in the footsteps of the Qin and Han dynasties by mounting large-scale campaigns of expansion in both Korea and Vietnam. Although the two lands responded differently to Chinese imperial expansion, both borrowed Chinese political and cultural traditions and used them in their own societies.

In the seventh century, Tang armies conquered much of Korea before the native Silla dynasty rallied. Both Tang and Silla authorities preferred to avoid a long and costly

The Silla Dynasty

conflict, so they agreed to a political compromise: Chinese forces withdrew from Korea, and the Silla king recognized the Tang emperor as his overlord.

Thus Korea entered into a tributary relationship with China. Envoys of the Silla kings regularly delivered gifts to Chinese emperors and performed the kowtow, but those concessions brought considerable benefits to the Koreans. In return for their recognition of Chinese supremacy, they received gifts more valuable than the tribute they delivered to China. Moreover, the tributary relationship opened the doors for Korean merchants to trade in China.

Meanwhile, the tributary relationship facilitated the spread of Chinese political and cultural influences to Korea. Korean rulers began to model their court along Chinese lines, and the Silla kings even built a new capital at Kumsong modeled on the Tang capital at Chang'an. Korean scholars went to China to study Chinese thought and literature and took copies of Chinese writings back to Korea. Their efforts helped to build elite

Chinese Influence in Korea

Image
Sokkuram Grotto

Korean interest in the Confucian tradition, and Chinese schools of Buddhism attracted widespread popular interest.

China and Korea differed in many respects. Most notably, perhaps, aristocrats and royal houses dominated Korean society much more than in China. Although the Korean monarchy sponsored Chinese schools and a Confucian examination system, Korea never established a bureaucracy based on merit, and political initiative remained firmly in the hands of the ruling classes. Nevertheless, extensive dealings with its powerful neighbor ensured that Korea reflected the influence of Chinese political and cultural traditions.

Chinese relations with Vietnam were far more tense than their relations with Korea. When Tang armies ventured into the land that Chinese called Nam Viet, they encountered spirited resistance on the part of the Viet people, who had settled in the region around the Red River. Tang forces soon won control of Viet towns and cities, and they launched efforts to absorb the Viets into Chinese society. The Viets readily adopted Chinese agricultural methods and irrigation systems as well as Chinese schools and administrative techniques. Like their Korean counterparts, Viet elites studied Confucian texts and took examinations based on a Chinese-style education, and Viet traders marketed their wares in China. Vietnamese authorities even entered into tributary rela-

China and Vietnam

Tang dynasty pottery figure of a Vietnamese dancer. Commercial and tributary relationships introduced southeast Asian performers to China, where sophisticated urban communities appreciated their exotic entertainment.

tionships with the Chinese court. Yet the Viets resented Chinese efforts to dominate them, and they mounted a series of revolts against Tang authorities. As the Tang dynasty fell during the early tenth century, the Viets won their independence and successfully resisted later Chinese efforts at imperial expansion to the south.

Like Korea, Vietnam differed from China in many ways. Although Buddhism won a large popular following, many Vietnamese retained their indigenous religions in preference to Chinese cultural traditions. Women played a much more prominent role in Vietnamese society and economy than did their Chinese counterparts. Southeast Asian women had dominated local and regional markets for centuries, and they participated actively in business ventures closed to women in the more rigidly patriarchal society of China. Nevertheless, Chinese traditions found a place in the southern land. Indeed, like Korea, Vietnam absorbed political and cultural influence from China and reflected the development of a larger east Asian society centered on China.

Early Japan

Chinese armies never invaded Japan, but Chinese traditions deeply influenced Japanese political and cultural development. The earliest inhabitants of Japan were nomadic peoples from northeast Asia. They migrated to Japan, perhaps across land bridges that formed during an ice age, about two hundred thousand years ago. Their language, material culture, and religion derived from their parent society in northeast Asia. Later migrants, who arrived in several waves from the Korean peninsula, introduced cultivation of rice, bronze and iron metallurgy, and horses into Japan. As the population of the Japanese islands grew and built a settled agricultural society, small states dominated by aristocratic clans emerged. By the middle of the first millennium C.E., several dozen states ruled small regions.

The establishment of the powerful Sui and Tang dynasties in China had repercussions in Japan, where they suggested the value of centralized imperial government. One of the aristocratic *Nara Japan* clans in Japan insisted on its precedence over the others, although in fact it had never wielded effective authority outside its own territory in central Japan. Nevertheless, inspired by the Tang example, this clan claimed imperial authority and introduced a series of reforms designed to centralize Japanese politics. The imperial house established a court modeled on that of the Tang, instituted a Chinese-style bureaucracy, implemented an equal-field system, provided official support for Confucianism and Buddhism, and in the year 710 moved to a new capital city at Nara (near modern Kyoto) that was a replica of the Tang capital at Chang'an. Never was Chinese influence more prominent in Japan than during the Nara period (710–794 C.E.).

Yet Japan did not lose its distinctive characteristics. While adopting Confucian and Buddhist traditions from China, for example, the Japanese continued to observe the

Shinto (SHIHN-toh)

rites of Shinto, their indigenous religion, which revolved around the veneration of ancestors and a host of nature spirits and deities.

The experiences of the Heian, Kamakura, and Muromachi periods clearly illustrate the distinctiveness of Japanese society. Under the *Heian Japan* Heian (794–1185 C.E.), local rulers on the island of Honshu mostly recognized the emperor as Japan's supreme political authority. Unlike their Chinese counterparts, however, Japanese emperors rarely ruled but, rather, served as ceremonial figureheads and symbols of authority. Effective power lay in the hands of the Fujiwara family, an aristocratic clan that controlled affairs from behind the throne through its influence over the imperial house and manipulation of its members. Indeed, since the Heian period the Japanese political order has almost continuously featured a split between a publicly recognized imperial authority and a separate agent of effective rule. This pattern helps to account for the remarkable longevity of the Japanese imperial house: because emperors have not ruled, they have not been subject to deposition during times of turmoil.

The cultural development of Heian Japan also reflected both the influence of Chinese traditions and the elaboration of peculiarly Japanese ways. Most literature imitated Chinese models and indeed was written in the Chinese language. Boys and young men who received a formal education in Heian Japan learned Chinese, read the classic works of China, and wrote in the foreign tongue. Officials at court conducted business and kept records in Chinese, and literary figures wrote histories and treatises in the style popular in China. Even Japanese writing reflected Chinese influence, since scholars borrowed many Chinese characters and used them to represent Japanese words. They also adapted some Chinese characters into a Japanese syllabic script, in which symbols represent whole syllables rather than a single sound, as in an alphabetic script.

In the late eleventh century, changes in the countryside brought an end to the Heian court. The equal-field system gradually fell into disuse, and aristocratic clans accumulated most of the islands' lands into vast estates. Two clans in particular—the Taira and the Minamoto—overshadowed the others. During the mid–twelfth century the two engaged in outright war, and in 1185 the Minamoto emerged victorious. Like the Fujiwara family, the Minamoto did not seek to abolish imperial authority in Japan but, rather, claimed to rule the land in the name of the emperor. They installed the clan leader as *shogun*—a military governor who ruled in place of the emperor—and established the seat of their government at Kamakura, near modern Tokyo, while the imperial court remained at Kyoto. For most of the next four centuries, one branch or another of the Minamoto clan dominated political life in Japan.

Medieval Japan

Historians refer to the Kamakura and Muromachi periods as Japan's medieval period: a middle era falling between the age of Chinese influence and court domination of political life in Japan, as represented by the Nara and Heian periods, and the modern age, inaugurated by the Tokugawa dynasty in the sixteenth century, when a centralized government unified and ruled all of Japan. During this middle era, Japanese society and culture took on increasingly distinctive characteristics.

In the Kamakura (1185–1333 C.E.) and Muromachi (1336–1573 C.E.) periods, Japan developed a decentralized political order in which provincial lords wielded effective power and authority in local regions *Political Decentralization* where they controlled land and economic affairs. As these lords and their clans vied for power and authority in the countryside, they found little use for the Chinese-style bureaucracy that Nara and Heian rulers had instituted in Japan and still less use for the elaborate protocol and refined conduct that prevailed at the courts. In place of etiquette and courtesy, they valued military talent and discipline. The mounted warrior, the *samurai,* thus played the most distinctive role in Japanese political and military affairs.

The samurai were professional warriors, specialists in the use of force and the arts of fighting. They served the provincial lords of Japan, *The Samurai* who relied on the samurai both to enforce their authority in their own territories and to extend their claims to other lands. In return for those police and military services, the lords supported the samurai from the agricultural surplus and labor services of peasants working under their jurisdiction. Freed of obligations to feed, clothe, and house themselves and their families, samurai devoted themselves to hunting, riding, archery, and martial arts.

Decline of Heian Japan

Heian (HAY-ahn)

shogun (SHOH-gun)
samurai (SAM-uhr-eye)

Thus, although it had taken its original inspiration from the Tang empire in China, the Japanese political order developed along lines different from those of the Middle Kingdom. Yet Japan clearly had a place in the larger east Asian society centered on China. Japan borrowed from China, among other things, Confucian values, Buddhist religion, a system of writing, and the ideal of centralized imperial rule. Though somewhat suppressed during later periods, these elements of Chinese society not only survived in Japan but also decisively influenced Japanese development over the long term.

Summary

The revival of centralized imperial rule in China had profound implications for all of east Asia and indeed for most of the eastern hemisphere. When the Sui and Tang dynasties imposed their authority throughout China, they established a powerful state that guided political affairs throughout east Asia. Tang armies extended Chinese influence to Korea, Vietnam, and central Asia. They did not invade Japan, but the impressive political organization of China prompted the islands' rulers to imitate Tang examples. Moreover, the Sui and Tang dynasties laid a strong political foundation for rapid economic development. Chinese society prospered throughout the postclassical era, partly because of technological and industrial innovation. Tang and Song prosperity touched all of China's neighbors, since it encouraged surging commerce in east Asia. Chinese silk, porcelain, and lacquerware were prized commodities among trading peoples from southeast Asia to east Africa. Chinese inventions such as paper, printing, gunpowder, and the magnetic compass found a place in societies throughout the eastern hemisphere as they diffused across the silk roads and sea lanes. The postclassical era was an age of religious as well as commercial and technological exchanges: Nestorian Christians, Zoroastrians, Manichaeans, and Muslims all maintained communities in Tang China, and Buddhism became the most popular religious faith in all of east Asia. During the postclassical era, Chinese social organization and economic dynamism helped to sustain interactions between the peoples of the eastern hemisphere on an unprecedented scale.

CHRONOLOGY

589–618	Sui dynasty (China)
602–664	Life of Xuanzang
604–618	Reign of Sui Yangdi
618–907	Tang dynasty (China)
627–649	Reign of Tang Taizong
669–935	Silla dynasty (Korea)
710–794	Nara period (Japan)
755–757	An Lushan's rebellion
794–1185	Heian period (Japan)
960–1279	Song dynasty (China)
960–976	Reign of Song Taizu
1024	First issuance of government-sponsored paper money

FOR FURTHER READING

Kenneth Ch'en. *Buddhism in China: A Historical Survey.* Princeton, 1964. A clear and detailed account by an eminent scholar.

Hugh R. Clark. *Community, Trade, and Networks: Southern Fujian Province from the Third to the Thirteenth Century.* Cambridge, 1991. Excellent scholarly study exploring the transformation of a region by trade and market forces.

Patricia Buckley Ebrey. *Chinese Civilization: A Sourcebook.* 2nd ed. New York, 1993. A splendid collection of documents in translation.

Mark Elvin. *The Pattern of the Chinese Past.* Stanford, 1973. A brilliant analysis of Chinese history, concentrating particularly on economic, social, and technological themes.

Jacques Gernet. *Daily Life in China on the Eve of the Mongol Invasion, 1250–1276.* Trans. by H. M. Wright. New York, 1962. Rich portrait of Southern Song China, emphasizing social history.

Ivan Morris. *The World of the Shining Prince: Court Life in Ancient Japan.* Harmondsworth, 1964. Vividly reconstructs the court life of Heian Japan.

Edward H. Schafer. *The Golden Peaches of Samarkand: A Study of T'ang Exotics.* Berkeley, 1963. Deals with relations between China and central Asian lands during the Tang dynasty.

H. Paul Varley. *Japanese Culture.* 4th ed. Honolulu, 2000. An authoritative analysis of Japanese cultural development from early times to the present.

Sally Hovey Wriggins. *Xuanzang: A Buddhist Pilgrim on the Silk Road.* Boulder, 1996. A fascinating and well-illustrated account of Xuanzang's journey to India and his influence on the development of Buddhism in China.

CHAPTER 13

India and the Indian Ocean Basin

Buzurg ibn Shahriyar was a tenth-century shipmaster from Siraf, a prosperous and bustling port city on the Persian Gulf coast. He probably sailed frequently to Arabia and India, and he may have ventured also to Malaya, the islands of southeast Asia, China, and east Africa. Like all sailors, he heard stories about the distant lands that mariners had visited, the different customs they observed, and the adventures that befell them during their travels. About 953 C.E. he compiled 136 such stories in his *Book of the Wonders of India*.

Buzurg's collection included a generous proportion of tall tales. He told of mermaids and sea dragons, of creatures born from human fathers and fish mothers, of serpents that ate cattle and elephants, of birds so large that they crushed houses, and of a talking lizard. Yet alongside the tall tales, many of Buzurg's stories accurately reflected the conditions of his time. One recounted the story of a king from northern India who converted to Islam and requested translations of Islamic law. Others reported on Hindu customs, shipwrecks, encounters with pirates, and slave trading.

Several of Buzurg's stories tempted readers with visions of vast wealth attainable through maritime trade. For example, Buzurg mentioned a Jewish merchant who left Persia penniless and returned from India and China with a shipload of priceless merchandise. Despite their embellishments, his stories faithfully reflected the trade networks that linked the lands surrounding the Indian Ocean in the tenth century. Although Buzurg clearly thought of India as a distinct land with its

OPPOSITE PAGE: *Kabir, the blind guru, weaves cloth while discussing religious matters with disciples.*

own customs, he also recognized a larger world of trade and communication that extended from east Africa to southeast Asia and beyond to China.

Just as China served as the principal inspiration of a larger east Asian society in the postclassical era, India influenced the development of a larger cultural zone in south and southeast Asia. Yet China and India played different roles in their respective spheres of influence. In east Asia, China was clearly the dominant power. In south and southeast Asia, however, there emerged no centralized imperial authority like the Tang dynasty in China. Indeed, although several states organized large regional kingdoms, no single state was able to extend its authority to all parts of the Indian subcontinent, much less to the mainland and islands of southeast Asia.

Though politically disunited, during the postclassical era India remained a coherent and distinct society as a result of powerful social and cultural traditions—especially the caste system and the Hindu religion. Beginning in the seventh century, Islam also began to attract a popular following in India, and after the eleventh century, Islam deeply influenced Indian society alongside the caste system and Hinduism.

Beyond the subcontinent Indian traditions helped to shape a larger cultural zone extending to the mainland and islands of southeast Asia. Throughout most of the region, ruling classes adopted Indian forms of political organization and Indian techniques of statecraft. Indian merchants took their Hindu and Buddhist faiths to southeast Asia, where they attracted sustained interest. Somewhat later, Indian merchants also helped introduce Islam to southeast Asia.

While Indian traditions influenced the political and cultural development of southeast Asia, the entire Indian Ocean basin began to move toward economic integration during the postclassical era, as Buzurg ibn Shahriyar's stories suggest. Indeed, innovations in maritime technology, the development of a well-articulated network of sea lanes, and the building of port cities enabled peoples living around the Indian Ocean to trade and communicate more actively than ever before. As a result, peoples from east Africa to southeast Asia and China increasingly participated in the larger economic, commercial, and cultural life of the Indian Ocean basin.

ISLAMIC AND HINDU KINGDOMS

Like the Han and Roman empires, the Gupta dynasty came under severe pressure from nomadic invaders.

From the mid–fourth to the mid–fifth century C.E., Gupta rulers resisted the pressures and preserved order throughout much of the Indian subcontinent. Beginning in 451 C.E., however, White Huns from central Asia invaded India, and by the mid–sixth century the Gupta state had collapsed. Effective political authority quickly devolved to invaders and independent regional power brokers. From the end of the Gupta dynasty until the sixteenth century, when a Turkish people known as the Mughals extended their authority to most of the subcontinent, India remained a politically divided land.

The Quest for Centralized Imperial Rule

Northern and southern India followed different political trajectories after the fall of the Gupta empire. In the north, local states contested for power and territory, and politics were turbulent and frequently violent. Nomadic Turkish-speaking peoples from central Asia contributed to this unsettled state of affairs by forcing their way into 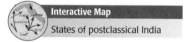 India. They eventually found niches for themselves in the caste system and became completely absorbed into Indian society. However, until processes of social absorption worked themselves out, the arrival of nomadic peoples caused additional disruption in northern India.

Even after the collapse of the Gupta dynasty, the ideal of centralized imperial rule did not entirely disappear. During the first half of the seventh century, King Harsha (reigned 606–648 C.E.) temporarily restored unified rule in most of northern India and sought to revive imperial authority. Using a massive military force from his kingdom in the lower Ganges valley, by about 612 Harsha had subdued those who refused to recognize his authority. *Harsha*

Yet even though Harsha was young, energetic, and an able ruler, he was unable to restore permanent centralized rule. Local rulers had established their authority too securely in India's regions for Harsha to overcome them. Ultimately, he fell victim to an assassin and left no heir to maintain his realm. His empire immediately disintegrated, and local rulers once again turned northern India into a battleground as they sought to enlarge their realms at the expense of their neighbors. *Collapse of Harsha's Kingdom*

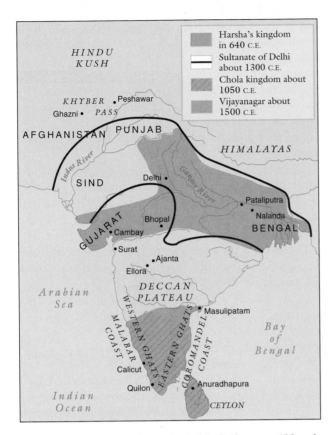

Map 13.1 Major states of postclassical India between 600 and 1600 C.E. Note the number of major rivers in northern India compared with the number of rivers in southern India. What effects might this difference have had on agriculture?

The Introduction of Islam to Northern India

Amid nomadic incursions and contests for power, northern India also experienced the arrival of Islam and the establishment of Islamic states. Islam reached India by several routes. One was mili-

The Conquest of Sind

tary: Arab forces entered India as early as the mid–seventh century, although their first expeditions were exploratory ventures rather than campaigns of conquest. In 711, however, a well-organized expedition conquered Sind, the Indus River valley in northwestern India, and incorporated it as a province of the expanding Umayyad empire. At midcentury, along with most of the rest of the *dar al-Islam,* Sind passed into the hands of the Abbasid caliphs. Although political elites eventually took advantage of their distance from the centers of Islamic power to reassert their control over most of

Sind, the region remained nominally under the jurisdiction of the caliphs until the collapse of the Abbasid dynasty in 1258.

While conquerors brought Islam to Sind, Muslim merchants took their faith to coastal regions in both northern and southern India. Indeed, Muslims dominated trade and transportation networks between India and western lands from the seventh through the fifteenth century. Muslim merchants formed small communities in all the major cities of coastal India, where they played a prominent role in Indian business and commercial life. They frequently married local women, and in many cases they also found places for themselves in Indian society. Thus Islam entered India's port cities in a more gradual but no less effective way than was the case in Sind.

Merchants and Islam

Islam also entered India by a third route: the migrations and invasions of Turkish-speaking peoples from central Asia. During the tenth century, several Turkish groups had become acquainted with Islam through their dealings with the Abbasid caliphate and had converted to the faith. Some of these Muslim Turks moved into Afghanistan, where they established an Islamic state.

Turkish Migrants and Islam

Mahmud of Ghazni, leader of the Turks in Afghanistan, soon turned his attention to the rich land to the south. Between 1001 and 1027 he mounted seventeen raiding expeditions into India. Taking advantage of infighting between local rulers, he annexed several states in northwestern India and the Punjab. For the most part, however, Mahmud had less interest in conquering India than in plundering the wealth stored in its many temples. Mahmud and his forces demolished hundreds of Hindu and Buddhist structures and frequently established mosques or Islamic shrines in their place. Not surprisingly, however, Mahmud's raids did not encourage Indians to turn to Islam.

Mahmud of Ghazni

During the late twelfth century, Mahmud's successors mounted a more systematic campaign to conquer northern India and place it under Islamic rule. By the early thirteenth century, they had conquered most of the Hindu kingdoms in northern India and established an Islamic state known as the sultanate of Delhi. The sultans established their capital at Delhi, a strategic site controlling access from the Punjab to the Ganges valley, and they ruled northern India at least in name for more than three centuries, from 1206 to 1526.

The Sultanate of Delhi

During the fourteenth century the sultans of Delhi commanded an army of three hundred thousand, and their state ranked among the most powerful in the Islamic world. Yet for the most part, the authority of the sultans did not extend far beyond Delhi. They had no permanent bureaucracy or administrative apparatus. Even in their immediate domain, they imposed a thin veneer of Islamic political and military authority on a land populated mostly by Hindus, and they depended on the goodwill of Hindu kings to carry out their policies and advance their interests in local regions. They did not even enjoy comfortable control of their own court: of the thirty-five sultans of Delhi, nineteen were killed by assassins. Nevertheless, the sultans prominently sponsored Islam and helped to establish a secure place for their faith in the cultural landscape of India.

Medieval fortress from the sultanate of Delhi, 14th C.

The Hindu Kingdoms of Southern India

Although it too remained politically divided, the southern part of the Indian subcontinent largely escaped the invasions, chronic war, and turmoil that troubled the north. Most Hindu rulers in the south presided over small, loosely administered states and did not engage in prolonged or frequent conflicts. Two kingdoms, however, were able to expand enough to exercise at least nominal rule over much of southern India. The first was the Chola kingdom, situated in the deep south, which

The Chola Kingdom

ruled the Coromandel coast for more than four centuries, from 850 to 1267 C.E. At its high point, during the eleventh century, Chola forces conquered Ceylon and parts of southeast Asia, and its navy dominated the waters from the South China Sea to the Arabian Sea.

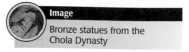
Bronze statues from the Chola Dynasty

Chola rulers did not build a tightly centralized state: they allowed considerable autonomy for local and village institutions as long as they maintained order and delivered tax revenues on time. By the twelfth century, however, revolts reduced the size and power of the Chola state, and it reverted to the status of one regional kingdom among many others in southern India.

The second state that dominated much of southern India was the kingdom of Vijayanagar, based in the northern Deccan. The kingdom owed its origin to efforts by the sultans of Delhi to extend their authority to southern India. Officials in Delhi dispatched two brothers, Harihara and Bukka, to represent the sultan and implement court policies in the south. Although they had converted from their native Hinduism to Islam, Harihara and Bukka recognized an opportunity to establish themselves as independent rulers. In 1336 they renounced Islam and proclaimed the establishment of an independent empire of Vijayanagar (meaning "city of victory"). Indeed, the Hindu kingdom of

The Kingdom of Vijayanagar

Vijayanagar (vih-juh-yuh-NUH-guhr)

The kings of Vijayanagar endowed their capital with splendid buildings and even provided these handsome domed stables for their elephants.

Vijayanagar was the dominant state in southern India from the mid–fourteenth century until 1565, when it fell to Mughal conquerors from the north.

As in northern India, then, political division and conflict between states in southern India characterized its political history in postclassical times. India did not generate the sort of large-scale, centralized, imperial state that guided the fortunes of postclassical societies in the eastern Mediterranean, southwest Asia, or China. Nevertheless, on the basis of trade, common social structures, and inherited cultural traditions, a coherent and distinctive society flourished in postclassical India.

PRODUCTION AND TRADE IN THE INDIAN OCEAN BASIN

As in the Mediterranean, southwest Asia, and China, agricultural yields increased significantly in postclassical India, enabling large numbers of people to devote themselves to trade and manufacturing rather than the production of food. Trade forged links between the various regions of the subcontinent and fostered economic development in southern India. Trade also created links between India and distant lands, as merchants and manufacturers transformed the Indian Ocean basin into a vast zone of communication and exchange. Yet even though the increasing prominence of trade and industry brought change to Indian society, caste identities and loyalties also remained strong, and the caste system continued to serve as the most powerful organizing feature of Indian society.

Agriculture in the Monsoon World

Because of the rhythms of the monsoons, irrigation was essential for the maintenance of a large, densely populated, agricultural society. During the spring and *Monsoons* summer, warm, moisture-laden winds from the southwest bring most of India's rainfall. During the autumn and winter, cool and very dry winds blow from the northeast. To achieve their agricultural potential, Indian lands required a good watering by the southern monsoon, supplemented by irrigation during the dry months. Light rain during the spring and summer months or short supplies of water for irrigation commonly led to drought, reduced harvests, and widespread famine.

In northern India, large rivers and plentiful surface water provided abundant opportunities to build irrigation systems. Indeed, irrigation had been a *Irrigation* fixture of the countryside in northern India *Systems* since Harappan times. For the most part, however, southern India is an arid land without rivers that can serve as sources for large-scale irrigation. Thus, as southern India became more densely populated, irrigation systems became crucial. Dams, reservoirs, canals, wells, and tunnels appeared in large numbers. Particularly impressive were monumental reservoirs lined with brick or stone that captured the rains of the spring and summer months and held them until the dry season, when canals carried them to thirsty fields. Projects of this size required enormous investments of human energy, both for their original construction and for continuing maintenance, but they led to significant increases in agricultural productivity.

As a result of this increased productivity, India's population grew steadily throughout the postclassical era. In 600 C.E., shortly after the fall *Population* of the Gupta dynasty, the subcontinent's *Growth* population stood at about 53 million. By 1000 it had grown 45 percent, to 79 million. During the following centuries the rate of growth slowed, but it took off again about 1500. By 1500, the population of the subcontinent had reached 105 million.

This demographic surge encouraged the concentration of people in cities. During the fourteenth century, the high point of the sultanate of *Urbanization* Delhi, the capital city had a population of about four hundred thousand, which made it second only to Cairo among Muslim cities. Many other cities—particularly ports and trading centers such as Cambay, Surat, Calicut, Quilon, and Masulipatam—had populations well over one hundred thousand.

Trade and the Economic Development of Southern India

Political fragmentation of the subcontinent did not prevent robust trade between the different states and regions of India. As the population grew, opportunities for specialized work became more numerous. Increased trade was a natural result of this process.

Most regions of the Indian subcontinent were self-sufficient in staple foods such as rice, wheat, barley, and millet. The case was different, *Internal Trade* however, with metals, salt, and specialized crops that grew well only in certain regions. Iron came mostly from the Ganges River valley near

Bengal, copper mostly from the Deccan Plateau, salt mostly from coastal regions, and pepper from southern India. These and other commodities sometimes traveled long distances to consumers in remote parts of the subcontinent.

Southern India and Ceylon benefited especially handsomely from this trade. As invasions and conflicts disrupted northern India, southern regions experienced rapid economic development. The Chola kingdom provided relative stability in the south, and Chola expansion in southeast Asia opened markets for Indian merchants and producers.

Temples and Society The Chola rulers allowed considerable autonomy to their subjects, and the towns and villages of southern India largely organized their own affairs. Public life revolved around Hindu temples, which organized agricultural activities, coordinated work on irrigation systems, and maintained reserves of surplus production for use in times of need. Temples often possessed large tracts of agricultural land, and they sometimes employed hundreds of people. To meet their financial obligations to employees, temple administrators collected a portion of the agricultural yield from lands subject to temple authority.

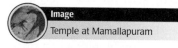
Image
Temple at Mamallapuram

Administrators were also responsible for keeping order in their communities and delivering tax receipts to the Cholas and other political authorities. In addition, temple authorities served as bankers, made loans, and invested in commercial and business ventures. They also frequently cooperated with the leaders of merchant guilds in seeking commercial opportunities to exploit. Temples thus grew prosperous and became crucial to the economic health of southern India.

Cross-Cultural Trade in the Indian Ocean Basin

Indian prosperity sprang partly from the productivity of Indian society, but it depended also on the vast wealth that circulated in the commercial world of the Indian Ocean basin. Trade in the Indian Ocean was not new in postclassical times: Indian merchants had already ventured to southeast Asia during the classical era, and they dealt regularly with mariners from the Roman empire who traveled to India in search of pepper. During the postclassical era, however, larger ships and improved commercial organization supported a dramatic surge in the volume and value of trade in the Indian Ocean basin.

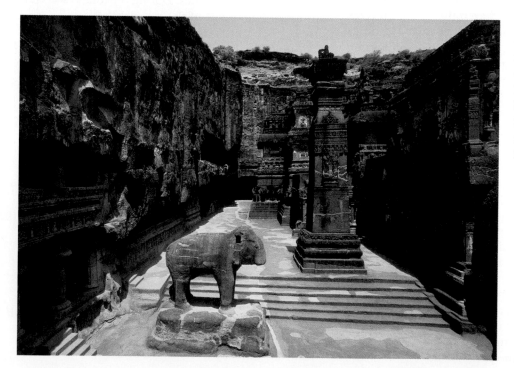

During the eighth century C.E., workers carved a massive temple out of sheer rock at Ellora in central India. Temple communities like the one that grew up at Ellora controlled enormous resources in postclassical India.

As larger, more stable ships came into use, mariners increasingly entrusted their crafts and cargoes to the reasonably predictable monsoons and sailed directly across the Arabian Sea and the Bay of Bengal. In the age of sail, however, it was impossible to make a round trip across the entire Indian Ocean without spending months at distant ports waiting for the winds to change, so merchants usually conducted their trade in stages.

Emporia   Because India stood in the middle of the Indian Ocean basin, it was a natural site for emporia and warehouses. Merchants coming from east Africa or Persia exchanged their cargoes at Cambay, Calicut, or Quilon for goods to take back west with the winter monsoon. Mariners from China or southeast Asia called at Indian ports and traded their cargoes for goods to ship east with the summer monsoon. Indeed, because of their central location, Indian ports became the principal clearinghouses of trade in the Indian Ocean basin, and they became remarkably cosmopolitan centers. Hindus, Buddhists,

Muslims, Jews, and others who inhabited the Indian port cities did business with counterparts from all over the eastern hemisphere.

Particularly after the establishment of the Umayyad and Abbasid dynasties in southwest Asia and the Tang and Song dynasties in China, trade in the Indian Ocean surged. Generally, Arabs and Persians dominated the carrying trade between India and points west. During the Song dynasty, Chinese junks also ventured into the western Indian Ocean and called at ports as far away as east Africa. To the east, in the Bay of Bengal and the China seas, Malay and Chinese vessels were most prominent.

As the volume of trade in the Indian Ocean basin increased, lands around the ocean began to engage in specialized production of commodities for the commercial market. Indian artisans, for example, built thriving local industries around the production of high-quality cotton textiles. These industries influenced the structure of the Indian economy: they created a demand

Specialized Production

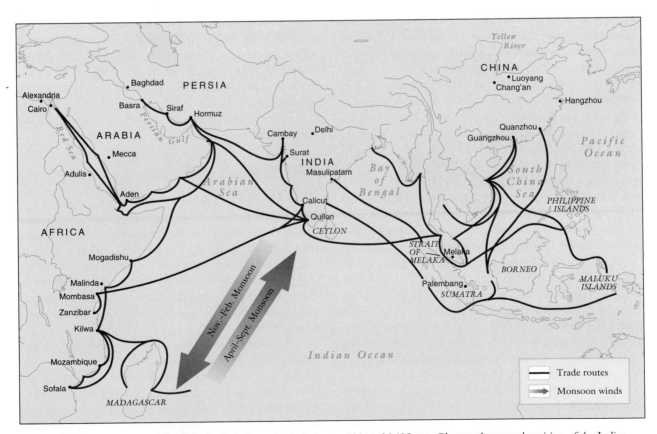

Map 13.2 Major trading routes of the Indian Ocean basin between 600 and 1600 C.E. Observe the central position of the Indian subcontinent in the Indian Ocean basin. In what ways might this have benefited the peoples of India, and who might have benefited most?

for specific agricultural products, provided a livelihood for thousands of artisans, and enabled consumers to import goods from elsewhere in the Indian Ocean basin.

Other lands concentrated on the production of different manufactured goods and agricultural commodities: China produced silk, porcelain, and lacquerware; southeast Asian lands provided fine spices; incense, horses, and dates came from southwest Asia; and east Africa contributed gold, ivory, and slaves. Thus trade encouraged specialized production and economic development in all lands participating in the trade networks of the Indian Ocean: cross-cultural trade in postclassical times influenced the structure of economies and societies throughout much of the eastern hemisphere.

Caste and Society

The political, economic, and social changes of the postclassical era brought a series of challenges for India's caste system. Migrations, the growing prominence of Islam, economic development, and urbanization all placed pressures on the caste system as it had developed during the Vedic and classical eras. But the caste system has never been a rigid, unchanging structure. Rather, individuals and groups have continuously adjusted it and adapted it to new circumstances. Adjustments and adaptations of the postclassical era resulted in a caste system that was more complex than in earlier ages and that also extended its geographic reach deeper into southern India than ever before. In the absence of strong central governments, the caste system helped maintain order in local communities by providing guidance on individuals' roles in society and their relationships with others.

The caste system closely reflected changes in Indian society. It adapted to the arrival of migrants, for *Caste and Migration* example, and helped to integrate them into Indian society. As Turkish peoples or Muslim merchants pursued opportunities in India, they gained recognition as distinct groups under the umbrella of the caste system. They established codes of conduct both for the regulation of behavior within their own groups and for guidance in dealing with members of other castes. Within a few generations their descendants had become absorbed into Indian society.

The caste system also accommodated the social changes brought about by trade and economic development. Even before the postclassical era, individuals

tended to identify most closely with their subcastes (*jati*), which were usually organized by occupation. In postclassical times, as merchants and manufacturers became increasingly important in the larger economy, they organized powerful workers' guilds to represent their interests. These guilds, however, were largely incorporated into the caste system as distinct *jati*. Thus merchants specializing in particular types of commerce, such as the silk, cotton, or spice trade, established themselves as subcastes, as did artisans working in particular industries, such as the iron, steel, or leather business.

Caste and Social Change

Besides becoming more complex, the caste system also extended its geographic reach. Caste distinctions first became prominent in northern India following the Aryan migrations. During the postclassical era, the caste system became securely established in southern India as well. Economic development aided this process by encouraging commercial relationships between southern merchants and their caste-conscious counterparts in the north. The emergence of merchant and craft guilds in southern regions strengthened the caste system, since guild members usually organized as a subcaste. Powerful temples also fostered caste distinctions, largely because of the influence of caste-conscious brahmins who supervised temple activities. As a result, by about the eleventh century C.E., caste had become the principal basis of social organization in southern India.

Expansion of the Caste System

THE MEETING OF HINDU AND ISLAMIC TRADITIONS

The Indian cultural landscape underwent a thorough transformation during the postclassical era. Jainism and Buddhism lost much of their popular following, although neither belief completely disappeared. In their place, Hindu and Islamic traditions increasingly dominated the cultural and religious life of India after 1000 C.E.

Hinduism and Islam differed profoundly. The Hindu pantheon made places for numerous gods and spirits, for example, whereas Islamic theology stood on the foundation of a firm and uncompromising monotheism. Yet both religions attracted large popular followings throughout the subcontinent, with Hinduism predominating in southern India and Islam in the north.

The Development of Hinduism

Toward the end of the first millennium C.E., Buddhism flourished in east Asia, central Asia, and parts of southeast Asia but came under great pressure in India. Like Mahayana Buddhism, both Hinduism and Islam promised salvation to devout individuals, and they gradually attracted Buddhists to their own communities. Invasions of India by Turkish peoples also hastened the decline of Buddhism because the invaders looted and destroyed Buddhist stupas and shrines. In 1196 Muslim forces overran the Buddhist schools in the city of Nalanda, torched the libraries, and killed or exiled thousands of monks. Buddhism soon became a minor faith in the land of its birth.

Hinduism benefited from the decline of Buddhism. One reason for the increasing popularity of Hinduism was the remarkable growth of *Vishnu and Shiva* devotional cults, particularly those dedicated to Vishnu and Shiva, two of the most important deities in the Hindu pantheon. Vishnu was the preserver of the world, a god who observed the universe from the heavens and

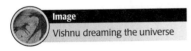

Image
Vishnu dreaming the universe

who occasionally entered the world in human form to resist evil or communicate his teachings. In contrast, Shiva was both a god of fertility and a destructive deity: he brought life but also took it away when its season had passed.

Hindus embraced the new cults warmly because they promised salvation. Devotional cults became especially popular in southern India, *Devotional Cults* where individuals or family groups went to great lengths to honor their chosen deities. Often cults originated when individuals identified Vishnu or Shiva with a local spirit or deity associated with a particular region or a prominent geographic feature. By venerating images of Vishnu or Shiva, offering them food and drink, and meditating on the deities and their qualities, Hindus hoped to achieve a mystic union with the gods that would bring grace and salvation.

The significance of Hinduism extended well beyond popular religion: it also influenced philosophy. Just as Buddhism, Christianity, and Islam influenced moral thought and philosophy in other lands, devo-

---

Buddhism (BOO-diz'm)
Vishnu (VIHSH-noo)
Shiva (SHIH-vuh)

Southern Indian artists often portrayed Shiva in bronze sculptures as a four-armed lord of dancers. In this figure from the Chola dynasty, Shiva crushes with his foot a dwarf demon symbolizing ignorance. One hand holds a bell to awaken his devotees, another bears the fire used by Shiva as creator and destroyer of the world, and a third gestures Shiva's benevolence toward his followers.

tional Hinduism guided the efforts of the most prominent philosophers in postclassical India. Brahmin philosophers such as Ramanuja took the Upanishads as a point of departure for subtle rea- *Shankara* soning and sophisticated metaphysics. Ramanuja, a devotee of Vishnu who was active during the eleventh and early twelfth centuries C.E., believed that genuine bliss came from salvation and identification of individuals with their gods. He followed the *Bhagavad Gita* in recommending intense devotion to Vishnu, and he taught that by placing themselves in the hands of Vishnu, devotees would win the god's grace and live forever in his presence. Thus, Ramanuja's philosophy pointed toward a Hindu theology of salvation. Indeed, his thought inspired the development of devotional cults throughout India, and it serves even today as a philosophical foundation for Hindu popular religion.

Islam and Its Appeal

The Islamic faith did not attract much immediate interest among Indians when it arrived in the subcontinent. It won gradual acceptance in merchant communities where foreign Muslim traders took local spouses and found a place in Indian society. Elsewhere, however, circumstances did not favor its adoption, since it often arrived with conquering peoples. Muslim conquerors generally reserved important political and military positions for their Arab, Persian, and Turkish companions. Only rarely did they allow Indians—even those who had converted to Islam—to hold sensitive posts. Because of that policy, conquerors offered little incentive for Indians to convert to Islam.

Conversion to Islam Gradually, however, many Indians converted to Islam. By 1500 C.E. Indian Muslims numbered perhaps twenty-five million—about one-quarter of the subcontinent's population. Some Indians adopted Islam in hopes of improving their positions in society: Hindus of lower castes, for example, hoped to escape discrimination by converting to a faith that recognized the equality of all believers. In fact, Hindus rarely improved their social standing by conversion. Often members of an entire caste or subcaste adopted Islam en masse, and after conversion they continued to play the same social and economic roles that they had before.

Sufis In India as elsewhere, the most effective agents of conversion to Islam were Sufi mystics. Sufis encouraged a personal, emotional, devotional approach to Islam. They did not insist on fine points of doctrine, and they sometimes even permitted their followers to observe rituals or venerate spirits not recognized by the Islamic faith. Because of their piety and sincerity, however, Sufi missionaries attracted individuals searching for a faith that could provide comfort and meaning for their personal lives. Thus, like Hinduism, Indian Islam emphasized piety and devotion. Even though Hinduism and Islam were profoundly different religions, they encouraged the cultivation of similar spiritual values that transcended the social and cultural boundary lines of postclassical India.

The Bhakti Movement In some ways the gap between Hinduism and Islam narrowed in postclassical India because both religions drew on long-established and long-observed cultural traditions. Sufis, for example, often attracted schools of followers in the manner of Indian gurus, spiritual leaders who taught Hindu values to disciples who congregated around them. Even more important was the development of the *bhakti* movement, a cult of love and devotion that ultimately sought to erase the distinction between Hinduism and Islam. The bhakti movement emerged in southern India during the twelfth century, and it originally encouraged a traditional piety and devotion to Hindu values. As the movement spread to the north, bhakti leaders increasingly encountered Muslims and became deeply attracted to certain Islamic values, especially monotheism and the notion of spiritual equality of all believers. Eventually, the bhakti movement rejected the exclusive features of both Hinduism and Islam, and some believers taught that Shiva, Vishnu, and Allah were all manifestations of a single, universal deity. The bhakti movement did not succeed in harmonizing Hinduism and Islam. Nevertheless, like the Sufis, bhakti teachers promoted values that helped build bridges between India's social and cultural communities.

THE INFLUENCE OF INDIAN SOCIETY IN SOUTHEAST ASIA

Just as China stood at the center of a larger east Asian society, India served as the principal source of political and cultural traditions widely observed throughout south and southeast Asia. For a millennium and more, southeast Asian peoples adapted Indian political structures and religions to local needs and interests. Although Indian armed forces rarely ventured into the region, southeast Asian lands reflected the influence of Indian society, as merchants introduced Hinduism, Buddhism, Sanskrit writings, and Indian forms of political organization. Beginning about the twelfth century, Islam also found solid footing in southeast Asia, as Muslim merchants, many of them Indians, established trading communities in the important port cities of the region. Over the next five hundred years, Islam attracted a sizable following and became a permanent feature in much of southeast Asia.

The States of Southeast Asia

Indian merchants visited the islands and mainland of southeast Asia from an early date, perhaps as early as 500 B.C.E. By the early centuries C.E., they had become

---

Sufis (SOO-fees)

bhakti (BHUK-tee)

The Bhagavata Purana *on Devotion to Vishnu*

With the development of devotional Hinduism in the postclassical era, religious leaders produced a body of literature known as the puranas, *texts that told stories about the gods and offered instructions in proper methods of worship. The most influential of these works is the* Bhagavata Purana *("Purana of the Lord"), composed about the eighth or ninth century C.E. In the following selection the god Vishnu sometimes refers to himself in the third person as "the lord" and sometimes speaks in the first person while instructing devotees how to worship him and support his cult.*

■ ■ ■

The teachers consider the utterance of the Lord's name as destructive of sin completely, even when the utterance is due to the name being associated with something else, or is done jocularly, or as a result of involuntary sound, or in derision. . . .

One should therefore resort to a teacher, desiring to know what constitutes the supreme welfare. . . . Taking the teacher as the deity, one should learn from him the practices characteristic of the Lord's devotees. . . . First, detachment from all undesirable associations, then, association with the good souls, compassion, friendliness, and due humility toward all beings, purity, penance, forbearance, silence, study of sacred writings, straightforwardness, continence, nonviolence, equanimity, seeing one's own Self and the Lord everywhere, seeking solitude, freedom from home, wearing clean recluse robes, satisfying oneself with whatever comes to one, faith in the scriptures of devotion and refraining from censure of those of other schools, subjugation of mind, speech, and action, truthfulness, quietude, restraint, listening to accounts of the Lord's advents, exploits, and qualities, singing of the Lord, contemplation of the Lord of wonderful exploits, engaging in acts only for His sake, dedicating unto the Lord everything—the rites one does, gifts, penance, sacred recital, righteous conduct and whatever is dear to one like one's wife, son, house, and one's own life—cultivating friendship with those who consider the Lord as their soul and master, service to the Lord and to the world and especially to the great and good souls, sharing in the company of fellow devotees the sanctifying glory of the Lord,

sharing with them one's delight, satisfaction and virtues of restraint, remembering oneself and reminding fellow-worshipers of the Lord who sweeps away all sin; bearing a body thrilled with devotion and ecstatic experience of the Lord, now in tears with some thought of the Lord, now laughing, now rejoicing, now speaking out, now dancing, now singing, now imitating the Lord acts, and now becoming quiet with the blissful experience of the Supreme—such are the devotees, who behave like persons not of this world. . . .

One should engage himself in singing of Me, praising Me, dancing with My themes, imitating My exploits and acts, narrating My stories or listening to them.

With manifold hymns of praise of Me, taken from the *Puranas* or from the local languages . . . , the devotee should praise and pray to Me that I bless him and prostrate himself completely before Me. With his head and hands at My feet, he should pray, "My lord, from the clutches of death [i.e., the cycle of birth and death], save me who have taken refuge under You." . . .

Whenever and wherever one feels like worshiping Me in images, etc., one should do so; I am, however, present in oneself and in all beings; for I am the Soul of everything. . . . Having consecrated an image of Me one should build a firm temple for Me, and beautiful flower gardens around for conducting daily worship and festivals. For the maintenance of My worship, etc., in special seasons as well as every day, one should bestow fields, bazaars, townships, and villages, and thereby attain to My own lordship.

- *Assess the extent to which the* Bhagavata Purana *builds on devotional teachings offered in the* Bhagavad Gita *discussed earlier.*

SOURCE: Ainslie T. Embree and Stephen Hay, eds. *Sources of Indian Tradition,* 2nd ed., 2 vols. New York: Columbia University Press, 1988, 1:325–26, 328.

In India as in other lands, Sufi mystics were the most effective Muslim missionaries. This eighteenth-century painting depicts the Sufi Khwaja Khidr, beloved in Muslim communities throughout northern India as one associated with springtime, fertility, and happiness.

familiar figures throughout southeast Asia, and their presence brought opportunities for the native ruling elites of the region. In exchange for spices and exotic products, Indian merchants brought textiles, beads, gold, silver, and manufactured metal goods. Southeast Asian rulers used the profits from this trade to consolidate their political control.

Indian Influence in Southeast Asia

Meanwhile, southeast Asian ruling elites became acquainted with Indian political and cultural traditions. Without necessarily giving up their own traditions, they borrowed Indian forms of political organization and accepted Indian religious faiths. On the model of Indian states, for example, they adopted kingship as the principal form of political authority, and they surrounded themselves with courts featuring administrators and rituals similar to those found in India.

Ruling elites also sponsored the introduction of Hinduism or Buddhism—sometimes both—into their courts. They embraced Indian literature such as the

Ramayana and the *Mahabharata*, which promoted Hindu values, as well as treatises that explained Buddhist views on the world. At the same time, however, they did not show much enthusiasm for the Indian caste system and continued to acknowledge the deities and nature spirits that southeast Asian peoples had venerated for centuries.

The first state known to have incorporated Indian influence into its own traditions was Funan, which dominated the lower reaches of the Mekong River (including parts of modern Cambodia and Vietnam) between the first and the sixth centuries C.E. Funan grew enormously wealthy because it dominated the Isthmus of Kra, the narrow portion of the Malay peninsula where merchants transported trade goods between China and India. (The short portage enabled them to avoid a long voyage around the Malay peninsula.) The rulers of Funan used the profits from this trade to construct an elaborate irrigation system that supported a highly productive agricultural economy in the Mekong delta.

Funan

As trade with India became an increasingly important part of Funan's economy, the ruling classes adopted Indian political, cultural, and religious traditions. They took the Sanskrit term *raja* ("king") for themselves and claimed divine sanction for their rule in the manner of Hindu rulers in India. They established positions for administrators and bureaucrats such as those found at Indian courts and conducted official business in Sanskrit. They introduced Indian ceremonies and rituals and worshiped Vishnu, Shiva, and other Hindu deities. They continued to honor local deities, but they eagerly welcomed Hinduism, which offered additional recognition and divine legitimacy for their rule. At first, Indian cultural and religious traditions were most prominent and most often observed at ruling courts. Over the longer term, however, those traditions extended well beyond ruling elites and won a secure place in southeast Asian society.

During the sixth century C.E., a bitter power struggle weakened Funan internally, and by late century it had passed into oblivion. After the fall of

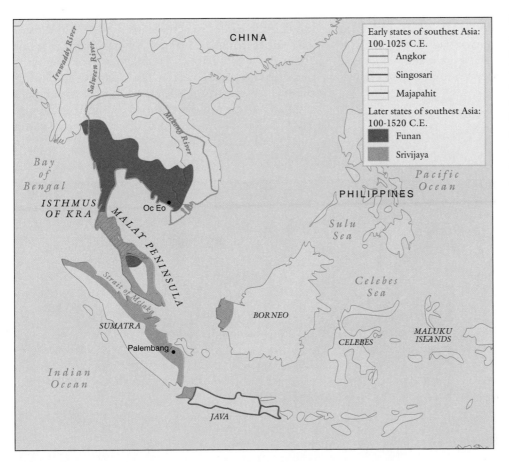

Map 13.3 **Major states of southeast Asia between about 100 and 1520 C.E.** Notice the strategic location of these southeast Asian states on the trade routes between China to the east and India to the west. How might this have affected the development of states in southeast Asia?

Srivijaya

Funan, political leadership in southeast Asia passed to the kingdom of Srivijaya (670–1025 C.E.) based on the island of Sumatra. The kings of Srivijaya built a powerful navy and controlled commerce in southeast Asian waters. They compelled port cities in southeast Asia to recognize their authority, and they financed their navy and bureaucracy from taxes levied on ships passing through the region. They maintained an all-sea trade route between China and India, eliminating the need for the portage of trade goods across the Isthmus of Kra. As the volume of trade with India increased in the postclassical era, the rulers of Srivijaya—like the rulers of Funan—borrowed heavily from Indian cultural traditions. Unlike their counterparts in Funan, however, the rulers of Srivijaya were most attracted to the teachings and practices associated with Buddhism. The Srivijaya kingdom prospered on the fruits of the Indian Ocean trade until the expansive Chola kingdom of southern India eclipsed it in the eleventh century. In the process, Srivijaya played an important role in facilitating cultural exchange in the Indian Ocean world.

With the decline of Srivijaya, the kingdoms of Angkor (889–1431 C.E.), Singosari (1222–1292 C.E.), and Majapahit (1293–1520 C.E.) dominated affairs in southeast Asia. Whereas Angkor had its base in Cambodia, Singosari and Majapahit were island states based on Java. Angkor made deep commitments to Buddhism; Majapahit was largely a Hindu state. Singosari represented a unique blend of Indian and indigenous traditions. Indeed, at the court of Singosari, religious authorities fashioned a cultural blend of Hindu, Buddhist, and indigenous values. Sculptures at the Singosari court depicted Hindu and Buddhist personalities, for example, but used them to honor local deities and natural spirits rather than Indian deities.

The magnificent monuments of Angkor testify eloquently to the influence of Indian traditions in southeast Asia. Beginning in the ninth century, the kings of the Khmers began to build a capital *Angkor* city at Angkor Thom. With the aid of brahmin advisors from India, the kings designed the city as a microcosmic reflection of the Hindu world order. At the center, they built a temple representing 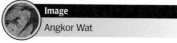 the Himalayan Mount Meru, the sacred abode of Shiva, and surrounded it with numerous smaller temples representing other parts of the Hindu universe.

As the Khmers turned to Buddhism during the twelfth and thirteenth centuries, they added Buddhist temples to the complex, though without removing the earlier structures inspired by Hinduism. The entire complex formed a square with sides of about three kilometers (two miles), surrounded by a moat filled from the nearby Tonle Sap River. During the twelfth century the Khmer kings constructed a smaller but even more elaborate temple center at Angkor Wat, about one kilometer (just over half a mile) from Angkor Thom.

Srivijaya (sree-vih-JUH-yuh)
Angkor (AHN-kohr)

Maritime trade flourished in southeast Asia during postclassical times. This ninth-century relief carving from the Buddhist temple at Borobodur in Java depicts a typical southeast Asian ship.

General view of the temple complex dedicated to Vishnu at Angkor Wat.

The Khmers abandoned Angkor in 1431 after Thai peoples invaded the capital and left much of it in ruins. Soon the jungle reclaimed both Angkor Thom and Angkor Wat, which remained largely forgotten until French missionaries and explorers rediscovered the sites in the mid–nineteenth century. Today the temple complexes of Angkor stand as vivid reminders of the influence of Indian political, cultural, and religious traditions in southeast Asia.

The Arrival of Islam

Muslim merchants had ventured into southeast Asia by the eighth century, but only during the tenth century did they become prominent in the region. Some came from southern Arabia or Persia, but most were Indians from Gujarat or the port cities of southern India. Thus Indian influence helped to establish Islam as well as Hinduism and Buddhism in southeast Asia.

For several centuries Islam maintained a quiet presence in southeast Asia. Small communities of foreign merchants observed their faith in the port cities of the region but attracted little interest on the part of the native inhabitants. Gradually, however, ruling elites, traders, and others who had regular dealings with foreign Muslims became interested in the faith.

Conversion to Islam

Like Hinduism and Buddhism, Islam did not enter southeast Asia as an exclusive faith. Ruling elites who converted to Islam often continued to honor Hindu, Buddhist, or native southeast Asian traditions. They adopted Islam less as an absolute creed than as a faith that facilitated their dealings with foreign Muslims and provided additional divine sanction for their rule. Rarely did they push their subjects to convert to Islam, although they allowed Sufi mystics to preach their faith before popular audiences. As in India, Sufis in southeast Asia appealed to a large public because of their reputation for sincerity and holiness. They allowed converts to retain inherited customs while adapting the message of Islam to local needs and interests.

During the fifteenth century the spread of Islam gained momentum in southeast Asia, largely because the powerful state of Melaka sponsored the faith throughout the region. Founded during *Melaka* the late fourteenth century by Paramesvara, a rebellious prince from Sumatra, Melaka took advantage of its strategic location in the Strait of Melaka, near modern Singapore, and soon became prominent in the trading world of southeast Asia. By the mid–fifteenth century, Melaka had built a substantial navy that patrolled the waters of southeast Asia and protected the region's sea lanes. Melakan fleets compelled ships to call at the port, where ruling authorities levied taxes on the value of their cargoes. Thus, like southeast Asian states of earlier centuries, Melaka became a powerful state through the control of maritime trade.

In one respect, though, Melaka differed significantly from the earlier states. Although it began as a

Melaka (may-LAHK-kah)

Hindu state, Melaka soon became predominantly Islamic. About the mid–fifteenth century the Melakan ruling class converted to Islam. It welcomed theologians, Sufis, and other Islamic authorities to Melaka and sponsored missionary campaigns to spread Islam throughout southeast Asia. By the end of the fifteenth century, mosques had begun to define the urban landscapes of Java, Sumatra, and the Malay peninsula, and Islam had made its first appearance in the spice-bearing islands of Maluku and in the southern islands of the Philippine archipelago.

Thus, within several centuries of its arrival, Islam was a prominent feature in the cultural landscape of southeast Asia. Along with Hinduism and Buddhism, Islam helped link southeast Asian lands to the larger cultural world of India and to the larger commercial world of the Indian Ocean basin.

SUMMARY

With respect to political organization, India differed from postclassical societies in China, southwest Asia, and the eastern Mediterranean basin: it did not experience a return of centralized imperial rule such as that provided by the Tang and Song dynasties, the Umayyad and Abbasid dynasties, and the Byzantine empire. In other respects, however, India's development was similar to that of other postclassical societies. Increased agricultural production fueled population growth and urbanization, while trade encouraged specialized industrial production and rapid economic growth. The vigorous and voluminous commerce of the Indian Ocean basin influenced the structure of economies and societies from east Asia to east Africa. It brought prosperity especially to India, which not only contributed cotton, pepper, sugar, iron, steel, and other products to the larger hemispheric economy but also served as a major clearinghouse of trade. Like contemporary societies, postclassical India experienced cultural change, and Indian traditions deeply influenced the cultural development of other lands. Hinduism and Islam emerged as the two most popular religious faiths within the subcontinent, and Indian merchants helped to establish Hinduism, Buddhism, and Islam in southeast Asian lands. Throughout the postclassical era, India participated fully in the larger hemispheric zone of cross-cultural communication and exchange.

CHRONOLOGY

1ST TO 6TH CENTURY	Kingdom of Funan
606–648	Reign of Harsha
670–1025	Kingdom of Srivijaya
711	Conquest of Sind by Umayyad forces
850–1267	Chola kingdom
889–1431	Kingdom of Angkor
1001–1027	Raids on India by Mahmud of Ghazni
11TH TO 12TH CENTURY	Life of Ramanuja
12TH CENTURY	Beginning of the bhakti movement
1206–1526	Sultanate of Delhi
1336–1565	Kingdom of Vijayanagar

FOR FURTHER READING

Aziz Ahmad. *Studies in Islamic Culture in the Indian Environment*. Oxford, 1964. A scholarly analysis of the arrival of Islam and its effects in India.

Buzurg ibn Shahriyar. *The Book of the Wonders of India: Mainland, Sea and Islands*. Trans. by G. S. P. Freeman-Grenville. London, 1981. Stories and tall tales of a tenth-century mariner who sailed frequently between Persia and India.

K. N. Chaudhuri. *Asia before Europe: Economy and Civilisation of the Indian Ocean from the Rise of Islam to 1750*. Cambridge, 1990. Controversial and penetrating analysis of economic, social, and cultural structures shaping societies of the Indian Ocean basin.

Ainslie T. Embree and Stephen Hay, eds. *Sources of Indian Tradition*. 2 vols. 2nd ed. New York, 1988. An important collection of primary sources in English translation.

Kenneth R. Hall. *Maritime Trade and State Development in Early Southeast Asia*. Honolulu, 1985. Examines the link between long-distance trade and state building in southeast Asia.

Charles Higham. *The Civilization of Angkor*. London, 2001. Draws usefully on recent archaeological research in placing Angkor in historical context.

S. M. Ikram. *Muslim Civilization in India*. Ed. by A. T. Embree. New York, 1964. Important survey of Islam and its impact in India.

Hermann Kulke and Dietmar Rothermund. *A History of India*. Totowa, N.J., 1986. A valuable interpretative synthesis of Indian history.

Patricia Risso. *Merchants and Faith: Muslim Commerce and Culture in the Indian Ocean*. Boulder, 1995. Surveys the activities of Muslim merchants in the Indian Ocean basin from the seventh to the nineteenth century.

Burton Stein. *Vijayanagara*. Cambridge, 1989. A study of the southern Hindu kingdom concentrating on political and economic history.

CHAPTER 14

The Foundations of Christian Society in Western Europe

In 802 C.E. a most unusual traveler made his way from Baghdad to Aachen (in modern Germany), capital of the western European empire ruled by Charlemagne. The traveler was an albino elephant named Abu al-Abbas, who was a diplomatic gift from the Abbasid caliph Harun al-Rashid to Charlemagne. From Baghdad the animal accompanied an embassy overland to Syria, then traveled by ship from Beirut to Malta and Rome, and finally went overland north to Charlemagne's court. Abu al-Abbas must have shivered through the cold, damp winters of western Europe, yet he overawed and amazed all who beheld him until his death in 810.

Charlemagne was not friendly to Islam. In fact, he himself had fought against Muslim forces in northern Spain. Nevertheless, in spite of his personal religious preferences, Charlemagne found it both necessary and convenient to have diplomatic dealings with Harun al-Rashid. Over the course of his rule (768–814 C.E.), Charlemagne dispatched at least three embassies to Baghdad and received three in return. The embassies dealt with several issues: the safety of Christian pilgrims and merchants traveling in Abbasid-controlled Syria and Palestine, relations between Charlemagne's realm and neighboring Muslim Spain, and policy toward the Byzantine empire, which stood between western Europe and the Abbasid caliphate.

Although Charlemagne's realm was weak and poor compared with the Abbasid empire, his dealings with Harun al-Rashid indicated that Charlemagne had the potential and the ambition to establish a centralized western

OPPOSITE PAGE: *An ivory book cover carved in the tenth century depicts Pope Gregory I at his writing desk.*

European empire similar to the Byzantine and Abbasid realms. Yet by the mid–ninth century, the empire Charlemagne had created was well on the way to dissolution less than a century after its foundation.

Historians refer to the era from about 500 to 1500 C.E. as the medieval period of European history—the "middle ages" falling between the classical era and modern times. During the early medieval period, from about 500 to 1000 C.E., European peoples recovered from the invasions that brought the Roman empire to an end and laid the political, economic, and cultural foundations for a new society. Those efforts took time, and like India during the postclassical era, early medieval Europe was a politically disunited and disorganized region. Unlike India, though, Europe mostly disengaged from hemispheric communication and exchange in this period. In fact, Europeans were able to reenter the larger trading world of the eastern hemisphere only about the tenth century, after effective political authority and a productive agricultural economy had been reestablished.

The early medieval period was important in western Europe, however, because political, economic, and social developments in that period laid the foundation for the emergence of a much more powerful European society after 1000 C.E. Three developments were particularly important in this regard. First, the peoples of western Europe restored political order in the wake of disruptions caused by invasions and depopulation. Unlike their counterparts in southwest Asia and China, they did not return to centralized imperial rule but, instead, resorted to a decentralized political order in which public authority was held by local and regional rulers. Second, European peoples began a process of economic recovery. They did not build large cities or generate a powerful industrial economy like those of the Byzantine, Abbasid, Tang, and Song empires. But they boosted agricultural production, which became the driving force behind increased trade and rapid economic development after the tenth century. Third, European peoples built an institutional framework that enabled the Christian church based in Rome to provide religious leadership and maintain cultural unity throughout western Europe. Thus, just as Confucianism, Buddhism, Hinduism, Islam, and eastern Christianity shaped cultural values in other lands, western Christianity emerged as the principal source of cultural authority in western Europe.

THE QUEST FOR POLITICAL ORDER

After toppling Rome's authority in the late fifth century C.E., Germanic invaders established successor states throughout the western Roman empire. From the fifth through the eighth century, continuing invasions and conflicts among the invaders themselves left western Europe in a shambles. For a brief moment during the late eighth and early ninth centuries, it looked as though one group of Germanic invaders, the Franks, might reestablish imperial authority in western Europe. If they had succeeded, they might have played a role similar to that of the Sui and Tang dynasties in China by reviving centralized imperial rule after a hiatus of several centuries. By the late ninth century, however, the Frankish empire had fallen victim to internal power struggles and a fresh series of invasions by Muslims, Hungarian Magyars, and Vikings. Political authority in early medieval Europe then devolved to local and regional jurisdictions, and Europeans fashioned a decentralized political order.

Germanic Successor States

Just a few decades after the Germanic general Odoacer deposed the last of the western Roman emperors in 476 C.E., the invaders had organized a series of Germanic kingdoms as successor states in place of the Roman empire. Visigoths conquered Spain during the 470s, for example, and established a kingdom there that survived until the Muslim invasions of the early eighth century. Ostrogoths dominated Italy from the fifth century until Justinian's forces reasserted imperial authority there during the 530s. Meanwhile, beginning about the mid–fifth century, Gaul fell under the control of other Germanic peoples, including the Burgundians, who settled in the southern and eastern regions, and the Franks, who brought the more northerly and westerly regions under their control. Angles, Saxons, and other Germanic peoples from Germany and Denmark crossed the English Channel and established regional kingdoms in Britain.

Germanic Kingdoms

Although Germanic peoples displaced the authority and institutions of Rome, they absorbed a great deal of Roman influence. Many of them converted to Christianity, for example, and others adapted Roman

Magyars (MAH-jahrs)

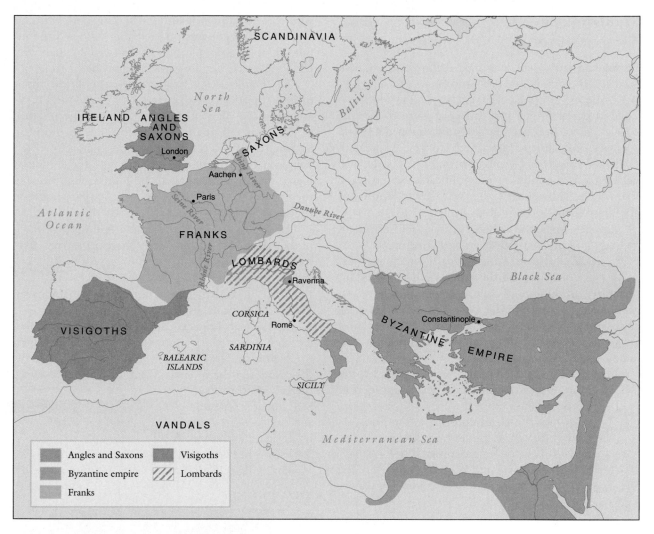

Map 14.1 Successor states to the Roman empire about 600 C.E. Compare this map with Map 8.4, which depicts the territories of the Roman empire about 147 C.E. How would the division of former Roman territories into so many smaller states have affected trade and politics in the Mediterranean?

law to the needs of their own societies. None of the Germanic peoples possessed the resources—much less the political and social organization—to dominate all the others and establish their hegemony throughout western Europe. Nevertheless, the Franks built an impressive imperial state that organized, at least temporarily, about half of the territories formerly embraced by the western Roman empire.

Even though their empire survived for only a short time, the Franks profoundly influenced the political, social, and cultural development of western Europe. For one thing, the Franks constructed a so-ciety that drew on the agricultural resources of continental Europe rather than on the commercial world of the Mediterranean basin. As a result, *The Franks* the center of gravity in western Europe shifted from Italy to the northern lands of France, Germany, and the Low Countries. Furthermore, the Franks oversaw the development of decentralized political institutions, which influenced European politics and society for a millennium and more. Finally, they made a firm alliance with the western Christian church and helped Roman Christianity maintain its cultural and religious primacy in western Europe.

The Franks and the Temporary Revival of Empire

As Roman authority crumbled during the late fifth century, the Franks seemed unlikely to play a prominent role in European affairs. They had little experience in government and little exposure to Roman society. Moreover, the Franks had developed a group identity only during the third century C.E., much later than the other Germanic peoples. Yet in the fifth century a strong military and political leader emerged from their midst. That leader was Clovis, who ruled the Franks from 481 until his death in 511.

Clovis   Under Clovis, the Franks became the preeminent military and political power in western Europe. During his lifetime, Clovis wiped out the last vestiges of Roman authority in Gaul, imposed his authority on the Franks themselves, and fought campaigns against neighboring Germanic peoples. By the time of Clovis's death, the Franks ranked as the most powerful and dynamic of the peoples building new states in western Europe.

Clovis's Conversion   One reason for the Franks' rapid rise had to do with religion. Originally, all the Germanic invaders of the Roman empire were polytheists who honored a pantheon of warlike gods. As they settled in and around the Roman empire, many Germanic peoples converted to Christianity. Unlike other Germanic peoples, however, the Franks remained mostly pagan until the time of Clovis, who converted to Roman Christianity along with his army. Clovis's conversion probably reflected the influence of his wife, Clotilda, a devout Christian who had long urged her husband to adopt her faith.

The Franks' conversion had great political implications. By adopting Roman Christianity, the Franks attracted the allegiance of the Christian population of the former Roman empire as well as recognition and support from the pope and the hierarchy of the western Christian church. Alliance with the church of Rome greatly strengthened the Franks, who became the most powerful of the Germanic peoples between the fifth and ninth centuries.

After Clovis's death the Frankish kings lost much of their authority, as aristocratic warriors seized effective control of affairs in their own regions. Nevertheless, Clovis's successors   *Charlemagne*   ruled the Frankish kingdom until the aristocratic clan of the Carolingians displaced the line of Clovis in 751. Under the Carolingians, the Frankish realm reached its high point during the reign of Charlemagne ("Charles the Great"), who ruled from 768 to 814. Like King Harsha in India, Charlemagne temporarily reestablished centralized imperial rule in a society disrupted by invasion and contests

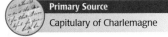
Primary Source
Capitulary of Charlemagne

for power between ambitious local rulers. Also like Harsha, Charlemagne possessed enormous energy,

A manuscript illustration depicts the baptism of Clovis witnessed by church officials (left) and Frankish nobles (right), while a dove descends from above, indicating divine approval of the event.

A bronze statue depicts Charlemagne riding a horse and carrying an orb symbolizing his imperial authority.

and the building of the Carolingian empire was in large measure his personal accomplishment. Although barely literate, Charlemagne was extremely intelligent. He spoke Latin, understood some Greek, and regularly conversed with theologians and other learned men. He maintained diplomatic relations with the Byzantine empire and the Abbasid caliphate. The gift of the white elephant Abu al-Abbas symbolized relations between the Carolingian and Abbasid empires, and the animal accompanied Charlemagne on many of his travels until its death.

When Charlemagne inherited the Frankish throne, his realm included most of modern France as well as the lands that now form Belgium, the Netherlands, and southwestern Germany. By the time of his death in 814, Charlemagne had extended his authority to northeastern Spain, Bavaria, and Italy as far south as Rome. He campaigned for thirty-two years to impose his rule on the Saxons of northern Germany and repress their rebellions. Beyond the Carolingian empire proper, rulers in eastern Europe and southern Italy paid tribute to Charlemagne as imperial overlord.

Charlemagne established a court and capital at Aachen (in modern Germany), but like Harsha in India, he spent most of his reign traveling throughout his realm to maintain his authority. In his absence, Charlemagne had to rely on aristocratic deputies, known as counts, who held political, military, and legal authority in local jurisdictions. However, the counts often had their own political ambitions, and they sometimes pursued policies contrary to the interests of the central government. In an effort to bring the counts under tighter control, Charlemagne instituted a new group of imperial officials known as *missi dominici* ("envoys of the lord ruler"), who traveled every year to all local jurisdictions and reviewed the accounts of local authorities.

Charlemagne's Administration

Although Charlemagne built the Frankish kingdom into an empire, he hesitated to call himself emperor. Charlemagne knew the title would constitute a

---

missi dominici (MEE-see doh-mee-NEE-chee)

Map 14.2 The Carolingian empire in 814 C.E. Note the location of Charlemagne's capital at Aachen, and also the extent of his empire's boundaries, which included parts of modern Spain and Italy as well as modern France and Germany. What kinds of geographical obstacles might Charlemagne have faced in his attempts to keep the empire together?

direct challenge to the authority of the Byzantine emperors, who regarded themselves as the only legitimate successors of the Roman emperors. In 800, however, Charlemagne did accept the title when Pope Leo III proclaimed him emperor during religious services on Christmas Day. It is not certain but it is at least possible that Charlemagne did not know of the pope's plan and that Leo surprised him with an impromptu coronation. In any case, Charlemagne had already built an imperial state, and his coronation constituted public recognition of his accomplishments.

Charlemagne as Emperor

Decline and Dissolution of the Carolingian Empire

If Charlemagne's empire had endured, Carolingian rulers might well have built a bureaucracy, used the *missi dominici* to enhance the authority of the central government, and permanently reestablished centralized imperial rule in western Europe. As it happened, however, internal disunity and external invasions brought the Carolingian empire to an early end.

Charlemagne's only surviving son, Louis the Pious (reigned 814–840), succeeded his father and kept the Carolingian empire together. Lacking Charlemagne's strong will and military skills, however, Louis lost control of the counts and other local authorities, who increasingly ignored the central government. Moreover, even before Louis's death his three sons disputed the inheritance of the empire and waged bitter wars against one another. In 843 they agreed to divide the empire into three roughly equal portions, and each of them took one portion to rule as king. Thus, less than a century after its creation, the Carolingian empire dissolved.

Louis the Pious

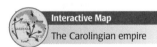

Interactive Map
The Carolingian empire

Even if internal disunity had not resulted in the dismemberment of the Carolingian empire, external pressures might well have brought it down. Beginning in the early ninth century, three groups of invaders pillaged the Frankish realm in search of wealth. From the south came Muslims, who raided towns, villages, churches, and monasteries in Mediterranean Europe from the mid–ninth to the late tenth century. Muslim invaders also seized Sicily as well as several territories in southern Italy and southern France. From the east came the Hungarian Magyars, who raided settlements in Germany, Italy,

Invasions

and southern France from the late ninth to the mid–tenth century. From the north came the Vikings, most feared of all the invaders, who began mounting raids in northern France even during Charlemagne's reign.

Viking invasions represented one dimension of a larger process of Norse expansion that began around 800 C.E. During the eighth century C.E., Norse mariners developed a remarkable set of shipbuilding techniques and seafaring skills that enabled them to travel safely and reliably through the open ocean. Venturing from their Scandinavian homelands of Norway, Denmark, and Sweden, they reconnoitered much of the north Atlantic Ocean and established settlements in the Shetland Islands, the Faeroes, Iceland, and Greenland. About the year 1000 C.E., a small group even established a colony at Newfoundland in modern Canada and explored the Atlantic coast of North America at least as far south as modern-day Maine in the United States. Those remarkable seafaring skills made it possible for Norse cultivators to migrate from their homelands and establish new agricultural communities in the north Atlantic basin.

Norse Expansion

Most Norse seafarers were merchants or migrants. Some, however, turned their maritime skills more toward raiding and plundering than trading or raising

The Oseberg ship, pictured here, is the best-preserved Viking vessel from the early middle ages. Built around 800 C.E., it served as a royal tomb until its discovery in 1903. A ship this size would accommodate about forty men.

crops. These were the Vikings. The Vikings sailed shallow-draft boats that could cross heavy seas but *The Vikings* then could also navigate the many rivers offering access to interior regions of Europe. Fleets of Viking boats could sail up a river, arrive unexpectedly at a village or monastery far from the sea, and then spill out crews of warriors who conducted lightning raids on unprepared victims. Sometimes large fleets of Viking ships even attacked sizable cities. In 885, for example, a Viking force consisting of at least 700 ships sailed up the Seine River and besieged Paris, and in 994 an armada of about 100 ships sprinted up the Thames River and raided London. Vikings also ventured into the Mediterranean, where they plundered sites in the Balearic Islands, Sicily, and southern Italy. Other Vikings made their way to Constantinople, which they raided at least three times during the ninth and tenth centuries.

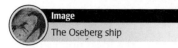

The Establishment of Regional Authorities

Because imperial authorities were unable to defend their territory against invaders such as the Muslims, the Magyars, and the Vikings, political and military initiative in western Europe passed increasingly to regional and local authorities who *England* could organize some means of defense. Yet local responses to ninth-century invasions took different forms in different lands. In England, which bore the brunt of the earliest Viking raids, invasions prompted the series of small kingdoms established earlier by various Germanic peoples to merge into a single larger realm. The leader of that effort was King Alfred (reigned 871–899), who built a navy to challenge the Vikings at sea and constructed fortresses on land to secure areas that he conquered from the invaders. As a result of those efforts, by the mid–tenth century Alfred's successors had established themselves as kings of all England.

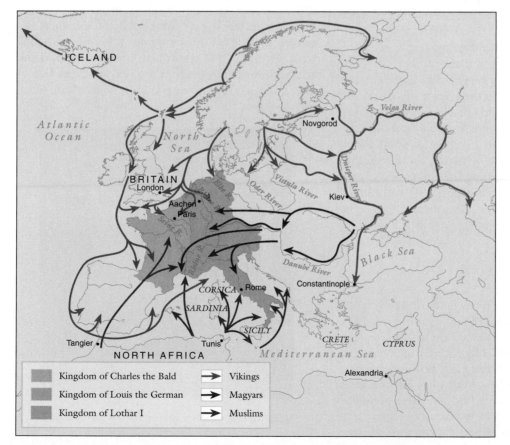

Map 14.3 The dissolution of the Carolingian empire in 843 C.E. and the invasions of early medieval Europe in the ninth and tenth centuries. Note the many routes of invasion taken by the Vikings, Magyars, and Muslims, and the extent to which these invasions reached both coastal and interior regions of Europe. How would these invasions have affected the social and economic life of Europe in this period?

In Germany, when Carolingian authorities were unable to prevent invasions by the Magyars, local lords took matters into their own hands. The most successful of them was King Otto I of Saxony (reigned 936–973). In 955 he inflicted a crushing defeat on a large Magyar army at Lechfeld near Augsburg, which effectively ended the Magyar threat. Otto also imposed his authority throughout Germany, and twice he led armies into Italy to support the papacy against Lombard magnates. On his second venture there in 962, the pope proclaimed him emperor and bestowed an imperial crown upon him. Otto's realm was really a German kingdom rather than an empire, but the imperial title survived until the nineteenth century, and later rulers of the Holy Roman Empire dated the foundation of their state to Otto's coronation in 962. In Germany, as in England, then, response to ninth-century invasions led to the organization of an effective regional state.

Germany

In France the end of Carolingian rule led instead to the proliferation of local authorities. Counts and other subordinates of the Carolingians withdrew allegiance from the central government, ruled their territories in their own interests, and usurped royal rights and prerogatives for themselves. They collected taxes, organized armed forces, built castles, and provided justice without reference to the Carolingians or other central authorities.

France

The emergence of effective regional kingdoms and local authorities prevented the return of centralized imperial rule like that of the Carolingians or postclassical societies in China, southwest Asia, and the eastern Mediterranean region. Like postclassical India, medieval Europe became a society of competing regional states. Yet by putting an end to the ninth-century invasions and establishing a stable political order, these states laid a foundation for social, economic, and cultural development.

EARLY MEDIEVAL SOCIETY

Historians once used the term *feudalism* to refer to the political and social order of medieval Europe. They spoke of a "feudal system" based on a neat hierarchy of lords and vassals, who collectively took charge of political and military affairs. Increasingly, however, scholars believe the term *feudalism* does not do justice to the complex, and often ad hoc, process by which local political and military elites organized their territories and maintained order in the absence of effective central authorities.

Organizing a Decentralized Society

After the dissolution of the Carolingian empire, European nobles took responsibility for maintaining order in their own territories. These nobles usually owed at least nominal allegiance to a higher authority, most often a descendant of the last Carolingian king. In fact, though, the nobles acted with growing independence: they collected rents and fees, administered local affairs, mobilized armed forces, and decided legal disputes.

To organize their territories the local nobles built military and political relationships with other prominent individuals in their territories. In doing so, they mobilized small private armies by attracting armed retainers into their service with grants of land or money. These grants enabled retainers to devote their time and energy to the service of their lords rather than the domestic tasks of cultivating food and providing for families. In exchange, retainers owed loyalty, obedience, respect, counsel, and military service to their lords.

Lords and Retainers

These relationships between lords and retainers became extremely important for the larger social order because retainers increasingly exercised political and legal rights over their holdings. Retainers became responsible for the organization of local public works projects, the resolution of disputes, and the administration of justice. As a result, political authorities and military specialists merged into a hereditary

Military retainers receive swords that indicate their close relationship with a local lord who accepts them as partners in authority.

noble class that lived off the surplus agricultural production it extracted from cultivators.

Potential for Instability — This decentralized political order developed into a complicated and sometimes even confusing network of relationships between lords and retainers. A lord with several retainers might himself be a retainer to a higher lord, who in turn might be one of several retainers to a yet greater lord in a web of relationships extending from local communities to a king. Although this decentralized political order had the potential to lead to chaos if retainers decided to pursue their own interests, in several places—including England, Germany, and France—high-ranking lords built powerful states on such foundations.

Serfs and Manors

The development of a decentralized political order accompanied fundamental changes in European society, particularly for slaves and free peasants. For sev-

Serfs — eral centuries after the fall of the western Roman empire, the population of western Europe consisted mostly of slaves and free peasants. As European society regained stability following the collapse of the Roman empire and the Germanic invasions, these slaves and free peasants worked at the same kinds of agricultural tasks and frequently intermarried. In addition, free peasants often sought protection from a lord and pledged their labor and obedience in exchange for security and land to cultivate. Beginning about the mid–seventh century, rulers and administrators recognized intermediate categories of individuals neither fully slave nor fully free. Though not chattel slaves subject to sale on a master's whim, these semifree individuals, known as *serfs*, owed obligations to the lords whose lands they cultivated.

Serfs usually had the right to work certain lands and to pass rights to those lands along to their heirs,

Serfs' Obligations — as long as they observed their obligations to landlords. Those obligations included both labor services and payments of rents in kind, such as a portion of a serf's own harvest at specified times during the year. Male serfs typically worked three days a week in the fields of their lords and provided additional labor services during planting and harvesting seasons, while women churned butter, made cheese, brewed beer, spun thread, wove cloth, or sewed clothes for the lords and their families. Because landlords provided them with land to cultivate and sometimes with tools and animals as well, serfs had little opportunity to move to different lands. In-

deed, they were able to do so only with the permission of their lord. They even had to pay a fee for the right to marry a serf who worked for a different lord.

During the early middle ages, the institution of serfdom encouraged the development of the manor as the principal form of agricultural organization in western Europe. A manor was a large estate *Manors* consisting of fields, meadows, forests, agricultural tools, domestic animals, and sometimes lakes or rivers, as well as serfs bound to the land. The lord of the manor was a prominent political or

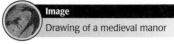
Image
Drawing of a medieval manor

military figure. He and his deputies provided government, administration, police services, and justice for the manor. Many lords had the authority to execute serfs for serious misconduct such as murder or other violent crimes.

By the Carolingian era, manors dominated rural regions in much of France, western Germany, and the Low Countries, as well as southern England and northern Italy. In the absence of thriving cities, manors became largely self-sufficient communities. Lords of the manors maintained mills, bakeries, breweries, and wineries, and serfs produced most of the iron tools, leather goods, domestic utensils, and textiles that the manorial community needed. During the high middle ages, craft skills developed on manors would help fuel an impressive round of economic development in western Europe.

The Economy of Early Medieval Europe

During the early middle ages, economic activity in western Europe was considerably slower than in China, India, southwest Asia, and the eastern Mediterranean region. Repeated invasions seriously disrupted European agriculture, and urban centers experienced diminished industrial production and trade. By the tenth century, however, political stability served as a foundation for economic recovery, and western Europeans began to participate more actively in the larger trading world of the eastern hemisphere.

With the establishment of the Frankish kingdom and the Carolingian empire, the European center of gravity shifted northward from the Medi- *Agriculture* terranean to the areas around modern France. Yet the small wooden plows that had worked well in light, well-drained Mediterranean soils made little headway in the heavy, moist soils of the north. In response, after the eighth century northern Europeans

Life on an Early Medieval Manor

Some useful insights into the lives and experiences of common people come from a decree known as the "Capitulary de Villis" issued by the emperor Charlemagne in 807 C.E. as a guide for stewards of Carolingian estates. The decree envisions a community with sophisticated agricultural and craft skills. Probably few estates observed all provisions of Charlemagne's decree, but the capitulary nonetheless communicates clearly how lords hoped to control their manors and profit from their production.

■   ■   ■

Each steward shall make an annual statement of all our income: an account of our lands cultivated by the oxen which our ploughmen drive and of our lands which the tenants of farms ought to plough; an account of the pigs, of the rents, of the obligations and fines; of the game taken in our forests without our permission; . . . of the mills, of the forest, of the fields, of the bridges, and ships; of the free men and the hundreds who are under obligations to our treasury; of markets, vineyards, and those who owe wine to us; of the hay, firewood, torches, planks, and other kinds of lumber; of the waste lands; of the fruits of the trees, of the nut trees, larger and smaller; of the grafted trees of all kinds; of the gardens; of the turnips; of the fish ponds; of the hides, skins, and horns; of the honey, wax; of the fat, tallow and soap; of the mulberry wine, cooked wine, mead, vinegar, beer, wine new and old; of the new grain and the old; of the hens and eggs; of the geese; the number of fishermen, [metal] smiths, sword-makers, and shoemakers; . . . of the forges and mines, that is iron and other mines; of the lead mines; . . . of the colts and fillies; they shall make all these known to us, set forth separately and in order, at Christmas, in order that we may know what and how much of each thing we have. . . .

[Stewards] must provide the greatest care, that whatever is prepared or made with the hands, that is, lard, smoked meat, salt meat, partially salted meat, wine, vinegar, mulberry wine, cooked wine . . . mustard, cheese, butter, malt, beer, mead, honey, wax, flour, all should be prepared and made with the greatest cleanliness. . . .

[Stewards should ensure] that in each of our estates, the chambers [living quarters] shall be provided with counterpanes, cushions, pillows, bed clothes, coverings for the tables and benches; vessels of brass, lead, iron and wood; andirons, chains, pot-hooks, adzes, axes, augers, cutlasses and all other kinds of tools, so that it shall never be necessary to go elsewhere for them, or to borrow them. And the weapons, which are carried against the enemy, shall be well cared for, so as to keep them in good condition; and when they are brought back they shall be placed in the chamber.

For our women's work they are to give at the proper time, as has been ordered, the materials, that is the linen, wool, woad, vermillion, madder, wool-combs, teasels, soap, grease, vessels and the other objects which are necessary.

Of the food products other than meat, two-thirds shall be sent each year for our own use, that is of the vegetables, fish, cheese, honey, mustard, vinegar, millet, panic [a grain similar to millet], dried and green herbs, radishes, and in addition of the wax, soap and other small products; and they shall tell us how much is left by a statement, as we have said above; and they shall not neglect this as in the past; because from those two-thirds, we wish to know how much remains.

Each steward shall have in his district good workmen, namely, blacksmiths, goldsmiths, silversmiths, shoemakers, [wood] turners, carpenters, sword-makers, fishermen, foilers [fine metalworkers], soap-makers, men who know how to make beer, cider, berry, and all other kinds of beverages, bakers to make pastry for our table, net-makers who know how to make nets for hunting, fishing and fowling, and the others who are too numerous to be designated.

- *On the basis of the "Capitulary de Villis," how would you characterize the conditions of material life in the Carolingian countryside?*

SOURCE: *Translations and Reprints from the Original Sources of European History,* vol. 2. Philadelphia: University of Pennsylvania Press, 1900. (Translation slightly modified.)

began to use a heavy plow equipped with iron tips that dug into the earth and with a mould-board to turn the soil. The heavy plow was a more expensive piece of equipment than the light Mediterranean plow, and it required cultivators to harness much more energy to pull it through moist northern soils. Once hitched to oxen or draft horses, however, the heavy plow contributed to significantly increased agricultural production.

Image
Limbourg Brothers
"February" & "March"

As the heavy plow spread throughout western Europe, cultivators also cleared new lands for cultivation. They constructed watermills, which enabled them to take advantage of a ready and renewable source of inanimate energy, and they experimented with new methods of rotating crops that allowed them to cultivate cleared land more intensively. Furthermore, they developed a special horse collar, which enabled them to rely less on slow-moving oxen and more on speedier horses to draw their heavy plows. As a result of those measures, agricultural production increased markedly in western Europe.

A Rural Society The agricultural surplus of early medieval Europe was not, however, substantial enough to support cities with large populations of artisans, crafts workers, merchants, and professionals. Whereas cities had thrived and trade had linked all regions of the Roman empire, early medieval Europe was almost entirely a rural society that engaged in little commerce. Manors and local communities produced most of the manufactured goods that they needed, and they provided both the materials and the labor for construction and other large-scale projects. Towns were few and sparsely populated, and they served as economic hubs for the areas immediately surrounding them rather than as vibrant centers integrating the economic activities of distant regions.

Yet trade did not entirely disappear from western Europe. Local markets and fairs offered opportunities for small-scale exchange, and itinerant peddlers shopped their wares from one settlement to another. Maritime trade flourished in the Mediterranean despite Muslim conquests in the region. Christian merchants from Italy and Spain regularly traded across religious boundary lines with Muslims of Sicily, Spain, and North Africa, who linked Europe indirectly with the larger Islamic world of communication and exchange. *Mediterranean Trade*

Maritime trade flourished also in the North Sea and the Baltic Sea. Most active among the early medieval merchants in the northern seas were Norse seafarers, kinsmen of the Vikings who raided lands from eastern Europe to the Mediterranean. By traveling down the Russian rivers to the Black Sea, they were able to trade actively in both the Byzantine and the Abbasid empires. Thus, like Mediterranean merchants, Norse mariners linked western Europe with the Islamic world. Indeed, the Carolingian empire depended heavily on the silver Norse merchants brought from the Abbasid empire, for it was a principal source of bullion used for minting coins and hence was a crucially important element of the western European economy. *Norse Merchant Mariners*

In this twelfth-century manuscript illustration, a peasant guides a heavy, wheeled plow while his wife prods the oxen that pull the plow.

By 900 the results of political stability and agricultural innovation were clearly evident in population figures as well as trade. In 200 C.E., before the Roman empire began to experience serious difficulties, the European population stood at about thirty-six million. By 600 it had fallen to twenty-six million—a decline that reflected both the ravages of epidemic diseases and the unsettled conditions of the early middle ages. Then, gradually, the population recovered. By 1000 European population once again amounted to thirty-six million—the level it had reached some eight centuries earlier. By the end of the early middle ages, western Europe was poised to experience remarkable economic and demographic expansion that vastly increased European influence in the eastern hemisphere.

Population

THE FORMATION OF CHRISTIAN EUROPE

By the time the Roman empire collapsed, Christianity was the principal source of religious, moral, and cultural authority throughout the Mediterranean basin. In the northern lands of Gaul, Germany, the British isles, and Scandinavia, however, Christianity had attracted few converts. Indeed, only after the conversion of Clovis and the Franks did Roman Christianity enjoy a powerful and energetic sponsor in lands beyond the Mediterranean rim. One of the most important developments of the early middle ages was the conversion of western Europe to Roman Christianity. The Franks, the popes, and the monasteries played important roles in bringing about this conversion. The adoption of Roman Christianity ensured that medieval Europe would inherit crucial cultural elements from classical Roman society, including the Latin language and the institutional Roman church.

The Politics of Conversion

Clovis and the Franks won the support of the church hierarchy as well as the Christian population of the former Roman empire when they converted to the Roman faith. Thereafter, a deep commitment to Roman Christianity became a hallmark of Frankish policy. Clovis, his successors, and the Carolingians viewed themselves as protectors of the papacy. In exchange for military and political support, the Carolingians received recogni-

The Franks and the Church

tion and backing from the popes, including the award of Charlemagne's imperial crown at the hands of Pope Leo III.

Charlemagne not only supported the papacy but also worked to spread Christianity in northern lands. In part, he achieved this through peaceful means, by ordering monasteries to establish elementary schools and to teach Christian doctrine. But Charlemagne also promoted the spread of Christianity by military force. Between 772 and 804, for example, he waged a bitter campaign against the Saxons, a pagan people inhabiting northern Germany. Along with claiming political hegemony, he insisted that the Saxons adopt Roman Christianity. Despite fierce Saxon resistance, Charlemagne prevailed: the Saxons not only acknowledged Charlemagne as their political lord but also replaced their pagan traditions with Christianity.

The Spread of Christianity

Although pagan ways persisted in some remote areas, by the year 1000 Christianity had won the allegiance of most people throughout western Europe and in the Nordic lands. By sponsoring the Roman church and its missionaries, Charlemagne helped establish Christianity as the dominant religious and cultural tradition in western Europe.

The Papacy

Apart from the political support it received from the Franks, the Roman church benefited from strong papal leadership. When the western Roman empire collapsed, the papacy survived and claimed spiritual authority over all the lands formerly embraced by the empire. Initially, the popes cooperated closely with the Byzantine emperors, who seemed to be the natural heirs to the emperors of Rome. Beginning in the late sixth century, however, the popes devoted their efforts to strengthening the western Christian church based at Rome and distinguishing it from the eastern Christian church based at Constantinople. The two churches differed on many issues by the eleventh century, and in 1054 the pope and patriarch excommunicated each other. After the eleventh century the two branches of Christianity formed distinct identities as the Roman Catholic and Eastern Orthodox churches.

The individual most responsible for providing the Roman church with its sense of direction was Pope Gregory I (590–604 C.E.), also known as Gregory the Great. As pope, Gregory faced an array of difficult challenges. Most important, Gregory strengthened the pope's control over

Pope Gregory I

church doctrine by reasserting papal primacy—the claim that the bishop of Rome was the ultimate authority in the Christian church. Gregory also made contributions as a theologian: he strongly emphasized the sacrament of penance, which required individuals to confess their sins to their priests and then to atone for their sins by penitential acts prescribed by the priests—a practice that enhanced the influence of the Roman church in the lives of individuals. In addition, Gregory strengthened the Roman church further by extending its appeal and winning new converts in western Europe through the efforts of missionaries. The most effective missionaries of Christianity in the early medieval period were monks. Indeed, Pope Gregory himself was a monk, and he relied heavily on the energies of his fellow monks in seeking converts throughout Europe.

Monasticism

Christian monasticism had its origin in the second century C.E. in Egypt, where devout Christians had

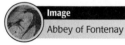
Image
Abbey of Fontenay

formed communes to devote themselves to the pursuit of holiness. When Christianity became legal during the fourth century, the monastic lifestyle became an increasingly popular alternative throughout the Roman empire. Monastic communities cropped up in Italy, Spain, Gaul, and the British isles as well as in the eastern Mediterranean region.

During the early days of monasticism, each community developed its own rules, procedures, and priorities. Some communities demanded that their inhabitants follow extremely austere lifestyles that sapped the energy of the monks, whereas others did not establish any clear expectations of their recruits. In response to those haphazard conditions, St. Benedict of Nursia (480–547 C.E.) strengthened the early monastic movement by

St. Benedict and the Rule

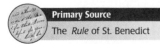
Primary Source
The *Rule* of St. Benedict

providing it with discipline and a sense of purpose. In 529 St. Benedict prepared a set of regulations known as Benedict's *Rule* for the monastic community that he had founded at Monte Cassino, near Rome. The *Rule* required monks to take vows to lead communal, celibate lives under the absolute direction of the abbot who supervised the monastery: poverty, chastity, and obedience became the prime virtues for Benedictine monks. The *Rule*

also called for monks to spend their time in prayer, meditation, and work.

Through the influence of St. Benedict's sister, the nun St. Scholastica (482–543), an adaptation of the *Rule* soon provided guidance for the religious life of women living in convents. *St. Scholastica* Within a century most European monasteries and convents observed the Benedictine *Rule*. Even today most Roman Catholic monasteries observe rules that reflect the influence of the Benedictine tradition.

Strengthened by the discipline that the Benedictine *Rule* introduced, monasteries became a dominant feature in the social and cultural life of western Europe throughout the middle ages. Monasteries helped to provide order in the countryside, for example, and to expand agricultural production. Monasteries accumulated large landholdings—as well as

Monasteries were the principal centers of literacy in western Europe during the early middle ages. In this manuscript illustration, one monk copies a manuscript, another makes geometric calculations, and a third cuts parchment, while two work on the building and one more rings the bells that call monks and members of the surrounding community to religious services.

authority over serfs working their lands—from the bequests of wealthy individuals, and on those lands they mobilized both monks and serfs to clear forests, drain swamps, and prepare lands for cultivation. Indeed, monasteries organized much of the labor that brought about the expansion of agricultural production in early medieval Europe.

Monasticism and Society   Like Buddhist monasteries in Asian lands and charitable religious foundations in Muslim lands, European monasteries provided a variety of social services. They served as inns, places of refuge, orphanages, and hospitals. They often set up schools, and large monasteries provided advanced instruction for those preparing for the priesthood or high ecclesiastical positions. Some monasteries maintained libraries and scriptoria, where monks copied works of classical literature and philosophy as well as the scriptures and other Christian writings. Almost all works of Latin literature that have come down to the present

survive because of copies made by medieval monks. Finally, monasteries served as a source of literate, educated, and talented individuals whose secretarial and administrative services were crucial for the organization of effective government in early medieval Europe.

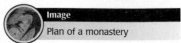

Image
Plan of a monastery

Because of the various roles they played in the larger society, monasteries were particularly effective agents in the spread of Christianity. While they organized life in the countryside and provided social services, monks also zealously preached Christianity and tended to the spiritual needs of rural populations. Monks patiently and persistently served the needs of rural populations, and over the decades and centuries they helped to instill Christian values in countless generations of European peasants.

SUMMARY

Like societies in China, India, southwest Asia, and the eastern Mediterranean region, western European society experienced enormous change during the postclassical era. In some ways western Europe had the most difficult experience of all the postclassical societies. In China, southwest Asia, and the eastern Mediterranean, societies were able to preserve or reestablish centralized imperial rule that maintained order and stability while also facilitating trade and encouraging economic development. India did not generate an imperial form of government, but because of the subcontinent's geographic location and productive capacity, India participated actively in the larger economic and commercial life of the eastern hemisphere. In contrast, rulers of early medieval Europe did not reinstate an imperial form of government—except for the short-lived Carolingian empire—and western Europeans did not participate actively in the larger trading world of the eastern hemisphere. The standards of material life in early medieval Europe—as measured by agricultural and industrial production, volume of trade, and the extent of urban settlement—stood well below those of other postclassical societies.

Yet, just as postclassical developments deeply influenced the evolution of societies in other lands, the early medieval era was a crucial period for the development of western Europe. In the absence of a durable centralized empire, western Europeans found ways to maintain relative order and stability by decentralizing political responsibilities and relying on local authorities for political organization. Over the longer term the decentralized political order of medieval Europe discouraged the revival of empire and encouraged the emergence of regional states that organized their communities into powerful societies. During the early middle ages, western Europeans experimented with agricultural techniques that enabled them to expand production dramatically, conduct increased trade, and rebuild urban centers. Finally, western Christianity preserved elements of classical Roman society and established a foundation for cultural unity in western Europe, just as Buddhism, Hinduism, Islam, and eastern Christianity served as sources of cultural authority in other societies.

CHRONOLOGY

476	Fall of the western Roman empire
480–547	Life of St. Benedict of Nursia
481–511	Reign of Clovis
482–543	Life of St. Scholastica
590–604	Reign of Pope Gregory I
751–843	Carolingian kingdom
768–814	Reign of Charlemagne
800	Coronation of Charlemagne as emperor
843	Dissolution of the Carolingian empire
936–973	Reign of King Otto I of Saxony
955	Battle of Lechfeld
962	Coronation of Otto I

FOR FURTHER READING

Robert-Henri Bautier. *The Economic Development of Medieval Europe*. New York, 1971. An excellent and well-illustrated survey, which examines the economic and social history of western Europe in the context of the larger Mediterranean basin.

Marc Bloch. *Feudal Society*. 2 vols. Trans. by L. A. Manyon. Chicago, 1961. A classic interpretation concentrating on social and economic history that has decisively influenced the way historians think about medieval Europe.

Peter Brown. *The Rise of Western Christendom: Triumph and Diversity*, A.D. *200–1000*. 2nd ed. Oxford, 2003. A landmark analysis of early Christian history that incorporates the findings of recent scholarship.

Patrick J. Geary, ed. *Readings in Medieval History*. Lewiston, N.Y., 1989. Offers substantial English translations of primary sources.

David Herlihy. *Opera Muliebra: Women and Work in Medieval Europe*. New York, 1990. Examines women's roles both in their own households and in the larger society of medieval Europe.

Richard Hodges and David Whitehouse. *Mohammed, Charlemagne, and the Origins of Europe: Archaeology and the Pirenne Thesis*. Ithaca, 1983. Draws on archaeological discoveries in placing the early medieval European economy in hemispheric context.

Gwyn Jones. *A History of the Vikings*. Rev. ed. Oxford, 1984. The best general work on Viking society and Viking expansion.

Michael McCormick. *Origins of the European Economy: Communications and Commerce*, A.D. *300–900*. Cambridge, Mass., 2001. A thorough and comprehensive analysis that emphasizes the participation of early medieval Europe in a larger Mediterranean economy.

Rosamond McKitterick. *The Frankish Kingdoms under the Carolingians, 751–987*. New York, 1983. Comprehensive survey of the Carolingian dynasty with special attention to political, cultural, and religious developments.

Susan Reynolds. *Fiefs and Vassals: The Medieval Evidence Reinterpreted*. Oxford, 1994. A powerful scholarly critique of the concept of feudalism.

The half millennium from 1000 to 1500 C.E. differed markedly from earlier eras. During classical and postclassical times, large, regional societies situated in China, India, southwest Asia, and the Mediterranean basin dominated the eastern hemisphere. From 1000 to 1500 C.E., however, nomadic Turkish and Mongol peoples overran settled societies and established vast transregional empires from China to eastern Europe.

Nomadic peoples toppled several postclassical states, most notably the Song empire in China and the Abbasid realm in southwest Asia. By building empires that transcended the boundaries of postclassical states, however, nomadic Turks and Mongols laid a political foundation for sharply increased trade and communication between peoples of different societies and cultural regions.

Increased trade in the Indian Ocean basin also promoted more intense cross-cultural communications. Maritime trade built on the political stability, economic expansion, and demographic growth of the postclassical era. This trade indicated a movement toward economic integration as societies of the Indian Ocean basin concentrated increasingly on cultivating crops or producing goods for export while importing foods or goods that they could not produce very well themselves.

Demographic growth, increased agricultural production, and economic expansion helped to underwrite rapid political development in sub-Saharan Africa and western Europe. Increasing volumes of trade favored a movement toward centralization in both areas, since taxes levied on trade helped to finance the professional bureaucrats and armed forces that centralized states required.

Although they did not participate in the demographic and economic expansion of the eastern hemisphere, the indigenous peoples of the Americas and Oceania also built larger and more centralized societies from 1000 to 1500 C.E. Centralized empires

4

appeared in Mesoamerica and Andean South
America, and agricultural societies emerged in
several regions of North America. Although Pacific islanders
had limited resources with which to build empires, within their own agricultural and
fishing societies they established tightly centralized kingdoms.

During the fourteenth and fifteenth centuries C.E., much of the eastern hemisphere
experienced difficulties not only because of warfare arising from the conquests of
nomadic peoples but also because of epidemic bubonic plague and global climatic
changes that brought cooler temperatures. Together with military destruction and

AN AGE OF CROSS-CULTURAL INTERACTION, 1000 TO 1500 C.E.

pandemic plague, reduced agricultural production led to political, social, and economic
problems throughout much of the eastern hemisphere.

Nevertheless, by the mid–fifteenth century, peoples from China to western Europe
were recovering from those difficulties and rebuilding prosperous societies. In their own
quest for prosperity, western European peoples unwittingly laid the foundations of a
new era in world history. While searching for sea routes to Asian markets, European
mariners happened upon the continents of North and South America. Their voyages
brought the world's various peoples for the first time into permanent and sustained
communication, and their interactions triggered a series of consequences that
profoundly influenced modern world history. Indeed, the European voyages that gave
rise to this interdependent and interconnected world took place precisely because of the
movement toward increasing interaction in the eastern hemisphere during the centuries
following 1000 C.E.

CHAPTER 15

Nomadic Empires and Eurasian Integration

Guillaume Boucher was a goldsmith who lived during the early and middle decades of the thirteenth century. During the 1230s, he left his native Paris and went to Budapest, which was then a part of the kingdom of Hungary. There he was captured by Mongol warriors campaigning in Hungary. The Mongols noticed and appreciated Boucher's talents, and when they left Hungary in 1242, they took him and other skilled captives to their central Asian homeland.

For at least the next fifteen years, Boucher lived at the Mongol capital at Karakorum. Though technically a slave, he enjoyed some prestige. He supervised fifty assistants in a workshop that produced decorative objects of gold and silver for the Mongol court. His most ingenious creation was a spectacular silver fountain in the form of a tree. Four pipes, con-

cealed by the tree's trunk, carried wines and other intoxicating drinks to the top of the tree and then dispensed them into silver bowls from which guests filled their cups. Apart from his famous fountain, Boucher also produced statues in gold and silver, built carriages, designed buildings, and even sewed ritual garments for Roman Catholic priests who conducted services for Christians living at Karakorum.

Boucher was by no means the only European living at the Mongol court. His wife was a woman of French ancestry whom Boucher had met and married in Hungary. The Flemish missionary William of Rubruck visited Karakorum in 1254, and during his sojourn there he encountered men and women from France, Russia, Greece, and England. Other European visitors to the Mongol

OPPOSITE PAGE: *Chabi, a Nestorian Christian and the favorite wife of Khubilai Khan, wearing the distincitve headgear reserved for Mongol women of the ruling class.*

court found Germans, Slavs, and Hungarians as well as Chinese, Koreans, Turks, Persians, and Armenians, among others. Many thirteenth-century roads led to Karakorum.

Nomadic peoples had made their influence felt throughout much of Eurasia as early as classical times. The Xiongnu confederation dominated central Asia and threatened the Han dynasty in China from the third to the first century B.C.E. During the second and third centuries C.E., the Huns and other nomadic peoples from central Asia launched migrations that helped bring down the western Roman empire, and later migrations of the White Huns destroyed the Gupta state in India. Turkish peoples ruled a large central Asian empire from the sixth through the ninth century, and the Uighur Turks even seized the capital cities of the Tang dynasty in the mid–seventh century.

Between the eleventh and fifteenth centuries, nomadic peoples became more prominent than ever before in Eurasian affairs. Turkish peoples migrated to Persia, Anatolia, and India, where they established new states. During the thirteenth and fourteenth centuries, the Mongols established themselves as the most powerful people of the central Asian steppes and then turned on settled societies in China, Persia, Russia, and eastern Europe. By the early fourteenth century, the Mongols had built the largest empire the world has ever seen, stretching from Korea and China in the east to Russia and Hungary in the west.

Most of the Mongol states collapsed during the late fourteenth and fifteenth centuries, but the decline of the Mongols did not signal the end of nomadic peoples' influence on Eurasian affairs. Although a native Chinese dynasty replaced the Mongol state in China, the Mongols continued to threaten its central Asian frontier. Moreover, from the fourteenth through the seventeenth century, Turkish peoples embarked on new campaigns of expansion that eventually brought most of India, much of central Asia, all of Anatolia, and a good portion of eastern Europe under their domination.

The military campaigns of nomadic peoples were sometimes exceedingly destructive. Nomadic warriors demolished cities, slaughtered urban populations, and ravaged surrounding agricultural lands. Yet those same forces also encouraged systematic peaceful interaction between peoples of different societies. Between the eleventh and fifteenth centuries, the imperial campaigns of Turkish and Mongol peoples forged closer links than ever before between Eurasian lands. By fostering cross-cultural communication and exchange on

an unprecedented scale, the nomadic empires integrated the lives of peoples throughout much of the eastern hemisphere.

TURKISH MIGRATIONS AND IMPERIAL EXPANSION

Turkish peoples never formed a single, homogeneous group but, rather, organized themselves into clans and tribes that often fought bitterly with one another. All Turkish peoples spoke related languages, and all were nomads or descendants of nomads. From modest beginnings they expanded their influence until they dominated not only the steppes of central Asia but also settled societies in Persia, Anatolia, and India.

Nomadic Economy and Society

Nomadic societies in central Asia developed by adapting to the ecological conditions of arid lands. Central Asia does not receive enough rain to support large-scale agriculture. Oases permit cultivation of limited regions, but for the most part only grasses and shrubs grow on the central Asian steppe lands, and there are no large rivers or other sources of water to support large-scale irrigation systems. Yet grazing animals thrive on grasses and shrubs, and the peoples of central Asia took advantage of this by herding sheep, horses, cattle, goats, and camels.

Nomadic peoples drove their herds and flocks to lands with abundant grass and then moved them along as the animals thinned the vegetation. They carefully followed migratory cycles that took account of the seasons and local climatic conditions and lived mostly off the meat, milk, and hides of their animals. They used animal bones for tools and animal dung as fuel. They made shoes and clothes out of wool from their sheep and skins from their other animals. Their dwellings—large tents called *yurts*—were fashioned with felt made from the wool of their sheep. They even prepared an alcoholic drink from their animals by fermenting mare's milk into a potent concoction known as *kumiss*.

Nomadic Peoples and Their Animals

The aridity of the climate and the nomadic lifestyle limited the development of human societies in central Asia. Intensive agriculture was impossible ex-

yurts (yuhrts)

cept in oases, and the need to regularly follow the herds made large-scale craft production impractical.

Nomadic and Settled Peoples   As a result, nomads avidly sought opportunities to trade with settled peoples. Much of that commerce took place on a small scale as nomads sought agricultural products and manufactured goods to satisfy their immediate needs. Often, however, nomads also participated in long-distance trade networks. Because of their mobility and their familiarity with large regions of central Asia, nomadic peoples were ideally suited to organize and lead the caravans that crossed central Asia and linked settled societies from China to the Mediterranean basin. During the postclassical era and later, Turkish peoples were especially prominent on the caravan routes of central Asia.

Nomadic society generated two social classes: nobles and commoners. Charismatic leaders won recognition as nobles and thereby acquired *Nomadic Society* the prestige needed to organize clans and tribes into alliances. Normally, nobles did little governing, since clans and tribes looked after their own affairs and resented interference. During times of war, however, nobles wielded absolute authority over the forces within their alliances.

The nobility was a fluid class. Leaders passed noble status along to their heirs, but the heirs could lose their status if they did not continue to provide appropriate leadership for their clans and tribes. Over the course of a few generations, nobles could return to the status of commoners. Meanwhile, commoners could win recognition as nobles by outstanding conduct, particularly by courageous behavior during war. Then, if they were clever diplomats, they could arrange alliances between clans and tribes and gain enough support to displace established leaders.

The earliest religion of the Turkish peoples revolved around shamans—religious specialists who possessed supernatural powers, communicated with the gods and nature spirits, and invoked *Nomadic Religion* divine aid on behalf of their communities. Yet many Turkish peoples became attracted to the religious and cultural traditions they encountered when trading with peoples of settled societies, and by the sixth century C.E. many Turks had converted to Buddhism, Nestorian Christianity, or Manichaeism. Partly because of their newly adopted religious traditions and partly

---

Nestorian (neh-STOHR-eeuhn)

A wall painting from a cave at Dunhuang, a major oasis on the silk roads, depicts a band of sword-wielding thieves (left) holding up a party of Turkish merchants (right). According to convention, the artist represented the Turks with pale skins, long noses, and deep-set eyes.

because of their prominence in Eurasian trade networks, Turkish peoples also developed a written script.

In the tenth century Turks living near the Abbasid empire began to turn to Islam. Their conversion had

Turkish Conversion to Islam

great significance. When Turkish peoples began to migrate into settled societies in large numbers, they helped spread Islam to new lands, particularly Anatolia and northern India. The boundaries of the Islamic world thus expanded along with the political and military influence of Turkish peoples.

This expansion took place when nomadic leaders organized vast confederations of peoples under the

Military Organization

leadership of a *khan* ("ruler"). In fact, khans rarely ruled directly, instead ruling through the leaders of allied tribes. Yet when organized on a large scale, nomadic peoples wielded enormous military power due mostly to their outstanding cavalry forces. Nomadic warriors had superior equestrian skills. Their arrows flew with deadly accuracy even when launched from the backs of galloping horses. Moreover, units of warriors coordinated their movements to outmaneuver and overwhelm their opponents. Indeed, few armies were able to resist the mobility and discipline of well-organized nomadic warriors. With such military capabilities, several groups of Turkish nomads began in the tenth century C.E. to seize the wealth of settled societies and build imperial states in the regions surrounding central Asia.

Turkish Empires in Persia, Anatolia, and India

Turkish peoples entered Persia, Anatolia, and India at different times and for different purposes. They approached Abbasid Persia much as Germanic peoples

Saljuq Turks and the Abbasid Empire

had earlier approached the Roman empire. From about the mid–eighth to the mid–tenth century, Turkish peoples lived mostly on the borders of the Abbasid realm. By the mid– to late tenth century, large numbers of Saljuq Turks served in Abbasid armies and lived in the Abbasid realm itself. By the mid–eleventh century the Saljuqs overshadowed the Abbasid caliphs so much that in 1055 the caliph recognized the Saljuq leader Tughril Beg as *sultan* ("chieftain"). Tughril first consolidated his hold on the

---

Abbasid (ah-BAH-sih)
Saljuqs (sahl-JYOOKS)

Abbasid capital at Baghdad, then he and his successors extended Turkish rule to Syria, Palestine, and other parts of the realm. For the last two centuries of the Abbasid state, the caliphs served only as figureheads: actual governance lay in the hands of the Turkish sultans.

Some Saljuq Turks began to turn their attention to the rich land of Anatolia, and in the early eleventh century they began migrating there in large numbers. In 1071 Saljuq forces inflicted a devastating defeat on the Byzantine army at Manzikert

Saljuq Turks and the Byzantine Empire

in eastern Anatolia and took the Byzantine emperor captive. Following that victory Saljuqs and other Turkish groups entered Anatolia almost at will. The peasants of Anatolia, who mostly resented their Byzantine overlords, tended to look upon the Saljuqs as liberators rather than as conquerors.

The migrants thoroughly transformed Anatolia. Turkish groups displaced Byzantine authorities and set up their own political and social institutions. They levied taxes on the Byzantine church, restricted its activities, and sometimes confiscated church property. Meanwhile, they welcomed converts to Islam and made political, social, and economic opportunities available to them. By 1453, when Ottoman Turks captured the Byzantine capital at Constantinople, Byzantine and Christian Anatolia had become largely a Turkish and Islamic land.

While the Saljuqs spearheaded Turkish migrations in Abbasid Persia and Byzantine Anatolia, in the early eleventh century Mahmud of Ghazni led the Turkish Ghaznavids of Af-ghanistan in raids on lucrative sites in northern India. Although their

Ghaznavid Turks and the Sultanate of Delhi

original goal was plunder, they gradually became more interested in permanent rule. They asserted their authority first over the Punjab and then over Gujarat and Bengal. By the thirteenth century the Turkish sultanate of Delhi claimed authority over all of northern India. Several of the Delhi sultans conceived plans to conquer southern India, but none was able to realize those ambitions. Indeed, the sultans faced constant challenges from Hindu princes in neighboring lands, and they periodically had to defend their northern frontiers from new Turkish or Mongol invaders. They maintained an enormous army with a large elephant corps, but those forces only enabled them to hold on to territories they already had.

Turkish rule had great social and cultural implications in India, as it did in Anatolia. Mahmud of Ghazni was a zealous foe of Buddhism and Hinduism alike,

Map 15.1 The Turkish empires and their neighbors about 1210 C.E. Compare this map with Map 11.1, which depicts the expansion of Islam in the seventh and eighth centuries C.E. In what ways did the boundaries of the Turkish empires overlap with the boundaries of Islam, and how might that overlap have affected the Turkish empires?

and his forces stripped Buddhist and Hindu establishments of their wealth, destroyed their buildings, and often slaughtered their residents and attendants as well. As Mahmud of Ghazni's forces repressed Buddhism and Hinduism, they encouraged conversion to Islam and enabled their faith to establish a secure presence in northern India.

Though undertaken by different groups and for different reasons, the Turkish conquests of Persia, Anatolia, and India represented part of a larger expansive movement by nomadic peoples. In all three cases the formidable military prowess of Turkish peoples enabled them to dominate settled societies. By the thirteenth century, the influence of nomadic peoples was greater than ever before in Eurasian history. Yet the Turkish conquests represented only a prelude to an astonishing round of empire building launched by the Mongols during the thirteenth and fourteenth centuries.

THE MONGOL EMPIRES

For most of history the nomadic Mongols lived on the high steppe lands of eastern central Asia. Like other nomadic peoples, they displayed deep loyalty to kin groups organized into families, clans, and tribes. They frequently allied with Turkish peoples who built empires on the steppes, but they rarely played a leading role in the organization of states before the thirteenth century. Strong loyalties to kinship groups made it difficult for the Mongols to organize a stable society on a large scale. During the early thirteenth century, however, Chinggis Khan (sometimes spelled "Genghis Khan") forged the various Mongol tribes into a powerful alliance that built the largest empire the world has ever seen. Although the vast Mongol realm soon dissolved into a series of smaller empires—most of which disappeared within a century—the Mongols' imperial venture brought the societies of Eurasia into closer contact than ever before.

Chinggis Khan and the Making of the Mongol Empire

The unifier of the Mongols was Temüjin, born about 1167 into a noble family. His father was a prominent warrior who forged an alliance between several Mongol clans and seemed likely to become a powerful leader. When Temüjin was about ten years old, however, rivals poisoned his father and destroyed the alliance. Abandoned by his father's allies, Temüjin led a precarious existence for some years. He lived in

Temüjin (TEM-oo-chin)

This painting by a Chinese artist depicts Chinggis Khan at about age sixty. Though most of his conquests were behind him, Chinggis Khan's focus and determination are readily apparent in this portrait.

poverty, since rivals seized the family's animals, and several times eluded enemies seeking to eliminate him. A rival once captured him and imprisoned him in a wooden cage, but Temüjin made a daring midnight escape and regained his freedom.

During the late twelfth century, Temüjin made an alliance with a prominent Mongol clan leader. He also

Chinggis Khan's Rise to Power mastered the art of steppe diplomacy, which called for displays of personal courage in battle, combined with intense loyalty to allies, a willingness to betray others to improve one's position, and the ability to entice other tribes into cooperative relationships. Temüjin gradually strengthened his position, sometimes by forging useful alliances, often by conquering rival contenders for power, and occasionally by turning suddenly against a troublesome ally. He eventually brought all the Mongol tribes into a single confederation, and in 1206 an assembly of Mongol leaders recognized Temüjin's supremacy by proclaiming him Chinggis Khan ("universal ruler").

Chinggis Khan's policies greatly strengthened the Mongol people. Earlier nomadic state builders had ruled largely through the leaders of allied tribes. But

Chinggis Khan mistrusted the Mongols' tribal organization, so he broke up the tribes and forced men of fighting age to join new military units with no tribal affiliations. He chose high military and political officials not on the basis of kinship or tribal status but because of their talents or their loyalty to him. Although he spent most of his life on horseback, Chinggis Khan also established a capital at Karakorum—present-day Har Horin, located about 300 kilometers (186 miles) west of the modern Mongo-

Mongol Political Organization

lian capital of Ulaanbaatar—where he built a luxurious palace. As command center of Chinggis Khan's empire, Karakorum symbolized a source of Mongol authority superior to the clan or tribe. Chinggis Khan's policies created a Mongol state that was not only much stronger than any earlier nomadic confederation but also less troubled by conflicts between clans and tribes.

The most important institution of the Mongol state was the army, which magnified the power of the small population. In the thirteenth century the Mongol population stood at about one million people—less than 1 percent of China's numbers. During Chinggis Khan's life, his army numbered only 100,000 to 125,000 Mongols, although allied peoples also contributed forces. How was it possible for so few people to conquer the better part of Eurasia?

Like earlier nomadic armies, Mongol forces relied on outstanding equestrian skills. In addition, their bows were short enough for archers to use while riding, and their arrows could *Mongol Arms* fell enemies at 200 meters (656 feet). Mongol horsemen were among the most mobile forces of the premodern world, sometimes traveling more than 100 kilometers (62 miles) per day to surprise an enemy. Furthermore, the Mongols understood the psychological dimensions of warfare and used them to their advantage. If enemies surrendered without resistance, the Mongols usually spared their lives, and they provided generous treatment for artisans, crafts workers, and those with military skills. In the event of resistance, however, the Mongols ruthlessly slaughtered whole populations, sparing only a few, whom they sometimes drove before their armies as human shields during future conflicts.

Once he had united the Mongols, Chinggis Khan turned his army and his attention to other parts of central Asia, particularly to nearby settled societies.

A Persian manuscript illustration depicts Chinggis Khan and his cavalry in hot pursuit of retreating forces.

He attacked the various Turkish peoples ruling in Tibet, northern China, Persia, and the central Asian steppes. Those conquests were important because they protected him against the possibility that other nomadic leaders might challenge his rule. But the Mongol campaigns in China and Persia had especially far-reaching consequences.

Chinggis Khan himself extended Mongol rule to northern China, dominated since 1127 C.E. by the nomadic Jurchen people, while the Song dynasty continued to rule in southern China. In 1211 C.E. Mongol raiding parties invaded the Jurchen realm, and by 1215 the Mongols had captured the capital near modern Beijing. This city, under the new name of Khanbaliq ("city of the khan"), also served as the Mongol capital in China. By 1220 the Mongols had largely established control over northern China.

Mongol Conquest of Northern China

Interactive Map
The Mongol empires

Next, Chinggis Khan led another force to Afghanistan and Persia, ruled at that time by a successor to the Saljuqs known as the Khwarazm shah. The mission was one of revenge, for in 1218 the Khwarazm shah had spurned a diplomatic envoy sent by Chinggis Khan by murdering the whole group. In response, the following year Chinggis Khan took his army west, pursued the Khwarazm shah to an island in the Caspian Sea (where he died), shattered his army, and seized control of his realm.

Mongol Conquest of Persia

Song (SOHNG)

To ensure that the shah's state would never constitute a challenge to his own empire, Chinggis Khan wreaked destruction on the conquered land. The Mongols ravaged one city after another, demolishing buildings and massacring hundreds of thousands of people. Some cities never recovered. The Mongols also destroyed the delicate *qanat* irrigation systems that sustained agriculture in the arid region, resulting in severely reduced agricultural production. For centuries after the Mongol conquest, Persian chroniclers cursed the invaders and the devastation they visited upon the land.

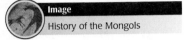
Image
History of the Mongols

By the time of his death in 1227, Chinggis Khan had laid the foundation of a vast and mighty empire. He had united the Mongols, established Mongol supremacy in central Asia, and extended Mongol control to northern China in the east and Persia in the west. But Chinggis Khan was a conqueror, not an administrator. He ruled the Mongols themselves through his control over the army, but he did not establish a central government for the lands that he conquered. Instead, he assigned Mongol overlords to supervise local administrators and to extract a generous tribute for the Mongols' own uses. Chinggis Khan's heirs continued his conquests, but they also undertook the task of designing a more permanent administration to guide the fortunes of the Mongol empire.

The Mongol Empires after Chinggis Khan

Chinggis Khan's death touched off a struggle for power among his sons and grandsons. Eventually, his heirs divided Chinggis Khan's vast realm into four regional empires. The great khans ruled China, the wealthiest of Mongol lands. Descendants of Chaghatai, one of Chinggis Khan's sons, ruled the khanate of Chaghatai in central Asia. Persia fell under the authority of rulers known as the ilkhans, and the khans of the Golden Horde dominated Russia. The great khans were nominally superior to the others, but they were rarely able to enforce their claims to authority. In fact, for as long as the Mongol empires survived, ambition fueled constant tension and occasional conflict among the four khans.

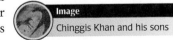
Image
Chinggis Khan and his sons

SOURCES FROM THE PAST

Marco Polo on Mongol Military Tactics

The Venetian Marco Polo traveled extensively through central Asia and China in the late thirteenth century, when Mongol empires dominated Asia. His book of travel writings is an especially valuable source of information about the Mongol age. Among other things, he described the Mongol way of making war.

Their arms are bows and arrows, sword and mace; but above all the bow, for they are capital archers, indeed the best that are known. . . .

When a Mongol prince goes forth to war, he takes with him, say, 100,000 men. Well, he appoints an officer to every ten men, one to every hundred, one to every thousand, and one to every ten thousand, so that his own orders have to be given to ten persons only, and each of these ten persons has to pass the orders only to another ten, and so on, no one having to give orders to more than ten. And every one in turn is responsible only to the officer immediately over him; and the discipline and order that comes of this method is marvellous, for they are a people very obedient to their chiefs. . . .

When they are going on a distant expedition they take no gear with them except two leather bottles for milk, a little earthenware pot to cook their meat in, and a little tent to shelter them from rain. And in case of great urgency they will ride ten days on end without lighting a fire or taking a meal. On such an occasion they will sustain themselves on the blood of their horses, opening a vein and letting the blood jet into their mouths, drinking till they have had enough, and then staunching it. . . .

When they come to an engagement with the enemy, they will gain the victory in this fashion.

They never let themselves get into a regular medley, but keep perpetually riding round and shooting into the enemy. And as they do not count it any shame to run away in battle, they will sometimes pretend to do so, and in running away they turn in the saddle and shoot hard and strong at the foe, and in this way make great havoc. Their horses are trained so perfectly that they will double hither and thither, just like a dog, in a way that is quite astonishing. Thus they fight to as good purpose in running away as if they stood and faced the enemy because of the vast volleys of arrows that they shoot in this way, turning round upon their pursuers, who are fancying that they have won the battle. But when the Mongols see that they have killed and wounded a good many horses and men, they wheel round bodily and return to the charge in perfect order and with loud cries, and in a very short time the enemy are routed. In truth they are stout and valiant soldiers, and inured to war. And you perceive that it is just when the enemy sees them run, and imagines that he has gained the battle, that he has in reality lost it, for the Mongols wheel round in a moment when they judge the right time has come. And after this fashion they have won many a fight.

- *In what ways do the military practices described by Marco Polo reflect the influence of the steppe environment on the Mongols?*

SOURCE: Marco Polo. *The Book of Ser Marco Polo*, 3rd ed. Trans. and ed. by Henry Yule and Henri Cordier. London: John Murray, 1921, pp. 260–63. (Translation slightly modified.)

Khubilai Khan

The consolidation of Mongol rule in China came during the reign of Khubilai (sometimes spelled Qubilai), one of Chinggis Khan's grandsons. Khubilai was perhaps the most talented of the great conqueror's descendants. He unleashed ruthless attacks against his enemies, but he also took an interest in cultural matters and worked to improve the welfare of his subjects. He actively promoted Buddhism, and he provided support also for Daoists, Muslims, and Christians in his realm. The famous Venetian

---

Buddhism (BOO-diz'm)

Map 15.2 The Mongol empires in 1300 C.E. Notice how the territories of the empires extended from Europe in the west to China in the east. Why would the existence of such vast empires have facilitated trade and travel across Eurasia?

traveler Marco Polo, who lived almost two decades at Khubilai's court, praised him for his generosity toward the poor and his efforts to build roads. From 1264 until his death in 1294, Khubilai Khan presided over the Mongol empire at its height.

Khubilai extended Mongol rule to all of China. From his base at Khanbaliq, he relentlessly attacked the

Mongol Conquest of Southern China

Song dynasty in southern China. The Song capital at Hangzhou fell to Mongol forces in 1276, and within three years Khubilai had eliminated resistance throughout China. In 1279 he proclaimed himself emperor and established the Yuan dynasty, which ruled China until its collapse in 1368.

Beyond China, Khubilai had little success as a conqueror. During the 1270s and 1280s, he launched several unsuccessful invasions of Vietnam, Cambodia, and Burma as well as a failed naval expedition against Java involving 500 to 1,000 ships and twenty thousand troops. In 1274 and again in 1281, Khubilai also attempted seaborne invasions of Japan, but on both occasions typhoons thwarted his plans. The storm of 1281 was especially vicious: it destroyed about 4,500 Mongol vessels carrying more than one hundred

thousand armed troops—the largest seaborne expedition before World War II.

As Khubilai consolidated his hold on east Asia, his cousins and brothers tightened Mongol control on lands to the west. Mongols of the group known as the Golden Horde

The Golden Horde

overran Russia between 1237 and 1241 and then mounted exploratory expeditions into Poland, Hungary, and eastern Germany in 1241 and 1242. Mongols of the Golden Horde prized the steppes north of the Black Sea as prime pastureland for their horses, and they used them to maintain a large army. They did not occupy Russia, which they regarded as an unattractive land of forests, but they extracted tribute from the Russian cities and agricultural provinces. The Golden Horde maintained its hegemony in Russia until the mid–fifteenth century, when the princes of Moscow built a powerful Russian state. By the mid–sixteenth century Russian conquerors had extended their control to the steppes, but Mongol khans descended from the Golden Horde continued to rule the Crimea until the late eighteenth century.

While the Golden Horde established its authority in Russia, Khubilai's brother Hülegü toppled the Abbasid empire and established the Mongol ilkhanate in Persia. In 1258 he captured the Abbasid capital of

Yuan (yoo-AHN)

Baghdad after a brief siege. His troops looted the city, executed the caliph, and massacred more than two hundred thousand residents. From Persia, Hülegü's army ventured into Syria, but Muslim forces from Egypt soon expelled them and placed a limit on Mongol expansion to the southwest.

The Ilkhanate of Persia

When the Mongols crushed ruling regimes in large settled societies, they discovered that they needed to become governors as well as conquerors. The Mongols had no experience administering complex societies, where successful governance required talents beyond the equestrian and military skills esteemed on the steppes. They had a difficult time adjusting to their role as administrators, and in fact most of their conquests fell out of their hands within a century.

The Mongols adopted different tactics in the different lands they ruled. In Persia they made important concessions to local interests. Although Mongols and their allies occupied the highest administrative positions, they basically allowed the Persians to run the ilkhanate as long as they delivered tax receipts and maintained order.

Mongol Rule in Persia

Over time, the Mongols even assimilated to Persian cultural traditions. The early Mongol rulers of Persia mostly observed their native shamanism, but

they tolerated all religions—including Islam, Nestorian Christianity, Buddhism, and Judaism. Gradually, however, the Mongols gravitated toward Islam. In 1295 Ilkhan Ghazan publicly converted to Islam, and most of the Mongols in Persia followed his example. Ghazan's conversion sparked large-scale massacres of Christians and Jews, and it signaled the absorption of the Mongols into Muslim Persian society.

In China, in contrast, the Mongol overlords stood aloof from their subjects, whom they scorned as mere cultivators. They outlawed intermarriage between Mongols and Chinese and forbade the Chinese to learn the Mongol language. Some of the victors went so far as to suggest that the Mongols exterminate the Chinese people and convert China itself into pastureland for their horses. In the end, the Mongols decided simply to extract as much revenue as possible from their Chinese subjects. Unlike their counterparts in Persia, the Mongols in China did not make much use of native administrative talent. Instead, they brought foreign administrators—including Arabs, Persians, and even Europeans—into China and placed them in charge.

Mongol Rule in China

The Mongols also resisted assimilation to Chinese cultural traditions. They ended the privileges enjoyed by the Confucian scholars, and they dismantled the

Ilkhanate (EEL-kahn-ate)

shamanism (SHAH-mah-niz'm)

The siege of Baghdad: a Persian manuscript illustration depicts Mongol forces camped outside the city walls while residents huddle within.

Confucian educational and examination system, which had produced untold generations of civil servants for the Chinese bureaucracy. They did not persecute Confucians, but they allowed the Confucian tradition to wither in the absence of official support. Meanwhile, although the Mongols mostly continued to follow their native shamanist cults, they tolerated all cultural and religious traditions in China, including Confucianism, Daoism, Buddhism, and Christianity. Of Khubilai Khan's four wives, his favorite was Chabi, a Nestorian Christian.

The Mongols and Eurasian Integration

In building their vast empire, the Mongols brought tremendous destruction to lands throughout much of the Eurasian landmass. Yet they also sponsored interaction among peoples of different societies and linked Eurasian lands more directly than ever before. Indeed, Mongol rulers positively encouraged travel and communication over long distances. Recognizing the value of regular communications for their vast empire, Chinggis Khan and his successors maintained a courier network that rapidly relayed news, information, and government orders. The network included relay stations with fresh horses and riders so that messages could travel almost nonstop throughout Mongol territories. The Mongols' encouragement of travel and communication facilitated trade, diplomatic travel, missionary efforts, and movements of peoples to new lands.

The Mongols and Trade As a nomadic people dependent on commerce with settled agricultural societies, the Mongols worked to secure trade routes and ensure the safety of merchants passing through their territories. The Mongol khans frequently fought among themselves, but they maintained reasonably good order within their realms and allowed merchants to travel unmolested through their empires. As a result, long-distance travel and trade became much less risky than in earlier times. Merchants increased their commercial investments, and the volume of long-distance trade across central Asia dwarfed that of earlier eras. Lands as distant as China and western Europe became directly linked for the first time because of the ability of individuals to travel across the entire Eurasian landmass.

Diplomatic Missions Like trade, diplomatic communication was essential to the Mongols, and their protection of roads and travelers benefited ambassadors as well as merchants. Throughout the Mongol era the great khans in China, the ilkhans in Persia, and the other khans maintained close communications by means of diplomatic embassies. They also had diplomatic dealings with rulers in Korea, Vietnam, India, and western Europe, and in other lands as well. Some diplomatic travelers crossed the entire Eurasian landmass. Several European ambassadors traveled to Mongolia and China to deliver

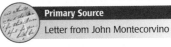

Primary Source
Letter from John Montecorvino

messages from authorities seeking to ally with the Mongols against Muslim states in southwest Asia. Diplomats also traveled west: Rabban Sauma, a Nestorian Christian monk born in Khanbaliq, visited Italy and France as a representative of the Persian ilkhan.

Missionary Efforts Like the silk roads in earlier times, Eurasian routes during the era of the Mongol empires served as highways for missionaries as well as merchants and diplomats. Sufi missionaries helped popularize Islam among Turkish peoples in central Asia, and Nestorian Christians found new opportunities to win converts when they went to China to serve as administrators for Mongol rulers. Roman Catholic Christians also mounted missionary campaigns in China. (See chapter 19 for further discussion of travel during the Mongol era.)

Resettlement Another Mongol policy that encouraged Eurasian integration was the practice of resettling peoples in new lands. As a nomadic people, the Mongols had limited numbers of skilled artisans and educated individuals, but the more their empire expanded, the more they needed the services of specialized crafts workers and literate administrators. Mongol overlords recruited the talent they needed largely from the ranks of their allies and the peoples they conquered, and they often moved people far from their homelands to sites where they could best make use of their services. Among the most important of the Mongols' allies were the Uighur Turks, who lived mostly in oasis cities along the silk roads. The Uighurs were literate and often highly educated, and they provided not only many of the clerks, secretaries, and administrators who ran the Mongol empires but also units of soldiers who bolstered Mongol garrisons.

Daoism (DOW-iz'm)

Uighurs (WEE-goors)

Arab and Persian Muslims were also prominent among those who administered the Mongols' affairs far from their homelands.

Conquered peoples also supplied the Mongols with talent. When they overcame a city, Mongol forces surveyed the captured population, separated out those with specialized skills, and sent them where there was demand for their services. After the 1230s the Mongols often took censuses of lands they conquered, partly to levy taxes and conscript military forces and partly to locate talented individuals. The Parisian goldsmith Guillaume Boucher was only one among thousands of foreign-born individuals who became permanent residents of the Mongol capital at Karakorum because of their special talents. Like their protection of trade and diplomacy, the Mongols' policy of resettling allies and conquered peoples promoted Eurasian integration by increasing communication and exchange between peoples of different societies.

Decline of the Mongols in Persia and China

Soon after the long and prosperous reign of Khubilai Khan, the Mongols encountered serious difficulties governing Persia and China. In Persia excessive spending strained the treasury, and overexploitation of the peasantry led to reduced revenues. When the ilkhan tried to resolve his financial difficulties by ordering the use of paper money in the 1290s, merchants refused to accept paper they regarded as worthless. Commerce ground to a halt until the ilkhan rescinded his order. Meanwhile, factional struggles plagued the Mongol leadership. When the last of the Mongol rulers died without an heir in 1335, the ilkhanate itself simply collapsed. Government in Persia devolved to local levels until late in the fourteenth century, when Turkish peoples reintroduced effective central government.

Collapse of the Ilkhanate

Mongol decline in China was a more complicated affair. As in Persia, it had an economic dimension. The Mongols continued to use the paper money that the Chinese had introduced during the Tang and Song dynasties, but they did not maintain adequate reserves of the bullion that backed up paper notes. The general population soon lost confidence in paper money, and its value plummeted. As in Persia, too, factions and infighting hastened Mongol decline in China. Beginning in the 1320s power struggles, im-

Decline of the Yuan Dynasty

perial assassinations, and civil war convulsed the Mongol regime in China.

Apart from financial difficulties and factional divisions, the Mongol rulers of China also faced an onslaught of epidemic disease. By facilitating trade and communications throughout Eurasia, the Mongols unwittingly expedited the spread of bubonic plague (discussed in chapter 19). During the 1330s plague erupted in southwestern China. From there it spread throughout China and central Asia, and by the late 1340s it had reached southwest Asia and Europe, where it became known as the Black Death. Bubonic plague sometimes killed half or more of an exposed population, particularly during the furious initial years of the epidemic, and it seriously disrupted economies and societies throughout much of Eurasia. In China depopulation and labor shortages that followed on the heels of epidemic plague weakened the Mongol regime.

Bubonic Plague

Because they treated their Chinese subjects as inferiors, the Mongols also faced a rebellious subject population in China. Beginning in the 1340s southern China became a hotbed of peasant rebellion and banditry, which the Mongols could not control. In 1368 rebel forces captured Khanbaliq, and the Mongols departed China en masse and returned to the steppes.

Despite the collapse of the Mongol regimes in Persia and China, Mongol states did not completely disappear. The khanate of Chaghatai continued to prevail in central Asia, and Mongols posed a threat to the northwestern borders of China until the eighteenth century. Meanwhile, the khanate of the Golden Horde continued to dominate the Caucasus and the steppe lands north of the Black Sea and Caspian Sea until the mid–sixteenth century, when a resurgent Russian state brought the Golden Horde down. Like Mongols in China, however, Mongols in Russia continued to threaten until the eighteenth century, and Mongols who had settled in the Crimean peninsula retained their identity until Josef Stalin forcibly moved them to other parts of the Soviet Union in the mid–twentieth century.

Surviving Mongol Khanates

AFTER THE MONGOLS

By no means did the decline of the Mongols signal the end of nomadic peoples' influence in Eurasia. As Mongol strength waned, Turkish peoples resumed the expansive campaigns that the Mongols had interrupted. During the late fourteenth and early fifteenth centuries, the Turkish conqueror Tamerlane built a central Asian empire rivaling that of Chinggis Khan himself. Although Tamerlane's empire foundered soon after his death, it deeply influenced three surviving Turkish Muslim states—the Mughal empire in India, the Safavid empire in Persia, and the Ottoman empire based in Anatolia—and embraced much of southwest Asia, southeastern Europe, and north Africa.

Tamerlane the Whirlwind

The Lame Conqueror The rapid collapse of the Mongol states left gaping power vacuums in China and Persia. While the native Ming dynasty filled the vacuum in China, a self-made Turkish conqueror named Timur moved on Persia. Because he walked with a limp, contemporaries referred to him as Timur-i lang—"Timur the Lame," an appellation that made its way into English as Tamerlane.

Born about 1336 near Samarkand, Tamerlane took Chinggis Khan as his model. Like Chinggis Khan,

---

Timur-i lang (tee-MOOR-yee LAHNG)

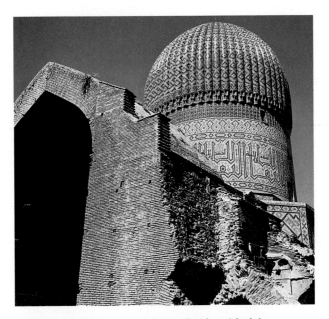

Spoils from Tamerlane's campaigns and raids enriched the conqueror's capital at Samarkand. They financed, among other buildings, the magnificent tomb where Tamerlane's remains still rest.

Tamerlane came from a family of the minor nobility and had to make his own way to power. Also like Chinggis Khan, he was a charismatic leader and a courageous warrior, and he attracted a band of loyal followers. During the 1360s

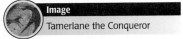
Image
Tamerlane the Conqueror

he eliminated rivals to power, either by persuading them to join him as allies or by defeating their armies on the battlefield, and he won recognition as leader of his own tribe. By 1370 he had extended his authority throughout the khanate of Chaghatai and had begun to build a magnificent imperial capital in Samarkand.

For the rest of his life, Tamerlane led his armies on campaigns of conquest. He turned first to the region between Persia and Afghanistan, and he took special care to establish his authority in the rich cities so that he could levy taxes on trade and agricultural production. Next he attacked the Golden Horde in the Caucasus region and Russia, and by the mid-1390s he had severely weakened it. During the last years of the century, he invaded India and subjected Delhi to a ferocious sack. Later Tamerlane campaigned along the Ganges, although he never attempted to incorporate India into his empire. He opened the new century with campaigns in southwest Asia and Anatolia. In 1404 he began preparations for an invasion of China, and he was leading his army east when he fell ill and died in 1405.

Like his model Chinggis Khan, Tamerlane was a conqueror, not a governor. He spent most of his adult life planning and fighting military campaigns. He did not create an imperial administration but, rather, ruled through tribal leaders who were his allies. He appointed overlords in the territories he conquered, but they relied on existing bureaucratic structures and simply received taxes and tributes on his behalf.

Tamerlane's Heirs Given its loose organization, it is not surprising that Tamerlane's empire experienced stresses and strains after the conqueror's death. Tamerlane's sons and grandsons engaged in a long series of bitter conflicts that resulted in the contraction of his empire and its division into four main regions. For a century after Tamerlane's death, however, they maintained control over the region from Persia to Afghanistan. When the last vestiges of Tamerlane's imperial creation disappeared, in the early sixteenth century, the Mughal, Safavid, and Ottoman empires that replaced it all clearly reflected the Turkish Muslim legacy of the lame conqueror.

Map 15.3 Tamerlane's empire about 1405 C.E. Note the overlap between Tamerlane's territories and those of the earlier ilkhanate of Persia in Map 15.2. What role did the cities in this area play in Tamerlane's ability to assert control over such a large area?

The Foundation of the Ottoman Empire

Chapter 25 will discuss the Mughal Empire in India and the Safavid Empire in Persia, both of which emerged during the early sixteenth century as Tamerlane's empire finally dissolved. The early stages of Ottoman expansion predated Tamerlane, however, and the foundation of the Ottoman empire throws additional light on the influence of nomadic peoples during the period 1000 to 1500 C.E.

After the Mongol conquest of Persia, large numbers of nomadic Turks migrated from central Asia to *Osman* the ilkhanate and beyond to the territories in Anatolia that the Saljuq Turks had seized from the Byzantine empire. There they followed charismatic leaders who organized further campaigns of conquest. Among those leaders was Osman, who during the late thirteenth and early fourteenth centuries carved a small state for himself in northwestern Anatolia. In 1299 Osman declared independence from the Saljuq sultan and launched a campaign to build a state at the expense of the Byzantine empire. After every successful operation Osman attracted more and more followers, who came to be known as Osmanlis or Ottomans.

During the 1350s the Ottomans gained a considerable advantage over their Turkish rivals when they established a foothold across the Dardanelles at Gallipoli on the Balkan peninsula. *Ottoman Conquests* The Ottomans quickly moved to expand the boundaries of their Balkan holdings. By the 1380s they had become by far the most powerful people in the Balkan peninsula, and by the end of the century they were poised to capture Constantinople and take over the Byzantine empire.

Tamerlane temporarily delayed Ottoman expansion in the Byzantine realm. In 1402 his forces crushed the Ottoman army, captured the sultan, and subjected the Ottoman state to the conqueror's authority. After Tamerlane's death, Ottoman leaders had to reestablish their rule in their own realm. Yet by the 1440s the Ottomans had recovered their balance and had begun again to expand in the Byzantine empire.

The campaign culminated in 1453 when Sultan Mehmed II, known as Mehmed the Conqueror, cap-

The Capture of Constantinople tured the Byzantine capital of Constantinople. After subjecting it to a sack, he made the city his own capital under the Turkish name of Istanbul. With Istanbul as a base, the Ottomans quickly absorbed the remainder of the Byzantine empire. By 1480 they controlled all of Greece and the Balkan region. They continued to ex-

pand throughout most of the sixteenth century as well, extending their rule to southwest Asia, southeastern Europe, Egypt, and north Africa. Once again, then, a nomadic people asserted control over a long-settled society and quickly built a vast empire.

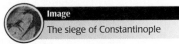
Image
The siege of Constantinople

SUMMARY

During the half millennium from 1000 to 1500 C.E., nomadic peoples of central Asia played a larger role than ever before in world history. As early as the second millennium B.C.E., they had periodically threatened states from China to the eastern Mediterranean region, and from classical times on they had traded regularly and actively with peoples of settled societies. From 1000 to 1500 their relations with neighboring peoples changed, as they dominated affairs in most of Eurasia through their conquests and their construction of vast transregional empires. Turkish peoples built the most durable of the nomadic empires, but the spectacular conquests of the Mongols most clearly demonstrated the potential of nomadic peoples to project their formidable military power to settled agricultural societies. By establishing connections that spanned the Eurasian landmass, the nomadic empires laid the foundation for increasing communication, exchange, and interaction among peoples of different societies and thereby fostered the integration of the eastern hemisphere. The age of nomadic empires, from 1000 to 1500 C.E., foreshadowed the integrated world of modern times.

CHRONOLOGY

1055	Tughril Beg named sultan
1071	Battle of Manzikert
1206–1227	Reign of Chinggis Khan
1211–1234	Mongol conquest of northern China
1219–1221	Mongol conquest of Persia
1237–1241	Mongol conquest of Russia
1258	Mongol capture of Baghdad
1264–1279	Mongol conquest of southern China
1264–1294	Reign of Khubilai Khan
1279–1368	Yuan dynasty
1295	Conversion of Ilkhan Ghazan to Islam
1336–1405	Life of Tamerlane
1453	Ottoman capture of Constantinople

FOR FURTHER READING

S. A. M. Adshead. *Central Asia in World History.* New York, 1993. A provocative essay on central Asia and its place in the larger world.

Thomas J. Barfield. *The Nomadic Alternative.* Englewood Cliffs, N.J., 1993. A sensitive study of nomadic societies in Africa and Eurasia by a leading anthropologist.

Charles J. Halperin. *Russia and the Golden Horde: The Mongol Impact on Medieval Russian History.* Bloomington, 1985. An insightful study of the Golden Horde and its influence on Russian society.

Halil Inalcik. *The Ottoman Empire: The Classical Age, 1300–1600.* Trans. by N. Itzkowitz and C. Imber. New York, 1973. The best short introduction to early Ottoman history.

Paul Kahn, ed. *The Secret History of the Mongols: The Origin of Chingis Khan.* Adapted from the translation of F. W. Cleaves. San Francisco, 1984. A translation of the Mongols' history of their own society, adapted for modern readers.

Adam T. Kessler. *Empires beyond the Great Wall: The Heritage of Genghis Khan.* Los Angeles, 1993. Well-illustrated survey of nomadic states in central Asia from the Xiongnu to the Mongols.

Beatrice Forbes Manz. *The Rise and Rule of Tamerlane.* Cambridge, 1989. Scholarly analysis of Tamerlane's career and his empire.

David Morgan. *Medieval Persia, 1040–1797.* London, 1988. A brief and insightful survey concentrating on the eras of Turkish and Mongol dominance in Persia.

———. *The Mongols.* Oxford, 1986. Lucid and witty study: the best short work on the Mongols.

Morris Rossabi. *Khubilai Khan: His Life and Times.* Berkeley, 1988. Excellent scholarly study of the greatest of the great khans.

CHAPTER 16

States and Societies of Sub-Saharan Africa

A remarkable oral tradition preserves the story of the lion prince Sundiata, thirteenth-century founder of the Mali empire in west Africa. Oral traditions include stories, histories, epics, and other accounts transmitted by professional singers and storytellers known in Africa as griots. Until scholars began to collect and publish African oral traditions in the middle of the twentieth century, the story of Sundiata was available only when a griot recited it.

According to the oral tradition, Sundiata's father ruled a small west African kingdom in the northeastern part of what is now Guinea. Despite his royal parentage, Sundiata had a difficult childhood, since a congenitally defective leg left him partially crippled. When the old king died, his enemies in-vaded the kingdom and killed the royal offspring, sparing Sundiata because they thought his physical condition would prevent him from posing a threat to their ambitions. But Sundiata overcame his injury, learned to use the bow and arrow, and strengthened himself by hunt-ing in the forest. As Sundiata grew stronger, his enemies began to fear him, and they forced him to seek refuge in a neighboring kingdom. While in exile, Sundiata distin-guished himself as a warrior and assembled a powerful cavalry force staffed by loyal followers and allies.

About 1235 Sundiata returned to his homeland and claimed the throne. His cavalry slashed through the countryside and de-feated his enemies. Within a few years he had overcome resistance, established the Mali empire, and

---

Sundiata (soon-JAH-tuh)
Mali (MAH-lee)

OPPOSITE PAGE: *A bronze plaque from the kingdom of Benin depicts a local chief flanked by warriors and attendants.*

consolidated his rule throughout the valley of the Niger River. Although he respected traditional religious beliefs and magical powers, Sundiata was a Muslim, and he welcomed Muslim merchants from north Africa into his realm. He built a capital city at Niani, which soon became a thriving commercial center. For two centuries after Sundiata's death about 1260, the lion prince's legacy shaped the lives of west African peoples and linked west Africa with north Africa and the Mediterranean basin.

From the classical era forward, peoples from east Asia to the Mediterranean basin established extensive networks of trade and communication. African peoples living south of the Sahara desert participated in the larger economy of the eastern hemisphere, though not as fully as their counterparts in north Africa. Geographic conditions help to explain why trade and communication networks did not embrace sub-Saharan Africa as readily as they did other regions: the Sahara desert poses a formidable challenge to overland travelers, the African coastlines offer few good natural harbors, and cataracts complicate travel up the continent's major rivers.

Nevertheless, like their Eurasian and north African counterparts, peoples of sub-Saharan Africa organized productive societies, built powerful states, and participated in large-scale networks of communication and exchange. Internal African processes drove much of this development. Between 1000 and 1500 C.E., in the wake of the Bantu and other migrations (discussed in chapter 2), population increases in sub-Saharan Africa led societies there to organize states, develop centers of economic specialization, and conduct interregional trade. Alongside these internal processes, relations with other peoples of the eastern hemisphere also profoundly influenced the development of African societies. From the early centuries C.E. to 1500 and later as well, trade with lands of the Mediterranean and the Indian Ocean basins encouraged African peoples to produce commodities desired by consumers throughout much of the eastern hemisphere. This trade promoted urban development, the organization of large states and empires, and the introduction of new food crops and new religious beliefs into sub-Saharan Africa.

EFFECTS OF EARLY AFRICAN MIGRATIONS

By 1000 C.E. Bantu-speaking peoples had settled in most parts of Africa south of the equator, and Kushite, Sudanese, Mande, and other peoples had also established communities in lands far from their original homes. For the next several centuries, African peoples built societies on the foundation of small communities that the Bantu and other migrations had generated.

Agriculture and Population Growth

The principal early result of the Bantu and other migrations was to spread agriculture and herding to almost all parts of Africa. As they established agricultural societies, cultivators and herders displaced or absorbed many of the hunting, gathering, and fishing peoples who previously inhabited sub-Saharan Africa. After about 500 B.C.E., most Bantu peoples possessed iron metallurgy, which enabled them to fashion iron tools that facilitated further clearing of lands and extension of agriculture. By the early centuries C.E., cultivation and herding had reached the southernmost parts of Africa. The expansion of agriculture, in turn, resulted in increased agricultural production, rising population, and pressure for continuing migration to new territories.

The introduction of bananas to Africa encouraged a fresh migratory surge. First domesticated in southeast Asia, bananas entered Africa by way of the Indian Ocean. Between about *Bananas* 300 and 500 C.E., Malay seafarers from the islands that make up modern Indonesia colonized the island of Madagascar and established banana cultivation there. From Madagascar, bananas easily made the jump to the east African mainland. By 500 C.E. several varieties of bananas had become well established in Africa.

Cultivation of bananas allowed the Bantu to expand into heavily forested regions where yams and millet did not grow well. Indeed, bananas increased the supply of available food, enriched the Bantu diet, and allowed sub-Saharan populations to expand more rapidly than before.

The population history of sub-Saharan Africa clearly reflects the significance of iron metallurgy and bananas. In 400 B.C.E., before iron working had deeply influenced the continent's *Population* societies, the population of sub-Saharan *Growth* Africa stood at about 3.5 million. By 800 C.E., after banana cultivation had spread throughout the continent, the sub-Saharan population had climbed to 17 million. And by 1000, when the Bantu migrations had introduced agriculture and iron metallurgy to most regions of sub-Saharan Africa, the population had passed 22 million.

African Political Organization

By 1000 C.E., the Bantu had approached the limits of their expansion. Because agricultural peoples already occupied most of the continent, migrating into new territories and forming new settlements was much more difficult than before. Instead of migrating in search of new lands to cultivate, then, African peoples developed increasingly complex forms of government that enabled them to organize their existing societies more efficiently.

Kin-Based Societies Most early Bantu societies did not depend on an elaborate hierarchy of officials or a bureaucratic apparatus to administer their affairs. Instead, Bantu peoples governed themselves mostly through family and kinship groups. Usually, Bantu peoples settled in villages with populations averaging about one hundred people. Male heads of families constituted a village's ruling council, which decided public affairs for the entire group. The most prominent of the family heads presided over the village as a chief and represented the settlement when it dealt with neighboring peoples. A group of villages constituted a district, which became the principal focus of loyalties. Usually, there was no chief or larger government for the district. Instead, village chiefs negotiated on matters concerning two or more villages. Meanwhile, within individual villages, family and kinship groups disciplined their own members as necessary.

Chiefdoms This type of organization lends itself particularly well to small-scale communities, but kin-based societies often grew to large proportions. After about 1000 C.E., kin-based societies faced difficult challenges as population growth strained resources. Conflicts between villages and districts became more frequent and more intense. Increased conflict encouraged Bantu communities to organize military forces for both offensive and defensive purposes, and military organization in turn encouraged the development of more formal structures of government.

Many districts fell under the leadership of powerful chiefs, who overrode kinship networks and imposed authority on their territories. Some of these chiefs conquered their neighbors and consolidated their lands into small kingdoms. These local kingdoms emerged in several regions of sub-Saharan Africa after about 1000 C.E. The kingdoms of Ife and Benin, for example, arose in the forested regions of west Africa. Both realms were city-states in which the court and urban residents controlled the surrounding countryside through family relationships and political alliances. Both Ife and Benin also produced magnificent

According to legend, this handsome terra-cotta head represents an ambitious warrior who usurped power in the small state of Ife (in modern Nigeria). Produced shortly after 1000 C.E., it testifies to the increasing tensions in sub-Saharan politics after the turn of the millennium.

sculptures that put human faces and figures to the early history of sub-Saharan Africa. Local kingdoms appeared also in southern Africa and central Africa.

Kingdom of Kongo One of the most active areas of political development was the basin of the Congo River (also known as the Zaire River). After about 1000 C.E. population pressures and military challenges encouraged kin-based societies in the Congo region to form small states embracing a few villages each. By 1200 conflict between these small states had resulted in the organization of larger, regional principalities that could better resist political and military pressures. One of the more prosperous of the Congolese states was the Kingdom of Kongo, which participated actively in trade networks involving copper, raffia cloth, and nzimbu shells from the Atlantic Ocean. During the fourteenth century the Kingdom of Kongo came to embrace much of the modern-day Republic of the Congo and Angola.

The central government of Kongo included the king and officials who oversaw military, judicial, and financial affairs (including a royal currency system based on cowry shells). Beneath the central government were six provinces administered by governors, each of whom supervised several districts administered by subordinate officials. Within the districts, villages ruled by chiefs provided local government. Though not the only kingdom in sub-Saharan Africa, Kongo was perhaps the most tightly centralized of the early Bantu kingdoms. The kingdom of Kongo provided effective organization from the fourteenth until the mid–seventeenth century, when Portuguese slave traders undermined the authority of the kings and the central government.

Kin-based societies did not disappear with the emergence of formal states. In fact, many survived well into the nineteenth century. Yet regional states and large kingdoms became increasingly prominent during the centuries after 1000 C.E. as Bantu and other African peoples responded to population pressures and military challenges facing their societies.

ISLAMIC KINGDOMS AND EMPIRES

While Bantu peoples organized societies on the basis of African traditions, merchants from north Africa and southwest Asia introduced their Islamic faith to sub-Saharan Africa. Islam arrived by two routes: it went to west Africa overland by trans-Saharan camel caravans, and it traveled to coastal east Africa over the sea lanes of the Indian Ocean in the vessels of merchant mariners. After the eighth century C.E., Islam profoundly influenced the political, social, and economic development of sub-Saharan Africa as well as its cultural and religious development.

Trans-Saharan Trade and Islamic States in West Africa

The Sahara desert has never served as an absolute barrier to communication between human societies. Small numbers of nomadic peoples have lived in the desert itself since about 5000 B.C.E. These nomads migrated around the desert and had dealings with other peoples settled on its fringes. In addition, merchants occasionally organized commercial expeditions across the desert even in ancient and classical times.

Yet travel across the Sahara quickened substantially with the arrival of the camel. Camels came to north

Africa from Arabia about the seventh century B.C.E. During the late centuries B.C.E., a special camel saddle, which took advantage of the animals' distinctive physical structure, also made its way to *Camels* north Africa. Because a caravan took seventy to ninety days to cross the Sahara and because camels could travel long distances before needing water, they proved to be extremely useful beasts of burden in such an arid region. After about 300 C.E. camels became the preferred transport animals throughout the Sahara.

When Arab conquerors established their Islamic faith in north Africa during the seventh and eighth centuries, they also integrated the region into a rapidly expanding zone of commerce and communication. Soon afterward, Muslims in north Africa began to explore the potential of trade across the Sahara. By the late eighth century, Islamic merchants had trekked across the desert and established commercial relations with societies in sub-Saharan west Africa. There they found a series of long-established trading centers such as Gao, a terminus of caravan routes across the Sahara that offered access to the Niger River valley, which was a flourishing market for copper, ironware, cotton textiles, salt, grains, and carnelian beads.

The principal state of west Africa at the time of the Muslims' arrival was the kingdom of Ghana (not related to the modern state of Ghana), situated between the Senegal and Niger *The Kingdom* rivers in a region straddling the border *of Ghana* between the modern states of Mali and Mauritania. Ghana emerged as a kingdom at an uncertain but early date: according to legends preserved by Arab travelers, as many as twenty-two kings ruled in Ghana before Muhammad and his companions embarked on the *hijra*. Ghana probably developed as a state during the fourth or fifth century C.E. when agricultural peoples sought to protect their societies from the raids of camel-riding nomads who increasingly came out of the Sahara. When Muslims arrived in west Africa, the kingdom of Ghana was a regional state much like others that were emerging elsewhere in sub-Saharan Africa.

As trade and traffic across the desert increased, Ghana underwent a dramatic transformation. It became the most important commercial site *Gold Trade* in west Africa because it was the center for trade in gold, which was in high demand throughout

Interactive Map
Kingdoms & empires of Africa

Ghana (GAH-nuh)

the eastern hemisphere. Muslim merchants flocked to camel caravans traveling across the Sahara to Ghana in search of gold for consumers in the Mediterranean basin and elsewhere in the Islamic world. Ghana itself did not produce gold, but the kings procured nuggets from lands to the south—probably from the region around the headwaters of the Niger, Gambia, and Senegal rivers, which enjoyed the world's largest supply of gold available at the time. By controlling and taxing trade in the precious metal, the kings both enriched and strengthened their realm. Apart from gold, merchants from Ghana provided ivory and slaves for traders from north Africa. In exchange, they received horses, cloth, small manufactured wares, and salt.

Integration into trans-Saharan trade networks brought enormous wealth and considerable power to Ghana. The kingdom's capital and prin-   *Koumbi-Saleh*
cipal trading site stood at Koumbi-Saleh, a small town today but a thriving commercial center with a population of some fifteen to twenty thousand people at its peak between the ninth and twelfth centuries. Al-Bakri, a Spanish Muslim traveler of the mid–eleventh century, described Koumbi-Saleh as a flourishing site with buildings of stone and more than a dozen mosques. From taxes levied on trade passing through Ghana, the kings financed a large army—al-Bakri reported that they could field two hundred thousand warriors—that protected the sources of gold, maintained order in the kingdom, kept allied and

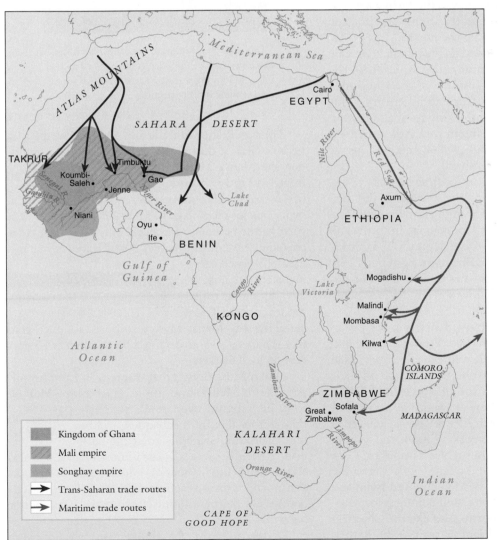

Map 16.1 Kingdoms, empires, and city-states of sub-Saharan Africa from **800 to 1500** C.E. Note both the trans-Saharan trade routes and the maritime trade routes that connected the Mediterranean region with west and east Africa. What role did these trade routes play in the creation of sub-Saharan cities and empires?

tributary states in line, and defended Ghana against no-madic incursions from the Sahara.

By about the tenth century, the kings of Ghana had converted to Islam. Their conversion led to improved relations with Muslim merchants from north Africa as well as Muslim nomads from the desert who transported trade goods across the Sahara. It also brought them recognition and support from Muslim states in north Africa. The kings of Ghana made no attempt to impose Islam forcibly on their society, nor did they accept Islam exclusively even for their own purposes. Instead, they continued to observe traditional religious customs: al-Bakri mentioned, for example, that native religious specialists practiced magic and kept idols in the woods surrounding the royal palace at Koumbi-Saleh. Even in the absence of efforts to impose Islam on Ghana, however, the faith attracted converts, particularly among those engaged in trade with Muslim merchants from the north.

Islam in West Africa

As the kingdom expanded to the north, it became vulnerable to attacks by nomadic peoples from the Sahara who sought to seize some of the kingdom's wealth. During the early thirteenth century, raids from the desert weakened the kingdom, and it soon collapsed. Political leadership in west Africa then fell to the powerful Mali empire, which emerged just as the kingdom of Ghana dissolved.

The lion prince Sundiata (reigned 1230–1255) built the Mali empire during the first half of the thirteenth century. Through alliances with local rulers, a reputation for courage in battle, and a large army dominated by cavalry, Sundiata had consolidated his hold on the Mali empire by about 1235. The empire embraced Ghana as well as other, neighboring kingdoms in the regions surrounding the Senegal and Niger rivers.

Sundiata

Mali benefited from trans-Saharan trade on an even larger scale than Ghana had. From the thirteenth until the late fifteenth century, Mali controlled and taxed almost all trade passing through west Africa. Enormous caravans with as many as twenty-five thousand camels linked Mali to north Africa. The capital city of Niani attracted merchants seeking gold, and market cities on the caravan routes such as Timbuktu, Gao, and Jenne grew crowded and wealthy. Like the earlier kings of Ghana, the rulers of Mali honored Islam and provided protection, lodging, and comforts for Muslim merchants from the north. Also like the Ghanaian kings, they did not force Islam on their realm. Rather, they encouraged its spread on a voluntary basis.

The Mali Empire and Trade

This terra-cotta sculpture from the thirteenth or fourteenth century depicts a helmeted and armored warrior astride a horse with elaborate harness and head protection.

The significance of trade and Islam for west Africa became clearest during the reign of Sundiata's grand-nephew Mansa Musa, who ruled Mali from 1312 to 1337, during the high point of the empire. Mansa Musa observed Islamic tradition by making his pilgrimage to Mecca in 1324–1325. His party formed a huge caravan that included thousands of soldiers, attendants, subjects, and slaves as well as a hundred camels carrying satchels of gold. In fact, during his three-month visit to Cairo along the way, Mansa Musa distributed so much gold that the metal's value declined by as much as 25 percent on local markets.

Mansa Musa

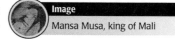
Mansa Musa, king of Mali

Mansa Musa drew great inspiration from his pilgrimage to Mecca, and upon returning to Mali he took his religion even more seriously than before. He built mosques, and he sent promising students to study with distinguished Islamic scholars in north Africa. He also established religious schools and brought in Arabian and north African teachers, including four descendants of Muhammad himself, to make Islam better known in Mali.

Mansa Musa and Islam

Within a century of Mansa Musa's reign, Mali was in serious decline: factions crippled the central

Sundiata and the Reconstruction of Niani

African griots tell many versions of an oral tradition dealing with Sundiata and his establishment of the Mali empire. Some dwell on Sundiata's cunning and clever strategy, others on his courage and physical valor. After recounting his birth, childhood, and campaign to conquer Mali, some oral traditions emphasize Sundiata's connections with his birthplace and capital city, Niani. The following selection deals with Sundiata's restoration of stability and prosperity and especially his services to Niani.

■ ■ ■

The troops were marching along singing the "Hymn to the Bow," which the crowd took up. New songs flew from mouth to mouth. Young women offered the soldiers cool water and cola nuts. And so the triumphal march across Mali ended outside Niani, Sundiata's city.

It was a ruined town which was beginning to be rebuilt by its inhabitants. A part of the ramparts had been destroyed and the charred walls still bore the marks of fire. From the top of the hill, Djata [a nickname for Sundiata] looked on Niani, which looked like a dead city. . . . The survivors of the catastrophe were standing in rows on the Mali road. The children were waving branches, a few young women were singing, but the adults were mute. . . .

With Sundiata peace and happiness entered Niani. Lovingly Sogolon's son [i.e., Sundiata] had his native city rebuilt. He restored in the ancient style his father's old enclosure where he had grown up. People came from all the villages of Mali to settle in Niani. The walls had to be destroyed to enlarge the town, and new quarters were built for each kin group in the enormous army. . . .

In their new-found peace the villages knew prosperity again, for with Sundiata happiness had come into everyone's home. Vast fields of millet, rice, cotton, indigo, and fonio surrounded the villages. Whoever worked always had something to live on. Each year long caravans carried the taxes in kind [in the form of grains] to Niani. You could go from village to village without fearing brigands. A thief would have his right hand chopped off and if he stole again he would be put to the sword [in accordance with Islamic law].

New villages and new towns sprang up in Mali and elsewhere. "Dyulas," or traders, became numerous and during the reign of Sundiata the world knew happiness.

There are some kings who are powerful through their military strength. Everybody trembles before them, but when they die nothing but ill is spoken of them. Others do neither good nor ill and when they die they are forgotten. Others are feared because they have power, but they know how to use it and they are loved because they love justice. Sundiata belonged to this group. He was feared, but loved as well. He was the father of Mali and gave the world peace. After him the world has not seen a greater conqueror, for he was the seventh and last conqueror. He had made the capital of an empire out of his father's village, and Niani became the navel of the earth. In the most distant lands Niani was talked of and foreigners said, "Travellers from Mali can tell lies with impunity," for Mali was a remote country for many peoples.

The griots, fine talkers that they were, used to boast of Niani and Mali saying: "If you want salt, go to Niani, for Niani is the camping place of the [trans-Saharan] caravans. If you want gold, go to Niani, for Bouré, Bambougou, and Wagadou [sources of west African gold] work for Niani. If you want fine cloth, go to Niani, for the Mecca road passed by Niani. If you want fish, go to Niani, for it is there that the fishermen of Maouti and Djenné come to sell their catches. If you want meat, go to Niani, the country of the great hunters, and the land of the ox and the sheep. If you want to see an army, go to Niani, for it [is] there that the united forces of Mali are to be found. If you want to see a great king, go to Niani, for it is there that the son of Sogolon lives, the man with two names."

- *To what extent was Sundiata's support for Islam an issue in the shaping of his reputation?*

SOURCE: D. T. Niane, ed. *Sundiata: An Epic of Old Mali.* Trans. by G. D. Pickett. Harlow, England: Longman, 1965, pp. 80–82.

Mansa Musa enjoyed a widespread reputation as the wealthiest king in the world. On this map, prepared in 1375 by a cartographer from the Mediterranean island of Majorca, Mansa Musa holds a gold nugget about the size of a grapefruit.

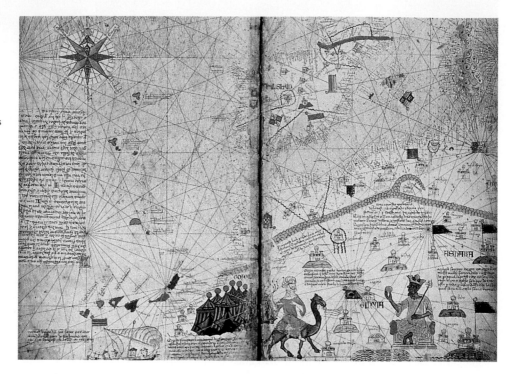

government, provinces seceded from the empire, and military pressures came both from neighboring kingdoms and from desert nomads. By the late fifteenth century, the Songhay empire had completely overcome Mali. Yet Mansa Musa and other Mali rulers had established a tradition of centralized government that the Songhay realm itself would continue, and they had ensured that Islam would have a prominent place in west African society over the long term.

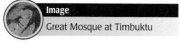

Image
Great Mosque at Timbuktu

The Indian Ocean Trade and Islamic States in East Africa

While trans-Saharan caravan traffic linked west Africa to the larger trading world of the eastern hemisphere, merchant mariners sailing the sea lanes of the Indian Ocean performed a similar service for Swahili societies in coastal east Africa. *Swahili* is an Arabic term meaning "coasters," referring to those who engaged in trade along the east African coast. Swahili society developed as a result of Bantu migrations to east Africa in the early centuries C.E. These migrants introduced

agriculture, cattle herding, and iron metallurgy to the region, and here, as elsewhere in sub-Saharan Africa, they founded complex societies governed by small, local states. As their population increased, Bantu peoples founded settlements on the coasts and offshore islands as well as the interior regions of east Africa. These coast dwellers supplemented their agricultural production with ocean fishing and maritime trade.

The Swahili dominated the east African coast from Mogadishu in the north to Kilwa, the Comoro Islands, and Sofala in the south. They spoke a Bantu language, also known as *The Swahili* Swahili, supplemented with words and ideas borrowed from Arabic. Swahili peoples developed different dialects, but they communicated readily among themselves because individuals frequently visited other Swahili communities in their oceangoing craft. Indeed, all along the east African coast, Swahili society underwent similar patterns of development with respect to language, religion, architecture, and technology.

In the tenth century, Swahili society attracted increasing attention from Islamic merchants. From the interior regions of east Africa, the Swahili obtained gold, slaves, ivory, and exotic local products, which they traded for pottery, glass, and textiles that Muslim merchants brought from Persia, India, and China.

Swahili (swah-HEE-lee)

The Swahili City-States

By the eleventh and twelfth centuries, trade had brought important changes to coastal east Africa, just as it had done in west Africa. By controlling and taxing trade within their jurisdictions, local chiefs grew wealthy, strengthened their own authority, and increased the influence of their communities. Gradually, trade concentrated at several coastal and island port cities that enjoyed especially convenient locations: Mogadishu, Lamu, Malindi, Mombasa, Zanzibar, Kilwa, Mozambique, and Sofala. Each of these sites developed into a powerful city-state governed by a king who supervised trade and organized public life in the region.

The cities themselves underwent an impressive transformation. Whereas most buildings were traditionally made of wood and dried mud, by about the twelfth century Swahili peoples began to construct large coral buildings, and by the fifteenth century the main Swahili towns boasted handsome stone mosques and public buildings. Meanwhile, urban Swahili elites dressed in silk and fine cotton clothes, and they set their tables with porcelain imported from China.

Kilwa

Travelers' reports and recent archaeological discoveries have thrown especially clear light on the development of Kilwa, one of the busiest city-states on the east African coast. With a population of about twelve thousand, Kilwa was a thriving city with many stone buildings and mosques. Residents imported cotton and silk textiles as well as perfumes and pearls from India, and archaeologists have

This fine piece of Chinese porcelain, probably produced in the fifteenth century, found its way into a Swahili tomb in modern Dar es Salaam, Tanzania.

unearthed a staggering amount of Chinese porcelain. Merchants of Kilwa imported these products in exchange for gold, slaves, and ivory obtained from interior regions. By the late fifteenth century, Kilwa exported about a ton of gold per year.

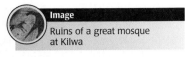

Ruins of a great mosque at Kilwa

Zimbabwe

The influence of long-distance trade also had important effects on the interior regions of east Africa. Indeed, trade and the wealth that it brought underwrote the establishment of large and powerful kingdoms in east and central Africa. The best known of these kingdoms was Zimbabwe. The term *zimbabwe* refers simply to the dwelling of a chief. About the early thirteenth century, interior peoples built a magnificent stone complex known as Great Zimbabwe near Nyanda in the modern state of Zimbabwe. Within stone walls 5 meters (16 feet) thick and 10 meters (32 feet) tall, Great Zimbabwe was a city of stone towers, palaces, and public buildings that served as the capital of a large kingdom. At the time of its greatest extent in the late fifteenth century, up to eighteen thousand people may have lived in the vicinity of Great Zimbabwe, and the kingdom stretched from the outskirts of the Swahili city of Sofala deep into the interior of south-central Africa.

Distant view of Great Zimbabwe

Kings residing at Great Zimbabwe controlled and taxed the trade between the interior and coastal regions. They organized the flow of gold, ivory, slaves, and local products from sources of supply to the coast. Their control over these products enabled them to forge alliances with local leaders and to profit handsomely from commercial transactions. Just as the trans-Saharan trade encouraged the building of states and empires in west Africa, the Indian Ocean trade generated wealth that financed the organization of city-states on the coast and large kingdoms in the interior regions of east and central Africa.

Islam in East Africa

In east Africa, as in west Africa, trade brought cultural as well as political changes. Like their counterparts in west Africa, the ruling elites and the wealthy merchants of east Africa converted to the Islamic faith. They did not necessarily give up their religious and cultural traditions but, rather, continued to observe them for

Zimbabwe (zihm-BAHB-way)

purposes of providing cultural leadership in their societies. By adopting Islam, however, they laid a cultural foundation for close cooperation with Muslim merchants. Moreover, Islam served as a fresh source of legitimacy for their rule, since they gained recognition from Islamic states in southwest Asia, and their conversion opened the door to political alliances with Muslim rulers in other lands. Even though the conversion of elite classes did not bring about the immediate spread of Islam throughout their societies, it enabled Islam to establish a presence in east Africa under the sponsorship of influential patrons. The faith eventually attracted interest in larger circles and became one of the principal cultural and religious traditions of east Africa.

AFRICAN SOCIETY AND CULTURAL DEVELOPMENT

By the eleventh century C.E., Africa was a land of enormous diversity. The peoples of sub-Saharan Africa spoke some eight hundred languages, and the continent supported a wide variety of societies and economies: mobile bands of hunting and gathering peoples, fishing peoples who lived alongside the continent's lakes and coasts, nomadic herders, subsistence farmers who migrated periodically to fresh lands, settled cultivators, and city-based societies that drew their livelihoods from mining, manufacturing, and trade. Although that diversity makes it difficult to speak of African society and cultural development in general terms, certain social forms and cultural patterns appeared widely throughout sub-Saharan Africa.

Social Classes

In kingdoms, empires, and city-states, such as Kongo, Mali, and Kilwa, respectively, African peoples developed complex societies with clearly defined classes: ruling elites, military nobles, administrative officials, religious authorities, merchants, artisans, peasants, and slaves. These societies more or less resembled those found in other settled, agricultural lands of Eurasia organized by powerful states.

In the small states and kin-based societies of sub-Saharan Africa, however, social structures were different. Small states often generated an aristocratic or ruling elite, and they always recognized a class of religious authorities. Yet in general, kinship, sex and gender expectations, and age groupings were the principal considerations that determined social position in such societies.

Extended families and clans served as the main foundation of social and economic organization in small-scale agricultural societies. The institution of privately owned property, found in most societies in north Africa and Eurasia, did not exist in sub-Saharan Africa. Instead, communities claimed rights to land and used it in common. The villages of sub-Saharan Africa, where most of the population lived, generally consisted of several extended family groups. Male heads of families jointly governed the village and organized the work of their own groups. They allocated portions of the communal lands for their relatives to cultivate and were responsible for distributing harvests equitably among all members of their groups.

Kinship Groups

Sex and gender relations also influenced the roles and occupations of individuals in society. Workers with special skills were mostly men. Leather tanning, for example, was the work of men who carefully guarded knowledge of their techniques and passed them down to their heirs. Iron working, which was highly prestigious, was also the work of men. Blacksmiths often served as community leaders, and like leather tanners, they passed knowledge of their craft down to their heirs. Men usually undertook the heavy labor of clearing land and preparing it for cultivation, although both men and women participated in the planting and harvesting of crops. Women's roles also included tending to domestic chores and taking primary responsibility for child rearing.

Sex and Gender Relations

As in other societies, men largely monopolized public authority. Yet women in sub-Saharan Africa generally had more opportunities open to them than did their counterparts in other lands. Women enjoyed high honor as the sources of life. On at least a few occasions, women made their ways to positions of power, and aristocratic women often influenced public affairs. Women merchants commonly traded at markets, and they participated actively in both local and long-distance trade in Africa. Sometimes women even engaged in combat and organized all-female military units.

Women's Roles

The arrival of Islam did not change the status of women in sub-Saharan Africa as dramatically as it did in Arabia and southwest Asia. South of the Sahara, early converts to Islam came mostly from the ranks of the ruling elites and the merchant classes. Because it did not become a popular faith for several centuries after its introduction, Islam did not deeply influence the customs of most Africans. Even at royal courts where Islam attracted eager converts, Muslims of sub-Saharan Africa simply did not honor the same social codes as their counterparts elsewhere. For the most part, Muslim women in sub-Saharan Africa socialized freely with men outside their immediate families, and they continued to appear and work openly in society. Thus Islam did relatively little to curtail the opportunities available to women or to compromise their status in sub-Saharan Africa.

Apart from kinship and expectations based on sex and gender roles, African society also made a place for *Age Grades* age groups that included all individuals within a given community born within a few years of one another. Members of age grades performed tasks appropriate for their levels of development, and they often bonded with one another to form tight circles of friends and political allies. Members of an age grade might provide labor for community projects, for example, or take joint responsibility for looking after village elders. They aided members who experienced adversities and helped one another at crucial junctures, such as marriage and the building of a new household. Thus age grades had the effect of establishing social ties that crossed the lines of family and kinship.

One class of individuals stood apart from the other social groups: slaves. As in other lands, the institution *Slavery* of slavery had had a place in Africa since antiquity. Most slaves were captives of war. Others came from the ranks of debtors, suspected witches, and criminals. Within Africa most slaves probably worked as agricultural laborers, although many also worked as construction laborers, miners, or porters. Slaves were an important form of personal wealth in sub-Saharan Africa. In the absence of private property, sub-Saharans could not become wealthy through the accumulation of landholdings. Instead, the accumulation of slaves enabled individuals or families to display their wealth, to enhance their positions in society, and also to increase their agricultural production. For those reasons, slave trading and slave holding were prominent features of sub-Saharan African society.

After about the ninth century C.E., the expansion of the trans-Saharan and Indian Ocean trade networks stimulated increased traffic in *Slave Trading* works stimulated increased traffic in African slaves. In previous centuries, eastern Europeans had been the main source of slaves in the trading networks of Muslim merchants. Yet the demand for slaves became greater than eastern Europe could supply. As a result, Muslim merchants turned increasingly to sub-Saharan Africa as an alternative source for slaves.

In response to that demand, slave raiding became an increasingly prominent activity within Africa itself. Rulers of large-scale states and empires began to make war on smaller, weaker states and kin-based societies in search of captives. In some years, ten to twenty thousand Africans left their homes as slaves. Indeed, although smaller than the Atlantic slave trade of modern times, the Islamic slave trade was a sizable affair: between 750 and 1500 C.E. the number of African slaves transported to foreign lands may have exceeded ten million. The high demand led to the creation of networks within Africa that supplied slaves and served as a foundation for the Atlantic slave trade in later centuries. Although records of the Islamic slave trade are scarce, a lengthy uprising known as the *Zanj* revolt allows a glimpse of the harsh conditions under which many of these slaves toiled. The term *Zanj* referred to black slaves from the Swahili coast, many of whom worked on sugarcane plantations or cleared land for cultivation in southern Mesopotamia by the seventh century C.E. Slave revolts were not uncommon, and about 869 a rebel slave named Ali bin Muhammad organized about fifteen thousand Zanj slaves into a massive force that captured Basra, the most important city of southern Mesopotamia. The rebels then proceeded to establish a state in the region, which was only defeated by the Abbasid rulers fourteen years later.

African Religion

Peoples of sub-Saharan Africa developed a wide range of languages, societies, and cultural traditions. Religious beliefs and practices in particular took many forms. The continent's peoples referred to their deities by different names, told different stories about them, and honored them with different rituals. Yet certain features were common to many religions of sub-Saharan Africa. In combination, these features offer considerable insight into the cultural and religious climate of sub-Saharan Africa in premodern times.

Many African peoples had held monotheistic beliefs from the early days of Sudanic agriculture. Although those beliefs were not static over time, many peoples recognized a single *Creator God* divine force or male god as the agent responsible for setting the world in motion and providing it with order. Some peoples believed that this god also sustained the world, intervening indirectly, through spirits, to influence the course of human affairs. Some considered this deity to be all-powerful, others regarded him as all-knowing, and many considered him both omnipotent and omniscient.

Apart from the superior creator god, Africans recognized many lesser gods and spirits often associated with the elements and with natural features. *Lesser Gods and Spirits* Unlike the creator god, these lesser deities participated actively in the workings of the world. They could confer or withhold benefits and bring favor or injury to humans. Similarly, most Africans believed that the souls of departed ancestors had the power to intervene in the lives of their descendants: the departed could bring good fortune to descendants who behaved properly and honored their ancestors, and they could also bring misfortune as punishment for evil behavior and neglect of their ancestors' memory. Much of the ritual of African religions focused on honoring deities, spirits, or ancestors' souls to win their favor or regain their goodwill. The rituals included prayers, animal sacrifices, and ceremonies marking important stages of life—such as birth, circumcision, marriage, and death.

Like other peoples of the world, Africans recognized classes of religious specialists—individuals who had the power to mediate between humanity and supernatural beings. *Diviners* Often referred to as diviners, they were intelligent people, usually men though sometimes women, who understood clearly the networks of political, social, economic, and psychological relationships within their communities. When afflicted by illness, sterility, crop failure, or some other disaster, individuals or groups consulted diviners to learn the cause of their misfortune. Diviners then consulted oracles, identified the causes of the trouble, and prescribed medicine, rituals, or sacrifices designed to eliminate the problem and bring about a return to normality.

For the most part, African religion concerned itself not with matters of theology but, rather, with the more practical business of explaining, predicting, and controlling the experiences of individuals and groups in the world. Thus African religion strongly emphasized morality and proper behavior as essential to the maintenance of an orderly world. Failure to observe high moral standards would displease deities, spirits, and departed ancestors and ensure that misfortune befell the negligent parties. Because proper moral behavior was so important to their fortunes, family and kinship groups took responsibility for policing their

Entrancing and enthralling masks like this one from Congo were essential to the proper observance of religious rituals, which often involved communicating with natural or animal spirits. Masks transformed diviners and provided them with powers not accessible to normal humans.

members and disciplining those who fell short of expected standards.

The Arrival of Christianity and Islam

Alongside religions that concentrated on the practical matter of maintaining an orderly world, two religions of salvation won converts in sub-Saharan Africa—Christianity and Islam. Both arrived in Africa as foreign faiths introduced by foreign peoples, but in time the sub-Saharan adherents adapted both faiths to the needs and interests of their societies.

Christianity reached Egypt and north Africa during the first century C.E., soon after the faith's appearance. Alexandria in Egypt became one of the most prominent centers of early Christian thought, and *Early Christianity in North Africa* north Africa was the home of St. Augustine, an important leader of the fledgling church.

About the middle of the fourth century C.E., Christianity established a foothold in the kingdom of Axum, located in the highlands of modern Ethiopia. The first Axumite converts were probably local merchants who traded with Mediterranean Christians calling at the port of Adulis on the Red Sea. As missionaries visited Ethiopia, the kings of Axum also

The Christian Kingdom of Axum

converted to Christianity. Indeed, the kings of Axum were some of the first royal converts to Christianity, adopting the faith shortly after the Roman emperor Constantine himself. Missionaries later established monasteries, translated the Bible into the Ethiopian language, and worked to popularize Christianity throughout the kingdom.

The fortunes of Christianity in Ethiopia reflected the larger political experience of the region. In the late seventh century C.E., the ruling house of Axum fell into decline, and during the next several centuries the expansion of Islam left an isolated island of Christianity in the Ethiopian highlands. During the twelfth century, however, a new ruling dynasty undertook a centralizing campaign and enthusiastically promoted Christianity as a faith that could provide cultural unity for the land. From the twelfth through the sixteenth century, Christianity enjoyed particular favor in Ethiopia. During the twelfth century, the Ethiopian kings ordered the carving of eleven massive churches out of solid rock—a monumental work of construction that required enormous resources. During the thirteenth century, rulers of Ethiopia's Solomonic dynasty claimed descent from the Israelite kings David and Solomon in an effort to lend additional biblical luster to their authority. The fictional work *Kebra Negast (The Glory of Kings),* which undertook to trace that lineage, has recently become popular among Rastafarians and devotees of reggae music in Ethiopia, Jamaica, and other lands. Meanwhile, Christianity retained its privileged status in Ethiopia until it fell out of favor following the socialist revolution of 1974.

During the centuries after the Islamic conquests of Egypt, the Sudan, and northern Africa, Ethiopian Christians had little contact with Christians

Ethiopian Christianity

in other lands. As a result, although Ethiopian Christianity retained basic Christian theology and rituals, it increasingly reflected the interests of its African devotees. Ethiopian Christians believed that a large host of evil spirits populated the world, for example, and carried amulets or charms for protection against these menacing spirits. The twelfth-century carved-rock churches themselves harked back to pre-Christian values, since rock shrines had long been a prominent feature in Ethiopian religion. Not until the sixteenth century, when Portuguese mariners began to visit Ethiopia en route to India, did Ethiopians reestablish relations with Christians from other

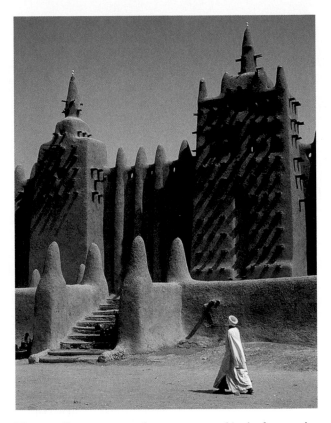

The magnificent mosque at Jenne, constructed in the fourteenth century, served as a principal center of Islamic education and scholarship in the Mali empire.

lands. By that time the Portuguese had introduced their Roman Catholic faith to the kingdom of Kongo, and Christianity began to win a place for itself elsewhere in sub-Saharan Africa.

Meanwhile, Islam appealed strongly to ruling elites and merchants in sub-Saharan west Africa and coastal east Africa because it served as a cultural foundation for their business relationships with Muslim merchants from north Africa and southwest Asia. Nonetheless, African ruling elites and merchants did not convert to Islam purely for mercenary reasons. On the contrary, the converts often took their new faith seriously. They built mosques, founded religious schools, invited experts in Islamic law into their lands, and displayed real enthusiasm for their adopted faith. Mansa Musa's pilgrimage to Mecca and his support of Islam in Mali represented a devotion to Islam shared by untold numbers of sub-Saharan Muslims.

Like Christianity, Islam in sub-Saharan Africa reflected the interests of local converts. Thus as in India, southeast Asia, and other lands, Islam in sub-Saharan

Africa made a place for the inherited traditions and beliefs of sub-Saharan Muslims. Africans who converted

African Islam   to Islam continued to take protective measures against the workings of evil spirits and witches, for example, and to participate in rituals designed to please nature deities and the spirits of departed ancestors.

Islam also had to accommodate African notions of proper relations between the sexes. When Ibn Bat-

Islam and African Society   tuta visited Mali in the mid–fourteenth century, he took deep offense at casual conversations that women had with men other than their husbands, and he became especially incensed when he observed women going about in public dressed only in loincloths. Yet African

Muslim hosts paid no heed to his railings and the lectures he delivered about the proper behavior and dress of women in Islamic society.

Indeed, during the early centuries after its introduction to the region, Islam supplemented rather than replaced the traditional religions of sub-Saharan Africa. West African merchants sometimes adopted Islam when they engaged actively in trade but returned to their inherited traditions when they turned from mercantile to other pursuits. And ruling elites routinely continued to honor inherited religious traditions, which provided powerful sanctions for their rule, long after adopting Islam for the various advantages it made available to them.

SUMMARY

States and societies of sub-Saharan Africa differed considerably from those in other parts of the eastern hemisphere. The foundations of most sub-Saharan societies were the agricultural economy and iron-working skills that Bantu and other peoples spread throughout most of the African continent. As these peoples migrated to new regions and established new communities, they usually based their societies on kin groups rather than the state structures that predominated elsewhere in the eastern hemisphere. When different societies came into conflict with one another, however, they increasingly established formal political authorities to guide their affairs. African peoples organized states of various sizes, some very small and others quite large. When they entered into commercial relationships with Muslim peoples in southwest Asia and north Africa, they also built formidable imperial states in west Africa and bustling city-states in coastal east Africa. These states had far-reaching implications for sub-Saharan societies because they depended on a regular and reliable flow of trade goods—particularly gold, ivory, and slaves—and they encouraged African peoples to organize themselves politically and economically to satisfy the demands of foreign Muslim merchants. Trade also had cultural implications because it facilitated the introduction of Islam, which together with native African traditions profoundly influenced the development of sub-Saharan societies. After the eighth century, ruling elites in both west Africa and coastal east Africa mostly accepted Islam and strengthened its position in their societies by building mosques, consulting Muslim advisors, and supporting Islamic schools. By 1500 C.E. African traditions and Islamic influences had combined to fashion a series of powerful, productive, and distinctive societies in sub-Saharan Africa.

CHRONOLOGY

4TH CENTURY C.E.	Introduction of bananas to Africa
11TH TO 13TH CENTURY	Kingdom of Ghana
11TH TO 15TH CENTURY	Swahili cities
12TH TO 15TH CENTURY	Kingdom of Great Zimbabwe
12TH TO 16TH CENTURY	Christian kingdom of Axum
13TH TO 15TH CENTURY	Mali empire
1230–1255	Reign of Sundiata
14TH TO 17TH CENTURY	Kingdom of Kongo
1312–1337	Reign of Mansa Musa
1324–1325	Mansa Musa's pilgrimage to Mecca

FOR FURTHER READING

Ibn Battuta. *Ibn Battuta in Black Africa*. Ed. and trans. by Said Hamdun and Noel King. Princeton, 1998. Translations of travel accounts of visits to coastal east Africa and the empire of Mali by a famous fourteenth-century Moroccan traveler.

Paul Bohannan and Philip D. Curtin. *Africa and Africans*. 3rd ed. Prospect Heights, Ill., 1988. Exploration of themes in African history, society, and culture by an anthropologist and a historian.

Christopher Ehret. *The Civilizations of Africa: A History to 1800*. Charlottesville, Va., 2002. An important contribution that views Africa in the context of world history.

J. F. P. Hopkins and N. Levtzion, eds. *Corpus of Early Arabic Sources for West African History*. Princeton, 2000. Translations of numerous important accounts by Muslim merchants and geographers who reported on conditions in west Africa before modern times.

Ali A. Mazrui. *The Africans: A Triple Heritage*. Boston, 1986. Emphasizes the legacies of indigenous, Islamic, and western influences on African history.

John S. Mbiti. *African Religions and Philosophy*. 2nd ed. London, 1990. A thorough and systematic study of traditional African religions in their cultural context.

Roderick James McIntosh. *The Peoples of the Middle Niger: The Island of Gold*. Oxford, 1998. Fascinating volume emphasizing the environmental context of west African history.

John Middleton. *The World of the Swahili: An African Mercantile Civilization*. New Haven, 1992. Rich scholarly analysis that places modern Swahili society and culture in its historical context.

D. T. Niane, ed. *Sundiata: An Epic of Old Mali*. Trans. by G. D. Pickett. London, 1965. Translation of the story of Sundiata, founder of the Mali empire, as preserved in African oral tradition.

Jan Vansina. *Paths in the Rainforests: Toward a History of Political Tradition in Equatorial Africa*. Madison, 1990. A brilliant synthesis of early African history by one of the world's foremost historians of Africa.

CHAPTER 17

Western Europe during the High Middle Ages

In 1260 C.E. two brothers, Niccolò and Maffeo Polo, traveled from their native Venice to Constantinople. The Polo brothers were jewel merchants, and while in Constantinople, they decided to pursue opportunities farther east. They went first to trading cities on the Black Sea and the Volga River and then spent three years in the great central Asian trading city of Bokhara. While in Bokhara, they received an invitation to join a diplomatic embassy going to the court of Khubilai Khan. They readily agreed and traveled by caravan to the Mongol court, where the great khan received them and inquired about their land, rulers, and religion.

Khubilai was especially interested in learning more about Roman Catholic Christianity. Thus he asked the Polo brothers to return to Europe and request the pope to send learned theologians

who could serve as authoritative sources of information on Christian doctrine. They accepted the mission and returned to Italy in 1269 as envoys of the great khan.

The Polo brothers were not able to satisfy the great khan's desire for expertise in Christian doctrine. The pope designated two missionaries to accompany the Polos, and the party set out in 1271, together with Niccolò's seventeen-year-old son, Marco Polo. Soon, however, the missionaries became alarmed at fighting along the route, and they decided to abandon the embassy and return to Europe. Only the Polos completed the journey, arriving at the Mongol court of Shangdu in 1274. Although they presented Khubilai with presents and letters from the pope rather than the requested missionaries, the great khan received them warmly. In fact, they remained in China in

OPPOSITE PAGE: *A street scene of fabric and furniture merchants.*

the service of the great khan for the next seventeen years. Their mission gave rise to Marco Polo's cele-

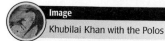
Khubilai Khan with the Polos

brated account of his travels, and it signaled the reintegration of Europe into the political and economic affairs of the larger eastern hemisphere.

During the early middle ages—from about 500 to 1000 C.E.—western Europe was a violent and disorderly land. The collapse of the western Roman empire and invasions by migratory peoples wrecked European society and the economy. The Germanic Carolingian empire—ruled most famously by Charlemagne—provided order in much of Europe only for a short time before a new series of invasions brought it down in 843 C.E. As a result of the turmoil and disarray that plagued Europe during the half millennium from 500 to 1000 C.E., western Europeans played little role in the development of a hemispheric economy during the era dominated by the Tang, Song, Abbasid, and Byzantine empires.

However, Europeans did begin to lay the foundations of a more dynamic society in the early middle ages. For example, regional states began to provide a stable political order. New tools and technologies led to increased agricultural production and economic growth. In addition, the western Christian church brought cultural and religious unity to most of Europe. Based on such political, economic, and cultural foundations, Europeans were able to build a vibrant and powerful society from about 1000 to 1300 C.E.—the period known in Europe as the "high middle ages."

Although the idea of empire continued to fascinate European leaders, no one managed to bring all of Europe under their control during the high middle ages. Instead, local rulers organized powerful regional states. Increased agricultural production fueled rapid population growth. Economic expansion led to increased long-distance trade, enriched cities, and helped to create new towns. Cultural and religious affairs also reflected a new dynamism, as European philosophers and theologians reconsidered traditional doctrines in light of fresh knowledge.

Political organization, demographic increase, and economic growth pushed Europeans once again into the larger world. European merchants began to participate directly in the commercial economy of the eastern hemisphere, sometimes traveling as far as China in search of luxury goods. Ambitious military and political leaders expanded the boundaries of Christendom by seizing Muslim-held territories in Spain and the Mediterranean islands. European forces even mounted a series of military crusades that sought to recapture Palestine and the city of Jerusalem from Muslim control. Those efforts clearly demonstrated that Europeans were beginning to play a much larger role in the world than they had for the previous half millennium.

THE ESTABLISHMENT OF REGIONAL STATES

Long after its disappearance the Roman empire inspired European leaders, who dreamed of a centralized political structure embracing all of Christian Europe. In the late tenth century, German princes formed the so-called Holy Roman Empire, which they viewed as a Christian revival of the earlier Roman empire. In fact, however, the Roman empire returned only in name. All attempts to extend its influence beyond Germany met stiff resistance from the popes and from the princes of other European lands. Meanwhile, independent monarchies emerged in France and England, and other authorities ruled the various regions of Italy and Spain. Thus medieval Europe was a political mosaic of independent and competing regional states. These states frequently clashed with one another, and they all faced perennial challenges from within. Yet they organized their own territories efficiently, and they laid the foundations for the emergence of powerful national states in a later era.

The Holy Roman Empire

As the Carolingian empire faded during the ninth century, local authorities took responsibility for providing order in their own regions. Gradually, some of them extended their influence beyond their own jurisdictions and built larger states. Otto of Saxony was particularly aggressive. By the mid–tenth century, he had established himself as king in northern Germany. He campaigned east of the Elbe River in lands populated by Slavic peoples, and twice he ventured into Italy to quell political disturbances, protect the church, and seek opportunities in the south. In appreciation for his aid to the church, Pope John XII proclaimed Otto emperor in 962 C.E. Thus was born the Holy Roman Empire.

Otto I

The imperial title had considerable cachet, and on several occasions energetic emperors almost transformed the Holy Roman Empire into a hegemonic state that might have reintroduced imperial unity to Europe. Conflict with the papacy, however, prevented

Map 17.1 Regional states of medieval Europe, about 1250 C.E. Note the large number of polities that claimed territories throughout Europe in this period. How would this variety of states have contributed to political instability in Europe? Were there also advantages to such an arrangement?

the emperors from building a strong and dynamic state. Although the popes crowned the medieval emperors, their relations were usually tense, since both popes and emperors made large claims to authority in Christian Europe. Relations became especially strained when emperors sought to influence the selection of church officials, which the popes regarded as their own prerogative, or when emperors sought to extend their authority into Italy, where the popes had long provided political leadership. Thus when the popes felt threatened by the pretensions of the Holy Roman Empire, they entered into alliances with other European authorities to check the power of the emperors. Because of that, the Holy Roman Empire remained an empire principally in name. Voltaire, the eighteenth-century French writer, once quipped that the Holy Roman Empire was "neither holy, nor Roman, nor an empire." Instead, it was a regional state that ruled Germany and occasionally sought to wield influence in eastern Europe and Italy.

Regional Monarchies in France and England

In the absence of an effective imperial power, regional states emerged throughout medieval Europe. In France and England, princes established regional monarchies on the basis of relationships between lords and their retainers.

The French monarchy grew slowly from humble beginnings. When the last of the Carolingians died, in 987 C.E., the lords of France elected *Capetian France* a minor noble named Hugh Capet to serve as king. Capet held only a small territory around Paris, and some of his retainers were far more powerful than he. Over the next three centuries, however, his descendants, known as the Capetian kings, gradually added to their resources, expanded their political influence, and established the right to administer justice throughout the realm. By the early fourteenth century, the Capetian kings had gradually centralized power and authority in France.

The English monarchy developed quite differently. Its founders were Normans—descendants of Vikings who carved out a state on the peninsula *The Normans* of Normandy in France during the ninth century. Though nominally subject to Carolingian and later to Capetian rulers, the dukes of Normandy in fact pursued their own interests with little regard for their lords. Within Normandy the dukes built a tightly centralized state in which all authority stemmed from the

Primary Source
Statutes of William the Conqueror

dukes themselves. The dukes also retained title to all land in Normandy and strictly limited the right of their retainers to grant land to others. In 1066 Duke William of Normandy invaded England, then ruled by descendants of the Angles, the Saxons, and other Germanic peoples. Following a speedy military victory, the duke, now known as William the Conqueror, introduced Norman principles of government and land tenure to England and quickly established a tightly centralized realm.

Both the Capetians and the Normans faced internal challenges from retainers seeking to pursue independent policies or enlarge their powers. Both dynasties also faced external challenges: indeed, they often battled each other, since the Normans periodically sought to expand their possessions in France. On the basis of relationships between lords and retainers, however, both the Capetians and the Normans managed to organize regional monarchies that maintained order and provided reasonably good government.

King Louis IX (reigned 1226–1270), also known as St. Louis, helped to consolidate the Capetian hold on the French monarchy. In this fourteenth-century manuscript illustration, he hears the petitions of humble subjects (right), while hanged criminals (left) serve as a reminder of felony's results.

Regional States in Italy and Iberia

Regional states emerged also in other lands of medieval Europe, though not on such a large scale as the monarchies of France and England. In Italy, for example, a *Church Influence in Italy* series of ecclesiastical states, city-states, and principalities competed for power and position. In central Italy the popes had provided political leadership since the Carolingian era and in fact ruled a good-sized territory known as the Papal States. In northern Italy, church bishops influenced political affairs and organized public life until the high middle ages, when wealthy lay classes displaced them as ruling authorities.

By about the twelfth century, a series of prosperous city-states—including Florence, Bologna, Genoa, *Italian States* Milan, and Venice—dominated not only their own urban districts but also the surrounding hinterlands. Meanwhile, in southern Italy, Norman adventurers invaded territories still claimed by the Byzantine empire and various Muslim states. With papal approval and support, they overcame Byzantine and Muslim authorities, brought southern Italy into the orbit of Roman Catholic Christianity, and laid the foundations for the emergence of the powerful kingdom of Naples.

As in Italy, a series of regional states competed for power on the Iberian peninsula. From the eighth to the eleventh century, Muslim conquerors ruled most of the peninsula except for a few small states in northern

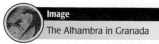
Image
The Alhambra in Granada

Spain. Beginning in the mid–eleventh century, though, Christian adventurers from these states began to attack Muslim territories and enlarge their own domains. By the late *Christian and Muslim States in Iberia* thirteenth century, the Christian kingdoms of Castile, Aragon, and Portugal controlled most of the Iberian peninsula, leaving only the small kingdom of Granada in Muslim hands.

With its Holy Roman Empire, regional monarchies, ecclesiastical principalities, city-states, and new states founded on conquest, medieval Europe might seem to present a stark contrast to a centralized, reunified land such as China. Moreover, European rulers constantly campaigned to enlarge their holdings at the expense of their neighbors and thus endlessly complicated medieval European politics. Yet the regional states of the high middle ages effectively tended to public affairs in limited regions. In doing so, they fashioned alternatives to a centralized empire as a form of political organization.

ECONOMIC GROWTH AND SOCIAL DEVELOPMENT

As regional states provided increasingly effective political organization, medieval Europe experienced dramatic economic growth and social development. The economic revival closely resembled the processes that in an earlier era had strengthened China, India, and the Islamic world. Increased agricultural production, urbanization, manufacturing, and trade transformed Europe and drew it once again into commercial relationships with distant lands.

Growth of the Agricultural Economy

As in China, India, and the Islamic world during the early postclassical era, a dramatic increase in agricultural yields was the foundation of economic growth and social development in medieval Europe. Several developments help to account for this increased agricultural production: the opening of new lands to cultivation, improved agricultural techniques, the use of new tools and technologies, and the introduction of new crops.

Expansion of Arable Land
Beginning in the late tenth century, as local lords pacified their territories, Europe began to experience population pressure. In response peasants cleared forests, drained swamps, and increased the amount of land devoted to agriculture. At first the lords opposed those efforts, but they gradually realized that increased agricultural production would yield higher taxes and increase their own wealth. By the early twelfth century, lords were encouraging the expansion of cultivation, and the process gathered momentum.

Improved Agricultural Techniques
Meanwhile, improved methods of cultivation and better agricultural technologies led to significantly higher productivity. During the high middle ages, European cultivators experimented with new crops and with different cycles of crop rotation to ensure the most abundant harvests possible without compromising the fertility of the soil. They increased cultivation especially of beans, which not only provided dietary protein but also enriched the land because of their property of fixing nitrogen in the soils where they grow. They kept more domestic animals, which not only served as beasts of burden and sources of food but also enriched fields with their droppings. By the thirteenth century, observation and experimentation with new crops and new techniques had vastly increased understanding of agricultural affairs. News of these discoveries circulated widely throughout Europe in books and treatises on household economics and agricultural methods, which in turn led to increased agricultural productivity.

During the high middle ages, European peoples expanded their use of watermills and heavy plows, which had appeared during the early middle ages, and

also introduced new tools. Two simple items in particular—the horseshoe and the horse collar—made it possible to increase sharply the amount of land that cultivators could work. Horseshoes helped to prevent softened and split hooves on horses that tramped through moist European soils. Horse collars placed the burden of a heavy load on an animal's chest and shoulders rather than its neck and enabled horses to pull heavy plows without choking. Thus Europeans could hitch their plows to horses rather than to slower oxen and bring more land under the plow. *New Tools and Technologies*

New Crops
Expansion of land under cultivation, improved methods of cultivation, and the use of new tools combined to increase both the quantity and the quality of food supplies. During the centuries from 1000 to 1300, European diets expanded from an almost complete reliance on grains to include meat, dairy products, fish, vegetables, and legumes such as beans and peas. Spain, Italy, and other Mediterranean lands benefited also from widespread cultivation of crops—such as hard durum wheat, rice, spinach, and citrus fruits—that had earlier been disseminated through the Islamic world.

Population Growth
As in other lands, increased agricultural productivity supported rapid population growth. In 800 C.E., during the Carolingian era, European population stood at about twenty-nine million. By 1000, when regional states had ended invasions and restored order, it had edged up to thirty-six million. By 1300, only three hundred years later, the population had reached seventy-nine million. Such rapid demographic growth in turn helped stimulate a vigorous revival of towns and trade in medieval Europe.

The Revival of Towns and Trade

Urbanization
With abundant supplies of food, European society was able to support large numbers of urban residents. Attracted by urban opportunities, people from the countryside flocked to established cities and founded new towns at strategically located sites. Cities founded during Roman times, such as Paris, London, and Toledo, became thriving centers of government and business, and new urban centers—such as Venice in northern Italy—also emerged. Northern Italy and Flanders (the northwestern part of modern Belgium) experienced especially strong urbanization. For the first time since the fall of the western Roman empire, cities began to play a major role in European economic and social development.

The growth of towns and cities brought about increasing specialization of labor, which in turn resulted in the dramatic expansion of manufacturing and trade. Manufacturing concentrated especially on the production of wool textiles. The cities of Italy and Flanders in particular became lively centers for wool production. Trade in wool products helped to fuel economic development, commercial exchange, and urbanization throughout Europe.

Textile Production

The revival of urban society was most pronounced in Italy, which was geographically well situated to participate in the trade networks of the Mediterranean basin. During the tenth century, for example, the cities of Amalfi and Venice served as ports for merchants engaged in trade with Byzantine and Muslim partners in the eastern Mediterranean. Italian merchants exchanged salt, olive oil, wine, wool fabrics, leather products, and glass for luxury goods such as gems, spices, silk, and other goods from India, southeast Asia, and China that Muslim merchants brought to eastern Mediterranean markets.

Mediterranean Trade

As trade expanded, Italian merchants established colonies in the major ports and commercial centers of the Mediterranean and the Black Sea. By the thirteenth century, Venetian and Genoese merchants maintained large communities in Constantinople, Alexandria, Cairo, Damascus, and the Black Sea ports of Tana, Caffa, and Trebizond. These trading posts enabled them to deal with Muslim merchants engaged in the Indian Ocean and overland trade with India, southeast Asia, and China. By the mid–thirteenth century some Italian merchants were beginning to venture as far as central Asia, India, and China in search of commercial opportunities.

Although medieval trade was most active in the Mediterranean basin, a lively commerce grew up also in the northern seas. The Baltic Sea and the North Sea were sites of a particularly well-developed trade network known as the Hanseatic League, or more simply as the Hansa—an association of trading cities stretching from Novgorod to London and embracing all the significant commercial centers of northern Europe. The Rhine, the Danube, and other major European rivers linked the Hansa trade network with that of the Mediterranean.

The Hanseatic League

As in postclassical China and the Islamic world, a rapidly increasing volume of trade encouraged the development of credit, banking, and new forms of business organization in Europe. Bankers issued letters of credit to merchants traveling to distant mar-

Improved Business Techniques

Venice, home of Marco Polo and a legion of merchants, drew enormous prosperity from trade. Street vendors, shopkeepers, and merchant ships figure prominently in this illustration from a fourteenth-century manuscript.

kets, which could then be exchanged for merchandise or cash in the local currency.

Meanwhile, merchants devised new ways of spreading and pooling the risks of commercial investments. They entered into partnerships with other merchants, and they limited the liability of partners to the extent of their individual investments. These arrangements encouraged the formation of commercial partnerships, thus further stimulating the European economy.

Social Change

Medieval social commentators frequently held that European society embraced three estates or classes: "those who pray, those who fight, and those who work." Those who prayed were clergy of the Roman Catholic Church. From lowly parish priests to bishops, cardinals, and popes, the clergy constituted a spiritual estate owing its loyalty to the church rather than secular rulers. The fighters came from the ranks of nobles. They inherited their positions in society and received an education that concentrated on equestrian skills and military arts. Finally, there were those who worked—the vast majority of the population—who mostly cultivated land as peasants.

The Three Estates

The formula dividing society neatly into three classes captures some important truths about medieval Europe. It clearly reflects a society marked by political, social, and economic inequality: although they did not necessarily lead lives of luxury, those who prayed and those who fought enjoyed rights and honors denied to those who worked.

Yet, though expressing some truths, the formula overlooks processes that brought considerable change to medieval European society. Within the ranks of the nobles, for example, an emphasis on chivalry and courtly behavior gradually introduced expectations of high ethical standards and refined manners that encouraged warriors to become cultivated leaders of society. Chivalry was an informal but widely recognized code of ethics and behavior considered appropriate for nobles. Church officials originally promoted the chivalric code in an effort to curb fighting within Christendom. By the twelfth century the ritual by which a young man became initiated into the nobility as a knight commonly called for the candidate to place his sword upon a church altar and pledge his service to God. Thus, the noble who observed the chivalric code would devote himself to the causes of order, piety, and the Christian faith.

Chivalry

Aristocratic women found the chivalric code much to their liking, and they went to some lengths to spread its values. Instead of emphasizing the code's religious dimensions, however, they promoted refined behavior and respectful relations between the sexes. Reflections of their interests survive in the songs and poems of the troubadours, a class of traveling poets, minstrels, and entertainers whom aristocratic women enthusiastically patronized. The troubadours, who were most active in southern France and northern Italy, drew inspiration from a long tradition of love poetry produced in nearby Muslim Spain. Enchanted by the refined songs and poems they heard in Spain, they began to produce similar verses for their own aristocratic patrons. Although troubadours' performances did not instantly transform rough warriors into polished courtiers, over the long term the code of chivalry they promoted helped to soften the manners of the nobility.

Troubadours

Social change also touched those who worked. By the twelfth century the ranks of workers included not only peasants but also increasing numbers of merchants, artisans, crafts workers, and professionals who filled the growing towns of medieval Europe. Because of their military power, lords could dominate these growing towns and tax their wealth. As towns grew larger, however, urban popula-

Independent Cities

tions were increasingly able to resist the demands of nobles and guide their own affairs. By the late eleventh century, inhabitants of prosperous towns were demanding that local lords grant them charters of incorporation that exempted them from political regulation and allowed them to manage their own affairs. Sometimes groups of cities organized leagues to advance their commercial interests, as in the case of the Hansa, or to protect themselves against the encroachments of political authorities.

The cities of medieval Europe were by no means egalitarian societies. Yet medieval towns and cities also reflected the interests and contributions of the working classes. Merchants and workers in all the arts, crafts, and trades organized guilds that regulated the production and sale of goods within their jurisdictions. By the thirteenth century the guilds had come to control much of the urban economy of medieval Europe. They established standards of quality for manufactured goods, they determined the prices at which members had to sell their products, and they regulated the entry of new workers into their groups.

Guilds

Guilds had social as well as economic significance in that they provided a focus for friendship and mutual support in addition to work. Guild members regularly socialized with one another, and prosperous guilds often built large halls where members held meetings, banquets, and sometimes boisterous drinking parties. Guilds often came to the aid of members and their families by providing financial and moral support for those

Women were prominent in the markets of medieval Europe and sometimes worked as bankers or tailors, as in this manuscript illustration.

Francesco Balducci Pegolotti on Trade between Europe and China

Francesco Balducci Pegolotti was an employee of a Florentine banking company. He traveled as far as London and Cyprus on bank business. Although he probably did not travel to Asia, Pegolotti learned about conditions that long-distance traders faced from many merchants who ventured far from home. About 1340 Pegolotti compiled their reports into a book of information and advice for merchants traveling to China from the port of Tana (modern Rostov) on the Sea of Azov.

In the first place, you must let your beard grow long and not shave. And at Tana you should furnish yourself with a dragoman [guide and interpreter]. And you must not try to save money in the matter of dragomen by taking a bad one instead of a good one. For the additional wages of the good one will not cost you so much as you will save by having him. And besides the dragoman it will be well to take at least two good men servants who are acquainted with the [Turkish] Cumanian tongue. . . .

The road you travel from Tana to Cathay [China] is perfectly safe, whether by day or by night, according to what the merchants say who have used it. Only if the merchant, in going or coming, should die upon the road, everything belonging to him will become the perquisite of the lord of the country in which he dies, and the officers of the lord will take possession of all. And in like manner if he die in Cathay. But if his brother be with him, or an intimate friend and comrade calling himself his brother, then to him they will surrender the property of the deceased, and so it will be rescued. . . .

Cathay is a province which contains a multitude of cities and towns. Among others there is one in particular, that is to say the capital city, to which is great resort of merchants, and in which there is a vast amount of trade; and this city is called Khanbaliq. And the said city hath a circuit of one hundred miles, and is all full of people and houses and of dwellers in the said city.

You may calculate that a merchant with a dragoman and two men servants and with goods to the value of twenty-five thousand golden florins

should spend on his way to Cathay from sixty to eighty ingots of silver, and not more if he manages well; and for all the road back again from Cathay to Tana, including the expenses of living and the pay of servants, and all other charges, the cost will be about five ingots per head of pack animals, or something less. And you may reckon the ingot to be worth five golden florins. . . .

Anyone from Genoa or Venice wishing to go to the places above named and to make the journey to Cathay should carry linens with him, and if he visits Urgench [in modern Uzbekistan] he will dispose of these well. In Urgench he should purchase ingots of silver, and with these he should proceed without making any further investment, unless it be some bales of the very finest stuffs which go in small bulk, and cost no more for carriage than coarser stuffs would do.

Whatever silver the merchants may carry with them as far as Cathay the lord of Cathay will take from them and put into his treasury. And to merchants who thus bring silver they give that paper money of theirs in exchange. This is of yellow paper, stamped with the seal of the lord aforesaid. And this money is called balishi; and with this money you can readily buy silk and all other merchandise that you have a desire to buy. And all the people of the country are bound to receive it. And yet you shall not pay a higher price for your goods because your money is of paper. And of the said paper money there are three kinds, one being worth more than another, according to the value which has been established for each by that lord.

• *On the basis of Pegolotti's report, how could you characterize the various commercial, financial, and economic risks faced by European merchants traveling to China and trading there?*

SOURCE: Henry Yule and Henri Cordier, eds. *Cathay and the Way Thither,* 2nd ed., 4 vols. London: Hakluyt Society, 1913–16, 3:151–55. (Translation slightly modified.)

who fell ill. They also arranged funeral services for their deceased and provided support for survivors. Thus guilds constituted a kind of social infrastructure that made it possible for medieval cities to function.

Urban Women Medieval towns and cities offered fresh opportunities for women as well as for men. Although few routes to public authority were open to women, in the larger towns and cities women worked alongside men as butchers, brewers, bakers, fishmongers, innkeepers, merchants, and occasionally physicians and pharmacists. Indeed, women dominated some occupations, particularly those involving textiles and decorative arts, such as sewing, spinning, weaving, and the making of hats, wigs, and fur garments.

Most guilds admitted women into their ranks, and some guilds had exclusively female memberships. In thirteenth-century Paris, for example, there were approximately one hundred guilds. Six of them admitted only women, but eighty others included women as well as men among their members. The increasing prominence of women in European society illustrates the significance of towns and cities as agents of social change in medieval Europe.

EUROPEAN CHRISTIANITY
DURING THE HIGH MIDDLE AGES

Roman Catholic Christianity guided European thought on religious, moral, and ethical matters. Representatives of the Roman church administered the rituals associated with birth, marriage, and death. Most of the art, literature, and music of the high middle ages drew inspiration from Christian doctrines and stories. Just as mosques and minarets defined the skylines of Muslim cities, the spires of churches and cathedrals dominated the landscape of medieval Europe, testifying visually to the importance of religion and the pervasive presence of the Roman Catholic church.

Western Christianity changed in several ways between 1000 and 1300. As the Roman Catholic church developed an identity distinct from the Eastern Orthodox church, western theologians became reacquainted with the works of Aristotle—mostly unknown to European scholars of the early middle ages—and they produced an impressive synthesis of Aristotelian philosophy and Christian values. Meanwhile, lay classes elaborated a rich tradition of popular religion. Although some popular religious movements posed challenges to Roman Catholicism, most remained within the bounds of Roman Catholic orthodoxy and represented an effort to express Christianity in meaningful terms.

Schools, Universities, and Scholastic Theology

Cathedral Schools During the early middle ages, European society was not stable and wealthy enough to support institutions of advanced education. As a result, early medieval scholars drew their inspiration from the Bible and from major spokesmen of the early Christian church such as St. Augustine of Hippo. During the high middle ages, however, economic development sharply increased the wealth of Europe and made more resources available for education. Meanwhile, an increasingly complex society created a demand for educated individuals who could deal with complicated political, legal, and theological issues. In response to such demand, by the eleventh century bishops and archbishops in France and northern Italy organized schools in their cathedrals and invited well-known scholars to serve as master teachers.

By the twelfth century the cathedral schools had established formal curricula. Instruction concentrated on the liberal arts, especially literature and philosophy. Students read the Bible and the writings of the church fathers, as well as classical Latin literature and the few works of Plato and Aristotle that were available in Latin translation. Some cathedral schools also offered advanced instruction in law, medicine, and theology.

Universities About the mid–twelfth century, students and teachers organized academic guilds and persuaded political authorities to grant charters guaranteeing their rights. Student guilds demanded fair treatment for students from townspeople and called on their teachers to provide rigorous, high-quality instruction. Faculty guilds sought to vest teachers with the right to bestow academic degrees, which served as licenses to teach in other cities,

Primary Source
Founding of the University of Heidelberg

and to control the curriculum in their own institutions. These guilds had the effect of transforming cathedral schools into universities. The first universities were those of Bologna, Paris, and Salerno, but by the late thirteenth century, universities had appeared also in Rome, Naples, Seville, Salamanca, Oxford, Cambridge, and other cities throughout Europe.

The evolution of the university coincided with the rediscovery of the works of Aristotle, which European scholars learned about through increased contacts with Byzantine as well as Muslim philosophers. During the

A manuscript illustration depicts a professor, at top left, lecturing in a medieval German university. About half the students listen and take notes diligently, while the others catch up on their sleep or chat with friends.

thirteenth century, Latin translations of Aristotle's works spread throughout Europe, and they profoundly influenced almost all branches of thought. The most notable result was the emergence of scholastic theology, which sought to synthesize the beliefs and values of Christianity with the logical rigor of Greek philosophy. The most famous of the scholastic theologians was St. Thomas Aquinas (1225–1274), who spent most of his career teaching at the University of Paris. While holding fervently to his Christian convictions, St. Thomas believed that Aristotle had understood and explained the workings of the world better than any other thinker. St. Thomas saw no contradiction between Aristotle and Christian revelation but, rather, viewed them as complementary: Aristotle explained the world according to human reason, and Christianity explained it as part of a divine plan. Thus, as expressed in the thought of St. Thomas Aquinas, scholastic theology represented the harmonization of Aristotle with Christianity and the synthesis of reason and faith. Like the neo-Confucianism of Zhu Xi or the Islamic philosophy of Ibn Rushd, scholastic theology reinterpreted inherited beliefs in light of the most advanced knowledge of the time.

Scholasticism: St. Thomas Aquinas

Popular Religion

St. Thomas and the other scholastic theologians addressed a sophisticated, intellectual elite rather than the common people of medieval Europe. The popular masses neither knew nor cared much about Aristotle. For their purposes, Christianity was important primarily as a set of beliefs and rituals that gave meaning to individual lives and that bound them together into coherent communities. Thus formal doctrine and theology did not appeal to popular audiences as much as the ceremonies and observances that involved individuals in the life of a larger community.

Popular piety generally entailed observance of the sacraments and devotion to the saints recognized by the Roman Catholic church. Sacraments are holy rituals that bring spiritual blessings on the observants. The church recognized seven sacraments, including baptism, matrimony, penance, and the Eucharist. By far the most popular was the Eucharist, during which priests offered a ritual meal commemorating Jesus' last meal with his disciples before his trial and execution by Roman authorities. Because the sacrament kept individuals in good standing with the church, conscientious believers observed it weekly, and the especially devout on a daily basis. Popular beliefs held that the sacrament would protect individuals from sudden death and advance their worldly interests.

Sacraments

Popular religion also took the form of devotion to the saints. According to church teachings, saints were human beings who had led such exemplary lives that God held them in special esteem. As a result, they enjoyed special influence with heavenly authorities and were able to intervene on behalf of individuals living in the world. Medieval Europeans frequently invoked the aid of saints, who had reputations for helping living people as well as souls of the dead. Tradition held that certain saints could cure diseases, relieve toothaches, and guide sailors through storms to a port.

Devotion to Saints

During the high middle ages, the most popular saint was always the Virgin Mary, mother of Jesus, who personified the Christian ideal of womanhood, love, and sympathy, and who reportedly lavished aid on her devotees. During the twelfth and thirteenth centuries, Europeans dedicated hundreds of churches and cathedrals to the Virgin, among them the splendid cathedral of Notre Dame ("Our Lady") of Paris.

The Virgin Mary

Medieval Europeans went to great lengths to express their adoration of the Virgin and other saints through veneration of their relics and physical remains, widely believed to retain the powers associated with the holy individuals themselves. Churches assembled vast collections of relics, such as clothes, locks of hair, teeth, and bones of famous

Saints' Relics

Architects and laborers sometimes worked more than a century to construct the massive gothic cathedrals of medieval Europe. Built during the twelfth and thirteenth centuries, the magnificent cathedral of Notre Dame in Paris honors the Virgin Mary.

saints. Especially esteemed were relics associated with Jesus or the Virgin, such as the crown of thorns that Jesus reportedly wore during his crucifixion or drops of the Virgin's milk miraculously preserved in a vial.

Some collections of relics became famous well beyond their own regions. Like Muslims making the hajj, *Pilgrimage* pilgrims trekked long distances to honor the saints the relics represented. The making of pilgrimages became so common during the high middle ages that a travel industry emerged to serve the needs of pilgrims. Inns dotted the routes leading to popular churches and shrines, and guides shepherded groups of pilgrims to religious sites and explained their significance. There were even guidebooks that pointed out the major attractions along pilgrims' routes and warned them of difficult terrain and unscrupulous scoundrels who took advantage of visitors.

Reform Movements and Popular Heresies

Although veneration of the saints and the making of pilgrimages indicated a deep reservoir of piety, popular religion also reflected the social and economic development of medieval Europe. As Europe's wealth increased, several groups of particularly devout individuals feared that European society was becoming excessively materialistic. Even Benedictine monasteries, in which monks originally observed the virtues of poverty, chastity, and obedience, had in many cases become comfortable retreats where privileged individuals led leisurely lives.

The devout responded to this state of affairs in several ways. Working within the Roman church, some in-dividuals organized movements designed to champion spiritual over materialistic values. Most prominent of them were St. Dominic (1170–1221) and St. Francis (1182–1226). During the thirteenth century St. Dominic and St. Francis founded orders of mendicants ("beggars"), known as the Dominican and Franciscan friars, who would have no personal possessions and would have to beg for their food and other needs from audiences to whom they preached.

Dominicans and Franciscans

Whereas the Dominicans and the Franciscans worked within the church, others rejected the Roman Catholic church altogether and organized alternative religious movements. *Popular Heresy* One example was the Waldensians, who were most active in southern France and northern Italy. Waldensians despised the Roman Catholic clergy as immoral and corrupt, and they advocated modest and simple lives. They also asserted the right of the laity to preach and administer sacraments—functions that the church reserved exclusively for priests. Although church authorities declared them heretical, the Waldensians continued to attract enthusiastic participants: a few Waldensians survive even today.

THE MEDIEVAL EXPANSION OF EUROPE

During the high middle ages, the relationship between western European peoples and their neighbors underwent dramatic change. Powerful states, economic expansion, and demographic growth all strengthened European society, while church officials encouraged the colonization of pagan and Muslim lands as a way to extend the influence of Roman Catholic Christianity. Beginning about the mid–eleventh century, Europeans embarked upon expansive ventures on several fronts: Atlantic, Baltic, and Mediterranean. All those ventures signaled clearly that Europeans were beginning to play a much larger role in the affairs of the eastern hemisphere than they had during the early middle ages.

Atlantic and Baltic Colonization

When regional states began to emerge and protect western Europe from Viking raids in the ninth and tenth centuries, Scandinavian seafarers turned their attention to the islands of the North Atlantic Ocean. They occupied Iceland beginning in the late ninth century, and by the end of the tenth century they had discovered Greenland and established a small colony there. About 1000 C.E. Leif Ericsson left the colony at Greenland and took an exploratory party south and west, arriving eventually at modern Newfoundland in Canada. Because of the wild grapes growing in the region, Leif called it Vinland. During the years following Leif's voyage, Greenlanders made several efforts to establish permanent colonies in Vinland. Ultimately, however, their efforts failed because they did not have the resources to sustain a settlement over the stormy seas of the North Atlantic Ocean. Nonetheless, the establishment of even a short-lived colony indicated a growing capacity of Europeans to venture into the larger world.

Vinland

While Scandinavians explored the North Atlantic, the Roman Catholic church drew Scandinavia itself into the community of Christian Europe. The kings of Denmark and Norway converted to Christianity in the tenth century. Conversion of their subjects came gradually and with considerable resistance, but royal support for the Roman Catholic church ensured that Christianity would have a place in Danish and Norwegian societies. Between the twelfth and fourteenth centuries, Sweden and Finland followed their neighbors into the Christian faith.

Christianity in Scandinavia

In the Baltic lands of Prussia, Livonia, and Lithuania, Christian authority arrived in the wake of military conquest. During the era of crusades, zealous Christians formed a series of military-religious orders. The most prominent were the Templars, Hospitallers, and Teutonic Knights, who pledged to devote their lives to the struggle against Muslims and pagans. The Teutonic Knights were most active in the Baltic region, where they waged military campaigns against the pagan Slavic peoples during the

Crusading Orders and Baltic Expansion

twelfth and thirteenth centuries. Aided by German missionaries, the Knights founded churches and monasteries in the territories they subdued. By the late thirteenth century, the Roman Catholic church had established its presence throughout the Baltic region, which progressively became absorbed into the larger society of Christian Europe.

The Reconquest of Sicily and Spain

The boundaries of Christian Europe also expanded in the Mediterranean basin. There Europeans came into conflict with Muslims, whose ancestors had conquered the major Mediterranean islands and most of the Iberian peninsula between the eighth and tenth centuries. As their society became stronger, Europeans undertook to reconquer those territories and reintegrate them into Christian society.

Most important of the islands was Sicily, which Muslims had conquered in the ninth century. During the eleventh century, Norman warriors returned Sicily to Christian hands after almost twenty years of conflict. Islam did not disappear immediately, and for some time Muslims continued to practice their faith privately. Over the longer term, however, as Muslims either left Sicily or converted to Christianity, Islam gradually disappeared from the island.

The Reconquest of Sicily

The reconquest of Spain—known as the *reconquista*—took a much longer time than the recapture of Sicily. Following the Muslim invasion and conquest of the early eighth century, the caliphate of Córdoba ruled almost all of the Iberian peninsula. A small Christian state survived in Catalonia in the far northeast, and the kingdom of León resisted Muslim advances in the far northwest. The process of *reconquista* began in the 1060s from these Christian toeholds. By 1150 Christian forces had recaptured Lisbon and established their authority over half of the peninsula. Their successes lured reinforcements from France and England, and in the first half of the thirteenth century a new round of campaigns brought most of Iberia into Christian hands. Only the kingdom of Granada in the far south of the peninsula remained Muslim. It survived as an outpost of Islam until 1492, when Christian forces mounted a campaign that conquered Granada and completed the *reconquista*.

The Reconquista of Spain

The political, economic, and demographic strength of Christian Europe helps to explain the reconquests

---

reconquista (ray-kohn-KEES-tah)

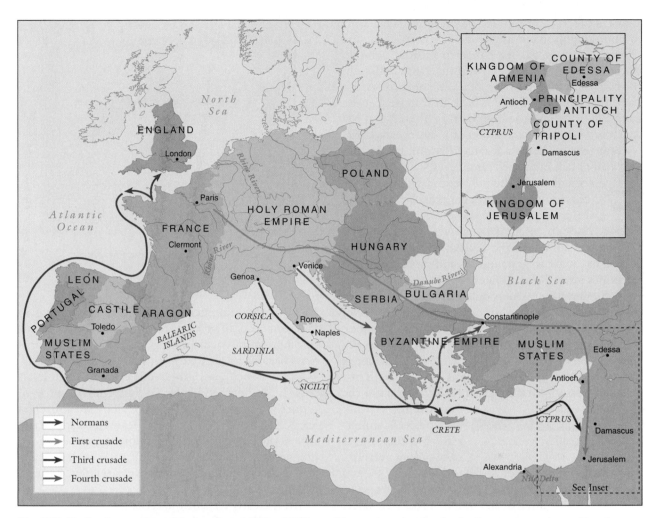

Map 17.2 Medieval expansion of Europe from 1000 to 1250 C.E. Observe the paths taken by the European crusaders and invaders. What does the distance of these paths tell you about the military and organizational capabilities of Europeans in the high middle ages?

of Sicily and Spain as military ventures. Especially in the case of Spain, however, it is clear that religious concerns also helped to drive the *reconquista*. The popes and other leading clergy of the Roman Catholic church regarded Islam as an affront to Christianity, and they enthusiastically encouraged campaigns against the Muslims. When reconquered territories fell into Christian hands, church officials immediately established bishoprics and asserted Christian authority. They also organized campaigns to convert local populations. As a result of those efforts, the Roman Catholic church began to displace Islam in conquered Spain.

The Crusades

The term *crusade* refers to a holy war. It derives from the Latin word *crux,* meaning "cross," the device on which Roman authorities had executed Jesus. When a pope declared a crusade, warriors would "take up the cross" as a symbol of their faith, sew strips of cloth in the form of a cross on the backs of their garments, and venture forth to fight on behalf of Christianity. The most famous of these crusades were the enormous expeditions that Roman Catholic Christians mounted in an effort to recapture Palestine and the holy city of Jerusalem from Muslim authorities.

Primary Source
Summons to the crusade

Pope Urban II launched these crusades in 1095. The response to Urban's appeal was immediate and enthusiastic. A zealous preacher named Peter the Hermit traveled throughout France, Germany, and the Low Countries whipping up support among popular audiences. Within a year of Pope

Urban II

Urban's call, the Hermit had organized a ragtag army of poor knights and enthusiastic peasants—including women—and set out for Palestine without training, discipline, weapons, supplies, or plans. Not surprisingly, the campaign was a disaster: many members of Peter's band died, and few made it back to Europe. Yet the campaign indicated the high level of interest that the crusading idea generated among the European public.

Shortly after Peter's ill-fated venture, French and Norman nobles organized a more respectable military expedition to the holy land. In late 1096 the crusading armies began the long trek to Palestine. In 1097 and 1098 they captured Edessa, Antioch, and other strategic sites. In 1099 Jerusalem itself fell to the crusaders, who then proceeded to extend their conquests and carve conquered territories into Christian states.

The First Crusade

Although the crusaders did not realize it, hindsight shows that their quick victories came largely because of division and disarray in the ranks of their Muslim foes. The crusaders' successes, however, encouraged Turks, Egyptians, and other Muslims to settle their differences, at least temporarily, in the interests of expelling European Christians from the eastern Mediterranean. By the mid–twelfth century the crusader communities had come under tremendous pressure. The crusader state of Edessa fell to Turks in 1144, and the Muslim leader Salah al-Din, known to Europeans as Saladin, recaptured Jerusalem in 1187. Crusaders maintained several of their enclaves for another century and even embarked on several more military expeditions, but Saladin's victories sealed the fate of Christian forces in the eastern Mediterranean.

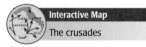

As holy wars intended to reestablish Roman Catholic Christianity in the eastern Mediterranean basin, the crusades were wars of military and political expansion. Yet in the long run, the crusades were much more important for their social, economic, commercial, and cultural consequences. Even as European armies built crusader states in Palestine and Syria, European scholars and missionaries dealt with Muslim philosophers and theologians, and European merchants traded eagerly with their Muslim counterparts. The result was a large-scale exchange of ideas, technologies, and trade goods that profoundly influenced

Consequences of the Crusades

A manuscript illustration depicts Muslims burning captured crusaders at the stake.

European development. Through their sojourns in Palestine and their regular dealings with Muslims throughout the Mediterranean basin, European Christians became acquainted with the works of Aristotle, Islamic science and astronomy, "Arabic" numerals (which Muslims had borrowed from India), and techniques of paper production (which Muslims had learned from China). They also learned to appreciate new food and agricultural products such as spices, granulated sugar, coffee, and dates as well as trade goods such as silk products, cotton textiles, carpets, and tapestries.

In the early days of the crusades, Europeans had little to exchange for those products other than rough wool textiles, furs, and timber. During the crusading era, however, Italian merchants seeking to meet the rising demand for luxury goods developed new products and marketed them in commercial centers and port cities. Thus Niccolò, Maffeo, and Marco Polo traded in gems and jewelry, and other merchants marketed fine woolen textiles or glassware. By the thirteenth century, large numbers of Italian merchants had begun to travel well beyond Egypt, Palestine, and Syria to avoid Muslim intermediaries and to deal directly with the producers of silks and spices in India, China, and southeast Asia. Thus, although the crusades largely failed as military ventures, they helped encourage the reintegration of western Europe into the larger economy of the eastern hemisphere.

SUMMARY

From 1000 to 1300 western Europe underwent thorough political and economic reorganization. Building on foundations laid during the early middle ages, political leaders founded a series of independent regional states. Despite the establishment of the Holy Roman Empire, they did not revive central imperial authority in western Europe. Regional states maintained good order and fostered rapid economic growth. Agricultural improvements brought increased food supplies, which encouraged urbanization, manufacturing, and trade. By the thirteenth century, European peoples traded actively throughout the Mediterranean, Baltic, and North Sea regions, and a few merchants even ventured as far away as China in search of commercial opportunities. In the high middle ages, as in the early middle ages, Roman Catholic Christianity was the cultural foundation of European society. The church prospered during the high middle ages, and advanced educational institutions reinforced the influence of Roman Catholic Christianity throughout Europe. Christianity even played a role in European political and military expansion, since church officials encouraged crusaders to conquer pagan and Muslim peoples in Baltic and Mediterranean lands. Thus between 1000 and 1300, western European peoples strengthened their own society and began in various ways to interact regularly with their counterparts in other regions of the eastern hemisphere.

CHRONOLOGY

962	Coronation of Otto I as Holy Roman Emperor
1066	Norman invasion of England
1096–1099	First crusade
1170–1221	Life of St. Dominic
1182–1226	Life of St. Francis
1187	Recapture of Jerusalem by Saladin
1225–1274	Life of St. Thomas Aquinas
1271–1295	Marco Polo's trip to China

FOR FURTHER READING

Robert Bartlett. *The Making of Europe: Conquest, Colonization, and Cultural Change, 950–1350.* Princeton, 1993. A well-documented examination of European expansion from a cultural point of view.

Robert-Henri Bautier. *The Economic Development of Medieval Europe.* New York, 1971. An excellent and well-illustrated survey that puts the economic and social history of western Europe in the context of the larger Mediterranean basin.

Rosalind Brooke and Christopher Brooke. *Popular Religion in the Middle Ages: Western Europe, 1000–1300.* London, 1984. Well-illustrated essays on the faith of the masses.

Georges Duby. *Rural Economy and Country Life in the Medieval West.* Trans. by C. Postan. Columbia, S.C., 1968. Authoritative and well-documented study of the medieval agrarian world by a distinguished scholar.

Patrick J. Geary, ed. *Readings in Medieval History.* Lewiston, N.Y., 1989. Offers substantial English translations of primary sources.

David Herlihy. *Opera Muliebra: Women and Work in Medieval Europe.* New York, 1990. Examines women's roles both in their own households and in the larger society of medieval Europe.

Benjamin Z. Kedar. *Crusade and Mission: European Approaches toward the Muslims.* Princeton, 1984. Insightful scholarly analysis of European policies toward Muslims during the crusading era.

Hans Eberhard Mayer. *The Crusades.* 2nd ed. Oxford, 1988. Perhaps the best short history of the crusades.

J. R. S. Phillips. *The Medieval Expansion of Europe.* Oxford, 1988. Excellent survey of European ventures in the larger world during the high and late middle ages.

Susan Reynolds. *Kingdoms and Communities in Western Europe, 900–1300.* Oxford, 1984. An imaginative study focusing on the political and social values that undergirded western European society.

CHAPTER 18

Worlds Apart:
The Americas and Oceania

In November 1519 a small Spanish army entered Tenochtitlan, capital city of the Aztec empire. Although they had heard many reports about the wealth of the Aztec empire, nothing prepared them for what they saw. Years after the conquest of the Aztec empire, Bernal Díaz del Castillo, a soldier in the Spanish army, described Tenochtitlan at its high point. The

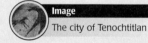
The city of Tenochtitlan

city itself sat in the water of Lake Texcoco, connected to the surrounding land by three broad causeways, and as in Venice, canals allowed canoes to navigate to all parts of the city. The imperial palace included many large rooms and apartments, and its armory was well stocked with swords, lances, knives, bows, arrows, slings, armor, and shields.

To Bernal Díaz the two most impressive sights were the markets and the temples of Tenochtitlan. The markets astonished him because of their size, the variety of goods they offered, and the order that prevailed there. In the principal market at Tlatelolco, a district of Tenochtitlan, Bernal Díaz found gold and silver jewelry, gems, feathers, embroidery, slaves, cotton, cacao, animal skins, maize, beans, vegetables, fruits, poultry, meat, fish, salt, paper, and tools. It would take more than two days, he said, to walk around the market and investigate all the goods offered for sale. His well-traveled companions-in-arms compared the markets favorably to those of Rome and Constantinople.

The temples also struck Bernal Díaz, though in a different way.

Tenochtitlan (teh-noch-tee-TLAHN)

OPPOSITE PAGE: *Cortez is greeted by Montezuma's messenger in 1519.*

Aztec temples were the principal sites of rituals involving human sacrifice. Bernal Díaz described interior rooms of the temple so encrusted with blood that their walls and floors had turned black. Some of the interior rooms held the dismembered limbs of sacrificial victims, and others were resting places for thousands of human skulls and bones.

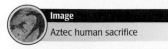
Image
Aztec human sacrifice

The contrast between Tenochtitlan's markets and temples challenged Bernal Díaz and his fellow soldiers. In the markets they witnessed peaceful exchange of the kind that took place all over the world. In the temples, however, they saw signs of human sacrifice on a scale rarely matched, if ever, anywhere else in the world. Yet by the cultural standards of the Aztec empire, both the commercial activity of the marketplaces and the human sacrifice of the temples had a place in the maintenance of the world: trade enabled a complex society to function, and sacrificial rituals pleased the gods and persuaded them to keep the world going.

Although the peoples of Africa, Asia, and Europe interacted regularly before modern times, before 1492 the indigenous peoples of the Americas had only fleeting and random dealings with their contemporaries across the oceans. Yet between 1000 and 1500 C.E. the peoples of North and South America, like their counterparts in the eastern hemisphere, organized large empires with distinctive cultural and religious traditions, and they created elaborate trade networks touching most regions of the Americas.

The indigenous peoples of Australia and the Pacific islands had irregular and sporadic dealings with peoples outside Oceania. Within Oceania itself, Pacific islanders did maintain links between various island groups by sailing over the open ocean. Yet to a greater extent than their counterparts in the eastern hemisphere, the indigenous peoples of Australia and the Pacific islands built self-sufficient societies that tended to their own needs. Even though they had extremely limited amounts of land and other natural resources to work with, by the thirteenth century C.E. they had established well-organized agricultural societies and chiefly states throughout the Pacific islands.

STATES AND EMPIRES IN MESOAMERICA AND NORTH AMERICA

Mesoamerica entered an era of war and conquest in the eighth century C.E. Great stores of wealth had accumulated in Teotihuacan, the largest early city in Mesoamerica. When Teotihuacan declined, it became a target for less-prosperous but well-organized forces from the countryside and northern Mexico. Attacks on Teotihuacan opened a long era of militarization and empire building in Mesoamerica that lasted until Spanish forces conquered the region in the sixteenth century. Most prominent of the peoples contesting for power in Mesoamerica were the Mexica, the architects of the Aztec empire.

The Toltecs and the Mexica

During the ninth and early tenth centuries, after the collapse of Teotihuacan, several regional states dominated portions of the high central valley of Mexico, the area surrounding Mexico City. Although these successor states and their societies shared the religious and cultural traditions of Teotihuacan, they fought relentlessly among themselves. Their capital cities all stood on well-defended hill sites, and warriors figured prominently in their works of art.

With the emergence of the Toltecs and later the Mexica, much of central Mexico again came under unified rule. The Toltecs began to migrate into the area from the arid land of northwestern *Toltecs* Mexico about the eighth century. They settled mostly at Tula, about 50 kilometers (31 miles) northwest of modern Mexico City. There, the Toltecs tapped the waters of the nearby River Tula to irrigate crops of maize, beans, peppers, tomatoes, chiles, and cotton. At its high point, from about 950 to 1150 C.E., Tula supported a population that might have reached sixty thousand people, and another sixty thousand lived in the surrounding region.

The Toltecs also built a compact regional empire with their large and powerful army, and they transformed their capital into a wealthy city with the tribute they exacted from subject peoples. Indeed, the city of Tula became an important center of weaving, pottery, and obsidian work, and residents imported large quantities of jade, turquoise, animal skins, exotic bird feathers, and other luxury goods from elsewhere in Mesoamerica. The Toltecs maintained close relations with societies on the Gulf coast as well as with the Maya of Yucatan. Indeed, Tula shared numerous architectural designs and art motifs with the Maya city of Chichén Itzá some 1,500 kilometers (932 miles) to the east.

Beginning about 1125 C.E. the Toltec empire faced serious difficulties as conflicts between the dif-

Yucatan (yoo-kuh-TAN)

ferent ethnic groups living at Tula led to civil strife. By the mid–twelfth century large numbers of migrants—mostly nomadic peoples from northwestern Mexico—had entered Tula and settled in the surrounding area. By 1175 the combination of civil conflict and nomadic incursion had destroyed the Toltec state.

Among the migrants drawn to central Mexico from northwestern regions was a people who called themselves the Mexica, often referred to as Aztecs because they dominated the alliance that built the Aztec empire in the fifteenth century. (The term *Aztec* derives from *Aztlán,* "the place of the seven legendary caves," which the Mexica remembered as the home of their ancestors.) The Mexica arrived in central Mexico about the middle of the thirteenth century. They had a reputation for making trouble by kidnapping women from nearby communities and seizing land already cultivated by others. On several occasions their neighbors became tired of their disorderly behavior and forced them to move. For a century they migrated around central Mexico, fighting with other peoples and sometimes surviving only by eating fly eggs and snakes.

The Mexica

About 1345 the Mexica settled on an island in a marshy region of Lake Texcoco and founded the city that would become their capital—Tenochtitlan, on top of which Spanish conquerors later built Mexico City. The site offered several advantages. The lake harbored plentiful supplies of fish, frogs, and waterfowl, and it also enabled the Mexica to develop the *chinampa* system of agriculture. The Mexica dredged the fertile muck from the lake's bottom and built it up into small plots of land known as *chinampas*. During the dry season, cultivators tapped water from canals leading from the lake to their plots, and in the temperate climate they grew crops year-round. *Chinampas* were so productive that cultivators were sometimes able to harvest seven crops per year. The lake also served as a natural defense: waters protected Tenochtitlan on all sides, and Mexica warriors patrolled the three causeways that eventually linked their capital to the surrounding mainland.

Tenochtitlan

By the early fifteenth century, the Mexica were powerful enough to overcome their immediate neighbors and demand tribute from their new subjects. During the middle decades of the century, the Mexica launched ambitious campaigns of imperial expansion. Under the rule of "the Obsidian Serpent" Itzcóatl (1428–1440) and Motecuzoma I (1440–1469), also known as Moctezuma or Montezuma, they first advanced against Oaxaca in southwestern Mexico. After conquering the city and

The Aztec Empire

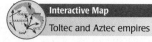
Interactive Map
Toltec and Aztec empires

slaying many of its inhabitants, they populated Oaxaca with colonists, and the city became a bulwark for the emerging Mexica empire.

The Mexica next turned their attention to the Gulf coast. Finally, they conquered the cities of the high plateaus between Tenochtitlan and the Gulf coast. About the mid–fifteenth century the Mexica joined forces with two neighboring cities, Texcoco and Tlacopan (modern Tacuba), to create a triple alliance that guided the Aztec empire. Dominated by the Mexica and Tenochtitlan, the allies imposed their rule on about twelve million people and most of Mesoamerica, excluding only the arid northern and western regions and a few small, independent states.

The main objective of the triple alliance was to exact tribute from subject peoples. From nearby peoples the Mexica and their allies received food crops and manufactured items. Tribute obligations were sometimes very oppressive for subject peoples. The annual tribute owed by the state of Tochtepec on the Gulf coast, for example, included 9,600 cloaks, 1,600 women's garments, 200 loads of cacao (the source of cocoa and chocolate), and 16,000 rubber balls. Ruling elites entrusted some of these tribute items to officially recognized merchants, who took them to distant lands and exchanged them for local products including luxury items such as translucent jade, tortoise shells, jaguar skins, parrot feathers, and seashells. The tropical lowlands also supplied vanilla beans and cacao, from which Mexica elites prepared tasty beverages.

Tribute and Trade

Unlike imperial states in the eastern hemisphere, the Aztec empire had no elaborate bureaucracy or administration. The Mexica and their allies simply conquered their subjects and assessed tribute, leaving local governance and the collection of tribute in the hands of the conquered peoples themselves. The allies did not even maintain military garrisons throughout their empire. Nor did they keep a permanent, standing army. Nevertheless, the Mexica in particular had a reputation for military prowess, and fear of reprisal kept most subject peoples in line.

At the high point of the Aztec empire in the early sixteenth century, tribute from some 489 subject territories flowed into Tenochtitlan, which was an enormously wealthy city. The Mexica capital had a population of about two hundred thousand people, and three hundred thousand more lived in nearby towns and suburban areas. The principal market had separate sections for merchants dealing in gold, silver,

Map 18.1 Toltec and Aztec empires from 950 to 1520 C.E. Note how the boundaries of the Aztec empire stretch from the Gulf coast to the Pacific coast. How would that have benefited Aztec abilities to control trade between lands to their north and south?

slaves, cloth, shoes, animal skins, turkeys, dogs, wild game, maize, beans, peppers, cacao, and fruits.

Mexica Society

More information survives about the Mexica and their subjects than about any other people of the pre-Columbian Americas. A few Mexica books survived the Spanish conquest of the Aztec empire, and they offer direct testimony about the Mexica way of life. Moreover, a great deal of information survives from interviews conducted by Spanish missionaries with priests, elders, and other leaders of the Mexica during the mid–sixteenth century. In combination, these sources shed considerable light on Mexica society.

Mexica society was rigidly hierarchical, with public honors and rewards going mostly to the military elite. *Social Structure* The Mexica looked upon all males as potential warriors, but for the most part the military elite came from the Mexica aristocracy. Men of noble birth received the most intense training in military affairs, and they enjoyed the best opportunities to display their talents on the battlefield.

The Mexica showered wealth and honors on the military elite. Accomplished warriors received extensive land grants as well as tribute from com-*Warriors* moners for their support. The most successful warriors formed a council whose members selected the ruler, discussed public issues, and filled government positions. They ate the best foods, and they consumed most of the luxury items that came into Mexica society by way of trade or tribute. Even dress reflected social status in Mexica society. Sumptuary laws required commoners to wear coarse, burlaplike garments made of henequen but permitted aristocrats to drape themselves in cotton. Successful warriors also enjoyed the right to don brightly colored capes and adorn themselves with lip plugs and eagle feathers.

Women played almost no public role in a society so dominated by military values, but they wielded influence within their families and enjoyed honor as mothers of warriors. *Mexica Women* Mexica women did not inherit property or hold official positions, and the law subjected them to the strict authority of their fathers and husbands. However, women were prominent in the marketplaces, as well as in crafts involving embroidery and needlework.

With the exception of a few who dedicated themselves to the service of a temple, all Mexica women married. Mexica values taught that their principal function was to bear children, and society recognized the bearing of children as equal to a warrior's capture of enemies in battle. Indeed, women who died in childbirth won the same fame as warriors who died valiantly on the battlefield.

Alongside the military aristocracy, a priestly class also ranked among the Mexica elite. Priests received a special education in calendrical and ritual lore, and

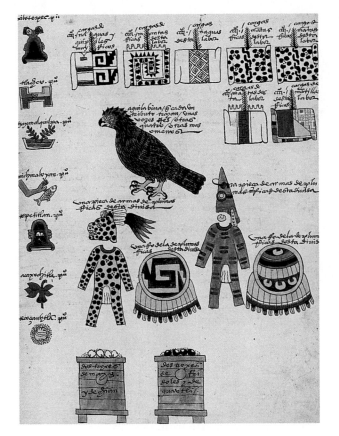

A Spanish copy of a Mexica list records tribute owed by six northwestern towns to the ruler Motecuzoma II. Each two years the towns delivered, among other items, women's skirts and blouses, men's shirts, warriors' armor and shields, an eagle, and various quantities of maize, beans, and other foods.

they presided over religious ceremonies that the Mexica viewed as crucial to the continuation of the world. *Priests* Priests read omens and explained the forces that drove the world, thereby wielding considerable influence as advisors to Mexica rulers. On a few occasions, priests even became supreme rulers of the Aztec empire: the ill-fated Motecuzoma II (reigned 1502–1520), ruler of the Aztec empire when Spanish invaders appeared in 1519, was a priest of the most popular Mexica cult.

The bulk of the Mexica population consisted of commoners who lived in hamlets cultivating lands allocated to their families by community *Cultivators and Slaves* groups known as *calpulli*. Originally, *calpulli* members claimed descent from common ancestors, but over time ancestry became less important than the fact that groups of families lived together in communities, organized their own affairs, and allocated community property to individual families. In addition to cultivating plots assigned by their *calpulli*, Mexica commoners also worked on the lands of aristocrats or warriors and contributed labor services to public works projects. Cultivators delivered periodic tribute payments to state agents, who distributed a portion of what they collected to the elite classes and stored the remainder in state granaries and warehouses. In addition to these cultivators of common birth, Mexica society included a large number of slaves, who usually worked as domestic servants. Most slaves were not foreigners, but Mexica who entered slavery because of financial distress or criminal behavior.

Skilled artisans, particularly those who worked with gold, silver, and other items destined for consumption by the elite, enjoyed considerable prestige in Mexica society. Merchants specializing in long-distance trade occupied an *Artisans and Merchants* important but somewhat more tenuous position in Mexica society. Indeed, although these merchants supplied important luxuries to the elite as well as political and military intelligence about the lands they visited, they often fell under suspicion as greedy profiteers.

Mexica Religion

When they migrated to central Mexico, the Mexica already spoke the Nahuatl language, which had been the prevalent tongue in the region since the time of the Toltecs. The Mexica soon adopted other cultural and religious traditions, some of which dated from the time of the Olmecs, shared by all the peoples of Mesoamerica. Most Mesoamerican peoples played a ball game in formal courts, for example, and maintained a complicated calendar based on a solar year of 365 days and a ritual year of 260 days. The Mexica enthusiastically adopted the ball game, and they also kept a sophisticated calendar.

The Mexica also absorbed the religious beliefs common to Mesoamerica. Two of their principal gods— Tezcatlipoca, "the Smoking Mirror," and *Mexica Gods* Quetzalcoatl, "the Feathered Serpent"— had figured in Mesoamerican pantheons at least since the time of Teotihuacan. Tezcatlipoca was a powerful figure, the giver and taker of life and the patron deity of warriors, whereas Quetzalcoatl supported arts, crafts, and agriculture. Like their predecessors, the Mexica believed that their gods had set the world in motion through acts of individual sacrifice. By letting

Quetzalcoatl (keh-tzahl-koh-AHTl)

In this manuscript illustration an aide stretches a victim over a sacrificial altar while a priest opens his chest, removes the still-beating heart, and offers it to Huitzilopochtli. At the bottom of the structure, attendants remove the body of an earlier victim.

their blood flow, the gods had given the earth the moisture it needed to bear maize and other crops. To win the favor of the gods and ensure the continuation of the world, the Mexica engaged in their own sacrificial bloodletting. Mexica priests regularly performed acts of self-sacrifice, piercing their earlobes or penises with cactus spines in honor of the primeval acts of their gods.

Ritual Bloodletting   Mexica priests also presided over the sacrificial killing of human victims. From at least the time of the Olmecs, Mesoamerican peoples had regarded the ritual sacrifice of human beings as essential to the world's survival. The Mexica, however, placed much more emphasis on human sacrifice than their predecessors had. To a large extent the Mexica enthusiasm for human sacrifice followed from their devotion to the god Huitzilopochtli as the patron deity of Mexica warriors. Military successes in the fourteenth century, when the Mexica subjected neighboring peoples to their rule, increasingly persuaded them of Huitzilopochtli's favor. As Mexica military successes mounted, the priests of Huitzilopochtli's cult demanded sacrificial victims to keep the war god appeased.

Huitzilopochtli (we-tsee-loh-POCK-tlee)

Some of the victims were Mexica criminals, and others came as tribute from neighboring peoples or from the ranks of warriors captured on the battlefield. In all cases the Mexica viewed human sacrifice not as a gruesome form of entertainment but, rather, as a ritual essential to the world's survival. They believed that the blood of sacrificial victims sustained the sun and secured a continuing supply of moisture for the earth, thus ensuring that human communities would be able to cultivate their crops and perpetuate their societies.

Peoples and Societies of the North

Beyond Mexico the peoples of North America developed a rich variety of political, social, and cultural traditions. Many North American peoples depended on hunting, fishing, and foraging. In the arctic and subarctic regions, for example, diets included whale, seal, and walrus supplemented by land mammals such as moose and caribou. Peoples in coastal regions consumed fish, and in interior regions they hunted large animals such as bison and deer. Throughout the continent nuts, berries, roots, and grasses supplemented the meat provided by hunters and fishers. Like their counterparts elsewhere, hunting, fishing, and foraging peoples of North America built societies on a relatively small scale, since food resources in the wild would not support dense populations.

In several regions of North America, agricultural economies enabled peoples to maintain settled societies with large populations. In what *Pueblo and Navajo Societies* is now the American southwest, for example, Pueblo and Navajo peoples tapped river waters to irrigate crops of maize, which constituted as much as 80 percent of their diets. Although the hot and dry environment periodically brought drought and famine, by about 700 C.E. the Pueblo and the Navajo had begun to construct permanent stone and adobe buildings. Archaeologists have discovered about 125 sites where agricultural peoples built such communities.

Large-scale agricultural societies emerged also in the woodlands east of the Mississippi River. Woodlands peoples began to cultivate maize *Iroquois Peoples* and beans during the early centuries C.E., and after about 800 these cultivated foods made up the bulk of their diets. By 1000 the Owasco people had established a distinct society in what is now upstate New York, and by about 1400 the five Iroquois nations (Mohawk, Oneida, Onondaga, Cayuga, and Seneca) had emerged from Owasco society. Women were in charge of Iroquois villages and longhouses, in which several related families lived together, and supervised cultivation of fields surrounding their settlements. Men took responsibility for affairs beyond the village—hunting, fishing, and war.

The most impressive structures of the woodlands were the enormous earthen mounds that dotted the countryside throughout the eastern half of North America. Woodlands *Mound-Building Peoples* peoples used these mounds as stages for ceremonies and rituals, as platforms for dwellings, and occasionally as burial sites. Although modern development has destroyed most of these mounds, several surviving examples demonstrate that they sometimes reached gigantic proportions.

The largest surviving structure is a mound at Cahokia near East St. Louis, Illinois. More than 30 meters (100 feet) high, 300 meters (1,000 feet) long, and 200 meters (650 feet) wide, it was *Cahokia* the third-largest structure in the western hemisphere before the arrival of Europeans. Only the temple of the sun in Teotihuacan and the temple of Quetzalcóatl in Cholula were larger. When 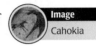 the Cahokia society was at its height, from approximately 900 to 1250 C.E., more than one hundred

---

Iroquois (EER-uh-kwah)

Cahokia (kuh-HOH-kee-uh)

Originally constructed about 1000 C.E., the Great Serpent Mound sits atop a ridge in modern Ohio. The serpent's coiled tail is visible at the left, while its open mouth holds an egg on the right.

smaller mounds stood within a few kilometers of the highest and most massive mound. Scholars have estimated that during the twelfth century, fifteen thousand to thirty-eight thousand people lived in the vicinity of the Cahokia mounds.

Trade   Because peoples north of Mexico had no writing, information about their societies comes almost exclusively from archaeological discoveries. Burial sites reveal that mound-building peoples recognized social classes, since they bestowed grave goods of differing quality and quantities on their departed kin. Archaeologists have shown, too, that trade linked widely separated regions and peoples of North America. An elaborate network of rivers—notably the Mississippi, Missouri, Ohio, and Tennessee rivers—facilitated travel and trade by canoe in the eastern half of North America. Throughout the eastern woodlands, archaeologists have turned up stones with sharp cutting edges from the Rocky Mountains, copper from the Great Lakes region, seashells from Florida, minerals from the upper reaches of the Mississippi River, and mica from the southern Appalachian mountains. Indeed, the community at Cahokia probably owed its size and prominence to its location at the hub of North American trade networks. Situated near the confluence of the Mississippi, Missouri, and Ohio rivers, Cahokia was most likely the center of trade and communication networks linking the eastern woodlands of North America with the lower Mississippi valley and lands bordering the Gulf of Mexico.

STATES AND EMPIRES IN SOUTH AMERICA

Like the peoples north of Mexico, South American peoples had no tradition of writing before the arrival of Spanish invaders in the early sixteenth century. As a result, the experiences of early South American societies have been reconstructed largely on the basis of archaeological evidence and information recorded by Spanish conquerors. As in Mesoamerica, cities and secular government in South America began to overshadow ceremonial centers and priestly regimes during the centuries from 1000 to 1500 C.E. Toward the end of the period, like the Mexica in Mesoamerica, the Incas built a powerful state, extended their authority over a vast region, and established the largest empire South America had ever seen.

The Coming of the Incas

After the disappearance of the Chavín and Moche societies, a series of autonomous regional states organized public affairs in Andean South America. The states frequently clashed, but rarely did one of them gain a long-term advantage over the others. For the most part they controlled areas either in the mountainous highlands or in the valleys and coastal plains.

In the highlands, people depended on the cultivation of potatoes and the herding of llamas and alpacas—camel-like beasts that were the only large domesticated animals anywhere in the Americas before the sixteenth century. After the twelfth century the kingdom of Chucuito dominated the highland region on the border between modern Peru and Bolivia. There, inhabitants built elaborately terraced fields where cultivators harvested potatoes of many different colors, sizes, and tastes.

Chucuito

Inhabitants of the coastal lowlands depended not on potatoes but on maize and sweet potatoes, which were grown with the aid of irrigation networks that tapped the rivers and streams flowing from the Andes mountains. Some lowland societies, such as the kingdom of Chimu, grew large and powerful in the half millennium before the emergence of the Incas in the mid–fifteenth century. Indeed, Chimu's capital city, Chanchan, had a population that exceeded fifty thousand and may have approached one hundred thousand.

Chimu

For several centuries, regional states such as Chucuito and Chimu maintained order in Andean South America. Yet within a period of about thirty years, they and other regional states fell under the domination of the dynamic and expansive society of the Incas. The word *Inca* originally was the title of the rulers of a small kingdom in the valley of Cuzco, but in modern usage the term refers more broadly to those who spoke the Incas' Quechua language, or even to all subjects of the Inca empire.

After a long period of migration in the highlands, the Incas settled in the highland region around Lake Titicaca about the mid–thirteenth century. At first they lived as one among many peoples inhabiting the region. About 1438, however, the Inca ruler Pachacuti (reigned 1438–1471) launched a series of military campaigns that vastly expanded the Incas' au-

The Inca Empire

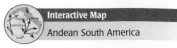
Interactive Map
Andean South America

Chanchan (CHAHN-chahn)

Map 18.2 **The Inca empire from 1471 to 1532 C.E.** Observe its long and narrow boundaries. What geographical features prevented the expansion of the Inca empire to the east?

the Inca empire easily ranked as the largest state ever built in South America.

The Incas ruled as a military and administrative elite. They led armies composed mostly of conquered peoples, and they staffed the bureaucracy that managed the empire's political affairs. But the Incas themselves were not numerous enough to overwhelm their subjects. Thus, they sought to encourage obedience among subject peoples by taking hostages from their ruling classes and forcing them to live at the Inca capital. Also, when conquered peoples became restive or uncooperative, the Incas sent loyal subjects to colonize the area and to establish military garrisons. When conquered peoples rebelled, Inca armies resettled them in distant parts of the empire.

Administration of the Inca empire rested with a large class of bureaucrats. In the absence of writing, bureaucrats relied on a mnemonic aid known as *quipu* to keep track of their responsibilities. Quipu consisted of an array of small cords of various colors and lengths, all suspended from one large, thick cord. Experts tied a series of knots in the small cords, which sometimes numbered a hundred or more, to help them remember certain kinds of information. Most quipu recorded statistical information having to

Quipu and Inca Administration

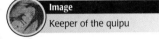

do with population, state property, taxes, and labor services that communities owed to the central government. Occasionally, though, quipu also helped experts to remember historical information having to do with the establishment of the Inca empire, the Inca rulers, and their deeds. Although much more unwieldy and less flexible than writing, quipu enabled Inca bureaucrats to keep track of information well enough to run an orderly empire.

The Inca capital at Cuzco served as the administrative, religious, and ceremonial center of the empire. At its high point in the late fifteenth century, Cuzco's population may have reached three hundred thousand. Most prominent of the residents were the Inca rulers and high nobility, the high priests of the various religious cults, and the hostages of conquered peoples who lived with their families under the watchful eyes of Inca guardians. Cuzco had many handsome buildings of red stone, and the most important temples and palaces sported gold facings.

Cuzco

thority. Pachacuti first extended Inca control over the southern and northern highlands and then turned his forces on the coastal kingdom of Chimu. Though well defended, Chimu had to submit to the Incas when Pachacuti gained control of the waters that supplied Chimu's irrigation system.

By the late fifteenth century, the Incas had built a huge empire stretching more than 4,000 kilometers (2,500 miles) from modern Quito to Santiago. It embraced almost all of modern Peru, most of Ecuador, much of Bolivia, and parts of Chile and Argentina. Only the tropical rain forests of the Amazon and other river valleys set a limit to Inca expansion to the east, and the Pacific Ocean defined its western boundary. With a population of about 11.5 million,

quipu (KEE-poo)

The different colors of quipu threads designated the different items recorded: population, animals, textiles, weapons, and perhaps even rulers and notable events of their reigns. People needed an advanced education to record and "read" information by quipu.

A magnificent and extensive road system enabled the central government at Cuzco to communicate *Inca Roads* with all parts of the far-flung Inca empire and to dispatch large military forces rapidly to distant trouble spots. Two roads linked the Inca realm from north to south—one through the mountains, the other along the coast. Scholars have estimated the combined length of these roads at 16,000 kilometers (9,944 miles). A corps of official runners carried messages along the roads so that news and information could travel between Cuzco and the most distant parts of the empire within a few days. When the Inca rulers desired a meal of fresh fish, they dispatched runners from Cuzco to the coast more than 320 kilometers (200 miles) away and had their catch within two days. Like roads in empires in other parts of the world, the Incas' roads favored their efforts at centralization.

Inca Society and Religion

Despite these splendid roads, Inca society did not generate large classes of merchants and skilled artisans. On the local level the Incas and their subjects bartered agricultural produce and handcrafted goods among *Trade* themselves. Long-distance trade, however, fell under the supervision of the central government. Administrators organized exchanges of agricultural products, textiles, pottery, jewelry, and craft goods, but the Inca state did not permit individuals to become independent merchants. In the absence of a market economy, then, there was no opportunity for a large class of professional, skilled artisans to emerge.

The main classes in Inca society were the rulers, aristocrats, priests, and peasant cultivators of common birth. The Incas considered their chief ruler a deity descended from the sun. In *Ruling Elites* theory, this god-king owned everything in the Inca realm, which he governed as an absolute and infallible ruler. Inca rulers retained their prestige even after death. Their descendants mummified the royal remains and regarded departed kings as intermediaries with the gods. Succeeding rulers often deliberated state policy in the presence of royal mummies so as to benefit from their counsel. Indeed, on the occasion of certain festivals, rulers brought out the mummified remains of their ancestors, dressed them in fine clothes, and presented them with offerings of food and drink to maintain cordial relations with former rulers.

Like the ruling elites, Inca aristocrats and priests led privileged lives. Aristocrats consumed fine foods and dressed in embroidered clothes provided by common subjects. Aristocrats also *Aristocrats and Priests* had the right to wear large ear spools that distended their lobes so much that Spanish conquerors referred to them as "big ears." Priests often came from royal and aristocratic families. They led celibate and ascetic lives, but they deeply influenced Inca society because of their education and their responsibility for overseeing religious rituals. The major temples supported hundreds of priests, along with attendants and virgin women devoted to divine service who prepared ceremonial meals and wove fine ritual garments for the priestly staff.

The cultivators were mostly peasants of common birth who lived in communities known as *ayllu*, similar to the Mexica's *calpulli*, which were the basic units of rural society. Ranging in size *Peasants* from small villages to larger towns, each *ayllu* consisted of several families who lived together, sharing land, tools, animals, crops, and work. Instead of paying taxes or tribute, peasants also worked on state lands administered by aristocrats. Much of the production from these state lands went to support the ruling, aristocratic, and priestly classes. The rest went into state storehouses for public relief in times of famine and for the support of widows, orphans, and others unable to cultivate land for themselves. Apart from agricultural work, peasants also owed compulsory labor services to the Inca state. Men provided the heavy labor required for the construction, main-

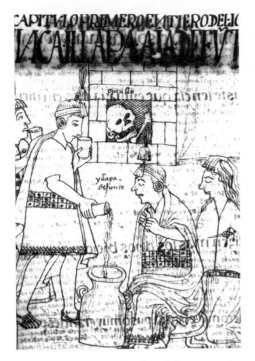

Descendants prepare a ritual meal for a mummified Inca ruler (depicted in the background).

tenance, and repair of roads, buildings, and irrigation systems. Women delivered tribute in the form of textiles, pottery, and jewelry. With the aid of quipu, Inca bureaucrats kept track of the labor service and tribute owed by local communities.

Members of the Inca ruling class venerated the sun as a god and as their major deity, whom they called *Inca Gods: Inti and Viracocha* Inti. They also recognized the moon, the stars, the planets, the rain, and other natural forces as divine. Some Incas, including the energetic ruler Pachacuti, also showed special favor to the god Viracocha, creator of the world, humankind, and all else in the universe. The cult of the sun, however, outshone all the others. In Cuzco alone some four thousand priests, attendants, and virgin devotees served Inti, whose temple attracted pilgrims from all parts of the Inca empire. Priests of all cults honored their deities with sacrifices, which in Inca society usually took the form of agricultural produce or animals such as llamas and guinea pigs rather than humans.

Alongside sacrifices and ritual ceremonies, Inca religion had a strong moral dimension. The Incas taught a concept of sin as a violation of the established social or natural order, and they believed in a life beyond death during which individuals would receive rewards or punishments based on the quality of their earthly lives. Sin, they believed, would bring divine disaster both for individuals and *Moral Thought* for their larger communities. The Incas also observed rituals of confession and penance by which priests absolved individuals of their sins and returned them to the good graces of the gods.

THE SOCIETIES OF OCEANIA

Inhabitants of Oceania did not interact with peoples of different societies as frequently or systematically as did their counterparts in the eastern hemisphere, but they built and maintained flourishing societies of their own. The aboriginal peoples of Australia ventured over vast stretches of their continent and created networks of trade and exchange between hunting and gathering societies. Meanwhile, throughout the Pacific Ocean, islanders built complex agricultural societies. By the time European mariners sailed into the Pacific Ocean in the sixteenth century, the larger island groups had sizable populations, hierarchical social orders, and hereditary chiefly rulers. In the central and western Pacific, mariners sailed regularly between island groups and established elaborate trade networks. Islanders living toward the eastern and western edges of the Pacific Ocean also had occasional dealings with American and Asian peoples, sometimes with significant consequences for Pacific island societies themselves.

The Nomadic Foragers of Australia

Although the aboriginal peoples of Australia learned how to expertly exploit the resources of the continent, they did not turn to agriculture as did their neighbors to the north in New Guinea. The inhabitants of New Guinea began to herd swine and cultivate root crops about 5000 B.C.E., and the inhabitants of islands in the Torres Strait 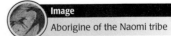 (which separates Australia from New Guinea) took up gardening soon thereafter. In contrast, the aboriginal peoples of northern Australia maintained nomadic, foraging societies until European peoples migrated to Australia in large numbers during the nineteenth and twentieth centuries.

As a result of their mobile and nomadic way of life, aboriginal Australians frequently interacted with

peoples of neighboring societies. Even though as nomads they did not accumulate large quantities of material goods, groups regularly exchanged surplus
food and small items when they met. Eventually,
this sort of small-scale exchange enabled trade goods
to spread throughout most of Australia. Pearly oyster
shells were among the most popular trade items. Archaeologists have turned up many of these shells fashioned into jewelry more than 1,600 kilometers (1,000
miles) from the waters where the oysters bred. Peoples
on the north coast also engaged in a limited amount of
trade with mariners from New Guinea and the islands
of southeast Asia. Australian spears and pearly shells
went north in exchange for items such as iron axes,
which were much coveted by aboriginal peoples who
had no tradition of metallurgy.

Trade

In spite of seasonal migrations, frequent encounters with peoples from other aboriginal societies, and
trade, the cultural traditions of Australian peoples did not diffuse much beyond the regions inhabited by individual
societies. Aboriginal peoples paid close
attention to the prominent geographic features of the
lands around them. Often they conducted religious
observances designed to ensure continuing supplies of
animals, plant life, and water. Given the intense concern of aboriginal peoples with their immediate environments, their cultural and religious traditions focused
on local matters and did not appeal to peoples from
other regions.

*Cultural and
Religious
Traditions*

The Development of Pacific Island Societies

By the early centuries C.E., human migrants had established agricultural societies in almost all the island
groups of the Pacific Ocean. About the middle of the
first millennium C.E., they ventured to the large islands of New Zealand—the last large, habitable region of the earth to receive members of the human
species. After 1000 C.E. Polynesians inhabiting the
larger Pacific islands grew especially numerous, and
their surging population prompted remarkable social
and political development.

In the central and western regions of the Pacific,
where several clusters of islands are relatively close to
one another, mariners linked island soci-
eties. Regional trade networks facilitated
exchanges of useful goods such as axes
and pottery, exotic items such as shells and decorative
ornaments, and sometimes even foodstuffs. Regional
trade within individual island groups served social and
political as well as economic functions, since it helped
ruling elites establish and maintain harmonious relations with one another. In some cases, trade crossed
longer distances and linked different island groups. Inhabitants of the Tonga, Samoa, and Fiji islands traded
mats and canoes, for example, and also intermarried,
thus creating political and social relationships.

*Trade between
Island Groups*

Elsewhere in Polynesia, vast stretches of deep
blue water made it much more complicated to travel

Map 18.3 Societies of Oceania. Note that the islands of the western Pacific are much closer to one another than are the islands of the eastern Pacific. How would such proximity or distance have affected the development of human societies in the Pacific?

A painting from 1825 shows several fishponds in active use near Honolulu in Hawai`i.

between different island groups and societies. As a result, regular trade networks did not emerge in the eastern Pacific Ocean. Nevertheless, mariners undertook lengthy voyages on an intermittent basis, sometimes with momentous results. After the original settlement of Easter Island about 300 C.E., for example, Polynesian mariners probably ventured to the western coast of South America, where they learned about the cultivation of sweet potatoes. Between about 400 and 700 C.E., mariners spread sweet potatoes throughout Polynesia and beyond. The new crop quickly became a prominent source of food in all the islands it reached. Thus long-distance voyages were responsible for the dissemination of sweet potatoes to remote islands situated thousands of kilometers from the nearest inhabited lands.

Long-Distance Voyaging

Another case of long-distance voyaging prompted social changes in the Hawaiian Islands. For centuries after the voyages that brought the original settlers to the islands in the early centuries C.E., there was little travel or communication between Hawai`i and other Polynesian societies. During the twelfth and thirteenth centuries, however, a series of two-way voyages linked Hawai`i with Tahiti and the Marquesas Islands. Memories of those voyages survive in oral traditions that relate the introduction into Hawai`i of new chiefly and priestly lines from Tahiti. Evidence for the voyages comes also from Hawaiian adoption of fishhook styles from Tahiti and words from the Tahitian language.

While undertaking regular or intermittent voyages over long distances, islanders throughout the Pacific Ocean also built productive agricultural and fishing societies. They cultivated taro, yams, sweet potatoes, bananas, breadfruit, and coconuts, and they kept domesticated pigs and dogs. They also fed on abundant supplies of fish. After about the fourteenth century, as their population increased, the inhabitants of Hawai`i built ingenious fishponds that allowed small fry to swim from the ocean through narrow gates into rock-enclosed spaces but prevented larger fish from escaping. Fishponds thus enabled Hawaiians to harvest large quantities of mature fish with relative ease. The establishment of agricultural and fishing societies led to rapid population growth in all the larger Pacific island groups. In Hawai`i, the most heavily populated of the Polynesian island groups, the human population may have exceeded five hundred thousand when European mariners arrived in the late eighteenth century.

Population Growth

Dense populations sometimes led to environmental degradation and social strife on small islands with limited resources. Easter Island in particular was the site of dramatic problems arising from overpopulation. Polynesian migrants originally settled Easter Island in the early centuries C.E., and during the era from about 1100 to 1500, their descendants numbered about ten

A massive wall constructed of basalt rock protects a burial site at Nan Madol in Pohnpei.

thousand. This population placed tremendous pressure on the island's resources. By 1500, islanders fought one another ferociously for those resources, engaging in brutal massacres of their enemies and the desecration of their bodies. As their society disintegrated, they sometimes resorted to cannibalism for lack of sufficient food.

In other lands, dense populations promoted social organization on a scale never before seen in Oceania. *Nan Madol* On Pohnpei in the Caroline Islands, for example, the Sandeleur dynasty built a powerful state and organized construction of a massive stone palace and administrative center at Nan Madol. Built mostly during the period from 1200 to 1600, the complex included ninety-three artificial islets protected by seawalls and breakwaters on three sides.

Indeed, beginning about the thirteenth century, expanding populations prompted residents of many *Development of Social Classes* Pacific islands to develop increasingly complex social and political structures. Especially on the larger islands, workers became more specialized: some concentrated on cultivating certain crops while others devoted their efforts to fishing or crafts production. Distinct classes emerged as well. The islands of Tonga, Tahiti, and Hawai`i had especially stratified societies with sharp distinctions between various classes of high chiefs, lesser chiefs, and commoners. Hawaiian society also recognized distinct classes of priests and skilled artisans as well as common classes.

In addition to distinct social classes, island societies generated strong political leadership. Ruling chiefs generally oversaw public affairs in portions of an island, in an entire island, or occasionally in several islands situated close to one another. In Tonga and Hawai`i, high chiefs frequently launched campaigns to bring additional islands under their control and create large centralized states. Rarely, however, were these militant chiefs able to overcome geographic and logistic difficulties and realize their expansionist ambitions before the nineteenth century. *The Formation of Chiefly States*

Nevertheless, high chiefs guided the affairs of complex societies throughout Polynesia. They allocated lands to families, mobilized labor for construction projects, and organized men into military forces. They commanded enormous respect within their societies. In Hawai`i, for example, the classes of high chiefs known as *ali`i nui* intermarried, ate the best fish and other foods that were *kapu* ("taboo") to commoners, and had the right to wear magnificent cloaks adorned with thousands of bright red and yellow bird feathers. Indeed, a *kapu* forbade commoners to approach or even cast a shadow on the *ali`i nui*.

High chiefs worked closely with priests, who served as intermediaries between human communities and the gods. Gods of war and agriculture were common throughout the Pacific islands, but individual islands and island groups recognized deities particular to their own regions and interests. The most distinctive architecture of early Pacific societies was the ceremonial precinct and temple structure known as *marae* (or *heiau* in Hawaiian). *Marae* often had several terraced floors, with a rock or coral wall designating the boundaries of the sacred space. In Tonga and Samoa, temples made of timber and thatched roofs served as places of worship, sacrifice, and communication between priests and the gods, whereas in eastern Polynesia religious ceremonies took place on platforms in open-air courtyards. *Polynesian Religion*

Pacific island societies did not enjoy access to the range of technologies developed by continental peoples until after the sixteenth century. Yet Pacific islanders cleverly exploited their environments, established productive agricultural economies, built elaborate, well-organized societies, and reached out when possible to engage in trade with their neighbors. Their achievements testify anew to the human impulses toward densely populated communities and interaction with other societies.

Moʻikeha's Migration from Tahiti to Hawaiʻi

A group of Polynesian oral traditions preserves memories of numerous two-way voyages between Tahiti and Hawaiʻi in the twelfth and thirteenth centuries. One of them has to do with Moʻikeha, a high chief who left Tahiti because of domestic difficulties and migrated to Hawaiʻi, where he founded a new chiefly line. The legend recounts several voyages between Tahiti and Hawaiʻi. The following excerpts deal with Moʻikeha's establishment as a chief in Hawaiʻi and the later arrival of his Tahitian son Laʻamaikahiki, who is credited with the introduction of Tahitian religious and cultural traditions to Hawaiʻi.

■ ■ ■

It was dark by the time they arrived [at the Hawaiian island of Kauaʻi], so they did not land, instead, mooring their canoe offshore. Early the next morning the people saw this double-hulled canoe floating offshore with the kapu sticks of a chief aboard. The canoe was brought ashore and the travelers got off. Meanwhile the locals were gathering in a crowd to go surf-riding. . . . Among them were the two daughters of the aliʻi nui [chief] of Kauaʻi, Hoʻoipoikamalanai and Hinauu.

Moʻikeha and his companions saw the crowd and followed along to take part in the morning exercise. Moʻikeha was a handsome man with dark reddish hair and a tall, commanding figure.

When Hoʻoipoikamalanai and her sister saw Moʻikeha, they immediately fell in love with him, and they decided to take him for their husband. Moʻikeha in the meantime was also struck with the beauty and grace of the two sisters, and he, too, fell in love with them and decided to take one of them to be his wife. After enjoying the surf for a time, Hoʻoipoikamalanai and her sister returned home and told their father about the new arrival and said: "We wish to take that young chief as a husband for one of us." The father approved.

Orders were issued that Moʻikeha be brought to the house of the two aliʻi women. Moʻikeha and his company were sent for and brought in the presence of the king [the aliʻi nui of Kauaʻi]. The love of these young people being mutual, Hoʻoipoikamalanai and Hinauu took Moʻikeha to be their husband. Moʻikeha became aliʻi nui of Kauaʻi after the death of his father-in-law. . . .

Moʻikeha worked to make his two wives and five children happy, giving his undivided attention to the bringing up of his boys. He thought no more of Luʻukia [his lover in Tahiti], but after a while, he began to feel a yearning desire to see his son Laʻamaikahiki, his child by his first wife Kapo. So he called his five sons together and said to them: "I'm thinking of sending one of you boys to bring your elder brother to Hawaiʻi.". . .

[After Moʻikeha's son Kila sailed to Tahiti and found his elder half-brother] Laʻamaikahiki immediately prepared to accompany his brother to Hawaiʻi, as Moʻikeha wished. Laʻamaikahiki took his priests and his god Lonoikaʻoualiʻi, and set sail for Hawaiʻi with the men who had come with Kila. When they were approaching Kauaʻi, Laʻamaikahiki began beating his drum. Moʻikeha heard his drum and ordered everything, the land as well as the house, to be made ready for the reception of the chief Laʻamaikahiki. Upon the arrival of Laʻamaikahiki and Kila, the high priest of Kauaʻi, Poloahilani, took Laʻamaikahiki and his god Lonoikaʻoualiʻi ("Lono at the Chiefly Supremacy") to the heiau [temple]. It is said that Laʻamaikahiki was the first person to bring a god (akua) to Hawaiʻi. . . .

[After returning to Tahiti, then sailing again to Hawaiʻi, Laʻamaikahiki] set sail again, going up the Kona coast [of Hawaiʻi Island]. . . . It was on this visit that Laʻamaikahiki introduced hula dancing, accompanied by the drum, to Hawaiʻi. . . .

Laʻamaikahiki stayed a long time on Kauaʻi teaching the people the art of dancing. From Kauaʻi Laʻamaikahiki visited all the other islands of this group and thus the drum dance (hula kaʻeke) spread to the other islands.

- *How would you characterize the political, social, and cultural significance of two-way voyaging between Tahiti and Hawaiʻi?*

SOURCE: Teuira Henry and others. *Voyaging Chiefs of Havaiʻi.* Ed. by Dennis Kawaharada. Honolulu: Kalamaku Press, 1995, pp. 138–39, 144–46.

SUMMARY

The original inhabitants of the Americas and Oceania lived in societies that were considerably smaller than those of the eastern hemisphere. Unlike their counterparts in the eastern hemisphere, they did not possess metallurgical technologies or transportation technologies based on wheeled vehicles and domesticated animals. Nevertheless, long before they entered into sustained interaction with European and other peoples, they built complex societies and developed sophisticated cultural and religious traditions. Indigenous peoples established foraging, fishing, and agricultural societies throughout the Americas, and they fashioned tools from wood, stone, and bone that enabled them to produce enough food to support sizable communities. In Mesoamerica and Andean South America, they also built imperial states that organized public affairs on a large scale.

The original inhabitants of Australia and the Pacific islands built societies on a smaller scale than did the peoples of the Americas, but they too devised effective means of exploiting the natural environment and organizing flourishing communities. Australia was a continent of foraging nomadic peoples, whereas the Pacific islands supported densely populated agricultural societies. Although they had limited communication with peoples of the Americas or the eastern hemisphere, the peoples of Oceania traded and interacted regularly with their neighbors, and inhabitants of the Pacific islands sometimes undertook lengthy voyages to trade with distant island groups.

CHRONOLOGY

AMERICAS	
950–1150	High point of the Toltec empire
1175	Collapse of the Toltec empire
1250	Inca settlement near Cuzco
1345	Foundation of Tenochtitlan by the Mexica
1400	Emergence of the five Iroquois nations
1428–1440	Reign of the Aztec ruler Itzcóatl
1438–1471	Reign of the Inca ruler Pachacuti
1440–1469	Reign of the Aztec ruler Motecuzoma I
1502–1520	Reign of the Aztec ruler Motecuzoma II
1519	Arrival of Spanish conquerors in Mexico
OCEANIA	
ELEVENTH CENTURY	Beginning of population growth in Pacific islands
THIRTEENTH CENTURY	Emergence of distinct social classes and chiefly states
FOURTEENTH CENTURY	Construction of fishponds in Hawai`i

FOR FURTHER READING

Peter Bellwood. *The Polynesians: Prehistory of an Island People.* Rev. ed. London, 1987. Well-illustrated popular account emphasizing the origins and early development of Polynesian societies.

Geoffrey Blainey. *Triumph of the Nomads: A History of Aboriginal Australia.* Melbourne, 1975. A sympathetic account of Australia before European arrival, well informed by archaeological discoveries.

Inga Clendinnen. *Aztecs: An Interpretation.* Cambridge, 1991. A brilliant recreation of the Mexica world, concentrating on cultural and social themes.

George A. Collier, Renato I. Rosaldo, and John D. Wirth, eds. *The Inca and Aztec States, 1400–1800: Anthropology and History.* New York, 1982. Seventeen well-focused essays represent approaches that scholars have taken to the Inca and Aztec empires.

Ben Finney. *Voyage of Rediscovery: A Cultural Odyssey through Polynesia.* Berkeley, 1994. Fascinating account of efforts to understand ancient Polynesian techniques of seafaring and to chart the courses of Polynesian migrations.

Patrick V. Kirch. *On the Road of the Winds: An Archaeological History of the Pacific Islands before European Contact.* Berkeley, 2000. A valuable synthesis of recent scholarship by the foremost contemporary archaeologist of the Pacific islands.

Miguel León-Portilla. *The Aztec Image of Self and Society: An Introduction to Nahua Culture.* Salt Lake City, 1992. An excellent guide to Mexica social and cultural history by the foremost student of the Mexica.

Lynda Norene Shaffer. *Native Americans before 1492: The Moundbuilding Centers of the Eastern Woodlands.* Armonk, N.Y., 1992. Places the societies of mound-building peoples in larger historical context.

Muriel Porter Weaver. *The Aztecs, Maya, and Their Predecessors: Archaeology of Mesoamerica.* 3rd ed. New York, 1993. An up-to-date survey based on historical and archaeological research.

CHAPTER 19

Reaching Out: Cross-Cultural Interactions

One of the great world travelers of all time was the Moroccan legal scholar Ibn Battuta. Born in 1304 at Tangier, Ibn Battuta followed family tradition and studied Islamic law. In 1325 he left Morocco to make a pilgrimage to Mecca. He traveled by caravan across north Africa and through Egypt, Palestine, and Syria, arriving at Mecca in 1326. After completing his hajj Ibn Battuta spent a year visiting Mesopotamia and Persia, then traveled by ship through the Red Sea and down the east African coast as far south as Kilwa. By 1330 he had returned to Mecca, but then soon set off for India when he learned that the sultan of Delhi offered handsome rewards to foreign legal scholars. In 1333 he arrived in Delhi after following a long and circuitous land route that took him

Primary Source
Ibn Battuta in China

through Egypt, Syria, Anatolia, Constantinople, the Black Sea, and the great trading cities of central Asia, Bokhara and Samarkand.

For the next eight years, Ibn Battuta remained in India, serving mostly as a *qadi* (judge) in the government of the sultan of Delhi. In 1341 Ibn Battuta began his travels again, this time making his way around southern India, Ceylon, and the Maldive Islands before continuing to China about 1345. He visited the bustling southern Chinese port cities of Quanzhou and Guangzhou, where he found large communities of Muslim merchants, before returning to Morocco in 1349 by way of southern India, the Persian Gulf, Syria, Egypt, and Mecca.

Still, Ibn Battuta's travels were not complete. In 1350 he made a

OPPOSITE PAGE: *A giraffe from east Africa sent as a present to China in 1414 and painted by a Chinese artist at the Ming zoo.*

short trip to the kingdom of Granada in southern Spain, and in 1353 he joined a camel caravan across the Sahara desert to visit the Mali empire, returning to Morocco in 1355. During his travels Ibn Battuta visited the equivalent of forty-four modern countries and logged more than 117,000 kilometers (73,000 miles). His account of his adventures stands with Marco Polo's book among the classic works of travel literature.

Between 1000 and 1500 C.E., the peoples of the eastern hemisphere traveled, traded, communicated, and interacted more regularly and intensively than ever before. The large empires of the Mongols and other nomadic peoples provided a political foundation for that cross-cultural interaction. When they conquered and pacified vast regions, nomadic peoples provided safe roads for merchants, diplomats, missionaries, and other travelers. Quite apart from the nomadic empires, improvements in maritime technology led to increased traffic in the sea lanes of the Indian Ocean and the South China Sea. As a result, long-distance travel became much more common than in earlier eras.

Merchants and travelers exchanged more than trade goods. They diffused technologies and spread religious faiths. They also exchanged diseases that caused deadly epidemics. During the middle decades of the fourteenth century, bubonic plague traveled the trade routes and spread through most of Eurasia. During its initial, furious onslaught, bubonic plague caused death and destruction on a huge scale and interrupted long-distance trade networks.

By the early fifteenth century, however, societies had begun to recover from the plague. Chinese and western European peoples in particular had restabilized their societies and begun to renew cross-cultural contacts. In Europe, this effort had profound consequences for modern world history. As they sought entry to the markets of Asia, European mariners sailed to the western hemisphere and the Pacific Ocean. Their voyages brought the peoples of the eastern hemisphere, the western hemisphere, and Oceania into permanent and sustained interaction with one another. Thus between 1000 and 1500, cross-cultural interactions pointed toward global interdependence, a principal characteristic of modern world history.

LONG-DISTANCE TRADE AND TRAVEL

Travelers embarked on long-distance journeys for a variety of reasons. Three of the more important motives for long-distance travel between 1000 and 1500

C.E. were trade, diplomacy, and missionary activity. The cross-cultural interactions that resulted helped spread technological innovations throughout the eastern hemisphere.

Patterns of Long-Distance Trade

Merchants engaged in long-distance trade relied on two principal networks of trade routes. Luxury goods of high value relative to their weight, such as silk textiles and precious stones, often traveled overland on the silk roads. Bulkier commodities, such as steel, stone, and building materials, traveled the sea lanes of the Indian Ocean, since it would have been unprofitable to transport them overland. The silk roads linked all of the Eurasian landmass, and trans-Saharan caravan routes drew west Africa into the larger economy of the eastern hemisphere. The sea lanes of the Indian Ocean served ports in southeast Asia, India, Arabia, and east Africa while also offering access via the South China Sea to ports in China, Japan, Korea, and the islands of southeast Asia. Thus, in combination, land and sea routes touched almost every corner of the eastern hemisphere.

As the volume of trade increased, the major trading cities and ports grew rapidly, attracting buyers, sellers, brokers, and bankers from parts near and far. When a trading or port *Trading Cities* city enjoyed a strategic location, maintained good order, and resisted the temptation to levy excessive customs fees, it had the potential to become a major emporium. A case in point is Melaka (in modern Malaysia). Founded in the 1390s, within a few decades Melaka became the principal clearinghouse of trade in the eastern Indian Ocean. The city's authorities policed the strategic Strait of Melaka and maintained a safe market that welcomed all merchants and levied reasonable fees on goods exchanged there. By the end of the fifteenth century, Melaka had a population of some fifty thousand people, and, according to one report, more than eighty languages could be heard in the city's streets.

Although the early period of Mongol conquest in the first half of the thirteenth century caused economic decline, especially in China and southwest Asia, eventually Mongol rule proved to be a boon for overland trade. Under Mongol rule, merchants traveling the silk roads faced less risk of banditry or political turbulence than in previous times. Meanwhile, strong

Melaka (may-LAH-kah)

economies in China, India, and western Europe fueled demand for foreign commodities.

The best-known long-distance traveler of Mongol times was the Venetian Marco Polo (1253–1324), *Marco Polo* who, with his father and his uncle, traveled and traded throughout Mongol lands in the late thirteenth century. When Marco Polo returned to Europe in 1295, stories of his adventures were compiled by a third party and circulated widely throughout Europe. In spite of occasional exaggerations and tall tales, Marco's stories about the textiles, spices, gems, and other goods he observed during his travels deeply influenced European readers eager to participate in the lucrative trade networks of Eurasia. Indeed, in the wake of the Polos came hundreds of others, whose travels helped to increase European participation in the larger economy of the eastern hemisphere.

Political and Diplomatic Travel

Marco Polo came from a family of merchants, and merchants were among the most avid readers of his stories. Yet his experiences also throw light on long-distance travel undertaken for political and diplomatic purposes. Khubilai Khan and the other Mongol rulers of China did not entirely trust their Chinese subjects and regularly appointed foreigners to administrative posts. Indeed, while in China Marco re-

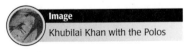
Khubilai Khan with the Polos

ported that Khubilai appointed him governor of the large trading city of Yangzhou, and that he represented Khubilai Khan's interests on diplomatic missions.

The emergence of elaborate trading networks and the establishment of vast imperial states created great *Mongol-Christian Diplomacy* demand for political and diplomatic representation during the centuries after 1000 C.E. The thirteenth century was a time of especially active diplomacy involving distant parties. During the 1240s and 1250s, for example, Pope Innocent IV dispatched a series of envoys who invited the Mongol khans to convert to Christianity and join Europeans in an alliance against the Muslims in control of Jerusalem. The khans declined the invitation, proposing in reply that the pope and European Christians submit to Mongol rule or face destruction.

Although the early round of Mongol-European diplomacy offered little promise of cooperation, the Mongols later initiated another effort. In 1287 the Mongol ilkhan of Persia planned to invade the

Muslim-held lands of southwest Asia and capture Jerusalem. In hopes of attracting support for the project, he dispatched Rabban Sauma, *Rabban Sauma* a Nestorian Christian priest of Turkish ancestry, as an envoy to the pope and European political leaders. Although his efforts did not succeed in garnering European support for Mongol plans, such diplomatic activity illustrates the complexity of political affairs in the eastern hemisphere and the need for diplomatic consultation over long distances.

The expansion of Islamic influence in the eastern hemisphere encouraged a different kind of politically motivated travel. Legal scholars and judges played a crucial role in Islamic societies, since the *sharia* prescribed religious observances and social relationships based on the Quran. Conversions to Islam and the establishment of Islamic states in India, southeast Asia, and sub-Saharan Africa created a demand for Muslims educated in Islamic law. After about the eleventh century, educated Muslims from southwest Asia and north Africa regularly traveled to recently converted lands to help instill Islamic values.

Best known of the Muslim travelers was Ibn Battuta (1304–1369). Islamic rulers governed most of the lands Ibn Battuta visited, but very few *Ibn Battuta* Muslims educated in the law were available in those lands. With his legal credentials Ibn Battuta had little difficulty finding government positions. As qadi and advisor to the sultan of Delhi, he supervised the affairs of a wealthy mosque and heard cases at law, which he strictly enforced according to Islamic standards of justice. On one occasion Ibn Buttuta sentenced a man to receive eighty lashes because he had drunk wine eight years earlier. Ibn Battuta also served as qadi in both east and west Africa, where he consulted with Muslim rulers and offered advice about government, women's dress, and proper relationships between the sexes. Like many other legal scholars whose stories went unrecorded, Ibn Battuta provided guidance in the ways of Islam in societies recently converted to the faith.

Missionary Campaigns

Islamic values spread not only through the efforts of legal scholars but also through the missionary activities of Sufi mystics. As in the early days of Islam, Sufis in the period from 1000 to 1500 ven- *Sufi Missionaries* tured to recently conquered or converted lands and sought to win a popular following for the faith in India, southeast Asia, and sub-Saharan Africa. Sufis did not insist on a strict, doctrinally

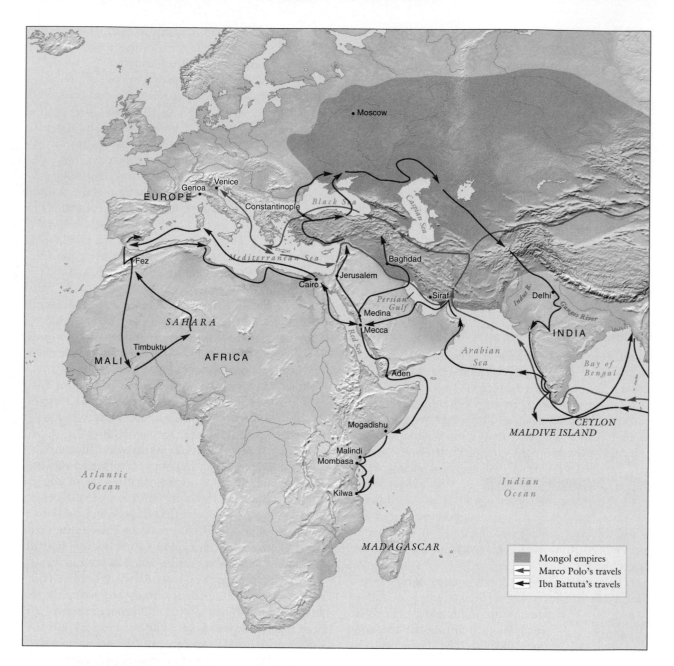

correct understanding of Islam but, rather, emphasized piety and devotion to Allah. They even tolerated continuing reverence of traditional deities. By taking a flexible approach to their missions, the Sufis spread Islamic values without facing the resistance that unyielding and doctrinaire campaigns might have provoked.

Meanwhile, Roman Catholic missionaries also traveled long distances in the interests of spreading Chris-

tianity. Missionaries accompanied the crusaders and other forces to all the lands where Europeans extended their influence after the year 1000. In lands where European conquerors maintained a long-term presence—such as the Baltic lands, the Balkan region, Sicily, and Spain—missionaries attracted converts in large numbers, and Roman Catholic Christianity became securely established.

Christian Missionaries

The most ambitious missions sought to convert Mongols and Chinese to Roman Catholic Christian-

Sufis (SOO-fees)

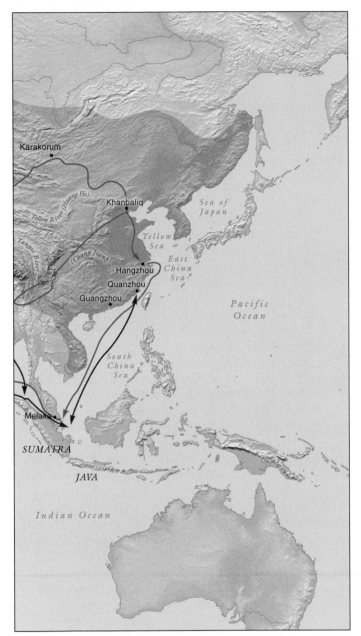

Map 19.1 Travel and trade routes from the twelfth to the fourteenth century. Note the routes of both Ibn Battuta and Marco Polo, and their travels across central Asia, the Indian Ocean, the Mediterranean, and the Sahara. What factors made it possible for them to travel so extensively, and how did they choose where to go?

Long-Distance Travel and Cross-Cultural Exchanges

Long-distance travel of all kinds, whether for commercial, political, diplomatic, or missionary purposes, encouraged cultural exchanges between peoples of different societies. Songs, stories, religious ideas, philosophical views, and scientific knowledge all passed readily among travelers who ventured into the larger world during the era from 1000 to 1500 C.E. The troubadours of western Europe, for example, drew on the poetry, music, and love songs of Muslim performers when developing the literature of courtly love. Similarly, European scientists avidly consulted their Muslim and Jewish counterparts in Sicily and Spain to learn about their understanding of the natural world. *Cultural Exchanges*

Large numbers of travelers also facilitated agricultural and technological diffusion during the period from 1000 to 1500. The magnetic compass, for example, invented in China during the Tang or Song dynasty, spread throughout the Indian Ocean basin during the eleventh century, and by the mid–twelfth century European mariners used compasses in the Mediterranean and the Atlantic Ocean. The compass was a boon to maritime trade, since it allowed mariners to sail over long stretches of deep water with confidence in their ability to find their destinations and return home safely.

Long-distance journeys enabled Muslim travelers to introduce new food and commercial crops—such as citrus fruits and Asian rice—to sub-Saharan Africa, which enriched west African diets after the eleventh century. Muslims also introduced cotton to west Africa, and by 1500 it was the principal textile produced in sub-Saharan Africa. *Spread of Crops*

Muslims were also instrumental in the continuing diffusion of sugarcane. Muslim merchants and other travelers had begun large-scale cultivation of sugarcane in southwest Asia and north Africa during the Abbasid caliphate. After the twelfth *Sugarcane*

ity. Yet even though Roman Catholic authorities in Europe dispatched many priests and missionaries to China during the early fourteenth century, they ultimately won few converts. In part, east Asia was just too distant for the resources available to the Roman Catholic church. Moreover, Christianity seemed to have little appeal to east Asian peoples, who already possessed sophisticated religious and cultural traditions.

Ibn Battuta on Customs in the Mali Empire

Long-distance travelers often encountered unfamiliar customs in foreign societies. The Moroccan traveler Ibn Battuta approved heartily when staying with hosts who honored the values of his own Muslim society, but he had little tolerance for those who did not. Here he describes what he witnessed at the sultan's court in the Mali empire.

The blacks are the most humble of men before their king and the most extreme in their self-abasement before him. They swear by his name, saying "Mansa Sulaimanki" [the law of Mansa Sulaiman, the Mali sultan]. When he calls one of them while he is in session . . . the man invited takes off his clothes and wears patched clothes, takes off his turban, puts on a dirty cap, and goes in raising his clothes and trousers up his legs halfway to his knees. He advances with humility looking like a beggar. He hits the ground with his elbows, he hits it hard. He stands bowed, like one . . . in prayer, listening to what the king says. When one of them speaks to the sultan and he gives him an answer, he removes his clothes from his back and throws dust on his head and back, as a person does when bathing with water. I used to wonder how they do not blind their eyes. . . .

Sometimes one of them would stand before him and recall what he had done in his [the sultan's] service, saying, "I did such and such on such a day," and, "I killed so and so on such a day." Those who know this confirm that he is telling the truth. Their confirmation is by pulling the strings of their bows and letting them go, as one does when one is shooting. If the sultan says to him that he has spoken the truth or thanks him, he takes off his clothes and dusts. This is good manners among them. . . .

Amongst their good qualities is the small amount of injustice amongst them, for of all people they are the furthest from it. . . .

Another of the good habits amongst them is the way they meticulously observe the times of the prayers and attendance at them, so also it is with regard to their congregational services and their beating of their children to instill these things in them.

When it is Friday, if a man does not come early to the mosque he will not find a place to pray because of the numbers of the crowd. It is their custom for every man to send his boy [i.e., servant] with his prayer mat. He spreads it for him in a place commensurate with his position and keeps the place until he comes to the mosque. . . .

Among their good qualities is their putting on of good white clothes on Friday. If a man among them has nothing except a tattered shirt, he washes and cleans it and attends the Friday prayer in it. Another of their good qualities is their concern for learning the sublime Quran by heart. . . .

Among the bad things which they do—their serving women, slave women and little daughters appear before people naked, exposing their private parts. I used to see many of them in this state in [the fasting month of] Ramadan, for it was the custom of the *farariyya* [commanders] to break the fast in the sultan's house. Everyone of them has his food carried in to him by twenty or more of his slave girls and they are naked, every one. Also among their bad customs is the way women will go into the presence of the sultan naked, without any covering; and the nakedness of the sultan's daughters—on the night of the twenty-seventh of Ramadan, I saw about a hundred slave girls coming out of his palace with food, with them were two of his daughters, they had full breasts and no clothes on. Another of their bad customs is their putting of dust and ashes on their heads as a sign of respect. . . . And another is that many of them eat animals not ritually slaughtered, and dogs and donkeys.

- *Discuss the various ways in which Islamic influences and established local customs came together in the Mali empire.*

SOURCE: Said Hamdun and Noel King, eds. *Ibn Battuta in Black Africa.* Princeton: Markus Wiener, 1998, pp. 49–50, 58–59.

A thirteenth-century manuscript illustration depicts two lute players: Muslim (left) and Christian (right). Muslim artists deeply influenced Christian poetry and music during the middle ages.

buchets to lob gunpowder bombs into cities under siege. Muslim armies soon developed similar weapons in response.

By the mid–thirteenth century gunpowder had reached Europe. By the early fourteenth century, armies from China to Europe possessed primitive cannons. Although not especially accurate, the weapons were powerful enough to blow holes in the defensive walls of cities under siege. Thus, with the assistance of Mongol warriors, gunpowder technology rapidly spread from its homeland in China across the entire Eurasian landmass and changed forever the nature of war.

Agricultural and technological diffusions of the era 1000 to 1500 were by no means unique processes in world history. For millennia, agricultural crops and technological skills had spread widely whenever peoples of different societies interacted with one another. Because of the particularly intense interactions of the period from 1000 to 1500, however, agricultural and technological diffusion profoundly influenced the lives of peoples throughout the eastern hemisphere on an unprecedented scale.

CRISIS AND RECOVERY

As Eurasian peoples traveled over long distances, they exchanged trade goods, agricultural crops, and technological expertise, and they also unwittingly spread disease pathogens. When diseases broke out among previously unexposed populations, they often caused widespread epidemics that severely disrupted whole societies. During the fourteenth century, bubonic plague erupted in epidemics that ravaged societies throughout most of Asia, Europe, and north Africa. Epidemic plague struck intermittently until the seventeenth century, but by the fifteenth century Chinese and western European societies in particular had begun to recover from its effects.

century, Muslims facilitated the westward spread of sugarcane by acquainting European crusaders with crystallized sugar refined from cane. Up to that time Europeans had little access to refined sugar, and they relied on honey and fruits as sweeteners. They immediately appreciated the convenience of refined sugar. Italian entrepreneurs began to organize sugarcane plantations on Mediterranean islands such as Sicily, Cyprus, Crete, and Rhodes, and investors began to seek suitable locations throughout the Mediterranean basin. The cultivation of sugarcane had deep social and economic implications. Like their Muslim predecessors, European sugar producers often staffed their plantations with slave laborers, and the growth of plantations fueled an increasing demand for Muslim war captives and black Africans who could supply labor services.

Although Muslim merchants and travelers were especially prominent agents of diffusion, Mongols also *Gunpowder* contributed to the process, notably by *Technologies* helping to spread gunpowder technologies west from China. Mongol invaders learned about gunpowder from Chinese military engineers in the early thirteenth century and soon incorporated gunpowder-based weapons into their arsenal. During the 1250s, as they campaigned in Persia and southwest Asia, the Mongols used catapults and tre-

Bubonic Plague

About 1300 C.E. a process of global climatic change caused temperatures to decline significantly throughout the world. For more than five hundred years, the

The Little Ice Age

earth experienced a "little ice age," when temperatures were much cooler than before. Markedly cooler temperatures meant shorter growing seasons, which caused agricultural production to decline in many lands. That, in turn, led to famine and sometimes even starvation. In some northerly lands, such as Greenland, agriculture ceased to be a practical possibility.

Just after the onset of the "little ice age," peoples in much of the eastern hemisphere suddenly encountered a new challenge in the form of

Origins of Epidemic Bubonic Plague

devastating epidemic disease. Bubonic plague spread from the Yunnan region of southwestern China, where it probably had been endemic for centuries. The plague bacillus infects rodents such as rats, squirrels, and prairie dogs, and fleas transmit the pathogen from one rodent to another. If rodent populations decline, fleas seek other hosts and sometimes spread the disease to human victims. In the early fourteenth century, Mongol military campaigns helped spread plague from Yunnan to China's interior, and by the 1350s it had spread to widely scattered regions of China. In some afflicted areas contemporaries reported that plague carried away two-thirds of the population.

During the 1340s Mongols, merchants, and other travelers helped spread the disease along trade routes

Spread of Plague

west of China. By 1346 it had reached the Black Sea ports of Caffa and Tana. In 1347 Italian merchants fled plague-infected Black

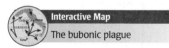

Interactive Map
The bubonic plague

Sea ports and unwittingly spread the disease throughout the Mediterranean basin. By 1348, following the trade routes, plague had sparked epidemics in most of western Europe.

Wherever it appeared, bubonic plague struck with frightful effects. Victims developed inflamed lymph nodes, particularly in the neck, armpit, and groin areas, and most died within a few days after the onset of symptoms. Internal hemorrhaging often discolored the inflammations known as buboes—which gave rise to the term *bubonic* plague—and because of the black or purple swellings, Europeans referred to the plague as the "Black Death." Bubonic plague typically killed 60 to 70 percent of its human victims. In some small villages and towns, disease wiped out

A painting of 1503 graphically communicates the horror felt by medieval Europeans when bubonic plague struck their communities. Here death takes away a cartload of victims, while others die beside the road.

the entire population. Plague also returned to claim new victims. In Europe plague erupted intermittently from the 1340s until the late seventeenth century.

Some parts of the eastern hemisphere did not suffer directly from plague epidemics. The long, cold winters of Scandinavia, for example, discouraged the proliferation of plague-bearing rodents and fleas. For reasons unknown, India also seems to have avoided the worst effects of the plague. In fact, Indian population grew from 91 million in the year 1300 to 97 million a century later. Epidemics also largely bypassed sub-Saharan Africa.

In lands hard hit by plague, however, it took a century and more to begin recovery from the demographic consequences of the disease. In

Population Decline

1300 China's population, already reduced by conflicts with the Mongols, stood at eighty-five million. In 1400, after about seventy years of epidemic plague, Chinese numbers amounted to only seventy-five million. A century later demographic recovery was under way, and China's population rebounded to one hundred million. European society also reeled from the effects of bubonic plague. From seventy-nine million in 1300, European population dropped by almost 25 percent to sixty million in 1400. As in China, demographic recovery in Europe was under way in 1500, when European population climbed to eighty-one million. Islamic societies in southwest Asia, Egypt, and north Africa also suffered devastating population losses, and demographic recovery took much longer there than in China and Europe. In Egypt human population probably did not reach pre-plague levels until the nineteenth century.

Because of its heavy demographic toll, bubonic plague disrupted societies and economies throughout Eurasia and north Africa. Such high death rates caused huge labor shortages, which in turn generated social unrest. In western Europe, for example, urban workers demanded higher wages, and many left their homes in search of better conditions. Political authorities responded by freezing wages and forbidding workers to leave their homes. Peasants in the countryside also sought to improve their circumstances by moving to regions where landlords offered better terms. Landlords responded to this challenge by restricting the freedom of peasants to move. As a result of sharply conflicting interests, disgruntled workers and peasants mounted a series of rebellions that rocked both the towns and the countryside of western Europe and were extinguished only after considerable social disruption and loss of life.

Social and Economic Effects

By the seventeenth century the plague had lost much of its ferocity. Epidemics occurred more sporadically, and they did not seriously diminish human populations. Since the 1940s antibiotic drugs have brought the disease largely under control among human populations, although it survives in rodent communities throughout much of the world.

Recovery in China: The Ming Dynasty

By the mid–fourteenth century the Mongol's Yuan dynasty was experiencing very difficult times. Financial mismanagement led to serious economic difficulties, and political conflicts led to factional fighting among the Mongols themselves. In 1368, with bubonic plague raging, the Yuan dynasty collapsed, and the Mongols departed China en masse, leaving China in a state of both demographic and political turmoil. However, an increasing birthrate soon helped to replenish human numbers, and political recovery accompanied the demographic rebound.

When the Yuan dynasty fell, the governance of China returned to Chinese hands. The new emperor came from a family so poor that he spent much of his youth as a beggar. Because of his size and strength, he came to the notice of military commanders, and he made his way through the ranks to lead the rebellious forces that toppled the Yuan dynasty. In 1368 he became Emperor Hongwu, and he proclaimed the establishment of the Ming ("brilliant") dynasty, which lasted until 1644.

Hongwu

Hongwu immediately set about eliminating all traces of Mongol rule and establishing a government on the model of traditional Chinese dynasties. Although Hongwu had little interest in scholarly matters, he reestablished the Confucian educational and civil service systems to ensure a supply of talented officials and bureaucrats. At the same time, he moved to centralize his authority. In 1380, when he suspected his chief minister of involvement in a treasonous plot, Hongwu executed the minister and his allies and then abolished the minister's position altogether. From that time forward the Ming emperors ruled directly, without the aid of chief ministers.

Ming Centralization

The Ming emperors insisted on absolute obedience to the policies and initiatives of the central government. They relied heavily on the mandarins, a special class of officials sent out as emissaries of the central government to ensure local compliance with imperial policy. The Ming emperors also relied more heavily on eunuchs than had any of their predecessors. Eunuchs had long been considered reliable because they could not generate families and build power bases that might challenge ruling houses. Yet Ming emperors intent on centralization placed even more importance on the service of eunuchs, since they expected that servants whose fortunes depended exclusively on the emperors' favor would work especially diligently to advance the emperors' interests.

Mandarins and Eunuchs

The tightly centralized administration instituted by the early Ming emperors lasted more than five hundred years. Although the dynasty fell in 1644 to Manchu invaders, who founded the Qing dynasty, the Manchus retained the administrative framework of the Ming state, which largely survived until the collapse of the Qing dynasty in 1911.

---

eunuchs (YOO-nihks)

Ming artisans won worldwide fame for their blue-and-white porcelain, which inspired the founders of the Delft porcelain factory in the Netherlands. This covered jar dates from the early fifteenth century.

While building a centralized administration, the Ming emperors also worked toward economic recovery. The new rulers conscripted laborers to rebuild irrigation systems that had fallen into disrepair, and agricultural production surged as a result. At the same time, they promoted the manufacture of porcelain, lacquerware, and fine silk and cotton textiles. They did not actively promote trade with other lands, but private Chinese merchants conducted a thriving business marketing Chinese products in ports and trading cities from Japan to the islands of southeast Asia. Meanwhile, domestic trade surged within China, reflecting increasing productivity and prosperity.

Economic Recovery

Alongside political and economic recovery, the Ming dynasty sponsored a kind of cultural revival in China. Emperor Hongwu tried to eradicate all signs of the recent nomadic occupation by discouraging the use of Mongol names and the wearing of Mongol dress. Ming emperors actively promoted Chinese cultural traditions, particularly the Confucian and neo-Confucian schools. Hongwu's successor, Yongle, even organized the preparation of a vast encyclopedia that com-

Cultural Revival

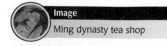

piled all significant works of Chinese history, philosophy, and literature. This *Yongle Encyclopedia* ran to almost twenty-three thousand manuscript rolls, each equivalent to a medium-size book, and was a clear signal of Ming interest in supporting native Chinese cultural traditions.

Recovery in Western Europe: State Building

Demographic recovery strengthened states in western Europe as it did in China. In Europe, however, political authority rested with a series of regional states rather than a centralized empire. By the late fifteenth century, states in Italy, Spain, France, and England had devised techniques of government that vastly enhanced their power.

During the later middle ages (1300–1500), internal problems as well as bubonic plague complicated European political affairs. The Holy Roman Empire survived in name, but effective authority lay with the German princes and the Italian city-states rather than the emperor. In Spain descendants of Muslim conquerors held the kingdom of Granada in the southern portion of the Iberian peninsula. Meanwhile, the kings of France and England sparred constantly over lands claimed by both.

By the late fifteenth century, however, regional states in western Europe had greatly strengthened their societies. The state-building efforts of the later middle ages involved two especially important elements. The first was the development of fresh sources of finance, usually through new taxes levied directly on citizens and subjects. The second was the maintenance of large standing armies, often composed of mercenary forces and equipped with gunpowder weapons, supported by state funds.

Taxes and Armies

The state-building process began in Italy, where profits from industrial production and trade enriched the major cities. Beginning in the thirteenth century, the principal Italian states—the city-states of Milan, Venice, and Florence, the papal state based in Rome, and the kingdom of Naples—began to finance their needs for military forces and larger bureaucracies by levying direct taxes and issuing long-term bonds that they repaid from treasury receipts. With fresh sources of finance, the principal Italian states strengthened their authority within their own boundaries as well as in their surrounding areas.

Italian States

During the fourteenth and fifteenth centuries, Italian administrative methods made their way be-

Yongle (YAWNG-leh)

yond the Alps. Partly because of the enormous expenses they incurred during wars against each other,

France and England

the kings of France and England began to levy direct taxes and assemble powerful armies. Rulers in both lands asserted the authority of the central government over the nobility. In France, King Louis XI (reigned 1461–1483) accomplished this by maintaining a permanent army of about fifteen thousand well-armed troops. Because the expense of maintaining such forces was beyond the means of the nobility, Louis and his successors enjoyed a decisive edge over ambitious subordinates seeking to challenge royal authority.

The process of state building was most dramatic in Spain, where the marriage in 1469 of Fernando of

Spain

Aragon and Isabel of Castile united the two wealthiest Iberian realms. Receipts from the sales tax, the primary source of royal income, supported a powerful standing army. Under Fernando and Isabel, popularly known as the Catholic Kings,

Image
Fernando and Isabel receive Boabdil

Christian forces completed the *reconquista* by conquering the kingdom of Granada and absorbing it into their state. The Catholic Kings also projected their authority beyond Iberia. When a French army threatened the kingdom of Naples in 1494, they seized southern Italy, and by 1559 Spanish forces had established their hegemony throughout most of the Italian peninsula.

Competition between European states intensified as they tightened their authority in their territories. This competition led to frequent small-scale wars between European states, and it encouraged the rapid development of military and naval technology. As states sought technological advantages over their neighbors, they encouraged the refinement and improvement of weapons, ships, and sails. When one state acquired powerful weapons—such as ships equipped with cannons—neighboring states sought to outdo their rivals with more advanced devices. Thus technological innovations vastly strengthened European armies just as they began to venture again into the larger world.

Recovery in Western Europe: The Renaissance

Demographic recovery and state-building efforts in western Europe coincided with a remarkable cultural

reconquista (ray-kohn-KEES-tah)

Brunelleschi's magnificent dome on the cathedral of Florence dominates the city's skyline even today.

flowering known as the Renaissance. The French word *renaissance* means "rebirth," and it refers here to a period of artistic and intellectual creativity from the fourteenth to the sixteenth century in western Europe. Painters, sculptors, and architects of the Renaissance era drew inspiration from classical Greek and Roman artists rather than from their medieval predecessors. In their efforts to revive classical aesthetic standards, they transformed European art. Meanwhile, Renaissance scholars known as humanists looked to classical rather than medieval literary models, and they sought to update medieval moral thought and adapt it to the needs of a bustling urban society.

Just as they pioneered new techniques of statecraft, the Italian city-states also pioneered Renaissance innovations in art and architecture. In

Italian Renaissance Art

search of realistic depictions, Italian artists studied the human form and represented the emotions of their subjects. Italian painters such as Leonardo da Vinci (1452–1519) relied on the technique of linear perspective to represent the three dimensions of real life

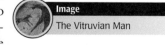
Image
The Vitruvian Man

on two-dimensional surfaces. Sculptors such as Donatello (1386–1466) and Michelangelo Buonarotti (1475–1564) sought to depict their subjects in natural poses that reflected the actual workings of human muscles rather than the awkward and rigid postures of earlier sculptures.

Renaissance architects designed buildings in the simple, elegant style preferred by their classical Greek and Roman predecessors. Their most impressive achievement was the construction of domed buildings.

Roman architects had built domes, but their technology and engineering did not survive the collapse of the Roman empire. In the early fifteenth century, however, the Florentine architect Filippo Brunelleschi (1377–1446) reinvented equipment and designs for a large dome. During the 1420s and 1430s, he oversaw the construction of a magnificent dome on the cathedral of Florence, which residents took as a symbol of the city's wealth and leadership in artistic and cultural affairs.

Renaissance Architecture

Like Renaissance artists and architects, scholars and literary figures known as humanists drew inspiration from classical models. The term *humanist* referred to scholars interested in the humanities—literature, history, and moral philosophy. Renaissance humanists were also deeply committed to Christianity. Several humanists worked diligently to prepare accurate texts and translations of the New Testament and other important Christian writings. Most notable of them was Desiderius Erasmus of Rotterdam (1466–1536), who in 1516 published the first edition of the Greek New Testament along with a revised Latin translation and copious annotations.

The Humanists

Humanists scorned the dense and often convoluted writing style of the scholastic theologians. Instead, they preferred the elegant and polished language of classical Greek and Roman authors and the early church fathers, whose works they considered more engaging and more persuasive than those of medieval philosophers and theologians. Thus humanists such as the Florentine Francesco Petrarca, known in English as Petrarch (1304–1374), traveled throughout Europe searching for manuscripts of classical works. In the monastic libraries of Italy, Switzerland, and southern France, they found hundreds of Latin writings that medieval scholars had overlooked. During the fifteenth century, Italian humanists became acquainted with Byzantine scholars and enlarged the body of classical Greek as well as Latin works available to scholars.

Classical Greek and Latin values encouraged the humanists to reconsider medieval ethical teachings. Medieval moral philosophers had taught that the most honorable calling was that of monks and nuns who withdrew from the world and dedicated their lives to prayer and contemplation, but the humanists drew inspiration from classical authors such as Cicero, who demonstrated that it was possible to lead a morally virtuous life while participating actively in

Humanist Moral Thought

the affairs of the world. Renaissance humanists argued that it was perfectly honorable for Christians to enter into marriage, business relationships, and public affairs. Humanist moral thought thus represented an effort to reconcile Christian values and ethics with the increasingly urban and commercial society of Renaissance Europe.

Quite apart from the conscious effort to draw inspiration from classical antiquity, Renaissance art and thought also reflected increasing European participation in the affairs of the eastern hemisphere. As merchants linked Europe to the larger hemispheric economy, European peoples experienced increased prosperity, which enabled them to invest resources in artistic production and support for scholarship. Renaissance painters filled their canvases with images of silk garments, lacquered wood, spice jars, and foreign peoples that had recently come to European attention. Princes and wealthy patrons commissioned hundreds of these paintings, which brought a cosmopolitan look to their palaces, residences, and places of business.

Renaissance Europe and the Larger World

EXPLORATION AND COLONIZATION

As peoples of the eastern hemisphere recovered from demographic collapse and restored order to their societies, they also sought to revive the networks of long-distance trade and communication that epidemic plague had disrupted. Most active in that effort were China and western Europe—the two societies that recovered most rapidly from the disasters of the fourteenth century. During the early Ming dynasty, Chinese ports accommodated foreign traders, and mariners mounted a series of enormous naval expeditions that visited almost all parts of the Indian Ocean basin. Meanwhile, by the end of the fifteenth century, Europeans not only had established sea lanes to India but also had made several return voyages to the American continents, thus inaugurating a process that brought all the world's peoples into permanent and sustained interaction.

The Chinese Reconnaissance of the Indian Ocean Basin

Having ousted the Mongols, the early Ming emperors were not eager to have large numbers of foreigners residing in China. Yet the emperors permitted foreign merchants to trade in the closely supervised ports of Quanzhou and Guangzhou, where they obtained Chinese silk, porcelain, and manufactured goods in exchange for pearls, gems, spices, and cotton fabrics. The early Ming emperors also refurbished the large Chinese navy built during the Song dynasty, and they allowed Chinese merchants to participate in overseas trading ventures in Japan and southeast Asia.

Moreover, for almost thirty years, the Ming government sponsored a series of seven unprecedented naval expeditions designed to establish a Chinese presence in the Indian Ocean basin. Emperor Yongle organized the expeditions for two main purposes: to impose imperial control over foreign trade with China and to impress foreign peoples with the power and might of the Ming dynasty. Indeed, he might well have hoped to extend the tributary system, by which Chinese dynasties traditionally recognized foreign peoples, to lands in the Indian Ocean basin.

Zheng He's Expeditions

The expeditions took place between 1405 and 1433. Leading them was the eunuch admiral Zheng He, a Muslim from Yunnan in southwestern China who became a trusted advisor of Yongle. Zheng He embarked on each voyage with an awesome fleet of vessels complemented by armed forces large enough to overcome resistance at any port where the expedition called. On the first voyage, for example, Zheng He's fleet consisted of 317 ships accompanied by almost twenty-eight thousand armed troops. Many of these vessels were mammoth, nine-masted ships with four decks capable of accommodating five hundred or more passengers. Measuring up to 124 meters (408 feet) long and 51 meters (166 feet) wide, these ships were by far the largest marine craft the world had ever seen.

On the first three voyages, Zheng He took his fleet to southeast Asia, India, and Ceylon. The fourth expedition went to the Persian Gulf and Arabia, and later expeditions ventured down the east African coast, calling at ports as far south as Malindi in modern Kenya. Throughout his travels, Zheng He liberally dispensed gifts of Chinese silk, porcelain, and other goods. In return he received rich and unusual presents, including African zebras and giraffes.

Zheng He generally sought to attain his goals through diplomacy, and for the most part he had little need to engage in hostilities. But a contemporary reported that Zheng He did not shrink from violence when he considered it necessary to impress foreign peoples with China's military might. He ruthlessly suppressed pirates

Chinese Naval Power

who had long plagued Chinese and southeast Asian waters. He also intervened in a civil disturbance to establish his authority in Ceylon, and he made displays of military force when local officials threatened his fleet in Arabia and east Africa. The seven expeditions established a Chinese presence and reputation in the Indian Ocean basin. Returning from his fourth voyage, Zheng He brought envoys from thirty states who traveled to China and paid their respects at the Ming court.

Yet suddenly, in the mid-1430s, the Ming emperors decided to end the expeditions. Confucian ministers, who mistrusted Zheng He and the eunuchs who supported the voyages, argued that resources committed to the expensive expeditions should go to better uses. Moreover, during the 1420s and 1430s the Mongols mounted a new military threat from the northwest, and land forces urgently needed financial support.

End of the Voyages

Thus in 1433, after Zheng He's seventh voyage, the expeditions ended. Chinese merchants continued to trade in Japan and southeast Asia, but imperial officials destroyed most of the nautical charts that Zheng He had carefully prepared. The decommissioned ships sat in harbors until they rotted away, and Chinese craftsmen forgot the technology of building such large vessels. Yet Zheng He's voyages demonstrated clearly that China could exercise military, political, and economic influence throughout the Indian Ocean basin.

European Exploration in the Atlantic and Indian Oceans

As Chinese fleets reconnoitered the Indian Ocean, European mariners were preparing to enter both the Atlantic and the Indian Ocean basins. Unlike Zheng He and his companions, however, Europeans ventured onto the seas not for diplomatic reasons but to expand the boundaries of Roman Catholic Christianity and to profit from commercial opportunities.

The experience of Portugal illustrates that mixture of motives. During the fifteenth century Prince Henrique of Portugal, often called Prince Henry the Navigator, embarked on an ambitious campaign to spread Christianity and increase Portuguese influence on the seas. In 1415 he watched as Portuguese forces seized the Moroccan city of Ceuta, which guarded the Strait of Gibraltar from the south. He regarded his victory both as a blow against Islam and as a strategic

Portuguese Exploration

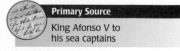

Primary Source

King Afonso V to his sea captains

Map 19.2 Chinese and European voyages of exploration from 1405 to 1498. Note the extensive nature of all of these voyages. What can the fact that these voyages took place at all tell us about the larger societies of China and Iberia in this period?

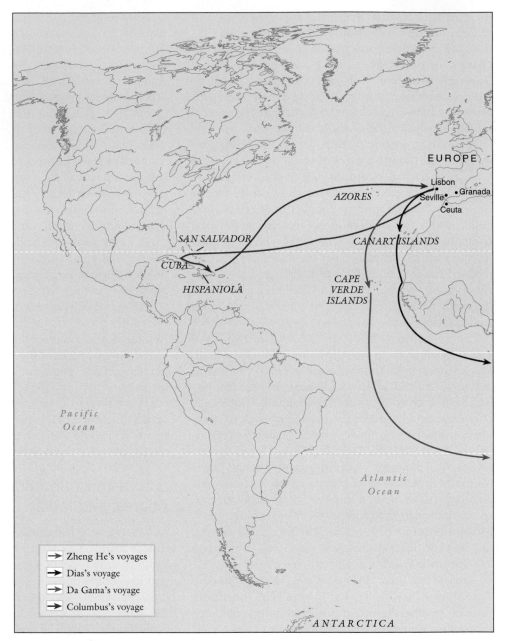

move enabling Christian vessels to move freely between the Mediterranean and the Atlantic.

Following the capture of Ceuta, Henrique encouraged Portuguese mariners to venture into the Atlantic. During their voyages they discovered the Madeiras and Azores Islands, all uninhabited, which they soon colonized. Later discoveries included the Cape Verde Islands, Fernando Po, São

Colonization of the Atlantic Islands

Tomé, and Principe off the west African coast. Because these Atlantic islands enjoyed fertile soils and a Mediterranean climate, Portuguese entrepreneurs soon began to cultivate sugarcane there, often in collaboration with Italian investors. Italians had financed sugar plantations in the Mediterranean islands since the twelfth century, and their commercial networks provided a ready means to distribute sugar to Europeans, who were rapidly developing a taste for sweets.

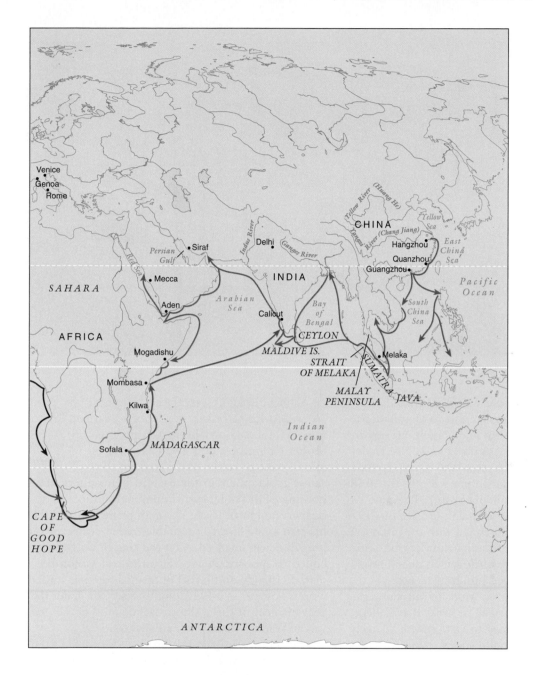

During the middle decades of the fifteenth century, a series of Portuguese fleets also explored the west African coast. Originally, the Portuguese traded guns, textiles, and other manufactured items for African gold and slaves. Soon, Portuguese traders changed the nature of the African slave trade by dramatically increasing its volume and by sending slaves to new destinations. In the mid–fifteenth century the Portuguese dispatched thousands of slaves annually to recently founded plantations in the Atlantic islands, where the slaves worked as laborers. The use of African slaves to perform heavy labor on commercial plantations soon became common practice, and it fueled the development of a huge, Atlantic-wide trade that delivered as many as twelve million enslaved Africans to destinations in North America, South America, and the Caribbean region.

Slave Trade

Although Christopher Columbus believed that he had sailed into Asian waters, later mariners soon realized that the Americas were continents unknown to geographers of the eastern hemisphere. This map, prepared in 1532 by the German cartographer Sebastian Münster, shows that by the early sixteenth century European geographers had acquired a rough but accurate understanding of South America but had reconnoitered only the Atlantic coastline of North America.

While some Portuguese mariners traded profitably in west Africa, others sought to eliminate the role of Muslim and Italian intermediaries in the Asian silk and spice trades by finding a sea lane from Europe around Africa and into the Indian Ocean. By 1488 Bartolomeu Dias had sailed around the Cape of Good Hope and entered the Indian Ocean. In 1497 Vasco da Gama departed Portugal with the intention of sailing to India. After rounding the Cape of Good Hope, he cruised up the east African coast and found a Muslim pilot who showed him how to take advantage of the seasonal monsoon winds to sail across the Arabian Sea to India. In 1498 he arrived at Calicut, and by 1499 he had returned to Lisbon with a hugely profitable cargo of pepper and spices.

Indian Ocean Trade

For most of the following century, Portuguese merchants and mariners dominated trade between Europe and Asia. Indeed, they attempted to control all shipping in the Indian Ocean by overpowering the vessels of Arabs, Persians, Indians, and southeast Asians. They did not have enough ships to oversee all trade in the region, but the entry of Portuguese mariners into the Indian Ocean signaled the beginning of European imperialism in Asia.

While Portuguese seafarers sought a sea route around Africa to India, the Genoese mariner Cristoforo Colombo, known in English as Christopher Columbus, conceived the idea of sailing west to reach Asian markets. Because geographers in the eastern hemisphere knew nothing of the Americas, Columbus's notion made a certain amount of sense, although many doubted that his plan could lead to profitable trade because of the long distances involved. After the king of Portugal declined to sponsor an expedition to test Columbus's plan, Fernando and Isabel of Spain agreed to underwrite a voyage. In 1492 Columbus set sail. Later that year his fleet of three ships reached land at San Salvador (Watling Island) in the Bahamas.

Christopher Columbus

Columbus returned to Spain without the gold, silk, and spices that he had expected to find, but he persistently held that he had reached islands near the Asian mainland and the markets of China and Japan. Yet although Columbus himself never acknowledged that his expeditions had not reached Asia, by the end of the fifteenth century other mariners who came to explore the Caribbean and the American continents realized that the western hemisphere constituted a world apart from Europe, Asia, and Africa.

SUMMARY

As European mariners ventured into the Indian and Atlantic Ocean basins, they unwittingly inaugurated a new era in world history. By 1500 the Indian Ocean served as a highway linking peoples from China to east Africa, and overland traffic kept the silk roads busy from China to the Mediterranean Sea. Trade goods, diplomatic missions, religious faiths, technological skills, agricultural crops, and disease pathogens all moved readily over the sea lanes and the silk roads, and they profoundly influenced the development of societies throughout the eastern hemisphere. In the western hemisphere, trading networks linked lands as distant as Mexico and the Great Lakes region, while Pacific islanders regularly traveled and traded between island groups. Never before, however, had peoples of the eastern hemisphere, the western hemisphere, and Oceania dealt with one another on a regular and systematic basis. The voyages of European mariners during the fifteenth and following centuries initiated a long-term process that brought all regions and peoples of planet earth into permanent and sustained interaction. The formation and reconfiguration of global networks of power, communication, and exchange that followed from these interactions rank among the most prominent themes of modern world history.

CHRONOLOGY

1253–1324	Life of Marco Polo
1287–1288	Rabban Sauma's embassy to Europe
1304–1369	Life of Ibn Battuta
1304–1374	Life of Francesco Petrarca
1330s	First outbreaks of bubonic plague in China
1347	Arrival of bubonic plague in the Mediterranean basin
1368–1644	Ming Dynasty
1405–1433	Zheng He's expeditions in the Indian Ocean
1466–1536	Life of Desiderius Erasmus of Rotterdam
1488	Bartolomeu Dias's voyage around Africa
1492	Christopher Columbus's first voyage to the western hemisphere
1497–1498	Vasco da Gama's voyage to India

FOR FURTHER READING

Janet L. Abu-Lughod. *Before European Hegemony: The World System, A.D. 1250–1350*. New York, 1989. An important study of long-distance trade networks during the Mongol era.

Jerry H. Bentley. *Old World Encounters: Cross-Cultural Contacts and Exchanges in Pre-modern Times*. New York, 1993. Studies cultural and religious exchanges in the eastern hemisphere before 1500 C.E.

Jerry Brotton. *The Renaissance Bazaar: From the Silk Road to Michelangelo*. Oxford, 2002. A provocative and well-illustrated study arguing that encounters in the larger world deeply influenced Renaissance cultural development in Europe.

K. N. Chaudhuri. *Asia before Europe: Economy and Civilisation of the Indian Ocean from the Rise of Islam to 1750*. Cambridge, 1990. Controversial and penetrating analysis of economic, social, and cultural structures shaping societies of the Indian Ocean basin.

Ross E. Dunn. *The Adventures of Ibn Battuta: A Muslim Traveler of the 14th Century*. Berkeley, 1986. Fascinating reconstruction of Ibn Battuta's travels and experiences.

Robert S. Gottfried. *The Black Death: Natural and Human Disaster in Medieval Europe*. New York, 1983. The best general study of bubonic plague and its effects in Europe.

John Larner. *Marco Polo and the Discovery of the World*. New Haven, 1999. Excellent study of Marco Polo and his significance, based on a thorough review of both textual evidence and recent scholarship.

Louise L. Levathes. *When China Ruled the Seas: The Treasure Fleet of the Dragon Throne, 1405–1433*. New York, 1994. Excellent popular account of Zheng He's voyages.

William D. Phillips Jr. and Carla Rahn Phillips. *The Worlds of Christopher Columbus*. New York, 1992. The best general work on Christopher Columbus.

Frances Wood. *The Silk Road: Two Thousand Years in the Heart of Asia*. Berkeley, 2002. A brilliantly illustrated volume discussing the history of the silk roads from antiquity to the twentieth century.

By 1500 C.E. peoples throughout the world had built well-organized societies with distinctive cultural traditions. Powerful agricultural societies dominated most of Asia, the Mediterranean basin, Europe, much of sub-Saharan Africa, Mexico, and the central Andean region. By 1500 peoples of the world had also established intricate transportation networks that supported travel, communication, and exchange. Although pioneered by merchants in the interests of trade, religion, food crops, animal stocks, and disease pathogens also traveled these routes.

Yet the commercial, cultural, and biological exchanges of premodern times prefigured much more intense cross-cultural interactions after 1500. Beginning in the fifteenth century, European mariners established trade routes linking the lands of the Indian, Atlantic, and Pacific Ocean basins. These routes in turn fostered direct contact between the peoples of the eastern hemisphere, the western hemisphere, and Oceania.

The establishment of links between all the world's regions and peoples gave rise to the early modern era of world history, approximately 1500 to 1800 C.E. The early modern era differed from the period from 1000 to 1500, when there were only sporadic contacts between peoples of the eastern hemisphere, the western hemisphere, and Oceania. It also differed from the modern era, from 1800 to the present, when national states, heavy industry, powerful weapons, and efficient technologies of transportation and communication enabled peoples of European ancestry to achieve political and economic dominance in the world.

During the early modern era, several global processes touched peoples in all parts of the world and influenced the development of their societies. One involved biological exchange: plants, animals, diseases, and human communities crossed the world's oceans and established themselves in new lands, where they dramatically affected both

the natural environment and established
societies. Another involved commercial exchange:
merchants took advantage of newly established sea lanes to
inaugurate a genuinely global economy. Yet another process involved the diffusion of
technologies and cultural traditions: printing and gunpowder spread throughout the
world, and Christianity and Islam attracted increasing numbers of converts.

These global processes had different effects for different peoples. In the Americas
and Oceania, diseases introduced from the eastern hemisphere ravaged indigenous
populations and sometimes led to the collapse of whole societies. In contrast, Europeans

THE ORIGINS OF GLOBAL INTERDEPENDENCE, 1500–1800

claimed vast stretches of land in the Americas, where they founded colonies and
cultivated crops for sale on the open market. In sub-Saharan Africa, millions of enslaved
individuals underwent a forced migration to the western hemisphere, where they
suffered both physical and psychological abuse. Meanwhile, east Asian and Islamic
peoples prospered from increased trade but restricted the introduction of foreign ideas
and technologies into their societies.

Although European peoples benefited from global processes of the period 1500
to 1800, by no means did they dominate world affairs in early modern times. Indeed,
most of the western hemisphere and Africa lay beyond their control until the nineteenth
century. Nevertheless, European peoples played a more prominent role in world affairs
than any of their ancestors, and their efforts helped foster the development of an
increasingly interdependent world.

CHAPTER 20

Transoceanic Encounters and Global Connections

On 8 July 1497 the Portuguese mariner Vasco da Gama led a small fleet of four armed merchant vessels with 170 crewmen out of the harbor at Lisbon. His destination was India, which he planned to reach by sailing around the continent of Africa and through the Indian Ocean. He carried letters of introduction from the king of Portugal as well as cargoes of gold, wool textiles, and other goods that he hoped to exchange for pepper and spices in India.

Before there would be an opportunity to trade, however, da Gama and his crew had a prolonged voyage through two oceans. They sailed south from Portugal to the Cape Verde Islands off the west coast of Africa, where they took on fresh provisions. On 3 August they headed southeast into the Atlantic Ocean to take advantage of the prevailing winds. For the next ninety-five days, the fleet saw no land. By October, da Gama had found westerly winds in the southern Atlantic, rounded the Cape of Good Hope, and entered the Indian Ocean. The fleet slowly worked its way up the east coast of Africa as far as Malindi, where da Gama secured the services of an Indian Muslim pilot to guide his ships across the Arabian Sea. On 20 May 1498—more than ten months after its departure from Lisbon—the fleet anchored at Calicut in southern India.

In India the Portuguese fleet found a wealthy, cosmopolitan society. The markets of Calicut offered not only pepper, ginger, cinnamon, and spices but also rubies, emeralds, gold jewelry, and

OPPOSITE PAGE: *A Chinese lacquer screen from the 17th century depicts Portuguese ships and sailors.*

fine cotton textiles. Alas, apart from gold and some striped cloth, the goods that da Gama had brought attracted little interest among merchants at Calicut. Nevertheless, da Gama managed to exchange gold for a cargo of pepper and cinnamon that turned a handsome profit when the fleet returned to Portugal in August 1499. Da Gama's expedition also opened the door to direct maritime trade between European and Asian peoples and helped to establish permanent links between the world's various regions.

Cross-cultural interactions have been a persistent feature of historical development. Even in ancient times mass migration, campaigns of imperial expansion, and long-distance trade deeply influenced societies throughout the world. Yet after 1500 C.E. cross-cultural interactions took place on a much larger geographic scale than ever before, and encounters were often more disruptive than in earlier centuries. Equipped with advanced technologies and a powerful military arsenal, western European peoples began to cross the world's oceans in large numbers during the early modern era. At the same time, Russian adventurers built an enormous Eurasian empire and ventured tentatively into the Pacific Ocean.

Europeans were not the only peoples who actively explored the larger world during the early modern era. In the early fifteenth century, the Ming emperors of China sponsored a series of seven enormous maritime expeditions that visited all parts of the Indian Ocean basin. In the sixteenth century Ottoman mariners also ventured into the Indian Ocean. Following the Ottoman conquest of Egypt in 1517, both merchant and military vessels established an Ottoman presence throughout the Indian Ocean basin.

Although other peoples also made their way into the larger world, only Europeans linked the lands and peoples of the eastern hemisphere, the western hemisphere, and Oceania. Because of that, European peoples benefited from unparalleled opportunities to increase their power, wealth, and influence. As a result, after 1500 European peoples became much more prominent in the larger world than before.

The expansion of European influence resulted in the establishment of global networks of transportation, communication, and exchange. Indeed, a worldwide diffusion of plants, animals, diseases, and human communities followed European ventures across the oceans, and intricate trade networks eventually gave birth to a global economy.

THE EUROPEAN RECONNAISSANCE OF THE WORLD'S OCEANS

Between 1400 and 1800, European mariners launched a remarkable series of exploratory voyages that took them to nearly all the earth's waters. Those voyages were very expensive affairs. Yet private investors and government authorities had strong motives to underwrite the expeditions and outfit them with the latest nautical technology. The voyages of exploration paid large dividends: they enabled European mariners to chart the world's ocean basins and develop an accurate understanding of world geography. On the basis of that knowledge, European merchants and mariners established global networks of communication, transportation, and exchange—and profited handsomely from their efforts.

Motives for Exploration

A complex combination of motives prompted Europeans to explore the world's oceans. Most important of those motives were the search for basic resources and lands suitable for the cultivation of cash crops, the desire to establish new trade routes to Asian markets, and the aspiration to expand the influence of Christianity.

Mariners from the relatively poor kingdom of Portugal were most prominent in the search for fresh resources and lands. Beginning in the thirteenth century, Portuguese seamen ventured away from the coasts and into the open Atlantic Ocean to supplement their own meager resources. By the early fourteenth century, they had discovered the uninhabited Azores and Madeiras Islands and called frequently at the Canary Islands, inhabited by the indigenous Guanche people. These Atlantic islands proved ideal for the cultivation of sugar, a product that enjoyed a strong European demand. In the fifteenth century, Italian investors—who had organized sugar plantations in the Mediterranean since the twelfth century—helped Portuguese mariners establish plantations in the Atlantic islands. Continuing Portuguese voyages also led to the establishment of plantations on the Cape Verde Islands, São Tomé, Principe, and Fernando Po.

Portuguese Exploration

The Lure of Trade   Even more alluring than the exploitation of fresh lands and resources was the goal of establishing maritime trade routes to the markets of Asia. During the era of the Mongol empires, European merchants often traveled overland as far as China to trade for Asian goods. When the Mongol empires collapsed and bubonic plague spread across Eurasia in the fourteenth century, however, travel on the silk roads became much more dangerous. As a result, Europeans relied on Muslim mariners to bring Asian goods through the Indian Ocean and the Red Sea to Cairo, where Italian merchants purchased them for distribution in western Europe. But prices at Cairo were high, and Europeans sought ever-larger quantities of Asian goods, particularly spices.

By the fourteenth century the wealthy classes of Europe regarded Indian pepper and Chinese ginger as expensive necessities, and they especially prized cloves and nutmeg from the spice islands of Maluku. Merchants and monarchs alike realized that by gaining direct access to Asian markets and eliminating Muslim intermediaries, they could increase the quantities of spices and other Asian goods available in Europe while making enormous profits.

African trade also beckoned to Europeans and called them to the sea. Since the twelfth century, Europeans had purchased west African gold, ivory, and slaves brought to north African ports by Muslim merchants. West African gold was especially important to Europeans because it was their principal form of payment for Asian luxury goods. As in the case of Asian trade, Europeans realized that they could profit from eliminating Muslim middlemen and establishing maritime routes that offered direct access to African markets.

Missionary Efforts   Alongside material incentives, the goal of expanding the boundaries of Christianity drove Europeans into the larger world. Like Buddhism and Islam, Christianity is a missionary religion that directs believers to spread the faith. Sometimes such efforts were attempted through peaceful persuasion. At other times the expansion of Christianity could be quite violent. Beginning in the eleventh century, for example, western Europeans launched a series of crusades against Muslims in Palestine, the Mediterranean islands, and Iberia. In Iberia, in fact, the Muslim kingdom of Granada fell to Spanish Christian forces just weeks before Christopher Columbus set sail on his famous first voyage to the western hemisphere in 1492. Whether through persuasion or violence, overseas voyages offered fresh opportunities for western Europeans to spread their faith.

In practice, the various motives for exploration combined and reinforced one another. When the Portuguese mariner Vasco da Gama reached the Indian port of Calicut in 1498, local authorities asked him what he wanted there. His reply: "Christians

Image
"Vasco da Gama in Calicut in 1498"

A detail from the Catalan Atlas, a magnificent illustrated representation of the known world produced about 1375, depicts a camel caravan traveling from China to Europe across the silk roads.

and spices." The goal of spreading Christianity thus became a powerful justification and reinforcement for the more material motives for the voyages of exploration.

The Technology of Exploration

Without advanced nautical technology and navigational skills, even the strongest motives would not have enabled European mariners to reconnoiter the world's oceans. They also needed sturdy ships, good navigational equipment, and knowledge of sailing techniques. These they devised by combining Chinese and Arabic technologies with their own inherited nautical technologies from the Mediterranean and northern Europe.

From their experiences in the rough coastal waters of the Atlantic, European sailors learned to con-

Ships and Sails

struct ships strong enough to brave most adverse conditions. Beginning about the twelfth century, they increased the maneuverability of their craft by building a rudder onto the stern. (The sternpost rudder was a Chinese invention that had diffused across the Indian Ocean.) They outfitted their vessels with two types of sails: square sails (which enabled them to take full advantage of a wind blowing from behind) and triangular lateen sails (which could catch winds from the side as well as from behind). With a combination of square and lateen sails, European ships were able to use whatever winds arose. Their ability to tack—to advance against the wind by sailing across it—was crucial for the exploration of regions with uncooperative winds.

The most important navigational equipment on board these vessels were magnetic compasses (which

Navigational Instruments

determined heading) and astrolabes (which determined latitude). The compass was a Chinese invention that had diffused throughout the Indian Ocean basin in the eleventh century and had reached European mariners by the mid–twelfth century. The astrolabe was a simplified version of an instrument used by Greek and Persian astronomers to measure the angle of the sun or the pole star above the horizon. In the late fifteenth century, however, Por-

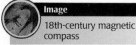
Image
18th-century magnetic compass

tuguese mariners encountered Arab sailors in the Indian Ocean using simpler and more serviceable instruments for determining latitude, which the Portuguese then used as models for the construction of cross-staffs and back-staffs.

By using cross-staffs to measure the angle of the sun or the pole star above the horizon, mariners could determine latitude.

European mariners' ability to determine direction and latitude enabled them to assemble a vast body of data about the earth's geography and to find their way around the world's oceans

Knowledge of Winds and Currents

with tolerable accuracy and efficiency. Equipped with advanced technological hardware, European mariners ventured into the oceans and gradually compiled a body of practical knowledge about winds and currents. Indeed, as they became familiar with the wind systems of the world's oceans, European mariners developed the ability to travel reliably to coastlines throughout the world.

Voyages of Exploration: From the Mediterranean to the Atlantic

Although European exploratory voyaging began as early as the thirteenth century, the pace quickened decisively after 1415. In that year, Prince Henry of Portugal (1394–1460), often called Prince Henry the Navigator, conquered the

Prince Henry of Portugal

Moroccan port of Ceuta and sponsored a series of voyages down the west African coast. Portuguese merchants soon established fortified trading posts at São Jorge da Mina (in modern Ghana) and other strategic locations. There they exchanged European horses and goods for gold and slaves. Portuguese explorations continued after Henry's death, and in 1488 Bartolomeu Dias rounded the Cape of Good Hope and entered the Indian Ocean. He did not proceed farther because of storms and a restless crew, but the route to India, China, and the spice-bearing islands of southeast Asia lay open. The sea route to the Indian Ocean offered European merchants the opportunity to buy silk, spices, and pepper at the source, rather than through

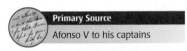

Primary Source

Afonso V to his captains

Muslim intermediaries, and to take part in the flourishing trade of Asia.

As we have already seen, in 1497 Vasco da Gama sought to do just that, departing Lisbon with a fleet of four armed merchant ships bound for India. His experience was not altogether pleasant. His fleet went more than three months without seeing land, and his cargoes excited

Vasco da Gama

Map 20.1 Voyages of European exploration in the Atlantic Ocean between 1486 and 1498. Observe the difference between Bartolomeu Dias's journey and Vasco da Gama's journey around the Cape of Good Hope. Why did da Gama go so far out into the Atlantic before rounding the Cape?

little interest in Indian markets. Moreover, less than half of his crew made it safely back to Portugal. Yet his cargo of pepper and cinnamon was hugely profitable, and Portuguese merchants began immediately to organize further expeditions. By 1500 they had built a trading post at Calicut, and Portuguese mariners soon called at ports throughout the Indian Ocean basin. By the late sixteenth century, English and Dutch mariners followed suit.

Christopher Columbus

While Portuguese navigators plied the sea route to India, the Genoese mariner Cristoforo Colombo, known in English as Christopher Columbus (1451–1506), proposed sailing to the markets of Asia by a western route. On the basis of wide reading in the existing geographical literature, Columbus believed that earth was a relatively small sphere with a circumference of about 17,000 nautical miles. (In fact, the earth's circumference is almost 25,000 nautical miles.) By Columbus's calculations, Japan should have been less than 2,500 nautical miles west of the Canary Islands. (The actual distance is more than 10,000 nautical miles.) This geography suggested that sailing west from Europe to Asian markets would be profitable, and Columbus sought royal sponsorship for a voyage to prove his ideas.

Eventually Fernando and Isabel of Spain agreed to underwrite Columbus's expedition, and in August 1492 his fleet of three ships departed southern Spain. He sailed south to the Canaries, picked up supplies, and then turned west with the trade winds. On the morning of 12 October 1492, he made landfall at an island in the Bahamas that the native Taino inhabitants called Guanahaní and that Columbus rechristened San Salvador (also known as Watling Island). Thinking that he had arrived in the spice islands known familiarly as the Indies, Columbus called the Tainos "Indians." He sailed around the Caribbean for almost three months in search of gold, and at the large island of Cuba he sent a delegation to seek the court of the emperor of China. When Columbus returned to Spain, he reported to his royal sponsors that he had reached islands just off the coast of Asia.

Hemispheric Links

Columbus never reached the riches of Asia, and he obtained very little gold in the Caribbean. Yet news of his voyage spread rapidly throughout Europe, and hundreds of Spanish, English, French, and Dutch mariners soon followed in his wake. Initially, many of them continued to seek the passage to Asian waters that Columbus himself had pursued. Over a longer term, however, it became clear that the American continents and the Caribbean islands themselves held abundant opportunities for entrepreneurs. Thus

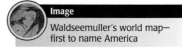
Image
Waldseemuller's world map—first to name America

A map prepared about 1512 by the Polish cartographer Jan Stobnicza shows eloquently that it took a long time for geographers to realize the extent of the Americas and the Pacific Ocean. Here "Cipangu" (Japan) lies just west of Mexico, with the Asian mainland nearby.

Christopher Columbus's First Impressions of American Peoples

Christopher Columbus kept journals of his experiences during his voyages to the western hemisphere. The journal of his first voyage survives mostly in summary, but it clearly communicates Columbus's first impressions of the peoples he met in the Caribbean islands. The following excerpts show that Columbus, like other European mariners, had both Christianity and commerce in mind when exploring distant lands.

■   ■   ■

Thursday, 11 October [1492]. . . .
I . . . in order that they would be friendly to us—because I recognized that they were people who would be better freed [from error] and converted to our Holy Faith by love than by force—to some of them I gave red caps, and glass beads which they put on their chests, and many other things of small value, in which they took so much pleasure and became so much our friends that it was a marvel. Later they came swimming to the ships' launches where we were and brought us parrots and cotton thread in balls and javelins and many other things, and they traded them to us for other things which we gave them, such as small glass beads and bells. In sum, they took everything and gave of what they had willingly.

But it seemed to me that they were a people very poor in everything. All of them go as naked as their mothers bore them; and the women also, although I did not see more than one quite young girl. And all those that I saw were young people, for none did I see of more than 30 years of age. They are very well formed, with handsome bodies and good faces. Their hair [is] coarse—almost like the tail of a horse—and short. They wear their hair down over their eyebrows except for a little in the back which they wear long and never cut. . . .

They do not carry arms nor are they acquainted with them, because I showed them swords and they took them by the edge and through ignorance cut themselves. They have no iron. Their javelins are shafts without iron and some of them have at the end a fish tooth and others of other things. All of them alike are of good-sized stature and carry themselves well. I saw some who had marks of wounds on their bodies and I made signs to them asking what they were; and they showed me how people from other islands nearby came there and tried to take them, and how they defended themselves and I believed and believe that they come here from *tierra firme* [the continent] to take them captive. They should be good and intelligent servants, for I see that they say very quickly everything that is said to them; and I believe that they would become Christians very easily, for it seemed to me that they had no religion. . . .

Monday, 12 November. . . .
They are very gentle and do not know what evil is; nor do they kill others, nor steal; and they are without weapons and so timid that a hundred of them flee from one of our men even if our men are teasing them. And they are credulous and aware that there is a God in heaven and convinced that we come from the heavens; and they say very quickly any prayer that we tell them to say, and they make the sign of the cross. So that Your Highnesses ought to resolve to make them Christians: for I believe that if you begin, in a short time you will end up having converted to our Holy Faith a multitude of peoples and acquiring large dominions and great riches and all of their peoples for Spain. Because without doubt there is in these lands a very great quantity of gold; for not without cause do these Indians that I bring with me say that there are in these islands places where they dig gold and wear it on their chests, on their ears, and on their arms, and on their legs; and they are very thick bracelets. And also there are stones, and there are precious pearls and infinite spicery. . . . And also here there is probably a great quantity of cotton; and I think that it would sell very well here without taking it to Spain but to the big cities belonging to the Grand [Mongol] Khan.

• *On the basis of Columbus's account, what inferences can you draw about his plans for American lands and peoples?*

SOURCE: Christopher Columbus. *The Diario of Christopher Columbus's First Voyage to America*. Trans. by Oliver Dunn and James E. Kelley Jr. Norman: University of Oklahoma Press, 1989, pp. 65–69, 143–45.

Map 20.2 Voyages of European exploration in the Pacific Ocean between 1519 and 1780. Note the vast expanses of blue water mariners had to cross in these voyages. What technologies made such extensive voyages possible?

Columbus's voyages to the western hemisphere had unintended but momentous consequences, since they established links between the eastern and western hemispheres and paved the way for the conquest, settlement, and exploitation of the Americas by European peoples.

Voyages of Exploration: From the Atlantic to the Pacific

While some Europeans sought opportunities in the Americas, others continued to seek a western route to Asian markets. However, in the early sixteenth century no one suspected the vast size of the Pacific Ocean, which covers one-third of the earth's surface.

The reconnaissance of the Pacific Ocean basin began with the Portuguese navigator Fernão de Magalhães (1480–1521), better known as Ferdinand Magellan. While sailing in the service of Portugal, Magellan had visited ports throughout the Indian Ocean basin and had traveled east as far as the spice islands of Maluku. He believed that the spice islands and Asian markets lay fairly close to the western coast of the Americas, and he decided to pursue Christopher Columbus's goal of establishing a western route to Asian waters. Because

Ferdinand Magellan

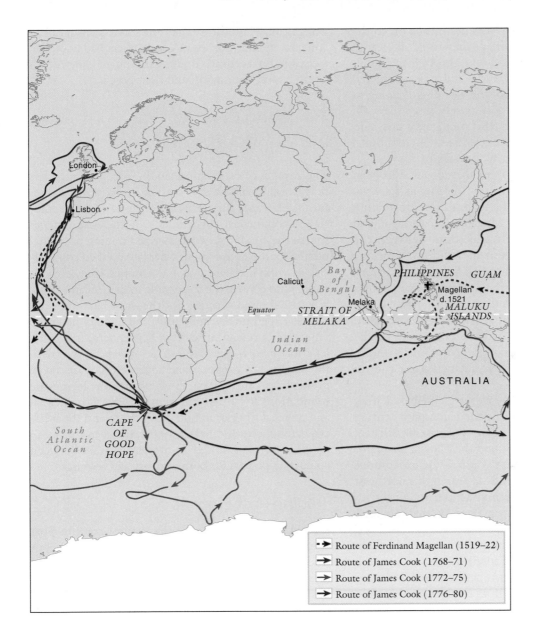

Portuguese mariners had already reached Asian markets through the Indian Ocean, they had little interest in Magellan's proposed western route. Thus, on his Pacific expedition and circumnavigation of the world (1519–1522), Magellan sailed in the service of Spain.

Magellan's voyage was an exercise in endurance. He began by probing the eastern coast of South America in search of a strait leading to the Pacific. Eventually he found and sailed through the treacherous Strait of Magellan near the southern tip of South America. His fleet then sailed almost four months before taking on fresh provisions at Guam.

The Circumnavigation

During that period crewmen survived on worm-ridden biscuits, ship's rats, leather they had softened in the ocean, and water gone foul. Lacking fresh fruits and vegetables in their diet, many of the crew fell victim to the dreaded disease of scurvy, which caused painful rotting of the gums, loss of teeth, abscesses, hemorrhaging, and in most cases death. Scurvy killed twenty-nine members of Magellan's crew during the Pacific crossing.

Conditions improved after the fleet called at Guam, but its ordeal had not come to an end. From Guam, Magellan proceeded to the Philippine Islands, where he and 40 of his crew were killed in a local political dispute. The survivors continued on to the spice islands of Maluku, where they took on a cargo of cloves. They then sailed home through the familiar waters of the Indian Ocean—and thus completed the first circumnavigation of the world—returning to Spain after a voyage of almost exactly three years. Of Magellan's five ships and 280 men, only one ship with 18 of the original crew returned. (An additional 17 crewmen returned later by other routes.)

The Pacific Ocean is so vast that it took European explorers almost three centuries to chart its features.

Exploration of the Pacific Spanish merchants built on information gleaned from Magellan's expedition and established a trade route between the Philippines and Mexico, but they did not continue to explore the ocean basin itself. English navigators, however, ventured into the Pacific in search of a northwest passage from Europe to Asia. While searching for a passage, English mariners established many of the details of Pacific geography. In the sixteenth century, for example, Sir Francis Drake scouted the west coast of North America as far north as Vancouver Island.

Russian expansion was mostly a land-based affair in early modern times, but by the eighteenth century Russians also were exploring the Pacific Ocean. Russian officials commissioned the Danish navigator Vitus Bering to undertake two maritime expeditions (1725–1730 and 1733–1742) in search of a northeast passage to Asian ports. Bering sailed through the icy Arctic Ocean and the Bering Strait, which separates Siberia from Alaska.

Other Russian explorers made their way from Alaska down the western Canadian coast to northern California. By 1800 Russian mariners were scouting the Pacific Ocean as far south as the Hawaiian Islands. Indeed, they built a small fort on the island of Kaua`i and engaged in trade there for a few years in the early nineteenth century.

Alongside Magellan, however, the most important of the Pacific explorers was Captain James Cook

Captain James Cook (1728–1779), who led three expeditions to the Pacific and died in a scuffle with the indigenous people of Hawai`i. Cook charted eastern Australia and New Zealand, and he added New Caledonia, Vanuatu, and Hawai`i to European maps of the Pacific. He probed the frigid waters of the Arctic Ocean and spent months at a time in the tropical islands of Tahiti,

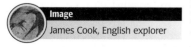
Image
James Cook, English explorer

Tonga, and Hawai`i. By the time Cook's voyages had come to an end, European geographers had compiled a reasonably accurate understanding of the world's ocean basins, their lands, and their peoples.

TRADE AND CONFLICT IN EARLY MODERN ASIA

The voyages of exploration taught European mariners how to sail to almost any coastline in the world and return safely. Once they arrived at their destinations, they sought commercial opportunities. In the eastern hemisphere they built a series of fortified trading posts that offered footholds in regions where established commercial networks had held sway for centuries. They even attempted to control the spice trade in the Indian Ocean, but with limited success. For the most part, they did not have the human numbers or the military power to impose their rule in the eastern hemisphere. In a parallel effort involving expansion across land rather than the sea, Russian explorers and adventurers established a presence in central Asia and Siberia, thus laying the foundations for a vast Eurasian empire. Commercial and political rivalries in both the eastern and the western hemispheres also led to conflict between European peoples, which resulted in numerous wars between competing powers for both territory and resources.

Trading-Post Empires

Portuguese mariners built the earliest trading-post empire. Their goal was not to conquer territories but to control trade routes by forcing merchant vessels to call at fortified trading sites and pay duties there. Vasco da Gama obtained permission from local authorities to establish a trading post at Calicut when he arrived there in 1498. By the mid–sixteenth century, Portuguese merchants had built more than fifty trading posts between west Africa and east Asia.

Portuguese Trading Posts

Equipped with heavy artillery, Portuguese vessels were able to overpower most other craft that they encountered, and they sometimes trained their cannon effectively onshore. The architect of their aggressive policy was Afonso d'Alboquerque, commander of Portuguese forces in the Indian Ocean during the early sixteenth century. Alboquerque's fleets seized Hormuz in 1508, Goa in 1510, and Melaka in 1511. From these strategic sites, Alboquerque sought to control Indian

Afonso d'Alboquerque

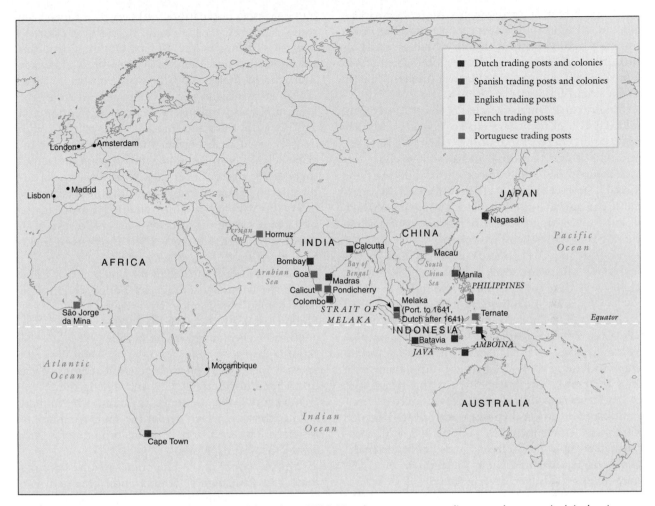

Map 20.3 European trading posts in Africa and Asia about 1700. Note how many more trading posts there were in Asia than in Africa. What accounts for the difference?

Ocean trade by forcing all merchant ships to purchase safe-conduct passes and present them at Portuguese trading posts. Ships without passes were subject to confiscation, along with their cargoes. Alboquerque's forces punished violators of his policy by executing them or cutting off their hands. Alboquerque was confident of Portuguese naval superiority and its ability to control trade in the Indian Ocean.

In reality, however, Portuguese forces did not have enough vessels to enforce their commander's orders. Arab, Indian, and Malay merchants continued to play prominent roles in Indian Ocean commerce, usually without taking the precaution of securing a safe-conduct pass. Indeed, Arab vessels continued to deliver shipments of pepper and spices through the Red Sea, which Portuguese forces never managed to control, to Cairo and Mediterranean trade routes.

By the late sixteenth century, Portuguese hegemony in the Indian Ocean was growing weak. Portugal was a small country with a small population—about one million in 1500—and was unable to sustain its large seaborne trading empire. In addition, by the late sixteenth century, investors in other lands began to organize their own expeditions to Asian markets. Most prominent of those who followed the Portuguese into the Indian Ocean were English and Dutch mariners.

Like their predecessors, English and Dutch merchants built trading posts on Asian coasts and sought to channel trade through them, but they did not attempt to control shipping on the high seas. They also occasionally seized Portuguese sites, although Portuguese authorities held many of their trading posts into the twentieth century. Meanwhile,

English and Dutch Trading Posts

English and Dutch entrepreneurs established parallel networks. English merchants concentrated on India and built trading posts at Bombay, Madras, and Calcutta, while the Dutch operated more broadly from Cape Town, Colombo, and Batavia (modern Jakarta on the island of Java).

English and Dutch merchants enjoyed two main advantages over their Portuguese predecessors. They sailed faster, cheaper, and more powerful ships, which offered both an economic and a military edge over their competitors. Furthermore, they conducted trade through an exceptionally efficient form of commercial organization—the joint-stock company—which enabled investors to realize handsome profits while limiting the risk to their investments.

The Trading Companies

English and Dutch merchants formed two especially powerful joint-stock companies: the English East India Company, founded in 1600, and its Dutch counterpart, the United East India Company, known from its initials as the VOC (Vereenigde Oost-Indische Compagnie), established in 1602. Private merchants advanced funds to launch these companies, outfit them with ships and crews, and provide them with commodities and money to trade. Although they enjoyed government support, the companies were privately owned enterprises. Unhampered by political oversight, company agents concentrated strictly on profitable trade. Their charters granted them the right to buy, sell, build trading posts, and even make war.

The English and Dutch companies experienced immediate financial success. In 1601, for example, five English ships set sail from London with cargoes mostly of gold and silver coins valued at thirty thousand pounds sterling. When they returned in 1603, the spices that they carried were worth more than one million pounds sterling. Because of their advanced nautical technology, powerful military arsenal, efficient organization, and relentless pursuit of profit, the English East India Company and the VOC contributed to the early formation of a global network of trade.

European Conquests in Southeast Asia

Following voyages of exploration to the western hemisphere, Europeans conquered indigenous peoples, built territorial empires, and established colonies settled by European migrants. In the eastern hemisphere, however, they were mostly unable to force their will on large Asian populations and powerful centralized states. With the decline of the Portuguese effort to control shipping in the Indian Ocean, Europeans mostly traded peacefully in Asian waters alongside Arab, Indian, Malay, and Chinese merchants.

Yet in two island regions of southeast Asia—the Philippines and Indonesia—Europeans conquered existing authorities and imposed their rule. Though densely populated, neither the Philippines nor Indonesia had a powerful state when Europeans arrived there in the sixteenth century. Nor did imperial authorities in China or India lay claim to the island regions. Heavily armed ships enabled Europeans to bring overwhelming force to bear and to establish imperial regimes that favored the interests of European merchants.

Conquest of the Philippines

Spanish forces approached the Philippines in 1565 under the command of Miguel López de Legazpi, who named the islands after King Philip II of Spain. Because the Philippines had no central government, there was no organized resistance to the intrusion. By 1575 Spanish forces controlled the coastal regions of the central and northern islands, and during the seventeenth century they extended their authority to most parts of the archipelago except the southern island of Mindanao, where a large Muslim community stoutly resisted Spanish expansion.

Manila

Spanish policy in the Philippines revolved around trade and Christianity. Manila soon emerged as a bustling, multicultural port city—an entrepôt for trade, particularly in silk—and it quickly became the hub of Spanish commercial activity in Asia. Chinese merchants were especially prominent in Manila. They occupied a specially designated commercial district of the city and supplied silk goods that Spanish traders shipped to Mexico in the so-called Manila galleons. Their commercial success brought suspicion on the Chinese community, however, and resentful Spanish and Filipino residents massacred Chinese merchants in several eruptions of violence over the next few hundred years. Meanwhile, the Spanish also sought to Christianize the Philippines. Spanish rulers and missionaries pressured prominent Filipinos to convert to Christianity in hopes of persuading others to follow their example. They opened schools to teach the fundamentals of Christian doctrine, along with basic literacy, in densely populated regions throughout the islands. Although Spanish missionaries initially faced resistance, over the long term Filipinos turned increasingly to Christianity, and by the nineteenth century the Philippines had become one of the most fervent Roman Catholic lands in the world.

Dutch mariners who imposed their rule on the islands of Indonesia did not worry about seeking con-*Conquest of Java* verts to Christianity but concentrated instead on the trade in spices, particularly cloves, nutmeg, and mace. The architect of Dutch policy was Jan Pieterszoon Coen, who in 1619 founded Batavia on the island of Java to serve as an entrepôt for the VOC. Coen's plan was to establish a VOC monopoly over spice production and trade, thus enabling Dutch merchants to reap enormous profits in European markets. Coen brought his naval power to bear on the small Indonesian islands and forced them to deliver spices only to VOC merchants. By the late seventeenth century, the VOC controlled all the ports of Java as well as most of the important spice-bearing islands throughout the Indonesian archipelago.

Dutch numbers were too few for them to rule directly over their whole southeast Asian empire. They made alliances with local authorities to maintain order in most regions, reserving for direct Dutch rule only Batavia and the most important spice-bearing islands. The Dutch did not embark on campaigns of conquest for purposes of adding to their holdings, but they uprooted spice-bearing plants on islands they did not control and mercilessly attacked peoples who sold their spices to merchants not associated with the VOC. Monopoly profits from the spice trade not only enriched the VOC but also made the Netherlands the most prosperous land in Europe throughout most of the seventeenth century.

Foundations of the Russian Empire in Asia

While western European peoples were building maritime empires, Russians were laying the foundations for a vast land empire that embraced most of northern Eurasia. This round of expansion began in the mid–sixteenth century, as Russian forces took over several Mongol khanates in central Asia. Those acquisitions resulted in Russian control over the Volga River and offered opportunities for trade with the Ottoman empire, Iran, and even India through the Caspian Sea. In the eighteenth century, Russian forces extended their presence in the Caspian Sea region by absorbing much of the Caucasus, a vibrant multiethnic region embracing the modern-day states of Georgia, Armenia, and Azerbaijan.

Far more extensive were Russian acquisitions in northeastern Eurasia. The frozen tundras and dense forests of Siberia posed formidable challenges, *Siberia* but explorers and merchants made their way into the region in a quest for fur. In the late sixteenth century, Russian explorers pushed into the interior regions of Siberia by way of the region's great rivers. By 1639 they had made their way across the Eurasian landmass and reached the Pacific Ocean.

Siberia was home to about twenty-six major ethnic groups that lived by hunting, trapping, fishing, or herding reindeer. These indigenous peoples varied widely in language and *Native Peoples of Siberia* religion, and they responded in different ways to the arrival of Russian adventurers who sought to exact tribute from them by coercing them to supply animal pelts on a regular basis. Some groups readily accepted iron tools, woven cloth, flour, tea, and liquor for the skins of fur-bearing animals such as otter, lynx, and especially sable. Others resented the ever-increasing demands for tribute and resisted Russian encroachment on their lands. For example, the Yakut people of the Lena and Aldan river

Harvesting mace on the island of Lontor in the Banda Islands.

valleys in central Siberia mounted a revolt against Russian oppression in 1642. The Russian response was brutal: over a period of forty years, Russian forces forced many Yakut out of their settlements and reduced their population by an estimated 70 percent. Quite apart from military violence, the peoples of Siberia reeled from epidemic diseases that reduced many populations by more than half.

The Russian Occupation of Siberia
Despite the region's harsh climate, Russian migrants—some of whom were social misfits or convicted criminals—gradually filtered into Siberia and thoroughly altered its demographic complexion. Small agricultural settlements grew up near many trading posts, particularly in the fertile Amur River valley. Over time, Siberian trading posts developed into Russian towns with Russian-speaking populations attending Russian Orthodox churches. By 1763 some 420,000 Russians lived in Siberia, nearly double the number of indigenous inhabitants. In the nineteenth century, large numbers of additional migrants moved east to mine Siberian gold, silver, copper, and iron, and the

Russian state was well on the way toward consolidating its control over the region.

European Commercial Rivalries

Exploration and imperial expansion led to conflicts not only between Europeans and Asians but also among Europeans themselves. Mariners competed vigorously for trade in Asia and the Americas, and their efforts to establish markets—and sometimes monopolies—led frequently to clashes with their counterparts from different lands.

Indeed, throughout the seventeenth and early eighteenth centuries, commercial and political rivalries led to running wars between ships flying different flags. Dutch vessels were most numerous in the Indian Ocean, and they enabled the VOC to dominate the spice trade. Dutch forces expelled most Portuguese merchants from southeast Asia and prevented English mariners from establishing secure footholds there. By the early eighteenth century, trade in Indian cotton and tea from

Competition and Conflict

Map 20.4 Russian expansion between 1462 and 1795. Observe how vast the empire became after it added the territory of Siberia. How did Russians exert their control over such a huge and unforgiving territory?

Ceylon had begun to overshadow the spice trade, and English and French merchants working from trading posts in India became the dominant carriers in the Indian Ocean. Fierce competition again generated violence: in 1746 French forces seized the English trading post at Madras, one of the three principal centers of British operations in India.

Commercial competition led to conflict also in the Caribbean and the Americas. English pirates and privateers preyed on Spanish shipping from Mexico, often seizing vessels carrying cargoes of silver. English and French forces constantly skirmished and fought over sugar islands in the Caribbean while also contesting territorial claims in North America. In addition, almost all conflicts between European states in the eighteenth century spilled over into the Caribbean and the Americas.

GLOBAL EXCHANGES

European explorers and those who followed them established links between all lands and peoples of the world. Interaction between peoples in turn resulted in an unprecedented volume of exchange across the boundary lines of societies and cultural regions. Some of that exchange involved biological species: plants, food crops, animals, human populations, and disease pathogens all spread to regions they had not previously visited. These biological exchanges had differing and dramatic effects on human populations, destroying some of them through epidemic diseases while enlarging others through increased food supplies and richer diets. Commercial exchange also flourished in the wake of the voyages of exploration as European merchants traveled to ports throughout the world in search of trade. Indeed, by the mid–eighteenth century they had established globe-girdling networks of trade and communication.

The Columbian Exchange

Processes of biological exchange were prominent features of world history well before modern times. The early expansion of Islam, for example, had facilitated *Biological Exchanges* the diffusion of plants and food crops throughout much of the eastern hemisphere during the period from about 700 to 1100 C.E., some of which helped spark demographic and economic growth in the lands where they took root. Yet the "Columbian exchange"—the global diffusion of plants, food crops, animals, human populations, and disease pathogens that took place after voyages of exploration by Christopher Columbus and other European mariners—had consequences much more profound than earlier rounds of biological exchange. Unlike earlier processes, the Columbian exchange involved lands with radically different flora, fauna, and diseases. For thousands of years the various species of the eastern hemisphere, the western hemisphere, and Oceania had evolved along separate lines. By creating links between these biological zones, the European voyages of exploration set off a round of biological exchange that permanently altered the world's human geography and natural environment.

Beginning in the early sixteenth century, infectious and contagious diseases brought sharp demographic losses to indigenous peoples of the Americas and the Pacific islands. The worst scourge was smallpox, but measles, diphtheria, whooping cough, and influenza also took heavy tolls. Before the voyages of exploration, none of the peoples of the western hemisphere or Oceania possessed inherited or acquired immunities to those pathogens. In the eastern hemisphere, these diseases were endemic: they claimed a certain number of victims from the ranks of infants and small children, but survivors gained immunity to the diseases through exposure at an early age. In some areas of Europe, for example, smallpox was responsible for 10 to 15 percent of deaths, but most victims were age ten or younger. Although its individual effects were tragic, smallpox did not pose a threat to European society as a whole because it did not carry away economically and socially productive adults.

When infectious and contagious diseases traveled to previously unexposed populations, however, they touched off ferocious epidemics that sometimes destroyed entire societies. Beginning in 1519, epidemic smallpox ravaged the Aztec *Epidemic Diseases and Population Decline* empire in combination with other diseases, and within a century the indigenous population of Mexico had declined by as much as 90 percent, from about 17 million to 1.3 million. By that time Spanish conquerors had imposed their rule on Mexico, and the political, social, and cultural traditions of the indigenous peoples had either disappeared or fallen under Spanish domination.

Imported diseases took their worst tolls in densely populated areas such as the Aztec and Inca empires, but they did not spare other regions. Smallpox and other diseases were so easily transmissible that they

Smallpox victims in the Aztec empire. The disease killed most of those it infected and left disfiguring scars on survivors.

raced to remote areas of North and South America and sparked epidemics well before the first European explorers arrived in those regions. By the 1530s smallpox may have spread as far from Mexico as the Great Lakes in the north and the pampas of Argentina in the south.

When introduced to the Pacific islands, infectious and contagious diseases struck vulnerable populations with the same horrifying effects as in the Americas. All told, disease epidemics sparked by the Columbian exchange probably caused the worst demographic calamity in all of world history. Between 1500 and 1800, upward of one hundred million people may have died of diseases imported into the Americas and Pacific islands.

Over a longer term, however, the Columbian exchange increased rather than diminished human population because of the global spread of *Food Crops and Animals* food crops and animals that it sponsored. For example, wheat, vines, horses, cattle, pigs, sheep, goats, and chickens went from Europe to the Americas, where they sharply increased supplies of food and animal energy. Food crops native to the Americas also played prominent roles in the Columbian exchange. American crops that took root in Africa, Asia, and Europe include maize, potatoes, beans, tomatoes, peppers, peanuts, manioc, papayas, guavas, avocados, tobacco, pineapples, and cacao, to name only a few. Residents of the eastern hemisphere only gradually developed a taste for American crops, but by the eighteenth century maize and potatoes had contributed to a sharply increased number of calories in Eurasian diets. In tropical regions, peanuts and manioc flourished in soils that otherwise would not produce large yields or support large populations.

The Columbian exchange of plants and animals fueled a surge in world population. In 1500, as Eurasian peoples were recovering from epidemic bubonic plague, world population *Population Growth* stood at about 425 million. By 1600 it had increased more than 25 percent, to 545 million. By 1750 human population stood at 720 million, and by 1800 it had surged to 900 million, having grown by almost 50 percent during the previous century. Much of the rise was due to the increased nutritional value of diets enriched by the global exchange of food crops and animals.

Alongside disease pathogens and plant and animal species, the Columbian exchange involved the spread of human populations through transoceanic *Migration* migration, whether voluntary or forced. During the period from 1500 to 1800, the largest contingent of migrants consisted of enslaved Africans transported involuntarily to the Americas. A smaller migration involved Europeans who traveled to the Americas and settled in lands depopulated by infectious and contagious diseases. During the nineteenth century, European peoples traveled in huge numbers to the western hemisphere and also to south Africa, Australia, and Pacific islands, and Asian peoples migrated to tropical and subtropical destinations throughout much of the world. In combination, those migrations have profoundly influenced modern world history.

The Origins of Global Trade

The trading-post empires established by Portuguese, Dutch, and English merchants linked Asian markets with European consumers and offered opportunities for European mariners to participate in the carrying trade within Asia. Indeed, by the late sixteenth century, European merchants carrying carpets, spices, silks, and silver were as prominent as Arabs in the trading world of the Indian Ocean basin.

Besides stimulating commerce in the eastern hemisphere, the voyages of European merchant mariners encouraged the emergence of a genuinely global trading system. As Europeans established colonies in the Caribbean and *Transoceanic Trade* the Americas, for example, trade networks extended to all corners of the Atlantic Ocean basin. European manufactured goods traveled west across the Atlantic in exchange for silver from Mexican and Peruvian mines and agricultural products such as sugar and tobacco, both of which were in high demand among European con-

Semen.
Flos
Fructus.
Papas
Radix

Bananas siue Ananas fructus Indicus occidentalis.
Papas Indorum germen, radix, caudex, et fructus.
Radix castanea quam Indiani Iuucas siue Ages nominant.

Illustrations in an early-seventeenth-century book depict pineapple, potatoes, and cassava—all plants native to the Americas and unknown to Europeans before the sixteenth century.

sumers. Trade in human beings also figured in Atlantic commerce. European manufactured goods went south to west Africa, where merchants exchanged them for African slaves, who then went to the tropical and subtropical regions of the western hemisphere to work on plantations.

The experience of the Manila galleons illustrates the early workings of the global economy in the Pacific Ocean basin. For 250 years, from 1565 to 1815, Spanish galleons—sleek, fast, heavily armed ships capable of carrying large cargoes—regularly plied the waters of the Pacific Ocean between Manila in the Philippines and Acapulco on the west coast of Mexico. From Manila they took Asian luxury goods to Mexico and exchanged them for silver. Most of the precious metal made its way to China, where a thriving domestic economy demanded increasing quantities of silver. Meanwhile, some of the Asian luxury goods from Manila remained in Mexico or went to Peru, where they contributed to a comfortable way of life for Spanish ruling elites. Most, however, went overland across Mexico and then traveled by ship across the Atlantic to Spain and European markets.

The Manila Galleons

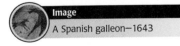

Image
A Spanish galleon—1643

As silver lubricated growing volumes of global trade, pressures increased on several animal species that had the misfortune to become commodities on the world market. Fur-bearing animals came under particularly intense pressure, as hunters sought their pelts for sale to consumers in China, Europe, and North America. During the seventeenth century, an estimated two hundred to three hundred thousand sable pelts flowed annually from Siberia to the global market, and during the eighteenth century, more than sixteen million North American beaver pelts fed consumers' demands for fur hats and cloaks. Wanton hunting of fur-bearing animals soon drove many species into extinction or near extinction, permanently altering the environments they had formerly inhabited. Early modern hunters also harvested enormous numbers of deer, codfish, whales, walruses, and seals as merchants sought to supply animal products for global consumers.

Environmental Effects of Global Trade

In the seventeenth and eighteenth centuries, the volume of global trade expanded rapidly. During the seventeenth century, for example, Dutch merchants imported, among other commodities, wheat from south Africa, cowry shells from India, and sugar from Brazil. The wheat fed domestic consumers, who increasingly worked as merchants, bankers, or manufacturers rather than as cultivators. English, Dutch, and other merchants eagerly purchased the cowry shells—which served as currency in much of sub-Saharan Africa—and exchanged them for slaves destined for plantations in the western hemisphere. The sugar went on the market at Amsterdam and found its way to consumers throughout Europe. And that was just the beginning. By 1750 all parts of the world except Australia participated in global networks of commercial relations in which European merchant mariners played prominent roles.

SUMMARY

Global commercial and biological exchanges arose from the efforts of European mariners to explore the world's waters and establish sea lanes that would support long-distance trade. Their search for sea routes to Asia led them to the western hemisphere and the vast expanse of the Pacific Ocean. The geographic knowledge that they accumulated enabled them to link the world's regions into a finely articulated network of trade. But commercial exchange was not the only result of this global network. Food crops, animal stocks, disease pathogens, and human migrants also traveled the sea lanes and dramatically influenced societies throughout the world. Transplanted crops and animal species led to improved nutrition and increasing populations throughout the eastern hemisphere. Epidemics sparked by unfamiliar disease pathogens ravaged indigenous populations in the Americas and the Pacific islands. Mass migrations of human communities transformed the social and cultural landscape of the Americas and encouraged increased mingling of the world's peoples. The European voyages of exploration, transoceanic trade networks, and the Columbian exchange pushed the world's regions toward interdependence and global integration.

CHRONOLOGY

1394–1460	Life of Prince Henry the Navigator of Portugal
1488	Bartolomeu Dias's voyage around the Cape of Good Hope into the Indian Ocean
1492	Christopher Columbus's first voyage to the western hemisphere
1497–1499	Vasco da Gama's first voyage to India
1519–1522	Ferdinand Magellan's circumnavigation of the world
1565–1575	Spanish conquest of the Philippines
1768–1780	Captain James Cook's voyages in the Pacific Ocean

FOR FURTHER READING

K. N. Chaudhuri. *Trade and Civilisation in the Indian Ocean: An Economic History from the Rise of Islam to 1750.* Cambridge, 1985. A brilliant analysis that places the European presence in the Indian Ocean in its larger historical context.

Christopher Columbus. *The* Diario *of Christopher Columbus's First Voyage to America.* Trans. by Oliver Dunn and James E. Kelley Jr. Norman, Okla., 1989. A careful translation.

Alfred W. Crosby. *The Columbian Exchange: Biological and Cultural Consequences of 1492.* Westport, Conn., 1972. Focuses on early exchanges of plants, animals, and diseases between Europe and America.

Philip D. Curtin. *Cross-Cultural Trade in World History.* New York, 1984. Focuses on the roles of cross-cultural brokers in facilitating trade between different societies.

Andre Gunder Frank. *ReORIENT: Global Economy in the Asian Age.* Berkeley, 1998. Important and challenging analysis of global economic integration in the early modern world.

Antonio Pigafetta. *Magellan's Voyage: A Narrative Account of the First Circumnavigation.* 2 vols. Trans. by R. A. Skelton. New Haven, 1969. Valuable account by a crewman on Magellan's circumnavigation of the world.

Kenneth Pomeranz. *The Great Divergence: China, Europe, and the Making of the Modern World Economy.* Princeton, 2000. Pathbreaking scholarly study that illuminates the economic history of the early modern world through comparison of economic development in Asian and European lands.

John F. Richards. *The Unending Frontier: An Environmental History of the Early Modern World.* Berkeley, 2003. Thoroughly explores the environmental effects of the global historical processes that shaped the early modern world.

Stuart B. Schwartz, ed. *Implicit Understandings: Observing, Reporting, and Reflecting on the Encounters between Europeans and Other Peoples in the Early Modern Era.* Cambridge, 1994. Fascinating collection of essays by specialists on cross-cultural perceptions in early modern times.

Yuri Slezkine. *Arctic Mirrors: Russia and the Small Peoples of the North.* Ithaca, N.Y., 1994. Thoughtful analysis of Russian relations with the hunting, fishing, and herding peoples of Siberia.

M · L

IN SILENCIO ET SPE ERIT FORTITVDO VESTRA

CHAPTER 21

The Transformation of Europe

In 1517 an obscure German monk posed a challenge to the Roman Catholic church. Martin Luther of Wittenberg denounced the church's sale of indulgences, a type of pardon that excused individuals from doing penance for their sins. Indulgences had been available since the eleventh century, but to raise funds for the reconstruction of St. Peter's basilica in Rome, church authorities began to market indulgences aggressively in the early sixteenth century. From their point of view, indulgences were splendid devices: they encouraged individuals to reflect piously on their behavior while also bringing large sums of money into the church's treasury.

To Martin Luther, however, indulgences were signs of greed, hypocrisy, and moral rot in the Roman Catholic church. Luther believed that no human being had the power to absolve individuals of their sins and grant them admission to heaven, so for him the sale of indulgences constituted a vast fraud. In October 1517, following academic custom, he offered to debate publicly with anyone who wished to dispute his views, and he denounced the sale of indulgences in a document called the *Ninety-five Theses*.

Luther did not nail his work to the church door in Wittenberg, although a popular legend credits him with that gesture, but news of the *Ninety-five Theses* spread instantly: within a few weeks, printed copies were available throughout Europe. Luther's challenge galvanized both strong support and severe criticism. Religious and political authorities seeking to maintain the established order were especially critical. Church officials judged Luther's views erroneous,

OPPOSITE PAGE: *Martin Luther at age forty-two, depicted as a conscientious and determined man by the German painter Lucas Cranach in 1525.*

and in 1520 Pope Leo X excommunicated him. In 1521 the Holy Roman emperor Charles V, a devout Roman Catholic, summoned Luther and demanded that he recant his views. Luther's response: "I cannot and will not recant anything, for it is neither safe nor right to act against one's conscience. Here I stand. I can do no other. God help me. Amen."

Martin Luther's challenge held enormous religious and political implications. Though expelled from the church, Luther still considered himself Christian, and he held religious services for a community of devoted followers. By the 1520s, religious dissent had spread through much of Germany and Switzerland. During the 1530s dissidents known as Protestants—because of their protest against the established order—organized movements also in France, England, the Low Countries, Italy, and Spain. By mid-century Luther's act of individual rebellion had mushroomed into the Protestant Reformation, which shattered the religious unity of western Christendom.

For all its unsettling effects, the Protestant Reformation was only one of several powerful movements that transformed European society during the early modern era. Another was the consolidation of strong centralized states, which took shape partly because of the Reformation. Between the sixteenth and eighteenth centuries, monarchs in western Europe took advantage of religious quarrels to tighten control over their societies. By the mid–eighteenth century, some rulers had concentrated so much power in their own hands that historians refer to them as absolute monarchs.

Alongside religious conflict and the building of powerful states, capitalism and early modern science profoundly influenced western European society in early modern times. Early capitalism encouraged European merchants and manufacturers to reorganize their businesses in search of maximum efficiency. Early modern science challenged traditional ways of understanding the world and the universe and prompted European intellectuals to seek an entirely rational understanding of human society as well as the natural world.

Thus between 1500 and 1800, western Europe underwent a thorough transformation. Although the changes were unsettling and often disruptive, they also strengthened European society. Indeed, by 1800 several European states had become especially powerful, wealthy, and dynamic. They stood poised to play major roles in world affairs during the nineteenth and twentieth centuries.

THE FRAGMENTATION OF WESTERN CHRISTENDOM

Although the peoples of western Europe spoke different languages and observed different customs, the church of Rome provided them with a common religious and cultural heritage. During the sixteenth and seventeenth centuries, however, revolts against the Roman Catholic church shattered the religious unity of western Europe. Followers of Martin Luther and other Protestant reformers established a series of churches independent of Rome, and Roman Catholic leaders strengthened their own church against the challengers. Throughout early modern times, religious controversies fueled social tensions.

The Protestant Reformation

Martin Luther (1483–1546) quickly attracted enthusiastic support from others who resented the policies of the Roman church. Luther was a talented writer, and he published scores of works condemning the Roman church. His cause benefited enormously from the printing press, which had first appeared in Europe in the mid–fifteenth century. A sizable literate public inhabited European cities and towns, and readers eagerly consumed printed works on religious as well as secular themes. Printed editions of Luther's writings appeared throughout Europe and sparked spirited debates on theological issues. His supporters and his critics took *Martin Luther*

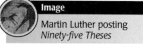

Image

Martin Luther posting *Ninety-five Theses*

their own works to the printers, and religious controversies kept the presses busy churning out pamphlets and treatises for a century and more.

Luther attacked the Roman church for a wide range of abuses and called for thorough reform of Christendom. He advocated the closure of monasteries, translation of the Bible from Latin into vernacular languages, and an end to priestly authority, including the authority of the pope himself. Most important, Luther believed that salvation could never be earned through good works or through the prayers of others. Instead, he argued, humans could be saved only through faith in the promises of God as revealed in the Bible. This idea of "justification by faith alone" became the core of Protestant belief. When opponents

---

vernacular (ver-NA-kyoo-lar)

pointed out that Luther's reform program ran counter to church policy, he rejected the authority of the church hierarchy and proclaimed that the Bible was the only source of Christian religious authority.

Luther's works drew an enthusiastic popular response, and in Germany they fueled a movement to reform the church along the lines of Luther's teachings. Lay Christians flocked to hear Luther preach in Wittenberg, and several princes of the Holy Roman Empire warmed to Luther's views—partly because of personal conviction but partly also because religious controversy offered opportunities for them to build their own power bases. During the 1520s and 1530s, many of the most important German cities—Strasbourg, Nuremberg, and Augsburg, among others—passed laws requiring all religious services to follow Protestant doctrine and procedures. By the mid–sixteenth century about half the German population had adopted Lutheran Christianity, and reformers had launched Protestant movements and established alternative churches in other lands as well. By the late 1520s the prosperous cities of Switzerland—Zurich, Basel, and Geneva—had fledgling Protestant churches. The heavily urbanized Low Countries also responded enthusiastically to Protestant appeals. Protestants appeared even in Italy and Spain, although authorities in those lands handily suppressed their challenge to the Roman church.

Reform outside Germany

Meanwhile, an even more influential reformation was taking shape in France and French-speaking Switzerland. The initiator was a French lawyer, John Calvin (1509–1564), who in the 1530s converted to Protestant Christianity. Because the French monarchy sought to suppress Protestants, Calvin moved to French-speaking Geneva in Switzerland, where he organized a tight-knit Protestant community. Calvin also composed an influential treatise, *Institutes of the Christian Religion* (first published in 1536), that presented Protestant teachings as a coherent and organized package. Although Calvin believed in the basic elements of Luther's Protestant teachings, his ideas differed from those of Luther in important ways. Most fundamentally, Calvin emphasized the awesome power of God more than Luther did. Indeed, he believed not only that humans could never earn salvation but also that God had in fact already determined which individuals would be saved from damnation before they were even born. These individuals, known as "the elect," were predestined to salvation regardless of their deeds on earth. This doc-

John Calvin

trine of "predestination," as it became known, grew increasingly important to the Calvinist church in the generations after Calvin's death.

Calvin's Geneva was based on a strict code of morality and discipline. Calvinists were supposed to dress simply, to study the Bible regularly, and to refrain from activities such as playing cards and dancing. It was, in effect, a model Protestant community. Geneva also became an important missionary center from which Calvinist doctrine spread to other parts of Europe. Calvinist missionaries were most active in France, where they attracted strong interest in the cities, but they ventured also to Germany, the Low Countries, England, Hungary, and—most successfully—the Netherlands and Scotland.

In England a reformation took place for political as well as religious reasons. Lutherans and other Protestants worked to build a following in England from the 1520s on, but they faced stout government resistance until King Henry VIII (reigned 1509–1547) came into conflict with the pope. Henry wanted to divorce his wife, who had not borne a male heir, but the pope refused to allow him to do so. Henry's response was to sever relations with the Roman church and make himself supreme head of the Anglican church—an English pope, as it were. While Henry reigned, the theology of the English church changed little, but his successors replaced Roman Catholic with Protestant doctrines and rituals. By 1560 England had permanently left the Roman Catholic community. Indeed, by the late sixteenth century, Lutherans, Calvinists, and Anglicans in Europe had built communities large enough that a return to religious unity in western Christendom was inconceivable.

The English Reformation

The Catholic Reformation

In response to the Protestant Reformation, Roman Catholic authorities undertook a wide-ranging reform effort of their own. Their purpose was to clarify differences between Roman and Protestant churches, to persuade Protestants to return to the Roman church, and to deepen the sense of spirituality and religious commitment in their own community. Taken together, their efforts constituted the Catholic Reformation.

Two institutions were especially important for defining the Catholic Reformation and advancing its goals—the Council of Trent and the Society of Jesus. The Council of Trent was an assembly of high church officials who met intermittently between 1545 and

Under inspiration of the Catholic Reformation, many devout individuals sought mystic union with God. One of the most famous of the mystics was St. Teresa of Avila (in Spain), who founded a strict order of nuns and often experienced religious visions. A famous sculpture by the Italian artist Gianlorenzo Bernini depicts St. Teresa in an ecstatic trance accompanied by an angel.

1563 to address matters of doctrine and reform. During the meetings, the council defined the elements of Roman Catholic theology in detail. The council also took steps to reform the church by demanding that church authorities observe strict standards of morality and requiring them to establish schools and seminaries to prepare priests properly for their roles.

The Council of Trent

While the Council of Trent dealt with doctrine and reform, the Society of Jesus sought to extend the boundaries of the reformed Roman church. The society's founder was St. Ignatius Loyola (1491–1556), a Basque nobleman and soldier who in 1521 suffered a leg wound

St. Ignatius of Loyola

that ended his military career. While recuperating he read spiritual works and popular accounts of saints' lives, and he resolved to put his energy into religious work. In 1540, together with a small band of disciples, he founded the Society of Jesus.

Ignatius required that members of the society, known as Jesuits, complete a rigorous and advanced education in theology, philosophy, languages, history, literature, and science. As a result of that preparation, the Jesuits made extraordinarily effective missionaries. They also acquired a reputation for discipline and determination, and often served as counselors to kings and other rulers. They also were the most prominent of the early Christian missionaries outside Europe: in the wake of the European reconnaissance of the world's oceans, Jesuits attracted converts in India, China, Japan, the Philippines, and the Americas, thus making Christianity a genuinely global religion.

The Society of Jesus

Witch-Hunts and Religious Wars

Europeans took religion seriously in the sixteenth century, and religious divisions helped to fuel social and political conflict. Apart from wars, the most destructive violence that afflicted early modern Europe was the hunt for witches, which was especially prominent in regions, such as the Rhineland, where tensions between Protestants and Roman Catholics ran high.

Like many other peoples, Europeans had long believed that certain individuals possessed unusual or supernatural powers. During the late fifteenth century, theologians developed a theory that some of these people were witches who derived their powers—such as the ability to fly through the night on brooms or pitchforks—from the devil. Theorists believed that witches regularly flew off to distant places to attend the "witches' sabbath," a gathering that featured devil worship and the concoction of secret potions and culminated in sexual relations with the devil himself. Indeed, witchcraft became a convenient explanation for any unpleasant turn of events—failure of a crop, an unexpected death, or inability to conceive a child.

In the sixteenth and seventeenth centuries, fears that individuals were making alliances with the devil sparked a widespread hunt for witches. About 110,000 individuals underwent trial as suspected witches, and about 60,000 of them died either by hanging or by burning at the stake. Most of the victims—perhaps 95 percent—were poor,

Witch-Hunting

old, single, or widowed women who lived on the margins of their societies and thus were easy targets for accusers. Although the fear of witches had largely diminished by 1700, the intermittent pursuit of witches for the better part of two centuries revealed clearly the stresses and strains—both secular and religious—that afflicted European society during early modern times.

Religious tensions also led to outright war between Protestant and Roman Catholic communities. Reli-

Religious Wars gious wars wracked France for thirty-six years (1562–1598), for example, and they also complicated relations between Protestant and Roman Catholic states. In 1588 King Philip II of Spain (reigned 1556–1598) attempted to force England to return to the Roman Catholic church by sending the Spanish Armada—a huge flotilla consisting of 130 ships and 30,000 men—to dethrone the Protestant Queen Elizabeth. The effort collapsed, however, when English forces disrupted the Spanish fleet by sending blazing, unmanned ships into its midst. Then a ferocious gale scattered Spanish vessels throughout the North Sea.

Religious convictions also aggravated relations between the Netherlands and Spain by fueling the revolt of the Dutch provinces from their overlord, the king of Spain. In 1567 resistance escalated into a full-scale rebellion. By 1610 the seven northern provinces (the modern Netherlands) had won their independence and formed a republic known as the United Provinces, leaving ten southern provinces (modern Belgium) under Spanish and later Austrian rule until the late eighteenth century.

The religious wars culminated in a great continental conflict known as the Thirty Years' War (1618–1648).

The Thirty Years' War The war opened after the Holy Roman emperor attempted to force his Bohemian subjects to return to the Roman Catholic church, and the main battleground was the emperor's territory in Germany. By the time the war ended, however, Spanish, French, Dutch, German, Swedish, Danish, Polish, Bohemian, and Russian forces had taken part in the conflict. The war itself was the most destructive European conflict before the twentieth century. Quite apart from violence and brutalities committed by undisciplined soldiers, the war damaged economies and societies throughout Europe and led to the deaths of about one-third of the German population. And though religious differences were not the only issues of the war, they complicated other issues and made them more difficult to resolve.

THE CONSOLIDATION OF SOVEREIGN STATES

Although fundamentally a religious movement, the Reformation had strong political implications, and centralizing monarchs readily made use of religious issues in their efforts to strengthen their states and enhance their authority. Indeed, after the devastation of the Thirty Years' War, rulers of these states devised a diplomatic system that sought to maintain order among the many independent and competitive European states.

The Attempted Revival of Empire

After the dissolution of the Carolingian empire in the ninth century C.E., there was no effective imperial government in western Europe. The so-called Holy Roman Empire emerged in the tenth century, but its authority extended only to Germany and northern Italy, and even there its power was contested. During the early sixteenth century, it seemed that Emperor Charles V (reigned 1519–1556) might establish the Holy Roman Empire as the preeminent political authority in Europe, but by midcentury it was clear that there would be no revival of empire. Thus, unlike China, India, and the Ottoman empire, early modern Europe developed as a region of independent states.

After 1438 the Habsburg family, with extensive dynastic holdings in Austria, dominated the Holy Roman Empire. Through marriage alli- *Charles V* ances, the Habsburgs accumulated rights and titles to lands throughout Europe and beyond. Indeed, when Charles V became emperor in 1519, his empire stretched from Vienna in Austria to Cuzco in Peru. In spite of his far-flung holdings, Charles did not extend his authority throughout Europe. Part of the reason was that throughout his reign Charles had to devote much of his attention and energy to the Lutheran movement and to putting down imperial princes who took advantage of religious controversy to assert their independence. Foreign difficulties also played a role, because Charles's neighbors to the west and east—in France and the Ottoman empire, respectively—actively opposed the creation of a powerful Holy Roman Empire.

To ensure that Charles's territories remained in disarray, for example, the Roman Catholic French kings aided German Lutherans in their rebellion against the Holy Roman Empire. The French kings even allied with the Muslim Ottoman Turks against the emperor.

Map 21.1 European states and territories in the sixteenth century. Note the extent of Habsburg territories, and the wide boundaries of the Holy Roman Empire. With such powerful territories, what prevented the Habsburgs from imposing imperial rule on most of Europe?

For their part, the Ottoman sultans did not want a powerful Christian empire to threaten their holdings in eastern Europe and the Mediterranean basin. With the encouragement of the French king, Turkish forces conquered Hungary in 1526, and three years later they even laid siege briefly to Vienna. Moreover, during the early sixteenth century Ottoman forces im-

posed their rule beyond Egypt and embraced almost all of north Africa.

Thus domestic and foreign problems prevented Charles V from establishing his vast empire as the supreme political authority in Europe. In 1556, disappointed especially in his inability to suppress the Lutherans in his territories, the emperor abdicated his throne and retired to a monastery in Spain. His empire did not survive. Charles bestowed his holdings in Spain, Italy, the Low Countries, and the Americas on his son, King Philip II of Spain, and his brother Ferdinand inherited the Habsburg family lands in Austria and the imperial throne.

The New Monarchs

In the absence of effective imperial power, public affairs fell to the various regional states that had emerged during the middle ages. In this period, however, the most powerful European states were the kingdoms of England, France, and Spain. During the late fifteenth and sixteenth centuries, rulers of these lands, known as the "new monarchs," marshaled their resources, curbed the nobility, and built strong centralized regimes.

The new monarchs included Henry VIII of England, Louis XI and Francis I of France, and Fernando and Isabel of Spain. All the new monarchs sought to enhance their treasuries by developing new sources of finance. The French kings levied direct taxes on sales, households, and the salt trade. A new sales tax dramatically boosted Spanish royal income in the sixteenth century, and English kings increased *Finance* revenues by raising fines and fees for royal services. Moreover, after Henry VIII severed ties between the English and Roman churches, he confiscated all church properties in England, which dramatically increased the size and wealth of the state.

With their increased income the new monarchs enlarged their administrative staffs, which enabled them to collect taxes and implement royal *State Power* policies more reliably than before. Increased wealth also allowed the new monarchs to raise powerful armies when the need arose. That, in turn, resulted in increased control over the nobility, who could no longer compete with the power and wealth of the state.

The debates and disputes launched by the Protestant Reformation also helped monarchs increase their power. Whereas monarchs in Protestant lands—including England, much of Germany, Denmark, and

When the Spanish Inquisition detected traces of Protestant heresy, the punishment could be swift and brutal. In this engraving of about 1560, a large crowd observes the execution of heretics (top right) by burning at the stake.

Sweden—expropriated church wealth to expand their powers, others relied on religious justifications to advance state ends. The Spanish Inquisition was the most distinctive institution of that kind. Fernando and Isabel founded the Spanish Inquisition in 1478, and they obtained papal license to operate the institution as a royal agency. Its original task was to ferret out those who secretly practiced Judaism or Islam, but Charles V charged it with responsibility also for detecting Protestant heresy in Spain.

The Spanish Inquisition

Inquisitors had broad powers to investigate suspected cases of heresy. Popular legends have created an erroneous impression of the Spanish Inquisition as an institution running amok, framing innocent victims and routinely subjecting them to torture. In fact, inquisitors usually observed rules of evidence, and they released many suspects after investigation. Yet when they detected heresy, inquisitors could be ruthless. They sentenced hundreds of victims to hang from the gallows or burn at the stake and imprisoned many others for extended periods of time. Fear of the inquisition deterred nobles from adopting Protestant views out of political ambition, and inquisitors also used their influence to silence those who threatened the Spanish monarchy. From 1559 to 1576, for ex-

ample, inquisitors imprisoned the archbishop of Toledo—the highest Roman Catholic church official in all of Spain—because of his political independence.

Constitutional States

During the seventeenth and eighteenth centuries, as they sought to restore order after the Thirty Years' War, European states developed along two lines. Rulers in England and the Netherlands shared authority with representative institutions and created constitutional states, whereas monarchs in France, Spain, Austria, Prussia, and Russia concentrated power in their own hands and created a form of state known as absolute monarchy.

During the seventeenth century the island kingdom of England and the maritime Dutch republic evolved governments that recognized rights pertaining to individuals and representative institutions. Their constitutional states took different forms: in England a constitutional monarchy emerged, whereas the Netherlands produced a republic based on representative government. In neither land did constitutional government come easily into being: in England it followed a civil war (1642–1649), and in the Nether-

Constitutional States

In this contemporary painting, the executioner holds up the just-severed head of King Charles I of England. The prospect of a royal execution overcomes one woman, who faints (at bottom).

lands it emerged after a long struggle for independence in the late sixteenth century. In both lands, however, constitutional government strengthened the state and provided a political framework that enabled merchants to flourish as never before in European experience.

Constitutional government came to England after political and religious disputes led to the English civil war. Politically, disputes arose between king and the parliament over the king's ability to institute new taxes without parliamentary approval, while religious tensions between the Anglican king and a vocal group of zealous, reform-minded Calvinists in Parliament created a deep rift between the two branches of government. By 1641 King Charles I and Parliament were at loggerheads. Both sides raised armies. In the conflicts that followed, Parliamentary forces captured Charles and in 1649 executed him for tyranny. Yet English problems of government continued through a dictatorial Puritan regime as well as the restoration of the monarchy in 1660, until in 1688 Parliament deposed King James II and invited his daughter Mary and her Dutch husband, William of Orange, to assume the throne. The resulting arrangement provided that kings would rule in cooperation with Parliament, thus guaranteeing that nobles, merchants, and other constituencies would enjoy representation in government affairs.

The English Civil War

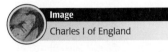

As in England, a combination of political and religious tensions led to conflict from which constitutional government emerged in the Netherlands. In the mid–sixteenth century, authority over the Low Countries, including modern-day Belgium as well as the Netherlands, rested with King Philip II of Spain. In 1566 Philip, a devout Roman Catholic, moved to suppress an increasingly popular Calvinist movement in the Netherlands—a measure that provoked large-scale rebellion against Spanish rule. In 1581 a group of Dutch provinces proclaimed themselves the independent United Provinces. Representative assemblies organized local affairs in each of the provinces, and on that foundation political leaders built a Dutch republic. Although Spain did not officially recognize the independence of the United Provinces until 1648, the Dutch republic was effectively organizing affairs in the northern Low Countries by the early seventeenth century.

The Dutch Republic

In both England and the Dutch republic, merchants were especially prominent in political affairs, and state policy in both lands favored maritime trade and the building of commercial empires overseas. The constitutional states allowed entrepreneurs to pursue their economic interests with minimal interference from public authorities, and during the late seventeenth and eighteenth centuries both states experienced extraordinary prosperity as a result of those policies. Indeed, in many ways the English and Dutch states represented an alliance between merchants and rulers that worked to the benefit of both. Merchants supported the state with the wealth that they generated through trade—especially overseas trade—and rulers followed policies that looked after the interests of their merchants.

Absolute Monarchies

Whereas constitutional states devised ways to share power and authority, absolute monarchies stood on a theoretical foundation known as the divine right of kings. This theory held that kings derived their authority from God and served as "God's lieutenants upon earth." There was no role in divine-right theory for common subjects or even nobles in public affairs: the king made law and determined policy. In fact, absolute monarchs always relied on support from nobles and other social groups, but the claims of divine-right theory clearly reflected efforts at royal centralization.

The most conspicuous absolutist state was the French monarchy. The architect of French absolutism was a prominent church official, Cardinal Richelieu, who served as chief minister to King Louis XIII from 1624 to 1642. Richelieu worked systematically to undermine the power of the nobility and enhance the authority of the king. He destroyed nobles' castles and ruthlessly crushed aristocratic conspiracies. As a counterweight to the nobility, Richelieu built a large bureaucracy staffed by commoners loyal to the king. He also appointed officials to supervise the implementation of royal policy in the provinces.

The ruler who best epitomized royal absolutism was King Louis XIV (reigned 1643–1715). In fact, Louis XIV once reportedly declared that he was himself the state: *"l'état c'est moi."* Known as *le roi soleil*— "the sun king"—Louis surrounded himself with splendor befitting one who ruled by divine right. During the 1670s he built a magnificent residence at Versailles, and in the 1680s he moved his court there. Louis's palace at Versailles was the largest building in Europe, with 230 acres of formal gardens and 1,400 fountains. All prominent nobles established residences at Versailles for their families

The Sun King

King Louis XIV and his entourage approach the main gate of Versailles (bottom right). Though only partially constructed at the time of this painting (1668), Versailles was already a spacious and luxurious retreat for Louis and his court.

and entourages. Louis strongly encouraged them to live at court, where he and his staff could keep an eye on them, and ambitious nobles gravitated there anyway in hopes of winning influence with the king. While nobles living at Versailles mastered the intricacies of court ritual and attended banquets, concerts, operas, balls, and theatrical performances, Louis and his ministers ran the state, maintained a huge army, waged war, and promoted economic development. In effect, Louis provided the nobility with luxurious accommodations and endless entertainment in exchange for absolute rule.

Image
Louis the XIV and Molière

Louis XIV was not the only absolute monarch of early modern Europe: Spanish, Austrian, and Prussian rulers embraced similar policies. Yet the potential of absolutism to increase state power was particularly conspicuous in the case of Russia, where tsars of the Romanov dynasty (1613–1917) tightly centralized government functions. Most important of the Romanov tsars was Peter I (reigned 1682–1725), widely known as Peter the Great, who inaugurated a thoroughgoing process of state transformation. Peter had a burning desire to transform Russia, a huge but underpopulated land, into a great military power like those that had recently emerged in western Europe. In 1697–1698 he led a large party of Russian observers on a tour of Germany, the Netherlands, and England to learn about western European administrative methods and military technology. His traveling companions often behaved crudely by western European standards: they consumed beer, wine, and brandy in quantities that astonished their hosts, and King William III sent Peter a bill for damages done by his entourage at the country house where they lodged in England.

Absolutism in Russia under Peter I

Versailles (vehr-SEYE)

Upon return to Moscow, Peter set Russia spinning. He reformed the army by providing his forces with extensive training and equipping them with modern weapons. He ordered aristocrats to study mathematics and geometry so that they could calculate how to aim cannons accurately, and he began the construction of a navy. He also overhauled the government bureaucracy to facilitate tax collection and improve administrative efficiency. He even commanded his aristocratic subjects to wear western European fashions and ordered men to shave their traditional beards. These measures provoked spirited protest among those who resented the influence of western European ways. Yet Peter was so insistent on the observance of his policies that he reportedly went into the streets and personally hacked the beards off recalcitrants' faces. Perhaps the best symbol of his policies was St. Petersburg, a newly built seaport that Peter opened in 1703 to serve as a magnificent capital city and a haven for Russia's fledgling navy.

Catherine II and the Limits of Reform

The most able of Peter's successors was Catherine II (reigned 1762–1796), also known as Catherine the Great. Like Peter, Catherine sought to make Russia a great power. She worked to improve governmental efficiency, and she promoted economic development in Russia's towns. For a while, she even worked to improve the conditions of Russia's oppressed peasantry by restricting the punishments—such as torture, beating, and mutilation—that noble landowners could inflict on the serfs who worked their lands.

However, Catherine's interest in social reform cooled rapidly when it seemed to inspire challenges to her rule. She faced a particularly unsettling trial in 1773 and 1774, when a disgruntled former soldier named Yemelian Pugachev mounted a rebellion in the steppe lands north of the Caspian Sea. Pugachev raised a motley army of adventurers, exiles, peasants, and serfs who killed thousands of noble landowners and government officials before imperial forces crushed the uprising. Government authorities took the captured Pugachev to Moscow in chains, beheaded him, quartered his body, and displayed his parts throughout the city as a warning against rebellion. Thereafter, Catherine's first concern was the preservation of autocratic rule rather than the transformation of Russia according to western European models.

Thus, in Russia as in other European lands, absolutist policies resulted in tight centralization and considerable strengthening of the state. The enhanced power that flowed from absolutism became dramatically clear in the period 1772 to 1797, when Austria, Prussia, and Catherine II's Russia picked the weak kingdom of Poland apart. In a series of three "partitions," the predatory absolutist states seized Polish territory and absorbed it into their own realms, ultimately wiping Poland entirely off the map. The lesson of the partitions was clear: any European state that hoped to survive needed to construct an effective government that could respond promptly to challenges and opportunities.

The European States System

Whether they relied on absolutist or constitutional principles, European governments of early modern times built states much more powerful than those of their medieval predecessors. This round of state development led to difficulties within Europe, since conflicting interests fueled interstate competition and war. In the absence of an imperial authority capable of imposing and maintaining order in Europe, sovereign states had to find ways to resolve conflicts by themselves.

The Peace of Westphalia

The Thirty Years' War demonstrated the chaos and devastation that conflict could bring. In an effort to avoid tearing their society apart, European states ended the Thirty Years' War with the Peace of Westphalia (1648), which laid the foundations for a system of independent, competing states. By the treaty's terms, the European states regarded one another as sovereign and equal. They also mutually recognized their rights to organize their own domestic and religious affairs

Interactive Map
The Peace of Westsphalia

and agreed that political and diplomatic affairs were to be conducted by states acting in their own interests. European religious unity had disappeared, and the era of the sovereign state had arrived.

The Peace of Westphalia did not bring an end to war. Indeed, war was almost constant in early modern Europe. Most conflicts were minor affairs, but some grew to sizable proportions. Most notable among them were the wars of Louis XIV and the Seven Years' War. Between 1668 and 1713, the sun king sought to expand his borders east into Germany and to absorb Spain and the Spanish Netherlands into his kingdom. That prospect prompted England, the United Provinces, and Austria to mount a coalition against Louis. Later the Seven Years' War (1756–1763) pitted France, Austria, and Russia against Britain and Prussia, and it merged with conflicts between France and Britain in India and North America to become a global war for imperial supremacy.

Map 21.2 European states and territories after the Peace of Westphalia in 1648. Compare this map with Map 21.1. How have the boundaries of the Holy Roman Empire changed, and why?

The Balance of Power

These shifting alliances illustrate the principal foundation of European diplomacy in early modern times—the balance of power. No ruler wanted to see another state dominate all the others. Thus, when any particular state began to wax strong, others formed coalitions against it. By playing balance-of-power politics, states-

men prevented the building of empires and ensured that Europe would be a land of independent, sovereign, competing states.

Frequent wars and balance-of-power diplomacy drained the resources of individual states but strengthened European society as a whole. European states competed vigorously and sought to develop the most expert military leadership and the most effective weapons for their arsenals. States organized military

Military Development

academies where officers received advanced education in strategy and tactics. Demand for powerful weapons stimulated the development of a sophisticated armaments industry. Gun foundries manufactured cannons of increasing size, range, power, and accuracy as well as small arms that allowed infantry to unleash withering volleys against their enemies.

In China, India, and Islamic lands, imperial states had little incentive to encourage similar technological innovation in the armaments industry. These states possessed the forces and weapons they needed to maintain order within their boundaries, and they rarely encountered foreign threats backed up with superior armaments. In Europe, however, failure to keep up with the latest improvements in arms technology could lead to defeat on the battlefield and decline in state power. Thus Europeans continuously sought to improve their military arsenals, and as a result, by the eighteenth century European armaments outperformed all others.

EARLY CAPITALIST SOCIETY

While the Protestant Reformation and the emergence of sovereign states brought religious and political change, a rapidly expanding population and economy encouraged the development of capitalism, which in turn led to a restructuring of European economy and society. Technologies of communication and transportation enabled businessmen to profit from distant markets, and merchants and manufacturers increasingly organized their affairs with the market rather than local communities in mind. Although capitalism generated considerable wealth, its effects were uneven and sometimes unsettling. Even in western Europe, where development and prosperity were most noticeable, early capitalism sometimes required painful adjustments to new conditions.

Population Growth and Urbanization

The foundation of European economic expansion in early modern times was a rapidly growing population, which reflected improved nutrition and decreasing mortality. The Columbian exchange enriched European diets by introducing new food crops to European

fields and tables. Most notable of the introductions was the potato, which provided a welcome and inexpensive source of carbohydrates for peasants and laborers all over Europe. Other American crops, such as tomatoes and peppers, added vitamins and tangy flavor to European diets.

American Food Crops

Since better-nourished populations are less susceptible to illness, new food crops also improved the overall resistance of Europeans to old diseases such as smallpox, dysentery, influenza, and typhus. Bubonic plague, a devastating epidemic killer during the fourteenth and fifteenth centuries, also

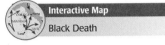

Interactive Map
Black Death

receded from European society. Although plague made periodic appearances throughout the early modern era, epidemics were rare and isolated events after the mid–seventeenth century.

Although European birthrates did not rise dramatically in early modern times, decreasing mortality resulted in rapid population growth. In 1500 the population of Europe, including Russia, was about 81 million. By 1700 the population had risen to 120

Population Growth and Urbanization

million, and in the next century it reached 180 million. Such rapid population growth drove a process of equally rapid urbanization. In the mid–sixteenth century, for example, the population of Paris was about 130,000, and London had about 60,000 inhabitants. A century later the populations of both cities had risen to half a million. Other European cities also experienced rapid growth, including Madrid, Amsterdam, Berlin, Copenhagen, Dublin, Stockholm, and Vienna, to name only a few.

Early Capitalism and Protoindustrialization

Population growth and rapid urbanization helped spur a round of remarkable economic development. That economic growth coincided with the emergence of capitalism—an economic system in which private parties make their goods and services available on a free market and seek

The Nature of Capitalism

to take advantage of market conditions to profit from their activities. Private parties own the land, machinery, tools, equipment, buildings, workshops, and raw materials needed for production. Private parties also hire workers and decide for themselves what to produce: economic decisions are the prerogative of capitalist businessmen, not governments or social superiors. The center of a capitalist system is the market in which businessmen compete with one another, and the forces of supply and demand determine the prices received for goods and services. The goal is to realize handsome profits from these activities.

Supply and Demand

The desire to accumulate wealth and realize profits was by no means new. Indeed, for several thousand years before the early modern era, merchants in China, southeast Asia, India, southwest Asia, the Mediterranean basin, and sub-Saharan Africa had pursued commercial ventures in hopes of realizing profits. During early modern times, however, European merchants and entrepreneurs transformed their society in a way that none of their predecessors had done. The capitalist economic order developed as businessmen learned to take advantage of market conditions in distant places via efficient networks of transportation and communication. For example, Dutch merchants might purchase cheap grain from Poland, store it in Amsterdam until they learned about a famine in the Mediterranean, and then transport it and sell it in southern France or Spain at an enormous profit.

Private parties organized an array of institutions and services to support early capitalism. Banks, for example, appeared in all the major commercial cities of Europe: they held funds on account for safekeeping and granted loans to merchants or entrepreneurs launching new business ventures. Insurance companies mitigated financial losses from risky undertakings such as transoceanic voyages, and stock exchanges provided markets where investors could buy and sell shares in joint-stock companies and trade in other commodities as well.

Joint-Stock Companies

Joint-stock companies were especially important institutions in early capitalist society. Large trading companies such as the English East India Company and its Dutch counterpart, the Vereenigde Oost-Indische Compagnie (VOC), spread the risks attached to expensive business enterprises and also took advantage of extensive communications and transportation networks. The trading companies organized commercial ventures on a larger scale than ever before in world history. They were the principal foundations of the global economy that emerged in early modern times, and they were the direct ancestors of contemporary multinational corporations.

Capitalism did not develop in a political vacuum. On the contrary, it emerged with the active support of government authorities who saw a capitalist order as the one best suited to their individual and collective interests. Merchants were especially influential in the affairs of the English and Dutch states, so it is not surprising that these lands adopted policies that were most favorable to capitalist enterprises throughout the early modern era. The English and Dutch states recognized individuals' rights to possess private property and protected their financial interests. They also authorized joint-stock companies to explore and colonize distant lands in search of commercial opportunities. Indeed, imperial expansion and colonial rule were crucial for the development of capitalism, since they enabled European merchants to gain access to the natural resources and commodities that they distributed so effectively through their transportation networks.

Politics and Empire

Quite apart from its influence on trade and the distribution of goods, capitalism also encouraged European entrepreneurs to organize new ways to manufacture goods. For centuries, craft guilds had monopolized the production of goods such as textiles and metalwares in European towns and cities. Guilds fixed prices and wages, and they regulated standards of quality. They sought not to realize profits so much as to protect markets and preserve their members' places in society. As a result, they actively discouraged competition.

Capitalist entrepreneurs seeking profits found the guilds inflexible, so they sidestepped them and moved production into the countryside. There, they organized a "putting-out system" by which they delivered unfinished materials such as raw wool to rural households. Men and women in the countryside would spin and weave the wool into cloth and then cut and assemble the cloth into garments. The entrepreneur picked up the finished goods, paid the workers, and sold the items on the market for a handsome profit. The putting-out system represented an early effort to organize efficient industrial production and remained a prominent feature of European society until the nineteenth century. In fact, some historians refer to the seventeenth and eighteenth centuries as an age of "protoindustrialization."

The Putting-Out System

Social Change in Early Modern Europe

Capitalist economic development brought unsettling change to European lands. In western Europe, the putting-out system introduced considerable sums of

An anonymous engraving depicts activity in a Dutch shipyard, where workers build a massive, oceangoing sailing ship. In the seventeenth century, Dutch ships were inexpensive to operate, yet they accommodated abundant cargoes.

money into the countryside, which tended to undermine long-established patterns of rural life even as it brought material benefits such as improved food, clothing, and furnishings to rural households. Increased wealth meant that individuals suddenly acquired incomes that enabled them to become financially independent of their families and neighbors, and many feared that these individuals—especially young adults and women—might abandon their kin and way of life altogether as a result.

In eastern Europe, the putting-out system did not become a prominent feature of production, but early capitalism prompted deep social change there as well. Eastern Europe had very few cities in early modern times, so in agrarian states such as Poland, Bohemia, and Russia, most people had no alternative to working in the countryside. Landlords took advantage of this situation by forcing peasants to work under extremely harsh conditions.

Russia in particular was a vast but sparsely populated empire with little trade or manufacturing. Out of *Serfdom in Russia* a concern to retain the allegiance of the powerful nobles who owned most of Russia's land, the Romanov tsars restricted the freedoms of most Russian peasants and tied them to the

land as serfs. The institution of serfdom had emerged in the early middle ages as a labor system that required peasants to provide labor services for landowners and prevented them from marrying or moving away without their landlords' permission. Although serfdom came to an end in western Europe after the fifteenth century, in eastern Europe landowners and rulers tightened restrictions on peasants during the sixteenth century. In Russia, for example, landlords commonly sold serfs to one another as if they were private property. In effect, the Romanovs won the support of the Russian nobles by ensuring them that laborers would be available to work their estates, which otherwise would have been worthless. Under these conditions, landlords operated estates with inexpensive labor and derived enormous incomes from the sale of agricultural products on the market.

These arrangements played crucial roles in the emergence of capitalism. In the larger economy of early modern Europe, eastern European lands produced agricultural products and raw materials based on semifree labor, which were then exported to western Europe to sustain its large and growing free wage labor force. Already by the early sixteenth century, consumers in the Netherlands depended for their survival on grains imported from Poland and Russia through the Baltic Sea. Thus it was possible for capitalism to flourish in western Europe only because the peasants and semifree serfs of eastern Europe provided inexpensive foods and raw materials that fueled economic development. From its earliest days, capitalist economic organization had implications for peoples and lands far removed from the centers of capitalism itself.

Profits and Ethics   Capitalism also posed moral challenges. Medieval theologians had regarded profit making as morally dangerous, since profiteers looked to their own advantage rather than the welfare of the larger community. But capitalism found advocates who sought to explain its principles and portray it as a socially beneficial form of economic organization. Most important of the early apostles of capitalism was the Scottish philosopher Adam Smith (1723–1790), who held that society would prosper when individuals pursued their own economic interests.

Nevertheless, prosperity was unattainable for all or even most early modern Europeans, which meant that the transition to capitalist economic practices was a long and painful process that generated deep social strains throughout Europe. Those strains often manifested themselves in violence: bandits plagued the countryside of early modern Europe, and muggers turned whole sections of large cities into danger zones. Some historians believe that witch-hunting activities reflected social tensions generated by early capitalism and that accusations of witchcraft represented hostility toward women who were becoming economically independent of their husbands and families.

The Nuclear Family   In some ways capitalism favored the nuclear family as the principal unit of society. Although for centuries European couples had set up independent households, early capitalism offered further opportunities for independent families to increase their wealth by producing goods for sale on the market. As nuclear families became more important economically, they also became more socially and emotionally independent. Love between a man and a woman became a more important consideration in the making of marriages than the interests of the larger extended families, and affection between parents and their children became a more important ingredient of family life. Capitalism did not necessarily cause these changes in family life, but it may have encouraged developments that helped to define the nature and the role of the family in modern European society.

SCIENCE AND ENLIGHTENMENT

While experiencing religious, political, economic, and social change, western Europe also underwent intellectual and cultural transformation. Astronomers and physicists rejected classical Greek and Roman authorities, whose theories had dominated scientific thought during the middle ages, and based their understanding of the natural world on direct observation and mathematical reasoning. During the seventeenth and eighteenth centuries, they elaborated a new vision of the earth and the larger universe in a process known as the scientific revolution. Some European intellectuals then sought to use scientific methods and reason to overhaul moral, social, and political thought. In the process, they weakened the influence of churches in western Europe and encouraged the development of secular values.

The Reconception of the Universe

The Ptolemaic Universe   Until the seventeenth century, European astronomers based their understanding of the universe on the work of the Greek scholar Claudius Ptolemy of Alexandria. In the middle of the second century C.E., Ptolemy produced a work known as the *Almagest*, which envisioned a motionless earth surrounded by a series of nine hollow, concentric spheres that revolved around it. Each of the first seven spheres had one of the observable heavenly bodies embedded in its shell. The eighth sphere held the stars, and an empty ninth sphere surrounded the whole cosmos and provided the spin that kept all the others moving. Beyond the spheres Christian astronomers located heaven, the realm of God.

Following Ptolemy, astronomers believed that the heavens consisted of a pure substance that did not experience change or corruption and was not subject to the physical laws that governed the world below the moon. They also held that heavenly bodies followed perfect circular paths in making their revolutions around the earth.

This cosmology, however, did not mesh readily with the erratic movements of the planets, which sometimes slowed down, stopped, or even turned back on

Ptolemaic (TAWL-oh-may-ihk)

Adam Smith on the Capitalist Market

Adam Smith devoted special thought to the nature of early capitalist society and the principles that made it work. In 1776 he published a lengthy book titled An Inquiry into the Nature and Causes of the Wealth of Nations, *a vastly influential work that championed free, unregulated markets and capitalist enterprise as the principal ingredients of prosperity. Smith's optimism about capitalism sprang from his conviction that society as a whole benefits when individuals pursue their own economic interests and trade on a free market.*

Every individual is continually exerting himself to find out the most advantageous employment for whatever capital he can command. It is his own advantage, indeed, and not that of the society, which he has in view. . . .

As every individual, therefore, endeavours as much as he can both to employ his capital in the support of domestic industry, and so to direct that industry that its produce may be of the greatest value, every individual necessarily labours to render the annual revenue of the society as great as he can. He generally, indeed, neither intends to promote the public interest, nor knows how much he is promoting it. By preferring the support of domestic to that of foreign industry, he intends only his own security; and by directing that industry in such a manner as its produce may be of the greatest value, he intends only his own gain, and he is in this, as in many other cases, led by an invisible hand to promote an end which was no part of his intention. Nor is it always the worse for the society that it was no part of it. By pursuing his own interest he frequently promotes that of the society more effectually than when he really intends to promote it. I have never known much good done by those who affected to trade for the public good. It is an affectation, indeed, not very common among merchants, and very few words need be employed in dissuading them from it.

What is the species of domestic industry which his capital can employ, and of which the produce is likely to be of the greatest value, every individual, it is evident, can, in his local situation, judge much better than any statesman or lawgiver can do for him. The statesman, who should attempt to direct private people in what manner they ought to employ their capitals, would not only load himself with a most unnecessary attention, but assume an authority which could safely be trusted, not only to no single person, but to no council or senate whatever, and which would nowhere be so dangerous as in the hands of a man who had folly and presumption enough to fancy himself fit to exercise it.

To give the monopoly of the home market to the produce of domestic industry, in any particular art or manufacture, is in some measure to direct private people in what manner they ought to employ their capitals, and must, in almost all cases, be either a useless or a hurtful regulation. If the produce of domestic can be brought there as cheap as that of foreign industry, the regulation is evidently useless. If it cannot, it must generally be hurtful. It is the maxim of every prudent master of a family, never to attempt to make at home what it will cost him more to make than to buy. The tailor does not attempt to make his own shoes, but buys them of the shoemaker. The shoemaker does not attempt to make his own clothes, but employs a tailor. The farmer attempts to make neither the one nor the other, but employs those different artificers. All of them find it for their interest to employ their whole industry in a way in which they have some advantage over their neighbours, and to purchase with a part of its produce, or, what is the same thing, with the price of a part of it, whatever else they have occasion for.

- *To what extent do you think Adam Smith's analysis reflected the experiences of his own times, and to what extent did they represent universally valid observations?*

SOURCE: Adam Smith. *An Inquiry into the Nature and Causes of the Wealth of Nations.* Edinburgh, 1863, pp. 198–200.

A woodcut illustration depicts the Ptolemaic universe with the earth at the center surrounded by spheres holding the planets and the stars.

their courses. Astronomers went to great lengths to explain planetary behavior as the result of perfect circular movements. The result was an awkward series of adjustments known as epicycles—small, circular revolutions that planets made around a point in their spheres, even while the spheres themselves revolved around the earth.

Planetary Movement

In 1543, however, the Polish astronomer Nicolaus Copernicus published *On the Revolutions of the Heavenly Spheres,* which broke with Ptolemaic theory. Copernicus argued that the sun rather than the earth stood at the center of the universe and that the planets, including the earth, revolved around the sun. Although this new theory harmonized much better with observational data, it did not receive a warm welcome. Copernicus's ideas not only challenged prevailing scientific theories but also threatened cherished religious beliefs, which held that the earth and humanity were unique creations of God.

The Copernican Universe

The Scientific Revolution

In time, though, Copernicus's theory inspired some astronomers to examine the heavens in fresh ways, using precise observational data and mathematical reasoning. Gradually, they abandoned the Ptolemaic in favor of the Copernican model of the universe. Some also began to apply their analytical methods to mechanics—the branch of science that deals with moving bodies—and by the mid–seventeenth century accurate observation and mathematical reasoning dominated both mechanics and astronomy. Indeed, reliance on observation and mathematics transformed the study of the natural world and brought about the scientific revolution.

The works of two mathematicians—Johannes Kepler of Germany and Galileo Galilei of Italy—rang the death knell for the Ptolemaic universe. Kepler (1571–1630) demonstrated that planetary orbits are elliptical, not circular as in Ptolemaic theory. Galileo (1564–1642) showed that the heavens were not the perfect, unblemished realm that Ptolemaic astronomers assumed. Using the recently invented telescope, Galileo was able to observe spots on the sun and mountains on the moon. He also caught sight of distant stars previously undetectable to the naked eye, which implied that the universe was much larger than anyone had previously suspected.

Galileo Galilei

The new approach to science culminated in the work of the English mathematician Isaac Newton (1642–1727), who depended on accurate observation and mathematical reasoning to construct a powerful synthesis of astronomy and mechanics. Newton outlined his views on the natural world in an epoch-making volume of 1687 titled *Mathematical Principles of Natural Philosophy.* Newton's work united the heavens and the earth in a vast, cosmic system. He argued that a law of universal gravitation regulates the motions of bodies throughout the universe, and he offered precise mathematical explanations of the laws that govern movements of bodies on the earth. His laws also allowed him to explain a vast range of seemingly unrelated phenomena, such as the ebb and flow of the tides and the eccentric orbits of planets and comets. Until the twentieth century, Newton's universe served as the unquestioned framework for the physical sciences.

Isaac Newton

Inspired by the dramatic discoveries of astronomers and physicists, other scientists began to construct fresh approaches to understanding the natural world. During the seventeenth and eighteenth centuries, anatomy, physiology, microbiology, chemistry, and botany underwent a thorough overhaul, as scientists tested their theories against direct observation of natural phenomena and explained them in rigorous mathematical terms.

The Enlightenment

Newton's vision of the universe was so powerful and persuasive that its influence extended well beyond science. His work suggested that rational analysis of human behavior and institutions could lead to fresh insights about the human as well as the natural world. From Scotland to Sicily and from Philadelphia to Moscow, European and Euro-American thinkers launched an ambitious project to discover natural laws that governed human society in the same way that Newton's laws regulated the universe. They went about this project in different ways. Some, such as John Locke (1632–1704), sought the natural laws of politics. Others, such as Adam Smith, sought to comprehend the laws of economics. Like the early modern scientists, however, they all abandoned Aristotelian philosophy and Christian religion as sources of authority in their quest to subject the human world to purely rational analysis. The result of their work was a movement known as the Enlightenment.

The center of Enlightenment thought was France, where prominent intellectuals known collectively as *philosophes* ("philosophers") advanced the cause of reason. The philosophes addressed their works more to the educated public than to scholars: instead of formal philosophical treatises, they mostly composed histories, novels, dramas, satires, and pamphlets on religious, moral, and political issues.

More than any other philosophe, François-Marie Arouet (1694–1778) epitomized the spirit of the Enlightenment. Writing under the pen name *Voltaire*, he championed individual freedom and attacked any institution sponsoring intolerant or oppressive policies. Targets of his often caustic wit included the French monarchy and the Roman Catholic church. When the king of France sought to save money by reducing the number of horses kept in royal stables, for example, Voltaire suggested that it would be more effective to get rid of the asses who rode the horses. Voltaire

Primary Source
Voltaire on nobility

also waged a long literary campaign against the Roman Catholic church, which he held responsible for fanaticism, intolerance, and incalculable human suffering. Indeed, Voltaire himself—like many other philosophes—was a deist and denied the supernatural teachings of Christianity. Instead, deists held that

Voltaire (vohl-TAIR)
deism (DEE-iz'm)

Socially prominent women deeply influenced the development of Enlightenment thought by organizing and maintaining salons—gatherings where philosophes, scientists, and intellectuals discussed the leading ideas of the day. Though produced in 1814, this painting depicts the Parisian salon of Mme. Geoffrin (center left), a leading patron of the French philosophes, about 1775. In the background is a bust of Voltaire, who lived in Switzerland at the time.

although a powerful god had created the universe, once created, the universe operated by itself according to rational and natural laws.

Most philosophes were optimistic about the future of the world and humanity. In fact, they believed *The Theory of Progress* that rational understanding of human and natural affairs would bring about a new era of progress and individual freedom and would lead to the construction of a prosperous, just, and equitable society. Although those fond wishes did not come to pass, the Enlightenment did indeed help to bring about a thorough cultural transformation of European society. For one thing, it weakened the influence of organized religion by encouraging the replacement of Christian values with a new set of secular values based on reason. Furthermore, the Enlightenment encouraged political and cultural leaders to subject society to rational analysis and intervene actively in its affairs in the interests of promoting progress and prosperity. In many ways the Enlightenment legacy continues to influence European and Euro-American societies.

SUMMARY

During the early modern era, European society experienced a series of profound and sometimes unsettling changes. The Protestant Reformation ended the religious unity of western Christendom and led to more than a century of religious conflict. Centralizing monarchs strengthened their realms and built a society of sovereign, autonomous, and intensely competitive states. Capitalist entrepreneurs reorganized the production and distribution of manufactured goods, and although their methods led to increased wealth, their quest for efficiency and profits clashed with traditional values. Modern science based on direct observation and mathematical explanations emerged as a powerful tool for the investigation of the natural world. Some people used scientific methods to investigate the human world and created a new moral thought based strictly on science and reason. At just the time that European merchants, colonists, and adventurers were seeking opportunities in the larger world, European society was becoming more powerful, more experimental, and more competitive than ever before.

CHRONOLOGY

1473–1543	Life of Nicolaus Copernicus
1478	Foundation of the Spanish Inquisition
1483–1546	Life of Martin Luther
1517	Publication of the *Ninety-five Theses*
1540	Foundation of the Society of Jesus
1545–1563	Council of Trent
1564–1642	Life of Galileo Galilei
1571–1630	Life of Johannes Kepler
1618–1648	Thirty Years' War
1632–1704	Life of John Locke
1642–1727	Life of Isaac Newton
1648	Peace of Westphalia
1694–1778	Life of Voltaire
1723–1790	Life of Adam Smith

FOR FURTHER READING

Fernand Braudel. *Civilization and Capitalism, 15th to 18th Century.* 3 vols. Trans. by S. Reynolds. New York, 1981–84. A rich analysis of early capitalist society by one of the greatest historians of the twentieth century.

Paul Dukes. *The Making of Russian Absolutism, 1613–1801.* 2nd ed. London, 1990. A succinct study of two disparate centuries, the seventeenth and eighteenth, and two influential tsars, Peter and Catherine.

Robert S. Duplessis. *Transitions to Capitalism in Early Modern Europe.* Cambridge, 1997. A valuable synthesis of recent research on early capitalism and protoindustrialization.

Margaret Jacob. *The Cultural Meaning of the Scientific Revolution.* New York, 1989. Explores the larger cultural and social implications of early modern science.

E. L. Jones. *The European Miracle: Environments, Economies, and Geopolitics in the History of Europe and Asia.* 2nd ed. Cambridge, 1987. Examines European politics and economic growth in comparative perspective.

Thomas S. Kuhn. *The Structure of Scientific Revolutions.* 3rd ed. Chicago, 1997. An influential theoretical work that views scientific thought in larger social and cultural context.

William H. McNeill. *The Pursuit of Power: Technology, Armed Force, and Society since A.D. 1000.* Chicago, 1982. Insightful analysis exploring the influence of sovereign states and early capitalism on military technology and organization.

Eugene F. Rice Jr. and Anthony Grafton. *The Foundations of Early Modern Europe, 1460–1559.* 2nd ed. New York, 1994. Excellent introduction to political, social, economic, and cultural developments.

Simon Schama. *The Embarrassment of Riches: An Interpretation of Dutch Culture in the Seventeenth Century.* New York, 1987. A marvelous popular study of the wealthy Dutch republic at its height.

Keith Thomas. *Religion and the Decline of Magic.* New York, 1971. A riveting analysis of popular culture in early modern times, especially strong on the explanation of magic and witchcraft.

CHAPTER 22

New Worlds: The Americas and Oceania

A remarkable young woman played a pivotal role in the Spanish conquest of Mexico. Originally called Malintzin, she is better known by her Spanish name, Doña Marina. Born about 1500 to a noble family in central Mexico, Doña Marina's mother tongue was Nahuatl, the principal language of the Aztec empire. When she was a girl, Doña Marina's family sent her to the Mexican coast as a slave. Her new family later passed her on to their neighbors on the Yucatan peninsula, where she also became fluent in the Maya language.

When Hernán Cortés arrived on the Mexican coast in 1519, only one of his soldiers could speak the Maya language spoken by coastal peoples. But he had no way to communicate with the Nahuatl-speaking peoples of central Mexico until a Maya chieftain presented him with twelve young women, including Doña Marina, as a token of alliance. Doña Marina's linguistic talents enabled Cortés to communicate through an improbable chain of languages—from Spanish to Maya to Nahuatl and then back again—while making his way to the Aztec capital of Tenochtitlan. (Doña Marina soon learned Spanish and thus eliminated the Maya link in the linguistic chain.)

Doña Marina provided Cortés with intelligence and diplomatic as well as linguistic services. On several occasions she learned of plans by native peoples to overwhelm and destroy the tiny Spanish army, and she alerted Cortés to the danger in time for him to forestall an attack. She also helped Cortés negotiate with emissaries from the major cities of central Mexico. Indeed, in the absence of Doña

OPPOSITE PAGE: *Doña Marina is depicted between a Tlaxcalan chief and Hernando Cortés.*

Marina's services, it is difficult to see how Cortés's small band could have survived to see the Aztec capital.

Apart from facilitating the Spanish conquest of the Aztec empire, Doña Marina also played a role in the formation of a new society in Mexico. In 1522 she gave birth to a son fathered by Cortés, and in 1526 she bore a daughter to a Spanish captain whom she had married. Her offspring thus symbolize the early emergence of a mestizo population in Mexico. Doña Marina died soon after the birth of her daughter, probably in 1527, but during her short life she contributed to the thorough transformation of Mexican society.

Until 1492 the peoples of the eastern and western hemispheres had few dealings with one another. Sporadic encounters between Europeans and North Americans did occur, and it is likely that an occasional Asian or Austronesian mariner reached the Pacific coast of the Americas before 1492. Yet travel between the eastern hemisphere, the western hemisphere, and Oceania was too irregular and infrequent to generate sustained interaction until the fifteenth century.

After 1492, however, the voyages of European mariners led to permanent and continuous contact between the peoples of all these areas. The resulting encounters brought profound and often violent change to both American and Pacific lands. European peoples possessed powerful weapons, horses, and ships that provided them with technological advantages over the peoples they encountered in the Americas and the Pacific islands. Moreover, most Europeans also enjoyed complete or partial immunity to diseases that caused devastating epidemics when introduced to the western hemisphere and Oceania. Because of their technological advantages and the depopulation that followed from epidemic diseases, European peoples were able to establish a presence throughout the Americas and much of the Pacific Ocean basin.

COLLIDING WORLDS

When European peoples first sought to establish their presence in the Americas, they brought technologies unavailable to the peoples they encountered in the western hemisphere. More important than technology, however, were the divisions between indigenous peoples that Europeans were able to exploit and the effects of epidemic diseases that devastated native societies. Soon after their arrival in the western hemisphere, Spanish conquerors toppled the Aztec and

Inca empires and imposed their own rule in Mexico and Peru. In later decades Portuguese planters built sugar plantations on the Brazilian coastline. French, English, and Dutch migrants displaced indigenous peoples in North America and established settler colonies under the rule of European peoples.

The Spanish Caribbean

The first site of interaction between European and American peoples was the Caribbean. When Spanish mariners arrived there, the Tainos (also known as Arawaks) were the most prominent people in the region. *Tainos* The Tainos cultivated manioc and other crops, and they lived in small villages under the authority of chiefs who allocated land to families and supervised community affairs.

Christopher Columbus and his immediate followers made the island of Hispaniola (which embraces modern Haiti and the Dominican Republic) the base of Spanish operations in the Caribbean. Columbus's original plan was to build forts and trading posts where merchants could trade with local peoples for products desired by European consumers. However, it soon became clear that the Caribbean region offered no silks or spices for the European market. If Spanish settlers wanted to maintain their presence in the Caribbean, they would need to find some way to make a living.

The settlers first attempted to support their society by mining gold. Spanish settlers were few in number and were not inclined to perform heavy labor, so they recruited the labor they needed from the ranks of the Tainos. This was done through an institution known as the *encomienda*, which gave Spanish settlers (*encomenderos*) the right to compel Tainos to work in their mines or fields. In return for

Image
Latin American slavery

labor, *encomenderos* were supposed to look after their workers' welfare and encourage their conversion to Christianity.

Conscription of Taino labor was a brutal business. *Encomenderos* worked their charges hard and punished them severely. Tainos occasionally organized rebellions, but their bows, arrows, and slings had little effect against Spanish steel. By about 1515, social disruption and physical abuse caused Taino popula-

Taino (tah-EE-noh)

encomienda (ehn-koh-MYEN-dah)

One of the earliest European depictions of native Americans was this engraving of 1505. The caption informed readers that American peoples lived in communal society, where men took several wives but none had private possessions, and that they routinely smoked and consumed the bodies of slain enemies.

tions to decline on the large Caribbean islands—Hispaniola, Jamaica, Puerto Rico, and Cuba—favored by Spanish settlers.

After 1518 serious demographic decline set in when smallpox reached the Caribbean and touched off devastating epidemics. To replace laborers lost to disease, *encomenderos* resorted to kidnapping and enslaving Tainos and other peoples. That tactic, however, only exposed additional victims to disease. As a result of epidemic disease, the native population of the Caribbean plummeted from about four million in 1492 to a few thousand in the 1540s. Entire native societies passed out of existence. By the middle of the sixteenth century, a few surviving words—*canoe, hammock, hurricane, barbecue, maize,* and *tobacco*—were all that was left of Taino society.

Smallpox

After the mid–sixteenth century, when it was clear that gold supplies in the region were thin, the Carib-bean became a sleepy backwater of the Spanish empire. In the 1640s, French, English, and Dutch settlers began to take the place of the Spanish and flocked to the Caribbean with the intention of establishing plantations. Indeed, they found that the Caribbean offered ideal conditions for the cultivation of cash crops, particularly sugar and tobacco. Meanwhile, because indigenous populations were extinct, planters imported several million slaves to provide labor. By 1700 Caribbean society consisted of a small class of European administrators and large numbers of African slaves.

From Mining to Plantation Agriculture

The Conquest of Mexico and Peru

Spanish interest shifted quickly from the Caribbean to the American mainland in the quest for resources.

During the early sixteenth century, Spanish *conquista-dores* ("conquerors") pressed west into Mexico and south into Panama and Peru. Between 1519 and 1521

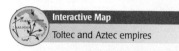
Interactive Map
Toltec and Aztec empires

Hernán Cortés and a small band of men brought down the Aztec empire in Mex-ico, and between 1532 and 1533 Francisco Pizarro and his followers toppled the Inca empire in Peru. Those conquests laid the foundations for colonial regimes that would transform the Americas.

In Mexico and Peru, Spanish explorers found so-cieties quite different from those of the Caribbean islands. Both Mexico and Peru had been sites of agri-cultural societies, cities, and large states for more than a millennium. In the early fifteenth century, both lands fell under the sway of powerful imperial states: the Mexica people and their allies founded the Aztec empire, which expanded to embrace most of Meso-america, and the Incas imposed their rule on a vast realm extending from modern Ecuador in the north to modern Chile in the south. (See chapter 18.)

The conquest of Mexico began in 1519 when Cortés led about 450 soldiers from Veracruz on the

Hernán Cortés   Gulf coast to the island city of Tenoch-titlan, the stunningly beautiful Aztec capital situated in Lake Texcoco. They seized the em-peror Motecuzoma II, who died in 1520 during a skirmish between Spanish forces and residents of Tenochtitlan. Aztec forces soon drove the conquista-dores from the capital, but Cortés built a small fleet of ships, placed Tenochtitlan under siege, and in 1521 starved the city into surrender.

Spanish weapons and horses offered Cortés and his soldiers some advantage over the forces they met and help to account for the Spanish conquest of the Aztec empire. Yet weaponry alone clearly was not enough to overcome such a large, densely populated society. Indeed, Cortés's expedition also benefited from divisions among the indigenous peoples of Mex-ico and made important alliances with peoples who resented Aztec domination. Native allies reinforced the small Spanish army with thousands of veteran warriors and provided Spanish forces with logistical support and secure bases in friendly territory.

Epidemic disease also aided Spanish efforts. Dur-ing the siege of Tenochtitlan, smallpox raged through

Epidemic Disease   the city, killing inhabitants by the tens of thousands. It then spread be-yond the capital and raced through Mexico, carrying

conquistadores (kon-kees-tah-DOH-rayz)

off so many people that Aztec society was unable to function. Only in the context of this enormous de-population is it possible to understand the Spanish conquest of Mexico.

Francisco Pizarro experienced similar results when he led a Spanish expedition from Central America to Peru. Pizarro set out in   *Francisco Pizarro*
1530 with 180 soldiers, later joined
by reinforcements to make a force of about 600. The conquistadores arrived in Peru just after a bitter dis-pute within the Inca ruling house, and it was easy for them to exploit differences between the factions. By 1533 they had taken

the Inca capital at Cuzco. Under pretext of holding a confer-

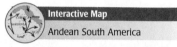
Interactive Map
Andean South America

ence, they called the Inca ruling elites together, seized them, and killed most of them. They spared the Inca ruler Atahualpa until he had delivered a large quantity of gold to Pizarro. Then they stran-gled him and decapitated his body. Pizarro and his conquistadores proceeded to loot gold and silver from Cuzco's temples and public buildings, and even to loot jewelry and ornaments from the embalmed bodies of deceased Inca rulers.

In this illustration from Felipe Guaman Poma de Ayala's letter of complaint to the Spanish king, conquistadores decapitate Atahualpa after executing him by strangulation in 1533.

First Impressions of Spanish Forces

As the Spanish army made its way to Tenochtitlan, Motecuzoma dispatched a series of emissaries to communicate with Cortés and learn his intentions. The reports that came back were not reassuring. They brought disturbing news about Spanish weapons, armor, horses, and dogs that were much larger and more aggressive than the small, barkless animals that were native to Mexico.

■ ■ ■

And when [Motecuzoma] had heard what the messengers reported, he was terrified, he was astounded. . . .

Especially did it cause him to faint away when he heard how the gun, at [the Spaniards'] command, discharged [the shot]; how it resounded as if it thundered when it went off. It indeed bereft one of strength; it shut off one's ears. And when it discharged, something like a round pebble came forth from within. Fire went showering forth; sparks went blazing forth. And its smoke smelled very foul; it had a fetid odor which verily wounded the head. And when [the shot] struck a mountain, it was as if it were destroyed, dissolved. And a tree was pulverized; it was as if it vanished; it was as if someone blew it away.

All iron was their war array. In iron they clothed themselves. With iron they covered their heads. Iron were their swords. Iron were their crossbows. Iron were their shields. Iron were their lances.

And those which bore them upon their backs, their deer [that is, horses], were as tall as roof terraces.

And their bodies were everywhere covered; only their faces appeared. They were very white; they had chalky faces; they had yellow hair, though the hair of some was black. Long were their beards; they also were yellow. They were yellow-headed. [The black men's hair] was kinky, it was curly.

And their food was like fasting food—very large, white, not heavy like [tortillas]; like maize stalks, good-tasting as if of maize stalk flour; a little sweet, a little honeyed. It was honeyed to eat; it was sweet to eat.

And their dogs were very large. They had ears folded over; great dragging jowls. They had fiery eyes—blazing eyes; they had yellow eyes—fiery yellow eyes. They had thin flanks—flanks with ribs showing. They had gaunt stomachs. They were very tall. They were nervous; they went about panting, with tongues hanging out. They were spotted like ocelots; they were varicolored.

And when Motecuzoma heard all this, he was much terrified. It was as if he fainted away. His heart saddened; his heart failed him.

- *In light of the reports that he received, what were Motecuzoma's options for dealing with the Spanish threat?*

SOURCE: Bernardino de Sahagún. *Florentine Codex: General History of the Things of New Spain,* 13 vols. Trans. by Arthur J. O. Anderson and Charles E. Dibble. Salt Lake City: University of Utah Press, 1950–82, 13:19–20. (Translation slightly modified.)

As Cortés's expedition had done to the Aztecs in Mexico, Pizarro's tiny force toppled the Inca empire by exploiting divisions among native peoples. Many Inca subjects despised their overlords and thus either allied with or did not resist Pizarro's forces. In addition, smallpox had spread to the Inca empire in the 1520s, long before Pizarro's arrival, and had already taken a heavy toll among Andean populations. As a result, by 1540 Spanish forces had established themselves securely as lords of the land.

Iberian Empires in the Americas

The conquests of Mexico and Peru were the results not of Spanish royal policy but, rather, of individual efforts by freelance adventurers. Gradually, however, the Spanish monarchy extended its control over the growing American empire, and by about 1570 it had established formal rule under the Spanish crown. Spanish administrators established two main centers of

Spanish Colonial Administration

authority in the Americas—Mexico (which they called New Spain) and Peru (known as New Castile)—each governed by a viceroy who was responsible to the king of Spain. In Mexico they built a new capital, Mexico City, on top of Tenochtitlan. In Peru they moved the seat of government from the high-altitude Inca capital of Cuzco to the Peruvian coast and in 1535 founded the new capital of Lima.

The viceroys were the king's representatives in the Americas, and they wielded considerable power. The kings of Spain attempted to hold them in check by subjecting them to the review of courts known as *audiencias* staffed by university-educated lawyers. The *audiencias* heard appeals against the viceroys' decisions and policies and had the right to address their concerns directly to the Spanish king. Furthermore, the *audiencias* conducted reviews of viceroys' performance at the end of their terms, and negative reviews could lead to severe punishment.

In many ways, Spanish administration in the Americas was a ragged affair. Transportation and communication difficulties limited the ability of viceroys to supervise their own extensive territories. The jurisdiction of the viceroyalty of New Spain, for example, reached from Mexico City as far as

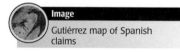
Gutiérrez map of Spanish claims

St. Augustine in Florida (founded in 1565). Distance also prevented Spanish monarchs from exercising much influence on American affairs. It often took two years for the central government in Spain to respond to a query from Mexico or Peru, and when viceroys received clear orders that they did not like, it was easy to procrastinate.

While the Spanish built a territorial empire in Mexico and Peru, Portuguese forces established an imperial presence in Brazil. The Portuguese presence came about by an odd twist of diplomatic convention. In 1494 Spain and Portugal signed the Treaty of Tordesillas, which divided the world along an imaginary north-south line 370 leagues west of the Azores and Cape Verde Islands. According to this agreement, Spain could claim any non-Christian lands west of that line, and Portugal gained the same rights for lands east of the line. Thus Portugal gained territory along the northeastern part of the South American continent, a region known as Brazil from the many brazilwood trees that grew along the coast, and the remainder of the western hemisphere fell under Spanish control. Brazil did not attract significant Portuguese interest, however, until entrepreneurs began establishing sugar plantations on

Portuguese Brazil

the coast after the mid–sixteenth century. Once it was clear the plantations would be profitable, Portuguese interest—and settlement—surged.

Both the Spanish and the Portuguese rapidly established cities throughout their territories. Like their compatriots in Europe, colonists preferred to live in cities even when they derived their income from the agricultural production of their landed estates, and they made every attempt to model their new cities along European lines. Away from urban areas, however, indigenous ways of life largely persisted. In places such as the Amazon basin and Paraguay, for example, where there were no mineral deposits to attract European migrants, European visitors learned to adapt to indigenous societies and customs: they ate bread made of manioc flour, made use of native hammocks and canoes, and communicated in the Guaraní and Tupí languages. Indeed, indigenous languages flourish even today throughout much of Latin America: among the more prominent are Nahuatl in Mexico, Quiché in Mexico and Guatemala, Guaraní in Paraguay, and Quechua in the Andean highlands of Peru, Ecuador, and Bolivia.

Colonial American Society

Spanish and Portuguese peoples always saw the western hemisphere more as a land to exploit and administer than as a place to settle and colonize. Nevertheless, upward of five hundred thousand Spaniards and one hundred thousand Portuguese settled permanently in the Americas between 1500 and 1800. Their presence contributed to the making of a new world—a world characterized by intense interaction between the peoples of Europe, Africa, and the Americas—in the western hemisphere.

Settler Colonies in North America

Throughout the sixteenth century, Spanish explorers sought opportunities north of Mexico and the Caribbean. They established towns, forts, and missions from modern Florida as far north as Virginia, and they scouted shorelines off Maine and Newfoundland. On the west coast they established a fort on Vancouver Island in modern Canada. By midcentury, however, French, English, and Dutch mariners were dislodging Spanish colonists north of Florida. Originally, they came in a fruitless search for a northwest passage to Asia. Instead, they found immense quantities of codfish, which they exploited from the banks off Labrador, Newfoundland, Nova Scotia, and New England.

More important, in the early seventeenth century they began to plant permanent colonies on the North

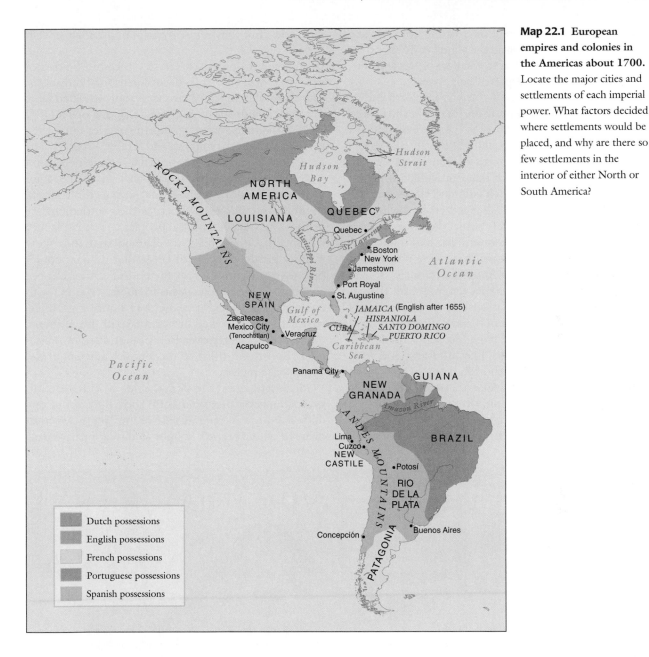

Map 22.1 European empires and colonies in the Americas about 1700. Locate the major cities and settlements of each imperial power. What factors decided where settlements would be placed, and why are there so few settlements in the interior of either North or South America?

Dutch possessions
English possessions
French possessions
Portuguese possessions
Spanish possessions

American mainland. French settlers established colonies at Port Royal (Nova Scotia) in 1604 and Quebec in 1608, and English migrants founded Jamestown in 1607 and the Massachusetts Bay Colony in 1630. Dutch entrepreneurs built a settlement at New Amsterdam in 1623, but in 1664 an English fleet seized and rechristened it New York and absorbed it into English colonial holdings. During the seventeenth and eighteenth centuries, French migrants settled in eastern Canada, and French explorers and traders scouted the St. Lawrence, Ohio, and Mississippi rivers, building forts

Foundation of Colonies

all the way to the Gulf of Mexico. Meanwhile, English settlers established colonies along the east coast of the present-day United States of America.

Life in those early settlements was extremely difficult. Most of the settlers hoped to sustain their communities not through farming but by producing valuable commodities such as fur, pitch, tar, or lumber, if not silver and gold. They relied heavily on provisions sent from Europe, and when supply ships did not arrive as expected, they sometimes avoided starvation only because indigenous peoples provided them with food. In Jamestown, food shortages and disease became so severe that only sixty of the colony's five hundred inhabitants survived the winter of 1609–1610. Some settlers went so far as to disinter corpses and consume the flesh of their departed neighbors.

Colonial Government

The French and English colonies in North America differed in several ways from Iberian territories to the south. Whereas Iberian explorations had royal backing, private investors played larger roles in French and English colonial efforts. Because of that, individuals retained much more control over their colonies' affairs than did their Iberian counterparts. Thus settlers in the English colonies—though ultimately subject to royal authority—maintained their own assemblies and influenced the choice of royal governors: there were no viceroys or *audiencias* in the North American colonies.

Relations with Indigenous Peoples

French and English colonies differed from Iberian territories also in their relationships with indigenous peoples. French and English migrants did not find large, densely settled, centralized states like the Aztec and Inca empires. Although many of the native societies in eastern North America practiced agriculture, most also relied on hunting and consequently moved their villages frequently in pursuit of game. They did not claim ownership of precisely bounded territories, but they regularly migrated between well-defined regions.

When European settlers saw forested lands not bearing crops, they staked out farms for themselves. The availability of fertile farmland soon attracted large numbers of European migrants. Upward of 150,000 English migrants moved to North America during the seventeenth century alone, and sizable French, German, Dutch, and Irish contingents soon joined them.

European migrants took pains to justify their claims to American lands. Some, such as the English, sought to provide legal cover for their settlements by negotiating treaties with the peoples whose lands they colonized. Other migrants claimed that they were making productive use of lands that native peoples only used as hunting parks. Such justifications did not convince native peoples, who frequently clashed with colonists over the right to use their hunting grounds, whether treaties existed or not. In 1622, for example, native peoples angry over European intrusions massacred almost one-third of the English settlers in the Chesapeake region.

Such attacks did not stem the tide of European migrants, however. Between 1600 and 1800, about one million European migrants arrived in North America, many of whom actively sought to displace native peo-

A painting of the English settlement at Jamestown in the early seventeenth century illustrates the precarious relations between European settlers and indigenous peoples. Note the heavy palisades and numerous cannons deployed within the fort, as well as the imposing figure of the native chief Powhatan depicted outside the settlement's walls.

ples from their lands. Violent conflict, indeed, took a heavy toll on native populations. Yet as in the Iberian territories, epidemic disease also dramatically reduced the indigenous population of North America in early modern times. In 1492 the native population of the territory now embraced by the United States was greater than five million, perhaps as high as ten million. By the mid–sixteenth century, however, smallpox and other diseases spread north from Mexico and ravaged native societies in the plains and eastern woodlands of North America. By 1800 only six hundred thousand indigenous peoples remained, as against almost five million settlers of European ancestry and about one million slaves of African ancestry. Although the settler colonies of North America differed markedly from the Iberian territorial empires, they too contributed greatly to the transformation of the western hemisphere.

COLONIAL SOCIETY IN THE AMERICAS

The European migrants who flooded into the western hemisphere interacted both with the native inhabitants and with African peoples whom they imported as enslaved laborers. Throughout the Americas, relations

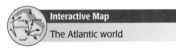

Interactive Map
The Atlantic world

between individuals of American, European, and African ancestry soon led to the emergence of mestizo populations. Yet European peoples and their Euro-American offspring increasingly dominated political and economic affairs in the Americas. They mined precious metals, cultivated cash crops such as sugar and tobacco, and trapped fur-bearing animals to supply capitalist markets that met the voracious demands of European and Asian consumers. Over time they also established their Christian religion as the dominant faith of the western hemisphere.

The Formation of Multicultural Societies

Many parts of the Americas remained outside European control until the nineteenth century. Only rarely did Europeans venture into the interior regions of the American continents in the sixteenth century, and those who did often found themselves at the mercy of

the native inhabitants. But even though their influence reached the American interior only gradually, European migrants radically transformed the social order in the regions where they established colonies.

In Spanish and Portuguese territories, society quickly became both multicultural and ethnically mixed, largely because of migration patterns. Indeed, more than 85 percent of Spanish migrants were men, and the percentage of men was even higher for the Portuguese. Because there were so few European women, Spanish and Portuguese migrants entered into relationships with native women, which soon gave rise to an increasingly mestizo society.

Mestizo Societies

This pattern was especially pronounced in the Portuguese colony of Brazil, where there were very few European women. There, Portuguese men entered into relationships with both native and African slave women. Brazil soon had large populations not only of mestizos but also of mulattoes, born of Portuguese and African parents; *zambos,* born of indigenous and African parents; and other combinations arising from these groups themselves. Indeed, marriages between members of different racial and ethnic communities became very common in colonial Brazil.

In both the Spanish and the Portuguese colonies, migrants born in Europe known as *peninsulares* (people from the Iberian peninsula) stood at the top of the social hierarchy, followed by *criollos,* or creoles, individuals born in the Americas of Iberian parents. As the numbers of mestizos grew, they also became essential contributors to their societies, especially in Mexico and Brazil. Meanwhile, mulattoes, zambos, and other individuals of mixed parentage became prominent groups in Brazilian society, although they were usually subordinate to peninsulares, creoles, and even mestizos. In all the Iberian colonies, imported slaves and native peoples stood at the bottom of the social hierarchy.

The Social Hierarchy

The social structure of the French and English colonies in North America differed markedly from that of the Iberian colonies. Women were more numerous, especially among the English migrants, and settlers mostly married within their own groups. Although French fur traders often associated with native women and

North American Societies

---

mestizo (mehs-TEE-soh)

zambos (SAHM-bohs)
peninsulares (pehn-IHN-soo-LAH-rayz)
criollos (KRYO-yohs)

generated *métis* (the French equivalent of mestizos) in regions around trading posts, such arrangements were less common in French colonial cities such as Port Royal and Quebec.

Mingling between peoples of different ancestry was least common in the English colonies of North America. Colonists regarded the native peoples they encountered as lazy heathens who did not exert themselves to cultivate the land. Later they also scorned African slaves as inferior beings. Those attitudes fueled a virulent racism, and English settlers worked to maintain sharp boundaries between themselves and peoples of American and African ancestry.

Yet English settlers readily borrowed useful cultural elements from other communities. From native communities, for example, they learned about American plants and animals, and they adapted moccasins and deerskin clothes. From their slaves they borrowed African food crops and techniques for the cultivation of rice. Yet, unlike their Iberian neighbors, English settlers strongly discouraged relationships between individuals of different ancestry and mostly refused to accept offspring of mixed parentage.

---

métis (may-TEE)

Mining and Agriculture in the Spanish Empire

From the Spanish perspective, the greatest attractions of the Americas were precious metals. Once the conquistadores had thoroughly looted the treasures of the Aztec and Inca empires, their followers opened mines to extract the mineral wealth of the Americas in a more systematic fashion.

Silver was the most abundant American treasure, and much of Spain's American enterprise focused on its extraction. Silver production con- *Silver Mining* centrated on two areas: the thinly populated Mexican north, particularly the region around Zacatecas, and the high central Andes, particularly the stunningly rich mines of Potosí. Both sites employed large numbers of indigenous laborers. Many laborers went to Zacatecas voluntarily to escape the pressures of conquest and disease. Over time they became professional miners, spoke Spanish, and lost touch with the communities of their birth.

Meanwhile, Spanish prospectors discovered a large vein of silver near Potosí in 1545 and began large-scale mining there in the 1580s. By 1600 Potosí had a booming population of 150,000. Such rapid growth

Mining operations at Potosí gave rise to a large settlement that housed miners and others who supplied food, made charcoal, fashioned tools, and supported the enterprise. In this illustration from the mid-1580s, llamas laden with silver ore descend the mountain (background) while laborers work in the foreground to crush the ore and extract pure silver from it.

created an explosive demand for labor. As in the Mexican mines, Spanish administrators relied mostly on voluntary labor, but they also adapted the Inca practice of requisitioning draft labor, known as the *mita* system, to recruit workers for particularly difficult and dangerous chores. Under the *mita* system, each native village was required to send one-seventh of its male population to work for four months in the mines at Potosí. Draft laborers received very little payment for their work, and conditions were extremely harsh. Death rates of draft laborers were high, and many native men sought to evade *mita* obligations by fleeing to cities or hiding in distant villages.

The Global Significance of Silver   The mining industries of Mexico and Peru powered the Spanish economy in the Americas and even stimulated the world economy of early modern times. Indeed, the Spanish government's share—one-fifth of all silver production, called the *quinto*—represented the principal revenue the crown derived from its American possessions. Most American silver made its way across the Atlantic to Spain, where it financed Spain's army and bureaucracy and lubricated markets throughout Europe. From Europe, merchants used it to trade for silk, spices, and porcelain in the markets of Asia. Silver also traveled from Acapulco on the west coast of Mexico across the Pacific in the Manila galleons, and from Manila it also made its way to Asian markets. No matter which direction it went, American silver powerfully stimulated global trade.

The Hacienda   Apart from mining, the principal occupations in Spanish America were farming, stock raising, and craft production. By the seventeenth century the most prominent site of agricultural and craft production in Spanish America was the estate, or hacienda, which produced goods for sale to local markets in nearby mining districts, towns, and cities. Bordering the large estates were smaller properties owned by Spanish migrants or creoles as well as sizable tracts of land held by indigenous peoples who practiced subsistence agriculture.

Labor Systems   The major source of labor for the haciendas was the indigenous population. As in the Caribbean, Spanish conquerors first organized native workforces under the *encomienda* system. Yet from the 1520s to the 1540s, this system led to rampant abuse, as Spanish landowners overworked

their laborers and skimped on their maintenance. After midcentury, *encomenderos* in agriculturally productive regions increasingly required their subject populations to provide tribute but not labor. That didn't solve the problem of labor, however, so Spanish landowners resorted to a system of debt peonage to recruit workers for their haciendas. Under this system, landowners advanced loans to native peoples so that they could buy seeds, tools, and supplies for their own farms. The debtors then repaid the loans with labor, but wages were so low that they were never able to pay off their debts. Thus, landowners helped create a cycle of debt that ensured them a dependent labor force to work their estates.

Resistance to Spanish Rule   The Spanish regimes in the Americas met considerable resistance from indigenous peoples. Resistance took various forms: armed rebellion, halfhearted work, and retreat into the mountains and forests. On some occasions, indigenous peoples turned to Spanish law in search of aid against oppressive colonists. In 1615, for example, Felipe Guaman Poma de Ayala, a native of Peru, fired off a 1,200-page letter to King Philip III of Spain asking for protection for native peoples against rapacious colonists. He wrote passionately of men ruined by overtaxation and women driven to prostitution, of Spanish colonists who grabbed the lands of native peoples and Spanish priests who seduced the wives of native men. Guaman Poma warned the king that if Philip wanted anything to remain of his Andean empire, he should intervene and protect the indigenous peoples of the land. Unfortunately for Guaman Poma, the king never saw the letter. Instead, it ended up in Denmark, where it remained unknown in a library until 1908.

Sugar and Slavery in Portuguese Brazil

Whereas the Spanish American empire concentrated on the extraction of silver, the Portuguese empire in Brazil depended on the production and export of sugar. The different economic and social foundations of the Spanish and Portuguese empires led to different patterns of labor recruitment. The Spanish forced native peoples to provide labor; the Portuguese relied instead on imported African slaves. Because of that, Africans and their descendants became the majority of the population in Brazil.

Colonial Brazilian life revolved around the sugar mill, or *engenho*, which came to represent a complex of

---

quinto (KEEN-toh)
hacienda (ah-SYEN-dah)

land, labor, buildings, animals, capital, and technical skills related to the production of sugar. Unlike other crops, sugarcane required extensive processing to yield molasses or refined sugar. Thus *engenhos* needed both heavy labor for the planting and harvesting of cane and specialized skills for the intricacies of processing.

The Engenho

Like their Spanish counterparts, Portuguese colonists first tried to enlist local populations as laborers. Unlike the inhabitants of Mexico and Peru, however, the peoples of Brazil were not sedentary cultivators. They resisted efforts to commandeer their labor and evaded the Portuguese simply by retreating to interior lands. In addition, in Brazil as elsewhere in the Americas, epidemic diseases devastated indigenous populations. After smallpox and measles ravaged the Brazilian coast in the 1560s, Portuguese settlers had a hard time even finding potential laborers, let alone forcing them to work.

The Search for Labor

Faced with those difficulties, the colonists turned to another labor source: African slaves. Portuguese plantation managers imported slaves as early as the 1530s, but they began to rely on African labor on a large scale only in the 1580s. The toll on slave communities was extremely heavy: arduous working conditions, mistreatment, poor nutrition, and inadequate housing combined to produce high rates of disease and mortality. Indeed, *engenhos* typically lost 5 to 10 percent of their slaves annually, so there was a constant demand for more slaves.

Slavery

Owners had little economic incentive to improve conditions for slaves or to encourage them to reproduce naturally. If a slave lived five to six years, the investment of the average owner doubled and permitted him to purchase a new and healthy slave without taking a monetary loss. Children required financial outlays for at least twelve years, which from the perspective of the owner represented a financial loss. To them the balance sheet of sugar production was about profit, not about slaves' lives. All told, the business of producing Brazilian sugar was so brutal that every ton of the sweet substance cost one human life.

Fur Traders and Settlers in North America

European mariners first frequented North American shores in search of fish. Over time, though, trade in furs became far more lucrative. After explorers found a convenient entrance to rich fur-producing regions through the Hudson Strait and Hudson Bay, they began to connect large parts of the North American interior by a chain of forts and trading posts. Indigenous peoples trapped animals for Europeans and exchanged the pelts for manufactured goods. The hides went mostly to Europe, where there was strong demand for beaver skin hats and fur clothing.

The Fur Trade

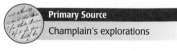
Primary Source
Champlain's explorations

The fur trade generated tremendous conflict between native groups. As overhunting caused American beaver populations to plummet, native trappers constantly had to push farther inland in search of hides. This frequently led native peoples to invade others' territories, which in turn often led to war. The fur trade also took place in the context of competition between European states. This competitive atmosphere contributed to further conflict, as indigenous peoples became embroiled in their patrons' rivalries.

Effects of the Fur Trade

European settler-cultivators posed an even more serious challenge to native ways of life than the fur traders, since they displaced indigenous peoples from the land and turned hunting grounds into plantations. And, as colonists' numbers increased, they sought to integrate their American holdings into the larger economy of the Atlantic Ocean basin by producing cash crops—such as tobacco, rice, and indigo—that they could market in Europe.

Settler Society

Primary Source
Conditions in the Virginia colony

Cash-crop plantations created high demand for cheap labor. Unlike their counterparts in the Spanish territories, indigenous peoples in North America could not be induced to labor in the colonists' fields. Instead, planters turned to indentured servants from Europe for their labor needs. Under this system, people who had little future in Europe—the chronically unemployed, orphans, criminals—received free passage across the Atlantic in exchange for providing four to seven years of labor. Although thousands of indentured servants came to the American colonies with high hopes for making a new start, the system was far from ideal—many died of disease or overwork before completing their terms of labor, and others found only marginal employment.

Indentured Labor

English settlers in North America also found uses for African slaves. In 1619 a group of about twenty Africans reached Virginia, where they worked along-

European moralists often denounced tobacco as a noxious weed, and they associated its use with vices such as drunkenness, gambling, and prostitution. Nevertheless, its popularity surged in Europe, and later in Africa and Asia as well, after its introduction from the Americas.

side European laborers as indentured servants. After about 1680, however, planters increasingly replaced indentured servants with African slaves. By 1750 some 120,000 black slaves tilled Chesapeake tobacco, and 180,000 others cultivated Carolina rice.

Slavery in North America

Slave labor was not prominent in the northern colonies, mostly because the land and the climate were not suitable for the cultivation of labor-intensive cash crops. Nevertheless, the economies of these colonies also profited handsomely from slavery. Many New England merchants traded in slaves destined for the West Indies: by the mid–eighteenth century, half the merchant fleet of Newport carried human cargo. The economies of New York and Philadelphia also benefited from the building and outfitting of slave vessels, and the seaports of New England became profitable centers for the distillation of rum. The chief ingredient of that rum was slave-produced sugar from the West Indies, and merchants traded much of the distilled spirits for slaves on the African coast. Thus, although the southern plantation societies became most directly identified with slavery, all the North American colonies participated in and profited from the slave trade.

Christianity and Native Religions in the Americas

Like Buddhists and Muslims in earlier centuries, European explorers, conquerors, merchants, and settlers took their religious traditions with them when they traveled overseas. The desire to spread Christianity was a prominent motive behind European ventures overseas, and missionaries soon made their way to the Americas.

From the beginning of Spanish colonization in Mexico and Peru, Franciscan, Dominican, and Jesuit missionaries campaigned to Christianize indigenous peoples. Over time, and despite considerable initial resistance, Christianity did win adherents in Spanish America. In the wake of conquest and epidemic disease, many native leaders in Mexico concluded that their gods had abandoned them and looked to the missionaries for spiritual guidance. When native peoples adopted Christianity, however, they blended their own interests and traditions with the faith taught by Spanish missionaries. When they learned about Roman Catholic saints, for example, they revered saints with qualities like those of their inherited gods or those whose feast days coincided with traditional celebrations.

Spanish Missionaries

In Mexico, Christianity became especially popular after the mid–seventeenth century, as an increasingly mestizo society took the Virgin of Guadalupe almost as a national symbol. According to legends, the Virgin Mary appeared before a peasant near Mexico City in 1531. The site of the apparition soon became a popular local shrine visited mostly by Spanish settlers. By the 1640s the shrine attracted pilgrims from all parts of Mexico, and the Virgin of Guadalupe gained a reputation for working miracles on behalf of individuals who visited her shrine. The popularity of the Virgin of Guadalupe helped to ensure that Roman Catholic Christianity would dominate cultural and religious matters in Mexico.

The Virgin of Guadalupe

French and English missionaries did not attract nearly as many converts to Christianity in North America as their Spanish counterparts did in Mexico and Peru, partly because French and English colonists

An eighteenth-century engraving depicts work on a plantation: African slaves prepare flour and bread from manioc (left) while others hang tobacco leaves to dry in a shed (right). A male turkey—a fowl native to the Americas—ignores the bustle and displays his feathers (right foreground).

did not rule over sedentary cultivators: it was much more difficult to conduct missions among peoples who frequently moved about the countryside than among those who lived permanently in villages, towns, or cities. Even so, French missionaries did work actively among native communities in the St. Lawrence, Mississippi, and Ohio river valleys and experienced modest success for their efforts. English colonists, in contrast, displayed little interest in converting indigenous peoples to Christianity, nor did they welcome native converts into their agricultural and commercial society. Yet even without native conversion to Christianity, the growing settlements of French and especially English colonists guaranteed that European religious traditions would figure prominently in North American society.

French and English Missions

EUROPEANS IN THE PACIFIC

Though geographically distant from the Americas, Australia and the Pacific islands underwent experiences similar to those that transformed the western hemisphere in early modern times. Like their American counterparts, the peoples of Oceania had no inherited or acquired immunities to diseases that were common to peoples throughout the eastern hemisphere, and their numbers plunged when epidemic disease struck their populations. For the most part, however, Australia and the Pacific islands experienced epidemic disease and the arrival of European migrants later than did the Americas. European mariners thoroughly explored the Pacific basin between the sixteenth and eighteenth centuries, but only in Guam and the Mariana Islands did they establish permanent settlements before the late eighteenth century. Nevertheless, their scouting of the region laid a foundation for much more intense interactions between European, Euro-American, Asian, and Oceanic peoples during the nineteenth and twentieth centuries.

Australia and the Larger World

At least from the second century C.E., European geographers had speculated about *terra australis incognita*—"unknown southern land"—that they thought must exist in the world's southern hemisphere to balance the huge landmasses north of the equator. Although Portuguese mariners most likely charted much of the western and northern coasts of Australia as early as the 1520s, Dutch sailors based in the Indonesian islands made the first recorded European sighting of the southern continent in 1606. The Dutch VOC authorized exploratory voyages, but mariners found little to encourage further efforts. In 1623, after surveying the landscape of western Australia, the Dutch mariner Jan Carstenzs described the land as "the most arid and barren region that could be found anywhere on earth."

Dutch Exploration

Nevertheless, Dutch mariners continued to visit Australia. By the mid–seventeenth century they had scouted the continent's northern, western, and southern coasts and had fleeting encounters with indigenous populations. Yet because those peoples were nomadic foragers rather than sedentary cultivators, Europeans mostly considered them wretched savages. In the absence of tempting opportunities to trade, European mariners made no effort to establish permanent settlements in Australia.

Only after James Cook charted the eastern coast in 1770 did European peoples become seriously interested in Australia. Cook dropped anchor for a week at Botany Bay (near modern Sydney) and reported that the region was suitable for settlement. In 1788 a British fleet arrived at Sydney carrying about one thousand passengers, eight hundred of them convicts, who established the first European settlement in Australia as a penal colony. For half a century Europeans in Australia numbered only a few thousand, most of them convicts. In fact, free settlers did not outnumber convicted criminal migrants

British Colonists

until the 1830s. Thus, despite early fleeting encounters between European and aboriginal Australian peoples, it was only in the nineteenth and twentieth centuries that a continuing stream of European migrants and settlers linked Australia more directly to the larger world.

The Pacific Islands and the Larger World

The entry of European mariners into the Pacific Ocean basin did not bring immediate change to most of the Pacific islands. In these islands, as in Australia, European merchants and settlers did not arrive in large numbers until the late eighteenth century. However, in Guam and the Mariana Islands, dramatic change was already under way by the sixteenth century.

Ferdinand Magellan and his crew became the first Europeans to cross the Pacific Ocean, in 1521. Before reaching the Philippines, they encountered only one inhabited island group—the Marianas, dominated by

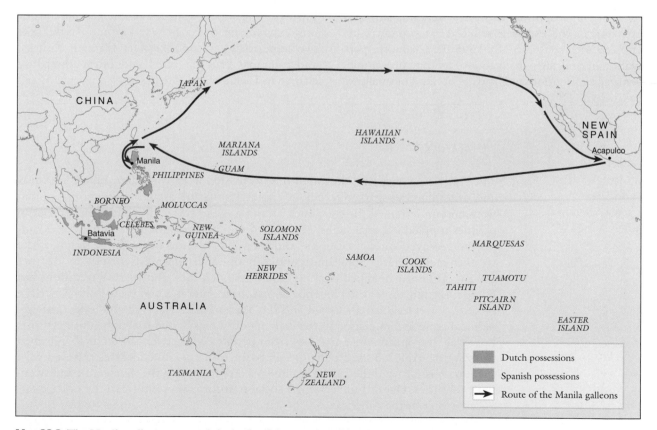

Map 22.2 The Manila galleon route and the lands of Oceania between 1500 and 1800. Note the route taken by the Manila galleons in relation to the majority of the Pacific islands. Why weren't Spanish mariners more interested in exploring the rest of the Pacific as they made their way to the Philippines?

Guam. In 1565 Spanish mariners inaugurated the Manila galleon trade between Manila and Acapulco.

Spanish Voyages in the Pacific

Because their primary goal was to link New Spain to Asian markets, they rarely went out of their way to explore the Pacific Ocean or to search for other islands. Although a few Spanish vessels visited some of the other Pacific islands in the sixteenth century, Spanish mariners found little to interest them and did not establish regular communications with island peoples.

The only Pacific islands that attracted substantial Spanish interest in the sixteenth century were Guam

Guam

and the Marianas. Manila galleons called regularly at Guam, which lay directly on the route from Acapulco to Manila. For more than a century, they took on fresh provisions and engaged in mostly peaceful trade with the indigenous Chamorro people. Then, in the 1670s and 1680s, Spanish authorities decided to bring the Mariana Islands under the control of the viceroy of New Spain in Mexico. They dispatched military forces to the islands to impose Spanish rule and subject the Chamorro to the spiritual authority of the Roman Catholic church. The Chamorro stoutly opposed those efforts, but a smallpox epidemic in 1688 severely reduced their numbers and crippled their resistance. By 1695 the Chamorro population had declined from about fifty thousand at midcentury to five thousand, mostly because of smallpox.

By the end of the seventeenth century, Spanish forces had established garrisons throughout the Mariana Islands and relocated surviving Chamorro into communities supervised by Spanish authorities.

By the late eighteenth century, growing European and Euro-American interest in the Pacific Ocean basin led to sharply increased interactions between islanders and mariners. English and French mariners explored the Pacific basin

Visitors and Trade

in search of commercial opportunities and the elusive northwest passage from Europe to Asia. They frequently visited Tahiti after 1767, and they soon began to trade with the islanders: European mariners received provisions and engaged in sexual relations with Tahitian women in exchange for nails, knives, iron tools, and textiles.

After 1778 the published writings of Captain James Cook, who happened across the Hawaiian Islands in that year, galvanized even greater interest in the Pacific. European whalers, missionaries, and planters came

Captain Cook and Hawai`i

in large numbers in search of opportunities. As a result, by the early nineteenth century, European and Euro-American peoples had become prominent figures in all the major Pacific island groups. In the next two centuries, interactions between islanders, visitors, and migrants brought rapid and often unsettling change to Pacific island societies.

SUMMARY

The Americas underwent thorough transformation in early modern times. Smallpox and other diseases sparked ferocious epidemics that devastated indigenous populations and undermined their societies. In the wake of severe depopulation, European peoples toppled imperial states, established mining and agricultural enterprises, imported enslaved African laborers, and founded colonies throughout much of the western hemisphere. Some indigenous peoples disappeared entirely as distinct groups. Others maintained their communities, identities, and cultural traditions but fell increasingly under the influence of European migrants and their Euro-American offspring. In Oceania only Guam and the Mariana Islands felt the full effects of epidemic disease and migration in the early modern era. By the late eighteenth century, however, European and Euro-American peoples with advanced technologies had thoroughly explored the Pacific Ocean basin, and epidemic diseases traveled with them to Australia and the Pacific islands. As a result, during the nineteenth and twentieth centuries, Oceania underwent a social transformation similar to the one experienced earlier by the Americas.

CHRONOLOGY

1492	First voyage of Christopher Columbus to the western hemisphere
1494	Treaty of Tordesillas
1518	Smallpox epidemic in the Caribbean
1519–1521	Spanish conquest of Mexico
1532–1540	Spanish conquest of Peru
1545	Spanish discovery of silver near Potosí
1604	Foundation of Port Royal (Nova Scotia)
1607	Foundation of Jamestown
1608	Foundation of Quebec
1623	Foundation of New Amsterdam
1630	Foundation of the Massachusetts Bay Colony
1688	Smallpox epidemic on Guam
1754–1763	French and Indian war in North America
1763	Transfer of French Canadian possessions to British rule
1768–1779	Captain James Cook's exploration of the Pacific Ocean
1788	Establishment of the first European colony in Australia

FOR FURTHER READING

Colin G. Callaway. *New Worlds for All: Indians, Europeans, and the Remaking of Early America.* Baltimore, 1997. Scholarly synthesis examining interactions and cultural exchanges between European and indigenous American peoples.

William Cronon. *Changes in the Land: Indians, Colonists, and the Ecology of New England.* New York, 1983. Brilliant study concentrating on the different ways English colonists and native peoples in colonial New England used the environment.

Philip D. Curtin. *The Rise and Fall of the Plantation Complex: Essays in Atlantic History.* 2nd ed. Cambridge, 1998. Examines plantation societies and slavery as institutions linking lands throughout the Atlantic Ocean basin.

K. R. Howe. *Where the Waves Fall: A New South Sea Island History from First Settlement to Colonial Rule.* Honolulu, 1984. A thoughtful survey of Pacific island history emphasizing interactions between islanders and visitors.

John E. Kicza. *Resilient Cultures: America's Native Peoples Confront European Colonization, 1500–1800.* Upper Saddle River, N.J., 2002. A comprehensive comparative study assessing the impact of colonization on indigenous American peoples as well as native influences on American colonial history.

Karen Ordahl Kupperman. *Indians and English: Facing Off in Early America.* Ithaca, N.Y., 2000. Fascinating reconstruction of the early encounters between English and indigenous American peoples, drawing on sources from all parties to the encounters.

Miguel León-Portilla. *The Broken Spears: The Aztec Account of the Conquest of Mexico.* Rev. ed. Boston, 1992. Offers translations of indigenous accounts of the Spanish conquest of the Aztec empire.

James Lockhart and Stuart B. Schwartz. *Early Latin America: A History of Colonial Spanish America and Brazil.* New York, 1982. The best survey of colonial Latin American history.

Gary B. Nash. *Red, White, and Black: The Peoples of Early America.* 3rd ed. Englewood Cliffs, N.J., 1992. Outstanding survey of early American history focusing on the interactions between peoples of European, African, and American ancestry.

Steve J. Stern. *Peru's Indian Peoples and the Challenge of Spanish Conquest.* 2nd ed. Madison, 1993. Scholarly analysis concentrating on the social history of indigenous peoples following the Spanish conquest of Peru.

Fig.2.

CHAPTER 23
Africa and the Atlantic World

Between 1760 and 1792, a west African man known as Thomas Peters crossed the Atlantic Ocean four times. In 1760 slave raiders captured Peters, whose original African name is unknown, marched him to the coast, and sold him to French slave merchants. He traveled in a slave ship to the French colony of Louisiana, where he probably worked on a sugar plantation. But Peters was not a docile servant. He attempted to escape at least three times, and his master punished him by beating him and branding him with a hot iron. During the 1760s his French master sold Peters to an English planter, and about 1770 a Scottish landowner in North Carolina bought him.

During the 1770s, as English colonists in North America prepared to rebel against the British government, slaves of African an-cestry considered their own prospects and looked for ways to obtain personal freedom. Peters was among them. When war broke out, he made his way with his wife and daughter to British lines and joined the Black Pioneers, a company of escaped slaves who fought to maintain British rule in the colonies. When the colonists won the war, Peters escaped to Nova Scotia with his family and many other former slaves.

Blacks were legally free in Nova Scotia, but the white ruling elites forced them to till marginal lands and live in segregated villages. In hopes of improving their lot, some two hundred black families sent Peters to London in 1790, where he promoted the establishment of a colony for former slaves in Sierra Leone. His efforts succeeded, and the next year he returned to Nova Scotia to seek

OPPOSITE PAGE: *An 18th-century engraving shows the slave trade in Africa, and the slaving ships that were used.*

recruits for the colony. In 1792 he led 1,196 blacks aboard a convoy of fifteen ships and began his fourth crossing of the Atlantic Ocean. The colonists arrived safely at Freetown, and Peters served as a leader of the black community there. Although he lived less than four months after arriving in Sierra Leone, his life and experiences personified the links connecting the lands of the Atlantic Ocean basin.

For the most part, the peoples of sub-Saharan Africa continued to follow established patterns of life in early modern times. They built states and organized societies based on kinship groups, and in west Africa and coastal east Africa they continued to trade regularly with Muslim merchants from north Africa and southwest Asia.

Yet the establishment of global trade networks brought deep change to sub-Saharan Africa. Commercial opportunities drew Europeans to the coasts of west Africa, and maritime trade soon turned west African attention to the Atlantic. Maritime commerce also helped promote the emergence of prosperous port cities and the establishment of powerful coastal kingdoms that traded through the ocean rather than the desert. In central Africa and south Africa, European merchants brought the first substantial opportunities for long-distance trade, since Muslim merchants had not ventured to those regions in large numbers.

Trade through the Atlantic profoundly affected African society because it involved human beings. Slavery had been a part of African societies for centuries, and Africans had long supplied slaves to Muslim merchants involved in trans-Saharan trade networks. The Atlantic slave trade, however, was vastly larger than the African and Islamic slave trades, and it had more serious consequences for African society. Between the fifteenth and the nineteenth centuries, it not only siphoned millions of people from their own societies but also provoked turmoil in much of sub-Saharan Africa.

The vast majority of Africans sold into the Atlantic slave trade went to the Caribbean or the Americas. Most worked on plantations cultivating cash crops for export, although some worked as domestic servants, miners, or laborers. Together they made up the largest migration in history before the nineteenth century and gave rise to an African diaspora in the western hemisphere. Under the restrictive conditions of slavery, they could not reconstitute African societies, but they preserved some African traditions and blended them with European and American traditions to create hybrid African-American societies.

AFRICAN POLITICS AND SOCIETY IN EARLY MODERN TIMES

At the start of the early modern era, African peoples lived under a variety of political organizations, including clans governed by kinship groups, regional kingdoms, city-states, and large imperial states that drew their power from the trans-Saharan trade. Under the influence of maritime trade, however, African patterns of state development changed. In west Africa, regional kingdoms replaced imperial states as peoples organized their societies to take advantage of Atlantic as well as trans-Saharan commerce. In east Africa, Swahili city-states fell under the domination of Portuguese merchant-mariners seeking commercial opportunities in the Indian Ocean basin. The extension of trade networks also led to the formation of regional kingdoms in central Africa and south Africa. As the volume of long-distance trade grew, both Islam and Christianity became more prominent in sub-Saharan African societies.

The States of West Africa and East Africa

Between the eighth and the sixteenth centuries, powerful kingdoms and imperial states ruled the savannas of west Africa. The earliest was the kingdom of Ghana, which originated as early as the fourth or fifth century and established its dominance in the region in the eighth century. By controlling and taxing the trans-Saharan trade in gold, the kings of Ghana gained the resources they needed to field a large army and influence affairs in much of west Africa. In the thirteenth century the Mali empire replaced Ghana as the preeminent power in west Africa and continued the Ghana policy of controlling trans-Saharan trade.

In the fifteenth century the expansive state of Songhay emerged to take Mali's place as the dominant power of the western grasslands. Based in the trading city of Gao, Songhay rulers built a flourishing city-state as early as the eighth century. In the early fifteenth century, they rejected Mali authority, and in 1464 the Songhay ruler Sunni Ali (reigned 1464–1493) conquered his neighbors and consolidated the Songhay empire (1464–1591). He brought the important trading cities of Timbuktu and Jenne under his control and used their wealth to dominate the central Niger valley.

The Songhay Empire

Timbuktu, the commercial and cultural center of the Mali and Songhay empires, as sketched by a French traveler in 1828. Though long in decline, the city's mosques, mud-brick dwellings, and crowds of people bespeak a prosperous community.

Sunni Ali built an elaborate administrative and military apparatus to oversee affairs in his realm. He instituted a hierarchy of command that turned his army into an effective military force. He also created an imperial navy to patrol the Niger River, which was an extremely important commercial highway. Songhay military might enabled Sunni Ali's successors to extend their authority north into the Sahara, east toward Lake Chad, and west toward the upper reaches of the Niger River.

Songhay Administration

The Songhay emperors presided over a prosperous land. The capital city of Gao had about seventy-five thousand residents, many of whom participated in the lucrative trans-Saharan trade that brought salt, textiles, and metal goods south in exchange for gold and slaves. The emperors were all Muslims: they supported mosques, built schools to teach the Quran, and maintained an Islamic university at Timbuktu. Like the rulers of Ghana and Mali, the Songhay emperors valued Islam as a cultural foundation for cooperation with Muslim merchants and Islamic states in north Africa.

The Songhay empire dominated west Africa for most of the sixteenth century, but it was the last of the great imperial states of the grasslands. In 1591 a musket-bearing Moroccan army trekked across the Sahara and opened fire on the previously invincible Songhay military machine. Songhay forces withered under the attack, and subject peoples took the opportunity to revolt against Songhay domination.

Fall of Songhay

As the Songhay empire crumbled, a series of small, regional kingdoms and city-states emerged in west Africa. On the coasts Diula, Mande, and other trading peoples established a series of states that entered into commercial relations with European merchant-mariners who called at west African ports after the fifteenth century. The increasing prominence of Atlantic trade in west African society worked against the interests of imperial states such as Mali and Songhay, which had relied on control of trans-Saharan trade to finance their empires.

While regional states displaced the Songhay empire in west Africa, the Swahili city-states of east Africa fell on hard times. In 1505 a huge Portuguese naval expedition subdued all the Swahili cities from Sofala to

Swahili (swah-HEE-lee)

Map 23.1 Major sub-Saharan African states between 1500 and 1650. Locate the three largest states of Songhay, Kongo, and Kanem-Bornu. What was it about their respective locations that favored the development of such large polities?

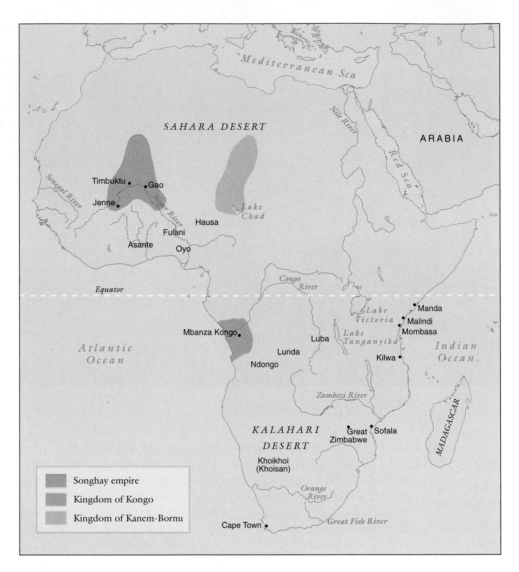

Songhay empire

Kingdom of Kongo

Kingdom of Kanem-Bornu

Swahili Decline

Mombasa. Portuguese forces built administrative centers at Mozambique and Malindi and constructed forts throughout the region in hopes of controlling trade in east Africa. They did not succeed in that effort, but they disrupted trade patterns enough to send the Swahili cities into a decline from which they never fully recovered.

The Kingdoms of Central Africa and South Africa

As trade networks multiplied and linked all regions of sub-Saharan Africa, an increasing volume of commerce encouraged state building in central and south Africa. In central Africa the principal states were the kingdoms of Kongo, Ndongo, Luba, and Lunda in the Congo River basin. Best known of them was the kingdom of Kongo, which emerged in the fourteenth century. Its rulers built a centralized state with officials overseeing military, judicial, and financial affairs, and by the late fifteenth century Kongo embraced much of the modern-day Republic of the Congo and Angola.

The Kingdom of Kongo

In 1483 a small Portuguese fleet initiated commercial relations with the kingdom of Kongo. Within a few years, Portuguese merchants had established a close political and diplomatic relationship with the kings of Kongo. They supplied the kings with advi-

Ndongo (n'DAWN-goh)

sors, provided a military garrison to support the kings and protect Portuguese interests, and brought artisans and priests to Kongo.

The kings of Kongo converted to Christianity as a way to establish closer commercial and diplomatic relations with the Portuguese. The kings appreciated the fact that Christianity offered a strong endorsement of their monarchical rule and found similarities between Roman Catholic saints and the spirits recognized in Kongolese religion. King Nzinga Mbemba of Kongo, also known as King Afonso I (reigned 1506–1542), became a devout Roman Catholic and sought to convert all his subjects to Christianity. Portuguese priests in Kongo reported that he attended religious services daily and studied the Bible so zealously that he sometimes neglected to eat.

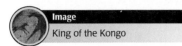

King of the Kongo

Slave Raiding in Kongo

Relations with Portugal brought wealth and foreign recognition to Kongo but also led eventually to the destruction of the kingdom. In exchange for their goods and services, Portuguese merchants sought high-value merchandise such as copper, ivory, and, most of all, slaves. They sometimes embarked on slaving expeditions themselves, but more often they made alliances with local authorities in interior regions and provided them with weapons in exchange for slaves. Such tactics undermined the authority of the kings, who appealed repeatedly for the Portuguese to cease or at least to limit their trade in slaves.

Over time, relations between Kongo and Portugal deteriorated, particularly after Portuguese agents began to pursue opportunities south of Kongo. In 1665 Portuguese colonists to the south even went to war with Kongo. Portuguese forces quickly defeated the Kongolese army and decapitated the king. Soon thereafter, Portuguese merchants began to withdraw from Kongo in search of more profitable business in the kingdom of Ndongo to the south. By the eighteenth century the kingdom of Kongo had largely disintegrated.

The Kingdom of Ndongo

Meanwhile, Portuguese explorers were developing a brisk slave trade to the south in the kingdom of Ndongo, which the Portuguese referred to as Angola from the title of the king, *ngola*. During the sixteenth century, Ndongo had grown from a small chiefdom subject to the kings of Kongo to a powerful regional kingdom, largely on the basis of the wealth it was able to attract by trading directly with Portuguese merchants rather than through Kongolese intermediaries. After 1611 the Portuguese steadily increased their influence inland by allying with neighboring peoples who delivered increasing numbers of war captives to feed the growing slave trade. Over the next several decades, Portuguese forces campaigned in Ndongo in an effort to establish a colony that would support large-scale trading in slaves.

Queen Nzinga

The conquest of Angola did not come easily. For forty years Queen Nzinga (reigned 1623–1663) led spirited resistance against Portuguese forces. Nzinga came from a long line of warrior kings. She dressed as a male warrior when leading troops in battle and insisted that her subjects refer to her as king rather than queen. She mobilized central African peoples against her Portuguese adversaries, and she allied with Dutch mariners who also traded on the African coast. Her aim was to drive the Portuguese from her land, then expel the Dutch, and finally create a central African empire embracing the entire lower Congo basin.

The Portuguese Colony of Angola

Although she was an effective military leader, Nzinga was unable to oust Portuguese forces from Ndongo. When Nzinga died, Portuguese forces faced less capable resistance, and they both extended and tightened their control over Angola, the first European colony in sub-Saharan Africa.

Regional Kingdoms in South Africa

In south Africa, as in central Africa, regional kingdoms dominated political affairs. Kingdoms had begun to emerge as early as the eleventh century, largely under the influence of trade. Merchants from the Swahili city-states of coastal east Africa sought gold, ivory, and slaves from the interior regions of south Africa. By controlling local commerce, chieftains increased their wealth, enhanced their power, and extended their authority. By 1300 rulers of one such kingdom had built a massive, stone-fortified city known as Great Zimbabwe, near the city of Nyanda in modern Zimbabwe, and they dominated the gold-bearing plain between the Zambesi and Limpopo rivers until the late fifteenth century.

Great Zimbabwe

After the fifteenth century a series of smaller kingdoms displaced the rulers of Great Zimbabwe, and Portuguese and Dutch mariners began to play a role in south African affairs. They became especially active

Zimbabwe (zihm-BAHB-way)

SOURCES FROM THE PAST

King Afonso I Protests Slave Trading in the Kingdom of Kongo

King Afonso I of Kongo wrote some twenty-four official letters to his fellow monarchs, the kings of Portugal. The letters touch on many themes—relations between Portugal and Kongo, Afonso's devotion to Christianity, and the slave trade. The following excerpts come from two letters of 1526, when Portuguese slave trading was causing serious disruption in Kongo, prompting Afonso to request help in controlling the activities of Portuguese merchants.

And we cannot reckon how great the damage [caused by Portuguese merchants] is, since the mentioned merchants are taking every day our natives, sons of the land and the sons of our noblemen and vassals and our relatives, because the thieves and men of bad conscience grab them wishing to have the things and wares of this Kingdom which they are ambitious of; they grab them and get them to be sold; and so great, Sir, is the corruption and licentiousness that our country is being completely depopulated, and Your Highness should not agree with this nor accept it as in your service. And to avoid it we need from [your] Kingdoms no more than some priests and a few people to teach in schools, and no other goods except wine and flour for the holy sacrament. That is why we beg of Your Highness to help and assist us in this matter, commanding your factors that they should not send here either merchants or wares, because it is *our will that in these Kingdoms there should not be any trade of slaves nor outlet for them.* Concerning what is referred [to] above, again we beg of Your Highness to agree with it, since otherwise we cannot remedy such an obvious damage. . . .

Moreover, Sir, in our Kingdoms there is another great inconvenience which is of little service to God, and this is that many of our people, keenly desirous as they are of the wares and things of your Kingdoms, which are brought here by your people, and in order to satisfy their voracious appetite, seize many of our people, freed and exempt men, and very often it happens that they kidnap even noblemen and the sons of noblemen, and our relatives, and take them to be sold to the white men who are in our Kingdoms. . . .

And as soon as they are taken by the white men they are immediately ironed and branded with fire, and when they are carried to be embarked, if they are caught by our guards' men the whites allege that they have bought them but they cannot say from whom, so that it is our duty to do justice and to restore to the freemen their freedom, but it cannot be done if your subjects feel offended, as they claim to be.

And to avoid such a great evil we passed a law so that any white man living in our Kingdoms and wanting to purchase goods [i.e., slaves] in any way should first inform three of our noblemen and officials of our court whom we rely upon in this matter, . . . who should investigate if the mentioned goods are captives or free men, and if cleared by them there will be no further doubt nor embargo for them to be taken and embarked. But if the white men do not comply with it they will lose the aforementioned goods. And if we do them this favor and concession it is for the part Your Highness has in it, since we know that it is in your service too that these goods are taken from our Kingdom, otherwise we should not consent to this.

- *On the basis of these letters, does it appear that King Afonso opposed all slave trading or only certain kinds of slave trading?*

SOURCE: Basil Davidson. *The African Past.* Boston: Little, Brown, 1964, pp. 191–93.

Queen Nzinga of Ndongo speaks with the Portuguese governor of Angola at his headquarters. The diplomat refused to provide Nzinga with a chair, so she seated herself on the back of a servant while her "concubines" looked on at the right.

after Dutch mariners built a trading post at Cape Town in 1652. With the aid of firearms, they claimed *European Arrival in South Africa* lands for themselves and commandeered the labor of indigenous Khoikhoi peoples. By 1700 large numbers of Dutch colonists had begun to arrive in south Africa, and by midcentury they had established settlements in the region. Their conquests laid the foundation for a series of prosperous Dutch and British colonies in sub-Saharan Africa.

Islam and Christianity in Early Modern Africa

Indigenous religions remained influential throughout sub-Saharan Africa in early modern times. Although many African peoples recognized a supreme, remote creator god, they devoted most of their attention to powerful spirits who were thought to intervene directly in human affairs. Some of those spirits were associated with geographic features such as mountains, waters, or forests, and others were believed to be the spirits of ancestors who roamed the world.

Although most Africans continued to observe their inherited religions, both Islam and Christianity attracted increasing interest in sub-Saharan Africa.

Islam was most popular in the commercial centers of west Africa and the Swahili city-states of east Africa. In the sixteenth century the trading city of Timbuktu had a prominent Islamic university and 180 schools that *Islam in Sub-Saharan Africa* taught the Quran. Students flocked to Timbuktu by the thousands from all parts of west Africa.

Most African Muslims blended Islam with indigenous beliefs and customs. The result was a syncretic brand of Islam that not only made a place for African beliefs but also permitted men and women to associate with one another on much more familiar terms than was common in north Africa and Arabia. This syncretic Islam frequently struck many devout Muslims as impure and offensive. Muslim merchants and travelers from north Africa and Arabia often commented on their shock at seeing women in tropical Africa who went out in public with bare breasts and socialized freely with men outside their own families.

Some Muslims in sub-Saharan Africa also shared these concerns about the purity of Islam. Most important of them were the Fulani of the west African savannas, who observed a strict form of Islam like that

---

Fulani (foo-LAH-nee)

practiced in north Africa and Arabia. Beginning about 1680 and continuing through the nineteenth century,

The Fulani and Islam

the Fulani led a series of military campaigns to establish Islamic states and impose their own brand of Islam in west Africa. They founded powerful states in what is now Guinea, Senegal, Mali, and northern Nigeria, and they promoted the spread of Islam beyond the cities to the countryside by establishing Islamic schools in remote towns and villages. Their campaigns did not stamp out African religions, but they strengthened Islam in sub-Saharan Africa and laid a foundation for new rounds of Islamic state-building and conversion efforts in the nineteenth and twentieth centuries.

Like Islam, Christianity blended with traditional beliefs and customs when it spread in sub-Saharan

Christianity in Sub-Saharan Africa

Africa and sometimes formed syncretic cults. A particularly influential syncretic cult was the Antonian movement in Kongo, which flourished in the early eighteenth century. The Antonian movement began in 1704 when an aristocratic woman named Doña Beatriz proclaimed that St. Anthony of Padua had possessed her and chosen her to communicate his messages. St. Anthony was a thirteenth-century Franciscan missionary and popular preacher, and he became the patron saint of Portugal. Doña Beatriz gained a reputation for working miracles and curing diseases, and she used her prominence to promote an African form of Christianity. She taught that Jesus Christ had been a black African man, that Kongo was the true holy land of Christianity, and that heaven was for Africans. She urged Kongolese to ignore European missionaries and heed her disciples instead, and she sought to harness the widespread popular interest in her teachings and use it to end the wars plaguing Kongo.

Doña Beatriz's movement was a serious challenge to Christian missionaries in Kongo. In 1706 they persuaded King Pedro IV of Kongo to arrest the charismatic prophetess on suspicion of heresy. Upon examining her, the missionaries determined that Doña Beatriz knowingly taught false doctrine. On their recommendation the royal government sentenced her to death and burned her at the stake. Yet the Antonian movement did not disappear: in 1708 an army of almost twenty thousand Antonians challenged King Pedro, whom they considered an unworthy ruler. Their efforts illustrate clearly the tendency of Kongolese Christians to fashion a faith that reflected their own needs and concerns as well as the interests of European missionaries.

Social Change in Early Modern Africa

Despite increased state-building activity and political turmoil, African society followed long-established patterns during the early modern era. Kinship groups, for example, continued to serve as the basis of social organization and sometimes political organization as well. Within agricultural villages throughout sub-Saharan Africa, clans under the leadership of prominent individuals organized the affairs of their kinship groups and disciplined those who violated community standards. Even in lands ruled by formal states, clan leaders usually implemented state policy at the village level.

Yet interaction with European peoples brought change to African society in early modern times. Trade brought access to European textiles and metal goods, which became popular as complements to native African wares. Trade also brought new food

American Food Crops in Sub-Saharan Africa

crops to sub-Saharan Africa. In the mid–sixteenth century, American crops such as manioc, maize, and peanuts arrived in Africa aboard Portuguese ships. These crops supplemented bananas, yams, rice, and millet, the principal staple foods of sub-Saharan Africa. The most important American crop was manioc because of its high yield and because it thrived in tropical soils not well suited to cultivation of the other crops.

Image
Asante Yam Festival

By the eighteenth century, bread made from manioc flour had become a staple food in much of west Africa and central Africa, where it helped to underwrite steady population growth.

Population Growth

In 1500 C.E. the population of sub-Saharan Africa was about thirty-four million. By 1600 it had increased to forty-four million, and it continued climbing to sixty million in 1800. This strong demographic expansion is all the more remarkable because it took place precisely when millions of Africans underwent an involuntary, forced migration to destinations in the Caribbean and the Americas.

THE ATLANTIC SLAVE TRADE

Of all the processes that linked Africa to the larger Atlantic world in early modern times, the most momentous was the Atlantic slave trade. From the fifteenth to the nineteenth century, European peoples looked to

Africa as a source of labor for large plantations that they established in the western hemisphere. In exchange for slaves, African peoples received European manufactured products—most notably firearms. Only in the nineteenth century did the Atlantic slave trade and, in most places, slavery itself come to an end.

Foundations of the Slave Trade

Until the nineteenth century many settled peoples of the world utilized slave labor in some form. Slavery was common throughout Africa after the Bantu migrations *Slavery in Africa* spread agriculture to all parts of the continent. As in other societies, most slaves in Africa were war captives, although criminals and individuals expelled from their clans also fell into slavery. Once enslaved, an individual had no personal or civil rights. Owners could punish slaves at will and sell them as chattel. African slaves usually worked as cultivators in societies far from their homes, although some worked as administrators, soldiers, or even highly placed advisors. The Songhay emperors, for example, often employed slaves as administrators and soldiers, since the rulers distrusted free nobles, whom they considered excessively ambitious and undependable.

Law and society made African slavery different from bondage in Europe, Asia, and other lands. African law did not recognize private property but, rather, vested ownership of land in communities. Thus wealth and power in Africa came not from the possession of land but from control over the human labor that made land productive. Slaves were thus an important means of measuring wealth. Those who controlled large numbers of individuals were able to harvest more crops and accumulate more wealth than others. Africans routinely purchased slaves to enlarge their families, and they often assimilated slaves into their kinship groups so that within a generation a slave might obtain both freedom and an honorable position in a new family or clan.

After the eighth century, Muslim merchants from north Africa, Arabia, and Persia sought African slaves for sale and distribution to destinations in *The Islamic Slave Trade* the Mediterranean basin, southwest Asia, India, and even southeast Asia and China. When traditional sources proved insufficient to satisfy the demand for slaves, merchants created new supplies by raiding villages and capturing innocent individuals. Merchants then transported the freshly recruited slaves across the Sahara desert or boarded them on ships at the Swahili port cities of east Africa.

Between the eighth and the twentieth centuries, as many as ten million Africans may have left their homeland to feed the Islamic slave trade.

By the time Europeans ventured to sub-Saharan Africa in the fifteenth and sixteenth centuries, traffic in slaves was a well-established feature of African society, and a system for capturing, selling, and distributing slaves had functioned effectively for more than five hundred years. After 1450 European peoples tapped existing networks and dramatically expanded commerce in African slaves even as they shifted its focus to the Atlantic Ocean basin. This Atlantic slave trade profoundly influenced the development of societies throughout the Atlantic Ocean basin.

Human Cargoes

The Atlantic slave trade began small, but it grew steadily and eventually reached enormous proportions. The earliest European slave traders were Portuguese explorers who, in 1441, seized twelve African men and took them to Portugal as slaves. Portuguese mariners encountered stiff resistance when they attempted to capture slaves, as African warriors fired thousands of poison-tipped arrows at gangs of would-be slave raiders. Soon, however, the mariners learned that they could purchase slaves rather than capture them. By 1460 they were delivering five hundred slaves per year to Portugal and Spain, where they usually worked as miners, porters, or domestic servants.

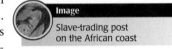
Image
Slave-trading post on the African coast

Slave traders also delivered their human cargoes to Portuguese island colonies in the Atlantic. There was no supply of labor to work plantations in the Azores, the Madeiras, the Cape Verde *The Early Slave Trade* Islands, and São Tomé, all of which were uninhabited when explorers discovered them in the fifteenth century. Sugar planters on the island of São Tomé in particular called for slaves in increasing quantities. By the 1520s some two thousand slaves per year went to São Tomé. By the 1530s Portuguese entrepreneurs had extended the use of slave labor to Brazil, which eventually became the wealthiest of the sugar-producing lands of the western hemisphere.

Spanish explorers and conquerors also sought laborers to work lands in the Caribbean and the Americas. As imported diseases ravaged indigenous populations, the conquerors found themselves with few laborers to work the land. Gradually Spanish settlers began to rely on imported African slaves as laborers. In 1518 the first shipment of slaves went directly from west Africa to the Caribbean, where they worked on recently established sugar plantations. By the early seventeenth century, English colonists had introduced slaves also to the North American mainland.

The demand for labor in the western hemisphere stimulated a profitable commerce known as the triangular trade, since European ships often undertook voyages of three legs. On the first leg they carried horses and European manufactured goods—especially firearms—which they exchanged in Africa for slaves. The second leg took Africans to Caribbean and American destinations.

Triangular Trade

Upon arrival merchants sold their human cargoes to plantation owners for two to three times what they had cost in Africa. In sugar-producing regions they often bartered slaves for sugar or molasses. Then they filled their vessels' hulls with American products before embarking on their voyage back to Europe.

At every stage of the process, the slave trade was a brutal and inhumane business. The original capture of slaves in Africa was almost always a violent affair. As European demand for slaves grew, some African chieftains organized raiding parties to seize individuals from neighboring societies. Others launched wars for the purpose of capturing victims for the slave trade. They often snatched individuals right out of their homes, fields, or villages: millions of lives changed instantly, as slave raiders grabbed their quarries and then immediately spirited them away in captivity. Bewilderment and anger was the lot not only of the captives but also of their family members, who would never again see their kin.

Following capture, enslaved individuals underwent a forced march to the coast, where they lived in holding pens until a ship arrived to transport them to the western hemisphere. Then they embarked on the dreadful "middle passage," the trans-Atlantic journey aboard filthy and crowded slave ships. Enslaved passengers traveled belowdecks in hideously cramped quarters. Conditions were so bad that many slaves attempted to starve themselves to death or mounted revolts. Ship crews often treated the unwilling passengers with cruelty and contempt. Crew members used tools to pry open the mouths of those who refused to eat and pitched sick individuals into the ocean rather than have them waste limited supplies of food.

The Middle Passage

Image
A slave ship

A bronze plaque from Benin offers an early African view of Europeans: it depicts a Portuguese soldier armed with a musket and accompanied by a dog.

Barring difficulties, the journey to Caribbean and American destinations took four to six weeks, during which heat, cold, and disease levied a heavy toll on the human cargo. During the early days of the slave trade, mortality could exceed 50 percent. As the volume of the trade grew, slavers provided better nourishment and facilities for their cargoes, and mortality eventually declined to about 5 percent per voyage. Over the course of the Atlantic slave trade, however, approximately one-quarter of individuals enslaved in Africa did not survive the middle passage.

The Impact of the Slave Trade in Africa

Before 1600 the Atlantic slave trade operated on a modest scale: on average about two thousand slaves left Africa annually during the late fifteenth and six-teenth centuries. During the seventeenth century, slave exports rose dramatically to twenty thousand per year. The high point of the slave trade came in the eighteenth century, when the number of slaves exported to the Americas averaged fifty-five thousand per year. During the 1780s slave arrivals averaged eighty-eight thousand per year, and in some individual years they exceeded one hundred thousand. From beginning to end the Atlantic slave trade brought about twelve mil-

Volume of the Slave Trade

lion Africans to the western hemisphere. An additional four million or more died before arriving.

The impact of the slave trade varied over time and from one African society to another. Some societies largely escaped the slave trade because their lands were distant from the major slave ports on the west African coast. Those societies that raided, took captives, and sold slaves to Europeans profited hand-somely from the trade, as did the port cities and the states that coordinated trade with European merchants. Asante, Dahomey, and Oyo peoples, for ex-ample, took advantage of the slave trade to obtain firearms from European merchants and build power-ful states in west Africa.

On the whole, however, Africa suffered serious losses from the slave trade. The Atlantic slave trade

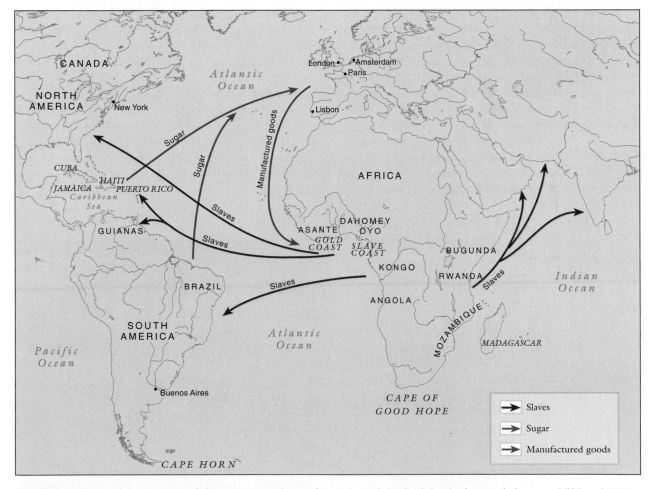

Map 23.2 Origins and destinations of slaves, sugar, and manufactured goods in the Atlantic slave trade between 1500 and 1800.
Note the "triangular" pattern of the Atlantic trade routes between Europe, Africa, and the Americas. Why were most slaves in the Atlantic system taken from west/central Africa, and where were they taken?

alone deprived African societies of about sixteen million individuals, in addition to several million others

Social Effects of the Slave Trade consumed by the continuing Islamic slave trade during the early modern era. Although total African population rose during the early modern era, partly because American food crops enriched diets, several individual societies experienced severe losses because of the slave trade. West African societies between Senegal and Angola were especially vulnerable to slave raiding because of their proximity to the most active slave ports.

While diverting labor from Africa to other lands, the slave trade also distorted African sex ratios, since approximately two-thirds of all exported slaves were males. Slavers preferred young men between fourteen and thirty-five years of age, since they had the best potential to provide heavy labor over an extended period of time. This preference for male slaves had social implications for lands that provided slaves. By the late eighteenth century, for example, women made up more than two-thirds of the adult population of Angola. This sexual imbalance encouraged Angolans to practice polygamy and forced women to take on duties that in earlier times had been the responsibility of men.

Apart from its demographic and social effects, the slave trade brought turmoil to African societies. Vio-

Political Effects of the Slave Trade lence escalated especially after the late seventeenth century, when African peoples increasingly exchanged slaves for European firearms. When the kingdom of Da-

homey obtained effective firearms, for example, its armies were able to capture slaves from unarmed neighboring societies and exchange them for more weapons. During the eighteenth century, Dahomey expanded rapidly and absorbed neighboring societies by increasing its arsenal of firearms and maintaining a constant flow of slaves to the coast. By no means did all African states take such advantage of the slave trade, but Dahomey's experience illustrates the potential of the slave trade to alter the patterns of African politics and society.

THE AFRICAN DIASPORA

Some slaves worked as urban laborers or domestic servants, and in Mexico and Peru many worked also as miners. The vast majority, however, provided agricultural labor on plantations in the Caribbean or the Americas. There they cultivated cash crops that made their way into commercial arteries linking lands throughout the Atlantic Ocean basin. Although deprived of their freedom, slaves often resisted their bondage, and they built hybrid cultural traditions compounded of African, European, and American elements. Most European and American states ended the slave trade and abolished slavery during the nineteenth century. By that time the African diaspora—the dispersal of African peoples and their descendants—had left a permanent mark throughout the western hemisphere.

Armed escorts march a group of freshly captured Africans to the coast for sale in slave markets.

Plantation Societies

Most African slaves went to plantations in the tropical and subtropical regions of the western hemisphere. Spanish colonists established the first of these plantations in 1516 on the island of Hispaniola (which embraces modern Haiti and the Dominican Republic) and soon extended them to Mexico as well. Beginning in the 1530s Portuguese entrepreneurs organized plantations in Brazil, and by the early seventeenth century English, Dutch, and French plantations had also appeared in the Caribbean and the Americas.

Many of these plantations produced sugar, which was one of the most lucrative cash crops of early modern times. But plantations produced other crops as well, including tobacco, rice, and indigo. By the eighteenth century many plantations concentrated on the cultivation of cotton, and coffee had begun to emerge as a plantation specialty.

Cash Crops

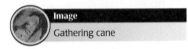

Image
Gathering cane

Regardless of the crops they produced, Caribbean and American plantations had certain elements in common. All of them specialized in the production and export of commercial crops. They all also relied almost exclusively on slave labor. Plantations also featured a sharp, racial division of labor: small numbers of European or Euro-American supervisors governed plantation affairs, and large numbers of African or African-American slaves performed most of the community's physical labor.

In spite of their structural similarities, plantation societies differed considerably from one region to another. In the Caribbean and South America, slave populations usually were unable to sustain their numbers by natural means. This was due partly to the impact of tropical diseases such as malaria and yellow fever, and partly to the brutal working conditions the slaves faced on the plantations. Moreover, since most slaves were male, slave communities did not reproduce quickly.

Regional Differences

Thus, in the Caribbean and South America, plantation owners demanded a continuous supply of slaves to maintain their workforces. Of all the slaves delivered from Africa to the western hemisphere, about half went to Caribbean destinations, and a third more went to Brazil.

Only about 5 percent of enslaved Africans went to North American destinations. Diseases there were less threatening than in the Caribbean and Brazil. More-over, North American planters imported larger numbers of female slaves and encouraged their slaves to form families and bear children.

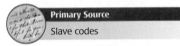

Primary Source
Slave codes

Their support for slave families was especially strong in the eighteenth century, when the prices of slaves direct from Africa rose dramatically.

No matter where they lived, slaves did not meekly accept their status but, like Thomas Peters, resisted it in numerous ways. Some forms of resistance were mild but costly to slave owners: slaves often worked slowly for their masters but diligently in their own gardens, for example. Sometimes they sabotaged plantation equipment or work routines. More seriously, slaves resisted by running away. Runaways known as maroons gathered in remote regions and built their own self-governing communities. Many maroons had gained military experience in Africa, and they organized escaped slaves into effective military forces. Maroon communities flourished throughout slave-holding regions of the western hemisphere, and some of them survived for centuries. In present-day Suriname, for example, the Saramaka people maintain an elaborate oral tradition that traces their descent from eighteenth-century maroons.

Resistance to Slavery

The most dramatic form of resistance to slavery was the slave revolt. Slaves far outnumbered others in most plantation societies, and thus slave revolts brought stark fear to plantation owners and supervisors. Yet slave revolts almost never brought slavery itself to an end, because the European and Euro-American ruling elites had access to military forces that extinguished most rebellions. Only in the French sugar colony of Saint-Domingue did a slave revolt abolish slavery as an institution (1793). Indeed, the slaves of Saint-Domingue declared independence from France, renamed the land Haiti, and established a self-governing republic (1804). The Haitian revolution terrified slave owners and inspired slaves throughout the western hemisphere, but no other slave rebellion matched its accomplishments.

Slave Revolts

The physical labor of African and African-American slaves made crucial contributions to the building of new societies in the Americas and also to the making of the early modern world as a whole. Slave labor cultivated many of the crops and extracted many of the minerals that made their way around the world in the global trade networks of the early modern era. Although slaves themselves did not enjoy the fruits of

Slavery and Economic Development

Slaves were vulnerable to cruel treatment that often provoked them to run away from their plantations or even mount revolts. A French visitor to Brazil in the early nineteenth century depicted a Portuguese overseer administering a brutal whipping to a bound slave on a plantation near Rio de Janeiro.

their labors, without them it would have been impossible for prosperous new societies to emerge in the Americas during the early modern era.

The Making of African-American Cultural Traditions

Enslaved Africans did not enjoy the luxury of maintaining their inherited cultural traditions in the western hemisphere. When packed in slave ships for the middle passage, they found themselves in the company of Africans from societies other than their own. When sold to masters in the Caribbean and the Americas, they joined societies shaped by European and American traditions. In those new circumstances, then, slaves constructed distinctive African-American cultural traditions.

African and Creole Languages European languages were the dominant tongues in the slave societies of the western hemisphere, but slave communities frequently spoke a creole tongue that drew on several African and European languages. In the low country of South Carolina and Georgia, for example, slaves made up about three-quarters of the population in the eighteenth century and regularly communicated in the creole languages Gullah and Geechee, respectively.

Like their languages, slaves' religions combined elements from different societies. Some slaves from Africa were Christians, and many others converted to Christianity after their arrival in the western *African-American Religions* hemisphere. Most Africans and African-Americans, however, practiced a syncretic faith that made considerable room for African interests and traditions. Because they developed mostly in plantation societies under conditions of slavery, these syncretic religions usually did not create an institutional structure or establish a hierarchy of priests and officials. Yet in several cases—most notably Vodou in Haiti, Santeria in Cuba, and Candomblé in Brazil—they became exceedingly popular.

All the syncretic African-American religions drew inspiration from Christianity: they met in parish churches, sought personal salvation, and made use of Christian paraphernalia such as holy water, candles, and statues. Yet they also preserved African traditions. They associated African deities with Christian saints and relied heavily on African rituals such as drumming, dancing, and sacrificing animals. They also preserved beliefs in spirits and supernatural powers: magic, sorcery, witchcraft, and spirit possession all played prominent roles in African-American religions.

African traditions also made their effects felt throughout much of the western hemisphere. Slaves introduced African foods to Caribbean and American societies and helped give rise to distinctive hybrid cuisines. They combined African okra, for example, with European-style sautéed vegetables and American shellfish to produce magnificent gumbos, which found their way to Euro-American as well as African-American tables. Slaves introduced rice cultivation to tropical and subtropical regions. They also built houses, fashioned clay pots, and wove grass baskets in west African styles. In many ways the African diaspora influenced the ways all peoples lived in plantation societies.

African-American Cultural Traditions

The End of the Slave Trade and the Abolition of Slavery

Almost as old as the Atlantic slave trade itself were voices calling for its abolition. The American and French revolutions, with their calls for liberty and universal human rights, stimulated the abolitionist cause. Africans also took up the struggle to abolish commerce in human beings. Frequent slave revolts in the eighteenth and nineteenth centuries made the institution of slavery an expensive and dangerous business. Some freed slaves contributed to the abolitionist cause by writing books that exposed the brutality of institutional slavery. Most notable of them was the west African Olaudah Equiano (1745–1797), who in 1789 published an autobiography detailing his experiences as a slave and a free man. Captured at age ten in his native Benin (in modern Nigeria), Equiano worked as a slave in the West Indies, Virginia, and Pennsylvania. He accompanied one of his masters on several campaigns of the Seven Years' War before purchasing his freedom in 1766. The book became a bestseller, and Equiano traveled throughout the British isles giving speeches and denouncing slavery as an evil institution. He lobbied government officials and members of Parliament, and his efforts strengthened the antislavery movement in England.

Olaudah Equiano

Quite apart from moral and political arguments, economic forces contributed to the end of slavery and the slave trade. Indeed, it gradually became clear that slave labor did not come cheap. The possibility of rebellion forced slave societies to maintain expensive military forces. Even in peaceful times slaves were often unwilling and unproductive workers. Further-

The Economic Costs of Slavery

Olaudah Equiano as depicted in the first edition of his autobiography (1789).

more, in the late eighteenth century a rapid expansion of Caribbean sugar production led to declining prices. About the same time, African slave traders and European merchants sharply increased the prices they charged for fresh slaves.

As the profitability of slavery declined, Europeans began to shift their investments from sugarcane and slaves to newly emerging manufacturing industries. Investors soon found that wage labor in factories was cheaper than slave labor on plantations. As an additional benefit, free workers spent much of their income on manufactured goods. Meanwhile, European investors realized that leaving Africans in Africa, where they could secure raw materials and buy manufactured goods in exchange, was good business.

In 1803 Denmark abolished trade in slaves, and other lands followed suit: Great Britain in 1807, the United States in 1808, France in 1814, the Netherlands in 1817, and Spain in 1845. The end of the slave trade did not abolish the institution of slavery itself, however, and as long as plantation slavery continued, a clandestine

End of the Slave Trade

trade shipped slaves across the Atlantic. British naval squadrons sought to prevent this trade by conducting search-and-seizure operations, and gradually the illegal slave trade ground to a halt. The last documented ship that carried slaves across the Atlantic arrived in Cuba in 1867.

The abolition of the institution of slavery itself was a long-drawn-out process: emancipation of all slaves came in 1833 in British colonies, 1848 in French colonies, 1865 in the United States, 1886 in Cuba, and 1888 in Brazil. Saudi Arabia and Angola abolished slavery in the 1960s. Officially, slavery no longer exists, but millions of people live in various forms of involuntary servitude even today. According to the Antislavery Society for the Protection of Human Rights, debt bondage, contract labor, sham adoptions, servile marriages, and other forms of servitude still oppress more than two hundred million people, mostly in Africa, south Asia, and Latin America. Meanwhile, the legacy of the Atlantic slave trade remains visible throughout much of the western hemisphere, where the African diaspora has given rise to distinctive African-American communities.

Summary

During the early modern era, the peoples of sub-Saharan Africa built states and traded with Islamic societies as they had since the eighth century C.E. Yet African peoples also experienced dramatic changes as they participated in the formation of an integrated Atlantic Ocean basin. The principal agents of change were European merchant-mariners who sought commercial opportunities in sub-Saharan Africa. They brought European manufactured goods and introduced American food crops that fueled population growth throughout Africa. But they also encouraged vast expansion of existing slave-trading networks as they sought laborers for plantations in the western hemisphere. The Atlantic slave trade violently removed at least sixteen million individuals from their home societies and caused political turmoil and social disruption throughout much of sub-Saharan Africa. Enslaved Africans and their descendants were mostly unable to build states or organize societies in the western hemisphere. But they formed an African diaspora that maintained some African traditions and profoundly influenced the development of societies in all slave-holding regions of the Caribbean and the Americas. They also collaborated with others to bring about an end to the slave trade and the abolition of slavery itself.

CHRONOLOGY

1441	Beginning of the Portuguese slave trade
1464–1493	Reign of Sunni Ali
1464–1591	Songhay Empire
1506–1542	Reign of King Afonso I of Kongo
1623–1663	Reign of Queen Nzinga of Ndongo
1706	Execution of Doña Beatriz
1745–1797	Life of Olaudah Equiano
1793–1804	Haitian revolution
1807	End of the British slave trade
1865	Abolition of slavery in the United States

FOR FURTHER READING

Michael L. Conniff and Thomas J. Davis. *Africans in the Americas: A History of the Black Diaspora*. New York, 1994. A comprehensive survey of African-European relations, the slave trade, and the African diaspora.

Philip D. Curtin. *The Rise and Fall of the Plantation Complex: Essays in Atlantic History*. 2nd ed. Cambridge, 1998. Examines plantation societies and slavery as institutions linking lands throughout the Atlantic Ocean basin.

———, ed. *Africa Remembered: Narratives by West Africans from the Era of the Slave Trade*. Madison, 1967. Translations of works in which ten enslaved Africans recounted their memories of early modern Africa.

Christopher Ehret. *The Civilizations of Africa: A History to 1800*. Charlottesville, Va., 2002. An important contribution that views Africa in the context of world history.

David Eltis. *The Rise of African Slavery in the Americas*. Cambridge, 1999. Emphasizes both the economic and the cultural foundations of Atlantic slavery.

Joseph E. Harris, ed. *Global Dimensions of the African Diaspora*. 2nd ed. Washington, 1993. A collection of scholarly essays on Africans in the Americas and the larger world.

Patrick Manning. *Slavery and African Life: Occidental, Oriental, and African Slave Trades*. Cambridge, 1990. Concentrates on the impact of the slave trade on Africa.

Sidney Mintz. *Sweetness and Power: The Place of Sugar in Modern History*. New York, 1985. Important study of sugar, slavery, politics, and society by a prominent anthropologist.

John Thornton. *Africa and Africans in the Making of the Atlantic World, 1400–1800*. 2nd ed. New York, 1997. A rich analysis of African peoples and their roles in the Atlantic Ocean basin.

Jan Vansina. *Paths in the Rainforest: Toward a History of Political Tradition in Equatorial Africa*. Madison, 1990. A thoughtful analysis that considers both native traditions and external influences on African history.

During the period from about 1750 to 1914, European peoples parlayed the profits they had gained from early modern trade, as well as their recent and advantageous domination of the Americas, into global hegemony. In stark contrast to the period from 1500 to 1800, by the late nineteenth century European powers controlled affairs in most of Asia and almost all of Africa, and their Euro-American cousins continued to dominate the Americas. Three historical developments—revolution, industrialization, and imperialism—help to explain how European and Euro-American peoples came to dominate so much of the world.

Revolution transformed societies in North America, France, Haiti, and South America during the late eighteenth and early nineteenth centuries. Although the results of each revolution were different, Enlightenment values of freedom, equality, and popular sovereignty played a large role in each. Revolutions also had a profound effect on the organization of societies in the Atlantic Ocean basin. First in Europe and later in the Americas as well, revolutions and the conflicts that followed from them encouraged the formation of national identities.

The idea of organizing states around national communities eventually influenced political development throughout the world. While organizing themselves into national states, western European and North American peoples also embarked on processes of industrialization. Although industrialization initially caused a great deal of discomfort and dislocation for workers, over time industrial societies became economically much stronger than agricultural societies, and industrial production brought about general improvement in material standards of living. After originating in Britain in the late

eighteenth century, industrialization spread
rapidly to western Europe and North America, and
by the late nineteenth century to Russia and Japan as well.

Alongside increased material standards of living, industrialization brought political, military, and economic strength. In western Europe, the United States, and Japan, industrialization helped underwrite processes of imperialism and colonialism. Railroads, steamships, telegraphs, and lethal weapons enabled industrial powers to impose their rule in most of Asia and Africa in the nineteenth century, just as Euro-American settlers relied on industrial technologies to drive the indigenous peoples of North

AN AGE OF REVOLUTION, INDUSTRY, AND EMPIRE, 1750–1914

America and South America onto marginal lands.

Revolution, industrialization, and imperialism had effects that were felt around the world. Western European and North American peoples vastly strengthened their position in the world by exercising political or economic influence over other societies. They also inspired sustained resistance among colonized peoples, which eventually led to the organization of anticolonial movements. Indeed, revolution, industry, and empire fueled conflict throughout the world in the nineteenth century, and in combination they forced the world's peoples to deal with one another more systematically than ever before in history.

CHAPTER 24

Tradition and Change in East Asia

I n January 1601 a mechanical clock chimed the hours for the first time in the city of Beijing. In the early 1580s, devices that Chinese called "self-ringing bells" had arrived at the port of Macau with Portuguese merchants. Reports of them soon spread to the emperor in Beijing. The Roman Catholic missionary Matteo Ricci conceived the idea of awing the emperor with mechanical clocks and then persuading him and his subjects to convert to Christianity. From his post at Macau, Ricci let imperial authorities know that he could supply the emperor with a chiming clock. When the emperor Wanli granted him permission to travel to Beijing and establish a mission, Ricci took with him a large mechanical clock intended for public display and a smaller clock for the emperor's personal use.

Chiming mechanical clocks enchanted Wanli and his court and soon became the rage in elite society throughout China. Wealthy Chinese merchants paid handsome sums for them, and Europeans often found that business went better if they presented clocks to the government officials they dealt with. By the eighteenth century the imperial court maintained a workshop to manufacture and repair mechanical clocks and watches. Although most Chinese could not afford to purchase mechanical clocks, commoners could admire the large, chiming clock Matteo Ricci installed outside his residence in Beijing.

Chiming clocks did not have the effect that Ricci desired. The emperor showed no interest in Christianity, and the missionaries attracted only small numbers of

Wanli (wahn-LEE)

OPPOSITE PAGE: *European-style buildings on the waterfront in eighteenth-century Guangzhou, where foreign merchants conducted their business.*

437

Chinese converts. Yet, by opening the doors of the imperial court to the missionaries, the self-ringing bells symbolized the increasing engagement between Asian and European peoples.

By linking all the world's regions and peoples, the European voyages of exploration inaugurated a new era in world history. Yet transoceanic connections influenced different societies in very different ways. In contrast to sub-Saharan Africa, where the Atlantic slave trade provoked turmoil, east Asian lands benefited greatly from long-distance trade, since it brought silver, which stimulated their economies. East Asian societies benefited also from American plant crops that made their way across the seas as part of the Columbian exchange.

Unlike societies in the Americas, where Europeans profoundly influenced historical development from the time of their arrival, east Asian societies largely controlled their own affairs until the nineteenth century. Because of its political and cultural preeminence, China remained the dominant power in east Asia. China was also a remarkably prosperous land. Indeed, with its huge population, enormous productive capacity, and strong demand for silver, China was a leading economic powerhouse driving world trade in early modern times. By the late eighteenth century, however, China was experiencing social and economic change that eventually caused instability.

During the seventeenth and eighteenth centuries, Japan also underwent major transformations. The Tokugawa shoguns unified the Japanese islands for the first time and laid a foundation for long-term economic growth. While tightly restricting contacts and relations with the larger world, Tokugawa Japan generated a distinctive set of social and cultural traditions. Those developments helped fashion a Japan that would play a decisive role in global affairs by the twentieth century.

THE QUEST FOR POLITICAL STABILITY

During the thirteenth and fourteenth centuries, China was ruled by the Yuan dynasty (1279–1368) of nomadic Mongol warriors. Mongol overlords ignored Chinese political and cultural traditions, and they displaced Chinese bureaucrats in favor of foreign administrators. When the Yuan dynasty came to an end, the

Tokugawa (TOH-koo-GAH-wah)
shogun (SHOH-gun)

Ming emperors who succeeded it sought to erase all signs of Mongol influence and restore traditional ways to China. Looking to the Tang and Song dynasties for inspiration, they built a powerful imperial state, revived the civil service staffed by Confucian scholars, and promoted Confucian thought. Rulers of the succeeding Qing dynasty were themselves Manchus of nomadic origin, but they too worked zealously to promote Chinese ways. Ming and Qing emperors alike were deeply conservative: their principal concern was to maintain stability in a large agrarian society, so they adopted policies that favored Chinese political and cultural traditions. The state they fashioned governed China for more than half a millennium.

The Ming Dynasty

When the Yuan dynasty collapsed, the Ming dynasty (1368–1644) restored native rule to China. Hongwu (reigned 1368–1398), founder of the Ming ("brilliant") dynasty, built a tightly centralized state. As emperor, Hongwu made extensive use of *Ming Government* mandarins, imperial officials who oversaw implementation of government policies throughout China. He also placed great trust in eunuchs on the assumption that they could not generate families who might one day challenge imperial authority. The emperor Yongle (reigned 1403–1424) launched a series of naval expeditions that went as far as Malindi in east Africa. Yongle's successors discontin-

Interactive Map
The Ming dynasty

ued the expeditions but maintained the centralized state that Hongwu had established.

The Ming emperors were determined to prevent new invasions. In 1421 Yongle moved the capital from Nanjing in the south to Beijing to *The Great Wall* keep closer watch on the Mongols and other nomadic peoples in the north. The later Ming emperors sought to protect their realm by building new fortifications, including the Great Wall of China, along the northern border. The Great Wall had precedents dating back to the fourth century B.C.E., but its con-

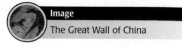
Image
The Great Wall of China

struction was a Ming-dynasty project. Workers by the hundreds of thousands labored throughout the late fifteenth and sixteenth centuries to build a stone and brick barrier

Qing (chihng)

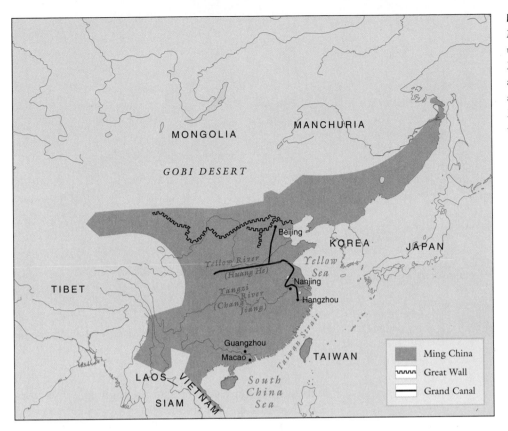

Map 24.1 Boundaries of Ming China from 1368 until 1644. Locate the old Ming capital at Nanjing and the new Ming capital at Beijing. Why would the Ming emperors have wanted to move so far north?

that ran some 2,500 kilometers (1,550 miles). The Great Wall was 10 to 15 meters (33 to 49 feet) high, and it featured watch towers, signal towers, and accommodations for troops deployed on the border.

The Ming emperors also set out to eradicate Mongol and other foreign influences and to create a stable society in the image of the Chinese past. Respect for Chinese traditions facilitated the restoration of institutions that the Mongols had ignored or suppressed. The government sponsored study of Chinese cultural traditions, especially Confucianism and the reestablishment of imperial academies and regional colleges. Most important, the Ming state restored the system of civil service examinations that Mongol rulers had neglected.

The vigor of early Ming rule did not survive beyond the mid–sixteenth century, when a series of problems weakened the dynasty. From the 1520s to the 1560s, pirates and smugglers operated almost at will along the east coast of China. Suppression of pirates took more than forty years, partly because of an increasingly inept imperial government.

Ming Decline

The later Ming emperors lived extravagantly in the Forbidden City, a vast imperial enclave in Beijing, and received news about the outside world only from eunuch servants and administrators. The emperors sometimes ignored government affairs for decades on end, while powerful eunuchs won favor by providing for their amusement. As the eunuchs' influence increased, corruption and inefficiency spread throughout the government and weakened the Ming state.

When a series of famines struck China during the early seventeenth century, the government was unable to organize effective relief efforts. During the 1630s peasants organized revolts throughout China. To complicate matters further, Manchu forces invaded from the north. In 1644 Chinese rebel forces captured the Ming capital at Beijing. Manchu invaders allied with an army loyal to the Ming, crushed the rebels, and recovered Beijing. The Manchus portrayed themselves as avengers who saved the capital from dangerous rebels, but they neglected to restore Ming rule. Instead, they moved their own capital to Beijing and displaced the Ming dynasty.

Ming Collapse

The emperor Yongle designed the Forbidden City as a vast, walled imperial retreat in central Beijing. Here a sculptured lion guards the Forbidden City's Gate of Supreme Harmony.

The Qing Dynasty

When the Ming dynasty fell, Manchus poured south into China from their homeland of Manchuria. The victors proclaimed a new dynasty, the Qing ("pure"), which ruled China until the early twentieth century (1644–1911). The Manchus mostly were pastoral nomads whose remote ancestors had traded with China since the Qin dynasty. During the late sixteenth and early seventeenth centuries, an ambitious chieftain named Nurhaci (reigned 1616–1626) unified Manchu tribes into a centralized state and organized a powerful military force. During the 1620s and 1630s, the Manchu army captured Korea and Mongolia and launched small-scale invasions into China. After their seizure of Beijing in 1644, the Manchus moved to extend their authority throughout China. By the early 1680s they had consolidated the Qing dynasty's hold throughout the land.

The Manchus

The establishment of the Qing dynasty was due partly to Manchu military prowess and partly to Chinese support for the Manchus. During the 1630s and 1640s, many Chinese generals and Confucian scholar-bureaucrats deserted the Ming dynasty because of its corruption and inefficiency. The Manchu ruling elites were schooled in Chinese language and Confucian thought, and they often enjoyed more respect from the scholar-bureaucrats than the high administrators of the Ming dynasty itself.

The Manchus were careful to preserve their own ethnic and cultural identity. They outlawed intermarriage between Manchus and Chinese and forbade Chinese to travel to Manchuria or to learn the Manchurian language. Qing authorities also forced Chinese men to shave the front of their heads and grow a Manchu-style queue as a sign of submission to the dynasty.

The long reigns of two particularly effective emperors, Kangxi (1661–1722) and Qianlong (1736–1795), helped mute the tensions between Manchus and Chinese and allowed the Manchus to consolidate their hold on China. Kangxi was a Confucian scholar as well as an enlightened ruler. He studied the Confucian classics and sought to apply their teachings through his policies. Thus, for example, he organized flood-control and irrigation projects on the Confucian precept that rulers should look after the welfare of their subjects and promote agriculture. He also generously patronized Confucian schools and academies.

Kangxi and His Reign

Kangxi was also a conqueror, and he oversaw the construction of a vast Qing empire. He conquered the island of Taiwan, where Ming loyalists had retreated after their expulsion from southern China, and absorbed it into his empire. Like his predecessors of the

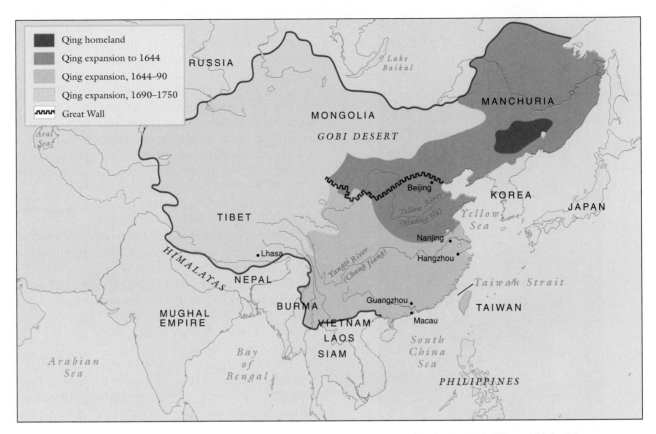

Map 24.2 **Boundaries of the Qing empire from 1644 until 1911.** Compare this map with Map 24.1. Why would the Qing emperors have wanted to incorporate such extensive territories in Mongolia and Tibet into their empire?

Han and Tang dynasties, Kangxi sought to forestall problems with nomadic peoples by projecting Chinese influence into central Asia. His conquests in Mongolia and central Asia extended almost to the Caspian Sea, and he imposed a Chinese protectorate over Tibet. Kangxi's grandson Qianlong continued this expansion of Chinese influence by consolidating Kangxi's conquests in central Asia and by making Vietnam, Burma, and Nepal vassal states of the Qing dynasty.

Qianlong's reign marked the height of the Qing dynasty. Like Kangxi, Qianlong was a sophisticated and learned man. During his long, sta-

Qianlong and His Reign

ble, and prosperous reign, the imperial treasury bulged so much that on four occasions Qianlong canceled tax collections. Toward the end of his reign, however, Qianlong delegated many responsibilities to his favorite eunuchs. His successors continued that practice, and by the nineteenth century the Qing dynasty faced serious difficulties. Throughout the reign of Qianlong, however, China remained a wealthy and well-organized land.

The Son of Heaven and the Scholar-Bureaucrats

Although Qing rulers usually appointed Manchus to the highest political posts, they relied on the same governmental apparatus that the Ming emperors had established. Indeed, for more than five hundred years, the autocratic state created by the Ming emperor Hongwu governed China's fortunes.

If the emperor of China during the Ming and Qing dynasties was not quite a god, he certainly was more than a mere mortal. Chinese tradition held that he was the "Son of Heaven," the human being designated by heavenly powers to

The Son of Heaven

maintain order on the earth. He led a privileged life within the walls of the Forbidden City. Hundreds of concubines resided in his harem, and thousands of eunuchs looked after his desires. Everything about his person and the institution he represented conveyed a sense of awesome authority. The imperial wardrobe and personal effects bore designs forbidden to all others, for

Though painted in the nineteenth century, this portrait depicts Kangxi in his imperial regalia as he looked at about age fifty.

Preparations for the examinations began at an early age, either in local schools or with private tutors. By the time students were eleven or twelve years old, they had memorized several thousand characters that were necessary to deal with the Confucian curriculum, including the *Analects* of Confucius and other standard works. They followed those studies with instruction in calligraphy, poetry, and essay composition.

The examinations consisted of a battery of tests administered at the district, provincial, and metropolitan levels. Stiff official quotas restricted the number of successful candidates in each examination—only three hundred students could pass metropolitan examinations—and students frequently took the examinations several times before earning a degree.

Civil Service Examinations

The possibility of bureaucratic service—with prospects for rich social and financial rewards—ensured that competition for degrees was ferocious at all levels. Yet a degree did not ensure government service. During the Qing dynasty the empire's one million degree holders competed for twenty thousand official civil service positions, and only those who passed the metropolitan examinations could look forward to powerful positions in the imperial bureaucracy.

The Examination System and Chinese Society

Yet the examination system was a pivotal institution. By opening the door to honor, power, and rewards, the examinations encouraged serious pursuit of a formal education. Furthermore, since the system did not erect social barriers before its recruits, it provided an avenue for upward social mobility. Finally, in addition to selecting officials for government service, the education and examination system molded the personal values of those who managed day-to-day affairs in imperial China. By concentrating on Confucian classics and neo-Confucian commentaries, the examinations guaranteed that Confucianism would be at the heart of Chinese education and that Confucians would govern the state.

ECONOMIC AND SOCIAL CHANGES

By modeling their governmental structure on the centralized imperial states of earlier Chinese dynasties, the Ming and Qing emperors succeeded in their goal of restoring and maintaining traditional ways in China. They also sought to preserve the traditional hierarchical and patriarchal social order. Yet, while the emperors promoted conservative political and social policies,

instance, and the written characters of the emperor's name were taboo throughout the realm. Individuals who had the rare privilege of a personal audience with the emperor had to perform the kowtow—three kneelings and nine head knockings. Those who gave even minor offense faced having their bare buttocks flogged with bamboo canes.

Day-to-day governance of the empire fell to scholar-bureaucrats appointed by the emperor. With few exceptions these officials came from the class of well-educated and highly literate men known as the scholar-gentry. These men had earned academic degrees by passing rigorous civil service examinations, and they dominated China's political and social life.

The Scholar-Bureaucrats

China experienced economic and social changes, partly as a result of influences from abroad. Agricultural production increased dramatically and fueled rapid population growth, and global trade brought China enormous wealth. These developments deeply influenced Chinese society and partly undermined the stability that the Ming and Qing emperors sought to preserve.

The Patriarchal Family

Moralists portrayed the Chinese people as one large family, and they extended family values to the larger society. Filial piety, for example, implied not only duties of children toward their fathers but also loyalty of subjects toward the emperor. Like the imperial government, the Chinese family was hierarchical, patriarchal, and authoritarian. The father was head of the household, and he passed leadership of the family to his eldest son. The veneration of ancestors, which the state promoted as a matter of Confucian propriety, strengthened the authority of the patriarchs by honoring the male line of descent. Filial piety was the cornerstone of family values. Children had the duty to look after their parents' happiness and well-being, especially in their old age. Young children heard stories of sons who went so far as to cut off parts of their bodies to ensure that their parents had enough to eat!

Filial Piety

The social assumptions of the Chinese family extended into patrilineal descent groups such as the clan. Clans—whose members sometimes numbered in the thousands—assumed responsibilities such as the maintenance of local order, organization of local economies, and provision for welfare. Clan-supported education gave poor but promising relatives the opportunity to succeed in the civil service examinations. Finally, clans served as a means for the transmission of Confucian values from the gentry leaders to all social classes within the clan.

Within the family, Confucian principles subjected women to the authority of men. The subordination of females began at an early age. Chinese parents preferred boys over girls. Whereas a boy might have the opportunity to take the official examinations and become a government official, parents regarded a girl as a social and financial liability. Under those circumstances it was not surprising that girls were the primary victims of infanticide.

Gender Relations

During the Ming and Qing dynasties, patriarchal authority over females probably became tighter than ever before in China. Since ancient times, relatives had discouraged widows from remarriage, but social pressures increased during the Ming dynasty. Friends and relatives not only encouraged widows to honor the memory of their departed husbands but also heaped posthumous honors on those who committed suicide and followed their spouses to the grave.

Moreover, foot binding, a custom that probably originated in the Song dynasty, became exceptionally popular during the late Ming and Qing dynasties. Tightly constrained and deformed by strips of linen, bound feet could not grow naturally and so would not support the weight of an adult woman. Bound feet were small and dainty, and they sometimes inspired erotic arousal among men. The practice of foot binding became most widespread among the wealthy classes, since it demonstrated an ability to support women who could not perform physical labor, but commoners sometimes bound the feet of especially pretty girls in hopes of arranging favorable marriages.

Foot Binding

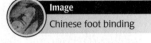

Image
Chinese foot binding

Marriage itself was a contractual affair whose principal purpose was to continue the male line of descent. A bride became a member of the husband's family, and her position there was one of unambiguous subservience. Women could not divorce their husbands, but men could put aside their wives in cases where there were no offspring or where the wife was guilty of adultery, theft, or disobedience.

Thus custom and law combined to strengthen patriarchal authority in Chinese families during the Ming and Qing dynasties. Yet, while family life continued to develop along traditional lines, the larger Chinese society underwent considerable change between the sixteenth and the eighteenth centuries.

Population Growth and Economic Development

China was a predominantly agricultural society, a fact that meshed agreeably with the Confucian view that land was the source of everything praiseworthy. Yet only a small fraction of China's land is suitable for planting: even today only about 11 percent is in cultivation. To feed the country's large population, China's farmers relied on intensive, garden-style agriculture that was highly productive. On its strong agrarian foundation, China supported a large population and built the most highly commercialized economy of the preindustrial world.

By intensively cultivating every available parcel of land, Chinese peasants increased their yields of traditional food crops—especially rice, wheat, and millet—until the seventeenth century. As peasants approached the upper limits of agricultural productivity, Spanish merchants coming by way of the Philippines introduced American food crops to China. American maize, sweet potatoes, and peanuts permitted Chinese farmers to take advantage of soils that previously had gone uncultivated. The introduction of new crops increased the food supply and supported further population growth.

American Food Crops

In spite of recurring epidemic diseases such as plague, China's population rose rapidly from 100 million in 1500 to 160 million in 1600. By 1750 it had surged to 225 million. However, this rapid demographic growth set the stage for future economic and social problems, since

Population Growth

agricultural production could not keep pace with population over a long term.

Although an increasing population placed pressure on Chinese resources, it offered opportunities for entrepreneurs. Indeed, entrepreneurs had access to a large labor force, which meant they were able to recruit workers readily at low cost. After the mid–sixteenth century the Chinese economy benefited also from the influx of Japanese and American silver, which stimulated trade and financed further commercial expansion.

Global trade brought tremendous prosperity to China, especially during the early Qing dynasty. Chinese workers produced vast quantities of silk, porcelain, lacquerware, and tea for consumers in the Indian Ocean basin, central Asia, and Europe. Chinese imports were relatively few, and thus the most important form of compensation for ex-

Foreign Trade

A Ming-era vase painting depicts a woman weaving silk as an attendant pours tea.

ports was silver bullion, which supported the silver-based Chinese economy and fueled manufacturing.

Economic growth and commercial expansion took place mostly in an atmosphere of tight government regulation. Although the Ming emperor Yongle had sponsored a series of maritime expeditions (1405–1433) in the Indian Ocean basin, his successors withdrew their support for such activities and even tried to prevent Chinese subjects from dealing with foreign peoples. In its effort to pacify southern China during the later seventeenth century, the Qing government tried to end maritime activity altogether. An imperial edict of 1656 forbade "even a plank from drifting to the sea," and in 1661 the emperor Kangxi ordered evacuation of the southern coastal regions. Those policies had only a limited effect, and when Qing forces pacified southern China in the 1680s, government authorities rescinded the strictest measures. Thereafter, however, Qing authorities closely supervised the activities of foreign merchants in China. Portuguese merchants were allowed to operate only at the port of Macau, and British agents had to deal exclusively with the official merchant guild in Guangzhou.

Government policies also discouraged the organization of large-scale commercial ventures by Chinese merchants. As a result, it was impossible to maintain shipyards that could construct large sailing ships capable of traveling long distances. Similarly, it was impossible to organize large trading firms like the English East India Company or the Dutch VOC.

Nevertheless, thousands of Chinese merchants worked either individually or in partnerships, plying the waters of the China seas to link China with global trade networks. Chinese merchants were especially prominent in Manila, where they exchanged silk and porcelain for American silver that came across the Pacific Ocean from Mexico. They were also frequent visitors at the Dutch colonial capital of Batavia, where they supplied the VOC with silk and porcelain in exchange for silver and Indonesian spices. Entrepreneurial Chinese merchants ventured also to lands throughout southeast Asia in search of exotic tropical products for Chinese consumers. Indeed, the early modern era was an age when merchants established a prominent Chinese presence throughout southeast Asia.

Trade and Migration to Southeast Asia

China's economic expansion took place largely in the absence of technological innovation. During the Tang and Song dynasties, Chinese engineers had produced a veritable flood of inventions, and China was the world's leader in technology. Yet by early Ming times, technological innovation had slowed. Part of the explanation for the slowdown has to do with role of the government. During the Tang and Song dynasties, the imperial government had encouraged technological innovation as a foundation of military and economic strength. In contrast, the Ming and Qing regimes favored political and social stability over technological innovation.

Government and Technology

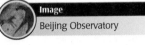
Image
Beijing Observatory

Alongside government policy, the abundance of skilled workers discouraged technological innovation. When employers wanted to increase production, they found that hiring additional workers was less costly than making investments in new technologies. In the short run this tactic kept most of China's population gainfully employed. Over the longer term, however, it meant that China lost technological ground to European peoples, who embarked on a round of stunning technological innovation beginning about the mid–eighteenth century.

Gentry, Commoners, Soldiers, and Mean People

Besides the emperor and his family, scholar-bureaucrats and gentry occupied the most exalted positions in Chinese society. Scholar-bureaucrats had much in common with the gentry: they came largely from gentry ranks, and after leaving government service they usually rejoined gentry society. The scholar-bureaucrats and the gentry functioned as intermediaries between the imperial government and local society. By organizing water-control projects and public security measures, they played a crucial role in the management of local society.

Privileged Classes

Scholar-bureaucrats and gentry were easy to identify. They wore distinctive clothing—black gowns with blue borders adorned with various rank insignia—and commoners addressed them with honorific terms. They also received favorable legal treatment and enjoyed immunity from corporal punishment as well as exemption from labor service and taxes.

Most of the gentry owned land, which was their major source of income. Some were also silent business partners of merchants and entrepreneurs. Their principal source of income, however, was the government service to which their academic degrees gave them access. In contrast to landed elites elsewhere, who

SOURCES FROM THE PAST

Qianlong on Chinese Trade with England

Qing administrators tightly restricted foreign trade. Foreign merchants had to deal with government-approved agents outside the city walls of Guangzhou and had to depart as soon as they had completed their business. In 1793 a British diplomat representing King George III of England bestowed gifts on the emperor Qianlong and petitioned for the right to trade at ports other than Guangzhou. In a letter to King George, Qianlong outlined his views on Chinese trade with England. His letter also bespeaks clearly the importance of government policy for commerce and economic affairs in China.

You, O king, from afar have yearned after the blessings of our civilization, and in your eagerness to come into touch with our influence have sent an embassy across the sea bearing a memorandum. I have already taken note of your respectful spirit of submission, have treated your mission with extreme favor and loaded it with gifts, besides issuing a mandate to you, O king, and honoring you with the bestowal of valuable presents. . . .

Yesterday your ambassador petitioned my ministers to memorialize me regarding your trade with China, but his proposal is not consistent with our dynastic usage and cannot be entertained. Hitherto, all European nations, including your own country's barbarian merchants, have carried on their trade with our Celestial Empire at Guangzhou. Such has been the procedure for many years, although our Celestial Empire possesses all things in prolific abundance and lacks no product within its own borders. There was therefore no need to import the manufactures of outside barbarians in exchange for our own produce. But as the tea, silk, and porcelain which the Celestial Empire produces are absolute necessities to European nations and to yourselves, we have permitted, as a signal mark of favor, that trading agents should be established at Guangzhou, so that your wants might be supplied and your country thus participate in our beneficence. But your ambassador has now put forward new requests which completely fail to recog-

nize our throne's principle to "treat strangers from afar with indulgence," and to exercise a pacifying control over barbarian tribes the world over. . . . Your England is not the only nation trading at Guangzhou. If other nations, following your bad example, wrongfully importune my ear with further impossible requests, how will it be possible for me to treat them with easy indulgence? Nevertheless, I do not forget the lonely remoteness of your island, cut off from the world by intervening wastes of sea, nor do I overlook your excusable ignorance of the usages of our Celestial Empire. I have consequently commanded my ministers to enlighten your ambassador on the subject, and have ordered the departure of the mission. . . .

If, after the receipt of this explicit decree, you lightly give ear to the representations of your subordinates and allow your barbarian merchants to proceed to Zhejiang and Tianjin, with the object of landing and trading there, the ordinances of my Celestial Empire are strict in the extreme, and the local officials, both civil and military, are bound reverently to obey the law of the land. Should your vessels touch the shore, your merchants will assuredly never be permitted to land or to reside there, but will be subject to instant expulsion. In that event your barbarian merchants will have had a long journey for nothing. Do not say that you were not warned in due time! Tremblingly obey and show no negligence! A special mandate!

- *What considerations might have prompted the Chinese government to take such a restrictive approach to foreign trade?*

SOURCE: J. O. P. Bland. *Annals and Memoirs of the Court of Peking.* Boston: Houghton Mifflin, 1914, pp. 325–31. (Translation slightly modified.)

This engraving depicts a peasant couple in harness pulling a plow. Note that the man wears the braided queue that Manchus required their male Chinese subjects to wear.

often lived on rural estates, China's gentry resided largely in cities and towns, where they tended to political, social, and financial affairs.

Confucian tradition ranked three broad classes of commoners below the gentry: peasants, artisans or workers, and merchants. By far the *Working Classes* biggest class consisted of peasants: a designation that covered everyone from day laborers to petty landlords. Confucian principles regarded peasants as the most honorable of the three classes, since they performed honest labor and supplied the entire population with food.

The category of artisans and workers encompassed a wide spectrum of occupations. Despite their lower status, crafts workers, tailors, barbers, and physicians generally enjoyed higher income than peasants did. Artisans and workers were usually employees of the state or of gentry and merchant families, but they also pursued their occupations as self-employed persons.

Merchants, from street peddlers to individuals of enormous wealth and influence, ranked at the bottom *Merchants* of the Confucian social hierarchy. Because moralists looked upon them as unscrupulous social parasites, merchants enjoyed little legal protection. Yet Chinese merchants often garnered official support for their enterprises through bribery of government bureaucrats or through profit-sharing arrangements with gentry families. Indeed, the participation of gentry families in commercial ventures such as warehousing, money lending, and pawnbroking blurred the distinction between gentry and merchants. In addition, merchants blurred the distinction further by preparing their sons for government examinations, which could result in appointment to civil service positions and promotion to gentry status.

Although China was still a basically agricultural land under the Ming and the Qing, the increasing prominence of artisans and merchants demonstrated that manufacturing and commerce had become much more economically important than in ancient times. As a result, those who could exploit opportunities had the potential to lead comfortable lives and even to climb into the ranks of the privileged gentry class. Yet Chinese merchants and artisans did not forge cooperative relationships with government authorities as their counterparts in England and the Netherlands did.

The principal concern of late Ming and Qing authorities was to preserve the stability of a large agrarian society, not to promote rapid economic development through trade. Thus Chinese authorities did not adopt policies designed to strengthen both merchants and the state by authorizing merchants to pursue their efforts aggressively in the larger world.

Beyond the Confucian social hierarchy were members of the military forces and the so-called mean people, such as slaves, indentured servants, *Lower Classes* entertainers, and prostitutes. Confucian moralists regarded armed forces as a wretched but necessary evil and attempted to avoid military dominance of society by placing civilian bureaucrats in the highest command positions, even at the expense of military effectiveness.

THE CONFUCIAN TRADITION AND NEW CULTURAL INFLUENCES

The Ming and Qing emperors looked to Chinese traditions for guidance in framing their cultural as well as their political and social policies. They provided generous support for Confucianism, and they ensured that formal education in China revolved around Confucian thought and values. Yet demographic and urban growth also encouraged the emergence of a vibrant popular culture in Chinese cities, and European missionaries acquainted the Chinese with Roman Catholic Christianity and European science and technology as well.

Neo-Confucianism and Pulp Fiction

Imperial sponsorship of Chinese cultural traditions meant primarily support for the Confucian tradition, especially as systematized by the Song dynasty scholar Zhu Xi, the most prominent architect of neo-Confucianism. Zhu Xi combined the moral, ethical, and political values of Confucius with the logical rigor and speculative power of Buddhist philosophy. He emphasized the values of self-discipline, filial piety, and obedience to established rulers, all of which appealed to Ming and Qing emperors seeking to maintain stability in their vast realm. To promote Confucian values, the Ming and Qing emperors supported educational programs at many levels throughout the land.

While the imperial courts promoted Confucianism, a lively popular culture took shape in the cities of China. *Popular Culture* Most urban residents did not have an advanced education and knew little about Confucius. Many were literate, however, and they found that popular novels met their needs for entertainment and diversion. Although Confucian scholars thought popular novels were crude, printing made it possible to produce them cheaply and in large numbers, and urban residents eagerly consumed them. Many of the novels had little literary merit, but their tales of conflict, horror, wonder, excitement, and sometimes unconcealed pornography appealed to readers.

Some popular novels, however, did offer thoughtful reflections on the world and human affairs. The historical novel *The Romance of the Three Kingdoms,* for example, explored the political intrigue that followed the collapse of the Han dynasty. *The Dream of the Red Chamber* told the story of cousins deeply in love who could not marry because of their families' wishes. Through the prism of a sentimental love story, the novel shed fascinating light on the dynamics of wealthy scholar-gentry families.

Popular Novels

The Return of Christianity to China

Nestorian Christians had established churches and monasteries in China as early as the seventh century C.E., and Roman Catholic communities were prominent in Chinese commercial centers during the Yuan dynasty. After the outbreak of epidemic plague and the collapse of the Yuan dynasty in the fourteenth century, however, Christianity disappeared from China. When Roman Catholic missionaries returned in the sixteenth century, they had to start from scratch in their efforts to win converts.

Founder of the mission to China was the Italian Jesuit Matteo Ricci (1552–1610), who had the ambitious goal of converting China to Christianity, beginning with the Ming emperor Wanli. Ricci was a brilliant and learned man as well as a polished diplomat, and he became a popular figure at the Ming court. Upon arrival at Macau in 1582, Ricci immersed himself in the study of the Chinese language and the Confucian classics. By the time he first traveled to Beijing and visited the imperial court in 1601, Ricci was able to write learned Chinese and converse fluently with Confucian scholars.

Matteo Ricci

Ricci's mastery of Chinese language and literature opened doors for the Jesuits, who then dazzled their hosts with European science, technology, and mechanical gadgetry such as glass prisms, harpsichords, and especially "self-ringing bells"—spring-driven mechanical clocks that chimed the hours.

The Jesuits sought to capture Chinese interest with European science and technology, but their ultimate goal was to win converts. Ricci, for example, tried to make Christianity seem familiar by arguing that the doctrines of Confucius and Jesus were very similar, if not identical. The Jesuits also held religious services in the Chinese language and allowed converts to continue the time-honored practice of venerating their ancestors.

Confucianism and Christianity

In spite of their tolerance, flexibility, and genuine respect for their hosts, the Jesuits attracted few converts in China. By the mid–eighteenth century, Chinese Christians numbered about 200,000—a tiny proportion of the Chinese population of 225 million. Many Chinese hesitated to adopt Christianity partly because of its exclusivity: like Islam, Christianity claimed to be the only true religion, so conversion implied that the time-honored traditions of Confucianism, Daoism, and Buddhism were fallacious creeds—a proposition most Chinese were unwilling to accept.

Ultimately, the Roman Catholic mission in China came to an end because of squabbles between the Jesuits and members of the Franciscan and Dominican orders, who also sought converts in China. Jealous of the Jesuits' presence at the imperial court, they complained to the pope about their rivals' tolerance of Chinese traditions. The pope sided with the critics and in the early eighteenth century issued several proclamations ordering missionaries in China to conduct services according to

End of the Jesuit Mission

Zhu Xi (ZHOO SHEE)
neo-Confucianism (NEE-oh kuhn-FYEW-shuhn-iz'm)

Buddhism (BOO-diz'm)

European standards. In response, the emperor Kangxi ordered an end to the preaching of Christianity in China. By the mid–eighteenth century, the mission had weakened so much that it had effectively come to an end.

The Roman Catholic mission to China did not attract large numbers of converts, but it nonetheless had important cultural effects. In letters, reports, and other writings distributed widely throughout Europe, the Jesuits described China as an orderly and rational society. The rational morality of Confucianism appealed to the Enlightenment philosophes, who sought alternatives to Christianity as the foundation for ethics and morality. Thus for the first time since Marco Polo, strong European interest in east Asian societies was stimulated.

THE UNIFICATION OF JAPAN

During the late sixteenth and early seventeenth centuries, the political unification of Japan ended an extended period of civil disorder. Like the Ming and Qing emperors in China, the Tokugawa shoguns

sought to lay a foundation for long-term political and social stability by promoting conservative values and tightly restricting foreign influence in Japan. As in China, however, demographic

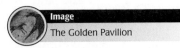

Image
The Golden Pavilion

expansion and economic growth fostered social and cultural change in Japan, and merchants introduced Chinese and European influences into Japan.

The Tokugawa Shogunate

From the twelfth through the sixteenth century, a *shogun* ("military governor") ruled Japan through retainers who received political rights and large estates in exchange for military services. Theoretically, the shogun ruled as a temporary stand-in for the Japanese emperor. In fact, however, the emperor was nothing more than a figurehead. After the fourteenth century the conflicting ambitions of shoguns and retainers led to constant turmoil, and by the sixteenth century Japan was in a state of civil war. Japanese historians often refer to the sixteenth century as the era of *sengoku*—"the country at war."

Map 24.3 Territories of Tokugawa Japan from 1600 to 1867. Consider Japan's position with regard to China, Korea, and Russia. Would it have been easy or difficult to enforce the ban on foreign trade during most of this period?

Toward the end of the sixteenth century, a series of military leaders brought about the unification of *Tokugawa Ieyasu* the land. In 1600 the last of those leaders, Tokugawa Ieyasu (reigned 1600–1616), established a military government known as the Tokugawa *bakufu* ("tent government," since it theoretically was only a temporary replacement for the emperor's rule). Ieyasu and his descendants ruled the bakufu as shoguns from 1600 until the end of the Tokugawa dynasty in 1867.

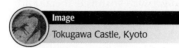

The principal aim of the Tokugawa shoguns was to prevent the return of civil war. Consequently, the shoguns needed to control the *daimyo* ("great names"), powerful territorial lords who ruled most of Japan from their vast, hereditary landholdings. Each maintained a government, an independent judiciary, and schools, and each circulated paper money. Moreover, after the mid–sixteenth century, many daimyo established relationships with European mariners, from whom they learned how to manufacture and use gunpowder weapons, which they turned against one another.

From the castle town of Edo (modern Tokyo), the shogun sought to extend his control over the daimyo *Control of* through the policy of "alternate atten- *the Daimyo* dance," which required daimyo to maintain their families at Edo and spend every other year at the Tokugawa court. This policy enabled the shoguns to keep an eye on the daimyo, and it encouraged daimyo to spend their money on comfortable lives in Edo rather than on military forces that could challenge the bakufu. The shoguns also discouraged the daimyo from visiting one another and even required daimyo to obtain permission to meet with the emperor.

In an effort to prevent European influences from destabilizing the land, the Tokugawa shoguns closely *Control of* controlled relations between Japan *Foreign Relations* and the outside world. A primary concern was that Europeans might threaten the bakufu by making alliances with daimyo and supplying them with weapons. Thus during the 1630s the shoguns issued a series of edicts sharply restricting Japanese relations with other lands.

The policy forbade Japanese to go abroad on pain of death and prohibited the construction of large ships. It expelled Europeans from Japan and prohib-

ited foreign merchants from trading in Japanese ports. The policy did, however, allow carefully controlled trade with Asian lands, and it also permitted small numbers of Chinese and Dutch merchants to trade under tight restrictions at the southern port city of Nagasaki. As a result, Japan was never completely isolated from the outside world.

Economic and Social Change

By ending civil conflict and maintaining political stability, the Tokugawa shoguns set the stage for economic growth in Japan. Ironically, peace and a booming economy encouraged social change that undermined the order that the bakufu sought to preserve. Economic growth had its roots in increased agricultural production, especially of rice, cotton, silk, and indigo. In many parts of Japan, villages moved away from subsistence farming in favor of production for the market.

Increased agricultural production brought about rapid demographic growth: during the seventeenth century the Japanese population rose by almost one-third, from twenty-two million *Population* to twenty-nine million. Thereafter, how- *Growth* ever, many families practiced population control to maintain or raise their standard of living. Between 1700 and 1850 the Japanese population grew only moderately, from twenty-nine million to thirty-two million. Contraception, late marriage, and abortion all played roles in limiting population growth, but the principal method of control was infanticide, euphemistically referred to as "thinning out the rice shoots." Japanese families resorted to these measures primarily because Japan was land poor, which made it easy for populations to strain available resources.

The Tokugawa era was an age of social as well as demographic change in Japan. Because of Chinese cultural influence, the Japanese social hier- *Social Change* archy followed Confucian precepts in ranking the ruling elites—including the daimyo and samurai warriors—as the most privileged class of society, followed by peasants and artisans. As in China, merchants ranked at the bottom. Yet the extended period of peace ushered in by Tokugawa rule undermined the social position of the ruling elites, who found their traditional role as local administrators redundant. Many of the ruling elite also fell into financial difficulty in this period because of rising prices and lavish lifestyles. As a result, many became indebted to rice brokers and gradually declined into genteel poverty.

daimyo (DEYEM-yoh)

Dutch sailing ships and smaller Japanese vessels mingle in Nagasaki harbor. Dutch merchants conducted their business on the artificial island of Deshima, at left.

Meanwhile, as in China, merchants in Japan became increasingly wealthy and prominent. Japanese cities flourished throughout the Tokugawa era—the population of Edo approached one million by 1700—and merchants prospered in the vibrant urban environment. Rice dealers, pawnbrokers, and sake merchants soon controlled more wealth than the ruling elites.

Neo-Confucianism and Floating Worlds

Japan had gone to school in China, and the influence of China continued throughout the Tokugawa era. Formal education began with study of Chinese language and literature. As late as the *Neo-Confucianism in Japan* nineteenth century, many Japanese scholars wrote their philosophical, legal, and religious works in Chinese. The common people embraced Buddhism, which had come to Japan from China, and Confucianism was the most influential philosophical system. Indeed, by the early

eighteenth century, neo-Confucianism had become the official ideology of the Tokugawa bakufu.

Yet even with Tokugawa sponsorship, neo-Confucianism did not dominate intellectual life in Japan. Some scholars sought to establish a sense of Japanese identity *Native Learning* that did not depend on cultural kinship with China. Particularly during the eighteenth century, scholars of "native learning" scorned neo-Confucianism and even Buddhism as alien cultural imports and emphasized instead the importance of folk traditions and the indigenous Shinto religion for Japanese identity. Many scholars of native learning viewed Japanese people as superior to all others and glorified the supposed purity of Japanese society before its adulteration by Chinese and other foreign influences.

Meanwhile, the emergence of a prosperous merchant class encouraged the development of a vibrant popular culture. During the seventeenth and eighteenth centuries, an exuberant middle-class culture flourished in cities such as Kyoto, Edo, and Osaka. In those and other cities, Japan's finest creative talents catered to middle-class appetites.

The centers of Tokugawa urban culture were the "floating worlds" *(ukiyo),* entertainment and pleasure quarters where teahouses, the- *Floating Worlds* aters, brothels, and public baths offered escape from the rigid rules of conduct that governed public behavior in Tokugawa society. In contrast to the solemn, serious proceedings of the imperial court and the bakufu, the popular culture of urban residents was secular, satirical, and even scatological. The main expressions of this lively culture were prose fiction and new forms of theater.

Ihara Saikaku (1642–1693), one of Japan's most prolific poets, helped create a new genre of prose literature, the "books of the floating world." Much of his fiction revolved around the theme of love. In *The Life of a Man Who Lived for Love,* for example, Ihara chronicled the experiences of a townsman who devoted his life to a quest for sexual pleasure. Ihara's treatment of love stressed the erotic rather than the aesthetic, and the brief, episodic stories that made up his work appealed to literate urban residents who were not inclined to pore over dense neo-Confucian treatises.

Beginning in the early seventeenth century, two new forms of drama became popular in Japanese cities. One was *kabuki* theater, which usually featured several

Shintoism (SHIHN-toh-iz'm)
kabuki (kah-BOO-kee)

A colored woodcut by Okumura Masanobu depicts the audience at a seventeenth-century kabuki theater. Enthusiastic actors often ran down wooden ramps and played their roles among the audience.

acts consisting of lively and sometimes bawdy skits where stylized acting combined with lyric singing, dancing, and spectacular staging. The other new dramatic form was *bunraku,* the puppet theater. In bunraku, chanters accompanied by music told a story acted out by puppets. Manipulated by a team of three, each puppet could execute the subtlest and most intricate movements, such as brushing a tear from the eye with the sleeve of a kimono. Both kabuki and bunraku attracted enthusiastic audiences in search of entertainment and diversion.

Christianity and Dutch Learning

Christian missionaries and European merchants also contributed their own distinctive threads to the cultural fabric of Tokugawa Japan. The Jesuit Francis

Christian Missions

Xavier opened the first Roman Catholic mission in 1549 and for a few decades experienced remarkable success. Several powerful daimyo adopted Christianity and ordered their subjects to do likewise. Many Japanese converts became enthusiastic Christians and worked to convert their compatriots to the new faith. By the 1580s about 150,000 Japanese had converted to Christianity, and by 1615 Japanese Christians numbered about 300,000.

Although Christians were only a tiny minority of the Japanese population, the popularity of Christianity

generated a backlash among those seeking to preserve Japanese religious and cultural traditions. The Tokugawa shoguns restricted European access to Japan largely because of concerns that Christianity might serve as a cultural bridge for alliances between daimyo and European adventurers, which in turn could threaten the bakufu. Meanwhile, Buddhist and Confucian scholars resented the Christian conviction that their faith was the only true doctrine.

Between 1587 and 1639, shoguns promulgated several decrees ordering a halt to Christian missions and commanding Japanese Christians to renounce their faith. In 1612 the shoguns began rigorous enforcement

Anti-Christian Campaign

of these decrees. They tortured and executed European missionaries who refused to leave the islands as well as Japanese Christians who refused to abandon their faith. The campaign was so effective that even some European missionaries abandoned Christianity. Most notable was the Por-

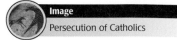

Image
Persecution of Catholics

tuguese Jesuit Christovão Ferreira, head of the Jesuit mission in Japan, who gave up Christianity under torture, adopted Buddhism, and interrogated many Europeans who fell into Japanese hands in the mid–seventeenth century. By the late seventeenth century, the anti-Christian campaign had claimed tens of thousands of lives, and Christianity survived only as a secret, underground religion.

Tokugawa policies ensured that Christianity would not soon reappear in Japan, but they did not entirely *Dutch Learning* prevent contacts between Europeans and Japanese. After 1639 Dutch merchants trading at Nagasaki became Japan's principal source of information about the world beyond east Asia. A small number of Japanese scholars learned Dutch to communicate with the foreigners. Their studies, which they called "Dutch learning," brought considerable knowledge of the outside world to Japan. After 1720 Tokugawa authorities lifted the ban on foreign books, and Dutch learning—especially European art and science—began to play a significant role in Japanese intellectual life. Indeed, by the mid-eighteenth century the Tokugawa shoguns themselves had become enthusiastic proponents of Dutch learning, and schools of European medicine and Dutch studies flourished in several Japanese cities.

SUMMARY

Both China and Japan controlled their own affairs throughout the early modern era and avoided the turmoil that afflicted societies in the Americas and much of sub-Saharan Africa. Rulers of the Ming dynasty built a powerful centralized state in China. They worked diligently to restore traditional ways by reviving Chinese political institutions and providing state sponsorship for neo-Confucianism. In the interest of stability, authorities also restricted foreign merchants' access to China and limited the activities of Christian missionaries. The succeeding Qing dynasty pursued similar policies. The Ming and Qing dynasties both brought political stability, but China experienced considerable social and economic change in early modern times. American food crops helped increase agricultural production, which fueled rapid population growth, and global trade stimulated the Chinese economy, which improved the position of merchants and artisans in society. The experience of the Tokugawa era in Japan was much like that of the Ming and Qing eras in China. The Tokugawa bakufu brought political order to the Japanese islands and closely controlled foreign relations, but a vibrant economy promoted social change that enhanced the status of merchants and artisans.

CHRONOLOGY

1368–1644	Ming dynasty (China)
1368–1398	Reign of Hongwu
1403–1424	Reign of Yongle
1552–1610	Life of Matteo Ricci
1572–1620	Reign of Emperor Wanli
1600–1867	Tokugawa shogunate (Japan)
1616–1626	Reign of Nurhaci
1642–1693	Life of Ihara Saikaku
1644–1911	Qing dynasty (China)
1661–1722	Reign of Kangxi
1736–1795	Reign of Qianlong
1793	British trade mission to China

FOR FURTHER READING

Timothy Brook. *The Confusions of Pleasure: Commerce and Culture in Ming China*. Berkeley, 1998. Fascinating social and cultural analysis of Ming China focusing on the role of commerce as an agent of social change.

Mark C. Elliott. *The Manchu Way: The Eight Banners and Ethnic Identity in Late Imperial China*. Stanford, 2001. Important scholarly study focusing on relations between Manchus and Chinese during the Qing dynasty.

Mark Elvin. *The Pattern of the Chinese Past: A Social and Economic Interpretation*. Stanford, 1973. A brilliant analysis of Chinese history concentrating on economic, social, and technological themes.

Ray Huang. *1587: A Year of No Significance*. New Haven, 1981. A very good history of the late Ming, with insights into daily life.

Susan Naquin and Evelyn S. Rawski. *Chinese Society in the Eighteenth Century*. New Haven, 1987. A lucid and well-organized discussion of Chinese social history.

Kenneth Pomeranz. *The Great Divergence: China, Europe, and the Making of the Modern World Economy*. Princeton, 2000. Pathbreaking scholarly study that illuminates the economic history of the early modern world through comparison of economic development in Asian and European lands.

Jonathan D. Spence. *The Death of Woman Wang*. New York, 1978. Engaging reconstruction of life in rural China during the early Qing dynasty.

Conrad Totman. *Early Modern Japan*. Berkeley, 1993. An outstanding survey of Tokugawa ecological, political, social, economic, and cultural history.

H. Paul Varley. *Japanese Culture*. 4th ed. Honolulu, 2000. Places the cultural history of the Tokugawa era in its larger historical context.

Frederic Wakeman Jr. *The Great Enterprise: The Manchu Reconstruction of the Imperial Order in Seventeenth-Century China*. 2 vols. Berkeley, 1985. Important scholarly analysis of early Qing history.

CHAPTER 25

The Islamic Empires

In 1635 Shah Jahan, the emperor of Mughal India, took his seat on the Peacock Throne. Seven years in the making, the Peacock Throne is probably the most spectacular seat on which any mortal human being has rested. Shah Jahan ordered the throne encrusted with ten million rupees' worth of diamonds, rubies, emeralds, and pearls. Atop the throne itself stood a magnificent, golden-bodied peacock with a huge ruby and a fifty-carat, pear-shaped pearl on its breast and a brilliant tail fashioned of sapphires and gems.

Yet, for all its splendor, the Peacock Throne ranks a distant second among Shah Jahan's artistic projects: pride of place goes to the incomparable Taj Mahal. Built over a period of eighteen years as a tomb for Shah Jahan's beloved wife, Mumtaz Mahal, who died during childbirth in 1631, the Taj Mahal is a graceful and elegant monument both to the departed empress and to Shah Jahan's Islamic faith.

The emperor and his architects conceived the Taj Mahal as a vast allegory in stone symbolizing the day when Allah would cause the dead to rise and undergo judgment. Its gardens represented the gardens of paradise, and the four water channels running through them symbolized the four rivers of the heavenly kingdom. The domed marble tomb of Mumtaz Mahal represented the throne of Allah. The main gateway to the structure features the entire text of the chapter promising that on the day of judgment, Allah will punish the wicked and gather the faithful into his celestial paradise.

The Peacock Throne and the Taj Mahal testify to the wealth of

OPPOSITE PAGE: *The Taj Mahal, a sumptuous mosque and tomb built between 1632 and 1649 by Shah Jahan in memory of his wife, Mumtaz Mahal.*

the Mughal empire, and the tomb of Mumtaz Mahal bespeaks also the fundamentally Islamic character of the ruling dynasty. But the Mughal realm was not the only well-organized Islamic empire of early modern times. The Ottoman dynasty ruled a powerful empire that expanded from its base in Anatolia to embrace much of eastern Europe, Egypt, and north Africa. The Safavid dynasty challenged the Ottomans for dominance in southwest Asia and prospered from its role in trade networks linking China, India, Russia, southwest Asia, and the Mediterranean basin.

All three Islamic empires of early modern times had dynasties that originated with nomadic, Turkish-speaking peoples from the steppes of central Asia. All three dynasties retained political and cultural traditions that their ancestors had adopted on the steppes, but they also adapted readily to the city-based agricultural societies that they conquered. The Ottoman dynasty made especially effective use of gunpowder weapons, and the Safavids and the Mughals also incorporated gunpowder weapons into their arsenals. All three dynasties officially embraced Islam and drew cultural guidance from Islamic values.

During the sixteenth and early seventeenth centuries, the three Islamic empires presided over expansive and prosperous societies. About the mid–seventeenth century, however, they all began to weaken. Each empire waged long, costly wars that drained resources without bringing compensating benefits. The empires also faced domestic difficulties. Each of them was an ethnically and religiously diverse realm, and each experienced tensions when conservative Muslim leaders lobbied for strict observance of Islam while members of other communities sought greater freedom for themselves. Furthermore, the Islamic empires made little investment in economic and technological development. By the mid–eighteenth century the Safavid empire had collapsed, and the Ottoman and Mughal realms were rapidly falling under European influence.

FORMATION OF THE ISLAMIC EMPIRES

The Islamic empires began as small warrior principalities in frontier areas. As they grew, they devised elaborate administrative and military institutions. Under the guidance of talented and energetic rulers, each empire organized an effective governmental apparatus and presided over a prosperous society.

The Ottoman Empire

The Ottoman empire was an unusually successful frontier state. The term *Ottoman* derived from Osman Bey, founder of the dynasty that continued in unbroken succession from 1289 until the dissolution of the empire in 1923. Osman was chief *(bey)* of a band of seminomadic Turks who migrated to northwestern Anatolia in the thirteenth century. Osman and his followers sought above all to become *ghazi,* Muslim religious warriors who fought on behalf of the faith.

Osman

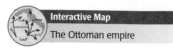

Interactive Map
The Ottoman empire

The Ottomans' location on the borders of the Byzantine empire afforded them ample opportunity to wage holy war. Their first great success came in 1326 with the capture of the Anatolian city of Bursa, which became the capital of the Ottoman principality. About 1352 they established a foothold in Europe when they seized the fortress of Gallipoli. The city of Edirne (Adrianople) became a second Ottoman capital and served as a base for further expansion into the Balkans. As warriors settled in frontier districts and pushed their boundaries forward, they took spoils and gathered revenues that enriched both the *ghazi* and the central government.

Ottoman Expansion

Driving Ottoman expansion was a formidable military machine, which included light cavalry, volunteer infantry, and—as the state grew larger—heavy cavalry. After expanding into the Balkans, the Ottomans created an important force composed of slave troops. Through an institution known as the *devshirme,* the Ottomans required the Christian population of the Balkans to contribute young boys to become slaves of the sultan. The boys received special training, learned Turkish, and converted to Islam. According to individual ability, they entered either the Ottoman civilian administration or the military. Those who became soldiers were known as Janissaries, from the Turkish *yeni cheri* ("new troops"). The Janissaries quickly gained a reputation for esprit de corps, loyalty to the sultan, and readiness to employ new military technology. The Ottomans also outfitted their forces with gunpowder weapons and used them effectively in battles and sieges.

The capture of Constantinople in 1453 by Mehmed II (reigned 1451–1481)—known as Mehmed the Con-

---

ghazi (GAH-zee)
Byzantine (BIHZ-uhn-teen)

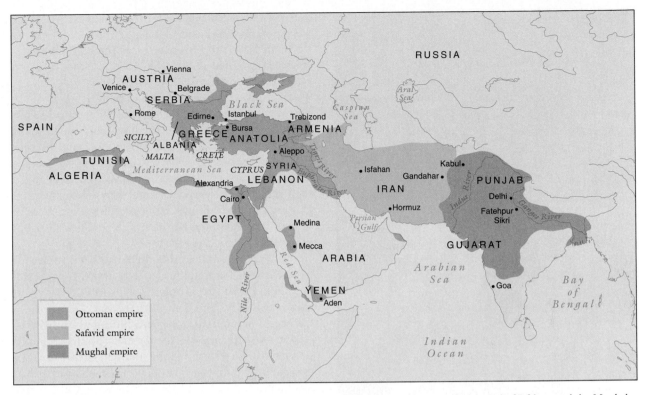

Map 25.1 Islamic empires from 1500 to 1800. Locate the Ottoman capital of Istanbul, the Safavid capital of Isfahan, and the Mughal capital of Delhi. What strategic or commercial purposes did each of these capitals fulfill, and how would their locations have aided or hindered imperial administration?

queror—opened a new chapter in Ottoman expansion. With its superb location and illustrious heritage, Constantinople became the new Ottoman capital, subsequently known as Istanbul. With the capture of the great city behind him, Mehmed presented himself not just as a warrior sultan but as a true emperor. He laid the foundations for a tightly centralized, absolute monarchy, and his army faced no serious rival. He completed the conquest of Serbia, moved into southern Greece and Albania, eliminated the last Byzantine outpost at Trebizond, captured Genoese ports in the Crimea, initiated a naval war with Venice in the Mediterranean, and reportedly hoped to march on Rome and capture the pope himself. Toward the end of his life, he launched an invasion of Italy and briefly occupied Otranto, but his successors abandoned plans for expansion in western Europe.

Mehmed the Conqueror

The Ottomans continued their expansion in the early sixteenth century by occupying Syria and Egypt. Ottoman imperialism climaxed in the reign of Süleyman the Magnificent (reigned 1520–1566). In 1534

Süleyman conquered Baghdad and added the Tigris and Euphrates valleys to the Ottoman domain. In Europe he kept the rival Habsburg empire on the defensive throughout his reign. He captured Belgrade in 1521, defeated and killed the king of Hungary at the battle of Mohács in 1526, and in 1529 subjected the Habsburgs' prized city of Vienna to a brief but nonetheless terrifying siege.

Süleyman the Magnificent

Under Süleyman the Ottomans also became a major naval power. In addition to their own Aegean and Black Sea fleets, the Ottomans inherited the navy of the Mamluk rulers of Egypt. A Turkish corsair, Khayr al-Din Barbarossa Pasha, placed his pirate fleet under the Ottoman flag and became Süleyman's leading admiral. With such resources and leadership, Süleyman was able to challenge Christian vessels throughout the Mediterranean as well as Portuguese fleets in the Red Sea and the Indian Ocean.

Süleyman (SOO-lehy-mahn)

Sultan Süleyman (center, on horse) leads Ottoman forces as they march on Europe.

The Safavid Empire

In 1499 a twelve-year-old boy named Ismail left the swamps of Gilan near the Caspian Sea, where he had hidden from the enemies of his family for five years, to seek his revenge. Two years later he entered Tabriz at the head of an army and laid claim to the ancient Persian imperial title of shah. The young Shah Ismail (reigned 1501–1524) also proclaimed that the official religion of his realm would be Twelver Shiism, and he proceeded to impose it, by force when necessary, on the formerly Sunni population. Over the next decade he seized control of the Iranian plateau and launched expeditions into the Caucasus, Anatolia, Mesopotamia, and central Asia.

Shah Ismail and his successors traced their ancestry back to Safi al-Din (1252–1334), leader of a Sufi religious order in northwestern Persia. The famous tomb and shrine of Safi al-Din at Ardabil became the home of Shah Ismail's family (named "Safavids" after the holy man himself), the headquarters of his religious movement, and the center of a determined, deliberate conspiracy to win political power for his descendants. The Safavids changed their religious preferences several times in the hope of gaining popular support before settling on a form of Shiism that appealed to the nomadic Turkish tribes who were moving into the area.   *The Safavids*

Twelver Shiism held that there had been twelve infallible imams (or religious leaders) after Muhammad, beginning with the prophet's cousin and son-in-law Ali. The twelfth, or   *Twelver Shiism*
"hidden," imam had gone into hiding about 874 to escape persecution, but the Twelver Shiites believed he was still alive and would one day return to take power and spread the true religion. Ismail's father had instructed his Turkish followers to wear a distinctive red hat with twelve pleats in memory of the twelve Shiite imams, and they subsequently became known as the *qizilbash* ("red heads"). Safavid propaganda also suggested that Ismail was himself the hidden imam, or even an incarnation of Allah. Although most Muslims would have regarded those pretensions as utterly blasphemous, the *qizilbash* enthusiastically accepted them, since they resembled traditional Turkish conceptions of leadership that associated military leaders with divinity. The *qizilbash* believed that Ismail would make them invincible in battle, and they became fanatically loyal to the Safavid cause.

Shah Ismail's curious blend of Shiism and Turkish militancy created some powerful enemies. Foremost among them were the staunchly Sunni Ottomans, who detested the Shiite Safavids and feared the spread of Safavid propaganda among the nomadic Turks in their own territory. As a result, Ottomans launched a full-scale invasion of Safavid territory in the early sixteenth century.

At a battle on the plain of Chaldiran (1514), the Ottomans deployed heavy artillery and thousands of

Shiism (SHEE-izm)
Sunni (SOON-nee)
Safavid (SAH-fah-vihd)
qizilbash (gih-ZIHL-bahsh)

Janissaries equipped with firearms behind a barrier of carts. Although the Safavids knew about gunpowder technology, they declined to use devices that they saw as unreliable and unmanly. Trusting in the protective charisma of Shah Ismail, the *qizilbash* cavalry fearlessly attacked the Ottoman line and suffered devastating casualties. Ismail had to slip away, and the Ottomans temporarily occupied his capital at Tabriz. The Ottomans badly damaged the Safavid state but lacked the resources to destroy it, and the two empires remained locked in intermittent conflict for the next two centuries.

Battle of Chaldiran

Shah Ismail and the *qizilbash*. This miniature painting from a Safavid manuscript depicts the shah and his *qizilbash* warriors wearing the distinctive red pleated cap that was their emblem of identity.

Later Safavid rulers prudently abandoned the extreme Safavid ideology that associated the emperor with Allah in favor of more conventional Twelver Shiism, from which they still derived legitimacy as descendants and representatives of the imams. In the late sixteenth century, Shah Abbas the Great (reigned 1588–1629) fully revitalized the Safavid empire. He moved the capital to the more central location of Isfahan, encouraged trade with other lands, and reformed the administrative and military institutions of the empire. With newly strengthened military forces, Shah Abbas led the Safavids to numerous victories. He attacked and defeated the nomadic Uzbeks in central Asia, expelled the Portuguese from Hormuz, and harassed the Ottomans mercilessly in a series of wars from 1603 to the end of his reign. His campaigns brought most of northwestern Iran, the Caucasus, and Mesopotamia under Safavid rule.

Shah Abbas the Great

The Mughal Empire

In 1523 Zahir al-Din Muhammad, known as Babur ("the Tiger"), a Chagatai Turk who claimed descent from both Chinggis Khan and Tamerlane, appeared in northern India. Unlike the Ottomans or Safavids, who fought on behalf of Islam, Babur made little pretense to be anything more than a soldier of fortune in the manner of his illustrious ancestors. His father had been the prince of Farghana, and Babur's great ambition was to transform his inheritance into a glorious central Asian empire. Yet envious relatives and Uzbek enemies frustrated his ambitions.

Babur

Unable to accomplish his goals in central Asia, Babur turned his attention to India. With the aid of gunpowder weapons, including artillery and firearms, Babur took Delhi in 1526. Ironically, Babur cared little for the land he had conquered. Many in his entourage wanted to take their spoils of war and leave the hot and humid Indian climate, which ruined their finely crafted compound bows, but Babur elected to stay. By the time of his death in 1530, Babur had built a loosely knit empire that stretched from Kabul through the Punjab to the borders of Bengal. He founded a dynasty called the *Mughal* (a Persian term for "Mongol"), which expanded to embrace almost all the Indian subcontinent.

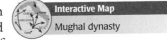

Mughal (MOO-guhl)

SOURCES FROM THE PAST

A Conqueror and His Conquests: Babur on India

Babur was a talented writer as well as a successful warrior. His memoirs make fascinating reading and provide a unique perspective on early Mughal India. His writings include his reflections on the territories he conquered in India, which he compared unfavorably to his central Asian homeland, and on his decision to stay in India and found an empire.

◼   ◼   ◼

Most of the inhabitants of India are infidels, called Hindus, believing mainly in the transmigration of souls; all artisans, wage-earners and officials are Hindus. In our countries the desert dwellers get tribal names; here people settled in the cultivated villages also get tribal names. Again, every artisan follows the trade handed down to him from his forefathers.

India is a country of few charms. The people lack good looks and good manners. They have no social life or exchange of visits. They have no genius or intelligence, no polite learning, no generosity of magnanimity, no harmony or proportion in their arts and crafts, no lead-wire or carpenter's square. They lack good horses and good dogs; grapes, melons, and any good fruit; ice and cold water; good food or good bread in the markets. They have no baths and no advanced educational institutions. . . . There are no running streams in their gardens or residences, no waters at all except the large rivers and the swamps in the ravines and hollows. Their residences have no pleasant and salubrious breezes, and in their construction [there is] no form or symmetry. . . .

Among the charms that India does possess is that it is a large country, with large quantities of gold and silver. Its air in the rainy season is very fine. Sometimes it rains ten or fifteen or even twenty times a day, and in such torrents that rivers flow where no water was previously. While it rains, and throughout the rainy season, the air is remarkably fine, not to be surpassed for mildness and pleasantness. Its only fault is its great humidity, which spoils bows. . . .

It was the hot season when we came to Agra. All the inhabitants had run away in terror. We could find neither grain for ourselves nor corn for our horses. The villages, out of hostility and hatred for us, had taken to thieving and highway-robbery, and it was impossible to travel on the roads. We had not yet the opportunity to distribute the treasure and to assign men in strength to each district. Moreover, the year was a very hot one, pestilential simooms [sandstorms] were striking people down in heaps, and masses were beginning to die off.

For all these reasons, most of the best warriors were unwilling to stay in India; in fact, they determined to leave. . . .

When I discovered this unsteadiness among my people, I summoned all the leaders and took counsel. I said, "Without means and resources there is no empire and conquest, and without lands and followers there is no sovereignty and rule. By the effort of long years, through much tribulation and the crossing of distant lands, by flinging ourselves into battle and danger, we have through God's favor overcome so many enemies and conquered such vast lands. And now, what force compels us, what necessity has arisen, that we should, without cause, abandon a country taken at such risk of life? And if we returned to Kabul, we would again be left in poverty and weakness. Henceforth, let no well-wisher of mine speak of such things! But let not those turn back from going who cannot bear the hardship and have determined to leave." With such words I reasoned with them and made them, willy-nilly, quit their fears.

•   *What does Babur's reaction to India suggest about his views of his own central Asian homeland?*

SOURCE: Babur. *The Babur-nama in English (Memoirs of Babur)*. Trans. by Annette Susannah Beveridge. London: Luzac, 1922. (Translation slightly modified.)

The real architect of the Mughal empire was Babur's grandson Akbar (reigned 1556–1605), a brilliant and charismatic ruler. During his reign, *Akbar* Akbar created a centralized administrative structure with ministries regulating the various provinces of the empire. His military campaigns consolidated Mughal power in Gujarat and Bengal. He destroyed the Hindu kingdom of Vijayanagar, thus laying the foundation for later Mughal expansion in southern India.

In addition to being an able ruler, Akbar was a thoughtful, reflective man deeply interested in religion and philosophy. He pursued a policy of religious toleration that he hoped would reduce tensions between Hindu and Muslim communities in India. Although illiterate (probably due to dyslexia), he was extremely intelligent and had books read to him daily. Instead of imposing Islam on his subjects, he encouraged the elaboration of a syncretic religion called the "divine faith" that focused attention on the emperor as a ruler common to all the religious, ethnic, and social groups of India.

The Mughal empire reached its greatest extent under Aurangzeb (reigned 1659–1707). During his *Aurangzeb* long reign, Aurangzeb waged a relentless campaign of expansion. By the early eighteenth century, Mughals ruled the entire subcontinent except for a small region at the southern tip. Although he greatly expanded Mughal boundaries, Aurangzeb presided over a troubled empire. Aurangzeb was a devout Muslim, and he broke with Akbar's policy of religious toleration. He demolished several famous

 Image Aurangzeb at prayer

Hindu temples and replaced them with mosques. He also imposed a tax on Hindus in an effort to encourage conversion to Islam. His promotion of Islam appealed strongly to Indian Muslims, but it provoked deep hostility among Hindus and enabled local leaders to organize movements to resist or even rebel against Mughal authority.

IMPERIAL ISLAMIC SOCIETY

Despite many differences, there were striking similarities in the development of Ottoman, Safavid, and Mughal societies. All relied on bureaucracies that drew inspiration from the steppe traditions of Turkish and Mongol peoples as well as from the heritage of Islam. They adopted similar economic policies and sought ways to maintain harmony in societies that embraced

This manuscript illustration from about 1590 depicts Akbar (at top, shaded by attendants) inspecting construction of a new imperial capital at Fatehpur Sikri.

many different religious and ethnic groups. Rulers of all the empires also sought to enhance the legitimacy of their regimes by providing for public welfare and associating themselves with literary and artistic talent.

The Dynastic State

The Ottoman, Safavid, and Mughal empires were all military creations, regarded by their rulers as personal possessions by right of conquest. The rulers exercised personal command of the armies, appointed and dismissed officials at will, and adopted whatever policies they wished. In theory, the emperors owned all land

and granted use of it in return for the payment of fixed taxes. The emperors and their families derived revenues from crown lands, and revenues from other lands supported military and administrative officials.

The Emperors and Islam

In the Ottoman, Safavid, and Mughal empires, the prestige and authority of the dynasty derived from the personal piety and the military prowess of the ruler and his ancestors. Devotion to Islam encouraged rulers to extend their faith to new lands. Moreover, the *ghazi* ideal of spreading Islam by fighting infidels or heretics resonated with the traditions of Turkish and Mongolian peoples, who were accustomed both to warfare and to leadership by warriors.

Steppe Traditions

The autocratic authority wielded by the rulers of the Islamic empires also reflected steppe traditions. The early emperors largely did as they pleased, irrespective of religious and social norms. The Ottoman sultans, for example, unilaterally issued numerous legal edicts, and Safavid and Mughal rulers unabashedly asserted their spiritual authority over their subjects. Yet steppe practices also brought problems to the Islamic empires, especially regarding succession issues. In the steppe empires the ruler's relatives often managed components of the states, and succession to the throne became a hot contest between competing members of the family. This was reflected in the Mughal empire, where conflicts among princes and rebellions of sons against fathers were recurrent features throughout its history. The Safavids also engaged in murderous struggles for the throne. Shah Abbas himself lived in fear that another member of the family would challenge him. He kept his sons confined to the palace and killed or blinded relatives he suspected, almost wiping out his family in the process.

Succession issues also became a problem for the Ottomans. After the fifteenth century, the sultans increasingly moved to protect their position by eliminating family rivals. Mehmed the Conqueror decreed that a ruler could legally kill off his brothers after taking the throne. His successors observed that tradition in Turko-Mongol style—by strangling victims with a silk bow string so as not to shed royal blood—until 1595, when the new sultan executed nineteen brothers, many of them infants, as well as fifteen expectant mothers. After that episode, sultans confined their sons in special quarters of the imperial harem and forbade them to go outside except to take the throne.

Even though Muslim theorists universally agreed that women should have no role in public affairs, women played important roles in managing the Islamic empires. Many Ottoman, Safavid, and Mughal emperors followed the example of Chinggis Khan, who revered his mother and his first wife.

Women and Politics

In the Islamic empires the ruler's mother and his chief wife or favorite concubine enjoyed special privileges and authority. Ottoman courtiers often complained loudly about the "rule of women," thus offering eloquent testimony to the power that women could wield. Süleyman the Magnificent, for example, became infatuated with Hürrem Sultana (also known as Roxelana), a concubine of Ukrainian origin. Süleyman elevated her to the status of a legal wife, consulted her on state policies, and deferred to her judgment even to the point of executing his eldest son when Hürrem wanted to secure the succession of her own child.

Women also played prominent political roles in the Safavid and Mughal empires. In Safavid Persia, Mahd-e Olya, the wife of one shah, was the de facto ruler. Her efforts to limit the power of the *qizilbash* so enraged them that they murdered her. The aunt of another shah scolded the ruler for neglecting his duties and used her own money to raise an army to put down a revolt. The Mughal emperor Jahangir was content to let his wife Nur Jahan run the government, and even the conscientious Muslim Aurangzeb listened to his daughter's political advice.

Agriculture and Trade

Food Crops

Productive agricultural economies were the foundations of all the Islamic empires. Each empire extracted surplus agricultural production and used it to finance armies and bureaucracies. Mostly the Islamic empires relied on crops of wheat and rice that had flourished for centuries in the lands they ruled. The Columbian exchange brought American crops to all the Islamic empires but without the same dramatic effects as in Europe, east Asia, and Africa. European merchants did introduce maize, potatoes, tomatoes, and other crops to the Islamic empires, however, and although the new arrivals did not become staples, they enlivened regional cuisines with new tastes and textures.

Two products of the Columbian exchange that caught on extremely well in both the Ottoman and the Safavid empires were coffee and tobacco. Although native to Ethiopia and cultivated in southern Arabia, coffee did not become popular in Islamic lands until the sixteenth century. Like sugar, coffee had traveled to Europe and from there to the Americas, where plantations specialized in the production of both tropical crops for the world market. By the eighteenth century, American producers and European merchants supplied Muslim markets with coffee as well as sugar.

Tobacco

According to the Ottoman historian Ibrahim Pechevi, English merchants introduced tobacco about 1600, claiming it was useful for medicinal purposes. Within a few decades it had spread throughout the Ottoman empire. The increasing popularity of coffee drinking and pipe smoking encouraged entrepreneurs to establish coffeehouses where customers could indulge their appetites for caffeine and nicotine at the same time. The popularity of coffeehouses provoked protest from moralists who worried that these popular attractions were dens of iniquity. Pechevi himself complained about the hideous odor of tobacco and the messy ashes, and religious leaders claimed that it was worse to frequent a coffeehouse than a tavern. Sultan Murad IV went so far as to outlaw coffee and tobacco and to execute those who continued to partake. That effort, however, was a losing battle. Both pastimes eventually won widespread acceptance, and the coffeehouse became a prominent social institution in the Islamic empires.

American food crops had less demographic effect in the Islamic empires than in other parts of the world. The population of India surged during early modern times, growing from 105 million in 1500 to 190 million in 1800. But population growth in India resulted more from intensive agriculture along traditional lines than from the influence of new crops. The Safavid population grew less rapidly, from 5 million in 1500 to 8 million in 1800. Ottoman numbers grew from 9 million in 1500 to about 24 million about 1800, but those numbers reflect territorial additions more than fertility increases. Even in the Ottoman heartland of Anatolia, population did not expand nearly as dramatically as it did in other lands in early modern times. From 6 million in 1500, the population of Anatolia rose to just 9 million in 1800.

Population Growth

The Islamic empires ruled lands that had figured prominently in long-distance trade for centuries and participated actively in global trade networks in early modern times. In the Ottoman empire, for example, the early capital at Bursa was also the terminus of a caravan route that brought raw silk from Persia to supply the Italian market. The Ottomans also granted special trading concessions to merchants from England and France to cement alliances against common enemies in Spain and central Europe, and the city of Aleppo became an emporium for foreign merchants engaged primarily in the spice trade.

Trade

Shah Abbas promoted Isfahan as a commercial center and extended trading privileges to foreign merchants to help create a favorable environment for trade. European merchants sought Safavid raw silk, carpets, and ceramics. The English East India Company, the

In this anonymous painting produced about 1670, Dutch and English ships lie at anchor in the harbor of the busy port of Surat in northwestern India.

French East India Company, and the Dutch VOC all traded actively with the Safavids. To curry favor, the English company even sent military advisors to help introduce gunpowder weapons to Safavid armed forces and provided a navy to help them retake Hormuz in the Persian Gulf from the Portuguese.

The Mughals did not pay as much attention to foreign trade as the Ottomans and the Safavids, partly because of the enormous size and productivity of the domestic Indian economy and partly because the Mughal rulers had little interest in maritime affairs. Nevertheless, the Mughal treasury derived significant income from foreign trade. The Mughals allowed the creation of trading stations and merchant colonies by Portuguese, English, French, and Dutch merchants. Meanwhile, Indian merchants formed trading companies of their own, venturing both overland as far as Russia and by sea to ports all over the Indian Ocean.

Religious Affairs in the Islamic Empires

Religious Diversity All the Islamic empires had populations that were religiously and ethnically diverse, and imperial rulers had the daunting challenge of maintaining harmony among different religious communities. The Ottoman empire included large numbers of Christians and Jews in the Balkans, Armenia, Lebanon, and Egypt. The Safavid empire embraced sizable Zoroastrian and Jewish communities as well as many Christian subjects in the Caucasus. The Mughal empire was especially diverse. Most Mughal subjects were Hindus, but large numbers of Muslims lived alongside smaller communities of Jains, Zoroastrians, Christians, and devotees of syncretic faiths such as Sikhism.

Akbar's Divine Faith In India, Akbar was especially tolerant of diverse religions and worked to find a religious synthesis that would serve as a cultural foundation for unity in his diverse empire. As part of that effort, he supported the early Sikhs, who combined elements of Hinduism and Islam in a new syncretic faith. He also attempted to elaborate his own "divine faith," which emphasized loyalty to the emperor while borrowing eclectically from different religious traditions. Akbar never explained his ideas systematically, but it is clear that they drew most heavily on Islam. The divine faith was strictly monotheistic, and it reflected the influence of Shiite and Sufi teachings.

But it also glorified the emperor: Akbar even referred to himself as the "lord of wisdom," who would guide his subjects to an understanding of god. The divine faith was tolerant of Hinduism, and it even drew inspiration from Zoroastrianism in its effort to bridge the gaps between Mughal India's many cultural and religious communities.

Status of Religious Minorities The Islamic empires relied on a long-established model to deal with subjects who were not Muslims. They did not require conquered peoples to convert to Islam but extended to them the status of a protected people (*dhimmi*). In return for their loyalty and payment of a special tax known as *jizya*, dhimmi communities retained their personal freedom, kept their property, practiced their religion, and handled their own legal affairs. In the Ottoman empire, for example, autonomous religious communities known as *millet* retained their own civil laws, traditions, and languages. *Millet* communities usually also assumed social and administrative functions in matters concerning birth, marriage, death, health, and education.

The situation in the Mughal empire was different, since its large number of religious communities made a *millet* system impractical. Mughal rulers reserved the most powerful military and administrative positions for Muslims, but in the day-to-day management of affairs, Muslims and Hindus cooperated closely. Some Mughal emperors, such as Akbar, worked particularly hard to forge links between religious communities and to integrate Muslim and Hindu elites. Indeed, in an effort to build bridges between the different religious communities of his realm, he abolished the *jizya* and sponsored discussions and debates between Muslims, Hindus, Jains, Zoroastrians, and Christians.

Promotion of Islam Policies of religious tolerance were not popular with many Muslims, who worried that toleration might lead to their absorption into Hindu society. They therefore insisted that Mughal rulers create and maintain an Islamic state based on Islamic law. When Aurangzeb reached the Mughal throne in 1659, that policy gained strength. Aurangzeb reinstated the *jizya* and promoted Islam as the official faith of Mughal India. His policy satisfied zealous Muslims but at the cost of deep bitterness among his Hindu subjects. Tension between Hindu and Muslim communities in India persisted throughout the Mughal dynasty and beyond.

Sikhs (SIHKS)

dhimmi (DIHM-mee)
jizya (JIHZ-yuh)

Cultural Patronage of the Islamic Emperors

As the empires matured, the Islamic rulers sought to enhance their prestige through public works projects and patronage of scholars. They competed to attract outstanding religious scholars, artists, and architects to their courts and lavished resources on public buildings.

Capital cities and royal palaces were the most visible expressions of imperial majesty. The Ottomans took *Istanbul* particular pride in Istanbul, which quickly revived after conquest and became a bustling, prosperous city of more than a million people. At its heart was the great Topkapi palace, which housed government offices and meeting places for imperial councils. At its core was the sultan's residence with its harem, gardens, pleasure pavilions, and a repository for the most sacred possessions of the empire, including the mantle of the prophet Muhammad. Sultan Süleyman the Magnificent was fortunate to be able to draw on the talents of the architectural genius Sinan Pasha (1489–1588) to create the vast religious complex called the Süleymaniye, which blended Islamic and Byzantine architectural elements. It combined tall, slender minarets with large domed buildings supported by half domes in the style of the Byzantine church Hagia Sofia (which the Ottomans converted into the mosque of Aya Sofya).

Shah Abbas made his capital, Isfahan, into one of the most precious jewels of urban architectural development anywhere in the world. Abbas *Isfahan* concentrated markets, the palace, and the royal mosque around a vast polo field and public square. Broad, shaded avenues and magnificent bridges linked the central city to its suburbs. Safavid architects made use of monumental entryways, vast arcades, spacious courtyards, and intricate, colorful decoration. Unlike the sprawling Ottoman and Mughal palaces, the Safavid palaces in Isfahan were relatively small and emphasized

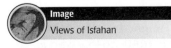
Views of Isfahan

natural settings with gardens, pools, and large, open verandas. The point was not only to enable the shah to observe outside activities but also to emphasize his visibility and accessibility, qualities long esteemed in the Persian tradition of kingship.

In India, Mughal architects skillfully blended central Asian traditions with elements of Hindu architecture, and they built on a scale that left no doubt about their wealth and resources. They constructed

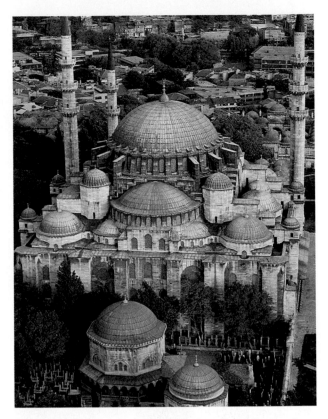

The massive Süleymaniye mosque built for Sultan Süleyman the Magnificent by the Ottoman architect Sinan Pasha in 1556.

scores of mosques, fortresses, and palaces and sometimes created entire cities.

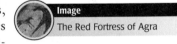
The Red Fortress of Agra

The best example was Fatehpur Sikri, a city planned and constructed by Akbar that served as his capital from 1569 to 1585. With its *Fatehpur Sikri* mint, records office, treasury, and audience hall, the new city demonstrated Akbar's strength and imperial ambitions. Fatehpur Sikri was also a private residence and retreat for the ruler, reproducing in stone a royal encampment with exquisite pleasure palaces where Akbar indulged his passions for music and conversation with scholars and poets. At yet another level, it was a dramatic display of Mughal piety and devotion, centered on the cathedral mosque and the mausoleum of Akbar's Sufi guru, Shaykh Salim Chisti. Despite their intensely Islamic character, many of the buildings consciously incorporated Indian elements, such as verandas supported by columns and decorations of stone elephants. Unfortunately, Akbar

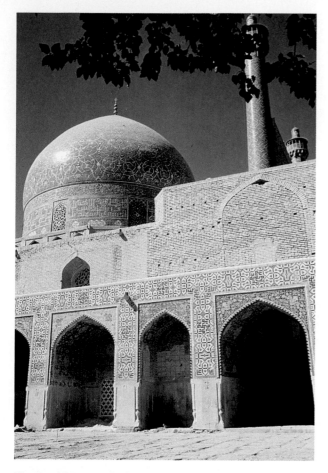

The Royal Mosque of Isfahan, centerpiece of the city as rebuilt by Shah Abbas at the end of the sixteenth century. With its combination of an open space flanked by markets, the palace, and religious structures, Isfahan stands as a unique example of urban planning in Islamic lands.

had selected a poor site for the city and soon abandoned it because of its bad water supply.

The most famous of the Mughal monuments—and one of the most prominent of all Islamic edifices—was *The Taj Mahal* the Taj Mahal. Shah Jahan had twenty thousand workers toil for eighteen years to erect the exquisite white marble mosque and tomb. He originally planned to build a similar mausoleum out of black marble for himself, but his son Aurangzeb deposed him before he could carry out the project. Shah Jahan spent his last years confined to a small cell with a tiny window, and only with the aid of a mirror was he able to catch the sight of his beloved wife's final resting place.

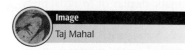

THE EMPIRES IN TRANSITION

The Islamic empires underwent dramatic change between the sixteenth and the eighteenth centuries. The Safavid empire disappeared entirely. In 1722 a band of Afghan tribesmen marched all the way to Isfahan, blockaded the city until its starving inhabitants resorted to cannibalism, forced the shah to abdicate, and executed thousands of Safavid officials as well as many members of the royal family. After the death of Aurangzeb in 1707, Mughal India experienced provincial rebellions and foreign invasions. By midcentury the subcontinent was falling under British imperial rule. By 1700 the Ottomans, too, were on the defensive: the sultans lost control over provinces such as Lebanon and Egypt, and throughout the eighteenth and nineteenth centuries European and Russian states placed political, military, and economic pressure on the shrinking Ottoman realm.

The Deterioration of Imperial Leadership

Strong and effective central authority was essential to the Islamic empires, and Muslim political theorists never tired of emphasizing the importance of rulers who were diligent, virtuous, and just. Weak, negligent, and corrupt rulers would allow the social order to break down. The Ottomans were fortunate in having a series of talented sultans for three centuries, and the Safavids and the Mughals produced their share of effective rulers as well.

Eventually, however, all three dynasties had rulers who were incompetent or irresponsible about tending to affairs of state. Moreover, all three *Dynastic Decline* dynasties faced difficulties because of suspicion and fighting among competing members of their ruling houses. In the Ottoman empire alone, notorious examples of problem rulers included Süleyman's successor, Selim the Sot (reigned 1566–1574) and Ibrahim the Crazy (reigned 1640–1648), who taxed and spent to such excess that government officials deposed and murdered him. Indeed, after the late seventeenth century, weak rule increasingly provoked mutinies in the army, provincial revolts, political corruption, and insecurity throughout the Ottoman realm.

Political troubles often arose from religious tensions. Conservative Muslim clerics had considerable influence in the Islamic empires because of their monopoly on education and their deep involvement in

Fatehpur Sikri, built by Akbar in the 1570s, commemorated the emperor's military conquests and housed the tomb of his religious guide. It included a palace, an audience hall where Akbar attended religious and philosophical debates, and a great mosque.

the everyday lives and legal affairs of ordinary subjects. The clerics mistrusted the emperors' interests *Religious Tensions* in unconventional forms of Islam such as Sufism, complained bitterly when women or subjects who were not Muslims played influential political roles, and protested any exercise of royal authority that contradicted Islamic law.

In the Ottoman empire, disaffected religious students often joined the Janissaries in revolt. A particularly serious threat came from the Wahhabi movement in Arabia, which denounced the Ottomans as dangerous religious innovators who were unfit to rule. Conservative Muslims fiercely protested the construction of an astronomical observatory in Istanbul and forced the sultan to demolish it in 1580. In 1742 they also forced the closure of the Ottoman printing press, which they regarded as an impious technology.

In the Safavid empire, rulers fell under the domination of conservative Shiite clerics. Shiite leaders pressured the shahs to persecute Sunnis, non-Muslims, and even the Sufis who had helped establish the dynasty. Religious tensions also afflicted Mughal India. In the mid–eighteenth century, as Aurangzeb struggled to claim the Mughal throne, he drew on conservative Islamic ideas when he required non-Muslims to pay the poll tax and ordered the destruction of Hindu temples. Those measures inflamed tensions between the various Sunni, Shiite, and Sufi branches of Islam and also fueled animosity among Hindus and other Mughal subjects who were not Muslims.

Economic and Military Decline

In the sixteenth century, all the Islamic empires had strong domestic economies and played prominent roles in global trade networks. By the eighteenth century, however, domestic economies were under great stress, and foreign trade had declined dramatically or had fallen under the control of European powers. The Islamic empires were well on their way to becoming marginal lands that depended on goods produced elsewhere.

The high cost of maintaining an expensive military and administrative apparatus helped to bring about economic decline in the Islamic empires. As long as the empires were expanding, they were able to finance their armies *Economic Difficulties* and bureaucracies with fresh resources extracted from newly conquered lands. When expansion slowed, ceased, or reversed, however, they faced the problem of supporting their institutions with limited resources.

Sufis (SOO-fees)

The long, costly, and unproductive wars fought by the Ottomans with the Habsburgs in central Europe, by the Safavids and Ottomans in Mesopotamia, and by Aurangzeb in southern India exhausted the treasuries of the Islamic empires without making fresh resources available to them.

As expansion slowed and the empires lost control over remote provinces, officials reacted to the loss of revenue by raising taxes, selling public offices, accepting bribes, or resorting to simple extortion. All those measures did long-term economic damage. To make matters worse, the governments viewed foreign trade as just another opportunity to bring in revenue. The Ottomans expanded the privileges enjoyed by foreign merchants, and the Mughals encouraged the establishment of Dutch and English trading outposts and welcomed the expansion of their business in India. In other words, imperial authorities were content to have foreign traders come to them. None made serious efforts to establish commercial stations abroad, although Indian merchants organized their own private trading companies.

As they lost initiative to western European peoples in economic and commercial affairs, the Islamic empires also did not seek actively to im-

Military Decline   prove their military technologies. During the sixteenth and early seventeenth centuries, the Islamic empires were able to purchase European weapons in large numbers and attract European expertise that kept their armies supplied with powerful gunpowder weapons. By about the mid–seventeenth century, however, European military technology was advancing so rapidly that the Islamic empires could not keep pace. None of the empires had a large armaments industry, so they had to rely on foreign suppliers. They still were able to purchase European weapons and expertise, but their arsenals became increasingly dated, since they depended on technologies that European peoples had already replaced. By the late eighteenth century, even the once-influential Ottoman navy was closing its shipbuilding operations and ordering new military vessels from foreign shipyards.

Cultural Conservatism

While experiencing economic and military decline, the Islamic empires also neglected cultural developments in the larger world. Europeans who visited the Islamic empires attempted to learn as much as possible about the language, religion, social customs, and history of the host countries. They published accounts of their travels that became extremely popular in their homelands, and they advocated serious study of Islamic lands.

Meanwhile, the Islamic empires expressed only limited interest in world affairs. In the sixteenth century, just as European mariners were scouting Atlantic waters, Ottoman mariners did   ***Piri Reis*** reconnoiter the Indian Ocean basin from east Africa to Indonesia. Ottoman geographers also manifested great interest in European knowledge of geography, some of which had considerable military value. The Ottoman admiral and cartographer Piri Reis produced several large-scale maps and a major navigational text, the *Book of Seafaring*, which drew on reports and maps from European mariners and explorers. Some of Piri Reis's maps included the Atlantic coast of North America and the lands visited by Columbus, which the cartographer probably learned

Ottoman cartographer Piri Reis drew on European charts when preparing this map of the Atlantic Ocean basin in 1513. Caribbean and South American coastlines are visible at left, and Iberian and west African coastlines appear in the upper right corner.

about from Spanish sailors captured in naval conflicts with Ottoman forces.

On the whole, however, few Muslims traveled willingly to the infidel lands of "the Franks." Muslim rulers and their Muslim subjects were confident that they had nothing to learn from Europeans. As a result, most Muslims remained largely oblivious to European cultural and technological developments. Not until 1703 was there an attempt to introduce European scientific instruments such as the telescope into astronomical observatories. Then conservative Muslim clerics soon forced the removal of the foreign implements, which they considered impious and unnecessary.

Cultural Conservatism

The early experience of the printing press in the Islamic empires illustrates especially well the resistance of conservative religious leaders to cultural imports from western Europe. Jewish refugees from Spain introduced the first printing presses to Anatolia in the late fifteenth century. Ottoman authorities allowed them to operate presses in Istanbul and other major cities as long as they did not print books in the Turkish or Arabic language. Not until 1729 did government authorities lift the ban on the printing of such books. During the next thirteen years, a Turkish press published seventeen books dealing mostly with history, geography, and language before conservative Muslims forced its closure in 1742. Only in 1784 did a new Turkish press open.

The Printing Press

Printing also caught on slowly in Mughal India. Jesuit missionaries in Goa published books, including translations of the Bible into Indian and Arabic languages, as early as the 1550s. Yet Mughal rulers displayed little interest in the press, and printing did not become prominent in Indian society until the establishment of British colonial rule in Bengal in the eighteenth century.

To some extent, aesthetic considerations stood in the way of the printing press: particularly in the Ottoman and Safavid empires, scholars and general readers alike preferred elegant handwritten books to cheaply produced printed works. Yet resistance to printing also reflected the concerns of conservative religious leaders that readily available printed books would introduce all manner of new and dangerous ideas to the public.

Thus, like imperial China and Tokugawa Japan, the Islamic empires resisted the introduction of cultural influences from western European societies. Rulers of the Islamic empires readily accepted gunpowder weapons as enhancements to their military and political power, but they and their subjects drew little inspiration from European religion, science, or ideas. Moreover, under the influence of conservative religious leaders, Islamic authorities actively discouraged the circulation of ideas that might pose unsettling challenges to the social and cultural order. Like the Ming, Qing, and Tokugawa rulers, the Ottoman, Safavid, and Mughal emperors preferred political and social stability to the risks that foreign cultural innovations might bring.

SUMMARY

Like China and Japan, the Islamic empires largely retained control of their own affairs throughout the early modern era. Ruling elites of the Ottoman, Safavid, and Mughal empires came from nomadic Turkish stock, and they all drew on steppe traditions in organizing their governments. But the rulers also devised institutions that maintained order over a long term. During the sixteenth and seventeenth centuries, all the Islamic empires enjoyed productive economies that enabled merchants to participate actively in the global trade networks of early modern times. By the early eighteenth century, however, these same empires were experiencing economic difficulties that led to political and military decline. Like the Ming, Qing, and Tokugawa rulers in east Asia, the Islamic emperors mostly sought to limit foreign and especially European influences in their realms. The Islamic emperors ruled lands that were religiously and ethnically diverse, and most of them worried that such influences would threaten political and social stability. They allowed their subjects to practice faiths other than Islam, and a few emperors actively worked to defuse religious tensions in their realms.

For the most part, however, rulers of the Islamic empires followed the advice of conservative Muslim clerics, who promoted Islamic values and fought the introduction of foreign cultural imports that might undermine their authority. By the late eighteenth century, the Safavid empire had collapsed, and economic difficulties and cultural insularity had severely weakened the Ottoman and Mughal empires.

CHRONOLOGY

1289–1923	Ottoman dynasty
1451–1481	Reign of Mehmed the Conqueror
1453	Ottoman conquest of Constantinople
1501–1524	Reign of Shah Ismail
1501–1722	Safavid dynasty
1514	Battle of Chaldiran
1520–1566	Reign of Süleyman the Magnificent
1526–1858	Mughal dynasty
1556–1605	Reign of Akbar
1588–1629	Reign of Shah Abbas the Great
1659–1707	Reign of Aurangzeb

FOR FURTHER READING

Esin Atil. *The Age of Sultan Süleyman the Magnificent.* Washington, 1987. Richly illustrated volume that emphasizes Süleyman's role as a patron of the arts.

Palmira Brummett. *Ottoman Seapower and Levantine Diplomacy in the Age of Discovery.* Albany, 1994. A scholarly study of Ottoman military strategy and diplomacy in the Mediterranean during the sixteenth century.

Stephen Frederic Dale. *Indian Merchants and Eurasian Trade, 1600–1750.* Cambridge, 1994. Examines the workings of an Indian trading community that conducted business in Persia, central Asia, and Russia.

Halil Inalçik. *The Ottoman Empire: The Classical Age, 1300–1600.* New York, 1973. A reliable survey by the foremost historian of the early Ottoman empire.

Çemal Kafadar. *Between Two Worlds: The Construction of the Ottoman State.* Berkeley, 1995. Studies the origins and early development of the Ottoman empire.

Bernard Lewis. *The Muslim Discovery of Europe.* New York, 1982. An important study that charts Muslim interest in European affairs.

Leslie Pierce. *The Imperial Harem: Women and Sovereignty in the Ottoman Empire.* Oxford, 1993. Challenges many stereotypes about the role of women in the imperial Ottoman elite.

John F. Richards. *The Mughal Empire.* Cambridge, 1993. A concise and reliable overview of Mughal history, concentrating on political affairs.

Roger Savory. *Iran under the Safavids.* Cambridge, 1980. A rich and authoritative survey of Safavid history, especially interesting for its views on Safavid origins, culture, and commercial relations.

CHAPTER 26

Revolutions and National States in the Atlantic World

Marie Gouze was a French butcher's daughter who educated herself by reading books, moved to Paris, and married a junior army officer. Under the name Olympe de Gouges she won some fame as a journalist, actress, and playwright. Gouges was as flamboyant as she was talented, and her well-publicized love affairs scandalized Parisian society.

Gouges was also a revolutionary and a strong advocate of women's rights. She responded enthusiastically when the French revolution broke out in July 1789, and she applauded in August when revolutionary leaders proclaimed freedom and equality for all citizens in the *Declaration of the Rights of Man and the Citizen*. It soon became clear, however, that freedom and equality pertained only to male citizens. Revolutionary leaders welcomed women's contributions to the revolution but refused to grant them political and social rights.

Gouges demanded that women share equal rights in family property and campaigned for equal education. She even appealed to Queen Marie Antoinette to use her influence to advance women's rights. In 1791 Gouges published a *Declaration of the Rights of Woman and the Female Citizen*, which claimed the same rights for women that revolutionary leaders had granted to men in August 1789. She insisted on the rights of women to vote, speak their minds freely, participate in the making of law, and hold public office.

Gouges's declaration attracted a great deal of attention but little support. Revolutionary leaders dismissed her appeal, and in 1793 they executed her because of her affection for Marie Antoinette

OPPOSITE PAGE: *Liberty, personified as a woman, leads the French people in a famous painting by Eugène Delacroix.*

475

and her persistent crusade for women's rights. Yet Gouges's campaign illustrated the power of the Enlightenment ideals of freedom and equality. Revolutionary leaders stilled her voice, but once they had proclaimed freedom and equality as universal human rights, they were unable to suppress demands to extend them to new constituencies.

A series of violent revolutions brought dramatic political and social change to lands throughout much of the Atlantic Ocean basin in the late eighteenth and early nineteenth centuries. Revolution broke out first in the British colonies of North America, where colonists founded a new republic. A few years later, revolutionaries abolished the French monarchy and thoroughly reorganized French society. Revolutionary ideas soon spread, prompting Latin American peoples to seek independence from Spanish and Portuguese colonial rule. In Saint-Domingue, revolution led to the abolition of slavery as well as independence from French rule. By the 1830s, peoples had reorganized political and social structures throughout western Europe and the Americas.

The revolutions of the late eighteenth and early nineteenth centuries had two results of deep global significance. First, they helped to spread a cluster of Enlightenment ideas concerning freedom, equality, and popular sovereignty. Revolutionary leaders argued that political authority arose from the people rather than the rulers and often sought to establish republican forms of government in which the people selected delegates to represent their interests. In fact, early revolutionaries extended political rights only to a privileged group of white men, but they justified their actions in general terms that prompted disenfranchised groups to seek freedom, equality, and a political voice as well. Indeed, such ideas spread globally in the nineteenth and twentieth centuries as social reformers and revolutionaries struggled to make freedom and equality a reality for oppressed groups throughout the world.

Second, while promoting Enlightenment values, revolutions encouraged the consolidation of national states as the principal form of political organization. As peoples defended their states from enemies and sometimes mounted attacks on foreign lands, they developed a powerful sense of identity with their compatriots. During the nineteenth century, strong national identities led to movements to build national states, which in turn profoundly influenced the political experiences of European states. During the late nineteenth and twentieth centuries, efforts to harness nationalist sentiments and form states based on national identity became one of the most powerful and dynamic movements in world history.

POPULAR SOVEREIGNTY AND POLITICAL UPHEAVAL

Drawing on Enlightenment ideals, revolutionaries of the eighteenth and nineteenth centuries sought to fashion equitable societies by instituting governments that were responsive to the peoples they governed. In justifying their policies, revolutionaries argued for popular sovereignty—the notion that legitimate political authority resides not in kings but, rather, in the people who make up a society. In North America, colonists declared independence from British rule and instituted a new government founded on the principle of popular sovereignty. Soon thereafter, French revolutionaries abolished the monarchy and revamped the social order. Yet revolutionaries in France were unable to devise a stable alternative to the monarchy. In the early nineteenth century, Napoleon Bonaparte imposed military rule on France and helped spread revolutionary ideas to much of western Europe.

Enlightened and Revolutionary Ideas

Throughout history kings or emperors ruled almost all settled agricultural societies. In justifying their rule, they often identified themselves with deities or claimed divine sanction for their authority. In imperial China, for example, dynastic houses claimed to rule in accordance with the "mandate of heaven," and in early modern Europe centralizing monarchs often asserted a "divine right of kings" to rule as absolute monarchs.

During the seventeenth and eighteenth centuries, philosophes and other advocates of Enlightenment ideas (discussed in chapter 21) began to question such notions and argued that *Popular Sovereignty* kings should be responsible to the people they governed. The English philosopher John Locke (1632–1704), for example, regarded government as a contract between rulers and ruled. In his *Second Treatise of Civil Government,* published in 1690, Locke held that individuals granted political rights to their rulers but retained personal rights to life, liberty, and property. Furthermore, according to Locke, rulers derived their authority from the consent of those they governed. If rulers broke the contract, the people had the right to replace their rulers. In effect, Locke's political thought relocated sovereignty, removing it from rulers as divine agents and vesting it in the people of a society.

Enlightenment thinkers addressed issues of freedom and equality as well as sovereignty. Philosophes *Individual* such as Voltaire (1694–1778) resented the *Freedom* persecution of religious minorities as well as royal censorship. Philosophes called for religious toleration and freedom to express their views openly. Thus, when censors prohibited the publication of their writings in France, they often published their books in Switzerland or the Netherlands and smuggled them across the border into France.

Many Enlightenment thinkers also called for equality. They argued that privileged aristocrats made *Political and* no more contribution to the larger so-*Legal Equality* ciety than peasants, artisans, or workers and recommended the creation of a society in which all individuals would be equal before the law. The most prominent advocate of political equality was the French-Swiss thinker Jean-Jacques Rousseau (1712–1778). In his influential book *The Social Contract* (1762), Rousseau argued that members of a society were collectively the sovereign. In an ideal society all individuals would participate directly in the formulation of policy and the creation of laws.

Most Enlightenment thinkers were of common birth but comfortable means. Though seeking to limit *Global Influence* the prerogatives of ruling and aristo-*of Enlightenment* cratic classes, they did not envision a *Values* society in which they would share political rights with women, children, peasants, laborers, or slaves. Nevertheless, Enlightenment thought constituted a serious challenge to long-established notions of political and social order. Although arguments for freedom, equality, and popular sovereignty originally served the interests of relatively privileged European and Euro-American men, many other groups made effective use of them in seeking the extension of political rights.

The American Revolution

In the mid–eighteenth century there was no sign that North America would become a center of revolution. Residents of the thirteen British colonies there regarded themselves as British subjects: they recognized British law, read English-language books, and benefited hand-somely from British rule. Trade brought prosperity to the colonies, and British military forces protected colonists' interests. From 1754 to 1763, for example, British forces waged an expensive

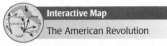

Interactive Map
The American Revolution

conflict in North America known as the French and Indian War. That conflict merged with a larger contest for imperial supremacy, the Seven Years' War (1756–1763), in which British and French forces battled each other in Europe and India as well as

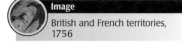

Image
British and French territories, 1756

North America. Victory in the Seven Years' War ensured that Britain would dominate global trade and that British North America would prosper.

After the mid-1760s, however, North American colonists became increasingly disenchanted with British imperial rule. Faced with staggering financial difficulties arising from the Seven Years' War, the British parliament expected that the North American colonies would bear a fair share of the cost *Tightened British Control of the Colonies* through new taxes. But new taxes proved extremely unpopular in North America. Colonists especially resented the imposition of taxes on molasses by the Sugar Act (1764), on publications and legal documents by the Stamp Act (1765), on a variety of imported items by the Townshend Act (1767), and on tea by the Tea Act (1773). Colonists also took offense at the Quartering Act (1765), which required them to provide housing and accommodations for British troops.

Colonists argued that they should pay such taxes only if the North American colonies were represented in the British parliament, arguing that there should be "no taxation without representation." They boycotted British products, physically attacked British officials, and mounted protests. They also organized the Continental Congress (1774), which coordinated the colonies' resistance to British policies. By 1775 tensions were so high that British troops and a colonial militia skirmished at the village of Lexington, near Boston. The war of American independence had begun.

On 4 July 1776 the Continental Congress adopted a document titled "The unanimous Declaration of the thirteen united States of America." This Declaration of Inde-*The Declaration of Independence* pendence drew deep inspiration from Enlightenment political thought in its insistence "that all men are created equal, that they are endowed by their Creator with certain unalienable

Rights, that among these are Life, Liberty, and the pursuit of Happiness." It echoed John Locke's contractual theory of government in arguing that governments derive their power and authority from "the consent of the governed." When any government infringes upon individuals' rights, the document continued, "it is the Right of the People to alter or abolish it, and to institute new Government." The Declaration of Independence presented a long list of specific abuses charged to the British crown and concluded by proclaiming the colonies "Free and Independent States."

It was one thing to declare independence, but a different matter to make independence a reality. Britain enjoyed many advantages over the rebels: a strong government, the most powerful navy in the world, a com-

petent army, and a sizable population of loyalists in the colonies. But the colonies were far away, and British opponents were many. In addition, many European states were eager to see Britain lose its colonies: France, Spain, the Netherlands, and several German principalities all contributed militarily and economically to the American quest for independence. Moreover, George Washington (1732–1799) provided strong and imaginative military leadership for the colonial army while local militias employed guerrilla tactics effectively against British forces.

By 1780 all combatants were weary of the conflict. In October 1781 British forces surrendered to American and French forces commanded by George Washington at Yorktown, Virginia. In September 1783 diplomats concluded the Peace of Paris, by

Map 26.1 The thirteen colonies that rebelled against the British during the American Revolution. Note the location of both the major towns and cities in the colonies and the location of the major battles that occurred during the revolution. Why were both situated so close to the eastern coast?

In this painting by American artist John Trumbull, authors of the Declaration of Independence, including John Adams, Thomas Jefferson, and Benjamin Franklin, stand before a desk at the Continental Congress in Philadelphia.

which the British government formally recognized American independence.

The leaders of the fledgling republic organized a state that reflected Enlightenment principles. In 1787 a constitutional convention drafted the Constitution of the United States, which emphasized the rights of individuals. American leaders based the federal government on popular sovereignty, and they agreed to guarantee individual liberties such as freedom of speech, of the press, and of religion. Full political and social rights, however, were accorded only to men of property: landless men, women, slaves, and indigenous peoples were not included. Over the long term, however, disenfranchised groups claimed and struggled for political and legal rights and helped broaden the implications of the Enlightenment values of freedom and equality as well as popular sovereignty.

Building an Independent State

The French Revolution

French revolutionaries also drew inspiration from Enlightenment political thought, but the French revolution was a more radical affair than its American counterpart. American revolutionary leaders sought independence from British imperial rule, but they were content to retain British law and much of their British social and cultural heritage. In contrast, French revolutionary leaders repudiated existing society, often referred to as the *ancien régime* ("the old order"), and sought to replace it with new political, social, and cultural structures.

Serious financial, political, and social problems put France on the road to revolution. When Louis XVI (reigned 1774–1793) became king, he inherited an enormous debt from his predecessors, most of which had been incurred during France's many wars in the seventeenth and eighteenth centuries. To make matters worse, the French government had spent large sums of money helping the Americans in their war of independence. As a result, by the 1780s half of the French royal government's revenues went to pay off the national debt, and an additional quarter supported the French armed forces. Although France was a wealthy country in the eighteenth century, it did not have a national banking system to finance loans, and it did not have an efficient system of tax collection. Even if it had, the wealthiest French classes—including the nobility and the clergy—were exempt from most taxes, which meant that nearly

The Estates General

all direct taxes had to be levied on the already poor and overburdened French peasantry.

By 1787 King Louis XVI was desperate for money. When he turned to the French nobility and clergy for help, however, they refused. They did so in part to protect their financial status, but they also wanted to demonstrate to the king their ability to act independently. If the king wanted their help, they argued, he was going to have to allow the nobility a larger share of power. This issue of power was one that the king and the nobles had clashed over repeatedly in the past, and it was one over which the king was not willing to compromise. In the hope that Louis would be forced to institute reforms to their liking, then, the nobility demanded that Louis summon the Estates General, an assembly that represented the entire French population through three groups, known as estates. The first estate consisted of about one hundred thousand Roman Catholic clergy, and the second included some four hundred thousand nobles. The third estate embraced the rest of the population—about twenty-four million serfs, free peasants, and urban residents. It had as many delegates as the other two estates combined.

The National Assembly

In May 1789 King Louis called the Estates General into session at the royal palace of Versailles in hopes that it would authorize new taxes. But the mood of many of the representatives was grim. People of the third estate, in particular, were extremely dissatisfied with Louis. The middle classes resented the assumption of the best jobs and offices by the nobility and were also influenced by

Versailles

calls for political reforms that were making their way through France and the Atlantic world. The poorer classes, meanwhile, resented the burden of taxation they had to carry and were in any case feeling desperate because of economic hardship brought about by extremely bad harvests in 1788.

It quickly became clear to the members of the third estate that the members of the first and second estates wanted to maintain control by insisting that each estate cast only one vote. Members of the third estate insisted, in contrast, that the estates vote together by head. Disillusioned by weeks of arguing, on 17 June 1789 representatives of the third estate took the dramatic step of seceding from the Estates General and proclaiming themselves to be the National Assembly. Three days later, members of the new Assembly swore not to disband until they had provided France with a new constitution. The next month, on 14 July 1789,

a Parisian crowd stormed the Bastille, a royal jail and arsenal, in search of weapons to defend themselves from what they feared would be a royal crackdown on supporters of the Assembly. The military garrison protecting the Bastille surrendered to the crowd but only after killing many of the attackers. To vent their rage, members of the crowd hacked the The Bastille defenders to death. News of the event soon spread, sparking insurrections in cities throughout France. Those insurrections grew even more intense when rumors spread that armed bands organized by nobles were moving through the countryside to restore order. This "Great Fear" prompted the peasantry all over France to burn monasteries, public records offices, and the houses of nobles.

Fearing that the revolution would swing out of their control unless they acted quickly, the National Assembly undertook a broad program of political and social reform. The *Declaration of the Rights of Man and the Citizen,* which the National Assembly promulgated in August 1789, articulated the guiding principles of the program. Reflecting the influence of American revolutionary ideas, the *Declaration of the Rights of Man and the Citizen* proclaimed the equality of all men, declared that sovereignty resided in the people, and asserted individual rights.

Liberty, Equality, and Fraternity

Between 1789 and 1791 the National Assembly reconfigured French society. Taking the Enlightenment ideals of "liberty, equality, and fraternity" as its goals, the Assembly abolished the old social order. It seized church lands, abolished the first estate, defined clergy as civilians, and required clergy to take an oath of loyalty to the state. It also produced a constitution that left the king in place but deprived him of legislative authority. France became a constitutional monarchy in which men of property—about half the adult male population—had the right to vote in elections to choose legislators.

The Convention

The revolution soon took a radical turn. Many Parisians who were supposed to be represented by the third estate felt that the changes effected by the revolution were not radical enough and favored transforming France into a republic. The desire for a more radical approach was further encouraged by the efforts of the French nobility to ally with foreign powers—especially Austria and Prussia—to help restore the ancien régime. Faced with this threat to the survival of the revolution, the Assem-

SOURCES FROM THE PAST

Declaration of the Rights of Man and the Citizen

While developing their program of reform, members of the National Assembly consulted closely with Thomas Jefferson, the principal author of the American Declaration of Independence, who was the U.S. ambassador to France in 1789. Thus it is not surprising that the Declaration of the Rights of Man and the Citizen *reflects the influence of American revolutionary ideas.*

■ ■ ■

First Article. Men are born and remain free and equal in rights. Social distinctions may be based only on common utility.

Article 2. The goal of every political association is the preservation of the natural and inalienable rights of man. These rights are liberty, property, security, and resistance to oppression.

Article 3. The principle of all sovereignty resides essentially in the nation. No body and no individual can exercise authority that does not flow directly from the nation.

Article 4. Liberty consists in the freedom to do anything that does not harm another. The exercise of natural rights of each man thus has no limits except those that assure other members of society their enjoyment of the same rights. These limits may be determined only by law.

Article 6. Law is the expression of the general will. All citizens have the right to participate either personally or through their representatives in the making of law. The law must be the same for all, whether it protects or punishes. Being equal in the eyes of the law, all citizens are equally eligible for all public honors, offices, and occupations, according to their abilities, without any distinction other than that of their virtues and talents.

Article 7. No person shall be accused, arrested, or imprisoned except in the cases and according to the forms prescribed by law. Any one soliciting, transmit-

ting, executing, or causing to be executed, any arbitrary order, shall be punished. But any citizen summoned or arrested in virtue of the law shall submit without delay, as resistance constitutes an offense.

Article 9. As all persons are held innocent until they shall have been declared guilty, if arrest shall be deemed indispensable, all harshness not essential to the securing of the prisoner's person shall be severely repressed by law.

Article 11. The free communication of thoughts and opinions is one of the most precious rights of man: every citizen may thus speak, write, and publish freely, but will be responsible for abuse of this freedom in cases decided by the law.

Article 13. For the maintenance of public military force and for the expenses of administration, common taxation is necessary: it must be equally divided among all citizens according to their means.

Article 15. Society has the right to require from every public official an accounting of his administration.

Article 16. Any society in which guarantees of rights are not assured and separation of powers is not defined has no constitution at all.

Article 17. Property is an inviolable and sacred right. No one may be deprived of property except when public necessity, legally determined, clearly requires it, and on condition of just and prearranged compensation.

• *In what ways do the principles established in the Declaration reflect the political transformations taking place throughout the age of Atlantic revolutions?*

SOURCE: *Déclaration des droits de l'homme et du citoyen.* Translated by Jerry H. Bentley.

bly declared war against Austria and Prussia in April 1792. In the following year, revolutionary leaders declared war on Spain, Britain, and the Netherlands. Fearing military defeat and counterrevolution, revo-

lutionary leaders created the Convention, a new legislative body elected by universal manhood suffrage, which abolished the monarchy and proclaimed France a republic. The Convention rallied the French

The guillotine was an efficient killing machine. In this contemporary print the executioner displays the just-severed head of King Louis XVI to the crowd assembled to witness his execution.

population by instituting the *levée en masse,* a "mass levy" that drafted people and resources for use in the war against invading forces. The Convention also rooted out enemies at home by making frequent use of the guillotine. In 1793 King Louis XVI and his wife, Queen Marie Antoinette, themselves went to the guillotine when the Convention found them guilty of treason to the principles of the revolution.

Revolutionary chaos reached its peak in 1793 and 1794 when Maximilien Robespierre (1758–1794) and the radical Jacobin party dominated the Convention. A lawyer by training, Robespierre had emerged during the revolution as a ruthless but popular radical known as "the Incorruptible," and he dominated the

Committee of Public Safety, the executive authority of the Republic. The Jacobins believed passionately that France needed complete restructuring, and they unleashed a campaign of terror to promote their revolutionary agenda. They sought to eliminate the influence of Christianity in French society by closing churches, forcing priests to take wives, and promoting a new, secular "cult of reason." They reorganized the calendar, replacing seven-day weeks with ten-day units that recognized no day of religious observance. The Jacobins also encouraged citizens to display their revolutionary zeal by wearing working-class clothes and granted increased rights to women by permitting them to inherit property and divorce their husbands.

The Jacobins made especially frequent use of the guillotine: in a yearlong "reign of terror" between the summer of 1793 and the summer of 1794, they executed about forty thousand people and imprisoned three hundred thousand others as suspected enemies of the revolution.

Eventually, such political purges undermined confidence in the regime itself. In July 1794 the Convention *The Directory* arrested Robespierre and his allies, convicted them of tyranny, and sent them to the guillotine. A group of conservative men of property then seized power and ruled France under a new institution known as the Directory (1795–1799). However, the Directory was unable to resolve the economic and military problems that plagued revolutionary France. In seeking a middle way between the ancien régime and radical revolution, they lurched from one policy to another, and the Directory faced constant challenges to its authority. It came to an end in November 1799 when a young general named Napoleon Bonaparte staged a coup d'état and seized power.

The Reign of Napoleon

Born to a minor noble family on the Mediterranean island of Corsica, Napoleon Bonaparte (1769–1821) studied at French military schools and became an officer in the army of King Louis XVI. A brilliant military leader, he became a general at age twenty-four. He was a fervent supporter of the revolution and defended the Directory against a popular uprising in 1795. In a campaign of 1796–1797, he drove the Austrian army from northern Italy and established French rule there. In 1798 he mounted an invasion of Egypt, but the campaign ended in a French defeat. Politically ambitious, Napoleon returned to France in 1799 and joined the Directory. When Austria, Russia, and Britain formed a coalition to attack France and end the revolution, he overthrew the Directory, imposed a new constitution, and named himself first consul. In 1802 he became consul for life, and two years later he crowned himself emperor.

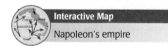
Interactive Map
Napoleon's empire

Napoleon brought political stability to a land torn by revolution and war. He made peace with the Roman *Napoleonic France* Catholic church and reversed the most radical religious policies of the Convention. In 1804 Napoleon promulgated the Civil Code, a revised body of civil law, which also helped stabilize French society. The Civil Code affirmed the political and legal equality of all adult men and established a merit-based society in which individuals advanced in education and employment because of talent rather than birth or social standing. The Civil Code confirmed many of the moderate revolutionary policies of the National Assembly but retracted measures passed by the more radical Convention. The code restored patriarchal authority in the family, for example, by making women and children subservient to male heads of households.

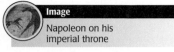
Image
Napoleon on his imperial throne

Although he approved of the Enlightenment ideal of equality, Napoleon was no champion of intellectual freedom or representative government. He limited free speech and routinely censored newspapers and other publications. He established a secret police force that relied heavily on spies and detained suspected political opponents by the thousands. He made systematic use of propaganda to manipulate public opinion. He ignored elective bodies and founded a dynasty that set his family above the people in whose name they ruled.

While working to stabilize France, Napoleon also sought to extend his authority throughout Europe. Napoleon's armies conquered the Iberian and Italian peninsulas, occupied the Neth- *Napoleon's Empire* erlands, and inflicted humiliating defeats on Austrian and Prussian forces. Napoleon sent his brothers and other relatives to rule the conquered and occupied lands, and he forced Austria, Prussia, and Russia to ally with him and respect French hegemony in Europe.

Napoleon's empire began to unravel in 1812, when he decided to invade Russia. Convinced that the tsar was conspiring with his British enemies, Napoleon led an army of six hundred thousand soldiers to Moscow. He captured the city, but the tsar withdrew and set Moscow ablaze, leaving Napoleon's vast army without adequate shelter or supplies. Napoleon ordered a retreat, but the bitter Russian winter destroyed his army, and only a battered remnant of thirty thousand soldiers managed to limp back to France.

Napoleon's disastrous Russian campaign emboldened his enemies. A coalition of British, Austrian, Prussian, and Russian armies converged on France and forced Napoleon to abdi- *The Fall of Napoleon* cate his throne in April 1814. The victors restored the French monarchy and exiled Napoleon to the tiny Mediterranean island of Elba. But in March 1815 Napoleon escaped from Elba, returned to France, and ruled France for a hundred days before a British army defeated him at Waterloo in Belgium. This time,

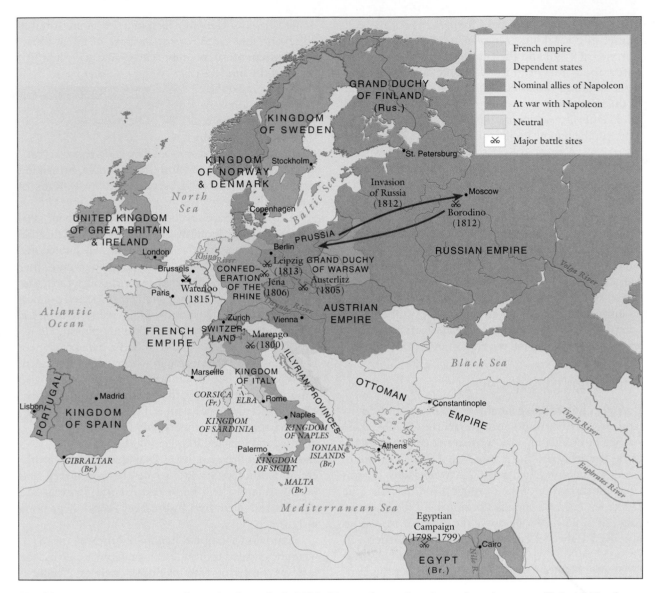

Map 26.2 Boundaries and states of Napoleon's empire in 1812. Observe the number of states dependent on or allied with Napoleon as opposed to those who were at war with him. Were there geographic conditions that allowed some states to resist Napoleon's efforts at conquest better than others?

European powers banished Napoleon to the remote and isolated island of St. Helena in the South Atlantic Ocean, where he died of natural causes in 1821.

THE INFLUENCE OF REVOLUTION

The Enlightenment ideals promoted by the American and French revolutions appealed to peoples throughout Europe and the Americas. In the Caribbean and Latin America, they inspired revolutionary movements: slaves in the French colony of Saint-Domingue rose

against their overlords and established the independent republic of Haiti, and Euro-American leaders mounted independence movements in Mexico, Central America, and South America. The ideals of the American and French revolutions also encouraged social reformers to organize broader programs of liberation for women and slaves of African ancestry.

The Haitian Revolution

The only successful slave revolt in history took place on the Caribbean island of Hispaniola. The Spanish colony of Santo Domingo occupied the eastern part of the island (modern Dominican Republic), and the French colony of Saint-Domingue occupied the western part (modern Haiti). Saint-Domingue was one of the richest of all European colonies in the Caribbean: sugar, coffee, and cotton produced there accounted for almost one-third of France's foreign trade.

Saint-Domingue Society In 1790 the population of Saint-Domingue included about forty thousand white French settlers, thirty thousand *gens de couleur* (free people of color), and some five hundred thousand black slaves, most of whom were born in Africa. Led by wealthy planters, white residents stood at the top of society. *Gens de couleur* farmed small plots of land, sometimes with the aid of a few slaves, or worked as artisans in the island's towns. Most of the colony's slaves toiled in the fields under brutal conditions. Many slaves ran away into the mountains to escape such treatment. By the late eighteenth century, Saint-Domingue had many large communities of maroons (escaped slaves).

The American and French revolutions prepared the way for a violent political and social revolution in Saint-Domingue. Because French policy supported North American colonists against British rule, colonial governors in Saint-Domingue sent about five hundred *gens de couleur* to fight in the American war of independence. They returned to Saint-Domingue

The slave rebellion in Saint-Domingue struck fear in the hearts of European and Euro-American peoples. This French print depicts outnumbered white settlers under attack on a plantation.

with the intention of reforming society. When the French revolution broke out in 1789, white settlers in Saint-Domingue sought the right to govern themselves, but they opposed proposals to grant political and legal equality to the *gens de couleur.* By May 1791 civil war had broken out between white settlers and *gens de couleur.*

The conflict expanded dramatically when a charismatic Vodou priest named Boukman organized a slave revolt. In August 1791 some twelve thou-

Slave Revolt

sand slaves began killing white settlers, burning their homes, and destroying their plantations. Within a few weeks the numbers of slaves in revolt grew to almost one hundred thousand. Saint-Domingue quickly descended into chaos as white, *gens de couleur,* and slave factions battled one another. Foreign armies soon complicated the situation: French troops arrived in 1792 to restore order, and British and Spanish forces intervened in 1793 in hopes of benefiting from France's difficulties.

Eventually, slave forces overcame white settlers, *gens de couleur,* and foreign armies. Their successes were due

Toussaint L'Ouverture

largely to the leadership of François-Dominique Toussaint (1744–1803), who after 1791 called himself Louverture— from the French *l'ouverture,* meaning "the opening." The son of slaves, he himself had been a free man since 1776. Toussaint was a skilled organizer, and by 1793 he had built a strong, disciplined army. He shrewdly played French, British, and Spanish forces against one another while also jockeying for power with other black and mulatto generals. By 1797 he led an army of twenty thousand that controlled most of Saint-Domingue. In 1801 he issued a constitution that granted equality and citizenship to all residents of Saint-Domingue. He stopped short of declaring independence from France, however, because he did not want to provoke Napoleon into attacking the island.

Nevertheless, in 1802 Napoleon dispatched forty thousand troops to restore French authority in Saint-

The Republic of Haiti

Domingue. Toussaint attempted to negotiate a peaceful settlement, but the French commander arrested him and sent him to France, where he died in jail of maltreatment in 1803. By the time he died, however, the black generals who succeeded Toussaint had defeated the remaining French troops and driven them out of the colony. Late in 1803 they declared independence, and on 1 January 1804 they proclaimed the establishment of Haiti, meaning "land of mountains," which became the second independent republic in the western hemisphere.

Wars of Independence in Latin America

Revolutionary ideals traveled beyond Saint-Domingue to the Spanish and Portuguese colonies in the Americas. Though governed by *peninsulares* (colonial officials from Spain or Portugal), the Iberian colonies all had a large, wealthy, and powerful class of Euro-

Latin American Society

American *criollos,* or creoles, individuals born in the Americas of Spanish or Portuguese ancestry. In 1800 the *peninsulares* numbered about 30,000, and the creole population was 3.5 million. The Iberian colonies also had a large population—about 10 million in all— of less privileged classes such as black slaves, indigenous peoples, mestizos, and mulattoes.

Creoles prospered during the eighteenth century as they established plantations in the colonies and participated in trade with Spain and Portugal. Yet the creoles also had grievances. Like British colonists in North America, the creoles resented administrative control and economic regulations imposed by the Iberian powers. Although they drew inspiration from Enlightenment political thought, the creoles desired neither radical social reform nor the establishment of an egalitarian society. Instead, they sought to displace the *peninsulares* but retain their privileged position in society. Between 1810 and 1825, creoles led movements that brought independence to all Spanish colonies in the Americas—except Cuba and Puerto Rico—and established creole-dominated republics.

The struggle for independence began in the wake of Napoleon's invasion of Spain and Portugal (1807), which weakened royal authority in the Iberian colonies. By 1810 revolts against Spanish rule had broken out in Ar-

Mexican Independence

gentina, Venezuela, and Mexico. The most serious was a peasant rebellion in Mexico led by a parish priest, Miguel de Hidalgo (1753–1811), who rallied indigenous peoples and mestizos against colonial rule. Conservative creoles who feared revolution by the masses soon captured Hidalgo and executed him, but his rebellion continued to flare for three years after his death. Hidalgo became the symbol of Mexican independence, and the day on which he proclaimed his revolt—16 September 1810—is Mexico's principal national holiday.

Colonial rule came to an end in 1821, when the creole general Augustín de Iturbide (1783–1824) de-

---

peninsulares (peh-neen-soo-LAH-rehs)

clared independence from Spain. In the following year, he declared himself emperor of Mexico. Iturbide was an incompetent administrator, however, and in 1823 creole elites deposed him and established a republic. Two years later the southern regions of the Mexican empire declared their own independence. They formed a Central American Federation until 1838, then split into the independent states of Guatemala, El Salvador, Honduras, Nicaragua, and Costa Rica.

In South America, creole elites such as Simón Bolívar (1783–1830) led the movement for independence. *Simón Bolívar* Born in Caracas (in modern Venezuela), Bolívar was a fervent republican steeped in Enlightenment ideas about popular sovereignty. Inspired by the example of George Washington, he took up arms against Spanish rule in 1811. In 1819, after many reversals, he assembled an army that surprised and crushed the Spanish army in Colombia. Later he campaigned in Venezuela, Ecuador, and Peru, coordinating his efforts with other creole leaders such as José de San Martín (1778–1850) in Argentina and Bernardo O'Higgins (1778–1842) in Chile. By 1825 creole forces had overcome Spanish armies and deposed Spanish rulers throughout South America.

Bolívar's goal was to weld the former Spanish colonies of South America into a confederation like the United States. During the 1820s independent Venezuela, Colombia, and Ecuador formed a repub-

lic called Gran Colombia, and Bolívar attempted to bring Peru and Bolivia into the confederation. By 1830, however, strong political and regional differences led to the breakup of Gran Colombia. As the confederation disintegrated, a bitterly disappointed Bolívar—who died shortly afterward—pronounced South America "ungovernable."

Independence came to Portuguese Brazil at the same time as to Spanish colonies, but by a different process. When Napoleon invaded Portu- *Brazilian* gal in 1807, the royal court fled Lisbon *Independence* and established a government-in-exile in Rio de Janeiro. In 1821 the king returned to Portugal, leaving his son Pedro in Brazil as regent. The next year Brazilian creoles called for independence from Portugal, and Pedro agreed to their demands. In 1822 Pedro declared Brazil's independence and accepted appointment as Emperor Pedro I (reigned 1822–1834).

In Brazil as in the former Spanish colonies, creole elites dominated both politics and society. Indeed, independence brought little social change in Latin America: although the *peninsulares* *Creole* returned to Europe, Latin American soci- *Dominance* ety remained stratified and unequal. The newly independent states granted military authority to local strongmen, known as caudillos, allied with creole elites. The new states also allowed the continuation of slavery, confirmed the wealth and authority of the Roman Catholic church, and repressed the lower orders. The principal beneficiaries of independence in Latin America were the creole elites.

The Emergence of Ideologies: Conservatism and Liberalism

While inspiring revolutions and independence movements in other lands, the American and French revolutions also prompted political and social theorists to crystallize the modern ideologies of conservatism and liberalism. An *ideology* is a coherent vision of human nature, human society, and the larger world that proposes some particular form of political and social organization as ideal. People who promote a given ideology seek to design a political and social order for their communities.

The modern ideology of conservatism arose as political and social theorists responded to the challenges of the American and especially *Conservatism* the French revolution. Conservatives believed that social change, if necessary at all, must be undertaken gradually and with respect for tradi-

Simón Bolívar, creole leader of the independence movement in Latin America, was a favorite subject of painters in the nineteenth century. This portrait depicts him as a determined and farsighted leader.

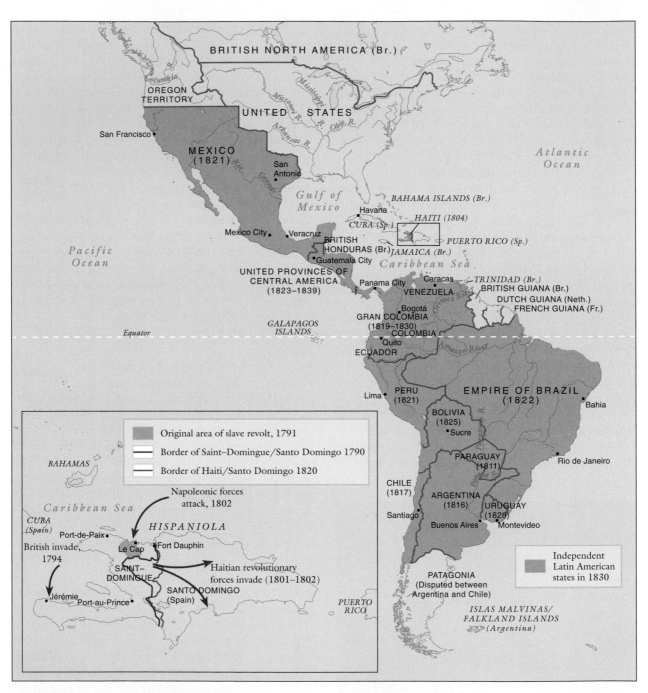

Map 26.3 States of Latin America in 1830. Note the dates each state won its independence. Since most states became independent in very close succession, what conditions prevented Latin American states from joining together in a federation like that in the United States?

tion. The English political philosopher Edmund Burke (1729–1797), for example, condemned radical or revolutionary change, which in his view could only lead to anarchy. Thus Burke approved of the American revolution, which he viewed as a natural and logical change, but he denounced the French

revolution as a chaotic and irresponsible assault on society.

In contrast to conservatives, liberals viewed change as the agent of progress. Conservatism, they argued, was just a means to justify the status quo and maintain the privileges enjoyed by favored classes. For liberals the trick was not to stifle change but, rather, to manage it in the best interests of society. Liberals such as

Liberalism the English political philosopher John Stuart Mill (1806–1873) championed the Enlightenment values of freedom and equality, which they believed would lead to higher standards of morality and increased prosperity for the whole society. They usually favored republican forms of government in which citizens elected representatives to legislative bodies, and they called for written constitutions that guaranteed freedom and equality for all citizens. Although some liberals, such as Mill, advocated universal suffrage (and in Mill's case even women's suffrage), many liberals during the nineteenth century did not go so far: for most, universal suffrage still seemed dangerous because it allowed the uneducated masses to participate in politics.

Testing the Limits of Revolutionary Ideals: Slavery and Women's Rights

The Enlightenment ideals of freedom and equality were watchwords of revolution in the Atlantic Ocean basin. Yet different revolutionaries understood the implications of freedom and equality in very different ways, and the Atlantic revolutions had produced widely varying results. Nevertheless, in the wake of the revolutions, social activists in Europe and the Americas considered the possibility that the ideals of freedom and equality would have further implications as yet unexplored. They turned their attention especially to the issues of slavery and women's rights.

The campaign to end the slave trade and abolish slavery began in the eighteenth century. Only after the

Movements to End the Slave Trade American, French, and Haitian revolutions, however, did the antislavery movement gain momentum. The leading spokesman of the movement was William Wilberforce (1759–1833), a prominent English philanthropist elected in 1780 to a seat in Parliament. There he tirelessly attacked slavery on moral and religious grounds. After the Haitian revolution he attracted supporters who feared that continued reliance on slave labor would result in more and larger slave revolts, and in 1807 Parliament passed Wilberforce's bill to end the slave trade. Under British pressure, other states also banned international commerce in slaves: the United States in 1808, France in 1814, the Netherlands in 1817, and Spain in 1845. The slave trade died slowly, but the British navy, which dominated the North Atlantic Ocean, patrolled the west coast of Africa to ensure compliance with the law.

The abolition of slavery itself was a much bigger challenge than ending the slave trade because owners had property rights in their slaves and strongly resisted efforts to alter the system. In some places, revolution hastened slavery's end: Haiti abolished the institution in 1801 and Mexico in 1829, and in South America Simón Bolívar freed slaves who joined his forces and provided constitutional guarantees of free status for all residents of Gran Colombia. In other areas slavery was abolished as a result of extensive campaigns by antislavery activists such as Wilberforce. In 1833, one month after Wilberforce's death, Parliament provided twenty million pounds sterling as compensation to slave owners and abolished slavery throughout the British empire. Other states followed the British example: France abolished slavery in 1848, the United States in 1865, Cuba in 1886, and Brazil in 1888.

Movements to Abolish Slavery

Abolition brought legal freedom for African and African-American slaves, but it did not bring political equality. In most places, African-American peoples were prevented from voting through property requirements, literacy tests, and campaigns of intimidation. Nor did emancipation bring social and economic improvements for former slaves and their descendants. White creole elites owned most of the property in the Americas, and they kept blacks in subordination by forcing them to accept low-paying work.

Freedom without Equality

Meanwhile, women who participated alongside men in the movement to abolish slavery came to believe that women suffered many of the same legal disabilities as slaves: they had little access to education, they could not enter professional occupations that required advanced education, and they were legally deprived of the right to vote. In making the case for their own rights, women drew on Enlightenment ideas about liberty and equality. For example, the English writer Mary Astell (1666–1731) used the political thought of John Locke to suggest that absolute sovereignty was no more appropriate in a family than in a state. Astell also reflected Enlightenment influence in asking why, if all men were born free, all women were born slaves? Mary Wollstonecraft (1759–1797), another British writer, similarly drew on Locke's ideas, especially in her 1792 essay titled *A Vindication of the Rights of Woman*. Like Astell, Wollstonecraft argued that women possessed all the rights that Locke had granted to men. She especially insisted on the right of women to education: it would make them better mothers and wives, she said, and would enable them

Enlightenment Ideals and Women

to contribute to society by preparing them for professional occupations and participation in political life.

Women played crucial roles in the revolutions of the late eighteenth and early nineteenth centuries, *Women and Revolution* from making bandages to managing farms to actively taking up arms. Yet even so, they did not win political or social rights. In France, where women did gain rights to property, education, and divorce in the early years of the revolution, they were consistently denied the right to vote or to hold public office. In the later years of the revolution, under the Directory and Napoleon's rule, women lost even the limited rights they had won earlier. In other lands, women never gained as much as they did in revolutionary France. In the United States and the independent states of Latin America, revolution brought legal equality and political rights only for adult white men, who retained patriarchal authority over their wives and families.

Nevertheless, throughout the nineteenth century social reformers pressed for women's rights as well as *Women's Rights Movements* the abolition of slavery. The American feminist Elizabeth Cady Stanton (1815–1902) was an especially prominent figure in this movement. In 1840 Stanton went to London to attend an antislavery conference but found that the organizers barred women from participation. Infuriated, Stanton returned to the United States and organized a conference of feminists who met at Seneca Falls, New York, in 1848. The conference passed twelve resolutions demanding that lawmakers grant women the right to vote, to attend public schools, to enter professional occupations, and to participate in public affairs. The women's rights movement experienced only limited success in the nineteenth century: some women gained access to education, but nowhere did they win the right to vote. Yet, by seeking to extend the promises of Enlightenment political thought to blacks and women as well as white men, social reformers of the nineteenth century laid a foundation that would lead to large-scale social change in the twentieth century.

THE CONSOLIDATION OF NATIONAL STATES IN EUROPE

The Enlightenment ideals of freedom, equality, and popular sovereignty inspired political revolutions in much of the Atlantic Ocean basin, and the revolutions in turn helped spread Enlightenment values. The wars of the French revolution and the Napoleonic era also inspired the development of a particular type of community identity that had little to do with Enlightenment values—nationalism. Revolutionary wars involved millions of French citizens in the defense of their country against foreign armies and the extension of French influence to neighboring states. Wartime experiences encouraged peoples throughout Europe to think of themselves as members of distinctive national communities. Throughout the nineteenth century, European nationalist leaders worked to fashion states based on national identities and mobilized citizens to work in the interests of their own national communities, sometimes by fostering jealousy and suspicion of other national groups. By the late nineteenth century, national identities were so strong that peoples throughout Europe responded enthusiastically to ideologies of nationalism, which promised glory and prosperity to those who worked in the interests of their national communities.

Nations and Nationalism

One of the most influential concepts of modern political thought is the idea of the nation. At various times and places in history, individuals have associated themselves primarily with families, clans, cities, regions, and religious faiths. Yet, during the nineteenth century, European peoples came to identify strongly with communities they called nations. Members of a nation considered themselves a distinctive people that spoke a common language, observed common customs, inherited common cultural traditions, held common values, and shared common historical experiences.

Intense feelings of national identity fueled ideologies of nationalism. Advocates of nationalism insisted that the nation must be the focus of political loyalty. Zealous nationalist leaders maintained that members of their national communities had a common destiny that they could best advance by organizing independent national states. Ideally, in their view, the boundaries of the national state embraced the territory occupied by the national community, and its government promoted the interests of the national group, sometimes through conflict with other peoples.

Early nationalist thought often sought to deepen appreciation for the historical experiences of the national community and foster pride in its cultural accomplishments. During the late eighteenth century, for example, Johann Gottfried von Herder (1744–1803) sang the praises of the German *Volk* ("people") and their powerful and expressive language. In reaction to

Cultural Nationalism

Enlightenment thinkers and their quest for a scientific, universally valid understanding of the world, early cultural nationalists such as Herder emphasized the uniqueness of their societies through the study of history, literature, and song.

During the nineteenth century, nationalist thought became much more strident. In lands where they were

Political Nationalism

minorities or where they lived under foreign rule, nationalists demanded loyalty and solidarity from the national group and sought to establish independent states. In Italy, for example, the nationalist activist Giuseppe Mazzini (1805–1872) formed a group called Young Italy that promoted independence from Austrian and Spanish rule and the establishment of an Italian national state. Austrian and Spanish authorities forced Mazzini to lead much of his life in exile, but he used the opportunity to encourage the organization of nationalist movements in new lands. By the mid–nineteenth century, Young Italy had inspired the development of nationalist movements in Ireland, Switzerland, and Hungary.

While it encouraged political leaders to work toward the establishment of national states for their

Nationalism and Anti-Semitism

communities, nationalism also had strong potential to stir up conflict between different groups of people. The more nationalists identified with their own national communities, the more they distinguished themselves both from peoples in other lands and from minority groups within their own societies. This divisive potential of nationalism helps to explain the emergence of Zionism, a political movement that holds that the Jewish people constitute a nation and have the right to their own national homeland. Unlike Mazzini's Italian compatriots, Jews did not inhabit a well-defined territory but, rather, lived in states throughout Europe. As national communities tightened their bonds, nationalist leaders often became distrustful of minority populations. Suspicion of Jews fueled violent anti-Semitism in many parts of Europe. In Russia and in the Russian-controlled areas of Poland, the persecution of Jews climaxed in a series of anti-Jewish riots called pogroms, which claimed the lives and property of thousands of Jews.

During the late nineteenth and twentieth centuries, millions of Jews migrated to other European lands or to North America to escape persecution and violence. Anti-Semitism was not as severe in France as

in central and eastern Europe, but it reached a fever pitch there after a military court convicted Alfred Dreyfus, a Jewish army officer, of spying for Germany in 1894. Although he was innocent of the charges and eventually had the verdict reversed on appeal, Dreyfus was the focus of bitter debates about the trustworthiness of Jews in French society. The trial also became a key event in the evolution of Zionism.

Among the reporters at the Dreyfus trial was a Jewish journalist from Vienna, Theodor Herzl (1860–1904). As Herzl witnessed mobs shouting "Death to the Jews" in the land of enlight-

Zionism

enment and liberty, he concluded that anti-Semitism was a persistent feature of human society that assimilation could not solve. In 1896 Herzl published the pamphlet *Judenstaat,* which argued that the only defense against anti-Semitism lay in the mass migration of Jews from all over the world to a land that they could call their own. In the following year, Herzl organized the first Zionist Congress in Basel, Switzerland, which founded the World Zionist Organization. The delegates at Basel formulated the basic platform of the Zionist movement, declar-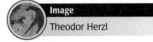ing that "Zionism seeks to establish a home for the Jewish people in Palestine," the location of the ancient kingdom of Israel. During the next half century, Jewish migrants trickled into Palestine, and in 1948 they won recognition for the Jewish state of Israel. Although it arose in response to exclusive nationalism in Europe, Zionism in turn provoked a resentful nationalism among Palestinians displaced by Jewish settlers. Conflicts between Jews and Palestinians continue to the present day.

The Emergence of National Communities

The French revolution and the wars that followed it heightened feelings of national identity throughout Europe. In France the establishment of a republic based on liberty, equality, and fraternity inspired patriotism and encouraged citizens to rally to its defense when foreign armies threatened it. Revolutionary leaders took the tricolored flag as a symbol of the French nation, and they adopted a rousing marching tune, the "Marseillaise," as an anthem that inspired pride and identity with the national community. In Spain, the Netherlands, Austria, Prussia, and Russia, national consciousness surged in reaction to the arrival of revolutionary and

Napoleonic armies. Opposition to Napoleon and his imperial designs also inspired national feeling in Britain.

The Congress of Vienna

After the fall of Napoleon, conservative political leaders feared that heightened national consciousness and ideas of popular sovereignty would undermine European stability. Meeting as the Congress of Vienna (1814–1815), representatives of Britain, Austria, Prussia, and Russia attempted to restore the prerevolutionary order. Under the guidance of the influential foreign minister of Austria, Prince Klemens von Metternich (1773–1859), the Congress dismantled Napoleon's empire, returned sovereignty to Europe's royal families, restored them to the thrones they had lost during the Napoleonic era, and created a diplomatic order based on a balance of power that prevented any one state from dominating the others. A central goal of Metternich himself was to suppress national consciousness, which he viewed as a serious threat to the multicultural Austrian empire. Yet the efforts of the Congress of Vienna to restore the ancien régime had limited success. Although the European balance of power established at Vienna survived for almost a century, it had become impossible to suppress national consciousness and ideas of popular sovereignty.

Nationalist Rebellions

From the 1820s through the 1840s, a wave of rebellions inspired by nationalist sentiments swept through Europe. The first uprising occurred in 1821 in the Balkan Peninsula, where the Greek people sought independence from the Ottoman Turks. With the aid of Britain, France, and Russia, the rebels won formal recognition of Greek independence in 1830. In the same year, liberal revolutionaries in France, Spain, Portugal, and some of the German principalities called for constitutional government based on popular sovereignty. In Belgium, Italy, and Poland, they demanded independence and the formation of national states as well as popular sovereignty. Revolution in Paris drove Charles X from the throne, and uprisings in Belgium resulted in independence from the Netherlands. In 1848 a new round of rebellions shook European states, where they brought down the French monarchy and seriously threatened the Austrian empire. Uprisings also rocked cities in Italy, Prussia, and German states in the Rhineland.

Wearing a white jacket, Otto von Bismarck (center) witnesses the crowning of King Wilhelm I of Prussia as German emperor. The coronation followed the victory of Prussia over France in 1871, and it took place in the royal palace at Versailles.

By the summer of 1849, the veteran armies of conservative rulers had put down the last of the rebellions. However, advocates of national independence and popular sovereignty remained active, and the potential of their ideals to mobilize popular support were crucial in the unification of two new European states: Italy by 1870 and Germany by 1871.

The Unification of Italy and Germany

The most striking demonstration of the power that national sentiments could unleash involved the unification of Italy and Germany. Since the fall of the Roman empire, Italy and Germany had been disunited lands. A variety of regional kingdoms, city-states, and ecclesiastical states ruled the Italian peninsula for more than a thousand years, and princes divided Germany into more than three hundred semi-autonomous jurisdictions.

The unification of Italy came about when practical political leaders such as Count Camillo di Cavour (1810–1861), prime minister to King Vittore Emmanuele II of Piedmont and Sardinia, combined forces with nationalist advocates of independence. Cavour was

a cunning diplomat, and the kingdom of Piedmont and Sardinia was the most powerful of the Italian states. In alliance with France, Cavour expelled Austrian authorities—who had gained control of the region through the Congress of Vienna—from most of northern Italy in 1859. Then he turned his attention to southern Italy, where Giuseppe Garibaldi (1807–1882), a dashing soldier of fortune and a passionate nationalist, led the unification movement. With an army of about one thousand men outfitted in distinctive red shirts, Garibaldi swept through Sicily and southern Italy, outmaneuvering government forces and attracting enthusiastic recruits. In 1860 Garibaldi met King Vittore Emmanuele near Naples. Not ambitious to rule, Garibaldi delivered southern Italy into Vittore Emmanuele's hands, and the kingdom of Piedmont and Sardinia became the kingdom of Italy. During the next decade the new monarchy absorbed several additional territories, including Venice, Rome, and their surrounding regions.

Cavour and Garibaldi

In Germany as in Italy, unification came about when political leaders harnessed nationalist aspirations. The Congress of Vienna created a German Confederation composed of thirty-nine states dominated by Austria. In 1862 King Wilhelm I of Prussia—one of the

Map 26.4 The unification of Germany. Locate the boundaries of Prussia between 1815 and 1816. Why was Prussia able to dominate the German Confederation in the period between 1866 and 1871?

thirty-nine states—appointed a wealthy landowner, Otto von Bismarck (1815–1898), as his prime minister. Bismarck was a master of Realpolitik ("the politics of reality") who argued that "the great questions of the day will not be settled by speeches or majority votes . . . but by blood and iron." It was indeed blood and iron that brought about the unification of Germany. As prime minister, Bismarck reformed and expanded the Prussian army. Between 1864 and 1870 he intentionally provoked three wars—with Denmark, Austria, and France—and whipped up German sentiment against the enemies. In all three conflicts Prussian forces quickly shattered their opponents, swelling German pride. In 1871 the Prussian king proclaimed himself emperor of the Second Reich—meaning the Second German Empire, following the Holy Roman Empire—which embraced almost all German-speaking peoples outside Austria and Switzerland in a powerful and dynamic national state.

Otto von Bismarck

The unification of Italy and Germany made it clear that when coupled with strong political, diplomatic, and military leadership, nationalism had enormous potential to mobilize people who felt a sense of national kinship. Italy, Germany, and other national states went to great lengths to foster a sense of national community. They adopted national flags to serve as symbols of unity, national anthems to inspire patriotism, and national holidays to focus public attention on individuals and events of special importance for the national community. They established bureaucracies that took censuses of national populations and tracked vital national statistics involving birth, marriage, and death. They built schools that instilled patriotic values in students, and they recruited young men into armies that defended national interests and sometimes went on the offensive to enhance national prestige. By the end of the nineteenth century, the national state had proven to be a powerful model of political organization in Europe.

SUMMARY

The Enlightenment ideals of freedom, equality, and popular sovereignty inspired revolutionary movements throughout much of the Atlantic Ocean basin in the late eighteenth and early nineteenth centuries. In North America colonists threw off British rule and founded an independent federal republic. In France revolutionaries abolished the monarchy, established a republic, and refashioned the social order. In Saint-Domingue rebellious slaves threw off French rule, established an independent Haitian republic, and granted freedom and equality to all citizens. In Latin America creole elites led movements to expel Spanish and Portuguese colonial authorities and found independent republics. During the nineteenth century, adult white men were the main beneficiaries of movements based on Enlightenment ideals, but social reformers launched campaigns to extend freedom and equality to African-Americans and women.

Meanwhile, as they fought one another in wars sparked by the French revolution, European peoples developed strong feelings of national identity and worked to establish states that advanced the interests of national communities. Nationalist thought was often divisive: it pitted national groups against one another and fueled tensions especially in large multicultural states. But nationalism also contributed to state-building movements that had the potential to unite. During the nineteenth and twentieth centuries, peoples throughout the world drew inspiration from Enlightenment ideals and national identities when seeking to build or restructure their societies.

CHRONOLOGY

1632–1704	Life of John Locke
1694–1778	Life of Voltaire
1712–1778	Life of Jean-Jacques Rousseau
1744–1803	Life of Toussaint Louverture
1748–1793	Life of Olympe de Gouges
1769–1821	Life of Napoleon Bonaparte
1774–1793	Reign of King Louis XVI
1775–1781	American Revolution
1783–1830	Life of Simón Bolívar
1789–1799	French Revolution
1791–1803	Haitian revolution
1799–1814	Reign of Napoleon
1810–1825	Wars of independence in Latin America
1814–1815	Congress of Vienna

FOR FURTHER READING

Benedict Anderson. *Imagined Communities: Reflections on the Origin and Spread of Nationalism.* Rev. ed. London, 1991. A pioneering work that analyzes the means and the processes by which peoples came to view themselves as members of national communities.

Bernard Bailyn. *The Ideological Origins of the American Revolution.* 2nd ed. Cambridge, Mass., 1992. A fundamental study of pamphlets and other publications that criticized British colonial policy in North America.

Aviva Chomsky and Aldo Lauria-Santiago, eds. *Identity and Struggle at the Margins of the Nation-State: The Laboring Peoples of Central America and the Hispanic Caribbean.* Durham, 1998. Discusses the impact that peasant action had on political and cultural development in different societies.

Linda Colley. *Britons: Forging the Nation, 1707–1837.* New Haven, 1992. A detailed analysis of the emergence of British national identity.

Susan Dunn. *Sister Revolutions: French Lightning, American Light.* New York, 1999. An accessible and stimulating work that traces the different legacies of the American and French revolutions of the eighteenth century.

Carolyn Fick. *The Making of Haiti: The Saint Domingue Revolution from Below.* Knoxville, 1990. A valuable study focusing on the role of slaves in the Haitian revolution.

François Furet. *Revolutionary France, 1770–1880.* Trans. by A. Nevill. Oxford, 1992. An influential interpretation emphasizing the ideological dimension of the French revolution.

Eric Hobsbawm. *Nations and Nationalism since 1780: Programme, Myth, and Reality.* 2nd ed. Cambridge, 1992. A brief interpretation of nationalism in Europe and the larger world.

Lester D. Langley. *The Americas in the Age of Revolution, 1750–1850.* New Haven, 1997. A comparative study of revolutions and wars of independence in the western hemisphere.

David Parker, ed. *Revolutions and the Revolutionary Tradition in the West, 1560–1991.* London and New York, 2000. In this comparative survey of revolutions—from the English revolution of 1649 to the revolutions within eastern Europe and the Soviet Union (1989–1991)—leading historians examine how a wider revolutionary tradition has shaped modern European history.

CHAPTER 27

The Making of Industrial Society

In 1827, shortly after marrying at the age of twenty-three, Betty Harris took a job as a drawer in a coal pit near Manchester, England. A drawer's job involved crawling down narrow mine shafts and hauling loads of coal from the bottom of the pit to the surface. Drawers performed unskilled labor for low wages, but their work was essential for obtaining the coal that fueled the factories and mills of early industrial society.

While working, Harris wore a heavy belt around her waist. Hitched to the belt was a chain that passed between her legs and attached to the coal cart that she pulled through the steep and slippery mine shafts, often on hands and knees. Every workday, even when she was pregnant, Harris strapped on her belt and chain at 6:00 A.M., removing her bindings only at the end of the shift twelve hours later.

Harris reported that drawing coal was "very hard work for a woman," and she did not exaggerate. The belts and chains worn by drawers often chafed their skin raw, and miners contributed to their physical discomfort by beating them for slow or clumsy work. The miners, many of whom worked naked in the hot, oppressive coal pits, also took sexual liberties with the women and girl drawers: Harris personally knew several illegitimate children conceived during forced sexual encounters in the mines.

Betty Harris faced her own sexual problems once she arrived home. Exhausted from twelve hours of work, with only a one-hour break for a lunch consisting of bread and butter, she often tried to discourage her husband's advances. Her husband had little patience, however, and Harris remarked that "my feller has beaten

OPPOSITE PAGE: *Young woman at work in a mechanized mill in the 1830s.*

me many a time for not being ready." Harris's work schedule made comfortable family life impossible. A cousin had to care for her two children during the day, and Harris tended to them and her husband at night. At age thirty-seven, after fourteen years in the mines, Harris admitted that "I am not so strong as I was."

Not all industrial workers worked in such difficult conditions, but Betty Harris's experience nonetheless illustrates some of the deep changes that industrialization wrought in patterns of work and family life. First in Britain, then in western Europe, North America, Russia, and Japan, machines and factories transformed agricultural societies into industrial societies. At the heart of this transformation were technological changes that led to the extensive use of machinery in manufacturing. Industrial machinery transformed economic production by turning out high-quality products quickly, cheaply, and efficiently. The process of industrialization encouraged rapid technological innovation and over the long term raised material standards of living in much of the world.

But the impact of industrialization went beyond economics, generating widespread and often unsettling social change as well. Early industrialists created a new work environment, the factory, which concentrated large numbers of workers under one roof to operate complicated machinery. By moving work outside the home, however, factories drew fathers, mothers, and children in different directions, altered traditional patterns of domestic life, and strained family relations in the industrial era.

Industrialization encouraged rapid urbanization and migration. New cities mushroomed to house workers who left the countryside for jobs in factories. Millions of migrants even crossed the seas in search of opportunities in new lands. Often, however, early industrial workers found themselves living in squalor and laboring under dangerous conditions.

Social critics and reformers worked to alleviate the problems of early industrial society. Despite their appeals, however, capitalism and industrialization flourished and spread rapidly from Britain to continental Europe, North America, and Asia. In some areas, notably western Europe and North America, industrialization was encouraged so that states could gain the economic advantages of industrialization. In other places, including Russia and Japan, industrialization was undertaken as part of a larger program of social, political, and economic reform to avoid domination by western European and American powers. Elsewhere, industrialization created a new international division of labor that made most of Africa, Asia, and Latin America economically dependent on the export of raw materials that supplied the factories and cities of the industrialized world. Thus, although industrialization and its effects spread unevenly and for different reasons, they profoundly influenced social and economic conditions all over the globe.

PATTERNS OF INDUSTRIALIZATION

Industrialization refers to a process that transformed agrarian and handicraft-centered economies into economies distinguished by industry and machine manufacture. The principal features of that process were technological and organizational changes that transformed manufacturing and led to increased productivity. Critical to industrialization were technological developments that made it possible to produce goods by machines rather than by hand and that harnessed inanimate sources of energy such as coal and petroleum. Also critical was the development of factory production, wherein workers assembled under one roof to produce goods in mass quantities. The need to invest in expensive factory equipment in turn encouraged the formation of large businesses: by the mid–nineteenth century many giant corporations had joined together to control trade through trusts and cartels.

Foundations of Industrialization

By the mid–eighteenth century, several areas of the world—Great Britain in western Europe, the Yangzi Delta in China, Japan—exhibited dynamic economies that shared many common features. High agricultural productivity resulted in significant population growth, and high population densities encouraged occupational specialization outside of agriculture. Navigable rivers and networks of canals facilitated trade and transport, and cities and towns supported sophisticated banking and financial institutions. At the same time, these sophisticated economies ran up against difficult ecological obstacles—especially soil depletion and deforestation—that threatened continued population growth and consumption levels. Despite their common features, Great Britain was the first to transcend these ecological constraints by exploiting coal deposits fortuitously found at home and natural resources found abroad.

Until the eighteenth century, wood had served as Great Britain's primary source of fuel for iron production, home heating, and cooking. Such extensive use of wood had resulted in serious wood shortages.

Coal and Colonies However, geographic luck had placed some of western Europe's largest coal deposits in Great Britain, within easy reach of water transport, centers of commerce, and pools of skilled labor. That fortunate conjunction encouraged the substitution of coal for wood, thus creating a promising framework for industrialization. Indeed, without easily accessible coal deposits, it was unlikely that the economy could have supported an expanding iron production and the application of steam engines to mining and industry—both crucial to the industrial process in Great Britain. In that respect Britain's experience differed from that of China, because the main coal-producing regions of northwest China were quite distant from the Yangzi Delta, China's most economically promising region for the development of industrialization. Thus, geography conspired against an important early shift from wood to coal in China.

The unique economic relationship between Europe and the Americas gave Great Britain additional ecological relief. The colonized lands of the Americas lifted European land constraints by supplying European societies with a growing volume of primary products. During the eighteenth century slave-based plantations supplied Europe with huge amounts of sugar and cotton; the former increased available food calories, and the latter kept emerging textile industries going. Neither of those products could have been grown in Europe. The significance of valuable American resources grew after 1830, when large amounts of grain, timber, and beef grown on colonial acreage traveled across the Atlantic to European destinations. In addition, American lands served as outlets for European manufactured goods as well as Europe's surplus population. Access to such overseas resources, in addition to coal deposits at home, provided a context—one not available to societies such as China—that increased the odds for an industrial breakthrough.

Industrial expansion in Britain began in the mid–eighteenth century with the textile industry, when consumer demand spurred a transformation of the British cotton industry. During the seventeenth century, English consumers had became fond of calicoes—inexpensive, brightly printed cotton textiles from India. Cotton cloth came into demand because it was lighter and easier to wash than wool, which was the principal fabric of European clothes before the nineteenth century. Although British wool producers tried to protect their industry through a series of laws designed to pro-hibit imports of cotton cloth in 1720 and 1721, they could not stifle public demand.

In fact, demand for cotton was so strong that producers had to speed up spinning and weaving to supply growing markets. To increase production they turned to inventions that rapidly mechanized the cotton textile industry. *Mechanization of the Cotton Industry* The first important technological breakthrough came in 1733 when Manchester mechanic John Kay invented the flying shuttle, which sped up the weaving process. Within a few years, inventors created several mechanical spinning devices, the most important of which was Samuel Crompton's "mule," built in 1779. In 1790 the mule was adapted for steam power, and it became the device of choice for spinning cotton. A worker using a steam-driven mule could produce a hundred times more thread than a worker using a manual spinning wheel.

The new spinning machines necessitated new weaving machines so that weavers could keep up with the production of thread. In 1785 Edmund Cartwright, a clergyman without experience in either mechanics or textiles, patented a water-driven power loom. Within two decades steam moved the power loom, and by the 1820s hand weavers were nearly obsolete. A young boy working on two power looms could produce fifteen times more cloth than the fastest hand weaver. Collectively, these technological developments permitted the mass production of inexpensive textile goods. By 1830 half a million people worked in the cotton business, Britain's leading industry, which accounted for 40 percent of exports.

The most crucial technological breakthrough of the early industrial era was the development of a general-purpose steam engine in 1765 by James Watt, an instrument maker at the University of Glasgow in Scotland. *Steam Power* Even before Watt's time, primitive steam engines had powered pumps that drew water out of coal mines, but those devices consumed too much fuel to be useful for other purposes. Watt's version relied on steam to force a piston to turn a wheel, whose rotary motion converted a simple pump into an engine. By 1800 more than a thousand of Watt's steam engines were in use in the British Isles. They were especially prominent in the textile industry, where they allowed greater productivity for manufacturers and cheaper prices for consumers.

The iron and steel industries also benefited from technological refinement, and the availability of inexpensive, high-quality iron and steel reinforced the move toward mechanization. After 1709 British smelters began to use coke (a purified form of coal) rather than more expensive charcoal as a fuel to pro-

Iron and Steel duce iron. As a result, British iron production skyrocketed during the eighteenth century, and prices to consumers fell.

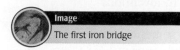

Inexpensive iron fittings and parts made industrial machinery stronger, and iron soon became common in bridges, buildings, and ships.

Steel is much harder, stronger, and more resilient than iron, but until the nineteenth century it was very expensive to produce. In 1856, however, Henry Bessemer built a refined blast furnace known as the Bessemer converter that made it possible to produce large quantities of steel cheaply. Steel production rose sharply, and steel quickly began to replace iron in tools, machines, and structures that required high strength.

Steam engineering and metallurgical innovations both contributed to improvements in transportation

Transportation technology. In 1815 George Stephenson, a self-educated Englishman, built the first steam-powered locomotive. In 1829 his Rocket won a contest by reaching a speed of 45 kilometers (28 miles) per hour. By the middle of the nineteenth century, refined steam engines of high efficiency also began to drive steamships.

Because they had the capacity to carry huge cargoes, railroads and steamships dramatically lowered transportation costs. They also contributed to the creation of transportation networks that linked remote interior regions and distant shores more closely than ever before in history. Between 1830 and 1870, British entrepreneurs laid about 20,000 kilometers (13,000 miles) of railroads, which carried some 322 million passengers as well as cargoes of raw materials and manufactured goods. Mean-

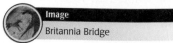

while, steamships proved their versatility by advancing up rivers to points that sailboats could not reach because of inconvenient twists or turns.

The Factory System

The factory system became the characteristic method of production in industrial economies. It began to emerge in the late eighteenth century, when technological advances transformed the British textile industry, and by the mid–nineteenth

The Factory

century most cotton production took place in factories. Many of the newly developed machines were too large and expensive for home use, so it became necessary to move work to centralized locations. That centralization of production brought together more workers doing specialized tasks than ever before.

The factory system with its new machines demanded a rational organization of job functions. Thus, the factory became associated with a new division of labor that called for a production process in which each worker performed a single task, rather than one in which a single worker completed the entire job, as was typical of handicraft traditions. This new division of labor allowed managers to improve worker productivity and realize spectacular increases in the output of manufactured goods. But the new environment also had unsettling effects on the nature of work. For instance,

Working Conditions

A woman working as a drawer in a British coal mine drags her coal cart with the aid of a belt and chain. Manually produced coal fueled the machines of early industrial society.

George Stephenson's North Star engine of 1837.

the factory system led to the emergence of an owner class whose capital financed equipment and machinery that were too expensive for workers to acquire. As a result, industrial workers became mere wage earners who depended on their employers for their livelihood. The repetitive and boring nature of many industrial jobs, moreover, left many workers alienated from their work and the products of their labor. In addition, any broad-range skills that workers may have previously acquired as artisans often became obsolete in the factory work environment. Between 1811 and 1816, that situation prompted organized bands of English handicraft workers known as Luddites to destroy textile machines that they blamed for their low wages and unemployment. Nevertheless, by hanging fourteen Luddites in 1813, the government served notice that it was unwilling to tolerate violence even against machines, and the movement gradually died out.

Equally disturbing was the new work discipline and the pace of work. Those accustomed to rural labor found that the seasons and fluctuations in the weather no longer dictated work routines. Instead, clocks, machines, and shop rules established new rhythms of work. Industrial workers commonly labored six days a week, twelve to fourteen hours a day. The factory whistle sounded the beginning and the end of each working day, and throughout the day workers had to keep pace with the movements of machines. At the same time, they faced strict and immediate supervision. Floor managers pressured men, women, and children to speed up production and punished them when they did not meet expectations.

In addition, dangerous work conditions often meant that early industrial workers faced the possibility of maiming or fatal accidents.

The Early Spread of Industrialization

For fifty years industrialization occurred only in Britain. Aware of their head start, British entrepreneurs and government officials forbade the export of machinery, manufacturing techniques, and skilled workers to other lands. Yet Britain's monopoly on industrialization did not last, because enterprising entrepreneurs ignored government regulations and sold machinery and technical know-how abroad. Moreover, European and North American businesspeople did not hesitate to bribe or even kidnap British engineers to learn the secrets of industrialization, and they also smuggled advanced machinery out of the British Isles.

As a result, by the mid–nineteenth century industrialization had spread to France, Germany, Belgium, and the United States. The earliest Continental center of industrial production was Belgium, where coal, iron, textile, glass, and armaments *Industrialization in Western Europe* production flourished in the early nineteenth century. About the same time, France also moved toward industrialization. By the mid–nineteenth century, French engineers and inventors were devising refinements and innovations that led to greater efficiencies, especially in metallurgical industries. Although German industrialization started off more slowly

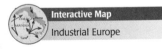

Interactive Map
Industrial Europe

than in France or Belgium, German coal and iron production soared after the 1840s, and by the 1850s an extensive railroad network was under construction. After unification in 1871, Bismarck's government sponsored rapid industrialization in Germany, especially of heavy industry.

Industrialization transformed North America as well as western Europe in the nineteenth century. American industrialization began in the 1820s when entrepreneurs lured *Industrialization in North America* British crafts workers to New England and built a cotton textile industry. By midcentury well over a thousand mills were producing fabrics from raw cotton grown in the southern states, and New England had emerged as a site for the industrial production also of shoes, tools, and handguns. In the

Map 27.1 Industrial Europe about 1850. Locate the places marked as emerging industrial areas. Are there any features those areas have in common? If so, what are they?

1870s heavy iron and steel industries emerged in areas such as western Pennsylvania and central Alabama where there were abundant supplies of iron ore and coal. By 1900 the United States had become an economic powerhouse, and industrialization had begun to spill over into southern Canada.

Industrial Capitalism

Cotton textiles were the major factory-made products during the early phase of industrialization, but the factory system soon spread to other industries. An important contribution to the evolving factory system came from the American inventor Eli Whitney (1765–1825). Though best

Mass Production

remembered as the inventor of the cotton gin (1793), Whitney also developed the technique of using machine tools to produce interchangeable parts in the making of firearms. This method meant that unskilled workers made only a particular part that fit every musket of the same model. Before long, entrepreneurs applied Whitney's method to the manufacture of everything from clocks and sewing machines to uniforms and shoes. By the middle of the nineteenth century, mass production of standardized articles was becoming the hallmark of industrial societies.

In 1913 Henry Ford improved manufacturing techniques further when he introduced the assembly line to automobile production. Instead of organizing production around a series of stations where workers assembled whole cars using standardized parts, Ford designed a conveyor system that allowed each worker to perform a specialized task at a fixed point on the assembly line. With the assembly line, workers churned out a complete chassis every 93 minutes instead of every 728 minutes under the old system. Such huge gains in productivity meant that car prices plummeted, allowing millions of ordinary people to purchase automobiles. The age of the motor car had arrived.

As the factory evolved, so too did the organization of business. Industrial machinery and factories were *The Corporation* expensive investments, and they encouraged businesses to organize on a large scale. During the 1850s and 1860s, government authorities in Britain and France laid the legal foundations for the modern corporation, which quickly became the most common form of business organization in industrial societies. A corporation was a private business owned by many investors who financed the business through the purchase of stocks representing shares in the company. When a corporation flourished, investors received dividends in proportion to their stake in the company. But if a corporation went bankrupt, laws protected shareholders from liability or financial loss beyond the extent of their investments—which made them extremely attractive to investors. By the late nineteenth century, corporations controlled most businesses requiring large investments in land, labor, or machinery.

To protect their investments, some big businesses of the late nineteenth century sought not only to outperform their competitors in the capitalist *Monopolies, Trusts, and Cartels* marketplace but also to eliminate competition. Business firms formed associations to restrict markets or establish monopolies in their industries. Large-scale business organizations formed trusts and cartels, both of which aimed to control the supply of a product and hence its price in the marketplace. Trusts commonly sought control of industries through vertical organization, by which they would dominate all facets of a single industry. John D. Rockefeller's Standard Oil Company and Trust, for example, controlled almost all oil drilling, processing, refining, marketing, and distribution in the United States.

Cartels, in contrast, tried to eliminate competition by means of horizontal organization, which involved the consolidation or cooperation of independent companies in the same business. Thus cartels sought to ensure the prosperity of their members by absorbing competitors, fixing prices, regulating production, or dividing up markets. By the end of the nineteenth century, some governments outlawed trusts and cartels. However, monopolistic practices continued well into the twentieth century.

INDUSTRIAL SOCIETY

Industrialization brought material benefits in its train: inexpensive manufactured products, rising standards of living, and population growth. Yet industrialization also unleashed dramatic social change. Immense internal and external migrations took place as people moved from the countryside to work in new industrial cities, and as Europeans crossed the Atlantic to seek opportunities in the western hemisphere. Industrialization also encouraged the emergence of new social classes and forced men, women, and children to adjust to distinctly new patterns of family and work life. Reformers sought to alleviate the social and economic problems that accompanied industrialization and worked toward the building of a more equitable and just society.

The Fruits of Industry

Industrialization brought efficiencies in production that flooded markets with affordable manufactured goods. Indeed, industrialization raised material standards of living in many ways. Industrial production led to dramatic reductions in the cost of clothing, for example, so by the early nineteenth century all but the desperately poor could afford several changes of clothes. Industrial factories turned out tools that facilitated agricultural work, and steam-powered locomotives delivered produce quickly and cheaply to distant markets. Consumers in early industrial Europe also filled their homes with more furniture, porcelain, and decorative objects than any but the most wealthy of their ancestors.

The populations of European and Euro-American peoples rose sharply during the eighteenth and nineteenth centuries, reflecting the rising prosperity and standards of living that came *Population Growth* with industrialization. Between 1700 and 1900 the population of Europe increased from 105 to 390 million. Demographic growth in the western hemisphere—fueled by migration from Europe—was even more remarkable. Between 1700 and 1900 the

Exhibitors from around the world displayed fine handicrafts and manufactured goods at the Crystal Palace exhibition of 1851 in London. Industrial products from Britain and the United States particularly attracted the attention of visitors to the enchanting and futuristic exhibition hall.

population of North America and South America rose from 13 million to 145 million.

The rapid population growth in Europe and the Americas reflected changing patterns of fertility and mortality. In most preindustrial societies fertility was high, but so was child mortality, which held population growth in check. High birthrates were common also in early industrializing societies, but death rates fell markedly because better diets and improved disease control reduced child mortality. By the late nineteenth century, better diets and improved sanitation led to declining levels of adult as well as child mortality. In combination, these two factors allowed populations to expand rapidly.

Beginning in the nineteenth century, however, industrializing lands experienced a social change known *The Demographic Transition* as the *demographic transition*. As industrialization transformed societies, fertility began a marked decline. In the short run, mortality fell even faster than fertility, so the populations of industrial societies continued to increase. Over time, however, declining birthrates led to lower population growth and relative demographic stability. The principal reason for declining fertility in industrial lands was voluntary birth control through contraception, perhaps because raising children cost more in industrial societies or because more children were likely to survive to adulthood than in the past.

Urbanization and Migration

Industrialization and population growth strongly encouraged migration and urbanization. Within industrial societies, migrants flocked from the countryside to urban centers in search of work. For example, in 1800 about one-fifth of the British population lived in towns and cities of 10,000 or more inhabitants. By 1900 three-quarters of the population worked and lived in cities. That pattern repeated itself elsewhere: by 1900 at least 50 percent of the population in industrialized lands lived in towns with populations of 2,000 or more. The increasing size of cities reflected this internal migration. In 1800 there were barely twenty cities in Europe with populations as high as 100,000, and there were none in the western hemisphere. By 1900 there were more than 150 large cities in Europe and North America combined.

With urbanization came intensified environmental pollution. Although cities have always been unsanitary places, the rapid increase in urban populations during the industrial age dramatically increased the magnitude and severity of water and air pollution. The widespread burning of fossil fuels fouled the air with vast quantities of chemicals and particulate matter. This

The Urban Environment

pollution led to occupational diseases in some trades. Chimney sweeps, for instance, contracted cancer of the scrotum from hydrocarbon deposits found in soot. Effluents from factories and mills as well as untreated sewage dirtied virtually every major river. No part of a city was immune to the constant stench coming from air and water pollution. Worse, tainted water supplies and unsanitary living conditions led to periodic epidemics of cholera and typhus. Until the latter part of the nineteenth century, urban environments remained dangerous places in which death rates commonly exceeded birthrates, and only the constant stream of new arrivals from the country kept cities growing.

Income determined the degree of comfort and security offered by city life. The wealthy typically tried to insulate themselves from urban discomforts by retreating to their elegant homes in newly growing suburbs. The working poor, in contrast, occupied overcrowded tenements lacking in comfort and amenities. The cramped spaces in apartments obliged many to share the same bed, increasing the ease of disease

transmission. The few open spaces outside the buildings were usually home to herds of pigs living in their own dung or were depositories for pools of stagnant water and human waste.

By the later nineteenth century, though, government authorities were tending to the problems of the early industrial cities. They improved municipal water supplies, expanded sewage systems, and introduced building codes that outlawed the construction of rickety tenements to accommodate poorly paid workers. Those measures made city life safer and brought improved sanitation. City authorities also built parks and recreational facilities to make cities more livable.

Rapid population growth in Europe also encouraged massive migration to the Americas, especially to the United States. During the nineteenth and early twentieth centuries, about fifty million Europeans migrated to the western hemisphere, which accounts for

Transcontinental Migration

much of the stunning demographic growth of the Americas. Many of the migrants intended to stay for only a few years and fully expected

Image
Immigration map, 1853

Squalid living conditions, ca. 1885. A group of people live in crowded conditions in one room, New York, USA.

to return to their homelands with a modest fortune made in the Americas. The vast majority, however, remained in the western hemisphere. They and their descendants transformed the Americas into Euro-American lands.

Industry and Society

Industrialization radically altered traditional social structures and helped bring new social classes into being. Enterprising businesspeople became fabulously *New Social Classes* wealthy and powerful enough to over-shadow the traditionally privileged classes. Less powerful than this new elite was the middle class, consisting of small business owners, factory managers, engineers, and professionals such as teachers, physicians, and attorneys. A large portion of industrial wealth flowed to the middle class, which benefited greatly from industrialization. Meanwhile, laborers who toiled in factories and mines constituted a new working class. Less skilled than the artisans and crafts workers of earlier times, the new workers tended to machines or provided heavy labor for low wages.

The most basic unit of social organization—the family—also underwent fundamental change during *Industrial Families* the industrial age. In preindustrial societies the family was the basic productive unit. Whether engaged in agriculture, domestic manufacturing, or commerce, family members worked together and contributed to the welfare of the larger group. Industrialization challenged the family economy and reshaped family life by moving economic production outside the home and introducing a sharp distinction between work and family life. Workers left their homes each day to labor an average of fourteen hours in factories, and family members led increasingly separate lives.

Men gained increased stature and responsibility in the industrial age as work dominated public life. *Men and the Industrial Revolution* Upper-class and middle-class men enjoyed especially increased prestige at home, since they usually were the sole providers who made their families' comfortable existence possible. Working-class men also enjoyed increased prestige because they tended to make wages far in excess of those of working-class women. As a result, their earnings usually constituted the bulk of their families' income.

Industrialization dramatically changed the terms of work for women. When industry moved produc-tion from the home to the factory, married women were unable to work unless they left their homes and children in someone else's care. Millions *Women and the Industrial Revolution* of working-class women had no choice but to work under such terms, but by the late nineteenth century middle-class society promoted the idea that respectable women should devote themselves to raising children, managing the home, and preserving family values rather than to paid labor.

For middle-class women, then, industrialization brought stringent confinement to the domestic sphere and pressure to conform to new models of behavior revolving around their roles as mothers and wives. Popular books such as *Woman in Her Social and Domestic Character* (1833) insisted that the ideal woman "knows that she is the weaker vessel" and takes pride in her ability to make the home a happy place. Meanwhile, in addition to working in factories, millions of working-class women worked as domestic servants for the growing middle class. In fact, one of every three European women became a domestic servant at some point in her life.

Industrialization profoundly influenced the childhood experience. Children in preindustrial societies had always worked in and around the *Child Labor* family home. However, industrial work, which took children away from home and parents for long hours with few breaks, made child labor seem especially pitiable and exploitative. Early reports from British textile mills described sensational abuses by overseers who forced children to work from dawn until dark and beat them to keep them awake. In the 1840s the British parliament began to pass laws regulating child labor and ultimately restricted or removed children from the industrial workforce. In the long term, urban industrial societies redefined the role of children. Motivated in part by the recognition that modern society demanded a skilled and educated labor force, governments established the legal requirement that education, and not work for monetary gain, was the principal task of childhood. In England, for instance, education for children aged five to ten became mandatory by 1881.

The Socialist Challenge

Among the most vocal and influential critics of early industrial society were the socialists, who worked to alleviate the social and economic problems generated by capitalism and industrialization. Socialists deplored economic inequalities, as represented by the vast difference in wealth between a captain of industry and a factory laborer, and they condemned the system that permitted the exploitation of laborers, especially women and children. Early socialists sought to expand the Enlightenment understanding of equality: they understood equality to have an economic as well as a political, legal, and social dimension, and they looked to the future establishment of a just and equitable society.

Most prominent of the nineteenth-century socialists were the German theorists Karl Marx (1818–1883) and Friedrich Engels (1820–1895). Marx and Engels believed that social problems of the nineteenth century were inevitable results of a capitalist economy. They held that capitalism divided people into two main classes, each with its own economic interests and social status: the capitalists, who owned industrial machinery and factories (which Marx and Engels called the means of production), and the proletariat, consisting of wageworkers who had only their labor to sell. Intense competition between capitalists trying to realize a profit resulted in ruthless exploitation of the working class. Moreover, according to Marx and Engels, the state and its coercive institutions, such as police forces and courts of law, functioned to enable capitalists to continue their exploitation of the proletariat. Even music, art, literature, and religion served the purposes of capitalists, according to Marx and Engels, since they amused the working classes and diverted attention from their misery.

Marx and Engels

Marx developed those views fully in a long, theoretical work called *Capital.* Together with Engels, Marx also wrote a short, spirited tract entitled *Manifesto of the Communist Party* (1848). In the *Manifesto* Marx and Engels aligned themselves with the communists, who worked toward the abolition of private property and the institution of a radically egalitarian society. The *Manifesto* asserted that all human history has been the history of struggle between social classes. It also argued that the future lay with the working class. Crises of overproduction, underconsumption, and diminishing profits would shake the foundations of the capitalist order. Meanwhile, members of the proletariat would come to view the forcible overthrow of the existing system as the only alternative available to them. Marx and Engels believed that a socialist revolution would result in a "dictatorship of the proletariat," which would abolish private property and destroy the capitalist

The Communist Manifesto

order. After the revolution was secure, the state would wither away. Coercive institutions would also disappear, since there would no longer be an exploiting class. Thus socialism would lead to a fair, just, and egalitarian society infinitely more humane than the capitalist order.

The doctrines of Marx and Engels came to dominate European and international socialism, and socialist parties grew rapidly throughout the nineteenth century. Political parties, trade unions, newspapers, and educational associations all worked to advance the socialist cause. Yet socialists disagreed strongly on the best means to reform society. Revolutionary socialists such as Marx and Engels urged workers to forcibly seize control of the state. In contrast, evolutionary socialists placed their hopes in representative governments and called for the election of legislators who supported socialist reforms.

Although socialists did not win control of any government until the Russian revolution of 1917, their critiques helped persuade government authorities to attack the abuses of early industrialization and provide more security for the working classes. In Britain, for example, Parliament prohibited underground employment for women and stipulated that children under the age of nine years not work more than nine hours a day. Beginning in 1832, a series of parliamentary acts also expanded the franchise for men by reducing property qualifications, preparing the way for universal male suffrage. In Germany in the 1880s, Otto von Bismarck introduced medical insurance, unemployment compensation, and retirement pensions to provide social security for working people in industrial society.

Social Reform

Trade unions also sought to advance the quest for a just and equitable society. As governments regulated businesses and enhanced social security, trade unions struggled to improve workers' lives by seeking higher wages and better working conditions for their members. Through most of the nineteenth century,

Trade Unions

Image
IWW demonstration

both employers and governments considered trade unions illegal associations whose purpose was to restrain trade. Yet trade unions persisted, and over the long run they improved the lives of working people and reduced the likelihood that a disgruntled proletariat would mount a revolution to overthrow industrial capitalist society.

Marx and Engels on Bourgeoisie and Proletarians

Karl Marx and Friedrich Engels were the most scathing critics of early industrial society. Indeed, their critique extended to industrial capitalism in general. In their view, contemporary society pitted capitalists (whom they called the bourgeoisie in their Manifesto of the Communist Party*) against proletarians. Marx and Engels argued that in the short term capitalists would exploit the proletarians, but that over the longer run proletarians would become aware of their misery, rise up, and destroy capitalist society.*

■   ■   ■

The history of all hitherto existing society is the history of class struggles.

Freeman and slave, patrician and plebeian, lord and serf, guild-master and journeyman, in a word, oppressor and oppressed, stood in constant opposition to one another, carried on an uninterrupted, now hidden, now open fight, a fight that each time ended, either in a revolutionary reconstitution of society at large, or in the common ruin of the contending classes. . . .

The modern bourgeois society that has sprouted from the ruins of feudal society has not done away with class antagonisms. It has but established new classes, new conditions of oppression, new forms of struggle in place of the old ones.

Our epoch, the epoch of the bourgeoisie, possesses, however, this distinctive feature: it has simplified the class antagonisms. Society as a whole is more and more splitting up into two great hostile camps, into two great classes directly facing each other: Bourgeoisie and Proletariat. . . .

The bourgeoisie has stripped of its halo every occupation hitherto honoured and looked up to with reverent awe. It has converted the physician, the lawyer, the priest, the poet, the man of science, into its paid wage-labourers. . . .

The need for a constantly expanding market for its products chases the bourgeoisie over the whole surface of the globe. It must nestle everywhere, settle everywhere, establish connexions everywhere. . . .

The weapons with which the bourgeoisie felled feudalism to the ground are now turned against the bourgeoisie itself.

But not only has the bourgeoisie forged the weapons that bring death to itself; it has also called into existence the men who are to wield those weapons—the modern working class—the proletarians.

In proportion as the bourgeoisie, i.e., capital, is developed, in the same proportion is the proletariat, the modern working class, developed—a class of labourers, who live only so long as they find work, and who find work only so long as their labour increases capital. These labourers, who must sell themselves piecemeal, are a commodity, like every other article of commerce, and are consequently exposed to all the vicissitudes of competition, to all the fluctuations of the market. . . .

The advance of industry, whose involuntary promoter is the bourgeoisie, replaces the isolation of the labourers, due to competition, by their revolutionary combination, due to association. The development of Modern Industry, therefore, cuts from under its feet the very foundation on which the bourgeoisie produces and appropriates products. What the bourgeoisie, therefore, produces, above all, is its own grave-diggers. Its fall and the victory of the proletariat are equally inevitable.

• *How did Marx and Engels's historical embrace of the concept of class struggle shape their understanding of the great forces clashing during this industrial age?*

SOURCE: Karl Marx and Friedrich Engels. *Manifesto of the Communist Party.* Trans. by Samuel Moore. London: W. Reeves, 1888.

Robert Koehler's painting *The Strike* depicts a situation verging on violence as workers mill about in a confrontation with factory owners and one angry laborer crouches to pick up a stone.

GLOBAL EFFECTS OF INDUSTRIALIZATION

Although early industrialization was a British, western European, and North American affair, it had deep global implications. In part this was because industrial powers used their tools, technologies, business organization, financial influence, and transportation networks to obtain raw materials from preindustrial societies around the world. Many lands that possessed natural resources were unable to maintain control over them because representatives of industrial countries dominated the commercial and financial institutions associated with their trade. Other societies, in particular Russia and Japan, saw the writing on the wall and embarked on huge industrialization programs of their own to stave off Euro-American domination.

The International Division of Labor

Industrialization influenced the economic and social development of many societies because it promoted a new international division of labor. Industrial societies needed minerals, agricultural products, and other raw materials to supply their factories, and they frequently obtained them from distant regions of the world.

Although large-scale global trade in agricultural products such as sugar, tea, and cotton was nothing new, industrial society fueled the demand for additional products as industrialists sought the natural resources and agricultural products of Africa, the Americas, Asia, Australia, and eastern Europe. The mechanization of the textile industry, for example, produced a demand for large quantities of raw cotton, which came mostly from India, Egypt, and the southern rim of the United States. Similarly, new industrial technologies increased demand for products such as rubber, the principal ingredient of the belts and tires that were essential to industrial machinery, which came from Brazil, Malaya, and the Congo River basin.

Economic Development

In some lands specialization in the production and export of primary goods paved the way for economic development and eventual industrialization. That pattern was especially noticeable in lands settled by European colonists, including Canada, Argentina, Uruguay, South Africa, Australia, and New Zealand, each of which experienced economic growth through the export of primary products and the infusion of foreign capital and labor. The same societies had an additional advantage in that they were high-wage economies. High incomes fostered economic development in two ways: they created flourishing markets, and they encouraged entrepreneurs to counteract high wages and labor security by inventing new labor-saving technologies.

Economic Dependence

In most of Latin America, sub-Saharan Africa, south Asia, and southeast Asia, however, dependence on exporting primary products such as sugar, cotton, and rubber resulted in little or no industrialization. Foreign investors owned and controlled the plantations that produced those crops, and most of the profits generated went abroad, depriving domestic economies of funds that might have contributed to the building of markets and industries. The low wages of plantation workers made the situation worse by dampening demand for manufactured goods. The result was the concentration of wealth in the hands of a small group of people, whether local or foreign, who contributed little to the creation of a domestic market. To compound the problem, both native and foreign financial interests adopted a free-trade policy that permitted unrestricted entry of foreign manufactures, further limiting opportunities for indigenous industrialization. Thus, although industrialization increasingly linked all the world's peoples in increasingly complex ways, its benefits and rewards went primarily to those who controlled the tools, capital, and trade rather than to those who provided the raw materials that made production possible.

The Continuing Spread of Industrialization: Russia and Japan

Industrialization brought great economic and military strength to societies that reconfigured themselves and relied on mechanized production. Their power encouraged other societies to seek their own paths to industrialization. Indeed, by the late nineteenth cen-

tury it had become clear to leaders in many preindustrial lands that unless they undertook programs of social, political, and economic reform, they would grow progressively weaker in relation to industrial powers. Faced with such a reality, after 1870 both Russia and Japan embarked on campaigns of rapid industrialization to strengthen their societies and enable them to resist military and economic pressures from western Europe and the United States.

Russia in 1870 was a multiethnic, multilingual, multicultural empire that stretched from Poland to the Pacific Ocean. The Romanov tsars ruled their diverse and sprawling realm through an autocratic regime in which all initiative came from the central administration. The tsars enjoyed the support of a powerful class of nobles who owned most of the land and were exempt from taxes and military duty. Peasants made up the vast majority of the population, and most of them were serfs bound to the lands that they cultivated.

Although the Russian army in the nineteenth century was huge, conflict with France and Britain in the Crimean War (1853–1856) clearly revealed the inability of Russian forces—based as they were on an agrarian economy—to compete with the industrial powers of western Europe. Military defeat compelled the tsarist autocracy to reevaluate the Russian social order and undertake an extensive program of reform along western European lines.

Emancipation of the Serfs

The key to social reform in Russia was emancipation of the serfs (1861), an institution many believed had become an obstacle to economic development. Indeed, Tsar Alexander II (reigned 1855–1881) emancipated the serfs partly with the intention of creating a mobile labor force for emerging industries, and the tsarist government encouraged industrialization as a way of strengthening the Russian empire. Thus, although Russian industrialization took place within a framework of capitalism, it differed from

Image
Tsar Alexander II

western European industrialization in that the motivation for development was political and military and the driving force was government policy rather than entrepreneurial initiative. Industrialization proceeded slowly at first, but it surged during the last two decades of the nineteenth century.

In Russia the tsarist government promoted industrialization by encouraging the construction of rail-

---

tsar (ZAHR)

Map 27.2 The Russian empire between 1801 and 1914. Note the sheer size of Russian territory in this period, and the fact that the state included parts of Europe, central Asia, and east Asia. How would straddling so much space and so many cultures have affected the processes of industrialization and nationalism in Russia?

roads to link the distant regions of the far-flung empire. In 1860 Russia had fewer than 1,100 kilometers *Railroads* (700 miles) of railroads, but by 1900 there were more than 58,000 kilometers (36,000 miles). Most impressive of the Russian railroads was the trans-Siberian line, constructed between 1891 and 1904, which stretched more than 9,000 kilometers (5,600 miles) and linked Moscow with the port of Vladivostok on the Pacific Ocean. Apart from drawing the regions of the Russian empire together, railroads stimulated the development of coal, iron, and steel industries and enabled Russia to serve as a commercial link between western Europe and east Asia.

Russian industry experienced explosive growth when Count Sergei Witte served as finance minister (1892–1903). Witte oversaw construction of the trans-Siberian railroad, and he worked to push Russian industrialization by reforming commercial law, protecting infant industries, supporting *The Witte System* steamship companies, and promoting nautical and engineering schools. He invited foreign investors to bring their capital and expertise to Russia, and he encouraged the establishment of savings banks to raise additional investment funds at home. By 1900 Russia produced half the world's oil, and Russian steel production ranked fourth in the world, behind that of the United States, Germany, and Britain. As a result of Witte's efforts, Russia also had enormous coal and iron industries, and government demand for weapons also supported a huge armaments industry.

Sergei Witte (SAYR-gay VIHT-tee)

Tsar Alexander II of Russia. After signing the Treaty of Paris in 1856, ending the Crimean War, Alexander abolished serfdom in the Russian empire.

Although Russia successfully began a program of industrialization, such efforts came at a high cost. As *Industrial Discontent* in other lands, industrial growth generated an urban working class, which endured miserable working and living conditions. Employers kept wages of overworked and poorly housed workers at the barest minimum. Moreover, economic exploitation and the lack of political freedom made workers increasingly receptive to socialist and revolutionary propaganda, which—when combined with further military defeat and political oppression—eventually undermined the Russian state itself in the early twentieth century.

In Japan, too, imperial authorities pushed industrialization, although under very different circumstances *Foreign Pressure* from those in Russia. Until 1853 Japan had largely closed itself off from interaction with European and American traders. The situation changed abruptly in that year, however, with the arrival of a U.S. naval squadron in Tokyo Bay. The American commander, Commodore Matthew C. Perry, trained his guns on the bakufu capital of Edo (modern Tokyo) and demanded that the shogun open Japan to diplomatic and commercial relations and sign a treaty of friendship. The shogun had no good alternative and so acquiesced to Perry's demands. Representatives of Britain, the Netherlands, and Russia soon won similar rights, all of which opened Japanese ports to foreign commerce, deprived the government of control over tariffs, and granted foreigners extraterritorial rights.

The sudden intrusion of foreign powers precipitated a domestic crisis in Japan that eventually resulted in the collapse of the Tokugawa bakufu and the restoration of imperial rule. After years of conflict and a brief civil war, the boy emperor Mutsuhito—known by his regnal name, Meiji ("Enlightened Rule")—took the reins of power on 3 January 1868.

The Meiji restoration returned authority to the Japanese emperor and marked the birth of a new Japan. Determined to gain parity with foreign powers, a conservative coalition of *The Meiji Restoration* daimyo, imperial princes, court nobles, and samurai formed a new government dedicated to the twin goals of prosperity and strength: "rich country, strong army." The Meiji government looked to the industrial lands of Europe and the United States to obtain the knowledge and expertise to strengthen Japan. The Meiji government sent many students and officials abroad to study everything from technology to constitutions, and it also hired foreign experts to facilitate economic development and the creation of indigenous expertise.

Economic initiatives were critical to the process of Meiji reconstruction. Convinced that a powerful economy was the foundation of national strength, the Meiji government created a *Economic Development* modern transportation, communications, and educational infrastructure. The establishment of telegraph, railroad, and steamship lines tied local and regional markets into a national economic network. Aiming to improve literacy rates, the government introduced a system of universal primary and secondary education. Universities provided advanced instruction for the best students, especially in scientific and technical fields. This infrastructure supported rapid industrialization and economic growth. Although most economic enterprises were privately owned, the government controlled military industries and established pilot programs to stimulate industrial development. During the 1880s the government sold most of its enterprises to private investors who had close ties to government officials. The result was a concentration of

---

Tokugawa (TOH-koo-GAH-wah)
Meiji (MAY-jee)
daimyo (DEYEM-yoh)

The Tomioka silk factory, established in the 1870s, was one of the earliest mechanized textile factories in Japan. In this factory, as in many textile mills in Europe and North America, male managers oversaw female factory workers.

enormous economic power in the hands of a small group of people, collectively known as *zaibatsu,* or financial cliques. By the early twentieth century, Japan had joined the ranks of the major industrial powers.

As in Russia, economic development came at a price, as the Japanese people bore the social and political costs of rapid industrialization. During this period, hundreds of thousands of rural families lived in destitution, haunted by malnutrition, starvation, and infanticide. In addition, those who took up work in the burgeoning industries learned that working

Costs of Economic Development

conditions were difficult and that the state did not tolerate labor organizations that promoted the welfare of workers.

Nevertheless, the desire to achieve political and economic equality with Euro-American industrial powers—and to avoid the domination and dependence experienced by preindustrial societies elsewhere—transformed Japan into a powerful industrial society in a single generation. Serving as symbols of Japan's remarkable development were the conclusion of an alliance with Britain as an equal power in 1902 and convincing displays of military prowess in victories over the Chinese empire (1894–1895) and the Russian empire (1904–1905).

zaibatsu (zeye-BAHT-soo)

SUMMARY

The process of industrialization involved the harnessing of inanimate sources of energy, the replacement of handicraft production with machine-based manufacturing, and the generation of new forms of business and labor organization. Along with industrialization came demographic growth, large-scale migration, and rapid urbanization, which increased the demand for manufactured goods by the masses of working people. Societies that underwent industrialization enjoyed sharp increases in economic productivity: they produced large quantities of high-quality goods at low prices, and their increased productivity translated into higher material standards of living. Yet industrialization brought costs as well as benefits. Family life changed dramatically in the industrial age as men, women, and children increasingly left their homes to work in factories and mines, often under appalling conditions. Socialist critics sought to bring about a more just and equitable society, and government authorities curtailed the worst abuses of the early industrial era. Meanwhile, industrialization increasingly touched the lives of peoples around the world. To avoid being dominated, Russia and Japan followed the lead of Britain, western Europe, and North America into industrialization, whereas many African, Asian, and Latin American lands became dependent on the export of raw materials to industrial societies.

CHRONOLOGY

1733	John Kay develops the flying shuttle
1765	James Watt patents an improved steam engine
1779	Samuel Crompton develops the spinning mule
1785	Edmund Cartwright develops the power loom
1797	Eli Whitney introduces interchangeable parts to the manufacturing process
1829	George Stephenson's locomotive, the Rocket, attains a speed of 45 kilometers (28 miles) per hour
1848	Karl Marx and Friedrich Engels publish *Manifesto of the Communist Party*
1849–1915	Life of Sergei Witte
1851	Crystal Palace exhibition in London
1853	Arrival of Commodore Perry in Japan
1853–1856	Crimean War
1855–1881	Reign of Tsar Alexander II
1856	Bessemer converter developed
1861	Emancipation of the Russian serfs
1868	Meiji restoration
1913	Henry Ford introduces the assembly line to the manufacture of automobiles

FOR FURTHER READING

William L. Blackwell. *The Industrialization of Russia: An Historical Perspective*. New York, 1982. A useful overview.

Daniel R. Headrick. *The Tentacles of Progress: Technology Transfer in the Age of Imperialism, 1850–1940*. New York, 1988. Concentrates on the political and cultural obstacles that hindered transfer of European technologies to colonial lands.

Marius B. Jansen and Gilbert Rozman, eds. *Japan in Transition: From Tokugawa to Meiji*. Princeton, 1986. Important collection of essays exploring economic and social change during the era of the Meiji restoration.

David S. Landes. *The Wealth and Poverty of Nations: Why Some Are So Rich and Some So Poor*. New York, 1998. A wide-ranging analysis arguing that social and cultural attitudes serve as the foundation of economic development.

Karl Marx and Friedrich Engels. *The Communist Manifesto*. Trans. by Samuel Moore. Harmondsworth, 1967. English translation of the most important tract of nineteenth-century socialism, with an excellent introduction by historian A. J. P. Taylor.

Kenneth Pomeranz. *The Great Divergence: China, Europe, and the Making of the Modern World Economy*. Princeton, 2000. Argues that the fortuitous location of coal deposits and access to the resources of the Americas created a uniquely advantageous framework for English industrialization.

Hans Rogger. *Russia in the Age of Modernisation and Revolution, 1881–1917*. New York, 1983. An important study of Russian social and economic development.

Peter N. Stearns. *The Industrial Revolution in World History*. Boulder, 1993. An excellent overview of industrialization, its European origins, its spread, and its effects in the larger world.

E. P. Thompson. *The Making of the English Working Class*. New York, 1966. A classic work that analyzes the formation of working-class consciousness in England from the 1790s to the 1830s.

Louise A. Tilly. *Industrialization and Gender Inequality*. Washington, D.C., 1993. A brief historiographical survey of debates on gender and industrialization in England, France, Germany, the United States, Japan, and China.

CHAPTER 28

The Americas in the Age of Independence

A village fish peddler, Fatt Hing Chin often roamed the coast of southern China in search of fish to sell at market. One day at the wharves, he heard a tale of mysterious but enticing mountains of gold beckoning young Chinese to cross the ocean. At nineteen years of age, Chin longed for the glittering mountains. He learned that he could purchase passage on a foreign ship, and in 1849 he boarded a Spanish ship to sail to California and join the gold rush.

Once at sea, Chin was surprised at the large number of young Chinese men crammed in with him in the ship's vomit-laden hold. Ninety-five difficult days and nights passed before the hills of San Francisco came into view. Upon arrival the travelers met Chinese veterans of life in the United States who explained the need to stick together if they were to survive and prosper.

Chin hired out as a gold miner, and after two years he accumulated his own little pile of gold. He wrote to his brothers and cousins, urging them to join him, and thus helped fuel the large-scale overseas migration of workers. Having made his fortune, though, Chin decided to return to China. Indeed, California gold provided him with the means to take a wife, build a house, and buy some land in his home country.

Although settled and prosperous, Chin longed for the excitement of California. Leaving his pregnant wife, he sailed for California again after only a year in China. He returned to mining with his brother, but the gold was more difficult to find. Inspired by the luck of another migrant, Tong Ling, who managed to get one

OPPOSITE PAGE: *Chinese immigrants employed to build the California railroads in the 1890s.*

dollar for each meal he sold, Chin's cousins in San Francisco decided to open a restaurant. Chin found the city much more comfortable than the mountains. "Let the others go after the gold in the hills," he said. "I'll wait for the gold to come to the city."

Fatt Hing Chin was one of the earliest Chinese migrants to settle in the Americas. His career path—from a miner in search of quick riches to an urban resident committed to a new homeland—was quite typical of Chinese migrants to the United States. Along with millions of others from Europe and Asia, Chinese migrants increased the ethnic diversity of American populations and stimulated political, social, and economic development in the western hemisphere.

During the late eighteenth and early nineteenth centuries, almost all the lands of the western hemisphere won their independence from European colonial powers. American peoples then struggled throughout the nineteenth century to build their own states and societies. The United States built the most powerful state in the western hemisphere and embarked on a westward push that brought most of the temperate regions of North America under U.S. control. Canada built a federal state under British Canadian leadership. The varied lands of Latin America built smaller states that often fell under the sway of local military leaders. One issue that most American peoples wrestled with, regardless of their region, was the legacy of the Enlightenment. The effort to build societies based on freedom, equality, and constitutional government was a monumental challenge that remained only partially realized. Indeed, Asian and European migrants joined freed slaves and native-born workers in labor systems—from plantations and factories to debt peonage—that often betrayed American promises of welcome and freedom.

The age of independence for the United States, Canada, and Latin America was a contentious era characterized by continuous mass migration and explosive economic growth, occasionally followed by deep economic stagnation, and punctuated with civil war, ethnic violence, class conflict, and battles for racial and sexual equality. Goals to build effective states, enjoy economic prosperity, and attain cultural cohesion were elusive throughout the nineteenth century and in many ways remain so even in the present day. Nevertheless, the histories of these first lands to win independence from colonial powers inspired other peoples who later sought freedom from imperial rule.

THE BUILDING OF AMERICAN STATES

After winning independence from Britain, the United States fashioned a government and began to expand rapidly to the west. Yet the United States was an unstable society composed of varied regions with diverse economic and social structures. Differences over slavery and the rights of individual states as opposed to the federal government sparked a bloody civil war in the 1860s. That conflict resulted in the abolition of slavery and the strengthening of the federal state. The experience of Canada was very different from that of the United States. Canada gained independence from Britain without fighting a war, and even though Canada also was a land of great diversity, it avoided falling into a civil war. Canada established a relatively weak federal government, which presided over provinces that had considerable power over local affairs. Latin American lands were even more diverse than their counterparts to the north, and there was never any real possibility that they could join together in a confederation. Throughout the nineteenth century Latin America was a politically fragmented region, and many individual states faced serious problems and divisions within their own societies.

The United States: Westward Expansion and Civil War

After gaining independence the United States faced the need to construct a government. During the 1780s leaders from the rebellious colonies drafted a constitution that entrusted responsibility for general issues to a federal government, reserved authority for local issues for individual states, and provided for the admission of new states and territories to the confederation. Originally, most states limited the vote to men of property, but the Enlightenment ideal of equality encouraged political leaders to extend the franchise: by the mid–nineteenth century almost all adult white men were eligible to vote.

While working to settle constitutional issues, Americans also began to expand to the west. After the American Revolution, Britain ceded to the new republic all lands between the Appalachian Mountains and the Mississippi River, and the United States doubled in size. In 1803 Napoleon Bonaparte allowed the United States to purchase France's Louisiana Ter-

Westward Expansion and Manifest Destiny

ritory, which extended from the Mississippi River to the Rocky Mountains. Overnight the United States doubled in size again. Between 1804 and 1806 a geographic expedition led by Meriwether Lewis and William Clark mapped the territory and surveyed its resources. Settlers soon began to flock west in search of cheap land to cultivate. By the 1840s many Americans spoke of a "manifest destiny" to occupy all of North America from the Atlantic to the Pacific Ocean.

Westward expansion brought settlers and government forces into conflict with the indigenous peoples of North America, who resisted efforts to push them from their ancestral lands and hunting grounds. However, U.S. officials and military forces supported Euro-American settlers and gradually forced the continent open to white expansion. With the Indian Removal Act of 1830, the United States government determined to move all Native Americans west of the Mississippi River into "Indian Territory" (Oklahoma). Among the tribes affected by this forced removal from the east were the

Conflict with Indigenous Peoples

Cherokees, who suffered a harrowing 800-mile migration from the eastern woodlands to Oklahoma on the Trail of Tears (1838–1839), so

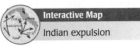

Interactive Map
Indian expulsion

known because thousands died from disease, starvation, and the difficulties of relocation.

After 1840 the site of conflict between Euro-American and indigenous peoples shifted to the plains region west of the Mississippi River. Settlers and ranchers in the trans-Mississippi west encountered peoples such as the Sioux, the Comanche, the Pawnee, and the Apache, who possessed firearms and outstanding equestrian skills. The native peoples of the plains offered effective resistance to encroachment by white settlers and at times won powerful victories over U.S. forces. In 1876, for example, thousands of Lakota Sioux and their allies annihilated an army under the command of Colonel George Armstrong Custer in the battle of Little Big Horn (in southern Montana). Ultimately, however, Native Americans on the plains lost

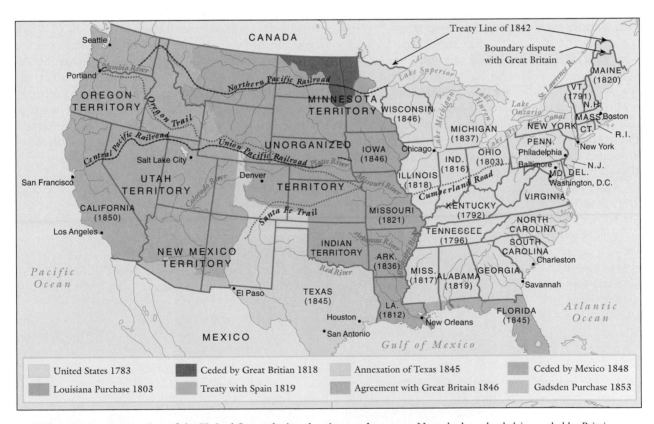

Map 28.1 Westward expansion of the United States during the nineteenth century. Note the large land claims ceded by Britain, France, and Mexico. Why were there no portions of North America purchased from or ceded by North American Indians?

the war against the forces of U.S. expansionism. U.S. forces employed cannons and deadly, rapid-fire Gatling guns against native peoples, which helped break native resistance and opened the western plains to U.S. conquest.

One last symbolic conflict took place in 1890 at Wounded Knee Creek in South Dakota. U.S. cavalry forces, hoping to suppress Sioux religious ceremonies that envisioned the disappearance of white people, chased the Sioux who were fleeing to safety in the South Dakota Badlands. At Wounded Knee Creek, a Sioux man accidentally shot off a gun, and the cavalry overreacted badly, slaughtering more than two hundred men, women, and children with machine guns. Emblematic of harsh U.S. treatment of native peoples, Wounded Knee represented the place where "a people's dream died," as a later native leader put it.

Westward expansion also generated tension between the United States and Mexico, whose territories included most of what is now the American southwest. Texas declared independence from Mexico in 1836, largely because the many American migrants who had settled there wanted to run their own affairs. In 1845 the United States accepted Texas as a new state—against vigorous Mexican protest— and moved to consolidate its hold on the territory. Those moves led to conflicts that rapidly escalated into the Mexican-American War (1845–1848). U.S. forces instigated the war and then inflicted a punishing defeat

The Mexican-American War

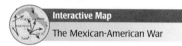

Interactive Map

The Mexican-American War

on the Mexican army. By the Treaty of Guadalupe Hidalgo (1848), the United States took possession of approximately one-half of Mexico's territory, paying a mere fifteen million dollars in exchange for Texas north of the Rio Grande, California, and New Mexico.

Westward expansion also created problems within the republic by aggravating tensions between regions. The most divisive issue had to do with slavery, which had vexed American politics since independence. The Enlightenment ideal of equality clearly suggested that the appropriate policy was to abolish slavery, but the framers of the Constitution recognized the sanctity of private property, including slaves. American independence initially promoted a surge of antislavery sentiment, and states from Delaware north abolished slavery within their jurisdictions. That move hardened divisions between slave and free states. Westward expansion aggravated tensions further by raising the question of whether settlers could extend slavery to newly acquired territories.

The election of Abraham Lincoln to the presidency in 1860 was the spark that ignited war between the states (1861–1865). Lincoln was an explicitly sectional candidate who *Sectional Conflict* was convinced that slavery was immoral and who was committed to free soil—territories without slavery. Although slavery stood at the center of the conflict, the Civil War also revolved around other important issues: the nature of the Union, states' rights as opposed to the federal government's authority, and the needs of a budding industrial-capitalist system against those of an export-oriented plantation economy.

This photograph of an 1890s Plains Indian camp in South Dakota offers an idealized, pastoral, and peaceful image of the disappearing indigenous societies in the United States.

The U.S. Civil War

Eleven southern states withdrew from the Union in 1860 and 1861, affirming their right to dissolve the Union and their support for states' rights. Northerners saw the situation differently. They viewed secession as illegal insurrection and an act of betrayal. They fought not only against slavery but also against the concept of a state subject to blackmail by its constituent parts. They also fought for a way of life—their emerging industrial society—and an expansive western agricultural system based on free labor.

Ultimately, the northern states prevailed. They brought considerable resources to the war effort—some 90 percent of the country's industrial capacity and approximately two-thirds of its railroad lines—but still they fought four bitter years against a formidable enemy. The consequences of that victory were enormous, for it ended slavery in the United States. Indeed, once Abraham Lincoln signed the Emancipation Proclamation on 1 January 1863, which made the abolition of slavery an explicit goal of the war, it was clear that a northern victory would entail radical changes in southern life. Moreover, the victory of the northern states ensured that the United States would remain politically united, and it enhanced the authority of the federal government in the American republic. Thus, as European lands were building powerful states on the foundations of revolutionary ideals, liberalism, and nationalism, the United States also forged a strong central government to supervise westward expansion and deal with the political and social issues that divided the American republic.

The Canadian Dominion: Independence without War

Autonomy and Division

Canada did not fight a war for independence, and in spite of deep regional divisions, it did not experience bloody internal conflict. Instead, Canadian independence came gradually as Canadians and the British government agreed on general principles of autonomy. The distinctiveness of the two dominant ethnic groups, the British Canadians and the French Canadians, ensured that the process of building an independent society would not be smooth, but intermittent fears about the possibility of a U.S. invasion from the south helped submerge ethnic differences. By the late nineteenth century, Canada was a land in control of its own destiny.

Originally colonized by trappers and settlers from both Britain and France, the colony of New France passed into the British empire after the British victory in the Seven Years' War (1756–1763). Until the late eighteenth century, however, French Canadians outnumbered British Canadians, so imperial officials made large concessions to their subjects of French descent to forestall unnecessary strife. After 1781, however, large numbers of British loyalists fled the newly formed United States and sought refuge in Canada, thus greatly enlarging the size of the English-speaking community there.

Ethnic divisions and political differences could easily have splintered Canada, but the War of 1812 stimulated a sense of unity against an external threat. The United States declared war on Britain in retaliation for

The grotesquely twisted bodies of dead northern soldiers lay near a fence outside Antietam, Maryland, in 1862. The Civil War was the most costly in U.S. history in number of lives lost.

encroachments on U.S. rights during the Napoleonic wars, and the British colony of Canada formed one of the front lines of the conflict. U.S. military leaders assumed that they could easily invade and conquer Canada to pressure Britain. Despite the greater resources of the United States, however, Canadian forces repelled U.S. incursions. Their victories promoted a sense of Canadian pride, and anti-U.S. sentiments became a means for covering over differences among French and British Canadians.

The War of 1812

After the War of 1812, Canada experienced an era of rapid growth. Expanded business opportunities drew English-speaking migrants, who swelled the population. This influx threatened the identity of Quebec, and discontent in Canada reached a critical point in the 1830s. The British imperial governors of Canada did not want a repeat of the American Revolution, so between 1840 and 1867 they defused tensions by expanding home rule in Canada and permitting the provinces to govern their own internal affairs.

Fear of U.S. expansion helped stifle internal conflicts among Canadians and prompted Britain to grant independence to Canada. The British North America Act of 1867 joined Quebec, Ontario, Nova Scotia, and New Brunswick and recognized them as the Dominion of Canada. Other provinces joined the Dominion later. Each province had its own seat of government, provincial legislature, and lieutenant governor representing the British crown. The act created a federal government headed by a governor-general, who acted as the British representative. An elected House of Commons and an appointed Senate rounded out the framework of governance. Without waging war, the Dominion of Canada had won control over all Canadian internal affairs, and Britain retained jurisdiction over foreign affairs until 1931.

Dominion

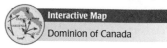

Interactive Map
Dominion of Canada

John A. Macdonald (1815–1891) became the first prime minister of Canada, and he moved to incorpo-

Map 28.2 The Dominion of Canada in the nineteenth century. Note the provinces that make up the modern state of Canada, and the dates in which they were incorporated into the Dominion. At what date were eastern and western Canada geographically united?

rate all of British North America into the Dominion. He negotiated the purchase of the huge Northwest Territories from the Hudson Bay Company in 1869, and he persuaded Manitoba, British Columbia, and Prince Edward Island to join the Dominion. Then, to strengthen the union, he oversaw construction of a transcontinental railroad, completed in 1885. The railroad facilitated transportation and communications throughout Canada and eventually helped bring new provinces into the Dominion: Alberta and Saskatchewan in 1905 and Newfoundland in 1949. Although maintaining ties to Britain and struggling to forge an identity distinct from its powerful neighbor to the south, Canada developed as a culturally diverse yet politically unified society.

Latin America: Fragmentation and Political Experimentation

Political unity was short-lived in Latin America. Simón Bolívar (1783–1830), hailed as the region's liberator, worked for the establishment of a large confederation that would provide Latin America with the political, military, and economic strength to resist encroachment by foreign powers. The wars of independence that he led encouraged a sense of solidarity in Latin America. But Bolívar once admitted, "I fear peace more than war," and after the defeat of the common colonial enemy, Latin America fragmented into numerous independent states.

Creole Elites and Political Instability Following the example of the United States, creole elites usually established republics with written constitutions for the newly independent states of Latin America. Yet Latin American leaders had less experience with self-government because Spanish and Portuguese colonial regimes were far more autocratic than was the British imperial government in North America. As a result, several Latin American lands lurched from one constitution to another as leaders struggled to create a machinery of government that would lead to political and social stability.

Creole elites also dominated the newly independent states and effectively prevented mass participation in public affairs. Less than 5 percent of the male population was active in Latin American politics in the nineteenth century, and millions of indigenous peoples lived entirely outside the political system. Those disillusioned with the system, then, had little choice beyond rebellion. To make matters worse, elites were divided by vocation—urban merchants versus rural landowners—as well as by ideology, whether liberalism, conservatism, secularism, or Roman Catholicism.

One thing elites agreed on was the policy of claiming land for agriculture and ranching by pushing aside indigenous peoples. Conflict was most intense on the plains of Argentina and Chile. During the mid–nineteenth century, as the United States was crushing native resistance to western expansion in North America, Argentine and Chilean forces brought modern weapons to bear in their campaign to conquer the indigenous peoples of the South American plains. By the 1870s colonists had pacified the most productive lands and forced indigenous peoples either to assimilate to Euro-American society or to retreat to marginal lands that were unattractive to cultivators and ranchers.

Conflicts with Indigenous Peoples

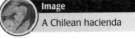
Image
A Chilean hacienda

Although creole elites agreed on the policy of conquering native peoples, division in the newly independent states helped *caudillos,* or regional military leaders, come to power in much of Latin America. The wars of independence had lasted well over a decade, and they provided Latin America with military rather than civilian heroes. After independence, military leaders took to the political stage by exploiting the discontent of the masses. One of the most notable caudillos was Juan Manuel de Rosas, who from 1835 to 1852 ruled an Argentina badly divided between the cattle-herding society of the pampas (the interior grasslands) and the urban elite of Buenos Aires. Rosas called for regional autonomy in an attempt to reconcile competing interests, but he worked to centralize the government he usurped. He quelled rebellions, but he did so in bloody fashion: one writer counted 22,404 victims murdered under Rosas's rule.

Caudillos

Rosas did what caudillos did best: he restored order. In doing so, however, he made terror a tool of the government, and he ruled as a despot through his own personal army. Yet although caudillo rule limited freedom and undermined republican ideals, it sometimes gave rise also to liberal opposition movements in favor of democratic forms of government.

Independent Mexico was a case in point. The Mexican-American War caused political turmoil in Mexico and helped the caudillo General Antonio López Santa Anna (1797–1876) come to power.

caudillos (KAHW-dee-yohs)

After the defeat and disillusion of the war, however, a liberal reform movement attempted to reshape Mexican society. Led by President Benito Juárez (1806–1872), a Mexican of indigenous ancestry, *La Reforma* of the 1850s aimed to limit the power of the military and the Roman Catholic church in Mexican society. The Constitution of 1857 set forth the ideals of *La Reforma*. It curtailed the prerogatives of priests and military elites, and it guaranteed universal male suffrage and other civil liberties, such as freedom of speech.

Mexico: War and Reform

La Reforma challenged the conservatism of Mexican elites, who led spirited opposition against it. In fact, divisions were so deep that conservatives forced the Juárez government out of Mexico City until 1861. During those difficult times, Juárez chose to suspend loan payments to foreign powers to lessen Mexico's financial woes, and that led to French, British, and Spanish intervention as Europeans sought to protect their investments in Mexico. France's Napoleon III even sent tens of thousands of troops to Mexico and proclaimed a Mexican empire.

Mexico: Revolution

Map 28.3 **The states of Latin America in the nineteenth century.** Note the many independent states that emerged from the independence movements early in the century. Why was it difficult for large, federated republics, such as the Republic of Colombia, founded by Simón Bolívar, to survive?

However, he was forced to withdraw French forces in 1867, and in the same year a Mexican firing squad killed the man he had appointed emperor, the Austrian archduke Maximilian (1832–1867). Juárez managed to restore a semblance of liberal government, but Mexico remained beset by political divisions.

By the early twentieth century, Mexico was a divided land moving toward civil war. The Mexican revolution (1911–1920), a bitter and bloody conflict, broke out when middle-class Mexicans joined with peasants and workers to overthrow the powerful dictator Porfirio Díaz (1830–1915). The revolt, which attempted to topple the grossly unequal system of landed estates—whereby fully 95 percent of all peasants remained landless—turned increasingly radical as rebels engaged in guerrilla warfare against government forces. The lower classes took up weapons and followed the revolutionary leaders Emiliano Zapata (1879–1919) and Francisco (Pancho) Villa (1878–1923), charismatic agrarian rebels who organized huge armies fighting for *tierra y libertad* (land and liberty). Zapata, the son of a mestizo peasant, and Villa, the son of a field worker, embodied the ideals and aspirations of the indigenous Mexican masses and enjoyed tremendous popular support. They discredited timid governmental efforts at reform and challenged governmental political control; Zapata himself confiscated hacienda lands and began distributing the lands to the peasants, while Villa attacked and killed U.S. citizens in retaliation for U.S. support of Mexican government officials.

Despite the power and popularity enjoyed by Zapata and Villa, they were unable to capture Mexico's major cities, and they did not command the resources and wealth of the government. The Mexican revolution came to an end soon after government forces ambushed and killed Zapata in 1919. Villa likewise was assassinated, on his ranch in 1923. Government forces regained control over a battered and devastated Mexico: as many as two million Mexicans may have died in the revolution. Although radicals such as Zapata and Villa were ultimately defeated, the Mexican Constitution of 1917 had already addressed some of the concerns of the revolutionaries by providing for land redistribution, universal suffrage, state-supported education, minimum wages and maximum hours for workers, and restrictions on foreign ownership of Mexican land and resources.

In the form of division, rebellion, caudillo rule, and civil war, instability and conflict plagued Latin America throughout the nineteenth century. Many

Zapata, hailing from the southern state of Morelos, was the very picture of a revolutionary leader, heavily armed and sporting his dashing, trademark moustache.

Latin American peoples lacked education, profitable employment, and political representation. Simón Bolívar himself once said that "independence is the only blessing we have gained at the expense of all the rest."

AMERICAN ECONOMIC DEVELOPMENT

During the nineteenth and early twentieth centuries, two principal influences—mass migration and British investment—shaped economic development throughout the Americas. But American states reacted in different ways to migration and foreign investment. The United States and Canada absorbed waves of migrants, exploited British capital, built industrial societies, and established economic independence. The fragmented states of Latin America were unable to follow suit, as they struggled with the legacies of colonialism, slavery, and economic dependence on single export crops. Throughout the Americas, however, life and labor for freed slaves, migrants, or industrial workers often proved arduous and at times heartbreaking, even as these American workers contributed to the economic development of the region.

Migration to the Americas

Underpinning the economic development of the Americas was the mass migration of European and Asian peoples to the United States, Canada, and Latin America. Gold discoveries in California and Canada drew prospectors hoping to make a quick fortune, but outnumbering gold prospectors were millions of European and Asian migrants who made their way to the factories, railroad construction sites, and plantations of the Americas. Following them were others who offered the support services that made life for migrant workers more comfortable and at the same time transformed the ethnic and cultural landscape of the Americas.

After the mid–nineteenth century, European migrants flocked to North America, where they filled the factories of the growing industrial economy of the United States. Their lack of skills made them attractive to industrialists seeking workers to operate ma-

chinery or perform heavy labor at low wages. By keeping labor costs down, migrants helped increase the profitability and fuel the expansion of U.S. industry. In the 1850s alone European migrants to the United States numbered 2.3 million—almost as many as had crossed the Atlantic during the half century from 1800 to 1850—and the volume of migration surged until the early twentieth century. In the first half of the century, migrants came mostly from Ireland, Scotland, Germany, and Scandinavia to escape high rents and indebtedness. By the late nineteenth century, most European migrants came from southern and eastern

Industrial Migrants

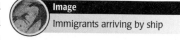
Image
Immigrants arriving by ship

Europe and included Poles, Russian Jews, Slavs, Italians, Greeks, and Portuguese. Without their labor, the remarkable industrial expansion that the United States experienced in the late nineteenth century would have been inconceivable.

Chinese migration grew rapidly after the 1840s, when British gunboats opened China to foreign influences. Between 1852 and 1875 some two hundred

Italian migrants construct a railway in New York. Italians were just one of many European groups coming to the Americas in the nineteenth century.

thousand Chinese migrated to California. Some, like Fatt Hing Chin, negotiated their own passage, but most traveled on indentured labor contracts that required them to cultivate crops or work on the Central Pacific Railroad. An additional five thousand Chinese entered Canada to search for gold in British Columbia or work on the Canadian Pacific Railroad.

Whereas migrants to the United States contributed to the development of an industrial society, those who

Plantation Migrants

went to Latin American lands mostly worked on agricultural plantations. Some Europeans figured among these migrants. About four million Italians sought opportunities in Argentina in the 1880s and 1890s, for example, and the Brazilian government paid Italian migrants to cross the Atlantic and work for coffee growers after the abolition of slavery there (1888).

Other migrants who worked on plantations in the western hemisphere came from Asia. More than fifteen thousand indentured laborers from China worked in the sugarcane fields of Cuba during the nineteenth century, and Indian migrants traveled to Jamaica, Trinidad, Tobago, and Guyana. Laborers from both China and Japan migrated to Peru, where they worked on cotton plantations, mined guano deposits, and helped build railroad lines. After the middle of the nineteenth century, expanding U.S. influence in the Pacific islands also led to Chinese, Japanese, Filipino, and Korean migrations to Hawai`i, where planters sought indentured laborers to tend sugarcane. About twenty-five thousand Chinese went to Hawai`i during the 1850s and 1860s, and later 180,000 Japanese also made their way to island plantations.

Economic Expansion in the United States

British investment capital in the United States proved crucial to the early stages of industrial development by helping businesspeople establish a textile industry.

British Capital

In the late nineteenth century, it also helped spur a vast expansion of U.S. industry by funding entrepreneurs who opened coal and iron ore mines, built iron and steel factories, and constructed railroad lines. The flow of investment monies was a consequence of Britain's own industrialization, which generated enormous wealth and created a need for investors to find profitable outlets for their funds.

Perhaps the most important economic development of the later nineteenth century was the construction of railroad lines that linked all U.S. regions and helped create an integrated national economy.

Railroads

Because of its enormous size and environmental diversity, the United States offered an abundance of natural resources for industrial exploitation. But vast distances made it difficult to maintain close economic ties between regions until a boom in railroad construction created a dense transportation, communication, and distribution network. Before the Civil War the United States had about 50,000 kilometers (31,000 miles) of railroad lines, most of them short routes east of the Mississippi River. By 1900 there were more than 320,000 kilometers (200,000 miles) of track, and the American rail network stretched from coast to coast.

Railroads decisively influenced American economic development. They provided cheap transportation for agricultural commodities, manufactured goods, and individual travelers. Railroads hauled grain, beef, and hogs from the plains states, cotton and tobacco from the south, lumber from the northwest, iron and steel from Pittsburgh, and finished products from the eastern industrial cities. Quite apart from the transportation services they provided, railroads spurred the development of other industries: they required huge amounts of coal, wood, glass, and rubber, and by the 1880s some 75 percent of U.S. steel went to the railroad industry. Railroads also required the development of new managerial skills to operate large, complicated businesses with multiple employees.

Railroads led to drastic changes in the landscape. Indeed, the westward expansion driven by the railroad led to large-scale land clearing and the extension of farming and mining lands

Space and Time

and brought about both human suffering for indigenous peoples and environmental damage through soil erosion and pollution. Railroads even shaped the American sense of time. Until rapid and regular rail transportation became available, communities set their clocks by the sun. As a result, New York time was eleven minutes and forty-five seconds behind Boston time. Those differences in local sun times created scheduling nightmares as well as the potential for train accidents. To simplify matters, in 1883 railroad companies divided the North American continent into four zones in which all railroad clocks read precisely the same time. The general public quickly adopted "railroad time," and in 1918 the U.S. government legally established the four time zones as the national standard.

In this lithograph of Frances F. Palmer's well-known painting *American Express Train* (ca. 1864), the railroad demonstrates its domination of the natural landscape and its role as the harbinger of change and industry.

AMERICAN EXPRESS TRAIN.

Led by railroads, the U.S. economy expanded at a blistering pace between 1870 and 1900. Inventors de-

Economic Growth

signed new products and brought them to market: electric lights, telephones, typewriters, phonographs, film photography, motion picture cameras, and electric motors all made their appearance during this era. Indeed, by the early twentieth century the United States had emerged as one of the world's major industrial powers.

Canadian Prosperity

British investment deeply influenced the development of the Canadian as well as the U.S. economy in the nineteenth and early twentieth centuries. Canadian leaders, like U.S. leaders, took advantage of British capital to industrialize without allowing their economy to fall under British control.

After the establishment of the Dominion, politicians started a program of economic development

The National Policy

known as the National Policy. The idea was to attract migrants, protect nascent industries through tariffs, and build national transportation systems. The centerpiece of the transportation network was the transcontinental Canadian Pacific Railroad, built largely with British investment capital and completed in 1885. The Canadian Pacific Railroad opened the western prairie lands to

commerce, stimulated the development of other industries, and promoted the emergence of a Canadian national economy. The National Policy created some violent altercations with indigenous peoples who resisted encroachment on their lands and with trappers who resented disruption of their way of life, but it also promoted economic growth and independence.

As a result of the National Policy, Canada experienced booming agricultural, mineral, and industrial production in the late nineteenth and early twentieth centuries. Canadian population surged as a result of both migration and natural increase. Migrants flocked to Canada's shores from Asia and especially from Europe: between 1903 and 1914 some 2.7 million eastern European migrants settled in Canada. Fueled in part by this population growth, Canadian economic expansion took place on the foundation of rapidly increasing wheat production and the extraction of rich mineral resources, including gold, silver, copper, nickel, and asbestos. Industrialists also tapped Canadian rivers to produce the hydroelectric power necessary for manufacturing.

Canada remained wary of its powerful neighbor to the south but did not keep U.S. economic influence entirely at bay. By 1918, Americans owned 30 percent of all Canadian in-

U.S. Investment

dustry, and thereafter the U.S. and Canadian economies became increasingly interdependent. Canada began to undergo rapid industrialization after the early twentieth century, as the province of Ontario benefited from the spillover of U.S. industry in the northeast.

Latin American Dependence

Latin American states did not undergo industrialization or enjoy economic development as did the United States and Canada. Colonial legacies are part of the explanation. Even when Spain and Portugal controlled the trade and investment policies of their American colonies, their home economies were unable to supply sufficient quantities of the manufactured goods that colonial markets demanded. As a result, they opened the colonies to British, French, and German trade, which in turn snuffed out local industries that could not compete with British, French, and German producers of inexpensive manufactured goods. Moreover, both in colonial times and after independence, Latin American elites retained control over local economies. Elites profited handsomely from European trade and investment and thus had little incentive to work toward economic diversification.

Foreign influence in Latin America generally took the form of investment, which brought handsome

British Investment profits and considerable control over Latin American economic affairs. In Argentina, for example, British investors encouraged the development of cattle and sheep ranching. After the 1860s and the invention of refrigerated cargo ships, meat became Argentina's largest export. British investors controlled the industry and reaped the profits, however, as Argentina became Britain's principal supplier of meat.

In a few lands, ruling elites made attempts to encourage industrialization, but with only limited suc-

Attempted Industrialization cess. The most notable of those efforts came when the dictatorial general Porfirio Díaz ruled Mexico (1876–1911). Díaz represented the interests of large landowners, wealthy merchants, and foreign investors. Under his rule, railroad tracks and telegraph lines connected all parts of Mexico and the production of mineral resources surged. A small steel industry produced railroad track and construction materials, and entrepreneurs also established glass, chemical, and textile industries. The capital, Mexico City, underwent a transformation during the Díaz years: it acquired paved streets, streetcar lines, and electric street lights. But the profits from Mexican enterprises did not support continuing industrial development. Instead, they went into

the pockets of the Mexican oligarchy and foreign investors who supported Díaz while a growing and discontented urban working class seethed with resentment at low wages, long hours, and foreign managers. Even as agriculture, railroad construction, and mining were booming, the standard of living for average Mexicans was declining in the late nineteenth century. Frustration with that state of affairs helps explain the sudden outbreak of violent revolution in 1911.

Despite a large proportion of foreign and especially British control, Latin American economies expanded rapidly in the late nineteenth century. Exports drove this growth: copper and silver from Mexico, bananas from Central America, rubber and coffee from Brazil, beef and wheat from Argentina, copper from Chile, and tobacco and sugar from Cuba. Other areas in the world also developed many of these same products for export, however, and competition for markets tended to drive prices down. As in the A coffee hacienda
United States and Canada, foreign investment in Latin America provided capital for development, but unlike the situation in the northern lands, control over industries and exports remained in foreign hands. Latin American economies were thus subject to decisions made in the interests of foreign investors, and unstable governments could do little in the face of strong foreign intervention. Controlled by the very elites who profited from foreign intervention at the expense of their citizens, Latin American governments helped promote the region's economic dependence, despite growth in industrial and export economies.

AMERICAN CULTURAL AND SOCIAL DIVERSITY

Much of the allure of the Americas derived from their vast spaces and diverse populations. While diversity distinguished the Americas, it also provided abundant fuel for conflicts between ethnic groups, social classes, and those segregated by race or gender. The social and cultural diversity of American societies challenged their ability to achieve cultural cohesion as well as democratically inclusive states. The lingering legacies of European conquest, slavery, migration, and patriarchy highlighted contradictions between the Enlightenment ideals of freedom and equality and the realities of life for native and African-American peoples as well as recent migrants and women. In efforts to maintain their own position and preserve social stability, the dominant political forces in the Americas often repressed demands for recognition by dispossessed groups.

Multicultural Society in the United States

By the late nineteenth century, the United States had become a boisterous multicultural society whose population included indigenous peoples, Euro-American settlers, African-American laborers, and growing numbers of migrants from Europe and Asia. The poet Walt Whitman described the United States as "not merely a nation but a teeming nation of nations." Yet political and economic power rested almost exclusively with white male elites of European ancestry. The United States experienced tension and occasional conflict as members of various constituencies worked for dignity, prosperity, and a voice in society.

As they expanded to the west, Euro-American settlers and ranchers pushed indigenous peoples onto *Native Peoples* reservations. Begrudging Native Americans even those meager lands, the United States embarked in the latter half of the nineteenth century on a policy designed to reduce native

autonomy even further through laws and reforms aimed at assimilating tribes to the white way of life. The U.S. government and private citizens acted to undermine or destroy outright the bases of native cultural traditions. For example, government officials removed native children from their families and tribes and enrolled them in white-controlled boarding schools. These schools, such as the Carlisle Indian School and the Toledo Indian School, illustrated the extent to which white society sought to eliminate tribal influences and inculcate Christian, U.S. values. Tribal languages as well as native dress and hair fashions were banned, further distancing the children from their cultures. Native Americans, however, resisted those forms of assimilation, and over the following decades tribes rebuilt and reaffirmed native identities.

The Civil War ended slavery, but it did not bring about equality for freed slaves and their African-American descendants. In an effort to *Freed Slaves* establish a place for freed slaves in American society, northern forces sent armies of occupation to the southern states and forced them to undergo a program of social and political reconstruction (1867–1877). They extended civil rights to freed slaves and provided black men with voting rights. People in

The Apache youths at the Carlisle Indian School offer stark faces to the camera, suggesting their discontent with reform efforts directed at assimilation through education.

A lithograph from *Harper's Weekly* after the Civil War. An artisan, a middle-class African-American, and a black Union soldier are in the process of voting, perhaps for the first time in their lives.

pursue careers over marriage. Yet meaningful economic and political opportunities for women awaited the twentieth century.

Migrants

Between 1840 and 1914 some twenty-five million European migrants landed on American shores, and in the late nineteenth century most of them hailed from southern and eastern European countries. Migrants introduced new foods, music, dances, holidays, sports, and languages to U.S. society and contributed to the cultural diversity of the western hemisphere. Yet white, native-born citizens of the United States began to feel swamped by the arrival of so many migrants. Indeed, concerns about growing numbers of migrants with different cultural and social traditions eventually led to the exclusion of new arrivals from Asian lands: the U.S. government ordered a complete halt to migration from China in 1882 and Japan in 1908.

Canadian Cultural Contrasts

Ethnic Diversity

British and French settlers each viewed themselves as Canada's founding people. That cleavage, which profoundly influenced Canadian political development, masked much greater cultural and ethnic diversity in Canada. French and British settlers displaced the indigenous peoples, who remain a significant minority of Canada's population today. Slavery likewise left a mark on Canada. Slavery was legal in the British empire until 1833, and many early settlers brought their slaves with them to Canada. After emancipation, blacks in Canada were free but not equal, segregated and isolated from the political and cultural mainstream. Chinese migrants also came to Canada: lured by gold rushes such as the Fraser River rush of 1858 and by opportunities to work on the Canadian Pacific Railway in the 1880s, Chinese migrants lived mostly in segregated Chinatowns in the cities of British Columbia, and like blacks they had little voice in public affairs. Between 1896 and 1914 three million migrants from Britain, the United States, and eastern Europe arrived in Canada, bringing even greater ethnic diversity with them.

Despite the heterogeneity of Canada's population, communities descended from British and French settlers dominated Canadian society, and conflict between the two communities was the most prominent source of ethnic tension throughout the nineteenth and twentieth centuries. After 1867, as British Canadians led the effort to settle the Northwest Territories

southern states elected biracial governments for the first time in U.S. history, and freed slaves participated actively in the political affairs of the republic.

After Reconstruction, however, the armies of occupation went home, and a violent backlash soon dismantled the reforms of Reconstruction. By the turn of the century, U.S. blacks faced violence and intimidation when they tried to vote. Southern states fashioned a rigidly segregated society that deprived the African-American population of educational, economic, and political opportunities. Although freedom was better than slavery, it was far different from the hopeful visions of the slaves who had won their emancipation.

Women

Even before the Civil War, a small but growing women's movement had emerged in the United States. At the Seneca Falls Convention in 1848, feminists issued a declaration arguing "that all men and women are created equal" and demanding equal political and economic rights. Women fought for equal rights throughout the nineteenth century, and new opportunities for education and employment offered alternatives to marriage and domesticity. Women's colleges, reform activism, and professional industrial jobs allowed some women to

SOURCES FROM THE PAST

The Meaning of Freedom for an Ex-Slave

Even before the conclusion of the Civil War brought slavery to an end in the United States, Jourdan Anderson had taken the opportunity to run away and claim his freedom. After the war his former master, Colonel P. H. Anderson, wrote a letter asking him to return to work on his Tennessee plantation. In responding from his new home in Dayton, Ohio, Anderson respectfully referred to the colonel as "my old master" and addressed him as "sir." Yet Anderson's letter makes it clear that his family's freedom and welfare were his principal concerns.

■ ■ ■

I want to know particularly what the good chance is you propose to give me. I am doing tolerably well here; I get $25 a month, with victuals and clothing; have a comfortable home for Mandy (the folks here call her Mrs. Anderson), and the children, Milly, Jane and Grundy, go to school and are learning well; the teacher says Grundy has a head for a preacher. They go to Sunday-School, and Mandy and me attend church regularly. We are kindly treated; sometimes we overhear others saying, "Them colored people were slaves" down in Tennessee. The children feel hurt when they hear such remarks, but I tell them it was no disgrace in Tennessee to belong to Col. Anderson. Many darkies would have been proud, as I used to was, to call you master. Now, if you will write and say what wages you will give me, I will be better able to decide whether it would be to my advantage to move back again.

As to my freedom, which you say I can have, there is nothing to be gained on that score, as I got my freepapers in 1864 from the Provost-Marshal-General of the Department at Nashville. Mandy says she would be afraid to go back without some proof that you are sincerely disposed to treat us justly and kindly—and we have concluded to test your sincerity by asking you to send us our wages for the time we served you. This will make us forget and forgive old scores, and rely on your justice and friendship in the future. I served you faithfully for thirty-two years and Mandy twenty years. At $25 a month for me, and $2 a week for Mandy, our earnings would amount to $11,680. Add to this the interest for the time our wages has been kept back and deduct what you paid for our clothing and three doctor's visits to me, and pulling a tooth for Mandy, and the balance will show what we are in justice entitled to. Please send the money by Adams Express, in care of V. Winters, esq, Dayton, Ohio. If you fail to pay us for faithful labors in the past we can have little faith in your promises in the future. We trust the good Maker has opened your eyes to the wrongs which you and your fathers have done to me and my fathers, in making us toil for you for generations without recompense. Here I draw my wages every Saturday night, but in Tennessee there was never any pay day for the negroes any more than for the horses and cows. Surely there will be a day of reckoning for those who defraud the laborer of his hire.

In answering this letter please state if there would be any safety for my Milly and Jane, who are now grown up and both good-looking girls. You know how it was with poor Matilda and Catherine. I would rather stay here and starve and die if it comes to that than have my girls brought to shame by the violence and wickedness of their young masters. You will also please state if there has been any schools opened for the colored children in your neighborhood, the great desire of my life now is to give my children an education, and have them form virtuous habits.

- *In what clever ways does Jourdan Anderson test the seriousness of his former owner's offer of employment, and what does his approach say about the meaning of black freedom?*

SOURCE: Leon F. Litwack. *Been in the Storm So Long: The Aftermath of Slavery.* New York: Knopf, 1979, pp. 334–35.

and incorporate them into the Dominion, frictions between the two groups intensified. Westward expansion brought British Canadian settlers and cultivators into conflict with French Canadian fur traders, lumberjacks, and métis of mixed French and Indian ancestry.

The Métis and Louis Riel

Indeed, a major outbreak of civil strife took place in the 1870s and 1880s. Native peoples and métis had moved west throughout the nineteenth century to preserve their land and trading rights, but the drive of British Canadians to the west threatened them. Louis Riel (1844–1885), who was himself a métis, emerged as the leader of the métis and indigenous peoples of western Canada. Of particular importance was his leadership in the resistance to the Canadian Pacific Railroad—and the white settlement it promised to bring—during the 1880s. In 1885 he organized a military force of métis and native peoples in the Saskatchewan river country and led an insurrection known as the Northwest Rebellion. Canadian forces quickly subdued the makeshift army, and government authorities executed Riel for treason. Although the Northwest Rebellion never had a chance of success, the execution of Riel nonetheless threatened to undermine the beginnings of Canadian national unity and foreshadowed a long term of cultural conflict between Canadians of British, French, and indigenous ancestry.

Ethnicity, Identity, and Gender in Latin America

The heritage of Spanish and Portuguese colonialism and the legacy of slavery inclined Latin American societies toward the establishment of hierarchical distinctions based on ethnicity and color. At the top of society stood the creoles, individuals of European ancestry born in the Americas; indigenous peoples, freed slaves, and their black descendants occupied the lowest rungs of the social ladder. In between were various groups of mixed ancestry, such as mestizos, mulattoes, zambos, and castizos. Although most Latin American states ended the legal recognition of these groups, the distinctions themselves persisted and limited their opportunities.

Large-scale migration brought cultural diversity to Latin America in the nineteenth century. Indentured laborers who went from Asian lands to Peru, Brazil, Cuba, and other Caribbean destinations carried with them many of their native cultural practices. When their numbers were relatively large, as in the case of Indian migrants to Trinidad and Tobago, they formed distinctive communities in which they observed their inherited cultural and social traditions.

Migration and Cultural Diversity

Migration of European workers to Argentina brought a lively diversity to the capital of Buenos Aires, which was perhaps the most cosmopolitan city of nineteenth-century Latin America. With its broad avenues, smart boutiques, and handsome buildings graced with wrought iron, Buenos Aires enjoyed a reputation as "the Paris of the Americas."

Gauchos

One prominent symbol of Latin American identity was Argentina's gauchos (cowboys). Most gauchos were mestizos or castizos, but there were also white and black gauchos. In fact, anyone who adopted gaucho ways became a gaucho, and gaucho society acquired an ethnic egalitarianism rarely found elsewhere in Latin America. Gauchos were most prominent in the Argentine pampas, but their cultural practices linked them to the cowboys, or vaqueros, found throughout the Americas. As pastoralists herding cattle and horses on the pampas, gauchos stood apart from both the indigenous peoples and the growing urban and agricultural elites who gradually displaced them with large landholdings and cattle ranches that spread to the pampas.

Male Domination

Even more than in the United States and Canada, male domination was a central characteristic of Latin American society in the nineteenth century. Women could not vote or hold office, nor could they work or manage estates without permission from their male guardians. In rural areas, women were liable to rough treatment and assault by gauchos and other men steeped in the values of *machismo*—a social ethic that honored male strength, courage, aggressiveness, assertiveness, and cunning. A few women voiced their discontent with male domination and machismo. Although Latin American lands did not generate a strong women's movement, they did begin to expand educational opportunities for girls and young women after the mid–nineteenth century. In large cities most girls received some formal schooling, and women usually filled teaching positions in the public schools that proliferated throughout Latin America in the late nineteenth century.

---

gauchos (GAHW-chohs)
vaqueros (bah-KEH-rohs)

SUMMARY

After gaining independence from European colonial powers, the states of the western hemisphere worked to build stable and prosperous societies. The independent American states faced difficult challenges as they sought to construct viable societies on the Enlightenment principles of freedom, equality, and constitutional government. The United States and Canada built large federal societies in North America, whereas a series of smaller states governed affairs in Latin America. Throughout the hemisphere descendants of European settlers subdued indigenous American peoples and built societies dominated by Euro-American peoples. They established agricultural economies, exploited natural resources, and in some lands launched processes of industrialization. They accepted streams of European and Asian migrants, who contributed to American cultural diversity. All American lands experienced tensions arising from social, economic, cultural, and ethnic differences, which led occasionally to violent civil conflict and often to smoldering resentments and grievances. The making of independent American societies was not a smooth process, but it reflected the increasing interdependence of all the world's peoples.

CHRONOLOGY

1803	Louisiana Purchase
1804–1806	Lewis and Clark expedition
1812–1814	War of 1812
1838–1839	Trail of Tears
1845–1848	Mexican-American War
1848	Seneca Falls Convention
1849	California gold rush
1850s	*La Reforma* in Mexico
1861–1865	U.S. Civil War
1867	Establishment of the Dominion of Canada
1867	French troops withdraw from Mexico
1867–1877	Reconstruction in the United States
1869	Completion of the transcontinental railroad line in the United States
1876	Battle of Little Big Horn
1876–1911	Rule of Porfirio Díaz in Mexico
1885	Completion of the Canadian Pacific Railroad
1885	Northwest Rebellion
1890	Massacre at Wounded Knee
1911–1920	Mexican revolution

FOR FURTHER READING

Colin G. Calloway. *First Peoples: A Documentary Survey of American Indian History.* Boston, 1999. A fine text on native American history, written by a knowledgeable scholar in the field.

Fernando Henrique Cardoso and Enzo Faletto. *Dependency and Development in Latin America.* Berkeley, 1979. A sophisticated treatment of economic development in Latin America.

William Cronon. *Nature's Metropolis: Chicago and the Great West.* New York, 1991. A valuable study exploring the role of Chicago in the economic development of the American west.

Tulio Halperín Donghi. *The Contemporary History of Latin America.* Trans. by J. C. Chasteen. Durham, 1993. An influential general history of Latin America from a Latin American point of view.

Ellen C. DuBois. *Feminism and Suffrage: The Emergence of an Independent Women's Movement in America, 1848–1869.* Ithaca, 1984. Traces the rise and character of the U.S. women's movement in the nineteenth century.

Patricia Nelson Limerick. *The Legacy of Conquest: The Unbroken Past of the American West.* New York, 1987. A provocative work exploring the influences of race, class, and gender in the conquest of the American west.

Leon F. Litwack. *Been in the Storm So Long: The Aftermath of Slavery.* New York, 1979. The best study of the promises and perils of life for freed slaves after the U.S. Civil War.

J. R. Miller. *Skyscrapers Hide the Heavens: A History of Indian-White Relations in Canada.* Toronto, 1989. An important study of Canadian policies toward indigenous peoples.

Walter Nugent. *Crossings: The Great Transatlantic Migrations, 1870–1914.* Bloomington, 1992. Provides an overview and analysis of the mass migrations to North America in the nineteenth and twentieth centuries.

Ronald Takaki. *A Different Mirror: A History of Multicultural America.* Boston, 1993. A spirited account of the contributions made by peoples of European, African, Asian, and Native American ancestry to the modern American society.

CHAPTER 29

The Building of Global Empires

F ew Europeans had traveled to south Africa by the mid–nineteenth century, but the discovery of diamonds and rich gold deposits brought European settlers to the region in large numbers. Among the arrivals was Cecil John Rhodes, an eighteen-year-old student at Oxford University, who in 1871 went to south Africa in search of a climate that would relieve his tuberculosis. While there, Rhodes bought claims in the diamond fields, and he bought the rights to others' claims when they looked promising. By 1889, at age thirty-five, he had almost monopolized diamond mining in south Africa, and he controlled 90 percent of the world's diamond production. With ample financial backing, Rhodes also built up a healthy stake in the gold-mining business and entered politics, serving as prime minister (1890–1896) of the British Cape Colony.

Yet Rhodes's ambitions went far beyond business and local politics. In his vision the Cape Colony would serve as a base of operations for the extension of British control to all of Africa. Under Rhodes's guidance, Cape Colony annexed Bechuanaland (modern Botswana) in 1885, and in 1895 it added Rhodesia (modern Zambia and Zimbabwe) to its holdings. But Rhodes's plan did not stop with Africa: he urged the expansion of the British empire until it embraced all the world, including the United States of America. Rhodes considered British imperial expansion as a duty to humankind: "We are the finest race in the world," he said in 1877, "and the more of the world we inhabit, the better it is for the human race." In his sense of superiority to other peoples, his compulsion to expand, and his craving to extract wealth from distant parts of the world, Rhodes

OPPOSITE PAGE: *The battle of Omdurman on the Nile River, 2 September 1898.*

represented well the views of European imperialists who carved the world into colonies during the nineteenth century.

From the days of ancient Mesopotamia and Egypt to the present, strong societies have often sought to dominate their weaker neighbors by subjecting them to imperial rule. Yet during the second half of the nineteenth century, a handful of western European states wrote a new chapter in the history of imperialism. Strong nationalist sentiments enabled them to mobilize their populations for purposes of overseas expansion. Industrialization equipped them with the most effective tools and the most lethal weapons available anywhere in the world. Three centuries of experience with maritime trade in Asia, Africa, the Americas, and Oceania provided them with unparalleled knowledge of the world and its peoples. With those advantages, western European peoples conquered foreign armies, dominated foreign economies, and imposed their hegemony throughout the world. Toward the end of the century, the United States and Japan joined European states as imperial powers.

The establishment of global empires had far-reaching effects. In many ways, imperialism tightened links between the world's societies. Imperial powers encouraged trade between dominant states and their overseas colonies, for example, and they organized mass migrations of laborers to work in agricultural and industrial ventures. Yet imperialism also fostered divisions between the world's peoples. Powerful tools, deadly weapons, and global hegemony tempted European peoples to consider themselves superior to their subjects throughout the world: modern racism is one of the legacies of imperialism. Another effect of imperialism was the development of both resistance and nationalism in subject lands. Thus, although formal empires almost entirely dissolved in the twentieth century, the influence of global imperialism continues to shape the contemporary world.

FOUNDATIONS OF EMPIRE

In nineteenth-century Europe, proponents of empire advanced a variety of political, economic, and cultural arguments to justify the conquest and control of foreign lands. The imperialist ventures that they promoted enjoyed dramatic success partly because of the increasingly sophisticated technologies developed by European industry.

Motives of Imperialism

The building of empires is an old story in world history. By the nineteenth century, however, European observers recognized that empires of their day were different from those of earlier times. Accordingly, about midcentury they began to speak of *imperialism,* and by the 1880s the recently coined term had made its way into popular speech and writing throughout western Europe. In contemporary usage, imperialism refers to the domination over subject lands in the larger world. Sometimes that domination came through formal imperialism, which involved military conquest and the establishment of political control. Frequently, however, it arose through what is known as informal imperialism: that is, the domination of trade, investment, and business activities that enabled imperial powers to profit from subject societies and influence their affairs without going to the trouble of exercising direct political control.

Modern Imperialism

Like the building of empires, the establishment of colonies in foreign lands is a practice dating from ancient times. In modern times, however, colonialism refers not just to the settlement of colonists in new lands but also to the political, social, economic, and cultural structures that enabled imperial powers to dominate subject lands. In some places, such as North America, Chile, Argentina, Australia, New Zealand, and South Africa, European powers established settler colonies populated largely by migrants from the home societies. Yet contemporary scholars also speak of European colonies in India, southeast Asia, and sub-Saharan Africa, even though European migrants did not settle there in large numbers. European agents, officials, and businesspeople effectively turned such places into colonies by controlling their domestic and foreign policies, integrating local economies into the network of global capitalism, and promoting European educational and cultural preferences.

Modern Colonialism

During the second half of the nineteenth century, many Europeans came to believe that imperial expansion and colonial domination were crucial for the survival of their societies. A wide range of motives encouraged European peoples to launch campaigns of domination, conquest, and control. Some advocates argued that imperialism was in the economic interests of European societies as well as individuals. They

Economic Motives of Imperialism

Cecil Rhodes resting in the goldfields of South Africa, about 1897.

pointed out that overseas colonies could serve as reliable sources of raw materials: rubber, tin, and copper were vital industrial products, for example, and by the late nineteenth century petroleum had also become a crucial industrial resource.

Geopolitical arguments were also important for justifying imperialism. Even if colonies were not economically beneficial, imperialists held that it was crucial for political and military reasons to maintain them. Some overseas colonies occupied strategic sites on the world's sea lanes, and others offered harbors or supply stations for commercial and naval ships. Advocates of imperialism sought to gain those advantages for their own states and to deny them to rivals.

Political Motives of Imperialism

Imperialism had its uses also for domestic politics. In an age when socialists and communists directly confronted industrialists, European politicians and national leaders sought to defuse social tension and inspire patriotism by focusing public attention on foreign imperialist ventures. Even spiritual motives fostered imperialism. Like the Jesuits in the early modern era, missionaries flocked to African and Asian lands in search of converts to Christianity, and their spiritual campaigns provided a powerful religious justification for imperialism. Furthermore, missionaries often facilitated communications between imperialists and subject peoples, and they sometimes provided European officials with information they needed to maintain control of overseas colonies.

While missionaries sought to introduce Christianity to subject peoples, their goals were compatible with those of other Europeans who sought to bring them "civilization" in the form of political order and social and cultural enlightenment. French imperialists routinely invoked the *mission civilisatrice* ("civilizing mission") as justification for their expansion into Africa and Asia, and other European powers routinely justified foreign intervention as their duty to civilize "backward" peoples.

Cultural Motives of Imperialism

Tools of Empire

Even the strongest motives would not have enabled imperialists to impose their rule throughout the world without the powerful technological advantages of industrialization. During the nineteenth century, industrialists devised effective technologies of transportation, communication, and war that enabled European imperialists to have their way in the larger world.

The most important innovations in transportation involved steamships and railroads. During the 1830s British naval engineers adapted steam power to military uses and built large, ironclad ships equipped with powerful guns. These steamships traveled much faster than any sailing vessel, and as an additional advantage they could ignore the winds and travel in any direction. Because of that, they could travel much farther upriver

Transportation Technologies

SOURCES FROM THE PAST

Rudyard Kipling on the White Man's Burden

Rudyard Kipling lived in northern India for the first six years of his life. He grew up speaking Hindi, and he mixed easily with Indian subjects of the British empire. After attending a boarding school in England, he returned to India in 1882 and became a journalist and writer. Many of his works express his deep enchantment with India, but he also believed strongly in imperial rule. Indeed, he wrote his famous poem titled "The White Man's Burden" to encourage the United States to impose colonial rule in the Philippines. Although recognizing the unpopularity of foreign rule, Kipling considered it a duty to bring order to colonial lands and to serve subject peoples.

■   ■   ■

Take up the White Man's burden—
    Send forth the best ye breed—
Go bind your sons to exile
    To serve your captives' need;
To wait in heavy harness,
    On fluttered folk and wild—
Your new-caught, sullen peoples,
    Half-devil and half-child.

Take up the White Man's burden—
    In patience to abide,
To veil the threat of terror
    And check the show of pride;
By open speech and simple,
    An hundred times made plain,
To seek another's profit,
    And work for another's gain.

Take up the White Man's burden—
    The savage wars of peace—
Fill full the mouth of Famine
    And bid the sickness cease;
And when your goal is nearest
    The end for others sought,
Watch Sloth and heathen Folly
    Bring all your hope to nought.

Take up the White Man's burden—
    No tawdry rule of kings,
But toil of serf and sweeper—
    The tale of common things.

The ports ye shall not enter,
    The roads ye shall not tread,
Go make them with your living,
    And mark them with your dead.
Take up the White Man's burden—
    And reap his old reward:
The blame of those ye better,
    The hate of those ye guard—
The cry of hosts ye humor
    (Ah, slowly!) toward the light;—
"Why brought ye us from bondage,
    "Our loved Egyptian night?"

Take up the White Man's burden—
    Ye dare not stoop to less—
Nor call too loud on Freedom
    To cloak your weariness;
By all ye cry or whisper,
    By all ye leave or do,
The silent, sullen peoples
    Shall weigh your Gods and you.

Take up the White Man's burden—
    Have done with childish days—
The lightly proffered laurel,
    The easy, ungrudged praise.
Comes now, to search your manhood
    Through all the thankless years,
Cold, edged with dear-bought wisdom,
    The judgment of your peers!

• *Compare and contrast the sorts of adjectives Kipling uses to describe native peoples as opposed to Europeans; how does his very language usage convey his sense of white superiority?*

SOURCE: Rudyard Kipling. "The White Man's Burden." *McClure's Magazine* 12, no. 4 (1899): 290–91.

than sailboats, which enabled imperialists to project power deep into the interior regions of foreign lands.

The construction of new canals enhanced the effectiveness of steamships. Both the Suez Canal (constructed 1859–1869) and the Panama Canal (constructed 1904–1914) facilitated the building and main-

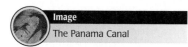

tenance of empires by enabling naval vessels to travel rapidly between the world's seas and oceans. They also lowered the costs of trade between imperial powers and subject lands.

Once imperialists had gained control of overseas lands, railroads helped them to maintain their hegemony and organize local economies to their own advantage. Rail transportation enabled colonial officials and armies to travel quickly through the colonies. It also facilitated trade in raw materials and the distribution of European manufactured goods in the colonies.

European industrialists also churned out enormous quantities of increasingly powerful weapons. By the middle of the nineteenth century, European armies were using breech-loading firearms with rifled bores that were far more accurate and reliable than any other firearm. By the 1870s Europeans were experimenting with rifled machine guns, and in the 1880s they adopted the Maxim gun, a light and powerful weapon that fired eleven bullets per second.

Military Technologies

These firearms provided European armies with an arsenal vastly stronger than any other in the world. Accurate rifles and machine guns devastated opposing overseas forces, enabling European armies to impose colonial rule against far more numerous opponents. In 1898, for example, a British army with twenty machine guns and six gunboats encountered a Sudanese force at Omdurman, near Khartoum on the Nile River. During five hours of fighting, the British force lost 368 men, whereas machine guns and explosive charges fired from gunboats killed some 11,000 Sudanese. The battle of Omdurman opened the door for British colonial rule in Sudan.

Communications also benefited from industrialization. In the 1830s it took as long as two years for a British correspondent to receive a reply to a letter sent to India by sailing ship. By the 1850s, after the introduction of steamships, correspondence could make the round-trip between London and Bombay

Communications Technologies

in four months. With the opening of the Suez Canal in 1869,

steamships traveled from Britain to India in less than two weeks.

The invention of the telegraph made it possible to exchange messages even faster. By 1870 submarine cables carried messages between Britain and India in about five hours. By 1902 cables linked all parts of the British empire throughout the world, and other European states maintained cables to support communications with their own colonies. Their monopoly on telegraphic communications allowed imperial officials to rapidly mobilize forces to deal with troubles, and the telegraph allowed merchants to respond quickly to developments of economic and commercial significance. Rapid communication was an integral structural element of empire.

EUROPEAN IMPERIALISM

Aided by powerful technologies, European states launched an unprecedented round of empire building in the second half of the nineteenth century. Imperial expansion began with the British conquest of India. Competition between imperial powers led to European intrusion into central Asia, the establishment of colonies in southeast Asia, and interference in the Ottoman and Qing empires in southwest and east Asia. Fearful that rivals might gain control over remaining regions, European states embarked on a campaign of frenzied expansion in the 1880s that brought almost all of Africa and Pacific Ocean territories into their empires.

The British Empire in India

The British empire in south Asia and southeast Asia grew out of the mercantile activities of the English East India Company, which enjoyed a monopoly on English trade with India. The East India Company obtained permission from the Mughal emperors of India to build fortified posts on the coastlines. In the seventeenth century, company merchants traded mostly for Indian pepper and cotton, Chinese silk and porcelain, and spices from southeast Asia. During the eighteenth century, tea and coffee became the most prominent trade items, and European consumers acquired a permanent taste for both beverages.

After the death of the emperor Aurangzeb in 1707, the Mughal state entered a period of decline.

Company Rule   The East India Company took advantage of Mughal weakness to strengthen and expand its trading posts. In the 1750s company merchants began campaigns of outright conquest in India, largely to protect their commercial interests. From their forts at Calcutta, Madras, and Bombay, the merchants extended their authority inland and won official rights to rule from the Mughal emperors and local authorities. They enforced their rule with armies composed mostly of Indian troops known as sepoys.

In 1857, following widespread campaigns of conquest that left most of the subcontinent under British control, the Indian sepoys of the Bengal army revolted. The Sepoy Rebellion, as it became known, was quickly augmented by civilian peasants and disgruntled elites in north-central India who were deeply dissatisfied with recent British policies regarding taxation and law. To regain control, the British waged a bloody campaign of retribution in which many thousands of Indians—including civilians not directly involved in the rebellion—lost their lives through summary hangings and the destruction of villages. Once order was restored in 1858, the British government abolished the East India Company and assumed direct rule over the subcontinent.

Under the new administration, Queen Victoria (reigned 1837–1901) assigned responsibility for Indian policy to the newly established office of secretary of state for India. A viceroy represented British royal authority and administered the colony through an elite Indian civil service staffed almost exclusively by the English. Indians served in *British Imperial Rule* low-level bureaucratic positions, but British officials formulated all domestic and foreign policy in India.

Under both company rule and direct colonial administration, British rule transformed India. To profit from India's enormous size and wealth, British officials cleared forests and encouraged the cultivation of crops, such as tea, coffee, and opium, that were especially valuable trade items. They restructured landholdings and ensured that land taxes financed the costs of British rule. They built extensive railroad and telegraph networks that tightened links between India and the larger global economy. They also constructed new canals, harbors, and irrigation systems to support commerce and agriculture.

Especially after 1857, British colonial authorities made little effort to promote Christianity. They did, however, establish English-style schools for the children of Indian elites, and they suppressed Indian customs that conflicted with European law or values. Most prominent of those customs were sati (the practice of widows burning themselves on their husbands' funeral pyres), infanticide, and slavery.

Mughal (MOO-guhl)

sati (suh-TEE)

Warships provide covering fire as British troops prepare to storm the Burmese port of Rangoon in 1824.

Imperialism in Southeast Asia

As the East India Company and British colonial agents tightened their grip on India, competition among European states kindled further empire-building efforts.

The Dutch East Indies   In southeast Asia, Dutch officials tightened their control and extended their authority throughout the Dutch East Indies, the archipelago that makes up the modern state of Indonesia. Along with cash crops of sugar, tea, coffee, and tobacco, exports of rubber and tin made the Dutch East Indies a valuable and productive colony.

In the interests of increasing trade between India, southeast Asia, and China, British imperialists moved in the nineteenth century to establish a presence in southeast Asia. By the 1880s they had established colonial authority in Burma, which became a source of teak, ivory, rubies, and jade. In 1824 Thomas Stamford Raffles founded the port of Singapore, which soon became the busiest center of trade in the Strait of Melaka. Administered by the colonial regime in India, Singapore served as the base for the British conquest of Malaya (modern Malaysia) in the 1870s and 1880s. Besides offering ports that enabled the British navy to control sea lanes linking the Indian Ocean with the South China Sea, Malaya provided abundant supplies of tin and rubber.

British Colonies in Southeast Asia

French imperialists built the large southeast Asian colony of French Indochina, consisting of the modern states of Vietnam, Cambodia, and Laos, between 1859 and 1893. Like their British counterparts in India,

Map 29.1 Boundaries of imperial territories in Asia about 1914 (dates in parentheses indicate year of conquest). Note the claims made by various industrial powers. Which territories remained unclaimed, and why? Which power claimed the most imperial territory in Asia?

French colonial officials introduced European-style schools and sought to establish close connections with native elites. Unlike their rivals,

French Indochina

French officials also encouraged conversion to Christianity, and as a result the Roman Catholic church became prominent throughout French Indochina, especially Vietnam. By century's end, all of southeast Asia had come under European imperial rule except for the kingdom of Siam (modern Thailand), which preserved its independence largely because colonial officials regarded it as a convenient buffer state between British-dominated Burma and French Indochina.

Informal Domination in the Ottoman and Qing Empires

As in India, the Indonesian islands, and Vietnam, European powers in the nineteenth century frequently seized territories outright and ruled them as colonies. More frequently, however, European (and later U.S.) forces used their economic and military power to force concessions out of militarily weak societies. They won rights for businesses to seek opportunities on favorable terms, gained influence in political affairs, and enabled industrial capitalists to realize huge profits without going to the trouble and expense of establishing formal colonies. In the last half of the nineteenth century, two formerly powerful societies—the Ottoman and the Qing empires—increasingly came under such informal domination as each struggled with military weakness and internal problems in contrast to the industrialized and competitive nation-states of Europe. Although reform movements emerged in both lands, the results were inadequate, and by the early twentieth century both empires were still firmly in the grip of foreign domination.

By the late seventeenth century, it was already clear that Ottoman forces lagged behind European armies

Military Decline

in strategy, tactics, weaponry, and training. Loss of military power translated into declining effectiveness of the central government, which was losing power in the provinces to its own officials. In addition, although the Ottoman government managed to maintain its authority in Anatolia as well as in Iraq, it suffered serious territorial losses in the Caucasus, central Asia, and the Balkan provinces of Greece (independent 1830) and Serbia (independent 1867).

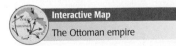

Interactive Map
The Ottoman empire

Most significant, however, was the loss of Egypt. In 1798 the ambitious French general Napoleon invaded Egypt in hopes of using it as a springboard for an attack on the British empire in India. His campaign was a miserable failure, but the invasion sparked turmoil in Egypt, as local elites battled to seize power after Napoleon's departure. The ultimate victor was the energetic general Muhammad Ali, who built a powerful army modeled on European forces and ruled Egypt from 1805 to 1848. He also launched a program of industrialization, concentrating on cotton textiles and armaments. Although he remained nominally subordinate to the Ottoman sultan, by 1820 he had established himself as the effective ruler of Egypt, which was the most powerful land in the Muslim world. He even invaded Syria and Anatolia, threatening to capture Istanbul and topple the Ottoman state. Indeed, the Ottoman dynasty survived only because British forces intervened out of fear that Ottoman collapse would result in a sudden and dangerous expansion of Russian influence.

Meanwhile, European textiles and manufactured goods began to flow into the Ottoman empire in the eighteenth and nineteenth centuries. Because these items were inexpensive and high-quality products, they placed consid-

Economic Difficulties

erable pressure on Ottoman artisans and crafts workers. Gradually, the Ottoman empire moved toward financial dependency on Europe. After the middle of the nineteenth century, economic development in the Ottoman empire depended heavily on foreign loans, as European capital financed the construction of railroads, utilities, and mining enterprises. Interest payments grew to the point that they consumed more than half of the empire's revenues. In 1882 the Ottoman state was unable to pay interest on its loans and had no choice but to accept European administration of its debts.

Nothing symbolized foreign influence more than the capitulations, agreements that exempted European visitors from Ottoman law and provided European powers with extraterritoriality—the right to exercise jurisdiction over

The Capitulations

their own citizens according to their own laws. Capitulations also served as instruments of economic penetration by European businesspeople who established tax-exempt banks and commercial enterprises in the Ottoman empire, and they permitted foreign governments to levy duties on goods sold in Ottoman ports.

In response to recurring and deepening crises, Ottoman leaders launched a series of reforms designed to strengthen and preserve the state. In the early nineteenth century, a significant period of reform occurred under the leadership of sultan Mahmud II (reigned 1808–1839). Mahmud's program remodeled Ottoman institutions along western European lines, especially in the creation of a more effective army. Before long, Ottoman recruits wore European-style uniforms and studied at military and engineering schools that taught European curricula. Equally important, Mahmud's government created a system of secondary education for boys to facilitate the transition from mosque schools, which provided most primary education, to newly established scientific, technical, and military academies. To make his authority more effective, the sultan established European-style ministries, constructed new roads, built telegraph lines, and inaugurated a postal service. By the time of Mahmud's death in 1839, the Ottoman empire had shrunk in size, but it was also more manageable and powerful than it had been since the early seventeenth century.

The Reforms of Mahmud II

Continuing defeats on the battlefield and the rise of separatist movements among subject peoples, however, prompted the ruling classes to undertake even more radical reforms during the Tanzimat ("reorganization") era (1839–1876). In designing their program, Tanzimat reformers drew considerable inspiration from Enlightenment thought and the constitutional foundations of western European states. One of their primary aims was to make Ottoman law more acceptable to Europeans so they could have the capitulations lifted and recover Ottoman sovereignty. Among the most important Tanzimat reforms were those that guaranteed public trials, rights of privacy, and equality before the law for all Ottoman subjects, whether Muslim or not. By 1869 educational reforms also provided free and compulsory primary education for all children. Yet even though reform and reorganization strengthened Ottoman society, the Tanzimat also provoked spirited opposition. Harsh criticism came from religious conservatives, who argued that reformers posed a threat to the empire's Islamic foundation. Perhaps most dangerously, the Ottoman bureaucracy itself criticized Tanzimat reforms because they believed that too much power was concentrated in the hands of the sultan.

The Tanzimat Era

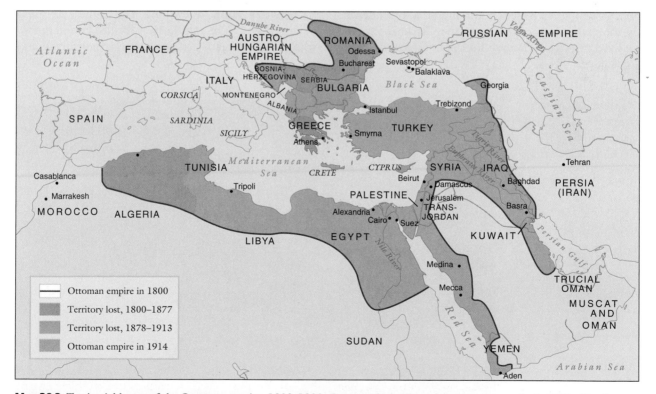

Map 29.2 Territorial losses of the Ottoman empire, 1800–1923. Compare the borders of the Ottoman empire in 1800 with what was left of the empire in 1914. What might have been the strategic value of the remaining Ottoman territories?

The despotic reign of Abdül Hamid II (reigned 1876–1909) only seemed to confirm such criticisms, and a variety of liberal opposition groups grew up to oppose his rule.

The Young Turks

Among the most articulate were those whose members were familiar with European society, and who believed above all else that Ottoman society was in dire need of a written constitution that defined and limited the sultan's power. The most active dissident organization was the Ottoman Society for Union and Progress, better known as the Young Turk Party. Founded in 1889 by exiled Ottoman subjects living in Paris, the Young Turk Party vigorously called for universal suffrage, equality before the law, freedom of religion, free public education, secularization of the state, and the emancipation of women. In 1908 the Young Turks inspired an army coup that forced Abdül Hamid to reinstate a constitution he had abandoned at the start of his reign. In 1909 they dethroned him and established Mehmed V Rashid (reigned 1909–1918) as a puppet sultan. Throughout the Young Turk era (1908–1918), Ottoman sultans reigned but no longer ruled.

Yet in spite of their efforts to shore up the ailing empire, reformers could not turn the tide of decline: Ottoman armies continued to lose wars, and subject peoples continued to seek autonomy or independence. By the early twentieth century, the Ottoman empire survived principally because European diplomats could not agree on how to dispose of the empire without upsetting the European balance of power.

The Chinese empire experienced even more difficulties than the Ottoman empire in the nineteenth century. Qing problems became serious in the early nineteenth century when *The Opium Trade* officials of the British East India Company began to trade in opium—rather than silver—in exchange for the Chinese silks, porcelains, and teas so coveted by Europeans. Trade in opium was illegal in China, but it expanded rapidly for decades because Chinese authorities made little effort to enforce the law. By the late 1830s, however, government officials had become aware that China had a trade problem and a drug problem as well. In 1839 the government took active steps to halt the trade, which included the destruction of some twenty thousand chests of opium.

Outraged, British commercial agents pressed their government into a military retaliation designed to reopen the opium trade. The ensuing conflict, known as the Opium War *The Opium War* (1839–1842), made plain the military power differential between Europe and China. The Chinese navy and infantry were no match for their British counterparts, who relied on steam power and modern firearms, and

Chinese opium smokers. Chinese efforts to stop opium imports led to a humiliating defeat in the Opium War.

in 1842 the Chinese government sued for peace. China experienced similar military setbacks throughout the second half of the nineteenth century in conflicts with Britain and France (1856–1858), France (1884–1885), and Japan (1894–1895).

In the wake of those confrontations came a series of pacts collectively known in China as unequal

Unequal Treaties treaties, which curtailed China's sovereignty. The Treaty of Nanjing (1842), which ended the British war against the Chinese, ceded Hong Kong Island in perpetuity to Britain, opened five Chinese ports to commerce and residence, compelled the Qing government to extend most-favored-nation status to Britain, and granted extraterritoriality to British subjects. In later years France, Germany, Denmark, the Netherlands, Spain,

Belgium, Austria-Hungary, the United States, and Japan concluded similar unequal treaties with China. By 1900 ninety Chinese ports were under the effective control of foreign powers, foreign merchants controlled much of the Chinese economy, Christian missionaries sought converts throughout China, and foreign gunboats patrolled Chinese waters.

To make matters more difficult, China was convulsed by several large-scale rebellions in the nineteenth century, all of which reflected the increasing poverty and discontent of the Chinese peasantry. After 1850, rebellions erupted throughout China: the Nian rebellion (1851–1868) in the northeast, the Muslim rebellion (1855–1873) in the southwest, and the Tungan rebellion (1862–1878) in the northwest. Most dangerous of all was the Taiping rebellion (1850–1864), which

Map 29.3 East Asia in the nineteenth century. Notice the division of China, which technically remained a sovereign nation, into spheres of influence by various European nations and Japan. What impact would such spheres of influence have had on the Chinese government in Beijing?

raged throughout most of China and brought the Qing dynasty to the brink of collapse.

The Taiping Rebellion

The village schoolteacher Hong Xiuquan provided both inspiration and leadership for the Taiping rebellion. He called for the destruction of the Qing dynasty and for the radical transformation of Chinese society, including the abolition of private property, the creation of communal wealth to be shared according to needs, the prohibition of foot binding and concubinage, free public education, simplification of the written language, literacy for the masses, and equality of the sexes. After sweeping through southeastern China, Hong and his followers in the Society of God Worshipers took Nanjing in 1853 and made it the capital of their Taiping ("Great Peace") kingdom. In 1855 a million Taipings were poised to attack Beijing, and in 1860 they threatened Shanghai. Although the rebellion was eventually crushed in 1864 with the aid of European advisors and weapons, in all it claimed between twenty and thirty million lives and devastated part of the Chinese countryside.

The Self-Strengthening Movement

The Taiping rebellion altered the course of Chinese history. Contending with aggressive foreign powers and lands ravaged by domestic rebellion, Qing rulers recognized that reforms were necessary for the empire to survive. Most imaginative of these programs was the Self-Strengthening Movement (1860–1895). While holding to Confucian values and seeking to reestablish a stable agrarian society, movement leaders built modern shipyards, constructed railroads, established weapons industries, opened steel foundries with blast furnaces, and founded academies to develop scientific expertise.

Yet the Self-Strengthening Movement did not introduce enough industry to bring real military and economic strength to China. It also did not prevent continuing foreign intrusion into Chinese affairs. During the latter part of the nineteenth century, foreign powers began to dismantle the Chinese system of tributary states. In 1885 France incorporated Vietnam into its colonial empire, and in 1886 Great Britain detached Burma from Chinese control. In 1895 Japan forced China to recognize the independence of Korea and cede the island of Taiwan and the Liaodong peninsula in southern Manchuria. By 1898 foreign powers had carved China itself into spheres of economic influence, and only distrust among them prevented the total dismemberment of the Middle Kingdom.

Taiping (TEYE-pihng)

The Hundred Days Reforms

These setbacks sparked the ambitious but abortive Hundred Days reforms of 1898, whose purpose was to turn China into a powerful modern industrial society. Impressed by the ideas of reform-minded scholars, the young and open-minded Emperor Guangxu launched a sweeping program to transform China into a constitutional monarchy, guarantee civil liberties, root out corruption, remodel the educational system, modernize military forces, and stimulate economic development. Yet these reform efforts produced a violent reaction from members of the imperial household, from their allies in the gentry, and especially from the young emperor's aunt, the ruthless and powerful empress dowager Cixi. After a period of 103 days, Cixi nullified the reform decrees, imprisoned the emperor in the Forbidden City, and executed six leading reformers.

The Boxer Rebellion

Cixi then threw her support behind an antiforeign uprising known as the Boxer rebellion, a violent movement spearheaded by militia units calling themselves the Society of Righteous and Harmonious Fists. The foreign press referred to the rebels as Boxers. In 1899 the Boxers organized to rid China of "foreign devils" and their influences. With the empress dowager's encouragement, the Boxers went on a rampage in northern China, killing foreigners and Chinese who had ties to foreigners. Confident that foreign weapons could not harm them, some 140,000 Boxers besieged foreign embassies in Beijing in the summer of 1900. They were crushed, however, by a heavily armed force of British, French, Russian, U.S., German, and Japanese troops. After the rebellion, the Chinese government was forced to allow foreign powers to station troops at their embassies in Beijing and along the route to the sea. When Cixi

died in 1908, anti-Qing revolutionary movements that sought alternative methods to deal with foreign and domestic crises were rife throughout China. Indeed, revolution broke out in the autumn of 1911, and by early 1912 the child Puyi—the last emperor of the Qing dynasty—had abdicated his throne.

The Scramble for Africa

Even as European powers sponsored informal imperialism in the Ottoman and Qing empires in the last half of the nineteenth century, they also embarked on a striking outburst of formal imperialism in Africa. This was all the more remarkable, since as late as 1875 European peoples maintained a limited presence in Africa: their only sizable possessions were the Portuguese colonies of Angola and Mozambique, the French settler colony in northern Algeria, and a cluster of settler colonies populated by British and Dutch migrants in south Africa.

Between 1875 and 1900, however, the relationship between Africa and Europe dramatically changed. Within a quarter century European imperial powers partitioned and colonized almost the entire African continent. Prospects of exploiting African resources and nationalist rivalries between European powers help to explain this frenzied quest for empire, often referred to as the "scramble for Africa."

The Belgian Congo In the 1870s King Leopold II of Belgium (reigned 1865–1909) employed the American journalist Henry Morton Stanley to help develop commercial ventures and establish a colony called the Congo Free State (modern-day Democratic Republic of the Congo) in the basin of the Congo River. To forestall competition from Belgium's much larger and more powerful European neighbors, Leopold announced that the Congo region would be a free-trade zone accessible to merchants and business-people from all European lands. In fact, however, he carved out a personal colony with the sole purpose of extracting lucrative rubber using forced labor. Working conditions in the Congo Free State were so brutal, taxes so high, and abuses so many that four to eight million Africans died under Leopold's personal rule. Once those abuses became public, humanitarian pressure induced the Belgian government to take control away from Leopold in 1908 and administer the colony directly.

As Leopold colonized central Africa, Britain established an imperial presence in Egypt. In an effort to build up their army, strengthen the economy, and distance themselves from Ottoman authority, Egypt's leaders had borrowed heavily from European lenders in the mid–nineteenth century. By the 1870s crushing debt forced Egyptian officials to impose high taxes, which provoked popular unrest and a military rebellion. Concerned over the status of their financial interests and the security of the Suez Canal, British forces occupied Egypt in 1882.

The British occupation of Egypt intensified tensions between those European powers who were seeking African colonies. To avoid war, delegates from fourteen European states and the United States—not a single

This 1912 photograph shows a stark portrait of the Belgian king's inhumane treatment of Africans in the Congo.

African was present—met at the Berlin West Africa Conference (1884–1885) to devise ground rules for the colonization of Africa. According to those rules, any European state could establish African colonies after notifying the others of its intentions and occupying previously unclaimed territory. *The Berlin Conference*

During the 1890s European imperialists sent armies to impose colonial rule on the African territories they claimed. Although resistance to colonial rule was often fierce, European cannons and machine guns rarely failed to defeat African forces. By the turn of the century, European colonies embraced all of Africa except for Ethiopia, where native forces fought off Italian efforts at colonization in 1896, and Liberia, a small republic in west Africa that was effectively a dependency of the United States.

In the wake of rapid conquest, Europeans struggled to identify the most cost-effective and efficient system of rule in Africa. By the early twentieth century, after some experimentation, most European governments *Direct and Indirect Rule* sought to establish their own rule, which took the form of either direct rule, typical of French colonies, or indirect rule, characteristic of British colonies.

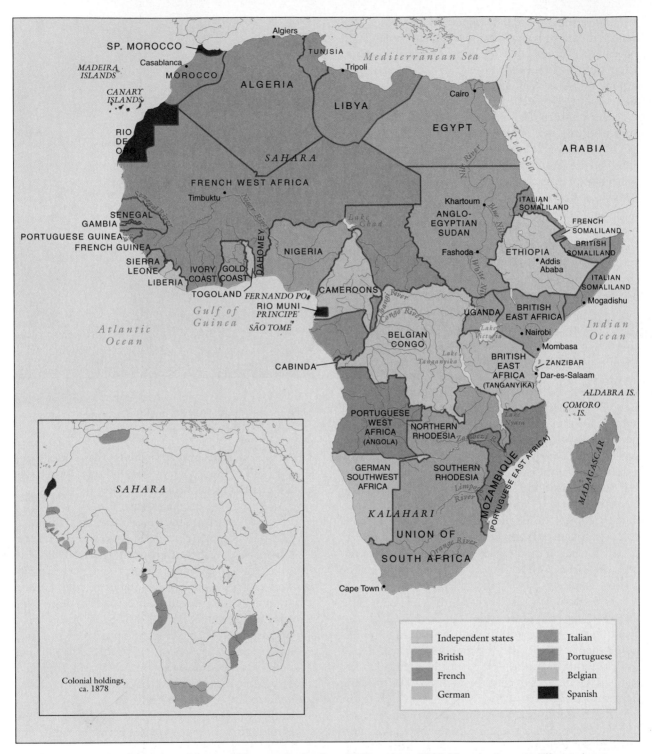

Map 29.4 Expansion of European claims to African territories from 1878 to about 1914. Note the dramatic difference between the map of 1878 and the later map. How was it possible that Europeans were able to claim so much territory in such a short span of time?

Under direct rule, colonies were headed by European personnel who assumed responsibility for tax collection, labor and military recruitment, and the maintenance of law and order. Administrative boundaries intentionally cut across existing African political and ethnic boundaries to divide and weaken potentially powerful indigenous groups. In contrast, indirect rule sought to exercise control over subject populations through indigenous institutions such as "tribal" authorities and "customary laws." Both methods of government were flawed: under direct rule, imperial powers struggled with a constant shortage of European personnel, which undermined the effectiveness of rule, and indirect rule imposed erroneous and rigid European ideas about what constituted tribal categories and boundaries onto African societies.

South Africa Although already inhabited by Europeans long before the scramble for Africa, still the southern tip of the African continent did not escape conflict at the close of the nineteenth century. In this case, however, the main antagonists were both of European descent: one side was composed of the descendants of Dutch settlers who had founded Cape Town in 1652 (called "Boers" or "Afrikaners"), and the other of British settlers who had taken control of the Cape in 1815. Relations between the two groups had never been good. When the British established themselves at the Cape, they subjected Afrikaners to British language and law—including the abolition of slavery when it became law in 1833. The abolition of slavery was particularly contentious, as Afrikaners believed that God had given them the right to exploit both the people and the resources of the Cape—the results of which left the indigenous Khoikhoi and Xhosa peoples decimated and virtually landless. Chafing under British rule, Afrikaners left their farms in Cape Colony and gradually migrated east in what they called the Great Trek. By the mid–nineteenth century, after fierce conflict with the Ndebele and Zulu peoples indigenous to the interior of the region, the Afrikaners created several independent republics: the Republic of Natal, annexed by the British in 1843; the Orange Free State in 1854; and in 1860 the South African Republic (Transvaal territories).

Britain's lenient attitude toward Afrikaner statehood took a drastic turn with the discovery of diamonds (1867) and gold (1886) in Afrikaner territories. The influx of thousands of British miners and prospectors led to tensions between British authorities and Afrikaners, culminating in the South African War (1899–1902; sometimes called the Boer War). Al-

though the brutal conflict pitted whites against whites, it also took a large toll on black Africans, who served both sides as soldiers and laborers. The internment of 100,000 black Africans in British concentration camps, for example, left more than 10,000 dead. The Afrikaners conceded defeat in 1902, and by 1910, the British government had reconstituted the four former colonies as provinces

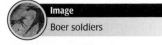
Image
Boer soldiers

in the Union of South Africa, a largely autonomous British dominion. British attempts at improving relations between English speakers and Afrikaners centered on shoring up the privileges of white colonial society and the domination of black Africans.

European Imperialism in the Pacific

While scrambling for Africa, European imperial powers did not overlook opportunities to establish their presence in the Pacific Ocean basin. Imperialism in the Pacific took two main forms. In Australia and New Zealand, European powers established settler colonies and dominant political institutions. In most of the Pacific islands, however, they sought commercial opportunities and reliable bases for their operations but did not wish to go to the trouble or expense of outright colonization. Only in the late nineteenth century did they begin to impose direct colonial rule on the islands.

Settler Colonies in the Pacific Settlers began to arrive in Australia in 1788, nearly two decades after Captain James Cook reported that the region would be suitable for settlement. In that year, a British fleet with about one thousand settlers, most of them convicted criminals, arrived at Sydney harbor and established the colony of New South Wales. By the 1830s voluntary migrants outnumbered convicts, and the discovery of gold in 1851 brought a surge in migration to Australia. European settlers established communities also in New Zealand, where the islands' fertile soils and abundant stands of timber drew large numbers of migrants.

European migration rocked the societies of Australia and New Zealand. Diseases such as smallpox and measles devastated indigenous peoples at the same time that European migrants flooded into their lands. The aboriginal population of Australia fell from about 650,000 in 1800 to 90,000 in 1900, whereas the European population rose from a few thousand to 3.75 million during the same period. Similarly, the population of indigenous Maori in New Zealand fell from about 200,000 in 1800 to 45,000 a century later, while European numbers climbed to 750,000.

Increasing migration also fueled conflict between European settlers and native populations. Large settler societies pushed indigenous peoples from their lands, often following violent confrontations. Because the nomadic foraging peoples of Australia did not occupy lands permanently, British settlers considered the continent *terra nullius*—"land belonging to no one"—that they could seize and put to their own uses. Despite native resistance, by 1900 the British had succeeded in brutally displacing most indigenous Australians from their traditional lands and dispersing them throughout the continent.

A similarly disruptive process transpired in New Zealand, where Maori leaders organized effective and long-lasting opposition to British attempts to usurp their land and sovereignty. Conflicts over land confiscations and disputed land sales, for example, helped to spark the New Zealand Wars, a series of confrontations between the Maori and the British that flared from the mid- to late nineteenth century. Despite that resistance, by the end of the century the British had managed to force many Maori into poor rural communities separated from European settlements.

On the smaller Pacific islands, the picture was quite different. Although indigenous peoples were ravaged

Maori (MAY-oh-ree)

by European diseases, the imperial powers had little interest in establishing direct colonial rule over the islands. Rather, they were content to use the islands as naval ports, as coaling stations, and sometimes as producers of primary products. The situation changed, however, in the late nineteenth century, as European nationalist rivalries encouraged the imperial powers to stake their claims in the Pacific as they had done in Africa. Thus, although France had established a protectorate in Tahiti, the Society Islands, and the Marquesas as early as 1841, it imposed direct colonial rule in 1880. Britain made Fiji a crown colony in 1874, and Germany annexed several of the Marshall Islands in 1876 and 1878. At the Berlin Conference, European diplomats agreed on a partition of Oceania as well as Africa, and Britain, France, Germany, and the United States proceeded to claim almost all the Pacific islands. By 1900 only the kingdom of Tonga remained independent, and even Tonga accepted British protection against the possibility of encroachments by other imperial powers.

Imperialists in Paradise

THE EMERGENCE OF NEW IMPERIAL POWERS

Nineteenth-century imperialism was mostly a European affair until the end of the century. At that point, two new imperial powers appeared on the world stage: the United States and Japan. Both lands experienced rapid

Map 29.5 Boundaries of imperial claims in Oceania about 1914. Observe the many small, distant islands of the Pacific. Why would imperial powers have thought it so important to claim these islands in the late nineteenth and early twentieth centuries?

industrialization in the late nineteenth century, and both built powerful armed forces. As European imperial powers planted their flags throughout the world, leaders of the United States and Japan decided that they too needed to establish a global imperial presence.

U.S. Imperialism in Latin America and the Pacific

The very existence of the United States was due to European imperialism. After the new republic had won its independence, U.S. leaders brought almost all the temperate regions of North America under their authority. In the process, they pushed indigenous peoples onto marginal lands and reservations. This domination of the North American continent was part of the larger story of European and Euro-American imperialism.

The fledgling United States also tried to wield power outside North America. In 1823 President James Monroe (in office 1817–1825) issued a proclamation that warned European states against imperialist designs in the western hemisphere. The Monroe Doctrine, as it came to be known, later served as a justification for U.S. intervention in hemispheric affairs.

As the United States consolidated its continental holdings, U.S. leaders became interested in acquiring territories beyond the temperate regions of North America. The United States purchased Alaska from Russia in 1867 and in 1875 claimed a protectorate over the islands of Hawai`i, where U.S. entrepreneurs had established highly productive sugarcane plantations. The Hawaiian kingdom survived until 1893, when a group of planters and businesspeople overthrew the last monarch, Queen Lili`uokalani (reigned 1891–1893), and invited the United States to annex the islands. In 1898 the pro-expansion president William McKinley (in office 1897–1901) agreed to acquire the islands.

The United States emerged as a major imperial and colonial power after the brief Spanish-Cuban-American War (1898–1899). War broke out as anticolonial tensions mounted in Cuba and Puerto Rico—the last remnants of Spain's American empire—where U.S. business interests had made large investments. In 1898 the U.S. battleship *Maine* exploded and sank in Havana harbor. U.S. leaders claimed sabotage and declared war on Spain. The United States easily defeated Spain and took control and possession of Cuba and Puerto Rico. After the U.S. navy destroyed the Spanish fleet at Manila in a single day, the United States also took possession of

The Spanish-Cuban-American War

Queen Lili`uokalani, last monarch of Hawai`i, before her deposition in 1893. Wearing a European dress, the queen sits on a throne covered with a traditional royal cape made of bird feathers.

Guam and the Philippines to prevent them from falling under German or Japanese control.

The consolidation of U.S. authority in the Philippines was an especially difficult affair. The Spanish-Cuban-American War coincided with a Filipino revolt against Spanish rule, and U.S. forces promised to support independence of the Philippines in exchange for an alliance against Spain. After the victory over Spain, however, President McKinley decided to bring the Philippines under American control instead. In response, Filipino rebels—led by Emilio Aguinaldo—turned their arms against the new intruders. The result was a bitter insurrection that raged until 1902 and claimed the lives of 4,200 American soldiers, 15,000 rebel troops, and some 200,000 Filipino civilians.

Instability and disorder also prompted the United States to intervene in the affairs of Caribbean and Central American lands, even those that were not U.S. possessions, to prevent rebellion and protect American business interests. In the early twentieth century, U.S. military forces occupied Cuba, the Dominican Republic, Nicaragua, Honduras, and Haiti.

The Panama Canal

To facilitate communication and transportation between the Atlantic and the Pacific oceans, the United States sought to build a canal across the Isthmus of Panama in northern Colombia. However, Colombia was unwilling to cede land for the project. Under President Theodore Roosevelt (in office 1901–1909), an enthusiastic champion of imperial expansion, the United States supported a rebellion against Colombia in 1903 and helped rebels establish the breakaway state of Panama. In exchange for that support, the United States won the right to build a canal across Panama and to control the adjacent territory, known as the Panama Canal Zone. Roosevelt then added a corollary to the Monroe Doctrine in 1904, which stated that the United States has the right to intervene in the domestic affairs of nations within the hemisphere if they demonstrate an inability to maintain the security deemed necessary to protect U.S. investments. The Roosevelt Corollary, along with the Panama Canal when it opened in 1914, strengthened U.S. military and economic claims.

Imperial Japan

Strengthened by rapid industrialization during the Meiji era, Japan joined the ranks of imperial powers in the late nineteenth century. Indeed, while founding representative political institutions to demonstrate their trustworthiness to American and European diplomats, Japanese leaders also made a bid to stand alongside the world's great powers by launching a campaign of imperial expansion.

Early Japanese Expansion

The Japanese drive to empire began in the east Asian islands. During the 1870s Japanese leaders consolidated their hold on Hokkaido and the Kurile Islands to the north, and they encouraged Japanese migrants to populate the islands to forestall Russian expansion there. By 1879 they had also established their hegemony over Okinawa and the Ryukyu Islands to the south.

The Sino-Japanese War

In 1876 Japan purchased modern warships from Britain, and the newly strengthened Japanese navy immediately began to flex its muscles in Korea. In 1894 conflict erupted between Japan and China over the status of Korea. When an antiforeign rebellion broke out in Korea in 1893, Qing rulers sent an army to restore order and reassert Chinese authority in Korea. However, Japanese businesses had built substantial interests in Korea, and Meiji leaders were unwilling to recognize Chinese control over such an economically important land. Thus in August 1894 they declared war on China. The Japanese navy quickly gained control of the Yellow Sea and demolished the Chinese fleet in a battle lasting a mere five hours. Within a few months the conflict was over. When the combatants made peace in April 1895, Qing authorities recognized the independence of Korea, thus making it essentially a dependency of Japan. They also ceded Taiwan, the Pescadores Islands, and the Liaodong peninsula, which strengthened Japanese control over east Asian waters. Alongside territorial acquisitions, Japan gained unequal treaty rights in China like those enjoyed by European and American powers.

The Russo-Japanese War

The unexpected Japanese victory startled European imperial powers, especially Russia. Tensions between Japan and Russia soon mounted, because both imperial powers had territorial ambitions in the Liaodong peninsula, Korea, and Manchuria. War broke out in 1904, and Japanese forces overran Russian installations before reinforcements could arrive from Europe. The Japanese navy destroyed the Russian Baltic fleet, which had sailed halfway around the world to support the war effort. By 1905 the war was over, and Japan won international recognition of its colonial authority over Korea and the Liaodong peninsula. Furthermore, Russia ceded the southern half of Sakhalin island to Japan, along with a railroad and economic interests in southern Manchuria. Victory in the Russo-Japanese War transformed Japan into a major imperial power.

LEGACIES OF IMPERIALISM

Imperialism and colonialism profoundly influenced the development of world history. In some ways they tightened links between the world's peoples: trade and migration increased dramatically as imperial powers exploited the resources of subject lands and recruited labor forces to work in colonies throughout the world. Yet imperialism and colonialism also brought peoples into conflict and heightened senses of difference between peoples. European, Euro-American, and Japanese imperialists all came to think of themselves as superior to the peoples they overcame. Meanwhile, foreign intrusion stimulated the development of resistance in colonized lands, which over time served as a foundation for anticolonial independence movements.

Japanese infantry charging during the Russo-Japanese war.

Empire and Economy

One of the principal motives of imperialism was the desire to gain access to natural resources and agricultural products. As imperial powers consolidated their hold on foreign lands, colonial administrators reorganized subject societies so they would become efficient suppliers of timber, rubber, petroleum, gold, silver, diamonds, cotton, tea, coffee, cacao, and other products. As a result, global trade in those commodities surged during the nineteenth and early twentieth centuries. The advantages of this trade went mostly to the colonial powers, whose policies encouraged subject lands to provide raw materials for processing in the industrialized societies of Europe, North America, and Japan.

Introduction of New Crops   In some cases, colonial rule led to the introduction of new crops that transformed both the landscape and the social order of subject lands. In the early nineteenth century, for example, British colonial officials introduced tea bushes from China to Ceylon and India. The effect on Ceylon was profound. British planters felled trees on much of the island, converted rain forests into tea plantations, and recruited Ceylonese women by the thousands to carry out the labor-intensive work of harvesting mature tea leaves.

Consumption of tea in India and Ceylon was almost negligible, but increased supplies met the growing demand for tea in Europe, where the beverage became accessible to individuals of all social classes. The value of south Asian tea exports rose from about 309,000 pounds sterling in 1866 to 6.1 million pounds sterling in 1900. Malaya and Sumatra underwent a similar social transformation after British colonial agents planted rubber trees there in the 1870s and established plantations to meet the growing global demand for rubber products.

Labor Migrations

Efforts to exploit the natural resources and agricultural products of subject lands led imperial and colonial powers to encourage mass migrations of workers during the nineteenth and early twentieth centuries. Two patterns of labor migration were especially prominent during the imperial and colonial era. European migrants went mostly to temperate lands, where they worked as free cultivators or industrial laborers. In contrast, migrants from Asia, Africa, and the Pacific islands moved largely to tropical and subtropical lands, where they worked as indentured laborers on plantations or manual laborers for mining enterprises or large-scale construction projects.

European Migration   Between 1800 and 1914 some fifty million European migrants left their homes and sought opportunities overseas. Most of those migrants left the relatively poor agricultural societies of southern and eastern Europe, especially Italy, Russia, and Poland, although sizable numbers came also from Britain, Ireland, Germany, and Scandinavia. A majority of the migrants—about thirty-two million—went to the United States. Settler colonies in Canada, Argentina, Australia, New Zealand, and south Africa also drew large numbers of European migrants.

Indentured Labor Migration   In contrast to their free European counterparts, migrants from Asia, Africa, and the Pacific islands generally traveled as indentured laborers. As the institution of slavery went into decline, planters sought laborers from poor and densely populated lands who could replace slaves. Between 1820 and 1914 about 2.5 million indentured laborers left their homes to work in distant parts of the world. Labor recruiters generally offered workers free passage to their destinations and provided them with food, shelter, clothing, and modest compensation for their services in exchange for a commitment to work for five to seven years.

The majority of the indentured laborers came from India, but sizable numbers also came from China, Japan, Java, Africa, and the Pacific islands. Indentured laborers went mostly to tropical and subtropical lands in the Americas, the Caribbean, Africa, and Oceania. Large numbers of Indian laborers went to work on rubber plantations in Malaya and sugar plantations in south Africa, the Pacific island of Fiji, the Guianas, and the Caribbean islands of Trinidad, Tobago, and Jamaica. After the Opium War, large numbers of Chinese laborers went to sugar plantations in Cuba and Hawai`i, guano mines in Peru, tin mines in Malaya, gold mines in south Africa and Australia, and railroad construction sites in the United States, Canada, and Peru. After the Meiji restoration in Japan, a large contingent of Japanese laborers migrated to Hawai`i to work on sugar plantations, and a smaller group went to work in guano mines in Peru. Indentured laborers from Africa went mostly to sugar plantations in Réunion, the Guianas, and Caribbean islands. Those from Pacific islands went mostly to plantations on other Pacific islands and in Australia.

All the large-scale migrations of the nineteenth century reflected the global influence of imperial powers.

Empire and Migration   European migrations were possible only because European and Euro-American peoples had established settler societies in temperate regions around the world. Movements of indentured laborers were possible because colonial officials were able to recruit workers and dispatch them to distant lands where their compatriots had already established plantations or opened mines. In combination the nineteenth-century migrations profoundly influenced societies around the world by depositing large communities of people with distinctive ethnic identities in lands far from their original homes.

Empire and Society

The policies adopted by imperial powers and colonial officials forced peoples of different societies to deal with one another on a regular and systematic basis.

Colonial Conflict   Their interactions often led to violent conflicts between colonizers and subject peoples. Indeed, the sepoy rebellion was only one among many insurrections organized by discontented Indian subjects between the mid–nineteenth and the mid–twentieth centuries. Colonized lands in southeast Asia and Africa also became hotbeds of resistance, as subject peoples revolted against foreign rule, the tyrannical behavior of colonial officials, the introduction of European schools and curricula, high

taxation, and requirements that subject peoples provide compulsory labor for colonists' enterprises.

Many rebellions drew strength from traditional religious beliefs, and priests or prophets often led resistance to colonial rule. In Tanganyika, for example, a local prophet organized the huge Maji Maji rebellion (1905–1906) to expel German colonial authorities from east Africa. Rebels sprinkled themselves with "magic water" *(maji-maji),* which they believed would protect them from German weapons. Although the rebellion failed and resulted in the deaths of as many as seventy-five thousand insurgents, it testified to the fact that rebellion was a constant threat to colonial rule. Even when subject peoples dared not revolt, they

Scientific racists often argued that Europeans had reached a higher stage of evolution than other peoples. An illustration from a popular book by Josiah Clark Nott and G. R. Glidden, *Indigenous Races of the Earth,* deliberately distorted facial and skull features to suggest a close relationship between African peoples and chimpanzees.

resisted colonial rule by boycotting European goods, organizing political parties and pressure groups, and pursuing anticolonial policies through churches and religious groups.

Social and cultural differences were the foundation of an academic pursuit known as scientific racism, which became prominent especially after the 1840s. Theorists such as the French nobleman Count Joseph Arthur de Gobineau (1816–1882) took race as the most important index of human potential. In fact, there is no such thing as a biologically pure race, but nineteenth-century theorists assumed that the human species consisted of several distinct racial groups. In his dense, four-volume *Essay on the Inequality of the Human Races* (1853–1855), Gobineau divided humanity into four main racial groups. Gobineau characterized Africans as unintelligent and lazy; Asians as smart but docile; the native peoples of the Americas as dull and arrogant; and Europeans as intelligent, noble, and morally superior to others. Throughout the later nineteenth and early twentieth centuries, racist thinkers sought to identify racial groups on the basis of skin color, bone structure, nose shape, cranial capacity, and other physical characteristics.

Scientific Racism

After the 1860s scientific racists drew heavily from the writings of Charles Darwin (1809–1882), an English biologist whose book *On the Origin of Species* (1859) argued that all living species had evolved over thousands of years in a ferocious contest for survival. Species that adapted well to their environment survived, reproduced, and flourished, according to Darwin, whereas others declined and went into extinction. The slogan "survival of the fittest" soon became a byword for Darwin's theory of evolution. Theorists known as social Darwinists seized upon those ideas, which Darwin had applied exclusively to biological matters, and adapted them to explain the development of human societies. The English philosopher Herbert Spencer (1820–1903) relied on theories of evolution to explain differences between the strong and the weak: successful individuals and races had competed better in the natural world and consequently evolved to higher states than did other, less fit peoples. On the basis of that reasoning, Spencer and others justified the domination of European imperialists over subject peoples as the inevitable result of natural scientific principles.

Racist views were by no means a monopoly of European imperialists: U.S. and Japanese empire builders also developed a sense of superiority over the peoples they conquered and ruled. U.S. forces in the Philippines disparaged the rebels they fought there as "gooks," and they did not hesitate to torture enemies in a conflict that was supposed to "civilize and Christianize" the Filipinos. In the 1890s Japanese newspapers portrayed Chinese and Korean peoples as dirty, backward, stupid, and cowardly. After their victory in the Russo-Japanese War, political and military leaders came to believe that Japan had an obligation to oversee the affairs of their backward neighbors and help civilize their little Asian brothers.

SUMMARY

The construction of global empires in the nineteenth century noticeably increased the tempo of world integration. Armed with powerful transportation, communication, and military technologies, European peoples imposed their rule on much of Asia and almost all of Africa. They wielded enormous influence throughout the world, even where they did not establish imperial control, because of their wealth and economic power. Toward the end of the nineteenth century, the United States and Japan joined European states as global imperialists. All the imperial powers profoundly influenced the development of the societies they ruled. They shaped the economies and societies of their colonies by pushing them to supply natural resources and agricultural commodities in exchange for manufactured products. They created multicultural societies around the world by facilitating the movement of workers to lands where there was high demand for labor on plantations or in mines. They also provoked subject peoples to resist colonial expansion, which over time led them to develop a sense of national identity. From the early twentieth century forward, much of global history has revolved around issues stemming from the world order of imperialism and colonialism.

CHRONOLOGY

1805–1848	Reign of Muhammad Ali in Egypt
1808–1839	Reign of Sultan Mahmud II
1809–1882	Life of Charles Darwin
1816–1882	Life of Count Joseph Arthur de Gobineau
1824	Founding of Singapore by Thomas Stamford Raffles
1839–1842	Opium War
1839–1876	Tanzimat Era
1850–1864	Taiping rebellion
1853–1902	Life of Cecil Rhodes
1857	Sepoy rebellion
1859–1869	Construction of the Suez Canal
1860–1864	Land wars in New Zealand
1860–1895	Self-Strengthening Movement
1884–1885	Berlin West Africa Conference
1894–1895	Sino-Japanese War
1897–1901	Term of office of U.S. president William McKinley
1898–1899	Spanish-Cuban-American War
1899–1902	South African War (Boer War)
1901–1909	Term of office of U.S. president Theodore Roosevelt
1904–1905	Russo-Japanese War
1904–1914	Construction of the Panama Canal
1905–1906	Maji Maji rebellion
1908–1918	Young Turk Era

FOR FURTHER READING

Michael Adas. *Machines as the Measure of Men: Science, Technology, and Ideologies of Western Dominance*. Ithaca, 1988. Argues that European imperialists judged other peoples on the basis of their technological expertise.

W. G. Beasley. *Japanese Imperialism, 1894–1945*. Oxford, 1987. The best study of the topic, emphasizing the relationship between Japanese industrialization and imperialism.

A. Adu Boahen. *African Perspectives on Colonialism*. Baltimore, 1987. A valuable synthetic work that examines African responses to imperial intrusions and colonial regimes.

Philip D. Curtin. *The World and the West: The European Challenge and the Overseas Response in the Age of Empire*. Cambridge and New York, 2000. A work that focuses on cultural change as it examines how various peoples have responded to the establishment of European empires.

John Gallagher. *The Decline, Revival, and Fall of the British Empire*. Ed. by Anil Seal. Cambridge, 1982. A collection of essays that have deeply influenced scholarship on the British empire.

Daniel R. Headrick. *The Tentacles of Progress: Technology Transfer in the Age of Imperialism, 1850–1940*. New York, 1988. Argues that imperial powers reserved the benefits of technological innovation for themselves by limiting the expertise that they shared with subject peoples.

Adam Hochschild. *King Leopold's Ghost: A Story of Greed, Terror, and Heroism in Colonial Africa*. Boston, 1998. A ghastly story of nearly forgotten greed and crime.

Peter Hopkirk. *The Great Game: The Struggle for Empire in Central Asia*. New York, 1992. Exciting account of the contest for power known as the Great Game.

David Northrup. *Indentured Labor in the Age of Imperialism, 1834–1922*. Cambridge, 1995. Careful study of indentured labor migrations and working conditions.

Thomas Pakenham. *The Scramble for Africa, 1876–1912*. New York, 1991. Detailed popular history of empire building in sub-Saharan Africa.

At the time the Great War erupted in 1914, Europeans and their descendants in North America dominated global affairs to an unprecedented extent, exercising political and economic control over peoples and their lands in most of Asia, nearly all of Africa, the Americas, and the Pacific islands. This global dominance was the outcome of three interconnected historical developments that took place between 1750 and 1914: the formation of national states, industrialization, and imperial expansion.

Those same historical developments, which encouraged national rivalries, colonial disputes, and nationalist aspirations, plunged Europe—and then much of the world—into war in 1914. By the time the war ended in 1918, all the major European powers had exhausted much of their economic wealth and global political primacy.

Global interdependence ensured that economic instability after the Great War affected much of the world. This was especially true in the Great Depression, when political turmoil and social misery paved the way to fascist dictatorships in Italy and Germany and to nationalist movements in Asia. Meanwhile, the Soviet Union embarked on a state-sponsored program of rapid industrialization that transformed it into a major international power.

Sparked as a result of the Great War and the Great Depression, World War II began in China in 1931 when Japanese forces established a colonial empire in Manchuria. The conflict spread to Europe in the late 1930s when the Nazi regime embarked on a policy of territorial expansion. By 1941 all the world's major powers had been sucked into a maelstrom of violence and suffering that engulfed most European societies, almost all of Asia and the Pacific, and parts of Africa.

7

World War II completed the economic and
political weakening of European societies and led to
the immediate outbreak of the cold war and the dismantling of
colonial empires, both of which realigned the world of the late twentieth and twenty-
first centuries. The cold war conflict between the forces of capitalism and communism
produced a new set of global relationships, shaping the foreign policies, economic
systems, and political institutions of nations throughout the world until
its abrupt end in the late 1980s.

In the three decades after World War II, an irresistible wave of independence

CONTEMPORARY GLOBAL REALIGNMENTS

movements swept away colonies and empires and led to the establishment of new nations
in Africa and Asia. However, the initial euphoria that accompanied freedom from
imperial control was tempered by neocolonial and postcolonial problems such as rapid
population growth, lack of economic development, and regional and ethnic conflicts.

Other forces that reshaped the twentieth- and twenty-first-century world include
globalization, a process that widened the extent and the forms of cross-cultural
interaction among the world's peoples. Technological advances dissolved old political,
social, and economic barriers. The resulting global integration encouraged similar
economic and political preferences and fostered common cultural values, but forces
promoting distinct cultural traditions and political identities also arose to challenge the
universalizing effects of globalization.

CHAPTER 30

The Great War:
The World in Upheaval

Archduke Francis Ferdinand (1863–1914) was aware that his first official visit to Sarajevo in 1914 was fraught with danger. That ancient city was the capital of Bosnia-Herzegovina, twin provinces that had been under Ottoman rule since the fifteenth century, then occupied in 1878, and finally annexed by Austria-Hungary in 1908. These provinces became the hotbed of pan-Serbian nationalism. Most Serbian nationalists hated the Austro-Hungarian dynasty and the empire represented by Ferdinand, the heir to the throne.

It was a warm and radiant Sunday morning when Ferdinand's motorcade made its way through the narrow streets of Sarajevo. Waiting for him along the designated route were seven assassins armed with bombs and revolvers, one of whom threw a bomb into the open car. Glancing off Ferdinand's arm, the bomb exploded near another vehicle and injured dozens of spectators.

Undeterred, Ferdinand went on to a reception at city hall; after the reception he instructed his driver to take him to the hospital where those wounded in the earlier attack were being treated. While Ferdinand was on his way to the hospital, a young Bosnian Serb named Gavrilo Princip (1894–1918) lunged at the archduke's car and fired a revolver. The first bullet blew a gaping hole in the side of Ferdinand's neck. A second bullet intended for the governor of Bosnia went wild and entered the stomach of the expectant Duchess Sophie, the wife of the archduke. Turning to his wife, the archduke pleaded: "Sophie, dear! Don't die! Stay alive for our children!" By the time medical

OPPOSITE PAGE: *Nurse, wounded soldier, and child.*

aid arrived, however, the archduke and the duchess were dead.

The assassination of the archduke and his wife brought to a head the tensions between the Austro-Hungarian empire and the neighboring kingdom of Serbia. As other European powers took sides, the stakes far outgrew Austro-Serbian conflicts. Nationalist aspirations, international rivalries, and an inflexible alliance system transformed that conflict into a general European war and ultimately into a global struggle involving thirty-two nations. Twenty-eight of those nations, collectively known as the Allies and the Associated Powers, fought the coalition known as the Central Powers, which consisted of Germany, Austria-Hungary, the Ottoman empire, and Bulgaria. The shell-shocked generation that survived the carnage called this clash of arms the Great War. A subsequent generation of survivors renamed the conflict World War I, because it was, sadly, only the first of two wars that engulfed the world in the first half of the twentieth century.

The Great War lasted from August 1914 to November 1918 and ushered in history's most violent century. In geographic extent the conflict surpassed all previous wars, compelling men, women, and children on five continents to participate directly or indirectly in a struggle that many did not understand. The Great War also had the distinction of being the first total war in human history, as governments mobilized every available human and material resource for the conduct of war. Moreover, the industrial nature of the conflict meant that it was the bloodiest in the annals of organized violence. The military casualties passed a threshold beyond previous experience: approximately fifteen million soldiers died, and an additional twenty million combatants suffered injuries.

The war of 1914–1918 did more than destroy individual lives. It seriously damaged national economies, it led to the redrawing of European boundaries, and it caused the demise of four dynasties and their empires—the Ottoman empire, the Russian empire, the Austro-Hungarian empire, and the German empire. The war also helped unleash the Bolshevik Revolution of 1917, which set the stage for an ideological conflict between capitalism and communism that endured to the end of the twentieth century. Finally, the Great War was responsible for an international realignment of power. It undermined the preeminence and prestige of European society, signaling an end to Europe's global primacy.

THE DRIFT TOWARD WAR

Although the catalyst for war was the assassination of Archduke Francis Ferdinand, the assassin's bullets would have had limited effect if there had not been deeper reasons for war. Indeed, the underlying causes for the war of 1914–1918 were many, including intense nationalism, abrasive colonial rivalries, and a general struggle over the balance of power in Europe and in the world at large. Between 1871 and 1914, European governments adopted foreign policies that increased steadily the danger of war. So as to not find themselves alone in a hostile world, national leaders sought alignments with other powers. The establishment and maintenance in Europe of two hostile alliances—the Allies and the Central Powers—helped spread the war from the Balkans.

Nationalist Aspirations

The nationalist fervor that spread throughout most of Europe in the nineteenth century had led many Europeans to rally behind the idea of *self-determination,* or the idea that peoples with the same ethnic origins, language, and political ideals had the right to form sovereign states. In fact, that idea helped inspire the nationalist movements that led to the creation of the new nations of Belgium (1830), Italy (1861), and Germany (1871). Yet at the end of the nineteenth century, the issue of nationalism remained unresolved in other areas of Europe, most notably in eastern Europe and the Balkans. There the nationalist aspirations of subject minorities threatened to tear apart the multinational empires of the Ottoman and Habsburg dynasties and with them the regional balance of power.

The Ottoman empire had controlled the Balkan peninsula since the fifteenth century, but after 1829 the Turkish empire shriveled, largely because of nationalist revolts. Greece was the first to gain independence (in 1830), but within a few decades Serbia, Romania, and Bulgaria followed suit. Austria-Hungary also confronted nationalism within its realms, especially the aspirations of Slavic peoples—Poles, Czechs, Slovaks, Serbs, Croats, and Slovenes. Most menacing and militant were the Serbs, who pressed for unification with the independent kingdom of Serbia. Russia and Germany added fuel to this volatile situation by supporting opposing sides. Russia supported Serbia and the notion of Slavic cultural unity, while Germany backed Austria-Hungary. Thus the stage was set for international conflict.

National Rivalries

Aggressive nationalism was also manifest in economic competition and colonial conflicts, fueling dangerous rivalries among the major European powers. All the industrialized nations of Europe competed for foreign markets and engaged in tariff wars, but the most unsettling economic rivalry involved Great Britain and Germany. By the twentieth century, Germany's rapid industrialization threatened Britain's long-standing economic predominance. Indeed, by 1914 Britain's share of global industrial output had declined to a level roughly equal to Germany's 13 percent. British reluctance to accept the relative decline of British industry vis-à-vis German industry strained relations between the two economic powers.

An expensive naval race further exacerbated tensions between the two nations. When Germany's political and military leaders announced their program to build a fleet with many large battleships, they seemed to undermine Britain's longtime mastery of the seas. The British government moved to meet the German threat through the construction of super battleships known as *dreadnoughts*. Rather than discouraging the Germans, the British determination to retain naval superiority stimulated the Germans to build their own flotilla of dreadnoughts. As the two nations raced to outdo each other, international hostilities boiled under the surface.

The Naval Race

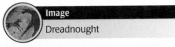

National rivalries also fomented colonial competition. During the late nineteenth and early twentieth centuries, European nations searched aggressively for new colonies or dependencies to bolster economic performance. In their haste to conquer and colonize, the imperial powers stumbled over one another, repeatedly clashing in one or the other corner of the globe: Britain and Russia faced off in Persia (modern-day Iran) and Afghanistan;

Colonial Disputes

Dissident cartoonist Walter Trier's satirical map of Europe in 1914.

Britain and France in Siam (modern-day Thailand) and the Nile valley; Britain and Germany in east and southwest Africa; Germany and France in Morocco and west Africa.

Between 1905 and 1914, a series of international crises and two local wars raised tensions and almost precipitated a general European war. The first crisis resulted from a French-German confrontation over Morocco in 1905. When the German government announced its support of Moroccan independence, which French encroachment endangered, the French responded by threatening war. An international conference in the following year prevented a clash of arms, but similar crises threatened the peace in subsequent years. Contributing to the growing tensions in European affairs were the Balkan wars. Between 1912 and 1913, the states of the Balkan peninsula—including Bulgaria, Greece, Montenegro, Serbia, and Romania—fought two wars for possession of European territories held by the Ottoman empire. The Balkan wars strained European diplomatic relations and helped shape the tense circumstances that led to the outbreak of the Great War.

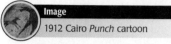
1912 Cairo *Punch* cartoon

Public pressure also contributed to national rivalries. New means of communication—especially cheap, mass-produced newspapers—nourished *Public Opinion* the public's desire to see their country "come in first," whether in the competition for colonies or in the race to the South Pole. However, public pressure calling for national greatness placed policymakers and diplomats in an awkward situation. Compelled to achieve headline-grabbing foreign policy successes, these leaders ran the risk of paying for short-lived triumphs with long-lasting hostility from other countries.

Understandings and Alliances

In addition to a basic desire for security, escalating national rivalries and nationalist aspirations of subject minorities spawned a system of entangling alliances. The complexity of those obligations could not hide the common characteristic underlying all the alliances: they outlined the circumstances under which countries would go to war to support one another. Intended to preserve the peace, rival alliance systems created a framework whereby even a small international crisis could set off a chain reaction leading to global war. By 1914 Europe's major powers had transformed themselves into two hostile camps—the Triple Alliance and the Triple Entente.

The Triple Alliance, also known as the Central Powers, grew out of the close relationship that developed between the leaders of Germany and Austria-Hungary during the last three *The Central Powers* decades of the nineteenth century. In 1879 the governments of the two empires formed the Dual Alliance, a defensive pact that ensured reciprocal protection from a Russian attack and neutrality in case of an attack from any other power. Fear of a hostile France motivated Germans to enter into this pact, whereas Austrians viewed it as giving them a free hand in pursuing their Balkan politics without fear of Russian intervention. Italy, fearful of France, joined the Dual Alliance in 1882, thereby transforming it into the Triple Alliance.

Meanwhile, the leaders of other nations viewed this new constellation of power with suspicion. This response was especially true of French leaders, who still remembered France's humiliating defeat during the Franco-Prussian War of 1870–1871. The tsarist regime of Russia was equally disturbed by the new alignment of powers, especially by Germany's support of Austria, and British leaders were traditionally suspicious of any arrangement that seemed to threaten the balance of power on the Continent. The result was that, in a series of agreements between 1904 and 1914, the most unlikely bedfellows formed the Triple Entente, a combination of nations commonly referred to as the Allies. The construction of such alliances made it difficult for diplomats to contain what otherwise might have been relatively small international crises.

The preservation of peace was also difficult because the military staffs of each nation had devised inflexible military plans and timetables to be carried *War Plans* out in the event of war. German war plans in particular played a crucial role in the events leading to the Great War. Germany's fear of encirclement by France and Russia encouraged its military planners to devise a strategy that would avoid a war on two fronts. It was based on a strategy developed in 1905 by General Count Alfred von Schlieffen (1833–1913). The Schlieffen plan called for a swift knockout of France, followed by defensive action against Russia. German planners predicated their strategy on the knowledge that the Russians could not mobilize their soldiers and military supplies as quickly as the French, thus giving

Triple Entente (ahn-TAHNT)

German forces a few precious weeks during which they could concentrate their full power on France. However, Germany's military strategy was a serious obstacle to those seeking to preserve the peace. In the event of Russian mobilization, Germany's leaders would feel compelled to stick to their war plans by attacking France first, thereby setting in motion a military conflict of major proportions.

GLOBAL WAR

In the capitals of Europe, people danced in the streets when their governments announced formal declarations of war. When the first contingents of soldiers left for the front, jubilant crowds threw flowers at the feet of departing men, who expected to return victorious after a short time. However, reality crushed any expectations of a short and triumphant war. On most fronts the conflict quickly bogged down and became a war of attrition in which the firepower of modern weapons slaughtered soldiers by the millions. For the first time in history, belligerent nations engaged in total war. Even in democratic societies, governments assumed dictatorial control to marshal the human and material resources required for continuous war. One result was increased participation of women in the labor force. Total war had repercussions that went beyond the borders of Europe.

Imperial ties drew millions of Asians, Africans, and residents of the British dominions into the war to serve as soldiers and laborers. Struggles over far-flung colonies further underlined the global dimension of this war. Last, the war gained a global flavor through the entry of Japan, the United States, and the Ottoman empire, nations whose leaders professed little direct interest in European affairs.

The Guns of August

The shots fired from Gavrilo Princip's revolver on that fateful day of 28 June 1914 set in motion a flurry of diplomatic activity that quickly escalated into war. Austrian leaders in Vienna were determined to teach the unruly Serbs a lesson, and on 23 July the Austrians issued an ultimatum to the government of Serbia. When the Serbian government rejected one of its terms, Austria-Hungary declared war on Serbia. The war had begun. The subsequent

Declarations of War

Image
Serbian ambulance tent

sequence of events was largely determined by two factors: complex mobilization plans and the grinding logic of the alliance system. Military planners were convinced that the timing of mobilization orders and adherence to precise timetables were crucial to the successful conduct of war.

On 29 July the Russian government mobilized its troops to defend its Serbian ally and itself from Austria. The tsar of Russia then ordered mobilization against Germany. Nicholas II (1868–1918) took that decisive step reluctantly and only after his military experts had convinced him that a partial mobilization might invite defeat should the Germans enter the war on the side of Austria. His action precipitated a German ultimatum to Russia on 31 July, demanding that the Russian army cease its mobilization immediately. Another ultimatum addressed to France demanded to know what France's intentions were in case Germany and Russia went to war. The Russians replied with a blunt "impossible," and the French never answered. Thus on 1 August the German government declared war on Russia, and France started to mobilize.

On 3 August the Germans declared war on France. On the same day, German troops invaded Belgium in accordance with the Schlieffen plan. Key to this plan was an attack on the weak left flank of the French army by an imposing German force through neutral Belgium. On 4 August the British government sent an ultimatum to Germany demanding that Belgian neutrality be respected. When Germany's wartime leaders refused, the British immediately declared war. A local conflict had become a general European war.

Mutual Butchery

Everyone expected the war to be brief. In the first weeks of August 1914, twenty million young men donned uniforms, took up rifles, and left for the front. Many of them looked forward to heroic charges, rapid promotions, and a quick homecoming. Some dreamed of glory and honor, and they believed that God was on their side. Similar attitudes prevailed among the political and military leaders of the belligerent nations, who were preoccupied by visions of sweeping assaults, envelopments, and, above all, swift triumphs. Their visions could hardly have been more wrong.

The initial German thrust toward Paris in August 1914 came to a grinding halt along the river Marne, after which each side tried to outflank the other in a race to the Atlantic coast. For the next three years, the battle lines remained virtually stationary, as both sides

The Western Front

dug in and slugged it out in a war of attrition that lasted until the late autumn of 1918. Each belligerent tried to wear down the enemy by inflicting continuous damage and casualties, only to have its own forces suffer heavy losses in return. Trenches on the western front ran from the English Channel to Switzerland. Farther south, Italy left the Triple Alliance to enter the war on the side of the Allies in 1915. Allied hopes that the Italians would pierce Austrian defenses quickly faded.

After a disastrous defeat at Caporetto in 1917, Italian forces maintained a defensive line only with the help of the French and the British.

Stalemate and New Weapons

The stalemate on the western and southern fronts reflected technological developments that favored defensive tactics. Barbed wire proved highly effective in frustrating the advance of soldiers across "no-man's-land," the deadly territory between opposing trenches. In addition, the rapid and continuous fire of machine

Map 30.1 The Great War in Europe and southwest Asia from 1914 to 1918. Note the locations of both the eastern and the western fronts in Europe during the war. Why didn't the same kind of trench warfare immobilize opposing armies on the eastern front the way it did on the western front?

Air raid warden in helmet and gas mask, holding a wooden gas attack rattle in his gloved hand.

guns turned infantry charges across no-man's-land into suicide missions. Both sides developed weapons to break the deadly stalemate and reintroduce movement into the war. Gas often proved lethal, and it caused its victims excruciating pain. Mustard gas, for example, rotted the body from both within and without. After blistering the skin and damaging the eyes, the gas attacked the bronchial tubes, stripping off the mucous membrane. Death could occur in four to five weeks. Yet although both sides suffered heavy casualties, totaling about 800,000 soldiers, gas attacks failed to deliver the promised strategic breakthroughs. Other novel weapons developed during the war included tanks and airplanes. Other weapons systems, such as the submarine, had made earlier appearances in warfare but were most effectively used by the German navy against Allied commercial shipping in the Great War.

No-Man's-Land The most courageous infantry charges, even when preceded by pulverizing artillery barrages and clouds of poisonous gas, were no match for determined defenders. Shielded by the dirt of their trenches and by barbed wire and gas masks, they unleashed a torrent of lethal metal with their machine guns and repeating rifles. In every sector of the front, those who fought rarely found the glory they sought. Instead, they encountered death. No-man's-land was strewn with shell craters, cadavers, and body parts. The grim realities of trench warfare—the wet, cold, waist-deep mud, gluttonous lice, and

corpse-fed rats—contrasted sharply with the ringing phrases of politicians and generals justifying the unrelenting slaughter.

Bloodletting Many battles took place, but some were so horrific, so devastating, and so futile that their names are synonymous with human slaughter. The casualty figures attested to this bloodletting. In 1916 the Germans tried to break the deadlock with a huge assault on the fortress of Verdun. The French rallying cry was "They shall not pass," and they did not—but at a tremendous cost: while the victorious French counted

Image
In the trenches at Verdun

315,000 dead, the defeated Germans suffered a loss of 280,000. To relieve the pressure on Verdun, British forces counterattacked at the Somme, and by November they had gained a few thousand yards at the cost of 420,000 casualties. The Germans suffered similar losses, although in the end neither side gained any strategic advantage.

The Eastern Front In eastern Europe and the Balkans, the battle lines were more fluid. After a staunch defense, a combination of Austrian and German forces overran Serbia, Albania, and Romania. Farther north, Russia took the offensive early by invading Prussia in 1914. The Central Powers recovered quickly, however, and in the summer of 1915, combined German-Austrian forces drove the Russian armies out of East Prussia and then out of Poland and established a defensive line extending from the Baltic to the Ukraine. Russian counterattacks in 1916 and 1917 collapsed in a sea of casualties. Those Russian defeats undermined the popularity of the tsar and his government and played a significant role in fostering revolutionary ferment within Russian society.

New Rules of Engagement Dying and suffering were not limited solely to combatants: the Great War established rules of engagement that made civilians targets of warfare, both from air attacks and from naval blockades. Indeed, military leaders on both sides used blockades to deny food to whole populations, hoping that starving masses would force their governments to capitulate. The British blockade of Germany during the war contributed to the deaths of an estimated half million Germans.

Total War: The Home Front

As the Great War ground on, it became a conflict of attrition in which the organization of material and

Mutilated body on the western front.

human resources was of paramount importance. War became total, fought between entire societies, and total victory was the only acceptable outcome that might justify the terrible sacrifices made by all sides. The nature of total war created a military front and a home front. The term *home front* expressed the important reality that the outcome of the war hinged on how effectively each nation mobilized its economy and activated its noncombatant citizens to support the war effort.

As the war continued beyond Christmas 1914 and as war weariness and a decline in economic capability *The Home Front* set in, the response of all belligerents was to limit individual freedoms and give control of society increasingly to military leaders. Initially, ministers and generals shrank from compulsive measures, even conscription of recruits, but they quickly changed their minds. Each belligerent government eventually militarized civilian war production by subordinating private enterprises to governmental control and imposing severe discipline on the labor process.

Economic measures were foremost in the minds of government leaders because the war created unprecedented demands for raw materials and manufactured goods. Planning boards reorganized entire industries, set production quotas and priorities, and determined what would be produced and consumed. Government authorities also established wage and price controls, extended work hours, and in some instances restricted the movement of workers. Because bloody battlefields

caused an insatiable appetite for soldiers, nations responded by extending military service. In Germany, for example, men between the ages of sixteen and sixty were eligible to serve at the front. By constantly tapping into the available male population, the war created an increasing demand for workers at home. Unemployment—a persistent feature of all prewar economies—vanished virtually overnight.

As men marched off to war, women marched off to work. Conscription took men out of the labor force, and wartime leaders exhorted women to fill the gaps in the work- *Women at War* force. A combination of patriotism and high wages drew women into many formerly "male" jobs in a wide variety of industries and public sectors. Perhaps the most crucial work performed by women during the war was the making of shells. Several million women, and sometimes children, put in long, hard hours in munitions factories. That work exposed them to severe dangers, not to mention death, from explosions and poisoning from long-term exposure to TNT.

Although some middle- and upper-class women reported that the war was a liberating experience in regard to personal and economic freedom, most working-class women found little that was liberating in war work. Most of the belligerent governments promised equal pay for equal work, but in most instances that promise remained unfulfilled. Moreover, substantial female employment was a transitory phenomenon. Once the war was over, many women workers—especially those in traditionally male occupations—found themselves forced to concede their jobs to men. Nevertheless, the extension of voting rights to women shortly after the war—in Britain (1918, for women thirty years and older), Germany (1919), and Austria (1919)—was in part due to the role women assumed during the Great War.

To maintain the spirit of the home front and to counter threats to national unity, governments resorted to the restriction of civil liberties, *Propaganda* censorship of bad news, and vilification of the enemy through propaganda campaigns. While some government officials busily censored war news, people who had the temerity to criticize their nation's war effort were prosecuted as traitors. Meanwhile, the propaganda offices of the belligerent nations tried to convince the public that military defeat would mean the destruction of everything worth living for, and to that end they did their utmost to discredit and dehumanize the enemy.

Dulce et Decorum Est

The Great War produced a wealth of poetry. The poetic response to war covered a range of moods from early romanticism and patriotism to cynicism, resignation, and the angry depiction of horror. Perhaps the greatest of all war poets was Wilfred Owen (1893–1918), whose poems are among the most poignant of the war. Owen, who enlisted for service on the western front in 1915, was injured in March 1917 and sent home. Declared fit for duty in August 1918, he returned to the front. German machine-gun fire killed him on 7 November, four days before the armistice, when he tried to cross the Sambre Canal.

■   ■   ■

Bent double, like old beggars under sacks,
Knock-kneed, coughing like hags, we cursed
    through sludge,
Till on the haunting flares we turned our backs
And towards our distant rest began to trudge.
Men marched asleep. Many had lost their boots
But limped on, blood-shod. All went lame; all
    blind;
Drunk with fatigue; deaf even to the hoots
Of gas-shells dropping softly behind.

Gas! GAS! Quick, boys!—An ecstasy of fumbling,
Fitting the clumsy helmets just in time;
But someone still was yelling out and stumbling
And floundering like a man in fire or lime.—
Dim, through the misty panes and thick green
    light
As under a green sea, I saw him drowning.

In all my dreams, before my helpless sight,
He plunges at me, guttering, choking, drowning.
If in some smothering dreams you too could pace
Behind the wagon that we flung him in,
And watch the white eyes writhing in his face,
His hanging face, like a devil's sick of sin;
If you could hear, at every jolt, the blood
Come gargling from the froth-corrupted lungs,
Obscene as cancer, bitter as the cud
Of vile, incurable sores on innocent tongues,—
My friend, you would not tell with such high zest
To children ardent for some desperate glory,
The old Lie: Dulce et decorum est
Pro patria mori.*

*Author's note: "Sweet and fitting is it to die for one's country" comes from a line by the Roman poet Horace (65–8 B.C.E.)

- *How does Owen poetically describe the effects of a gas attack? Is his literary depiction more or less effective than detached descriptions of war's effects?*

SOURCE: Edmund Blunden, ed. *The Poems of Wilfred Owen.* London: Chattus & Windus, 1933, p. 66.

German propaganda depicted Russians as semi-Asiatic barbarians, and French authorities chronicled the atrocities committed by the German "Hun" in Belgium. In 1917 the *Times* of London published a story claiming that Germans converted human corpses into fertilizer and food. In Germany, one widely distributed poster invoked images of bestial black Allied soldiers raping German women to suggest the horrors that would follow if the nation's war effort failed. Most atrocity stories were patently false, and they eventually engendered public skepticism and cynicism. Ironically, public disbelief of wartime propaganda led to an inability to believe in the abominations perpetrated in later wars.

Conflict in East Asia and the Pacific

The Great War quickly turned from a European war into a global conflict. There were three reasons for the war's expansion. First, European governments carried their animosities into their colonies, embroiling them—especially African societies—in their war.

"The Heroes of Belgium 1914." French propaganda poster expresses outrage at the German invasion of Belgium.

An Indian gun crew in the Somme area, 1916.

Second, because Europe's human reserves were not enough to satisfy the appetite of war, the British and the French augmented their ranks by recruiting men from their colonies. Millions of Africans and Asians were drawn into the war. Behind their trenches the French employed laborers from Algeria, China, and French Indochina, and the British did not hesitate to draft Indian and African troops for combat. The British in particular relied on troops furnished by the dominion lands, including Australia, New Zealand, Canada, Newfoundland, and South Africa. Third, the Great War assumed global significance because of the entrance into the war of Japan, the United States, and the Ottoman empire.

On 15 August 1914 the Japanese government sent an ultimatum to Germany demanding the hand-over of the German-leased territory of Jiaozhou (northeastern China) to Japanese authorities without compensation. The same note also demanded that the German navy unconditionally withdraw its warships from Japanese and Chinese waters. When the Germans refused to comply, the Japanese entered the war on the side of the Allies on 23 August 1914. Japanese

forces then proceeded to seize German territories in China and—aided by forces from New Zealand and Australia—in the Pacific. Next, Japan shrewdly exploited Allied support and European preoccupation to advance its own imperial interests in China. On 18 January 1915 the Japanese presented the Chinese government with twenty-one secret demands. The terms of that ultimatum, if accepted, would have reduced China to a protectorate of Japan. Chinese diplomats leaked the note to the British authorities, who spoke up for China, thus preventing total capitulation. The Twenty-One Demands reflected Japan's determination to dominate east Asia and served as the basis for future Japanese pressure on China.

Battles in Africa and Southwest Asia

The geographic extent of the conflict also broadened beyond Europe when the Allies targeted German colonies in Africa. When the war of 1914–1918 erupted in Europe, all of sub-Saharan Africa (except Ethiopia and Liberia) consisted of European colonies, with the Germans controlling four: Togoland, the Cameroons, German Southwest Africa, and German East Africa. Unlike the capture of German colonies in the Pacific, which allied forces accomplished during the first three months of the war with relative ease, the conquest of German colonies in Africa was difficult. Fighting took place on land and sea; on lakes and rivers; in deserts, jungles, and swamps; and in the air. Indeed, the German flag did not disappear from

Africa until after the armistice took effect on 11 November 1918.

The most extensive military operations outside Europe took place in the southwest Asian territories of the Ottoman empire, which was aligned with the Central Powers at the end of 1914. Seeking a way to break the stalemate on the western front, Winston Churchill (1874–1965), first lord of the Admiralty (British navy), suggested that an Allied strike against the Ottomans—a weak ally of the Central Powers—would hurt the Germans. Early in 1915 the British navy conducted an expedition to seize the approach to the Dardanelles Strait in an attempt to open a warm-water supply line to Russia through the Ottoman-controlled strait. The campaign was a disaster. Turkish defenders, ensconced in the cliffs above, quickly pinned down the Allied troops on the beaches. Trapped between the sea and the hills, Allied soldiers dug in and engaged in their own version of trench warfare. The resulting stalemate produced a total of 250,000 casualties on each side. Despite the losses, Allied leaders took nine months to admit that their campaign had failed.

THE END OF THE WAR

The war produced strains within all the belligerent nations, but most of them managed, often ruthlessly, to cope with food riots, strikes, and mutinies. In the Russian empire, the war amplified existing stresses to such an extent that the Romanov dynasty was forced to abdicate in favor of a provisional government in the spring of 1917. Eight months later, the provisional government yielded power to Bolshevik revolutionaries, who took Russia out of the war early in 1918. This blow to the Allies was more than offset by the entry of the United States into the conflict in 1917, which turned the tide of war in 1918. The resources of the United States finally compelled the exhausted Central Powers to sue for peace in November 1918.

In 1919 the victorious Allies gathered in Paris to hammer out a peace settlement that turned out to be a compromise that pleased few of the parties involved. The most significant consequence of the war was Europe's diminished role in the world. The war of 1914–1918 undermined Europe's power and simultaneously promoted nationalist aspirations among colonized peoples, who clamored for self-determination

Romanov (ROH-mah-nahv)
Bolshevik (BOHL-shih-vehk)

and national independence. For the time being, however, the major imperialist powers kept their grip on their overseas holdings.

Revolution in Russia

The Great War had undermined the Russian state. In the spring of 1917, disintegrating armies, mutinies, and food shortages provoked a series of street demonstrations and strikes in Petrograd (St. Petersburg). The inability of police forces to suppress the uprisings, and the subsequent mutiny of troops garrisoned in the capital, persuaded Tsar Nicholas II (reigned 1894–1917), to abdicate the throne.

After its success in Petrograd, this "February Revolution" spread throughout the country, and political power in Russia shifted to two new agencies: the provisional government and the Petrograd soviet of Workers' and Soldiers' Deputies. Soviets, which were revolutionary councils organized by socialists, surfaced all over Russia in 1917, wielding considerable power through their control of factories and segments of the military. The period between February and October witnessed a political struggle between the provisional government and the powerful Petrograd soviet. At first the new government enjoyed considerable public support as it eliminated the repressive institutions of the tsarist state, but it failed to satisfy popular demands for an end to war and for land reform. It claimed that, being provisional, it could not make fundamental changes such as confiscating land and distributing it among peasants. The government also promised to continue the war and to bring it to a victorious conclusion. The Petrograd soviet, in contrast, called for an immediate peace.

The Struggle for Power

Into this tense political situation stepped Vladimir Ilyich Lenin (1870–1924), a revolutionary Marxist and the leader of the small but radical Bolshevik socialist party. Although Lenin had been living in enforced exile in Switzerland, early in 1917 the German High Command helped him return to Russia in the hope that he would foment revolution and bring about Russia's withdrawal from the war. He did. Already in April 1917 Lenin began calling for the transfer of legal authority to the soviets and advocated uncompromising opposition to the war.

Lenin

Under Lenin's leadership, the Bolsheviks eventually gained control of the Petrograd soviet. Crucial to this development was the provisional government's insistence on continuing the war, its inability to feed the population, and its refusal to undertake land reform.

Vladimir Lenin makes a speech in Red Square on the first anniversary (1918) of the Bolshevik revolution.

Workers and peasants became increasingly convinced that their problems could be solved only by the soviets. In September, Lenin persuaded the Central Committee of the Bolshevik party to organize an armed insurrection and seize power in the name of the All-Russian National Congress of Soviets, which was then convening in Petrograd. During the night of 24 October and the following day, armed workers, soldiers, and sailors stormed the Winter Palace, the home of the provisional government. By the afternoon of 25 October, the virtually bloodless insurrection had run its course, and power passed from the provisional government into the hands of Lenin and the Bolshevik Party.

The Bolshevik rulers then ended Russia's involvement in the Great War by signing the Treaty of Brest-Litovsk with Germany on 3 March 1918. *Treaty of Brest-Litovsk* The treaty gave the Germans possession or control of one-third of Russia's territory (the Baltic States, the Caucasus, Finland, Poland, and the Ukraine) and one-quarter of its population. Although the terms of the treaty were harsh and humiliating, taking Russia out of the war gave the new government an opportunity to deal with internal problems. Russia's departure from the war also meant that Germany could concentrate all its resources on the western front.

U.S. Intervention and Collapse of the Central Powers

The year 1917 was crucial for another reason: it marked the entry of the United States into the war on the side of the Allies. In 1914 the American public firmly opposed intervention in a European war. That sentiment soon changed. After the outbreak of the war, the United States pursued a neutrality that favored the Allies, and as the war progressed, the United States became increasingly committed economically to an Allied victory.

The official factor in the United States' decision to enter the war, however, was Germany's resumption of unrestricted submarine warfare in February 1917—a practice that had aroused *America Declares War* American outrage in the early years of the war. Germany's leaders took this decisive step because they were desperate to break the British blockade that threatened to starve the Central powers and hoped to use their submarines to break it. German military experts calculated that submarine attacks against the ships of Great Britain and all the ships headed to Great Britain would bring about the defeat of Great Britain in six months. By that time, however, both the American public and its leadership were invested in an Allied victory, and thus Germany's decision brought the United States into the war in April 1917.

The corrosive effects of years of bloodletting showed. For the first two years of the conflict, most people supported their governments' war efforts, but the continuing ravages of war *Collapsing Fronts* took their toll everywhere. The Central Powers suffered from food shortages as a result of the British blockade, and increasing numbers of people took to the streets to demonstrate against declining food rations. Food riots were complemented by strikes as prewar social conflicts reemerged. Governments reacted harshly to these challenges, pouncing on strikers, suppressing demonstrators, and jailing dissidents. Equally dangerous was the breakdown of military discipline on both sides. In France, for example, a mutiny in the spring of 1917 involved 50,000 soldiers, resulting in 23,385 courts-martial and 432 death sentences.

Against that grim background, Germany took the risk of throwing its remaining might at the western front in the spring of 1918. The gamble failed, and as the offensive petered out, the Allies—strengthened by fresh U.S. troops—broke through the front and started pushing the Germans back. By that time Germany had effectively exhausted its human and material means to wage war. Meanwhile, Bulgaria capitulated to the invading Allies on 30 September, the Ottomans concluded an armistice on 30 October, and Austria-Hungary surrendered on 4 November. Finally, the Germans accepted an armistice, which took effect on 11 November 1918. At last the guns went silent.

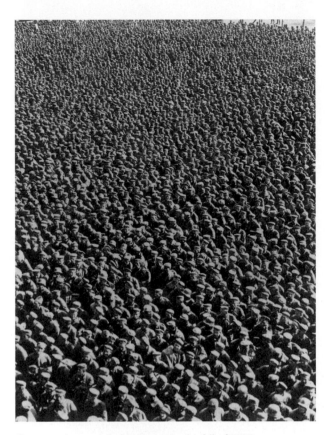

German prisoners taken in France in the fall of 1918.

The Paris Peace Conference

The immediate effects of the Great War were all too obvious. Aside from the physical destruction, which was most visible in northern France and Belgium, the war had killed, disabled, orphaned, or rendered homeless millions of people. Conservative estimates suggest that the war killed fifteen million people and wounded twenty million others. In the immediate postwar years, millions more succumbed to the effects of starvation, malnutrition, and epidemic diseases.

Before the costs of the war were assessed fully, world attention shifted to Paris. There, in 1919, the victorious powers convened to arrange a postwar settlement and set terms for the defeated nations. At the outset, people on both sides of the war had high hopes for the settlement, but in the end it left a bitter legacy. Ultimately, Georges Clemenceau (1841–1929), David Lloyd George (1863–1945), and Woodrow Wilson—the representative leaders of France, Great Britain, and the United States—dominated the deliberations. The Allies did not permit representatives of the Central Powers to participate, and the Soviet Union was not invited to the conference. Throughout this time the

British blockade of Germany remained in effect, adding a sense of urgency to the proceedings.

One year before the opening of the Paris Peace Conference, in January 1918, U.S. president Woodrow Wilson had forwarded a proposal for a just and enduring postwar peace settlement. Wilson's postwar vision subsequently prompted the defeated Central Powers to announce their acceptance of his so-called Fourteen Points as the basis for the armistice. They also expected the Allies to use them as the foundation for later peace treaties. Key among Wilson's Fourteen Points were the following recommendations: open covenants (agreements) of peace, openly arrived at; absolute freedom of navigation upon the seas in peace and war; the removal of all economic barriers and the establishment of an equality of trade conditions among all nations; adequate guarantees for a reduction in national armaments; adjustments of colonial disputes to give equal weight to the interests of the controlling government and the colonial population; and a call for "a general association of nations."

Wilson's Fourteen Points

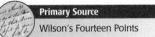
Primary Source
Wilson's Fourteen Points

The idealism expressed in the Fourteen Points gave Wilson a position of moral leadership among the Allies. Those same allies also opposed various points of Wilson's peace formula, because those points compromised the secret wartime agreements by which they had agreed to distribute among themselves territories and possessions of the defeated nations. The defeated powers, in turn, later felt betrayed when they faced the harsh peace treaties that so clearly violated the spirit of the Fourteen Points.

The final form of the treaties represented a series of compromises among the victors. The hardest terms originated with the French, who desired the destruction or the permanent weakening of German power. Thus, in addition to requiring Germany to accept sole responsibility and guilt for causing the war, the victors demanded a reduction in the military potential of the former Central Powers. In addition, the Allies prohibited Germany and Austria from entering into any sort of political union. The French and the British agreed that the defeated Central Powers must pay for the cost of the war and required the payment of reparations either in money or in kind.

The Peace Treaties

The Paris Peace Conference resulted in additional treaties with Bulgaria, Austria, Hungary, and the Ottoman empire. Whereas Bulgaria lost only small portions of territory as a result, the Austro-Hungarian empire was destroyed: in separate treaties both Austria and Hungary suffered severe territorial losses.

Arrangements between the defeated Ottoman empire and the Allies proved to be a more complicated and protracted affair that involved two treaties. In 1920 the Treaty of Sèvres effectively dissolved the empire, calling for the surrender of Ottoman Balkan and Arab provinces and the occupation of eastern and southern Anatolia by foreign powers. However, Turkish nationalists—led by the war hero Mustafa Kemal—set out to defy those terms. Kemal organized a national army that drove out Allied occupation forces, abolished the sultanate, and replaced it with the Republic of Turkey, with Ankara as its capital. In a great diplomatic victory for Turkish nationalists, the Allied powers officially recognized the Republic of Turkey in a final peace agreement, the Treaty of Lausanne (1923).

Although the war was over, the peace settlement that resulted from it was weak. To be sure, some efforts to avoid future conflicts were made. At the urging of U.S. president Woodrow Wilson, the Covenant of the League of Na-

The League of Nations

tions was made an integral part of the peace treaties, and every signatory to a peace treaty had to accept this new world organization. However, the league suffered from fundamental weaknesses that made it unable to enforce its decisions. Over the next two decades, it became clear that the league could not stop the aggression that would lead to World War II, and the institution closed its doors in 1940. Nevertheless, the league did establish the pattern for a permanent international organization and served as a model for its successor, the United Nations.

Another weakness of the peace was the uneven way in which key ideas of the peace-making process—especially the idea of national self-determination—were put into practice around the world. In Europe, the peacemakers in Paris did in fact try to apply the principle of self-determination and nationality to a variety of peoples, such as Slavs, Czechs, and Slovaks, although the results were far from perfect. Yet in other instances

Self-Determination

Map 30.2 Territorial changes that occurred in Europe after the Great War. Observe the territories ceded by the Central Powers and the Soviet Union. Which power lost the most territory, and why?

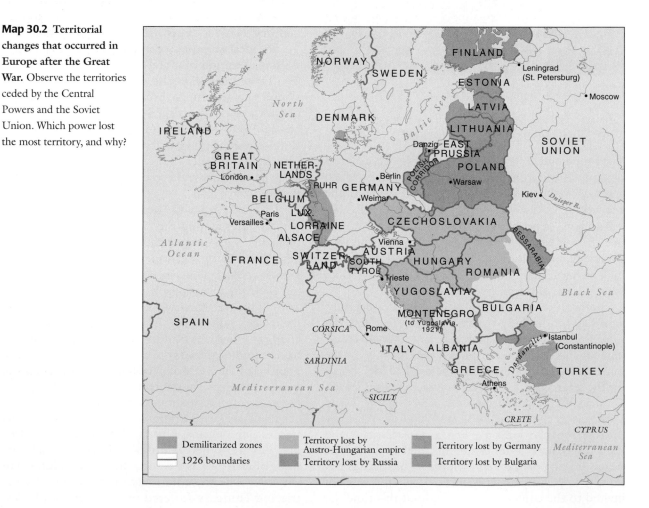

peacemakers pushed the principle aside for strategic and security reasons, such as in Austria and Germany, whose peoples were denied the right to form one nation.

However imperfect the results, the peacemakers at Paris tried to apply the principle of self-determination and nationality throughout Europe. Else-where, however, they did not do so. The unwillingness to apply the principle of self-determination became most obvious when the victors confronted the issue of what to do with Germany's former colonies and the Arab territories of the Ottoman empire. Because the United States rejected the establishment of old-fashioned colonies, the European powers came up with the enterprising idea of trusteeship. Article 22 of the Covenant of the League of Nations referred to the colonies and territories of the former Central Powers as areas "inhabited by peoples not yet able to stand by themselves under the strenuous conditions of the modern world." As a result, "The tutelage of such peoples should be entrusted to the advanced nations who . . . can best undertake this responsibility." The administration of the mandates fell to the victorious powers of the Great War.

The Mandate System

The Germans interpreted the mandate system as a division of colonial booty by the victors, who had conveniently forgotten to apply the tutelage provision to their own colonies. German cynicism was more than matched by Arab outrage. The establishment of mandates in the former territories of the Ottoman empire violated promises (made to Arabs) by French and British leaders during the war. They had promised Arab nationalists in-dependence from the Ottoman empire and had promised Jewish nationalists in Europe a homeland in Palestine. Where the Arabs hoped to form independent states, the French (in Lebanon and Syria) and the British (in Iraq and Palestine) established mandates. The Allies viewed the mandate system as a reasonable compromise between the reality of imperialism and the ideal of self-determination. To the peoples who were directly affected, the mandate system smacked of continued imperial rule draped in a cloak of respectability.

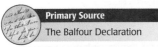

Primary Source

The Balfour Declaration

Challenges to European Preeminence

When the war ended, it seemed to most Europeans that their global hegemony was more secure than ever. But the Great War did irreparable damage to European power and prestige and set the stage for a process of decolonization that gathered momentum during and after the Second World War. The decline in European power was closely related to diminished economic stature, a result of the commitment to total war. Nothing was more indicative of Europe's reduced economic might than the reversal of the economic relationship between Europe and the United States. Whereas the United States was a debtor nation before 1914, owing billions of dollars to European investors, by 1919 it was a major creditor.

The war also weakened the European hold over colonial territories. Colonial subjects in Africa, Asia, and the Pacific tended to view the Great War as a civil war among the European nations, a bloody spectacle in which the haughty bearers of an alleged superior society vilified and slaughtered one another. Because Europe seemed weak, divided, and vulnerable, the white overlords no longer appeared destined to rule over colonized subjects. The colonials who returned home from the war in Europe and southwest Asia reinforced those general impressions with their own firsthand observations. In particular, they were less inclined to be obedient imperial subjects.

The war also helped spread revolutionary ideas to the colonies. The U.S. war aims spelled out in the Fourteen Points raised the hopes of peoples under imperial rule and promoted nationalist aspirations. The peacemakers repeatedly invoked the concept of self-determination, and Wilson publicly proposed that in all colonial questions "the

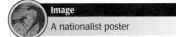

Image

A nationalist poster

interests of the native populations be given equal weight with the desires of European governments." Nationalists struggling to organize anti-imperialist resistance also sought inspiration from the Soviet Union, whose leaders denounced all forms of imperialism and pledged their support to independence movements. Taken together, those messages were subversive to imperial control and had a great appeal for colonial peoples. Although nationalist movements endured many setbacks, the days of European global dominance were numbered.

Summary

The assassination of the Austrian archduke Francis Ferdinand had a galvanizing effect on a Europe torn by national rivalries, colonial disputes, and demands for self-determination. In the summer of 1914, inflexible war plans and a tangled alliance system transformed a local war between Austria-Hungary and Serbia into a European-wide clash of arms. With the entry of the Ottoman empire, Japan, and the United States, the war of 1914–1918 became a global conflict. Although many belligerents organized their societies for total war and drew on the resources of their overseas empires, the war remained at a bloody stalemate until the United States entered the conflict in 1917. The tide turned, and the combatants signed an armistice in November 1918. The Great War, a brutal encounter between societies and peoples, inflicted ghastly human casualties, severely damaged national economies, and discredited established political and cultural traditions. The war also altered the political landscape of many lands as it destroyed four dynasties and their empires and fostered the creation of several new European nations. In Russia the war served as a backdrop for the world's first successful socialist revolution. In the end the Great War sapped the strength of European colonial powers while it promoted nationalist aspirations among colonized peoples.

CHRONOLOGY

1914	Assassination of Archduke Francis Ferdinand
1915	Japan makes twenty-one demands on China
1915	Gallipoli campaign
1916	Battles at Verdun and the Somme
1917	German resumption of unrestricted submarine warfare
1917	United States declaration of war on Germany
1917	Bolshevik Revolution
1918	Treaty of Brest-Litovsk
1918	Armistice suspends hostilities
1919	Paris Peace Conference
1920	First meeting of the League of Nations

FOR FURTHER READING

Joanna Bourke. *Dismembering the Male: Men's Bodies, Britain, and the Great War.* Chicago, 1996. A study that examines the most intimate site of the war—the bodies of the men who fought it.

Belinda Davis. *Home Fires Burning: Food, Politics, and Everyday Life in World War I Berlin.* Chapel Hill, 2000. Effectively covers daily life in wartime and also offers insights into how government policies during the war affected the reconstruction of society following it.

Niall Ferguson. *The Pity of War: Explaining World War I.* New York, 2000. A stimulating example of revisionist history that shifts the blame for the war away from Germany and onto England.

Paul Fussell. *Great War and Modern Memory.* Oxford, 1975. An original and deeply moving piece of cultural history.

James Joll. *The Origins of the First World War.* 2nd ed. London, 1991. The most lucid and balanced introduction to a complex and controversial subject.

John Keegan. *The First World War.* New York, 1999. A comprehensive and a stunningly vivid account of the Great War.

John Maynard Keynes. *The Economic Consequences of the Peace.* New York, 1920. A classic and devastating critique of the Versailles treaty.

John H. Morrow. *The Great War: An Imperial History.* New York, 2003. A global history of the Great War that places the conflict squarely in the context of imperialism.

Erich Remarque. *All Quiet on the Western Front.* New York, 1958. A fictional account of trench warfare.

Barbara Tuchman. *The Guns of August.* New York, 1962. Spellbinding narrative of the coming of the war.

CHAPTER 31
An Age of Anxiety

orn on a lovely spring day in 1889, in a quaint Austrian village, he was the apple of his mother's eye. He basked in Klara's warmth and indulgence as a youth, enjoying the fine life of a middle-class child. As he grew older, however, he sensed a tension between the competing expectations of his parents. Contented with the dreamy indolence allowed by Klara, he bristled at the demands of his father, Alois, who expected him to study hard and enter the Austrian civil service. He had no desire to become a bureaucrat. In fact, he envisioned a completely different life for himself. He wanted to be an artist.

Alois's unexpected death in 1903 freed him from a future as a bureaucrat. He left school in 1905, not at all dissatisfied with having achieved only a ninth-grade education, because now he could pursue an education as an artist. He followed his ambitions to Vienna, only to find bitter disappointment when the Vienna Academy of Fine Arts rejected him as an art student in 1907. His beloved Klara died the following year, and he meandered the city streets of Vienna, admiring the architecture of the city and attending the opera when his funds permitted.

Eventually, he hit bottom and began staying at a homeless shelter. It was interesting, though, to hear the different political points of view spouted by the shelter's other inhabitants. They discussed compelling issues of the day, and he listened intently to those who hailed the supremacy of the Aryan race and the inferiority of the Jews. He came to hate Jews and Marxists, who he thought had formed an evil union with the

OPPOSITE PAGE: *Edvard Munch,* Anxiety, *1896.*

581

goal of destroying the world. He also despised liberalism and democracy.

In 1913 he left his Austrian homeland and found refuge in Munich, Germany. In Germany he volunteered for service in the army, which had just embarked on the greatest war ever fought. He discovered in himself a real talent for military service, and he remained in the army for the duration of the war, 1914–1918. Twice wounded and decorated for bravery, he nonetheless found himself in despair at war's end. An impotent rage coursed through him when he learned of Germany's defeat. He knew with all his being that the Jews were responsible for this humiliation, and he also knew that he had to enter the political arena in his chosen fatherland and save the nation. Adolf Hitler had finally found his mission in life.

Hitler (1889–1945) stood as just one personification of Europe's age of anxiety in the early decades of the twentieth century. Embittered by a sense of dislocation and fear stemming from the enormous changes engulfing the society around him, Hitler dedicated himself to discovering a way out of the anxiety for Germany. Ultimately, his solutions brought about more rather than less anxiety, but the novelty and cruelty of his political and military agendas reflected brilliantly the traumatic consequences of the Great War and the Great Depression.

Just as Adolf Hitler changed as a result of his life experiences in the early twentieth century, so too did European society as a whole. Badly shaken by the effects of war, Europeans experienced a shock to their system of values, beliefs, and traditions. Profound scientific and cultural transformations in the postwar decades also contributed to a sense of loss and anxiety. Then, as peoples in Europe and around the world struggled to come to terms with the aftermath of war, an unprecedented economic contraction gripped the international community.

Against the background of the Great Depression, dictators in Russia, Italy, and Germany tried to translate blueprints for utopias into reality. Those political innovations unsettled many Europeans and much of the world, contributing significantly to the anxiety of the age. Moreover, such innovations matched in their radicalness, however strangely, the vast alterations taking place in the intellectual and cultural realms of European society after the Great War.

PROBING CULTURAL FRONTIERS

The Great War discredited established social and political institutions and long-held beliefs about the superiority of European society. Writers, poets, theologians, and other intellectuals lamented the decline and imminent death of their society. While some wrote obituaries, however, others embarked on bold new cultural paths that established the main tendencies of contemporary thought and taste.

The discoveries of physicists undermined the Newtonian universe, in which a set of inexorable natural laws governed events, with a new and disturbing cosmos. Equally discomfiting were the insights of psychoanalysis, which suggested that human behavior was fundamentally irrational. Disquieting trends in the arts paralleled developments in science and psychology. Especially in painting, an aversion to realism and a pronounced preference for abstraction heralded the arrival of new aesthetic standards.

This is one of the few known photographic images of a young Adolf Hitler, taken in 1923.

Postwar Pessimism

"You are all a lost generation," noted Gertrude Stein (1874–1946) to her fellow American writer Ernest Hemingway (1899–1961). Stein had given a label to the group of American intellectuals and literati who congregated in Paris in the postwar years. This "lost generation" expressed in poetry and fiction the malaise and disillusion that characterized U.S. and European thought after the Great War. The brutal realities of industrialized warfare left no room for heroes or glory, and during the 1920s artists and intellectuals spat out their revulsion in a host of war novels, such as Hemingway's *A Farewell to Arms* (1929) and Erich Maria Remarque's *All Quiet on the Western Front* (1929)—works overflowing with images of meaningless death and suffering. Postwar writers lamented the decline of Western society. A retired German schoolteacher named Oswald Spengler (1880–1936) made headlines when he published *The Decline of the West* (1918–1922). In this work, which might have been seen as an obituary of civilization, Spengler proposed that all societies pass through a life cycle of growth and decay comparable to the biological cycle of living organisms. His analysis of the history of western Europe led him to conclude that European society had entered the final stage of its existence. All that remained was irreversible decline, marked by imperialism and warfare.

Theologians joined the chorus of despair. In 1919 Karl Barth (1886–1968), a notable Christian theologian, published a religious bombshell titled *Epistle to the Romans*. In his work Barth sharply attacked the liberal Christian theology that embraced the idea of progress, that is, the tendency of European thinkers to believe in limitless improvement as the realization of God's purpose. The Augustinian, Lutheran, and Calvinist message of original sin—the depravity of human nature—fell on receptive ears as many Christians refused to accept the idea that contemporary human society was in any way a realization of God's purpose. The Russian orthodox thinker Niokolai Berdiaev (1874–1948) summed up those sentiments: "Man's historical experience has been one of steady failure, and there are no grounds for supposing it will be ever anything else."

The Great War destroyed long-cherished beliefs, such as belief in the universality of human progress. Many idols of nineteenth-century progress came under attack, especially science and technology. The scientists' dream of leading humanity to a beneficial conquest of nature seemed to have gone awry, because scientists had spent the war making poisonous gas and high explosives. Democracy was another fallen idol. The idea that people should have a voice in selecting the leaders of their government enjoyed widespread support in European societies. By the early twentieth century, such sentiments had led to universal male suffrage in most societies, and after the Great War many societies also extended the franchise to women. However, many intellectuals abhorred what they viewed as weak political systems that championed the tyranny of the average person. In Germany, for example, a whole school of conservatives lamented the "rule of inferiors."

Revolutions in Physics and Psychology

The postwar decade witnessed a revolution in physics that transformed the character of science. Albert Einstein (1879–1955) struck the first blow with his theory of special relativity (1905), showing that there is no single spatial and chronological framework in the universe. According to the theory, it no longer makes

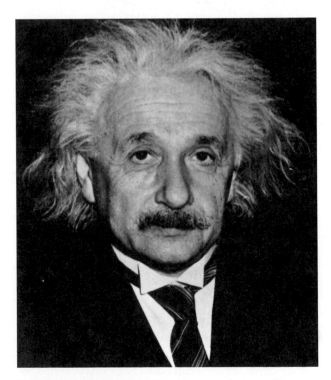

One of the best-known faces of the twentieth century, Albert Einstein was the symbol of the revolution in physics.

sense to speak of space and time as absolutes, because the measurement of those two categories always varies with the motion of the observer. That is, space and time are relative to the person measuring them. To the layperson such notions suggested that a commonsense universe had vanished, to be replaced by a radically new one in which reality or truth was merely relative.

More disquieting even than Einstein's discoveries was the theory formulated by Werner Heisenberg (1901–1976), who in 1927 established the "uncertainty principle." According to Heisenberg, it is impossible to specify simultaneously the position and the velocity of a subatomic particle. The more accurately one determines the position of an electron, the less precisely one can determine its velocity, and vice versa. In essence, scientists cannot observe the behavior of electrons objectively, because the act of observation interferes with them.

The Uncertainty Principle

It quickly became evident that the uncertainty principle had important implications beyond physics. Indeed, Heisenberg's theory called into question established notions of truth. Likewise, objectivity as it was understood was no longer a valid concept, because the observer was always part of the process under observation. Accordingly, any observer—an anthropologist studying another society, for instance—had to be alert to the fact that his or her very presence became an integral part of the study.

As equally unsettling as the advances in physics were developments in psychology that challenged established concepts of morality and values. Beginning in 1896, the Austrian medical doctor Sigmund Freud (1856–1939) embarked on research that focused on psychological rather than physiological explanations of mental disorders. Through his clinical observations of patients, Freud identified a conflict between conscious and unconscious mental processes that lay at the root of neurotic behavior. That conflict, moreover, suggested to him the existence of a repressive mechanism that keeps painful memories away from the conscious mind. Freud believed that dreams held the key to the deepest recesses of the human psyche. Using the free associations of patients to guide him in the interpretation of dreams, he identified sexual drives and fantasies as the most important source of repression. For example, Freud claimed to have discovered a so-called Oedipus complex, in which male children develop an erotic attachment to their mother and hostility toward their father.

Freud's Psychoanalytic Theory

A striking painted portrait of Sigmund Freud.

In the end, Freudian doctrines shaped the psychiatric profession and established a powerful presence in literature and the arts. During the 1920s, novelists, poets, and painters acknowledged Freud's influence as they focused on the inner world of their characters. The creators of imaginative literature used Freud's bold emphasis on sexuality as a tool for the interpretation and understanding of human behavior.

Experimentation in Art and Architecture

The roots of contemporary painting go back to nineteenth-century French avant-garde artists who disdained realism and instead were concerned with freedom of expression. The aversion to visual realism was heightened by the spread of photography. When everyone could create naturalistic landscapes or portraits with a camera, it made little sense for artists to do the same with paint and brush. Thus painters began to think that the purpose of a painting was not to mirror reality but to create it.

At the beginning of the twentieth century, this new aesthetic led to the emergence of a bewildering variety of pictorial schools, all of which promised an entirely new art. Regardless of whether they called themselves expressionists, cubists, abstractionists, dadaists, or surrealists, artists generally agreed on a program "to abolish the sovereignty of appearance." Paintings no longer depicted recognizable objects from the everyday world, and beauty was expressed in pure color or shape. Some painters sought to express feelings and emotions through violent distortion of forms and the use of explosive colors; others, influenced by Freudian psychology, tried to tap the subconscious mind to communicate an inner vision or a dream.

The artistic heritages of Asian, Pacific, and African societies fertilized various strains of contemporary painting. Nineteenth-century Japanese prints, for example, influenced French impressionists such as Edgar Degas (1834–1917). The deliberate violation of perspective by Japanese painters and their stress on the flat, two-dimensional surface of the picture, their habit of placing figures off center, and their use of primary colors encouraged European artists to take similar liberties with realism. In Germany a group of young artists *Artistic Influences*

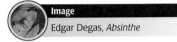
Image
Edgar Degas, *Absinthe*

known as the "Bridge" made a point of regularly visiting the local ethnographic museum to be inspired by the boldness and power of indigenous art. The early works of Pablo Picasso (1881–1973), the leading

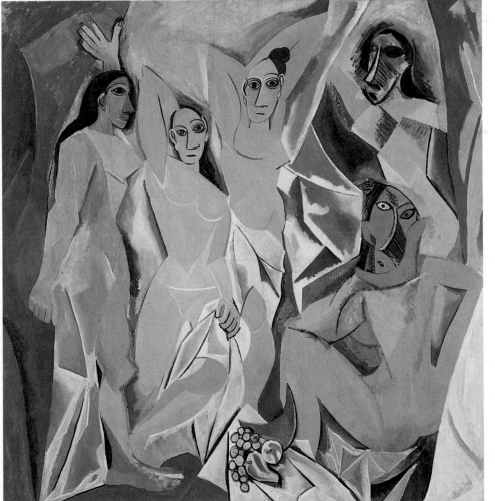

Pablo Picasso's *Les Demoiselles d'Avignon* (1907) was the first of what would be called cubist works. This image had a profound impact on subsequent art.

proponent of cubism, displayed the influence of African art forms.

By the third decade of the twentieth century, it was nearly impossible to generalize about contemporary painting. All artists were acknowledged to have a right to their own reality, and generally accepted standards that distinguished between "good" and "bad" art disappeared.

GLOBAL DEPRESSION

After the horrors and debilitating upheavals of the Great War, much of the world yearned for a return to normality and prosperity. By the early 1920s the efforts of governments and businesses to rebuild damaged economies seemed to be bearing fruit. Prosperity, however, was short-lived. In 1929 the world plunged into an economic depression that was so long-lasting, so severe, and so global that it has become known as the Great Depression. The old capitalist system of trade and finance collapsed, and until a new system took its place after 1945, a return to worldwide prosperity could not occur.

The Great Depression

By the middle of the 1920s, most countries seemed on the way to economic recovery, and industrial productivity had returned to prewar levels. But that prosperity was fragile, perhaps false, and many serious problems and dislocations remained in the international economy.

The economic recovery and well-being of Europe, for example, was tied to a tangled and interdependent financial system. In essence, the governments of Austria and Germany relied on U.S. loans and investment capital to finance reparation payments to France and England. The French and British governments, in turn, depended on those reparation payments to pay off loans taken out in the United States during the Great War. Strain on any one part of the system, then, inevitably strained them all.

Economic Problems

There were other problems as well. Improvements in industrial processes reduced worldwide demand for certain raw materials, which had devastating consequences for export-dependent areas. Technological advances in the production of automobile tires, for instance, permitted the use of reclaimed rubber. The resulting glut of natural rubber badly damaged the economies of the Dutch East Indies, Ceylon, and Malaysia, which relied on rubber exports. Similarly, the increased use of oil undermined the coal industry, and the growing adoption of artificial nitrogen virtually ruined the nitrate industry of Chile.

One of the nagging weaknesses of the global economy in the 1920s was the depressed state of agriculture. During the Great War, when Europe's agricultural output declined significantly, farmers in the United States, Canada, Argentina, and Australia expanded their own production. At the end of the war, European farmers resumed their agricultural activity, thereby contributing to worldwide surpluses. As production increased, prices collapsed throughout the world. By 1929 the price of a bushel of wheat was at its lowest level in four hundred years, and farmers everywhere became impoverished. The reduced income of farm families contributed to high inventories of manufactured goods, which in turn caused businesses to cut back production and to dismiss workers.

The United States enjoyed a boom after the Great War, which prompted many people in the United States to invest their earnings and savings in speculative and risky financial ventures, particularly in stocks. By October 1929, warnings from experts that stock prices were overvalued prompted investors to pull out of the market. On Black Thursday (24 October), a wave of panic selling on the New York Stock Exchange caused stock prices to plummet. Investors who had overextended themselves through speculative stock purchases watched in agony. Thousands of people, from poor widows to industrial tycoons, lost their life savings, and by the end of the day eleven financiers had committed suicide. The crisis deepened when lenders called in loans, thereby forcing more investors to sell their securities at any price.

The Crash of 1929

In the wake of this financial chaos came a drastic decrease in business activity, wages, and employment. When businesses realized that shrinking consumer demand meant they could not sell their inventories, they responded with layoffs. With so many people unemployed, demand plummeted further, causing more business failures and soaring unemployment. In 1930 the slump deepened, and by 1932 industrial production had fallen to half of its 1929 level. National income had dropped by approximately half, and 44 percent of U.S. banks were out of business. Because much of the world's prosperity depended on the export of U.S. capital and the strength of U.S. import markets, the con-

Economic Contraction Spreads

traction of the U.S. economy created a ripple effect that circled the globe.

Most societies experienced economic difficulties throughout the 1930s. Virtually every industrialized society saw its economy shrivel, but nations that relied on exports of manufactured goods to pay for imported fuel and food—Germany and Japan in particular—suffered the most. The depression also spread to primary producing economies in Latin America, Africa, and Asia. Hardest hit were countries that depended on the export of a few primary products such as coffee, sugar, minerals, ores, and rubber.

U.S. investors, shaken by the collapse of stock prices, tried to raise money by calling in loans and liquidating investments, and Wall Street banks refused to extend short-term loans as they became due. Banking houses in Austria and Germany became vulnerable to collapse, because they had been major recipients of U.S. loans. Devastated by the loss of U.S. capital, the German economy experienced a precipitous economic slide that by 1932 resulted in 35 percent unemployment and a 50 percent decrease in industrial production. As the German economy—which had remained a leading economic power in Europe throughout the postwar years—ground to a virtual halt, the rest of Europe sputtered and stalled with it. Likewise, because of its great dependence on the U.S. market, the Japanese economy felt the depression's effects almost immediately. Unemployment in export-oriented sectors of the economy skyrocketed as companies cut back on production.

Economic Nationalism The Great Depression destroyed the international financial and commercial network of the capitalist economies. As international cooperation broke down, governments turned to their own resources and practiced economic nationalism. By imposing tariff barriers, import quotas, and import prohibitions, politicians hoped to achieve self-sufficiency. Yet economic nationalism invariably backfired. Each new measure designed to restrict imports provoked retaliation by other nations whose interests were affected. After the U.S. Congress passed the Smoot-Hawley Tariff Act in 1930, which raised duties on most manufactured products to prohibitive levels, the governments of dozens of other nations retaliated by raising tariffs on imports of U.S. products. The result was a sharp drop in international trade. Between 1929 and 1932, world production declined by 38 percent and trade dropped by more than 66 percent.

Despair and Government Action

By 1933 unemployment in industrial societies had reached thirty million, more than five times higher than in 1929. Both men and women lost their jobs, and over the course of the depression most governments enacted policies restricting female employment, especially for married women. Indeed, the notion that a woman's place was in the home was widespread, and some—such as the French physician Charles Richet (1850–1935)—even insisted that removing women from the workforce would solve the problem of male unemployment.

The Great Depression caused enormous personal suffering. The stark statistics documenting the failure of economies do not convey the anguish and despair of those who lost their jobs, savings, and homes. For millions of people the struggle for food, clothing, and shelter grew desperate. Shantytowns appeared overnight in urban areas, and breadlines stretched for blocks. Marriage, childbearing, and

Image
A depression-era breadline

Dorothea Lange, *Migrant Mother, Nipomo California* (1936). A famous photograph of the Great Depression.

"Hoovervilles"

divorce rates declined, and suicide rates rose. Those simply trying to survive came to despise the wealthy, who, despite their own reduced incomes, remained shielded from the worst impact of the economic downturn. Adolescents completing their schooling faced an almost nonexistent job market.

Economic Experimentation

Classical economic thought held that capitalism was a self-correcting system that operated best when left to its own devices. Thus, in the initial stages of the depression most governments did nothing, hoping that the crisis would resolve itself. Faced with such human misery, however, some governments assumed more active roles, pursuing deflationary measures by balancing national budgets and curtailing public spending. Rather than lifting national economies out of the doldrums, however, those remedies only worsened the depression's impact. Far from self-correcting, capitalism seemed to be dying. Many people called for a fundamental revision of economic thought.

John Maynard Keynes (1883–1946), the most influential economist of the twentieth century, offered a novel solution. In his seminal work, *The General Theory of Employment, Interest, and Money* (1936), he argued that the fundamental cause of the depression was not excessive supply but inadequate demand. Accordingly, he urged governments to stimulate the economy by increasing the money supply, thereby lowering interest rates and encouraging investment. He also *Keynes* advised governments to undertake public works projects to provide jobs and redistribute incomes through tax policy. Such intervention would result in reduced unemployment and increased consumer demand, which would lead to economic revival. These measures were necessary even if they caused governments to run deficits and maintain unbalanced budgets.

Although Keynes's theories did not become influential with policymakers until after World War II, the administration of U.S. president Franklin Delano Roosevelt (1882–1945) antici- *The New Deal* pated his ideas. Roosevelt took aggressive steps to reinflate the economy and ease the worst of the suffering caused by the depression. His program for dealing with the national calamity—called the New Deal—included legislation designed to prevent the collapse of the banking system, to provide jobs and farm subsidies, to guarantee minimum wages, and to provide social security in old age. Its fundamental premise,

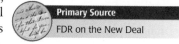
Primary Source
FDR on the New Deal

that the federal government was justified in protecting the social and economic welfare of the people, represented a major shift in U.S. government policy and started a trend toward social reform legislation that continued long after the depression years.

CHALLENGES TO THE LIBERAL ORDER

Amid the gloom and despair of the Great Depression, some voices proclaimed the promise of a better tomorrow. Marxists believed that capitalist society was on its deathbed, and they had faith that a new and better system based on rule by the proletariat was being born out of the ashes of the Russian empire. The new rulers of Russia, Vladimir Ilyich Lenin and then Joseph Stalin, transformed the former tsarist empire into the world's first socialist society, the Union

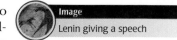
Image
Lenin giving a speech

of Soviet Socialist Republics (1922). Other people, uncomfortable with socialism, found solace in fascist movements, which seemed to offer revolutionary answers to the economic, social, and political problems of the day. Among these fascist movements, the Italian and German ones figured most prominently.

Human faces of the Great Depression: children bathing in the Ozark Mountains, Missouri, 1940.

SOURCES FROM THE PAST

Franklin Delano Roosevelt: Nothing to Fear

Franklin Delano Roosevelt (1882–1945) assumed the presidency of the United States on 4 March 1933, during the very depths of the Great Depression. In his inaugural address to the nation, he conveyed both the anxiousness of the times and the seemingly unquenchable optimism that carried him—and his nation—through hard times. A vastly wealthy man serving as president during a time of devastating penury, Roosevelt nonetheless gained the admiration and respect of the people because of his warm eloquence and compassion. Although he hid his condition quite successfully during his time in public, FDR had contracted polio in the 1920s and had lost the use of his legs. This "crippled" president became a metaphor for the United States' economic collapse but also for its ability to overcome fear itself.

I am certain that my fellow Americans expect that on my induction into the Presidency I will address them with a candor and a decision which the present situation of our Nation impels. This is preeminently the time to speak the truth, the whole truth, frankly and boldly. Nor need we shrink from honestly facing conditions in our country today. This great Nation will endure as it has endured, will revive and will prosper. So, first of all, let me assert my firm belief that the only thing we have to fear is fear itself—nameless, unreasoning, unjustified terror which paralyzes needed efforts to convert retreat into advance. In every dark hour of our national life a leadership of frankness and vigor has met with that understanding and support of the people themselves which is essential to victory. I am convinced that you will again give that support to leadership in these critical days.

In such a spirit on my part and on yours we face our common difficulties. They concern, thank God, only material things. Values have shrunken to fantastic levels; taxes have risen; our ability to pay has fallen; government of all kinds is faced by serious curtailment of income; the means of exchange are frozen in the currents of trade; the withered leaves of industrial enterprise lie on every side; farmers find no markets for their produce; the savings of many years in thousands of families are gone.

More important, a host of unemployed citizens face the grim problem of existence, and an equally great number toil with little return. Only a foolish optimist can deny the dark realities of the moment. . . .

Happiness lies not in the mere possession of money; it lies in the joy of achievement, in the thrill of creative effort. The joy and moral stimulation of work no longer must be forgotten in the mad chase of evanescent profits. These dark days will be worth all they cost us if they teach us that our true destiny is not to be ministered unto but to minister to ourselves and to our fellow men.

- *How does Roosevelt believe U.S. citizens can profit from the dark days of the Great Depression, and why is it that all they have to fear is fear itself?*

SOURCE: Franklin D. Roosevelt, First Inaugural Address, 4 March 1933, available at The Avalon Project at http://www.yale.edu/lawweb/avalon/president/inaug/froos1.htm.

Communism in Russia

In 1917 Lenin and his fellow Bolsheviks had taken power in the name of the Russian working class, but socialist victory did not bring peace and stability to the lands of the former Russian empire. After seizing power, Lenin and his supporters had to defend the world's first "dictatorship of the proletariat" against numerous internal and external enemies.

Opposition to the Bolshevik Party—by now calling itself the Russian Communist Party—erupted into a civil war that lasted from 1918 to 1920. In response, Lenin's government began a policy of terror in which 200,000 suspected

Civil War

anticommunists (known as Whites) were arrested, tried, and executed. In July 1918 the Bolsheviks executed Tsar Nicholas II, Empress Alexandra, and their five children because they feared that the Romanov family could strengthen counterrevolutionary forces. White terror was often equally as brutal as Red terror. The peasantry, although hostile to the communists, largely supported the Bolsheviks, fearing that a victory by the Whites would result in the return of the monarchy.

Meanwhile, foreign powers in Britain, France, Japan, and the United States, angry over Russia's withdrawal from the Great War and inflamed by anticommunism, supported the Whites and sent a limited number of troops and supplies to aid them. Their efforts failed, however, and in 1920 the Red Army defeated the Whites. The costs of war were devastating: estimates place the number of lives lost in the civil war at ten million, mostly from disease and starvation. Moreover, the political system that emerged from the civil war bore the imprint of political oppression, which played a significant role in the later development of the Soviet state.

Over the course of the civil war, the new rulers of Russia transformed the economy by embarking on a hasty and unplanned course of nationalization, known as war communism. After officially annulling private property, the Bolshevik government assumed control of banks, industry, and other privately held commercial properties. Landed estates and the holdings of monasteries and churches also became national property. Private trade was abolished, and the party seized crops from peasants to feed people in the cities. This last measure proved especially unpopular and caused peasants to drastically reduce their production. By 1920 industrial production had fallen to about one-tenth of its prewar level and agricultural output to about half its prewar level.

War Communism

In 1921, as the Reds consolidated their military victories after the civil war, the Soviet economy was in a shambles. Workers were on strike, cities were depopulated, and factories were destroyed. Faced with economic paralysis, in the spring of 1921 Lenin decided on a radical reversal of war communism. In its place he implemented the New Economic Policy (NEP), which temporarily restored the market economy and some private enterprise in Russia. Large industries and banks remained under state control, but the government re-

The New Economic Policy

turned small-scale industries to private ownership. The government also allowed peasants to sell their surpluses at free-market prices. Other features of the NEP included a vigorous program of electrification and the establishment of technical schools to train technicians and engineers. Lenin did not live to see the success of the NEP. After suffering three paralytic strokes, he died in 1924.

After a bitter political struggle for power, Joseph Stalin (1879–1953), general secretary of the Communist Party, emerged as the new leader of the Soviet Union in 1928. A Georgian by birth, an Orthodox seminarian by training, and a Russian nationalist by conviction, Stalin indicated his unified resolve to gain power in his surname, which meant "man of steel." His first economic program, which replaced Lenin's NEP, was both ambitious and ruthless. Indeed, Stalin's First Five-Year Plan, implemented in 1929, aimed at nothing less than transforming the Soviet Union from a predominantly agricultural country to a leading industrial power. The First Five-Year Plan set targets for increased productivity in all spheres of

Joseph Stalin

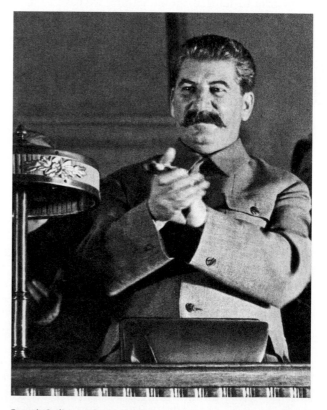

Joseph Stalin at a Soviet congress in 1936.

the economy but emphasized heavy industry—especially steel and machinery—at the expense of consumer goods. As the rest of the world teetered on the edge of economic collapse, Stalin's plan offered a bold alternative to market capitalism. Stalin repeatedly stressed the urgency of this monumental endeavor, telling his people, "We are 50 to 100 years behind the advanced countries. Either we do it, or we shall go under."

Integral to the drive for industrialization was the collectivization of agriculture. The Soviet state expropriated privately owned land to create collective, or cooperative, farm units whose profits were shared by all farmers. Stalin and his regime viewed collectivization as a means of increasing the efficiency of agricultural production and ensuring that industrial workers would be fed.

Collectivization of Agriculture

In some places, outraged peasants reacted to the government's program by slaughtering their livestock and burning their crops. Faced with enforced collectivization, millions of farmers left the land and migrated to cities in search of work. Those who stayed behind were often unable to meet production quotas and starved to death on the land they once owned. When Stalin called a halt to collectivization in 1931, half the farms in the Soviet Union had been collectivized. Estimates of the cost in number of peasant lives lost have fluctuated wildly, but even the most cautious place it at three million. Among them, the *kulaks*—relatively wealthy peasants who had risen to prosperity during the NEP—were nearly eliminated.

The Soviet leadership proclaimed the First Five-Year Plan a success after only four years. The Soviet Union industrialized under Stalin even though the emphasis on building heavy industry first and consumer industries later meant that citizens postponed the gratifications of industrialization. However, the scarcity or nonexistence of such consumer goods as refrigerators, radios, and automobiles was to some degree balanced by full employment, low-cost utilities, and cheap housing and food. Set against the economic collapse of the capitalist world, the ability of a centrally planned economy to create more jobs than workers could fill made it appear an attractive alternative.

Nevertheless, the disaster of collectivization and the ruthlessness with which it was carried out had raised doubts about Stalin's administration. As the Communist Party prepared for its seventeenth congress in 1934, the "Congress of

The Great Purge

Victors," Stalin learned of a plan to bring more pluralism back into leadership. The Congress of Victors quickly became the "Congress of Victims" as Stalin purged two-thirds of the delegates from the Communist Party. Between 1935 and 1938 Stalin removed from posts of authority all persons suspected of opposition, including more than half the army's high-ranking officers. In 1939 eight million Soviet citizens faced long-term suffering in labor camps, and three million were dead as a result of the "cleansing," as Stalin's supporters termed this process.

The outside world watched the events unfolding within the Soviet Union with a mixture of contempt, fear, and admiration. The establishment of the world's first dictatorship of the proletariat challenged the values and institutions of liberal society all over the world and seemed to demonstrate the viability of communism as a social and political system.

The Fascist Alternative

While socialism was transforming the former Russian empire, another political force swept across Europe after the Great War. Fascism, a political movement and ideology that sought to create a new type of society, developed as a reaction against liberal democracy and the spread of socialism and communism. In 1919 Benito Mussolini founded the first fascist party. Movements comparable to Italian fascism subsequently developed in many European societies, most notably in Germany in the guise of National Socialism (Nazism). Although fascism enjoyed widespread popularity in many European countries, it rarely threatened the political order and overthrew parliamentary systems only in Italy and Germany. Although potential fascist movements sprang up during the 1930s in Japan, China, and South Africa; in Latin American societies such as Brazil and Argentina; and in several Arab lands, fascism nevertheless remained basically a European phenomenon in the era between the two world wars.

During the 1920s and 1930s, fascism attracted millions of followers and proved especially attractive to middle classes and rural populations. Those groups became radicalized by economic and social crises and were especially fearful of the perceived threat from the political left. Fascism also proved attractive to nationalists of all classes. Asserting that society faced a profound crisis, fascists sought to create a new national community, which they defined either as a nation-state or as a unique ethnic or racial group. Although each fascist movement had its own unique characteristics, most nevertheless shared certain common features, such as the veneration of the state, a devotion to a strong leader, and an emphasis on ultranationalism, ethnocentrism, and militarism.

Fascist ideology consistently invoked the primacy of the state, which stood at the center of the nation's life and history. Strong and charismatic leaders, such as Benito Mussolini in Italy and Adolf Hitler in Germany, embodied the state and claimed indisputable authority. Consequently, fascists were hostile to liberal democracy, which they viewed as weak and decadent. Fascism was also extremely hostile to socialism and communism. Fascist movements emphasized a belligerent form of nationalism (chauvinism) and a fear of foreign people (xenophobia), which they frequently linked to an exaggerated ethnocentrism. The typical fascist state also embraced militarism, a belief in the rigors and virtues of military life as an individual and national ideal. In practice, militarism meant that fascist regimes maintained large and expensive military establishments, tried to organize much of public life along military lines, and generally showed a fondness for uniforms, parades, and monumental architecture.

Italian Fascism

The first fascist movement grew in Italy after the Great War. Conditions conducive to the rise of fascism included a widespread disillusionment with uninspired political leadership and ineffective government, extensive economic turmoil and social discontent, and a growing fear of socialism. In addition, there was vast disappointment over Italy's skimpy territorial spoils from the peace settlement after the Great War.

The guiding force behind Italian fascism was Benito Mussolini, a former socialist who turned, after the *Benito Mussolini* Great War, to a political program that emphasized virulent nationalism, demanded repression of socialists, and called for a strong political leader. In 1919 he established the Fasci Italiani di Combattimento (Italian Combat Veteran League). Mussolini's movement gained widespread support after 1920, and by 1921 his league managed to have thirty-five fascists elected to the Italian parliament. Much of the newly found public support resulted from the effective use of violence against socialists by fascist armed squads known as Blackshirts. In 1922 Mussolini and his followers decided the time was ripe for a fascist seizure of power, and on 28 October they staged a march on Rome. While Mussolini

stayed safely in Milan, thousands of his black-shirted troops converged on Rome. Rather than calling on the military to oppose the fascist threat, King Victor Emmanuel III hastily asked Mussolini on 29 October to become prime minister and form a new government. Mussolini inaugurated a fascist regime in 1922.

Between 1925 and 1931, Italy's fascists consolidated their power through a series of laws that transformed the nation into a one-party dictatorship. In 1926 Mussolini seized   *The Fascist State* total power as dictator and subsequently ruled Italy as Il Duce ("the leader"). The regime moved quickly to eliminate all other political parties, curb the freedom of the press, and outlaw free speech and association. A Special Tribunal for the Defense of the State, supervised by military officers, silenced political dissent. Marked as antifascist "subversives," thousands of Italians found themselves imprisoned or exiled on remote islands, and some faced capital punishment. Allying himself and his movement with business and

Italian dictator Benito Mussolini strikes a dramatic pose on horseback in 1940.

landlord interests, Il Duce also crushed labor unions and prohibited strikes. In 1932, on the tenth anniversary of the fascist seizure of power, Mussolini felt confident enough to announce that "the twentieth century will be a century of fascism, the century of Italian power."

Although racism and anti-Semitism were never prominent components of Italian fascism, in 1938 the government suddenly issued a series of anti-Semitic laws. That development may have been occasioned by Mussolini's newly found friendship with fellow dictator Adolf Hitler. In 1936 Mussolini told his followers that from now on, world history would revolve around a Rome-Berlin axis. In May 1939 the leaders of fascist Italy and Nazi Germany formalized their political, military, and ideological alliance by signing a ten-year Pact of Steel.

German National Socialism

After Adolf Hitler's postwar political awakening, he came into contact with an obscure political party sympathetic to his ideas. In 1921 he became chairman of *Hitler and the Nazi Party* the party now known as the National Socialist German Workers' Party. National Socialism (the Nazi movement) made its first major appearance in 1923 when party members and Hitler attempted to overthrow the democratic Weimar Republic, which had replaced the German empire in 1919. The revolt was a failure, however, and Hitler was jailed. When Hitler emerged from prison in 1924, he resolved to gain power legally through the ballot box and, once successful, to discard the very instrument of his success.

National Socialism made rapid gains after 1929 because it had broad appeal. Hitler attracted disillu-*The Struggle for Power* sioned people, many of whom blamed the young German democracy for Germany's misfortunes: a humiliating peace treaty— the Treaty of Versailles—that identified Germany as responsible for the Great War and assigned reparation payments to the Allies; the hyperinflation of the early 1920s that wiped out the savings of the middle class; and the suffering brought on by the Great Depression. Adolf Hitler promised an end to all those misfortunes by creating a new order that would lead to greatness for Germany. By stressing racial doctrines, particularly anti-Semitism, the Nazis added a unique and frightening twist to their ideology. Although the Nazis

avoided class divisions by recruiting followers from all strata of society, National Socialism in the main appealed to the members of the lower-middle classes: ruined shopkeepers, impoverished farmers, discharged white-collar workers, and disenchanted students.

As Germany slipped into the Great Depression, the government's inability to find solutions to unemployment and impoverishment radicalized the electorate and caused them to lose faith in the democratic system. Between 1930 and 1932 the Nazi Party became the largest party in parliament, and the reactionary and feeble president, Paul von Hindenburg (1847–1934), decided to offer Hitler the chancellorship. Hitler lost little time in transforming the dying republic into a single-party dictatorship. He promised a German *Reich*, or empire, that would endure for a thousand years.

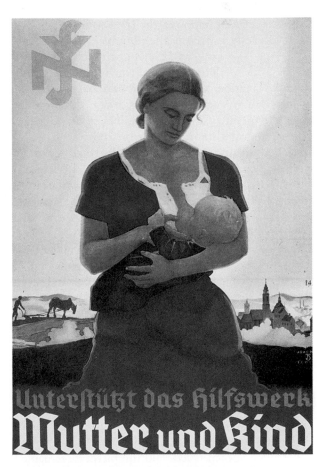

"Mother and Child" was the slogan on this poster, idealizing and encouraging motherhood. The background conveys the Nazi predilection for the wholesome country life, a dream that clashed with the urban reality of German society.

Under the guise of a state of national emergency, the Nazis used all available means to impose their rule.

Consolidation of Power

They began by eliminating all working-class and liberal opposition. The Nazis suppressed the German communist and socialist parties and abrogated virtually all constitutional and civil rights. Subsequently, Hitler made the National Socialist Party the only legal party. Between 1933 and 1935 the regime replaced Germany's federal structure with a highly centralized state. The National Socialist

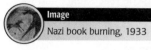
Nazi book burning, 1933

state then guided the destruction of trade unions and the elimination of collective bargaining, subsequently prohibiting strikes and lockouts. The Nazis also purged the judiciary and the civil service, took control of all police forces, and removed enemies of the regime—both real and imagined—through incarceration or murder.

Once securely in power, the Nazi regime translated racist ideology, especially the notions of racial superiority and racial purity, into practice.

The Racial State

The leaders of the Third Reich pursued the creation of a race-based national community by introducing eugenic measures designed to improve both the quantity and the "quality" of the German "race." Alarmed by declining birthrates, the Nazis launched a campaign to increase births of "racially valuable" children. Through tax credits, special child allowances, and marriage loans, the authorities tried to encourage marriage and, they hoped, procreation among young people. At the same time, the regime outlawed abortions, restricted birth control devices, and made it difficult to obtain information about family planning. The Nazis also became enamored of pronatalist (to increase births) propaganda and set in motion a veritable cult of motherhood. Annually on 12 August—the birth date of Hitler's mother—women who bore many children received the Honor Cross of the German Mother in three classes: bronze for those with more than four children, silver for those with more than six, and gold for those with more than eight. By August 1939 three million women carried this prestigious award, which many Germans cynically called the "rabbit decoration." In the long term, however, any efforts by the Nazis to increase the fecundity of German women failed, and the birthrate remained below replacement level.

The quantity of offspring was not the only concern of the new rulers, who were obsessed with "qual-ity." Starting in 1933, the regime initiated a compulsory sterilization program for men and women whom the regime had identified as having "hereditarily determined" sicknesses, including schizophrenia, manic depression, hereditary blindness, hereditary deafness, and serious physical deformities. Between 1934 and 1939 more than thirty thousand men and women underwent compulsory sterilization. The mania for "racial health" culminated in a state-sponsored euthanasia ("mercy killing") program that was responsible for the murder of approximately two hundred thousand women, men, and children. Between 1939 and 1945 the Nazis systematically killed those people judged useless to society, especially the physically and mentally handicapped.

Anti-Semitism, or prejudice against Jews, was a key element in the designs to achieve a new racial order. Immediately after coming to power in 1933, the Nazis initiated systematic measures to suppress Germany's Jewish population. A flood of discriminatory laws and directives designed to humiliate, impoverish, and segregate Jews from the rest of society followed. In 1935 the notorious Nuremberg Laws deprived German Jews of their citizenship and prohibited marriage and sexual intercourse between Jews and other Germans. The Nazi party, in cooperation with government agencies, banks, and businesses, took steps to eliminate Jews from economic life and expropriate their wealth. Party authorities also supervised the liquidation of Jewish-owned businesses or argued for their purchase—at

A Nazi "racial expert" uses a caliper to measure the racial purity of a German.

much less than their true value—by companies owned or operated by non-Jews.

The official goal of the Nazi regime was Jewish emigration. Throughout the 1930s thousands of Jews left Germany, depriving the nation of many of its leading intellectuals, scientists, and artists. The exodus gained urgency after what came to be known as "the night of broken glass" *(Kristallnacht)*. During the night of 9–10 November 1938, the Nazis arranged for the destruction of thousands of Jewish stores, the burning of most synagogues, and the murder of more than one hundred Jews throughout Germany and Austria. This *pogrom* (a Yiddish term for devastation) was a signal that the position of Jews in Hitler's Reich was about to deteriorate dramatically. Indeed, approximately 250,000 Jews had left Germany by 1938. Those staying behind, especially the poor and the elderly, contemplated an uncertain destiny.

SUMMARY

In the decades after the Great War, European intellectuals questioned and challenged established traditions. While scientists and social thinkers conceived new theories that reshaped human knowledge and perceptions, artists forged a contemporary aesthetic. In an age of global interdependence, the U.S. stock market crash of 1929 ushered in a period of prolonged economic contraction and social misery that engulfed much of the world. As most of the industrialized world reeled under the impact of the Great Depression, the leadership of the Soviet Union embarked on a state-sponsored program of rapid industrialization that, despite causing widespread suffering, transformed the Soviet Union into a major industrial and military power.

Italians under the leadership of Mussolini rebuilt their state through fascist policies and imperial expansion. In Germany the effects of the Great Depression paved the way for the establishment of the Nazi state, which was based on the principle of racial inequality. Although many different peoples suffered under the new regime, Jews were the principal victims of the Nazi racial state. Adolf Hitler's mission in life, envisioned in the wake of the Great War, was coming to a spectacular conclusion that culminated in another world war. That war brought both the fulfillment and the destruction of the goals and dreams he had crafted in an age of anxiety.

CHRONOLOGY

1905	Einstein publishes special theory of relativity
1907	Picasso paints *Les Demoiselles d'Avignon*
1918–1920	Civil war in Russia
1919	Mussolini launches fascist movement in Italy
1921–1928	Lenin's New Economic Policy
1927	Heisenberg establishes "uncertainty principle"
1928–1932	First Soviet Five-Year Plan
1929	U.S. stock market crash
1929	Beginning of Great Depression
1929	Hemingway and Remarque publish antiwar novels
1933–1945	Hitler is ruler in Germany
1935–1938	Stalin's "Great Purge" in the Soviet Union

FOR FURTHER READING

Martin Broszat. *The Hitler State: The Foundation and Development of the Internal Structure of the Third Reich*. New York, 1981. An account that does justice to the complexity of the Nazi movement and its rule.

Robert Conquest. *Stalin: Breaker of Nations*. New York, 1991. A compelling and absorbing biography.

Sheila Fitzpatrick. *The Russian Revolution, 1917–1932*. 2nd ed. New York, 1984. This work stands out for the author's ability to make complex processes accessible to the general reader and still instruct the specialist.

George Gamow. *Thirty Years That Shook Physics*. Garden City, N.Y., 1966. A leading physicist engagingly tells the story of modern physics.

Peter Gay. *Freud: A Life for Our Time*. New York, 1988. A balanced biography of one of the most influential social thinkers of the twentieth century.

George Heard Hamilton. *Painting and Sculpture in Europe, 1880–1940*. 6th ed. New Haven, 1993. A classic that presents a discerning overview of the subject.

Ian Kershaw. *The Nazi Dictatorship: Problems and Perspectives of Interpretation*. 2nd ed. London, 1989. A superb assessment that also provides the best introduction to the enormous literature on the Third Reich.

A. J. H. Latham. *The Depression and the Developing World, 1914–1939*. London, 1981. One of the few works that look beyond the industrialized world to give a global perspective on the subject.

Robert Paxton. *The Anatomy of Fascism*. New York, 2004. A groundbreaking and fascinating history of fascism.

Richard Pipes. *The Russian Revolution*. New York, 1990. When the Communist Party collapsed in 1991, this sweeping study was quickly translated into Russian and became a national best seller.

CHAPTER 32

Nationalism and Political Identities in Asia, Africa, and Latin America

Shanfei lived in politically exciting times. The daughter of a wealthy Chinese landowner, she grew up amid luxury and opportunity. Shanfei, however, matured into a woman who rejected the rich trappings of her youth. Her formative years were marked by the unsettling political and cultural changes that engulfed the globe in the wake of the Great War. The rise of nationalism and communism in China after the revolution of 1911 and the Russian revolution in 1917 guided the transformation of Shanfei—from a girl ruled by tradition and privilege, she became an active revolutionary.

With the exception of Shanfei's father, the members of her family in Hunan province took in the new spirit of the first decades of the twentieth century. Her brothers returned from school with compelling ideas, including

some that challenged the subordinate position of women in China. Shanfei's mother, to all appearances a woman who accepted her subservience to her husband, listened quietly to her sons as they discussed new views and then applied them to her daughter. She used every means at her disposal to persuade her husband to educate their daughter. He relented but still insisted that Shanfei receive an old-fashioned education and submit to foot binding and childhood betrothal.

When Shanfei was eleven years old, her father suddenly died. Shanfei's mother took the opportunity to rip the bandages off Shanfei's feet and send her to a modern school. In the lively atmosphere of her school, Shanfei bloomed into an activist. At sixteen she incited a student strike against the administration of her

OPPOSITE PAGE: *In this cigarette advertisement from 1935, Chinese women are shown challenging traditions. They are "new women," affected by the radical changes in identity and behavior taking place after the Great War and during the Great Depression.*

school, transferred to a more modern school, and became famous as a leader in the student movement. She broke tradition in both her personal and her political life. In 1926 Shanfei abandoned her studies to join the Communist Youth, and she gave up her fiancé for a free marriage to the man she loved: a peasant leader in the communist movement.

The twists of fate that altered the destiny of Shanfei had parallels throughout the colonial world after 1914. Two major events, the Great War and the Great Depression, defined much of the turmoil of those years. Disillusion and radical upheaval marked areas in Asia, Africa, and Latin America. In Japan the ravages of the Great Depression prompted militarist leaders to build national strength through imperial expansion. Latin American states worked to alter the economic domination of their "good neighbor" to the north, and African peoples suffered a contraction in living standards along with their imperial overlords.

European empires still appeared to dominate global relations, but the Great War opened fissures within the European and American spheres of influence. Beneath colonial surfaces, resistance to foreign rule and a desire for national unity were stronger than ever. This situation was especially true in India and China, but it also pertained to those in Africa and Latin America who struggled against the domination of imperial powers.

ASIAN PATHS TO AUTONOMY

The Paris peace settlement barely altered the prewar colonial holdings of Europeans, yet indirectly the Great War affected relations between Asian peoples and the imperial powers. In the decades following the Great War, nationalism developed into a powerful political force in Asia, especially in India and China. Achieving the twin ideals of independence from foreign powers and national unity became a dream of intellectuals and a goal of new political leaders. In their search for new identities untainted by the dependent past, Asians transformed and adapted European ideologies such as nationalism and socialism to fit indigenous traditions. In that sense, peoples in India and China followed in the footsteps of Japan, which had already adapted European and American economic strategies to its own advantage. Still dissatisfied with its status, Japan used militarism and imperial expansion in the interwar years to enhance its national identity.

Indian, Chinese, and Japanese societies underwent a prolonged period of disorder and struggle until a new order emerged. In India the quest for national identity focused on gaining independence from British rule but was complicated by sectarian differences between Hindus and Muslims. The Chinese path to national identity was fraught with foreign and civil war as two principal groups—the Nationalist and Communist parties—contended for power. Japanese militarists made China's quest for national unity more difficult, because Japan struggled to overcome its domestic problems through conquests that focused on China.

India's Quest for Home Rule

By the beginning of the twentieth century, Indian nationalism threatened the British empire's hold on India. The construction of a vast railway network across India to facilitate the export of raw materials contributed to national unity by bringing the people of the subcontinent within easy reach of one another. Moreover, the British had created an elite of educated Indian administrators to control and administer the vast subcontinent. A European system of education familiarized this elite with the political and social values of European society. Those values, however—democracy, individual freedom, and equality—were the antithesis of empire, and they promoted nationalist movements.

Of all the associations dedicated to the struggle against British rule, the most influential was the Indian National Congress, founded in 1885. This organization, which enlisted the support of many prominent Hindus *Indian National Congress* and Muslims, at first stressed collaboration with the British to bring self-rule to India, but after the Great War the congress pursued that goal in opposition to the British.

During the Great War, large numbers of Indians rallied to the British cause, and nationalist movements remained inactive. But as the war led to scarcities of goods and food, social discontent with British rule led to an upsurge in nationalist activity. Indian nationalists also drew encouragement from ideas emanating from Washington, D.C., and St. Petersburg. They read Woodrow Wilson's Fourteen Points, which called for national self-determination, and Lenin's appeal for a united struggle by proletarians and colonized peoples. The British government responded to increased nationalism in this period with a series of repressive measures that precipitated a wave of violence and disorder throughout the Indian subcontinent.

Mohandas K. Gandhi

Into this turmoil stepped Mohandas Karamchand Gandhi (1869–1948), one of the most remarkable and charismatic leaders of the twentieth century. Gandhi grew up in a prosperous and pious Hindu household, married at thirteen, and left his hometown in 1888 to study law in London. In 1893 he went to South Africa to accept a position with an Indian firm, and there he quickly became involved in organizing the local Indian community against a system of racial segregation that made Indians second-class citizens. During the twenty-five years he spent in South Africa, Gandhi embraced a moral philosophy of tolerance and nonviolence *(ahimsa)* and developed the technique of passive resistance that he called *satyagraha* ("truth and firmness"). His belief in the virtue of simple living led him to renounce material possessions, dress in the garb of a simple Indian peasant, and become a vegetarian.

Returning to India in 1915, Gandhi became active in Indian politics and succeeded in transforming the Indian National Congress from an elitist institution into a mass organization. Gandhi's unique mixture of spiritual intensity and political activism appealed to a broad section of the Indian population, and in the eyes of many he quickly achieved the stature of a political and spiritual leader, their Mahatma, or "great soul." Although he was himself a member of the merchant caste, Gandhi was determined to eradicate the injustices of the caste system. He fought especially hard to improve the status of the lowest classes of society, the casteless Untouchables, whom he called *harijans* ("children of God").

Under Gandhi's leadership the congress launched two mass movements: the Non-Cooperation Movement of 1920–1922 and the Civil Disobedience Movement of 1930. Convinced that economic self-sufficiency was a prerequisite for self-government, Gandhi called on the Indian people to boycott British goods and return to wearing homespun cotton clothing. Gandhi furthermore admonished his people to boycott institutions operated by the British in India, such as schools, offices, and courts. Despite Gandhi's cautions against the use of force, violence often accompanied the protest movement. The British retaliated with arrests. That the British authorities could react brutally was shown in 1919 in the city of Amritsar, where colonial troops fired on an unarmed crowd, killing 379 demonstrators.

Gandhi marches to the sea to make salt

The India Act

In the face of sustained nationalist opposition and after years of hesitation, the British parliament enacted the Government of India Act, which gave India the institutions of a self-governing state. The legislation allowed for the establishment of autonomous legislative bodies in the provinces of British India, the creation of a bicameral (two-chambered) national legislature, and the formation of an executive arm under the control of the British government. Upon the urging of Gandhi, the majority of Indians approved the measure, which went into effect in 1937.

The India Act proved unworkable, however, because India's six hundred nominally sovereign princes refused to cooperate and because Muslims feared that Hindus would dominate the national legislature. Muslims had reason for concern because they already faced economic control by Hindus, a fact underlined during the Great Depression, which had a severe impact on India. Indeed, since Muslims constituted the majority of indebted tenant farmers, during the Great Depression they found themselves increasingly unable to pay rents and debts to their Hindu landlords. As a result, many Muslims felt that they had been economically exploited by Hindus, which exacerbated tensions between the two groups. Muhammad Ali Jinnah (1876–1948), an eloquent and brilliant lawyer who headed the Muslim League—a separate nationalist organization founded in 1906 that focused on the needs of Indian Muslims—warned that a unified India represented nothing less than a threat to the Muslim faith and its Indian community. In place of one India, he proposed two states, one of which would be the "land of the pure," or Pakistan. Jinnah's proposal reflected an uncomfortable reality that society in India was split by hostility between Hindus and Muslims.

China's Search for Order

As Shanfei's life story suggested, during the first half of the twentieth century China was in a state of almost continual revolutionary upheaval. The conflict's origins dated from the nineteenth century, when the Chinese empire came under relentless pressure from imperialist powers (see chapter 29). As revolutionary

Satyagraha (suh-TYA-gruh-hah)

and nationalist uprisings gained widespread support, a revolution in 1911 forced the Xuantong emperor, still a child (also known as Puyi), to abdicate. The Qing empire fell with relative ease. Dr. Sun Yatsen (1866–1925), a leading opponent of the old regime, proclaimed a Chinese republic in 1912 and assumed the office of president.

Yet the revolution of 1911 did not establish a stable government. Indeed, the republic soon plunged *The Republic* into a state of political anarchy and economic disintegration marked by the rule of warlords, who were disaffected generals from the old imperial Chinese army. Although the central government in Beijing ran the post office and a few other services, the warlords established themselves as provincial rulers. Because the warlords were responsible for the neglect of irrigation projects, for the revival of the opium trade, and for the decline of economic investments, they contributed to the deterioration and instability of Chinese society. Yet warlords were just one symbol of the disintegration of the political order. The relationship between native authority and foreign powers was another. Since the nineteenth century, a collection of treaties, known in China as the unequal treaties, had established a network of foreign control over the Chinese economy that permitted foreigners to intervene in Chinese society. Foreigners did not control the state, but through their privileges they impaired its sovereignty.

After the Great War, nationalist sentiment developed rapidly in China. Youths and intellectuals, who *Chinese Nationalism* had looked to Europe and the United States for models and ideals on Chinese reform, eagerly anticipated the results of the 1919 peace conference in Paris. They expected the U.S. government to support the termination of the treaty system and the restoration of full Chinese sovereignty. Instead, the peacemakers approved increasing Japanese interference in China. That decision gave rise to the May Fourth Movement. Spearheaded by students and intellectuals in China's urban areas, all classes of Chinese protested against foreign, especially Japanese, interference. In speeches, newspapers, and novels, the movement's leaders—including student leaders such as Shanfei—pledged themselves to rid China of imperialism and reestablish national unity.

Disillusioned by the cynical self-interest of the United States and the European powers, some Chinese became interested in Marxist thought and the social and economic experiments under way in the Soviet Union. The anti-imperialist rhetoric of the Soviet lead-

ership prompted the founding of the Chinese Communist Party (CCP) in Shanghai in 1921. Among its early members was Mao Zedong (1893–1976), a former teacher and librarian who viewed a Marxist-inspired social revolution as the cure for China's problems.

The most prominent nationalist leader at the time, Sun Yatsen, did not share the communists' enthusiasm for a dictatorship of the proletariat. *Sun Yatsen* Rather, Sun's basic ideology called for elimination of special privileges for foreigners, national reunification, economic development, and a democratic republican government based on universal suffrage. To realize those goals, he was determined to bring the entire country under the control of his Nationalist People's Party, or *Guomindang*. In 1923 members of the small CCP began to augment the ranks of the Guomindang and by 1926 made up one-third of the Guomindang's membership. Both organizations availed themselves of the assistance offered by the Soviet Union, whose advisors helped reorganize the Guomindang and the CCP into effective political organizations. In the process, the Soviets bestowed upon China the basis of a new political system.

After the death of Sun Yatsen in 1925, the leadership of the Guomindang fell to Jiang Jieshi (Chiang Kai-shek, 1887–1975), a young general who had been trained in Japan and the So- *Civil War* viet Union. Before long, Jiang Jieshi launched a political and military offensive, known as the Northern Expedition, that aimed to unify the nation and bring China under Guomindang rule. Toward the end of his successful campaign, in 1927, Jiang Jieshi brutally and unexpectedly turned against his former communist allies, bringing the alliance between the Guomindang and the CCP to a bloody end. In the following year, nationalist forces occupied Beijing, set up a central government in Nanjing, and declared the Guomindang the official government of a unified and sovereign Chinese state. Meanwhile, the badly mauled communists retreated to a remote area of southeastern China to reconstitute and reorganize their forces.

The nationalist government had to deal with many concerns, but Chinese leaders evaded one major global crisis—the Great Depression. Foreign trade in such items as tea and silk, which did decline, made up only a small part of China's economy, which was otherwise dominated by its large domestic markets. Although the new government in China gener-

---

Guomindang (GWOH-mihn-dahng)

Map 32.1 Struggle for control in China between 1927 and 1936. Compare the continental territories controlled by Japan and the Guomindang in 1934. How would the size of Japan's territories in Manchuria and Korea influence Chinese abilities to challenge Japanese expansion?

ally avoided having to contend with global economic devastation, it did have to confront three major problems during the 1930s. First, the nationalists actually controlled only part of China, leaving the remainder of the country in the hands of warlords. Second, in the early 1930s communist revolution was still a major threat. Third, the Guomindang faced increasing Japanese aggression.

In dealing with those problems, Jiang Jieshi gave priority to eliminating the CCP. No longer able to ward off the relentless attacks of nationalist forces, the communists took flight in October 1934 to avoid annihilation, and some eighty-five thousand troops and auxiliary personnel of the Red Army began the legendary Long March, an epic journey of 10,000 kilometers (6,215 miles). After traveling across difficult terrain and fighting for survival against hunger, disease, and Guomindang forces, those marchers who had not perished arrived in a remote area of Shaanxi province in northwestern China in October 1935 and established headquarters at Yan'an. During the Long March, Mao Zedong emerged as the leader and the principal theoretician of the Chinese communist movement. He came up with a Chinese form of Marxist-Leninism, or Maoism, an ideology grounded in the conviction that peasants rather than urban proletarians were the foundation for a successful revolution in China.

Adversaries in the struggle for power in China: at left, Jiang Jieshi (Chiang Kai-shek); at right, Mao Zedong.

Imperial and Imperialist Japan

After the Great War, Japan achieved great-power status and appeared to accept the international status quo that the major powers fashioned in the aftermath of war. After joining the League of Nations as one of the "big five" powers, in 1922 the Japanese government entered into a series of international agreements whereby Japan agreed to limit naval development, pledged to evacuate Shandong province of China, and guaranteed China's territorial integrity. In 1928 the Japanese government signed the Kellogg-Briand Pact, which renounced war as an instrument of national policy. Concerns about earlier Japanese territorial ambitions in China receded from the minds of the international community.

Japan's limited involvement in the Great War gave a dual boost to its economy. Japanese businesses profited from selling munitions and other goods to the Allies throughout the war, and they gained a bigger foothold in Asia as the war led Europe's trading nations to neglect Asian markets. Economic prosperity was short-lived, however, as the postwar economy of Japan faced a series of recessions that culminated in a giant economic slump caused by the Great Depression.

Economic contraction set the stage for social unrest and radical politics. Public demands for sweeping political and social reforms figured prominently in Japanese domestic politics throughout the 1920s. Yet conservatives blocked any major advances beyond the suffrage law of 1925, which established universal male suffrage. By the early 1930s an increasingly frustrated

and disenchanted public blamed its government for the nation's continuing economic problems. Right-wing political groups called for an end to party rule, while xenophobic nationalists argued for the preservation of a unique Japanese culture and the eradication of "Western" influences. A campaign of assassinations, targeting political and business leaders, culminated in the murder of Prime Minister Inukai Tsuyoshi (1855–1932).

Politicians who supported Japan's role in the international industrial-capitalist system faced increasing opposition from those who were inclined toward a militarist vision of a self-sufficient Japan that would dominate east Asia. Indeed, the hardships of the depression only seemed to discredit the internationalist position and make the militarist vision of self-sufficiency more attractive.

Meanwhile, militarists were setting their sights on expansion in China, where political instability made it an inviting target. In 1931 Japan's military forces began their campaign of expansion in Manchuria, which had historically been Chinese territory. The choice of Manchuria was no accident: the Japanese had significant economic interests there by the twentieth century, not least of which was the Manchurian Railroad, which they had built in 1906 and continued to maintain.

On the night of 18 September 1931, Japanese troops used explosives to blow up a few feet of rail on the Japanese-built South Manchuria Railway north of Mukden, then accused the Chinese of attacking their railroad. This "Mukden incident" became the pretext for war between Japanese and Chinese troops. Although the civilian government in Japan tried to halt *The Mukden Incident* this military incursion, by 1932 Japanese troops controlled all of Manchuria. The Japanese established a puppet state called Manchukuo, but in reality Japan had absorbed Manchuria into its empire, challenged the international peace system, and begun a war. In response to the Manchurian invasion, the Guomindang (Nationalist

Party) leader Jiang Jieshi appealed to the League of Nations to halt Japanese aggression. The league eventually called for the withdrawal of Japanese forces and for the restoration of Chinese sovereignty. The Japanese responded by leaving the league, and nothing was done to stop the aggression. That reaction set the pattern for future responses to the actions of expansionist nations like Japan. Embarking on conquests in east Asia, Japanese militarists found a sure means of promoting a new militant Japanese national identity. They also helped provoke a new global conflagration.

AFRICA UNDER COLONIAL DOMINATION

The Great War and the Great Depression similarly complicated quests for national independence and unity in Africa. The colonial ties that bound African colonies to European powers ensured that Africans became participants in the Great War, willing or not. European states transmitted their respective animosities and their military conflicts to African soil and drew on their colonies for soldiers and carriers. The forced recruitment of military personnel led some Africans to raise arms against their colonial overlords, but Europeans generally prevailed in putting down those uprisings. African contributions to the Great War and the wartime rhetoric of self-determination espoused by U.S. president Woodrow Wilson led some Africans to anticipate a different postwar world. The peacemakers in Paris, however, ignored African pleas for social and political reform.

In the decades following the peace settlement of 1919, colonialism grew stronger on the African continent as European powers focused on the economic exploitation of their colonies. The imposition of a rapacious form of capitalism destroyed the self-sufficiency

of many African economies, and African economic life became more thoroughly enmeshed in the global economy. During the decades following the Great War, African intellectuals searched for new national identities and looked forward to the construction of nations devoid of European domination and exploitation.

Africa and the Great War

The Great War had a profound impact on Africa. The conflict of 1914–1918 affected Africans because many belligerents were colonial powers with colonies in Africa. Except for Spanish-controlled territories, which remained neutral, every African colony as well as the two independent states of Ethiopia and Liberia took sides in the war.

Although Germany had been a latecomer in the race for overseas colonies, German imperialists had managed to carve out an African empire *War in Africa* in Togo, Cameroon, German Southwest Africa, and German East Africa. Thus, one immediate consequence of war for Africans in 1914 was that the Allies invaded those German colonies. Badly outnumbered by French and British-led troops, the Germans could not hope to win the war in Africa. Yet, by resorting to guerrilla tactics, some fifteen thousand German troops tied up sixty thousand Allied forces and postponed defeat until the last days of the war.

More than one million African soldiers participated directly in military campaigns, in which they witnessed firsthand the spectacle of white people fighting one another. The colonial powers also encouraged their African subjects in uniforms to kill the enemy "white man," whose life until now had been sacrosanct because of his skin color. Even more men, as well as women and children, served as carriers to support European armies, many of them serving involuntarily. In French colonies, military service became compulsory for all males between the ages of twenty and twenty-eight, and by the end of the war over 480,000 colonial troops had served in the French army. In British colonies, a compulsory service order in 1915 made all men aged eighteen to twenty-five liable for military service. In the Congo, the Belgians impressed more than half a million porters. Ultimately, more than 150,000 African soldiers and carriers lost their lives, and many suffered injury or became disabled.

While the world's attention was focused on the slaughter taking place in Europe between 1914 and 1918, Africans mounted bold challenges to European

A Senegalese regiment of the French Colonial Infantry on parade in Africa during the Great War.

colonial authority. Indeed, opportunities for rebellion and protest increased when the already thin European presence in Africa grew even thinner as commercial and administrative personnel left the colonies in large numbers to serve the war effort. The causes of those revolts varied. In some cases, as in Libya, revolts simply represented continued resistance to European rule. In other instances, religious opposition manifested itself in uprisings. The Mumbo cult in Kenya, for example, targeted Europeans and their Christian religion, declaring that "all Europeans are our enemies, but the time is shortly coming when they will disappear from our country." The major inspiration for most revolts, however, stemmed from the resentment and hatred engendered by the compulsory conscription of soldiers and carriers. No matter the cause, colonial authorities responded ruthlessly to put down the revolts.

Challenges to European Authority

The Colonial Economy

The decades following the Great War witnessed a thorough transformation of African economic life. Colonial powers pursued two key economic objectives in Africa: they wanted to make sure that the colonized paid for the institutions—bureaucracies, judiciary, police, and military forces—that kept them in subjugation; and they developed export-oriented economies characterized by the exchange of raw materials or cash crops for manufactured goods from abroad. In pursuit of those goals, colonial authorities imposed economic structures that altered, subordinated, or destroyed African economies by making them increasingly dependent on a European-dominated global economy. One result of this integration was that global economic downturns could spell disaster for African economies. During the Great Depression, for example, as international markets for primary products shrank, prices for African raw materials and cash crops dropped sharply and trade volume often fell by half. This, in turn, wreaked havoc on economies that had been geared almost completely toward the production of a single resource or crop.

Part of the process of global economic integration involved investment in infrastructures such as port facilities, roads, railways, and telegraph wires. Efficient transportation and communication networks not only facilitated conquest and rule but also linked the agricultural or mineral wealth of a colony to the outside world. Although Europeans later claimed that they had given Africa its first modern infrastructure, Europeans and their businesses were usually its main beneficiaries. Even though Africans paid for the infrastructure with their labor and taxes, Europeans designed such systems with their own needs, rather than the needs of Africans, in mind.

Infrastructure

Colonial taxation was used as an important tool to drive Africans into the labor market. To earn the money to pay colonial taxes, African farmers had to become cash-crop farmers or seek wage labor on plantations and in mines. In most colonies, farmers specialized in one or two crops destined for export to the country governing them, among them peanuts from Senegal and northern Nigeria, cotton from Uganda, cocoa from the Gold Coast, rubber from the Congo, and palm oil from the Ivory Coast and the Niger delta. In areas with extensive white settlement, such as in Kenya, Rhodesia, and South Africa, settlers expropriated African lands and grew cash crops—using African labor—themselves. In British-controlled Kenya, for example, four thousand white farmers seized seven million acres in the Kikuyu highlands, the colony's richest land.

Farming and Mining

In South Africa, the government reserved 88 percent of all land for whites, who made up just 20 percent of the total population. Colonial mining enterprises geared toward the extraction of copper, gold, and diamonds loomed large in parts of central and southern Africa. These enterprises depended on the labor of African men who were recruited from rural areas and were paid minimal wages. Such recruitment practices set in motion a vast pattern of labor migration that persisted throughout the twentieth century. In many cases, the absence of male labor and the payment of minimal wages had the effect of impoverishing rural areas, where the women left behind could not grow enough food to feed their children and elderly relatives.

Where taxation failed to create a malleable native labor force, colonial officials resorted to outright forced labor and barely disguised variants of slavery. Indeed, the construction of railways and roads often depended on forced-labor regimes. When the French undertook the construction of the Congo-Ocean railway from Brazzaville to the port at Point-Noir, for example, they rounded up some ten thousand workers annually. Within a few years, between fifteen

Labor Practices

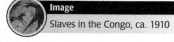
Image
Slaves in the Congo, ca. 1910

and twenty thousand African laborers had perished from starvation, disease, and maltreatment. A white settler in Kenya candidly expressed the view held by many colonial administrators: "We have stolen his land. Now we must steal his limbs. Compulsory labor is the corollary to our occupation of the country."

African Nationalism

In the decades following the Great War, many Africans were disappointed that their contributions to that conflict went unrewarded. In place of anticipated social reforms or some degree of greater political participation came an extension and a consolidation of

A European colonialist takes advantage of African labor and is "Traveling in Hammock," as this 1912 photograph's title suggests.

the colonial system. Nevertheless, ideas concerning self-determination, articulated by U.S. president Woodrow Wilson during the war, gained adherents among a group of African nationalists. Those ideas influenced the growth of African nationalism and the development of incipient nationalist movements. An emerging class of native urban intellectuals, frequently educated in Europe, became especially involved in the formation of ideologies that promised freedom from colonialism and promoted new national identities.

Colonialism prompted the emergence of a new African social class, sometimes called the "new elite."
Africa's New Elite
This elite derived its status from European-style education and employment in the colonial state, in foreign companies, or in Christian missions. The upper echelons of this elite were high-ranking civil servants, physicians, lawyers, and writers who had studied abroad in western Europe or the United States. A case in point was Jomo Kenyatta (1895–1978), who spent almost fifteen years in Europe, during which time he attended various schools, including the London School of Economics. An immensely articulate nationalist, Kenyatta later led Kenya to independence from the British. Below men such as Kenyatta in status stood teachers, clerks, and interpreters who had obtained a European-derived primary or secondary education. All members of the elite, however, spoke and understood the language of the colonizer and outwardly adopted the cultural norms of the colonizer, such as wearing European-style clothes or adopting European names. It was within the ranks of this new elite that ideas concerning African identity and nationhood germinated.

Because colonialism had introduced Africans to European ideas and ideologies, African nationalists frequently embraced the European concept
Forms of Nationalism
of the nation as a means of forging unity—as well as colonial resistance—among disparate African groups. Some nationalists looked to the precolonial past for inspiration. There they found identities based on ethnicity, religion, and languages, and they believed that any future nation must reconstitute distinctively African spiritual and political institutions. Race had provided colonial powers with one rationale for conquest and exploitation; hence it was not surprising that some nationalists used the concept of an African race as a foundation for identity, solidarity, and nation building. Indeed, race figured prominently in a strain of African nationalism known as pan-Africanism, which originated in the western hemisphere among the descendants of slaves. Representative of this pan-Africanism was the Jamaican nationalist leader Marcus Garvey (1887–1940), who thought of all Africans as members of a single race and who promoted the unification of all people of African descent into a single African state. Still other nationalists looked for an African identity rooted in geography rather than in race.
That approach commonly translated into a desire to build the
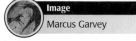
Image
Marcus Garvey
nation on the basis of borders that defined existing colonial states. Collectively those ideas influenced the development of nationalist movements during the 1930s and 1940s, which, after World War II, translated into demands for independence from colonialism.

LATIN AMERICAN STRUGGLES WITH NEOCOLONIALISM

The postcolonial history of Latin American states in the early twentieth century offered clues about what the future might hold for those areas in Asia and Africa still seeking independence from colonial rule. Having gained their independence in the nineteenth century, most sovereign nations in Latin America thereafter struggled to achieve political and economic stability in the midst of interference from foreign powers. The era of the Great War and the Great Depression proved crucial to solidifying and exposing to view the neocolonial structures that guided affairs in Latin America. Generally seen as a more subtle form of imperial control, neocolonialism refers to foreign economic domination, as well as military and political intervention, in states that have already achieved independence from colonial rule. In Central and South America, as well as in the Caribbean, this new imperial influence came not from former colonial rulers in Spain and Portugal but, rather, from wealthy, industrial-capitalist powerhouses such as Great Britain and the United States. Neocolonialism impinged on the political and economic development of Latin American states, but it did not fully prevent nationalist leaders from devising strategies to combat the newfound imperialism.

The Impact of the Great War and the Great Depression

The Great War, the Russian revolution, and the Mexican revolution spread radical ideas and the promise of new political possibilities throughout Latin America. The disparate ideals emerging from this time of politi-

SOURCES FROM THE PAST

Africa for Africans

Marcus Garvey (1887–1940) is best remembered as a pivotal figure in black nationalism, one who inspired nationalist movements as well as many African leaders. A powerful orator, Garvey preached the greatness of the African heritage and called on European colonial powers to leave Africa. Convinced that blacks in the diaspora could never secure their rights as minorities, this "Black Moses" rejected the idea of integration and instead championed a "Back to Africa" movement. According to Garvey, a Jamaican who garnered notoriety during his time in the United States, only in ancestral Africa would it be possible to establish an autonomous black state that featured its own unique culture.

■ ■ ■

George Washington was not God Almighty. He was a man like any Negro in this building, and if he and his associates were able to make a free America, we too can make a free Africa. Hampden, Gladstone, Pitt and Disraeli were not the representatives of God in the person of Jesus Christ. They were but men, but in their time they worked for the expansion of the British Empire, and today they boast of a British Empire upon which "the sun never sets." As Pitt and Gladstone were able to work for the expansion of the British Empire, so you and I can work for the expansion of a great African Empire. Voltaire and Mirabeau were not Jesus Christs, they were but men like ourselves. They worked and overturned the French Monarchy. They worked for the Democracy which France now enjoys, and if they were able to do that, we are able to work for a democracy in Africa. Lenin and Trotsky were not Jesus Christs, but they were able to overthrow the despotism of Russia, and today they have given to the world a Social Republic, the first of its kind. If Lenin and Trotsky were able to do that for Russia, you and I can do that for Africa. Therefore, let no man, let no power on earth, turn you from this sacred cause of liberty. I prefer to die at this moment rather than not to work for the freedom of Africa. If liberty is good for certain sets of humanity it is good for all. Black men, Colored men, Negroes have as much right to be free as any other race that God Almighty ever created, and we desire freedom that is unfettered, freedom that is unlimited, freedom that will give us a chance and opportunity to rise to the fullest of our ambition and that we cannot get in countries where other men rule and dominate.

We have reached the time when every minute, every second must count for something done, something achieved in the cause of Africa. . . . It falls to our lot to tear off the shackles that bind Mother Africa. Can you do it? You did it in the Revolutionary War. You did it in the Civil War; You did it at the Battles of the Marne and Verdun; You did it in Mesopotamia. You can do it marching up the battle heights of Africa. Let the world know that 400,000,000 Negroes are prepared to die or live as free men. Despise us as much as you care. Ignore us as much as you care. We are coming 400,000,000 strong. We are coming with our woes behind us, with the memory of suffering behind us—woes and suffering of three hundred years—they shall be our inspiration. My bulwark of strength in the conflict of freedom in Africa, will be the three hundred years of persecution and hardship left behind in this Western Hemisphere.

• *In his speech, how does Marcus Garvey convey the significance of Africa for both Africans and those involved in the black diaspora?*

SOURCE: Amy Jacques Garvey, compiler. *Philosophy and Opinions of Marcus Garvey or Africa for Africans.* London: Frank Cass and Co., 1967, pp. 73–74.

cal ferment found receptive audiences in Latin America, especially during the global economic crisis of the Great Depression. Marxism, Vladimir Lenin's theories on capitalism and imperialism, and a growing concern for the impoverished Indian masses as well as exploited peasants and workers in Latin American societies informed the outlooks of many disgruntled intellectuals and artists. The Enlightenment-derived liberalism that had shaped independence movements and the political systems of many post-independence nations no longer served as the only form of political legitimacy.

Some of the most radical responses to U.S. economic domination came from Latin American universities, whose students became increasingly politicized in this period. Many took their inspiration from the Mexican and Russian revolutions—both of which were inimical to the ideas of the United States. Indeed, universities became training grounds for future political leaders, including Cuba's Fidel Castro (1926–). In many Latin American countries, radicalism also expressed itself in the formation of political parties that either openly espoused communism or otherwise adopted rebellious agendas for change.

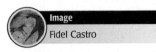

The ideological transformations apparent in Latin America became stunningly and publicly visible in the murals painted by famed Mexican artist Diego Rivera (1886–1957). Artistically trained in Mexico in his youth, Rivera went to study in Europe in 1907 and did not return to Mexico until 1921. Influenced by indigenous art forms as well as the European Renaissance artists and Cubists, Rivera's paintings reflected the turmoil and shifting political sensibilities taking place during the Great War and its aftermath. He blended his artistic and political visions in vast public murals in Mexico's cities, because he believed that art should be on display for working people.

Diego Rivera and Radical Artistic Visions

As a political activist, Rivera also used his art to level a pointed critique of the economic dependency and political repressiveness engendered by U.S. neocolonialism in Latin America. In the painting *Imperialism,* for example, Rivera depicted massive guns and tanks extending over the New York Stock Exchange. In the foreground and at the edges of the stock exchange are a variety of Latin American victims of this monied-military oppression. Indeed, Rivera made visible the

Diego Rivera's *Imperialism* was one in a series of paintings on the United States and offered a visual critique of U.S. neocolonialism in Latin America.

impact of U.S. imperialism on Latin American societies, and by doing so he helped spread political activism in the Americas.

The Evolution of Economic Imperialism

Latin American states were no strangers to foreign economic domination in the nineteenth and early twentieth centuries. Their export-oriented economies had long been tied to global finances and had been subject to controls imposed by foreign investors, largely those from Great Britain and the United States. The major evolution in economic neocolonialism during this period concerned the growing predominance of the United States in the economic affairs of Latin American nations, which was sealed by the Great War. Between 1924 and 1929, U.S. banks and businesses more than doubled their financial interests in Latin America as investments grew from $1.5 billion to $3.5 billion.

That U.S. neocolonialism was meant to be largely economic became evident in the policies of President William Howard Taft (1857–1931). In his final address to Congress in 1912, Taft argued that the United States should substitute "dollars for bullets" in its foreign policy. He wanted businesses to develop foreign markets through peaceful commerce and believed that expensive military intervention should be avoided as much as possible. This new vision of U.S. expansion abroad, dubbed "dollar diplomacy" by critics, encapsulated the gist of what those in Latin America perceived as "Yankee imperialism."

The economic crisis of the Great Depression demonstrated the extent to which Latin America had become integrated in the world economy. Indeed, the Great Depression halted fifty years of economic growth in Latin America and illustrated the region's susceptibility to global economic crises. For one thing, U.S. capital investments for nascent industries and other financial concerns during the 1920s could not be

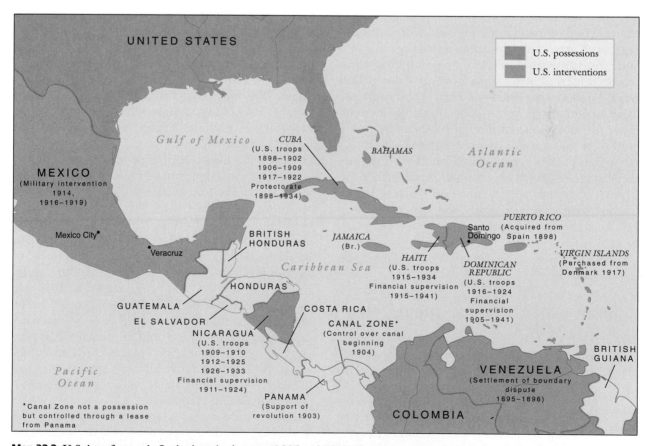

Map 32.2 U.S. interference in Latin America between 1895 and 1941. Note the number of states where U.S. troops intervened in local politics. On what basis did U.S. policymakers justify those interventions?

maintained during this disastrous economic downturn. Moreover, most Latin American states, because they exported agricultural products or raw materials, suffered from plummeting prices. Indeed, the prices of sugar from the Caribbean, coffee from Brazil and Colombia, wheat and beef from Argentina, tin from Bolivia, nitrates from Chile, and many other products fell sharply after 1929. Throughout Latin America unemployment rates increased rapidly. The drastic decline in the price of the region's exports and the drying-up of foreign capital prompted Latin American governments to raise tariffs on foreign products and impose various other restrictions on foreign trade.

Although the weaknesses of export-oriented economies and industrial development financed by foreigners became evident during the Great Depression, the international crisis also allowed Latin American nations to take alternative paths to economic development. Economic policy stressing internal economic development was most visible in Brazil, where dictator-president (1930–1945, 1950–1954) Getúlio Dornelles Vargas (1883–1954) turned his nation into an *estado novo* (new state). Ruling with the backing of the military but without the support of the landowning elite, Vargas and his government during the 1930s and 1940s embarked on a program of industrialization that created new enterprises. Key among them was the iron and steel industry. The Vargas regime also implemented protectionist policies that shielded domestic production from foreign competition, which pleased both industrialists and urban workers. Social welfare initiatives accompanied industrial development, protecting workers with health and safety regulations, minimum wages, limits on working hours, unemployment compensation, and retirement benefits. Thus the Great Depression contributed in many ways to the evolution of both economic neocolonialism and economic experimentation within Latin American states.

Conflicts with a "Good Neighbor"

The pressures of the Great Depression and the instability of global politics led to a reassessment of U.S. foreign policy in Latin America during the late 1920s and 1930s. U.S. leaders realized the *The "Good* costliness and the ineffectiveness of *Neighbor Policy"* direct interventions in Latin America, especially when committing U.S. marines as peacekeeping forces. To extricate U.S. military forces and

rely more fully on "dollar diplomacy," policymakers instituted certain innovations that nonetheless called into question any true change of heart among U.S. neocolonialists. They approved "sweetheart treaties" that guaranteed U.S. financial control in the Caribbean economies of Haiti and the Dominican Republic, for example, and the U.S. Marines provided training for indigenous police forces to keep the peace and maintain law and order. This revamped U.S. approach to relations with Latin America became known as the "Good Neighbor Policy," and it was most closely associated with the administration of Franklin D. Roosevelt (1882–1945).

Interactive Map
The U.S. in Latin America

Under Roosevelt, the Good Neighbor Policy evolved into a more conciliatory U.S. approach to Latin American relations. The interventionist corollary to the Monroe Doctrine enunciated previously by President Theodore Roosevelt (1859–1919) was formally renounced in December 1933, when Secretary of State Cordell Hull attended the Seventh International Conference of American States in Montevideo, Uruguay. Hull signed the Convention on the Rights and Duties of States, which held that "no state has the right to intervene in the internal or external affairs of another." That proposition faced a severe challenge in March 1938 when Mexican president Lázaro Cárdenas (1895–1970) nationalized the oil industry, much of which was controlled by foreign investors from the United States and Great Britain.

Given the history of tempestuous relations between the United States and Mexico, including multiple U.S. military incursions into Mexico during the revolution, it seemed there was little chance for a peaceful resolution to this provocative move on the part of Cárdenas. The reluctance of U.S. and British oil companies to grant concessions to Mexican oil workers prompted him to this drastic act. Yet despite calls for a strong U.S. and British response, Roosevelt and his administration officials resisted the demands of big businesses and instead called for a cool, calm response and negotiations to end the conflict. This plan prevailed, and the foreign oil companies ultimately had to accept only $24 million in compensation rather than the $260 million that they initially demanded.

Although the nationalization crisis in Mexico ended in a fashion that suggested the strength of the Good Neighbor Policy, a good deal of the impetus for this policy came from economic and political concerns

This Hollywood publicity photo of Carmen Miranda features the type of lively costuming that made her a colorful favorite in both the United States and Latin America.

associated with the Great Depression and the deterioration of international relations in the 1930s. The United States wanted to cultivate Latin American markets for its exports, and it wanted to distance itself from the militarist behavior of Asian and European imperial powers. The U.S. government knew it needed to improve relations with Latin America, if only to secure those nations' support in the increasingly likely event of another global war. Widespread Mexican migration to the United States during and after the Great

War suggested the attractiveness of the United States for at least some Latin Americans.

Filling the migration void left by Europeans prevented from coming to the United States by the war and by the U.S. immigration restriction laws of the 1920s, Mexican men, women, and children entered the United States in the hundreds of thousands to engage in agricultural and industrial work. The migrants suffered the animosity of some U.S. citizens, who considered them "cheap Mexican labor," but the political power of agribusinesses prevented the government from instituting legal restrictions on Mexican migration. Federal and local officials managed, however, to deport thousands of Mexicans during the Great Depression.

Trying to contribute to the repairing of relations and the promoting of more positive images of Latin American and U.S. relations, Hollywood adopted a Latin American singing and dancing sensation, Carmen Miranda (1909–1955). Born in Portugal but raised from childhood in Brazil, Miranda found fame on a Rio de Janeiro radio station and recorded hundreds of hit songs. In the United States, she gained her greatest visibility in films produced during World War II, such as *Down Argentine Way* (1940). Carmen Miranda appeared as an exotic Latin American woman, usually clothed in sexy, colorful costumes that featured headdresses adorned with the fruits grown in Latin America—such as bananas. She softened representations of Latin Americans for audiences in the United States, providing a less threatening counterpoint to laboring migrants or women guerrilla fighters in Mexico's revolution. She also became a source of pride for Brazilians, who reveled in her Hollywood success. Hollywood's espousal of Roosevelt's Good Neighbor Policy proved a success.

SUMMARY

In the decades after the Great War, and in the midst of the Great Depression, intellectuals and political activists in Asia, Africa, and Latin America challenged the ideological and economic underpinnings of empire and neocolonialism. Often embracing the ideas and theories that disseminated around the globe as a result of the war, including self-determination, socialism, communism, and anti-imperialism, radicals and nationalists revised understandings of political identity in the colonial and neocolonial worlds.

Japanese and U.S. imperial practices incited military and civil discord within their respective spheres, while European colonial rulers continued to limit, often brutally, the freedom of peoples in India and Africa. Like Shanfei, young intellectuals and older political leaders alike emerged transformed in these years. Their efforts to inspire nationalism and to achieve economic and political autonomy came to fruition later—after another world war had come and gone.

CHRONOLOGY

1912	Taft establishes "dollar diplomacy" as U.S. foreign policy
1914–1918	2.5 million African troops and carriers serve in the Great War
1919	May Fourth Movement in China
1920	Non-Cooperation Movement in India
1921	Rivera returns to Mexico to paint
1928	Socialist Party of Peru is founded
1929	Beginning of Great Depression
1930	Civil Disobedience Movement in India
1931	Japanese invasion of Manchuria
1933	Roosevelt begins practice of the Good Neighbor Policy
1934	Long March by Chinese communists
1935	Government of India Act is passed
1938	Cárdenas nationalizes oil industry in Mexico

FOR FURTHER READING

A. Adu Boahen, ed. *Africa under Colonial Domination, 1880–1935.* Berkeley, 1985. Part of the ambitious UNESCO General History of Africa (vol. 7), this work reflects how different Africans view their own history.

Tulio Halperin Donghi. *The Contemporary History of Latin America.* Translated and edited by John Charles Chasteen. Durham, 1993. An exhaustive historical survey of Latin American social and political change.

Cynthia Enloe. *Bananas, Beaches & Bases: Making Feminist Sense of International Politics.* Berkeley, 1989. A gendered analysis of U.S. and other foreign policies through such categories as tourism and diplomats' spouses.

Robert E. Hannigan. *The New World Power: American Foreign Policy, 1898–1917.* Philadelphia, 2002. A detailed account of U.S. foreign relations that links class, race, and gender influences to policymakers.

John Iliffe. *Africans: The History of a Continent.* New York, 1995. A well-written introductory text that is organized thematically rather than chronologically.

Jim Masselos. *Indian Nationalism: A History.* 3rd ed. Columbia, 1998. A keen work that remains the standard, most readable introduction to Indian leaders and movements.

Michael E. Parish. *Anxious Decades: America in Prosperity and Depression, 1920–1941.* New York, 1992. A detailed portrait of the United States between the world wars, featuring treatments of foreign relations with Latin America.

Jonathan D. Spence. *Mao Zedong.* New York, 1999. Blending history with cultural analysis, this intimate portrait of Mao is informative despite its brevity.

Odd Arne Westad. *Decisive Encounters: The Chinese Civil War, 1946–1950.* Stanford, 2003. An engagingly written work that introduces the reader to the salient political and military events that led to the eventual defeat of the Guomindang.

Louise Young. *Japan's Total Empire: Manchuria and the Culture of Wartime Imperialism.* Berkeley, 1999. An important and penetrating work on the nature of Japanese imperialism.

CHAPTER 33

New Conflagrations: World War II

On 6 August 1945, as he listened to the armed services radio on Saipan (a U.S.-controlled island in the North Pacific), U.S. marine Victor Tolley heard the president of the United States announce that a "terrible new weapon" had been deployed against the city of Hiroshima, Japan. Tolley and the other marines rejoiced, realizing that the terrible new weapon—the atomic bomb—might end the war. A few days later Tolley heard that the city of Nagasaki had also been hit with an atomic bomb and that radio announcers suggested it might be decades before either city would be inhabitable.

Imagine Tolley's astonishment when he was assigned to the U.S. occupation forces in Nagasaki just a few weeks after the Japanese surrender. Assured that Nagasaki was "very safe," Tolley lived there for

three months, during which he became very familiar with the devastation wrought by the bomb. Tolley also became acquainted with some of the Japanese survivors in Nagasaki, which proved to be an eye-opening experience. After seeing "young children with sores and burns all over," Tolley, having become separated from his unit, befriended a young boy who took Tolley home to meet his surviving family. Tolley recalled that while speaking to the boy's father about his missing son-in-law, "it dawned on me that they suffered the same as we did. They lost sons and daughters and relatives, and they hurt too."

Before his chance meeting with this Japanese family, Tolley had felt nothing except contempt for the Japanese. He pointed out, "We were trained to kill them. They asked for it and now we're

OPPOSITE PAGE: *A Japanese child crouches and cries in the rubble of Hiroshima in the aftermath of the atomic bombing, expressing the profound sadness of war and its devastating weapons.*

gonna give it to 'em. That's how I felt until I met this young boy and his family." But after coming face-to-face with his enemies, Tolley saw only their common humanity, their suffering, and their hurt.

The civility that reemerged at the end of the war was little evident during the war years. The war began and ended with Japan. In 1931 Japan invaded Manchuria, and the United States concluded hostilities by dropping atomic bombs on Hiroshima and Nagasaki. By 1941 World War II was a truly global war. Hostilities spread from east Asia and the Pacific to Europe, north Africa, and the Atlantic. Beyond its immense geographic scope, World War II exceeded even the Great War (1914–1918) in demonstrating the willingness of societies to make enormous sacrifices in lives and other resources to achieve complete victory. Moreover, World War II redefined gender roles and relations between colonial peoples and their colonizers. The cold war and the atomic age that began almost as soon as World War II ended also inaugurated a new global order. In particular, the United States and the Soviet Union gained geopolitical strength during the early years of the cold war as they competed for global influence.

ORIGINS OF WORLD WAR II

In 1941 two major alliances squared off against each other. Japan, Germany, and Italy, along with their conquered territories, formed the Axis powers. The Allied powers included France and its empire; Great Britain, its empire, and its Commonwealth allies (such as Canada, Australia, and New Zealand); the Soviet Union; China; and the United States and its allies in Latin America. Driven in part by a desire to revise the peace settlements that followed the Great War and compelled by the economic distress of the worldwide depression, Japan, Italy, and Germany engaged in a campaign of territorial expansion that ultimately broke apart the structure of international cooperation that had kept the world from violence in the 1920s. These revisionist powers, so called because they revised or overthrew the terms of the post–Great War peace, confronted nations that were committed to the avoidance of another world war. To expand their global influence, the revisionist nations remilitarized and conquered territories they deemed central to their needs. The Allies acquiesced to the revisionist powers' early aggressive actions, but in the late 1930s and early 1940s they decided to engage the Axis powers in a total war.

Japan's War in China

The global conflict opened with Japan's attacks on China in the 1930s: the conquest of Manchuria between 1931 and 1932 was the first step in the revisionist process of expansionism and aggression. In 1933, after the League of Nations condemned its actions in Manchuria, Japan withdrew from the league and followed an ultranationalist and promilitary policy. Four years later, Japan launched a full-scale invasion of China. Japanese troops first took Beijing and then moved south toward Shanghai and Nanjing, the capital of China. Japanese naval and air forces bombed

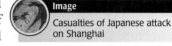

Casualties of Japanese attack on Shanghai

Shanghai, killing thousands of civilians, and secured it as a landing area for armies bound for Nanjing. By December 1937 Shanghai and Nanjing had fallen, and during the following six months Japanese forces won repeated victories.

China became the first nation to experience the horrors of World War II: brutal warfare against civilians and repressive occupation. Chinese civilians were among the first to feel the effects of aerial bombing of urban centers; the people of Shanghai died by the tens of thousands when Japanese bombers attacked the city. What became known as the Rape of Nanjing demonstrated the brutality of the war as the residents of Nanjing became victims of Japanese troops inflamed by war passion and a sense of racial superiority. Over the course of two months, Japanese soldiers raped seven thousand women, murdered hundreds of thousands of unarmed soldiers and civilians, and burned one-third of the homes in Nanjing. Four hundred thousand Chinese lost their lives as Japanese soldiers used them for bayonet practice and machine-gunned them into open pits. *The Rape of Nanjing*

Despite Japanese military successes, Chinese resistance persisted throughout the war. Japanese aggression aroused feelings of nationalism among the Chinese that continued to grow as the war wore on. By September 1937 nationalists and communists had agreed on a "united front" policy against the Japanese, uniting themselves into standing armies of some 1.7 million soldiers. Although Chinese forces failed to defeat the Japanese, who retained naval and air superiority, they tied up half the Japanese army, 750,000 soldiers, by 1941. *Chinese Resistance*

Throughout the war, the coalition of nationalists and communists threatened to fall apart as the two groups competed for control of enemy territory and

Japanese soldiers execute
Chinese prisoners.

for political control within China. Those clashes rendered Chinese resistance less effective. While the nationalists shied away from direct military confrontation with Japanese forces and kept the Guomindang government alive by moving inland to Chongqing, the Chinese communists carried on guerrilla operations against the Japanese invaders. The guerrillas did not defeat the Japanese, but they captured the loyalty of many Chinese peasants through their resistance to the Japanese and their moderate policies of land reform. At the end of the war, the communists were poised to lead China.

The Japanese invasion of China met with intense international opposition, yet other world powers, distracted by depression and military aggression in Europe, could offer little in the way of an effective response to Japanese actions. The government of Japan aligned itself with the other revisionist nations, Germany and Italy, by signing a ten-year military and economic pact, the Tripartite Pact, in September 1940. Japan also cleared the way for further empire building in Asia and the Pacific basin by concluding a neutrality

pact with the Soviet Union in April 1941, thereby precluding hostilities in Manchuria. Japan did not face determined opposition to its expansion until it ran into conflict with the United States in December 1941.

Italian and German Aggression

Italy's expansionism helped destabilize the post–Great War peace. Italians suffered tremendously in World War I. Six hundred thousand Italian soldiers died, and the national economy was badly damaged. Many Italians expected far greater recompense and respect than they received at the conclusion of the Great War.

Benito Mussolini promised to bring glory to Italy through the acquisition of territories that it had been denied after the Great War. Italy's conquest of *Italy* Ethiopia in 1935 and 1936, when added to the previously annexed Libya, created an overseas empire. Italy also intervened in the Spanish Civil War (1936–1939) on the side of General Francisco Franco (1892–1975), and it annexed Albania in 1939. The invasion and conquest of Ethiopia in particular infuriated other

Ethiopian soldiers train with outmoded equipment that proves no match for Italian forces.

nations, but as with Japan's invasion of Manchuria, the League of Nations offered little effective opposition.

What angered nonrevisionists about Italy's conquest of Ethiopia was not just the broken peace but also the excessive use of force. Mussolini sent an army of 250,000 soldiers armed with tanks, poison gas, artillery, and aircraft to conquer the Ethiopians, who were entirely unprepared for the assault. The mechanized Italian troops mowed them down. Italy lost 2,000 soldiers, whereas 275,000 Ethiopians lost their lives.

Japan and Italy were the first nations to challenge the post–World War I settlements through territorial conquest, but it was Germany that systematically undid the Treaty of Versailles and the fragile peace of the interwar years. Most Germans deeply resented the harsh terms imposed on their nation in 1919. Adolf Hitler (1889–1945) came to power in 1933, riding a wave of public discontent with Germany's postwar powerlessness and the suffering caused by the Great Depression. Hitler referred to the signing of the 1918 armistice as the "November crime" and blamed it on those he viewed as Germany's internal enemies: Jews, communists, and liberals of all sorts. Hitler's scheme for ridding Germany of its enemies and reasserting its power was remilitarization—which was legally denied to Germany under the Versailles Treaty. Hitler's aggressive foreign policy helped relieve the German public's feeling of war shame and depression trauma. After withdrawing Germany from the League of Nations in 1933, his government carried out a large-scale plan to strengthen the German armed forces. Hitler reinstated universal

Germany

military service in 1935, and in the following year his troops entered the previously demilitarized Rhineland, which bordered France. In 1938 Hitler began the campaign of expansion that ultimately led to the outbreak of World War II in Europe.

Germany's forced *Anschluss* ("union") with Austria took place in March 1938. Hitler justified this annexation as an attempt to reintegrate all Germans into a single homeland. Europe's major powers, France and Britain, did nothing in response, thereby enhancing Hitler's reputation in the German military and deepening his contempt for the democracies. Soon thereafter, using the same rationale, the Nazis attempted to gain control of the Sudetenland, the western portion of Czechoslovakia, which was inhabited largely by ethnic Germans. In September 1938 Hitler demanded the immediate cession of the Sudetenland to the German Reich. Against the desires of the Czechoslovak government, the leaders of France and Britain accommodated Hitler and allowed Germany to annex the Sudetenland. Neither the French nor the British were willing to risk a military confrontation with Germany to defend Czechoslovakian territory.

At the Munich Conference, held in September 1938, European politicians formulated the policy that came to be known as appeasement. In conceding demands to Hitler, or "appeasing" him, the British and French governments extracted a promise that Hitler would cease further efforts to expand German territorial claims. Their goal was to keep peace in Europe, even if it meant making major concessions. Britain's prime minister, Neville Chamberlain (1869–1940), arrived home from Munich to announce that the meeting had achieved "peace for our time." Unprepared for war and distressed by the depression, nations sympathetic to Britain and France also embraced peace as an admirable goal in the face of aggression by the revisionist nations.

Hitler, however, refused to be bound by the Munich agreement, and in the next year German troops occupied most of Czechoslovakia. As Hitler next threatened Poland, it became clear that the policy of appeasement was a failure, which caused Britain and France to abandon it by guaranteeing the security of Poland. By that time Joseph Stalin (1879–1953) was convinced that British and French leaders were conspiring to deflect German aggression toward the Soviet Union, which made him seek an accommodation with the Nazi regime. In August 1939 the foreign ministers of the Soviet Union and Germany signed the Russian-German Treaty of Nonaggression, an agreement that promised neutrality in the event of war with a third party and prevented the possibility of a war on two fronts. Additionally, a secret protocol divided eastern Europe into German and Soviet spheres of influence. Hitler was ready to conquer Europe.

TOTAL WAR: THE WORLD UNDER FIRE

Two months after the United States became embroiled in World War II, President Franklin Roosevelt (1882–1945) delivered one of his famous radio broadcasts, known as fireside chats. In it he explained: "This war is a new kind of war. It is warfare in terms of every continent, every island, every sea, every air lane." There was little exaggeration in FDR's analysis. Before World War II was over, almost every nation had participated in it, and virtually every weapon known to humanity had been used. More so than the Great War, this was a conflict in which entire societies engaged in warfare and mobilized every available material and human resource.

The war between Japan and China had been in progress for eight years when European nations stormed into battle in 1939. By 1941 nations outside Europe were also drawn into the conflict, including the French and British colonies in Africa and India, as well as Canada, Australia, and New Zealand. As the war dragged on, only eleven countries avoided direct involvement: Afghanistan, Greenland, Iceland, Ireland, Mongolia, Portugal, Spain, Sweden, Switzerland, Tibet, and Yemen.

Blitzkrieg: Germany Conquers Europe

During World War II it became common for aggressor nations to avoid overt declarations of war. Instead, the new armed forces relied on surprise and swiftness for their conquests. Germany demonstrated the advantages of that strategy in Poland, when their air force and *Panzer* ("armored") columns moved into Poland unannounced on 1 September 1939. Within a month they had subdued its western expanses while the Soviets took the eastern sections in accordance with the Nazi-Soviet pact. The Germans stunned the world with their *Blitzkrieg* ("lightning war") and sudden victory.

Nazi rallies in Nuremberg

With Poland subdued, Germany prepared to break through European defenses. In April 1940 the Germans occupied Denmark and Norway, then launched a full-scale attack on western Europe. Their offensive against Belgium, France, and the Netherlands began in May, and again the Allies were jolted by Blitzkrieg tactics. Belgium and the Netherlands fell first, and the French signed an armistice in June. After the fall of France, Italy's Benito Mussolini entered the conflict in the hopes of reaping any potential benefits his partnership with the Germans might offer.   *The Fall of France*

Before the battle for France, Hitler had boasted to his staff, "Gentlemen, you are about to witness the most famous victory in history!" Given France's rapid fall, Hitler was not far wrong. In a moment of exquisite triumph, Hitler had the French sign their armistice in the very railroad car in which the Germans had signed the armistice in 1918. Meanwhile, the British, in an attempt to rescue the remaining Allied troops in France, engineered a stunning retreat from Dunkirk across the English Channel, but it could not hide the bleak failure of the Allied troops. Britain now stood alone against the German forces.

Germany therefore launched the Battle of Britain, led by its air force, the Luftwaffe. "The Blitz," as the British called this air war, rained bombs on heavily populated metropolitan areas, especially London, and killed more than forty   *The Battle of Britain* thousand British civilians. The Royal Air Force staved off defeat, however, forcing Hitler to abandon plans to

Adolf Hitler proudly walks through conquered Paris in 1940, with the Eiffel Tower as a backdrop.

invade Britain. Yet despite the setback in Britain, Hitler had plenty of reasons to be happy by the summer of 1941, for the swastika-bedecked Nazi flag waved from the streets of Paris to the Acropolis in Athens, and he had succeeded beyond his dreams in his quest to reverse the outcome of World War I.

The German Invasion of the Soviet Union

Flush with victory in the spring of 1941, Hitler turned his sights on the Soviet Union. This land was the ultimate German target, from which Jews, Slavs, and Bolsheviks could be expelled or exterminated to create more Lebensraum ("living space") for resettled Germans. Believing firmly in the bankruptcy of the Soviet system, Hitler was confident that in the Soviet Union

---

Lebensraum (LAY-behnz-rahwm)

"you only have to kick in the door, and the whole rotten structure will come crashing down."

On 22 June 1941, Adolf Hitler ordered the initiation of Operation Barbarossa, the invasion of the Soviet Union. For that, the German military assembled the largest and most powerful invasion force in history, attacking with 3.6 million soldiers, thirty-seven hundred tanks, twenty-five hundred planes, and thirty divisions from the governments of Hungary, Finland, and Romania. The invasion along a front of 3,000 kilometers (1,900 miles) took Stalin by surprise and caught the Red Army off guard. By December 1941 German troops had reached the gates of Moscow. Germany seemed assured of victory. *Operation Barbarossa*

However, German Blitzkrieg tactics that had earlier proved so effective in Poland and western Europe failed the Germans in the vast expanses of Russia. Hitler and his military leaders underestimated Soviet personnel reserves and industrial capacity. Within a matter of weeks, for example, the 150 German divisions faced 360 divisions of the Red Army. By the time the German forces reached the outskirts of Moscow, fierce Soviet resistance had produced eight hundred thousand German casualties.

The arrival of winter—the most severe in decades— also helped Soviet military efforts. So sure of an early victory were the Germans that they did not bother to supply their troops with winter clothing and boots. One hundred thousand soldiers suffered frostbite, and two thousand of them underwent amputation. The Red Army, in contrast, prepared for winter and found further comfort in the thirteen million pairs of felt-lined winter boots sent by their allies in the United States. By early December, Soviet counterattacks along the entire front had stopped German advances.

In the spring of 1942 the Germans briefly regained the military initiative, and by June they were approaching the city of Stalingrad. As the Germans came upon Stalingrad in September, the Russians dug in. "Not a step back," Stalin ordered. The Russians did indeed hold Stalingrad, but only at the price of waging a bloody street-by-street defense of the city until the Red Army could regroup for a counterattack.

Battles in Asia and the Pacific

Before 1941 the United States was inching toward greater involvement in the war. In 1939 it instituted a cash-and-carry policy of supplying the British, in which the British paid cash and carried the materials on their own ships. More significant was the lend-lease program initiated in 1941, in which the United States "lent" destroyers and other war goods to the British in return for the lease of naval bases. The program later extended such aid to the Soviets, the Chinese, and many others.

German victories in 1940 and Great Britain's precarious military position in Europe encouraged the Japanese to project their influence into southeast Asia in their quest for raw materials such as tin, rubber, and petroleum. Between September 1940 and July 1941, and with the blessings of the German-backed Vichy government of France, Japanese forces occupied French Indochina (now Vietnam, Laos, and Cambodia). The government of the United States—supported by Great Britain, the Commonwealth of Nations, and the Dutch East Indies—responded to this situation by freezing Japanese assets in the United States and by imposing a complete embargo on oil. To Japanese militarists faced with the alternative either of succumbing to U.S. demands—which included the withdrawal of Japanese forces from China and southeast Asia—or of engaging the United States in war, war seemed the lesser of two evils.

The Japanese hoped to destroy American naval capacity in the Pacific with an attack at Pearl Harbor. On 7 December 1941, "a date which will live in infamy," as Franklin Roosevelt concluded, more than 350 Japanese bombers, fighters, and torpedo planes struck in two waves, sinking or disabling eighteen ships and destroying more than two hundred. Except for the U.S. aircraft carriers, which were out of the harbor at the time, American naval power in the Pacific was devastated.

Pearl Harbor

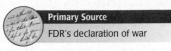
Primary Source
FDR's declaration of war

On 11 December 1941, though not compelled to do so by treaty, Hitler and Mussolini declared war on the United States. That move provided the United States with the only reason it needed to declare war on Germany and Italy. The United States, Great Britain, and the Soviet Union came together in a coalition that linked two vast and interconnected theaters of war, the European and Asian-Pacific theaters, and ensured the defeat of Germany and Japan. Winston Churchill (1874–1965), prime minister of Britain, expressed a vast sense of relief when he said: "So we had won after all!"

Flames consumed U.S. battleships in Pearl Harbor after the Japanese attack on 7 December 1941.

Japanese Victories

Yet after Pearl Harbor the Japanese swept on to one victory after another. The Japanese coordinated their strike against Pearl Harbor with simultaneous attacks against the Philippines, Guam, Wake Island, Midway Island, Hong Kong, Thailand, and British Malaya. For the next year the Japanese military maintained the initiative in southeast Asia and the Pacific, capturing Borneo, Burma, the Dutch East Indies, and several Aleutian islands off Alaska. Australia and New Zealand were now within striking distance. Moreover, the humiliating surrender of British-held Singapore in February 1942 dealt a blow to British prestige and shattered any myths of European military invincibility.

The slogan under which Japan pursued expansion in Asia was "Asia for Asians," according to which the Japanese would lead Asian peoples to independence from the despised European imperialists. In this struggle for Asian independence, Japan required the region's resources, arguing that this was necessary to build a "Greater East Asia Co-Prosperity Sphere." The appeal to Asian independence at first struck a responsive chord among Asians, but conquest and brutal occupation soon made it obvious to most Asians that the real agenda was "Asia for the Japanese." Proponents of the Greater East Asia Co-Prosperity Sphere advocated Japan's expansion in Asia and the Pacific while cloaking their territorial and economic designs with the idealism of Asian nationalism.

Map 33.1 The high tide of Axis expansion in Europe and north Africa between 1942 and 1943. Observe the number of nations occupied by or allied with the Axis powers. Given Axis dominance in Europe, what factors finally allowed the Allies to turn the tide of war in their favor?

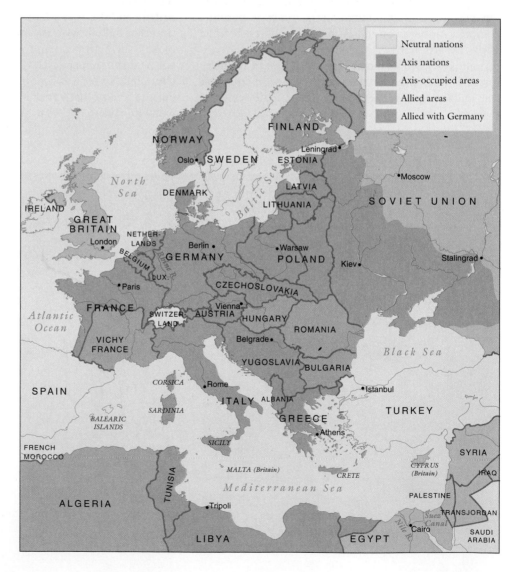

Defeat of the Axis Powers

The entry of the Soviet Union and the United States into the war in 1941 was decisive, because personnel reserves and industrial capacity were the keys to the Allied victories in the European and Asian-Pacific theaters. The U.S. automotive industry alone, for instance, produced more than four million armored, combat, and supply vehicles of all kinds during the war. Not until the United States joined the struggle in 1942 did the tide in the battle for the Atlantic turn in favor of the Allies.

By 1943 German forces in Russia faced bleak prospects. Moscow never fell, and the battle for Stalingrad, which ended in February 1943, resulted in the first large-scale victory for Soviet forces. The Red Army, drawing on enormous personnel and material reserves, then pushed the German invaders out of Russian territory. By April 1945 the Soviets had reached the suburbs of Berlin. At that point, the Soviets had inflicted more than six million casualties on the German enemy—twice the number of the original German invasion force. The Red Army had broken the back of the German war machine.

Allied Victory in Europe

With the eastern front disintegrating under the Soviet onslaught, British and U.S. forces attacked the Germans from North Africa and then through Italy. In August 1944 the Allies forced Italy to withdraw from the Axis and to join them. In the meantime, the Germans also prepared for an Allied offensive in the west, where the British and U.S. forces opened a front in France. On D-Day, 6 June 1944, British and U.S. troops landed on the French coast of Normandy and overwhelmed the Germans. With the two fronts collapsing around them and round-the-clock strategic bombing by the United States and Britain leveling German cities, German resistance faded. Indeed, the British firebombing raid on Dresden alone killed 135,000 people in February 1945. As Germans and Russians engaged in a brutal street-by-street battle in Berlin and U.S. and British forces advanced through western Germany, the Germans surrendered unconditionally on 8 May 1945. A week earlier, on 30 April, as fighting flared right outside his Berlin bunker, Hitler committed suicide. He therefore did not live to see the Soviet red flag flying over the Berlin Reichstag, Germany's parliament building.

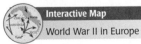

Interactive Map
World War II in Europe

The turning point in the Pacific war came at Midway (4 June 1942), the last U.S.-controlled island in the Pacific. The victory was accomplished by a code-breaking operation known as *Magic*, which enabled a cryptographer to discover the plan to attack Midway. On the morning of 4 June, thirty-six carrier-launched dive-bombers attacked the Japanese fleet, sinking three Japanese carriers in one five-minute strike and a fourth one later in the day. After Midway, the Allies took the offensive in the Pacific. They adopted an island-hopping strategy, capturing islands from which they could make direct air assaults on Japan. Deadly, tenacious fighting characterized these battles in which the United States and its allies gradually retook islands in the Marianas and the Philippines and then, early in 1945, moved toward areas more threatening to Japan: Iwo Jima and Okinawa.

Turning the Tide in the Pacific

The fighting on Iwo Jima and Okinawa was savage. On Okinawa the Japanese introduced the kamikaze—pilots who volunteered to fly planes with just enough fuel to reach an Allied ship and dive-bomb into it. In the two-month battle for Okinawa, the Japanese flew nineteen hundred kamikaze missions, sinking dozens of ships and killing more than five thousand U.S. soldiers. The kamikaze, and the defense mounted by Japanese forces and the 110,000 Okinawan civilians who died refusing to surrender, convinced many people in the United States that the Japanese would never capitulate.

The fall of Saipan in July 1944 and the subsequent conquest of Iwo Jima and Okinawa brought the Japanese homeland within easy reach of U.S. strategic bombers. The release of napalm firebombs during low-altitude sorties at night met with devastating success. The firebombing of Tokyo in March 1945 destroyed 25 percent of the city's buildings and annihilated approximately one hundred thousand people. The final blows came on 6 and 9 August 1945, when the United States used its revolutionary new weapon, the atomic bomb, against the cities of Hiroshima and Nagasaki. The atomic bombs either instantaneously vaporized or slowly killed by radiation poisoning upward of two hundred thousand people. The Soviet Union declared war on Japan on 8 August 1945, and that new threat, combined with the devastation caused by the bombs,

Japanese Surrender

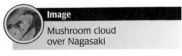

Image
Mushroom cloud over Nagasaki

---

kamikaze (kah-mih-KAH-zee)

Map 33.2 Progress of World War II in Asia and the Pacific. Compare the geographical conditions of the Asian-Pacific theater with those of the European theater. What kinds of resources were necessary to win in the Asian-Pacific theater as opposed to the European theater?

persuaded Emperor Hirohito (1901–1989) to surrender unconditionally on 15 August. On 2 September 1945, the war officially ended.

LIFE DURING WARTIME

The widespread bombing of civilian populations during World War II, from its beginning in China to its end in Hiroshima and Nagasaki, meant that there was no safe home front during the war. So too did the arrival of often brutal occupation forces in the wake of Japanese and German conquests in Asia and Europe. In this total war, civilian death tolls far exceeded military casualties. In spite of the war's brutality, however, the human spirit endured, personified in the contributions of resistance groups and mobilized women, and in the survivors of bombings or concentration camps.

A Hiroshima Maiden's Tale

Yamaoka Michiko, at fifteen years of age, worked as an operator at a telephone exchange in Hiroshima and attended girls' high school. Many young women had been mobilized for work during World War II, and they viewed even civilian work on telephone exchanges as a means of helping to protect Japan during wartime. On the morning of 6 August 1945, when the first U.S. atomic bomb used in battle devastated Hiroshima, Yamaoka Michiko had just started off for work.

That morning I left the house at about seven forty-five. I heard that the B-29s [U.S. bomber planes] had already gone home. Mom told me, "Watch out, the B-29s might come again." My house was one point three kilometers from the hypocenter [the exact point of the atomic bomb's impact]. My place of work was five hundred meters from the hypocenter. I walked toward the hypocenter. . . . I heard the faint sound of planes. . . . The planes were tricky. Sometimes they only pretended to leave. I could still hear the very faint sound of planes. . . . I thought, how strange, so I put my right hand above my eyes and looked up to see if I could spot them. The sun was dazzling.

That was the moment. There was no sound. I felt something strong. It was terribly intense. I felt colors. It wasn't heat. You can't really say it was yellow, and it wasn't blue. At that moment I thought I would be the only one who would die. I said to myself, "Goodbye, Mom."

They say temperatures of seven thousand degrees centigrade hit me. You can't really say it washed over me. It's hard to describe. I simply fainted. I remember my body floating in the air. That was probably the blast, but I don't know how far I was blown. When I came to my senses, my surroundings were silent. There was no wind. I saw a threadlike light, so I felt I must be alive. I was under stones. I couldn't move my body. I heard voices crying, "Help! Water!" It was then I realized I wasn't the only one. . . .

"Fire! Run away! Help! Hurry up!" They weren't voices but moans of agony and despair. "I have to get help and shout," I thought. The person who rescued me was Mom, although she herself had been buried under our collapsed house. Mom knew the route I'd been taking. She came, calling out to me. I

heard her voice and cried for help. Our surroundings were already starting to burn. Fires burst out from just the light itself. It didn't really drop. It just flashed. . . .

My clothes were burnt and so was my skin. I was in rags. I had braided my hair, but now it was like a lion's mane. There were people, barely breathing, trying to push their intestines back in. People with their legs wrenched off. Without heads. Or with faces burned and swollen out of shape. The scene I saw was a living hell.

Mom didn't say anything when she saw my face and I didn't feel any pain. She just squeezed my hand and told me to run. She was going to rescue my aunt. Large numbers of people were moving away from the flames. My eyes were still able to see, so I made my way toward the mountain, where there was no fire, toward Hijiyama. . . .

I spent the next year bedridden. All my hair fell out. When we went to relatives' houses later they wouldn't even let me in because they feared they'd catch the disease. There was neither treatment nor assistance for me. . . . It was just my Mom and me. Keloids [thick scar tissue] covered my face, my neck. I couldn't even move my neck. One eye was hanging down. I was unable to control my drooling because my lip had been burned off. . . .

The Japanese government just told us we weren't the only victims of the war. There was no support or treatment. It was probably harder for my Mom. Once she told me she tried to choke me to death. If a girl had terrible scars, a face you couldn't be born with, I understand that even a mother could want to kill her child. People threw stones at me and called me Monster. That was before I had my many operations.

- *What did Yamaoka Michiko's psychological and physical reactions to the atomic bombing of Hiroshima suggest about the nature of these new weapons? Why did friends and relatives treat her as if she were a "monster"?*

SOURCE: Yamaoka Michiko. "Eight Hundred Meters from the Hypocenter." In Haruko Taya Cook and Theodore F. Cook, *Japan at War: An Oral History.* New York: The New Press, 1992, pp. 384–87.

Occupation, Collaboration, and Resistance

The administration imposed on conquered territories by Japanese and German forces varied in character. In territories such as Manchukuo, Japanese-controlled China, Burma, and the Philippines, Japanese authorities installed puppet governments. Other conquered territories either were considered too unreliable for "self-rule" or were deemed strategically too important to be left alone. Thus territories such as Indochina, Malaya, the Dutch East Indies, Hong Kong, Singapore, Borneo, and New Guinea came under direct military control.

In Europe, Hitler's racist ideology played a large role in determining how occupied territories were administered. Hitler intended that most areas of western and northern Europe—populated by racially valuable people, according to him—would become part of a Greater Germanic Empire. Accordingly, Denmark retained its elected government and monarchy under German supervision. In Norway and Holland, the Germans left the civilian administration intact. Though northern France and the Atlantic coast came under military rule, the so-called Vichy government remained the civilian authority in the unoccupied southeastern part of the country. In contrast, most conquered territories in eastern Europe and the Balkans came under direct military rule as a prelude for harsh occupation, economic exploitation, and German settlement.

Japanese and German authorities administered their respective empires for economic gain and pro-
Exploitation   ceeded to ruthlessly exploit the resources of the lands under their control for their own benefit. The most notorious form of economic exploitation involved the use of slave labor. In Poland, the Soviet Union, France, Italy, and the Balkan nations, German occupiers forced millions of people to labor in work camps and war industries, and the Japanese did likewise in China and Korea. These slave laborers worked under horrific conditions and received little in the way of sustenance.

Reaction to Japanese and German occupation varied from willing collaboration and acquiescence to
Collaboration and Resistance   open resistance. In both Asia and Europe, local notables often joined the governments sponsored by the conquerors because collaboration offered them the means to gain power or because they thought native rule was better than foreign rule. Businesspeople and companies often collaborated because they prospered financially from foreign rule. Still other people assisted occupation forces to get revenge for past grievances.

Nevertheless, occupation and exploitation created an environment for resistance that took various forms. The most dramatic forms of resistance were campaigns of sabotage, armed assaults on occupation forces, and assassinations. Resistance fighters as diverse as Filipino guerrillas and Soviet partisans blew up ammunition dumps and destroyed communication and transportation facilities. More quietly, other resisters gathered intelligence or hid and protected refugees.

Resistance also comprised simple acts of defiance such as scribbling anti-German graffiti or walking out of bars and restaurants when Japanese soldiers entered. German and Japanese citizens faced different decisions about resistance than conquered peoples did, since they had no antiforeign axe to grind. Moreover, many institutions that might have formed the core of resistance in Japan and Germany, such as political parties, labor unions, and churches, were weak or had been destroyed. As a result, there was little or no opposition to the state and its policies in Japan, while in Germany resistance remained generally sparse and ineffective.

Occupation forces reacted swiftly and brutally to resistance. When in May 1942 members of the Czech resistance assassinated the Nazi official Reinhard Heydrich, the Nazis eliminated the en-   *Atrocities* tire village of Lidice as punishment. Likewise, when a group of officers and civilians tried to kill Adolf Hitler in July 1944, many of the conspirators were hanged with piano wire suspended from meat hooks, a process recorded on film for Hitler. The Japanese were equally brutal. After eight hundred Chinese slave laborers were captured after escaping from their camp in the small Japanese town of Hanaoka, at least fifty were beaten and tortured to death as they hung by their thumbs from the ceiling of the town hall. Yet despite such deadly retaliation meted out to people who resisted occupation, widespread resistance movements grew throughout the war.

The Holocaust

By the end of World War II, the Nazi regime and its accomplices had physically annihilated millions of Jews, Slavs, Gypsies, homosexuals, Jehovah's Witnesses, communists, and others targeted as undesirables. Jews were the primary target of Hitler's racially motivated genocidal policies, and the resulting Holocaust nearly wiped out the Jewish population of Europe.

Titled "Abyss of Human Horror," this photograph shows a survivor of the concentration camp at Nordhausen, Germany, upon its liberation by Allies in 1945.

The murder of European Jews was preceded by centuries of anti-Semitism in Europe, where Jews were routinely marked as outsiders. Thus Europeans' passive acceptance of anti-Semitism, combined with Nazi determination to destroy the Jewish population, laid the groundwork for genocide. Initially, the Nazi regime encouraged Jewish emigration. Although tens of thousands of Jews availed themselves of the opportunity to escape from Germany and Austria, many more were unable to do so because most European nations limited the migration of Jewish refugees and because German victories in Europe brought an ever-larger number of Jews under Nazi control. Early in the war, Nazi "racial experts" toyed with the idea of mass deportation of Jews, but that idea proved to be impractical as well as threatening, since the concentration of Jews in one area led to the dangerous possibility of the creation of a separate Jewish state, hardly a solution to the so-called Jewish problem in the Nazi view.

The Final Solution The German occupation of Poland in 1939 and the invasion of the Soviet Union in the summer of 1941 gave Hitler an opportunity to solve what he considered the problem of Jews throughout Europe. When German armies invaded the Soviet Union in June 1941, the Nazis dispatched three thousand troops in mobile detachments known as SS *Einsatzgruppen* ("action squads") to kill entire populations of Jews and Roma (Gypsies), and many non-Jewish Slavs in the newly occu-

pied territories. By the end of 1941, the special units had killed 1.4 million Jews.

Sometime during 1941 the Nazi leadership committed to the "final solution" of the Jewish question, which entailed the attempted murder of every Jew living in Europe. At the Wannsee Conference, on 20 January 1942, fifteen leading Nazi

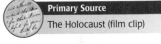

Primary Source
The Holocaust (film clip)

bureaucrats agreed to evacuate all Jews from Europe to camps in eastern Poland, where they would be worked to death or exterminated. Soon German forces—aided by collaborating authorities in foreign countries—rounded up Jews and deported them by rail to specially constructed concentration camps in occupied Poland. The Jewish victims packed into those suffocating railway cars never knew their destinations, but rumors of mass deportations and mass deaths spread among Jews remaining at large and among the Allied government leaders, who were apparently apathetic to the fate of Jews.

In camps such as Belzec, Treblinka, and Auschwitz, the final solution took on an organized and technologically sophisticated character. Nazi camp personnel subjected victims from all corners of Europe to industrial work, starvation, medical experiments, and outright extermination. The German commandant of Auschwitz—the largest camp, where at least one million Jews perished—explained proudly how his camp became the most efficient at killing Jews: by using the fast-acting

Map 33.3 The major concentration, extermination, and euthanasia sites of the Holocaust in Europe. Observe the geographical locations of the concentration and extermination camps. Why were there more concentration camps in Germany and more extermination camps in Poland?

crystallized prussic acid Zyklon B as the gassing agent, by enlarging the size of the gas chambers, and by lulling victims into thinking they were going through a delousing process. At Auschwitz and elsewhere, the Germans also constructed large crematories to incinerate the bodies of gassed Jews and hide the evidence of their crimes. Even though Jews put up fierce resistance throughout the war, by 1945 approximately 5.7 million Jews had perished in the Holocaust.

Women and the War

Observing the extent to which British women mobilized for war, the U.S. ambassador to London noted, "This war, more than any other war in history, is a woman's war." While hundreds of thousands of women in Great Britain and the United States joined the armed forces or entered war industries, women around the world were affected by the war in a variety of ways. In some nations, such as the Soviet Union

and China, women took up arms. So, too, did female members of resistance groups, who often excelled at resistance work because they were less suspect in the eyes of occupying security forces and less subject to searches. Nazi forces did not discriminate, though, when rounding up Jews for transport and extermination: Jewish women and girls died alongside Jewish men and boys.

Although women's roles changed during the war, often in dramatic ways, those new roles were temporary. After the war, women warriors and workers were expected to return home and assume their traditional roles as wives and mothers. In the meantime, though, women made the most of their opportunities. In Britain, more than half a million women joined British military services, and approximately 350,000 women did the same in the United States.

Women's experiences in war were not always ennobling or empowering. The Japanese army forcibly conscripted as many as three hundred thousand

A WAVE recruitment poster proclaims "It's A Woman's War Too!"

women aged fourteen to twenty to serve in military brothels, called "comfort houses" or "consolation centers." Most of the women came from Japanese colonies such as Korea, Taiwan, and Manchuria and from occupied territories in the Philippines and elsewhere in southeast Asia. Eighty percent of the women came from Korea.

Once forced into this imperial prostitution service, "comfort women" catered to between twenty and thirty men each day. Some were killed by Japanese soldiers, especially if they tried to escape or contracted venereal diseases. At the end of the war, soldiers massacred large numbers of comfort women to cover up the operation. The impetus behind the establishment of comfort houses came from the horrors of Nanjing, where Japanese soldiers had engaged in the mass rape of Chinese women. In trying to avoid such atrocities, however, the Japanese army created another. Comfort women who survived the war experienced deep shame and hid their past or faced shunning by their families. They found little comfort or peace after the war.

NEITHER PEACE NOR WAR

The end of World War II produced moving images of peace, including those of Soviet and U.S. soldiers clasping hands in camaraderie at the Elbe River, celebrating their victory over the Germans. Indeed, the Soviet Union and the United States emerged as the two strongest powers after the war, and each played a central role in shaping, influencing, and rebuilding the postwar world. It quickly became clear that both powers sought to create a world in their own image. Initially, the struggle to align postwar nations on one side or the other centered on areas liberated at the end of the war. Ultimately, however, it spread to the whole world.

Postwar Settlements and Cold War

Although the peoples of victorious nations danced in the streets on Victory in Europe (V-E) Day and Victory in Japan (V-J) Day, they also gazed at a world transformed by war. At least sixty million people perished in World War II. The Soviets lost more than twenty million, one-third of whom were soldiers; fifteen million Chinese, mostly civilians, died; Germany and Japan suffered the deaths of four million and two million people, respectively; six million Poles were also dead; in Great Britain four hundred thousand people died; and the United States lost three hundred thousand. The Holocaust claimed the lives of almost six million European Jews. In Europe and Asia tens of millions of displaced persons further contributed to the difficulty of rebuilding areas destroyed by war.

At the same time, the cold war between the Soviet Union and the United States began. That long-drawn-out conflict (1947–1991) divided humans and nations as sympathetic either to the Soviet Union or to the United States. The cold war came to define the postwar era as one of political, ideological, and economic hostility between the two superpowers and affected nations around the globe.

Throughout most of World War II, Hitler had believed that the alliance of the communist Soviet Union, the imperialist Great Britain, and the unwarlike U.S. democracy would break up over ideological differences. Yet Hitler underestimated the extent to which opposition to his regime could unite such unusual allies. Winston Churchill had put it like this: "If Hitler invaded Hell, I would at least make favorable reference to the Devil in the House of Commons."

The Origins of the Cold War

Comfort women playing
mah-jongg.

The necessity of defeating the Axis nations glued the Allies together, although there were tensions among them. Some of those tensions began to surface at the second wartime conference between the Allied leaders, at Yalta (4–11 February 1945), but they became obvious at the third and final wartime conference, at Potsdam (16 July–2 August 1945). By the time of the Yalta Conference, the Soviets were 64 kilometers (40 miles) from Berlin, and they controlled so much territory that Churchill and Roosevelt could do little to alter Stalin's plans for eastern Europe. They attempted to persuade Stalin to allow democracy in Poland, but Stalin's plans for Soviet-occupied nations prevailed. The Soviets suppressed noncommunist political parties and prevented free elections in Poland, Czechoslovakia, Hungary, Romania, and Bulgaria. They also installed a communist government in Poland and took similar steps elsewhere in eastern Europe.

At Yalta Stalin ensured that the Red Army's presence would dictate the future of states liberated by the Soviets, and at Potsdam Truman initiated the pro-capitalist, pro-democracy stance of the United States. The successful test of the atomic bomb while Truman was at Potsdam stiffened the president's re-

solve, and tensions over postwar settlements intensified. Having just fought a brutal war to guarantee the survival of their ways of life, neither the United States nor the Soviet Union would easily forgo the chance to remake occupied territories as either capitalist or communist allies.

In the end, all the Allies agreed on was the dismemberment of the Axis states and their possessions. The Soviets took over the eastern sections of Germany, and the United States, Britain, and France occupied the western portions. The capital city of Berlin, deep within the Soviet area, remained under the control of all four powers. In 1946, Churchill proclaimed that an "iron curtain" had come down on Europe, separating the Soviet-controlled nations of eastern Europe from the capitalist nations of western Europe. A somewhat similar division occurred in Asia. Whereas the United States alone occupied Japan, Korea remained occupied half by the Soviets and half by the Americans.

The enunciation of the Truman Doctrine on 12 March 1947 crystallized the new U.S. perception of a world divided between free and enslaved peoples. Articulated partly in response to crises in Greece and Turkey, where communist movements seemed to threaten democracy and U.S. strategic interests, the Truman Doctrine starkly drew the battle lines of the cold war. As Truman explained to the U.S. Congress: "I believe that it must be the policy of the United States to support free peo-

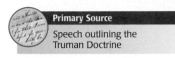

Primary Source

Speech outlining the Truman Doctrine

ples who are resisting attempted subjugation by armed minorities or by outside pressures." Thus the United States committed itself to an interventionist foreign policy, dedicated to the "containment" of communism, which meant preventing any further expansion of Soviet influence. As a result, the world was polarized into two armed camps, each led by a superpower that provided economic and military aid to nations within its sphere of influence.

Global Reconstruction and the United Nations

As an economic adjunct to the Truman Doctrine, the U.S. government developed a plan to help shore up the destroyed infrastructures of western Europe. The Eu-

The Marshall Plan

ropean Recovery Program, commonly called the Marshall Plan after U.S. secretary of state George C. Marshall (1880–1959), proposed to rebuild European economies to forestall Soviet influence in the devastated nations of Europe. Beginning in 1948, the Marshall Plan provided more than $13 billion to reconstruct western Europe.

In response, the Soviet Union countered with a plan for its own satellite nations. The Soviet Union established the Council for Mutual Economic Assistance (COMECON) in 1949, offering increased trade within the Soviet Union and eastern Europe as an alternative to the Marshall Plan.

The creation of the U.S.-sponsored North Atlantic Treaty Organization (NATO) and the Soviet-controlled Warsaw Pact signaled the militarization of the cold war.

In 1949 the United States established NATO as a regional military alliance against Soviet aggression. The original members included Bel-

NATO and the Warsaw Pact

gium, Canada, Denmark, France, Great Britain, Iceland, Italy, Luxembourg, the Netherlands, Norway, Portugal, and the United States. The intent of the alliance was to maintain peace in postwar Europe through collective defense. When NATO admitted West Germany and allowed it to rearm in 1955, the Soviets formed the Warsaw Pact as a countermeasure. A military alliance of seven communist European nations, the Warsaw Pact matched the collective defense policies of NATO.

Despite their many differences, the superpowers were among the nations that agreed to the creation of the United Nations (UN), a supranational

The United Nations

organization dedicated to keeping world peace. The commitment to establish a new international organization derived from Allied cooperation during the war, and in 1945 the final version of the United Nations charter was hammered out by delegates from fifty nations at the United Nations Conference in San Francisco. The United Nations was dedicated to maintaining international peace and security and promoting friendly relations among the world's nations. It offered an alternative for global reconstruction that was independent of the cold war.

It rapidly became clear, however, that international peace and security eluded both the United Nations and the superpowers. The cold war dominated postwar reconstruction efforts. It remained cold for the most part, characterized by ideological and propaganda campaigns, but it became "hot" in places, such as Korea between 1950 and 1953, and it had the potential to escalate into a war more destructive than World War II. The Soviet Union broke the U.S. monopoly on the atomic bomb in September 1949, and from that point on the world held its collective breath at the possibility of a nuclear war.

SUMMARY

At the end of World War II, it was possible for a U.S. marine to enjoy the hospitality of a Japanese family in Nagasaki, but not for Soviet and U.S. troops to continue embracing in camaraderie. World War II was a total global war that forced violent encounters between peoples and radically altered the political shape of the world. Beginning with Japan and China in 1931, this global conflagration spread to Europe and its empires and to the Pacific Ocean and the rest of Asia. Men, women, and children throughout the world became intimate with war as victims of civilian bombing campaigns, as soldiers and war workers, and as slave laborers and comfort women. When the Allies defeated the Axis powers in 1945, destroying the German and Japanese empires, the world had to rebuild as the cold war began. The cold war helped determine the new shape of the world as nations reconstructed under the auspices of either the United States or the Soviet Union, the two superpowers of the postwar era.

CHRONOLOGY

1937	Invasion of China by Japan
1937	The rape of Nanjing
1938	German *Anschluss* with Austria
1939	Nazi-Soviet pact
1939	Invasion of Poland by Germany
1940	Fall of France, Battle of Britain
1941	German invasion of the Soviet Union
1941	Attack on Pearl Harbor by Japan
1942	U.S. victory at Midway
1943	Soviet victory at Stalingrad
1944	D-Day, Allied invasion at Normandy
1945	Capture of Berlin by Soviet forces
1945	Atomic bombing of Hiroshima and Nagasaki
1945	Establishment of United Nations
1947	Truman Doctrine
1948	Marshall Plan
1949	Establishment of NATO
1955	Establishment of Warsaw Pact

FOR FURTHER READING

Ian Buruma. *The Wages of Guilt: Memories of War in Germany and Japan*. New York, 1995. A moving account of how societies deal with the war crimes of World War II.

Haruko Taya Cook and Theodore F. Cook. *Japan at War: An Oral History*. New York, 1992. Views of World War II in the words of the Japanese who witnessed it.

John Dower. *War without Mercy: Race and Power in the Pacific War*. New York, 1986. An insightful and important work on how race influenced the Japanese and U.S. war in the Pacific.

Paul Fussell. *Understanding and Behavior in the Second World War*. Oxford, 1989. A dissection of the culture of war; see the author's similar treatment of World War I.

Margaret Higgonet, Jane Jenson, Sonya Michel, and Margaret Weitz, eds. *Behind the Lines: Gender and the Two World Wars*. New Haven, 1987. A penetrating series of articles on women in both world wars, focusing generally on U.S. and European experiences.

Raul Hilberg. *The Destruction of the European Jews*. New York, 1967. One of the most important works on the Holocaust.

Akira Iriye. *The Origins of the Second World War in Asia and the Pacific*. New York, 1987. An examination of the Asian and Pacific origins of the war by one of the field's leading scholars.

Studs Terkel. *"The Good War": An Oral History of World War II*. New York, 1984. A valuable collection of oral histories on the war from a U.S. perspective.

Sun, You-Li. *China and the Origins of the Pacific War, 1931–1941*. New York, 1993. An account of the origins of the war in which China takes center stage.

Gerhard Weinberg. *A World at Arms: A Global History of World War II*. Cambridge, 1994. An exhaustive look at the war from a global perspective.

CHAPTER 34
The Bipolar World

In the summer of 1959, the world was treated to a verbal slugfest—subsequently known as the kitchen debate—between United States vice president Richard M. Nixon (1913–1994) and Soviet premier Nikita S. Khrushchev (1894–1971). In July of that year, Nixon arrived in Moscow to open the American National Exhibition, a rare display of U.S. goods on Russian soil. Khrushchev, however, was not in a welcoming mood: the U.S. Congress had just passed the "captive nations" resolution, which openly criticized the Soviet Union for mistreating its satellite nations, and Khrushchev was convinced that Nixon's visit to Moscow was timed to humiliate the Soviet leader. Before visiting the exhibit, Khrushchev and Nixon met privately and exchanged heated words about captive nations. Ac-

cording to Nixon's memoirs, the colorful and candid Soviet premier initiated the conversation by remarking: "It stinks like fresh horse shit, and nothing smells worse than that." The equally frank Nixon—aware that Khrushchev had tended pigs in his youth—quickly replied: "There is something that smells worse than horse shit and that is pig shit." Having thus set the mood, Nixon and Khrushchev descended on the exhibit, where they continued their barbed exchange.

The high point of their vocal showdown took place in the kitchen of a U.S. model house built expressly for the exhibit. Without hesitation, Khrushchev mocked the many modern appliances in the kitchen. In his opinion they epitomized "the capitalist attitude toward women." Besides, he argued, the working class could

OPPOSITE PAGE: *The visceral beauty of nuclear explosions, such as this one in the Marshall Islands in 1954, masked the terror and tensions that beset the Soviet Union, the United States, and the rest of the world during the cold war.*

never afford such useless gadgets. In response, Nixon poked a finger at the chest of the Soviet premier and declared that any U.S. steelworker could purchase this $14,000 home. What followed was an unrehearsed polemical discourse on communism and capitalism that climaxed with a debate on the relative merits of everything from dishwashers to missiles.

The kitchen debate between Nixon and Khrushchev took place at the height of the cold war and illustrated how deep the rift between the United States of America and the Union of Soviet Socialist Republics (USSR) had grown since 1945. The cold war was a strategic struggle that developed after World War II between the United States and its allies on the one hand and the USSR and its allies on the other. Yet the confrontation was more than great-power rivalry; it was also an encounter between rival social and economic systems and competing political ideologies. This clash in turn gave rise to a new set of global relationships, shaping the foreign policies, economic systems, and political institutions of nations throughout the world.

The geopolitical and ideological rivalry between the Soviet Union and the United States lasted almost five decades and affected every corner of the world. The cold war was responsible for the formation of military and political alliances, the creation of client states, and an arms race of unprecedented scope. In the end, however, the United States and the Soviet Union always avoided a direct clash of arms, hence the term *cold war*. Nevertheless, the ideological exchanges of the cold war inspired significant changes in social and economic practices in both the Soviet Union and the United States.

THE FORMATION OF A BIPOLAR WORLD

By the time Germany surrendered in the spring of 1945, the wartime alliance between the Soviet Union and the United States was disintegrating. With the advent of peace, the one-time partners increasingly sacrificed cooperation for their own national interests. The competing ideologies of capitalism and communism shaped the postwar aims of the two superpowers, and their mutual hostility resulted in a divided world.

The Cold War in Europe

Among the first manifestations of the cold war was the division of the European continent into competing political, military, and economic blocs—one dependent on the United States and the other subservient to the USSR—separated by what Winston Churchill called an "iron curtain." In essence, both blocs adopted the political institutions, economic systems, and foreign policies of the two superpowers. Thus western European nations that were tied to the United States embraced parliamentary political systems and capitalist economic structures and

Interactive Map
The cold war

Soviet premier Nikita Khrushchev and U.S. vice president Richard Nixon sharing a rare "lighter" moment during the kitchen debate.

adjusted their foreign policies to the U.S. vision of the postwar world. On the other hand, the governments of eastern European states adopted Soviet political and economic institutions and supported Moscow's foreign policy goals.

The fault lines of cold war Europe were most visible in Germany. After the collapse of Hitler's Third

A Divided Germany

Reich, the forces of the United States, the Soviet Union, Britain, and France occupied Germany and its capital, Berlin, both of which they divided into four administrative zones. Specific travel corridors running through the Soviet occupation zone of Germany gave the French, British, and Americans access from their zones of occupation in western Germany to their sectors in Berlin, which lay deep within Soviet territory. Tensions mounted between Soviet authorities and their Western counterparts in 1947–1948 after the Western powers decided to merge their occupation zones in Germany into a single economic unit and to introduce a new currency, the German mark, throughout their occupation zones and in their sectors of Berlin.

The Soviets retaliated by blockading all road, rail, and water links between Berlin and western Germany. The Soviet Union maintained that Western economic

measures violated wartime agreements and, on 24 June 1948, announced that the four-power administration of Berlin was no longer in effect and that the Allies no longer had any jurisdiction there. Two days later, in the

Blockade and Airlift

first serious test of the cold war, the Americans and British responded with an airlift designed to keep the city's inhabitants fed and warm. For eleven months, American and British aircrews flew around-the-clock missions to supply West Berlin with the necessities of life. Finally, the Soviet leadership called off the blockade in May 1949, though the airlift continued until September. The blockade failed to force the British, French, and Americans to vacate Berlin. In May 1949 the U.S., British, and French zone of occupation coalesced to form the Federal Republic of Germany (West Germany). In October the German Democratic Republic (East Germany) emerged out of the Soviet zone of occupation. A similar process repeated itself in Berlin: the Soviet sector formed East Berlin and became the capital of the new East Germany, and the remaining three sectors united to form West Berlin.

By 1961 the communist East German state was hemorrhaging from a steady drain of refugees who preferred life in capitalist West Germany. Much to the

Map 34.1 Boundaries of occupied Germany between 1945 and 1949. Locate the city of Berlin in Soviet-controlled territory. How was it possible for the British, American, and French to maintain their zones of control in Berlin, given such geographical distance from western Germany?

Barbed wire and a concrete wall in front of the Brandenburg Gate in Berlin symbolized the cold war division of Europe.

embarrassment of East Germany's communist leaders, between 1949 and 1961 nearly 3.5 million East Ger-

Berlin Wall

mans—many of them young and highly skilled—left their homeland. To remedy the problem, in August 1961 the communists built a fortified wall—replete with watchtowers, searchlights, antipersonnel mines, and border guards ordered to shoot to kill—dividing the city of Berlin. In subsequent years several thousand East Germans escaped to West Germany, but several hundred others paid with their lives for attempting to do so.

A central feature of the cold war world was a costly arms race and the terrifying proliferation of nuclear

The Nuclear Arms Race

weapons. The struggle between the United States and the Soviet Union led to the creation of two military blocs: the North Atlantic Treaty Organization, or NATO (1949), and the Warsaw Treaty Organization, or Warsaw Pact (1955). Because the United States was determined to retain military superiority and because the Soviet Union was equally determined to reach parity with the

United States, both sides amassed enormous arsenals of thermonuclear weapons

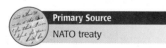

Primary Source
NATO treaty

and developed a multitude of systems for deploying those weapons. By 1970 both superpowers had ac-

quired the capacity for mutually assured destruction, or MAD. Yet the balance of terror restrained the contestants and stabilized their relationship, with two important exceptions.

Confrontations in Korea and Cuba

With the unforeseen outbreak of hostilities on the Korean peninsula in the summer of 1950, the focus of the cold war shifted from Europe to east Asia. At the end of World War II, the leaders of the Soviet Union and the United States had partitioned Korea along the thirty-eighth parallel of latitude into a northern Soviet zone and a southern U.S. zone. Because the superpowers were unable to agree on a framework for the reunification of the country, in 1948 they consented to the establishment of two separate Korean states: in the south, the Republic of Korea, with Seoul as its capital and the conservative anticommunist Syngman Rhee (1875–1965) as its president; in the north, the People's Democratic Republic of Korea, with Pyongyang as its capital and the revolutionary communist Kim Il Sung (1912–1995) as its leader. After arming their respective clients, each of which claimed sovereignty over the entire country, U.S. and Soviet troops withdrew.

Early on the morning of 25 June 1950, the unstable political situation in Korea came to a head. Determined to unify Korea by force, the Pyongyang regime ordered more

The Korean War

than one hundred thousand troops across the thirty-eighth parallel in a surprise attack, capturing Seoul on 27 June. Convinced that the USSR had sanctioned the invasion, and armed with UN support, the U.S. military went into action. Within two weeks U.S. forces had pushed North Koreans back to the thirty-eighth parallel. However, sensing an opportunity to unify Korea under a pro-U.S. government, they pushed on into North Korea, occupied Pyongyang, and made advances toward the Chinese border. Those advances caused the government of the People's Republic of China to issue a warning: the U.S. incursion across the thirty-eighth parallel threatened Chinese national interests and could result in Chinese intervention in the Korean conflict.

When U.S. leaders gave no indication of heeding China's warning, some three hundred thousand Chinese soldiers surged into North Korea. A combined force of Chinese and North Koreans pushed U.S. forces and their

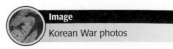

Image
Korean War photos

allies back into the south, and the war settled into a protracted stalemate near the original border at the thirty-eighth parallel. After two more years of fighting that resulted in three million deaths—mostly Korean civilians—both sides finally agreed to a cease-fire in July 1953.

Beyond the human casualties and physical damage it wrought, the Korean conflict also encouraged the globalization of containment. After Korea, the U.S. government extended military protection and economic aid to the noncommunist governments of Asia to bolster them against communism. It also entered into security agreements that culminated in the creation of the Southeast Asian Treaty Organization (SEATO), an Asian counterpart of NATO. In 1954 U.S. president Dwight D. Eisenhower (1890–1969) accepted the famous "domino theory," which rationalized worldwide U.S. intervention on the assumption that if one country became communist,

The Globalization of Containment

In August 1950, U.S. troops marched toward North Korea while South Koreans moved in the opposite direction to escape the fighting.

neighboring ones would collapse as well. Subsequent U.S. administrations extended the policy of containment to real or imagined communist threats in Central and South America, Africa, and Asia.

Ironically, the cold war confrontation that came closest to unleashing nuclear war took place not at the expected flashpoints in Europe or Asia but on the island of Cuba. In 1959 a revolutionary movement headed by Fidel Castro Ruz (1926–) overthrew the autocratic Fulgencio Batista y Zaldivar (1901–1973), whose regime had gone to great lengths to maintain the country's traditionally subservient relationship with the United States. Denouncing Yankee imperialism, Castro seized foreign properties and businesses, most of which were U.S. owned. He also accepted assistance from the Soviet Union. The U.S. government promptly retaliated by cutting off Cuban sugar imports to the U.S. market and imposing a severe export embargo of U.S. goods on Cuba. U.S. officials also cut diplomatic relations with Cuba and secretly began planning an invasion of the island.

Cuba: Nuclear Flashpoint

The severing of ties between Cuba and the United States gave the Soviet Union an unprecedented opportunity to contest the dominant position of the United States in its own hemisphere. Castro's regime accepted a Soviet offer of extensive military and economic aid, including an agreement to purchase half of Cuba's sugar production. In return for the Soviet largesse, Castro loudly declared his support for the USSR's foreign policy at the UN General Assembly on 26 September 1960.

Cuba's alignment with the Soviet Union spurred newly elected president John F. Kennedy (1917–1963) to approve a plan to invade Cuba and overthrow Castro. In April 1961 a force of 1,500 anti-Castro Cubans trained, armed, and transported by the Central Intelligence Agency (CIA) landed on Cuba at a place called the Bay of Pigs. The invasion, however, was a complete failure and actually strengthened Castro's position in Cuba as well as his commitment to communism. It also likely encouraged Castro to accept and the Soviets to deploy nuclear missiles in Cuba as a deterrent to any future invasion.

The Bay of Pigs

On 22 October 1962 President Kennedy went on national television to inform the public about the U.S. discovery of offensive nuclear missiles and launch sites in Cuba. The Soviet government apparently took that bold step to protect the Castro government, give the USSR greater diplomatic leverage vis-à-vis the United States,

The Cuban Missile Crisis

undermine U.S. credibility in the region, and gain more influence in Latin America. Whatever the precise motives, the deployment of nuclear missiles in Cuba represented an unacceptable threat to U.S. national security. In response, President Kennedy delivered a public ultimatum calling on the Soviets to 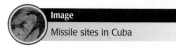 withdraw all missiles from Cuba and stop the arrival of additional nuclear armaments. To back up his demand, Kennedy imposed an air and naval quarantine on the island, which went into effect two days later. The superpowers seemed poised for nuclear confrontation, and for a week the world's peoples held their collective breath.

Understanding the seriousness of a nuclear showdown over Cuba, Nikita Khrushchev agreed to Kennedy's demand that he withdraw the missiles on the condition that the United States pledge not to invade Cuba. He also received a private promise from Kennedy

that U.S. missiles in Turkey would be removed. Khrushchev informed the public of the end of the crisis in a worldwide radio broadcast on 28 October, and global tension finally began to ebb.

Cold War Societies

The global political arena after World War II resounded with clashes stemming from the cold war and decolonization. The conflicts emanating from those dual forces naturally had repercussions in societies around the world. Postwar social transformations demonstrated how domestic policies and international affairs often become linked, particularly as peoples living in disparate parts of the world discover commonalities and differences, mutual sympathies and antipathies.

When Nikita Khrushchev and Richard Nixon squared off in the kitchen debate in Moscow, their argument highlighted the different ways that capitalist

Map 34.2 Allies of the United States and the Soviet Union between 1949 and 1962. Note the size of the territories and the number of states allied to both sides. Were these alliances a source of global stability or global instability?

and communist societies understood the importance of women and domesticity. Citizens of the United States, like Nixon, celebrated the home appliances that made the lives of house- wives so comfortable and that distin- guished them from their toiling Soviet counterparts. Women did not need to work, as they did in the Soviet Union, because their husbands earned enough to support the family in sub- urban splendor and because a mother's most impor- tant job was keeping the family happy and loyal.

Domestic Containment and Female Liberation

Indeed, in the United States cold war concerns about the spread of communism reached into the do- mestic sphere. Politicians, FBI agents, educators, and social commentators warned of communist spies try- ing to undermine the institutions of U.S. life. Thus, many believed that U.S. women best served their families and their nation by staying home and rear- ing patriotic, anticommunist children. The idea of families providing the best defense against commu- nist infiltration has been dubbed by scholars as "do- mestic containment," indicating its similarity to the U.S. foreign policy of containment.

Women were deeply affected by the restraints im- posed by domestic containment. Not all women aspired to the domestic ideals being showcased on new tele- vision shows such as *Leave It to Beaver* (1957–1963), and female discontent with postwar domesticity in the United States helped to fuel the modern femi- nist movement. In 1963 U.S. author Betty Friedan (1921–2006) published *The Feminine Mystique,* lay- ing bare the severe unhappiness of women who pre- sumably enjoyed the best life the United States could offer. Aligning themselves to some extent with women in societies such as the Soviet Union and taking inspi- ration from women in Asia and Africa who fought for their independence from the colonial powers, women activists adopted the language and terms of Marxism and anticolonialism in their own quest for equality and independence. They referred to women as an "op- pressed class" and argued for "women's liberation." Support for domestic containment, and containment itself, wavered.

As the ideals of domestic containment clearly indi- cate, cross-fertilization between domestic and foreign policies took place throughout the early cold war years. Another arena in which those links could be seen was the coincid- ing of the cold war with the modern civil rights move- ment in the United States. The Soviet Union could and did use the appalling conditions of African- Americans to expose the weaknesses of the capitalist

Black Nationalism

system in the United States. In virtually every sphere of life, southern U.S. states institutionalized segregation, a system of laws and customs designed to separate blacks and whites. African-Americans contended with segre- gation and the loss of voting rights, widespread discrim- ination, and extralegal violence. Discrimination was less pronounced in northern states, but informal segrega- tion practices also influenced northern society. U.S. politicians and lawmakers recognized the adverse prop- aganda value of this institutionalized racism during the cold war, and in 1954 the U.S. Supreme Court ruled segregation in the schools illegal in *Brown v. the Board of Education.* However, it was direct action on the part of African-Americans—through the civil rights move- ment—that brought segregation down.

Indeed, the civil rights movement was first and foremost a challenge to segregation. In 1955, when Rosa Parks, an African-American woman living in Montgomery, Ala- bama, refused to give up her seat on a bus to a white man—as required by law—she accel- erated a civil rights revolution that resulted in major advances for blacks in the United States. African- Americans in Montgomery refused to ride city buses until they were desegregated, and the Montgomery bus boycott—led by Dr. Martin Luther King Jr. (1929–1968)—proved the effectiveness of Mohandas Gandhi's methods of nonviolence in a new social con- text. King went on to lead numerous marches and demonstrations and, despite the violence visited on him and his followers, to win major civil rights battles. Until his assassination in 1968, King clung to his dream of black equality in the United States, a nation pressured by the cold war and African liberation move- ments to accede rights to its black population.

The Civil Rights Movement

The United States fell short in cold war ideologi- cal battles in its treatment of African-Americans, but the Soviet Union had difficulty match- ing the United States and its allies in the provision of material wealth, leisure, and consumer goods. Like women and domesticity, con- sumerism became a means of distinguishing commu- nist and capitalist societies.

Cold War Consumerism

The contrasting economic and social conditions of western and eastern Europe after World War II dem- onstrated the different lifestyles that emerged in Eu- rope during the cold war. Western European nations experienced what many people termed an economic miracle, recovering swiftly from the war's devastation. Starting with an infusion of $13 billion from the U.S. Marshall Plan between 1948 and 1952, west European government leaders rebuilt their nations by

Nikita Khrushchev on the Capitalist Iron Curtain

In early 1946 Winston Churchill (1874–1965) delivered his "Iron Curtain" speech, stirring audiences with its image of a Europe firmly and frighteningly divided between communist nations and marking, for some, the beginning of the cold war. Fifteen years after Churchill delivered his speech, Nikita Khrushchev (1894–1971) acknowledged the power of Churchill's imagery by using it in his own speech to the Communist Party Congress. In his 1961 "Report to the Communist Party Congress," Soviet premier Khrushchev blasted capitalism with the same force Churchill had employed in his earlier condemnation of communism.

■ ■ ■

Comrades! The competition of the two world social systems, the socialist and the capitalist, has been the chief content of the period since the 20th Party Congress [February 1956]. It has become the pivot, the foundation of world development at the present historical stage. Two lines, two historical trends, have manifested themselves more and more clearly in social development. One is the line of social progress, peace and constructive activity. The other is the line of reaction, oppression and war.

In the course of the peaceful competition of the two systems, capitalism has suffered a profound moral defeat in the eyes of all peoples. The common people are daily convinced that capitalism is incapable of solving a single one of the urgent problems confronting mankind. It becomes more and more obvious that only on the paths to socialism can a solution to these problems be found. Faith in the capitalist system and the capitalist path of development is dwindling. Monopoly capital, losing its influence, resorts more and more to intimidating and suppressing the masses of the people, to methods of open dictatorship in carrying out its domestic policy and to aggressive acts against other countries. But the masses of the people offer increasing resistance to reaction's acts.

The ruling circles of some imperialist powers have elevated subversive activities against the socialist countries to the level of state policy. With cynical frankness, the United States of America is spending hundreds of millions of dollars on espionage and subversion against socialist countries and organizing so-called "guerrilla units," assembling

in them criminal elements and cut-throats prepared to undertake the vilest crimes for money. For several successive years the United States has been holding provocational "captive nations weeks." The hired agents of the monopolies call "captive" all those peoples who have liberated themselves from imperialist bondage and taken the path of free development. Truly, imperialist demagogy and hypocrisy know no bounds!

Our society is open to those people who come to us from abroad with open hearts. It is open to honest trade, to scientific, technical and cultural exchanges, to the exchange of truthful information. If it's an iron curtain we're talking about, where it really exists is in the world of capitalism, which, though dubbing itself the "free world," every now and then fearfully slams its gates shut to Soviet people, one moment to our cooks, the next to our chess players. There was a case where one state, which calls itself the "most open," was afraid to let in Soviet dancers. Can they really have feared that Russian folk dancing might shake the foundations of the capitalist world?!

We have long proposed to the capitalist world that we compete not in an arms race but in improving the working people's lives. We are confident that capitalism cannot stand up under that kind of competition! We are confident that in the end all peoples will make the correct choice, will give their preference to the truly free world of communism and turn their backs on the so-called "free world" of capitalism.

- *Why did Khrushchev contend that faith in capitalism had dwindled and that the true "iron curtain" closed capitalist nations to outside contacts?*

SOURCE: Nikita Khrushchev. "Report to the Communist Party." In *Current Soviet Policies IV,* ed. Charlotte Saikowski and Leo Gruliow, from the translations of *The Current Digest of the Soviet Press.* 1962.

encouraging economic growth and by providing social services that outpaced those in the United States—including, over time, the guarantee of a thirty-day paid vacation. Western Europeans also enjoyed increased access to consumer goods such as automobiles, supermarkets, and record albums.

In contrast, the peoples of the Soviet Union and eastern European nations experienced less economic

The Space Race

growth and enjoyed far fewer consumer items and far less leisure than did their counterparts in western Europe and North America. They could, however, take pride and some comfort from the technological triumphs enjoyed by the Soviet Union in the late 1950s and early 1960s. Soviet experts demonstrated to the world their apparent superiority in science and technology when they tested a workable intercontinental ballistic missile (ICBM) in

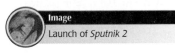

Launch of *Sputnik 2*

the late 1950s. That success was overshadowed on 4 October 1957 by the more spectacular Soviet launching into space of the first satellite, *Sputnik.* Between the ICBM and *Sputnik,* the Soviets grabbed the initiative in the newly dubbed space race, an extraterrestrial form of the cold war. The Soviet head start in that race provoked panic among U.S. citizens and politicians, which intensified in April 1961 when the Soviets rocketed cosmonaut Yuri Gagarin (1934–1968) into space, where he became the first man to orbit the earth.

The United States soon copied those Soviet successes in space with its own—launching the satellite *Explorer I* in 1958 and sending astronaut John Glenn (1921–) into orbit in 1962. When John F. Kennedy became president, he dedicated himself and the National Aeronautics and Space Administration (NASA) to the task of landing a man on the moon. That came to fruition on 20 July 1969 when *Apollo XI* gently set down on the moon's Sea of Tranquility. The moon landing reassured U.S. citizens of their world status, but the earlier years of the cold war had left them insecure about missile gaps and diminished scientific ingenuity in a society relentlessly devoted to consumerism.

Societies in the Soviet Union and the United States may have resembled each other in their space racing, in

Peaceful Coexistence

their pursuit of nuclear superiority, and in their quest for cold war supremacy, but they also resembled each other in their basic humanity: a fact that may have prevented the ultimate tipping of the balance of terror. A few weeks after the famous kitchen debate, Khrushchev became the first

Soviet leader to visit the United States. Despite some tense moments, Khrushchev's tour of the United States contributed to a thaw in the cold war, however brief. In his September 1959 travels, which included stops in New York, California, and Iowa, he showed himself to be a warm and witty man. Television coverage of his trip allowed millions in the United States to see the previously demonized Soviet premier as a human being as he talked with U.S. farmers and thanked his U.S. hosts for their hospitality. That encounter between a Soviet leader and a U.S. audience suggested the ever-shifting possibilities for peace in the perilous cold war world.

CHALLENGES TO SUPERPOWER HEGEMONY

The global preeminence of the two new superpowers evoked challenges from several quarters. In western Europe, French politicians sought to free their nation from superpower dominance by transforming Europe into an independent strategic bloc. Eastern European states also tried to become their own masters, or at least to gain a measure of autonomy from the Soviet Union. The leadership of the People's Republic of China mounted the most serious challenge to Soviet hegemony within the communist world when a quarrel over national interests and disagreements concerning ideology grew into a schism. Finally, in Vietnam and Afghanistan, respectively, the United States and the Soviet Union suffered serious political and military setbacks that signaled the decline of superpower hegemony.

Defiance, Dissent, and Intervention in Europe

The first direct assault on the bipolar world emanated from France under the leadership of President Charles de Gaulle (1890–1970), who dreamed of a Europe that could act as a third force in world affairs. In particular, de Gaulle regarded subservience to U.S. author-

France under de Gaulle

ity and unqualified support for U.S. global objectives intolerable, because he believed that France could never regain great-power status if it depended for security on U.S. military protection. Moreover, military dependence carried with it the risk that a nuclear confrontation between the superpowers over issues unrelated to European interests could engulf Europe by virtue of its alliance with the United States.

The focus of French policy under de Gaulle was disengagement from the U.S.-dominated NATO and the development of an independent nuclear strike force, which became a realistic proposition in 1964 when the French detonated their first atomic bomb in the Sahara desert. Four years later the French military put together a nuclear delivery system consisting of long-range bombers and land- and submarine-based missiles. French military doctrine and capability failed to persuade Europeans to leave the protective fold of the United States, however, and by the time de Gaulle left office in 1969 his vision for France and Europe had nearly disappeared.

There were many challenges to the hegemonic position of the Soviet Union during the cold war decades.

Tito's Yugoslavia   The first opposition from within the communist world emanated from Yugoslavia, where a postwar communist regime under Josip Broz, known as Marshal Tito (1892–1980), came to power without the assistance of the Soviet Union. Tito's resistance to Soviet control led to a major split with Stalin, and in 1948 Stalin expelled Yugoslavia from the Soviet bloc.

Developments within the Soviet Union caused more serious changes in eastern Europe. Three years *De-Stalinization* after Stalin's death in 1953, Nikita Khrushchev attacked Stalin and questioned his methods of rule during a secret speech at the Twentieth Party Congress. Khrushchev subse-

quently embarked on a policy of de-Stalinization, that is, the end of the rule of terror and the partial liberalization of Soviet society. Government officials removed portraits of Stalin from public places, renamed localities bearing his name, and commissioned historians to rewrite textbooks to deflate Stalin's reputation. The de-Stalinization period, which lasted from 1956 to 1964, also brought a "thaw" in government control and resulted in the release of millions of political prisoners. One of those was Alexandr Solzhenitsyn (1919–), who, thanks to Khrushchev, was able to publish his novel *One Day in the Life of Ivan Denisovich* (1962), a moving description of life in a Siberian forced-labor camp. With respect to foreign policy, Khrushchev emphasized the possibility of "peaceful coexistence" between different social systems and the recognition that a nuclear war was more likely to lead to mutual annihilation than to victory. The peaceful coexistence that Khrushchev fostered with the United States appeared to apply to domestic Soviet and eastern European societies also and tempted communist leaders in eastern Europe to experiment with domestic reforms and seek a degree of independence from Soviet domination.

The most serious challenge to Soviet control in eastern Europe came in 1956 from nationalist-minded communists in Hungary. When the communist regime in Hungary embraced the process of de-Stalinization, *The Hungarian Challenge* large numbers of Hungarian citizens demanded democracy and the breaking of ties to Moscow and

Czech citizens confront Warsaw Pact troops in Prague during the Soviet invasion in the spring of 1968.

the Warsaw Pact. In the wake of huge street demonstrations joined by the Hungarian armed forces, communist Imre Nagy (1896–1958) gained power and visibility as a nationalist leader who announced Hungary's withdrawal from the Warsaw Pact. Yet there were limits to Soviet tolerance for reform: viewing Hungary's demands as a threat to national security, Soviet officials sent tanks into Budapest and crushed the uprising in the late autumn of 1956.

The Prague Spring Twelve years after the Hungarian uprising, Soviets again intervened in eastern Europe, this time in Czechoslovakia. In 1968 the Communist Party leader, Alexander Dubček (1921–1992), launched a liberal movement known as the "Prague Spring" and promised his fellow citizens "socialism with a human face." But Khrushchev's successor, Leonid Ilyich Brezhnev (1906–1982), fearful that such reforms might undermine Soviet control in eastern Europe, sanctioned military intervention by the Soviet army and brought an end to the Prague Spring. Brezhnev justified the invasion of Czechoslovakia by the Doctrine of Limited Sovereignty, better known as the "Brezhnev doctrine," which reserved the right to invade any socialist country that was deemed to be threatened by internal or external elements "hostile to socialism." The destruction of the Prague Spring served to reassert Soviet control over its satellite nations in eastern Europe and led to tightened controls within the Soviet Union.

The People's Republic of China

The birth of a communist China further transformed the cold war. With the defeat of Japan in 1945, the civil war in China resumed. By mid-1948 the strategic balance favored the communists, who inflicted heavy military defeats on the nationalists throughout 1948 and 1949. Faced with communist control, the national government under Jiang Jieshi (Chiang Kaishek) fled to the island of Taiwan, all the while continuing to claim its legitimacy as the government of all China. Nevertheless, Mao Zedong, the chairman of the Chinese Communist Party, proclaimed the establishment of the People's Republic of China on 1 October 1949. That declaration brought to an end the long period of imperialist intrusion in China and spawned a close relationship between the world's largest and most powerful socialist states.

Although the new Chinese constitution that took effect in 1954 created a national assembly chosen by popular election, it was the Communist Party that monopolized political power through a central committee and a politburo, chaired by Mao. To protect its authority, the government orchestrated campaigns to remove from power—by execution as well as through forced-labor camps—all of those likely to be a threat to the new leaders.

Next came the economic and social transformations of Chinese society, which centered on rapid industrialization and the collectivization of agriculture. Emulating the Soviet experiment of 1929, the Chinese introduced their first Five-Year Plan in 1955, which was designed to speed up economic development and expand heavy industry at the expense of consumer goods. A series of agrarian laws confiscated the landholdings of rich peasants and landlords and redistributed the land so that virtually every peasant had at least a small plot of land. After the government took over the grain market and prohibited farmers from marketing their crops, however, collective farms replaced private farming. Health care and primary education anchored to collectives permitted the extension of social services to a larger part of the population. Social reforms challenged and often eliminated Chinese family traditions, including child and forced marriages. Women also gained equal access to divorce as well as legal abortions. Foot binding, a symbol of women's subjugation, became a practice of the past.

Social and Economic Transformations

Moscow and Beijing drew closer during the early years of the cold war. That relationship was hardly astonishing because the leaders of both communist states felt threatened by a common enemy, the United States, which sought to establish anticommunist bastions throughout Asia, especially in Japan, South Korea, and Taiwan. In the early 1950s the Chinese-Soviet partnership took on a distinct form when Beijing recognized Moscow's authority in world communism in exchange for Russian military equipment and economic aid. In return, Soviet diplomats instigated a campaign in the United Nations to transfer the Chinese seat in the Security Council from Taiwan to the communist government on the mainland.

Fraternal Cooperation

As the Chinese embarked on a crash program of industrialization, the Soviet Union rendered valuable assistance in the form of economic aid and technical advisors. Before long, however, cracks appeared in the Soviet-Chinese alliance. From the Chinese perspective, Soviet aid programs were far too modest and had too many strings attached. For example, Soviet military aid to China

Cracks in the Alliance

during the Korean War had to be repaid in full at a time when China was in desperate need of capital. Another source of friction was the conflict between China and India over Tibet. After forcibly restoring Chinese sovereignty over Tibet in 1950, the Chinese ruthlessly quelled an armed insurrection in favor of Tibetan independence eleven years later. Beijing accused the government of India of fomenting the revolt, and the two sides subsequently became involved in border clashes in the Himalayas. Most infuriating to the Chinese, however, was Moscow's announcement of neutrality in the conflict, which the Soviets belied by giving a loan to India that exceeded any similar loan ever granted to China.

By the end of 1964, the rift between the Soviet Union and the People's Republic of China had become embarrassingly public, with both sides engaging in name-calling and in open competition for influence among the newly independent nations of Africa and Asia.

Détente and the Decline of Superpower Influence

In the late 1960s the leaders of the Soviet Union and the United States agreed on a policy of *détente,* or a reduction in hostility, trying to cool the costly arms race and slow their competition in developing countries. Although détente did not resolve the deep-seated antagonism between the superpowers, it did signal the relaxation of cold war tensions and prompted a new spirit of cooperation.

Between 1972 and 1974, U.S. and Soviet leaders exchanged visits and signed agreements calling for co-operation in areas such as health research, *An Era of Cooperation* environmental protection, space ventures, and cultural exchange programs. However, the spirit of détente was most visible in negotiations designed to reduce the threat posed by strategic nuclear weapons. In 1972 U.S. and Soviet negotiators concluded their Strategic Arms Limitations Talks (SALT) with two agreements and reached another accord in 1979. The two cold war antagonists cooperated despite the tensions caused by the U.S. incursion into Vietnam, Soviet involvement in Angola and other African states, and continued Soviet repression of dissidents in eastern Europe.

Ironically, the era of détente coincided with a marked decline in superpower influence and prestige. This became clearly evident in the military and political setbacks experienced by the United States in Vietnam. After the Vietnamese defeated their French colonizers

in 1954, the United States extended aid to noncommunist Vietnamese in the south as a way of countering the influence of communists who had installed themselves in the north. *The U.S. Defeat in Vietnam* Thereafter, U.S. involvement in South Vietnam steadily escalated and militarized under Presidents Eisenhower, Kennedy, and Lyndon B. Johnson (1908–1973), until by 1968 more than half a million U.S. troops served in-country in defense of South Vietnam. Heavy bombing campaigns were also unleashed on North Vietnam. Yet even with such a major U.S. presence, U.S. and South Vietnamese military leaders and troops could only achieve a stalemate in their struggles against communists in both North and South Vietnam. In the face of such a 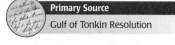 stalemate as well as mounting U.S. casualties, militant protests against the U.S. role in Vietnam spread in the United States, signaling a public distancing from U.S. cold war policy.

Recognizing his country's distaste for the U.S. role in the Vietnam War, presidential candidate Richard Nixon pledged in 1968 to end the war. After escalation of the conflict in 1969 and 1970, U.S. troops began to withdraw, leaving the war in the hands of the South Vietnamese. In January 1973 the U.S. phase of the Vietnam War ended with the Paris Peace Accords. Within two years, however, the North Vietnamese, with help from the communist National Liberation Front in the south, had torn up the peace accords and defeated South Vietnam. In 1976 they unified the nation. In addition to being a bloody and expensive conflict, the Vietnam War severely damaged U.S. prestige at home and abroad.

Although the Vietnam War caused tension between the United States and the Soviet Union, it did not destroy the détente. By the early 1980s, however, relations between the *Soviet Setbacks in Afghanistan* superpowers had deteriorated notably, in large part due to another conflict—this time between the Soviet Union and Afghanistan. Until 1978 Muslim Afghanistan had quietly remained aloof from the cold war as a nonaligned nation. In that year, however, a pro-Soviet coup drew the republic into the cold war, precipitated foreign intervention, and fomented civil war. Once in power, the leftist People's Democratic Party of Afghanistan (PDPA) wasted little time in introducing radical social and legal reforms, which quickly caused a backlash. Especially in rural areas, Islamic religious and ethnic leaders objected to rapid

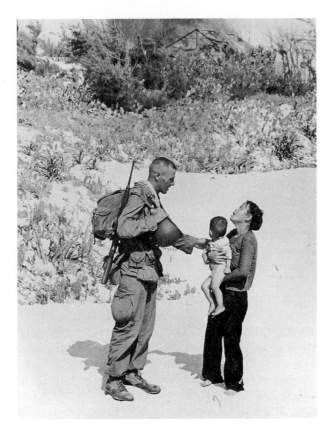

The Vietnam War: with her home going up in flames behind her, a Vietnamese woman pleads with a U.S. soldier.

social change and to the PDPA's brutal methods and called for armed resistance. By the summer of 1979, antigovernment rebels controlled much of the Afghan countryside. At that point the Soviet Union intervened, installing the Marxist Babrak Karmal as president. This Soviet-backed government was highly unpopular, and a national resistance movement spread throughout the country.

For nine years, well-equipped Soviet forces fought a brutal, unsuccessful campaign against Afghan mujahideen, or Islamic warriors, who gradually gained control of most of the countryside. Weapons and money from the United States, Saudi Arabia, Iran, Pakistan, and China sustained the mujahideen in their struggle. In 1986 the Kremlin decided to pull its troops out of the costly, unpopular, and unwinnable war. A cease-fire negotiated by the United Nations in 1988 led to a full Soviet withdrawal in 1989. However, the shared Islamic identity that mobilized and unified the mujahideen in their struggle against Soviet forces gave way to tribal, ethnic, and religious rival-

ries. In 1994 the Taliban, an organization claiming to be an army of religious students, began a campaign to unify the Afghan lands. In 1996 they captured the capital of Kabul after an eleven-month siege and proclaimed the Islamic State of Afghanistan.

Like the U.S. involvement in Vietnam, the Soviet experience in Afghanistan taxed the nation financially and also caused internal dissatisfaction with cold war politics. And as the Vietnam conflict had done to the United States, the war in Afghanistan undermined Soviet prestige and exposed the hollowness of its claims to military superiority.

Indeed, anxiety about nuclear weapons and doubts about cold war policies flourished in the 1960s and 1970s, and the world's youth formed the vanguard in a countercultural revolution that challenged the basic *Countercultural Protests* political and cultural precepts of post–World War II societies. Disturbed by their nations' apparent commitment to war and social conformity, European and American students in particular took to the streets in massive demonstrations designed to promote peace, end the nuclear arms race and the war in Vietnam, and abolish unfair university rules and restrictions. In the United States, students at the University of California at Berkeley formed the Free Speech Movement in 1964 to encourage free political expression on campus; four years later, students in France erected barricades in Paris reminiscent of nineteenth-century French revolts.

THE END OF THE COLD WAR

Between 1989 and 1991 the Soviet system in Europe collapsed with stunning speed. During most of the 1980s, U.S. president Ronald Reagan (in office 1981–1989) reinvigorated cold war animosities, zeroing in on communism and the 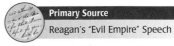 USSR, which he called "the evil empire." In addition, Reagan called for enormous military spending to stay ahead of the Soviets.

Yet although Reagan's cold war rhetoric and budgets challenged détente and the Soviet ability to match U.S. spending, internal changes in the Soviet Union and eastern Europe worked most effectively to end communism and the cold war. Between 1989 and 1990, through a series of mostly nonviolent revolutions, the peoples of eastern and central Europe

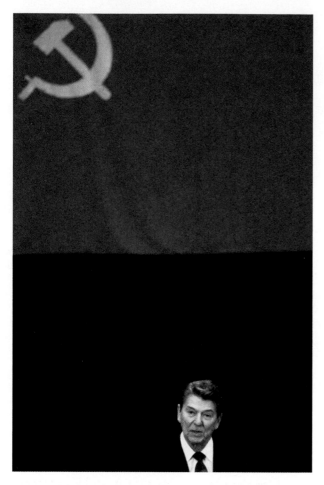

At a U.S./USSR summit in 1985, a Soviet flag served as a dramatic backdrop and counterpoint to U.S. president Ronald Reagan's speech.

tegration by restructuring the economy and liberalizing society. Caught between the rising tide of radical reforms and the opposition of entrenched interests, however, he could do little except watch as events unfolded beyond his control. By the time the Soviet Union collapsed in 1991, the cold war system of states and alliances had become irrelevant to international relations.

Revolutions in Eastern and Central Europe

The inability to connect communism with nationalism left communist regimes vulnerable throughout eastern and central Europe. Those regimes were born in Moscow, transplanted by the Soviet army, and shored up by tanks and bayonets. To most eastern and central Europeans, the Soviet-imposed governments lacked legitimacy from the beginning, and despite the efforts of local communist leaders, the regimes never became firmly established. Moreover, the brutal Soviet interventions in 1956 (Hungary) and 1968 (Czechoslovakia) dashed the aspirations and dreams of reformers who had hoped to establish less harsh, more enlightened forms of communist rule. Thus, by the early 1970s, intellectuals and dissidents had abandoned all hope for a humane socialism. The Polish intellectual Leszek Kolakowski echoed the sentiments of many reformers when he complained in 1971 that "the dead and by now also grotesque creature called Marxist-Leninism still hangs at the necks of the rulers like a hopeless tumor."

Despite economic stagnation, an accelerated arms race with the Reagan administration that further strained the Soviet economy, and obvious signs of discontent, the rulers of eastern and central Europe were reluctant to restructure their ailing systems. It remained for a new Soviet leader, Mikhail S. Gorbachev, to unleash the forces that resulted in the disappearance of the Soviet empire in Europe. By the time Gorbachev visited East Berlin in 1989 on the fortieth anniversary of the German Democratic Republic, he had committed himself to a restructuring of the Soviet Union and to unilateral withdrawal from the cold war. In public interviews he surprised his grim-faced hosts with the announcement that the Brezhnev doctrine was no longer in force and that from then on each country would be responsible for its own destiny. The new Soviet orientation led in rapid succession to the collapse or overthrow of regimes in Poland, Bulgaria, Hungary, Czechoslovakia, Romania, and East Germany.

regained their independence, instituted democratic forms of government, and adopted market-based economies.

The downfall of communist regimes in Europe was the direct consequence of interrelated economic and political developments. The economic weakness of the communist regimes in eastern and central Europe and the Soviet Union became so apparent as to require reforms. The policies espoused by Soviet leader Mikhail Gorbachev (1931–), who came to power in 1985, represented an effort to address this economic deterioration, but they also unleashed a tidal wave of revolution that brought down governments from Czechoslovakia to the Soviet Union. As communism unraveled throughout eastern and central Europe, Gorbachev desperately tried to save the Soviet Union from disin-

The end of communism came first in Poland, where Solidarity—a combined trade union and nationalist movement—put pressure on the crumbling rule of the Communist Party. The Polish government legalized the previously banned Solidarity movement and agreed to multiparty elections in 1989 and 1990. The voters favored Solidarity candidates, and Lech Walesa (1943–), the movement's leader, became president of Poland. In Bulgaria popular unrest forced Todor Zhivkov (1911–1998), eastern Europe's longest-surviving communist dictator, to resign in November 1989. Two months later a national assembly began dismantling the communist state. In 1990 Hungarians also held free elections and launched their nation on the rocky path toward democracy and a market economy.

The disintegration of communism continued elsewhere in eastern Europe. In Czechoslovakia a "velvet revolution"—so called because it entailed little violence—swept communists out of office and restored

***

Lech Walesa (LEHK wah-LEHN-sah)

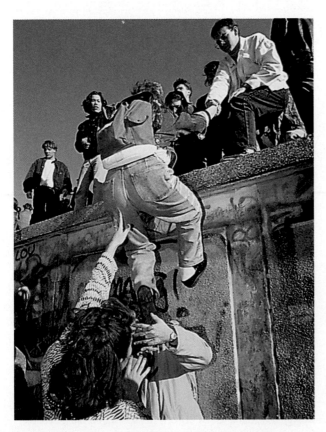

Berliners climb the wall after it fell on 9 November 1989.

democracy by 1990. In 1993 disagreements over the time frame for shifting to a market economy led to a "velvet divorce," breaking Czechoslovakia into two new nations, the Czech Republic and Slovakia. In Romania, in contrast, the regime of dictator Nicolae Ceauşescu (1918–1989) savagely repressed demonstrations, setting off a national uprising that ended within four days and left Ceauşescu and his wife dead.

East Germany had long been a staunchly communist Soviet satellite. Its aging leader, Erich Honecker (1912–1994), openly clung to Stalinist policies. It was too late for anything other than radical changes, however. Honecker's own party removed him from power and decided to open the Berlin Wall to intra-German traffic on 9 November 1989. The end to a divided Berlin was in sight, literally, as thousands of East and West Berliners tore down the Berlin wall in the last weeks of 1989. In 1990 the two Germanies, originally divided by the cold war, formed a united nation.

The Collapse of the Soviet Union

The desire to concentrate attention and resources on urgent matters at home motivated Gorbachev's decision to disengage his nation from the cold war and its military and diplomatic extensions. Although he never intended to abolish the existing political and economic system, it proved impossible to fix parts of the system without undermining the whole. The desire of the Communist Party to control every aspect of the system precluded partial reforms.

Gorbachev's reform efforts focused on the ailing economy. Antiquated industrial plants and obsolete technologies resulted in shoddy and outmoded products, and in any case the diversion of crucial resources to the military *Gorbachev's Reforms* made it impossible to produce enough consumer goods. The failure of state and collective farms to feed the population compelled the Soviet government to import grains from the United States, Canada, and elsewhere. By 1990 the government had imposed rationing to cope with the scarcity of essential consumer goods and food. Economic stagnation in turn contributed to the decline of the Soviet standard of living and the disintegration of the state-sponsored health care system. Funding of the educational system dropped precipitously, and pollution threatened to engulf the entire country. Demoralization affected ever-larger numbers of Soviet citizens as divorce rates climbed, corruption intensified, and alcoholism became more widespread.

When it was clear that the old methods of boosting productivity through bureaucratic exhortation and harassment would not work, Gorbachev contemplated different kinds of reform, using the term *perestroika*, or "restructuring," to describe his efforts to decentralize the economy. To make perestroika work, the Soviet leader linked it to *glasnost*, the opening of Soviet society to public criticism and admission of past mistakes.

Perestroika and Glasnost

Perestroika proved more difficult to implement than Gorbachev had imagined, and glasnost unleashed a torrent of criticism that shook the Soviet state to its foundations. When Gorbachev pushed economic decentralization, the profit motive and the cost-accounting methods he instituted engendered the hostility of those whose privileged positions depended on the old system. Many of Gorbachev's comrades and certain factions of the military objected to perestroika and worked to undermine or destroy it. Moreover, as glasnost allowed discontent with Soviet life to burst into the open, long-repressed ethnic and nationalist sentiments bubbled to the surface, posing a threat to the multiethnic Soviet state.

By the summer of 1990, it was clear that Gorbachev's reforms could not halt the downward slide of industrial and agricultural production or control skyrocketing inflation. As the Soviet economy disintegrated, many minorities contemplated secession from the Soviet Union. The Baltic peoples—Estonians, Latvians, and Lithuanians—were first into the fray, declaring their independence in August 1991. In the following months the remaining twelve republics of the Soviet Union followed suit. The largest and most prominent of the Soviet republics, the Russian Soviet Federated Socialist Republic, and its recently elected president, Boris N. Yeltsin (1931–), led the drive for independence. Soviet leaders vacillated between threats of repression and promises of better treatment, but neither option could stop the movement for independence.

perestroika (payr-eh-STROY-kuh)
glasnost (GLAHS-nohst)

Map 34.3 Collapse of the Soviet Union and the European communist regimes. Note the number of states suddenly created by the breakup of the Soviet Union. How would this affect the ability of each to survive, both economically and politically?

Some did try. While Gorbachev was vacationing in the Crimea in August 1991, a group of conspirators—including discontented party functionaries, disillusioned KGB (secret police) officials, and dissatisfied military officers—decided to seize power. Gorbachev's former friend and ally, the flamboyant Boris Yeltsin, crushed the coup with the help of loyal Red Army units. Gorbachev emerged unscathed from house arrest, but his political career had ended. He watched from the sidelines as Yeltsin dismantled the Communist Party and pushed the country toward market-oriented economic reforms. On 25 December 1991 the Soviet flag fluttered for the last time atop the Kremlin, and by the last day of that year the Union of Soviet Socialist Republics had ceased to exist.

Toward an Uncertain Future

In many ways the cold war provided comfort to the world—however cold that comfort seemed at the time. World War II left most of the major imperialist, fascist, and militarist nations in shambles, and the United States and the Soviet Union stepped into what could have been an uncomfortable vacuum in global leadership. Perilous and controlling it may have been, but the cold war that resulted from the ideological contest between the superpowers ordered and defined the world for almost fifty years. The cold war also shaped how the nations and peoples of the world perceived themselves—as good capitalists fighting evil communists, as progressive socialists battling regressive capitalists, or as nonaligned peoples striving to follow their own paths. Although those perceptions placed constraints on the choices open to them, particularly given the control exerted by the United States and the USSR at the peak of their power, the choices nonetheless were familiar. At the end of the cold war, those easy choices disappeared.

The most immediate and obvious loss that accompanied the end of the cold war involved the alliance systems built by the two former superpowers. Indeed, many observers praised the cold war system for providing peace and security around the world despite the nuclear balance of terror. The loss of deterrence against global disorder and violence was matched by a corresponding lack of certainty regarding the future and by a declining sense of purpose in an era no longer characterized by ideological struggle.

The disappearance of communist regimes in eastern Europe, the dissolution of the Soviet Union, and the increasing market orientation of the People's Republic of China virtually guaranteed the diminishing popularity of the communist model. To be sure, a few states, such as Cuba and North Korea, clung to communism, but without the support once furnished by the Soviet Union their long-term viability as communist regimes was doubtful. The end of the cold war suggested the possibility of a radical shift in power relations, a global realignment that marked a new era of world history devoid of the categories embraced during the cold war.

Summary

The cold war defined much of the global political landscape after World War II. The United States and the Soviet Union stepped into the void created by the disappearance of European empires after 1945, and global encounters between these proponents of democracy and communism stretched from a divided Europe to Korea, Cuba, Vietnam, and Afghanistan. Adding elements of tension to these conflicts were the increasingly sophisticated nuclear weapons and delivery systems that threatened human annihilation. The cold war evolved from mutual hostility to peaceful coexistence and détente, finally reaching extinction at the close of the twentieth century. Facing opposition at home and military humiliation abroad, the superpowers relinquished their hegemonic dreams of world control. From its beginning to its end, the cold war suggested powerful new global forces at work in the wake of World War II. The process of decolonization—itself complicated by the cold war—also symbolized that same phenomenon of radical postwar alterations in the global balance of power.

CHRONOLOGY

1948–1949	Berlin blockade and airlift
1949	Division of Berlin and Germany
1949	Establishment of People's Republic of China
1950–1953	Korean War
1956	Uprising in Hungary
1959	Castro comes to power in Cuba
1961	Bay of Pigs invasion
1961	Construction of Berlin Wall
1962	Cuban missile crisis
1964	Sino-Soviet rift
1965–1973	U.S. troops to Vietnam
1968	Prague Spring
1973	U.S. defeat in Vietnam
1989	Soviet withdrawal from Afghanistan
1989	Fall of Berlin Wall
1990	Reunification of Germany
1991	Collapse of the Soviet Union
1991	End of the cold war

FOR FURTHER READING

David Calleo. *Beyond American Hegemony: The Future of the Western Alliance.* New York, 1987. A broad treatment of Europe during and after the cold war.

John Lewis Gaddis. *Strategies of Containment: A Critical Appraisal of Postwar American National Security Policy.* New York, 1982. Insightful work that traces the U.S. policy of containment from its inception to the late 1970s.

Margot A. Henriksen. *Dr. Strangelove's America: Society and Culture in the Atomic Age.* Berkeley, 1997. Analyzes the crucial role the bomb played in shaping postwar U.S. society.

Akira Iriye. *The Cold War in Asia: A Historical Introduction.* Englewood Cliffs, N.J., 1974. A leading diplomatic historian provides an excellent introduction to the subject.

Madeline Kalb. *The Congo Cables: The Cold War in Africa—from Eisenhower to Kennedy.* New York, 1982. Proper attention for an often neglected aspect of the cold war.

Bruce Kuniholm. *The Origins of the Cold War in the Near East.* Princeton, 1980. A dissection of great power diplomacy and conflicts that focuses on Greece, Turkey, and Iran.

Walter Lafeber. *America, Russia, and the Cold War, 1945–1992.* 7th ed. New York, 1993. A standard work that emphasizes the corrosive effects the cold war had on democratic values in the United States.

Elaine Tyler May. *Homeward Bound: American Families in the Cold War Era.* New York, 1988. An insightful analysis of how the cold war and the atomic age affected family and gender roles in U.S. society.

William Taubman. *Stalin's American Policy: From Entente to Détente to Cold War.* New York, 1982. An important work that focuses on the Soviet perspective of the cold war.

Stephen Whitfield. *The Culture of the Cold War.* Baltimore, 1991. An in-depth analysis of how the cold war and domestic anti-communism shaped U.S. culture from the 1940s to the early 1960s.

CHAPTER 35

The End of Empire and the Emergence of a World without Borders

"Hé Ram" were the last words that escaped his lips after three bullets savagely ripped through his frail body. Roughly translated, he uttered "O! God" and then died. It had begun as a day much like any other in the life of Mohandas K. Gandhi (1869–1948), or "Bapuji" as he was fondly called—a dear father of the country of India. On 30 January 1948, a few months after India gained its independence from Great Britain, he awakened at 3:00 A.M. to work on a draft of a new constitution for the Indian National Congress. The draft emphasized his major concerns for the newly independent India: that villages be empowered, that discrimination based on the caste system be abolished, and that religious intolerance and violence between Hindus and Muslims cease. Still distraught over the partition-

ing of his land into a Hindu India and a Muslim Pakistan, he had weakened himself after independence through fasts and hunger strikes to protest the killings of Hindus and Muslims that had ensued. He weighed a mere 107 pounds that day.

Alternating between working, talking with visitors, and napping, Gandhi finally took a meal at 4:30 P.M. A little over half an hour later, he made his way to the evening prayer meeting he was to lead. As he approached the dais, he stopped to press his palms together, offering the traditional Hindu greeting to the waiting crowd. At that moment, out of the crowd stepped the Hindu extremist Nathuram Godse, who suddenly pulled a Beretta pistol from his pants pocket and fired the three shots that ended the life of the man many credited with

OPPOSITE PAGE: *This saintly image of Mohandas K. Gandhi captures his spiritual significance to the independence movement in India both before and after his death.*

Indian independence, the man seen as the very soul and conscience of India.

Gandhi's murder suggested the troubles and traumas faced by nations and peoples adjusting to independence from colonial rule. Yet despite the hazards of life in a world without empires, peoples in the colonial world fought tenaciously for independence and then for national unity after World War II. In conjunction with the cold war, decolonization reshaped the world in the latter half of the twentieth century. Indeed, the end of empire was one of the most important outcomes of World War II, as dozens of new, independent nations emerged from the British, French, Dutch, Spanish, and Portuguese empires established in previous centuries. With the emergence of two superpowers dedicated to the overthrow of empire, the stage was set for a wholesale overturning of colonial rule. As cold war animosities deepened, however, emerging nations were often confronted by the demand that they take sides and choose between capitalism and communism. At times that demand compromised their newly won independence, particularly in nations deemed strategically important by the superpowers.

In the years between the end of World War II and 1980, more than ninety nations gained independence. Nations achieved independence at different times: whereas India and Pakistan became independent in 1947, for example, Zimbabwe (Southern Rhodesia) became independent only in 1980. Algerians in North Africa fought a long, hard war against the French for freedom, whereas others followed less torturous routes to independence. Vietnam became deeply embroiled in the cold war even as it successfully fought French imperial domination; other countries managed to avoid such entanglement. Regardless of freedom's timetable, new and developing nations around the world discovered, as Gandhi had, that independence was just the first step on a much longer, and often much more difficult, road to national unity and social and economic stability.

With the end of empires and also of the cold war, a new world order emerged: one without borders. One pronounced feature of that world was an increased level of economic interaction and integration between countries. The forces driving the world economy in that direction, often referred to as *globalization,* included advances in communications technology, an enormous expansion of international trade, and the emergence of new international organizations that favored market-oriented economics. Many of these same forces have also driven global cultural integration through consumer goods, television, computers, and popular culture. Although global economic and cultural integration are not new, the more recent phenomenon of globalization has been different and unprecedented both in scope and in speed, and it has transformed the social and political as well as the economic contours of the world. Some of those transformations have taken the form of global problems—such as poverty, terrorism, and environmental degradation—that now face all of humanity. Whatever the transformations, one thing is increasingly clear: the national borders so long fought for, and fought over, are no longer as significant as they once were.

INDEPENDENCE IN ASIA

In the wake of World War II, the power of Asian nationalism was irrepressible. New nations emerged throughout Asia, from India and Pakistan in south Asia to diverse Arab nations in southwest Asia and to Vietnam, Cambodia, and Laos in southeast Asia. These lands encountered different conditions in their quests for independence and freedom from imperial control, but everywhere Asian nationalists rallied their people against colonialism and imperialism.

India's Partitioned Independence

After World War II, it became painfully obvious to the British government that it could not continue to bear the financial burden of governing India, particularly since nationalists made it clear that they would accept nothing less than complete independence. As the probability of Indian independence became more pronounced, the issue of Muslim separatism grew in importance, and Muslims increasingly feared their minority status in a free India dominated by Hindus. Muhammad Ali Jinnah (1876–1948), leader of the Muslim League, felt no qualms about frankly expressing Muslim concerns and desires for a separate Muslim state, even as Congress Party leaders such as Jawaharlal Nehru (1889–1964) and Gandhi urged all Indians to act and feel as one nation, undivided by what came to be known as communalism—emphasizing religious over national identity.

The Coming of Self-Rule

Jinnah had his way, however, and when the British withdrew from India in 1947 two new flags were raised in place of the British Union Jack. Gandhi condemned

Zimbabwe (zihm-BAHB-way)

the division as a "vivisection" of his homeland and prophesied that "rivers of blood" would flow in its

Partition and Violence

wake. His vision came true as the terms of partition were announced and hundreds of thousands of Muslim and Hindu refugees migrated to either Muslim Pakistan (divided between parts of Bengal in the east and Punjab in the west) or Hindu India to escape religious per-

secution. By mid-1948 an estimated ten million refugees had made the tortuous journey to one or the other state, and between half a million and one million people had died in the violence that accompanied those mass migrations. Through it all, Gandhi continually urged all Indians

Image
Partition of India

Map 35.1 Decolonization in Asia. (Date is year of independence.) Note the dates of independence for the colonies of Great Britain, the Netherlands, the United States, and France. Why did independence occur in such a short span of time for most of these colonies?

and Pakistanis to adhere to the practice of nonviolence. When Gandhi was shot he became a martyr to his own cause, killed by the violence he so abhorred.

Though mired in violence, Indian independence became a reality, with momentous consequences for the process of decolonization. Just as Gandhi's nonviolent resistance to British rule inspired nationalists around the globe before and after World War II, independence in India and Pakistan further encouraged anti-imperial movements throughout Asia and Africa. Moreover, once India left the British empire, there could be little doubt about the fate of Britain's remaining imperial possessions.

Unlike the Dutch and the French, who at times tenaciously battled to maintain imperial control in Asia, the British recognized that Europeans could not rule in Asia without the cooperation of colonial peoples. Also unlike the Dutch and the French, the British could rely on their own models of decolonization, previously tested in Canada. Like Canada, India and Pakistan gained independence yet retained ties to Britain, becoming Dominion members in the British Commonwealth and adopting English as their official language.

Another way in which Indian independence inspired other nations and set a pattern for grappling *Nonalignment* with decolonization in the midst of a cold war was through Nehru's promotion of a nonalignment strategy. Nehru proved instrumental in fashioning a compelling position for newly independent nations caught in the cold war and in the superpower tug-of-war contests for the loyalties of new nations. He became one of the impassioned defenders of nonalignment, arguing that "each country has not only the right to freedom but also to decide its own policy and way of life."

Nehru made that assertion at the Bandung Conference, where in April 1955 leaders from twenty-three Asian and six African nations met in Bandung, Indonesia, to discuss alternatives to choosing between the United States and the Soviet Union. Besides neutrality in the cold war, the Bandung Conference stressed the struggle against colonialism and racism. Bandung was the precursor of the broader Nonaligned Movement, which held occasional meetings so that its members could discuss their relations with the United States and the Soviet Union. The movement's primary goal was to maintain formal neutrality. However, although theoretically nonaligned with either cold war superpower, many member states had close ties to one or the other, and that situation caused dissension within the movement. For example, the Philippines and Cuba clearly supported the U.S. and Soviet camps, respectively. Nevertheless, other individual states avoided becoming pawns in the cold war by announcing the policy of nonalignment advocated by Nehru.

Since winning its independence, India has stood out among decolonized nations not just for its advocacy of nonalignment but also for its ability to maintain its political stability and its democratic system. Indeed, even though India has faced many of the same crises that have shaken other developing nations—ethnic and religious conflict, wars, poverty, political assassinations, and overpopulation—Nehru's heirs have remained committed to free elections and a critical press.

Nationalist Struggles in Vietnam

In contrast to India, Vietnam could not keep its nationalist struggle for independence separate from the complications of the cold war. Rather, Vietnam became deeply enmeshed in the contest between capitalism and communism, which meant that decolonization there was a long and bloody process.

Vietnam's nationalist communist leader, Ho Chi Minh (1890–1969), had been struggling for autonomy from French imperialism for two decades when World War II broke out in Europe. Thus the Japanese invasion of his homeland after the fall of France in 1940 seemed to Ho like the replacement of 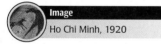 one imperialist power with another. During the war, Ho fought against the Japanese and in the waning days of the war helped oust them from Vietnam altogether. With both the French and the Japanese gone, Ho took the opportunity to establish himself as leader of an independent Vietnam, complete with a Declaration of Independence modeled on the U.S. declaration.

However, the French, humiliated by their country's easy defeat and occupation by the Germans, sought to reclaim their imperial possessions as a way of regaining their world-power status. In 1945 they invaded Vietnam, and by 1947 they seemed to have secured their power. However, that security proved to be temporary. Much like the Chinese communists in their battles against the Japanese and then against the nationalists in the postwar years, the Vietnamese resistance forces, led by Ho Chi Minh and General Vo Nguyen Giap (1911–), mounted a campaign of guerrilla warfare. The Vietnamese communists increasingly regained control of their country, especially after 1949, when communist China sent aid and arms to the Viet Minh. Thus strengthened, they defeated the French at their fortress in Dienbienphu in 1954. The French had to sue for peace at the conference table.

The peace conference, held in Geneva in 1954, determined that Vietnam should be temporarily divided at the seventeenth parallel; North Vietnam would be controlled by Ho Chi Minh and the communist forces, whereas South Vietnam remained in the hands of noncommunists. Leaving all of Vietnam in the hands of Ho's communists was unthinkable for the United States, especially after the globalization of the cold war that had accompanied the Korean War. The United States had already aided the French in their struggle against Ho—now they did the same for the government of South Vietnam. Violating the terms of the Geneva Agreements, which required elections that would likely have brought Ho to power, South Vietnam's leaders, with U.S. support, avoided elections and sought to build a government that would prevent the spread of communism in South Vietnam and elsewhere in Asia. However, the leaders of South Vietnam did not have the support of the people, who quickly grew discontented enough to resort to arms.

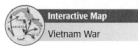
Interactive Map
Vietnam War

In 1960 South Vietnamese nationalists—with the aid of weapons and troops from the north—formed the National Liberation Front to fight for freedom from South Vietnamese rule. In turn, the government in the north received economic and military assistance from the Soviet Union and China. This ensured that the war would be a long, bloody, and expensive stalemate. Ultimately, United States forces withdrew from this unwinnable war in 1975, and in 1976 North Vietnam conquered the south, united the country, and at long last declared independence.

Although the Vietnamese ultimately did achieve their long-awaited independence, their experience demonstrated what could occur when independence movements became entangled with the politics and logic of the cold war.

Arab National States and the Problem of Palestine

With one exception, the Arab states of southwest Asia—including Syria, Iraq, Lebanon, and Jordan—had little difficulty freeing themselves from the colonial powers of France and Britain by the end of World War II. The issue of Palestinian independence, however, highlighted the difficulties of decolonization in an area where more than one group claimed the right to establish a nation.

Great Britain served as the mandate power in Palestine after the Great War, and before and during its mandate made conflicting promises both to Palestinian Arabs and to Jews who hoped to establish a secure homeland in Palestine. With the Balfour Declaration of 1917, the British government committed itself to the support of a Jewish homeland. The declaration was due in part to pressure by Zionists, who were dedicated to combating the violent anti-

Primary Source
The Balfour Declaration

Semitism prevailing in central and eastern Europe by establishing a national Jewish state. Zionists received an additional boost when their aims were supported by the Allies at the Paris Peace Conference in 1919. Thus the British were compelled to allow Jewish migration to Palestine under their mandate, but they also had to allay the fears of those in possession of the land—the Palestinian Arabs.

This British attempt to balance the causes of two conflicting groups was unsuccessful, and large-scale violence was prevented only through the use of imperial military forces. The Palestinian Muslims perceived the Jews as alien interlopers in their own land. At the same time, European Jews were dangerously under attack by the Nazis, and Zionists in Palestine armed themselves to protect Jewish settlers against Arab reprisals. At the end of World War II, a battle brewed. As Arab states around Palestine gained their freedom from imperial rule, they developed a pan-Arab nationalism

Ho Chi Minh, leader of North Vietnam from 1945 to 1969 and one of southeast Asia's most influential communist leaders.

sparked by support for their fellow Arabs in Palestine and opposition to the possibility of a Jewish state there. The Holocaust, however, intensified the Jewish commitment to build a state capable of defending the world's remaining Jews.

While the Arabs in Palestine insisted on complete independence under Arab rule, in 1945 the Jews embarked on a course of violent resistance to the British to compel recognition of Jewish demands for self-rule. The British could not resolve the dispute and instead gave up. In 1947 they turned the region over to the newly created United Nations, which came up with a plan, in November 1947, to divide Palestine into two distinct states. Both Arabs and Jews found the terms unacceptable and began to battle each other. In May 1948 the Jews in Palestine further provoked Arab outrage when they announced the creation of the independent state of Israel. In response, the Arab states of Egypt, Jordan, Syria, Leb-

anon, and Iraq joined Palestinians in a war to destroy the new state.

However, Arab attacks and campaigns, although boldly fought, were uncoordinated, and the Israelis managed to achieve a stunning victory, gaining territories far larger than those that would have been granted to the Jewish state under the United Nations partition plan. A truce went into effect in early 1949 under UN auspices, and the partition of Palestine resulted. Jerusalem and the Jordan River valley were divided between the new Israeli state and the Kingdom of Jordan, and Israel controlled the coastal areas of Palestine and the Negev Desert to the Red Sea.

The problem of Palestine, then, demonstrated the difficulties and dangers of decolonization in contested areas. In the case of Palestine, it seems safe to say that the transfer of power from the British mandate system resulted in an outcome that has created long-term instability and mutual hatreds.

Map 35.2 Arab-Israeli conflict between 1949 and 1982. Compare the boundaries proposed by the UN partition of Palestine with those claimed by Israel after 1948–49. What were the strategic advantages of the extra territories claimed by Israel in 1948–49?

DECOLONIZATION IN AFRICA

In the 1950s the superpowers' influence intensified. For African lands, that situation often meant delays in decolonization. Also complicating the decolonization process were internal divisions in African societies, which undermined attempts to forge national or pan-African identities. Tribal, ethnic, religious, and linguistic divides within and between state boundaries, all of which colonial rulers had exploited, posed a challenge to African leaders, particularly once independence came and the imperial enemy departed. Given the variety of barriers to African independence, then, it is not astonishing that independence came more slowly in Africa than in other regions of the world.

Forcing the French out of North Africa

In Africa as in southeast Asia, the French resisted decolonization. In Algeria the French fought a bloody war that began in 1954, the year France suffered its defeat at Dienbienphu. Somewhat iron-

France in Africa

ically, while it focused its efforts on Algeria in the 1950s and 1960s, France allowed all its other territories in Africa to gain independence. In

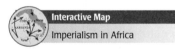
Interactive Map
Imperialism in Africa

1956 France granted independence to its colonies in Morocco and Tunisia, and thirteen French colonies in west and equatorial Africa won

their independence in 1960, a year that came to be known as "the year of Africa."

In Algeria, however, France was determined to remain in control. The two million French settlers who lived there by the mid-1940s demanded that the government in Paris defend their cause in north Africa. Yet after World War II, Algerians embarked on a revitalized campaign for independence from France and for freedom from domination by white settlers. The event that touched off the Algerian revolt came in May 1945. French colonial police in the town of Sétif fired shots into an otherwise peaceful demonstration in support of Algerian and Arab nationalism. The resulting melee killed more than eight thousand Algerian Muslims and approximately one hundred French.

In 1954 the Algerian war of liberation began in earnest under the command of the Front de Libération Nationale (National Liberation Front, or FLN). France sent thousands of

War in Algeria

troops to Algeria to put down the revolution, and by 1958 it had committed half a million soldiers to the war. The war became ugly and brutal: Algerians serving with the French had to kill fellow Algerians or be killed by them; Algerian civilians became trapped in the crossfire of war, often accused of and killed for aiding FLN guerrillas; thousands of French soldiers died. By the time Algerians finally gained independence from France in 1962, hundreds of thousands of Algerians had lost their lives. Thereafter, thanks in large part to the writings of the West Indian Frantz Fanon (1925–1961), who became an Algerian revolutionary, the Algerian war of liberation became synonymous

French paratroopers search for terrorists near Algiers, January 1957.

with the utility of using whatever violent means necessary to achieve independence from colonial oppressors.

Black African Nationalism and Independence

Before and during World War II, nationalism flourished in sub-Saharan Africa. African nationalists celebrated their blackness and Africanness in contrast to their European colonial rulers. Drawing from the pan-African movements that emerged in the United States and the Caribbean, African intellectuals, especially in French-controlled west Africa, established a movement to promote *Négritude* ("Blackness"). Reviving Africa's great traditions and cultures, poets and writers expressed a widely shared pride in Africa.

This celebration of African culture was accompanied by grassroots protests against European imperialism. However, although most Europeans came to believe in the inevitability of decolonization in the decades after World War II, their beliefs about the incapacities of Africans for self-government convinced them that the transition to independence would be very slow indeed. Also complicating the process of decolonization in sub-Saharan Africa were the presence of white settlers in certain African colonies as well as cold war politics, which allowed imperial powers to justify oppressive actions in the name of rooting out a subversive communist presence. Despite the delays, however, sub-Saharan states slowly but surely won their independence.

Growth of African Nationalism

Agitation for independence in sub-Saharan Africa took on many forms, peaceful and violent, and decolonization occurred at a different pace in different nations. Ghana became independent in 1957, but independence came much later to Angola (1975) and Zimbabwe, formerly Southern Rhodesia (1980). In many instances, African nations sealed their severance from imperial control by adopting new names that shunned the memory of European rule and drew from the glory of Africa's past empires. Ghana set the pattern, and the map of Africa soon featured similar references to precolonial African places: Zambia, Malawi, Zimbabwe.

African Independence

Freedom and Conflict in Sub-Saharan Africa

Ghana's success in achieving its freedom from British rule in 1957 served as a hallmark in Africa's end of empire. Under the leadership of Kwame Nkrumah (1909–1972), political parties and strategies for mass action took shape. Although the British initially subjected Nkrumah and other nationalists to jail terms and repressive control, gradually they allowed reforms and negotiated the peaceful transfer of power in their Gold Coast colony. After it became independent in 1957, Ghana emboldened and inspired other African nationalist movements. Nkrumah, as a leader of the first sub-Saharan African nation to gain independence from colonial rule, became a persuasive spokesperson for pan-African unity.

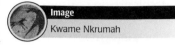
Kwame Nkrumah

The process of attaining independence did not always prove as nonviolent as in Ghana. The battle that took place in the British colony of Kenya in east Africa demonstrated the complexity and difficulty of African decolonization. The situation in Kenya turned tense and violent in a clash between powerful white settlers and nationalists, especially the Kikuyu, one of Kenya's largest ethnic groups. Beginning in 1947, Kikuyu rebels embarked on a violent campaign against Europeans and African collaborators. The settlers who controlled the colonial government in Nairobi refused to see the uprisings as a legitimate expression of discontent with colonial rule. Rather, they branded the Kikuyu tribes as radicals—calling them Mau Mau subversives or communists—bent on a racial struggle for primacy. As one settler put it, "Why the hell can't we fight these apes and worry about the survivors later?"

Anticolonial Rebellion in Kenya

In reality, Kikuyu radicalism and violence had much more to do with nationalist opposition to British colonial rule, especially land policies in Kenya. In the 1930s and 1940s, white settlers had pushed many Kikuyu off the most fertile highland farm areas and reduced them to the status of wage slaves or relegated them to overcrowded "tribal reserves." Resistance began in the early 1940s with labor strikes and violent direct-action campaigns, but attacks on white settlers and black collaborators escalated in the 1950s. In 1952 the British established a state of emergency to crush the anticolonial guerrilla movement. Unable or unwilling to distinguish violent activism from nonviolent agitation, the British moved to suppress all nationalist groups and jailed Kenya's nationalist leaders, including Jomo Kenyatta (1895–1978), in 1953. Amid growing resistance to colonial rule, the British mounted major military offenses against rebel forces, supporting their army troops with artillery, bombers, and jet fighters. By 1956 the British had effectively

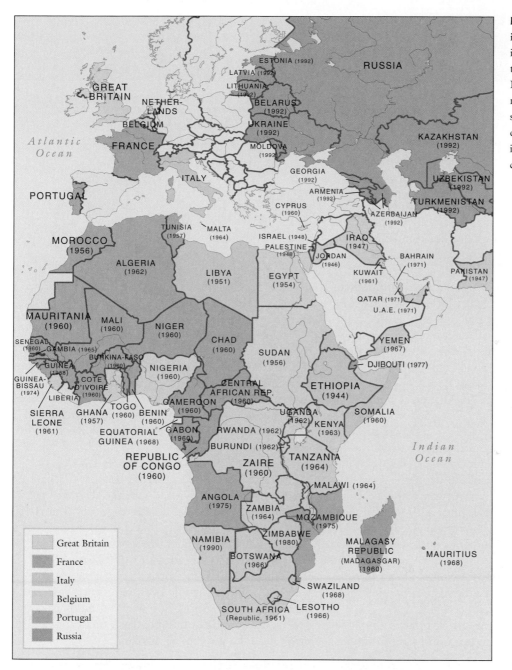

Map 35.3 Decolonization in Africa. (Date is year of independence.) Compare this map with Map 29.4. How do the borders of the newly independent African states compare with those drawn by European powers in the late nineteenth century?

crushed all military resistance in a conflict that claimed the lives of twelve thousand Africans and one hundred Europeans.

Despite military defeat, Kikuyu fighters broke British resolve in Kenya and gained increasing international recognition of African grievances. The British resisted the radical white supremacism and political domineering of the settlers in Kenya and instead responded to calls for Kenya's independence. In 1959

the British lifted the state of emergency, and as political parties formed, nationalist leaders such as Kenyatta reemerged to lead those parties. By December 1963 Kenya had negotiated its independence.

The experience of some African countries also demonstrated the dangers of becoming entangled in cold war politics. That was the case in the land once known as the Belgian Congo, which was reconfigured as Zaire in 1971 and renamed the Democratic Republic of the

SOURCES FROM THE PAST

Kwame Nkrumah on African Unity

As the leader of the first African nation to gain independence, Kwame Nkrumah (1909–1972) became a respected spokesperson for African unity as a strategy for dealing with decolonization during the cold war. In his book I Speak of Freedom: A Statement of African Ideology *(1961), Nkrumah made an eloquent case for an African solution for the problems of African independence during a global cold war.*

■ ■ ■

It is clear that we must find an African solution to our problems, and that this can only be found in African unity. Divided we are weak; united, Africa could become one of the greatest forces for good in the world.

Never before have a people had within their grasp so great an opportunity for developing a continent endowed with so much wealth. Individually, the independent states of Africa, some of them potentially rich, others poor, can do little for their people. Together, by mutual help, they can achieve much. But the economic development of the continent must be planned and pursued as a whole. A loose confederation designed only for economic cooperation would not provide the necessary unity of purpose. Only a strong political union can bring about full and effective development of our natural resources for the benefit of our people.

The political situation in Africa today is heartening and at the same time disturbing. It is heartening to see so many new flags hoisted in place of the old; it is disturbing to see so many countries of varying sizes and at different levels of development, weak and, in some cases, almost helpless. If this terrible state of fragmentation is allowed to continue it may well be disastrous for us all.

Critics of African unity often refer to the wide differences in culture, language and ideas in various parts of Africa. This is true, but the essential fact remains that we are all Africans, and have a common interest in the independence of Africa. The difficulties presented by questions of language, culture and different political systems are not insuperable. If the need for political union is agreed by us all, then the will to create it is born; and where there's a will there's a way.

The greatest contribution that Africa can make to the peace of the world is to avoid all the dangers inherent in disunity, by creating a political union which will also by its success, stand as an example to a divided world. A union of African states will project more effectively the African personality. It will command respect from a world that has regard only for size and influence.

We have to prove that greatness is not to be measured in stock piles of atom bombs. I believe strongly and sincerely that with the deep-rooted wisdom and dignity, the innate respect for human lives, the intense humanity that is our heritage, the African race, united under one federal government, will emerge not as just another world bloc to flaunt its wealth and strength, but as a Great Power whose greatness is indestructible because it is not built on fear, envy and suspicion, nor won at the expense of others, but founded on hope, trust, friendship and directed to the good of all mankind.

• *How does Nkrumah's call for African unity rather than fragmentation reflect the tensions between decolonization and the ongoing cold war?*

SOURCE: Kwame Nkrumah. *I Speak of Freedom: A Statement of African Ideology.* New York: Frederick A. Praeger, 1961, x–xii.

Congo in 1997. The region won independence from Belgium in 1960 under the popular leadership of Patrice Lumumba (1925–1961), who was also a Maoist Marxist. The general Mobutu Sese Seko (1930–1997), a contender for power, killed Lumumba the very next year in a military coup supported by the United States. Although Mobutu ruled Zaire as a dictator and devastated the economy in the process of enriching himself, his government continued to receive support from the United States and other European

Rebel suspects in a British internment camp, Nairobi, Kenya.

democracies hoping to quell the growth of communism in Africa. Thus the convergence of decolonization with the politics of the cold war helped to undermine the possibilities for lasting stability in an independent Zaire.

The Democratic Republic of the Congo

AFTER INDEPENDENCE: LONG-TERM STRUGGLES IN THE POSTCOLONIAL ERA

Political and economic stability often proved elusive after independence, particularly in those developing nations struggling to build political and economic systems free from the domination of more powerful nations. The legacies of imperialism, either direct or indirect, hindered the creation of democratic institutions in many parts of the world. In Asia and the Islamic world, some governments staved off interference by relying on tightly centralized rule, as in China, or on religion, as in Iran after the 1979 revolution. Few developing or newly industrialized countries, however, escaped the disruption of war or revolution that also characterized the postcolonial era.

Communism and Democracy in Asia

Except for Japan and India, the developing nations in south, southeast, and east Asia adopted some form of authoritarian or militarist political system, and many of them followed a communist or socialist path of political development. Under Mao Zedong (1893–1976), China served as a guide and inspiration for those countries seeking a means of political development distinct from the ways of their previous colonial masters. Mao reunified China for the first time since the collapse of the Qing dynasty, transforming European communist ideology into a distinctly Chinese form. After 1949 he embarked on programs designed to accelerate development in China and to distinguish Chinese communism from Soviet communism. Unfortunately, the Great Leap Forward (1958–1961) and the Great Proletarian Cultural Revolution (1966–1976) hampered the political and economic development that Mao so urgently sought.

Mao's China

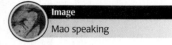

Mao envisioned his Great Leap Forward as a way to overtake the industrial production of more developed nations, and to that end he worked to collectivize all land, business, and industrial enterprises. Private ownership was abolished, and farming and industry became largely rural and communal. The Great Leap Forward—or "Giant Step Backward" as some have dubbed it—failed. Most disastrous was its impact on agricultural production in China: peasants could not meet quotas, and a series of bad harvests contributed to one of the deadliest famines in history, resulting in the deaths of as many as twenty million people between 1959 and 1962.

In 1966 Mao tried to reignite the revolutionary spirit with the inauguration of the Great Proletarian Cultural Revolution. Designed to root out the revisionism Mao perceived in Chinese life, the Cultural Revolution subjected millions of people to humiliation, persecution, and death. The elite—intellectuals, teachers, professionals, and managers—constituted the major targets of the Red Guards, youthful zealots empowered to cleanse Chinese society of opponents to Mao's rule. Victims were beaten and killed, jailed, or sent to corrective labor camps or to toil in the countryside. The Cultural Revolution, which cost China years of stable development and gutted its educational system, did not end until after Mao's death in 1976. It fell to one of Mao's heirs, Deng Xiaoping—himself a one-time victim of the Cultural Revolution—to heal the nation.

Deng came to power in 1981, and the 1980s are often referred to as the years of "Deng's Revolution." Deng moderated Mao's commitment to Chinese self-sufficiency and isolation and engineered China's entry into the international financial and trading system. In

A 1966 poster shows Mao Zedong inspiring the people to launch the Great Proletarian Cultural Revolution.

addition, Deng sent tens of thousands of Chinese students to foreign universities to rebuild the professional, intellectual, and managerial elite needed for modern development. These students were exposed to the democratic societies of western Europe and the United States. However, when they staged pro-democracy demonstrations in Beijing's Tiananmen Square in 1989, Deng approved a bloody crackdown. Indeed, having successfully negotiated a path that halted imperial interference, China entered the global economy facing the issue of how (or whether) to reap economic benefits without compromising its identity and its authoritarian political system.

Deng's Revolution

Islamic Resurgence in Southwest Asia and North Africa

The geographic convergence of the Arab and Muslim worlds in southwest Asia and north Africa encouraged the development of Arab nationalism in states of those regions that gained independence after World War II.

Whether in Libya, Algeria, or Egypt in north Africa or in Syria, Saudi Arabia, or Iraq in southwest Asia, visions of Arab nationalism, linked to the religious force of Islam, dazzled nations that wished to fend off European and U.S. influence. In north Africa, Egypt's Gamal Abdel Nasser provided the leadership for this Arab nationalism, and Arab-Muslim opposition to the state of Israel held the dream together.

The hopes attached to pan-Arab unity did not materialize. Although Arab lands shared a common language and religion, divisions were frequent and alliances shifted over time. The cold war split the Arab-Muslim world as some states allied themselves with the United States and others associated with the Soviet Union. Religious divisions also complicated the attainment of Arab unity, because Sunni and Shia Muslims followed divergent theologies and foreign policies.

Muslim Revival and Arab Disunity

In southwest Asia, peace seemed a distant prospect, given the political turmoil caused by the presence of Israel in the midst of Arab-Islamic states, many of which allied themselves with the Soviet Union as Israel became a staunch ally of the United States. Intermittent Arab-Israeli wars also greatly intensified the tensions in the region. Although Egyptian president Anwar Sadat (1918–1981) did in fact make significant progress in improving relations between Egypt and Israel, those efforts also raised the ire of the other Arab states and ultimately resulted in Sadat's assassination in 1981 by anti-Israeli opponents.

In Palestine, violence between Israelis and Palestinians—under the leadership of Yasser Arafat's (1929–2004) Palestinian Liberation Organization (PLO)—continued into the 1990s. However, in 1993 and 1995 Arafat and Israeli prime minister Yitzhak Rabin (1922–1995) signed peace treaties that advanced the notion of limited Palestinian self-rule in Israeli-occupied territories. Yet the assassination of Rabin in 1995 by a Jewish extremist who opposed the peace agreements, as well as other hurdles, blocked the peace process.

Elsewhere in southwest Asia and north Africa, a revival of Muslim traditions found expression in Islamism. At the heart of Islamism was the desire for the reassertion of Islamic values in Muslim politics. Many Muslims had become skeptical about European and American models of economic development and political and cultural norms, which they blamed for economic and political failure as well as the breakdown of traditional social and re-

Islamism

ligious values. The solution to the problems faced by Muslim societies lay, according to Islamists, in the revival of Islamic identity, values, and power. Although the vast majority of Islamic activists have sought to bring about change through peaceful means, an extremist minority has called for violent transformations. Convinced that the Muslim world is under siege, extremists use the concept of *jihad*—the right and duty to defend Islam and the Islamic community from unjust attack—to rationalize and legitimize violence and revolution.

The Iranian Revolution

The Iranian revolution of 1979 demonstrated the power of Islam as a means of staving off secular foreign influences. Islamist influences grew in Iran during the lengthy regime of Shah Mohammed Reza Pahlavi (1919–1980), whom the CIA helped bring to power in 1953. Money from Iran's lucrative oil industry helped finance industrialization under the shah, and the United States provided Iran with the necessary military equipment to fight communism in the region. By the late 1970s, however, opposition to the shah's government came from many quarters. Shia Muslims despised the shah's secular regime, Iranian small businesses detested the influence of U.S. corporations on the economy, and leftist politicians rejected the shah's repressive policies. The shah fled the country in early 1979, and power was captured by the Islamist movement under the direction of Ayatollah Ruhollah Khomeini (1900–1989).

The revolution took on a strongly anti-U.S. cast, partly because the shah was allowed to travel to the United States for medical treatment. In retaliation, Shia militants captured sixty-nine hostages at the U.S. embassy in Tehran, fifty-five of whom remained captives until 1981. In the meantime, Iranian leaders shut U.S. military bases and confiscated U.S.-owned economic ventures. This Islamic power play against a developed nation such as the United States inspired other Muslims to undertake terrorist actions.

The Iran-Iraq War

The resurgent Islam of Iran did not lead to a new era of Islamic solidarity, however. Instead, Iran's neighbor Iraq—led by President Saddam Hussein (in office 1979–2003)—attempted to take advantage of the revolution to invade Iran. Although Iraqi troops were initially successful, they faced a determined counterattack by Iranian forces, and the conflict became a war of attrition—as many as one million soldiers were killed—that did not end until 1988.

Although Hussein's bid to conquer Iran was unsuccessful, Iraq continued on a militant course. Two years after the end of the Iran-Iraq War, Hussein's troops invaded Kuwait (1990) and incited the Gulf War (1991). Hussein suffered another defeat, creating further hardship for Iraqis and much of southwest Asia. His troubles deepened in the wake of the 11 September 2001 terrorist attacks against the United States as President George W. Bush (1946–) vastly expanded his nation's war on terror. A coalition of forces aligned with the United States launched a preemptive invasion of Iraq in 2003 to destroy Hussein's "weapons of mass destruction" and Iraq's capacity to harbor global terrorists. Iraqi military units suffered defeat and coalition forces captured Saddam Hussein in December 2003.

Iranians show their devotion to the Ayatollah Khomeini at his funeral in 1989.

A WORLD WITHOUT BORDERS

The United States' war on terror, which legitimized the invasion of Iraq in 2003, offered a telling testament to the emergence of a new world order. By the turn of the twenty-first century, empires had given way to a multiplicity of national states, and the collapse of the Soviet system had destroyed the bipolar world. Even the name of the conflict—the war on terror—does not feature nation-states or locations: rather, it denotes a more far-reaching, extensive conflict that could be anywhere, at any time. It implies connections between civilians all over the world who could be victims of terrorism in their home countries, while moving from place to place, or even on their computers. It is a global conflict in an increasingly globalized world.

Indeed, the problem of terrorism highlights one of the darker sides of the new international order, in which small groups, connected across borders by financial flows and communications technology, can utilize resources to control or combat the actions of even the most powerful nations. Yet there is far more to this new, globalized world than terrorism. The world's peoples have become connected in many other ways—economically through global trade networks, and culturally through mass media and consumerism. The world's peoples are also connected through the global problems that now face all of humanity, including overpopulation, environmental degradation, and poverty. Opinions differ as to the costs and benefits of this new globalized world, but few can deny its realities. It is somewhat ironic, however, that within a few decades of nearly all the world's peoples achieving independence from colonial rule and creating long-wished-for nation-states, national borders have become increasingly vulnerable to supranational influences such as global financial networks, corporations, and media. And although the joys of independence and decolonization were surely real, it is nevertheless the case that many of the world's newest nations have found that they receive few dividends in this new world order.

Economic Globalization

The early origins of economic globalization derived from the establishment of international organizations such as the International Monetary Fund (IMF). Founded in 1944, the IMF began the promotion of market economies, free trade, and high growth rates.

In addition to the IMF, U.S. politicians and business leaders wanted to establish an international trading system that suited their interests, and they pushed for the elimination of restrictive trading practices that stood in the way of free trade across national borders. The main vehicle for the promotion of unrestricted global trade was the General Agreement on Tariffs and Trade (GATT), which was signed by the representatives of twenty-three noncommunist nations in 1947. After the round of negotiations that ended in 1994, the member nations of GATT (now totaling 123) signed an agreement to establish the World Trade Organization (WTO), which took over the activities of GATT in 1995. The WTO has developed into a forum for settling international trade disputes, with the power to enforce its decisions. Numbers tell the story of the fortunes of free trade. World trade (exports and imports) grew by 6.6 percent annually between 1948 and 1966 and by 9.2 percent annually between 1966 and 1977. Although trade slowed in the 1980s, by 1990 world trade exceeded six trillion U.S. dollars, roughly double the figure for 1980.

GATT and WTO

The emergence of a new breed of corporation played another key role in the development of the new economic order. Global corporations have increasingly replaced the more traditional international or multinational forms of corporate enterprises. International companies were born out of the desire to extend business activities across borders in pursuit of specific activities such as importation, exportation, and the extraction of raw materials. International companies evolved into multinationals, which conducted their business in several countries but had to operate within the confines of specific laws and customs of a given society. During the last twenty-five years, the transformation of the corporate landscape has resulted in the birth of some fifty thousand global corporations. In contrast to the multinational, the typical global corporation relies on a small headquarters staff while dispersing all other corporate functions across the globe in search of the lowest possible operating costs. For example, global corporations move jobs from high-wage facilities to foreign locations where wages are low and environmental laws are weak or nonexistent. Global corporations treat the world as a single market and act as if the nation-state no longer exists. Many multinational corporations, such as General Motors, Siemens AG, and Nestlé, have transformed themselves into global enterprises, both benefiting from and contributing to the ongoing process of globalization.

Global Corporations

One response to the increasingly competitive global economy has been the creation of national economic alliances designed to achieve advantages and greater strength for their partners. One of the earliest and most successful of these alliances was the Organization of Petroleum Exporting Countries (OPEC), a producer cartel established in 1960 by the oil-producing states of Iran, Iraq, Kuwait, Saudi Arabia, and Venezuela and later joined by Qatar, Libya, Indonesia, Abu Dhabi, Algeria, Nigeria, Ecuador, and Gabon. The mostly Arab and Muslim member states of OPEC sought to raise the price of oil through cooperation, but OPEC demonstrated during the Arab-Israeli War of 1973 that cooperation had political as well as economic potential. The cartel ordered an embargo on oil shipments to the United States, Israel's ally, and quadrupled the price of oil between 1973 and 1975. The huge increase in the cost of petroleum triggered a global economic downturn.

Trading Blocs

OPEC's policies therefore demonstrated that the alliance could exert control over the developed world and its financial system. The most famous and most strongly integrated regional bloc is the European Union, which is characterized by a common market and free trade. In March 1957 representatives of six nations—France, West Germany, Italy, the Netherlands, Belgium, and Luxembourg—took a significant step in this direction by establishing the European Economic Community (renamed the European Community in 1967). At the heart of this new community of nations lay the dismantling of tariffs and other barriers to free trade among member nations. Subsequent treaties creating political institutions such as the Council of Ministers and the European Parliament facilitated the long-range goal of European political integration. The development of a supranational organization dedicated to increasing European economic and political integration culminated in the Maestricht Treaty of 1993, which established the European Union. Fifteen European nations have submerged much of their national sovereignty in the European Union, and since 1999 eleven members have adopted a common currency. In the future, this tight economic integration is expected to lead to a European Political Union.

Cross-Cultural Exchanges and Global Communications

Like trade and business organizations, cultural practices have become increasingly globalized, thriving on a continuous flow of information, ideas, tastes, and values. At the turn of the twentieth century, local traditions—commonly derived from gender, social class, or religious affiliation—still determined the cultural identity of the vast majority of people. At the end of the twentieth century, thanks in part to advances in technology and communications, information and cultural practices were becoming truly global.

One of the hallmarks of this new global cultural integration is consumption. Although the desire to consume is hardly novel, one of the tendencies of the modern consumer culture is toward the homogenization of cultural products. Critics sometimes refer to the homogenizing aspect of global culture as the "Americanization" or "McDonaldization" of the world. Those terms suggest that the consumer culture that developed in the United States during the mid–twentieth century has been exported throughout the world, principally through advertising. Thus it is no accident that young people clad in blue jeans and T-shirts sing the same Usher or Eminem lyrics in San Francisco, Sarajevo, and Beijing. Still, nothing symbolizes the global marketing of U.S. mass culture more than the spread of its food and beverage products. While Pepsi and Coca-Cola fight battles over the few places on earth that their beverages have not yet dominated, fast-food restaurants such as Burger King, McDonalds, and Pizza Hut sell their standardized foods throughout the world. The closing of many bistros and cafés in France, for instance, is the result of more French people opting for fashionable fast food instead of taking the time for more traditional and lengthy lunches. So successful has the global spread of U.S. mass culture been that it seems to threaten local or indigenous cultures everywhere.

Consumption and Cultural Interaction

The export of U.S. products and services is not the sole determinant of global cultural practices, however. Indeed, the experiences in the Americas demonstrate that U.S. patterns of cultural consumption have not simply dominated the globe without competition or critical evaluation. One example in Latin America is Music Television (MTV) Latino, perceived by many critics as another case of foreign cultural intrusion, where Latin video deejays speak "Spanglish" or "Chequenos" ("check us out"), mixing Spanish and English. Yet, whereas Latin Americans once had called for protection against such alien influence, by the 1990s many had relaxed their guard. They see evidence of increased cultural sharing among Latin societies, noting that MTV and cable television have come to serve as a means of communication and unity by making the

A citizen of Kuwait lugs a television through streets filled with European and U.S. consumer products. From tennis shoes to automobiles to English-language signs, cultural interpenetration is occurring around the globe.

nations of Latin America more aware of one another. Although the sheer dominance and size of the U.S. entertainment-technology industry keeps cultural sharing lopsided, cultural dominance is also limited by those societies' ability to blend and absorb a variety of foreign and indigenous practices.

Global Problems in a Borderless World

One of the consequences of a globalized world is the rapid development of global problems, which in turn demand global solutions. One of the most important of those problems is the rapid growth of the human population and attendant questions about human poverty and the environmental capacity of the earth. Indeed, in the past three hundred years the world has experienced a fivefold population increase: from 500 million people in 1650 to 2.5 billion in 1950. After World War II the widespread and successful use of vaccines, antibiotics, and insecticides, along with improvements in water supplies and increased agricultural yields, caused a dramatic decline in worldwide death rates. By 1994 roughly 5.5 billion people shared the planet, and the population division of the United Nations has estimated that the earth's population will stabilize around 11.6 billion in 2200.

A large population changes the earth and its environment, raising an important question: How many people can the earth support? The exact carrying capacity of the planet is, of course, a matter of debate, but by many measures the earth seems to strain already to support the current population. Scientists and concerned citizens have become increasingly convinced that human society cannot infinitely expand beyond the physical limits of the earth and its resources.

The prodigious growth of the human population is also at the root of many environmental problems. As people are born, pollution levels increase, more habitats and animal and plant species disappear, and more natural resources are consumed. This process, in turn, contributes to the atmospheric pollution that causes global warming. Indeed, if global warming caused even a modest rise of one to three degrees Celsius in the temperature of the atmosphere, that could allow sea levels to rise to levels that would inundate low-lying islands and coastal areas on all continents.

Global poverty—caused by a combination of overpopulation and an unequal distribution of global wealth—is another serious problem of the contemporary world. Several hundred million people, especially in the developing areas of eastern Europe, Africa, Latin America, and Asia, struggle daily for sufficient food, clean water, adequate shelter, and other basic necessities. Poverty has correlated strongly with higher-than-average infant mortality rates and lower-than-average life expectancies.

It is no accident that many of the poorest areas in the world share a legacy of colonialism, defined by the appropriation of labor and natural resources. Indeed, pervasive poverty characterizes many former colonies and dependencies. All of these developing societies have tried to raise income levels and eliminate poverty through diversified economic development, but only a few, such as South Korea, Singapore, Malaysia, and Indonesia, have accomplished their aims. In the meantime, economic globalization has generated unprecedented wealth for developed nations, creating an even deeper divide between rich and poor countries.

The global economy—and the globalized world more generally—is still very much a work in progress, and it not clear what the long-term effects will be on the societies it touches. To its supporters, the global economy delivers markets that operate with maximum efficiency. Proponents of globalization also argue that the new economy is the only way to bring prosperity to the developing world. To its critics, the global economy is a force that rewards the few and impoverishes the many. Specifically, antiglobalization groups assert that globalization diminishes the sovereignty of local and national governments and transfers the power to shape economic and political destinies to transnational corporations and global institutions such as the IMF and the WTO. Detractors of globalization also claim that the hallmark of globalization—rapid economic development—is responsible for the destruction of the environment, the widening gap between rich and poor societies, and the worldwide homogenization of local, diverse, and indigenous cultures.

SUMMARY

In the years immediately before and after World War II, a few nations controlled the political and economic destiny of much of the world. The decades following 1945 witnessed the stunning reversal of that state of affairs, as European empires fell and dozens of newly independent nations emerged. Decolonization changed the world's political, economic, and social landscape in often radical ways, and the peoples of these newly free countries thereafter labored to reshape their own national identities and to build workable political and economic systems. The effervescence of liberty and independence at times gave way to a more sober reality in the days, years, and decades after liberation. Religious and ethnic conflict, political instability, economic dependency, and foreign interference dampened spirits and interfered with the ability of nations to achieve peace and stability. Yet the global balance of power had been irrevocably altered by this attainment of worldwide independence. The fall of those age-old empires, along with the disappearance of the superpowers' bipolar cold war world, reshaped the world's landscape once again and intensified the globalization of economies and cultures around the world. National boundaries became increasingly irrelevant and ushered in a world order based more than ever on connections and encounters. This new world order is replete with problems, and in contemporary times those problems are shared by all humanity.

CHRONOLOGY

1947	Partition of India
1947	Establishment of GATT
1948	Creation of Israel
1954	French defeat at Dienbienphu
1954–1962	Algerian war of liberation
1955	Bandung Conference
1957	Ghana gains independence
1958–1961	Great Leap Forward in China
1960	Creation of OPEC
1967	Birth of European Community
1973	Arab-Israeli War
1979	Revolution in Iran
1980–1988	Iran-Iraq war
1990–1991	Gulf War
1995	WTO supersedes GATT
2000	World population at 6 billion
2001	Terrorist attacks against the United States

FOR FURTHER READING

Franz Ansprenger. *The Dissolution of the Colonial Empires.* New York, 1989. A discerning and thorough treatment of the dismantling of European empires and colonies.

Mark Borthwick, ed. *Pacific Century: The Emergence of Modern Pacific Asia.* Boulder, 1992. An excellent source for an overview of southeast and east Asia.

Michael J. Cohen. *Palestine and the Great Powers 1945–48.* 2nd ed. Princeton, 1992. An evenhanded assessment of the role played by the great powers in the partition of Palestine and the creation of Israel.

Basil Davidson. *The Black Man's Burden: Africa and the Curse of the Nation State.* New York, 1992. A critical postindependence account that emphasizes the shortcomings of nationalism and the national state.

Thomas L. Friedman. *The Lexus and Olive Tree.* New York, 1999. A readable overview that does justice to the complexities of globalization.

Sunil Khilani. *The Idea of India.* New York, 1988. A lively and incisive analysis of the contracts between India and Pakistan.

Naomi Klein. *No Space, No Choice, No Jobs, No Logo: Taking Aim at the Brand Bullies.* New York, 2000. Part cultural analysis and part political manifesto, this work makes an angry case against multinational corporations.

J. R. McNeill. *Something New under the Sun: An Environmental History of the Twentieth-Century World.* New York, 2000. A brilliant but dark tale of the past century's interaction between humans and the environment.

Robert A. Mortimer. *The Third World Coalition in International Politics.* New York, 1980. Surveys the political evolution of the nonaligned world.

Jeffrey N. Wasserstrom and Elizabeth J. Perry, eds. *Popular Protest and Political Culture in Modern China.* 2nd ed. Boulder, 1994. A collection of essays in which scholars from various disciplines take a critical look at contemporary China.

Glossary and Pronunciation Guide

A	short *a* sound, as in *asp, fat, parrot*
AH	*a* sound, as in *car, father*
AHW	diphthong *au* in Romance languages, similar to vowel sound in *ouch*
AHY	diphthong *ai* in Romance languages, similar to vowel sound in *die*
AW	diphthong *a* sound, as in *awful, paw, law*
AY	long *a* sound, as in *ape, date, play*
EE	long *e* sound, as in *even, meet, money*
EH	short *e* sound, as in *ten, elf, berry, how, bow*
EHY	diphthong *ei* in Romance languages, similar to "ay" in *day*
EW	diphthong *iu* in Romance languages, similar (but shorter than) *you*
EYE	long *i* sound, as in *ice, high, bite*
IH	short *i* sound, as in *fit, his, mirror*
KH	hard *h* sound
OH	long *o* sound, as in *open, go, tone*
OHI	diphthong *oi* in Romance languages, similar to "oy" in *toy*
OO	long *o* sound, as in *ooze, tool, crew*
'R	tapped *r* like *dd* or *tt* in *latter* and *butter*
RR	trilled *r* (repeated taps)
UH	short *u* sound, as in *up, cut, color*
WA	diphthong *ua* in Romance languages, similar to the "wa" in *want* and *waffle*
WE	diphthong *ui* in Romance languages, similar to the word *we*
Y	like *ll* in *million* or *ny* in *canyon*
YA	diphthong *ia* in Romance languages, similar to "ya" in *yacht*
YE	diphthong *ie* in Romance languages, similar to "ye" in *yet*
YO	diphthong *io* in Romance languages, similar to "yo" in the suffix *yoke*

Note on emphasis: Syllables in capital letters receive the stress. If there is no syllable in capitals, then all syllables get equal stress.

Abbasid (ah-BAH-sihd) Cosmopolitan Arabic dynasty (750–1258) that replaced the Umayyads; founded by Abu al-Abbas and reaching its peak under Harun al-Rashid.

Abolitionism Antislavery movement.

Absolutism Political philosophy that stressed the divine right theory of kingship: the French king Louis XIV was the classic example.

Abu Bakr (ah-BOO BAHK-uhr) First caliph after the death of Muhammad.

Achaemenid empire (ah-KEE-muh-nid) First great Persian empire (558–330 B.C.E.), which began under Cyrus and reached its peak under Darius.

Aeschylus (ES-kuh-luhs) Greek tragedian, author of the *Oresteia.*

Age grades Bantu concept in which individuals of roughly the same age carried out communal tasks appropriate for that age.

Agricultural transition The gradual transition from a dependence on hunting and gathering for subsistence to a dependence on cultivation and animal husbandry. First evidence of transition is from around 12,000 B.C.E.

Ahimsa (uh-HIM-suh) Jain term for the principle of nonviolence to other living things or their souls.

Ahmosis (AH-moh-sis) Egyptian pharaoh (c. 1500 B.C.E.), founder of the New Kingdom.

Ahura Mazda (uh-HOORE-uh MAHZ-duh) Main god of Zoroastrianism who represented truth and goodness and was perceived to be in an eternal struggle with the malign spirit Angra Mainyu.

Al-Andalus (al-ahn-dah-LOOS) Islamic Spain.

Allah (AH-lah) God of the monotheistic religion of Islam.

Aliæi nui Hawaiian class of high chiefs.

Amon-Re (AH-mohn RRAY) Egyptian god, combination of the sun god Re and the air god Amon.

Ancestor worship Belief that dead ancestors can influence one's fortunes in this life. People who practice ancestor worship characteristically practice rituals and ceremonies to the memory or remains of their ancestors.

Ancien régime The political structure of prerevolutionary France, characterized by an absolute monarchy, a feudal aristocracy, and a vast class of powerless peasants.

Angkor (AHN-kohr) Southeast Asian Khmer kingdom (889–1432) that was centered around the temple cities of Angkor Thom and Angkor Wat.

Anti-Semitism Term coined in late nineteenth century that was associated with a prejudice against Jews and the political, social, and economic actions taken against them.

Antonianism African syncretic religion, founded by Doña Beatriz, that taught that Jesus Christ was a black African man and that heaven was for Africans.

Apartheid (ah-PAHR-teyed) South African system of "separateness" that was implemented in 1948 and that maintained the black majority in a position of political, social, and economic subordination.

Appeasement British and French policy in the 1930s that tried to maintain peace in Europe in the face of German aggression by making concessions.

Arianism Early Christian heresy that centered around teaching of Arius (250–336 C.E.) and contained the belief that Jesus was a mortal human being and not coeternal with God; Arianism was the focus of Council of Nicaea.

Artha Hindu concept for the pursuit of economic well-being and honest prosperity.

Arthashastra (UHRR-th-sha-strrah) Ancient Indian political treatise from the time of Chandragupta Maurya; its authorship was traditionally ascribed to Kautalya, and it stressed that war was inevitable.

Aryans (AYR-ee-uhns) Indo-European tribes who settled in India after 1500 B.C.E.; their union with indigenous Dravidians formed the basis of Hinduism.

Association of Southeast Asian Nations (ASEAN.) Regional alliance established in 1967 by Thailand, Malaysia, Singapore, Indonesia, and the Philippines; the alliance was designed to promote economic progress and political stability; it later became a free-trade zone.

Assyrians (uh-SEER-ee-uhns) Southwest Asian people who built an empire that reached its height during the eighth and seventh centuries B.C.E.; it was known for a powerful army and a well-structured state.

Astrolabe Navigational instrument for determining latitude.

Aten Monotheistic god of Egyptian pharaoh Akhenaten (r. 1353–1335 B.C.E.) and arguably the world's first example of monotheism.

Audiencias Spanish courts in Latin America.

Australopithecus (ah-strah-loh-PIHTH-uh-kuhs) "Southern ape," oldest known ancestor of humans; it lived from around four million down to around one million years ago, and it could walk on hind legs, freeing up hands for use of simple tools.

Austronesians People who, by as early as 2000 B.C.E., began to explore and settle islands of the Pacific Ocean basin.

Avesta Book that contains the holy writings of Zoroastrianism.

Aztec empire Central American empire constructed by the Mexica and expanded greatly during the fifteenth century during the reigns of Itzcoatl and Motecuzoma I.

Axum African kingdom centered in Ethiopia that became an early and lasting center of Coptic Christianity.

Balfour Declaration British declaration from 1917 that supported the creation of a Jewish homeland in Palestine.

Bantu (BAHN-too) African peoples who originally lived in the area of present-day Nigeria; around 2000 B.C.E. they began a centuries-long migration that took them to most of sub-Saharan Africa; the Bantu were very influential, especially linguistically.

Bedouins (BEHD-oh-ihnz) Nomadic Arabic tribespeople.

Benefice Grant from a lord to a vassal, usually consisting of land, which supported the vassal and signified the relationship between the two.

Berlin Conference Meeting organized by German chancellor Otto von Bismarck in 1884–1885 that provided the justification for European colonization of Africa.

Bhagavad Gita (BHUHG-vuhd GEE-tuh) "Song of the Lord," an Indian short poetic work drawn from the lengthy *Mahabharata* that was finished around 400 C.E. and that expressed basic Hindu concepts such as karma and dharma.

Bhakti (BHUK-tee) Indian movement that attempted to transcend the differences between Hinduism and Islam.

Black Hand Pre–World War I secret Serbian society; one of its members, Gavrilo Princip, assassinated Austrian archduke Francis Ferdinand and provided the spark for the outbreak of the Great War.

Blitzkrieg German style of rapid attack through the use of armor and air power that was used in Poland, Norway, Denmark, Belgium, the Netherlands, and France in 1939–1940.

Boddhisatvas (BOH-dih-SAT-vuhs) Buddhist concept regarding individuals who had reached enlightenment but who stayed in this world to help people.

Bolshevik (BOHL-shih-vehk) Russian communist party headed by Lenin.

Bourgeoisie Middle class in modern industrial society.

Boyars (BOY-ahrs) Russian nobles.

Brahmins (BRAH-minz) Hindu caste of priests.

Brezhnev Doctrine Policy developed by Leonid Brezhnev (1906–1982) that claimed for the Soviet Union the right to invade any socialist country faced with internal or external enemies; the doctrine was best expressed in Soviet invasion of Czechoslovakia.

Bubonic plague Epidemic that swept Eurasia, causing devastating population loss and economic disruption. It was known as the Black Death in Europe after around 1350 C.E.

Buddha (BOO-duh) The "enlightened one," the term applied to Siddhartha Gautama after his discoveries that would form the foundation of Buddhism.

Buddhism (BOO-diz'm) Religion, based on Four Noble Truths, associated with Siddhartha Gautama (563–483 B.C.E.), or the Buddha; its adherents desired to eliminate all distracting passion and reach nirvana.

Bunraku (boon-RAH-koo) Japanese puppet theater.

Bushido (BOH-shee-DOH) The "way of the warrior," the code of conduct of the Japanese samurai that was based on loyalty and honor.

Byzantine (BIHZ-uhn-teen) Long-lasting empire centered at Constantinople; it grew out of the end of the Roman empire and carried legacy of Roman greatness and was the only classical society to survive into the early modern age; it reached its early peak during the reign of Justinian (483–565).

Caesaropapism Concept relating to the mixing of political and religious authority, as with the Roman emperors, that was central to the church versus state controversy in medieval Europe.

Cahokia (kuh-HOH-kee-uh) Large structure in modern Illinois that was constructed by the mound-building peoples; it was the third largest structure in the Americas before the arrival of the Europeans.

Caliph (KAH-leef) "deputy," Islamic leader after the death of Muhammad.

Capetian (cah-PEE-shuhn) Early French dynasty that started with Hugh Capet.

Capitalism An economic system with origins in early modern Europe in which private parties make their goods and services available on a free market.

Capitulation Highly unfavorable trading agreements that the Ottoman Turks signed with the Europeans in the nineteenth century that symbolized the decline of the Ottomans.

Carolingians Germanic dynasty that was named after its most famous member, Charlemagne.

Carthage Northern African kingdom, main rival to early Roman expansion, that was defeated by Rome in the Punic Wars.

Caste A social class system with distinctions that are transferred through generations or through occupation. Restrictions are placed on marriage, occupation, handling of food, and other matters, according to caste. Caste usually refers to the social system of India.

Çatal Hüyük Important Neolithic settlement in Anatolia (7250–6150 B.C.E.).

Cathars Medieval heretics, also known as the Albigensians, who considered the material world evil; their followers renounced wealth and marriage and promoted an ascetic existence.

Catholic Reformation Sixteenth-century Catholic attempt to cure internal ills and confront Protestantism; it was inspired by the reforms of the Council of Trent and the actions of the Jesuits.

Caudillos (kahw-DEE-yohs) Latin American term for nineteenth-century local military leaders.

Central Powers World War I term for the alliance of Germany, Austria-Hungary, and the Ottoman empire.

Chaghatai One of Chinggis Khan's sons, whose descendants ruled central Asia through the Chaghatai khanate.

Chan Buddhism (CHAHN BOO-diz'm) Most popular branch of Buddhism in China, with an emphasis on intuition and sudden flashes of insight instead of textual study.

Chan Chan (chahn chahn) Capital of the pre-Incan, South American Chimu society that supported a large population of fifty thousand.

Chavín cult Mysterious but very popular South American religion (1000–300 B.C.E.).

Chimu Pre-Incan South American society that fell to Incas in the fifteenth century.

Chinampas Style of agriculture used by Mexica (Aztecs) in which fertile muck from lake bottoms was dredged and built up into small plots.

Chivalry European medieval concept, a code of conduct for the knights based on loyalty and honor.

Chola Southern Indian Hindu kingdom (850–1267), a tightly centralized state that dominated sea trade.

Christianity Religious doctrine that emerged in southeast Asia in the first century C.E. and then spread through Europe, north Africa, parts of Asia, and eventually to the Americas. Central to the religion is the belief that Jesus was the son of God and sacrificed himself on behalf of humankind.

Chucuito (choo-CWE-toh) Pre-Incan South American society that rose in the twelfth century and fell to the Incas in the fifteenth century.

City-state Urban areas that controlled surrounding agricultural regions and that were often loosely connected in a broader political structure with other city-states.

Cohong Specially licensed Chinese firms that were under strict government regulation.

Collectivization Process beginning in the late 1920s by which Stalin forced the Russian peasants off their own land and onto huge collective farms run by the state; millions died in the process.

Columbian Exchange The trans-Atlantic exchange of plants, animals, and diseases that followed European contact with the Americas at the end of the fifteenth century.

COMECON The Council for Mutual Economic Assistance, which offered increased trade within the Soviet Union and eastern Europe; it was the Soviet alternative to the United States's Marshall Plan.

Communalism A term, usually associated with India, that placed an emphasis on religious rather than national identity.

Communism Philosophy and movement that began in middle of the nineteenth century with the work of Karl Marx; it has the same general goals as socialism, but it includes the belief that violent revolution is necessary to destroy the bourgeois world and institute a new world run by and for the proletariat.

Confucianism (kuhn-FEW-shuhn-iz'm) Philosophy, based on the teachings of the Chinese philosopher Kong Fuzi (551–479 B.C.E.), or Confucius, that emphasizes order, the role of the gentleman, obligation to society, and reciprocity.

Congress of Vienna Gathering of European diplomats in Vienna, Austria, from October 1814 to June 1815. The representatives of the "great powers" that defeated Napoleon—Britain, Austria, Prussia, and Russia— dominated the proceedings, which aimed to restore the prerevolutionary political and social order.

Conquistadores (kohn-kees-tah-DOH-rays) Spanish adventurers like Cortes and Pizarro who conquered Central and South America in the sixteenth century.

Conservatism A political philosophy that emphasizes gradual change, continuity of traditions and established authority. Although the word has taken on many shades of meaning, nineteenth-century conservatives generally opposed democracy and supported traditional institutions such as church, monarchy, and nobility.

Constitutionalism Movement in England in the seventeenth century that placed power in Parliament's hands as part of a constitutional monarchy and that increasingly limited the power of the monarch; the movement was highlighted by the English Civil War and the Glorious Revolution.

Containment Concept associated with the United States and specifically with the Truman Doctrine during the cold war that revolved around the notion that the United States would contain the spread of communism.

Corporation A concept that reached mature form in 1860s in England and France; it entailed private business owned by thousands of individual and institutional investors who financed the business through the purchase of stocks.

Corpus iuris civilis (KOR-poos EW-rees sih-BEE-lees) *Body of the Civil Law,* the Byzantine emperor Justinian's attempt to codify all Roman law.

Cossacks (KAW-sacks) Russian "free men" recruited by Ivan III to settle conquered land in return for their freedom; the strategy eventually played a key role in Russian expansion eastward.

Criollos (KRYO-yohs) Creoles, people born in the Americas of Spanish or Portuguese ancestry.

Cro-Magnon (CROH MAHG-nohn) *Homo sapiens sapiens,* who appeared forty thousand years ago during the Paleolithic age and were the first human beings of the modern type.

Cross staff Device that sailors used to determine latitude by measuring the angle of the sun or pole star above the horizon.

Cuneiform Written language of the Sumerians, probably the first written script in the world.

Daimyo (DEYEM-yoh) Powerful territorial lords in early modern Japan.

Dao Key element in Chinese philosophy that means the "way of nature" or the "way of the cosmos."

Daodejing (DOW-DAY-JIHNG) Book that is the fundamental work of Daoism.

Daoism (DOW-i'zm) Chinese philosophy with origins in the Zhou dynasty; it is associated with legendary philosopher Laozi, and it called for a policy of inaction.

Dar al-Islam The "house of Islam," a term for the Islamic world.

Declaration of Independence Drafted by Thomas Jefferson in 1776; the document expressed the ideas of John Locke and the Enlightenment, represented the idealism of the American rebels, and influenced other revolutions.

Declaration of the Rights of Man and Citizen Document from the French Revolution (1789) that was influenced by the American Declaration of Independence and in turn influenced other revolutionary movements.

Decolonization Process by which former colonies achieved their independence, as with the newly emerging African nations in the 1950s and 1960s.

Deism (DEE-iz'm) An Enlightenment view that accepted the existence of a god but denied the supernatural aspects of Christianity; in deism, the universe was an orderly realm maintained by rational and natural laws.

Demographic transition Adjustments in the rate of births and deaths that usually accompany industrialization. The demographic transition is often triggered by improvements in health and nutrition, which result in lower death rates. Birthrates remain high initially, but after a period of rapid population growth, birthrates fall in response to the lower death rates. Eventually, in highly industrialized societies, birthrates and death rates stabilize at low levels.

Descamisados "Shirtless ones," Argentine poor who supported Juan and Eva Perón.

Détente A reduction in cold war tension between the United States and the Soviet Union from 1969 to 1973.

Devshirme Ottoman requirement that the Christians in the Balkans provide young boys to be slaves of the sultan.

Dharma (DHUHR-muh) Hindu concept of obedience to religious and moral laws and order.

Dhimmi (DIHM-mee) Islamic concept of a protected people that was symbolic of Islamic toleration during the Mughal and Ottoman empires.

Dhow Indian, Persian, and Arab ships, one hundred to four hundred tons, that sailed and traded throughout the Indian Ocean basin.

Diaspora People who have settled far from their original homeland but who still share some measure of ethnic identity.

Dionysus Greek god of wine, also known as Bacchus; Greek plays were performed in his honor.

Dravidians Peoples who produced the brilliant Harappan society in India, 3000–1500 B.C.E.

Dreadnoughts A class of British battleships whose heavy armaments made all other battleships obsolete overnight.

Duma Russian parliament, established after the Revolution of 1905.

Dutch learning European knowledge that reached Tokugawa Japan.

East India Company British joint-stock company that grew to be a state within a state in India; it possessed its own armed forces.

Eastern Orthodox Christianity An eastern branch of Christianity that evolved after the division of the Roman Empire and the subsequent development of the Byzantine Empire in the east and the medieval European society in the west. The Eastern Orthodox Church acknowledged what became known as the Byzantine rite and recognized the primacy of the patriarch of Constantinople.

Eight-legged essay Eight-part essays that an aspiring Chinese civil servant had to compose, mainly based on a knowledge of Confucius and the Zhou classics.

Encomienda (ehn-koh-MYEN-dah) System that gave the Spanish settlers (*encomenderos*) the right to compel the indigenous peoples of the Americas to work in the mines or fields.

Engenho (ehn-GEN-yo) Brazilian sugar mill; the term also came to symbolize the entire complex world relating to the production of sugar.

Enlightenment Eighteenth-century philosophical movement that began in France; its emphasis was on the preeminence of reason rather than faith or tradition; it spread concepts from the Scientific Revolution.

Epicureans (ehp-ih-KYOOR-eeuhns) Hellenistic philosophers who taught that pleasure—as in quiet satisfaction—was the greatest good.

Equal-field system Chinese system during the Han dynasty in which the goal was to ensure an equitable distribution of land.

Essenes Jewish sect that looked for the arrival of a savior; they were similar in some of their core beliefs to the early Christians.

Etruscans (ih-TRUHS-kuhns) Northern Italian society that initially dominated the Romans; the Etruscans helped convey Greek concepts to the expanding Romans.

Eunuchs (YOO-nihks) Castrated males, originally in charge of the harem, who grew to play major roles in government; eunuchs were common in China and other societies.

European Community (EC) Organization of European states established in 1957; it was originally called the European Economic Community and was renamed the EC in 1967; it promoted economic growth and integration as the basis for a politically united Europe.

European Union Established by the Maastricht Treaty in 1993, a supranational organization for even greater European economic and political integration.

Fascism Political ideology and mass movement that was prominent in many parts of Europe between 1919 and 1945; it sought to regenerate the social, political, and cultural life of societies, especially in contrast to liberal democracy and socialism; fascism began with Mussolini in Italy, and it reached its peak with Hitler in Germany.

Fief (FEEF) A grant of land from a lord to a vassal.

Five Pillars The foundation of Islam; (1) profession of faith, (2) prayer, (3) fasting during Ramadan, (4) alms, and (5) pilgrimage, or hajj.

Five-year plans First implemented by Stalin in the Soviet Union in 1928; five-year plans were a staple of communist regimes in which every aspect of production was determined in advance for a five-year period; five-year plans were opposite of the free market concept.

Four Noble Truths The foundation of Buddhist thought: (1) life is pain, (2) pain is caused by desire, (3) elimination of desire will bring an end to pain, (4) living a life based on the Noble Eightfold Path will eliminate desire.

Free trade Economic doctrine, first argued by Adam Smith in the late eighteenth century, of unrestricted trade between nations without protective tariffs or duties. Smith and his followers argue that, through free trade and competition, the forces of supply and demand will ensure that the best product is available at the best price. Free trade has gained wide acceptance since World War II.

Front de Libération Nationale (FLN) The Algerian organization that fought a bloody guerilla war for freedom against France.

Fulani (foo-LAH-nee) Sub-Saharan African people who, beginning in the seventeenth century, began a series of wars designed to impose their own strict interpretation of Islam.

Gathas (GATH-uhs) Zoroastrian works believed to be compositions by Zarathustra.

Gauchos (GAHW-chohs) Argentine cowboys, highly romantic figures.

General Agreement on Tariffs and Trade (GATT) Free trade agreement first signed in 1947; by 1994 it had grown to 123 members and formed the World Trade Organization (WTO).

Ghana (GAH-nuh) Kingdom in west Africa during the fifth through the thirteenth centuries whose rulers eventually converted to Islam; its power and wealth was based on dominating trans-Saharan trade.

Ghaznavids Turkish tribe under Mahmud of Ghazni who moved into northern India in the eleventh century and began a period of greater Islamic influence in India.

Ghazi (GAH-zee) Islamic religious warrior.

Gilgamesh Legendary king of the Mesopotamian city-state of Uruk (ca. 3000 B.C.E.), subject of the *Epic of Gilgamesh,* world's oldest complete epic literary masterpiece.

Glasnost (GLAHS-nohst) Russian term meaning "openness" introduced by Mikhail Gorbachev in 1985 to describe the process of opening Soviet society to dissidents and public criticism.

Globalization The breaking down of traditional boundaries in the face of increasingly global financial and cultural trends.

Global warming The emission of greenhouse gases, which prevents solar heat from escaping the earth's atmosphere and leads to the gradual heating of the earth's environment.

Golden Horde Mongol tribe that controlled Russia from the thirteenth to the fifteenth centuries.

Greater East Asia Co-Prosperity Sphere Japanese plan for consolidating Asia under their control during World War II.

Great Game Nineteenth-century competition between Great Britain and Russia for the control of central Asia.

Great Zimbabwe Large sub-Saharan African kingdom in the fifteenth century.

Greenpeace An environmental organization founded in 1970 and dedicated to the preservation of earth's natural resources.

Guild Organizations whose membership is based on occupation. They often regulate the production and sale of goods and serve as mutual aid societies for their members. They were particularly powerful in medieval European cities.

Guomindang (GWOH-mihn-dahng) Chinese nationalist party founded by Sun Yat-sen (1866–1925) and later led by Jiang Jieshi; it has been centered in Taiwan since the end of the Chinese civil war.

Gupta (GOOP-tah) Indian dynasty (320–550 C.E.) that briefly reunited India after the collapse of the earlier Mauryan dynasty.

Hacienda (ah-SYEN-dah) Large Latin American estates.

Hagia Sophia (HAH-yah soh-FEE-uh) Greek orthodox temple constructed by the Byzantine emperor Justinian and later converted into a mosque.

Hajj (HAHJ) Pilgrimage to Mecca.

Hammurabi's Code (hahm-uh-RAH-beez cohd) Sophisticated law code associated with the Babylonian king Hammurabi (r. 1792–1750 B.C.E.).

Harappan (huh-RUHP-puhn) Early brilliant Indian society centered around Harappa and Mohenjo-Daro.

Harijans "Children of God," Gandhi's term for the Untouchables.

Hebrews Semitic-speaking nomadic tribe influential for monotheistic belief in Yahweh.

Heian (HAY-ahn) Japanese period (794–1185), a brilliant cultural era notable for the world's first novel, Murasaki Shikibu's *The Tale of Genji.*

Hellenic Era First phase in Greek history (ca. 2000–328 B.C.E.), which was highlighted by the Golden Age of Athens in the fifth century B.C.E.

Hellenistic Era Second phase in Greek history (328–146 B.C.E.), from the conquest of Greece by Philip of Macedon until Greece's fall to the Romans; this era was a more cosmopolitan age facilitated by the conquests of Alexander the Great.

Hieroglyphics (heye-ruh-GLIPH-iks) Ancient Egyptian written language.

Hijra Muhammad's migration from Mecca to Medina in 622, which is the beginning point of the Islamic calendar and is considered to mark the beginning of the Islamic faith.

Hinayana (HEE-nah-yah-nuh) Branch of Buddhism known as the "lesser vehicle," also known as Theravada Buddhism; its beliefs include a strict, individual path to enlightenment, and it is popular in south and southeast Asia.

Hinduism Main religion of India, a combination of Dravidian and Aryan concepts; Hinduism's goal is to reach spiritual purity and union with the great world spirit; its important concepts include dharma, karma, and samsara.

Holocaust German attempt in World War II to exterminate the Jews of Europe.

Holy Roman Empire A confederation of states mostly in central and western Europe. It began in 962 C.E. with the crowning of Otto I by the pope.

Humanism Cultural movement during the Renaissance that drew inspiration from the humanities, that is, literature, history, philosophy, and the arts. In contrast to medieval theologians, humanists argued that one could live a moral life and still be actively engaged in the affairs of the world.

Home front Term made popular in World War I and World War II for the civilian "front" that was symbolic of the greater demands of total war.

Hominid (HAW—mih-nihds) A creature belonging to the family Hominidae, which includes human and humanlike species.

Homo erectus (HOH-moh ee-REHK-tuhs) "Upright-walking human," which existed from 1.5 million to two hundred thousand years ago; *Homo erectus* used cleavers and hand axes and learned how to control fire.

Homo sapiens (HOH-moh SAY-pyans) "Consciously thinking human," which first appeared around two hundred fifty thousand years ago and used sophisticated tools.

Homo sapiens sapiens (HOH-moh SAY-pyans SAY-pyans) First human being of the modern type, which appeared roughly one hundred thousand years ago; Cro-Magnon falls into this category.

Huitzilopochtli (we-tsee-loh-POCK-tlee) Sun god and patron deity of the Aztecs.

Hundred Days of Reform Chinese reforms of 1898 led by Kang Youwei and Liang Qichao in their desire to turn China into a modern industrial power.

Hunting/gathering culture Any culture whose primary means of subsistence is through hunting and gathering from the environment. Humans survived this way for millions of years before the agricultural transition, and some hunting/gathering cultures persisted into the twenty-first century C.E.

Hyksos (HICK-sohs) Invaders who seized the Nile delta and helped bring an end to the Egyptian Middle Kingdom.

Iconoclasts (eye-KAHN-oh-klasts) Supporters of the movement, begun by the Byzantine Emperor Leo III (r. 717–741), to destroy religious icons because their veneration was considered sinful.

Ilkhanate (EEL-kahn-ate) Mongol state that ruled Persia after abolition of the Abbasid empire in the thirteenth century.

Imperialism Term associated with the expansion of European powers and their conquest and colonization of African and Asian societies, mainly from the sixteenth through the nineteenth centuries.

Inca empire Powerful South American empire that would reach its peak in the fifteenth century during the reigns of Pachacuti Inca and Topa Inca.

Indentured labor Labor source in the Americas; wealthy planters would pay the European poor to sell a portion of their working lives, usually seven years, in exchange for passage.

Indo-Europeans Series of tribes from southern Russia who, over a period of millennia, embarked on a series of migrations from India through western Europe; their greatest legacy was the broad distribution of Indo-European languages throughout Eurasia.

Indra Early Indian god associated with the Aryans; Indra was the king of the gods and was associated with warfare and thunderbolts.

Intelligentsia Refers to an educated and literate class in Russia that often advocated social and political reform. In the late nineteenth century the Russian intelligentsia became frustrated when reform efforts failed, and many turned to anarchism and violence. Some members of the intelligentsia supported the Bolshevik rise to power in the revolution of 1917.

Investiture (ihn-VEHST-tih-tyoor) The granting of church offices by a lay leader; one aspect of the medieval European church versus state controversy.

Iroquois (EER-uh-kwah) Eastern American Indian confederation made up of the Mohawk, Oneida, Onondaga, Cayuga, and Seneca tribes.

Islam Monotheistic religion of the prophet Muhammad (570–632); influenced by Judaism and Christianity, Muhammad was considered the final prophet because the earlier religions had not seen the entire picture; the Quran is the holy book of Islam.

Jainism (JEYEN-iz'm) Indian religion associated with the teacher Vardhamana Mahavira (ca. 540–468 B.C.E.) in which

every physical object possessed a soul; Jains believe in complete nonviolence to all living beings.

Jati Indian word for a Hindu subcaste.

Jihad Arabic word meaning "struggle." In Islam this word is understood to be one's duty to struggle on behalf of the faith. Although this struggle might be a personal and spiritual effort, it has frequently been a call for holy war against perceived enemies. In recent years, radical Islamists such as al-Qaeda have called for a *jihad* against the United States and other "nonbelievers."

Jizya (JIHZ-yuh) Tax in Islamic empires that was imposed on non-Muslims.

Joint-stock companies Early forerunner of the modern corporation; individuals who invested in a trading or exploring venture could make huge profits while limiting their risk.

Judaism The monotheistic religion of the Jewish people that traces its origins to Abraham (ca. 2000 B.C.E.). It emerged in the Middle East, and constitute a majority, believers were widespread in Europe, north Africa, and southeast Asia.

Ka'ba (KAH-bah) Main shrine in Mecca, goal of Muslims embarking on the hajj.

Kabuki (kah-BOO-kee) Japanese theater in which actors were free to improvise and embellish the words.

Kama Hindu concept of the enjoyment of physical and sexual pleasure.

Kamikaze (KAH-mih-kah-zee) A Japanese term meaning "divine wind" that is related to the storms that destroyed Mongol invasion fleets; the term is symbolic of Japanese isolation and was later taken by suicide pilots in World War II.

Kanun (KUH-noon) Laws issued by the Ottoman Süleyman the Magnificent, also known as Süleyman Kanuni, "the Lawgiver."

Kapu Hawaiian concept of something being taboo.

Karma (KAHR-mah) Hindu concept that the sum of good and bad in a person's life will determine his or her status in the next life.

Khoikhoi Sub-Saharan African society referred to pejoratively as the Hottentots by Europeans.

Kin-based society A society that governs itself primarily through family and clan relationships; many existed in sub-Saharan Africa throughout history.

Kongo Central African state that began trading with the Portuguese around 1500; although their kings, such as King Affonso I (r. 1506–1543), converted to

Christianity, they nevertheless suffered from the slave trade.

Koumbi-Saleh Important trading city along the trans-Saharan trade route from the eleventh to the thirteenth centuries.

Kshatriayas (SHUHT-ree-uhs) Hindu caste of warriors and aristocrats.

Kulaks Land-owning Russian peasants who benefited under Lenin's New Economic Policy and suffered under Stalin's forced collectivization.

Kush Nubian African kingdom that conquered and controlled Egypt from 750 to 664 B.C.E.

Lamaist Buddhism (LAH-muh-ihst BOO-diz'm) Branch of Buddhism that was similar to shamanism in its acceptance of magic and supernatural powers.

La Reforma Political reform movement of Mexican president Benito Juárez (1806–1872) that called for limiting the power of the military and the Catholic church in Mexican society.

Latifundia (lah-tee-FOON-dya) Huge state-run and slave-worked farms in ancient Rome.

League of Nations Forerunner of the United Nations, the dream of American president Woodrow Wilson, although its potential was severely limited by the refusal of the United States to join.

Lebensraum (LAY-behnz-rahwm) German term meaning "living space"; the term is associated with Hitler and his goal of carving out territory in the east for an expanding Germany.

Legalism Chinese philosophy from the Zhou dynasty that called for harsh suppression of the common people.

Levée en Masse (leh-VAY ahn MAS) A term signifying universal conscription during the radical phase of the French revolution.

Lex talionis (lehks tah-LYO-nihs) "Law of retaliation," laws in which offenders suffered punishments similar to their crimes; the most famous example is Hammurabi's Laws.

Li (LEE) Confucian concept, a sense of propriety.

Liberalism A political philosophy inspired by John Locke and the ideals of the Enlightenment that advocated individual liberty, constitutional government, and free trade. Nineteenth-century liberals favored representative government but not necessarily democracy.

Liberation theology The beliefs of Christian thinkers and social activists who emphasize Jesus' role in helping those who were oppressed, a view that gained wide support in Latin America in the late twentieth century. Liberation theologians question the historic role of the church in supporting traditional regimes.

Linear A Minoan written script.

Linear B Early Mycenaean written script, adapted from the Minoan Linear A.

Luddites Early-nineteenth-century artisans who were opposed to new machinery and industrialization.

Machismo (mah-CHEEZ-moh) Latin American social ethic that honored male strength, courage, aggressiveness, assertiveness, and cunning.

Madrasas (MAH-drahs-ahs) Islamic institutions of higher education that originated in the tenth century.

Magyars (MAH-jahrs) Hungarian invaders who raided towns in Germany, Italy, and France in the ninth and tenth centuries.

Mahabharata (mah-hah-BAH-rah-tah) Massive ancient Indian epic that was developed orally for centuries; it tells of an epic civil war between two family branches.

Mahayana (mah-huh-YAH-nah) The "greater vehicle," a more metaphysical and more popular northern branch of Buddhism.

Majapahit Southeast Asian kingdom (1293–1520) centered on the island of Java.

Mali (MAH-lee) West African kingdom founded in the thirteenth century by Sundiata; it reached its peak during the reign of Mansa Musa.

Manchus Manchurians who conquered China, putting an end to the Ming dynasty and founding the Qing dynasty (1644–1911).

Mandate of Heaven Chinese belief that the emperors ruled through the mandate, or approval, of heaven contingent on their ability to look after the welfare of the population.

Mandate system System that developed in the wake of World War I when the former colonies ended up mandates under European control, a thinly veiled attempt at continuing imperialism.

Manichaeism (man-ih-KEE-iz'm) Religion founded by the prophet Mani in the third century C.E., a syncretic version of Zoroastrian, Christian, and Buddhist elements.

Manifest destiny The idea, popular in the United States in the mid-nineteenth century, that the North American continent was intended by God to be settled by white Americans. This notion helped justify the Mexican war of 1846–1848 and the Indian wars of the 1870s and 1880s.

Manor Large estates of the nobles during the European middle ages, home for the majority of the peasants.

Maori (MAY-oh-ree) Indigenous peoples of New Zealand.

Marathon Battlefield scene of the Athenian victory over the Persians in 490 B.C.E.

Marae Polynesian temple structure.

Maroons Runaway African slaves.

Marshall Plan U.S. plan, officially called the European Recovery Program, that offered financial and other economic aid to all European states that had suffered from World War II, including Soviet bloc states.

Mauryan empire Indian dynasty (321–185 B.C.E.) founded by Chandragupta Maurya and reaching its peak under Ashoka.

Maya (MAH-uh) Brilliant Central American society (300–1100) known for math, astronomy, and a sophisticated written language.

May Fourth Movement Chinese movement that began 4 May 1919 with a desire to eliminate imperialist influences and promote national unity.

Medes (meeds) Indo-European branch that settled in northern Persia and eventually fell to another branch, the Persians, in the sixth century.

Meiji Restoration (MAY-jee) Restoration of imperial rule under Emperor Meiji in 1868 by a coalition led by Fukuzawa Yukichi and Ito Hirobumi; the restoration enacted western reforms to strengthen Japan.

Melaka (may-LAHK-ah) Southeast Asian kingdom that was predominantly Islamic.

Mesopotamia Term meaning "between the rivers," in this case the Tigris and Euphrates; Sumer and Akkad are two of the earliest societies.

Mestizo (mehs-TEE-soh) Latin American term for children of Spanish and native parentage.

Metallurgy The process of extracting metal from ores, or purifying metals, and of creating objects from metals.

Métis (may-TEE) Canadian term for individuals of mixed European and indigenous ancestry.

Millet An autonomous, self-governing community in the Ottoman empire.

Ming Chinese dynasty (1368–1644) founded by Hongwu and known for its cultural brilliance.

Minoan (mih-NOH-uhn) Society located on the island of Crete (ca. 2000–1100 B.C.E.) that influenced the early Mycenaeans.

Missi dominici (MEE-see doh-mee-NEE-chee) "Envoys of the lord ruler," the noble and church emissaries sent out by Charlemagne.

Mithraism (MIHTH-rah-iz'm) Mystery religion based on worship of the sun god Mithras; it became popular among the Romans because of its promise of salvation.

Mochica (moh-CHEE-kah) Pre-Incan South American society (300–700) known for their brilliant ceramics.

Moksha Hindu concept of the salvation of the soul.

Monotheism (mah-noh-THEE-iz'm) Belief in only one god, a rare concept in the ancient world.

Monroe Doctrine American doctrine issued in 1823 during the presidency of James Monroe that warned Europeans to keep their hands off Latin America and that expressed growing American strength and also growing American imperialistic views regarding Latin America.

Mughals (MOO-guhls) Islamic dynasty that ruled India from the sixteenth through the eighteenth centuries; the construction of the Taj Mahal is representative of their splendor; with the exception of the enlightened reign of Akbar, the increasing conflict between Hindus and Muslims was another of their legacies.

Muhammad (muh-HAHM-mahd) Prophet of Islam (570–632).

Muslim A follower of Islam.

Mycenaean (meye-suh-NEE-uhn) Early Greek society on the Peloponese (1600–1100 B.C.E.) that was influenced by the Minoans; the Mycenaeans' conflict with Troy is immortalized in Homer's *Odyssey*.

Nara era Japanese period (710–794), centered around city of Nara, that was the highest point of Chinese influence.

National Policy Nineteenth-century Canadian policy designed to attract migrants, protect industries through tariffs, and build national transportation systems.

NATO The North Atlantic Treaty Organization, which was established by the United States in 1949 as a regional military alliance against Soviet expansionism.

Ndongo (n'DAWN-goh) Angolan kingdom that reached its peak during the reign of Queen Nzinga (r. 1623–1663).

Neandertal (nee-ANN-duhr-tawl) Early humans (100,000 to 35,000 years ago) who were prevalent during the Paleolithic period.

Negritude (NEH-grih-tood) "Blackness," a term coined by early African nationalists as a means of celebrating the heritage of black peoples around the world.

Neo-Confucianism (nee-oh-kuhn-FYEW-shuhn-iz'm) Philosophy that attempted to merge certain basic elements of Confucian and Buddhist thought; most important of the early Neo-Confucianists was the Chinese thinker Zhu Xi (1130–1200).

Neolithic New Stone Age (10,000–4000 B.C.E.), which was marked by the discovery and mastery of agriculture.

Nestorian (neh-STOHR-eeuhn) Early branch of Christianity, named after the fifth-century Greek theologian Nestorius, that emphasized the human nature of Jesus Christ.

New Economic Policy (NEP) Plan implemented by Lenin that called for minor free market reforms.

Nirvana (nihr-VAH-nuh) Buddhist concept of a state of spiritual perfection and enlightenment in which distracting passions are eliminated.

Noble Eightfold Path Final truth of the Buddhist Four Noble Truths that called for leading a life of balance and constant contemplation.

North American Free Trade Agreement (NAFTA) Regional alliance established in 1993 between the United States, Canada, and Mexico; it formed world's second largest free-trade zone.

Nubia (NOO-bee-uh) Area south of Egypt; the kingdom of Kush in Nubia invaded and dominated Egypt from 750 to 664 B.C.E.

Oceania Term referring to the Pacific Ocean basin and its lands.

Olmecs Early Central American society (1200–100 B.C.E.) that centered around sites at San Lorenzo, La Venta, and Tres Zapotes and that influenced later Maya.

Oprichnina (oh-PREEK-nee-nah) A Russian term meaning the "land apart," Muscovite territory that the Russian Tsar Ivan IV (r. 1533–1584) demanded to control; the tsar created a new class of nobles called the *oprichniki* for this territory.

Oracle bones Chinese Shang dynasty (1766–1122 B.C.E.) means of foretelling the future.

Organization of African Unity (OAU) An organization started in 1963 by thirty-two newly independent African states and designed to prevent conflict that would lead to intervention by former colonial powers.

Organization of Petroleum Exporting Countries (OPEC) An organization begun in 1960 by oil-producing states originally for purely economic reasons but that later had more political influence.

Osiris Ancient Egyptian god that represented the forces of nature.

Ottoman empire Powerful Turkish empire that lasted from the conquest of Constantinople (Istanbul) in 1453 until 1918 and reached its peak during the reign of Süleyman the Magnificent (r. 1520–1566).

Paleolithic Old Stone Age, a long period of human development before the development of agriculture.

Palestinian Liberation Organization (PLO) Organization created in 1964 under the leadership of Yasser Arafat to champion Palestinian rights.

Paris Peace Accords Agreement reached in 1973 that marked the end of the United States's role in the Vietnam War.

Parsis (pahr-SEES) Indian Zoroastrians.

Parthians Persian dynasty (247 B.C.E.–224 C.E.) that reached its peak under Mithradates I.

Pater familias (PAH-tehrr fah-MEE-lyas) Roman term for the "father of the family," a theoretical implication that gave the male head of the family almost unlimited authority.

Patriarch (PAY-tree-ahrk) Leader of the Greek Orthodox church, which in 1054 officially split with the Pope and the Roman Catholic church.

Patriarchy A system of social organization in which males dominate the family and in which the public institutions and descent and succession are traced through the male line.

Patricians Roman aristocrats and wealthy classes.

Pax Americana "American Peace," a term that compares American domination in the years after World War II with the power of Rome at its peak.

Pax Romana (Pahks roh-MAH-nah) "Roman Peace," a term that relates to the period of political stability, cultural

brilliance, and economic prosperity beginning with unification under Augustus and lasting through the first two centuries C.E.

Peninsulares (peh-neen-soo-LAH-rehs) Latin American officials from Spain or Portugal.

Perestroika (PAYR-eh-stroy-kuh) "Restructuring," a Russian term associated with Gorbachev's effort to reorganize the Soviet state.

Pharaohs (FARE-ohs) Egyptian kings considered to be gods on earth.

Plebeians (plih-BEE-uhns) Roman common people.

Polis (POH-lihs) Greek term for the city-state.

Popol Vuh (poh-pohl VOO) Mayan creation epic.

Prehistory The period before the invention of writing.

Proletariat Urban working class in a modern industrial society.

Protestant Reformation Sixteenth-century European movement during which Luther, Calvin, Zwingli, and others broke away from the Catholic church.

Putting-out system Method of getting around guild control by delivering unfinished materials to rural households for completion.

Ptolemaic (tawl-oh-MAY-ihk) Term used to signify both the Egyptian kingdom founded by Alexander the Great's general Ptolemy and the thought of the philosopher Ptolemy of Alexandria (second century C.E.), who used mathematical formulas in an attempt to prove Aristotle's geocentric theory of the universe.

Qadis Islamic judges.

Qanat (kah-NAHT) Persian underground canal.

Qi (chee) Chinese concept of the basic material that makes up the body and the universe.

Qin (chihn) Chinese dynasty (221–207 B.C.E.) that was founded by Qin Shihuangdi and was marked by the first unification of China and the early construction of defensive walls.

Qing (chihng) Chinese dynasty (1644–1911) that reached its peak during the reigns of Kangxi and Qianlong.

Qizilbash (gih-ZIHL-bahsh) Term meaning "red heads," Turkish tribes that were important allies of Shah Ismail in the formation of the Safavid empire.

Quetzalcoatl (keh-tzahl-koh-AHT'l) Aztec god, the "feathered serpent," who was borrowed originally from the Toltecs; Quetzalcoatl was believed to have been defeated by another god and exiled, and he promised to return.

Quinto (KEEN-toh) The one-fifth of Mexican and Peruvian silver production that was reserved for the Spanish monarchy.

Quipu (KEE-poo) Incan mnemonic aid comprised of different colored strings and knots that served to record events in the absence of a written text.

Quran (koorr-AHN) Islamic holy book that is believed to contain the divine revelations of Allah as presented to Muhammad.

Ramayana (rah-MAHY-yuh-nah) Ancient Indian masterpiece about the hero Rama that symbolized the victory of *dharma* (order) over *adharma* (chaos).

Rape of Nanjing Japanese conquest and destruction of the Chinese city of Nanjing in the 1930s.

Realpolitik (ray-AHL-poh-lih-teek) The Prussian Otto von Bismarck's "politics of reality," the belief that only the willingness to use force would actually bring about change.

Reconquista (ray-kohn-KEES-tah) Crusade, ending in 1492, to drive the Islamic forces out of Spain.

Reconstruction System implemented in the American South (1867–1877) that was designed to bring the Confederate states back into the union and also extend civil rights to freed slaves.

Renaissance The cultural flowering of western Europe in the fourteenth and fifteenth centuries. Arts and literature of this period reflected greater individualism and secularism than in the medieval period and often drew inspiration from classical models.

Repartimiento (ray-pahrr-tee-MYEN-toh) Spanish labor system in Latin America, supposed to replace the *encomienda* system, in which native communities were compelled to provide laborers for the farms or mines and the Spanish employers were expected to pay fair wages.

Romanov (ROH-mah-nahv) Russian dynasty (1610–1917) founded by Mikhail Romanov and ending with Nicholas II.

Rubaiyat (ROO-beye-aht) "Quatrains," famous poetry of Omar Khayyam that was later translated and transformed by Edward Fitzgerald.

Safavid (SAH-fah-vihd) Later Persian empire (1501–1722) that was founded by Shah Ismail and that became a center for Shiism; the empire reached its peak under Shah Abbas the Great and was centered around the capital of Isfahan.

Sakk Letters of credit that were common in the medieval Islamic banking world.

Saljuqs (sahl-JYOOKS) Turkish tribe that gained control over the Abbasid empire and fought with the Byzantine empire.

Samsara (suhm-SAH-ruh) Hindu term for the concept of transmigration, that is, the soul passing into a new incarnation.

Samurai (SAM-uhr-eye) A Japanese warrior who lived by the code of *bushido*.

Sasanids (suh-SAH-nids) Later powerful Persian dynasty (224–651) that would reach its peak under Shapur I and later fall to Arabic expansion.

Sati (suh-TEE) Also known as *suttee*, Indian practice of a widow throwing herself on the funeral pyre of her husband.

Satraps (SAY-traps) Persian administrators, usually members of the royal family, who governed a satrapy.

Satyagraha (suh-TYA-gruh-hah) "Truth and firmness," a term associated with Gandhi's policy of passive resistance.

Scholar-bureaucrats Describes the administrative apparatus of China created by the Ming dynasty (1368–1644) and continued by the Qing dynasty (1644–1911). Under this system, Confucian scholars, chosen through a highly competitive series of examinations, ran the country. This system meant that China was a meritocracy, but a very conservative one.

Scholasticism Medieval attempt of thinkers like St. Thomas Aquinas to merge the beliefs of Christianity with the logical rigor of Greek philosophy.

Scientific racism Nineteenth-century attempt to justify racism by scientific means; an example would be Gobineau's *Essay on the Inequality of the Human Races.*

Self-determinism Belief popular in World War I and after that every people should have the right to determine their own political destiny; the belief was often cited but ignored by the Great Powers.

Self-strengthening movement Chinese attempt (1860–1895) to blend Chinese cultural traditions with European industrial technology.

Seleucids (sih-LOO-sihds) Persian empire (323–83 B.C.E.) founded by Seleucus after the death of Alexander the Great.

Semitic (suh-MIHT-ihk) A term that relates to the Semites, ancient nomadic herders who spoke Semitic languages; examples of Semites were the Akkadians, Hebrews, Aramaics, and Phoenicians, who often interacted with the more settled societies of Mesopotamia and Egypt.

Sepoys Indian troops who served the British.

Seppuku A Japanese term for ritual suicide committed by the samurai when he had been dishonored.

Serfs Peasants who, while not chattel slaves, were tied to the land and who owed obligation to the lords on whose land they worked.

Shamanism (SHAH-mah-niz'm) Belief in shamans or religious specialists who possessed supernatural powers and who communicated with the gods and the spirits of nature.

Sharia (shah-RREE-ah) The Islamic holy law, drawn up by theologians from the Quran, and accounts of Muhammad's life.

Shia (SHEE-ah) Islamic minority in opposition to the Sunni majority; their belief is that leadership should reside in the line descended from Ali.

Shintoism (SHIHN-toh-iz'm) Indigenous Japanese religion that emphasizes purity, clan loyalty, and the divinity of the emperor.

Shiva (SHIH-vuh) Hindu god associated with both fertility and destruction.

Shogun (SHOH-gun) Japanese military leader who ruled in place of the emperor.

Shudras (SHOO-druhs) Hindu caste of landless peasants and serfs.

Siddhartha Gautama (sih-DHAR-thuh GAHW-tah-mah) Indian *kshatriya* who achieved enlightenment and became known as the Buddha, the founder of Buddhism.

Sikhs (SIHKS) Indian syncretic faith that contains elements of Hinduism and Islam.

Silk roads Ancient trade routes that extended from the Roman empire in the west to China in the east.

Social Darwinism Nineteenth-century philosophy, championed by thinkers such as Herbert Spencer, that attempted to apply Darwinian "survival of the fittest" to the social and political realm; adherents saw the the elimination of weaker nations as part of a natural process and used the philosophy to justify war.

Socialism Political and economic theory of social organization based on the collective ownership of the means of production; its origins were in the early nineteenth century, and it differs from communism by a desire for slow or moderate change compared to the communist call for revolution.

Solidarity Polish trade union and nationalist movement in the 1980s that was headed by Lech Walesa.

Song (SOHNG) Chinese dynasty (960–1279) that was marked by an increasingly urbanized and cosmopolitan society.

Soviets Russian elected councils that originated as strike committees during the 1905 St. Petersburg disorders; they represented a form of local self-government that went on to become the primary unit of government in the Union of Soviet Socialist Republics. The term was also used during the cold war to designate the Soviet Union.

Spanish Inquisition Institution organized in 1478 by Fernando and Isabel of Spain to detect Protestant heresy and the secret practice of Judaism or Islam.

Spheres of influence A region dominated by an outside power. Generally refers to the intrusion of western imperial powers into China in the late nineteenth century. China, although technically a sovereign state, was divided into "spheres," each one occupied by a European state that had license to conduct business without any interference.

Srivijaya (sree-vih-JUH-yuh) Southeast Asian kingdom (670–1025), based on the island of Sumatra, that used a powerful navy to dominate trade.

Stateless societies Term relating to societies such as those of sub-Saharan Africa after the Bantu migrations that featured decentralized rule through family and kinship groups instead of strongly centralized hierarchies.

Stoics (STOH-ihks) Hellenistic philosophers who encouraged their followers to lead active, virtuous lives and to aid others.

Stoicism A Hellenistic philosophy that emphasized strict adherence to duty and

personal self-discipline. It became very popular among the Roman upper classes.

Strabo (STRAH-boh) Greek geographer (first century C.E.).

Strategic Arms Limitations Talk (SALT) Agreement in 1972 between the United States and the Soviet Union.

Stupas (STOO-pahs) Buddhist shrines.

Sufis (SOO-fees) Islamic mystics who placed more emphasis on emotion and devotion than on strict adherence to rules.

Sui (SWAY) Chinese dynasty (589–618) that constructed Grand Canal, reunified China, and allowed for the splendor of the Tang dynasty that followed.

Süleyman (SOO-lehy-mahn) Ottoman Turkish ruler Süleyman the Magnificent (r. 1520–1566), who was the most powerful and wealthy ruler of the sixteenth century.

Sumerians (soo-MEHR-ee-uhns) Earliest Mesopotamian society.

Sundiata (soon-JAH-tuh) Founder of the Mali empire (r. 1230–1255), also the inspiration for the *Sundiata,* an African literary and mythological work.

Sunni (SOON-nee) "Traditionalists," the most popular branch of Islam; Sunnis believe in the legitimacy of the early caliphs, compared to the Shiite belief that only a descendent of Ali can lead.

Suu Kyi, Aung San (SOO KEE, AWNG SAHN) Opposition leader (1945–) in Myanmar; she was elected leader in 1990 but she was not allowed to come to power; she was a Nobel Peace Prize recipient in 1991.

Swahili (swah-HEE-lee) East African city-state society that dominated the coast from Mogadishu to Kilwa and was active in trade.

Taino (tah-EE-noh) A Caribbean tribe who were the first indigenous peoples from the Americas to come into contact with Christopher Columbus.

Taiping rebellion (TEYE-pihng) Rebellion (1850–1864) in Qing China led by Hong Xiuquan, during which twenty to thirty million were killed; the rebellion was symbolic of the decline of China during the nineteenth century.

Taliban Strict Islamic organization that ruled Afghanistan from 1996 to 2002.

Tang Taizong (TAHNG TEYE-zohng) Chinese emperor (r. 627–649) who founded the Tang dynasty (618–907).

Tanzimat "Reorganization" era (1839–1876), an attempt to reorganize

the Ottoman empire on Enlightenment and constitutional forms.

Temnjin (TEM-oo-chin) Mongol conqueror (ca. 1167–1227) who later took the name Chinggis Khan, "universal ruler."

Tenochtitlan (teh-noch-tee-TLAHN) Capital of the Aztec empire, later Mexico City.

Teotihuacan (tay-oh-tee-wa-KAHN) Central American society (200 B.C.E.–750 C.E.); its Pyramid of the Sun was the largest structure in Mesoamerica.

Teutonic Knights Crusading European order that was active in the Baltic region.

Third Rome Concept that a new power would rise up to carry the legacy of Roman greatness after the decline of the Second Rome, Constantinople; Moscow was referred to as the Third Rome during the fifteenth century.

Three Principles of the People Philosophy of Chinese Guomindang leader Sun Yat-sen (1866–1925) that emphasized nationalism, democracy, and people's livelihood.

Tian (TEE-ehn) Chinese term for heaven.

Tikal (tee-KAHL) Maya political center from the fourth through the ninth centuries.

Timur-i lang (tee-MOOR-yee LAHNG) "Timur the Lame," known in English as Tamerlane (ca. 1336–1405), who conquered an empire ranging from the Black Sea to Samarkand.

Tokugawa (TOH-koo-GAH-wah) Last shogunate in Japanese history (1600–1867); it was founded by Tokugawa Ieyasu who was notable for unifying Japan.

Toltecs Central American society (950–1150) that was centered around the city of Tula.

Trail of Tears Forced relocation of the Cherokee from the eastern woodlands to Oklahoma (1837–1838); it was symbolic of U.S. expansion and destruction of indigenous Indian societies.

Triangular trade Trade between Europe, Africa, and the Americas that featured finished products from Europe, slaves from Africa, and American products bound for Europe.

Triple Alliance Pre–World War I alliance of Germany, Austria-Hungary, and Italy.

Triple Entente (ahn-TAHNT) Pre–World War I alliance of England, France, and Russia.

Truman Doctrine U.S. policy instituted in 1947 by President Harry Truman in which the United States would follow an interventionist foreign policy to contain communism.

Tsar (ZAHR) Old Russian term for king that is derived from the term *caesar.*

Twelver Shiism (SHEE'i'zm) Branch of Islam that stressed that there were twelve perfect religious leaders after Muhammad and that the twelfth went into hiding and would return someday; Shah Ismail spread this variety through the Safavid empire.

Uighurs (WEE-goors) Turkish tribe.

Ukiyo Japanese word for the "floating worlds," a Buddhist term for the insignificance of the world that came to represent the urban centers in Tokugawa Japan.

Ulama (oo-lah-MAH) Islamic officials, scholars who shaped public policy in accordance with the Quran and the *sharia.*

Ulaanbaatar (OO-lahn-bah-tahr) Mongolian city.

Umayyad (oo-MEYE-ahd) Arabic dynasty (661–750), with its capital at Damascus, that was marked by a tremendous period of expansion to Spain in the west and India in the east.

Umma (UM-mah) Islamic term for the "community of the faithful."

United Nations (UN) Successor to the League of Nations, an association of sovereign nations that attempts to find solutions to global problems.

Upanishads (oo-pan-NIH-shuhds) Indian reflections and dialogues (800–400 B.C.E.) that reflected basic Hindu concepts.

Urdu (OOR-doo) A language that is predominant in Pakistan.

Uruk (OO-rook) Ancient Mesopotamian city from the fourth millennium B.C.E. that was allegedly the home of the fabled Gilgamesh.

Vaishyas (VEYESH-yuhs) Hindu caste of cultivators, artisans, and merchants.

Vaqueros (bah-KEH-rohs) Latin American cowboys, similar to the Argentine gaucho.

Varna (VUHR-nuh) Hindu word for caste.

Varuna (vuh-ROO-nuh) Early Aryan god who watched over the behavior of mortals and preserved the cosmic order.

Vedas (VAY-duhs) "Wisdom," early collections of prayers and hymns that provide information about the Indo-European Aryans who migrated into India around 1500 B.C.E.; *Rig Veda* is most important collection.

Velvet revolution A term that describes the nonviolent transfer of power in Czechoslovakia during the collapse of Soviet rule.

Venta, La (BEHN-tah, lah) Early Olmec center (800–400 B.C.E.).

Venus figurines Small Paleolithic statues of women with exaggerated sexual features.

Vernacular (ver-NA-kyoo-lar) The language of the people; Martin Luther translated the Bible from the Latin of the Catholic church into the vernacular German.

Versailles (vehr-SEYE) Palace of French King Louis XIV.

Viet Minh North Vietnamese nationalist communists under Ho Chi Minh.

Vijayanagar (vih-juh-yuh-NUH-guhr) Southern Indian kingdom (1336–1565) that later fell to the Mughals.

Vishnu (VIHSH-noo) Hindu god, preserver of the world, who was often incarnated as Krishna.

Vodou (VOO-doo) Syncretic religion practiced by African slaves in Haiti.

Volksgeist (FOHLKS-geyest) "People's spirit," a term that was coined by the German philosopher Herder; a nation's volksgeist would not come to maturity unless people studied their own unique culture and traditions.

Volta do mar (VOHL-tah doh MAHR) "Return through the sea," a fifteenth-century Portuguese sea route that took advantage of the prevailing winds and currents.

Voltaire (vohl-TAIR) Pen name of French philosophe Francois-Marie Arouet (1694–1778), author of *Candide.*

Walesa, Lech (WAH-lehn-sah, LEHK) Leader of the Polish Solidarity movement.

Waldensians Twelfth-century religious reformers who criticized the Roman Catholic church and who proposed that the laity had the right to preach and administer sacraments; they were declared heretics.

Wanli (wahn-LEE) Chinese Ming emperor (r. 1572–1620) whose refusal to meet with officials hurried the decline of Ming dynasty.

War Communism The Russian policy of nationalizing industry and seizing private land during the civil war.

Warsaw Pact Warsaw Treaty Organization, a military alliance formed by Soviet bloc nations in 1955 in response to rearmament of West Germany and its inclusion in NATO.

Wind wheels Prevailing wind patterns in the Atlantic and Pacific Oceans north and south of the equator; their discovery made sailing much safer and quicker.

Witte, Sergei (VIHT-tee, SAYR-gay) Late-nineteenth-century Russian minister of finance who pushed for industrialization.

World Health Organization (WHO) United Nation organization designed to deal with global health issues.

World Trade Organization (WTO) An organization that was established in 1995 with more than 120 nations and whose goal is to loosen barriers to free trade.

Wuwei (woo-WAY) Daoist concept of a disengagement from the affairs of the world.

Xia (shyah) Early Chinese dynasty (2200–1766 B.C.E.) that is known mainly from legend.

Xianyang (SHYAHN-YAHNG) Capital city of Qin empire.

Xiao (SHAYOH) Confucian concept of respect for one's parents and ancestors.

Xinjiang (shin-jyahng) Western Chinese province.

Xuanzang (SHWEN-ZAHNG) Seventh-century Chinese monk who made a famous trip to India to collect Buddhist texts.

Yahweh (YAH-way) God of the monotheistic religion of Judaism that influenced later Christianity and Islam.

Yangshao (YAHNG-shahw) Early Chinese society (2500–2200 B.C.E.).

Yangzi (YAHNG-zuh) River in central China.

Yongle (YAWNG-leh) Chinese Ming emperor (r. 1403–1424) who pushed for foreign exploration and promoted cultural achievements such as the *Yongle Encyclopedia.*

Young Turks Nineteenth-century Turkish reformers who pushed for changes within the Ottoman empire, such as universal suffrage and freedom of religion.

Yu (yoo) Legendary founder of the Xia dynasty (ca. 2200 B.C.E.).

Yuan (yoo-AHN) Chinese dynasty (1279–1368) that was founded by the Mongol ruler Khubilai Khan.

Yucatan (yoo-kah-TAN) Peninsula in Central America, home of the Maya.

Yurts (yuhrts) Tents used by nomadic Turkish and Mongol tribes.

Zaibatsu (zeye-BAHT-soo) Japanese term for "wealthy cliques," which are similar to American trusts and cartels but usually organized around one family.

Zambos (SAHM-bohs) Latin American term for individuals born of indigenous and African parents.

Zamudio, Adela (sah-MOO-dyo, ah-DEH-lah) Nineteenth-century Bolivian poet, author of "To Be Born a Man."

Zarathustra (zar-uh-THOO-struh) Persian prophet (ca. 628–551 B.C.E.) who founded Zoroastrianism.

Zen Buddhism Japanese version of Chinese Chan Buddhism, with an emphasis on intuition and sudden flashes of insight instead of textual study.

Zhou (JOH) Chinese dynasty (1122–256 B.C.E.) that was the foundation of Chinese thought formed during this period: Confucianism, Daoism, Zhou Classics.

Zhu Xi (ZHOO-SHEE) Neo-Confucian Chinese philosopher (1130–1200).

Ziggurats (ZIG-uh-rahts) Mesopotamian temples.

Zimbabwe (zihm-BAHB-way) Former colony of Southern Rhodesia that gained independence in 1980.

Zemstvos (ZEHMST-voh) District assemblies elected by Russians in the nineteenth century.

Zoroastrianism (zohr-oh-ASS-tree-ahn-iz'm) Persian religion based on the teaching of the sixth-century B.C.E. prophet Zarathustra; its emphasis on the duality of good and evil and on the role of individuals in determining their own fate would influence later religions.

Credits

p. 613, Courtesy Everett Collection
Chapter 33 p. 616, © Bettmann/Corbis;
p. 619, © Hulton-Deutsch Collection/
Corbis; p. 620, © Popperfoto; p. 622,
© Harwood/Getty Images; p. 623, 629,
© Bettmann/Corbis; p. 631, Library of
Congress; p. 632, © Bettmann/Corbis
Chapter 34 p. 636, © Corbis; p. 638,
© Authenticated News/Getty Images;
p. 640, © Fritz Henle/Photo Researchers,
Inc.; p. 641, © UPI/Corbis; p. 646,
© Josef Koudelka/Magnum Photos;
p. 649, © James Pickerell/Camera Press,
London/Retna, Ltd.; p. 650, © Peter
Turnley/Corbis; p. 651, © Tom Stoddart/
Katz Pictures/Woodfin Camp and Associates **Chapter 35** p. 656, © Bettmann/
Corbis; p. 661, © Baldwin H. Ward/
Corbis; p. 663, © UPI/Corbis; p. 667,
© Bert Hardy/Getty Images; p. 668,
© Sovfoto; p. 669, © Alexandra Avakian/
Woodfin Camp and Associates; p. 672,
© Bruno Barbey/Magnum Photos

TEXT CREDITS

Chapter 1 Pritchard, James, *Ancient Near
Eastern Texts Relating to the Old Testament.* Third Edition with Supplement.
© 1950, 1955, 1969, renewed 1978 by
Princeton University Press. Reprinted by
permission of Princeton University Press.
Chapter 2 Miriam Lichtheim, ed., *Ancient Egyptian Literature.* Three volumes.
Berkeley: University of California Press,
1973. Vol. 1, pp. 25–27. Reprinted by
permission of the University of California
Press. **Chapter 4** Reprinted with permission of Simon & Schuster Adult Publishing
Group, from *Popul Vuh: The Definitive
Edition of the Mayan Book of the Dawn of
Life.* Translated by Dennis Tedlock. Copyright © 1985, 1996 by Dennis Tedlock.
All rights reserved. **Chapter 10** From *The
Alexiad of Anna Comnena.* Translated by
E. R. A. Sewter (Penguin Classics, 1969)
copyright © E. R. A. Sewter, 1969.
Pp. 496–505. Reproduced by permission
of Penguin Books Ltd. **Chapter 13** From
Sources of Indian Tradition. Volume 1,
pp. 325–26, 328 edited by Ainslie T.
Embree and Stephen Hay. © 1988 Columbia University Press. **Chapter 16** From
D. T. Niane, *Sundiata: An Epic of Old
Mali,* pp. 80–82. © Pearson Education
Limited, 1965. Used by permission of
Pearson Education Limited. **Chapter 18**
Teuira Henry and others, Dennis
Kawaharada, ed., *Voyaging Chiefs of
Havai'i.* Copyright 1995. pp. 138–39,
144–46. Kalamaku Press. Reprinted by
permission of Kalamaku Press. **Chapter 19**
From Said Hamdun and Noel King, *Ibn
Battuta in Black Africa.* Princeton: Markus
Wiener Publishers, 1994, pp. 49–50,
58–59. Reprinted by permission. **Chapter
20** Christopher Columbus, *The Diario of
Christopher Columbus's First Voyage to
America.* Trans. By Oliver Dunn and

James E. Kelley, Jr. Norman: University
of Oklahoma Press, 1989, pp. 65–69,
143–45. Reprinted by permission of the
University of Oklahoma Press. **Chapter 22**
Bernardino de Sahagun, *Florentine Codex:
General History of the Things of New Spain.*
13 vols. Trans. By Arthur J. O. Anderson
and Charles E. Dibble. Salt Lake City:
University of Utah Press, 1950–82,
13:19–20. Used by permission of the
University of Utah Press. **Chapter 23**
Copyright © 1964 by Basil Davidson.
Reprinted by permission of Curtis Brown,
Ltd. **Chapter 28** From *Been in the Storm
So Long* by Leon F. Litwack, copyright
© 1979 by Leon F. Litwack. Used by
permission of Alfred A. Knopf, a division
of Random House, Inc. **Chapter 32** Amy
Jacques Garvey, compiler, *Philosophy and
Opinions of Marcus Garvey or Africa for
Africans.* Reprinted courtesy of The
Majority Press Inc. PO Box 538, Dover,
MA 02030. **Chapter 33** Haruko Taya
Cook and Theodore F. Cook, *Japan
at War.* Copyright © 1993. Reprinted
by permission of The New Press. www.
thenewpress.com. **Chapter 34** Nikita
Khrushchev, "Report to the Communist
Party," in *Current Soviet Policies IV,* ed.
Charlotte Saikowski and Leo Gruliow,
from the translations of *The Current Digest
of the Soviet Press,* 1962. Used by permission of the Current Digest of the Post-
Soviet Press.

Index

Subheadings are arranged under headings chronologically rather than alphabetically. The date ranges after names of people refer to life spans, unless otherwise stated.

The italicized word "map" following page numbers refers to maps, and "source document" refers to primary source material. The italicized abbreviation "illus." following page numbers refers to illustrations. "B.C.E." following dates refers to "Before the Common Era". "C.E." following dates refers to "Common Era". Dates without qualifiers are in the Common Era.

Abbasid dynasty, 202–6, 208, 233, 259, 270, 271 *(map)*
Abbas the Great, Shah of Safavid empire (reigned 1588–1629), 461, 464, 467, 468 *(illus.)*
Abdül Hamid II, Ottoman sultan (reigned 1876–1909), 546
abolition of slavery, 431–32, 489, 520–21
absolute monarchies, 385–87, 386 *(illus.)*
Abu al-Abbas (722–754), 202
Abu Bakr (573–634), 200–201
academic guilds, 309
Achaemenid empire (558–330 B.C.E.), 84–87, 85 *(map)*, 86 *(illus.)*, 87 *(illus.)*, 94, 137. *See also* Persia
Actium, battle of (31 B.C.E.), 147
Admonitions for Women, 110
Aeschylus (fifth century B.C.E.), 143
Afghanistan: spread of Islam in, 233, 270; in Tamerlane empire, 279, 280 *(map)*; Britain and Russia in, prior to World War I, 565; Soviet

Union in, 648–49. *See also* Bactria
Afonso I (Nzinga Mbemba), King of Kongo (reigned 1506–1542), 421, 422 *(source document)*
Africa: early agriculture in, 7, 26–28, 27 *(map)*, 28 *(illus.),* 38–39; climatic change in, 26–28; ancient Egypt and Nubia, 26–37, 27 *(map)*, 28 *(illus.),* 31 *(map);* iron metallurgy in, 34; Bantu speakers in, 37–39, 38 *(map);* Christianity in, 261, 296–97; Kongo kingdom, 287–88, 294, 296 *(illus.),* 297, 420–21, 420 *(map);* Islam in west Africa, 288–92, 289 *(map);* trans-Saharan trade in, 288–92, 289 *(map)*, 419; Islam in east Africa, 292–94; kingdom of Zimbabwe, 293; Swahili city-states, 293; slave trade and diaspora, 428–32, 430 *(illus.),* 431 *(illus.);* European imperialism in, 548–51, 550 *(map)*, 572–73; Belgian Congo, 549, 549 *(illus.),* 550 *(map)*, 605, 665–67; Berlin West Africa Conference (1884–1885), 549; indentured labor migrations from, 556; in World War I, 572, 605–6, 606 *(illus.);* Great Depression in, 587, 606; revolts against colonial powers, 606; nationalism in, 607–8, 609 *(source document);* independence in, 608, 658, 664–67, 665 *(map)*, 666 *(source document). See also* east Africa; north Africa; south Africa; sub-Saharan Africa; west Africa
African Americans: American Revolution and Black Pioneers, 417; cultural traditions under slavery, 430–31,

431 *(illus.);* equality for, 489; civil rights of, 530–31, 531 *(illus.),* 532 *(source document);* segregation, 531; Black nationalism, 643. *See also* slave revolts; slavery
Afrikaners, 551
age groups, in sub-Saharan Africa, 295
agriculture: early complex societies and, 2–3, 6; neolithic, 7–8; in Mesopotamia, 8–10; in early African societies, 26–28, 27 *(map)*, 28 *(illus.),* 37–39; in early China, 44, 51–52, 58–59; in Indus River valley, 44–45; in Olmec culture, 65–66; drainage systems in, 67; in Maya culture, 67, 69; in Teotihuacan, 70; in early Andean societies, 72–73; in classical Persia, 91, 92; in Han dynasty China, 110; in classical Greece, 133, 139, 139 *(illus.);* in Roman Empire, 149; in early Islamic world, 203–4, 204 *(illus.);* equal-field system, 214–15; in Tang and Song dynasties, 217–18, 217 *(illus.);* in India, 235; in medieval Europe, 257–59, 259 *(illus.),* 305; Aztec *chinampa* system, 319; in early North America, 323; cross-cultural exchanges in, 339, 341, 372, 389; sugarcane production, 339, 341, 348, 371–73, 401, 409–10; Columbian exchange, 371–72, 372 *(illus.),* 464; in American colonies, 400–401, 406, 409; cash-crop plantations in North America, 410, 412 *(illus.);* American food crops in sub-Saharan Africa, 424; in

Ming and Qing dynasties, 443–44, 447 *(illus.);* in Islamic empires, 464–65; imperialism and, 529, 555; fertilizer impacts on, 586; collectivization of, 591, 647; in British India, 601; immigrant Mexican labor in United States, 613; in People's Republic of China, 667. *See also* irrigation
Aguinaldo, Emilio, 553
ahimsa (nonviolence), 122–23, 125, 601
Ahura Mazda (god), 93–95, 93 *(illus.)*
air war, 621–22
Akbar, Mughal emperor (reigned 1556–1605), 463, 463 *(illus.),* 466–67
Akhenaten, Pharaoh (reigned 1353–1335 B.C.E.), 36
Akkad (Mesopotamia), 10–11
al-Andalus, 205–6. *See also* Spain
Alaric, King of Visigoths (c. 370–410), 170
Alaska, purchased by United States, 553
Albania, annexation by Italy, 619
d'Alboquerque, Afonso (sixteenth century), 366–67
Aleppo, Spain, 465
Alexander II, Tsar of Russia (reigned 1855–1881), 510, 512 *(illus.)*
Alexander of Macedon (Alexander the Great, 356–323 B.C.E.): in Persia, 88–89, 135; Zoroastrianism and, 94; in India, 116, 118–19, 137; conquest of Mediterranean region by, 137; extent of empire, 138 *(map);* death of, 137
Alexandria (Egypt), 138, 138 *(map)*
Alexandrian Library (Egypt), 138
Alexandrian Museum (Egypt), 138